Complete Technical

Information and Tools

for Creating Custom

Applications with

Microsoft Word

Microsoft®
Word
Developer's Kit
Third Edition

Microsoft Press

PUBLISHED BY
Microsoft Press
A Division of Microsoft Corporation
One Microsoft Way
Redmond, Washington 98052-6399

Library of Congress Cataloging-in-Publication Data
Microsoft Word developer's kit. -- 3rd ed.
      p.   cm.
   Includes index.
   ISBN 1-55615-880-7
   1. Microsoft Word for Windows. 2. Word processing. 3. IBM
 -compatible computers--Programming. I. Microsoft Corporation.
Z52.5.M523M49 1995
652.5'536--dc20   95-38729
                                          CIP

Printed and bound in the United States of America.

1 2 3 4 5 6 7 8 9 QMQM 0 9 8 7 6 5

Distributed to the book trade in Canada by Macmillan of Canada, a division of Canada Publishing
Corporation.

A CIP catalogue record for this book is available from the British Library.

Microsoft Press books are available through booksellers and distributors worldwide. For further information
about international editions, contact your local Microsoft Corporation office. Or contact Microsoft Press
International directly at fax (206) 936-7329.

Acquisitions Editor: Casey D. Doyle
Project Editor: Brenda L. Matteson

Contents

About This Book   xiii
Organization   xiv
      Part 1, "Learning WordBasic"   xiv
      Part 2, "WordBasic Reference"   xv
      Part 3, "Appendixes"   xv
Typographic Conventions   xvi

Part 1   Learning WordBasic

Chapter 1   Introduction   3
Features of WordBasic   3
Tips on How to Learn WordBasic   4
Sample Files   5
      Loading the Sample Files   6
      Accessing the Macro Examples   7
Other Resources   7
      Microsoft Product Support Services   7
      Product Training and Consultation   9
      Books   9

Chapter 2   Getting Started with Macros   11
Recording a Macro   11
      Starting the Recording   12
      Assigning the Macro   13
      Recording the Macro Actions   15
Running a Macro   16
Editing a Macro   19
      Examining the Macro   19
      Editing the BoldItalic Macro   20
      Getting Help on WordBasic   21
      The Macro Toolbar   22
      Running the Macro from the Macro-Editing Window   23
      Error Checking in the Macro-Editing Window   24
      The Macro Text Style   25
      View Options for Macro-Editing Windows   26
      The Record Next Command Button   26

Macros and Templates   26
    Why Store Macros in Different Templates?   28
    Making Templates Global   28
    Priority Among Templates   29
Saving a Macro   29
    Using the Save Template Command   30
    Using the Save Copy As Command   30
Macro Housekeeping   30
Modifying a Word Command   31
    An Example   32
    Restoring a Modified Command   34
Auto Macros   35
    Auto Macro Examples   36

Chapter 3   WordBasic Fundamentals   39
A Simple Macro   39
Statements and Functions   41
    Statements   42
    Functions   43
Strings and Numbers   44
Variables   46
    Assigning Values to Variables   46
    Changing Strings to Numbers and Numbers to Strings   48
Expressions   48
Conditionals and Loops   49
    What Is a Condition?   50
    The If Conditional   53
    The While…Wend Loop   55
    Compound Expressions in Conditional Statements   56
    The NOT Operator   57
Displaying Messages and Requesting Information   58
    Print   58
    MsgBox and MsgBox()   59
    InputBox$()   60
    Input   61
Common WordBasic Techniques   61
    Inserting Text into a Document   62
    Working on Part of a Document   63
    Reading Text from a Document   64
    Testing for the End of a Document   65

Some Sample Macros   66
    Delete to the Beginning of a Sentence   66
    Remove Excess Paragraph Marks   67
    Determine How Many Days Until a Future Date   67
    Count How Many Times a Word Appears   68

Chapter 4   Advanced WordBasic   71
More Conditionals and Loops   71
    The For…Next Loop   71
    The Select Case Conditional   74
    The Goto Statement   76
Array Variables   77
    Defining an Array   78
    Assigning Values to an Array   78
    Resizing an Array   79
    Arrays with More Than One Dimension   80
    Sorting Arrays   81
Subroutines and User-Defined Functions   82
    Subroutines   82
    User-Defined Functions   83
    Sharing Values Among Subroutines and Functions   84
    Using Subroutines and Functions from Other Macros   88
Working with Dialog Records   91
    Defining a Dialog Record   92
    Retrieving and Changing Dialog Box Settings   92
    Using a Dialog Record to Toggle a Check Box   93
    Displaying a Dialog Box   95

Chapter 5   Working with Custom Dialog Boxes   99
Dialog Box Controls   99
    OK, Cancel, and Push Buttons   100
    List Boxes, Drop-Down List Boxes, and Combo Boxes   100
    Check Boxes   100
    Text Boxes and Text   101
    Option Buttons and Group Boxes   101
    Pictures and File Preview   101

Using the Dialog Editor to Create a Dialog Box   102
    Starting the Dialog Editor   102
    Adding Items to a Dialog Box   102
    Positioning and Sizing Items   105
    Deleting Items   110
    Changing Labels and Identifiers   110
    Copying a Dialog Box to a Macro   111
    Exiting the Dialog Editor   112
    Editing an Existing Dialog Box   112
    Tips for Using the Dialog Editor   112
Using Custom Dialog Boxes   115
    The Dialog Box Definition   115
    Creating a Dialog Record   117
    Placing Values into a Dialog Box   117
    Displaying the Dialog Box   120
    Retrieving Values from the Dialog Box   121
Using Dynamic Dialog Boxes   123
    What Can You Do with a Dynamic Dialog Box?   123
    How to Make a Dialog Box Dynamic   125
    Dialog Function Techniques   131
    Statements and Functions Used in Dialog Functions   142

Chapter 6   Debugging   145
Common WordBasic Errors   145
    Syntax Error   146
    Type Mismatch   147
    Wrong Number of Parameters   147
    Unknown Command, Subroutine, or Function   147
    Undefined Dialog Record Field   147
    Bad Parameter   148
    Duplicate Label   148
Ways to Avoid WordBasic Errors   148
    Use the Record Next Command Button   148
    Copy Syntax from Help   149
    Store Instructions as AutoText Entries   150

Debugging Tools   150
    Trace   150
    Step   151
    Step Subs   152
    Show Variables   152
    Add/Remove REM   153
    Statements Useful for Debugging   154
An Example: Debugging the InsertTab Macro   155

Chapter 7   The Well-Behaved Macro   157
Handling Errors   157
    WordBasic and Word Errors   158
    Error-Handling Instructions   159
Bulletproofing   162
Cleaning Up   163

Chapter 8   Communicating with Other Applications   165
Using Dynamic Data Exchange   165
    Clients, Servers, and Conversations   166
    Application Names, Topics, and Items   166
    Initiating a DDE Conversation   168
    Requesting Information   171
    Sending Information   172
    Sending Commands   173
    Terminating DDE Conversations   174
    Using Microsoft Excel as a Server   174
    Using Microsoft Access as a Server   177
    Using Word as a Server   179
Using OLE Automation with Word   182
    Accessing Word   183
    Using WordBasic Statements and Functions   184
    Accessing an Embedded Word Object   186
    Retrieving Word Dialog Box Settings   188
    Running Word Macros and Displaying Dialog Boxes   189
    Using Positional Arguments in Visual Basic Version 3.0   191
Using MAPI and AOCE   193

Chapter 9   More WordBasic Techniques   195

Storing Values When a Macro Ends   196

Settings Files   196

Using the WIN.INI File   199

Accessing WINWORD6.INI and Word Settings (6)   199

Accessing the Windows Registry   200

Document Variables   201

Document Properties   203

AutoText Entries   205

Using Sequential File Access   205

Opening a File for Sequential Access   206

Writing to a File   207

Reading from a File   208

Closing a File   210

Other Sequential Access Statements and Functions   210

Automating Forms   212

Example   215

Creating a Wizard   218

Wizard Templates   219

The StartWizard Macro   219

The Wizard Interface   221

Managing the Dialog Box Panels   224

Storing Wizard Settings   226

Calling Routines in DLLs   228

Declaring a DLL Routine   228

Calling a DLL Routine   229

Special Considerations When Declaring DLL Routines   230

Calling DLL Routines with Specific Variable Types   231

Converting Common Declarations   233

Developing Macros for More Than One Platform   234

Using Platform-Specific Instructions and Arguments   235

Handling Platform-Level Differences   237

Moving a Cross-Platform Macro Between Platforms   241

Distributing Macros   242

Distributing Macros with a Local Template   243

Distributing Macros with a Global Template   244

Distributing Macros Without a Template   245

Distributing Macros Internationally   245

Optimizing Macros   247

Part 2   WordBasic Reference

Language Differences Across Versions of Word   253

Statements and Functions Used Only in the Windows Versions of Word 253

Statements and Functions Used Only in Word Version 6.0 for the Macintosh   255

Statements and Functions Used Only in Word Version 7.0   256

Statements with Version-Specific Arguments   258

Statements and Functions with Version-Specific Behavior   259

Language Summary   265

Address Book   265

Application Control   265

AutoCorrect   266

AutoText   266

Basic File Input/Output   266

Bookmarks   267

Borders and Frames   267

Branching and Control   267

Bullets and Numbering   267

Character Formatting   268

Customization   268

Date and Time   269

Definition and Declaration   269

Dialog Box Definition and Control   269

Disk Access and Management   270

Documents, Templates, and Add-ins   270

Document Properties   271

Drawing   272

Dynamic Data Exchange (DDE)   273

Editing   273

Electronic Mail and Routing   274

Environment   274

Fields   275

Finding and Replacing   275

Footnotes, Endnotes, and Annotations   276

Forms   276

Help   276

Macros   277
Mail Merge   277
Moving the Insertion Point and Selecting   278
Object Linking and Embedding   279
Outlining and Master Documents   279
Paragraph Formatting   280
Proofing   280
Section and Document Formatting   281
Strings and Numbers   281
Style Formatting   282
Tables   282
Tools   282
View   283
Windows   284

Statements and Functions   285

Operators and Predefined Bookmarks   889
Operators   889
        Operator Precedence   889
        Arithmetic Operators   890
        The String Concatenation Operator   891
        Comparison Operators   891
        Logical Operators   891
        True, False, and Bitwise Comparisons   892
Predefined Bookmarks   895

Error Messages   897
WordBasic Error Messages   897
Word Error Messages   901

Part 3   Appendixes

Appendix A   Workgroup Extensions for Microsoft Word   925
Loading the Workgroup Extensions   926
Understanding the Workgroup Extensions   926
    Understanding Mail Sessions   927
    Understanding Messages   927
        The Current Messages   927
        Recipients   928

Working with MAPI Data Types   928
Handle   928
MapiFile   929
MapiMessage   929
MapiRecip   929
WordBasic MAPI Functions   930

Appendix B   ODBC Extensions for Microsoft Word   969
Understanding the ODBC Extensions   970
The ODBC Extensions and SQL   971
ODBC SQL Data Types   973
Before You Begin   973
Installing ODBC Drivers   974
Setting Up Data Sources   974
Installing and Loading WBODBC.WLL   976
Using the ODBC Extensions   976
Declaring the Functions   976
Sequence of Use   977
Mapping the Structure of a Database   977
Checking for Error Conditions   977
ODBC Examples   977
Example of Automating Forms Using ODBC   980
WordBasic ODBC Functions   982

Appendix C   Microsoft Word Application Programming Interface   1003
Why Use the Word API?   1003
What You Need to Know   1004
Requirements   1004
Installation   1004
Overview of Add-ins and WLLs   1005
What Is a Word Add-in Library?   1005
WordBasic and the Word API   1006
Loading a WLL   1007
Calling Word from a WLL   1008
The wdCommandDispatch Function   1008
Step by Step Through the Parameters   1009
Platform-Specific Notes About wdCommandDispatch   1010
The Word Operator (WDOPR)   1013
Step by Step Through the Data Structure   1014
Specifics on Arrays   1016

Techniques for Successful Calling   1017
    Handling Errors   1017
    Allocating Memory   1018
    Deallocating Memory   1018
    Working with Strings   1018
Using the CAPILIB Functions   1019
    The Word Command Buffer (WCB)   1019
    Functions in CAPILIB   1019
    Building Word Operators with CAPILIB   1025
    Passing Arrays with CAPILIB   1026
    Customizing Word with CAPILIB   1027
Calling Word from Another Application   1029
Word API Functions   1030
    General Functions   1030
    Timer Messages   1031
    WLL Windows   1031
Word API Errors   1032

Appendix D   AppleScript   1035
Supported Suites   1036
Object Hierarchy   1037
Extensions to Supported Suites   1040
    Word Objects   1040
    Word Event   1041
    Word Properties   1042
Extending WordBasic with AppleScript   1048
    Recording Scripts   1048
    Using the Do Script Event   1049
    Attaching Scripts   1050

Appendix E   Microsoft Word Operating Limits   1051
  WordBasic Limits   1051
  Word Limits   1051

Index   1053

About This Book

The *Microsoft Word Developer's Kit* includes introductory and advanced material about programming macros in WordBasic and complete reference information about the WordBasic language in Microsoft® Word version 6.0 and 7.0. Additional information about WordBasic extensions and the Word application programming interface (Word API) is included in the appendixes.

The Microsoft Word Developer's Kit disk provided in this book includes files for use with WordBasic, the function libraries of extensions to WordBasic described in the appendixes, and the C programming tools required to program custom function libraries with the Word API. For information about installing files from the Microsoft Word Developer's Kit disk, see the following:

- For information about installing templates of WordBasic examples, as well as text files with more WordBasic information, see Chapter 1, "Introduction," in Part 1, "Learning WordBasic."

- For information about installing the workgroup extensions, see Appendix A, "Workgroup Extensions for Microsoft Word," in Part 3, "Appendixes."

- For information about installing the ODBC extensions, see Appendix B, "ODBC Extensions for Microsoft Word," in Part 3, "Appendixes."

- For information about installing the Word API programming tools and the files for a sample WLL, see Appendix C, "Microsoft Word Application Programming Interface," in Part 3, "Appendixes."

All WordBasic macro examples in Part 2, "WordBasic Reference," are available directly from the online Help available with the Microsoft Word package. For information about copying and using these examples, see Chapter 2, "Getting Started with Macros," in Part 1, "Learning WordBasic."

Note Setup does not install WordBasic Help in the Typical installation. If you selected the Typical installation during Setup, you must rerun Setup to add WordBasic Help to your existing installation.

Organization

The book is divided into three parts:

- Part 1, "Learning WordBasic," gets you started programming in WordBasic or learning the details of WordBasic if you already know another Basic programming language.

- Part 2, "WordBasic Reference," documents all the statements and functions in the WordBasic language.

- Part 3, "Appendixes," provides information about advanced topics such as workgroup and ODBC extensions, the Word API, and AppleScript™.

Part 1, "Learning WordBasic"

This part includes the following:

- Chapter 1, "Introduction," presents a brief overview of WordBasic as well as suggestions on learning how to program.

- Chapter 2, "Getting Started with Macros," presents step-by-step procedures to get you started recording macros.

- Chapter 3, "WordBasic Fundamentals," gives an overview of the primary elements of WordBasic.

- Chapter 4, "Advanced WordBasic," completes the discussion of the language.

- Chapter 5, "Working with Custom Dialog Boxes," gives tips on designing dialog boxes with the Dialog Editor and shows you how to use dialog functions in your macros to create dynamic dialog boxes.

- Chapter 6, "Debugging," explains techniques for testing and troubleshooting your macros.

- Chapter 7, "The Well-Behaved Macro," shows you how to make your macros robust and stable.

- Chapter 8, "Communicating with Other Applications," shows you how to integrate applications using dynamic data exchange (DDE) and OLE Automation.

- Chapter 9, "More WordBasic Techniques," illustrates ways to develop powerful macros and custom wizards using WordBasic.

Part 2, "WordBasic Reference"

This part includes the following:

- "Language Differences Across Versions of Word" identifies WordBasic statements and functions that operate differently or are not available in one or more versions of Word.

- "Language Summary" presents the WordBasic language in lists of related statements and functions.

- "Statements and Functions" is an alphabetic reference for WordBasic, with thorough examples.

- "Operators and Predefined Bookmarks" describes all the available mathematical operators and built-in bookmarks.

- "Error Messages" is a comprehensive list of the Word and WordBasic error messages and their associated numbers, which you can use to handle errors in your macros.

Part 3, "Appendixes"

This part includes the following:

- Appendix A, "Workgroup Extensions for Microsoft Word," describes the MAPI functions provided in WBMAPI.DLL (a library of functions included on the Microsoft Word Developer's Kit disk), which you can use to integrate WordBasic macros with electronic mail programs such as Microsoft Mail on any Windows® platform.

- Appendix B, "ODBC Extensions for Microsoft Word," presents the ODBC functions available in the WBODBC.WLL add-in library (provided on the Microsoft Word Developer's Kit disk) for adding enhanced database functionality to WordBasic macros on any Windows platform.

- Appendix C, "Microsoft Word Application Programming Interface," is a guide to using the Word API, the tools provided on the Microsoft Word Developer's Kit disk, and a programming language such as Microsoft Visual C++™ to create your own Word add-in libraries of custom functions, which you can access directly from Word or a WordBasic macro.

- Appendix D, "AppleScript," describes the unique AppleScript scripting commands available for controlling Word with scripts on the Apple® Macintosh®.

- Appendix E, "Microsoft Word Operating Limits," documents Word and WordBasic operating limits.

Typographic Conventions

In general, this book uses the following typographic conventions. For details on syntax and notation conventions for the WordBasic reference, see "Statements and Functions" in Part 2, "WordBasic Reference."

Example of convention	Explanation
If, Then, ChDir, FileName$( ), **.Path =**	In syntax, characters in bold indicate keywords and symbols that must be typed in macro instructions.
	In descriptive text, all WordBasic statement and function names appear in bold.
Message$, *Save*, *text*, *number*	In syntax, words in italic indicate placeholders for variable information you supply.
	In descriptive text, words in italic either refer to placeholders in syntax or introduce new terms.
[**Else**], [*Save*], [**, .Password** = *text*], [*Filename$*]	In syntax, bold and italic items inside square brackets are optional.

`If count = 13 Then`
`    MsgBox "Count reached 13."`
`    count = 1`
`End If`
	In WordBasic examples, text in this monospace font indicates literal macro instructions.

	Characters in this monospace font within descriptive text refer to the same characters in the example under discussion.
NORMAL.DOT, MACRO EXAMPLES	Words in all capital letters indicate filenames.
ENTER, ALT, CTRL+F9, COMMAND	Words in small capital letters indicate literal key names; a plus sign between two key names indicates that the keys must be pressed in combination.
rich-text format (RTF), dynamic data exchangc (DDE)	Abbreviations are spelled out the first time they are used.

A Note About Versions

The *Microsoft Word Developer's Kit* documents WordBasic as it is supported by the following versions of Microsoft Word:

- Microsoft Word version 7.0, which runs in Windows 95 and Windows NT™ version 3.51 or later.

- Microsoft Word version 6.0 for Windows, which runs in the Microsoft Windows family of operating systems: Windows version 3.1 or later, Windows for Workgroups version 3.1 or later, Windows 95, and Windows NT version 3.1 or later.

- Microsoft Word version 6.0 for the Macintosh, which runs in Apple Macintosh System 7 or later on any Apple Macintosh computer with at least a 68020 processor, or in System 7.5 or later on any Apple Power Macintosh™.

- Microsoft Word version 6.0 for Windows NT, which runs in Windows NT version 3.5 or later and Windows 95.

This book uses the phrases "in Windows" and "on the Macintosh" to describe behavior that differs across those platforms. The phrase "in Windows" refers to Word version 7.0, Word version 6.0 for Windows, and Word version 6.0 for Windows NT.

In a few cases, the phrase "in Windows 95" is used to describe behavior specific to Word version 7.0. Also, the phrase "in Windows NT" is used to describe behavior specific to Word version 6.0 for Windows NT. Behavior described with the phrase "in Windows 95" or "in Windows NT" does not occur in Word version 6.0 for Windows, even when it is running in Windows 95 or Windows NT.

PART 1

Learning WordBasic

CHAPTER 1

Introduction

Welcome to "Learning WordBasic." This part of the *Microsoft Word Developer's Kit* introduces the tools Word provides for writing and testing macros, the elements of the WordBasic language itself, and techniques useful for various tasks. This chapter provides a brief overview of the WordBasic macro language, some tips on how to approach learning WordBasic, a description of the sample files provided on the Microsoft Word Developer's Kit disk with instructions for loading them, and references to resources for additional information.

Features of WordBasic

WordBasic is a structured programming language originally modeled on the Microsoft QuickBasic™ language. It combines a subset of the instructions available in standard Basic languages with statements and functions based on the Word user interface. You can use WordBasic to modify any Word command or to write your own. You can assign your macros to menus, toolbars, and shortcut keys so that they look and function like regular Word commands.

WordBasic includes the following features for developing macros.

Macro-editing environment The macro editing environment includes tools for testing and debugging macros. For example, buttons on the Macro toolbar can step and trace through macros, show current variable values in a paused macro, and "comment out" instructions (Chapter 2, "Getting Started with Macros," and Chapter 6, "Debugging").

Control structures WordBasic supports most of the standard Basic control structures, including **If…Then…Else**, **For…Next**, **While…Wend**, and **Select Case** (Chapter 3, "WordBasic Fundamentals," and Chapter 4, "Advanced WordBasic").

Subroutines and user-defined functions By writing subroutines and defining functions, you can create modular code that is easy to test. You can also store libraries of subroutines and functions that can be used in more than one macro (Chapter 4, "Advanced WordBasic").

Dialog Editor You can use the Dialog Editor included with Word to design custom dialog boxes that support most of the standard dialog box controls in the Microsoft Windows family of operating systems and the Apple Macintosh System 7 operating system. The Dialog Editor automatically creates the WordBasic instructions that define your custom dialog box (Chapter 5, "Working with Custom Dialog Boxes").

DDE and OLE Automation To communicate with other applications, Word supports dynamic data exchange (DDE) and provides partial support for OLE Automation (Chapter 8, "Communicating with Other Applications").

Extensibility In Windows, you can extend WordBasic's capabilities by calling functions stored in dynamic-link libraries (DLLs) and Word add-in libraries (WLLs), as well as functions available through the Windows application programming interface (API). On the Macintosh, you can call functions stored in Word add-in libraries, and you can run AppleScript scripts from within WordBasic (Chapter 9, "More WordBasic Techniques").

Tips on How to Learn WordBasic

Here are some suggestions for getting the most from the time you spend learning WordBasic.

Learn Word first

The more you know about Word, the better prepared you will be to venture into WordBasic. Most macros perform a sequence of actions in Word, and most instructions in a macro are equivalent to commands or actions in Word. So working with WordBasic is a little like working with Word without a user interface; instead of commands and dialog boxes, you use WordBasic instructions. The statements and functions you use to write instructions are much easier to understand if you're familiar with the features of Word they represent.

Also, if you know Word well, you can better answer the question you're likely to ask when writing a macro: "What's the best way to do this?" People have been known to write long macros for tasks that could be handled by a single Word command.

Learn what you need

Learn what you need for the task at hand. WordBasic can seem overwhelming at first, particularly if you haven't had experience with a macro programming language. A great way to learn the language is to investigate how to implement a particular macro idea you have. As you gain experience writing different types of macros, you'll cover a lot of ground.

Use the macro recorder

The macro recorder can record the WordBasic instruction for virtually every action you take in Word. You can use the macro recorder to see how actions in Word translate into WordBasic instructions, and vice versa. Also, you'll find recording part of a macro is often faster and easier than writing out the instructions.

Use Help

Help is a powerful tool for learning WordBasic. In a macro-editing window, you can type a WordBasic instruction and press F1 (Windows), or HELP or COMMAND+/ (Macintosh), to immediately display the Help topic for that statement or function. The Help topic for most statements and functions includes an example you can copy and paste into your macro.

Read the first four chapters

After reading the first four chapters of "Learning WordBasic," you'll have a solid base from which to launch your macro explorations. The other chapters in "Learning WordBasic" provide information about WordBasic capabilities or techniques you may need for a particular application.

Sample Files

The Microsoft Word Developer's Kit disk includes several files that are referred to in "Learning WordBasic."

File	Description
EXAMPLES.DOT (MACRO EXAMPLES on the Macintosh disk)	A template containing the sample macros described in "Learning WordBasic."
INVOICE2.DOT (INVOICE FORM on the Macintosh disk)	The invoice form template described in Chapter 9, "More WordBasic Techniques."

File	Description
NWIND.XLS (NORTHWIND DATABASE on the Macintosh disk)	A Microsoft Excel workbook used by the invoice form described in Chapter 9, "More WordBasic Techniques."
POSITION.TXT (not available on the Macintosh disk)	A text file that lists the order of arguments for WordBasic statements and functions. This file is useful if you are using a Visual Basic® version 3.0 application to send WordBasic instructions through OLE Automation. For more information about using OLE Automation with Word, see "Using OLE Automation" in Chapter 8, "Communicating with Other Applications."
STARTER.WIZ (STARTER WIZARD on the Macintosh disk)	A blank wizard that contains the routines shared by all Word wizards, as described in Chapter 9, "More WordBasic Techniques."
MKWIZARD.WIZ (WIZARD MAKER WIZARD on the Macintosh disk)	A wizard that makes a wizard according to your specifications.
WIN16API.TXT and WIN32API.TXT (not available on the Macintosh disk)	A text file containing prewritten **Declare** instructions for calling Windows application programming interface (API) functions from WordBasic; for more information about using Windows API functions, see "Calling Routines in DLLs" in Chapter 9, "More WordBasic Techniques."

Loading the Sample Files

The sample files referred to in "Learning WordBasic" are located in the WRDBASIC folder on the Windows disk and the WORDBASIC folder on the Macintosh disk. To use them, you need to copy the files to your hard disk.

Windows

- Copy the templates (EXAMPLES.DOT and INVOICE2.DOT) and wizards (STARTER.WIZ and MKWIZARD.WIZ) into your template folder, which is the path specified for User Templates on the File Locations tab in the Options dialog box (Tools menu).
- Copy the database file NWIND.XLS into your Microsoft Excel program folder. If you have not installed Microsoft Excel, you cannot use this file.
- Copy POSITION.TXT, WIN16API.TXT, and WIN32API.TXT into your document folder.

Macintosh

- Copy the templates (MACRO EXAMPLES and INVOICE FORM) and wizards (STARTER WIZARD and WIZARD MAKER WIZARD) into your template folder, which is the folder specified for User Templates on the File Locations tab in the Options dialog box (Tools menu).

- Copy the database file NORTHWIND DATABASE into your Microsoft Excel program folder. If you have not installed Microsoft Excel, you cannot use this file.

Accessing the Macro Examples

To run the macros in the EXAMPLES.DOT template (Windows) or MACRO EXAMPLES template (Macintosh), you can use the Templates command (File menu) to load the template as a global template. When the template is loaded as a global template, you can use the Macro command (Tools menu) to run the macros. You can also use the Organizer dialog box (Macro command, Tools menu) to copy the macros to another template. To view or edit the macros, you can open the template directly or copy the macros to another open template, and then use the Macro command (Tools menu) to open a macro in a macro-editing window.

Other Resources

The resources described in this section provide additional information about Word macros and programming with WordBasic.

Microsoft Product Support Services

Microsoft offers a variety of support options to help you get the most from your Microsoft product. For more information about Microsoft Product Support Services, see "Technical Support" in Help.

If you have questions concerning programming techniques and solutions, refer to the following electronic services. These services are available 24 hours a day, 7 days a week, including holidays.

The Microsoft Network In Word version 7.0, you can use The Microsoft Network™ to interact with other users or access the Microsoft Knowledge Base to get product information. From the Help menu, choose The Microsoft Network. Select where you want to go, and then choose Connect.

CompuServe, America Online, and GEnie The Microsoft Knowledge Base (KB) and Microsoft Software Library (MSL) are available on the CompuServe®, America Online®, and GEnie™ information services. CompuServe also hosts Microsoft forums where you can interact with other users and Microsoft support personnel.

Service	Access
CompuServe	To access the Microsoft Knowledge Base, type **go mskb** at any ! prompt.
	To access the Microsoft Software Library, type **go msl** at any ! prompt.
	To access Microsoft forums, type **go microsoft** at any ! prompt.
America Online	To access the Microsoft Knowledge Base, click Keyword on the Go To menu, type **microsoft** in the Enter Word(s) box, and then click Go. In the Microsoft Resource Center, click Knowledge Base.
GEnie	To access the Microsoft Knowledge Base, type **m505** at the GEnie system prompt.

Internet

Access the Microsoft Software Library (MSL) and the Microsoft Knowledge Base (KB) at any of the following Internet sites:

- Microsoft World Wide Web site, located at www.microsoft.com
- Microsoft Gopher site, located at gopher.microsoft.com
- Microsoft FTP site (which supports anonymous logon), located at ftp.microsoft.com

The KB at the World Wide Web and Gopher sites provides full-text searches and automatic links to files on the MSL so you can download files directly from KB articles.

Microsoft Download Service (206) 936-6735 via modem. Access the Driver Library and the most current technical notes (1200, 2400, 9600, or 14,400 baud; no parity; 8 data bits; 1 stop bit).

Product Training and Consultation

Microsoft Solution Providers are independent organizations that provide consulting, integration, customization, development, technical support and training, and other services for Microsoft products. These companies are called Solution Providers because they apply technology and provide services to help solve real-world problems.

To find out more about Microsoft Solution Providers:

- In the United States and Canada, call 1-800-SOL-PROV between 6:30 A.M. and 5:30 P.M. Pacific time, Monday through Friday, excluding holidays.

- Outside North America, contact your local Microsoft office.

Books

Learn Basic Now, Michael Halvorson and David Rygmyr (Microsoft Press®, 1989) and *Learn Basic for the Apple Macintosh Now,* Michael Halvorson and David Rygmyr (Microsoft Press, 1990). If you have little or no experience with a programming language, these books may be a helpful starting point. They use the Microsoft QuickBasic programming language, on which WordBasic was modeled. ISBN 155615240X and ISBN 1556153147

Hacker's Guide to Word for Windows (2nd ed.), Woody Leonhard, Vincent Chen, and Scott Krueger (Addison-Wesley Publishing Company, 1994). An insider's guide to Word and WordBasic. ISBN 0201407639

C H A P T E R   2

Getting Started with Macros

This chapter introduces the tools you need to create macros: the macro recorder and the macro-editing window. The macro recorder provides an easy way to record simple, "playback" macros and to start building more complex ones. The macro-editing window is a window with special capabilities for writing, editing, and testing macros in the Word macro language, WordBasic. This chapter includes a series of practices in which you record and then edit a very simple macro that applies bold and italic formatting.

The chapter goes on to discuss the relationship between macros and templates and how to store macros. Finally, the last two sections discuss modifying Word commands and creating "auto" macros that run automatically in response to such actions as creating a new document.

In this chapter:

- Recording a macro
- Running a macro
- Editing a macro
- Macros and templates

- Saving a macro
- Macro housekeeping
- Modifying a Word command
- Auto macros

Recording a Macro

You can create a macro by recording it with the macro recorder, writing it in WordBasic, or both. For many macros, even complex ones, a good technique is to start by recording as much of the macro as possible and then finish by writing the parts of the macro that can't be recorded.

Starting the Recording

To begin recording a macro, choose the Macro command from the Tools menu and then choose the Record button in the Macro dialog box, or simply double-click "REC" on the status bar. Word displays the Record Macro dialog box, in which you can name, describe, and assign the macro you are about to record.

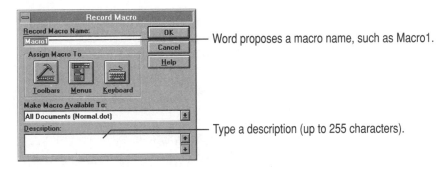

Word proposes a macro name, such as Macro1.

Type a description (up to 255 characters).

The Record Macro dialog box

Word provides two ways to identify macros: the macro name and its description text. Although you may be tempted to accept the macro name that Word proposes, and get on with recording your macro, it's a good idea to get into the habit of giving meaningful names to macros right away. A macro with a descriptive name is easy to identify. Macro names cannot include spaces, commas, or periods. If you want to include two or more words together in a macro name, you can begin each word with a capital letter to make the name easy to read. For example, "TransposeCharacters" or "OpenSalesReport" are readable macro names. If you assign a macro to a toolbar button, the macro name is displayed in a ToolTip when the mouse pointer is positioned over the toolbar button. When a macro name is displayed in a ToolTip, a space is placed before capital letters; for example, the ToolTip for a macro named "OpenSalesReport" would be "Open Sales Report."

It's also worth taking the time to write a short description in the Description box. As you accumulate macros over time, you may find it difficult to remember what each one does. A macro description provides a helpful reminder. If you assign a macro to a menu or to a toolbar button, its description appears in the status bar when you select the menu item or position the mouse pointer over the toolbar button. A macro description can be up to 255 characters long, although only about 100 characters appear on most status bars (the length of the status bar depends on screen resolution).

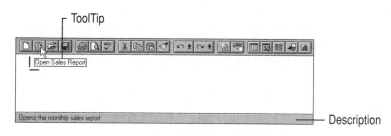

ToolTip

Description

When you position the mouse pointer over a toolbar button
assigned to a macro, the macro name is displayed in a ToolTip
and the macro description appears in the status bar.

By default, macros you record are stored in the Normal template. If a different
template is attached to the active document, you can also store a macro in that
template. For more information on storing macros in different templates, see
"Macros and Templates" later in this chapter.

▶ **To start recording the BoldItalic macro**

The BoldItalic macro, a macro that applies bold and italic formatting to a
selection, is the practice macro you will create in this chapter. Of course, you can
easily apply bold and italic separately by pressing CTRL+B and CTRL+I (Windows)
or COMMAND+B and COMMAND+I (Macintosh). But if you often format text as
bold italic, it's convenient to have a quick way to apply both formats at once.

1. Do one of the following:
    - From the Tools menu, choose Macro, and then choose the Record button.
    - Double-click "REC" on the status bar.
2. In the Record Macro Name box, type **BoldItalic**.
3. In the Description box, type **Applies bold and italic formatting to selected
    text**.

The next step is to assign the BoldItalic macro to a shortcut key. This procedure is
described in the next section.

Assigning the Macro

Even before you begin to record your macro, you can assign it to a menu, toolbar,
or shortcut key. You could wait until after you've recorded it, but if you assign
the macro right away, you can try it out after you've finished recording. Also,
fewer steps are needed to assign it at this point. If the macro you're recording
doesn't work out, you can easily delete it; any assignments you've made for it are
removed also.

There are advantages and disadvantages to each kind of assignment. A menu item provides the highest visibility, but menus have limited space. A toolbar button is slightly more accessible than a menu item, but its purpose is less obvious. A shortcut key is hidden, but provides the quickest access.

▶ **To assign the BoldItalic macro to a shortcut key**

Because the BoldItalic macro is a short macro that must run quickly to be worth running at all, it makes sense to assign it to a shortcut key for quick access.

1. In the Record Macro dialog box, choose the Keyboard button.

   Word displays the Customize dialog box with the BoldItalic macro name selected.

2. Position the insertion point in the Press New Shortcut Key box, and do one of the following:

   - In Windows, press CTRL+SHIFT+B.

   - On the Macintosh, press COMMAND+SHIFT+B.

3. Choose the Assign button.

   By default, this duplicate shortcut key was assigned to the Bold command. When you choose the Assign button, the shortcut key is assigned to the BoldItalic macro. Later, if you remove this assignment, the shortcut key will be reassigned to the Bold command.

4. Choose the Close button.

Now you're ready to take the actions you want the macro recorder to record. This procedure is described in the next section.

Press a shortcut key for the macro.

The Customize dialog box

Recording the Macro Actions

When you've named your macro and assigned it, you're ready to begin recording. After you close the Record Macro dialog box, the macro recorder records every action you take in Word until you turn the recorder off.

When the macro recorder is on, the Macro Record toolbar is displayed. It contains the Stop and Pause buttons, which you can use to stop and pause the macro recorder. If you click the Pause button to pause the recorder—perhaps to arrange something for your macro that you didn't set up in advance—the button remains in the down position. You can click it again to resume recording.

When the macro recorder is on, a recorder graphic attaches to the mouse pointer when it is positioned over a document window. In addition, the abbreviation "REC" (for "record") is highlighted in the status bar. You can double-click it to stop recording. (When the macro recorder is not on, you can double-click "REC" to start recording.)

When you stop recording, the Macro Record toolbar disappears automatically.

Here are a few things to be aware of when you're recording macros:

- You can use the mouse to choose commands or click the scroll bar, but you can't use the mouse to move the insertion point or select text in your document. The macro recorder does not record mouse movements in a document window.

- If you choose the Cancel button to dismiss a dialog box, Word does not record the command.

- If you use the BACKSPACE key (Windows) or the DELETE key (Macintosh) when you're typing, Word does not record the characters you delete or the backspacing action. In other words, it's as if you had never typed those characters.

- Word cannot record the following: printer setup options specific to a particular printer, document statistics, and any actions taken from the Find File dialog box (File menu) after the first search.

▶ **To record the actions of the BoldItalic macro**

1. From the Format menu, choose Font. In the Font dialog box, select Bold Italic in the Font Style list, and then choose OK.

2. Click the Stop button on the Macro Record toolbar.

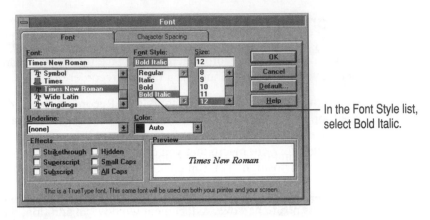

In the Font Style list,
select Bold Italic.

The Font dialog box

Running a Macro

You can run macros using the Macro dialog box (Tools menu), or you can run
them using menu, toolbar, and shortcut key assignments. To use the Macro dialog
box to run a macro, select the one you want to run, and then choose the Run
button.

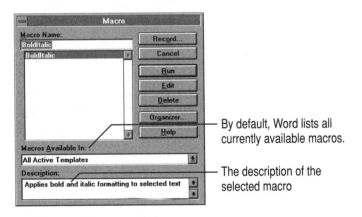

By default, Word lists all
currently available macros.

The description of the
selected macro

The Macro dialog box

The list of macros displayed depends on the setting in the Macros Available In
box. By default, the list shows all available macros, which includes the macros
stored in the Normal template and any other open templates. If you choose, you
can list just the macros stored in a particular template. You can also list all the
built-in Word commands. If you have removed a macro or Word command from
its menu, toolbar, or shortcut key assignment, you can still run it using the Macro
dialog box.

Because you've already assigned the BoldItalic macro to a key combination, there's no need to use the Macro dialog box; you can run the macro directly from your document.

▶ **To run the BoldItalic macro**

1. Select some text in a document.

2. Press CTRL+SHIFT+B (Windows) or COMMAND+SHIFT+B (Macintosh).

The bold and italic formats are applied.

When you select text and run the BoldItalic macro ..

the bold and italic formats are appliod.

Now try an experiment. With the text still selected, choose Undo from the Edit menu. Apply a different font to the selection, and then press the shortcut keys assigned to the BoldItalic macro (CTRL+SHIFT+B in Windows; COMMAND+SHIFT+B on the Macintosh).

When you change the font and run the BoldItalic macro again ...

the font returns to the font the text had when the macro was recorded

Notice that the font changes back to whichever font the text had when you recorded the macro. This happens because the macro recorder records all the settings in a dialog box when it records a command. In this case, it recorded the current font when you recorded the macro, so now when you run the macro, it applies that font to the selected text.

What you want the macro to do is just apply bold and italic formatting and ignore any other character formatting. To achieve this result, you need to edit the macro. This process is described in the next section, "Editing a Macro."

Other Ways to Run Macros

You can run macros in several other ways, most of them in response to specific events that can trigger macros.

- The command line. In Windows, you can add the name of a macro to the Word command line so that the macro will run when Word starts. You can modify the Word command line by selecting the Word icon in Program Manager (Windows 3.x and Windows NT) or the Word shortcut icon in the Programs subfolder in the Start Menu folder (Windows 95) and choosing the Properties command from the File menu. Here is the syntax for starting a macro using the command line:

   winword /**m***MacroName*

   MacroName is the name of the macro that runs when Word starts. Each icon in Program Manager or shortcut icon on the Start Menu can have a different command line, so you can create different Word icons that launch different macros when Word starts.

   The Macintosh does not provide a command line, but you can use the Word Settings (6) file to designate a macro to run when Word starts. You can access this file through the ToolsAdvancedSettings command. (To run the command, select ToolsAdvancedSettings from the list of Word commands in the Macro dialog box (Tools menu), and then choose the Run button.) In the Advanced Settings dialog box, select Microsoft Word from the Categories list, and then type **WordSwitches** in the Option box; in the Setting box, type /**m***MacroName* where *MacroName* is the name of the macro to run when Word starts. Then choose the Set button.

- Auto macros. Auto macros are macros that run automatically when you create a new document, open an existing document, and so on. For more information, see "Auto Macros" later in this chapter.

- MACROBUTTON fields. These fields launch macros when they are double-clicked, and can be inserted anywhere in a document.

- Form fields. A form field can trigger a macro when the field is selected ("on entry") and after it has been modified ("on exit"). For information on running macros from form fields, see "Automating Forms" in Chapter 9, "More WordBasic Techniques."

Editing a Macro

You can edit an existing macro or write a new macro from scratch using a macro-editing window. Macro-editing windows have several special properties:

- The Macro toolbar is displayed whenever you open a macro-editing window. This toolbar provides quick access to several commands for running and testing macros.

- When you run a macro in the macro-editing window, Word highlights any line containing certain kinds of errors.

- You can position the insertion point on a line containing a WordBasic instruction and get Help for that instruction by pressing F1 (Windows), or HELP or COMMAND+/ (Macintosh).

- Formatting is controlled by the Macro Text style. You can use this style to set character and paragraph formatting for text in all macro-editing windows.

To begin writing a new macro, choose Macro from the Tools menu, type a name for the macro in the Macro Name box, and then choose the Create button.

A new macro-editing window

When the macro-editing window appears, the instructions Sub MAIN and End Sub (between which all the other instructions must appear) are already on the screen with the insertion point positioned between them.

To open and edit an existing macro, select the one you want to edit from the list of macros in the Macro dialog box, and then choose the Edit button (the Create button becomes the Edit button when an existing macro is selected).

▶ **To open the BoldItalic macro for editing**

- From the Tools menu, choose the Macro command. Then select the BoldItalic macro and choose the Edit button.

Examining the Macro

The Word macro recorder does not record keystrokes, as some macro recorders do; it records *actions*, which are translated into the Word macro language, WordBasic. So when you open a recorded macro in the macro-editing window, the window displays a series of WordBasic instructions.

```
BoldItalic
Sub MAIN
FormatFont .Points = "12", .Underline = 0, .Color = 0, .Strikeout = 0, .Superscript = 0, .Subscript = 0,
.Hidden = 0, .SmallCaps = 0, .AllCaps = 0, .Spacing = "0 pt", .Position = "0 pt", .Kerning = 0,
.KerningMin = "", .Tab = "0", .Font = "Times New Roman", .Bold = 1, .Italic = 1
End Sub
```

The BoldItalic macro-editing window

Consider the text of the BoldItalic macro, beginning with Sub MAIN and ending with End Sub. These two statements begin and end every WordBasic macro. "Sub" stands for *subroutine*, which is a subsection of a larger program. The larger program in this case is Word itself. From the perspective of WordBasic, a macro is a small task within a larger task—the task of running Word. "MAIN" indicates that this is the main subroutine of the macro. In the case of the BoldItalic macro, it's also the only subroutine in the macro.

Now consider the lines sandwiched between Sub MAIN and End Sub:

```
FormatFont .Points = "12", .Underline = 0, .Color = 0, .Strikethrough =
0, .Superscript = 0, .Subscript = 0, .Hidden = 0, .SmallCaps = 0,
.AllCaps = 0, .Spacing = "0 pt", .Position = "0 pt", .Kerning = 0,
.KerningMin = "", .Tab = "0", .Font = "Times New Roman", .Bold = 1,
.Italic = 1
```

These lines form a single *statement,* the **FormatFont** statement. A statement is a WordBasic instruction that tells the macro to do something. The **FormatFont** statement corresponds to the Font dialog box (Format menu). Each word in the statement that begins with a period corresponds to an option in the dialog box. These words, such as .Points, .Strikethrough, and .Hidden, are called *arguments* —they qualify the statement. (Note that if you recorded your macro on the Macintosh, the **FormatFont** statement includes two additional arguments— .Outline and .Shadow—that are valid only on the Macintosh.)

Every argument in a statement has a *value*, which corresponds to the setting of the option in the dialog box. For example, the Font dialog box contains several check boxes which can be either selected or cleared. Likewise, the WordBasic arguments that correspond to those check boxes can have one of two values. If the Strikethrough check box is selected, for example, the WordBasic argument would read .Strikethrough = 1. If the check box were not selected, the argument would read .Strikethrough = 0.

Editing the BoldItalic Macro

The BoldItalic macro you recorded earlier in this chapter didn't work properly as it was recorded. The only thing you wanted the macro to do was apply bold and italic formatting. Unfortunately, it also applied other character formats such as font and font size. With the macro open in a macro-editing window, you can correct that problem by removing the irrelevant arguments from the **FormatFont** statement.

▶ **To edit the FormatFont statement**

- With the macro open in a macro-editing window, select and delete every argument except .Bold and .Italic.

The edited BoldItalic macro should look like this:

```
Sub MAIN
FormatFont .Bold = 1, .Italic = 1
End Sub
```

Getting Help on WordBasic

In a macro-editing window, you can immediately get reference information about any WordBasic instruction by positioning the insertion point on the same line as the instruction and pressing F1 (Windows), or HELP or COMMAND+/ (Macintosh).

▶ **To get Help for the FormatFont statement**

- Position the insertion point anywhere in the **FormatFont** statement, and then press F1 (Windows), or HELP or COMMAND+/ (Macintosh).

Position the insertion point in the statement ...

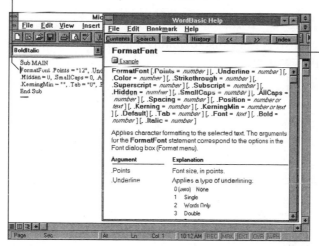

and then press F1 (Windows), or SHIFT or COMMAND+\ (Macintosh), to access Help on that statement.

For many WordBasic instructions, Help provides examples you can copy. You can click Example in the Help topic to display the examples. You can choose the Copy button (Word version 6.0) or choose Copy from the shortcut menu (Word version 7.0) in the example window to copy the text of the code example onto the Clipboard. You can then paste the example into your own macro or document.

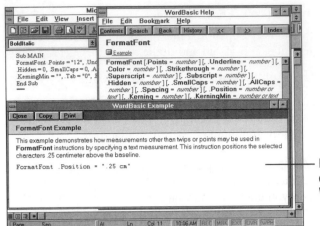

In Windows, WordBasic Help examples are displayed in he WordBasic Example window

You can also use the Help menu in Word to access Help topics about WordBasic. Help provides a language summary that groups WordBasic statements and functions by category, as well as information on predefined bookmarks and error messages. All the reference information contained in Part 2, "WordBasic Reference," is available in Help.

The Macro Toolbar

Whenever you open a macro-editing window, the Macro toolbar is displayed, if it isn't displayed already.

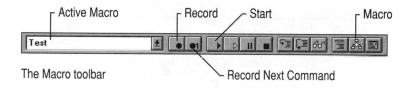

The Macro toolbar

Many of the buttons on the toolbar are used for testing, but several of the buttons can be used for running and recording macros:

Active Macro   This box lists the macros open in macro-editing windows. If more than one macro is open, you can use the Active Macro box to select which macro runs when you click the Start button.

Record   Displays the Record Macro dialog box, so that you can begin recording a macro.

Record Next Command   Records a single command or action in Word and inserts the resulting WordBasic instruction in the active macro-editing window (or the most recently active one, if a document window is active). For more information, see "The Record Next Command Button" later in this section.

Start   Runs the macro selected in the Active Macro box. By default, this is the macro in the active macro-editing window (or the most recently active one, if a document window is active).

Macro   Displays the Macro dialog box. Clicking this button is a shortcut for choosing the Macro command from the Tools menu.

For information on the Trace, Continue, Stop, Step, Step Subs, Show Variables, and Add/Remove REM buttons, see Chapter 6, "Debugging." For information on the Dialog Editor button, see Chapter 5, "Working with Custom Dialog Boxes."

Running the Macro from the Macro-Editing Window

You can use the Start button on the Macro toolbar to run the macro in the active macro-editing window. Some macros, however, will not run unless a document window is active. For example, if you run the BoldItalic macro when its macro-editing window is active, an error occurs, because the Font command (Format menu) is not available when a macro-editing window is active.

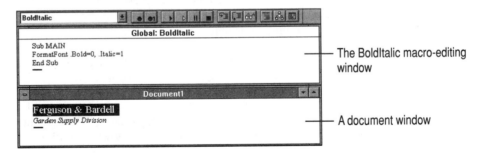

Running the BoldItalic macro from a macro-editing window produces an error.

If you browse through the menus when a macro-editing window is active, you can see that many commands are unavailable—they are commands for tasks that aren't useful for editing macros.

If you have a document window open in addition to a macro-editing window, you can choose the Arrange All command from the Window menu to display both the document window and the macro-editing window. To run the BoldItalic macro now, you can just click in the document window to make it active, and then click the Start button on the Macro toolbar.

The BoldItalic macro-editing window

A document window

Error Checking in the Macro-Editing Window

Whenever you run a macro, Word automatically checks the *syntax* of each WordBasic command. In programming, syntax refers to the rules governing the spelling of arguments, the number of arguments, and so on. Word also checks to make sure the arguments have appropriate values. If a macro-editing window is open and Word discovers an instruction with a problem, it highlights the instruction and presents an error message.

To see how Word identifies syntax errors, you can alter the syntax of the BoldItalic macro. Try deleting the comma between the .Bold and .Italic arguments so that the **FormatFont** statement looks like the following:

```
FormatFont .Bold = 1 .Italic = 1
```

Now try running the macro.

```
BoldItalic                    ● ●|  |▶ ▷ || ■  ⬚⬚⬚⬚ ⬚⬚ ⬚
                    Global: BoldItalic
Sub MAIN
FormatFont .Bold = 0 .Italic = 1
End Sub
```

When WordBasic encounters a syntax error, it displays an error
message box.

Another common error is to type an argument without the period in front of it.
It's easy to make these errors, but by highlighting the line containing the error,
the macro-editing window helps you find them.

The Macro Text Style

The Macro Text style determines the formatting of text in macro-editing
windows. You can't apply direct formatting to text in a macro-editing window,
but you can modify the Macro Text style. The Macro Text style is a special style
that is stored in the Normal template. It affects every macro-editing window,
regardless of whether the macro displayed in a macro-editing window is stored
in the Normal template or in another template.

You use the Style command (Format menu) to modify the Macro Text style.
A document window must be active when you choose the Style command;
you cannot choose the Style command when a macro window is active.

Note   When you modify the Macro Text style, Word updates the style definition
displayed in the Style dialog box (Format menu) only for the document that is
active and for the Normal template. This means that when other documents and
documents based on other templates are active, the Macro Text style definition
displayed in the Style dialog box may not be current.

To find out the current, correct style definition of Macro Text, create a document
based on the Normal template. Choose Style from the Format menu, and then
select the Macro Text style in the Styles list (if necessary, select All Styles in the
List box to see the Macro Text style in the Styles list); the Description box will
show the current style definition.

View Options for Macro-Editing Windows

You can use the View tab in the Options dialog box to set view options for macro-editing windows. View options you set for macro-editing windows do not affect view options for document windows. For example, you can hide the status bar in macro-editing windows but not in document windows.

The Record Next Command Button

Sometimes, you want to record one or two commands to insert into an existing macro you're working on, but you don't want to record a new macro. The Record Next Command button on the Macro toolbar provides this capability. When you have a macro-editing window open, you can use the Record Next Command button to record the next Word command you choose or action you take (such as scrolling through a document). Word inserts the equivalent WordBasic instruction at the insertion point in the macro-editing window.

If a macro window is active and you want to record a command that isn't available in macro-editing windows, switch to a document window before clicking the Record Next Command button. If you click the Record Next Command button and then switch to a document window, Word will record your switching windows rather than the command you want to record.

Stopping or Pausing a Macro

When a macro is running, you can stop or pause it by pressing the ESC key. Word displays a message stating that the macro was interrupted. If the macro is open in a macro-editing window, you can click the Continue button on the Macro toolbar to continue running the macro, or you can press the ESC key again or click the Stop button on the Macro toolbar to stop the macro. If the macro is not open in a macro-editing window when you press the ESC key, Word simply stops the macro.

Macros and Templates

Word stores macros in templates, just as it does styles and AutoText entries. When you create a new macro, it is stored by default in the Normal template and is available "globally"—that is, you can always run or edit the macro, even if the active document is based on a different template. When you store a macro in a template other than the Normal template, you can run or edit it only when the template itself or a document based on the template is the active document.

Whether or not a macro stored in a template other than Normal is available depends on which document is active. For example, if you choose the Macro command when a document attached to a template other than Normal is active, any macros stored in that template, as well macros stored in the Normal template, are available in the list of macros. But if you switch to a document attached to the Normal template and choose the Macro command again, the macros stored in the other template are not listed.

The same holds true for new macros that you create. To store a new macro in a given template, either the template itself or a document attached to the template must be active when you create the macro:

- If you are creating a new macro using the Macro dialog box, you select the appropriate template name in the Macros Available In box and then choose the Create button to open a new macro-editing window.

- If you are recording a new macro, you select the appropriate template name in the Make Macro Available To box in the Macro Record dialog box.

Neither the Normal template nor a document based on the Normal template needs to be active to store new macros globally. You can store new macros in the Normal template even if no documents attached to the Normal template are open.

Note that you choose which template to store a macro in when you create it, rather than when you first save it. Once you've stored a macro in a particular template, you can use the Organizer dialog box to move or copy it to another template. For more information, see "Macro Housekeeping" later in this chapter.

When you open a macro, notice that the title of the macro-editing window includes either the name of the template in which the macro is stored or "Global" if the macro is stored in the Normal template.

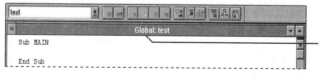

"Global" in the title bar indicates the macro is stored in the Normal template.

Why Store Macros in Different Templates?

Since macros stored in the Normal template are always available and macros stored in other templates are less widely available, you might wonder about the advantages of storing macros in other templates.

One advantage is that macros designed to work with a particular type of document can be stored in the template used to produce that document. Another reason to store macros in different templates is that the Normal template can get crowded. The more macro instructions you store in Normal, the longer it takes to save the template. You won't notice a difference if you have ten or twenty macros stored in Normal, but as you add macros, Normal will gradually take longer to save.

Together, macros and templates can be used to create a Word "application"—a highly customized version of Word designed to accomplish a particular task or set of tasks. For example, a group of macros and templates could be designed to automate the creation of forms and other documents a company uses. Because the macros used in the application are stored within one or more custom templates, the application is relatively simple to distribute; it's just a matter of copying the templates. If the application's macros were stored in the Normal template, it would be much more complicated to install the application on another machine, which already has its own Normal template.

Making Templates Global

Sometimes it's useful to make a macro or set of macros available temporarily. For example, you may create a set of macros for a task you perform only occasionally. Rather than storing them in the Normal template, you can store them in another template and load that template as a global template when you want to run them.

You use the Templates command (File menu) to load templates as global templates. You can also store a template in the Startup folder (specified on the File Locations tab in the Options dialog box (Tools menu)) to load it automatically as a global template each time you start Word. When a template is loaded globally, its macros become available in the same way macros stored in the Normal template are available. A document based on a loaded global template doesn't need to be active for you to run the macros stored there.

One important difference between loaded global templates and the Normal template, however, is that you cannot edit macros or add new ones to a global template. In effect, a global template is available on a read-only basis.

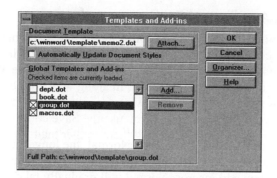

The Templates And Add-ins dialog box

Priority Among Templates

In the case of a naming conflict (that is, when you select a macro to run when more than one macro with the same name is stored in the available templates), macros stored in the template attached to the active document have priority over other macros. Next in priority are macros stored in the Normal template. Lowest in priority are the macros stored in other global templates (assuming global templates are loaded); priority among other global templates is determined by the alphabetical order of the template names.

Naming conflicts occur most often with "auto" macros, specially named macros that run automatically (for example, when a document is created or opened). For more information on auto macros, see "Auto Macros" later in this chapter.

Naming conflicts may also arise if you modify Word commands. For more information, see "Modifying a Word Command" later in this chapter.

Saving a Macro

When a macro-editing window is active, the Save and Save As commands on the File menu change to the Save Template and Save Copy As commands.

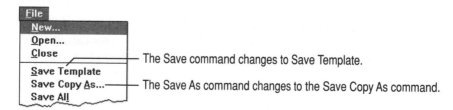

The Save command changes to Save Template.

The Save As command changes to the Save Copy As command.

Using the Save Template Command

You can think of the Save Template command as the "save macros" command—that's what the command is designed to do and why it's available only when a macro-editing window is active. The command is called Save Template because it saves the templates the macros are stored in along with all the other items stored in there, such as autotext entries and styles. Use the Save Template command to save macros as you edit them, just as you use the Save command to save documents as you're writing or revising them, rather than waiting until your work is completed.

Using the Save Copy As Command

The Save Copy As command is designed to make it easy to save a macro as a text file, which is useful if you want to store macros apart from the template. When you choose the Save Copy As command, Word displays the Save As dialog box. In Windows, Word proposes the macro name with a .TXT extension as the filename. On the Macintosh, Word proposes the macro name alone as the filename. In either case, you can change the name Word proposes and even select a different file format if you want to.

Macro Housekeeping

Macro housekeeping includes renaming, copying, moving, and deleting macros. You can use the Organizer dialog box for all these tasks. To display the Organizer dialog box, choose Macro from the Tools menu, and then choose the Organizer button. If the templates you want to work with are not open, you can use the Open File buttons to open them.

The Organizer dialog box

You can select more than one macro to copy or delete in the Organizer dialog box. To select a series of macros, hold down SHIFT and click the first and last items in the series. To select individual macros, hold down CTRL (Windows) or COMMAND (Macintosh) and click each item.

Modifying a Word Command

You can modify most Word commands by turning them into macros. For example, you can modify the Open command on the File menu so that instead of displaying a list of Word document files (in Windows, files ending with the .DOC filename extension), Word displays every file in the current folder.

To display the list of built-in Word commands in the Macro dialog box, you select Word Commands in the Macros Available In box. Every menu command and every command available on a toolbar or through shortcut keys is listed. Menu commands begin with the menu name associated with the command. For example, the Save command on the File menu is listed as FileSave. This is the same convention used by WordBasic statements. The WordBasic statement equivalent to the Save command, for example, is **FileSave**.

You can run any one of these commands by selecting it and choosing the Run button in the Macro dialog box. For example, if you select the FileSave command and choose the Run button, Word saves the current document, just as if you had chosen Save from the File menu.

When Word Commands is selected in the Macros Available In box, the Create button is disabled.

The list of Word commands in the Macro dialog box

Note, however, that the Create button is disabled when Word Commands is selected in the Macros Available In box. You cannot edit the commands themselves, but by giving a macro the same name as a Word command, you can replace the Word command with a macro. Then, whenever you choose the Word command using a menu, toolbar, or shortcut keys, Word runs the replacement macro instead. For example, if you create a macro called FileSave, Word runs this macro when you choose the Save command from the File menu, click the Save button on the Standard toolbar, or press CTRL+S (Windows) or COMMAND+S (Macintosh).

To replace a Word command, you can either type its name in the Macro Name box or select it from the list of Word commands. You then select the template in which you would like to store the macro that replaces the command—either the Normal template or the one attached to the active document—and choose the Create button. Word displays a macro-editing window for the new macro.

An Example

This example takes you through the steps needed to modify the Close command on the File menu. In this example, you'll store the macro that replaces the FileClose command in the Normal template, so that the command will be modified globally—that is, for every document.

▶   **To modify the FileClose command**

1. From the Tools menu, choose Macro.

2. In the Macros Available In box, select Word Commands.

3. In the Macro Name box, select FileClose.

4. In the Macros Available In box, select either Normal.dot (Global Template) in Windows or Normal (Global Template) on the Macintosh.

5. Choose the Create button.

The FileClose macro now appears in a macro-editing window.

```
FileClose
    Sub MAIN
    FileClose
    End Sub
```

The FileClose macro, which replaces the Close command on the
File menu

As the previous illustration shows, Word automatically inserts the instruction
FileClose in the new macro. Any macro with the same name as a Word command
initially contains one or more lines that run the Word command the macro
replaces. (The macro also inherits the Word command's description, which
appears in the Description box in the Macro dialog box.)

You can edit the new macro in many ways. For example, you could add a
FileSave instruction:

```
Sub MAIN
    FileSave
    FileClose
End Sub
```

To test the new command, open an existing document, change it in some way, and
then close it (using the Close command on the File menu). The original Word
command would prompt you to save your document if it contained any unsaved
changes. The new macro avoids that prompt by saving changes automatically.

Note that you could remove the **FileClose** instruction from the macro if you
wanted to:

```
Sub MAIN
    MsgBox "Sorry, the Close command is disabled."
End Sub
```

Now, when you choose the Close command, Word does not close the document
window, but displays the following message box.

```
        Microsoft Word
Sorry, the Close command is disabled.

            OK
```

In fact, you could remove every instruction from the macro, so that only `Sub MAIN` and `End Sub` remain:

```
Sub MAIN
End Sub
```

Now, when you choose the Close command, nothing happens at all. In this way, you can not only modify Word commands but disable them. Disabling commands can be useful if you are creating an environment for a particular kind of document and don't want the user to be able to run certain commands. (Note that you can also disable a Word command by removing it from its menu, toolbar, and shortcut key assignments.)

If you want to run a modified command in another macro, you use a **ToolsMacro** instruction to run the macro that replaces the original command. For example, to run the FileClose macro, you would use the following instruction:

```
ToolsMacro .Name = "FileClose", .Run
```

Note that you could not include this instruction inside the FileClose macro, because Word does not allow a macro to run itself.

Modifying Commands that Display Dialog Boxes

To modify commands that display dialog boxes (the Open command on the File menu, for example), it's helpful to understand how to work with dialog records. For information on dialog records and modifying commands that display dialog boxes, see "Working with Dialog Records" in Chapter 4, "Advanced WordBasic."

Restoring a Modified Command

Since modifying a Word command involves creating a macro with the same name as the command you want to modify, globally restoring an original Word command is simply a matter of deleting or renaming the macro that replaced it in the active or Normal template.

In other cases, you might want to modify a command globally, but restore the original command for a particular template. For example, you could modify the Open command on the File menu (FileOpen) so that it lists every file in a folder instead of just the Word document files. But perhaps a particular template only uses Word document files. It would make sense to restore the original Open command for that template.

To restore an original Word command only for a particular template, you create a second replacement macro that overrides the replacement macro stored in the Normal template. This second replacement macro just runs the original Word command. To create this replacement macro, you follow the same steps used to create the first replacement macro: specify the command you want to restore from the list of Word commands, select the template name in the Macros Available In box, and then choose the Create button to create the new macro.

The trick to this procedure is that even though you don't want to modify the command, *you must still make some change to the second replacement macro.* Otherwise, Word will not save it when you close it. You can simply add a space to the command and delete the space. This action "dirties" the macro so that Word will save it when you choose the Save Template command or close the macro-editing window. The requirement that you change the macro in some way is a safeguard to prevent you from opening a macro and replacing a Word command without intending to.

Auto Macros

Word recognizes the following five macro names that run automatically.

Macro name	When it runs
AutoExec	When you start Word
AutoNew	Each time you create a new document
AutoOpen	Each time you open an existing document
AutoClose	Each time you close a document
AutoExit	When you quit Word

You create an auto macro just as you do a regular macro. The only difference is that you must give the macro one of the special auto macro names that Word recognizes. Just like other macros, auto macros can be defined either globally or for a particular template. The only exception is the AutoExec macro, which must be stored either in the Normal template or in a template in the Startup folder (the Startup folder is specified on the File Locations tab in the Options dialog box (Tools menu)).

In the case of a naming conflict, Word always runs the auto macro stored in the template attached to the active document. For example, if you define an AutoNew macro as a global macro stored in the Normal template, Word runs that macro whenever you create a new document, unless the new document is attached to a template that contains an AutoNew macro; in that case, Word runs the AutoNew macro stored in the attached template.

Auto Macro Examples

The following examples are intended to demonstrate some of the ways auto macros can be used. Don't worry if you don't understand the WordBasic instructions at this point. Chapters 3 and 4 describe the WordBasic language elements used in these examples.

AutoExec

By default, Word creates a new document based on the Normal template whenever you start Word. The following AutoExec macro replaces the new document based on the Normal template with one based on the LETTER template.

```
Sub MAIN
    FileNew .Template = "LETTER"
End Sub
```

AutoOpen

When you open a document, the following AutoOpen macro displays a prompt to ask if you would like to turn on revision marks; if you choose the Yes button, the macro turns on revision marks. You could modify this macro to test for different conditions. For example, you might want to turn on revision marks only if you aren't the author of the document you are opening. The macro could test for this condition and display or not display the prompt accordingly. For information on testing for conditions, see Chapter 3, "WordBasic Fundamentals."

```
Sub MAIN
    answer = MsgBox("Do you want to turn on revision marks?", 36)
    If answer = - 1 Then
        ToolsRevisions .MarkRevisions = 1
    End If
End Sub
```

AutoNew

The following AutoNew macro displays the Save As dialog box when you create a new document based on the template in which the AutoNew macro is stored. The comments (preceded by apostrophes) describe the purpose of each instruction; they have no effect when the macro runs.

```
Sub MAIN
    Dim FSArec as FileSaveAs           'Create the dialog record "FSArec"
    GetCurValues FSArec                'Place current values into FSArec
    choice = Dialog(FSArec)            'Display FileSaveAs dialog box
    If choice = -1 Then FileSaveAs FSArec    'If user chose OK, run FSA
End Sub
```

AutoClose

When a document is closed, the following AutoClose macro makes a backup copy by copying the document to a file server. On the Macintosh, the path "E:\DOCS\BACKUP" would change to a Macintosh path, such as "BACKUP SERVER:DOCUMENTS:BACKUP."

```
Sub MAIN
    file$ = FileName$()                          'Store filename in "file$"
    FileClose 1                                  'Close and save the file
    CopyFile .FileName = file$, .Directory = "E:\DOCS\BACKUP"    'Backup
End Sub
```

AutoExit

You probably have certain view options you prefer; for example, you may generally like to work with the Standard and Formatting toolbars displayed. The following AutoExit macro resets those settings, so that when you start Word again you have the environment you want, regardless of what was displayed or hidden when you last quit Word. This particular example displays the Standard and Formatting toolbars, but of course you could edit the macro to specify any settings you wanted.

```
Sub MAIN
    ViewToolbars .Toolbar = "Standard", .Show
    ViewToolbars .Toolbar = "Formatting", .Show
End Sub
```

C H A P T E R   3

WordBasic Fundamentals

This chapter introduces the fundamental elements of WordBasic that you need to write macros or add to macros you record. The building blocks WordBasic provides are simple, but you can use them to produce macros that perform almost any word-processing task.

In this chapter:

- A simple macro
- Statements and functions
- Strings and numbers
- Variables
- Expressions
- Conditionals and loops
- Displaying messages and requesting information
- Common WordBasic techniques
- Some sample macros

A Simple Macro

A good way to get started with WordBasic is to look at a simple macro. This one transposes characters (for example, to change "teh" to "the"). The following table illustrates the actions that the macro takes and the corresponding WordBasic instructions.

What happens on the screen	WordBasic instruction	Explanation
Rogre|		Before the macro begins, the insertion point is positioned after the letters to be switched.
Rogre	CharLeft 1, 1	First, the macro moves the insertion point to the left by one character and selects that character.
Rogr|	EditCut	Then it cuts the selected letter.
Rogr|	CharLeft 1	Then it moves the insertion point to the left by one character.
Roger|	EditPaste	Next, it pastes the character that was cut.
Roger|	CharRight 1	Finally, it moves the insertion point to the right by one character—back to where it was before the macro began.

You can easily record this macro by starting the macro recorder and performing the actions described in the table. (Remember, while recording a macro, you need to use the keyboard to move the insertion point and select text.) If you do so and then choose the Macro command (Tools menu) to open the macro in a macro-editing window, you'll see the following instructions:

```
Sub MAIN
CharLeft 1, 1
EditCut
CharLeft 1
EditPaste
CharRight 1
End Sub
```

As explained in the previous chapter, Sub MAIN and End Sub begin and end every macro. Notice that each instruction within the macro is on a separate line. You can place more than one instruction on the same line, but only if you separate each instruction with a colon (:). Generally, macros are easier to read if each instruction is on a separate line.

Also, notice the pattern of capitalization. When Word saves a macro, it gives the proper capitalization to every word that it recognizes as part of the WordBasic "vocabulary." You do not have to worry about typing instructions with the correct capitalization because WordBasic is not *case-sensitive*—it recognizes instructions typed in any combination of uppercase and lowercase letters.

Two of the instructions, CharLeft and CharRight, move the insertion point and optionally select text. The other two instructions, EditCut and EditPaste, correspond to the Cut and Paste commands on the Edit menu. In Word, virtually every action you can take has an equivalent WordBasic instruction.

Comments

Comments explain a macro to others and remind you of the purpose of the macro or of particular instructions. Word ignores comments when it runs the macro.

You can use the **REM** statement to insert a comment in a macro. For example:

```
REM This is a comment
```

Or you can use an apostrophe:

```
'This is also a comment
```

Both ways of commenting have advantages. The **REM** statement helps to make comments visible. But **REM** and the comment that follows it must be on their own line. You can use an apostrophe to place a comment on the same line as an instruction. Word interprets any text after the apostrophe until the end of the line as a comment. For example, you could add comments to these instructions from the macro that transposes characters described earlier in this chapter:

```
CharLeft 1, 1            'Select character to the left
EditCut                  'Cut selected character
```

You can use the Add/Remove REM button on the Macro toolbar to easily add or remove **REM** statements. For more information about using the Add/Remove REM button, see Chapter 6, "Debugging."

Statements and Functions

WordBasic instructions are composed of statements and functions, which are defined as follows:

- A *statement* carries out an action. For example, opening a file, selecting text, and scrolling through a document are all actions. Virtually every action you can perform in Word has an equivalent WordBasic statement.

- A *function* retrieves information. A function sometimes also performs an action, but the primary purpose of a function is to return information to the macro. A function can determine the character formatting of selected text, whether a document is in outline view, whether a toolbar is displayed, and many other things.

When you begin working with WordBasic, it's very helpful to get a sense of the different statements and functions available to you. A good way to do this is to browse through "Language Summary" in Part 2, "WordBasic Reference," which classifies WordBasic statements and functions according to the tasks they accomplish.

Statements

Most WordBasic statements are equivalent to Word commands. For example, the following instruction, which uses the **EditFind** statement, is equivalent to choosing the Find command from the Edit menu and searching for "Yours truly":

```
EditFind .Find = "Yours truly", .Direction = 0, \
        .MatchCase = 0, .WholeWord = 0, .PatternMatch = 0,\
        .SoundsLike = 0, .FindAllWordForms = 0, .Format = 0, .Wrap = 1
```

Each option in the Find dialog box has a corresponding *argument* in the **EditFind** statement. For example, the Match Case check box is represented by the `.MatchCase` argument. Arguments that correspond to dialog box options begin with a period (.) and are separated by commas (,). Each argument has a *value* associated with it, which may be a number or text enclosed by quotation marks. For example, `.MatchCase` takes a numeric value, while `.Find` takes a text value.

The syntax for each statement in Part 2, "WordBasic Reference," indicates the values that arguments require. You can see the same entry in Help by positioning the insertion point in the **EditFind** statement in the macro-editing window and pressing F1 (Windows) or HELP or COMMAND+/ (Macintosh). In the entry for **EditFind**, the syntax line shows all the available arguments for the statement with the values they require:

EditFind [**.Find** = *text*] [, **.Replace** = *text*] [, **.Direction** = *number*]
[, **.WholeWord** = *number*] [, **.MatchCase** = *number*]
[, **.PatternMatch** = *number*] [, **.SoundsLike** = *number*] [, **.FindAllWordForms** = *number*] [, **.Format** = *number*] [, **.Wrap** = *number*]

The syntax also indicates which arguments are necessary and which are optional; brackets ([ ]) enclose optional arguments. For complete information on how to interpret syntax lines, see the introduction to "Statements and Functions" in Part 2, "WordBasic Reference."

Controlling Where Lines Break in Long Instructions

In a WordBasic macro, every instruction ends with a paragraph mark. Most instructions are less than a line long, but some WordBasic statements have many arguments and can't fit on a single line. When you record one of these instructions, Word wraps it onto a second or third line as needed. For example, if you record changing information on the User Info tab in the Options dialog box (Tools menu), Word inserts an instruction like the following one in the macro you're recording:

```
ToolsOptionsUserInfo .Name = "Lucie Caselli", .Initials = "LC",
.Address = "Aperture Film"
```

You can make multiple-line instructions such as this one more readable by adding line breaks. To do so, place the insertion point at the location where you want to break the line, type the backslash (\) character to indicate to Word that the instruction continues into the next paragraph, and then press ENTER. For example, here's how you could rearrange the preceding **ToolsOptionsUserInfo** instruction by inserting a line break and some tab characters:

```
ToolsOptionsUserInfo .Name = "Lucie Caselli", .Initials = "LC", \
                .Address = "Aperture Film"
```

Functions

WordBasic functions do not correspond to Word commands as neatly as statements do, but they provide many types of information about documents and the current state of Word. For example, the **Font$()** function returns the name of the font where the insertion point is located. Often, the information that a function returns is placed in a *variable*, which is a kind of storage container. Variables are described in the "Variables" section later in this chapter.

A function is easily distinguished from a statement because it ends with parentheses. Here are some examples:

```
Font$()
Selection$()
CharColor()
CountStyles()
ViewOutline()
BookMarkName$()
```

Note that some functions include a dollar sign ($) character just before the ending parentheses. These functions return information in the form of text, or strings. The other functions return numbers. Strings and numbers are described in the following section.

Strings and Numbers

In addition to statements and functions, a macro contains data, or information. For example, if a macro includes a **FileOpen** statement to open a file, it also needs to know the name of the file to open. The filename is considered to be a piece of information. In WordBasic, information must be in the form of either a *string* or a *number*.

- A *string* is a series of characters treated as a single piece of information. A string can include letters, numbers, spaces, and punctuation marks—any characters. A double quotation mark is used to indicate the beginning and end of a string. A string can be as long as 65,280 characters, unless there isn't enough memory available to hold it.

- A *number* can include a decimal value and can accommodate as many as 14 digits (not including an exponent value if one is included).

Here are some examples of strings and numbers.

Strings	Numbers
"Please type your name"	52.6
"Lucida Sans Type"	.12345678901234
"3,500"	3500
"10"	10

Note that you can include numbers in a string, but WordBasic does not interpret them as numeric values. For example, the string "42" simply represents the characters "4" and "2," not the value 42.

Numbers in WordBasic can include a period as a decimal separator, but not other separators. For example, the number 3,500 generates an error. Note that in WordBasic the decimal separator must be a period, regardless of the decimal separator specified with the International option in Control Panel (Windows) or the keyboard layout specified with the Keyboard control panel (Macintosh).

Note Large numbers can be expressed as *mmm*E*eee*, in which *mmm* is the mantissa and *eee* is the exponent (a power of 10). The highest positive number allowed is 1.7976931348623E+308, which represents $1.7976931348623 \times 10^{308}$. (Technically, WordBasic numbers are double-precision floating-point numbers and occupy 8 bytes of memory.)

Including Quotation Marks and Special Characters in Strings

You can include any character in a string, but double quotation marks and special characters must be handled in a special way. A double quotation mark (") is used to mark the beginning and end of a string, so if you want to include one *within* a string, you must indicate that it is not intended to end or begin the string. To do so, you use the **Chr$()** function, which returns a character corresponding to the character code you specify. The code for a double quotation mark is 34. For example, the following instruction assigns the string "The word "cool" appears twice." to the variable result$:

```
result$ = "The word " + Chr$(34) + "cool" + Chr$(34) + \
          " appears twice."
```

Word provides a shortcut for typing instructions that include quotation marks within strings. If you type two double quotation marks in a row ("") where a double quotation mark should appear within a string, Word splits the string at those places and inserts + Chr$(34) + between each segment when you first run the instruction or save the macro. For example, consider the following line typed in a macro-editing window:

```
result$ = "The word ""cool"" appears twice."
```

When you run or save the macro for the first time, Word automatically converts the instruction so it looks like the previous example with **Chr$()**.

You also use **Chr$()** to include a nonprinting character such as a tab or newline character. For more information, see **Chr$()** in Part 2, "WordBasic Reference."

Variables

A *variable* is a storage container for a string or a number. A macro can change the contents of a variable as it is running. In other words, the value of a variable—the string or number it contains—can vary, which is why a variable is so named.

Variables provide the means for flexible and powerful macros. For example, to avoid overusing the word "cool," you could write a macro to calculate how many times the word appears in your document or in a paragraph. This macro may be useful, but it is not very flexible because it counts only the word "cool." Using a variable, you can modify the macro to calculate how frequently *any* word that you specify appears in a document. For a discussion of this macro, see "Some Sample Macros" at the end of this chapter.

WordBasic supports *string variables* and *numeric variables* to store strings and numbers. A string variable is identified by a dollar sign ($) ending character. A numeric variable does not end with a dollar sign character. Here are some examples of possible string and numeric variable names.

Examples of string variable names	Examples of numeric variable names
MyName$	Total
SearchText$	count
answer$	size

When creating a variable name, keep the following rules in mind:

- It must begin with a letter.
- It can contain only letters, numbers, and underscore (_) characters; punctuation marks and spaces are not allowed.
- It cannot be longer than 40 characters.
- It cannot be a *reserved word*. A reserved word is a word that already has a defined meaning in WordBasic. These words include statements, functions, arguments, and operators (such as AND and MOD).

Assigning Values to Variables

A variable has no value until you assign it one. In effect, it is an empty container waiting to be filled by a string or numeric value.

In some programming languages, you have to "declare" variables before you can assign values to them. In other words, before you write the body of your program, you must specify all the words that are going to be used as variable names. You do not have to declare variables in WordBasic, so often a variable appears in your macro for the first time when you assign it a value. But for complex macros that use many variables, you can make the macro more readable by declaring all the variables at the beginning of the macro. You use the **Dim** statement to declare a variable. For information, see **Dim** in Part 2, "WordBasic Reference."

To assign a value to a variable, you use an equal sign (=), placing the variable name on the left side and the value you are assigning it on the right side. The following example assigns the string "Willie" to the variable MyName$:

```
MyName$ = "Willie"
```

Don't try to place the value you are assigning on the left side of the equal sign—this doesn't work. The following example produces a syntax error:

```
"Willie" = MyName$          'Produces a syntax error
```

Once you have assigned a value to a variable, you can use that variable just as you would use a string or number. If the variable is numeric, you can use it in mathematical expressions. The first line of the following example assigns to counter a value of 6. The second line assigns to counter the result of the expression counter + 1, or 7:

```
counter = 6
counter = counter + 1
```

You cannot assign numeric values to string variables or string values to numeric variables. The following statements are not acceptable (either statement would prevent a macro from running and cause Word to display the message "Type mismatch"):

```
strg$ = 3.14159          'Produces an error
number = "hi, there"     'Produces an error
```

Variables often act as containers for information returned by a function. For example:

```
firstdoc$ = FileName$()
```

In this example, firstdoc$ stores the filename of the current document.

Changing Strings to Numbers and Numbers to Strings

Sometimes you need to change a string value to a numeric value, or vice versa. You use the **Val()** function to convert a string to a number and the **Str$()** function to convert a number to a string. For example, the following input box asks the user to type the number of files the macro should open.

The **InputBox$()** function, which displays the input box, returns a string value. So the **Val()** function is used to convert the string value to the NumFiles numeric value:

```
NumFilesString$ = InputBox$("How many files do you want to list?")
NumFiles = Val(NumFilesString$)
```

On the other hand, the **MsgBox** statement accepts only string values. So if you want to use **MsgBox** to display a numeric value, you must first convert it into a string with the **Str$()** function. For example:

```
NumFiles$ = Str$(NumFiles)
MsgBox "You have chosen to list" + NumFiles$ + " files."
```

These instructions display the following message box.

The **Str$()** function adds a space before positive numbers. The space accommodates the minus sign (−) for negative numbers. You can use the **LTrim$()** function to remove the space. For an example, see **LTrim$()** in Part 2, "WordBasic Reference." For more information on **InputBox$()** and **MsgBox**, see "Displaying Messages and Requesting Information" later in this chapter.

Expressions

An *expression* is a formula that can include either strings or numbers. A numeric expression consists of numbers or numeric variables linked together by *operators* to perform a mathematical calculation. For example, 2+2 is an expression.

WordBasic supports the following standard mathematical operators.

Operator	Function
+	Addition
–	Subtraction
*	Multiplication
/	Division
MOD	Modular division

The MOD operator performs a special type of division in which the whole-number part of the division result is discarded and the remainder is returned. For example, the result of 7 MOD 3 is 1 (1 is the remainder when you divide 7 by 3).

You can use just one mathematical operator—the plus sign (+)—in string expressions because, while it doesn't make sense to multiply, divide, or subtract strings, it's often useful to "add" or combine them. For example:

```
Word$ + " was found" + Str$(count) + " times in your document."
```

For more examples of combining strings, see "Some Sample Macros" at the end of this chapter. For detailed information on WordBasic operators, see "Operators and Predefined Bookmarks" in Part 2, "WordBasic Reference."

Conditionals and Loops

Conditionals and loops are key elements for building powerful and flexible macros. They are defined as follows:

- A *conditional* statement tells the macro to run a group of instructions only if a specified condition is met. The logic of a conditional statement is simple and familiar. "If it's raining, I'll put on my raincoat" is an example of a conditional statement.

- A *loop* statement tells the macro to repeat a group of statements either a specified number of times or until a condition is met. The equivalent in everyday life might be "Beat the egg whites until they are fluffy." In Word, a loop might be "Format every paragraph until you reach the end of the document."

Conditional and loop statements are often referred to as *control structures* because they control when and how other statements are run. Generally, a control structure is composed of a beginning instruction and an ending one, with the instructions being controlled in the middle.

WordBasic offers more than one conditional statement and more than one way to create a loop. This chapter covers the **If** conditional and the **While...Wend** loop; the next chapter covers the **Select Case** conditional and the **For...Next** loop.

What Is a Condition?

A *condition* is an expression that is either true or false. WordBasic uses conditions to determine whether or not to run the statements in an **If** conditional or a **While...Wend** loop.

Consider the statement "Today is Monday." This statement is either true or false: either today is Monday or it isn't. The statement becomes a condition when it is put into a conditional sentence: "If today is Monday, I'll go to work." This conditional says that if the condition ("today is Monday") is true, the second part of the sentence will occur ("I'll go to work").

In WordBasic and other programming languages, you express a condition by comparing values. For example, if you say "Today is Monday," you are comparing today to Monday and saying that Monday and today are the same. In WordBasic, you compare values by using *relational operators*—symbols that state how values stand in relation to each other (they're equal, one is greater than the other, and so on). The symbols in the following table are probably familiar to you from math, although some might look a little different (for example, >= rather than ≥).

Relational operator	Meaning
=	Equal to
<>	Not equal to
>	Greater than
<	Less than
>=	Greater than or equal to
<=	Less than or equal to

Word evaluates conditions—expressions that use relational operators—as either true or false. Here are some examples.

Condition	Evaluation
7 = 35	False
7 <> 6	True
7 <= 7	True

You can also compare strings.

Condition	Evaluation
`"Bob" = "Bob"`	True
`"Bob" = "bob"`	False
`"Bob" <> "Jerry"`	True
`"Blue" < "Green"`	True
`"love" > "life"`	True

Most often, string comparisons are used to determine whether two strings match. For example, a macro might contain a condition such as `StyleName$()` = `"Heading 2"` which tests whether the current style name is "Heading 2." As the condition `"Bob"` = `"bob"` (which evaluates as false) reveals, the case of letters is significant in string comparisons; an uppercase "B" does not match a lowercase "b." You can use the WordBasic functions **LCase$()** and **UCase$()**, which return strings in lowercase and uppercase characters, to equalize case when doing string comparisons where case should be ignored.

How Word Evaluates String Comparisons

You can use the > or < operator to compare whether one string is "greater than" or "less than" another. This sort of comparison is rare, but if you do use it, you need to know a little more about how string comparisons are evaluated. Word evaluates string comparisons character by character until it finds characters that don't match; the alphabetic or character code values for each character are then compared.

If the characters are letters in the alphabet, Word evaluates them according to which letter is first in the alphabet. For example, "B" follows "A" in the alphabet, so "B" is evaluated as greater than "A." Likewise, an uppercase "B" follows a lowercase "a" in alphabetic order, so "B" is evaluated as greater than "a," even though the character code for "B" (66) is less than the character code for "a" (97). (The character codes for all lowercase letters are higher than the character codes for all uppercase letters; for that reason "b" is evaluated as greater than "B.") If the characters are nonalphabetic, Word evaluates them according to their character code value. For example, a period (.) is greater than a comma (,) because 46, the code for a period, is greater than 44, the code for a comma.

Thus, `"Blue" < "Green"` is true because "B" comes before "G" in the alphabet. In the condition `"love" > "life"`, both strings begin with "l," so Word evaluates the second characters in the strings; "o" comes after "i" in the alphabet, so the first string is evaluated as greater than the second one.

Note You can use numbers to represent "true" and "false". In a conditional, false can be represented as 0 (zero), and true can be represented as –1. Therefore, if the result of a conditional expression is 0 (zero), it is evaluated as false. If the result is any nonzero number (not just –1), it is evaluated as true. See "The While...Wend Loop" later in this chapter for an example of a macro that uses this capability.

An Example

You can create a macro that is the WordBasic equivalent of the sentence "If today is Monday, I'll go to work."

To start with, create a series of numeric variables corresponding to the days of the week:

```
Sunday = 1
Monday = 2
Tuesday = 3
Wednesday = 4
Thursday = 5
Friday = 6
Saturday = 7
```

Next, add this instruction:

```
ThisDay = WeekDay(Today())
```

The numeric variable `ThisDay` holds the value returned by the WordBasic functions **Today()** and **WeekDay()**. **Today()** returns a serial number that represents the current date; **WeekDay()** converts that serial number into a number from 1 to 7, where 2 represents Monday, just like the variables you've set up. Now the macro is ready for the following conditional statement:

```
If ThisDay = Monday Then MsgBox "Time to go to work!"
```

The **MsgBox** statement displays a message box, so if the day happens to be Monday and you run the macro, you'll get this message box on your screen.

The If Conditional

You can write the **If** conditional in several different ways, depending on how complex your control structure needs to be. The previous example used the shortest form, or syntax, as shown here:

If *condition* **Then** *instruction*

This syntax says that if the *condition* is true, the *instruction* will run. Generally, this form is used just for a single instruction because every instruction that is part of this form of the **If** conditional must be on the same line. In the following example, if the text is bold, bold formatting is removed:

```
If Bold() = 1 Then Bold 0
```

You could add instructions on the same line, separating each one with a colon (:). In the following example, if the text is bold, bold formatting is removed and italic applied:

```
If Bold() = 1 Then Bold 0 : Italic 1
```

But if you want to include more than one instruction within the **If** control structure, you generally use the following syntax:

If *condition* **Then**
    Series of instructions
End If

All the *instructions* between **If** and **End If** are dependent on the *condition*. In the following example, **If** evaluates, or "tests," the condition to determine whether selected text is formatted as bold. If it is, the instructions remove the bold formatting and apply italic and underline formatting:

```
If Bold() = 1 Then          'If the selected text is bold, then
    Bold 0                  'remove bold formatting
    Italic 1                'apply italic formatting
    Underline 1             'apply underline formatting
End If
```

If control structures can include an **Else** instruction. Instructions subject to **Else** run if the condition is not true:

If *condition* **Then**
    Series of instructions to run if condition is true
Else
    Series of instructions to run if condition is false
End If

The following example toggles bold formatting. That is, if the selected text is formatted as bold, the first **Bold** instruction removes bold formatting; if the text is not bold, the second **Bold** instruction applies bold formatting (this is how the Bold button on the Formatting toolbar works):

```
If Bold() = 1 Then          'If the selected text is bold, then
    Bold 0                  'remove bold formatting
Else                        'otherwise
    Bold 1                  'apply bold formatting
End If
```

An abbreviated, one-line version of the **If...Then...Else** syntax is available without the ending **End If**:

If *condition* **Then** *instruction* **Else** *instruction*

Again, this one-line structure works well for conditionals where only one or two instructions are involved. For example:

```
If Bold() = 1 Then Bold 0  Else Bold 1
```

For cases where multiple instructions are involved, the full syntax with **End If** works better.

The most complex form of the **If** conditional includes the **ElseIf** instruction:

If *condition1* **Then**
    Series of instructions to run if condition1 is true
ElseIf *condition2* **Then**
    Series of instructions to run if condition2 is true
Else
    Series of instructions to run if no condition is true
End If

ElseIf is a second **If** conditional contained within a single **If** control structure. You could add an **ElseIf** instruction to the "days of the week" example presented earlier. In English, the conditional could be expressed as "If today is Saturday or Sunday, I'll stay at home; otherwise, I'll go to work." In WordBasic, the conditional might look like the following:

```
If ThisDay = Saturday Then
    MsgBox "Stay at home!"
ElseIf ThisDay = Sunday Then
    MsgBox "Stay at home!"
Else
    MsgBox "Go to work!"
End If
```

You can add as many **ElseIf** instructions to an **If** conditional as you need. For example, you could use **ElseIf** to test a condition for every day of the week (although this wouldn't be a very efficient technique).

The While...Wend Loop

You can think of a **While...Wend** loop as a conditional that can run the statements it controls more than once. Here's the syntax for the **While...Wend** loop:

While *condition*
> *Series of instructions to run if condition is true*

Wend

As with the **If** conditional, the instructions within a **While...Wend** loop will not run unless *condition* is true. If *condition* is true, the instructions repeat until the condition is no longer true. If the condition never changes, an "endless loop" occurs—the instructions within the loop repeat endlessly until someone interrupts the macro by pressing ESC or clicking the Stop button on the toolbar. This is not usually an effect you want to achieve, so when you create a **While...Wend** loop, you must build into it a means of changing the condition that starts the loop from true to false. This may sound difficult, but in practice it usually isn't. Consider the following example:

```
Sub MAIN
StartOfDocument
TRUE = - 1
EditFind .Find = "cool", .Direction = 0, .MatchCase = 0, \
    .WholeWord = 0, .PatternMatch = 0, .SoundsLike = 0, \
    .FindAllWordForms = 0, .Format = 0, .Wrap = 0
count = 0
While EditFindFound() = TRUE
    count = count + 1
    RepeatFind
Wend
MsgBox "Cool was found" + Str$(count) + " times."
End Sub
```

This macro moves the insertion point to the start of the document and then searches for the word "cool." It uses a **While...Wend** loop to continue searching for "cool" until every instance of the word has been found. The macro then reports how many times it found the word in the document.

The condition `EditFindFound() = TRUE` controls the **While...Wend** loop. The **EditFindFound**() function returns a value of –1 if the result of the most recent search using **EditFind** was successful. If the search wasn't successful, **EditFindFound**() returns 0 (zero). In a condition, a result of 0 (zero) corresponds to "false," and –1 corresponds to "true." So if the search is not successful, **EditFindFound**() returns 0 (zero) and the condition is no longer true. Note that the variable TRUE, defined earlier as –1, is used instead of –1 to make the condition easier to read.

Compound Expressions in Conditional Statements

You can link two or more conditions together into a compound expression that is evaluated as a single condition. To link conditions together, you use the *logical operators* AND and OR, described as follows:

- When two conditions are linked by AND, *both* conditions must be true in order for the compound expression to be true.

- When two conditions are linked by OR, the compound expression is true if *either* condition is true.

The following table provides some examples of compound expressions.

Compound expression	Evaluation
`10 > 5 And 100 < 200`	True
`3 < 6 And 7 > 10`	False
`8 < 7 Or 90 > 80`	True
`2 < 1 Or 3 > 60`	False
`"Y" > "N" And "yes" <> "no"`	True
`"Y" < "N" Or 4 <> 4`	False

Earlier in this section, the **ElseIf** instruction was used in an **If** control structure to express the conditional "If today is Saturday or Sunday, I'll stay at home; otherwise, I'll go to work." The following example uses a compound expression instead:

```
If ThisDay = Saturday Or ThisDay = Sunday Then
    MsgBox "Stay home today!"
Else
    MsgBox "Time to go to work!"
End If
```

The compound expression is more efficient in this case than using **ElseIf**—fewer instructions are needed to accomplish the same task and the instructions are also easier to understand, since they're closer to the way you would express the condition in English.

Note that the following instruction would not work properly:

```
If ThisDay = Saturday OR Sunday      'Produces the wrong result
```

Although this instruction reads like English, and you might therefore expect it to work, it does not. The expression `ThisDay = Saturday` is one condition and, on the other side of OR, `Sunday` is the other condition. WordBasic reads the compound expression as something like "If today is Saturday or if Sunday is Sunday." Because `Sunday` is always `Sunday`, the compound expression is always evaluated as true, no matter what day it is.

When WordBasic evaluates compound expressions, it proceeds from left to right; all conditions are evaluated first, then all compound expressions with AND, then all compound expressions with OR. You can use parentheses to control the order of evaluation, as in mathematical expressions.

Note The AND and OR operators can be tricky. It is easy in some cases to use an OR operator when you need to use an AND. If you have any uncertainty over which one to use, test your macro.

The NOT Operator

A third logical operator available in WordBasic is NOT. The NOT operator negates the expression that follows it. The following table shows some examples.

Expression	Evaluation
Not (5 > 10)	True
Not (8 < 7 Or 90 > 80)	False
Not (0)	True

The logic of the last example may not be immediately obvious. Because 0 (zero) is evaluated as false, `Not (0)` means "not (false)," or true.

The NOT operator is useful as a way to make a condition easier to read. For example, compare the following two instructions:

```
If ViewOutline() = 0 Then ViewOutline
If Not ViewOutline() Then ViewOutline
```

The instructions have the same effect, but the second one is closer to the way the conditional would be expressed in English: "If the document is not in outline view, then switch to outline view."

Note The NOT operator works well with functions such as **ViewOutline**() that return –1 (true) or 0 (false); it can reverse either value the function returns. It is usually not appropriate to use NOT with functions that can return other values. For more detailed information on NOT, see "Operators and Predefined Bookmarks" in Part 2, "WordBasic Reference."

Displaying Messages and Requesting Information

WordBasic includes several statements and functions you can use to communicate with the user. This section explains the **Print**, **MsgBox**, **MsgBox**(), **InputBox$**(), and **Input** statements and functions, each of which provides a different way to display a message or to request information. Here's a brief overview of the capabilities of each one:

- Print displays a message in the status bar. It is useful for displaying status messages while the macro is running. It doesn't require any response from the user.

- The **MsgBox** statement displays a message box that the user must acknowledge before the macro can continue. The **MsgBox**() function displays a message box and also returns a value. You can use **MsgBox**() to ask the user a question that requires a "yes" or "no" answer.

- InputBox$() displays a dialog box in which the user can type a response to a prompt.

- **Input** displays a prompt in the status bar where the user can type a response.

You can also create your own dialog boxes with check boxes, list boxes, and other features. For more information, see Chapter 5, "Working with Custom Dialog Boxes."

Note **Print** and **Input** can also be used to insert information into or read information from text files. For information on using **Print** and **Input** in this way, see "Using Sequential File Access" in Chapter 9, "More WordBasic Techniques."

Print

The **Print** statement displays a message in the status bar. Its most common use is to display a message describing the status of the macro. For example, if a macro needs time to perform a task, you might use the **Print** statement to display the message "Working…" in the status bar so the user understands that something is indeed happening.

The instruction `Print "Working..."` displays the following message in the status bar.

The **Print** statement accepts strings, string variables, numbers, and numeric variables, and allows you to mix them together. Here are some examples of valid **Print** instructions:

```
Print "Hello"
Print Name$
Print 365.25
Print Total
```

The **Print** statement can also display multiple items separated by commas or semicolons. When you use commas as delimiters, Word inserts a predefined tab space between the items. When you use semicolons as delimiters, the next item starts immediately after the previous one. For example:

```
Print "Hello, "; Name$, "The total is "; Total
```

MsgBox and MsgBox()

The **MsgBox** statement displays a message in a message box that the user must acknowledge before the macro can continue. You can provide a title for the message box and specify a symbol that identifies the type of message you want to display. For example:

```
MsgBox "The macro is finished.", "Sample Macro", 64
```

This instruction displays the following message box.

In the previous **MsgBox** instruction, `"Sample Macro"` is the message box title and `64` is a number that controls which symbol and buttons are displayed. For more information on using these arguments, see **MsgBox** in Part 2, "WordBasic Reference."

The **MsgBox()** function is just like the **MsgBox** statement, except that you can use it to give the user a choice or to ask the user a question. For example:

```
answer = MsgBox("OK to reformat?", "Two Column Macro", 292)
```

This instruction displays the following message box.

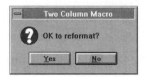

If the user chooses the Yes button, **MsgBox()** returns one value; if the user chooses the No button, **MsgBox()** returns a different value. The values are placed in the variable answer. The numeric argument 292 specifies the symbol and buttons displayed.

InputBox$()

InputBox$() displays an input box in which the user can type a response to a prompt. You can provide a title for the input box, a prompt, and a default response. For example:

```
DocName$ = InputBox$("Name of the file to open?", "Open Macro", \
        "Latest memo")
```

This instruction displays the following input box.

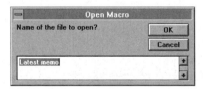

The user can replace the default response or accept it. The response is placed in the variable DocName$. Note that the user can type more than one line in an input box and can type ENTER to begin a new line. If the user presses ENTER to begin a new line, either Chr$(11) + Chr$(10) (Windows) or just Chr$(11) (Macintosh) is included in the string **InputBox$()** returns. In Windows, the Chr$(11) + Chr$(10) combination is interpreted as two paragraph marks when inserted into a document; in effect, an extra paragraph mark is inserted. You can use the **CleanString$()** function to remove the extra paragraph mark, as shown in the following example:

```
Address$ = InputBox$("Please type an address:", "Letter Macro")
Insert CleanString$(Address$)
```

Input

The **Input** statement uses the status bar to prompt the user for information. Because it's easy to overlook a prompt in the status bar, **InputBox$()** is generally preferred over **Input**. However, **Input** is a little more flexible than **InputBox$()**. **Input** can assign the user's response to numeric or string variables, whereas **InputBox$()** only returns strings. For example:

```
Input "What point size for the headline", Size
```

This instruction displays the following prompt. Notice that **Input** adds a question mark to the prompt.

The user's response is placed in the numeric variable Size.

You can prompt for a list of variables by separating each one with a comma. For example:

```
Input ItemNumber, Quantity
Input UserName$, ID
```

The user must respond with appropriate values separated by commas. The following are examples of acceptable responses:

```
1234,3
Mark Kyle, 6823
```

Input always attempts to divide the user's response at a comma. If you want to allow responses that contain commas, use a **Line Input** instruction. **Line Input** works like **Input**, but with one important difference: You can specify only a single string variable. For example:

```
Line Input Address$
```

If Word encounters a comma in the response, it returns the comma as part of the string that is assigned to Address$.

Common WordBasic Techniques

So far, this chapter has presented the building blocks needed to construct macros with WordBasic. This section describes a few widely used WordBasic techniques that employ some of those building blocks.

Inserting Text into a Document

To insert text, special characters, and even nonprinting characters like tab characters, you use the **Insert** statement. The **Insert** statement is the macro equivalent of typing at the keyboard; anything you can type, a macro can insert with **Insert**. For example, the following instruction inserts the phrase "Sincerely yours" into a document:

```
Insert "Sincerely yours"
```

Notice that the statement doesn't specify where "Sincerely yours" is to be inserted. Just as when you type, the phrase is inserted into the active document wherever the insertion point is currently located. If there is a selection, **Insert** will replace it (assuming the Typing Replaces Selection check box on the Edit tab in the Options dialog box (Tools menu) is selected).

The **Insert** statement inserts plain text into a document. The text you insert takes on the formatting of the text that precedes it. If you want to insert text with a different format, you place instructions to apply that formatting before the **Insert** instruction, just as you would turn on formatting before typing text. The following example turns on italic formatting just before inserting text and turns it off just afterward:

```
Italic 1                            'Turn on italic
Insert "Love's Labour's Lost,"      'Insert text
Italic 0                            'Turn off italic
Insert " by William Shakespeare"    'Insert more text
```

You can insert many special characters and nonprinting characters with **Insert** by typing them and enclosing them in quotation marks, as you would other text. For example, the following instruction inserts a tab character:

```
Insert "    "                       'Insert a tab character
```

Just looking at this instruction, though, it's difficult to tell whether you intend to insert a tab character or several spaces. In general, it's a better practice to use the **Chr$()** function with **Insert** to insert nonprinting characters:

```
Insert Chr$(9)                      'Insert a tab character
```

To insert paragraph marks, use **InsertPara**.

If you want to insert text into a document that isn't active, you include statements in your macro to open the document or switch to it. The following example activates the document associated with the variable LetterDoc$ and moves the insertion point to a bookmark called "Closing" before inserting text:

```
Activate LetterDoc$                 'Switch to the LetterDoc$ window
EditGoTo "Closing"                  'Move the insertion point to a bookmark
Insert "Sincerely yours"            'Insert text
```

Working on Part of a Document

Quite often, you want a macro to operate on only part of a document. For example, a macro that creates a table and inserts information into the table should operate just within the table. Or a macro may be designed to perform a series of formatting and editing operations on a particular paragraph.

The most useful tool Word provides for identifying discrete parts of documents is bookmarks. A simple use for bookmarks is just to mark a selection or location in a document. The following instruction marks the current selection (or the current location of the insertion point if there is no selection) with the bookmark "temp":

```
EditBookmark .Name = "temp", .Add
```

You can also use bookmarks to select text between two arbitrary locations in a document, as shown in the following example. It marks the current location with the bookmark "temp" and then pastes text from the Clipboard into the next paragraph. The **ExtendSelection** instruction activates extend mode, and the **EditGoto** instruction returns to the "temp" bookmark, selecting all the text between the end of the inserted text and "temp" as it does so.

```
EditBookmark .Name = "temp", .Add      'Insert bookmark "temp"
ParaDown                               'Move to next paragraph
EditPaste                              'Paste from Clipboard
ExtendSelection                        'Activate extend selection
EditGoto "temp"                        'Return to "temp"; select text
```

Word provides a set of predefined bookmarks for macros. These bookmarks do not appear in the list of bookmarks that appears in the Bookmark and Go To dialog boxes (Edit menu), but a macro can use them in the same way it can use other bookmarks. Here is the list of predefined bookmarks.

Bookmark	Description
\Sel	Current selection or the insertion point
\PrevSel1	Most recent location where editing occurred
\PrevSel2	Second most recent location where editing occurred
\StartOfSel	Start of the current selection
\EndOfSel	End of the current selection
\Line	Current line or the first line of the current selection
\Char	Current character or the character following the insertion point if there is no selection
\Para	Current paragraph or the first paragraph of the selection
\Section	Current section or the first section in the selection
\Doc	Entire contents of the active document

Bookmark	Description
\Page	Current page or the first page of the selection
\StartOfDoc	Beginning of the document
\EndOfDoc	End of the document
\Cell	Current cell or the first cell in the selection
\Table	Current table or the entire first table of the selection
\HeadingLevel	The heading that contains the insertion point or selection, plus any subordinate headings and text

For a more detailed description of the predefined bookmarks, see "Operators and Predefined Bookmarks" in Part 2, "WordBasic Reference."

The following example places a tab character in front of every paragraph in a table cell. The first instruction uses the predefined bookmark "\Cell" to select the current cell (assuming the insertion point is already within a cell). The **EditReplace** instruction then replaces every paragraph mark with a paragraph mark and a tab character. After the replace operation, each paragraph except the first paragraph (since it isn't preceded by a paragraph mark) begins with a tab character. The **CharLeft** instruction then moves the insertion point to the start of the cell and inserts a tab character in front of the first paragraph.

```
EditGoTo "\Cell"
EditReplace .Find = "^p", .Replace = "^p^t", .Direction = 0, \
            .ReplaceAll, .Format = 0, .Wrap = 0
CharLeft
Insert Chr$(9)
```

You can use the **SelInfo()** function to test whether the insertion point is within a table. The following example uses **SelInfo()** to control a **While** loop that moves through a table and inserts information into each cell. When the macro reaches the last cell of the table, it stops.

```
EditGoTo .Destination = "t"              'Go to next table
While SelInfo(12) = - 1
    'Series of instructions to run while in the table
Wend
```

For more information, see **SelInfo()** in Part 2, "WordBasic Reference."

Reading Text from a Document

Frequently, a macro needs to "read" text from a document. For example, if a macro is moving through a document, it may need to check its location by checking the contents of a selection.

You use the **Selection$()** function to return the contents of the current selection. If no text is selected, **Selection$()** returns the character following the insertion point. The following example determines whether or not a paragraph contains text or just consists of a paragraph mark. If the selection is just a paragraph mark (Chr$(13) is equivalent to a paragraph mark), the message "This paragraph is empty" is displayed.

```
EditGoto "\Para"                        'Select paragraph
If Selection$() = Chr$(13) Then          'Test selection
    MsgBox "This paragraph is empty."
Else
    MsgBox "This paragraph contains text."
End If
```

You can also use the **GetBookmark$()** function to return text marked by a bookmark. For more information, see **Selection$()** and **GetBookmark$()** in Part 2, "WordBasic Reference."

Testing for the End of a Document

You often need macros to perform a series of operations on every instance of a particular element in a document. For example, you might want a macro to change the capitalization of every heading formatted with the Heading 5 style. A common way to set up this sort of macro is to have the macro start at the beginning of the document and stop when it reaches the end of the document.

Word provides several ways to test for the end of the document. The most straightforward is the **AtEndOfDocument()** function, which returns a true value, −1, when the insertion point is at the end of the document. The following loop operates until the insertion point reaches the end of the document:

```
While AtEndOfDocument() <> -1
    'Series of instructions to run until the end of the document
Wend
```

The **LineDown()** and **ParaDown()** functions return a false value, 0 (zero), when they are unable to move the insertion point, which occurs only when they are at the end of a document. The following loop moves through the document a paragraph at a time until the insertion point reaches the end of the document:

```
While ParaDown()
    'Series of instructions to run until the end of the document
Wend
```

The end of a document is defined as the location just in front of the final paragraph mark in the document. The functions **AtEndOfDocument()**, **LineDown()**, and **ParaDown()** will not return a value indicating the end of a document unless the insertion point is at that location. It is not enough for the insertion point to be somewhere on the last line or somewhere in the last paragraph of a document.

You can also use **CmpBookmarks()** to test for the end of of the document, as shown in the following example:

```
While CmpBookmarks("\Sel", "\EndOfDoc")
    'Series of instructions to run until the end of the document
Wend
```

The **EditFind** and **EditReplace** instructions do not directly test for the end of a document, but you can use them to perform a task for as long as something is found. The following example changes the capitalization of each Heading 5 paragraph in a document. After the first search for a heading, the **While…Wend** loop repeats the search until no more headings formatted with the Heading 5 style are found:

```
StartOfDocument
EditFindClearFormatting
EditFindStyle .Style = "Heading 5"
EditFind .Find = "", .Direction = 0, .Format = 1, .Wrap = 0
While EditFindFound() = - 1
    ChangeCase 2            'Capitalize first letter of each word
    RepeatFind
Wend
```

Some Sample Macros

This section provides some macro ideas and demonstrates ways you can use some of the WordBasic elements introduced in this chapter.

The macros described in this section are available on the Microsoft Word Developer's Kit disk in EXAMPLES.DOT (Windows) or MACRO EXAMPLES (Macintosh). For information about installing the files on the disk, see Chapter 1, "Introduction."

Delete to the Beginning of a Sentence

Here's a simple macro to delete the text between the insertion point, positioned within a sentence, and the beginning of the sentence. The macro capitalizes the first letter of the remaining text:

```
Sub MAIN
    SentLeft 1, 1           'Move to start of sentence; select text
    EditCut                 'Cut selected text
    ChangeCase 4            'Capitalize first letter of remaining text
End Sub
```

Remove Excess Paragraph Marks

When you're typing in Word and you reach the end of a line, Word automatically moves the insertion point to the next line. You press ENTER only when you reach the end of a paragraph. But many other sources of text include a paragraph mark at the end of every line. This text is difficult to work with in Word because Word treats each line as a separate paragraph and does not wrap the text. The solution is to remove the excess paragraph marks, leaving only the ones that end each paragraph. You can do this by hand, using the Replace command (Edit menu), but it is faster to record the process and run a macro such as the following:

```
Sub MAIN
StartOfDocument
EditReplace .Find = "^p^p", .Replace = "@#$#", \
        .Direction = 0, .ReplaceAll, .Format = 0, .Wrap = 0
FileSave
EditReplace .Find = "^p", .Replace = " ", .ReplaceAll, \
        .Format = 0, .Wrap = 0
FileSave
EditReplace .Find = "@#$#", .Replace = "^p^p", .ReplaceAll, \
        .Format = 0, .Wrap = 0
End Sub
```

This macro assumes that two consecutive paragraph marks signify the end of a paragraph. When you remove paragraph marks from text, you usually want to preserve separate paragraphs. For that reason, this macro replaces two consecutive paragraph marks with the placeholder "@#$#". It then replaces each remaining paragraph mark with a space. Finally, it replaces the "@#$#" placeholder with two paragraph marks.

Determine How Many Days Until a Future Date

The following macro uses two WordBasic time and date functions, **DateValue**() and **Today**(), to count the number of days between today and a future date that you specify. An **InputBox$**() instruction prompts you to specify a future date; a **MsgBox** instruction displays a message box that indicates the number of days between the current date and the specified date. For a complete listing of time and date functions, see "Language Summary" in Part 2, "WordBasic Reference."

```
Sub MAIN
    enddate$ = InputBox$("Please enter future date:")
    serialenddate = DateValue(enddate$)
    numdays = serialenddate - Today()
    MsgBox "The number of days between now and " + enddate$ + \
        " is" + Str$(numdays) + "."
End Sub
```

Count How Many Times a Word Appears

The first version of this macro (see "The While...Wend Loop" earlier in this chapter) counted the number of times the word "cool" appeared in a document. You can modify this macro so that it counts the number of times *any* word appears in a document:

```
Sub MAIN
TRUE = - 1
searchtext$ = InputBox$("Please type a word to search for:")
StartOfDocument
EditFind .Find = searchtext$, .Direction = 0, .MatchCase = 0, \
    .WholeWord = 0, .PatternMatch = 0, .SoundsLike = 0, \
    .FindAllWordForms = 0, .Format = 0, .Wrap = 0
count = 0
While EditFindFound() = TRUE
        count = count + 1
        RepeatFind
Wend
MsgBox searchtext$ + " was found" + Str$(count) + " times."
End Sub
```

The first line of the macro uses the **InputBox$()** function to prompt the user for the text to search for. The user's response is placed in the variable searchtext$.

When the macro is finished, it displays a message box indicating how many times searchtext$ was found.

You could further improve this macro by presenting different messages according to whether the text was not found, found just once, or found more than once. To do so, you can replace the **MsgBox** instruction in the example with the following **If** conditional:

```
If count = 0 Then
    MsgBox searchtext$ + " was not found."
ElseIf count = 1 Then
    MsgBox searchtext$ + " was found once."
Else
    MsgBox searchtext$ + " was found" + Str$(count) + " times."
End If
```

This conditional tests for two specific conditions: count = 0 (the text was not found) and count = 1 (the text was found only once). All other cases (the text was found more than once) are handled by **Else**. If count = 0, the macro will display a message box similar to the following one.

You can make one more refinement to this macro by changing the **MsgBox** instructions so that when the word being counted is displayed, it is enclosed by quotation marks. Because quotation marks cannot be used inside a string, you need to use the **Chr$()** function: Chr$(34) produces a double quotation mark. In the following example, quote$ is assigned the result of Chr$(34). In the **MsgBox** instruction, quote$ is used in strings wherever a double quotation mark should appear:

```
quote$ = Chr$(34)
If count = 0 Then
    MsgBox quote$ + searchtext$ + quote$ + " was not found."
ElseIf count = 1 Then
    MsgBox quote$ + searchtext$ + quote$ + " was found once."
Else
    MsgBox quote$ + searchtext$ + quote$ + " was found" + \
    Str$(count) + " times."
End If
```

This example displays a message box similar to the following one.

For more information on the **Chr$()** function, see **Chr$()** in Part 2, "WordBasic Reference."

C H A P T E R   4

Advanced WordBasic

This chapter introduces the advanced elements of the WordBasic language, which you can use to create complex, powerful macros.

In this chapter:

- More conditionals and loops
- Array variables
- Subroutines and user-defined functions
- Working with dialog records

More Conditionals and Loops

The previous chapter introduced the **If** conditional and the **While...Wend** loop. This chapter introduces the following control structures, which are typically useful in more complex macros:

- The **For...Next** loop
- The **Select Case** conditional
- The **Goto** statement

The For...Next Loop

You use the **For...Next** loop when you want to carry out a group of instructions a specific number of times. Here is the syntax (the arguments in brackets are optional):

For *CounterVariable = Start* **To** *End* [**Step** *Increment*]
    Series of instructions
Next [*CounterVariable*]

Word carries out the *instructions* between **For** and **Next** as many times as it takes for the *CounterVariable* to increment from the *Start* value to the *End* value. The *CounterVariable* is incremented each time Word runs the **Next** instruction following the *instructions*. The *Increment* indicates how much to increment the counter; if this is omitted, as is often the case, the counter is incremented by 1.

Examples

The following example displays in the status bar the numbers from 1 to 12, one at a time:

```
For dozen = 1 To 12        'Loop 12 times
    Print dozen            'Display the value in the status bar
Next dozen                 'Return to the For statement to repeat loop
```

The initial value of dozen is 1, as set in the **For** instruction. During the first iteration, the **Print** statement displays 1 (the value of dozen) in the status bar; during the next iteration, it displays 2; during the next, 3; and so on until month reaches 12—the end of the loop and the last number displayed in the status bar.

The following example creates a document with a sample sentence formatted in each available font:

```
For count = 1 To CountFonts()        'Loop for the number of fonts
    fname$ = Font$(count)            'Place a font name in "fname$"
    Font fname$                      'Apply formatting with this font
    Insert "This is " + fname$ + "." 'Insert sentence
    InsertPara                       'Insert paragraph mark
Next count
```

The **CountFonts()** function returns the number of available fonts. Because this value is the end value of the loop, the number of times the loop will repeat is equivalent to the number of available fonts. The **Font$()** function returns the name of the current font from the list of available fonts. In the example, the instruction Font$(count) returns the font whose position in the list of fonts corresponds to the value of count.

Several functions begin with "Count" and work much like **CountFonts()** does: They return the number of macros, AutoText entries, styles, and so on. These functions are often used to control **For...Next** loops just as **CountFonts()** does in the previous example.

You can nest a **For...Next** loop by placing it within another **For...Next** loop. The following example uses a nested loop to create a simple calendar based on a 360-day year:

```
For months = 1 To 12              'Loop 12 times
    For days = 1 To 30            'Loop 30 times
        Insert Str$(days)        'Insert "days" as a string
    Next days                    'Return to "For days = 1..."
    InsertPara                   'Insert a paragraph mark
Next months                      'Return to "For months = 1..."
```

The outside loop repeats 12 times, corresponding to the months of the year. Then, for each month, the inside loop repeats for the 30 days in the month. The **Insert** instruction uses the **Str$()** function to convert the value stored in the numeric variable day into a string, then inserts it into a document (you cannot use the **Insert** statement to insert a numeric value).

You can set up **For**...**Next** statements in many ways. The following table provides some examples of different start and end values and their possible increment values.

Example	Result
For dozens = 0 To 144 Step 12	The variable dozens increments from 0 (zero) to 144 in steps of 12.
For countdown = 10 To 1 Step -1	The variable countdown decrements from 10 to 1 in steps of −1.
For loop = start To finish Step size	The variable loop increments or decrements from the value of the variable start to the value of the variable finish in steps equal to the variable size.
For count = count To count + 10	The initial value of the variable count is increased by 10 in steps of 1 (the default increment).

Note that the **For**...**Next** loop increment (the value after **Step**) can be a positive or negative number—positive numbers increase the counter, and negative numbers decrease it. If the end value is larger than the start value (for example, For x = 1 To 10), the increment must be positive. Likewise, if the end value is smaller (for example, For x = 10 To 1), the increment must be negative.

The Select Case Conditional

Select Case is useful when you want to test many different conditions or a range of conditions. It's similar to the **If** conditional, but is more efficient for testing multiple conditions. Here is the syntax (arguments in brackets are optional):

Select Case *Expression*
   Case *CaseExpression*
      Series of instruction(s)
   [**Case Else**
      Series of instruction(s)]
End Select

A **SelectCase** conditional can contain any number of **Case** instructions. The result of the *Expression* is compared with the *CaseExpression* values in every given **Case** instruction until a match is found. If a match is found, the instructions following the appropriate **Case** instruction are carried out. If there is no match, the instructions following **Case Else** are carried out. If there is no **Case Else** instruction and no match is found, Word displays an error message. To be safe, you should include a **Case Else** instruction—even if no statements follow it and it has no effect—to ensure that Word doesn't generate an error, regardless of the value of *Expression*. In *CaseExpression*, you can use the **Is** keyword when you want to use logical operators to compare *Expression* with a value. For example, Case Is > 5. You use the **To** keyword to test for a range of values. For example, Case 10 To 20 (10 and 20 are included in the range).

Examples

A macro that creates a calendar needs to determine how many days are in each month. Four of the months contain 30 days, February has 28 (in non-leap years), and the remaining months have 31 days. In the following example, the **Select Case** instruction tests the value of the month variable and then assigns the appropriate value to the lastday variable. The month variable is a number from 1 to 12 that corresponds to a month of the year.

```
Select Case month           'Select the value of month
    Case 4,6,9,11           'If month is 4,6,9, or 11
        lastday = 30        'the month has 30 days
    Case 2                  'If month is 2 (February)
        lastday = 28        'the month has 28 days
    Case Else               'Otherwise
        lastday = 31        'the month has 31 days
End Select
```

Note that the first **Case** instruction has several values, separated by commas. If month equals any one of these values, the instruction following the **Case** instruction (lastday = 30) is carried out.

The following example uses the **StyleName$()** function to return the name of the style applied to the paragraph that contains the insertion point. Each **Case** instruction proposes a style name to match the one returned by **StyleName$()**. If the style name matches the proposed style, the instruction following the **Case** instruction is carried out.

```
Select Case StyleName$()                'Select the current stylename
    Case "ListItem1"                     'If it's "ListItem1"
        ToolsBulletsNumbers .Type = 0    'add a bullet
    Case "ListItem2"                     'If it's "ListItem2"
        StartOfLine                      'go to the start of the line
        Insert "-" + Chr$(9)             'and insert a hyphen and a tab
    Case Else                            'Otherwise
        MsgBox "Not a list style"        'display a message
End Select
```

The following example demonstrates how you can use the **Is** and **To** keywords in **Case** instructions to test for a range of values. The example uses the **Rnd()** function to generate a random number from 0 (zero) to 10. The **Case** instructions test the number generated by **Rnd()** and display a corresponding message.

```
Select Case Int(Rnd() * 10)      'Select a random number from 0 to 10
    Case 0,1,3                    'If it is 0, 1, or 3
        Print "0, 1, or 3"       'print this message
    Case Is > 8                   'If it is greater than 8
        Print "Greater than 8"   'print this message
    Case 4 To 8                   'If it is between 4 and 8
        Print "Between 4 and 8"  'print this message
    Case Else                     'Otherwise
        Print "It's 2"            'print this message
End Select
```

The second **Case** instruction uses the **Is** keyword and the greater than (>) operator to test for any value greater than 8. The third **Case** instruction uses the **To** keyword to test for a value that falls in the range of values between 4 and 8.

The Goto Statement

Goto isn't a conditional or a loop, but it is included in this section because, like a conditional or loop, it controls the flow of a macro—the order in which Word interprets a macro's instructions. **Goto** tells Word to go to a line in the macro and carry out the instructions from that line forward. Among programmers, **Goto** is infamous for having the potential to create difficult-to-read code, often referred to as "spaghetti code" because it can make the flow of a program tangled and difficult to follow. Used sparingly, though, **Goto** can be useful in some situations. Also, it is usually necessary in WordBasic to use **Goto** with error-handling instructions (for information on error handling, see Chapter 7, "The Well-Behaved Macro").

Here is the syntax for **Goto**:

Goto *Label*

Word goes to the line in the macro that starts with *Label*, which must be within the same subroutine or user-defined function as the **Goto** instruction (see "Subroutines and User-Defined Functions" later in this chapter). A line label must begin at the start of a line (it cannot be preceded by a space or tab character) and end with a colon (:). The rules for *Label* names are the same as those for variable names (see "Variables" in Chapter 3, "WordBasic Fundamentals").

You can also use a line number with a **Goto** instruction instead of a label, although it's unusual to use line numbers in WordBasic macros. Line numbers are supported primarily for compatibility with old Basic programs in which line numbers were required. Like a label, a line number must begin at the start of a line; the line number can be as high as 32759. Unlike a text label, a line number does not need a colon following it.

The following example uses the **InputBox$()** function to request a social security number, then tests to see whether the number typed by the user is longer than 11 characters. If it is, the example displays a message box that asks the user to try entering the social security number again.

```
tryagain:
answer$ = InputBox$("Please enter your social security number: ")
If Len(answer$) > 11 Then
    MsgBox "Too many characters. Please try again."
    Goto tryagain
End If
```

The **Goto** instruction sends Word to the `tryagain:` label, so that the entire sequence of instructions is repeated. Note that when the **Goto** instruction refers to the `tryagain:` label, the ending colon (:) is dropped.

Nesting Conditionals and Loops

It's often useful to *nest* conditionals and loops—that is, to place a conditional or loop within another conditional or loop. The following example uses an **If** conditional within a **Select Case** conditional to assign 29 to the lastday variable if month is 2 (February) and it's a leap year:

```
Select Case this month            'Select the value of month
    Case 4,6,9,11                 'If month is 4,6,9, or 11
        lastday = 30              'the month has 30 days
    Case 2                        'If month is 2 (February)
        If leapyear = 1 Then      'If it's a leap year
            lastday = 29          'the month has 29 days
        Else                      'Otherwise
            lastday = 28          'the month has 28 days
        End If                    'End of If conditional
    Case Else                     'Otherwise
        lastday = 31              'the month has 31 days
End Select
```

WordBasic supports up to 16 levels of nesting. Generally, though, it's best to limit nesting to no more than three or four levels; the more levels you use, the more obscure the logic of the macro can become.

Array Variables

An *array variable* gives a single name to a group of related values and organizes them in a list or table. Here are some of the advantages that using an array can provide over using regular variables:

- A group of related variables can be easier to work with when ordered within an array.

- A **For...Next** loop can be used with an array to assign values efficiently to many variables.

- By changing the size of an array, a macro can create variables as it runs, so you don't need to know in advance how many variables your macro may need. For example, if you want to create a variable for the name of each style in a document, you cannot know how many variables will be needed (different documents can store different numbers of styles). If you use an array, your macro can create the necessary number of variables to store the values each time it runs.

Arrays are not difficult to use or understand, but they're not usually used in simple macros. Unless your macro needs to handle a lot of values, you probably don't need to use an array. The most common use for arrays in WordBasic is to list items in a custom dialog box. For more information on using arrays in custom dialog boxes, see Chapter 5, "Working with Custom Dialog Boxes."

Defining an Array

Each variable within an array is called an *element* and shares a common name—the array name. Elements are distinguished from each other by a *subscript*, a unique number assigned to each element. Before you can assign values to the elements of an array, you must specify how many elements the array contains. To do so, you use the **Dim** statement. Here is the syntax:

Dim *ArrayVariableName*(*LastElementNumber*)

The first element of a WordBasic array is always numbered 0 (zero). This can be confusing because it means that the subscript number of the last element is one less than the number of elements. For example:

```
Dim Months$(11)                     'Define an array with 12 elements
```

This instruction defines an array with 12 elements to hold the names of the months of the year. Because the first element is numbered 0 (zero), the twelfth element is numbered 11.

An array variable can be defined to hold either numbers or strings—a single array cannot hold *both*. The name of an array that contains string values must end with the dollar sign ($), just like a regular string variable.

Assigning Values to an Array

After you have used the **Dim** statement to define an array, you can assign values to the elements within it. You can assign values to array elements just as you do to regular variables. Here is an example:

```
Dim FourWinds$(3)                   'Define an array with four elements
FourWinds$(0) = "East"
FourWinds$(1) = "West"
FourWinds$(2) = "North"
FourWinds$(3) = "South"
```

Sometimes, it's useful to ignore an array's first element, numbered 0 (zero), so that you can assign your first value to the element whose subscript is 1, the second value to the element whose subscript is 2, and so on. The following example assigns string values to the array Weekdays$(7) so that the subscripts of elements 1 through 7 correspond to a number returned by the **Weekday**() function:

```
Dim Weekdays$(7)                         'Define an array with eight elements
Weekdays$(0) = ""                        'Assign no value to first element
Weekdays$(1) = "Sunday"
Weekdays$(2) = "Monday"
Weekdays$(3) = "Tuesday"
Weekdays$(4) = "Wednesday"
Weekdays$(5) = "Thursday"
Weekdays$(6) = "Friday"
Weekdays$(7) = "Saturday"
MsgBox "Today is " + Weekdays$(WeekDay(Today()))
```

You can use a **For...Next** loop to assign values to some arrays. The following
example first defines an array that has as many elements as the number of
available fonts, a value returned by the **CountFonts()** function. Then a
For...Next loop inserts the names of all the fonts into the array. Note that the
array is dimensioned so that the number of the last element is CountFonts() - 1,
since **CountFonts()** starts its count at 1, whereas (as noted earlier) array subscript
numbering starts at 0 (zero).

```
Dim fontnames$(CountFonts() - 1)            'Define an array
For count = 0 To (CountFonts() - 1)        'Repeat CountFont() times
     fontnames$(count) = Font$(count + 1)  'Assign font name Font$()
Next
```

You could use the fontnames$() array to present the list of font names in a
custom dialog box. For information on using arrays in this way, see Chapter 5,
"Working with Custom Dialog Boxes."

Resizing an Array

At times, it's useful for a macro to change the size of an array. For example, a
macro that defines an array to hold all the fonts available on the current printer
could later select another printer and reuse the original array to hold the new list
of fonts. Because the second printer could have a different number of fonts
available, the macro should resize the array before reusing it.

You use the **Redim** statement to resize an array. The syntax for **Redim** is exactly
the same as for **Dim**:

Redim *ArrayVariableName*(*LastElementNumber*)

Note that when you resize an array, you also clear its contents. If you try to use
the **Dim** statement to resize an existing array, Word generates an error.

Arrays with More Than One Dimension

The examples presented so far use arrays to order variables in a list. But you can also use arrays to order variables in a table. Suppose, for example, you wanted to create a variable for each day of the year. One way would be to define an array that lists 365 variables. For example:

```
Dim Year(364)                    'Define an array with 365 variables
```

However, you could give more structure to these variables by placing them in a table. You could order them, for example, so that each row of a table represented a month and each column corresponded to a day:

```
Dim Year(11,30)                  'Define an array with 12 rows and 31 columns
```

This kind of array is called a *two-dimensional* array, while those presented earlier in the chapter are *one-dimensional* arrays. You can create arrays with three or more dimensions—as many as there is room for in memory—but in practice, arrays with more than two dimensions are rare.

You define an array with more than one dimension by listing the number of elements in each dimension in the standard **Dim** statement. Here is the syntax for a two-dimensional array:

Dim *ArrayVariableName*(*LastElementNumber1*, *LastElementNumber2*)

In the following example of a two-dimensional array, both dimensions have five elements:

```
Dim MailingList$(4,4)            'Define a 5-by-5 two-dimensional array
```

Here is a visual representation of the 25 elements contained in the array.

0, 0	0, 1	0, 2	0, 3	0, 4
1, 0	1, 1	1, 2	1, 3	1, 4
2, 0	**2, 1**	2, 2	2, 3	2, 4
3, 0	3, 1	3, 2	3, 3	3, 4
4, 0	4, 1	4, 2	4, 3	4, 4

— MailingList(2,1)

Each cell in the table represents an element in the array—a slot for a string, because `Dim MailingList$(4,4)` defines a string array variable. Each pair of numbers represents the subscript for an element of the array. For example, `MailingList$(2,1)` indicates the second element in the third row. You could use this array to store five names, each with its own street address, city, state or province, and postal code. The first column would list the names, the second column would list the street addresses, and so on.

The following example creates a two-dimensional array that contains a multiplication table up to, and including, the number 10, and inserts the table into the active document:

```
Dim MultTable(10,10)
For N = 1 to 10
    For M = 1 to 10
        MultTable(N,M) = N * M
        Insert Str$(MultTable(N,M)) + Chr$(9)
    Next
    EditClear -1
    InsertPara
Next
```

In the example, the inner loop multiplies N and M, assigns the value to the element MultTable(N,M), and then inserts the product and a tab character into the active document. At the end of each row, the macro deletes the last tab character in the row and inserts a paragraph mark to start a new row.

Sorting Arrays

You can use the **SortArray** statement to sort arrays in alphabetical or numerical order. The following example assigns the available font names to the array fontnames$() and sorts the array:

```
Dim fontnames$(CountFonts() - 1)              'Define an array
For count = 0 To (CountFonts() - 1)           'Repeat CountFont() times
    fontnames$(count) = Font$(count + 1)      'Assign font name Font$()
Next
SortArray fontnames$()                        'Sort font names
```

For detailed information, see **SortArray** in Part 2, "WordBasic Reference."

Subroutines and User-Defined Functions

As your macros become more complicated, you can split the code into self-contained units called *subroutines* and *user-defined functions*. A subroutine carries out a task; it is like a custom-made statement. A user-defined function returns information and may also carry out a task. Subroutines and functions offer at least two advantages:

- Instructions stored in a subroutine or function are reusable. A complex macro may need to carry out a task more than once. Rather than duplicating the instructions, you can store them in a subroutine or function that the macro "calls" when needed. Moreover, subroutines and functions are available not just to the current macro but to other macros that might need them.

- Subroutines and functions allow you to break down complex tasks into smaller pieces. Instead of developing your macro in terms of one long process, you can break it down into manageable parts. Each subroutine or function can be tested separately, so you can more easily isolate problems and test the macro as a whole.

Subroutines

A subroutine is a kind of macro within a macro. It carries out a particular task, just as the macro as a whole does. Virtually any part of a macro can be placed in a subroutine, but usually it only makes sense to create a subroutine for a part that is self-contained or that will be used more than once. For this reason, subroutines are generally not needed in simple macros.

Every macro has a main subroutine that begins with the instruction Sub MAIN. A subroutine that you create is defined in the same way as the main subroutine, but requires a different name:

Sub *SubroutineName*[(*ArgumentList*)]
    Series of instructions
End Sub

The *SubroutineName* is whatever name you choose that isn't a reserved word or a variable name. The limitations are the same as those for variable names (see "Variables" in Chapter 3, "WordBasic Fundamentals"). *ArgumentList* is a list of variables, separated by commas, that accept values passed to the subroutine. See "Sharing Values Among Subroutines and Functions" later in this chapter.

The **Sub...End Sub** instructions cannot be placed within the main subroutine or within any other subroutine. In other words, you cannot nest subroutines as you can WordBasic control structures, such as **For...Next** loops or **If** conditionals.

On the other hand, the instruction that runs, or "calls," the subroutine *is* placed within another subroutine. You can use the **Call** statement to run a subroutine, or you can use just the name of the subroutine as the instruction. (The **Call** keyword makes the macro easier to read—it's clear that a subroutine and not a built-in WordBasic statement is being run.) After the instructions in the subroutine have been carried out, control reverts to the routine that called the subroutine, as shown in the following diagram.

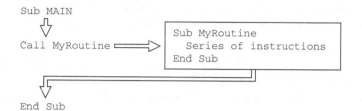

In the following example, the BeepMsgExit subroutine is called if the user chooses the Yes button in a message box that asks if he or she wants to quit Word:

```
Sub MAIN
    response = MsgBox("Do you want to quit Word?", 4)
    If response = -1 Then
        Call BeepMsgExit
    End If
End Sub

Sub BeepMsgExit
    Beep
    MsgBox("Quitting Word now...", -8)
    FileExit 1
End Sub
```

User-Defined Functions

User-defined functions are similar to subroutines—they are self-contained units of code that are called from one or more subroutines. But unlike a subroutine, a user-defined function returns a value, just as built-in WordBasic functions do. The rules for using functions you create are the same as those for built-in functions. Generally, you define a function because WordBasic does not include a function designed to return the particular value you need.

You define new functions in a manner similar to subroutines, except that instead of using the **Sub** instruction, you use the **Function** instruction. The syntax is as follows:

Function *FunctionName*[(*ArgumentList*)]
 Series of instructions
 FunctionName = value
End Function

The *ArgumentList* is a list of variables, separated by commas, that accept values passed to the function. The function returns a value by assigning it to the function name itself, using the syntax *FunctionName = value*. A user-defined function can return either a numeric or string value. Functions that return string values have function names that end with the dollar sign ($).

In the following example, the `MyDateTime$` function is called by the main subroutine to display the date and time in a message box. Note that no arguments are passed to this function, so it does not end with parentheses as a built-in Word function would (for example, **Font$()**); it looks just like a variable.

```
Sub MAIN
    MsgBox "The date and time is: " + MyDateTime$
End Sub

Function MyDateTime$
    mDate$ = Date$()
    mTime$ = Time$()
    MyDateTime$ = mDate$ + " " + mTime$
End Function
```

Sharing Values Among Subroutines and Functions

By default, a variable is available only within the subroutine or function in which it is initially used. However, subroutines and functions often need to exchange or share values. The following two methods are available:

- You can use a **Dim Shared** instruction to declare a *shared* variable.

- You can *pass* values to a specific subroutine or function.

Shared Variables

A shared variable can be used in any subroutine or function in the macro. Here is the syntax for declaring a shared variable:

Dim Shared *Var*, *Var1*, *Var2*...

A single **Dim Shared** instruction can be used to declare several shared variables. Every type of variable, including number, string, and array variables, can be declared as shared. A **Dim Shared** instruction is not placed inside a subroutine or function since it applies to all the subroutines and functions within the macro. Generally, you declare shared variables at the beginning of a macro, before the main subroutine.

In the following example, the variable num is declared as shared:

```
Dim Shared num                      'Declare "num" as a shared variable
Sub MAIN
    num = 6                         'Set the value of num
    AddTenRoutine                   'Call the routine
End Sub

Sub AddTenRoutine
    num = num + 10                  'Increase the value of num by 10
    Print num                       'Display the new value of num
End Sub
```

The main subroutine sets num equal to 6, and then calls the AddTenRoutine subroutine. The subroutine adds 10 to num and then displays the value 16. If num was not declared as a shared variable, the value displayed would be 10, because num would have no value at the start of the AddTenRoutine subroutine.

Any subroutine can affect the value of a shared variable. If you have many subroutines, shared variables can be a source of problems. For example, you might intend to use a variable named "count" in two subroutines. Later on, if you forget that you've already used "count" and you use it in a new subroutine, you could create an error that might be difficult to find. You can avoid this problem by passing variable values through subroutine or function arguments.

Passing Values to Subroutines and Functions

You can pass values from one subroutine or user-defined function directly to another through *arguments*. Arguments are variables in a subroutine or function that initially receive their values from the calling subroutine or function. Unlike shared variables, whose values can be affected by any subroutine or function, values passed to subroutines and user-defined functions can be affected only by the subroutines or functions involved.

Here is the syntax for subroutine arguments in the **Call** statement:

[**Call**] *SubroutineName* [*argument1*, *argument2*, …]

The syntax for passing values to a user-defined function is similar; the main difference is that the arguments are enclosed in parentheses:

FunctionName[(*argument1*, *argument2*, …)]

Note that you can pass any number of values, each separated by a comma.

Here is an example of passing a value to the AddTenRoutine shown earlier:

```
Sub MAIN
    num = 6                 'Set the value of num
    AddTenRoutine num       'Call the routine and specify "num"
End Sub

Sub AddTenRoutine(var1)
    var1 = var1 + 10        'Increase the value of var1 by 10
    Print var1              'Display the new value of var1
End Sub
```

The following example uses a function called FindAverage() to average two numbers. The variables a and b, defined as 6 and 10, are passed to the FindAverage() function, which averages the two values. The main subroutine then displays the result.

```
Sub MAIN
    a = 6
    b = 10
    Print FindAverage(a, b)
End Sub

Function FindAverage(firstnum, secondnum)
    FindAverage = (firstnum + secondnum) / 2
End Function
```

Note that the variable names in the subroutine or user-defined function do not have to match the names of the variables passed to it, but the order of the arguments must match. In the previous example, the value of the a variable is passed to the firstnum variable, and the value of b is passed to secondnum.

You can pass strings, numbers, and arrays to subroutines and user-defined functions. In the following example, the fontnames$() array is passed to the FillFontArray subroutine, which fills the array with the list of available font names.

```
Sub MAIN
    lastelement = CountFonts() - 1
    Dim fontnames$(lastelement)
    FillFontArray$(fontnames$(), lastelement)
End Sub

Sub FillFontArray(array$(), maxcount)
    For arraycount = 0 To maxcount
        array$(arraycount) = Font$(arraycount + 1)
    Next
End Sub
```

Passing Arguments "by Value"

Normally, when you pass a variable to a subroutine or user-defined function, the subroutine or function can change the value of that variable not only within the subroutine or function itself but also in the calling subroutine. This is known as passing an argument "by reference." In the following example, the `greeting$` variable is passed to the `ChangeGreeting` subroutine by reference. The main subroutine then displays the greeting, which the `ChangeGreeting` subroutine has changed from "Hello" to "What's up?"

```
Sub MAIN
    greeting$ = "Hello"
    ChangeGreeting greeting$
    MsgBox greeting$
End Sub


Sub ChangeGreeting(change$)
    change$ = "What's up?"
End Sub
```

You can pass an argument and ensure that its value in the calling subroutine remains unchanged by passing the argument "by value." To pass an argument by value in WordBasic, you enclose it in parentheses.

In the following example, the `greeting$` argument is passed by value, so when the main subroutine displays the greeting, the greeting remains "Hello."

```
Sub MAIN
    greeting$ = "Hello"
    ChangeGreeting (greeting$)
    MsgBox greeting$
End Sub

Sub ChangeGreeting(change$)
    change$ = "What's up?"
End Sub
```

In the following example, the variable a is passed by reference, while b is passed by value:

```
Sub MAIN
    a = 6
    b = 10
    OnePlusAverage a,(b)
    MsgBox "a =" + Str$(a) + " and b =" + Str$(b)
End Sub
```

```
Sub OnePlusAverage(firstval, secondval)
    firstval = firstval + 1
    secondval = secondval + 1
    avg =  (firstval + secondval) / 2
    Print avg
End Sub
```

The OnePlusAverage subroutine adds 1 to each value passed to it, and then displays the average of the two values in the status bar. When the OnePlusAverage subroutine ends and control returns to the main subroutine, the main subroutine displays the following message box, which shows that the argument passed "by reference" changed, while the argument passed "by value" did not.

Note that if you are passing more than one argument to a subroutine and you want to pass the first argument by value, you must enclose the list of arguments in parentheses. For example, if you wanted to pass a by value and b by reference, you would specify the following instruction:

```
OnePlusAverage((a),b)
```

This issue doesn't arise when you're passing arguments to a user-defined function, since the list of arguments passed to a function must always be enclosed in parentheses.

Using Subroutines and Functions from Other Macros

You can call subroutines and functions that are stored in other macros. This technique lets you create libraries of subroutines and functions so that you can avoid copying or rewriting code you use often.

To call a subroutine stored in another macro, use the following syntax:

[**Call**] *MacroName*.*SubroutineName*[(*ArgumentList*)]

MacroName is the name of the macro containing the subroutine, and *SubroutineName* is the name of the subroutine you want to use. The optional *ArgumentList* is the list of values to be passed to the subroutine in the same way values are passed within the same macro. You can pass string and numeric values and arrays, just as you can within a macro.

The template in which the specified macro is stored can be the active template, the Normal template, or a loaded global template. Subroutines and functions stored in the Normal template are always available. For information on loading a template as a global template, see "Macros and Templates" in Chapter 2, "Getting Started with Macros."

The following example is a subroutine contained in a macro called Library:

```
Sub MyBeep
    Beep : Beep : Beep                  'Beep three times
    For t = 1 to 100 : Next             'Pause
    Beep : Beep : Beep                  'Beep three times again
End Sub
```

Here's an example of a macro that calls the MyBeep subroutine:

```
Sub MAIN
    YES = -1
    answer = Msgbox("Listen to MyBeep?", 36) 'Prompt user
    If answer = YES Then Library.MyBeep      'If yes, run MyBeep
End Sub
```

To use a function stored in another macro, use the following syntax: *MacroName.FunctionName* [(*ArgumentList*)]. For example, suppose the following function is stored in the Library macro:

```
Function MyDateTime$
    mDate$ = Date$()
    mTime$ = Time$()
    MyDateTime$ = mDate$ + " " + mTime$
End Function
```

In a macro called CheckDateTime, you could call this function as follows:

```
Sub MAIN
    MsgBox "The date and time is: " + Library.MyDateTime$
End Sub
```

Running Another Macro from Within Your Macro

In addition to being able to call subroutines and functions stored in other macros, you can run entire macros from within your macro. It can be useful to call a macro for a specific task from within a larger macro that performs several tasks. You can call a macro in the same way you call a subroutine or function, with or without the optional **Call** keyword. For example, to call a macro named ChangeSettings, you can use the following instruction:

```
Call ChangeSettings
```

Or you can omit the **Call** keyword:

```
ChangeSettings
```

You can also use **ToolsMacro** to run a macro:

```
ToolsMacro .Name = "ChangeSettings", .Show = 3, .Run
```

One advantage of using **ToolsMacro** to run a macro is that you can specify the template where the macro you want to run is stored. In the previous example, **ToolsMacro** will run the ChangeSettings macro stored in the template attached to the active document. When you use the **Call** statement, Word looks for the called macro first in the template that contains the calling macro. Only if the macro is not found there does Word look in other templates. This distinction between **ToolsMacro** and **Call** can make a difference if different available templates contain macros with the same names.

Here are some points to be aware of when calling subroutines or functions from another macro:

- Shared variables declared in one macro are not available in another. Each time a macro calls a subroutine or function from another macro, any shared variables declared in the macro being called are reinitialized.

- You can pass values to a macro's main subroutine just as you can pass values to any other subroutine. Note, however, that the main subroutine must be set up to receive values. For example, a main subroutine or function set up with the instruction Sub MAIN(a, b) requires two values from a macro that calls it. If you set up a main subroutine to accept values in this way, you can only run the macro that contains it by calling it from another macro.

- A macro cannot use the syntax for calling a subroutine or function in another macro to call a subroutine or function within itself. For example, if the macro CheckDateTime contained the MyBeep subroutine within it, the instruction `Call CheckDateTime.MyBeep` would generate an error. Similarly, a subroutine or function called from another macro cannot call a subroutine or function from the macro that is calling it.

- Limit calls between macros to four or five levels of nesting. For example, when macro A calls a subroutine in macro B that in turn calls a subroutine in macro C that calls macro D, three levels of nesting are involved.

- If more than one macro with a specified name is available, Word first looks for the macro stored in the same template as the calling macro. For example, suppose the Normal template and another template called Sample both contain a macro called Welcome. If a macro stored in the Normal template opens a document attached to the Sample template and then calls a subroutine within Welcome, Word runs the subroutine in the Welcome macro stored in the Normal template, even though Sample is the active template (since it is attached to the active document). If the called subroutine does not exist in the Welcome macro stored in Normal, Word generates an error (Word does not look for the subroutine in the Sample template's Welcome macro).

Important   You cannot call a subroutine or user-defined function stored in another macro if the name of the subroutine or function is the same as the name of an argument for a WordBasic statement that corresponds to a dialog box. For example, `Library.Wrap` generates an error because `.Wrap` is an argument for the **EditFind** statement.

Working with Dialog Records

You can create a special variable called a *dialog record* that stores the settings of a Word dialog box. You can use dialog records for Word dialog boxes in the following two ways:

- To retrieve or change the settings of dialog box options without displaying the dialog box.

- To display a Word dialog box and change the settings of options in the dialog box. Generally, when you display a dialog box, its settings reflect the current state of the active document or of Word itself. But you might want to change the settings displayed in a dialog box. For example, the Summary Info dialog box (File menu) normally shows the name of the document's original author. A macro can place a value in a dialog record for the Summary Info dialog box so that when the dialog box is displayed, the original author's name is automatically replaced with a different name.

Defining a Dialog Record

You use the **Dim** statement to define a dialog record. Here is the syntax:

Dim *DialogRecord* **As** *DialogBoxName*

DialogRecord can be any name you choose that isn't a reserved word. The limitations are the same as those for string and numeric variables (see "Variables" in Chapter 3, "WordBasic Fundamentals"). *DialogBoxName* can be any WordBasic statement name that corresponds to a dialog box. For example, the WordBasic statement that corresponds to the Open dialog box on the File menu is **FileOpen**, so "FileOpen" is a valid *DialogBoxName*. If you're not sure what the valid *DialogBoxName* for a dialog box is, see "Language Summary" and "Statements and Functions" in Part 2, "WordBasic Reference."

Here are some examples of dialog records:

```
Dim FPrec As FormatParagraph      'Define a dialog record "FPrec" for
                                  'the FormatParagraph dialog box

Dim Fontrecord As FormatFont      'Define a dialog record "Fontrecord"
                                  'for the FormatFont dialog box

Dim TOVrec As ToolsOptionsView    'Define a dialog record "TOVrec"
                                  'for the ToolsOptionsView dialog box
```

As the last example shows, you can sometimes specify the tab as well as the dialog box name for dialog boxes that contain tabs. That is, you can specify "ToolsOptionsView," not merely "ToolsOptions." To check whether you can specify a tab in this way for a particular dialog box, see the entry for the statement that corresponds to the dialog box in Part 2, "WordBasic Reference."

Retrieving and Changing Dialog Box Settings

Once you define a dialog record for a dialog box, you use the **GetCurValues** statement to place the current values of the dialog box into the dialog record. The following example copies the current settings of the View tab in the Options dialog box (Tools menu) into the TOVrec dialog record:

```
Dim TOVrec As ToolsOptionsView    'Define a dialog record "TOVrec"
GetCurValues TOVrec               'Get the current values
```

You can change or retrieve the values of the dialog box settings stored in a dialog record by referring to them with the following syntax:

DialogRecord.DialogBoxOption

DialogBoxOption is an argument for the WordBasic statement that corresponds to the dialog box whose options are stored in *DialogRecord*. For the list of valid arguments, see the entry for the corresponding WordBasic statement in Part 2, "WordBasic Reference."

The following example retrieves the current setting of the Picture Placeholders check box on the View tab in the Options dialog box (Tools menu) and places it in the variable `picture`:

```
Dim TOVrec As ToolsOptionsView
GetCurValues TOVrec
picture = TOVrec.PicturePlaceHolders
```

You change the value of an option in a dialog record by assigning it a value, just as you assign a value to any other variable. For example:

```
Dim TOVrec As ToolsOptionsView
GetCurValues TOVrec
TOVrec.PicturePlaceHolders = 1
ToolsOptionsView TOVrec
```

In this example, the `.PicturePlaceHolders` argument is given a value of 1, which corresponds to selecting the Picture Placeholders check box. The final instruction in the example (`ToolsOptionsView TOVrec`) puts the values stored in the `TOVrec` into effect. This instruction is required because changing values in a dialog record does not in itself cause changes to occur in Word. Only the WordBasic statement that corresponds to the dialog box can put the changes into effect.

The following WordBasic instruction is equivalent to the four instructions in the previous example:

```
ToolsOptionsView .PicturePlaceHolders = 1
```

As you can see, it's not very efficient to use a dialog record to change the value of a single option in a dialog box. But if you create a dialog record to retrieve dialog box values, you can use the dialog record to change a value conditionally. The most common use of this technique is to "toggle" a dialog box option.

Using a Dialog Record to Toggle a Check Box

To *toggle* something means to reverse its current "state" or value. You can toggle a check box in a dialog box because it has two "opposite" values—selected and cleared. The same is true of some Word commands. For example, when you choose the Ruler command from the View menu, Word hides the ruler if it was displayed or displays the ruler if it was hidden. The current state of the ruler (displayed or hidden) is reversed each time.

Using the appropriate dialog record, you can create a macro to toggle any check box. You can then assign the macro to a shortcut key or menu for quick access. The following macro toggles the Paragraph Marks check box on the View tab in the Options dialog box (Tools menu) to show or hide paragraph marks:

```
Sub MAIN
    Dim TOVrec As ToolsOptionsView      'Define a dialog record "TOVrec"
    GetCurValues TOVrec                 'Get the current values
    If TOVrec.Paras = 1 then            'If on
        TOVrec.Paras = 0                'turn off
    Else                                'Otherwise
        TOVrec.Paras = 1                'turn on
    End If
    ToolsOptionsView TOVrec             'Reset the dialog
End Sub
```

The following macro uses a slightly different technique to show or hide hidden text:

```
Sub MAIN
    Dim TOVrec As ToolsOptionsView            'Define a record "TOVrec"
    GetCurValues TOVrec                       'Get the current values
    TOVrec.Hidden = Abs(TOVrec.Hidden - 1)    'Reverse state
    ToolsOptionsView TOVrec                   'Reset the dialog
End Sub
```

This macro uses the expression Abs(TOVrec.Hidden - 1) to toggle the value of the Hidden Text check box on the View tab in the Options dialog box. Here's how it works. The Hidden Text check box can have the value 0 (zero) if it is not selected or 1 if it is selected:

- If the check box is not selected, then TOVrec.Hidden - 1 is equivalent to 0–1, or –1. The **Abs()** function makes the negative number positive, so the final result of Abs(TOVrec.Hidden - 1) is 1, which selects the check box.

- If the check box is selected, then TOVrec.Hidden - 1 is equivalent to 1–1, or 0 (zero). The **Abs()** function has no effect in this case, and the final result of Abs(TOVrec.Hidden - 1) is 0 (zero), which clears the check box.

Displaying a Dialog Box

Once you have created a dialog record, you can use the **Dialog** statement or **Dialog**() function to display the corresponding dialog box. This is useful if you want your macro to present a dialog box so that a user can set the options he or she wants before the macro continues. The following example displays the Options dialog box (Tools menu) with the View tab showing and then runs **ToolsOptionsView** after the user closes the dialog box.

```
Dim TOVrec As ToolsOptionsView    'Define a dialog record "TOVrec"
GetCurValues TOVrec               'Place current values in record
Dialog TOVrec                     'Display dialog box
ToolsOptionsView TOVrec           'Run ToolsOptionsView with new settings
```

Note that the **GetCurValues** instruction is necessary. Without this instruction, the macro would display the dialog box with no values—it would not reflect the current state of Word. The **ToolsOptionsView** instruction is necessary for the settings that the user chooses in the dialog box to have an effect. If this instruction were left out, the user could change settings and then choose the OK button, but Word would not carry out the command.

If you want to modify dialog box settings before displaying the dialog box for the user, you just change the settings of the dialog record options before running **Dialog** or **Dialog**(). The following example creates a dialog record for the Summary Info dialog box (File menu) and changes the contents of the Author box:

```
Dim FSIrecord as FileSummaryInfo     'Define a dialog record "FSIrecord"
GetCurValues FSIrecord               'Get the current values
FSIrecord.Author = "Louis Caspary"   'Place a name in the Author box
Dialog FSIrecord                     'Display Summary Info dialog box
FileSummaryInfo FSIrecord            'Do FileSummaryInfo instruction
```

The **Dialog** instruction displays the Summary Info dialog box with the name "Louis Caspary" in the Author box, as shown in the following illustration.

Checking How a Dialog Box Is Closed

When a macro displays a dialog box, it also needs to test how the user closes the dialog box. If the user chooses the OK button, the macro should carry out the command associated with the dialog box. If the user chooses the Cancel button, the macro should not carry out the command. The way you check how a dialog box is closed depends on whether you use the **Dialog** statement or the **Dialog()** function to display a dialog box:

- If a dialog box is displayed with the **Dialog()** function, the **Dialog()** function returns a value corresponding to the button used to dismiss the dialog box. You can then use that value in a conditional statement to determine how the macro should proceed.

- If a dialog box is displayed with the **Dialog** statement and the user chooses the OK button or the Close button, Word moves to the next statement in the macro. But if the user chooses the Cancel button, Word generates an error that you can handle with an **On Error** statement.

Here is an example that uses the **Dialog()** function and an **If** conditional to test whether the user chooses the OK button or the Cancel button to dismiss a dialog box:

```
Dim FSIrecord as FileSummaryInfo     'Define a dialog record "FSIrecord"
GetCurValues FSIrecord               'Get the current values
FSIrecord.Author = "Louis Caspary"   'Place a name in the Author box
choice = Dialog(FSIrecord)           'Display dialog and return button
If choice = -1 Then                  'If "OK" then
    FileSummaryInfo FSIrecord        'do FileSummaryInfo with changes
End If
```

The OK button returns a value of –1; the Cancel button returns 0 (zero). In this example, the value returned by Dialog(FSIrecord) is stored in the variable choice. If the user chooses the OK button, then the macro runs the **FileSummaryInfo** statement—the WordBasic statement corresponding to the Summary Info dialog box. Otherwise, nothing happens.

In the following example, the **On Error Goto** statement is used to trap the error generated by the Cancel button when the **Dialog** statement is used to display the Open dialog box:

```
Dim FOrecord as FileOpen          'Define a dialog record "FOrecord"
GetCurValues FOrecord             'Get the current values
On Error Goto trap                'Go to the "trap" label if the user
                                  'chooses the Cancel button
Dialog FOrecord                   'Display the Open dialog box
FileOpen FOrecord                 'Carry out FileOpen with changes
Goto bye                          'Go to the "bye" label
trap:                             'Label for On Error Goto statement
MsgBox "Macro cannot proceed."    'Error message
bye:                              'Label for Goto statement
```

This more elaborate example uses an **On Error Goto** instruction to present a message to the user if he or she chooses the Cancel button. The **MsgBox** instruction informs the user that the macro cannot continue because the user did not open a file. For more information on error trapping, see Chapter 7, "The Well-Behaved Macro."

CHAPTER 5

Working with Custom Dialog Boxes

You can create custom dialog boxes for your macros. This chapter describes how to design a custom dialog box with the Dialog Editor and then use the dialog box in a macro. The last section of the chapter deals with dynamic dialog boxes— dialog boxes that can respond to user actions while they are displayed. These dialog boxes are more complex to set up but deliver many useful capabilities.

In this chapter:

- Dialog box controls
- Using the Dialog Editor to create a dialog box
- Using custom dialog boxes
- Using dynamic dialog boxes

Dialog Box Controls

WordBasic supports most of the standard Windows and Macintosh dialog box controls. This section introduces the controls available for custom dialog boxes and provides guidelines for using them.

OK, Cancel, and Push Buttons

Every custom dialog box must contain at least one "command" button—an OK button, a Cancel button, or a push button. WordBasic includes separate dialog box definition statements for each of these three types of buttons. A common use for a push button is to display another dialog box.

List Boxes, Drop-Down List Boxes, and Combo Boxes

You use a list box, drop-down list box, or combo box to present a list of items from which the user can select. A drop-down list box saves space (it can drop down to cover other dialog box controls temporarily). A combo box allows the user either to select an item from the list or type a new item. The items displayed in a list box, drop-down list box, or combo box are stored in an array that is defined before the instructions that define the dialog box.

Check Boxes

You use a check box to make a "yes or no" or "on or off" choice. For example, you could use a check box to display or hide a toolbar or to apply or remove formatting for selected text.

Text Boxes and Text

A text box control is a box in which the user can enter text while the dialog box is displayed. By default, a text box holds a single line of text, but you can also size it to hold multiple lines of text (text wraps within a multiple-line text box, and the user can also press ENTER to start a new line). A text control displays text that the user cannot change. It is often used to label a text box.

Option Buttons and Group Boxes

You use option buttons to allow the user to choose one option from several. Typically, you use a group box to surround a group of option buttons, but you can also use a group box to set off a group of check boxes or any related group of controls.

Pictures and File Preview

A custom dialog box can include graphics, or "pictures," and a file preview box, which displays a thumbnail representation of any Word document. A dialog box can include only one file preview box. A graphic can be stored as a file, an AutoText entry, an item marked with a bookmark in a document, or an item on the Clipboard.

Using the Dialog Editor to Create a Dialog Box

You can use the Dialog Editor to create a new dialog box or to edit an existing one. Here's the sequence for creating and using a custom dialog box:

1. Design the dialog box using the Dialog Editor application.

2. Select the completed dialog box and copy it into the macro in which you want to use it.

3. Add the instructions needed to display the dialog box and to retrieve information from it.

Starting the Dialog Editor

The Dialog Editor is a separate application included in the Word package. If you chose not to install the Dialog Editor when you set up Word, you can run the Word Setup program again to install it.

The Dialog Editor button (Macro toolbar)

To start the Dialog Editor, click the Dialog Editor button on the Macro toolbar. In Windows, you can also run the Dialog Editor from Program Manager or File Manager. On the Macintosh, you can run the Dialog Editor by double-clicking the Dialog Editor icon in the Word folder.

Note In Windows, the Dialog Editor does not support 3-D dialog effects. However, when a WordBasic macro displays a dialog box created with the Dialog Editor in Windows, the dialog box has the same 3-D look as built-in Word dialog boxes, assuming the 3-D Dialog And Display Effects check box is selected on the General tab in the Options dialog box (Tools menu).

Adding Items to a Dialog Box

When you start the Dialog Editor, it displays an empty dialog box to which you can add dialog box controls such as buttons, text, and list boxes. In the Dialog Editor, controls are called *items*. You use the Item menu to add them to the dialog box.

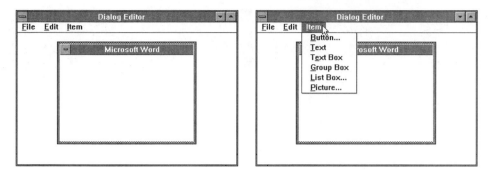

When you start the Dialog Editor, it presents an empty dialog box.

The Item menu in the Dialog Editor

After you have used the Item menu to insert an item, the item remains selected. You can press ENTER to create a copy of the selected item. For example, when a check box is selected you can press ENTER to insert another check box. When an OK button or push button is selected and you press ENTER, the Dialog Editor inserts a Cancel button if there isn't one already; likewise, when a Cancel button or a push button is selected and you press ENTER, the Dialog Editor inserts an OK button if there isn't one already. If both an OK button and a Cancel button are present, pressing ENTER when any command button is selected inserts a new push button.

When an item is selected, you can press ENTER to create copies.

When an OK button is selected, ENTER inserts a Cancel button.

Adding a Group of Option Buttons

An easy way to create a group of option buttons is to insert a group box, press ENTER to insert the first option button, and continue to press ENTER to insert additional option buttons. To insert a group box, choose Group Box from the Item menu. Immediately after creating each option button, type a name for it. (When an option button is selected, you can replace the default text, "Option Button," by typing new text.)

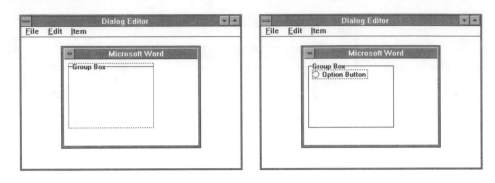

With the group box selected ...   press ENTER to insert the first option button.

Adding a Picture Item

Using the Picture command on the Item menu, you can add graphics to your dialog boxes. When you choose the Picture command from the Item menu, it displays the New Picture dialog box, in which you can indicate how the graphic you're adding is stored—as a file, an AutoText entry, an item marked with a bookmark, or an item on the Clipboard. In the Text$ box of the Information dialog box (Info command, Edit menu) for the picture item, type the path and filename of the graphics file, the name of the AutoText entry, or the name of the bookmark, or just type **Clipboard**. The Dialog Editor does not display the graphic, but you can position and size the picture item just as you can any other item. Don't worry if you don't know the name of the file or the picture type; you can specify it later.

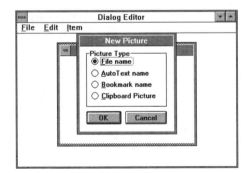

In the New Picture dialog box, select the type   The Dialog Editor inserts a picture placeholder.
of graphic you want to display, and choose the
OK button.

Adding a Multiple-Line Text Box

When you use the Dialog Editor to insert a text box control, the text box is sized to hold a single line of text. To make the text box into a multiple-line text box, you change the text box's height so that it can accommodate more than one line. Initially, however, the Dialog Editor doesn't allow you to change a text box's height. This is to prevent you from accidentally changing the height as you change the width. To change the height, you have to double-click the text box to display the Information dialog box, which displays settings pertinent to the selected dialog box item, and then clear the Auto check box next to Height. You can then adjust the height of the text box to make it into a multiple-line text box.

Adding a File Preview Box

The Dialog Editor does not have a command to insert a File Preview box. However, you can use another item that can be sized in a similar way as a placeholder. A group box, for example, makes a good placeholder. When you paste the dialog box into your macro, you can then change the name of the item's instruction to **FilePreview**. Keep in mind that a dialog box can include only one File Preview box; also, when a dialog box includes a File Preview box, it must call a dialog function. For information on dialog functions, see "Using Dynamic Dialog Boxes" later in this chapter. For more information, see **FilePreview** in Part 2, "WordBasic Reference."

Positioning and Sizing Items

Once you have added an item, you can use the mouse to position and size it.

The mouse pointer for positioning

Positioning   You can position an item by dragging it with the mouse. When the mouse pointer is positioned over an item, the pointer changes to a four-headed arrow.

The dotted lines indicate where the item will be positioned when you release the mouse button.

The mouse pointers
for sizing

Sizing You can size an item by dragging its borders with the mouse. When the mouse pointer is positioned over a border, the pointer changes to a double-headed arrow.

You can drag the lower-right corner of an item to
size it horizontally and vertically at the same time.

Positioning and Sizing Precisely

Using the SHIFT key to align If you hold down the SHIFT key just before you move an item, you can drag only vertically or only horizontally, depending on which direction you first move the mouse.

Using the arrow keys You can use the arrow keys to position or size a selected item. You can position an item by pressing an arrow that corresponds to the direction you want to move the item. To size an item, hold down the SHIFT key and press an arrow key. In Windows, the selected item is moved or sized by four X or Y units each time you press an arrow key. To move or size the item by just one X or Y unit, hold down the CTRL key while moving or sizing. For example, to increase the width of a selected item by one X unit in Windows, you could press CTRL+SHIFT+RIGHT ARROW. In Windows, you must press ENTER to finish moving or sizing an item; you can press ESC to cancel. On the Macintosh, the selected item is moved or sized one X or Y unit each time you press an arrow key; you can hold down the OPTION key to move or size an item by four X or Y units each time you press an arrow key. For example, to increase the width of a selected item by one X unit on the Macintosh, you could press SHIFT+RIGHT ARROW.

Using the Information dialog box   The Information dialog box displays the exact position and size of an item, so that you can set it precisely. You can also see at a glance whether or not an item is precisely aligned with another item. For example, if you want to align two items horizontally, a good technique is to do it first by eye and then use the Information dialog box to get the Y coordinates of the items; if one of them is off by one or two Y units, you can adjust its position accordingly. To display the Information dialog box for an item, double-click the item, or select it and choose Info from the Edit menu.

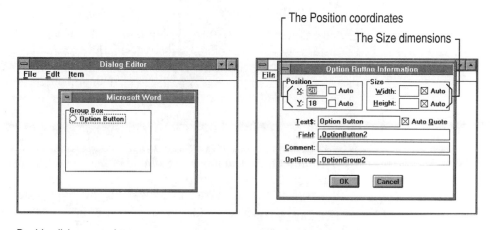

The Position coordinates

The Size dimensions

Double-click a control ...   to display the Information dialog box for that item.

What Do X and Y Represent?

The Dialog Editor positions and sizes items in X units for horizontal positioning and width, and Y units for vertical positioning and height. Because monitors have different resolutions, these units are defined in relative rather than absolute terms. X units are increments of 1/8 of the System font in Windows or the dialog font on the Macintosh. Y units are increments of 1/12 of the System font in Windows or the dialog font on the Macintosh.

Note that in Windows, the System font is not the same as the font used to display text in a custom dialog box. Generally, the dialog font and the System font are scaled in proportion to each other, but some display drivers install a System font that is easier to read and disproportionately large. For example, the Windows Super VGA 1024 x 768 (large fonts) display driver uses this technique. When one of these display drivers is installed, the Word dialog font does not expand to the degree the System font does. This means that dialog boxes and controls, whose size is dependent on the System font, expand more than dialog box text, which appears a little shrunken. Likewise, if you design a dialog box with a large-fonts display driver installed and then display the dialog box with a small- or normal-fonts display driver installed, dialog box text may be truncated (since dialog box controls shrink more than the text they contain).

To avoid this problem, either design your dialog boxes with a standard VGA resolution driver installed or, if you're designing with a large-fonts display driver installed, make sure that controls containing text (such as text label and option button controls) are a little larger than necessary so that text has room to expand when displayed with a different display driver.

Selecting Multiple Items

You can select more than one item by holding down the SHIFT key and clicking the additional items you want to select. This is useful if you want to move several items as a group. You can select every item in a dialog box by using the Select All Items command on the Edit menu.

Selecting a Group

When you move option buttons or other items within a group box, you typically want to move them as a group. The Dialog Editor provides a Select Group command to select all the items within a group box, including the group box. A group box is most often used to group option buttons, but you can include any item within it.

Positioning and Sizing Automatically

The Dialog Editor automatically positions or sizes some items. When an Auto check box is selected for an item, you cannot change the item's position or size. Automatic sizing is a useful way to fix the size of items you generally don't want to resize, such as OK buttons and Cancel buttons. To select or clear automatic positioning and sizing for any item, double-click the item and select or clear the appropriate Auto check boxes in the Information dialog box.

Note that if you select Auto for the position of an item you've already moved, it returns to the position where the Dialog Editor originally inserted it; this may conflict with the position of other items you have moved. However, you can set automatic positioning for an item just after inserting it to force it to move with the item that precedes it. For example, if you select Auto for the position of a text box inserted beneath a text item, you can move them together by dragging only the text item.

Sizing the Dialog Box

When you have added all the items the dialog box will contain, you can drag the borders of the dialog box (Windows) or drag the sizing box at the bottom-right corner (Macintosh) to fit the items. You can also choose the Resize command from the Edit menu or double-click the dialog box border (Windows) or click the zoom box (Macintosh) to have the Dialog Editor size the dialog box for you.

You can double-click a dialog box border...   to resize the dialog box.

Deleting Items

You can delete one or more selected items by choosing Clear from the Edit menu. In Windows, you can also press the DELETE key; on the Macintosh, you can press either DEL or COMMAND+DELETE (on the Macintosh, the DELETE key deletes text in an item label, not the item itself). To delete all of the items in a dialog box, select the dialog box itself or choose Select All Items from the Edit menu before deleting. To start from scratch with a new, empty dialog box with the default label and default size and position, choose New from the File menu.

Changing Labels and Identifiers

When you insert an item, it has a default label such as "Check Box," "Option Button," or "Text." Immediately after you've inserted an item, while it is selected, you can replace the default label by typing the one you want. Once you have changed the default text, you can select the item and use the BACKSPACE key (Windows) or the DELETE key (Macintosh) to delete what you typed, or you can use the Information dialog box to edit it.

To display the Information dialog box, double-click the item or select the item and choose the Info command from the Edit menu. In the Information dialog box, you edit the label by changing the text in the Text$ box. The Auto Quote check box is selected by default; it inserts quotation marks around the item's label when you paste the dialog box definition into a macro. If you want to use a variable name as a label, you can clear the Auto Quote check box (since a variable name should not be enclosed in quotation marks). On the Macintosh, the Auto Quote check box is not included in the Dialog Editor.

Many dialog box items are designed to return a value to the macro that displays the dialog box. In your macro, you use an item's *identifier* to access the value associated with that dialog box item. The Dialog Editor assigns these items default identifiers such as .CheckBox1 or .ListBox2. You can use the .Field box in the Information dialog box to change an item's identifier to something less generic. The .Field box is so named because the values returned by dialog box items are stored in a dialog record. In programming terminology, values stored in a record are "fields." In this book, the term "identifier" is used instead because identifiers serve not only to indicate fields within records but also to identify dialog box items to other instructions within a macro.

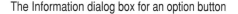

The Information dialog box for an option button

Comments   In the Comment box, you can add a comment that will appear in the dialog box definition when the dialog box is copied from the Dialog Editor into a macro. In your macro, the comment will be located on the same line as the WordBasic instruction associated with the item.

Access keys   Access keys allow quick keyboard access to items in a dialog box. When an access key is defined for an item in a custom dialog box, the user can press ALT+the specified letter (Windows) or COMMAND+the specified letter (Macintosh) to activate a text box, select or clear a check box, or choose a command button, for example. In the Information dialog box, you define an access key for an item by including an ampersand (&) character before a letter in the Text$ box. In the dialog box, the letter appears underlined. (Note that on the Macintosh, you must hold down the COMMAND key for a second or two before the letter appears underlined.) To define an access key for a text box, you define one for a text item associated with the text box. To associate a text item with a text box, insert the text item first, then insert a text box. In the dialog box definition created when the dialog box is pasted into a macro, the **Text** instruction must immediately precede the **TextBox** instruction.

Copying a Dialog Box to a Macro

When you're ready to insert a dialog box into the macro that will display it, you select the dialog box in the Dialog Editor and copy it. You don't have to select each item in the dialog box; you just select the dialog box itself. You can do this by clicking the dialog box title bar or by choosing the Select Dialog command from the Edit menu.

When the dialog box is selected, choose the Copy command from the Edit menu to copy it. In Word, open the macro and position the insertion point where you want to insert the dialog box definition. Then paste the dialog box definition. It will appear as a series of instructions enclosed by a **Begin Dialog**...**End Dialog** instruction.

In the Dialog Editor, click the title bar or choose Select Dialog from the Edit menu to select the dialog box.

In Word, paste the dialog box definition into the macro-editing window.

Exiting the Dialog Editor

In the Dialog Editor, choose Exit (Windows) or Quit (Macintosh) from the File menu. If you've created a new dialog box or changed an existing one and have not copied your work, the Dialog Editor asks if you want to copy it to the Clipboard. If you want to use the dialog box in Word, choose the Yes button. If you choose the No button, the new dialog box or any changes made to an existing one will be lost.

Editing an Existing Dialog Box

You can change a custom dialog box in any macro by copying the dialog box definition from the macro to the Clipboard and then pasting it from the Clipboard into the Dialog Editor. You can then edit the dialog box in the Dialog Editor. Note that when you select a dialog box definition, the selection must start with the **Begin Dialog** instruction and end with the **End Dialog** instruction.

Tips for Using the Dialog Editor

The following tips can save you time and effort when building custom dialog boxes with the Dialog Editor.

Build a dialog box from top to bottom and from left to right   Within the Dialog Editor, everything is relative to the upper-left corner of the dialog box. When you resize a dialog box, items aligned with the top and left borders of the dialog box will keep their position relative to the top and left borders, but items aligned with the bottom and right borders will lose their position.

Use the SHIFT key to align items with the mouse   If you hold down the SHIFT key before moving an item with the mouse, you will only be able to move the item in the direction you first move it. You can confidently position the item without worrying that you'll accidentally move it out of alignment in the other direction. You can also use the SHIFT key to select multiple items and move them together so they maintain their positions relative to each other.

Select an item, then add an item below it   You can minimize the amount of rearranging you have to do if you keep in mind that when you add an item, the Dialog Editor positions it below the currently selected item. For example, if you know you want to add a text box with a text label, add the text label first, then add the text box (assuming that you want the text label to appear above the text box, as it usually does).

Add a group box first   If you want to enclose items such as option buttons or check boxes within a group box, add the group box first. If you add the check boxes or option buttons first, the group box will hide rather than enclose them.

Use a group box to create a rectangle   A group box normally includes a text label, but if you delete the label, the group box forms a rectangle that you can use as a design element.

Use the arrow keys to make small adjustments   In Windows, when you press an arrow key, you move the selected dialog box item four X or Y units; when you press CTRL+an arrow key, you move the item one X or Y unit. To size an item, press SHIFT+an arrow key or CTRL+SHIFT+an arrow key. Press ENTER to complete positioning or sizing or ESC to cancel it.

On the Macintosh, when you press an arrow key, you move the selected item one X or Y unit; when you press OPTION+an arrow key, you move the item four X or Y units. To size an item, hold down SHIFT and press an arrow key or OPTION+an arrow key.

Always include a command button   A dialog box must include at least one command button. That is, it must include either an OK button, a Cancel button, or a push button. Otherwise, Word will generate an error when you run the macro to display the dialog box.

Avoid a "value out of range" error   Sometimes when you insert a large item such as a group box into a dialog box, the item's boundaries fall outside the dialog box border. If you paste the dialog box into a macro and run it, Word will display a "value out of range" error. You can avoid this error by simply repositioning the item that causes the error. A macro can't display an item in a dialog box unless it lies entirely within the dialog box. (Drop-down list boxes can drop slightly outside the dialog box, but no more than an eighth of an inch or so.)

A Glossary of Dialog Box Terms

The vocabulary associated with dialog boxes can be confusing. Here's a glossary of terms.

Custom dialog box   A dialog box defined by WordBasic instructions. Usually, the Dialog Editor is used to design a custom dialog box, which is then copied into a macro. A custom dialog box is used to display and return information. Also known as a user-defined dialog box.

Dialog box control   An element of a dialog box such as a command button, check box, text label, or list box. Within the Dialog Editor, a dialog box control is referred to as an "item." For descriptions of the dialog box controls available for custom dialog boxes, see "Dialog Box Controls" earlier in this chapter.

Dialog box control identifier   A string used to identify a particular dialog box control. The identifier is used with a dialog record to insert and retrieve values from dialog boxes and to reference dialog box controls.

Dialog box definition   The set of WordBasic instructions used in a macro to define a custom dialog box. These instructions are enclosed within a **Begin Dialog…End Dialog** instruction. The Dialog Editor automatically generates a dialog box definition.

Dialog function   A special user-defined function that can be called while a custom dialog box is displayed. The dialog function can make a custom dialog box "dynamic" by responding to events while the dialog box is displayed. See "Using Dynamic Dialog Boxes" later in this chapter.

Dialog record   A variable that contains the values returned by a Word dialog box or by a custom dialog box. Each setting in a dialog box is stored in a field within the record associated with the dialog box. For more information, see "Working with Dialog Records" in Chapter 4, "Advanced WordBasic."

Dynamic dialog box   A custom dialog box whose contents can change dynamically in response to user actions while the dialog box is displayed. See "Using Dynamic Dialog Boxes" later in this chapter.

Word dialog box   A dialog box built into Word. Most dialog boxes are displayed by choosing a menu command, but some, like the Organizer dialog box, are available only by choosing buttons in other dialog boxes.

Using Custom Dialog Boxes

A custom dialog box is designed to display and return information. Once you have built a dialog box in the Dialog Editor and copied it into a macro, you need to add instructions to put information into the dialog box, display the dialog box, and retrieve information from it. Here's an overview of the steps involved:

1. Define the dialog box. You use the Dialog Editor to define the dialog box. The instructions the Dialog Editor generates are called a *dialog box definition*.

2. Create a dialog record. You use a **Dim** statement to create a dialog record for a custom dialog box, just as you do for a built-in dialog box.

3. Put values into the dialog box. If the dialog box includes a list box, drop-down list box, or combo box, you probably want to fill it with items. You may also want to place default text in a text box or select check boxes before displaying the dialog box.

4. Display the dialog box. You use a **Dialog** instruction to display the dialog box. As with built-in dialog boxes, you can use either the **Dialog** statement or the **Dialog**() function.

5. Retrieve values from the dialog box. The settings of dialog box controls are stored in the dialog record, so you retrieve information from the dialog record after the dialog box is closed.

The Dialog Box Definition

A dialog box definition is the set of instructions that defines the contents of a dialog box as well as its size and position. When you create a dialog box in the Dialog Editor, it generates these instructions.

Dialog box definition instructions are enclosed within the **Begin Dialog…End Dialog** statement. Here is the syntax:

Begin Dialog UserDialog [*HorizPos, VertPos,*] *Width, Height, Title$*
[, *.DialogFunction*]
   Series of instructions to define controls in the dialog box
End Dialog

The optional *HorizPos* and *VertPos* arguments position the dialog box; if they are omitted, Word displays the dialog box at the center of the Word window. *Width* and *Height* size the dialog box. The *Title$* argument is the text that appears in the dialog box title bar. If you do not specify *HorizPos* and *VertPos*, you can omit *Title$*; you can omit *Title$* even if you specify *HorizPos* and *VertPos* if you also specify *.DialogFunction*. If you omit *Title$*, "Microsoft Word 6.0" appears in the title bar. The *.DialogFunction* argument is used only if you want to create a dynamic dialog box. For information on dynamic dialog boxes, see "Using Dynamic Dialog Boxes" later in this chapter. For complete information, see **Begin Dialog…End Dialog** in Part 2, "WordBasic Reference."

The following dialog box includes every dialog box control.

Here is the dialog box definition that defines the dialog box:

```
Begin Dialog UserDialog 612, 226, "Every Dialog Box Control", \
        .DlgFunction
    ComboBox 8, 76, 176, 111, MyList$(), .ComboBox1
    CheckBox 198, 79, 180, 16, "&Check Box", .CheckBox1
    ListBox 195, 102, 189, 83, MyList$(), .ListBox1
    DropListBox 417, 5, 179, 108, MyList$(), .DropListBox1
    Text 417, 186, 35, 13, "&Text"
    TextBox 417, 199, 179, 18, .TextBox1
    GroupBox 7, 4, 177, 65, "&Group Box"
    OptionGroup  .OptionGroup1
        OptionButton 17, 16, 148, 16, "Option Button &1"
        OptionButton 17, 33, 148, 16, "Option Button &2"
        OptionButton 17, 50, 148, 16, "Option Button &3"
    Picture 199, 7, 181, 62, "BIRD", 1, .Picture1
    FilePreview 417, 31, 179, 148, .fileprev
    PushButton 10, 199, 108, 21, "&PushButton"
    CancelButton 131, 199, 108, 21
    OKButton 253, 199, 108, 21
End Dialog
```

Note that each dialog box control has its own instruction within the dialog box definition. The first pair of numbers that follows each instruction for a control positions the control relative to the upper-left corner of the dialog box; the second pair defines the control's width and height.

Controls that store a value, such as combo boxes and check boxes, include in their instructions identifiers that begin with a period. For example, the **CheckBox** instruction includes the identifier .CheckBox1. These identifiers are used to access the control's value or setting in a dialog record.

To see the full syntax for a dialog box definition statement such as **CheckBox** or **ListBox**, see the corresponding entry in Part 2, "WordBasic Reference."

Creating a Dialog Record

A dialog record stores the values that you put into and retrieve from a dialog box. A dialog record for a custom dialog box is defined in much the same way as one for a built-in Word dialog box:

Dim *DialogRecord* **As UserDialog**

The *DialogRecord* argument can be any variable name. **As UserDialog** identifies the dialog record as the record for a custom dialog box (just as As FormatFont in a **Dim** instruction identifies a dialog record for the Font dialog box). You can include as many custom dialog boxes in a macro as you need, but you can define only one **UserDialog** record at a time.

Placing Values into a Dialog Box

It's often necessary to place initial values into a custom dialog box and to specify the default settings of some controls before the dialog box is displayed. The values you can place in a dialog box and the settings you can control include the following:

- The items in a list box, drop-down list box, or combo box
- The default text in a text box
- Check box values
- The initial focus (the item that has the focus when the dialog box is first displayed)

Placing Items into a List Box, Drop-Down List Box, or Combo Box

The items displayed in a list box, drop-down list box, or combo box control are stored as elements of an array. Therefore, before you display a dialog box containing one of these controls, you must define an array and fill it with the items to be listed; you then refer to the array in the instruction for the control in the dialog box definition. For example, if you want a dialog box to present a list of fonts, as in the following illustration, you first create an array to hold the font names.

Here are the instructions that define and fill an array, FontArray$(), for the font names:

```
lastElement = CountFonts() - 1
Dim FontArray$(lastElement)             'Define the array
For count = 0 To lastElement            'Fill the array
    FontArray$(count) = Font$(count + 1)
Next
```

To place the array elements into a list box, you refer to the array in the **ListBox** instruction. For example:

```
ListBox 10, 25, 160, 84, FontArray$(), .ListBox1
```

Putting it all together, here are the complete instructions for displaying the Show Font List dialog box in the preceding illustration. The array is defined first, then the dialog box, and finally the dialog record used in the **Dialog**() instruction to display the dialog box.

```
lastElement = CountFonts() - 1
Dim FontArray$(lastElement)             'Define the array
For count = 0 To lastElement            'Fill the array
    FontArray$(count) = Font$(count + 1)
Next
Begin Dialog UserDialog 362, 122, "Show Font List"
    ListBox 10, 9, 206, 100, FontArray$(), .FontList
    OKButton 265, 7, 88, 21
    CancelButton 265, 31, 88, 21
End Dialog
Dim dlg As UserDialog                   'Define the dialog record
buttonchoice = Dialog(dlg)              'Display the dialog box
```

Placing Default Text in a Text Box and Setting Check Box Values

A text box—a box in which the user can enter text—is usually empty when the dialog box is first displayed. But in some cases, you may want to place default text in a text box. For example, in the following dialog box the user is prompted to type his or her name and phone number. Most of the time that text will not change, so rather than force the user to type the text each time the dialog box is displayed, you can make the name and phone number default text.

You place default text in a text box (or combo box) by assigning it to the dialog identifier that corresponds to the text box. Recall that the dialog record contains a value corresponding to the identifier for each dialog box control that can return a value. The identifier is part of the instruction that defines the control. The following instructions define the text boxes in the Personal Info dialog box shown in the previous illustration:

```
TextBox 7, 21, 160, 18, .Name$
TextBox 7, 64, 160, 18, .Phone$
```

Note that .Name$ and .Phone$ are the identifiers for the text boxes (the dollar signs ($) aren't necessary, but indicate that the fields in the dialog record corresponding to these identifiers hold string values). You could use the following instructions to assign default text to these identifiers, where PersonalInfoDlgRec is the name of the dialog record:

```
PersonalInfoDlgRec.Name = "Michel Gabor"
PersonalInfoDlgRec.Phone = "(206) 555-1234"
```

Of course, you must define a dialog record before you can assign values to identifiers within it. Here are the complete instructions to display the dialog box:

```
Begin Dialog UserDialog 320, 102, "Personal Info"
    Text 7, 5, 89, 13, "Your &Name:"
    TextBox 7, 21, 160, 18, .Name$
    TextBox 7, 64, 160, 18, .Phone$
    Text 7, 47, 157, 13, "Your &Phone Number:"
    OKButton 225, 3, 88, 21
    CancelButton 225, 27, 88, 21
End Dialog
Dim PersonalInfoDlgRec As UserDialog       'Define dialog record
PersonalInfoDlgRec.Name$ = "Michel Gabor"  'Assign value to .Name$
PersonalInfoDlgRec.Phone$ = "(206) 555-1234" 'Assign value to .Phone$
x = Dialog(PersonalInfoDlgRec)             'Display dialog box
```

You can use the same method of assigning values to text boxes to specify the initial setting of a check box. After defining the dialog record, you assign one of three values to the identifier for the check box: 0 (zero) to clear the check box (this is the default), 1 to select the check box, and -1 to make it indeterminate.

Setting the Initial Focus and Tab Order

When a control is active, it is said to have the *focus*, which means that you can act on it. For example, if a text box has the focus, you can type in it. You can use the TAB key to move the focus and activate controls in a dialog box. The *tab order* is the order in which controls become active when you use the TAB key to move to them. The TAB key is particularly useful for dialog boxes that contain more than one text box; if you're typing in a text box, it's natural to use the TAB key to move to the next text box.

The control that has the focus when the dialog box is first displayed is said to have the initial focus. The initial focus is important in dialog boxes in which the user is prompted to type something. For example, in the dialog box shown in the following illustration, the initial focus should be on the Fax Number text box. If it isn't and the user starts typing, nothing will happen; the dialog box will seem not to work properly.

The order of the instructions within the dialog box definition determines the initial focus and the tab order: The first control in a dialog box definition has the initial focus, the second control has the focus next, and so on. Items that cannot be active, such as the text control, are ignored. (On the Macintosh, only text box and combo box controls can have the focus.)

Here are the instructions for the Fax Info dialog box shown in the previous illustration. Note that the first instruction is a **Text** instruction. Since a text control cannot have the focus, the initial focus is on the text box defined by the **TextBox** instruction.

```
Begin Dialog UserDialog 370, 92, "Fax Info"
    Text 14, 7, 96, 13, "Fax Number:"
    TextBox 14, 23, 160, 18, .TextBox1
    CheckBox 14, 57, 211, 16, "Add To Fax Number List", .FaxList
    OKButton 270, 6, 88, 21
    CancelButton 270, 30, 88, 21
End Dialog
Dim dlg As UserDialog
buttonchoice = Dialog(dlg)
```

Displaying the Dialog Box

You use the **Dialog** statement or the **Dialog**() function to display a custom dialog box in the same way that you can use them to display a dialog box built into Word.

In general, the **Dialog**() function rather than the **Dialog** statement is the best choice for custom dialog boxes. If you use the **Dialog** statement, Word generates an error if the user chooses the Cancel button in the dialog box. You can use the **On Error** statement to handle this error, but you can avoid it entirely by using the **Dialog**() function. Also, if your dialog box contains a push button, you need to use the **Dialog**() function to determine whether the push button was chosen (or which one was chosen if the dialog box contains more than one).

For complete information on the **Dialog** statement and the **Dialog**() function, see the entry in Part 2, "WordBasic Reference."

The Default Command Button

You can use the *DefaultButton* argument of the **Dialog** statement or the **Dialog**() function to determine the default command button. The default command button is the button that is highlighted when the dialog box is first displayed. It is also the command button that is chosen if a control other than a command button has the focus when the user presses ENTER. Unless you specify otherwise, the OK button is the default command button.

For the *DefaultButton* argument to have any effect, the instruction for the specified button must be preceded in the dialog box definition by an instruction for a non-command button dialog box control that can receive the focus, such as a list box or check box. (Note that because a text control cannot receive the focus, it does not meet this criterion.) Otherwise, the first button in the dialog box definition is the default command button.

Retrieving Values from the Dialog Box

Once a custom dialog box has been displayed and the user has closed it, the macro can retrieve the settings of the dialog box controls. These values are stored in the dialog record, so retrieving values is a matter of accessing the appropriate identifiers in the dialog record.

The following table shows the values that different dialog box controls store in the dialog record.

Control	Value stored in the dialog record
Check box	If the check box is selected, 1; if the check box is clear, 0 (zero); if the check box is indeterminate, −1
Option group	A number corresponding to the option button selected
List box or drop-down list box	The number of the item chosen, beginning with 0 (zero)
Combo box	A text string (what the user typed or selected in the list of items)
Text box	A text string

Examples

The following example tests the value of the Add To Fax Number List check box in the Fax Info dialog box (shown in the following illustration) to determine whether the user selected that control.

Two nested **If** conditionals are used to test two conditions. The first **If** instruction uses the condition buttonchoice = -1 to test whether the user chose the OK button to dismiss the dialog box (**Dialog()** returns –1 if the user chose the OK button). If this condition is true, the second **If** instruction tests the value of the Add To Fax Number List check box, which is stored in dlg.FaxList. If the check box is selected, meaning the fax number should be added to the list of fax numbers, the dialog record identifier for the check box is equal to 1. The macro then runs the instructions to add the fax number to the list of numbers.

```
Begin Dialog UserDialog 370, 92, "Fax Info"
    Text 14, 7, 96, 13, "Fax Number:"
    TextBox 14, 23, 160, 18, .TextBox1
    CheckBox 14, 57, 211, 16, "Add To Fax Number List", .FaxList
    OKButton 270, 6, 88, 21
    CancelButton 270, 30, 88, 21
End Dialog
Dim dlg As UserDialog
buttonchoice = Dialog(dlg)
If buttonchoice = -1 Then
    If dlg.CheckBox1 = 1 Then
        'Series of instructions to add fax number to list.
    End If
End If
```

The following example formats the selected text with the font selected in the Show Font List dialog box shown in the following illustration.

As in the previous example, the **If** instruction tests whether the user chose the OK button to dismiss the dialog box (rather than the Cancel button to indicate that the dialog box should not carry out an action). If the user chose the OK button, the instruction Font FontArray$(dlg.FontList) formats the selection with or prepares to insert text in the font the user selected in the dialog box. The FontArray$() array stores the names of the fonts displayed in the dialog box. The dlg.FontList setting in the dialog record contains the number of the font selected in the list box.

```
Begin Dialog UserDialog 362, 122, "Show Font List"
    ListBox 10, 9, 206, 100, FontArray$(), .FontList
    OKButton 265, 7, 88, 21
    CancelButton 265, 31, 88, 21
End Dialog
Dim dlg As UserDialog                    'Define the dialog record
buttonchoice = Dialog(dlg)               'Display the dialog box
If buttonchoice = - 1 Then
    Font FontArray$(dlg.FontList)        'Format selected text
End If
```

Using Dynamic Dialog Boxes

A *dynamic* dialog box is one whose contents can change while it is displayed. Many dialog boxes built into Word are dynamic in this sense. For example, the Open dialog box (File menu) is a dynamic dialog box: If you double-click a folder, Word updates the list of files to show the files in the folder you double-clicked.

What Can You Do with a Dynamic Dialog Box?

Here are some examples that demonstrate the capabilities of dynamic dialog boxes. The macros that produce the sample dialog boxes shown in this section are stored in the EXAMPLES.DOT template (Windows) and the MACRO EXAMPLES template (Macintosh) on the Microsoft Word Developer's Kit disk.

Change button names and other text   It can be useful to change the names of buttons and other controls in a dialog box in response to an action. When you choose the Start button in the StopWatch custom dialog box shown in the following illustration, the Start button becomes the Stop button, and the Pause button is enabled. While the dialog box is displayed, the text label that displays the time is updated every second.

After you choose the Start button ...

the Start button becomes the Stop button and the Pause button is enabled.

Update lists   In a dynamic dialog box, the list of items in a list box can change in response to a user's actions. For example, in the File Browser custom dialog box, shown in the following illustration, the user can double-click a directory in the Directories list box, and the list of files and directories changes in the two list boxes.

Double-click the CLIPART directory ...

to display the files stored in that directory.

Show or hide parts of the dialog box   You can create a dialog box with more than one "panel" of controls, in which one panel is displayed and one or more other panels are hidden. This sort of dialog box is similar to the dialog boxes built into Word that have "tabs" with which you can display different controls. In the Master Document Macro custom dialog box, you can click the Master Document or Subdocuments option buttons to display two different panels of controls.

The options in the Subdocuments panel ...

and the Master Document panel

Display a built-in dialog box   It is sometimes useful to provide access from within a custom dialog box to a dialog box built into Word. In the Close File custom dialog box, shown in the following illustration, you can choose the Word Count button to check the word count of the file before closing it. When you dismiss the Word Count dialog box, you return to the Close File dialog box. Note that you cannot display a second custom dialog box while the Close File dialog box is displayed; only one custom dialog box can be displayed at a time.

Choose the Word Count button ...

to display the Word Count dialog box built into Word. Choose the Close button to return to the custom dialog box.

Enable and disable controls   With a dynamic dialog box, you can enable and disable controls as appropriate. In the Add File custom dialog box shown in the following illustration, the Info To Record option buttons are disabled by default but are enabled if the user selects the Record Addition In Log check box.

If the user selects the Record Addition In Log check box ...

the Info To Record option buttons are enabled.

How to Make a Dialog Box Dynamic

A dynamic dialog box begins with a standard dialog box definition. You then add three elements to make the dialog box dynamic:

- A *dialog function.* The dialog function responds to events and changes the appearance of the dialog box. The dialog function, in short, is what makes a dialog box dynamic. All the instructions that are carried out while the dialog box is displayed are either placed within this function or in subroutines and user-defined functions called from this function.

- A dialog function argument in the **Begin Dialog** instruction that calls the dialog function.

- Identifiers for any dialog box controls that the dialog function acts on or gets information from. Most of the instructions in a custom dialog box definition already include identifiers for the controls they describe.

How a Dialog Function Works

When Word reads the **Dialog** or **Dialog**() instruction that displays the dialog box, it calls the dialog function and begins initializing the dialog box. Initialization happens between the time the dialog function is called and the time the dialog box appears on the screen. Word calls the dialog function and says, in effect, "Is there anything you'd like to do before the dialog box is displayed?" The dialog function can do nothing or can respond in some way.

Typical actions that a dialog function might take during initialization include disabling or hiding dialog box controls. By default, dialog box controls are enabled, so if you want a control to be disabled when a dialog box is first displayed, it must be disabled during initialization. Likewise, all dialog box controls are shown by default rather than hidden, so if you want to create a dialog box with more than one panel of controls, any controls that you don't want to show when the dialog box is first displayed must be hidden during initialization.

After initialization, Word displays the dialog box. When the user takes an action, such as selecting an option button, Word calls the dialog function and passes values to the function to indicate the kind of action taken and the control that was acted upon. For example, if the dialog box contains a list of graphics filenames, and you click one of the filenames, the dialog function will be called and could respond by displaying the selected graphics file in a picture control.

Word also calls the dialog function when the dialog box is "idle"—that is, while the user is not acting on the dialog box. In fact, as soon as the dialog box begins initializing and for as long as it is displayed, Word sends a continuous stream of idle messages to the dialog function—more than one a second. This stream is interrupted only when the user acts on the dialog box in some way. Most dialog functions are designed to ignore idle messages, but they can be used to continuously update a dialog box (as in the StopWatch custom dialog box example described earlier in this section).

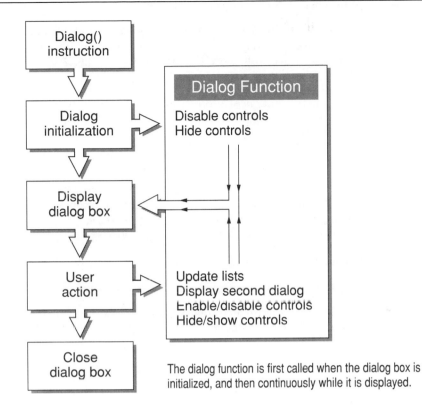

The dialog function is first called when the dialog box is initialized, and then continuously while it is displayed.

Calling the Dialog Function

The link between the dialog box and its function is established in the dialog box definition. Specifically, a *.FunctionName* argument is added to the **Begin Dialog** instruction, where *.FunctionName* matches the name of the dialog function. Here's the syntax for the instruction:

Begin Dialog UserDialog [*HorizPos, VertPos,*] *Width, Height, Title$,* *.FunctionName*

Dialog Box Control Identifiers

A dialog function needs an identifier for each dialog box control that it acts on or gets information from. Normally, the dialog function uses string identifiers, but it can also use numeric identifiers. For information on numeric identifiers, see "Numeric Identifiers," which follows.

String identifiers are the same as the identifiers used with a dialog record. If you use the Dialog Editor to create a dialog box, the Dialog Editor automatically creates an identifier for any control that can store a value in a dialog record. For example, in the following instruction, .CheckBox1 is the string identifier created by the Dialog Editor:

```
CheckBox 398, 24, 109, 16, "Check Box", .CheckBox1
```

Don't confuse a dialog box control's *label* and its identifier. An identifier begins with a period (.) and is the last argument in a dialog box control instruction. In the previous instruction, "Check Box" is a check box label and .CheckBox1 is its identifier.

Unlike other elements of WordBasic, string identifiers are *case-sensitive*. When an instruction in a dialog function refers to an identifier, it must match the case of the identifier.

Numeric Identifiers

Numeric identifiers are an alternative way of referring to dialog box controls. You can use numeric identifiers to improve the performance of a dialog function when a dialog box contains many controls. But instructions that use numeric identifiers are more difficult to read than instructions that use string identifiers.

Numeric identifiers are numbers, starting at 0 (zero), that correspond to the positions of dialog box control instructions within a dialog box definition. The following example shows the numeric identifiers for four dialog box controls. Note that the numeric identifier is not included in the instruction for a dialog box control; the number associated with a control is determined by the control's place within the dialog box definition. If the position of the control changes, so does its numeric identifier. For example, in the following dialog box definition, the **Text** instruction is first and so has a numeric identifier of 0 (zero). If you moved the instruction so that it was the last one in the dialog box definition, it would have an identifier of 3 (assuming no new instructions were added).

```
Begin Dialog UserDialog 370, 92, "Fax Info"
    Text 14, 7, 96, 13, "Fax Number:"        'Numeric identifier is 0
    TextBox 14, 23, 160, 18, .Fax$           'Numeric identifier is 1
    OKButton 270, 6, 88, 21                  'Numeric identifier is 2
    CancelButton 270, 30, 88, 21             'Numeric identifier is 3
End Dialog
```

Dialog Function Syntax

A dialog function is just like any other user-defined function except that it takes three required arguments. The syntax is as follows:

Function *FunctionName(ControlID$,* *Action,* *SuppValue)*
    Series of instructions to determine a value
    FunctionName = value
End Function

The function will generate an error if one of the three mandatory arguments— *ControlID$, Action,* and *SuppValue*—is missing or if an additional argument is added. The arguments are variables, however, and you can use any variable name you want. For example, you could use id$ instead of ControlID$ as the name for the first argument.

A dialog function returns a value when the user chooses a command button—the OK button, Cancel button, or a push button. Word acts on the value returned by either closing the dialog box associated with the function or continuing to display it. By default, the dialog function returns 0 (zero), which causes Word to close the dialog box, regardless of which button was chosen. But if you assign a nonzero value to the dialog function, the dialog box remains displayed. By keeping the dialog box displayed, the dialog function allows the user to carry out more than one command from the same dialog box. For examples, see "Responding to a Double-Click" and "Responding to a Push Button" later in this chapter.

The DialogFunctionDemo macro, stored in the EXAMPLES.DOT template (Windows) and the MACRO EXAMPLES template (Macintosh) on the Microsoft Word Developer's Kit disk, displays the values of the arguments passed to a dialog function while a custom dialog box is displayed. You may find this macro, along with the following discussion, a useful starting place when you begin to work with dialog functions.

Here is a closer look at each dialog function argument.

ControlID$*   Receives the identifier string of the dialog box control associated with a call to the dialog function. For example, if the user selects a check box, the dialog function is called and the *ControlID$ argument receives the identifier for the check box.

Action   Identifies the action that calls the dialog function. There are six possible actions that can call the dialog function, each with a corresponding *Action* value.

Action value	Meaning
1	Corresponds to dialog box initialization. This value is passed before the dialog box becomes visible.
2	Corresponds to choosing a command button or changing the value of a dialog box control (with the exception of typing in a text box or combo box). When *Action* is 2, *ControlID$* corresponds to the identifier for the control that was chosen or changed.
3	Corresponds to a change in a text box or combo box. This value is passed when a control loses the focus (for example, when the user presses the TAB key to move to a different control) or after the user clicks an item in the list of a combo box (an *Action* value of 2 is passed first). Note that if the contents of the text box or combo box do not change, an *Action* value of 3 is not passed. When *Action* is 3, *ControlID$* corresponds to the identifier for the text box or combo box whose contents were changed.
4	Corresponds to a change of control focus. When *Action* is 4, *ControlID$* corresponds to the identifier of the control that is gaining the focus. *SuppValue* corresponds to the numeric identifier for the control that lost the focus. A dialog function cannot display a message box or dialog box in response to an *Action* value of 4.

Action value	Meaning
5	Corresponds to an idle state. As soon as the dialog box is initialized, Word continuously passes an *Action* value of 5 while no other action occurs. If the dialog function responds to an *Action* value of 5, the dialog function should return a nonzero value. (If the dialog function returns 0 (zero), Word continues to send idle messages only when the mouse moves.) When *Action* is 5, *ControlID$* is an empty string (""); *SuppValue* corresponds to the number of times an *Action* value of 5 has been passed so far.
6	Corresponds to the user moving the dialog box. This value is passed only when screen updating is turned off (using a **ScreenUpdating** instruction). When screen updating is turned off and the user moves the dialog box, the screen is refreshed once. As a result, any changes that were made by the macro after screen updating was turned off will suddenly appear. A dialog function can prevent this problem by responding to an *Action* value of 6 and controlling what will be displayed when the screen refreshes. For example, if a new document (created after screen updating was turned off) deactivates the visible document, the dialog function could activate the visible document again. Note that Word does not refresh the screen until after an *Action* value of 6 has been passed and the dialog function has ended. When *Action* is 6, *ControlID$* is an empty string (""); *SuppValue* is equal to 0 (zero).

SuppValue Receives supplemental information about a change in a dialog box control. The information *SuppValue* receives depends on which control calls the dialog function. The following *SuppValue* values are passed when *Action* is 2 or 3.

Control	*SuppValue* passed
List box, drop-down list box, or combo box	Number of the item selected, where 0 (zero) is the first item in the list box, 1 is the second item, and so on
Check box	1 if selected, 0 (zero) if cleared
Option button	Number of the option button selected, where 0 (zero) is the first option button within a group, 1 is the second option button, and so on
Text box	Number of characters in the text box
Combo box	If *Action* is 3, number of characters in the combo box
Command button	A value identifying the button chosen. This value is not often used, since the same information is available from the *ControlID$* value. If the OK button is chosen, *SuppValue* is 1; if the Cancel button is chosen, *SuppValue* is 2. The *SuppValue* for push buttons is an internal number used by Word. This number is not the same as the numeric identifier for a push button, but it does change if the instruction that defines the push button changes position within the dialog box definition.

Dialog Functions and Variables

Like variables in other user-defined functions, variables defined in a dialog function lose their values when the function ends. A dialog function is available for as long as a dialog box is displayed, so it's easy to imagine that variables in the dialog function last that long as well. But the dialog function is called not once but many times while the dialog box is displayed, and the dialog function's variables lose their values after each call. If you need variables used in a dialog function to last as long as a dialog box is displayed, you must use the **Dim** statement to declare them as shared variables.

Pressing ESC to Cancel a Dynamic Dialog Box

Normally, you can press ESC to cancel a dialog box—to cancel any settings you might have changed and close the dialog box. If you press ESC while a dynamic dialog box is displayed, however, Word interrupts the macro. (In Windows, the dialog box remains displayed when the macro is interrupted; on the Macintosh, it disappears, but will reappear if you choose the Continue button on the Macro toolbar to continue running the macro.) You can include a **DisableInput** instruction to allow the ESC key to cancel a dynamic dialog box. The **DisableInput** instruction must run before the ESC key is pressed. If you only want to disable the macro-interrupting capability of the ESC key while the dynamic dialog box is displayed, a good strategy is to place a DisableInput 1 instruction immediately before the **Dialog()** instruction that displays the dialog box and a DisableInput 0 instruction immediately after it. For example:

```
DisableInput 1          'Prevent ESC key from interrupting
choice = Dialog(dlg)    'Display dynamic dialog box
DisableInput 0          'Allow ESC key to interrupt
```

Dialog Function Techniques

This section provides examples that demonstrates how to carry out common dialog function tasks. These examples use a set of WordBasic statements and functions used only within dialog functions. You can recognize these statements and functions in that they all begin with "Dlg." For example, **DlgEnable** and **DlgFocus** are two statements used only in dialog functions. For a complete list of these statements and functions, see "Statements and Functions Used in Dialog Functions" later in this chapter. The macros shown in this section are stored in the EXAMPLES.DOT template (Windows) and the MACRO EXAMPLES template (Macintosh) on the Microsoft Word Developer's Kit disk.

Responding to Clearing or Selecting a Check Box

When the user selects or clears a check box, Word calls the dialog function. In the following example, a dialog function causes an option button group to be enabled or disabled when the user selects or clears the Record Addition In Log check box.

The option group disabled ...   and enabled

Word passes these values to the dialog function when the user selects or clears a check box: an *Action* value of 2, a *ControlID$* value containing the identifier for the check box, and a *SuppValue* that indicates whether the check box is selected or cleared.

The following dialog function uses a **Select Case** control structure to check the value of *Action*. (The *SuppValue* is ignored in this function.) An **If** conditional then checks the value of the *ControlID$*. If the identifier is "RecordAddition"— the identifier assigned to the Record Addition In Log check box—**DlgEnable** either enables or disables the option buttons. Because the option buttons are disabled when the dialog box is first displayed and the check box is cleared, selecting the check box corresponds to enabling the option buttons.

```
Sub MAIN
Begin Dialog UserDialog 376, 158, "Add File ", .EnableFunction
    Text 8, 10, 73, 13, "Filename:"
    TextBox 8, 26, 160, 18, .Filenametext
    CheckBox 8, 56, 203, 16, "Record Addition in Log", .RecordAddition
    GroupBox 8, 79, 356, 70, "Info to Record:", .Group
    OptionGroup .InfoChoice
        OptionButton 18, 100, 189, 16, "Author Information", .Authorinf
        OptionButton 18, 118, 159, 16, "File History", .History
    OKButton 277, 8, 88, 21
    CancelButton 277, 32, 88, 21
End Dialog
Dim dlg As UserDialog
DisableInput 1
x = Dialog(dlg)
DisableInput 0
End Sub
```

```
Function EnableFunction(id$, action, suppval)
Select Case action
Case 1                                 'Dialog box initializes
    DlgEnable "Group", 0               'Disable group box
    DlgEnable "InfoChoice", 0          'Disable option buttons
Case 2                                 'User selects a dialog box option
    If id$ = "RecordAddition" Then
        DlgEnable "Group"              'Enable/disable group box
        DlgEnable "InfoChoice"         'Enable/disable option buttons
    End If
Case Else
End Select
End Function
```

Responding to Selecting an Item in a List Box, Drop-Down List Box, or Combo Box

Word calls the dialog function associated with a dialog box when the user selects an item in a list box, drop-down list box, or combo box. The dialog function can identify the item selected and act accordingly. In the following example, the dialog box presents a list of graphics and displays the graphic corresponding to the selected name. When the user selects a different name, the dialog function changes the graphics display.

The graphic displayed corresponds
to the filename selected.

In the following dialog function, the **If** conditional tests for an *Action* value of 2, which indicates that the user has acted on a control. A nested **If** conditional then tests *ControlID$* to see if the user acted on the list box, which has the identifier "ListBox1." Then the **DlgText$()** function is used to return the text of the item selected in the list box. The text is the name of a graphic stored in an AutoText entry, which the **DlgSetPicture** instruction then displays. The dialog box definition that defines the dialog box is not shown in this example.

```
Function ShowPicture(id$, action, suppval)
If action = 2 Then   'The user selects a control
    If id$ = "ListBox1" Then
        picturename$ = DlgText$("ListBox1")
        DlgSetPicture "Picture1", picturename$, 1
    End If
End If
End Function
```

Responding to a Double-Click

In most built-in dialog boxes in Word, you can double-click an option button or an item in a list to close the dialog box and carry out the settings of the dialog box. Double-clicking is usually a shortcut for selecting an item and then choosing the OK button. Custom dialog boxes work this way by default.

In some Word dialog boxes, though, double-clicking an item in a list does not close the dialog box. For example, in the Open dialog box (File menu), when you double-click a folder, Word displays the files in that folder and does not close the dialog box. Using a dialog function, you can make a custom dialog box behave in the same way. The following example shows how a custom dialog box allows the same action.

The File Browser dialog box shows the list of files and subdirectories in the current directory.

Double-clicking a subdirectory displays the list of files and subdirectories in that directory.

Here is the dialog function, with some instructions removed for clarity:

```
Function FileBrowserFunction(id$, action, suppval)
If action = 2 Then
    If id$ = "OK" And DlgFocus$() = "listdirs" Then
        'Series of instructions to update the directory and file lists
        FileBrowserFunction = 1
    End If
End If
End Function
```

The first **If** conditional tests for an *Action* value of 2, meaning that the user has acted on a control. The nested **If** conditional then tests for two conditions: when the *ControlID$* value is "OK" (the identifier for the OK button) and when the focus is on the Directories list box (whose identifier is "listdirs"). This compound condition is met only when the user double-clicks an item in the Directories list box (if the user clicks just once, the *ControlID$* is "listdirs" rather than "OK").

The final key instruction is `FileBrowserFunction = 1`. By default, when the user chooses a command button such as the OK button, Cancel button, or a push button, Word closes the dialog box. In this case, when the user double-clicks an item in a list box, it has the same effect. But a dialog box remains displayed if the dialog function returns a nonzero value; that is the purpose of the `FileBrowserFunction = 1` instruction.

The technique described here works not only with the OK button, but with any default command button specified with the *DefaultButton* argument of a **Dialog()** instruction. The dialog box does not need to contain an OK button. For more information on setting a default command button, see "Displaying the Dialog Box" earlier in this chapter or **Dialog** in Part 2, "WordBasic Reference."

Responding to a Push Button

In the following example, the user can choose the Word Count button to display the built-in Word Count dialog box; the Close File custom dialog box remains displayed and will be available when the user closes the Word Count dialog box. Note that you cannot display a second custom dialog box while the Close File dialog box is displayed; only one custom dialog box can be displayed at a time.

Choose the Word Count button ...   to display the Word Count dialog box built into Word. Choose the Close button to return to the custom dialog box.

Here is the dialog function, with some instructions removed for clarity. The key instruction that allows the Close File dialog box to remain displayed after the Word Count button is chosen is `CloseFileFunction = 1`, which causes the dialog box to remain displayed.

```
Function CloseFileFunction(id$, action, suppval)
If action = 2 Then
    If id$ = "wordcount" Then
        'Series of instructions to display the Word Count dialog box
        CloseFileFunction = 1
    End If
End If
End Function
```

Responding to Typing in a Text Box or Combo Box

After the user types in a text box or combo box and uses the mouse or the TAB key to move to a different dialog box control, Word calls the dialog function and passes the following values:

- A *ControlID$* value equal to the identifier of the text box or combo box

- An *Action* value of 3 (rather than 2, as with all the other controls)

- A *SuppValue* value indicating the number of characters the user typed

In the following example, the dialog function is called when the user leaves the first text box. If the user does not type a valid social security number, the dialog function displays a message box.

When the Social Security Number text box loses the focus …

a message is displayed if the number entered is not valid.

Here is the dialog function:

```
Function TestNumber(id$, action, suppval)
    If action = 3 Then
            If id$ = "socsecnum" And suppval <> 11 Then
                MsgBox "Not a valid " + Chr$(13) + \
                        "social security number."
                wrongnumberflag = 1
            End If
    ElseIf action = 4 Then
            If wrongnumberflag = 1 Then
                DlgFocus "socsecnum"
                wrongnumberflag = 0
            End If
    End If
End Function
```

Note that the function tests for *Action* values 3, corresponding to a text change, and 4, corresponding to a change of focus. When an *Action* 3 value is passed, the function uses the *SuppValue* argument to test the number of characters in the text box. If the number of characters doesn't correspond to the number required for a correct social security number, the dialog function displays a message box and sets the variable wrongnumberflag to 1. Immediately after the *Action* 3 value is passed, an *Action* value of 4 is passed. If wrongnumberflag is set to 1, the dialog function returns the focus to the social security text box and resets wrongnumberflag to 0 (zero). You cannot use the **DlgFocus** statement when *Action* has a value of 3, because the *Action* 4 value that follows overrides it, changing the focus back to wherever the user intended to move it. Hence the wrongnumberflag variable is needed to indicate whether the focus should be changed when the *Action* 4 value is passed.

Responding to a Change in the Focus

Whenever the user moves the focus from one dialog box control to another, Word calls the dialog function and passes the following values:

- A *ControlID$* value equal to the identifier for the control that is gaining the focus

- An *Action* value of 4

- A *SuppValue* value corresponding to the numeric identifier for the control that lost the focus

In the following example, the dialog function changes the "banter" text (the text that appears at the bottom of the dialog box) according to which control has the focus. For example, when the focus is on the Phone Number text box, the dialog function changes the banter text to read "Please enter a phone number."

When the focus is on the Social Security Number text box, the banter text reads "Please enter a social security number."

When the focus is on the Phone Number text box, the banter text changes.

The following instructions would be added to the *Action* 4 instructions in the TestNumber dialog function (shown in the previous example) to include the banter text functionality:

```
If id$ = "socsecnum" Then
    DlgText$ "Text1", "Please enter a social security number."
ElseIf id$ = "phone" Then
    DlgText$ "Text1", "Please enter a phone number."
End If
```

Displaying More Than One Panel of Controls

Dialog functions let you define more than one panel of controls in a dialog box. By organizing controls into panels, you can present a large number of controls in a single dialog box. This example shows a two-panel dialog box.

To create a two-panel dialog box, you use the Dialog Editor to design two separate dialog boxes corresponding to the two panels of the single dialog box; you then merge the two dialog box definitions into a single definition. When Word first displays the dialog box, one of the panels must be hidden; you'll have a mess if both panels are displayed at the same time.

When the dialog box in the following illustration is first displayed, it shows the Subdocuments controls, which means that the Master Document controls must be hidden while the dialog box is being initialized.

The options in the Subdocuments panel ...   and the Master Document panel

To hide the controls in the Master Document panel, the dialog function calls a subroutine named ShowHidePanel:

```
Sub ShowHidePanel(FirstCtrl, LastCtrl, ShowOrHide)
For count = FirstCtrl To LastCtrl
    DlgVisible count, ShowOrHide
Next
End Sub
```

In this subroutine, a **For…Next** loop and a **DlgVisible** instruction are used to show or hide controls in a panel. The instructions to define the Master Document controls are grouped together in the dialog box definition. They have the numeric identifiers 13 through 18 (the first Master Document control is the thirteenth instruction within the dialog box definition). The **For…Next** loop counts from FirstCtrl to LastCtrl—13 to 18, in this case. For each iteration, the **DlgVisible** instruction shows or hides the control with the numeric identifier count. If the ShowOrHide variable is 1, **DlgVisible** shows the controls; if it is 0 (zero), **DlgVisible** hides them.

In Word version 6.0 for the Macintosh and Windows NT and in Word version 7.0, a single **DlgVisible** instruction can be used to show or hide a range of controls, so a separate subroutine such as ShowHidePanel is not needed. For example, to hide the Master Document controls in the preceding example, the dialog function would simply run the following instruction:

```
DlgVisible 13, 18, 0
```

For more information, see **DlgVisible** in Part 2, "WordBasic Reference."

To switch panels while the dialog box is displayed, the dialog function must hide the panel of controls currently displayed and show the other panel. Here is the **If** conditional that checks which panel is selected. Note that Case 2 matches an *Action* value of 2, which indicates that the user has acted on a control.

```
Case 2
    If identifier$ = "masterdocs" Then
        ShowHidePanel 13, 10, 1          'Show master doc controls
        ShowHidePanel 7, 12, 0           'Hide subdoc controls
    ElseIf identifier$ = "subdocs" Then
        ShowHidePanel 13, 18, 0          'Hide master doc controls
        ShowHidePanel 7, 12, 1           'Show subdoc controls
    End If
```

The **If** conditional calls the ShowHidePanel subroutine and uses it to show or hide the panels as appropriate.

Numeric identifiers and **For…Next** loops provide an efficient way to manipulate panels of controls. Since the numeric identifier of a control depends on its place within the dialog box definition, you must be careful about changing the order of instructions within the dialog box definition.

The wizards that come with Word use this technique to manage the panels of a wizard dialog box. For a detailed description of managing panels in wizards, see "Creating a Wizard" in Chapter 9, "More WordBasic Techniques."

Tip Many Word dialog boxes with tabs "remember" which tab was selected when the dialog box was last closed. The theory is that the user is most likely to want to use the panel of controls that was last displayed. You can achieve this effect in WordBasic by storing the final dialog box setting in a settings file. For information on using settings files, see Chapter 9, "More WordBasic Techniques."

Updating Text Continuously in a Dialog Box

You can use a dialog function to update a dialog box continuously. In the example shown and described here, the dialog function updates the text item displaying the time elapsed every second.

The dialog box before choosing   and after
the Start button ...

Here is the dialog function, with all but one **Case** in the **Select Case** control structure removed for clarity:

```
Function Stopwatch(id$, action, suppval)
Select Case action
    Case 5
        If startflag = 1 Then
            newnow = (Now() - oldnow)
            thissecond$ = LTrim$(Str$(Second(newnow)))
                If thissecond$ <> thissecondold$ Then
                    thishour$ = Str$(Hour(newnow))
                    thisminute$ = LTrim$(Str$(Minute(newnow)))
                    fullstring$ = thishour$ + ":" + thisminute$ + ":"\
                                        + thissecond$
                    DlgText$ "Text1", fullstring$
                    thissecondold$ = thissecond$
                End If
        End If
        Stopwatch = 1
    Case Else
End Select
End Function
```

Word begins sending "idle" (*Action* 5) messages to the dialog function as soon as the dialog box is initialized. As long as no other action takes place, Word continues sending this idle message until the dialog box is closed. However, the text should only update after the user chooses the Start button. Therefore, all the statements following Case 5 depend on whether startflag is equal to 1 (earlier in the dialog function, startflag is set to 1 when the user chooses the Start button); if startflag is not equal to 1, the text is not updated.

A second point to observe is that Word sends idle messages to the dialog function at the rate of more than one a second. If the text were updated each time it received the idle message, the text would be jittery. The second **If** conditional therefore tests whether the time has changed and only updates the text every second. Note that startflag and thissecondold$ must be declared as shared variables before the main subroutine; if they were not declared as shared variables, they would lose their value each time the dialog function was called.

Storing and Loading Dynamic Dialog Box Settings

It's often useful to store a dialog box's settings when the user closes it and to load the settings the next time the dialog box is displayed so that the settings are the same as the ones the user last saw. For example, the dialog box for the Master Document macro, shown in the following illustration, contains a number of check boxes whose settings it would be useful to save.

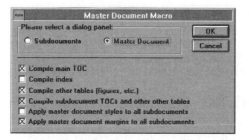

In Windows, you use the **SetPrivateProfileString** and **GetPrivateProfileString$()** instructions to store dialog box settings. For information on using these instructions, see "Using Settings Files and Document Variables" in Chapter 9, "More WordBasic Techniques."

On the Macintosh, you can use the **DlgStoreValues** and **DlgLoadValues**() instructions to store and load settings. Unlike **SetPrivateProfileString** and **GetPrivateProfileString$**(), which require a separate instruction for each setting stored or loaded, a single **DlgStoreValues** or **DlgLoadValues**() instruction can store or load all of the settings in a dialog box. For dialog boxes with a large number of settings to store and load, **DlgStoreValues** or **DlgLoadValues**() offer a significant improvement in performance. **DlgStoreValues** and **DlgLoadValues**() require a dialog function; if you want to use them with a dialog box that would not otherwise need a dialog function, you can simply create a dialog function just for these intstructions.

The following dialog function (with some instructions removed for clarity) shows how **DlgStoreValues** and **DlgLoadValues**() can be used to store and load check-box settings:

```
Function MyDlgFunction(id$, action, suppval)
Select Case action
    Case 1
        success = DlgLoadValues("Dialog Settings", "MasterDocDialog")
    Case 2
        If id$ = "OK" Then
            DlgStoreValues "Dialog Settings", "MasterDocDialog")
        End If
    Case Else
End Select
End Function
```

The **DlgLoadValues**() instruction runs when the dialog box is initialized (*Action* 1). The **DlgStoreValues** instruction runs when the the user closes the dialog box by choosing the OK button. Note that if the user closes the dialog box by choosing the Cancel button, the dialog box settings are not stored. By default, **DlgStoreValues** and **DlgLoadValues**() store and load most dialog box settings, but you can also control whether or not individual settings are stored and loaded. For more information, see **DlgStoreValues** and **DlgLoadValues**() in Part 2, "WordBasic Reference."

Statements and Functions Used in Dialog Functions

WordBasic includes a set of statements and functions that are used only within dialog functions. The statements act on dialog box controls and the dialog functions return information about them. For example, you use the **DlgVisible** statement to hide or display a dialog box control; **DlgVisible**() returns a value determined by whether the control is displayed or hidden.

For complete information on these statements and functions, see the corresponding entries in Part 2, "WordBasic Reference."

Statement or function	Action or result
DlgControlId()	Returns the numeric equivalent of *Identifier$*, the string identifier for a dialog box control.
DlgEnable, DlgEnable()	The **DlgEnable** statement is used to enable or disable a dialog box control. When a control is disabled, it is visible in the dialog box, but is dimmed and not functional. **DlgEnable()** is used to determine whether or not the control is enabled.
DlgFilePreview, DlgFilePreview$()	The **DlgFilePreview** statement is used to display a file in the file preview item. **DlgFilePreview$()** returns the path and filename of the document displayed.
DlgFocus, DlgFocus$()	The **DlgFocus** statement is used to set the focus on a dialog box control. (When a dialog box control has the focus, it is highlighted.) **DlgFocus$()** returns the identifier of the control that has the focus.
DlgListBoxArray, DlgListBoxArray()	The **DlgListBoxArray** statement is used to fill a list box or combo box with the elements of an array. It can be used to change the contents of a list box or combo box while the dialog box is displayed. **DlgListBoxArray()** returns an item in an array and the number of items in the array.
DlgLoadValues()	Loads dialog box settings. Available on the Macintosh only.
DlgSetPicture	Sets the graphic displayed in the **Picture** dialog box control.
DlgStoreValues	Stores dialog box settings. Available on the Macintosh only.
DlgText, DlgText$()	The **DlgText** statement is used to set the text or text label for a dialog box control. The **DlgText$()** function returns the text or label of a control.
DlgUpdateFilePreview	Updates a file preview item.
DlgValue, DlgValue()	The **DlgValue** statement is used to select or clear a dialog box control. The **DlgValue()** function returns the setting of a control.
DlgVisible, DlgVisible()	The **DlgVisible** statement is used to hide or show a dialog box control. The **DlgVisible()** function is used to determine whether a control is visible or hidden.

CHAPTER 6

Debugging

According to one of the most famous anecdotes in computing lore, computer pioneer Grace Hopper couldn't get her program to run one day and discovered that the problem was caused by a moth. The moth had become lodged in one of the computer's switches. When the moth was removed, Hopper reported that she had "debugged" the computer—hence the terms "bug," which has come to mean any error in a program, and "debugging," which means tracking down errors and removing them.

Debugging plays a part in developing all but the simplest macros. This chapter describes the kinds of errors you're likely to encounter and the debugging tools Word provides.

In this chapter:

- Common WordBasic errors
- Ways to avoid WordBasic errors
- Debugging tools

Common WordBasic Errors

The WordBasic errors described in this section are errors that prevent a macro from running. These errors occur when an instruction breaks one of the rules that govern the way you can use the WordBasic language. Word displays an error message as soon as it encounters a line containing an error. If you have the macro open in a macro-editing window, Word highlights the offending line in red. Every WordBasic error message box contains a Help button. When you choose the Help button, Word provides suggestions about what may have caused the error.

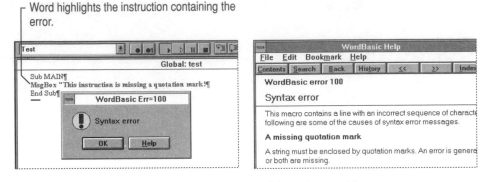

Word highlights the instruction containing the error.

Choose the Help button...   for information about the error.

Note Word does not highlight all the errors in a macro at once. If you have many typos or syntax errors in your macro, you will get an error message each time you run your macro, until all the errors are corrected.

Syntax Error

This is by far the most common error message. The following are some of the causes of syntax error messages.

A missing quotation mark A string must be enclosed by quotation marks. An error is generated if one or both are missing.

A missing, misplaced, or extra comma Each argument for a statement or function must be separated by a comma. A missing, misplaced, or extra comma generates an error.

A missing period Each argument for a statement that corresponds to a dialog box must begin with a period. For example, .FileName is an argument for the **FileOpen** statement.

A missing parenthesis at the end of a function A function is always followed by an opening and closing parenthesis. A syntax error is generated if one or both are missing.

A missing reserved word Some WordBasic instructions include more than one reserved word. For example, an **If...Then...Else** instruction must include the **Then** reserved word.

A reserved word name conflict WordBasic generates a syntax error if you create a variable name that matches a reserved word. For example, a variable named "Then" conflicts with the reserved word **Then**, which is part of the **If...Then...Else** statement.

Type Mismatch

This error occurs when an instruction requires a particular data type but doesn't get it. Because there are only two data types in WordBasic—strings and numbers—the error means that a string was used when a number was required, or vice versa. In the following example, pet is meant to be a string variable, but it is missing a dollar sign ($), so Word interprets it as a numeric variable and generates an error:

```
pet = "poodle"          'Should be: pet$ = "poodle"
```

This error is also generated when you provide a function with an argument of the wrong type. Here is an example:

```
a$ = Str$("4")          'Should be: a$ = Str$(4)
```

Wrong Number of Parameters

This error is generated when a statement or function has too many or too few arguments (also known as "parameters"). Here are some examples:

```
a$ - Chr$()             'Chr$() requires an argument
a$ = Str$()             'Str$() requires an argument
a$ = Selection$(1)      'Selection$() does not take an argument
MsgBox                  'MsgBox requires an argument
ChDir                   'ChDir requires an argument
```

Unknown Command, Subroutine, or Function

This error message usually means that you have misspelled a function or statement name. It can also occur if you omit the dollar sign ($) from a function that returns a string. Each of the following instructions generates this error message:

```
MgsBox "Hello"          'Should be: MsgBox "Hello"
EditFnd "muskrat"       'Should be: EditFind "muskrat"
quote$ - Chr(34)        'Should be: quote$ = Chr$(34)
```

In addition, this error can occur if an instruction that should be two words is typed as one—EndDialog, for example, instead of End Dialog (though both EndIf and End If are accepted).

Undefined Dialog Record Field

This error message is displayed if you misspell the argument for a statement that corresponds to a dialog box, as in the following example:

```
EditFind "sasquatch", .WhleWord = 1          'Should be: .WholeWord = 1
```

The error also occurs if you include an argument that doesn't belong, as in the following:

```
EditFind "skunk", .WholeWord = 1, .Musk = 1  '"Musk" is not valid
```

Bad Parameter

This message is displayed if the value for an argument is outside the range of accepted values, as in the following example:

```
ChangeCase 50                          '"50" is too large a value
```

Duplicate Label

This error occurs if the macro includes two subroutines or user-defined functions with the same name. It also occurs if you create two **Goto** labels that have the same name.

Ways to Avoid WordBasic Errors

Whenever you type a new instruction, you run the risk of misspelling a reserved word or leaving out a comma or a period and thereby creating an error. The techniques described in this section can help you reduce errors by reducing the number of instructions you type from scratch.

Use the Record Next Command Button

The Record Next
Command button

If you need to include an unfamiliar statement in your macro and can't remember the names for the arguments you need, use the Record Next Command button on the Macro toolbar to record the instruction. The Record Next Command button turns on the macro recorder and records the next command you choose; Word then inserts the corresponding instruction in the macro-editing window. If a macro-editing window is not open, the Record Next Command button does nothing.

To use the Record Next Command button, position the insertion point in a macro-editing window at the place where you want to insert the instruction. If the command you want to record is not available in the macro-editing window, switch to a document window. Click the Record Next Command button, and then choose the command you want to record. If the command has a dialog box associated with it, set the options you want in the dialog box and then choose the OK or Close button (if you choose the Cancel button, the command is not recorded).

File	Edit	View	Insert	Format	Tools	Table	Wind

Test

Font...
Paragraph...
Tabs...
Borders and Shading...
Columns...
Change Case...
Drop Cap...
Bullets and Numbering...
Heading Numbering...
AutoFormat...
Style Gallery...
Style...
Frame...
Picture...
Drawing Object...

Sub MAIN

End Sub

File	Edit	View	Insert	Format	Tools	Table	Wind

Test

Document1

Global: test

Sub MAIN
FormatParagraph .LeftIndent = "0" + Chr$(34), .RightIndent = "0"
"0 pt", .LineSpacingRule = 0, .LineSpacing = "", .Alignment = 0, .
0, .KeepTogether = 0, .PageBreak = 0, .NoLineNum = 0, .DontHyp
+ Chr$(34)
End Sub

After clicking the Record Next Command button, choose the command you want to record.

After you complete the command, Word inserts the corresponding instruction in the macro-editing window.

If you need to switch to a document window to record a command, be sure to switch before clicking the Record Next Command button. Otherwise, Word will record your switch to the document window rather than recording the command you choose. Of course, if the command is available in the macro-editing window, you do not have to switch to a document window.

Copy Syntax from Help

As useful as the Record Next Command button is, you can't use it to record WordBasic functions, nor can you record statements that do not correspond to Word commands. For these statements and functions, copying from Help is the solution.

If you know the statement or function name, you can type it in a macro-editing window and then, with the insertion point on the same line, press F1 (Windows) or HELP or COMMAND+/ (Macintosh) to display the Help topic for that statement or function. The Help topic for each statement and function includes its complete syntax. You can use the syntax simply to jog your memory or you can copy it directly into your macro. Many topics offer examples you can copy as well.

Store Instructions as AutoText Entries

Another way to minimize errors is to store frequently used instructions as AutoText entries. The capitalized letters in statement and function names lend themselves to a consistent and easy-to-remember naming system. You could store the **EndOfLine** statement, for example, in an AutoText entry named "eol." You may also want to store frequently used control structures such as **If** conditionals. As a further refinement, you could record a macro that not only inserts an **If** conditional, but also moves the insertion point to an appropriate place within the control structure so that you can begin typing immediately. If you create AutoText entries as you're working on a macro, it's not much of a chore, and in a short time you'll have a collection of entries that can help you put macros together very quickly.

Debugging Tools

The Macro toolbar is displayed whenever you open a macro-editing window, and it provides a number of debugging tools. In addition, WordBasic includes some statements used primarily for debugging. This section describes these debugging tools and statements.

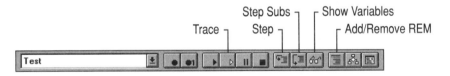

The Macro toolbar

Trace

The Trace button

When you click the Trace button, Word runs the active macro and highlights each instruction as it runs it. Tracing happens very quickly because the macro runs at approximately its normal speed. Tracing can be useful for macros with many conditionals and loops, in which the flow is complex. You can use tracing to quickly determine, for example, whether a particular branch of an **If** control structure is run.

Of course, the macro-editing window must be visible, or you cannot see the instructions as they are highlighted. You can use the Arrange All command on the Window menu to layer a document window and a macro-editing window horizontally. You may also want to arrange the windows vertically, as in the following illustration, so that you can see more macro instructions at the same time.

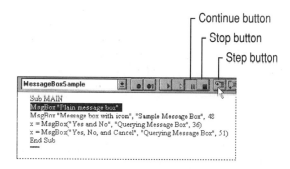

A document window and a macro-editing window arranged for tracing

Step

The Step button, along with its close relative the Step Subs button, is probably the most useful debugging tool. You can use the Step button to run a macro literally step by step. Each time you click the Step button, Word highlights an instruction and pauses; when you click the Step button again, Word runs the instruction and highlights the next one. In this way, you can monitor the effect of each instruction in your macro. This capability is especially useful for macros that move the insertion point in complex ways.

The Step button

Click the Step button to run the highlighted instruction.

As you're stepping through a macro, you can click the Stop button to stop running the macro or the Continue button to run the remaining instructions consecutively without pausing.

Note   If the active macro calls a subroutine or function in another macro, Word steps through the called subroutine or function as well. To see Word step through the instructions, open the macro or macros being called and arrange the macro-editing windows so they are all visible in the Word window before clicking the Step button.

Stepping through long macros can be inefficient, particularly if most of the macro works fine and you're stepping through a lot of instructions just to get to the one in which the problem occurs. The solution is to use a **Stop** instruction to pause the macro just before the point where the error occurs, and then use the Step button to step through the instructions that generate the error. For more information on using **Stop**, see "Statements Useful for Debugging" later in this section.

Step Subs

The Step Subs button

The Step Subs button works just like the Step button except that it doesn't step through subroutines or user-defined functions; it only steps through the main subroutine. This button is useful when you know that the problem you're trying to isolate is not contained in a macro's subroutines or user-defined functions. For macros with only a main subroutine, choosing this button has the same effect as choosing the Step button.

Show Variables

The Show Variables button

The Show Variables button displays the Macro Variables dialog box, in which you can see and change the values of variables. The Show Variables button is active only when the macro is paused. You can pause a macro by using the Step button to step through it, or you can use a **Stop** instruction to pause it at a certain point.

The Macro Variables dialog box can display variables defined in the main subroutine, variables defined in subroutines and user-defined functions, and variables shared by all subroutines; variables in the active subroutine are listed first. Variable names are preceded by the name of the subroutine or function for which they are defined, separated by an exclamation point. For example, in the following illustration, the string variable searchtext$ in the main subroutine is listed as MAIN!SEARCHTEXT$. The string variable owner$ in the FindAddress subroutine is listed as FINDADDRESS!OWNER$. The shared variable animal$ is listed as !ANIMAL$.

> Macro Variables
>
> Variables: | Set... | Close | Help |
>
> FINDADDRESS!TRAINER$=Carmen Jones
> FINDADDRESS!OWNER$=James Gilmour
> FINDADDRESS!HOMEPHONE$=(206)555-1234
> MAIN!SEARCHTEXT$=cat
> MAIN!COUNT=0
> !ANIMAL$=cat
> !APPOINTMENT$=6/7/93

— Variables in the FindAddress subroutine

— Variables in the main subroutine

— Global (shared) variables

Variables in the active subroutine are listed first.

You can use the Set button in the Macro Variables dialog box to display the Set Variable dialog box, where you can change the value of the selected variable. It's particularly useful to change the values of variables that control loops. After running the loop enough times to test it, you can change the value of the controlling variable so that the macro can escape from the loop early.

> Macro Variables
>
> Set Variable
>
> Set Variable to: | OK |
> dog | Cancel |
> | Help |

You can use the Set Variable dialog box to change the value of the selected variable.

Note   The Macro Variables dialog box does not display the values of array variables or dialog records. Use the **MsgBox** or **Print** statements to display the values of array elements.

Add/Remove REM

The Add/Remove REM button

One of the most useful debugging techniques is to deactivate part of your macro by "commenting it out." You do so by turning instructions into comments, either by placing an apostrophe (') in front of them or by placing a **REM** instruction in front of the line. The Add/Remove REM button does the latter.

For example, you may want to test a macro that includes an instruction to print a document, but you probably don't want to print each time you test the macro. The solution is to comment out the **FilePrint** instruction as follows:

```
REM    FilePrint "LETTER.DOC"
```

When you've finished testing the macro, you can select the instructions you commented out, and then click the Add/Remove REM button again to remove the **REM** statements and reactivate the instructions.

Statements Useful for Debugging

The following are WordBasic statements you can insert as instructions in your macro to assist in debugging.

Stop

When Word is running a macro and it encounters a **Stop** instruction, it pauses the macro at the **Stop** instruction. You can use a **Stop** instruction to pause a macro just before or after the place where you suspect a problem.

By default, the **Stop** statement produces a message box to notify you that it has paused the macro.

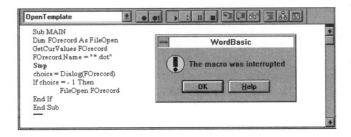

Word displays a message box and pauses the macro when it encounters a **Stop** instruction.

This message box is unnecessary if the macro-editing window is visible because Word highlights the **Stop** instruction in red. You can add an argument to the **Stop** instruction so that it does not display a message box—the instruction Stop -1 suppresses the message box.

ShowVars

This statement displays the Macro Variables dialog box. It's the equivalent of pausing the macro and choosing the Show Variables button at a given point in your macro.

MsgBox

Although you can check the status of most variables using the Macro Variables dialog box, that dialog box does not display array variables or dialog records. You can use the **MsgBox** statement to display and monitor these values. The **MsgBox** statement does not display numeric values, but you can use the **Str$()** function to convert numeric values into strings.

Print

The **Print** statement is useful for the same reasons **MsgBox** is, but it does not interrupt the macro as a message box does. You can also use it to display numeric values—you don't have to convert them to strings first, as you do with the **MsgBox** statement.

An Example: Debugging the InsertTab Macro

The InsertTab macro in this example is meant to insert a tab character in front of every paragraph in a selection. It uses the **CopyBookmark** statement to mark the selection with a bookmark called "temp." Then it goes to the start of the selection and moves the insertion point paragraph by paragraph through the document, inserting a tab character in front of each paragraph until it moves outside the area marked with the "temp" bookmark. The macro uses CmpBookmarks("\Sel", "temp") to compare the location of the insertion point (represented by the predefined bookmark "\Sel") with the "temp" bookmark, which marks the original selection. When the insertion point is no longer within the original selection, the macro should end. Here are the macro instructions:

```
Sub MAIN
CopyBookmark "\Sel", "temp"                   'Copy selection into bookmark
ParaUp                                        'Go to start of first paragraph
While CmpBookmarks("\Sel", "temp") <> 1
    Insert Chr$(9)                            'Insert tab character
    ParaDown                                  'Go to next paragraph
Wend
End Sub
```

When tested, the macro sometimes inserts an additional tab character in front of the first paragraph after the selection. For some reason, the CmpBookmarks("\Sel", "temp") <> 1 condition doesn't always trigger the end of the **While**...**Wend** loop at the right time.

When these paragraphs are selected before the macro begins...

the macro inserts a tab character in front of the first paragraph after the selection.

Because the problem has something to do with the CmpBookmarks("\Sel", "temp") <> 1 condition, a good way to start investigating it would be to check the value returned by the **CmpBookmarks()** function with each iteration of the **While...Wend** loop. You can do this by inserting the following instruction inside the **While...Wend** loop and then using the Step button to step through the macro:

```
MsgBox Str$(CmpBookmarks("\Sel", "temp"))
```

Using this technique, you can discover that when the original selection includes the paragraph mark of the last paragraph in the selection, CmpBookmarks("\Sel", "temp") returns a value of 10 at the beginning of the next paragraph, rather than 1 as expected. When **CmpBookmarks()** returns a value of 10, it means that the two bookmarks being compared end at the same place but the second bookmark is longer. In this example, that means the insertion point and the "temp" bookmark end at the same place and "temp" marks more text than "\Sel," which only marks the insertion point.

When the insertion point is here, **CmpBookmarks()** returns 10.

The corrected macro needs to exit the **While...Wend** loop when **CmpBookmarks()** returns either 10 or 1:

```
Sub MAIN
CopyBookmark "\Sel", "temp"          'Copy selection into bookmark
ParaUp                               'Go to start of first para in selection
While CmpBookmarks("\Sel", "temp") <> 1 And \
        CmpBookmarks("\Sel", "temp") <> 10
    Insert Chr$(9)
    ParaDown
Wend
End Sub
```

C H A P T E R   7

The Well-Behaved Macro

The well-behaved macro is one that can anticipate and respond to a variety of situations. Good macro behavior encompasses preventing errors, handling them when they do occur, being stable enough to perform under various conditions, and not leaving a mess behind for the user to clean up.

In this chapter:

- Handling errors
- Bulletproofing
- Cleaning up

Handling Errors

When Word is asked to do something it can't do, an error condition occurs, and Word displays an error message box. An error condition is different from the WordBasic language errors described in the previous chapter; those errors are errors in the way a macro is written. However, a macro can be thoroughly debugged and still encounter error conditions. Here are some macro actions that can cause errors:

- Trying to open a file that isn't available
- Trying to create a bookmark with an invalid name
- Trying to use a command that isn't available—for example, trying to use the Annotations command (View menu) when the document doesn't contain annotations

When you encounter these errors as you're working on documents in Word, you just close the error message box and continue working. But when a macro encounters an error, it stops, and the rest of the instructions in the macro are not carried out—unless you include instructions to *trap*, or *handle*, the error. When a macro handles an error, it can respond to it and continue. WordBasic includes several statements you can use to handle errors.

WordBasic and Word Errors

When you're working on documents in Word, the only errors you encounter are Word errors. A macro, however, can also generate WordBasic errors. Some WordBasic errors, such as syntax errors (discussed in the previous chapter), prevent a macro from running. Others—the ones you might want to trap— occur only when a macro is running in specific situations.

The distinction between WordBasic and Word errors is important because a macro can prevent a WordBasic error message box from being displayed, but cannot prevent a Word error message box from being displayed.

For example, if you run a macro that includes a command that is not available, WordBasic displays a WordBasic error message box, as shown in the following illustration. If you include instructions in your macro to handle that error, the error message box will not be displayed; the macro will carry out the error-handling instructions. The error-handling instructions could move the insertion point to a context in which the command is available, for example.

A WordBasic error message box

On the other hand, if a macro tries to move the insertion point to a bookmark that doesn't exist, Word generates a Word error and will display an error message box whether or not the macro includes error-handling instructions. The error-handling instructions do make a difference, however. Without them, Word stops the macro where the error occurs. With them, the macro can continue after the user closes the error message box, and the macro can respond to the error, perhaps by requesting the name of another bookmark.

A Word error message box

Every error has a number. WordBasic errors have numbers below 1000; Word errors have numbers of 1000 or above. You can use these numbers in a macro to test for and respond to different types of errors. There are a few WordBasic errors, such as "Syntax error" and "Unknown Command, Subroutine, or Function," that prevent a macro from running and that you cannot trap.

For a complete list of WordBasic and Word error messages, see "Error Messages" in Part 2, "WordBasic Reference."

Error-Handling Instructions

WordBasic provides three forms of the **On Error** statement; the special variable **Err**; and the **Error** statement for handling errors in your macros.

On Error Goto *Label*

This form of the **On Error** statement enables error handling. It must be placed before the instruction that can generate an error. When an error occurs, Word goes to the line indicated by *Label*.

The following example displays an input box in which the user can type the name of a file to open. If the user chooses the Cancel button when the input box is displayed, a WordBasic error is generated. (You may not consider choosing the Cancel button an error, but WordBasic does.)

To trap the error, you place the **On Error Goto** *Label* instruction before the instruction that displays the input box. If the user chooses the Cancel button, the error is trapped, and Word goes to the line indicated by *Label*. In this case the label is bye, which is at the end of the macro. So if the user chooses the Cancel button in the input box, the macro ends without displaying an error message box.

```
Sub MAIN
On Error Goto bye
ans$ = InputBox$("Please type the name of a file to open:")
FileOpen ans$
'Series of instructions that operate on the file that was opened
bye:
End Sub
```

On Error Goto *Label* places the number of the error generated when the user chooses the Cancel button in the special variable **Err**, described later in this section.

On Error Resume Next

This form of the **On Error** statement allows a macro to trap errors and ignore them. When an error occurs, the macro simply resumes and goes to the next instruction as if nothing had happened. Using **On Error Resume Next** is sometimes the simplest way to deal with an error.

The following version of the previous example shows another way to deal with the error that occurs if the user chooses the Cancel button to close an input box. In this example, if the user chooses the Cancel button, the error is ignored. The **If** conditional tests whether a value was placed in the `ans$` variable. No value is placed in it if the user chooses Cancel, so the **FileOpen** instruction doesn't run in that case.

```
Sub MAIN
On Error Resume Next
ans$ = InputBox$("Please type the name of a file to open:")
If ans$ <> "" Then FileOpen ans$
'Series of instructions that operate on the file that was opened
End Sub
```

After an **On Error Resume Next** instruction, Word continues to ignore any errors that might occur until the macro ends or until it encounters an instruction that disables error trapping, such as **On Error Goto 0**. As useful as it can be to have Word ignore specific errors, such as the one generated by the Cancel button, to have *all* errors ignored can cause problems: A macro may not work properly after an unexpected error occurs. So it's a good idea to disable error trapping (or use **On Error Goto** *Label* to reset error trapping) after using **On Error Resume Next**.

On Error Resume Next sets the value of the special variable **Err** to 0 (zero). **Err** is described later in this section.

On Error Goto 0

This form of the **On Error** statement is used to disable error trapping. While both **On Error Goto** *Label* and **On Error Resume Next** allow the macro to continue when an error occurs, **On Error Goto 0** ensures that if an error is encountered, an error message is displayed and the macro stops.

You can use **On Error Goto 0** to limit error handling to a specific part of your macro. In the following example, **On Error Goto 0** is used to disable the error handling enabled by **On Error Resume Next**. Because the rest of the macro is meant to operate on an open file, the macro should end if no file is opened. **On Error Goto 0** ensures that the macro is stopped if the **FileOpen** instruction generates an error.

```
Sub MAIN
On Error Resume Next
ans$ = InputBox$("Please type the name of a file to open:")
On Error Goto 0
If ans$ <> "" Then FileOpen ans$
'Series of instructions that operate on the file that was opened
End Sub
```

Err

When error trapping is enabled with **On Error Goto** *Label*, the number of any error that occurs is stored in the special variable **Err**. By testing this value, the macro can take different actions according to the type of error that occurs.

In the following example, the `On Error Goto trap` instruction enables error handling. The error-handling instructions, beginning after the label `trap`, test for three different values. If **Err** is equal to 102, it means that the user chose the Cancel button in the input box, in which case the `Goto bye` instruction ends the macro. If **Err** is equal to 1078 or 1177, the user typed either an invalid filename or the name of a file that isn't stored in the current folder. In either case, the macro displays a message box that asks the user if he or she would like to try to open the file again. If the user chooses the Yes button, the macro resets **Err** to 0 (zero) and goes to the `tryagain` label.

By default, **Err** has a value of 0 (zero). Once an error occurs and **Err** is assigned a nonzero value, error trapping is disabled until **Err** is reset to 0 (zero). In the following example, **Err** must be reset to 0 (zero) or error trapping will not work when the instructions after the `tryagain` label are repeated:

```
Sub MAIN
tryagain:
    On Error Goto trap
    ans$ = InputBox$("Please type the name of a file to open:")
    FileOpen ans$
    'Series of instructions that operate on the file that was opened
    Goto bye
trap:
    If Err = 102 Then Goto bye          'User cancels input box
    If Err = 1078 Or Err = 1177 Then    'Not found/invalid filename
        response = MsgBox("Couldn't open the file. Try again?", 4)
                If response = -1 Then
                Err = 0
                Goto tryagain
        End If
    End If
bye:
End Sub
```

You can look up the number that corresponds to any Word or WordBasic error message in "Error Messages" in Part 2, "WordBasic Reference."

Error

You can use the **Error** statement to generate an error so that you can test whether your error trap works as intended, without having to create an actual error situation. Here is an example:

```
On Error Goto trap
Error 502                      'Simulate error 502
trap:
If Err = 502 Then MsgBox "Error was trapped."
```

If error trapping is not enabled before an **Error** instruction runs, Word highlights the **Error** instruction in the macro-editing window and stops the macro. If the error you specified is a WordBasic error, Word displays the corresponding error message box; if it is a Word error, no message is displayed.

Bulletproofing

Many macros are fragile initially: Everything must be just so, or they won't run properly. Fragile macros are fine if you're the only one who uses them. But if you're writing a macro others might use, you have to consider all the conditions in which someone might run it. *Bulletproofing* is the process of making a macro less dependent on a particular set of conditions.

The following is a checklist of questions to consider.

Where is the insertion point or selection when the macro begins?   A macro that uses editing statements may not work correctly if the insertion point or selection is in a table or a frame. If the insertion point or selection is in a macro-editing window or a header, footer, footnote, or annotation pane, a macro may not run because many commands are not available. You can use the **SelInfo( )** function to determine whether the insertion point or selection is in a macro-editing window or a pane.

Is there a selection?   Often, macros that are designed to help with editing assume that text is either selected or not selected. A bulletproofed macro would use the **SelType( )** function to test that assumption and quit if the selection were inappropriate.

Which view is the document in?   A macro that runs properly in normal view may not work in outline view or page layout view.

Is a window open? Most Word commands are unavailable when no document window is open.

What are the current Word settings? The settings in the Options dialog box (Tools menu) can often determine whether a macro runs properly. For example, a macro that pastes text onto or types over a selection depends on whether the Typing Replaces Selection check box on the Edit tab is selected. If a macro searches for or edits hidden text, hidden text must be visible; however, if a macro repaginates (or compiles an index or table of contents), page numbering may be thrown off if hidden text is visible. Use the WordBasic statements that control the Options dialog box to ensure the current settings are appropriate for your macro.

Could the macro trigger an auto macro? If the macro performs any of the actions that can trigger an auto macro (such as opening an existing document or creating a new one), it may be disrupted or perform unnecessary actions. You can disable auto macros using the **DisableAutoMacros** statement.

What if the user interrupts the macro? Usually, it's convenient to be able to cancel a macro by pressing the ESC key. But if a macro is carrying out a critical operation, canceling it could create problems. You can use the **DisableInput** statement to prevent the user from canceling a macro.

> ### Bulletproofing and Speed
> Every bulletproofing precaution slows your macro down. For long, complex macros, the added robustness is well worth a slight delay at the start. For short, quick macros, however, speed may be critical—if they take too long, they're not worth using. Use your judgment as to what level of bulletproofing is appropriate for a given macro.

Cleaning Up

The well-behaved macro cleans up after itself. In the course of carrying out its various tasks, a macro may open and close documents, change the settings of various options, and make other modifications before it is finished. Some of these changes may not be desirable to the user after the macro is done. For example, a macro designed to work on selected text may create a bookmark to mark an area of the document. The macro needs this bookmark, but the user doesn't; the macro should remove the bookmark when it's no longer needed.

Here's a checklist of possible cleanup tasks for your macro:

- Close any documents the macro opened that the user doesn't need.
- Save a document with changes that should be saved.
- Close a document without saving it if the macro made changes that should not be saved. If the document should be open but unchanged when the macro ends, close it without saving changes, and then reopen it.
- Restore the settings of any options the macro may have changed for its own purposes. For example, if hidden text was not displayed when the macro began, it should not be displayed when the macro ends (unless that is part of the purpose of the macro).
- Delete any temporary bookmarks created by the macro.
- Restore the original selection or return the insertion point to the appropriate location.
- Restore the original size of the document window.
- Re-enable auto macros if the macro disabled them. Auto macros remain disabled for the entire Word session if the macro does not re-enable them before it ends.
- Return to the original folder.

C H A P T E R   8

Communicating with Other Applications

Word supports several ways of communicating and sharing information with other applications. The simplest is through the Clipboard, using the standard Cut, Copy, and Paste commands (Edit menu). A more useful technique for WordBasic macros is dynamic data exchange (DDE), a protocol your macro can use to extract information from other applications, automatically update them with new information, and even send commands or keystrokes to manipulate them by remote control.

Word also offers limited support for object linking and embedding (OLE) Automation. OLE Automation is the successor to DDE and offers additional capabilities. An application such as Microsoft Excel can use OLE Automation to control Word and request information.

In Windows, you can use the messaging application programming interface (MAPI) to integrate Word with applications that support MAPI, such as Microsoft Mail. On the Macintosh, you can use built-in WordBasic statements and functions that support Apple Open Collaboration Environment (AOCE) messaging.

In this chapter:

- Using dynamic data exchange
- Using OLE Automation with Word
- Using MAPI and AOCE

Using Dynamic Data Exchange

Dynamic data exchange (DDE) is a mechanism supported by Microsoft applications in Windows and on the Macintosh that enables two applications to "talk" to each other. DDE automates the manual cutting and pasting of information between applications, providing a faster vehicle for updating information.

More specifically, DDE provides three capabilities:

- You can request information from an application. For example, in a DDE conversation with Microsoft Excel, a Word macro can request the contents of a cell or range of cells in a Microsoft Excel worksheet.

- You can send information to an application. In a DDE conversation with Microsoft Excel, a Word macro can send text to a cell or range of cells.

- You can send commands to an application. For example, in a DDE conversation with Microsoft Excel, a Word macro can send a command to open a worksheet from which it wants to request information. Commands sent to an application must be in a form the application can recognize.

Note Not all applications support DDE. Consult the documentation for your other applications to see if they support DDE.

Clients, Servers, and Conversations

Two applications exchange information by engaging in a DDE *conversation*. In a DDE conversation, the application that initiates and controls the conversation is the *client* and the application that responds is the *server*. The client application requests information from the server and sends information and commands to it. The server application, as its name implies, serves the needs of the client application by returning information, accepting information, and carrying out commands. There is nothing special about an application that makes it a client or a server; these are simply roles an application can adopt. In fact, an application can be engaged in several DDE conversations at the same time, acting as the client in some and the server in others. Each conversation is identified by a separate *channel* number.

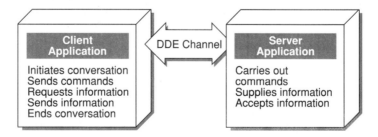

Application Names, Topics, and Items

When a client application begins a DDE conversation, it must specify two things:

- The name of the application it wants to talk to (the server)
- The subject of the conversation (the *topic*)

When a server application receives a request for a conversation concerning a topic it recognizes, it responds and the conversation is started. Once established, a conversation cannot change applications or topics. The combination of application and topic uniquely identifies the conversation, and the combination remains constant for the duration of the conversation. If either the client or the server changes the application or the topic, the conversation is terminated.

During the conversation, the client and server may exchange information concerning one or more *items*. An item is a reference to data that is meaningful to the server application. Either the client or the server can change the item during the conversation.

Together, the application name, topic, and item uniquely identify the information that is being passed between the applications. Each of these is discussed in detail in the sections that follow.

Application Names

Every application that supports DDE has a unique DDE application name. The following are application names for some Microsoft applications.

Application	DDE application name
Microsoft Access	MSAccess
Microsoft Excel for Windows	Excel
Microsoft Excel for the Macintosh	Excel
Microsoft FoxPro® for Windows	FoxPro
Microsoft Project for Windows	WinProj
Microsoft Project for the Macintosh	MSProject
Microsoft Word for Windows	WinWord
Microsoft Word for the Macintosh	MSWord or WinWord
Microsoft Windows 3.x Program Manager	ProgMan

Note   Visual FoxPro™ 3.0 can act as both a server and a client to send data to and receive data from other applications such as Word. For more information see "DDE Functions" in Microsoft Visual FoxPro Help.

Topics

Every DDE conversation is with both a server application and a topic the server application supports. Most applications support the names of open files as topics. Some possible topics are a Microsoft Excel worksheet (for example, "DAILYORD.XLS"), a Word document (for example, "SALESREP.DOC"), or an object in a Microsoft Access database (for example, "NORTHWIND.MDB;TABLE Shippers").

A special topic that many applications recognize is "System." Unlike other topics, which may or may not be available depending on whether a file is open, the System topic is always available and provides a list of the other topics that are currently available as well as other information about the application.

Items

With the server's application name and a topic name, a client can initiate a DDE conversation. But for a client to exchange information with the server, one other essential piece of information is needed: the items available in the topic of the DDE conversation. An item is a kind of subtopic that identifies the information *actually being exchanged* during the DDE conversation. For example, Microsoft Excel recognizes cell references (such as R1C1) as items in a conversation. In Word, a bookmark is an item. Microsoft Access recognizes several items, including SQL statements.

Initiating a DDE Conversation

A key requirement for a DDE conversation is that both applications be running. If an application isn't running, a client can't initiate a DDE conversation with it. For that reason, a macro that initiates a DDE conversation usually includes instructions that carry out the following three steps:

1. Determine whether the application you want to talk to is running

2. Start the application if it isn't already running

3. Initiate the DDE conversation

Step One: Determine Whether the Application Is Running

You can use the **AppIsRunning**( ) function to determine whether an application is running. Here is the syntax:

AppIsRunning(*Title$*)

In Windows, *Title$* is the name of the application as it appears in the title bar of the application window (*Title$* also appears in the Task List). For example, to determine if Microsoft Excel is running, you can use the following instruction:

```
status = AppIsRunning("Microsoft Excel")
```

Note that the *Title$* is not the same as the DDE application name. Word does not generate an error if you specify the wrong name for an **AppIsRunning**( ) instruction, but the instruction will give unexpected results.

On the Macintosh, *Title$* is the application name. You can also use the **MacID$**( ) function to specify an application's signature instead of the application name. For example:

```
status = AppIsRunning(MacID$("XCEL"))
```

Note In Windows, when a document window is maximized, the document window name is included in the title bar of the application window, but you don't have to specify the document window part of the title. For example, if Microsoft Excel is running and "BUDGET.XLS" is opened in a maximized document window, the application window title is "Microsoft Excel - BUDGET.XLS." But you can specify just "Microsoft Excel" for *Title$*.

Step Two: Start the Application If Necessary

If the server application is not running, you can use the **Shell** statement to start it. Here is the syntax:

Shell *Application$* [, *WindowStyle*]

Application$ must be the actual application filename. For example, "EXCEL.EXE" is acceptable in Windows; on the Macintosh, "Microsoft Excel" is accepted. In Windows, the optional *WindowStyle* argument specifies how the application window is displayed (for example, as an icon or a maximized window); on the Macintosh, *WindowStyle* specifies whether the application should be activated. If the application you want to start is not in the current folder, or not on a path recognized by the operating system, you must specify the path as well as the filename. Here is a Windows example:

```
Shell "C:\EXCEL\EXCEL.EXE", 0          'Start Excel minimized
```

Here is the same example on the Macintosh:

```
Shell "HD1:EXCEL:Microsoft Excel", 0     'Start Excel and activate
```

On the Macintosh, it's a good idea to use the **MacID$()** function to specify an application signature rather than a specific application filename, since it isn't uncommon for Macintosh users to change application filenames. The application signature provided by **MacID$()** ensures that the **Shell** statement will run the specified application, regardless of the filename. Here is an example:

```
Shell MacID$("XCEL"), 0
```

To open a document at the same time you start the application, you can specify a document filename with the application filename or just the document filename, assuming the operating system can associate the filename with the application you want to start. Here is a Windows example:

```
Shell "C:\EXCEL\EXAMPLES\BUDGET.XLS", 0
```

Here is the same example on the Macintosh:

```
Shell "HD1:EXCEL:My Budget", 0
```

Here's how you might use **AppIsRunning()** and **Shell** together in Windows:

```
If AppIsRunning("Microsoft Excel") = 0 Then Shell "EXCEL.EXE", 0
```

In Windows, the **AppIsRunning()** instruction is necessary because with most applications, **Shell** starts a second instance of the application if one instance is already running — not usually the effect you want. On the Macintosh, **Shell** does not start a second instance of an application. If the application is already running, **Shell** either activates it or has no effect, depending on the value of the *WindowStyle* argument. Here's an example:

```
Shell MacID$("XCEL"), 4
```

The *WindowStyle* argument of 4 specifies that Microsoft Excel is not to be activated; if Microsoft Excel is already running, this instruction has no effect.

Note In Word version 6.0 for Windows NT and Word version 7.0, you cannot depend on a program started with **Shell** to be finished loading before the instructions following the **Shell** statement in your macro are run. A **DDEInitiate** instruction that tries to communicate with an application that has not finished loading will generate errors. To avoid this problem, you can use a **For...Next** loop to delay the **DDEInitiate** instruction until the other application is loaded. For example:

```
If AppIsRunning("Microsoft Access") = 0 Then
    Shell "MSACCESS.EXE", 0
    For i = 1 To 2000
        x = i
    Next i
End If
chan = DDEInitiate("MSAccess", "System")
```

Step Three: Initiate the DDE Conversation

When you have established that the application you want to talk to is running, you are ready to initiate a DDE conversation with **DDEInitiate()**. Here is the syntax:

DDEInitiate(*Application$*, *Topic$***)**

Application$* is the DDE application name of the application you want to initiate a conversation with. *Topic$ is the name of a topic the application currently supports. For example, the following instruction initiates a conversation with Microsoft Excel for Windows or Microsoft Excel for the Macintosh on the System topic:

```
chan = DDEInitiate("Excel", "System")
```

If **DDEInitiate**() is successful in initiating a conversation with the specified server application and topic, it returns a channel number. You use this channel number as an argument in other DDE statements and functions to refer to this DDE conversation.

An error occurs if the application isn't running or if the application doesn't recognize the topic. For example, if you specify "SALES.XLS" as the topic, but SALES.XLS isn't open, an error is generated.

Requesting Information

Once you have initiated a conversation with another application, you can use the **DDERequest$**() function to obtain information from an item within the specified topic. Here is the syntax:

DDERequest$(*ChanNum*, *Item$*)

ChanNum is the number of a channel returned by the **DDEInitiate**() instruction. *Item$* is an item supported by the topic of the DDE conversation.

You can use **DDERequest$**() to query the System topic in Microsoft Excel to get a list of the currently supported topics, as shown in the following Windows example:

```
If AppIsRunning("Microsoft Excel") = 0 Then Shell "EXCEL.EXE", 4
chan = DDEInitiate("Excel", "System")
topics$ = DDERequest$(chan, "Topics")
```

Here is the same example on the Macintosh:

```
If AppIsRunning(MacID$("XCEL")) = 0 Then Shell MacID$("XCEL"), 4
chan = DDEInitiate("Excel", "System")
topics$ = DDERequest$(chan, "Topics")
```

"Topics" is an item in the System topic that lists all the topics currently available. You can add an **Insert** instruction such as the following:

```
Insert topics$
```

This instruction inserts the list of topics in a document.

```
[SALES.XLS]Sales Report          [SALES.XLS]Sheet2       [SALES.XLS]Sheet3
[SALES.XLS]Sheet4        [SALES.XLS]Sheet5      [SALES.XLS]Sheet6
[SAMPLES.XLS]Advanced           [SAMPLES.XLS]Amortization Table
[SAMPLES.XLS]CONTENTS          [SAMPLES.XLS]Control Structures
[SAMPLES.XLS]Moving [SAMPLES.XLS]Worksheet Functions      System
```

Topic names are separated by tab marks. In this example, [SALES.XLS]Sales Report and [SAMPLES.XLS]Amortization Table are the names of Microsoft Excel worksheets that can be accessed as topics in DDE conversations.

If the specified channel number doesn't refer to an active DDE conversation, **DDERequest$()** generates an error. You'll also get an error if the specified item is not recognized by the other application.

Note that since **DDERequest$()** is a string function, information is always returned to the Word macro in the form of a string. For an example that retrieves information from a range of cells in Microsoft Excel, see "Using Microsoft Excel as a Server" later in this chapter.

You can use **InStr()** to determine whether a file is currently open. The following Windows example determines if SALES.XLS is an available DDE topic (the file is open):

```
If AppIsRunning("Microsoft Excel") = 0 Then Shell "EXCEL.EXE", 4
chan = DDEInitiate("Excel", "System")
topics$ = DDERequest$(chan, "Topics")
If InStr(topics$, "SALES.XLS") <> 0 Then
    Print "File is Open"
End If
```

Sending Information

Although the client in a DDE conversation usually obtains information from the server, the client can supply information to the server as well. To do so, you use the **DDEPoke** statement. Here is the syntax:

DDEPoke *ChanNum*, *Item$*, *Data$*

ChanNum is the channel number returned by the **DDEInitiate()** instruction that began the DDE conversation. *Item$* is the name of an item supported by the topic of the DDE conversation. *Data$* is the information—in the form of a string—that you want to "poke" (or insert) into the item. To send a number, you must first convert it into a string.

The following example pokes the numeric value 100 into the first cell of the Microsoft Excel worksheet that is the topic of the DDE conversation. The **Str$()** function is used to convert the value into a string:

```
DDEPoke chan1, "R1C1", Str$(100)
```

Sending Commands

You can use the **DDEExecute** statement to send a command recognized by the server application:

DDEExecute *ChanNum*, *Command$*

ChanNum is the channel number returned by the **DDEInitiate()** instruction that began the DDE conversation. In Microsoft Excel and many other applications that support DDE, *Command$* is a statement or function in the application's macro language. For example, in Microsoft Excel the XLM macro statement that creates a new worksheet is NEW(1). (Microsoft Excel does not accept Visual Basic instructions through DDE.) To send the same command through a DDE channel, you would use the following instruction:

```
DDEExecute chan1, "[NEW(1)]"
```

Many applications, including Microsoft Excel, require that each command received through a DDE channel be enclosed in brackets. You can use a single **DDEExecute** instruction to send more than one command, with each command enclosed in brackets. For example, the following instruction tells Microsoft Excel to open and then close a worksheet:

```
DDEExecute chan1, "[NEW(1)][FILE.CLOSE(0)]"
```

Note that there must be no spaces between bracketed commands in a single **DDEExecute** instruction; otherwise, an error will occur. The preceding instruction is equivalent to the following two instructions:

```
DDEExecute chan1, "[NEW(1)]"
DDEExecute chan1, "[FILE.CLOSE(0)]"
```

Many commands require arguments in the form of strings enclosed in quotation marks. Because the quotation mark indicates the beginning and end of a string in WordBasic, you must use `Chr$(34)` to include a quotation mark in a command string. For example, to send the Microsoft Excel macro instruction `OPEN("SALES.XLS")`, you would use the following instruction:

```
DDEExecute chan1, "[OPEN(" + Chr$(34) + "SALES.XLS" + Chr$(34) + ")]"
```

Terminating DDE Conversations

DDE channels are not closed automatically until you exit Word. If you don't close a channel, it remains open, even after the macro has ended. Because each channel uses some system resources, you should always close channels when you no longer need them. You terminate a DDE conversation with **DDETerminate**. Here is the syntax:

DDETerminate *ChanNum*

ChanNum is the channel number returned by the **DDEInitiate**() instruction that began the conversation.

When you close Word, it automatically terminates all active DDE conversations. However, you might want to terminate all conversations without closing Word. To do so, you could use several consecutive **DDETerminate** statements or a loop. However, WordBasic provides **DDETerminateAll** as a shortcut. **DDETerminateAll** terminates all active DDE conversations that Word has initiated (it does not terminate DDE conversations that another application may have initiated with Word as the server). If you are debugging a macro that performs DDE and are often interrupting and restarting the macro, it's a good idea to use **DDETerminateAll** periodically to close any channels you may have inadvertently left open.

Using Microsoft Excel as a Server

Here are some points to keep in mind about DDE conversations with Microsoft Excel:

- The DDE application name for Microsoft Excel in Windows and on the Macintosh is Excel.

- Microsoft Excel supports the standard System topic, which supports the following items.

Item	Description
SysItems	Provides a list of the items in the System topic
Topics	Provides a list of the currently valid topics, including all open documents

Item	Description
Status	Indicates whether Microsoft Excel is ready to receive DDE messages ("Busy" or "Ready")
Formats	Provides the list of formats supported
Selection	Indicates the currently selected cell or range of cells
Protocols	Not applicable
EditEnvItems	Not applicable

- Any open document is a valid DDE topic in Microsoft Excel.

- A cell or range of cells is an item within a worksheet, macro sheet, or slide-show document. To specify a cell or range of cells as an item, you can use a name defined in Microsoft Excel that identifies them, or you can indicate the cells themselves. You must use the "R1C1" convention to refer to cells rather than the "A1" convention. For example, to refer to a cell in the second column of the fourth row, you specify "R4C2" rather than "D2." Note that you don't need to change the corresponding Workspace option in Microsoft Excel.

- Using the **DDEExecute** statement, you can send Microsoft Excel XLM macro commands enclosed in brackets. You can send more than one command with a single **DDEExecute** statement; each macro command must be enclosed in brackets.

  Microsoft Excel does not accept Visual Basic instructions through a DDE channel. However, you can send an XLM macro command to run an available XLM macro or Visual Basic procedure. For example, the following instruction runs a Visual Basic procedure called FormatCells stored in a module called VBAMacros:

  ```
  DDEExecute chan, "[run(" + Chr$(34) + "VBAMacros!FormatCells" + \
          Chr$(34) + ")]"
  ```

- You cannot initiate a DDE link if the formula bar in Microsoft Excel is active. If you try to initiate a link when the formula bar is active, WordBasic will display an error message saying that the application does not respond.

- Microsoft Excel includes an option to prevent other applications from initiating DDE conversations with it. To check the setting of this option, choose Options from the Tools menu in Microsoft Excel, and select the General tab. If the Ignore Other Applications check box is selected, you cannot initiate a DDE conversation. If you try to initiate a conversation when the Ignore Other Applications check box is selected, Word will display a message saying that the "remote data" is not accessible and will ask if you want to start another instance of Microsoft Excel. To initiate a DDE conversation successfully at that point, you must first clear the Ignore Other Applications check box in Microsoft Excel.

Example

The following example initiates a DDE conversation with SALES.XLS (a sample workbook supplied with Microsoft Excel), requests some sales figures, and inserts them into a Word document:

```
chan = DDEInitiate("Excel", "[SALES.XLS]Sales Report")
figures$ = DDERequest$(chan, "R4C2:R8C4")
Insert figures$
DDETerminate chan
```

You could also use a name defined in Microsoft Excel to refer to the cell range R4C2:R8C3. For example, if the cells were defined with the name "JanuarySales," you could use the following instruction:

```
figures$ = DDERequest$(chan, "JanuarySales")
```

Note that when the figures are inserted into Word, each cell is delimited by a tab character and each row by a paragraph mark, as shown in the following illustration. A paragraph mark is inserted after the last row in Windows, but not on the Macintosh.

```
Region→January→February¶
North → 10111 → 13400¶
South → 22100 → 24050¶
East  → 13270 → 15670¶
West  → 10800 → 21500¶
¶
```

Since **DDERequest()** returns the figures as a string, they lose any formatting that was applied in Microsoft Excel. Instead, they acquire the formatting of the paragraph in which the insertion point is located in Word.

You can use the following instructions to have the preceding macro select the figures after it inserts them and convert them into a table. The first instruction creates a temporary bookmark at the location where the figures from Microsoft Excel will be inserted. The remaining instructions select the figures and convert them into a table.

```
CopyBookmark "\Sel", "temp"
Insert figures$
ExtendSelection
EditGoTo "temp"
TableInsertTable .ConvertFrom = 1
```

Note that you cannot have the macro pour the figures into the selected cells of an existing table, as you can when you use the Paste command (Edit menu) to copy cells from Microsoft Excel using the Clipboard.

Using Microsoft Access as a Server

Microsoft Access version 7.0 provides a wide variety of topics to allow you to access tables and queries. You can also send SQL statements to a database and launch macros. For information on the topics and items supported, see the Microsoft Access Help topic "Using Microsoft Access as a DDE Server."

Here are some other points to keep in mind when using Microsoft Access as a server:

- The DDE application name for Microsoft Access is MSAccess.
- Microsoft Access supports the standard System topic, which supports the following items.

Item	Description
SysItems	Provides a list of the items in the System topic
Topics	Provides a list of all open databases
Status	Indicates whether Microsoft Access is ready to receive DDE messages ("Busy" or "Ready")
Formats	Provides a list of formats Microsoft Access can copy to the Clipboard

- The Topics item in the System topic does not provide a comprehensive list of the topics available in Microsoft Access; it lists only the open databases. For a complete list of the available topics, see the Microsoft Access Help topic "Using Microsoft Access as a DDE Server."
- Like Microsoft Excel, Microsoft Access includes an option to prevent another application from initiating a DDE conversation. To check the setting of this option, choose Options from the Tools menu in Microsoft Access, and then click the Advanced tab. If the Ignore DDE Requests check box is selected, Microsoft Access will not respond to **DDEInitiate( )**. You must clear the check box before initiating a DDE conversation.

- You can use the **DDEExecute** statement to run a macro in the active database or carry out an action in Visual Basic using one of methods of the DoCmd object. You can also use the OpenDatabase and CloseDatabase actions to open or close a database.

- You cannot use **DDEPoke** to send information to Microsoft Access.

- You cannot send a parameter query to Microsoft Access.

Examples

The following example inserts the contents of the Shippers table into a Word document. The Shippers table is a table in the NORTHWIND.MDB sample database included with Microsoft Access version 7.0. Note that Microsoft Access has its own internal syntax for specifying a table in a database as a topic, and this differs from the syntax used to specify a worksheet in Microsoft Excel, for example. This syntax is described in the Microsoft Access Help topic "Using Microsoft Access as a DDE Server."

```
Sub MAIN
chan1 = DDEInitiate("MSAccess", "System")
DDEExecute chan1, "[OpenDatabase
C:\MSOffice\Access\Samples\NORTHWIND.MDB]"
chan2 = DDEInitiate("MSAccess", "NORTHWIND;TABLE Shippers ")
figures$ = DDERequest$(chan2, "All")
Insert figures$
DDETerminateAll
End Sub
```

As with figures imported from Microsoft Excel worksheets, fields are separated by tab characters and records by paragraph marks (although the last record does not end with a paragraph mark).

You can also access queries in a Microsoft Access database using the Query topic. For example:

```
chan = DDEInitiate("MSAccess", "NORTHWIND;QUERY Ten Most Expensive
Products")
```

The following example sends an SQL statement to the NORTHWIND database to return a list of customers stored in the database:

```
Sub MAIN
chan1 = DDEInitiate("MSAccess", "System")
DDEExecute chan1, "[OpenDatabase
C:\MSOffice\Access\Samples\NORTHWIND.MDB]"chan2 = DDEInitiate("MSAccess"
, "NORTHWIND;SQL SELECT DISTINCTROW" + \
  " Customers.CompanyName FROM Customers" + \
  " ORDER BY Customers.CompanyName;")
list$ = DDERequest$(chan2, "Data")
Insert list$
DDETerminateAll
End Sub
```

An easy way to create SQL statements is to first create the query in Microsoft Access, and then copy the SQL statement into your Word macro. To see the SQL statement for a query in Microsoft Access, open the query in Design mode and choose SQL from the View menu to display the SQL dialog box.

Using Word as a Server

So far, this chapter has described Word as the client application, but Word can also be used as a DDE server. Here are some points to keep in mind when using Word as a server:

- In Windows, the DDE application name for Word is WinWord; on the Macintosh, it is MSWord or WinWord.

- Word supports the standard System topic, which supports the following items:

Item	Description
SysItems	Provides a list of the items in the System topic
Topics	Provides a list of the currently valid topics, including all open documents
Formats	Provides a list of all the Clipboard formats supported by Word

- Word supports all open documents, macros, and templates as topics. A template is considered to be open if it is attached to an open document, if it is loaded as a global template, or if it is open in a document window. It's best to include the complete path when specifying a document or template as a topic; otherwise, Word won't find the document if it isn't located in the current folder.

- In documents and templates, Word supports bookmarks as items. Three of the predefined bookmarks are supported as items: "\StartOfDoc," "\EndOfDoc," and "\Doc." An error will occur if an application requests an "empty" bookmark—one that marks a location in a document but not any text. For example, the predefined bookmark "\StartOfDoc" does not mark any text and so an error will occur if an application requests it. You can, however, poke information into an empty bookmark; you could use the "\StartOfDoc" bookmark to poke information into the beginning of a document.

- You do not have to write any WordBasic code to use Word as a server. For example, if you want to use Microsoft Excel or Microsoft Access as the client and Word as the server, you write a procedure in Visual Basic; you don't have to write a Word macro.

- The client application can use its equivalent of the **DDEExecute** statement to send WordBasic instructions to Word. The following Visual Basic instruction sends instructions to open two documents in Word:

```
DDEExecute chan%, "[FileOpen ""JOE.DOC""][FileOpen ""REPORT.DOC""]"
```

Note that each WordBasic instruction is enclosed in brackets and that you can send more than one WordBasic instruction with a single Visual Basic **DDEExecute** instruction. Visual Basic uses a pair of quotation marks to indicate one quotation mark within a string.

You can also send macro names to have Word start a macro. For example, the following Visual Basic instruction runs the Word macro SortHeadings:

```
DDEExecute chan%, "[SortHeadings]"
```

Do not send instructions that display dialog boxes in Word—Word will not become the active application window, and the DDE conversation will time out, waiting for the user to respond to the dialog box.

- Word can open a DDE channel with another instance of itself. One instance of Word becomes the client and the other becomes the server. Word can even open a DDE channel to a single instance of itself (although it cannot poke information into itself when only one instance is running). This capability can be useful for testing macros.

Examples

The following Microsoft Excel procedure opens a Word document, retrieves the text marked by a bookmark, and places it in a series of cells in a worksheet. First it defines `returnlist` as an object variable equivalent to six cells. Then it opens a DDE channel to the Word System topic and uses the **DDEExecute** method to send the WordBasic instruction `FileOpen "TEST.DOC"`. Note that the instruction is enclosed in brackets and that `"TEST.DOC"` is enclosed in pairs of quotation marks, which Visual Basic uses to indicate quotation marks within a string. Once TEST.DOC is open, the macro closes the DDE channel to the System topic and opens a new one to the TEST.DOC topic. Finally, it uses the **DDERequest** method to request the text marked by the bookmark "listitems," which is returned to the object variable `returnlist`.

```
Sub ReturnWordBookmarkText()
    Dim returnList As Object
    Set returnList = ActiveSheet.Range(Cells(1, 1), Cells(6, 1))
    channelNumber = Application.DDEInitiate("WinWord", "System")
    Application.DDEExecute channelNumber, "[FileOpen ""TEST.DOC""]"
    Application.DDETerminate channelNumber
    channelNumber = Application.DDEInitiate("WinWord", "TEST.DOC")
    returnList.value = Application.DDERequest(channelNumber, "listitems")
    Application.DDETerminate channelNumber
End Sub
```

The following WordBasic macro establishes a DDE conversation with the same instance of Word and displays a message box, such as the one that follows, showing the list of currently valid topics. The **While...Wend** loop replaces the tab characters between topics with paragraph marks so that the list is easier to read. Note that a WordBasic message box cannot display more than 255 characters, so the macro displays a message if the list of topics is too long.

```
Sub MAIN
chan = DDEInitiate("winword", "system")
topics$ = DDERequest$(chan, "topics")
tab$ = Chr$(9)
para$ = Chr$(13)
While InStr(topics$, tab$)
    tab = InStr(topics$, tab$)
    leftside$ = Left$(topics$, tab - 1)
    rightside$ = Right$(topics$, Len(topics$) - tab)
    topics$ = leftside$ + para$ + rightside$
Wend
msg$ = "The topics available are: " + para$ + para$ + topics$
If Len(msg$) > 255 Then
    MsgBox "Sorry, the list of topics is too long to display " + \
           "in a message box. (255 characters is the maximum.)"
Else
    MsgBox msg$, "Word DDE Topics"
End If
DDETerminate chan
End Sub
```

The topics available are:

System
C:\WINWORD\TEMPLATE\NORMAL.DOT
Global: DDESystemTest
Document1

Using OLE Automation with Word

OLE Automation is a protocol intended to replace DDE. As with DDE, an application can use OLE Automation to share data or control another application.

In OLE Automation, Word provides another application (called the "container" application) with an *object*—a unit of information similar to a topic in DDE. Word supports a single object called "WordBasic" for OLE Automation. You use the "WordBasic" object to send WordBasic instructions to Word. The technique is similar to sending commands to Word through DDE, but with OLE Automation, WordBasic instructions can return numbers or strings directly to the container application. This makes it possible to use WordBasic instructions as an extension of the container application's macro or programming language.

Note that Word can provide an object to another application for OLE Automation, but it cannot use OLE Automation to access objects in other applications. In other words, applications that support OLE Automation, such as Microsoft Excel or a Visual Basic application, can use OLE Automation to access Word, but Word cannot use OLE Automation to access them. (In DDE terms, Word can act as a server for another application but cannot act as the client.)

Microsoft Visual FoxPro version 3.0 includes an OLE Automation client example. For information about how to run and view the code associated with the OLE Automation example, see "OLE Automation Sample" in Microsoft Visual FoxPro Help.

Note   Throughout this section, the term "Visual Basic" is used to refer to either Visual Basic version 3.0 or later (Windows) or Visual Basic in Microsoft Access version 7.0 (Windows) and Microsoft Excel version 5.0 or later (Windows or Macintosh), unless otherwise indicated.

Accessing Word

The first step toward making Word available to a container application is to define an object variable that will reference the "WordBasic" object in Word. In Visual Basic, you declare a variable of type **Object**. For example:

```
Dim WordObj As Object
```

You then make the "WordBasic" object available to the container application by "creating" it for the application and assigning it to the object variable. In Visual Basic, you use the **CreateObject** function to create an object and the **Set** keyword to assign to the object variable. Here is the syntax:

Set *ObjectVar* = **CreateObject("***Application.ObjectType***")**

For example, in Visual Basic you could use the following instruction:

```
Set WordObj = CreateObject("Word.Basic")
```

This instruction makes the "WordBasic" object in Word available to the container application for OLE Automation.

If Word version 6.0 is not running when another application needs to access it, OLE Automation starts a visible instance of Word. You don't need to include a separate instruction to start Word, as you do with DDE. An error occurs if Word cannot be found. While a visible instance is useful for debugging a Visual Basic procedure, you may want to hide the instance in the final macro. To do so, use the WordBasic **AppHide** statement:

```
Set WordObj = CreateObject("Word.Basic")
WordObj.AppHide
```

If Word version 7.0 is not running when another application needs to access it, OLE Automation starts a hidden instance of Word. While a hidden instance is useful for the final macro, you may want to make the instance visible while debugging the Visual Basic procedure. To do so, use the WordBasic **AppShow** statement:

```
Set WordObj = CreateObject("Word.Basic")
WordObj.AppShow
```

Applications that fully support OLE Automation make their documents available as objects. Since Word supports only the "WordBasic" object for OLE Automation, you cannot use OLE Automation to directly access a Word document as an object (unless the document is embedded in the container application; see "Accessing an Embedded Word Object" later in this chapter). For example, you cannot use the **GetObject** function in Visual Basic to access a Word document. Instead, you use WordBasic instructions to access Word and to act on Word documents, as described in the following section.

If OLE Automation starts a Word session, OLE Automation will close Word when the object variable that references the "WordBasic" object expires—when either the procedure ends or the container application is closed. In Visual Basic, you can use the **Set** statement with the **Nothing** keyword to clear an object variable, which has the same effect as closing the container application.

Note that the "WordBasic" object does not support a method to close itself. That is, if Word is running when OLE Automation starts, you cannot close Word through OLE Automation; you can only close a Word session if you also used OLE Automation to start it.

Using WordBasic Statements and Functions

Once you have made the "WordBasic" object available to the container application, you can use most WordBasic statements or functions to act on Word and Word documents. You use WordBasic instructions in OLE Automation in the same way you use them in Word macros.

WordBasic statements and functions not available to OLE Automation include the following: control structures, such as **While…Wend** and **If…Then…Else**; declaration statements such as **Dim**; statements associated with custom dialog boxes; the **FileExit** statement; and statements or functions that require array variables as arguments.

WordBasic functions that return strings end in a dollar sign ($). When using these functions in OLE Automation, you can either leave off the dollar sign or enclose it in brackets. The following instruction shows the **GetBookmark$()** function as it might appear in a WordBasic macro:

```
mark$ = GetBookmark$("Address")
```

In Visual Basic, the same instruction might be specified as either of the following two instructions, where `mark` is a string variable:

```
mark = WordObj.[GetBookmark$]("Address")
mark = WordObj.GetBookmark("Address")
```

Note The following WordBasic functions that return strings require the dollar sign and must be enclosed in brackets: **Font$()**, **GetSystemInfo$()**, and **Language$()**. These WordBasic functions have the same keywords as WordBasic statements (for example, there is a **Font** statement as well as a **Font$()** function); without the dollar sign WordBasic has no way to distinguish them from WordBasic statements.

The following example opens the Word document LETTER.DOC and then uses a WordBasic **GetBookmark$()** instruction to retrieve the text of the "Address" bookmark in LETTER.DOC and display it in a message box:

```
Dim mark As String
Dim WordObj As Object
Set WordObj = CreateObject("Word.Basic")
WordObj.FileOpen Name:= "LETTER.DOC"
mark = WordObj.GetBookmark("Address")
MsgBox mark
```

The following example retrieves the list of bookmarks from the active document and displays their contents in a series of message boxes. These instructions use WordBasic instructions just as if they were part of the Visual Basic language. In effect, these instructions extend the functionality of Visual Basic. The only difference is that since WordBasic is not an object oriented language with methods and properties like those of Visual Basic, the syntax of the WordBasic instructions does not match Visual Basic syntax.

```
Dim WordObj As Object
Set WordObj = CreateObject("Word.Basic")
Dim count As Integer, countmarks As Integer
countmarks = WordObj.CountBookmarks()
If countmarks <> 0 Then
    ReDim bmarks$(1 To countmarks)
    For count = 1 To countmarks
        bmarks$(count) = WordObj.BookmarkName(count)
    Next count
    For count = 1 To countmarks
        MsgBox bmarks$(count)
    Next
End If
```

In the following example, the instructions toggle the bold formatting of the selected paragraph in Word:

```
Dim WordObj As Object
Set WordObj = CreateObject("Word.Basic")
WordObj.EditGoto "\Para"     'Select the current paragraph
If WordObj.Bold() <> 0 Then
    WordObj.Bold 0              'Remove bold from the selected text
Else
    WordObj.Bold 1             'Apply bold to the selected text
End If
```

What Does the Instruction Act On?

A significant difference between Visual Basic and WordBasic is that in Visual Basic, whatever a statement (or "method") acts on is specified in the statement itself. In WordBasic, however, that is not always the case. For example, an **EditCut** WordBasic instruction might cut anything from a single character to an entire document: it cuts whatever is selected in the active document when the instruction runs. Most WordBasic formatting and editing instructions work this way. If you're used to the Visual Basic way of doing things, keep in mind that when using WordBasic instructions, you usually need to be aware of the current selection or location of the insertion point.

Accessing an Embedded Word Object

So far, this section has described accessing Word as a separate application. But you can also access a Word object such as a Word document or Word picture embedded in the container application. In Visual Basic, you use the Object property to access the document or picture and to use WordBasic statements and functions to act on it. Here is the syntax for Visual Basic version 3.0 or later (not available on the Macintosh):

Set *ObjectVar* = *OLEControlName*.**Object.Application.WordBasic**

ObjectVar is a previously declared object variable; *OLEControlName* is the name of the OLE control in which the Word object is embedded. For example, you could use the following instructions to access a document embedded in an OLE control called OLE1:

```
Dim WordObj As Object
Set WordObj = OLE1.Object.Application.WordBasic
```

In Microsoft Excel Visual Basic, you use the OLEObjects method to return the embedded Word object. The following example accesses a Word document object with the name Picture 1 (the name given to the object in Microsoft Excel, not a document filename) in the active worksheet:

```
Dim WordObj As Object
Set WordObj = ActiveSheet.OLEObjects("Picture 1")
```

In Microsoft Access Visual Basic, you use the Object property to access an embedded Word document. For example, you could use the following instructions to access a document embedded in an OLE control called OLE1:

```
Dim WordObj As Object
Set WordObj = Me!OLE1.Object.Application.WordBasic
```

The embedded object must be activated before it can be accessed. You can either include an instruction to activate the OLE control, or you can assume the object is activated in some other way (for example, the user double-clicks it). In Visual Basic version 3.0, you can use the Action property to activate OLE control. For example:

```
OLE1.Action = 7
```

In this instruction, OLE1 is the name of the OLE control in which the Word object is embedded.

In Visual Basic version 4.0, you can activate an OLE control using the Action property or the DoVerb method. For example, the following two instructions are equivalent:

```
OLE1.DoVerb(vbOLEShow)
OLE1.Action = 7
```

In Microsoft Excel Visual Basic, you use the Activate method to activate the Word object. In the following example, WordObj is an object variable in which the Word document object is stored:

```
WordObj.Activate
```

In Microsoft Access Visual Basic, you use the Action property to activate the Word object. For example:

```
Me!OLE1.Action = acOLEActivate
```

The following example accesses a Word object embedded in a Visual Basic version 4.0 container application. Then it uses the WordBasic **EditSelectAll** statement to select all the text, and the WordBasic **Bold** statement to format it as bold. The Check1.SetFocus instruction deactivates the embedded Word object and returns the focus to a checkbox named "Check1."

```
Dim WordObj As Object
OLE1.DoVerb(vbOLEShow)
Set WordObj = OLE1.Object.Application.WordBasic
WordObj.EditSelectAll
WordObj.Bold
Check1.SetFocus
Set WordObj = Nothing
```

Here is the same example using Microsoft Excel Visual Basic. The final instruction, Range("B6").Activate, deactivates the embedded Word object and activates cell B6 in the active worksheet.

```
Dim WordObj As Object
Set WordObj = ActiveSheet.OLEObjects("Picture 1")
WordObj.Activate
With WordObj.Object.Application.WordBasic
    .EditSelectAll
    .Bold
End With
Range("B6").Activate
```

Here is the same example using Microsoft Access Visual Basic. The final instruction, DoCmd.GoToControl "Check1", activates the check box named "Check1."

```
Dim WordObj As Object
Set WordObj = Me!OLE1.Object.Application.WordBasic
Me!OLE1.Action = acOLEActivate
WordObj.EditSelectAll
WordObj.Bold
DoCmd.GoToControl "Check1"
Set WordObj = Nothing
```

Retrieving Word Dialog Box Settings

You can retrieve Word dialog box settings when you're using OLE Automation to access either Word itself (through the "Basic" object) or an embedded Word document. To do so, you first create an object variable to hold the settings, and then place the settings in the object variable. For example:

```
Dim TOVvar As Object
Set TOVvar = WordObj.CurValues.FileOpen
```

The first instruction defines an object variable to hold the dialog box settings. The second instruction assigns the variable the current settings of the dialog box—in this case, the settings of the Open dialog box (File menu). WordObj is the object variable defined to access WordBasic. **CurValues** returns the dialog box settings from the dialog box specified. To specify a dialog box, you use the name of the WordBasic statement that corresponds to a Word dialog box. For example, **FileOpen** is the name of the WordBasic statement that corresponds to the Open dialog box (File menu). If you don't know the name to use for a dialog box, see "Language Summary" and "Statements and Functions" in Part 2, "WordBasic Reference."

Once you have placed the dialog box settings in an object variable, you use the following syntax to access them:

DialogObjectVar.DialogBoxSettingName

DialogBoxSettingName is the name of an argument for the WordBasic statement that corresponds to the dialog box whose settings are stored in *DialogObjectVar*. For the list of valid arguments, see the entry for the WordBasic statement in Part 2, "WordBasic Reference."

The following Visual Basic example toggles the Draft Font setting on the View tab in the Options dialog box (Tools menu). Note that if you are using Visual Basic version 3.0, you cannot use the instruction WordObj.ToolsOptionsView DraftFont := 0 since DraftFont is a named argument. Instead, you specify the argument positionally, as described in "Using Positional Arguments in Visual Basic Version 3.0" later in this chapter.

```
Dim WordObj As Object
Dim TOVvar As Object
Set WordObj = CreateObject("Word.Basic")
Set TOVvar = WordObj.CurValues.ToolsOptionsView
If TOVvar.DraftFont = 1 Then
    WordObj.ToolsOptionsView DraftFont := 0
Else
    WordObj.ToolsOptionsView DraftFont := 1
End If
```

Running Word Macros and Displaying Dialog Boxes

You can run a Word macro through OLE Automation, just as you can from within another Word macro. After the macro runs, control returns to the procedure that called it. You use the WordBasic **ToolsMacro** statement to run a macro. For example, the following instruction runs a macro called CountOpenWindows:

```
WordObj.ToolsMacro "CountOpenWindows", True
```

Word must be the active application if the macro displays a dialog box, message box, input box, or anything that requires a response from the user before the macro can continue. If Word is not the active application, the macro comes to a halt and eventually an OLE Automation error occurs. To make Word the active application, you can use an instruction similar to the WordBasic **AppActivate** statement in the container application's macro or programming language.

You can't directly define and display a dialog box through OLE Automation, but you can run a Word macro to display the dialog box. If the dialog box is a dialog box built into Word, you can then use the **CurValues** method to retrieve its settings. If the dialog box is a custom dialog box, the macro that displays the dialog box can save the dialog box settings so that they remain after the macro is finished. For example, the macro could save the settings in a settings file. For information on settings files, see "Using Settings Files and Document Variables" in Chapter 9, "More WordBasic Techniques."

Passing Values to a Word Macro

You cannot directly pass arguments to a Word macro or macro subroutine through OLE Automation. Within WordBasic, you can use the syntax *MacroName.Subroutine* [(*ArgumentList*)] to call subroutines in other macros and pass arguments to them, but this syntax is not supported by OLE Automation. If you want your Visual Basic code to run a WordBasic macro and to pass values to that macro, you must store those values in a location the macro can access. For example, you could store values in a settings file or in Word document variables. For information on settings files and document variables, see "Using Settings Files and Document Variables" in Chapter 9, "More WordBasic Techniques."

The following Visual Basic example runs a Word macro called CreateAndSaveNewDoc and displays a message when the macro is finished. The Visual Basic **AppActivate** statement is used to activate Word before the macro runs, since the macro will display the Save As dialog box.

```
Dim WordObj As Object
Set WordObj = CreateObject("Word.Basic")
AppActivate "Microsoft Word"
WordObj.ToolsMacro "CreateAndSaveNewDoc", True
MsgBox "The CreateAndSaveNewDoc macro is done."
```

You can also run this example in a Visual Basic version 3.0 application, but the Visual Basic version 3.0 **AppActivate** statement requires as an argument the same text that appears in the Word application window title bar. This text may change if a document window is maximized, so you need to add an **If** conditional to check whether this is the case and change the text specified in **AppActivate** accordingly. The following conditional uses the WordBasic functions **CountWindows**, **DocMaximize()**, and **WindowName$()** to accomplish this task:

```
If WordObj.CountWindows( ) > 0 Then
    If WordObj.DocMaximize( ) = True Then
        AppActivate "Microsoft Word - " + WordObj.WindowName( )
    Else
        AppActivate "Microsoft Word"
    End If
Else
    AppActivate "Microsoft Word"
End If
```

Here is the CreateAndSaveNewDoc macro:

```
Sub MAIN
AppMaximize "Microsoft Word"
On Error Goto bye
FileNew
FileSave
AppActivate "Microsoft Excel"
bye:
End Sub
```

This macro maximizes the Word window (in case Word is minimized when the macro is called), then creates a new file and uses the **FileSave** statement to display the Save As dialog box (File menu). (This dialog box is displayed because the file has never been saved.) The **AppActivate** instruction at the end of the macro activates Microsoft Excel so that control returns to the routine that called the macro. If you are using Visual Basic version 4.0, you can use the AppActivate statement with the text from the application title bar (i.e. AppActivate "Form1")

Using Positional Arguments in Visual Basic Version 3.0

WordBasic statements that correspond to Word dialog boxes use named arguments—arguments whose values are associated with names. For example, .Font is the named argument in the following instruction:

```
FormatDropCap .Font = "Arial"
```

In Visual Basic version 4.0, Microsoft Excel Visual Basic, and Microsoft Access Visual Basic, you can call WordBasic instructions using named arguments, as shown in the following example:

```
WordObj.FormatDropCap Font:="Arial"
```

You cannot call a WordBasic instruction from Visual Basic version 3.0 using named arguments. Instead, you identify arguments by position. The following example shows a WordBasic instruction as it could appear in a Word macro:

```
FormatDropCap .Position = 1, .Font = "Arial", .DropHeight = 3,
.DistFromText = 6
```

To use this instruction in a Visual Basic version 3.0 procedure, you would write the following:

```
WordObj.FormatDropCap 1, "Arial", 3, 6
```

In this instruction, WordObj is an object variable that refers to WordBasic. If you want to leave out an argument, you must indicate the missing argument with a comma, as shown in the following instruction:

```
WordObj.FormatDropCap , "Arial", , 6
```

Trailing commas can be omitted (for example, WordObj.FormatDropCap 1, "Arial" is valid; it isn't necessary to specify WordObj.FormatDropCap 1, "Arial", , ,).

Boolean "true" and "false" values are used to specify command buttons. For example, the following WordBasic instruction runs the macro CountOpenWindows:

```
ToolsMacro .Name = "CountOpenWindows", .Run
```

where .Run is the named argument equivalent to the Run button in the Macro dialog box. In a Visual Basic version 3.0 procedure, the instruction might appear as follows:

```
WordObj.ToolsMacro "CountOpenWindows", True
```

A true value is equivalent to choosing a command button; false is equivalent to not choosing it. The following instruction opens the CountOpenWindows macro for editing:

```
WordObj.ToolsMacro "CountOpenWindows", False, True
```

In WordBasic, the third argument is .Edit, so in Visual Basic version 3.0 a true value in the third position is equivalent to choosing the Edit button. Omitting a command button argument is equivalent to giving it a value of false.

Note   The syntax line for most statement and function entries in WordBasic Help describes the correct positional order of arguments. There are some exceptions, however. For a complete list of these exceptions and the correct order of their arguments, see POSITION.TXT on the Microsoft Word Developer's Kit disk (Windows).

Using MAPI and AOCE

In Windows, you can use the messaging application programming interface (MAPI) to provide a macro with the same kind of access to Microsoft Mail—and other mail applications that support MAPI—as it has to Word through WordBasic. Using MAPI, a macro can extract messages, retrieve names from the Microsoft Mail Address Book, send or read messages, and so on.

MAPI uses data types that WordBasic doesn't support—they are similar to WordBasic dialog records in that they combine values of different types (strings, numbers, and others). So WordBasic requires extensions of the MAPI functions to make the data available in a way that WordBasic can access it. These extensions are provided in WBMAPI.DLL on the Microsoft Word Developer's Kit disk. For more information on integrating Word and Microsoft Mail with WBMAPI.DLL, see Appendix A, "Workgroup Extensions for Microsoft Word," in Part 3, "Appendixes."

On the Macintosh, you can access Apple Open Collaboration Environment (AOCE) services from within WordBasic by using a set of WordBasic statements and functions provided for that purpose. For a list of these messaging statements and functions, see "Language Summary" in Part 2, "WordBasic Reference."

C H A P T E R   9

More WordBasic Techniques

The first two sections of this chapter introduce different ways macros can store and retrieve information. Settings files, document variables, document properties, and AutoText entries, described in the first section, provide storage for variable values after a macro has run. Sequential file access, described in the second section, provides quick access to text files.

The third section of the chapter describes how you can use macros to automate forms. The fourth section documents the STARTER.WIZ template (Windows) or the STARTER WIZARD template (Macintosh) supplied on the Microsoft Word Developer's Kit disk. This template is a starting point for developing wizards and provides the basic interface shared by every Word wizard.

The fifth section describes techniques for successfully calling routines from dynamic-link libraries (DLLs), which you can use to increase the capabilities of your WordBasic macros.

The last sections describe developing WordBasic macros that work across all the platforms that support WordBasic (Windows 3.x, Windows 95, Windows NT, and the Macintosh) and techniques for distributing and optimizing macros.

In this chapter:

- Storing values when a macro ends
- Using sequential file access
- Automating forms
- Creating a wizard
- Calling routines in DLLs and WLLs
- Developing macros for more than one platform
- Distributing macros
- Optimizing macros

Storing Values When a Macro Ends

When a macro ends, the values stored in its variables are lost. If a macro needs to preserve a value, it must store that value outside itself, preferably in a place from which the value can be easily retrieved. Consider, for example, a document-numbering macro that runs each time a document is created and assigns a unique number to the new document. Each time a document is created, the macro must "remember" the number it assigned to the previous document the last time it ran, so that it can generate an appropriate new number. Then the macro must store the new number so that the number can be referenced the next time the macro runs.

This section describes how a macro can use a settings file, document variables, document properties, or AutoText entries to store information.

Settings Files

A settings file is a file used by programs and macros to store values; you can think of a setting as a variable stored in a file. In Windows terminology, WIN.INI, the settings file used by Microsoft Windows 3.*x* and many 16-bit Windows-based applications, is a "public" settings file because it can be used by more than one application. Settings files created for use by particular applications are "private" settings files. In Windows, settings files are text files and can be opened by a text editor like any other text file. On the Macintosh, settings files are not text files; they can only be edited directly using the ResEdit™ program.

WordBasic provides the **SetPrivateProfileString** statement and the **GetPrivateProfileString$()** function for accessing private settings files. You use **SetPrivateProfileString** to assign a setting to a private settings file. Here is the syntax:

SetPrivateProfileString *Section$*, *KeyName$*, *Setting$*, *Filename$*

Section$* is the name of a section within the settings file. *KeyName$ is the name of the "key"—the equivalent of a variable name. *Setting$* is the value you are assigning to the key. *Filename$* is the name of the settings file. If the file doesn't exist, **SetPrivateProfileString** creates it. Here's what a typical Windows settings file might look like if you opened it in a text editor.

```
[Directories Macro]                                          ── Section name
directory 1=C:\WINWORD
directory 2=C:\WINWORD\TEMPLATE
directory 3=C:\WINWORD\DOCUMENT\LETTERS ──────               ── Setting

[Document Numbering Macro]                                   ── Key name
current number=000234
```

The settings files for Windows-based applications usually have filenames with the .INI filename extension. ("INI" is short for "initialization"; a settings file is also known as an initialization file because an application that is starting up, or initializing, can use its initialization file to retrieve settings from the last time it ran.) Although you can give any extension to the Windows settings files you create, using the .INI extension helps to make their purpose clear. On the Macintosh, it's similarly useful to include "Settings" in a settings filename. One advantage of creating a settings file with **SetPrivateProfileString** is that the file is stored automatically in the Windows folder in Windows or in the Preferences folder on the Macintosh (assuming you don't specify a path for *Filename$*). Since the instruction doesn't specify the name of the Windows or Preferences folder, your macro isn't dependent on a particular folder name or structure, and you can distribute it to other users without modification.

WordBasic does not include statements or functions to handle numeric values in settings files. To store a numeric value, first use the **Str$()** function to convert it to a string. To retrieve the value, use the **Val()** function to convert the string setting back to a number.

You use **GetPrivateProfileString$()** to retrieve the value of the specified *KeyName$* stored in a settings file. Here is the syntax:

GetPrivateProfileString$(***Section$*, ***KeyName$***, ***Filename$***)**

Section$*, *KeyName$, and *Filename$* are used in the same way as the arguments in the **SetPrivateProfileString** statement.

You can use any number of settings files, but it's best to avoid using more files than necessary. In fact, you can use a single settings file for all your macros. Section headings provide a way to group settings and prevent key-name conflicts. For example, two different macros can both use a key called "Directory 1" without conflict, assuming the two key names are associated with different section names. In Windows, a settings file is just a text file, so you're not restricted to only using WordBasic instructions to access it. If you've forgotten what you've stored, you can always use Word to open a Windows settings file in a document window. On the Macintosh, you can use the ResEdit program to edit a settings file.

Examples

Here is a simple document-tracking macro that assigns a number to every new document. The macro is an AutoNew macro that runs whenever a new document is created. The macro uses **GetPrivateProfileString$()** to retrieve the current document number, increments it by 1, and then uses **SetFormResult** to insert the number in a form field. Finally, the macro uses **SetPrivateProfileString** to store the new number in the settings file.

```
Sub MAIN
docnum$ = GetPrivateProfileString$("DocTracker", "DocNum", "MACRO.INI")
docnum$ = Str$((Val(docnum$) + 1))
SetFormResult "DocNumField", docnum$
SetPrivateProfileString "DocTracker", "DocNum", docnum$, "MACRO.INI"
End Sub
```

Using a **For...Next** loop to retrieve or assign a large number of settings is a very useful technique. The following subroutine uses a **For...Next** loop to retrieve a list of seven folder names from a settings file and load them into an array. The key names for the folder names include numbers: "Dir 1" for the first key, "Dir 2" for the second key, and so on. The loop uses these numbers to enumerate the key names so that, instead of requiring a separate **GetPrivateProfileString$()** for each key name, the subroutine can use just one instruction.

```
Sub GetDirNames
For count = 1 To 7
    dirListname$ =  "Dir" + LTrim$(Str$(count - 1))
    dirNames$(count - 1) = GetPrivateProfileString$("DirList", \
                              dirListname$, "MACRO.INI")
Next
End Sub
```

This subroutine is used in the ChangeDirectory macro provided in the EXAMPLES.DOT (Windows) or MACRO EXAMPLES (Macintosh) template supplied on the Microsoft Word Developer's Kit disk. The macro displays the dialog box shown in the following illustration. By selecting one of the folders listed, the user can quickly move to that folder.

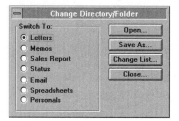

Using the WIN.INI File

WIN.INI is the "public" settings file used by Windows 3.*x*. Using the **SetProfileString** statement and **GetProfileString$()** function, you can store information in and retrieve information from the WIN.INI file in the same way you can with private settings files.

In addition to Windows 3.*x*, 16-bit Windows-based applications such as Word version 6.0 for Windows store settings information in WIN.INI, and this can lead to a large, inefficient file. For this reason, it's usually best not to store private settings in the WIN.INI file. But **SetProfileString** and **GetProfileString$()** can be useful for retrieving and changing Windows environment settings in WIN.INI.

Note Windows 95 and Windows NT do not use the WIN.INI file. Instead, they store settings in the registry. **SetProfileString** and **GetProfileString$()** are available in Windows 95 and Windows NT, but there is no reason to use them, as they do not affect settings in the registry; in effect, they become limited versions of **SetPrivateProfileString** and **GetPrivateProfileString$()** that work with just one settings file that happens to be called WIN.INI.

Example

This Word version 6.0 example checks the Windows 3.*x* "long date" format. If the format doesn't match "dddd d MMMM yyyy" (for example, "Sunday 23 May 1993"), **SetProfileString** changes the setting to that format.

```
format$ = GetProfileString$("intl", "sLongDate")
If format$ <> "dddd d MMMM yyyy" Then
    SetProfileString "intl", "sLongDate", "dddd d MMMM yyyy"
End If
```

Accessing WINWORD6.INI and Word Settings (6)

Word version 6.0 for Windows settings are stored in a settings file called WINWORD6.INI; in Word version 6.0 for the Macintosh, they're stored in the Word Settings (6) file. In Windows, you can use **GetPrivateProfileString$()** and **SetPrivateProfileString** to retrieve and change settings. On the Macintosh, you can use **GetProfileString$()** and **SetProfileString** to change settings in the Word Settings (6) file. For example, the following Word version 6.0 for Windows instruction sets the Word DDETimeOut setting to 100 seconds in WINWORD6.INI:

```
SetPrivateProfileString "Microsoft Word", "DDETimeOut", \
    "100", "WINWORD6.INI"
```

Here is the equivalent instruction for Word version 6.0 for the Macintosh:

```
SetProfileString "Microsoft Word", "DDETimeOut", "100"
```

Accessing the Windows Registry

In Windows 95 and Windows NT, the registry is a system-wide database used for storing software and hardware configuration settings. The registry is created during system setup and is updated whenever you add or remove software or hardware. Windows 95 and Windows NT store settings in the registry instead of the WIN.INI file. You can view and edit the contents of the registry using the Registry Editor (REGEDIT.EXE in Windows 95, REGEDT32.EXE in Windows NT).

While most settings for Word version 6.0 for Windows are stored in WINWORD6.INI, most settings for Word version 6.0 for Windows NT and Word version 7.0 are stored in the registry under the following key: HKEY_CURRENT_USER\Software\Microsoft\Word\6.0 (or 7.0).

From WordBasic, you can access the registry information using the **GetPrivateProfileString$()** function. You use an empty string ("") instead of the name of a settings file to specify the registry. For example, the following instruction assigns the Word version 7.0 document path (DOC-PATH) from the registry to the variable a$:

```
key$ = "HKEY_CURRENT_USER\Software\Microsoft\Word\7.0\Options"
a$ = GetPrivateProfileString$(key$, "DOC-PATH", "")
```

You can also modify information in the registry using the **SetPrivateProfileString** statement. Note that even though you can use **SetPrivateProfileString** to add keys to the registry, macro settings are best stored in a private settings file to avoid corrupting important application settings.

Example

The DateFormat setting in the registry sets the default date format for Word version 7.0. This example uses the **SetPrivateProfileString** statement to set the date format to "dddd d MMMM yyyy." A future date is calculated and the result is then displayed in the new date format.

```
Sub MAIN
key$ = "HKEY_CURRENT_USER\Software\Microsoft\Word\7.0\Options"
SetPrivateProfileString(key$, "DateFormat", "dddd d MMMM yyyy", "")
MsgBox Date$(Now() + 7)
End Sub
```

Document Variables

A document variable is a variable stored as part of a document. It is available only when the document in which it is stored is the active document. Document variables are similar to key names in a settings file; they are accessed through the complementary **SetDocumentVar** statement and **GetDocumentVar$()** function. Here is the syntax for **SetDocumentVar**:

SetDocumentVar *VariableName$*, *Text$*

VariableName$* is the name of the document variable and *Text$ is the string value you are assigning to the variable. Document variables accept only string values. Here is the syntax for **GetDocumentVar$()**:

GetDocumentVar$(***VariableName$*)**

Document variables are available only through WordBasic instructions, so the user cannot inadvertently change them. And since they are contained within the document, they travel with it: If you move the document to another computer, for example, the document variables remain available. A document can contain any number of document variables.

If you add document variables to a template, the variables, including their values, will be stored in all new documents that are subsequently based on the template.

Note   Document variables are not saved when a document is saved in rich-text format (RTF).

If you plan to store a document variable in a document that may contain other document variables, you should ensure that the variable name you are planning to use does not already exist in the document. Two functions are provided for this purpose: **CountDocumentVars()** and **GetDocumentVarName$()**. **CountDocumentVars()** returns the number of document variables stored in the active document. Given a number between 1 and the value returned by **CountDocumentVars()**, **GetDocumentVarName$()** returns the name of the corresponding document variable. For example, the following instructions determine whether a document variable named "TrackingNum" already exists in a document:

```
For count = 1 To CountDocumentVars()
    If GetDocumentVarName$(count) = "TrackingNum" Then
        MsgBox "TrackingNum already exists."
        Goto bye
    End If
Next
bye:
```

Deleting a Document Variable

WordBasic does not include a command to delete document variables, but if you set a document variable to an empty string, the document variable is removed. For example, the following instruction removes a document variable called `ReminderMsg`:

```
SetDocumentVar ReminderMsg, ""
```

The following instructions remove all of the document variables from a document:

```
For count = 1 To CountDocumentVars()
    SetDocumentVar GetDocumentVarName$(1), ""
Next
```

Another way to remove all of the document variables in a document is to save the document in rich-text format (RTF). Since document variables are not saved in RTF, they will no longer be in the document.

Example

This macro displays a dialog box showing the revision history for a document and providing a text box in which the user can type a new entry. Each entry in the revision history is stored in a document variable. Before displaying the dialog box, the macro retrieves the revision entries from the document variables and loads them into an array that will be displayed in a list box. If the user creates a new revision entry, the macro adds the current date as a prefix and stores the entry in a new document variable.

```
Sub MAIN
If CountDocumentVars() > 0 Then
    Dim docVarArray$(CountDocumentVars() - 1)
    For count = 1 To CountDocumentVars()
        docVarArray$(count - 1) = \
                    GetDocumentVar$(GetDocumentVarName$(count))
    Next
Else
    Dim docVarArray$(0)
End If
Begin Dialog UserDialog 508, 214, "Revision History"
    Text 12, 133, 105, 13, "New Revision", .Text2
    TextBox 12, 149, 453, 18, .NewRevision
    OKButton 380, 186, 88, 21
```

```
        CancelButton 282, 186, 88, 21
        Text 12, 6, 80, 13, "Revisions:", .Text1
        ListBox 12, 21, 473, 106, docVarArray$(), .ListBox1
End Dialog
Dim dlg As UserDialog
x = Dialog(dlg)
If dlg.NewRevision <> "" Then
    revVarName$ = "rev" + LTrim$(Str$(CountDocumentVars()))
    revText$ = Date$() + " - " + dlg.NewRevision
    SetDocumentVar revVarName$, revText$
End If
End Sub
```

Here is the dialog box, showing some sample revisions.

Document Properties

Like document variables, document properties allow you to store information along with a document. Document properties can be viewed and modified in the Properties dialog box (File menu). Unlike document variables, document properties can be inserted into a document using the DOCPROPERTY field.

Note Document properties are available only in Word version 7.0.

Document properties are defined using the **SetDocumentProperty** statement. Here is the syntax for **SetDocumentProperty**:

SetDocumentProperty *Name$, Type, Value[$], CustomOrBuiltIn*

Name$ is the name of the document property and *Type* specifies the data type you want to store in the document property. *Value[$]* is the number, string, or date you are assigning to the document property. *CustomOrBuiltIn* specifies whether you are defining a custom or built-in property. (Document properties include custom properties that you add as well as built-in properties such as "Company.")

Examples

This example prompts for a company name and then set the results in the built-in "Company" document property.

```
CompanyName$ = InputBox$("Type your company name", "Company Name")
SetDocumentProperty("Company", 0, CompanyName$, 1)
```

The text you type appears as the company name on the Summary tab in the Properties dialog box (File menu).

The following macro displays a dialog box showing the built-in and custom document properties for the active document. Prior to displaying the dialog box, the macro retrieves the document property names and stores them in an array. If the user chooses OK, the contents of the selected property are inserted into the document.

```
Sub MAIN
Dim prop$(CountDocumentProperties() - 1)
For count = 1 To CountDocumentProperties()
    prop$(count - 1) = DocumentPropertyName$(count)
Next
Begin Dialog UserDialog 340, 144, "Document Properties"
    OKButton 229, 104, 88, 21
    CancelButton 131, 104, 88, 21
    ListBox 24, 12, 293, 84, prop$(), .property
End Dialog
Dim dlg As UserDialog
n = Dialog(dlg)
If prop$(dlg.property) <> "" And n = - 1 Then
    Insert prop$(dlg.property) + ":" + Chr$(9)
    type = DocumentPropertyType(prop$(dlg.property))
    Select Case type
        Case 0, 2, 3
            text$ = GetDocumentProperty$(prop$(dlg.property))
            Insert text$
        Case 1
            Num = GetDocumentProperty(prop$(dlg.property))
            Insert LTrim$(Str$(Num))
        Case Else
    End Select
End If
End Sub
```

The previous macro inserts document properties as plain text. You can also insert document properties using the DOCPROPERTY field. For example, the following instruction inserts a field that references the "Company" document property:

```
InsertField .Field = "DOCPROPERTY Company"
```

The DOCPROPERTY field ensures that the latest property information appears in your document when the field is updated.

AutoText Entries

AutoText entries can be used to store information in a template. The **SetAutoText** statement defines a text-only AutoText entry. Here is the syntax:

SetAutoText *Name$, Text$* [*, Context*]

Name$* is the AutoText entry name, *Text$ is the text defined with the AutoText entry, and *Context* indicates where the AutoText entry is stored (the active template or the Normal template). The complementary **GetAutoText$()** function retrieves the contents of an AutoText entry.

Example

The following macro defines an entry named INVOICE# in the active template (a template other than Normal). Each time the macro is run, the invoice number in the INVOICE# AutoText entry is incremented by one. If this macro were named AutoNew and stored in a special invoice template, the macro would automatically insert an invoice number with each new invoice created.

```
Sub MAIN
number = Val(GetAutoText$("INVOICE#", 1)) + 1
InvoiceNum$ = LTrim$(Str$(number))
SetAutoText "INVOICE#", InvoiceNum$, 1
Insert "Invoice: " + invoicenum$
End Sub
```

Using Sequential File Access

WordBasic includes a set of statements and functions you can use to access text files without opening them in a document window. This kind of interaction is called *file input and output*, or *file I/O*. Using file input, a macro can "read" a file to retrieve information from it ("input" refers to input from the file into the macro). Using file output, a macro can "write" to a file to store information ("output" refers to output from the macro to the file). WordBasic supports *sequential* file I/O, or sequential file access, a kind of file I/O supported by most varieties of the Basic programming language. In sequential file access, the information in the file is usually read or written in sequence, from the beginning of the file to the end.

Sequential file access is used most often to provide a macro with information. For example, a macro designed to work on a series of files can use sequential file access to retrieve a list of filenames from a text file.

The advantage of sequential file access is that it's fast. If a macro needs to read or store information, sequential file access can do it more quickly than statements that open a file in a document window. The disadvantage, of course, is that sequential file access is more rigid than working with a file in a document window. It's difficult to go directly to a specific place in a file, and you can't read from a file and write to it at the same time.

Note Sequential file-access statements and functions are designed to work with text-only files, not Word document files. While it is possible to open a Word document for sequential access, it isn't useful to do so because Word documents contain formatting codes that make the file very difficult to read from or write to through sequential access. To work with a Word document, open it in a document window.

Opening a File for Sequential Access

When you open a file for sequential access, you specify whether you want to read from the file or write to it. If a macro needs both to read from and write to a file, it must open the file to read from it, close it, and then reopen the file to write to it. A macro can have as many as four files open at a time for sequential access.

To open a file for sequential access, you use the **Open** statement, which has the following syntax:

Open *Name$* **For** *Mode* **As** [#]*FileNumber*

Name$ is the name of the file to open and *FileNumber* is a number between 1 and 4 that other sequential access instructions use to refer to the open file. *Mode* indicates how the file is to be used: for input, output, or appending. The modes are described as follows.

Mode	Explanation
Input	Opens the text file so that data may be read from the file into the macro. When you open a file for input you can use **Read**, **Input**, **Line Input**, and **Input$()** instructions to read from the file. If the specified text file isn't found, an error occurs.
Output	Opens the text file so that data may be written from the macro to the file. When you open a file for output, you can use **Write** and **Print** instructions to write to the file. Opening a file for output deletes the existing contents of the file, even if you do not write to the file. If the specified text file isn't found, a new file is created.
Append	Opens the text file so that data may be written from the macro to the file. When you open a file to append, you can use **Write** and **Print** instructions to write to the file. The existing contents of the file remain and the information you write is added to the end of the file. If the specified text file isn't found, a new file is created.

The following diagram shows the relationship between a macro and a text file in the different modes, along with the sequential file-access statements and functions available in those modes.

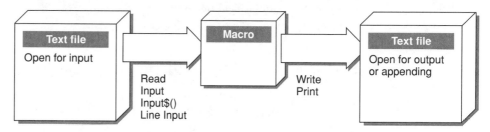

Writing to a File

WordBasic includes two statements for writing to a file: **Write** and **Print**. You can use these statements to write both strings and numbers. Each instruction creates a single line in a text file. In Windows, each line of the text file ends with the carriage-return and linefeed characters (character codes 13 and 10); on the Macintosh, each line ends with a single carriage-return (character code 13). You can think of each line as a single data record that can have multiple fields containing different values. Each **Write** and **Print** instruction writes sequentially to the text file, adding one line of data after another for as long as the file is open.

Write

The **Write** statement is designed to write data that can be easily read by the complementary **Read** statement. The syntax of **Write** is as follows:

Write #*FileNumber*, *Expression1*[*$*] [, *Expression2*[*$*]] [, ...]

FileNumber refers to the number you assigned to the file when you opened it. An *Expression* contains the data you're writing to the file. Usually, *Expression* is a string or numeric variable, but it could also be a numeric expression or a function that returns a string or number. For example, the following instruction writes the currently selected text to a file:

```
Write #1, Selection$()
```

Write places quotation marks around string values, but not around numeric values; it places a comma between each value as a delimiter. For example, the instruction

```
Write #1, name$, age, employeeNum
```

creates a line such as the following in the text file:

```
"John Jones", 32, 12345
```

Print

Unlike **Write**, the **Print** statement does not have a complementary statement designed to read whatever it writes. **Print** is most useful if you want to write data to a file that may be read by another application. You can also use **Print** to write information to be read by the **Line Input** statement. The syntax for **Print** is as follows:

Print #*FileNumber*, *Expression1*[*$*] [*; or* , *Expression2*[*$*]] [*; or* , ...]

FileNumber refers to the number you assigned to the file when you opened it. *Expression* contains the data you're writing to the file, usually a variable, number, or string.

String and numeric values can be separated by either a semicolon or a comma. Values separated by a semicolon are joined together in the text file with a space inserted before numbers. For example, the instruction

```
Print #1, name$; age; employeeNum
```

creates a line such as the following in the text file:

```
John Jones 32 12345
```

Values separated by a comma are separated by a tab character in the text file. For example, the instruction

```
Print #1, "Jones", "123 1st Street"
```

results in the following line, with a tab character between "Jones" and "123 1st Street":

```
Jones    123 1st Street
```

None of the WordBasic sequential access instructions that read files recognize tab characters as delimiters, but many applications support file formats that use tab characters as delimiters. For example, you could use **Print** to create a tab-delimited file for a database program.

Reading from a File

The sequential file-access statements **Write** and **Print** write information sequentially, adding one line of information after another for as long as the file is open. The information is read in the same way; after one instruction reads information, the next instruction begins reading the next piece of information, in sequence. All the statements and functions that read sequential files read a line at a time (delimited by a paragraph mark), except **Input$()**, which reads a specified number of characters.

Read

The **Read** statement is designed to read information written with **Write**. Here is the syntax:

Read #_FileNumber_**,** _Variable1_[$] [**,** _Variable2_[$]] [**,** _Variable3_[$]] [**,** …]

Read can read both numeric and string values and can read multiple values from a single line when the values are delimited by commas. It removes quotation marks from string values (placed there by **Write**) and can also accept strings that are not enclosed in quotation marks. **Read** can accept a string with as many as 65,280 characters; longer strings are truncated. The following example reads values into one string variable and two numeric variables:

```
Read #1, name$, age, employeeNum
```

Input

Like **Read**, the **Input** statement can read multiple values from a single line when the values are delimited by commas. However, **Input** does not remove quotation marks from strings, so it doesn't work well with **Write**, which places quotation marks around string values. **Input** uses the same syntax as **Read**, as shown in this example:

```
Input #1, name$, age, employeeNum
```

Line Input

The **Line Input** statement reads an entire line, including commas or other delimiters, and places it into a string variable. Here is the syntax:

Line Input #_FileNumber_**,** _Variable_$

Variable must be a string variable, even if the line contains numbers only. A line is delimited by a paragraph mark. **Line Input** can accept lines as long as 65,280 characters; longer lines are truncated.

Input$()

With the **Input$()** statement, you specify exactly how many characters to read. Here is the syntax:

Input$(_NumChars_**,** [**#**]_FileNumber_**)**

NumChars is the number of characters **Input$()** reads from the file identified by _FileNumber_. **Input$()** can read any number of lines (as many lines as are contained in the specified number of characters) and returns every character within the specified range of characters, including delimiters such as commas and carriage returns.

Input\$() is generally not as useful as the other statements that read sequential files, but you can use it to read a file that uses delimiters that the other sequential file-access statements and functions don't support.

In the following example, **Input\$()** is used to read a file in which values are delimited by a space character. The file contains 20 employee numbers, which **Input\$()** reads into an array. Each employee number is five characters long and is separated from the following number by a space. Each time **Input\$()** reads five characters, it also moves the point at which data is read five characters ahead, so that the next **Input\$()** instruction begins reading the next character. Because there is a space between each number, the macro includes the instruction space$ = Input$(1, #1), whose purpose is just to read the space preceding the next number. Otherwise, the second **Input\$()** instruction would begin by reading the space character and miss part of the next employee number.

```
Dim empNums(19)
Open "EMPNUMS.DAT" For Input As #1
    For count = 0 To 19
        empNums(count) = Val(Input$(5, #1))
        space$ = Input$(1, #1)
    Next
Close #1
```

Closing a File

As mentioned earlier, once you've opened a file in a specific mode—for input, output, or appending—you have to close it before you can open it in a different mode. For example, if a macro opens a file to read some information from it and then needs to overwrite the existing information or append additional information, it must close the file and then reopen it in the appropriate mode. Here is the syntax of the **Close** statement:

Close [[#]*FileNumber*]

FileNumber is the number of the file to close. If *FileNumber* is not specified, all files opened with the **Open** statement are closed.

Other Sequential Access Statements and Functions

WordBasic includes four other sequential file-access statements and functions: **Eof()**, **Lof()**, **Seek**, and **Seek()**.

Eof()

The **Eof()** function returns a value of –1 when the end of a file has been reached. Typically, **Eof()** is used to control a **While...Wend** loop that reads a file until it reaches the file's end. Here is the syntax for **Eof()**:

Eof([#]*FileNumber*)

FileNumber is the number assigned to the file when it was opened. The following example reads a list of Word document filenames from a text file. For each document filename, the corresponding file is opened, the DoFormattingRoutine subroutine (not shown here) performs various formatting actions, and the file is closed. The **Eof()** function controls a **While...Wend** loop, so that every filename in FILES.TXT is read until the end of the file is reached.

```
Sub MAIN
Open "FILES.TXT" For Input As #1
While Not Eof(#1)
    Read #1, file$
    FileOpen file$
    DoFormattingRoutine
    FileClose 1
Wend
Close #1
End Sub
```

Lof()

The **Lof()** function returns the length of a file, in bytes, opened with an **Open** instruction. Each byte corresponds to one character in the file. Among other things, you can use **Lof()** to determine whether a file contains any information. Here is the syntax for **Lof()**:

Lof([#]*FileNumber***)**

FileNumber is the number you assigned to the file when you opened it. The following example determines whether a file contains any information before opening it for output and overwriting it. After the file is opened for input, the **Lof()** function is used to determine whether or not the file already contains information. If it does, a message box is displayed, asking if you want to overwrite the file. If you choose the Yes button in the message box, the file is closed and then reopened for output.

```
YES = - 1
Open "EMPNUMS.DAT" For Input As #1
If Lof(#1) > 0 Then
    answer = MsgBox("Do you want to overwrite this file?", 4)
    If answer = YES Then
        Close #1
        Open "EMPNUMS.DAT" For Output As #1
        'Series of instructions to write information to the file
    End If
End If
Close #1
```

Seek, Seek( )

The **Seek** statement changes the point in a file at which information is retrieved or stored. Here is the syntax:

Seek [#]*FileNumber*, *Count*

The **Seek( )** function returns the point in the file where information will next be retrieved or stored. Here is the syntax:

Seek([#]*FileNumber*)

Usually the **Seek** statement and **Seek( )** function are used together. You use the **Seek( )** function to return the position of an item; then you use the **Seek** statement to move directly to that location.

You can use **Seek** with other sequential access statements and functions to write information into the middle of a file rather than appending it at the end, but this technique has limited use. Whatever is written to the file overwrites the corresponding number of characters in the same position in the file.

The following example is part of a macro to sort mail messages by sender and by subject. The text file MSGS.TXT contains sender names and subject categories. This example searches for the heading "Monthly Reports" in the file, records its position in the variable readposition, and then closes the file. Next, the file is opened to append information to the file, and then closed again. Finally, the file is reopened for input and the instruction Seek #1, readposition moves directly to the position where the "Monthly Reports" heading is located.

```
Open "MSGS.TXT" For Input As #1
While Not Eof(#1) And searchtext$ <> "Monthly Reports"
    readposition = Seek(#1)
    Line Input #1, searchtext$
Wend
Close #1
Open "MSGS.TXT" For Append As #1
    'Series of instructions to append data to the file
Close #1
Open "MSGS.TXT" For Input As #1
Seek #1, readposition
```

Automating Forms

Macros can be used to automate the process of filling in Word forms. Information that would otherwise have to be typed manually can be filled in automatically. Custom commands can be created that are appropriate for a particular form.

Several types of macros are useful for automating forms. They include the following:

- "On-entry" and "on-exit" macros. Every form field in a form can have an on-entry macro, triggered when the field is activated, and an on-exit macro, triggered when the user moves to another field.

- Auto macros. Auto macros such as AutoNew and AutoClose provide a useful starting point for automation. For example, an AutoNew macro, triggered when a new form document is created, can run a series of other macros to guide the user through filling in the form. For more information on auto macros, see Chapter 2, "Getting Started with Macros."

- Macros assigned to a menu or a toolbar. Users filling in forms customized for a particular task can often benefit from custom commands. Turning macros into custom commands and placing them on menus or a toolbar gives them accessibility and visibility.

- MACROBUTTON fields. These fields, which trigger macros, provide another way to embed macros within a form. For example, you could use a MACROBUTTON field to insert a bitmap of a dialog box button that says "Click Here to Print." A button embedded in a form makes an important command hard to miss.

A form should be made into a template so that whenever a user wants to fill in a new form, he or she creates a new document based on the form template. The new form inherits the form's boilerplate text and formatting. Any macros used to automate the form can be stored in the template. If the template is protected for forms, so are new documents based on it.

Here are some other points to keep in mind when automating a form:

- A drop-down form field can contain no more than 25 items. Use a dialog box when you want to present more items.

- You can use the **EditGoTo** statement to move to a form field. The following instruction selects the form field named "Check1":

```
EditGoTo "Check1"
```

"Check1" is the default bookmark name for the first check box form field inserted in a form. You can change a bookmark name for a form field by unprotecting the form and double-clicking the field.

- For items that the macro will insert into the form—such as an invoice number or part number on an invoice—you can use either bookmarks or form fields to mark where the items are to be inserted. If you use form fields, you can use the **SetFormResult** statement to set the result of a form field. The following instruction inserts "Hello" into the "Text1" form field.

```
SetFormResult "Text1", "Hello"
```

A form field isn't necessary unless you also want to allow the user to insert the information. Even when a document is protected for forms, a macro can insert information into any part of the document (unlike a user, who can type in form fields only). For example, the following instructions insert "Hello" at the beginning of the document:

```
StartOfDocument
Insert "Hello"
```

- Some WordBasic statements, such as **InsertFormField**, are not available when a document is protected for forms. In this case, the macro needs to unprotect the document, run the statement and then protect the document for forms. The following instructions unprotect the document, insert a text form field at the top of the document, and then protect the document for forms:

```
If DocumentProtection() = 1 Then
    ToolsUnprotectDocument
    StartOfDocument
    InsertFormField .TextType = 0
    ToolsProtectDocument .Type = 2, .NoReset = 1
End If
```

If the .NoReset argument is not specified in a **ToolsProtectDocument** statement, unlocking and locking a document resets the form fields to their default results. If .NoReset is set to 1, Word does not reset form fields to their default results when a document is protected for forms (.Type = 2).

In Word version 7.0, the **DocumentProtection**() function returns a number indicating the type of document protection. In Word version 6.0, use the **CommandValid**() function to determine whether a document is protected.

- You can connect a form to a database in several ways. For example, the invoice form described in this section uses dynamic data exchange (DDE) to query a Microsoft Excel database and then displays the information— customer names or products—in a dialog box. If you're working with a large number of items, however, loading them into the dialog box can be slow. Another solution would be to open the database within Microsoft Excel itself: to make it the active application, in other words. A Microsoft Excel macro could then send the information selected in the database to the form in Word.

Another possibility would be to use the open database connectivity (ODBC) extensions for WordBasic to work with a database. A Word macro could then place the selected information in the appropriate field in the form. For information on using the ODBC extensions, see Appendix B, "ODBC Extensions for Microsoft Word," in Part 3, "Appendixes." Note that the ODBC extensions described in Appendix B are not available on the Macintosh.

- When the Save Data Only For Forms option is selected (Save tab, Options dialog box, Tools menu), the Save As command (File menu) creates a comma-delimited record of the setting of every form field in a document. The record is the same as a record created with the **Write** instruction. You can write a macro to retrieve this record and add it to a database file.

- You can use the **SetFormResult** statement to set the default result for a form field. A form field's default result is displayed each time a document is protected for forms. If you create a new document based on a protected template, the new document displays the default results of the form fields it contains.

- You can use the **SetFormResult** statement without the *Result[$]* argument to update a calculation form field. For example, the following instruction updates the "Total" calculation form field:

```
SetFormResult "Total"
```

For a complete list of form statements and functions, see "Language Summary" in Part 2, "WordBasic Reference."

Example

This form, including the macros described here, is available as INVOICE2.DOT (Windows) or INVOICE FORM (Macintosh) on the Microsoft Word Developer's Kit disk.

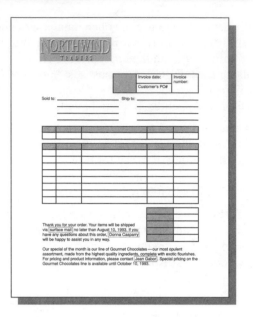

When a salesperson creates a new invoice, an AutoNew macro inserts a number for the Invoice Number and Customer's P.O. Number, and updates fields that indicate the Invoice Date, Date Ordered, and Date Shipped.

The new document is protected for forms, so the salesperson can type in form fields only and can't inadvertently disturb other parts of the form. Because the form is protected, the salesperson can use the tab key to move from one form field to another.

When the new invoice is created, the first form field—the New Customer check box—is automatically selected. When the user moves to the first form field in the address, an on-entry macro runs. The on-entry macro evaluates whether the New Customer check box is selected or cleared. If the check box is selected, indicating a new customer, the macro displays the New Customer dialog box as shown in the following illustration.

The New Customer dialog box

If the New Customer check box is cleared, indicating an existing customer, the macro displays a dialog box that allows the salesperson to query a Microsoft Excel database for the customer's address. He or she can type any part of the customer's name to get a list of customer names that match.

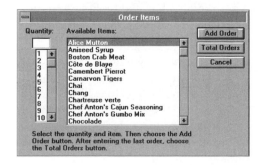

If a match is found, the macro displays a dialog box in which the salesperson can select the address he or she wants.

The macro then places the information in the Sold To area of the form. The salesperson can select the type of terms and shipping method from drop-down form field lists.

When the salesperson moves into the Quantity column, an on-entry macro displays the following dialog box showing a list of the items available.

When the salesperson selects the item and quantity, the macro then inserts this information into the form, along with the corresponding part number, unit price, and total amount. Each item selected by the salesperson is entered on a separate line of the form.

When the salesperson has entered all the items ordered in the invoice, he or she then chooses the Total Orders button in the Order Items dialog box. The macro adds the figures in the Total Amount column, calculates the sales tax (if any), and inserts the appropriate figures.

When the salesperson has completed the form, it is printed out and the data is saved. The modified Close command (File menu) sends the form data to a Microsoft Excel database that stores a record for every invoice.

Creating a Wizard

A wizard is a macro (or a set of macros) that creates a document or carries out a task as directed by the user.

Like most computer programs, a wizard has two parts: the user interface that requests information from the user, and the behind-the-scenes part that carries out the actions necessary to accomplish the task. The behind-the-scenes part of a wizard varies according to what the wizard is designed to accomplish; every wizard is different in that respect. But the wizards that come with Word share a common user interface, which is described in this section.

The Microsoft Word Developer's Kit disk includes two wizards, the Starter Wizard (STARTER.WIZ on the Windows disk, STARTER WIZARD on the Macintosh disk) and the Wizard Maker Wizard (MKWIZARD.WIZ on the Windows disk, WIZARD MAKER WIZARD on the Macintosh disk), to help you get started creating your own wizards. The Starter Wizard is a "blank" wizard that contains routines (common to all wizards) that manage the user interface. The Wizard Maker Wizard constructs a wizard using the same routines as those contained in the Starter Wizard. You can then complete the new wizard, adding more controls to the wizard dialog box and including routines to carry out the task you want the wizard to accomplish.

Note This section assumes a familiarity with dynamic custom dialog boxes. If you're not familiar with custom dialog boxes and dynamic dialog boxes, see Chapter 5, "Working with Custom Dialog Boxes."

Wizard Templates

A wizard is stored in a template. In Windows, a wizard is stored in a template saved with the filename extension .WIZ rather than .DOT. When you save a template with the extension .WIZ in your template folder, Word identifies the template as a wizard in the list of templates and wizards displayed in the New dialog box (File menu). On the Macintosh, a wizard is a Word template with the file type WIZ! (you can use the **SetFileCreatorAndType** statement to change a template's file type). The wizard's filename is the name that appears in the list of templates and wizards displayed in the New dialog box (File menu). To be displayed in the New dialog box, a wizard must be saved in the template folder.

Every Word wizard contains an AutoNew macro that runs when the user creates a new document based on the wizard. The AutoNew macro calls the StartWizard macro, which does all the wizard's work. In effect, the StartWizard macro *is* the wizard; the template is just the container in which it's stored.

The StartWizard Macro

The StartWizard macro provided in the Starter Wizard template has the same design as the StartWizard macros in the wizard templates provided with Word. Its structure separates those parts of the macro that may need to be modified for a particular wizard from those parts that can be used by every wizard without modification. The following diagram shows how the macro code is organized.

```
'Global variables used by all wizards
        'Variable declarations
'Global wizard-specific variables
        'Variable declarations
```

```
Sub MAIN
        'Dialog box definition
End Sub
```

```
'** Wizard-specific subroutines and user-defined functions
        'Subroutines and functions here

'** Subroutines and user-defined functions used by all wizards
        'Subroutines and functions here
```

```
Function DialogCtrl(id$, action, sval)
        'Dialog function goes here
End Function
```

Many routines categorized as "wizard-specific" are shared by all wizards and are included in the Starter Wizard. These routines often do not need to be customized, but they can be. Some of these routines are described in detail later in the chapter, but it isn't necessary to understand how most of the routines work to take advantage of them in wizards you develop.

The following table lists all the wizard-specific routines included in the Starter Wizard and other Word wizards.

Name	Description
DoButtonClick	Responds to the user choosing a button or selecting an option on a dialog box panel.
GetHintName$()	Returns the AutoText name for the current panel's hint. Can be customized to return different AutoText names for different controls on the same panel.
NextPanel	Determines which panel is displayed next.
PrevPanel	Determines which panel was displayed previously.
RstDialog	Retrieves the wizard dialog box settings. Can call RstDlgPref, RstDlgValPref, and RstDlgMultiLinePref.
SaveDialog	Saves wizard settings. Can call SaveDlgPref, SaveDlgValPref, and SaveDlgMultiLinePref.

The following table lists the routines in the Starter Wizard and other Word wizards that are exactly the same in every wizard; they are not designed to be customized.

Name	Description
ChangePanel	Changes the wizard dialog box panel. Calls ShowHideControls.
DisplayHint	Displays a hint when the user chooses the Hint button. Calls the GetHintName$() function.
EnableControls	Enables and disables standard wizard controls. For example, if the last panel is displayed, the Next button is disabled.
ItemsInPanel	Stores the number of controls in a panel, plus the total number of previous controls in the PanelControls array.
RstDlgPref	Retrieves a string setting. Calls xFetchPref$().
RstDlgMultiLinePref	Retrieves a multiple-line text box setting. Calls xFetchPref$().
RstDlgValPref	Retrieves a numeric setting (for example, a check box setting). Calls xFetchPref$().

Name	Description
SaveDlgPref	Saves a string setting. Calls xStorePref.
SaveDlgValPref	Saves a numeric setting (for example, a check box setting). Calls xStorePref.
SaveDlgMultiLinePref	Saves a multiple-line text box setting. Calls xStorePref.
ShowHideControls	Shows or hides the controls in a panel. (Not used on the Macintosh or in Windows NT.)
xFetchPref$()	Retrieves settings from a settings file.
xStorePref	Stores settings in a settings file.

Note   The names of some routines in the Starter Wizard are slightly different from the names of those in the wizards that ship with Word. For example, the ShowHideControls subroutine is called SHControls in the Word wizards. The Starter Wizard uses the term "panel" to refer to a set of dialog box controls displayed at the same time, because that term is used in this book; the wizards that ship with Word use the term "state." Thus, subroutines in the Starter Wizard such as NextPanel and PrevPanel are called NextState and PrevState in the Word wizards.

The Wizard Interface

The interface shared by all the wizards included with Word consists of a dialog box with several panels. Each panel in the dialog box has its own set of controls, and each panel also shares a set of controls used to move between panels and to dismiss the dialog box. These standard controls are shown in the following illustration.

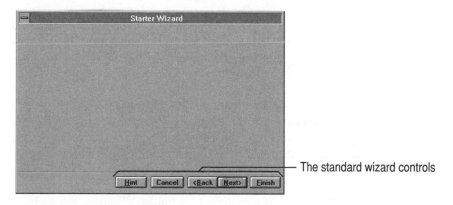

The standard wizard controls

The Wizard Dialog Box Definition

A dialog box definition defines all the controls in a dialog box. Definitions for dialog boxes with more than one panel, such as wizard dialog boxes, are quite long because the definition must include the controls for all the dialog box panels.

In the wizard dialog box definition, the instructions defining the standard controls shared by every panel are defined first, followed by the controls for the first panel, the controls for the second panel, and so on.

Here is the dialog box definition in in the Starter Wizard's StartWizard macro:

```
Begin Dialog UserDialog 628, 276, wizname$, .DlgControl
'Controls shown in every panel: 0-8
    Picture 0, 238, 500, 11, "LinePic", 1, .LinePicA          '0
    Picture 128, 238, 500, 11, "LinePic", 1, .LinePicB        '1
    OKButton 11, 215, 73, 21                                  '2
    PushButton 229, 250, 73, 19, "&Hint", .Hint               '3
    CancelButton 313, 250, 80, 19                             '4
    PushButton 401, 250, 71, 19, "<&Back", .Back              '5
    PushButton 471, 250, 71, 19, "&Next>", .Next              '6
    PushButton 550, 250, 75, 19, "&Finish", .FastForward      '7
    FilePreview 16, 12, 250, 214, .Preview                    '8
    StateItems(0) = 9
'Panel 1
    'Controls for the first panel go here
    ItemsInPanel 0   'The number of controls in 1st panel
'Panel 2
    'Controls for the second panel go here
    ItemsInPanel 0   'The number of controls in 2nd panel
'Panel 3
    'Controls for the third panel go here
    ItemsInPanel 0   'The number of controls in 3rd panel
End Dialog
```

The dialog box definition in the StartWizard macro is set up with nine standard controls. All these controls—except the file preview box and the OK button—are displayed in every panel of the wizard dialog box. The file preview box is included in the standard controls because there can be only one per dialog box, and when a Word wizard uses this control in a panel, the control is always in the same location in the dialog box. Note that in Windows the line graphic displayed by the two picture controls is stored as two AutoText entries in the wizard template, rather than in a separate file. This ensures that the graphic is always available. (Two picture controls are necessary to create a line that extends the full width of the dialog box. On the Macintosh, only one picture control is needed, and the graphic is stored in a Macintosh resource fork.) The rest of the dialog box definition has placeholders for three panels, but you can add more panels as you need them.

Two other instructions within the dialog box definition require explanation:
`PanelItems(0) = 9` and `ItemsInPanel 0`. `PanelItems()` is an array defined (before
the dialog box definition) with as many elements as the dialog box has panels.
Each element of the array will store the number of controls in its corresponding
panel, plus the total number of controls defined for previous panels. The standard
controls that are defined first are stored in the element numbered 0 (zero), the
controls for the first panel are stored in the element numbered 1, and so on. The
instruction `PanelItems(0) = 9` indicates that there are nine standard controls (or
"items").

For the other panels, the subroutine `ItemsInPanel` is used to assign the number
of items to the `PanelItems()` array. The `ItemsInPanel` subroutine increments the
array index number and adds the number of controls stored in the current panel to
the total number of controls defined to that point in the dialog box definition. For
example, if there are two controls in the first panel, the number 2 is added to the
number of standard controls, 9, for a total of 11 controls. Other subroutines in the
macro will be able to manipulate this array to hide or show the items in a panel,
which is the most important task in managing the different panels. Here is the
`ItemsInPanel` subroutine:

```
Sub ItemsInPanel(howMany)
LastPanel = LastPanel + 1
PanelItems(LastPanel) = howMany + PanelItems(LastPanel - 1)
End Sub
```

The global variable `LastPanel` stores the index number of the `PanelItems()` array.
The variable `howMany` is the number of items in the current panel, which is passed
to the subroutine when it is called.

Numeric Identifiers

The order of the controls in the StartWizard dialog box definition is important
because the instructions in the dialog function that display and hide these controls
use numeric identifiers. The numeric identifier for a control is determined by its
position within the dialog box definition. Numeric identifiers are used because
they are much faster than string identifiers in dialog boxes with many controls.
Numeric identifiers are also efficient because you can use loops to operate on a
group of controls. In wizards, loops are used to hide and display all the controls
in a dialog box panel.

As you're developing a wizard, you should use string identifiers rather than
numeric ones, so that you can add and delete controls from the dialog box
definition without having to change all the instructions that act on those controls.
Then, when you have finished the dialog box, you can convert to numeric
identifiers for better performance.

Managing the Dialog Box Panels

Each time the user chooses a button to move to a different panel, the controls in the current panel must be hidden and the controls in the new panel must be displayed. In addition, if the user moves to the first panel, the Back button must be disabled; if the user moves to the last panel, the Next button must be disabled. The task of managing panels is shared among the various subroutines described here.

Before turning to those subroutines, though, consider a portion of the dialog function that determines which action to take if a user chooses one of the standard wizard buttons. Each **Case** instruction in the following **Select Case** control structure corresponds to the numeric identifier of one of the wizard's standard buttons. Note that Case 5 and Case 6 correspond to the user choosing the Back and Next buttons. In both cases, the ChangePanel subroutine is called.

```
Select Case idnum
    Case 3              'Hint
        DisplayHint
    Case 4              'Cancel, so exit dialog box
        fRet = 0
    Case 5              '<Back
        ChangePanel(Panel, PrevPanel(Panel))
    Case 6              'Next>
        ChangePanel(Panel, NextPanel(Panel))
    Case 7              'Finish, so exit dialog box
        fRet = 0
    Case Else
        'Shouldn't happen...
End Select
```

The ChangePanel subroutine takes two arguments: Panel (the number of the current panel) and PrevPanel(Panel) if the Back button is chosen or NextPanel(Panel) if the Next button is chosen. PrevPanel() and NextPanel() are user-defined functions that determine which panel is the next panel. Usually, this is simply Panel + 1 or Panel - 1. Here is the NextPanel() function:

```
Function NextPanel(oldPanel)     'Determine the panel following oldPanel
If oldPanel = LastPanel Then
    NextPanel = oldPanel         'Safeguard -- do not modify
Else
    NextPanel = oldPanel + 1     'The normal, default case
End If
End Function
```

ChangePanel

The ChangePanel subroutine calls the ShowHideControls subroutine to hide the current panel and display the new one. Also, ChangePanel either hides or shows the FilePreview control and calls the EnableControls subroutine. The old argument corresponds to the current panel that will be hidden; the new argument indicates the new panel that will be displayed.

```
Sub ChangePanel(old, new)
ShowHideControls(PanelItems(old - 1), PanelItems(old), 0)
DlgVisible "preview", 1 - HideFilePreview(new)
ShowHideControls(PanelItems(new - 1), PanelItems(new), 1)
Panel = new
EnableControls
End Sub
```

ShowHideControls

This subroutine is called to hide the current panel and display the new one. (This subroutine is only necessary in Word version 6.0 for Windows. In Word version 6.0 for the Macintosh and Windows NT, and in Word version 7.0, a single **DlgVisible** instruction can show or hide a range of dialog box controls.) If ShowHideVal is equal to 1, the controls are shown; if it's equal to 0 (zero), they're hidden. The variables FirstControl and LastControl are the key values. They control the **For…Next** loop, which hides or shows all the controls in a panel: FirstControl corresponds to the numeric identifier of the first control in a panel and (LastControl - 1) corresponds to the numeric identifier of the last control in a panel.

When the ChangePanel subroutine calls ShowHideControls to hide the current panel, it passes PanelItems(old - 1) as FirstControl. Each element in the array PanelItems( ), you recall, corresponds to a panel in the dialog box. The number assigned to each element is the total number of dialog box controls defined up through the last control on the corresponding panel. For example, if 25 controls are defined for the first two panels (including the standard controls), PanelItems(2) is assigned the value of 25. If the third panel has 10 items, PanelItems(3) is assigned a value of 35. One final piece of the puzzle: WordBasic assigns numeric identifiers to dialog box controls starting with 0 (zero). So if a dialog box definition contains 35 controls, the last control is numbered 34. To hide the 10 controls in the third panel, you could write a loop that iterates from 25 to 35−1:

```
For i = 25 To (35 - 1)
    DlgVisible i, 0
Next
```

That is just what the ShowHideControls subroutine does:

```
Sub ShowHideControls (FirstControl, LastControl, ShowHideVal)
For i = FirstControl To LastControl - 1
    DlgVisible i, ShowHideVal
Next
End Sub
```

EnableControls

This subroutine controls which wizard button has the focus and which buttons are enabled. When the first panel is displayed, the Next button gets the focus and the Back button is disabled. When the last panel is displayed, the Next button is disabled and the Finish button gets the focus. Otherwise, both the Back button and the Next button are enabled, and the focus remains on the button chosen last.

```
Sub EnableControls
    If Panel = 1 Then
        DlgFocus 6                    'Give the Next> button the focus
        DlgEnable 5, 0                'Disable the <Back button
    ElseIf Panel = 2 Then
        DlgEnable 5, 1                'Enable the <Back button
    ElseIf Panel = LastPanel - 1 Then
        DlgEnable 6, 1                'Enable the Next> button
    ElseIf Panel = LastPanel Then
        DlgFocus 7                    'Give the Finish button the focus
        DlgEnable 6, 0                'Disable the Next> button
    EndIf
End Sub
```

Storing Wizard Settings

Every wizard contains a set of subroutines that save and retrieve settings, so the wizard can "remember" the user's choices and present them as defaults the next time the user runs the wizard. Some of the subroutines are designed to be customized for different wizards and some remain the same in every wizard.

On the Macintosh, **DlgStoreValues** and **DlgLoadValues()** are used to save and retrieve multiple settings. These instructions are not available in Windows, so the subroutines to save and retrieve settings are more complex. This section describes the Windows subroutines.

The SaveDialog subroutine saves the wizard dialog box settings. You can call three subroutines from the SaveDialog subroutine: SaveDlgValPref to save numeric values such as check box settings; SaveDlgPref to save the contents of a text box; and SaveDlgMultiLinePref to save the contents of a multiple-line text box. Each of these subroutines takes as an argument the string identifier of the control whose setting is to be saved. For example, the following instruction saves the setting of the control with the identifier Panel4CheckBox:

```
SaveDlgValPref "Panel4CheckBox"
```

Here is the framework of the SaveDialog subroutine:

```
Sub SaveDialog
'Panel 1
'Statements to save settings in panel 1 go here
'Panel 2
'Statements to save settings in panel 2 go here
'Panel 3
'Statements to save settings in panel 3 go here
'Panel 4
'Statements to save settings in panel 4 go here
End Sub
```

Likewise, there are three corresponding subroutines you can call from the RstDialog subroutine to restore settings to a newly opened wizard dialog box: RstDlgValPref, RstDlgPref, and RstDlgMultiLinePref. Each subroutine takes two arguments: the string identifier of the control whose setting is to be restored and a default setting. The default setting is used only when there is no value to restore (the first time the wizard is used). For example, the following instruction restores the setting of the control with the identifier Panel4CheckBox; the default value is 0 (zero), which means the check box is cleared:

```
RstDlgValPref "Panel4CheckBox", 0
```

The following example restores the setting of a text box with the identifier "Panel2TextBox"; the default text is an empty string (leaving an empty text box):

```
RstDlgPref "Panel2TextBox", ""
```

Here is the framework of the RstDialog subroutine:

```
Sub RstDialog
'Panel 1
'Statements to restore settings in panel 1 go here
'Panel 2
'Statements to restore settings in panel 2 go here
'Panel 3
'Statements to restore settings in panel 3 go here
'Panel 4
'Statements to restore settings in panel 4 go here
End Sub
```

Calling Routines in DLLs

In Windows, a macro can call routines in a *dynamic-link library* (DLL) or Word add-in library (WLL) to access capabilities that aren't directly available in WordBasic. Calls are often made to Windows API (application programming interface) routines, but they can be made to routines in any DLL that makes routines available for other programs. WLLs are a special kind of DLL written specifically for Word; WordBasic can call routines in a WLL in the same way it calls routines from a DLL.

On the Macintosh, DLL files are not available, but you can call routines stored in WLLs. In this section, the term DLL is used to refer to DLLs in Windows and Word add-in libraries in Windows or on the Macintosh.

Note   For information about writing Word add-in libraries using the Word API, see Appendix C, "Microsoft Word Application Programming Interface," in Part 3, "Appendixes."

Because DLL routines reside in files that are external to Word, you must let WordBasic know where it can find the routines you want to use. You provide this information with the **Declare** statement. Once you have declared a DLL routine, you can use it in your code like any other routine (although you have to be especially careful about the arguments that you pass to DLL routines).

There are two steps to using a DLL routine:

1. Tell WordBasic about the routine by using a **Declare** statement.
2. Make the actual call.

You declare a DLL routine only once in a macro. You then can call it any number of times from any subroutine or user-defined function used in the macro.

Declaring a DLL Routine

To declare a DLL routine, place a **Declare** statement outside a subroutine or user-defined function. Typically, **Declare** statements are placed at the start of the macro before any other statements.

If the routine does not return a value, declare it as a subroutine. For example:

```
Declare Sub SetWindowTextA Lib "User32" (hWnd As Long,\
    lpString As String)
```

If the routine returns a value, declare it as a function. For example:

```
Declare Function GetSystemMetrics Lib "User32" (num As Long) \
    As Long
```

In Windows 95 and Windows NT, function names are case-sensitive and must be declared exactly as they appear in the DLL.

Here are the same declarations in Word version 6.0 for Windows:

```
Declare Sub SetWindowText Lib "User" (hWnd As Integer, \
    lpString As String)
Declare Function GetSystemMetrics Lib "User" (num As Integer) As Integer
```

Note the **Lib** keyword in the **Declare** statement. The **Declare** statement can also contain an optional **Alias** keyword. The use of these keywords is explained under "Special Considerations When Declaring DLL Routines" later in this section.

For the complete syntax of the **Declare** statement, see Part 2, "WordBasic Reference."

Calling a DLL Routine

Once a routine is declared, you can then call it just as you would a WordBasic statement or function. The following example uses the GetSystemMetrics Windows API routine to determine whether a mouse is installed. The value 19 assigned to SM_MOUSEPRESENT is one of a number of values that can be passed to the GetSystemMetrics function. These values are listed in the Microsoft Win32® Software Development Kit.

```
Declare Function GetSystemMetrics Lib "User32" (num As Long) \
    As Long

Sub MAIN
    SM_MOUSEPRESENT = 19
    If GetSystemMetrics(SM_MOUSEPRESENT) Then MsgBox "Mouse installed"
End Sub
```

Important WordBasic can't verify that you are passing correct values to a DLL routine. If you pass incorrect values, the routine may fail, which may cause unexpected behavior or errors in Word or the operating system. Take care when experimenting with DLL routines, and save your work often.

Special Considerations When Declaring DLL Routines

As you have probably realized, the declarations for DLL routines can be quite complex. The Microsoft Word Developer's Kit disk for Windows includes the text files WIN16API.TXT and WIN32API.TXT, which list WordBasic DLL routine declarations for the Windows API. You can search for the declarations you want in the text files, copy them, and paste them into your macro.

Once you have pasted the appropriate DLL routine declarations into your code, you simply call the routines like any other routine in your application. Because you have to take extra care when passing values to DLL routines, however, you should first read "Calling DLL Routines with Specific Variable Types" later in this section.

If you are attempting to call a routine in a DLL that is not part of the operating environment, you should consult the documentation for the DLL to determine the proper declaration for it.

Specifying the Library

The **Lib** *LibName$* clause in the **Declare** statement tells WordBasic where to find the dynamic-link library. For the Windows 95 and Windows NT operating environment DLLs, this is either "User32," "GDI32," "Kernel32," or one of the other system DLLs such as "MMSystem." For Windows 3.*x*, this is either "User," "GDI," "Kernel," or one of the other system DLLs. For other DLLs, the *LibName$* is a file specification that can include a path. For example:

```
Declare Function EnvString Lib "C:\WIN\STRINGS.DLL" (stringbuffer$, \
    stringnum As Long) As Long
```

If you are declaring a function in a loaded DLL or WLL, you do not need to specify the path.

Using an Alias

You can use the **Alias** keyword to call a routine by a different name within a macro. You may need to do this if the routine name is not a valid subroutine or function name in WordBasic. If a routine has a long name, you can use **Alias** to substitute a shorter one. For example, this **Declare** statement substitutes the name WinDir for the routine's longer name (GetWindowsDirectory):

```
Declare Function WinDir Lib "Kernel32" Alias "GetWindowsDirectoryA" \
    (stringbuffer$, stringnum As Long) As Long
```

Note that the routine's real name, GetWindowsDirectoryA, follows the **Alias** keyword and that the alias WinDir (the name given to the routine within the macro) follows the **Function** keyword.

Here is the same **Declare** statement for Windows 3.*x*:

```
Declare Function WinDir Lib "Kernel" Alias "GetWindowsDirectory" \
    (stringbuffer$, stringnum As Integer) As Integer
```

Now you can use this shorter name to call the GetWindowsDirectory routine:

```
WinPath$ = String$(145, "*")
worked = WinDir(WinPath$, Len(WinPath$))
MsgBox WinPath$
```

Calling DLL Routines with Specific Variable Types

Many DLL routines require or return variable types that are not supported in WordBasic. WordBasic, in turn, supports variable-length strings, which are not supported by most DLL routines. Therefore, you must take care when passing variables to and receiving variables from DLL routines.

DLL Routines That Use Strings

Windows 95 or Windows NT functions that use strings are typically available in two versions, ANSI and Unicode. Word version 7.0 and Word version 6.0 for Windows NT are ANSI applications and must, therefore, use ANSI versions of the API functions. The ANSI API functions have an "A" appended to the function name. For instance, the Windows 3.*x* function GetWindowsDirectory is GetWindowsDirectoryA in Windows 95 and Windows NT.

DLL Routines That Modify Strings

A DLL routine can modify a WordBasic string variable it receives as an argument. (Strings are always passed to DLL routines by reference.) Be careful when calling a DLL routine that modifies a string. A DLL cannot increase the length of a WordBasic string; it simply writes beyond the end of the string if it is not long enough. This corrupts other areas of memory. You can avoid this problem by making the string argument long enough that the DLL routine can never write past the end of it.

For example, the GetWindowsDirectory routine returns the path for the Windows folder in its first argument:

```
Declare Function GetWindowsDirectoryA Lib "Kernel32" \
    (stringbuffer As String, stringnum As Long) As Long
```

A safe way to call this routine is to make the returned argument at least 255 characters long by filling it with characters—in this case, asterisk (*) characters—before it is passed by reference to the DLL routine:

```
path$ = String$(255, "*")
worked = GetWindowsDirectory(path$, Len(path$))
```

Most DLL routines (and all the routines in the Windows API) expect standard C strings, which end in a "null character" (ANSI 0). Word converts all strings that it passes to DLL routines to null-terminated strings. Visual Basic includes the **ByVal** keyword to specify that a string should be passed as a null-terminated string, but this keyword is not supported (or necessary) in WordBasic.

Note Windows DLL routines generally do not return strings longer than 255 characters. While this is true of many other libraries, always consult the documentation for the routine in question.

The Double, Integer, and Long Variable Types

Two variable types are supported within WordBasic: strings and numbers (double-precision floating-point numbers). But in the **Declare** statement only, WordBasic supports two additional types, **Integer** and **Long**:

- An **Integer** variable stores an integer value between -32,768 and 32,767 or between 0 and 65,535.

- A **Long** variable stores a value between -2,147,483,648 and -2,147,483,647 or 0 and 4,294,967,295.

Integer and **Long** variables are used to export values from and import values to WordBasic. When WordBasic receives an **Integer** or **Long** value from a DLL routine, the value is converted into a double-precision floating-point value, the standard WordBasic numeric type.

If a function in Windows 3.*x* uses the type **Integer**, the corresponding function in Windows 95 and Windows NT uses **Long**.

In addition, the variable type **Double** is available in **Declare**. **Double** is a double-precision floating-point number equivalent to the standard WordBasic numeric type. When you define a variable as **Double** in a **Declare** instruction, it is the same as defining it as a numeric variable elsewhere in WordBasic.

Structured Variable Limitation

Some DLL routines take or receive variables referred to as "structures" in C, as "records" in Pascal, or as "user-defined types" in Visual Basic. DLL documentation often uses the C terminology. WordBasic does not support structured variables (other than dialog records), so these routines calling DLL routines that return or require structured variables may cause unpredictable results.

Arrays

You can pass individual elements of an array in the same way you pass any variable. For example, you can use the sndPlaySound routine to play a series of .WAV files stored in an array:

```
Declare Function sndPlaySoundA Lib "WINMM"(sound$, flag As Integer) \
    As Long

Sub MAIN
WAVEFILECOUNT = 10
Dim WaveFile$(WAVEFILECOUNT - 1)
For i = 0 To WAVEFILECOUNT - 1
    worked = sndPlaySoundA(WaveFile$(i), 0)
Next i
End Sub
```

WordBasic does not support passing entire arrays to DLL routines.

Converting Common Declarations

The routines in DLLs are most commonly documented using C language syntax. To call them from WordBasic, you must translate them into valid **Declare** statements and call them correctly. When translating, you may find the following table useful; it lists common C language declarations and their WordBasic equivalents.

C language declaration	In WordBasic declare as	Call with
Pointer to a string (LPSTR)	S **As String** or S$	A string variable
Pointer to an integer (LPINT)	L **As Long**	A long variable
Pointer to a long integer (LPDWORD)	L **As Long**	A long variable
Pointer to a structure (for example, LPRECT)	No equivalent	No equivalent

C language declaration	In WordBasic declare as	Call with
Integer (INT, UINT, WORD, BOOL)	L **As Long** (I **As Integer** in Windows 3.*x*)	A long variable (an integer variable in Windows 3.*x*)
Handle (hWnd, hDC, hMenu, and so on)	h **As Long** (h **As Integer** in Windows 3.*x*)	A long variable (an integer variable in Windows 3.*x*)
Long (DWORD, LONG)	L **As Long**	A long variable
Pointer to an array of integers	No equivalent	No equivalent
Pointer to a void (void *)	No equivalent	No equivalent

If the routine's return value is void, it should be declared as a subroutine (see "Declaring a DLL Routine" earlier in this section).

Developing Macros for More Than One Platform

The WordBasic macro language is shared across platforms, but there are a few things to take into account when developing cross-platform macros. This section organizes cross-platform issues into three areas:

- Using platform-specific instructions and arguments
- Handling platform-level differences
- Moving cross-platform macros between platforms

Most of this section deals with differences between the Macintosh and Windows platforms. There are very few WordBasic differences between the Windows 3.*x*, Windows 95, and Windows NT versions of Word. For the most part, you don't need to worry about Windows differences unless you're declaring external functions, which may need to be declared differently in Windows 95 and Windows NT (see "Using the Declare Statement to Call External Routines" later in this section).

You use the **AppInfo$()** function to return the name of the current platform. In Windows, AppInfo$(1) returns a string containing "Windows," "Windows 95," or "Windows NT" and the version number; on the Macintosh, it returns a string containing "Macintosh" and the system software version number. After you've determined the platform, you use a control structure to run the appropriate block of instructions for that platform.

The following example uses **InStr()** to determine whether the string returned by AppInfo$(1) contains the word "Macintosh"; if it does, the flag variable, MacintoshFlag, is set to 1. A control structure then tests the value of the MacintoshFlag variable to determine whether to run instructions for Windows or for the Macintosh.

```
If Instr(AppInfo$(1), "Macintosh") <> 0 Then MacintoshFlag = 1
If MacintoshFlag = 0 Then
    ChDir "C:\WINWORD6\TEMPLATE"
    FileOpen "ARTICLE.DOT"
Else
    ChDir "HD:MICROSOFT WORD 6:TEMPLATES"
    FileOpen "ARTICLE TEMPLATE"
End If
```

Using Platform-Specific Instructions and Arguments

WordBasic includes a number of statements and functions that are specific to a particular platform. A statement or function intended for use on one platform only will produce an error if run on another platform. In addition, some dialog-equivalent statements take arguments that are valid on one platform only. Once you use **AppInfo()** to determine which platform the macro is running on, you can use a control structure to ensure that platform-specific statements, functions, and arguments run only when the macro is running on the appropriate platform.

The following paragraphs describe significant areas where Windows and Macintosh statements differ. For a complete list of Macintosh- and Windows-specific statements and functions, see "Language Differences Across Versions of Word" in Part 2, "WordBasic Reference."

Differences in Page Setup

Because of differences in printing and page setup in Windows and on the Macintosh, the **FilePageSetup** statement is available only in Windows. A separate set of statements is provided for page setup on the Macintosh: **FileDocumentLayout**, **FileMacPageSetup**, **FileMacCustomPageSetupGX**, and **FileMacPageSetupGX**. On a Macintosh with QuickDraw™ GX installed, use **FileMacCustomPageSetupGX** and **FileMacPageSetupGX** instead of **FileMacPageSetup**.

You can use the **GetSystemInfo$()** function to determine whether QuickDraw GX is installed. The return value of GetSystemInfo$(519) is "Yes" if QuickDraw GX is installed and "No" if it is not.

Custom Dialog Box Accelerators

When you display a custom dialog box on the Macintosh, accelerators specified in the dialog box definition do not appear with an underline. However, the accelerators do work as expected. After the user presses the COMMAND key, an underline appears under the specified characters.

To automatically display accelerators in a dialog box (without the user pressing the COMMAND key), add a **MenuMode** instruction to the macro before displaying the custom dialog box, as shown in the following macro:

```
Sub MAIN
MenuMode
Begin Dialog UserDialog 320,144, "Microsoft Word"
    OKButton 10, 6, 88, 21
    CancelButton 10, 30, 88, 21
    CheckBox 150, 84, 100, 18, "C&heck Box", .CheckBox1
End Dialog
Dim dlg As UserDialog
n = Dialog(dlg)
End Sub
```

Differences in WordBasic Sort Order

The ANSI character sort order differs between the Macintosh and Windows. The specific sort order of ANSI characters is relevant when you write WordBasic macros that compare strings. The sort order is predictable for alphabetic and numeric characters (for example, "A" comes before "B" and "3" comes before "4"). However, the sort order for the remaining characters is not predictable. To determine whether "!" is greater than or less than "?" on the current platform, you can create an array of those characters and use the **SortArray**() function to sort them.

Screen Updating

In Windows, the **ScreenUpdating** statement turns off screen updating so that changes to document and application windows are not displayed on the screen. On the Macintosh, changes within document windows are not displayed, but changes to the document window frame are displayed. For example, if a document window is moved while screen updating is turned off, the document window frame is shown in the new position. Likewise, if a document is opened while screen updating is turned off, the document's window frame will be displayed (the document itself will appear blank until screen updating is turned on, or until the macro ends).

Using SendKeys

On the Macintosh, a **SendKeys** instruction can send no more than 10 keystrokes, and can send them only to Word; **SendKeys** cannot be used to send keystrokes to another application. You can send a SHIFT key combination using the plus sign (+), but you cannot send key combinations including OPTION or COMMAND. For a list of keystrokes supported by **SendKeys**, see Part 2, "WordBasic Reference."

Differences in Custom Dialog Box Capabilities

On the Macintosh, you can store the picture displayed in a picture dialog box control in a "resource fork" (you can use **Picture** or **DlgSetPicture** to specify a resource fork as the storage place). Also available on the Macintosh are two instructions, **DlgStoreValues** and **DlgLoadValues()**, with which you can store and load custom dialog box settings. In Word version 6.0 for the Macintosh, Word version 6.0 for Windows NT, and Word version 7.0, you can use a single **DlgVisible** instruction to show or hide a range of controls (in Windows 3.*x*, a single **DlgVisible** instruction can affect one control only).

The **DlgFocus** statement does not change the focus in a Word version 6.0 for the Macintosh custom dialog box.

The following commands, which control the size or position of custom dynamic dialog boxes in the Windows versions of Word, are not available and generate errors in Word version 6.0 for the Macintosh: **AppSize**, **AppMove**, **AppWindowHeight**, **AppWindowWidth**, **AppWindowPosTop**, **AppWindowPosLeft**

Making a Network Connection

In Windows, you can use the **Connect** statement to connect to a network drive; on the Macintosh, you can use the **MountVolume** statement. You can use **Connect** to display the Connect dialog box; **MountVolume** does not have a dialog box associated with it.

Handling Platform-Level Differences

Even when a WordBasic statement or function has the same result on all platforms, the code may need to be different. Different platforms have different system-specific functionality such as file-naming conventions that need to be considered in cross-platform macros.

Specifying Filenames and Paths

In Windows, you use the question mark (?) and asterisk (*) wildcards to specify a group of files. Wildcards are not accepted on the Macintosh, but you can use the **MacID$()** function to specify files of a certain type. A Macintosh file type is a unique four-letter label assigned to every file created by a Macintosh application (you can use the **FileType$()** function to determine a file's type).

The following example creates a list of all the text files in a folder (the `MacintoshFlag` variable has been set earlier in the macro):

```
If MacintoshFlag = 0 Then
    textfilename$ = Files$("*.TXT")
Else
    textfilename$ = Files$(MacID$("TEXT"))
End If
Insert textfilename$
While textfilename$ <> ""
    textfilename$ = Files$()
    Insert textfilename$
Wend
```

MacID$() can also be used to specify file types with the **FileOpen** and **Kill** statements. The following instructions display the Open dialog box showing a list of all the template files in a folder (the `MacintoshFlag` variable has been set earlier in the macro):

```
Dim dlg as FileOpen
GetCurValues dlg
If MacintoshFlag = 0 Then
    Chdir "C:\WINWORD\TEMPLATE"
    dlg.Name = "*.DOT"
Else
    Chdir "HD1:WORD:TEMPLATES"
    dlg.Name = MacID$("WTBN")
End If
choice = Dialog(dlg)
If choice Then FileOpen dlg
```

Note Although **MacID$()** appears to return a string, it actually returns a value that doesn't correspond to any WordBasic data type. Consequently, **MacID$()** should be used only with the statements described here that accept the internal value it returns. In addition, you cannot concatenate the value returned by **MacID$()** with a path string; instead, you use **ChDir** to change the current folder.

You can use **MacID$()** with a Macintosh application signature to specify an application. **MacID$()** can be used to specify an application with the following instructions: **AppActivate**, **AppClose**, **AppCount**, **AppGetNames**, **AppGetNames()**, **AppIsRunning()**, and **Shell**. **MacID$()** provides a more reliable way to specify an application than the application name, because the user may change the application name but is not likely to change the Macintosh application signature. The following example uses **MacID$()** with **AppIsRunning()** and **Shell** to determine whether Microsoft Excel is running, and to start it if it isn't.

```
If AppIsRunning(MacID$("XCEL")) = 0 Then Shell MacID$("XCEL")
```

Note that you don't need to specify a path or folder when you use **MacID$()** to specify an application.

Using Settings Files

There are a few differences to be aware of when working with settings files in Windows 3.*x* and on the Macintosh.

- If you don't specify a path in the filename for **SetPrivateProfileString** or **GetPrivateProfileString**, Word stores or looks for the file in the Windows folder in Windows or the Preferences folder on the Macintosh.

- In Windows, settings files are text files and they can be opened by a text editor like any other text file. On the Macintosh, settings files are not text files; they can be edited directly using the **ToolsAdvancedSettings** command or the ResEdit program.

- The Macintosh does not include an equivalent of the Windows WIN.INI file that can be accessed by **SetProfileString** and **GetProfileString$()**.

- In Word version 6.0 for Windows, settings are stored in a settings file called WINWORD6.INI; in Word version 6.0 for the Macintosh, they're stored in a file called Word Settings (6). You can use **SetPrivateProfileString** and **GetPrivateProfileString$()** to change settings in WINWORD6.INI or Word Settings (6). For example:

```
a$ = GetPrivateProfileString$("Microsoft Word", "USER-DOT-PATH", \
    "Word Settings (6)")
```

Note   Windows 95 and Windows NT do not use the settings files WIN.INI and WINWORD6.INI. Instead, settings are stored in the registry. For information about returning and setting values in the registry, see "Accessing the Windows Registry" earlier in this chapter.

Working with DDE

When an application runs on more than one platform, the same application may have a different application name in Windows and on the Macintosh. For example, in Windows, the DDE application name for Microsoft Word is "WinWord," whereas on the Macintosh, it's "MSWord," although "WinWord" is also accepted.

The instructions used to initiate DDE conversations are the same in Windows and on the Macintosh, but since DDE application names may be different on different platforms, separate instructions may be necessary for each platform. Also, it's a good idea to use **MacID$()** to specify an application on the Macintosh if you use the **AppIsRunning()** and **Shell** instructions when initiating a DDE conversation. In the following example, a different block of instructions for each platform is used to initiate a DDE conversation with Microsoft Excel (the MacintoshFlag variable has been set earlier in the macro). Note that Microsoft Excel has the same DDE application name in Windows and on the Macintosh, so separate **DDEInitiate()** instructions are not needed.

```
If MacintoshFlag = 0 Then
    If AppIsRunning("Microsoft Excel") = 0 Then Shell "EXCEL.EXE", 4
    chan = DDEInitiate("Excel", "System")
Else
    If AppIsRunning(MacID$("XCEL")) = 0 Then Shell MacID$("XCEL"), 4
    chan = DDEInitiate("Microsoft Excel", "System")
End If
chan = DDEInitiate("Excel", "System")
topics$ = DDERequest$(chan, "Topics")
Insert topics$
```

Using the Declare Statement to Call External Routines

In Windows, you can use the **Declare** statement to call routines stored in a dynamic-link library (DLL) or a Word add-in library (WLL). On the Macintosh, only routines stored in a WLL can be called. When a macro created in a Windows version of Word is converted to Word version 6.0 for the Macintosh, any **Declare** statements that refer to Windows DLLs will return the WordBasic error 543, "Unable to open specified library."

Declare instructions in macros ported from Word version 6.0 for Windows to Word version 7.0 or Word version 6.0 for Windows NT need to be modified. Because you cannot declare an external routine in a 16-bit library from a 32-bit application, such as Word version 7.0 or Word version 6.0 for Windows NT, you must update macros that declare routines in 16-bit libraries to identify the 32-bit versions of those libraries. Also the names, locations, and parameters of many Windows 3.x operating system routines (often referred to as API calls) changed in Windows 95 and Windows NT. You must update macros that declare Windows 3.x API calls to declare the correct routines in Windows 95 or Windows NT. Windows 95 and Windows NT function libraries are documented in the Microsoft Win32 Software Development Kit.

Unlike routine names in Windows 3.*x*, routine names are case-sensitive in Windows 95 and Windows NT. In addition, some routines need to be declared with different variable types in Windows 95 or Windows NT: INT return values or parameters must be declared as LONG; handles must be declared as LONG. For more information on using the **Declare** statement, see "Calling Routines in DLLs" earlier in this chapter.

Moving a Cross-Platform Macro Between Platforms

There are two potential problems that can occur when you move a macro with platform-specific instructions between Word version 6.0 for Windows and Word version 6.0 for the Macintosh. These problems occur when one version of Word does not recognize instructions that are supported in another version. Specifically, Word version 6.0, 6.0a, and 6.0c for Windows do not support the Macintosh-specific WordBasic statements and functions available in Word version 6.0 for the Macintosh. In this situation, the following two problems can occur:

- If you develop a macro in Word version 6.0, 6.0a, or 6.0c for Windows and then move the macro to Word version 6.0 for the Macintosh, instructions specific to the Macintosh version of Word will produce an error—error 124, "Unknown command, subroutine, or function"—until the macro is edited on the Macintosh (the macro must be "dirtied").

- If you develop a macro in Word version 6.0 for the Macintosh, move the macro to Word version 6.0 or 6.0a for Windows, and then edit and save the macro in Windows, Macintosh-specific keywords will be removed from the macro; they will not be restored if the macro is moved back to the Macintosh. (The macro should still run correctly in Windows, since the Macintosh-specific instructions should not run on the Windows platform anyway. But the macro will no longer run correctly if it is moved back to the Macintosh.) Note that this problem does not occur in Word version 6.0c for Windows.

Note   These problems do not occur if you develop cross platform macros in Word version 7.0 or Word version 6.0 for Windows NT.

Typically, a cross-platform macro is developed on one platform and then tested on the other platforms for which it is intended. If you're working with Word version 6.0 or 6.0a for Windows, you need to avoid editing the macro on more than one platform. That is, once you choose a platform for developing a Word 6.0 or 6.0a cross-platform macro, you must stick with it; if you edit the macro on more than one platform, you may encounter problems.

If you develop cross-platform macros in Word for Windows, you need to make sure the macros run properly on the Macintosh before you distribute them. You may want to distribute your cross-platform macros in execute-only format so that they cannot be edited (you use the **MacroCopy** statement to make a macro execute-only). If you don't want to distribute your cross-platform macros in execute-only format (that is, if you don't want to disable editing), you run the risk that a user will edit the macro.

Moving a Macro with Extended Characters Between Platforms

In Windows and on the Macintosh, different character codes are used to represent international characters. If you create a macro that contains string values with international characters in them (for example, á, ç, and ö), these characters will change when the macro is opened or run on another platform. To avoid this result, use the following steps to move the macro between platforms:

1. Copy the text of the macro from the macro-editing window into a new document and save the document.

2. Open the document on the other platform, save it in Text Only format, close it, and then open it again.

3. Copy the text from the document into a new macro-editing window.

Note that distributing a macro as execute-only does not correct this behavior. If you need to distribute a macro with extended characters in string values, you must create separate templates with unique versions of the macro for each platform.

Distributing Macros

Once you've created a few macros, you may want to distribute your macros to other Word users. The way in which you distribute your macros depends on how you intend others to store, run, or modify them. There are also important issues to consider before distributing a macro for use in another language version of Word.

Distributing Macros with a Local Template

Distributing your macros to others can be as easy as distributing the template where your macros are stored. For example, if you've created a template for an automated form or a Wizard, you can distribute your macros by giving the template to others. They can then copy the template to their User Templates location specified on the File Locations tab in the Options dialog box (Tools menu). Alternatively, you can write a setup macro or program that automatically copies the template to the appropriate location using the **CopyFile** statement. You can use the **GetPrivateProfileString$()** function to retrieve the User Templates location from the system settings file or the registry.

Note Most users have a Normal template on their computer, so if your macros are currently stored in your Normal template you shouldn't distribute them by giving others your Normal template. Instead, create a new template and use the Organizer to copy the appropriate macros into the new template. Save and distribute the new template instead of your Normal template.

Prior to distributing a macro, you can make it "execute-only" so that other people can only run your macro. When a macro is execute-only, the Edit button in the Macro dialog box (Tools menu) is unavailable (dimmed) when the macro name is selected. The execute-only format is best used when you don't want other people to be able to view or edit your macro. To make a macro execute-only, use the **MacroCopy** statement in another macro. Be sure to make a backup copy of your macro prior to making it execute-only. Once the macro is execute-only, you won't be able to view or edit the instructions.

If you're working in a workgroup setting and want everyone to have access to your macros, you can copy your template to the Workgroup Templates location specified on the File Locations tab in the Options dialog box (Tools menu). The Workgroup Templates location allows multiple users to access a group of templates from one network share. Templates that are used by everyone in the workgroup are copied to this location. Templates from the User Templates and Workgroup Templates locations are available in the New dialog box (File menu). When you update your macros, you can copy the updated template to the Workgroup Templates location. This distribution technique ensures that everyone is using the latest version of your macros.

Distributing Macros with a Global Template

If the macros you want to distribute are not specific to a particular type of document, users may want to run your macro from any document (regardless of the attached template). To be run this way, the macro needs to be stored in a loaded global template. Users can temporarily load a global template by selecting the template in the Templates And Add-ins dialog box (Templates command, File menu). Alternatively, you can write a setup macro that uses the **AddAddIn** statement to load a template as a global template. The template is not, however, permanently loaded as a global template.

Templates stored in the Startup folder are automatically loaded as global templates when Word starts. If you want your global template loaded automatically, you can ask users to manually copy the file to their Startup folder, or you can write a setup macro. The setup macro can copy the template to the Startup folder using the **CopyFile** statement (use the **GetPrivateProfileString$()** function to retrieve the Startup folder location from the system settings file or the registry).

Loading templates globally consumes memory. A way to control this is to allow the user to dynamically load or unload the template at the click of a button. As a result, the template is only loaded into memory when the user needs to run the macros in the template. The following macro uses the **AddInState** statement to load or unload a global template.

```
Sub MAIN
state = AddInState("agenda.dot")     'check current state
If state = 1 Then
    AddInState "agenda.dot", 0       'load template
Else
    AddInState "agenda.dot", 1       'unload template
End If
End Sub
```

During an installation macro, this macro can be copied to the user's Normal template and assigned to a toolbar button. Use the **MacroCopy** or the **Organizer** statement to copy a macro to the Normal template, and use **AddButton** to add a toolbar button.

Another distribution technique is to write an AutoOpen macro that copies macros from the current template to the user's Normal template. Use the **MacroCopy** or **Organizer** statement to copy macros between templates. However, because users may have a number of macros already in their in Normal template or may have macros with the same names as the macros you want to copy, this technique is not the preferred way of distributing macros.

Distributing Macros Without a Template

If you want to distribute a macro without a template, you can save your macro as a text file. Open your macro in a macro-editing window and choose Save Copy As from the File menu. Type a file name and then choose Save. You can send the text file to another Word user. To run the macro, the user can copy the instructions from the text file into a new macro.

Distributing Macros Internationally

Microsoft Word is available in many different languages. At some point, you may need to distribute your macro to someone using a different language version of Word. Functionally, the programs are the same, but distributing macros between different language versions of Word requires some forethought.

WordBasic macros that are stored in templates are stored in a "tokenized" format. Macro keywords (statements and arguments such as "EditFind" and ".Name") are compressed and stored as three-byte tokens. When you edit a macro, the tokens are decoded into keywords for the current language of Word. For example, if a macro is written in the English (US) version of Word and then opened in the German version of Word, the WordBasic keywords will appear in German. The command to open a new document appears as "FileNew" in the English version of Word and "DateiNeu" in the German version of Word.

While macro keywords are translated, string values are not translated between languages. The following table demonstrates how English instructions are translated into German. The text enclosed in quotation marks is not translated.

English Instruction	Instruction translated into German
Insert "Hello World"	Einfügen "Hello World"
Style "Tag Line"	Formatvorlage "Tag Line"
EditGoTo "Bookmark2"	BearbeitenGeheZu "Bookmark2"
MsgBox "Insert Disk A"	MsgBox "Insert Disk A"

To run in multiple language versions of Word, your macro must determine the current language version and then use the appropriate string values for that version. Use the **AppInfo$()** function to determine the current language version, as shown in the following example.

```
Sub MAIN
lang$ = AppInfo$(16)              'Determine the language version
Select Case lang$
Case "English (US)"              'English version
    sometext$ = "Hello World"
Case "Deutsch"                   'German version
    sometext$ = "Hallo Welt"
Case Else
End Select
Insert sometext$
End Sub
```

For a list of language names returned by the **AppInfo$()** function, see **ToolsLanguage** in Part 2, "WordBasic Reference."

Tip Macros that use numerous strings can either use arrays to store strings for each language or return strings stored in a text file by using sequential file access.

The default measurement unit specified on the General tab in the Options dialog box (Tools menu) and the decimal separator in most languages is different from the defaults in the English (US) version of Word. Because of this, measurements you specify in statements such as **FormatParagraph** and **FilePageSetup** may not work as expected or may cause syntax errors when the macro is run in another language version of Word.

You can use the same technique described earlier for creating message string values to create measurement unit string values.

```
Sub MAIN
lang$ = AppInfo$(16)              'Determine the language version
Select Case lang$
Case "English (US)"              'English version
    points$ = "pt"
Case "Español"                   'Spanish version
    points$ = "pto"
Case Else
End Select
FormatParagraph .LeftIndent = "36" + points$
End Sub
```

An alternative is to specify a numeric value for arguments that accept either a numeric or string value, because the default measurement unit of a numeric value for a given argument is the same across multiple language versions of Word. For example, the default unit for a numeric value specified for the .LeftIndent argument of **FormatParagraph** is points. Therefore, the following statement works in any language version of Word.

```
FormatParagraph .LeftIndent = 36          '36 points in any language
```

For information about the default measurement units of numeric values for an argument of a specific statement, see the corresponding entry in Part 2, "WordBasic Reference."

The English (US) version of Word uses a period (.) for a decimal separator, while most European countries use a comma (,). You can use the **AppInfo$()** function to determine the decimal separator. Once you know the character, you can create a string that includes the decimal separator ("12.5" or "12,5" in the following example).

```
dec$ = AppInfo$(18)     'Get the decimal separator
FormatParagraph .LeftIndent = "12" + dec$ + "5 pt"
```

No matter which language version of Word you are using, if you specify a numeric value for an argument that accepts either a numeric or string value, you must use a period for the decimal separator. A comma decimal separator generates a syntax error. For example, if the following statements in an English (US) macro were opened in the German version of Word, the translated versions would be equivalent:

```
FormatParagraph .LeftIndent = "12,5 pt"
FormatParagraph .LeftIndent = 12.5
```

Optimizing Macros

When you first start to write macros, you'll probably be satisfied with simply getting the job done. However, when you write a macro that will be used many times or that will be used by other people, you should consider *optimizing* the macro so that it requires less time and memory to run. The following techniques will help you write smaller, faster macros.

- Specify only the arguments you need. The macro recorder explicitly sets all available arguments. For example, the macro recorder records the following instruction when you close the Paragraph dialog box.

```
FormatParagraph .LeftIndent = "0" + Chr$(34), .RightIndent = "0" +
Chr$(34), .Before = "0 pt", .After = "0 pt", .LineSpacingRule = 2,
.LineSpacing = "", .Alignment = 0, .WidowControl = 1, .KeepWithNext =
0, .KeepTogether = 0, .PageBreak = 0, .NoLineNum = 0, .DontHyphen =
0, .Tab = "0", .FirstIndent = "0" + Chr$(34)
```

However, if you only want to change the line spacing to double, you can delete the additional arguments from the **FormatParagraph** instruction. For example:

```
FormatParagraph .LineSpacingRule = 2
```

- A macro that changes the appearance of a document—such as a macro that changes the formatting of every table in a large document—will run faster when screen updating is turned off. Use the **ScreenUpdating** statement at the beginning of your macro to prevent screen updates while the macro is running. You can use the Print statement to let the user know the progress of the macro (for example, `Print "Working..."`).

If you want to show changes on the screen while a macro is running, you can improve performance by switching to normal view, using picture placeholders, disabling background repagination, and using the draft font, all of which are accomplished by the following instructions:

```
ViewNormal
ToolsOptionsView .PicturePlaceHolders = 1, .DraftFont = 1
ToolsOptionsGeneral .Pagination = 0
```

At the end of the macro, be sure to restore the settings back to the user's original settings.

- Minimize the use of global variables. Reuse local or temporary variables instead of defining additional variables. Also, reuse arrays and dialog records by using the **Redim** statement to reset the variables.

- Keep variable names, label names, and text between quotation marks short. These items don't "tokenize" when a macro is run and can slow down processing time. Remark statements (**REM**) and blank lines also don't tokenize and can slow down a macro.

  Note that while these tips may improve performance, your macro will lose readability. For this reason, it may be best to make these changes just before distributing a macro.

- The **Select Case** control structure executes faster than a complex **If...Then...Else** condition. The **For...Next** loop is faster than the **While...Wend** loop.

- The **GetText$()** function is faster than selecting text and using the **Selection$()** function. You can often use **GetSelStartPos()**, **GetSelEndPos()**, and **SetSelRange** instead of bookmarks. These commands are faster than setting and using bookmarks.

- Calling a subroutine in another macro is slower than calling a subroutine in the same macro. You may want to copy frequently called subroutines into the same macro.

- You cannot turn off the Undo or Redo commands on the Edit menu, nor can you change the maximum number of actions Word stores in the Undo or Redo lists (Word stores up to approximately 100 or the total number of actions in one document). If you are experiencing out-of-memory errors or slow performance, try periodically clearing the Undo and Redo lists by calling the following subroutine.

```
Sub ClearUndoList
Dim Dlg As ToolsRevisions
GetCurValues Dlg
ToolsRevisions .MarkRevisions = Abs(Dlg.MarkRevisions - 1)
ToolsRevisions .MarkRevisions = Dlg.MarkRevisions
End Sub
```

- If you are experiencing out-of-memory errors with a macro that makes extensive edits to a document, save the document periodically without fast saves active. For example, the following macro replaces all semicolons with tabs in a document. The **If** statement and count variable are used to save the document after every 50 replacements.

```
Sub MAIN
ToolsOptionsSave .FastSaves = 0
StartOfDocument
count = 0
EditFindClearFormatting
EditFind .Find = ";", .Direction = 0
While EditFindFound()
    count = count + 1
    EditClear
    Insert Chr$(9)
    If count = 50 Then
        FileSave
        count = 0
    End If
    RepeatFind
Wend
End Sub
```

- If possible, move commonly used routines into a Word add-in library (WLL). Word add-in libraries are faster and more efficient than thier equivalent WordBasic macros. For information on creating Word add-in libraries, see Appendix C, "Microsoft Word Application Programming Interface."

PART 2

WordBasic Reference

Language Differences Across Versions of Word

The *Microsoft Word Developer's Kit* documents the WordBasic programming language for the following versions of Microsoft Word:

- Microsoft Word versions 6.0, 6.0a, and 6.0c for Windows (referred to as Microsoft Word version 6.0 for Windows)
- Microsoft Word version 6.0 for the Macintosh
- Microsoft Word version 6.0 for Windows NT
- Microsoft Word for Windows 95 (referred to as Microsoft Word version 7.0)

All these versions of Word share a majority of WordBasic's functionality. However, there are a handful of differences in WordBasic between each version. For example:

- Word version 6.0 for the Macintosh cannot run statements such as **AppActivate** and **AppSendMessage** that rely on Windows features, while the Windows versions of Word cannot run statements such as **EditPublish** and **EditSubscribe** that rely on Macintosh features.
- None of the versions of Word earlier than Word version 7.0 can run statements and functions for Word features that were added to Word for Windows 95.
- In Word version 6.0 for Windows NT and Word version 7.0, the arguments for **GetPrivateProfileString$()** and **SetPrivateProfileString** changed to allow setting and returning values in the registry.

The following sections list these and other differences in detail. You can use this information along with the cross-platform programming guidelines in Chapter 9, "More WordBasicTechniques," (Part 1, "Learning WordBasic") to develop WordBasic macros that run without error in any version of Word listed earlier.

Statements and Functions Used Only in the Windows Versions of Word

The following table lists WordBasic statements and functions that rely on Windows features and therefore cannot be run in Word version 6.0 for the Macintosh.

Statement or function	Description
AppActivate; **AppClose**; **AppCount()**; **AppGetNames**, **AppGetNames()**; **AppHide**; **AppIsRunning()**; **AppMaximize**, **AppMaximize()**; **AppMinimize**, **AppMinimize()**; **AppMove**; **AppRestore**, **AppRestore()**; **AppSendMessage**; **AppShow**; **AppSize**; **AppWindowHeight**, **AppWindowHeight()**; **AppWindowPosLeft**, **AppWindowPosLeft()**; **AppWindowPosTop**, **AppWindowPosTop()**; **AppWindowWidth**, **AppWindowWidth()**	Control application windows
Connect	Connects to a disk or directory shared across the network
ControlRun	Runs the Clipboard or Control Panel
Environ$()	Returns a string associated with an MS-DOS environment variable
ExitWindows	Exits Windows
FilePrintSetup	Changes the active printer or its options
HelpWordPerfectHelp; **HelpWordPerfectHelpOptions**	Control the Help For WordPerfect™ Users feature
MicrosoftAccess; **MicrosoftPublisher**; **MicrosoftSchedule**; **RunPrintManager**	Start the specified application
ToggleScribbleMode	Toggles hand annotation mode on and off

Statements and Functions Used Only in Word Version 6.0 for the Macintosh

The following table lists WordBasic statements and functions that rely on Macintosh features and therefore cannot be run in any of the Windows versions of Word.

Statement or function	Description
AOCEAddRecipient; AOCEAuthenticateUser(); AOCEClearMailerField; AOCECountRecipients(); AOCEGetRecipient$(); AOCEGetSender$(); AOCEGetSubject$(); AOCESendMail; AOCESetSubject; FileAOCEAddMailer; FileAOCEDeleteMailer; FileAOCEExpandMailer; FileAOCEForwardMail; FileAOCENextLetter; FileAOCEReplyAllMail; FileAOCEReplyMail; FileAOCESendMail	Send and receive letters through PowerTalk™ and return information about the active letter
DlgStoreValues; DlgLoadValues, DlgLoadValues()	Save or retrieve custom dialog box settings
EditCopyAsPicture	Copies the selected text or object to the Clipboard as a picture
EditCreatePublisher; EditPublishOptions; EditSubscribeOptions; EditSubscribeTo	Use the publishing and subscribing features in Word for the Macintosh

Statement or function	Description
EditFindBorder; **EditFindFrame**; **EditFindTabs**; **EditReplaceBorder**; **EditReplaceFrame**; **EditReplaceTabs**	Specify additional formats in find and replace operations
FileCreator$(); **FileType$()**; **SetFileCreatorAndType**	Set and determine Macintosh application signatures and file types
FileDocumentLayout; **FileMacCustomPageSetupGX**; **FileMacPageSetup**; **FileMacPageSetupGX**	Control page formatting for the entire document or specified sections
FilePrintOneCopy	Prints a single copy of the active document
FileQuit	Exits Word
MacID$()	Converts a Macintosh application signature or file type to a value for use with **AppActivate**, **AppClose**, **AppCount**, **AppGetNames**, **AppGetNames()**, **AppIsRunning()**, **Files$()**, **FileOpen**, **Kill**, or **Shell**
MacScript, MacScript$()	Runs an AppleScript script
MountVolume	Connects to a disk or folder shared across the network
Outline, Outline(); **Shadow, Shadow()**	Apply additional character formats
ShowClipboard	Displays the Clipboard and its contents

Statements and Functions Used Only in Word Version 7.0

The following statements and functions were added to Word version 7.0 and therefore cannot be run in earlier versions of Word. For more detailed lists and descriptions of each new WordBasic statement and function, see "What's New in WordBasic" in Word version 7.0 Help.

Statement or function	Description
CountAutoCorrectExceptions(); **GetAutoCorrectException$()**; **IsAutoCorrectException()**; **ToolsAutoCorrectCapsLockOff**, **ToolsAutoCorrectCapsLockOff()**; **ToolsAutoCorrectExceptions**	Control new AutoCorrect features
AddAddress; **GetAddress$()**; **InsertAddress**; **MailMergeUseAddressBook**	Add addresses to or return addresses from the default MAPI address book

Statement or function	Description
Highlight; HighlightColor, HighlightColor()	Apply highlighting format
CountDocumentProperties(); DeleteDocumentProperty; DocumentPropertyExists(); DocumentPropertyName$(); DocumentPropertyType(); FileProperties; GetDocumentProperty(), GetDocumentProperty$(); IsCustomDocumentProperty(); IsDocumentPropertyReadOnly(); SetDocumentProperty; SetDocumentPropertyLink	Set and access built-in and custom document properties
EditFindHighlight; EditFindNotHighlight; EditReplaceHighlight; EditReplaceNotHighlight	Specify additional formats in find and replace operations
AutomaticChange; HelpMSN; ShowMe; TipWizard	Use new Help features
DocumentHasMisspellings(); NextMisspelling; SpellChecked, SpellChecked(); ToolsSpellingRecheckDocument	Control background spelling features
DocumentProtection()	Indicates the level of protection for the active document
FilePost	Posts the active document to a public folder in Microsoft Exchange
MailCheckNames; MailHideMessageHeader; MailMessageDelete; MailMessageForward; MailMessageMove; MailMessageNext; MailMessagePrevious; MailMessageProperties; MailMessageReply; MailMessageReplyAll; MailSelectNames	Manage Word Mail messages

Statements with Version-Specific Arguments

The following statements, which correspond to Word dialog boxes, have arguments that are ignored or are not available in every version of Word.

Statement	Version-specific arguments
ConvertObject	The .IconFilename and .DisplayIcon arguments are ignored in Word version 6.0 for the Macintosh.
DlgVisible	The *LastIdentifier* argument is not valid in Word version 6.0 for Windows.
EditFindFont	The .Outline and .Shadow arguments are valid in Word version 6.0 for the Macintosh only.
EditReplaceFont	The .Outline and .Shadow arguments are valid in Word version 6.0 for the Macintosh only.
FileFind	The .ShowFolders argument is valid in Word version 6.0 for the Macintosh only.
	The .SearchName, .Options, .PatternMatch, .View, .SortBy, .ListBy, .SelectedFile, .ShowFolders, .Add, and .Delete arguments are ignored in Word version 7.0.
FilePrint	The .OutputPrinter argument is valid in Word version 6.0 for the Macintosh only.
FilePrintSetup	The .DoNotSetAsSysDefault argument is valid in Word version 7.0 only.
FormatBordersAndShading	The .FineShading argument is ignored in the Windows versions of Word.
FormatFont	The .Outline and .Shadow arguments are valid in Word version 6.0 for the Macintosh only.
HelpTipOfTheDay	The .StartupTips argument is not valid in Word version 7.0.
InsertObject	The .IconFilename and .DisplayIcon arguments are ignored in Word version 6.0 for the Macintosh.
ToolsAutoCorrect	The .CapsLock argument is valid in Word version 7.0 only.
ToolsOptionsAutoFormat	The .ApplyBulletedLists, .ReplaceOrdinals, .ReplaceFractions, .ApplyBorders, .ApplyNumberedLists, and .ShowOptionsFor arguments are valid in Word version 7.0 only.

Statement	Version-specific arguments
ToolsOptionsCompatibility	The .ShowBreaksInFrames, .SwapBordersFacingPages, .SuppressTopSpacingMac5, .SpacingWholePoints, .PrintBodyTextBeforeHeader, .NoLeading, and .MWSmallCaps arguments are not valid in Word version 6.0 for Windows.
	The .NoSpaceForUL, .NoExtraLineSpacing, .TruncateFontHeight, and .SubFontBySize arguments are valid in Word version 7.0 only.
ToolsOptionsEdit	The .TabIndent argument is valid in Word version 7.0 only.
ToolsOptionsGeneral	The .Effects3D argument is ignored in Word version 7.0.
	The .ConfirmConversions and .TipWizardActive arguments are valid in Word version 7.0 only.
ToolsOptionsPrint	The .Draft and .Background arguments are ignored in Word version 6.0 for the Macintosh.
ToolsOptionsRevisions	The .HighlightColor argument is valid in Word version 7.0 only.
ToolsOptionsSpelling	The .AutomaticSpellChecking, .HideSpellingErrors, and .RecheckDocument arguments are valid in Word version 7.0 only.
ToolsOptionsView	The .Highlight argument is valid in Word version 7.0 only.
ViewToolbars	The .ToolTipsKey argument is valid in Word version 7.0 only.

Statements and Functions with Version-Specific Behavior

The following statments and functions exhibit different behavior depending on the version of Word in which they are run.

Statement or function	Version-specific behavior
AppInfo$()	The strings returned by the values 9 and 10 are meaningful only in Word version 6.0 for Windows running in Windows 3.*x* and Word version 6.0 for the Macintosh.
	The value 26 is valid in Word version 7.0 only.
Beep	In the Windows versions of Word, the sound produced by **Beep** is determined by the *ErrorType* argument; in Word version 6.0 for the Macintosh, **Beep** always produces the sound selected in the Sound control panel.

Statement or function	Version-specific behavior
DDEExecute	In Word version 6.0 for the Macintosh, you cannot use **DDEExecute** to send keystrokes to another application.
Declare	In Word version 6.0 for Windows, you can only declare external functions in 16-bit libraries.
	In Word version 6.0 for the Macintosh, you can only declare external functions in Word add-in libraries (WLLs).
	In Word version 6.0 for Windows NT and Word version 7.0, you can only declare external functions in 32-bit libraries. In addition, external function names are case-sensitive.
	For detailed information about using **Declare** in all versions of Word, see "Calling Routines in DLLs" in Chapter 9, "More WordBasic Techniques" (Part 1, "Learning WordBasic").
DlgSetPicture	In Word version 6.0 for the Macintosh, *PictureName$* accepts a value to indicate a PICT file stored in the resource fork of the template containing the macro.
DOSToWin$(), WinToDos$()	In Word version 6.0 for the Macintosh, these statements perform no translation and return the original string unchanged.
FileFind	In Word version 6.0 for the Macintosh, you use the .ShowFolders argument to group filenames by folder.
	In Word version 7.0, you cannot specify multiple folders with .SearchPath, and you cannot display the Find File dialog box using a **Dialog** or **Dialog()** instruction.
FileNameInfo$()	In Word version 6.0 for the Macintosh, FileNameInfo$(3) and FileNameInfo$(4) return the same value (since Macintosh filenames do not have "extensions").
	In Word version 6.0 for the Macintosh, FileNameInfo$(6) returns a string that begins with the zone and computer name where the specified file is stored.

Statement or function	Version-specific behavior
FileOpen	In Word version 6.0 for the Macintosh, you can use this statement to open only one file at a time.
	In Word version 6.0 for the Macintosh, if you open a document with **FileOpen**, the case of the document window's title will match the case of text specified by the .Name argument. For example, the instruction `FileOpen .Name = "my file"` opens a document called "My File" in a document window with the title "my file."
Files$()	In the Windows versions of Word, the question mark (?) and asterisk (*) wildcards are accepted as file specifiers. On the Macintosh, wildcards are not accepted; **MacID$()** is used instead.
GetAttr()	In Word version 6.0 for the Macintosh, the System and Archive attributes are not supported.
GetPrivateProfileString$()	In Word version 6.0 for Windows and Word version 6.0 for the Macintosh, the arguments specify sections and key names in a particular settings file. In Word version 6.0 for Windows NT and Word version 7.0, the arguments can specify keys and values in the registry.
GetSystemInfo, GetSystemInfo$()	In the Windows versions of Word, *Type* is a value from 21 to 32, and the size of the array filled by **GetSystemInfo** is 12 elements. In Word version 6.0 for the Macintosh, *Type* is a value from 512 to 523, and the size of the array is 15 elements.
	The strings returned by the values 23, 25 and 27 are meaningful only in Word version 6.0 for Windows running in Windows 3.*x*.
HelpExamplesAndDemos, HelpQuickPreview	In Word version 6.0 for Windows NT and Word version 7.0, the examples, demonstrations, and previews are not available and these statements generate errors.
InputBox$()	In the Windows versions of Word, if the user presses ENTER in an input box, **InputBox$()** returns `Chr$(11)+Chr$(10)`; in Word version 6.0 for the Macintosh, `Chr$(13)` is returned.
InsertSound	In the Windows versions of Word, starts Sound Recorder; in Word version 6.0 for the Macintosh, starts Microsoft Voice Annotation.
Kill	In the Windows versions of Word, the question mark (?) and asterisk (*) wildcards are accepted. On the Macintosh, wildcards are not accepted; **MacID$()** is used instead.

Statement or function	Version-specific behavior
ListCommands	This statement is not valid in Word version 6.0 for Windows.
MailMergeCreateDataSource; MailMergeDataSource$(); MailMergeEditDataSource; MailMergeOpenDataSource; MailMergeQueryOptions	ODBC functionality is not supported in Word version 6.0 for the Macintosh.
MsgBox, MsgBox()	In the Windows versions of Word, a *Type* value of 32 produces a question symbol; in Word version 6.0 for the Macintosh, it produces an information symbol. In Word version 6.0 for the Macintosh, a message box will not have a title bar if *Title$* is an empty string ("").
Name	In the Windows versions of Word, you can use this statement to move a file to another directory; in Word version 6.0 for the Macintosh, **Name** does not provide this capability.
Picture	In Word version 6.0 for the Macintosh, *PictureName$* accepts a value to indicate a PICT file stored in the resource fork of the template containing the macro.
ScreenUpdating	In Word version 6.0 for the Macintosh, the contents of document windows are not updated when screen updating is turned off, but document frames remain visible.
SendKeys	In Word version 6.0 for the Macintosh, you can use **SendKeys** to send keystrokes (10 or fewer) only to Word; you cannot use **SendKeys** to send keystrokes to other applications. Also, you can send a key combination that includes SHIFT by using the plus sign (+), but you cannot send key combinations that include OPTION or COMMAND.
SelInfo()	The value 37 is valid in Word version 7.0 only.
SetAttr	In Word version 6.0 for the Macintosh, the System and Archive attributes are not supported.
SetPrivateProfileString	In Word version 6.0 for Windows and Word version 6.0 for the Macintosh, the arguments specify settings, sections, and key names in a particular settings file. In Word version 6.0 for Windows NT and Word version 7.0, the arguments can specify settings, keys, and values in the registry.
ShadingPattern, ShadingPattern()	In Word version 6.0 for the Macintosh, shading pattern values 35 through 61 apply shading patterns in 2.5% increments.

Statement or function	Version-specific behavior
Shell	In the Windows versions of Word, the *WindowStyle* argument determines how an application started by **Shell** is displayed; in Word version 6.0 for the Macintosh, *WindowStyle* determines whether or not the application is activated. In Word version 6.0 for the Macintosh, you can use **MacID\$( )** to specify an application name.
ToolsAdvancedSettings	In Word version 6.0 for Windows NT and Word version 7.0, you cannot use this statement to modify settings in the registry.
ToolsCustomizeKeyboard	The Windows CTRL key is equivalent to the Macintosh COMMAND key; the Windows ALT key is equivalent to the Macintosh OPTION key. An additional value is available to assign the Macintosh CONTROL key.

Language Summary

WordBasic keywords are listed here by category. Refer to this section when you know what you want to do but not which commands you need to accomplish the task, or when you want to learn about related statements and functions. Keywords appear alphabetically in each list; some keywords appear in more than one category.

Address Book

AddAddress

GetAddress$()

InsertAddress

MailMergeUseAddressBook

Application Control

AppActivate

AppClose

AppCount()

AppGetNames, AppGetNames()

AppHide

AppInfo$()

AppIsRunning()

AppMaximize, AppMaximize()

AppMinimize, AppMinimize()

AppMove

AppRestore, AppRestore()

AppSendMessage

AppShow

AppSize

AppWindowHeight,
AppWindowHeight()

AppWindowPosLeft,
AppWindowPosLeft()

AppWindowPosTop,
AppWindowPosTop()

AppWindowWidth,
AppWindowWidth()

ControlRun

DDEExecute

DDEInitiate()

DDEPoke

DDERequest$()

DDETerminate

DDETerminateAll

DialogEditor

ExitWindows

FileExit

FileQuit

GetSystemInfo, GetSystemInfo$()

MacID$()

MacScript, MacScript$()

Microsoft*Application*

RunPrintManager

SendKeys

Shell

ShowClipboard

AutoCorrect

CountAutoCorrectExceptions()

GetAutoCorrect$()

GetAutoCorrectException$()

IsAutoCorrectException()

ToolsAutoCorrect

ToolsAutoCorrectCapsLockOff,
ToolsAutoCorrectCapsLockOff()

ToolsAutoCorrectDays,
ToolsAutoCorrectDays()

ToolsAutoCorrectExceptions

ToolsAutoCorrectInitialCaps,
ToolsAutoCorrectInitialCaps()

ToolsAutoCorrectReplaceText,
ToolsAutoCorrectReplaceText()

ToolsAutoCorrectSentenceCaps,
ToolsAutoCorrectSentenceCaps()

ToolsAutoCorrectSmartQuotes,
ToolsAutoCorrectSmartQuotes()

AutoText

AutoText

AutoTextName$()

CountAutoTextEntries()

EditAutoText

GetAutoText$()

InsertAutoText

Organizer

SetAutoText

Basic File Input/Output

Close

Eof()

Input

Input$()

Line Input

Lof()

Open

Print

Read

Seek, Seek()

Write

Bookmarks

BookmarkName$()

CmpBookmarks()

CopyBookmark

CountBookmarks()

EditBookmark

EmptyBookmark()

ExistingBookmark()

GetBookmark$()

SetEndOfBookmark

SetStartOfBookmark

Borders and Frames

BorderBottom, BorderBottom()

BorderInside, BorderInside()

BorderLeft, BorderLeft()

BorderLineStyle, BorderLineStyle()

BorderNone, BorderNone()

BorderOutside, BorderOutside()

BorderRight, BorderRight()

BorderTop, BorderTop()

FormatBordersAndShading

FormatDefineStyleBorders

FormatDefineStyleFrame

FormatFrame

InsertFrame

RemoveFrames

ShadingPattern, ShadingPattern()

ViewBorderToolbar

Branching and Control

Call

For...Next

Function...End Function

Goto

If...Then...Else

On Error

OnTime

Select Case

Stop

Sub...End Sub

While...Wend

Bullets and Numbering

DemoteList

FormatBullet

FormatBulletDefault,
FormatBulletDefault()

FormatBulletsAndNumbering

FormatDefineStyleNumbers

FormatMultilevel

FormatNumber

FormatNumberDefault,
FormatNumberDefault()

PromoteList

RemoveBulletsNumbers

SkipNumbering, SkipNumbering()

ToolsBulletListDefault

ToolsBulletsNumbers

ToolsNumberListDefault

Character Formatting

AllCaps, AllCaps()

Bold, Bold()

CharColor, CharColor()

CopyFormat

CountFonts()

CountLanguages()

DottedUnderline, DottedUnderline()

DoubleUnderline, DoubleUnderline()

Font, Font$()

FontSize, FontSize()

FontSizeSelect

FontSubstitution

FormatAddrFonts

FormatChangeCase

FormatDefineStyleFont

FormatDefineStyleLang

FormatFont

FormatRetAddrFonts

GrowFont

GrowFontOnePoint

Hidden, Hidden()

Highlight

HighlightColor, HighlightColor()

Italic, Italic()

Language, Language$()

NormalFontPosition

NormalFontSpacing

Outline, Outline()

PasteFormat

ResetChar, ResetChar()

Shadow, Shadow()

ShrinkFont

ShrinkFontOnePoint

SmallCaps, SmallCaps()

Strikethrough, Strikethrough()

Subscript, Subscript()

Superscript, Superscript()

SymbolFont

ToolsLanguage

Underline, Underline()

WordUnderline, WordUnderline()

Customization

AddButton

ChooseButtonImage

CopyButtonImage

CountKeys()

CountMenuItems()

CountMenus()

CountToolbarButtons()

CountToolbars()

DeleteButton

EditButtonImage   PasteButtonImage
KeyCode()   RenameMenu
KeyMacro$()   ResetButtonImage
ListCommands   SizeToolbar
MenuItemMacro$()   ToolbarButtonMacro$()
MenuItemText$()   ToolbarName$()
MenuMode   ToolbarState()
MenuText$()   ToolsCustomize
MoveButton   ToolsCustomizeKeyboard
MoveToolbar   ToolsCustomizeMenuBar
NewToolbar   ToolsCustomizeMenus

Date and Time

Date$()   Now()
DateSerial()   OnTime
DateValue()   Second()
Day()   Time$()
Days360()   TimeSerial()
Hour()   TimeValue()
InsertDateField   Today()
InsertDateTime   ToolsRevisionDate()
InsertTimeField   ToolsRevisionDate$()
Minute()   Weekday()
Month()   Year()

Definition and Declaration

Declare   Let
Dim   Redim

Dialog Box Definition and Control

Begin Dialog...End Dialog   ComboBox
CancelButton   Dialog, Dialog()
CheckBox

DialogEditor

FilePreview

DlgControlId()

GetCurValues

DlgEnable, DlgEnable()

GroupBox

DlgFilePreview, DlgFilePreview$()

InputBox$()

DlgFocus, DlgFocus$()

ListBox

DlgListBoxArray, DlgListBoxArray()

MsgBox, MsgBox()

DlgLoadValues, DlgLoadValues()

OKButton

DlgSetPicture

OptionButton

DlgStoreValues

OptionGroup

DlgText, DlgText$()

Picture

DlgUpdateFilePreview

PushButton

DlgValue, DlgValue()

Text

DlgVisible, DlgVisible()

TextBox

DropListBox

Disk Access and Management

ChDefaultDir

Kill

ChDir

MkDir

Connect

MountVolume

CopyFile

Name

CountDirectories()

PathFromMacPath$()

DefaultDir$()

PathFromWinPath$()

Files$()

RmDir

GetAttr()

SetAttr

GetDirectory$()

Documents, Templates, and Add-ins

AddAddIn, AddAddIn()

CountAddIns()

AddInState, AddInState()

CountDocumentVars()

ClearAddIns

CountFiles()

Converter$()

CountFoundFiles()

ConverterLookup()

DeleteAddIn

CopyFile

DisableInput

DocClose

DocumentStatistics

FileClose

FileCloseAll

FileConfirmConversions,
FileConfirmConversions()

FileCreator$()

FileDocumentLayout

FileFind

FileList

FileMacCustomPageSetupGX

FileMacPageSetup

FileMacPageSetupGX

FileName$()

FileNameFromWindow$()

FileNameInfo$()

FileNew

FileNewDefault

File*Number*

FileOpen

FilePageSetup

FilePrint

FilePrintDefault

FilePrintOneCopy

FilePrintPreview,
FilePrintPreview()

FilePrintPreviewFullScreen

FilePrintPreviewPages,
FilePrintPreviewPages()

FilePrintSetup

FileQuit

FileRoutingSlip

Files$()

FileSave

FileSaveAll

FileSaveAs

FileSendMail

FileSummaryInfo

FileTemplates

FileType$()

FoundFileName$()

GetAddInID()

GetAddInName$()

GetAttr()

GetDocumentVar$()

GetDocumentVarName$()

InsertFile

Kill

LockDocument, LockDocument()

MacroFileName$()

Name

Organizer

PathFromMacPath$()

PathFromWinPath$()

SaveTemplate

SelectionFileName$()

SetAttr

SetDocumentVar, SetDocumentVar()

ToolsOptionsFileLocations

ToolsOptionsPrint

Document Properties

CountDocumentProperties()

DeleteDocumentProperty

DocumentPropertyExists()

DocumentPropertyName$()

DocumentPropertyType()

GetDocumentProperty(),
GetDocumentProperty$()

IsCustomDocumentProperty()

IsDocumentPropertyReadOnly()

SetDocumentProperty

SetDocumentPropertyLink

Drawing

DrawAlign

DrawArc

DrawBringForward

DrawBringInFrontOfText

DrawBringToFront

DrawCallout

DrawClearRange

DrawCount()

DrawCountPolyPoints()

DrawDisassemblePicture

DrawEllipse

DrawExtendSelect

DrawFlipHorizontal

DrawFlipVertical

DrawFreeformPolygon

DrawGetCalloutTextbox

DrawGetPolyPoints

DrawGetType()

DrawGroup

DrawInsertWordPicture

DrawLine

DrawNudgeDown

DrawNudgeDownPixel

DrawNudgeLeft

DrawNudgeLeftPixel

DrawNudgeRight

DrawNudgeRightPixel

DrawNudgeUp

DrawNudgeUpPixel

DrawRectangle

DrawResetWordPicture

DrawReshape

DrawRotateLeft

DrawRotateRight

DrawRoundRectangle

DrawSelect, DrawSelect()

DrawSelectNext

DrawSelectPrevious

DrawSendBackward

DrawSendBehindText

DrawSendToBack

DrawSetCalloutTextbox

DrawSetInsertToAnchor

DrawSetInsertToTextbox

DrawSetPolyPoints

DrawSetRange, DrawSetRange()

DrawSnapToGrid

DrawTextBox

DrawUngroup

DrawUnselect

EditCopyAsPicture

FormatCallout

FormatDrawingObject

FormatPicture

InsertDrawing   ToggleScribbleMode
SelectDrawingObjects   ViewDrawingToolbar

Dynamic Data Exchange (DDE)

DDEExecute   FileCreator$( )
DDEInitiate( )   FileType$( )
DDEPoke   MacID$( )
DDERequest$( )   SendKeys
DDETerminate   SetFileCreatorAndType
DDETerminateAll

Editing

AutoMarkIndexEntries   EditUndo
Cancel   ExtendMode( )
ChangeCase, ChangeCase( )   Insert
CopyText   InsertAddCaption
DeleteBackWord   InsertAutoCaption
DeleteWord   InsertBreak
EditClear   InsertCaption
EditCopy   InsertCaptionNumbering
EditCopyAsPicture   InsertColumnBreak
EditCut   InsertCrossReference
EditFind   InsertIndex
EditGoTo   InsertPageBreak
EditLinks   InsertPageNumbers
EditObject   InsertSpike
EditPaste   InsertSymbol
EditPasteSpecial   InsertTableOfAuthorities
EditPicture   InsertTableOfContents
EditRedo   InsertTableOfFigures
EditRepeat   MarkCitation
EditReplace   MarkIndexEntry
EditTOACategory

MarkTableOfContentsEntry

Overtype, Overtype( )

MoveText

Spike

OK

ToolsOptionsEdit

Electronic Mail and Routing

AOCEAddRecipient

FileAOCESendMail

AOCEAuthenticateUser( )

FilePost

AOCEClearMailerField

FileRoutingSlip

AOCECountRecipients( )

FileSendMail

AOCEGetRecipient$( )

MailCheckNames

AOCEGetSender$( )

MailHideMessageHeader

AOCEGetSubject$( )

MailMessageDelete

AOCESendMail

MailMessageForward

AOCESetSubject

MailMessageMove

FileAOCEAddMailer

MailMessageNext

FileAOCEDeleteMailer

MailMessagePrevious

FileAOCEExpandMailer

MailMessageProperties

FileAOCEForwardMail

MailMessageReply

FileAOCENextLetter

MailMessageReplyAll

FileAOCEReplyAllMail

MailSelectNames

FileAOCEReplyMail

Environment

AppInfo$( )

IsExecuteOnly( )

Beep

IsMacro( )

CommandValid( )

IsTemplateDirty( )

DOSToWin$( )

LockDocument, LockDocument( )

Environ$( )

MacroFileName$( )

Err

MicrosoftSystemInfo

Error

ScreenRefresh

GetPrivateProfileString$( )

ScreenUpdating, ScreenUpdating( )

GetProfileString$( )

SelInfo( )

GetSystemInfo, GetSystemInfo$( )

SelType, SelType( )

IsDocumentDirty( )

SetDocumentDirty

SetPrivateProfileString,
SetPrivateProfileString()

SetProfileString

SetTemplateDirty

ViewMenus()

WaitCursor

WinToDOS$()

Fields

CheckBoxFormField

CountMergeFields()

DoFieldClick

DropDownFormField

EnableFormField

FormFieldOptions

GetFieldData$()

GetMergeField$()

InsertDateField

InsertDateTime

InsertField

InsertFieldChars

InsertFormField

InsertMergeField

InsertPageField

InsertTimeField

LockFields

MergeFieldName$()

NextField, NextField()

PrevField, PrevField()

PutFieldData

TextFormField

ToggleFieldDisplay

ToolsManageFields

UnlinkFields

UnlockFields

UpdateFields

UpdateSource

ViewFieldCodes, ViewFieldCodes()

Finding and Replacing

EditFind

EditFindBorder

EditFindClearFormatting

EditFindFont

EditFindFound()

EditFindFrame

EditFindHighlight

EditFindLang

EditFindNotHighlight

EditFindPara

EditFindStyle

EditFindTabs

EditReplace

EditReplaceBorder

EditReplaceClearFormatting

EditReplaceFont

EditReplaceFrame

EditReplaceHighlight

EditReplaceLang

EditReplaceNotHighlight

EditReplacePara

EditReplaceStyle

EditReplaceTabs

RepeatFind

Footnotes, Endnotes, and Annotations

AnnotationRefFromSel$()

EditConvertAllEndnotes

EditConvertAllFootnotes

EditConvertNotes

EditSwapAllNotes

GoToAnnotationScope

InsertAnnotation

InsertFootnote

NoteOptions

ResetNoteSepOrNotice

ShowAnnotationBy

ViewAnnotations, ViewAnnotations()

ViewEndnoteArea,
ViewEndnoteArea()

ViewEndnoteContNotice

ViewEndnoteContSeparator

ViewEndnoteSeparator

ViewFootnoteArea,
ViewFootnoteArea()

ViewFootnoteContNotice

ViewFootnoteContSeparator

ViewFootnotes, ViewFootnotes()

ViewFootnoteSeparator

Forms

AddDropDownItem

CheckBoxFormField

ClearFormField

DocumentProtection()

DropDownFormField

EnableFormField

FormFieldOptions

FormShading, FormShading()

GetFormResult(), GetFormResult$()

InsertFormField

RemoveAllDropDownItems

RemoveDropDownItem

SetFormResult

TextFormField

ToolsProtectDocument

ToolsProtectSection

ToolsUnprotectDocument

Help

Help

HelpAbout

HelpActiveWindow

HelpContents

HelpExamplesAndDemos

HelpIndex

HelpKeyboard

HelpMSN

HelpPSSHelp

HelpQuickPreview

HelpSearch

HelpTipOfTheDay

HelpTool

HelpUsingHelp

HelpWordPerfectHelp

HelpWordPerfectHelpOptions

ShowMe

TipWizard

Macros

CommandValid()

CountMacros()

DisableAutoMacros

IsExecuteOnly()

IsMacro()

KcyMacro$()

MacroCopy

MacroDesc$()

MacroFileName$()

MacroName$()

MacroNameFromWindow$()

MenuItemMacro$()

OnTime

Organizer

PauseRecorder

REM

ShowVars

ToolbarButtonMacro$()

ToolsMacro

Mail Merge

CountMergeFields()

GetMergeField$()

InsertMergeField

MailMerge

MailMergeAskToConvertChevrons,
MailMergeAskToConvertChevrons()

MailMergeCheck

MailMergeConvertChevrons,
MailMergeConvertChevrons()

MailMergeCreateDataSource

MailMergeCreateHeaderSource

MailMergeDataForm

MailMergeDataSource$()

MailMergeEditDataSource

MailMergeEditHeaderSource

MailMergeEditMainDocument

MailMergeFindRecord

MailMergeFirstRecord

MailMergeFoundRecord()

MailMergeGotoRecord,
MailMergeGotoRecord()

MailMergeHelper

MailMergeInsertAsk

MailMergeInsertFillIn

MailMergeInsertIf

MailMergeInsertMergeRec

MailMergeInsertMergeSeq

MailMergeInsertNext

MailMergeInsertNextIf

MailMergeInsertSet

MailMergeInsertSkipIf

MailMergeLastRecord

MailMergeMainDocumentType,
MailMergeMainDocumentType( )

MailMergeNextRecord

MailMergeOpenDataSource

MailMergeOpenHeaderSource

MailMergePrevRecord

MailMergeQueryOptions

MailMergeReset

MailMergeState( )

MailMergeToDoc

MailMergeToPrinter

MailMergeUseAddressBook

MailMergeViewData,
MailMergeViewData( )

MergeFieldName$( )

ToolsAddRecordDefault

ToolsRemoveRecordDefault

Moving the Insertion Point and Selecting

AtEndOfDocument( )

AtStartOfDocument( )

Cancel

CharLeft, CharLeft( )

CharRight, CharRight( )

ColumnSelect

EditSelectAll

EndOfColumn, EndOfColumn( )

EndOfDocument, EndOfDocument( )

EndOfLine, EndOfLine( )

EndOfRow, EndOfRow( )

EndOfWindow, EndOfWindow( )

ExtendMode( )

ExtendSelection

GetSelEndPos( )

GetSelStartPos( )

GetText$( )

GoBack

GoToAnnotationScope

GoToHeaderFooter

GoToNext*Item*

GoToPrevious*Item*

HLine

HPage

HScroll, HScroll( )

Insert

LineDown, LineDown( )

LineUp, LineUp( )

NextCell, NextCell( )

NextField, NextField( )

NextObject

NextPage, NextPage( )

NextWindow

OtherPane

PageDown, PageDown( )

PageUp, PageUp( )

ParaDown, ParaDown( )

ParaUp, ParaUp( )

PrevCell, PrevCell( )

PrevField, PrevField( )

PrevObject

PrevPage, PrevPage()

PrevWindow

SelectCurAlignment

SelectCurColor

SelectCurFont

SelectCurIndent

SelectCurSentence

SelectCurSpacing

SelectCurTabs

SelectCurWord

SelType, SelType()

SentLeft, SentLeft()

SentRight, SentRight()

SetSelRange

ShrinkSelection

StartOfColumn, StartOfColumn()

StartOfDocument, StartOfDocument()

StartOfLine, StartOfLine()

StartOfRow, StartOfRow()

StartOfWindow, StartOfWindow()

TableSelectColumn

TableSelectRow

TableSelectTable

VLine

VPage

VScroll, VScroll()

WordLeft, WordLeft()

WordRight, WordRight()

Object Linking and Embedding

ActivateObject

ConvertObject

EditCreatePublisher

EditLinks

EditObject

EditPasteSpecial

EditPicture

EditPublishOptions

EditSubscribeOptions

EditSubscribeTo

FileClosePicture

InsertChart

InsertDatabase

InsertEquation

InsertExcelTable

InsertObject

InsertPicture

InsertSound

InsertWordArt

Outlining and Master Documents

CreateSubdocument

DemoteToBodyText

InsertSubdocument

MergeSubdocument

OpenSubdocument

OutlineCollapse

OutlineDemote

OutlineExpand

OutlineLevel()

OutlineMoveDown

OutlineMoveUp

OutlinePromote

OutlineShowFirstLine,
OutlineShowFirstLine( )

OutlineShowFormat

RemoveSubdocument

ShowAllHeadings

ShowHeading*Number*

SplitSubdocument

ViewMasterDocument,
ViewMasterDocument( )

ViewOutline, ViewOutline( )

ViewToggleMasterDocument

Paragraph Formatting

CenterPara, CenterPara( )

CloseUpPara

CopyFormat

FormatDefineStylePara

FormatDefineStyleTabs

FormatDropCap

FormatParagraph

FormatTabs

HangingIndent

Indent

InsertPara

JustifyPara, JustifyPara( )

LeftPara, LeftPara( )

NextTab( )

OpenUpPara

ParaKeepLinesTogether,
ParaKeepLinesTogether( )

ParaKeepWithNext,
ParaKeepWithNext( )

ParaPageBreakBefore,
ParaPageBreakBefore( )

ParaWidowOrphanControl,
ParaWidowOrphanControl( )

PasteFormat

PrevTab( )

ResetPara, ResetPara( )

RightPara, RightPara( )

SpacePara1, SpacePara1( )

SpacePara15, SpacePara15( )

SpacePara2, SpacePara2( )

TabLeader$( )

TabType( )

UnHang

UnIndent

Proofing

CountToolsGrammarStatistics( )

DocumentHasMisspellings( )

NextMisspelling

SpellChecked, SpellChecked( )

ToolsGetSpelling, ToolsGetSpelling( )

ToolsGetSynonyms,
ToolsGetSynonyms( )

ToolsGrammar

ToolsGrammarStatisticsArray

ToolsHyphenation

ToolsHyphenationManual

ToolsOptionsGrammar

ToolsOptionsSpelling

ToolsSpelling

ToolsSpellingRecheckDocument

ToolsSpellSelection

ToolsThesaurus

Section and Document Formatting

CloseViewHeaderFooter

FileDocumentLayout

FileMacCustomPageSetupGX

FileMacPageSetup

FileMacPageSetupGX

FormatAutoFormat

FormatColumns

FormatHeaderFooterLink

FormatHeadingNumber

FormatHeadingNumbering

FormatPageNumber

FormatSectionLayout

GoToHeaderFooter

InsertSectionBreak

ShowNextHeaderFooter

ShowPrevHeaderFooter

ToggleHeaderFooterLink

ToggleMainTextLayer

TogglePortrait

ToolsOptionsAutoFormat

ViewFooter, ViewFooter( )

ViewHeader, ViewHeader( )

Strings and Numbers

Abs( )

Asc( )

Chr$( )

CleanString$( )

InStr( )

Int( )

LCase$( )

Left$( )

Len( )

LTrim$( )

Mid$( )

Right$( )

Rnd( )

RTrim$( )

Selection$( )

Sgn( )

SortArray

Str$( )

String$( )

UCase$( )

Val( )

Style Formatting

CountStyles()

FormatDefineStyleBorders

FormatDefineStyleFont

FormatDefineStyleFrame

FormatDefineStyleLang

FormatDefineStyleNumbers

FormatDefineStylePara

FormatDefineStyleTabs

FormatStyle

FormatStyleGallery

NormalStyle

Organizer

Style

StyleDesc$()

StyleName$()

Tables

FieldSeparator$, FieldSeparator$()

InsertExcelTable

NextCell, NextCell()

PrevCell, PrevCell()

TableAutoFormat

TableAutoSum

TableColumnWidth

TableDeleteCells

TableDeleteColumn

TableDeleteRow

TableFormula

TableGridlines, TableGridlines()

TableHeadings, TableHeadings()

TableInsertCells

TableInsertColumn

TableInsertRow

TableInsertTable

TableMergeCells

TableRowHeight

TableSelectColumn

TableSelectRow

TableSelectTable

TableSort

TableSortAToZ

TableSortZToA

TableSplit

TableSplitCells

TableToText

TableUpdateAutoFormat

TextToTable

Tools

DocumentProtection()

ToolsAdvancedSettings

ToolsCalculate, ToolsCalculate()

ToolsCompareVersions

ToolsCreateEnvelope

ToolsCreateLabels

ToolsCustomize

ToolsHyphenation

ToolsHyphenationManual

ToolsLanguage

ToolsMergeRevisions

ToolsOptions

ToolsOptionsAutoFormat

ToolsOptionsCompatibility

ToolsOptionsEdit

ToolsOptionsFileLocations

ToolsOptionsGeneral

ToolsOptionsPrint

ToolsOptionsRevisions

ToolsOptionsSave

ToolsOptionsUserInfo

ToolsOptionsView

ToolsProtectDocument

ToolsProtectSection

ToolsRepaginate

ToolsReviewRevisions

ToolsRevisionAuthor$()

ToolsRevisionDate()

ToolsRevisionDate$()

ToolsRevisions

ToolsRevisionType()

ToolsShrinkToFit

ToolsUnprotectDocument

ToolsWordCount

View

ClosePreview

CloseViewHeaderFooter

FilePrintPreview, FilePrintPreview()

FilePrintPreviewFullScreen

FilePrintPreviewPages,
FilePrintPreviewPages()

Magnifier, Magnifier()

ShowAll, ShowAll()

ShowNextHeaderFooter

ShowPrevHeaderFooter

ToggleFull

TogglePortrait

ToolsOptionsView

ViewAnnotations, ViewAnnotations()

ViewBorderToolbar

ViewDraft, ViewDraft()

ViewDrawingToolbar

ViewEndnoteArea,
ViewEndnoteArea()

ViewEndnoteContNotice

ViewEndnoteContSeparator

ViewEndnoteSeparator

ViewFieldCodes, ViewFieldCodes()

ViewFooter, ViewFooter()

ViewFootnoteArea,
ViewFootnoteArea()

ViewFootnoteContNotice

ViewFootnoteContSeparator

ViewFootnotes, ViewFootnotes()

ViewFootnoteSeparator

ViewHeader, ViewHeader()

ViewMasterDocument,
ViewMasterDocument()

ViewMenus()

ViewNormal, ViewNormal()

ViewOutline, ViewOutline()

ViewPage, ViewPage()

ViewRibbon, ViewRibbon()

ViewRuler, ViewRuler()

ViewStatusBar, ViewStatusBar()

ViewToggleMasterDocument

ViewToolbars

ViewZoom

ViewZoom100

ViewZoom200

ViewZoom75

ViewZoomPageWidth

ViewZoomWholePage

Windows

Activate

AppActivate

AppClose

AppCount()

AppGetNames, AppGetNames()

AppHide

AppMaximize, AppMaximize()

AppMinimize, AppMinimize()

AppMove

AppRestore, AppRestore()

AppShow

AppSize

AppWindowHeight,
AppWindowHeight()

AppWindowPosLeft,
AppWindowPosLeft()

AppWindowPosTop,
AppWindowPosTop()

AppWindowWidth,
AppWindowWidth()

ClosePane

CountWindows()

DocClose

DocMaximize, DocMaximize()

DocMinimize, DocMinimize()

DocMove

DocRestore

DocSize

DocSplit, DocSplit()

DocWindowHeight,
DocWindowHeight()

DocWindowPosLeft,
DocWindowPosLeft()

DocWindowPosTop,
DocWindowPosTop()

DocWindowWidth,
DocWindowWidth()

ExitWindows

FileNameFromWindow$()

HelpActiveWindow

IsMacro()

NextWindow

OtherPane

PrevWindow

Window()

WindowArrangeAll

WindowList

WindowName$()

WindowNewWindow

Window*Number*

WindowPane()

Statements and Functions

Statements and functions are listed alphabetically. Each statement or function name appears as a bold heading in the margin. One or more syntax statements follow the bold heading. Here is a syntax example:

CharLeft [*Count*] [*, Select*]

When you type an instruction, you must include all the items in the syntax that are formatted in bold. Items enclosed in brackets are optional. Do not type the brackets when including an optional item. Italic formatting indicates argument names or value placeholders that you replace with actual values or variables to which you've already assigned values.

For example, you could use any of the following **CharLeft** instructions in a macro:

```
CharLeft
CharLeft 1
CharLeft 1, 1
```

If you assigned acceptable values to the numeric variables move and extend, you could use the following **CharLeft** instruction:

```
CharLeft move, extend
```

Note that you must separate arguments with commas. The acceptable values for arguments are listed in the remarks following the syntax, usually in a table. Some syntax examples include required arguments. For example:

EditReplaceStyle .Style = *text*

To use this statement, you must include the .Style argument—note the period preceding the argument name. You must type all the text that appears in bold and supply a specific value or variable for the italic placeholder, as in the following examples:

```
EditReplaceStyle .Style = "Heading 1"
EditReplaceStyle .Style = "Normal"
```

Other statements and functions include a mixture of required and optional arguments:

EditAutoText .Name = *text* [, **.Context** = *number*] [, **.InsertAs** = *number*] [, **.Insert**] [, **.Add**] [, **.Delete**]

According to this syntax, you must include the first argument and a value, but the remaining arguments are optional. As the syntax indicates, every argument in your final macro instruction must be separated by a comma. For example:

```
EditAutoText .Name = "disclaimer", .Context = 1, .Add
```

For more information about WordBasic syntax, see Part 1, "Learning WordBasic," which includes many examples of the correct use of WordBasic statements and functions. WordBasic Help and most entries in this reference also include examples of how to use specific statements and functions. For more information about typographic conventions used in this book, see "About This Book" in the front matter.

Abs()

Syntax   **Abs(***n***)**

Remarks   Returns the absolute value of *n*. For example, Abs(-5) returns the value 5.

Example   This example toggles the display of hidden text. You can use this example as a model for toggling any check box in Word. In a Word dialog box, a selected check box has a value of 1; a cleared check box has a value of 0 (zero). The example reverses the current value of the check box by subtracting 1 from it and using **Abs()** to return the absolute value of the result.

```
Dim dlg As ToolsOptionsView
GetCurValues dlg
dlg.Hidden = Abs(dlg.Hidden - 1)
ToolsOptionsView dlg
```

See Also   **Int()**, **Rnd()**, **Sgn()**

Activate

Syntax   **Activate** *WindowTitle$* [, *PaneNum*]

Remarks   Activates the window with the specified *WindowTitle$*. You can use the **WindowName$()** function to store the name of a window in a variable and then use this variable with **Activate** when you need to activate that window. *WindowTitle$* must match a window name on the Window menu.

Argument	Explanation
WindowTitle$	The name of the window to activate, as it appears on the Window menu
PaneNum	The number of the pane to activate:
	1 or 2 Top pane
	3 or 4 Bottom pane

Example   This example stores the name of the active window, opens a document, and then reactivates the original window:

```
firstwin$ = WindowName$()
FileOpen "CHAP2.DOC"
Activate firstwin$
```

See Also   **DocSplit**, **NextWindow**, **OtherPane**, **PrevWindow**, **WindowList**, **WindowName$()**, **Window***Number*, **WindowPane()**

ActivateObject

Syntax   **ActivateObject**

Remarks   Activates the selected embedded object for editing, or plays the sound or video
file associated with the selected icon (for example, a sound file associated with
the microphone icon). **ActivateObject** is equivalent to double-clicking the
selected embedded object.

Example   This example moves the insertion point to the next Microsoft WordArt object and
activates it for editing:

```
EditGoTo "o'MSWordArt.2'"
ActivateObject
```

See Also   **EditGoTo**, **EditObject**

AddAddln, AddAddln()

Syntax   **AddAddIn** *AddIn$* [, *Load*]

AddAddIn(*AddIn$* [, *Load*])

Remarks   The **AddAddIn** statement adds a template or Word add-in library (WLL) to the
list of global templates and add-ins in the Templates And Add-ins dialog box
(Templates command, File menu).

Argument	Explanation
AddIn$	The path and filename of the template or WLL
Load	Specifies whether to load the template or add-in after adding it to the list:
	0 (zero) Does not load the template or add-in
	1 or omitted Loads the template or add-in

The **AddAddIn**() function behaves the same as the statement and also returns a
value corresponding to the position of the global template or add-in in the list,
where 1 is the first template or add-in, 2 is the second, and so on. This value may
be used with other add-in statements and functions.

You can use functions defined in a loaded WLL in a macro. Functions that take no arguments may be used just like WordBasic statements; you can return the names of these functions using **CountMacros()** and **MacroName$()**. Functions in the WLL that take arguments must be declared using the **Declare** statement.

For more information on loading global templates and add-ins, see "add-in programs" in Help. For more information on using functions in WLLs, see Chapter 9, "More WordBasic Techniques," in Part 1, "Learning WordBasic."

Example

These examples use **AddAddIn()** to load a global template and define the variable id as a numeric identifier for the template:

```
id = AddAddIn("C:\MYDOT\MYLIB.DOT", 1)          'Windows example
id = AddAddIn("HD:TEMPLATES:LIB TEMPLATE", 1)   'Macintosh example
```

The following example fills an array with the names of functions in loaded WLLs that can be called from a macro just like Word commands:

```
nonaddins = CountMacros(0) + CountMacros(1)
loaded = CountMacros(0, 0, 1)
size = loaded - 1
If size >= 0 Then
    Dim loaded$(size)
    For count = 0 To size
        pos = (count + 1) + nonaddins
        loaded$(count) = MacroName$(pos, 0, 1)
    Next count
End If
```

See Also

AddInState, ClearAddIns, CountAddIns(), CountMacros(), DeleteAddIn, GetAddInID(), GetAddInName$(), MacroName$()

AddAddress

Syntax

AddAddress *AddressProperties$( )*

Remarks

Adds a new address to the default address book. **AddAddress** is available only if Windows 95 and either Microsoft Exchange or Schedule+ version 2.0 are installed. In Word version 6.0, **AddAddress** is unavailable and generates an error.

Argument	Explanation
AddressProperties$( )	A predefined two-dimensional array that contains the information for the new address you want to add.
	The following example demonstrates how the array should be defined:
	`Dim addrprop$(numprops - 1, 1)`
	where `numprops` is the number of properties you want to specify for the address.
	The first dimension of each two-dimensional element (for example, `addrprop$(0, 0)`) specifies a valid property name. The second dimension (for example, `addrprop$(0, 1)`) specifies the text value for that property.
	For a complete list of valid property names available in the Personal Address Book in Microsoft Exchange, see the table of properties later in this topic.
	For more information about how to create a two-dimensional array, see **Dim**.

The following is a list of the most common address book properties used to get or define address information. These property names correspond to the options in the Properties dialog box of the Personal Address Book in Microsoft Exchange. You can also use the hexadecimal identifier for any MAPI property supported by Microsoft Exchange or any other application that supports MAPI address books. For a complete list of the MAPI properties and their hexadecimal identifiers, see your MAPI software development kit documentation.

Property	Explanation
PR_ADDRTYPE	The addressee's electronic mail address type
PR_BEEPER_TELEPHONE_NUMBER	The addressee's beeper telephone number
PR_BUSINESS_FAX_NUMBER	The addressee's business fax number
PR_CAR_TELEPHONE_NUMBER	The addressee's car telephone number
PR_CELLULAR_TELEPHONE_NUMBER	The addressee's cellular telephone number
PR_COMMENT	The text included on the Notes tab for the address entry
PR_COMPANY_NAME	The name of the addressee's company
PR_COUNTRY	The addressee's country
PR_DEPARTMENT_NAME	The name of the addressee's department within the company

Property	Explanation
PR_DISPLAY_NAME	The name displayed in the Address Book dialog box
PR_EMAIL_ADDRESS	The addressee's electronic mail address
PR_GIVEN_NAME	The addressee's given name, or first name
PR_HOME_FAX_NUMBER	The addressee's home fax number
PR_HOME_TELEPHONE_NUMBER	The addressee's home telephone number
PR_INITIALS	The addressee's initials
PR_LOCALITY	The addressee's city or locality
PR_LOCATION	The addressee's location, in the format *buildingnumber /roomnumber*; for example, "16/3000" represents room 3000 in building 16
PR_OFFICE_LOCATION	The addressee's office location
PR_OFFICE_TELEPHONE_NUMBER	The addressee's office telephone number
PR_OFFICE2_TELEPHONE_NUMBER	The addressee's second office telephone number
PR_OTHER_TELEPHONE_NUMBER	The addressee's alternate telephone number (other than home or office)
PR_POSTAL_CODE	The addressee's postal code
PR_PRIMARY_FAX_NUMBER	The addressee's primary fax number
PR_PRIMARY_TELEPHONE_NUMBER	The addressee's primary telephone number
PR_RADIO_TELEPHONE_NUMBER	The addressee's radio telephone number
PR_STATE_OR_PROVINCE	The addressee's state or province
PR_STREET_ADDRESS	The addressee's street address
PR_SURNAME	The addressee's surname, or last name
PR_TITLE	The addressee's job title

Example

This example creates a two-dimensional array with valid MAPI address book properties and their respective values, and it adds the new address to the default address book.

```
Dim addressText$(6,1)
addressText$(0,0) = "PR_SURNAME"
addressText$(0,1) = "Smith"
addressText$(1,0) = "PR_GIVEN_NAME"
addressText$(1,1) = "Phil"
addressText$(2,0) = "PR_STREET_ADDRESS"
addressText$(2,1) = "12345 55th Avenue #5432"
addressText$(3,0) = "PR_LOCALITY"
addressText$(3,1) = "New York"
addressText$(4,0) = "PR_STATE_OR_PROVINCE"
addressText$(4,1) = "NY"
addressText$(5,0) = "PR_POSTAL_CODE"
addressText$(5,1) = "10023"
addressText$(6,0) = "PR_DISPLAY_NAME"
addressText$(6,1) = "Phil Smith"
AddAddress addressText$()
```

See Also   **GetAddress$()**, **InsertAddress**, **ToolsCreateEnvelope**, **ToolsCreateLabels**

AddButton

Syntax   **AddButton** *Toolbar$*, *Position*, *Category*, *Name$* [, *ButtonTxtOrImageNum*[$]] [, *Context*] [, *CommandValue$*]

Remarks   Adds to a toolbar a button that runs a built-in command or macro, applies a font or style, or inserts an AutoText entry.

Argument	Explanation
Toolbar$	The name of the toolbar as listed in the Toolbars dialog box (View menu).
Position	A number corresponding to the position on the specified toolbar at which to add the button, where 1 is the first position, 2 is the second position, and so on. Note that a list box or space counts as one position.
Category	The type of item to be assigned: 1 Built-in commands 2 Macros 3 Fonts 4 AutoText entries 5 Styles
Name$	The name of the built-in command, macro, font, AutoText entry, or style to associate with the button. To add a space to a toolbar, specify an empty string ("").

Argument	Explanation
ButtonTxtOrImageNum[$]	The text you want to appear on the button, or a number corresponding to an image for the button in the built-in set of buttons, where 0 (zero) is no image (for a blank button), 1 is the first image, 2 is the second image, and so on. For a list of button images and their associated numbers, see "Toolbar Button Images and Numbers" in Help.
Context	Determines where the new toolbar assignment is stored:
	0 (zero) or omitted Normal template
	1 Active template
CommandValue$	Additional text, if any, required for the command specified by *Name$*. For example, if *Name$* is "Color," *CommandValue$* specifies the color. For more information, see the second table in **ToolsCustomizeMenus**.

Example

This example replaces the button at position 11 on the Formatting toolbar with button image 80. The built-in command assigned to the button is Color, which requires that an additional value be specified (in this case, "2" for the color blue).

```
DeleteButton "Formatting", 11, 0
AddButton "Formatting", 11, 1, "Color", 80, 0, "2"
```

See Also

ChooseButtonImage, CopyButtonImage, DeleteButton, EditButtonImage, MoveButton, PasteButtonImage, ResetButtonImage

AddDropDownItem

Syntax

AddDropDownItem *BookmarkName$, ItemText$*

Remarks

Adds an item to a drop-down form field. A drop-down form field can hold as many as 25 items; if you attempt to add more than 25 items, an error occurs.

Argument	Explanation
BookmarkName$	The name of the bookmark that marks the drop-down form field. If you specify a bookmark that does not mark a drop-down form field, an error occurs.
ItemText$	The item to add to the drop-down form field.

Example

This example adds three items to the drop-down form field marked by the bookmark "Dropdown1":

```
AddDropDownItem "Dropdown1", "Red"
AddDropDownItem "Dropdown1", "Blue"
AddDropDownItem "Dropdown1", "Green"
```

See Also

DropDownFormField, RemoveAllDropDownItems, RemoveDropDownItem

AddInState, AddInState()

Syntax

AddInState *AddIn*, *Load*

AddInState *AddIn$*, *Load*

AddInState(*AddIn*)

AddInState(*AddIn$*)

Remarks

The **AddInState** statement loads or unloads the specified global template or add-in listed in the Templates And Add-ins dialog box (Templates command, File menu). You can specify the global template or add-in as a number or as text.

Argument	Explanation
AddIn	A number corresponding to the global template or add-in's position in the list of global templates and add-ins, where 1 is the first template or add-in, 2 is the second, and so on
AddIn$	The path and filename of the global template or add-in
Load	Specifies whether to load or unload the global template or add-in:
	0 (zero) Unloads the template or add-in
	1 Loads the template or add-in

The **AddInState()** function returns the following values. Note that the return values are additive. For example, if the specified add-in is loaded, a WLL, and in the Startup folder, **AddInState()** returns 7 (the sum of 1, 2, and 4).

Value	Explanation
0 (zero)	If none of the following descriptions are true of the global template or add-in.
1	If the global template or add-in is loaded.
2	If it is a Word add-in library (WLL).
4	If the global template or add-in loads automatically; templates and add-ins in the folder specified by the Startup option on the File Locations tab in the Options dialog box (Tools menu) load automatically.

See Also

AddAddIn, **ClearAddIns**, **CountAddIns()**, **DeleteAddIn**, **GetAddInID()**, **GetAddInName$()**

AllCaps, AllCaps()

Syntax   **AllCaps** [*On*]

AllCaps()

Remarks   The **AllCaps** statement adds or removes the all caps character format for the current selection, or controls all caps formatting for characters to be inserted at the insertion point.

Argument	Explanation
On	Specifies whether to add or remove the all caps format:
	1 Formats the selection as all caps
	0 (zero) Removes the all caps format
	Omitted Toggles the all caps format

The **AllCaps()** function returns the following values.

Value	Explanation
0 (zero)	If none of the selection is formatted as all caps
−1	If part of the selection is formatted as all caps
1	If all the selection is formatted as all caps

Example   This example applies the all caps format to the entire selection if part of the selection is formatted as all caps:

```
If AllCaps() = -1 Then AllCaps 1
```

See Also   **FormatFont**

AnnotationRefFromSel$()

Syntax   **AnnotationRefFromSel$()**

Remarks   Returns the annotation mark associated with the insertion point or the beginning of the selection. The insertion point must be immediately before an annotation mark in the document window or within an annotation in the annotation pane; otherwise, the characters "[0]" are returned.

Note that because Word treats an entire annotation mark as an individual character, you cannot return the characters within an annotation mark using the **Selection$()** function.

Example   This example goes to the next annotation mark and sets the variable `mark$` to the characters in the annotation mark:

```
EditGoTo "a"
mark$ = AnnotationRefFromSel$()
```

See Also   **EditGoTo**, **GoToAnnotationScope**, **GoToNext***Item*, **GoToPrevious***Item*, **ShowAnnotationBy**

AOCEAddRecipient

Syntax   **AOCEAddRecipient** *Recipient$* [, *AddressType*] [, *MailSlot$*]

Remarks   Adds the specified recipient address to the mailer attached to the active document. **AOCEAddRecipient** is available only on the Macintosh and only if PowerTalk™ is installed.

Argument	Explanation
Recipient$	The address of the recipient
AddressType	Specifies the list to add the recipient to:
	13 or omitted "To" list
	14 "Cc" list
	15 "Bcc" list (the recipient's name appears in neither the "To" nor "Cc" lists)
MailSlot$	Specifies how the user will receive the document (for example, "AppleTalk®" or "Fax")

See Also   **AOCECountRecipients()**, **AOCEGetRecipient$()**, **FileAOCEAddMailer**

AOCEAuthenticateUser()

Syntax   **AOCEAuthenticateUser(**[*AllowPrompt*]**)**

Remarks   Returns −1 if the user has logged on to PowerTalk and 0 (zero) if not. A mailer need not be attached to the active document for this function to work. **AOCEAuthenticateUser()** is available only on the Macintosh and only if PowerTalk is installed.

Argument	Explanation
AllowPrompt	If the user has not logged on to PowerTalk, specifies whether or not to display a dialog box prompting the user to type an access code to unlock the key chain:
	0 (zero) No dialog box appears.
	1 or omitted The dialog box appears.

See Also   **AOCEGetSender$()**

AOCEClearMailerField

Syntax

AOCEClearMailerField *FieldNumber*

Remarks

Clears the specified field in the mailer attached to the active document.
AOCEClearMailerField is available only on the Macintosh and only if
PowerTalk is installed.

Argument	Explanation
FieldNumber	The field in the mailer you want to clear:
	20 "Recipient" field
	22 "Subject" field
	26 "Enclosures" field
	The "From" field cannot be cleared.

See Also

FileAOCEDeleteMailer

AOCECountRecipients()

Syntax

AOCECountRecipients(*AddressType*)

Remarks

Returns the number of recipients in the mailer attached to the active document.
AOCECountRecipients() is available only on the Macintosh and only if
PowerTalk is installed.

Argument	Explanation
AddressType	The type of recipients to count:
	0 (zero) All recipients
	13 "To" recipients
	14 "Cc" recipients
	15 "Bcc" recipients

See Also

AOCEAddRecipient, AOCEGetRecipient$()

AOCEGetRecipient$()

Syntax

AOCEGetRecipient$(*RecipientNumber* [, *AddressType*])

Remarks

Returns the address of the specified recipient. **AOCEGetRecipient$**() is
available only on the Macintosh and only if PowerTalk is installed.

Argument	Explanation
RecipientNumber	A number between 1 and **AOCECountRecipients**(*AddressType*) specifying the recipient whose address you want to return.
AddressType	Specifies the list from which you want to return an address:
	13 or omitted "To" list
	14 "Cc" list
	15 "Bcc" list

See Also   **AOCEAddRecipient**, **AOCECountRecipients**(), **AOCEGetSender$**(), **AOCEGetSubject$**()

AOCEGetSender$()

Syntax   **AOCEGetSender$**()

Remarks   Returns the address in the "From" field in the mailer attached to the active document. **AOCEGetSender** is available only on the Macintosh and only if PowerTalk is installed.

See Also   **AOCEAuthenticateUser**(), **AOCEGetSubject$**(), **AOCEGetRecipient$**()

AOCEGetSubject$()

Syntax   **AOCEGetSubject$**()

Remarks   Returns the text in the "Subject" field in the mailer attached to the active document. **AOCEGetSubject$**() is available only on the Macintosh and only if PowerTalk is installed.

See Also   **AOCEGetRecipient$**(), **AOCEGetSender$**(), **AOCESetSubject**

AOCESendMail

Syntax   **AOCESendMail** [*SignLetter*] [, *Priority*] [, *SendAppleMail*] [, *SendImage*] [, *SendWordDoc*] [, *Format$*]

Remarks   Sends the active document to the recipients specified in the attached mailer. **AOCESendMail** is available only on the Macintosh and only if PowerTalk is installed.

Argument	Explanation
SignLetter	If 1, the sender is prompted to select a signer file.
Priority	Sets a priority:
	1 Normal
	2 Low
	3 High
Format$	If *SendWordDoc* is 1, the name of the format, as listed under Save File As Type in the Save As dialog box (File menu). Word Document is the default format.

You can specify one or more of the following formats.

Argument	Explanation
SendAppleMail	If 1, the recipient may open the letter from the standard interchange, or "AppleMail," format.
SendImage	If 1, the recipient may open the letter from image, or "Snapshot," format.
SendWordDoc	If 1, the recipient may open the letter from the file format specified by *Format$*.

See Also   **FileAOCEForwardMail, FileAOCESendMail, FileSendMail**

AOCESetSubject

Syntax   **AOCESetSubject** *Subject$*

Remarks   Inserts the specified text in the "Subject" field of the mailer attached to the active document. **AOCESetSubject** is available only on the Macintosh and only if PowerTalk is installed.

See Also   **AOCEGetSubject$()**

AppActivate

Syntax   **AppActivate** *WindowName$* [, *Immediate*]

Remarks   Activates a running application.

Argument	Explanation
WindowName$	In Windows, the name of the application window to activate, as it appears in the title bar or Task List. It is not necessary to specify the entire window name. For example, to indicate a window named "Notepad - FILES.TXT," you can specify "Notepad - FILES.TXT," "Notepad," or even "Note." The first window name in the Task List that matches the beginning of the specified string is affected. The case of characters is not significant in *WindowName$*.
	On the Macintosh, *WindowName$* is the application name or the signature returned by the **MacID$()** function. It is generally preferable to use the signature instead of the application name (for example, `MacID$("XCEL")` instead of `"Microsoft Excel"`) because, unlike the application name, the signature never changes.
Immediate	Specifies when to switch to the other application:
	0 (zero) or omitted If Word is not active, Word flashes its title bar or icon, waits for the user to activate Word, and then activates the other application.
	1 Word immediately activates the other application, even if Word is not the active application.

Example

This Windows example activates File Manager if it is running and starts File Manager if it is not running:

```
If AppIsRunning("File Manager") Then
    AppActivate "File Manager"
Else
    Shell "WINFILE.EXE"
End If
```

This Macintosh example activates Microsoft Excel if it is running and starts Microsoft Excel if it is not running.

```
If AppIsRunning(MacID$("XCEL") Then
    AppActivate MacID$("XCEL")
Else
    Shell MacID$("XCEL")
End If
```

Note that the Macintosh example could be shortened to `Shell MacID$("XCEL")` because, unlike in Windows, **Shell** on the Macintosh does not start a second instance of an application if it is already running.

See Also

AppClose, **AppGetNames**, **AppIsRunning()**, **MacID$()**, **Microsoft***Application*, **Shell**

AppClose

Syntax   **AppClose** [*WindowName$*]

Remarks   Closes the specified application.

Argument	Explanation
WindowName$	In Windows, a string that matches the beginning of an application window name, as it appears in the title bar or Task List. If omitted, Word is assumed. On the Macintosh, *WindowName$* is either the application name or the signature returned by **MacID$()**. For more information on *WindowName$*, see **AppActivate**.

Example   This example closes Microsoft Excel if it is running:

```
If AppIsRunning("Microsoft Excel") Then
    AppClose "Microsoft Excel"
End If
```

On the Macintosh, you can rewrite the previous example as follows, using **MacID$()** to specify the Microsoft Excel signature. This ensures the example will work even if the user has changed the filename for Microsoft Excel.

```
If AppIsRunning(MacID$("XCEL")) Then
    AppClose MacID$("XCEL")
End If
```

See Also   **AppActivate, AppIsRunning(), FileExit, FileQuit, MacID$(), Shell**

AppCount()

Syntax   **AppCount()**

Remarks   Returns the number of open applications (including hidden applications that do not appear in the Task List (Windows) or on the Application menu (Macintosh)). For an example, see **AppGetNames**.

See Also   **AppGetNames**

AppGetNames, AppGetNames()

Syntax

AppGetNames *ArrayVariable$( )*

AppGetNames(*ArrayVariable$( )*)

Remarks

The **AppGetNames** statement fills a previously defined string array with the names of open application windows (including hidden application windows that do not appear in the Task List (Windows) or on the Application menu (Macintosh)). If *ArrayVariable$( )* has fewer elements than the number of open applications, the array is filled with as many names as there are elements, and an error does not occur.

The **AppGetNames()** function carries out the same action and also returns the number of open application windows (including hidden application windows that do not appear in the Task List (Windows) or on the Application menu (Macintosh)). **AppGetNames()** returns the same value as **AppCount()**.

Example

This example inserts a list of application window names at the insertion point:

```
size = AppCount() - 1
Dim winnames$(size)
AppGetNames winnames$()
For i = 0 To size
    Insert winnames$(i)
    InsertPara
Next
```

See Also

AppActivate, AppClose, AppCount(), AppIsRunning()

AppHide

Syntax

AppHide [*WindowName$*]

Remarks

In Windows, hides the specified application and removes its window name from the Task List. On the Macintosh, **AppHide** is not available and generates an error.

Argument	Explanation
WindowName$	A string that matches the beginning of an application window name, as it appears in the title bar or Task List. If omitted, Word is assumed. For more information on *WindowName$*, see **AppActivate**.

See Also

AppClose, AppShow

AppInfo$()

Syntax   **AppInfo$(***Type***)**

Remarks   Returns one of 24 types of information about the Word application. Note that the
GetSystemInfo$() function returns similar information. Also, you can use the
GetSystemInfo statement to fill an array with system information.

Type is one of the following numeric codes, specifying the type of information to
return.

Type	**Explanation**
1	Environment (for example, "Windows 3.10" or "Macintosh 7.1").
2	Word version number (for example, "6.0").
3	Returns 1 if Word is in a special mode (for example, **CopyText** or **MoveText** mode).
4	In Windows, distance from the left edge of the screen to the left border of the Word window, in points (72 points = 1 inch). Note that when Word is maximized, AppInfo$(4) returns a negative value to indicate the borders are beyond the edge of the screen (this value varies depending on the width of the borders). On the Macintosh, AppInfo$(4) returns −1.
5	In Windows, distance from the top of the screen to the top border of the Word window, in points. Note that when Word is maximized, AppInfo$(5) returns a negative value to indicate the borders are beyond the edge of the screen (this value varies depending on the width of the borders). On the Macintosh, AppInfo$(5) returns 1.
6	Width of the workspace, in points. In Windows, the width increases as you widen the Word window. Note that increasing the zoom percentage decreases the return value, and vice versa.
7	Height of the workspace, in points; the height increases as you hide Word screen elements or, in Windows, increase the height of the Word window. Note that increasing the zoom percentage decreases the return value, and vice versa.
8	Returns 1 if the application is maximized (on the Macintosh, this is always the case).
9	Total memory, in kilobytes. In Windows 95 and Windows NT, this value returns 0 (zero).
10	Available memory, in kilobytes. In Windows 95 and Windows NT, this value returns 0 (zero).
13	Returns −1 if a math coprocessor is installed.
14	Returns −1 if a mouse is installed.
15	Available disk space, in kilobytes.
16	Returns the language version of Word. For example, returns "Français" for the French version of Word. For a list of languages, see **ToolsLanguage**.

Type	Explanation
17	Returns the list separator setting.
18	Returns the decimal setting.
19	Returns the thousands separator.
20	Returns the currency symbol.
21	Returns the clock format.
22	Returns the A.M. string.
23	Returns the P.M. string.
24	Returns the time separator.
25	Returns the date separator.
26	In Windows NT, returns 1 if the A.M. and P.M. strings are displayed before time values or 0 (zero) if they are displayed after. In Windows 95, returns 0 (zero). In Word version 6.0, this value is not available and generates an error.

Example

This example displays a message box containing the version number of Word:

```
ver$ = AppInfo$(2)
MsgBox ver$, "Microsoft Word Version", 64
```

The following macro shows how you might use a user-defined function to check the current platform before running an instruction. This technique is useful for macros designed to run both in Windows and on the Macintosh.

```
Sub Main
    If fMac Then MsgBox "Current platform is Macintosh"
End Sub

Function fMac
    a = InStr(AppInfo$(1), "Macintosh")
    If a Then fMac = -1
End Function
```

See Also

AppGetNames, GetSystemInfo

ApplsRunning()

Syntax   **AppIsRunning**(*WindowName$*)

Remarks   Returns –1 if the specified application is running or 0 (zero) if it is not.

Argument	Explanation
WindowName$	In Windows, a string that matches the beginning of an application window name, as it appears in the title bar or Task List. On the Macintosh, *WindowName$* is either the application name or the signature returned by **MacID$( )**. For more information on *WindowName$*, see **AppActivate**.

For an example, see **AppActivate**.

See Also   **AppActivate**, **AppClose**, **MacID$( )**, **MicrosoftApplication**

AppMaximize, AppMaximize()

Syntax   **AppMaximize** [*WindowName$*] [, *State*]

AppMaximize([*WindowName$*])

Remarks   In Windows, the **AppMaximize** statement maximizes or restores the specified application.

Argument	Explanation
WindowName$	A string that matches the beginning of an application window name, as it appears in the title bar or Task List (Windows). If omitted, Word is assumed. For more information on *WindowName$*, see **AppActivate**.
State	Specifies whether to maximize or restore the application: 0 (zero) Restores the application 1 Maximizes the application Omitted Toggles between restored and maximized states If the state of the application changes, it is activated. If the state does not change (for example, if you run the instruction AppMaximize "Microsoft Excel", 1 and Microsoft Excel is already maximized), the application is not activated.

The **AppMaximize**( ) function returns the following values.

Value	Explanation
–1	If the application is maximized
0 (zero)	If the application is not maximized

On the Macintosh, **AppMaximize** and **AppMaximize**( ) are not available and generate errors.

See Also   **AppMinimize**, **AppMove**, **AppRestore**, **AppSize**, **DocMaximize**

AppMinimize, AppMinimize()

Syntax   **AppMinimize** [*WindowName$*] [, *State*]

AppMinimize([*WindowName$*])

Remarks   In Windows, the **AppMinimize** statement minimizes or restores the specified application.

Argument	Explanation
WindowName$	A string that matches the beginning of an application window name, as it appears in the title bar or Task List (Windows). If omitted, Word is assumed. For more information on *WindowName$*, see **AppActivate**.
State	Specifies whether to minimize or restore the application: 0 (zero) Restores the application. 1 Minimizes the application. Omitted Toggles between restored and minimized states. If the application is restored from an icon, it is activated. If the state does not change or if the application is minimized, the application is not activated.

Note If an untrapped error occurs in a macro while Word is minimized, the macro halts and the Word icon flashes. When Word is restored, it displays a message indicating the nature of the error.

The **AppMinimize**( ) function returns the following values.

Value	Explanation
–1	If the application is minimized
0 (zero)	If the application is not minimized

On the Macintosh, **AppMinimize** and **AppMinimize**( ) are not available and generate errors.

See Also   **AppMaximize, AppMove, AppRestore, AppSize, DocMinimize**

AppMove

Syntax   **AppMove** [*WindowName$*,] *HorizPos*, *VertPos*

Remarks   In Windows, moves the specified application window or icon to a position relative to the upper-left corner of the screen. If the application is maximized, an error occurs. On the Macintosh, **AppMove** is not available and generates an error.

Argument	Explanation
WindowName$	A string that matches the beginning of an application window or icon name, as it appears in the title bar or Task List (Windows). If omitted, Word is assumed. For more information on *WindowName$*, see **AppActivate**.
HorizPos, *VertPos*	The horizontal (*HorizPos*) and vertical (*VertPos*) distance from the upper-left corner of the screen to the upper-left corner of the application window or icon, in points (72 points = 1 inch). Negative measurements are allowed only if you specify *WindowName$*.

Example   This Windows example starts Microsoft Excel if it is not running and then arranges Word and Microsoft Excel into nonoverlapping windows, each one-half the height of the screen:

```
If AppIsRunning("Microsoft Excel") = 0 Then MicrosoftExcel
AppRestore
AppMove 0, 0
AppSize 480, 180
AppRestore "Microsoft Excel"
AppMove "Microsoft Excel", 0, 180
AppSize "Microsoft Excel", 480, 180
```

See Also   **AppRestore, AppSize, AppWindowPosLeft, AppWindowPosTop, DocMove**

AppRestore, AppRestore()

Syntax   **AppRestore** [*WindowName$*]

AppRestore([*WindowName$*])

Remarks   In Windows, the **AppRestore** statement restores the specified application from a maximized or minimized state and activates the application. If the specified application is already restored, **AppRestore** has no effect.

Argument	Explanation
WindowName$	A string that matches the beginning of an application window name, as it appears in the title bar or Task List (Windows). If omitted, Word is assumed. For more information on *WindowName$*, see **AppActivate**.

The **AppRestore()** function returns the following values.

Value	Explanation
−1	If the application is restored
0 (zero)	If the application is not restored

For an example, see **AppMove**.

On the Macintosh, **AppRestore** and **AppRestore()** are not available and generate errors.

See Also   **AppMaximize**, **AppMinimize**, **AppMove**, **AppSize**, **DocRestore**

AppSendMessage

Syntax   **AppSendMessage** [*WindowName$,*] *Message,* *Wparam,* *Lparam*

Remarks   Sends a Windows message and its associated parameters to the application specified by *WindowName$*. On the Macintosh, **AppSendMessage** is not available and generates an error.

Argument	Explanation
WindowName$	A string that matches the beginning of an application window name, as it appears in the title bar or Task List (Windows). If omitted, Word is assumed. For more information on *WindowName$*, see **AppActivate**.
Message	A decimal number corresponding to the message you want to send. If you have the Microsoft Windows 3.1 Software Development Kit or the Microsoft Win32 Software Development Kit, you can look up the name of the message in WINDOWS.H and then convert the associated hexadecimal number to a decimal number using Calculator.

Argument	Explanation
Wparam, Lparam	Parameters appropriate for the message you are sending. For information on what these values represent, see the reference topic for the message in the *Microsoft Windows 3.1 Programmer's Reference, Volume 3,* available in the Microsoft Windows 3.1 Software Development Kit or from Microsoft Press, or in the *Programmer's API Reference, Volume 5*, available in the Microsoft Win32 Software Development Kit or from Microsoft Press. To retrieve the appropriate values, you may need to use the Spy utility (which comes with the Microsoft Windows 3.1 SDK or the Microsoft Win32 SDK).

Example

This Windows 3.*x* example starts the Windows Help application and then sends it a message that displays the Open dialog box. The number 273 is the decimal value associated with the message WM_COMMAND and 1101 is the parameter that specifies the Open command. *Lparam* is ignored in this case, but must still be specified as 0 (zero).

```
Shell "WINHELP.EXE"
AppSendMessage "Windows Help", 273, 1101, 0
```

See Also

AppActivate, AppIsRunning(), DDEExecute, DDEPoke

AppShow

Syntax

AppShow [*WindowName$*]

Remarks

In Windows, makes visible and activates an application previously hidden with **AppHide** and restores the application window name to the Task List. If the application is not hidden, **AppShow** has no effect. On the Macintosh, **AppShow** is not available and generates an error.

Argument	Explanation
WindowName$	A string that matches the beginning of an application window name, as it would appear in the title bar or Task List (Windows) if the application were visible. If omitted, Word is assumed. For more information on *WindowName$*, see **AppActivate**.

See Also

AppActivate, AppHide

AppSize

Syntax

AppSize [*WindowName$*,] *Width*, *Height*

Remarks

In Windows, sizes an application window to a specified width and height. If the application is maximized or minimized, an error occurs. On the Macintosh, **AppSize** is not available and generates an error.

Argument	Explanation
WindowName$	A string that matches the beginning of an application window name, as it appears in the title bar or Task List (Windows). If omitted, Word is assumed. For more information on *WindowName$*, see **AppActivate**.
Width, *Height*	The width and height of the application window, in points (72 points = 1 inch).

For an example, see **AppMove**.

See Also   **AppMove**, **AppRestore**, **AppWindowHeight**, **AppWindowWidth**, **DocSize**

AppWindowHeight, AppWindowHeight()

Syntax   **AppWindowHeight** [*WindowName$***,**] *Height*

AppWindowHeight([*WindowName$*])

Remarks   In Windows, the **AppWindowHeight** statement adjusts the height of an application window to a specified number of points (if *WindowName$* is omitted, Word is assumed). **AppWindowHeight** allows you to change the height of a window without affecting its width (unlike **AppSize**). The **AppWindowHeight**() function returns the height of an application window, in points. For argument descriptions, see **AppSize**.

On the Macintosh, **AppWindowHeight** and **AppWindowHeight()** are not available and generate errors.

See Also   **AppSize**, **AppWindowPosLeft**, **AppWindowPosTop**, **AppWindowWidth**

AppWindowPosLeft, AppWindowPosLeft()

Syntax   **AppWindowPosLeft** [*WindowName$***,**] *HorizPos*

AppWindowPosLeft([*WindowName$*])

Remarks   In Windows, the **AppWindowPosLeft** statement moves an application window or icon to a horizontal position specified in points (if *WindowName$* is omitted, Word is assumed). **AppWindowPosLeft** allows you to change the horizontal position of
a window or icon without affecting its vertical position (unlike **AppMove**). The **AppWindowPosLeft**() function returns the horizontal position of an application window or icon, in points. For argument descriptions, see **AppMove**.

On the Macintosh, **AppWindowPosLeft** and **AppWindowPosLeft()** are not available and generate errors.

See Also   **AppMove**, **AppWindowHeight**, **AppWindowPosTop**, **AppWindowWidth**

AppWindowPosTop, AppWindowPosTop()

Syntax   **AppWindowPosTop** [*WindowName$,*] *VertPos*

AppWindowPosTop([*WindowName$*])

Remarks   In Windows, the **AppWindowPosTop** statement moves an application window or icon to a vertical position specified in points (if *WindowName$* is omitted, Word is assumed). **AppWindowPosTop** allows you to change the vertical position of a window or icon without affecting its horizontal position (unlike **AppMove**). The **AppWindowPosTop**() function returns the vertical position of an application window or icon, in points. For argument descriptions, see **AppMove**.

On the Macintosh, **AppWindowPosTop** and **AppWindowPosTop**() are not available and generate errors.

See Also   **AppMove, AppWindowHeight, AppWindowPosLeft, AppWindowWidth**

AppWindowWidth, AppWindowWidth()

Syntax   **AppWindowWidth** [*WindowName$,*] *Width*

AppWindowWidth([*WindowName$*])

Remarks   In Windows, the **AppWindowWidth** statement adjusts the width of an application window to a specified number of points (if *WindowName$* is omitted, Word is assumed). **AppWindowWidth** allows you to change the width of a window without affecting its height (unlike **AppSize**). The **AppWindowWidth**() function returns the width of an application window, in points. For argument descriptions, see **AppSize**.

On the Macintosh, **AppWindowWidth** and **AppWindowWidth**() are not available and generate errors.

See Also   **AppSize, AppWindowHeight, AppWindowPosLeft, AppWindowPosTop**

Asc()

Syntax   **Asc**(*a$*)

Remarks   Returns the character code of the first character in *a$*. Although "Asc" is short for ASCII, **Asc**() actually returns ANSI codes. The function name is preserved for compatibility purposes. You can use the syntax **Asc(Selection$())** to return the code for the character to the right of the insertion point (for example, to test for a paragraph mark).

Example   This example moves to the beginning of the next paragraph and checks the character to the right of the insertion point. If the character is a paragraph mark, indicating an empty paragraph, a message box is displayed.

```
ParaDown
If Asc(Selection$()) = 13 Then
    ans = MsgBox("Empty paragraph. Continue?", 4)
End If
```

See Also   **Chr$(), Len()**

AtEndOfDocument()

Syntax   **AtEndOfDocument()**

Remarks   Returns −1 if the insertion point is at the end of the document or 0 (zero) if it is not. Unlike the **EndOfDocument()** function, **AtEndOfDocument()** does not move the insertion point.

See Also   **AtStartOfDocument(), EndOfDocument**

AtStartOfDocument()

Syntax   **AtStartOfDocument()**

Remarks   Returns −1 if the insertion point is at the beginning of the document or 0 (zero) if it is not. Unlike the **StartOfDocument()** function, **AtStartOfDocument()** does not move the insertion point.

See Also   **AtEndOfDocument(), StartOfDocument**

AutoMarkIndexEntries

Syntax   **AutoMarkIndexEntries** *ConcordanceFilename$*

Remarks   Automatically indexes the active document using *ConcordanceFilename$*, the path and filename of a concordance file. A concordance file is a Word document containing a two-column table with terms to index in the first column and index entries in the second column. The **AutoMarkIndexEntries** statement inserts an XE (Index Entry) field with the appropriate entry text after each occurrence of the terms listed in the first column of the concordance file.

See Also   **MarkIndexEntry**

AutomaticChange

Syntax   **AutomaticChange**

Remarks   Performs an AutoFormat action when there is a change suggested by the TipWizard. The **AutomaticChange** statement corresponds to the Change button on the TipWizard toolbar. In Word version 6.0, **AutomaticChange** is unavailable and generates an error.

See Also   **Help**, **ShowMe**

AutoText

Syntax   **AutoText**

Remarks   Displays the AutoText dialog box if there is a selection (and proposes up to the first 32 characters of the selection for the unique entry name) or, if there is no selection, attempts to match the text before or surrounding the insertion point with an AutoText entry and insert the entry (including its formatting, if any). Word looks for the entry first in the active template, then in the Normal template, and finally in each loaded global template in the order listed in the Templates And Add-ins dialog box (File menu). If no match can be made, an error occurs. **AutoText** corresponds to the AutoText button on the Standard toolbar.

See Also   **AutoTextName$()**, **CountAutoTextEntries()**, **EditAutoText**, **GetAutoText$()**, **InsertAutoText**, **SetAutoText**

AutoTextName$()

Syntax   **AutoTextName$(***Count* [*, Context*]**)**

Remarks   Returns the name of an AutoText entry in the specified context.

Argument	Explanation
Count	The number of the AutoText entry, from 1 to the total number of AutoText entries defined in the given context (you can obtain the total using **CountAutoTextEntries()**). AutoText entries are listed in alphabetic order.
Context	The context in which to return the name of an AutoText entry:
	0 (zero) or omitted Normal template and any loaded global templates
	1 Active template
	Note that if *Context* is 1 and the active template is the Normal template, **AutoTextName$()** generates an error.

Example

This example creates a new document that lists all AutoText entries in the Normal template and any loaded global templates. Entry names are inserted with bold formatting and are followed by the contents of the entry.

```
FileNewDefault
For count = 1 To CountAutoTextEntries()
    a$ = AutoTextName$(count)
    Bold 1 : Insert a$
    InsertPara
    Bold 0 : EditAutoText .Name = a$, .Insert
    InsertPara : InsertPara
Next
```

See Also

AutoText, CountAutoTextEntries(), EditAutoText, GetAutoText$(), InsertAutoText, SetAutoText

Beep

Syntax

Beep [*ErrorType*]

Remarks

Causes the computer's speaker to produce a sound. A typical use of **Beep** is to signal the end of a long process or to indicate that an error has occurred.

In Windows, **Beep** produces the sound associated with the specified error type. You associate sounds with error types using the Sound option in Control Panel. If there isn't a sound device installed, **Beep** produces the default sound through the computer speaker, regardless of the value of *ErrorType*.

On the Macintosh, **Beep** produces the sound selected in the Sound control panel, regardless of the value of *ErrorType*.

Argument	Explanation
ErrorType	In Windows, the type of sound, as specified in Control Panel.
	-1 Default sound from the computer speaker
	0 (zero) or omitted Default sound
	16 Critical stop
	32 Question
	48 Exclamation
	64 Asterisk
	If there is no sound associated with the specified error type, Word produces the default sound.

Note In Windows 3.*x*, a beep will not sound if the [Windows] section of WIN.INI includes the line Beep = No. In Windows NT, a beep will not sound if the Beep setting has the value "No" in the HKEY_CURRENT_USER\Control Panel\Sound key.

Examples

This example produces a beep immediately before displaying an input box:

```
Beep
name$ = InputBox$("The macro has finished running. " + \
                        "Save document as:")
```

The following example makes the computer beep three times. The second **For**...**Next** loop nested within the first one provides a delay between beeps. In effect, the delay loop makes Word count to a thousand before producing the next beep. Without the delay loop, Word would produce beeps so quickly that they would sound like a single, continuous beep. You can vary the delay between beeps by increasing or decreasing the end value of the second **For**...**Next** loop. For example, changing the end value to 5000 would increase the delay between beeps; changing it to 100 would decrease the delay.

```
Sub BeepThreeTimes
    For x = 1 to 3
        Beep
        For timer = 1 To 1000    'Delay loop between beeps
        Next timer
    Next x
End Sub
```

Begin Dialog...End Dialog

Syntax

Begin Dialog UserDialog [*HorizPos*, *VertPos*,] *Width*, *Height*, *Title$* [, *.DialogFunction*]
    Series of dialog box definition instructions
End Dialog

Remarks

Encloses the instructions that define a dialog box you create within a macro. A dialog box definition consists of a series of instructions that define different elements of the dialog box, such as the OK button, Cancel button, and so on. Dialog box elements are also known as *dialog box controls*.

The easiest way to create a dialog box is to use the Dialog Editor. With the Dialog Editor, you can use the mouse to design the dialog box. The Dialog Editor then creates the WordBasic code needed to define the dialog box. For information on creating and working with dialog boxes, see Chapter 5, "Working with Custom Dialog Boxes," in Part 1, "Learning WordBasic."

Note Every custom dialog box must contain at least one command button so the user can close the dialog box. For that reason, a dialog box definition must include either an **OKButton**, a **CancelButton**, or a **PushButton** instruction; otherwise, a WordBasic error will occur when the macro is run.

Argument	Explanation
HorizPos, *VertPos*	The horizontal and vertical distance of the upper-left corner of the dialog box from the upper-left corner of the Word window, in increments of 1/8 and 1/12 of the System font (Windows) or the dialog font (Macintosh). If *HorizPos* and *VertPos* are not specified, Word centers the dialog box within the Word window.
Width, *Height*	The width and height of the dialog box, in increments of 1/8 and 1/12 of the System font (Windows) or the dialog font (Macintosh).
Title$	The text that is displayed in the title bar of the dialog box. If you do not specify *HorizPos* and *VertPos*, or if you do specify *.DialogFunction*, you can omit *Title$*. If *Title$* is not specified, the application name is used.
.DialogFunction	The name of a dialog function associated with the dialog box; used for dialog boxes that update dynamically while the dialog box is displayed.

You can use the tab key to move between controls in a dialog box. The order of the instructions in a dialog box definition determines the tabbing order in the dialog box. By default, the dialog control represented by the first instruction in the dialog box definition will be selected when the dialog box is displayed. However, you can override this default by using the **DlgFocus** statement in a dialog function. You can also use the **Dialog** statement to specify the default button for a dialog box.

Example

This example defines and displays a dialog box (shown after the instructions) that includes every dialog box control available. Note that the **Picture** instruction refers to a Windows metafile graphic in the CLIPART folder, installed by Word. On the Macintosh, substitute the path and filename HD:WORD 6:CLIP ART:BIRD.

Once you have defined a dialog box with **Begin Dialog...End Dialog**, you need two additional instructions to display it: a **Dim** instruction that defines a dialog record in which the dialog box's values are stored, and a **Dialog** instruction that displays the dialog box. Note that a dialog function is required to display a document in the **FilePreview** control. For information on dialog functions, see Chapter 5, "Working with Custom Dialog Boxes," in Part 1, "Learning WordBasic."

```
Sub MAIN
Dim MyList$(2)
MyList$(0) = "Blue"
MyList$(1) = "Green"
MyList$(2) = "Red"
Begin Dialog UserDialog 612, 226, "Every Dialog Box Control", \
    .DlgFunction
    ComboBox 8, 76, 176, 111, MyList$(), .ComboBox1
```

```
            CheckBox 198, 79, 180, 16, "&Check Box", .CheckBox1
            ListBox 195, 102, 189, 83, MyList$(), .ListBox1
            DropListBox 417, 5, 179, 108, MyList$(), .DropListBox1
            Text 417, 186, 35, 13, "&Text"
            TextBox 417, 199, 179, 18, .TextBox1
            GroupBox 7, 4, 177, 65, "&Group Box"
            OptionGroup  .OptionGroup1
                OptionButton 17, 16, 148, 16, "Option Button &1"
                OptionButton 17, 33, 148, 16, "Option Button &2"
                OptionButton 17, 50, 148, 16, "Option Button &3"
            Picture 199, 7, 181, 62, "C:\WINWORD\CLIPART\BIRD.WMF", 0, .Picture1
            FilePreview 417, 31, 179, 148, .fileprev
            PushButton 10, 199, 108, 21, "&PushButton"
            CancelButton 131, 199, 108, 21
            OKButton 253, 199, 108, 21
        End Dialog
        Dim sampleDlg As UserDialog
        DisableInput 1
        button = Dialog(sampleDlg)
        DisableInput 0
        End Sub
        Function DlgFunction(identifier$, action, suppvalue)
            'A dialog function is required to display
            'a document in the FilePreview control.
        End Function
```

See Also   **CancelButton**, **CheckBox**, **ComboBox**, **Dialog**, **Dim**, **DropListBox**,
FilePreview, **GroupBox**, **ListBox**, **OKButton**, **OptionButton**, **OptionGroup**,
Picture, **PushButton**, **Text**, **TextBox**

Bold, Bold()

Syntax

Bold [*On*]

Bold()

Remarks

The **Bold** statement adds or removes the bold character format for the current selection, or controls bold formatting for characters to be inserted at the insertion point.

Argument	Explanation
On	Specifies whether to add or remove the bold format:
	1 Formats the selection as bold
	0 (zero) Removes the bold format
	Omitted Toggles the bold format

The **Bold**() function returns the following values.

Value	Explanation
0 (zero)	If none of the selection is formatted as bold
–1	If part of the selection is formatted as bold
1	If all the selection is formatted as bold

Example

This example applies the bold format to the entire selection if part of the selection is formatted as bold:

```
If Bold( ) = -1 Then Bold 1
```

See Also

FormatFont

BookmarkName$()

Syntax

BookmarkName$(*Count*)

Remarks

Returns the name of the bookmark specified by *Count*.

Argument	Explanation
Count	The number of the bookmark, from 1 to the total number of bookmarks defined for the active document (you can obtain the total using **CountBookmarks**()). The order of bookmark names is determined by the order of the bookmarks in the document.
	You must specify *Count*; otherwise, the function returns an error. For example, a$ = BookmarkName$( ) generates an error.

Example   This example puts a list of every bookmark name in a document into the array
mark$(). You could use this array to present a list of bookmark names in a dialog
box. Note that the size of the array is one less than the number of bookmarks
because the subscript for the first array element is 0 (zero), not 1.

```
numBookmarks = CountBookmarks()
arraySize = numBookmarks - 1
Dim mark$(arraySize)
For n = 0 To arraySize
    mark$(n) = BookmarkName$(n + 1)
Next
```

See Also   **CountBookmarks()**, **GetBookmark$()**

BorderBottom, BorderBottom()

Syntax   **BorderBottom** [*On*]

BorderBottom()

Remarks   The **BorderBottom** statement applies or removes a bottom border for the selected
paragraphs, table cells, or graphic. Note that when you apply a bottom border to a
series of paragraphs or table rows, the border appears only beneath the last
paragraph or row in the series. If you want a border to separate each paragraph or
row, use **BorderInside**.

Argument	Explanation
On	Specifies whether to apply or remove a bottom border:
	1 Applies the border
	0 (zero) Removes the border
	Omitted Toggles the border

The **BorderBottom**() function returns the following values.

Value	Explanation
0 (zero)	If at least one of the selected items has no bottom border or if the selection contains a mixture of items (for example, a paragraph and a table cell)
1	If each item in the selection is of the same type and has a bottom border

Example	This example applies a bottom border using one of two line styles, depending on whether the selection is within a table. If the selection is within a table, a double border is applied; otherwise, a thick, single border is applied.

```
If SelInfo(12) = - 1 Then
    BorderLineStyle 8
    BorderBottom 1
Else
    BorderLineStyle 4
    BorderBottom 1
End If
```

See Also	**BorderInside, BorderLeft, BorderLineStyle, BorderNone, BorderOutside, BorderRight, BorderTop, FormatBordersAndShading, ShadingPattern**

BorderInside, BorderInside()

Syntax	**BorderInside** [*On*]
	BorderInside( )
Remarks	The **BorderInside** statement applies or removes inside borders for the selected paragraphs or table cells. The following illustrations show inside borders within a series of paragraphs and a table.

Inside borders for paragraphs   Inside borders for a table

The **BorderInside**() function returns either 0 (zero) or 1, depending on whether all the selected paragraphs or table cells are formatted with an inside border. Note that **BorderInside**() returns 0 (zero) if the selection is a single table cell, regardless of the borders applied to the surrounding group of cells; a single table cell can have bottom, left, right, and top borders, but not inside borders.

For complete descriptions of arguments and return values, see **BorderBottom**.

See Also	**BorderBottom, BorderLeft, BorderLineStyle, BorderNone, BorderOutside, BorderRight, BorderTop, FormatBordersAndShading, ShadingPattern**

BorderLeft, BorderLeft()

Syntax   **BorderLeft** [*On*]

BorderLeft()

Remarks   The **BorderLeft** statement applies or removes left borders for the selected paragraphs, table cells, or graphic. The **BorderLeft**() function returns either 0 (zero) or 1, depending on whether the selected graphic or all the selected paragraphs or table cells are formatted with a left border.

For complete descriptions of arguments and return values, see **BorderBottom**.

See Also   **BorderBottom**, **BorderInside**, **BorderLineStyle**, **BorderNone**, **BorderOutside**, **BorderRight**, **BorderTop**, **FormatBordersAndShading**, **ShadingPattern**

BorderLineStyle, BorderLineStyle()

Syntax   **BorderLineStyle** *Style*

BorderLineStyle()

Remarks   The **BorderLineStyle** statement specifies the line style for subsequent **BorderBottom**, **BorderInside**, **BorderLeft**, **BorderOutside**, **BorderRight**, and **BorderTop** instructions.

Argument	Explanation
Style	One of 13 line styles:
	0 (zero) None
	1 ————
	2 ———
	3 ———
	4 ———
	5 ■■■■
	6 ■■■
	7 ═══
	8 ═══
	9 ═══
	10 ··············
	11 - - - - - -
	12 ————
	Style 12, which corresponds to the Hairline option, is available only on the Macintosh.

For an example that uses **BorderLineStyle**, see **BorderBottom**.

The **BorderLineStyle**() function returns a number from 0 (zero) to 12 that corresponds to the line style that will be applied by subsequent border instructions. Note that this line style does not necessarily match the line style of borders in the selected paragraphs, table cells, or graphic.

See Also   **BorderBottom**, **BorderInside**, **BorderLeft**, **BorderNone**, **BorderOutside**, **BorderRight**, **BorderTop**, **FormatBordersAndShading**, **ShadingPattern**

BorderNone, BorderNone()

Syntax   **BorderNone** [*Remove*]

BorderNone()

Remarks   The **BorderNone** statement removes or applies all borders (left, right, top, bottom, and inside) for the selected items. You can remove or apply all borders for a series of paragraphs or table rows, but not a combination of paragraphs and table rows. To remove or apply borders for a graphic, you must first select only that graphic.

Argument	Explanation
Remove	Specifies whether to remove or apply all borders for the selection:
	0 (zero) Applies borders
	1 or omitted Removes borders

The **BorderNone**() function returns 0 (zero) if the selection contains at least one border and 1 if the selection contains no borders.

See Also   **BorderBottom**, **BorderInside**, **BorderLeft**, **BorderLineStyle**, **BorderOutside**, **BorderRight**, **BorderTop**, **FormatBordersAndShading**, **ShadingPattern**

BorderOutside, BorderOutside()

Syntax   **BorderOutside** [*On*]

BorderOutside()

Remarks   The **BorderOutside** statement applies or removes outside borders for the selected paragraphs, table cells, or graphic. The following illustrations show outside borders applied to a series of paragraphs and an entire table.

Lorem ipsum dolor sit amet
Lorem ipsum dolor sit amet
Lorem ipsum dolor sit amet

Lorem ipsum	Lorem ipsum
Lorem ipsum	Lorem ipsum
Lorem ipsum	Lorem ipsum

Outside borders for paragraphs   Outside borders for a table

The **BorderOutside()** function returns either 0 (zero) or 1, depending on whether the selected graphic or all the selected paragraphs or table cells are formatted with an outside border.

For complete descriptions of arguments and return values, see **BorderBottom**.

See Also   **BorderBottom, BorderInside, BorderLeft, BorderLineStyle, BorderNone, BorderRight, BorderTop, FormatBordersAndShading, ShadingPattern**

BorderRight, BorderRight()

Syntax   **BorderRight** [*On*]

BorderRight()

Remarks   The **BorderRight** statement applies or removes right borders for the selected paragraphs, table cells, or graphic. The **BorderRight()** function returns either 0 (zero) or 1, depending on whether the selected graphic or all the selected paragraphs or table cells are formatted with a right border.

For complete descriptions of arguments and return values, see **BorderBottom**.

See Also   **BorderBottom, BorderInside, BorderLeft, BorderLineStyle, BorderNone, BorderOutside, BorderTop, FormatBordersAndShading, ShadingPattern**

BorderTop, BorderTop()

Syntax   **BorderTop** [*On*]

BorderTop()

Remarks   The **BorderTop** statement applies or removes a top border for the selected paragraphs, table cells, or graphic. Note that when you apply a top border to a series of paragraphs or table rows, the border appears only above the first paragraph or row in the series. If you want a border to separate each paragraph or row, use **BorderInside**.

The **BorderTop()** function returns either 0 (zero) or 1, depending on whether the selected graphic or all the selected paragraphs or table cells are formatted with a top border.

For complete descriptions of arguments and return values, see **BorderBottom**.

See Also   **BorderBottom, BorderInside, BorderLeft, BorderLineStyle, BorderNone, BorderOutside, BorderRight, FormatBordersAndShading, ShadingPattern**

Call

Syntax

[**Call**] [*MacroName*][**.**][*SubName*] [*ArgumentList*]

Remarks

Transfers control to a subroutine in the running macro or another macro. To specify a subroutine in another macro, use the syntax *MacroName.SubName*. If *SubName* is not specified, the Main subroutine in *MacroName* runs. **Call** is optional; it can help distinguish subroutine names from WordBasic keywords when you read and edit macros. Each variable in the comma-delimited *ArgumentList* must correspond to a value that the subroutine being called is prepared to receive.

Note When you call another macro, Word looks for the macro in available templates in the following order: the template containing the **Call** instruction, the active template, the Normal template, and loaded global templates. For example, suppose USER.DOT and NORMAL.DOT both contain a DisplayMessage macro. The following macro in USER.DOT:

```
FileNew .Template = "Normal"
DisplayMessage
```

runs the DisplayMessage macro in USER.DOT, even though a document based on NORMAL.DOT is active when the **Call** instruction is run.

For more information about using subroutines, including how to share variables and pass arguments between subroutines, see Chapter 4, "Advanced WordBasic," in Part 1, "Learning WordBasic."

Example

This example calls the subroutine FindName twice; each line, with or without **Call**, has the same effect:

```
Call FindName          'Transfer control to the subroutine FindName
FindName               'Transfer control to the subroutine FindName
```

See Also

Sub…End Sub

Cancel

Syntax

Cancel

Remarks

Cancels a mode activated by the **ColumnSelect**, **CopyFormat**, **CopyText**, or **ExtendSelection** statements.

Example

This example pastes the contents of the Clipboard into a document, selects the pasted text, and then places the text of the selection into a variable. To accomplish this task, the macro inserts a bookmark at the insertion point, pastes the text, and then, using **ExtendSelection**, selects the pasted text. The **Cancel** statement turns off extend mode, so that when the last instruction moves the insertion point to the end of the document, no text is selected.

```
CopyBookmark "\Sel", "temp"
EditPaste
ExtendSelection
EditGoTo "temp"
pasted$ = Selection$()
Cancel
EndOfDocument
```

See Also   **OK**

CancelButton

Syntax   **CancelButton** *HorizPos*, *VertPos*, *Width*, *Height* [, *.Identifier*]

Remarks   Creates a Cancel button in a custom dialog box. A user chooses the Cancel button to close the dialog box without taking any action.

Argument	Explanation
HorizPos, *VertPos*	The horizontal and vertical distance of the upper-left corner of the Cancel button from the upper-left corner of the dialog box, in increments of 1/8 and 1/12 of the System font (Windows) or the dialog font (Macintosh).
Width, *Height*	The width and height of the Cancel button, in increments of 1/8 and 1/12 of the System font (Windows) or the dialog font (Macintosh).
.Identifier	An optional identifier used by statements in a dialog function that act on the Cancel button, such as **DlgEnable** and **DlgVisible**. If omitted, "Cancel" is the default identifier.

If you use the **Dialog** statement to display the dialog box and the user chooses the Cancel button, WordBasic generates an error, which you can trap with **On Error**.

If you use the **Dialog()** function to display the dialog box and the user chooses the Cancel button, the function returns 0 (zero) rather than generating an error.

To see an example of **CancelButton** in a dialog box definition, see **Begin Dialog…End Dialog**.

See Also   **Begin Dialog…End Dialog**, **Dialog**, **Err**, **Error**, **OKButton**, **On Error**, **PushButton**

CenterPara, CenterPara()

Syntax

CenterPara

CenterPara( )

Remarks

Centers the selected paragraphs.

The **CenterPara( )** function returns the following values.

Value	Explanation
0 (zero)	If none of the selection is centered
−1	If part of the selection is centered or there is a mix of alignments
1	If all the selection is centered

See Also

FormatParagraph, **JustifyPara**, **LeftPara**, **RightPara**

ChangeCase, ChangeCase()

Syntax

ChangeCase [*Type*]

ChangeCase( )

Remarks

The **ChangeCase** statement sets the case of the selected text to sentence case, lowercase, uppercase, or initial capital letters. **ChangeCase** does not change the character formats associated with the selected text, as do the **SmallCaps** and **AllCaps** statements. **ChangeCase** corresponds to the Change Case command (Format menu).

Argument	Explanation
Type	Specifies the change in case:
	Omitted If the selection is one sentence or less, alternates the case of the selection among all lowercase, all uppercase, and initial capital letters. If the selection is more than one sentence, alternates among all lowercase, all uppercase, and sentence case.
	0 (zero) Sets the text to all lowercase
	1 Sets the text to all uppercase
	2 Capitalizes the first letter of each selected word
	3 Capitalizes the first letter of the selection
	4 Capitalizes the first letter of each selected sentence
	5 Toggles the case of each selected letter (for example, "Word" becomes "wORD")

If there is no selection, Word selects the word nearest the insertion point, and then changes the case of the selected word.

The **ChangeCase()** function returns the following values.

Value	Explanation
0 (zero)	If none of the selected text is in uppercase
1	If all of the selected text is in uppercase
2	If the text is in a mixture of uppercase and lowercase

Example

This example selects the current paragraph (using the predefined bookmark "\Para") and capitalizes the first letter of each sentence:

```
EditGoTo "\Para"
ChangeCase 4
```

See Also

AllCaps, FormatChangeCase, LCase$(), SmallCaps, UCase$()

CharColor, CharColor()

Syntax

CharColor *Color*

CharColor()

Remarks

The **CharColor** statement sets the character color of the selection to the specified color, where *Color* is one of the following numeric codes.

Color	Explanation
0 (zero)	Auto
1	Black
2	Blue
3	Cyan
4	Green
5	Magenta
6	Red
7	Yellow
8	White
9	Dark Blue
10	Dark Cyan
11	Dark Green
12	Dark Magenta
13	Dark Red
14	Dark Yellow
15	Dark Gray
16	Light Gray

The **CharColor()** function returns the same number codes set by the **CharColor** statement or –1 if all the selected text is not the same color.

Example

This example selects the current paragraph (using the predefined bookmark "\Para") and applies magenta character color formatting if it contains the string "Comments: ".

```
EditGoTo "\Para"
If InStr(Selection$(), "Comments: ") Then CharColor 5
```

See Also

FormatFont, **SelectCurColor**

CharLeft, CharLeft()

Syntax

CharLeft [*Count*] [, *Select*]

CharLeft([*Count*] [, *Select*])

Remarks

The **CharLeft** statement moves the insertion point or the active end of the selection (the end that moves when you press SHIFT+LEFT ARROW) to the left by the specified number of characters.

Argument	Explanation
Count	The number of characters to move. If less than one or omitted, 1 is assumed.
Select	Specifies whether to select text:
	0 (zero) or omitted Text is not selected. If there is already a selection, **CharLeft** moves the insertion point *Count*–1 characters to the left of the selection.
	Nonzero Text is selected. If there is already a selection, **CharLeft** moves the active end of the selection toward the beginning of the document.
	In a typical selection made from left to right, where the active end of the selection is closer to the end of the document, **CharLeft** shrinks the selection. In a selection made from right to left, it extends the selection.

If there is a selection, CharLeft 1 changes the selection to an insertion point positioned at the left end of the original selection.

The **CharLeft()** function behaves the same as the statement and also returns the following values.

Value	Explanation
0 (zero)	If the insertion point or the active end of the selection cannot be moved to the left.
–1	If the insertion point or the active end of the selection is moved to the left by any number of characters, even if less than *Count*. For example, CharLeft(10) returns –1 even if the insertion point is only three characters from the start of the document.

Examples

This example moves the insertion point five characters to the left. The **If** conditional determines whether there is a selection. If there is a selection, the CharLeft 1 instruction changes the selection to an insertion point at the left end of the selection before moving the insertion point five characters to the left. This ensures that the insertion point is moved five characters whether or not there is a selection.

```
If SelType() = 2 Then
    CharLeft 1
    CharLeft 5
Else
    CharLeft 5
End If
```

The following example selects the current paragraph and then shrinks the selection by one character, so that the paragraph text is selected, but not the paragraph mark. You might want to do this if you need to copy the text of a paragraph but not its paragraph formatting, which is stored in the paragraph mark.

```
EditGoTo "\Para"
CharLeft 1, 1
```

See Also

CharRight, **SentLeft**, **SentRight**, **WordLeft**, **WordRight**

CharRight, CharRight()

Syntax

CharRight [*Count*] [, *Select*]

CharRight([*Count*] [, *Select*])

Remarks

The **CharRight** statement moves the insertion point or the active end of the selection (the end that moves when you press SHIFT+RIGHT ARROW) to the right by the specified number of characters.

Argument	Explanation
Count	The number of characters to move. If less than one or omitted, 1 is assumed.
Select	Specifies whether to select text:

0 (zero) or omitted   Text is not selected. If there is already a selection, **CharRight** moves the insertion point *Count*–1 characters to the right of the selection.

Nonzero   Text is selected. If there is already a selection, **CharRight** moves the active end of the selection toward the end of the document.

In a typical selection made from left to right, where the active end of the selection is closer to the end of the document, **CharRight** extends the selection. In a selection made from right to left, it shrinks the selection.

If there is a selection, CharRight 1 changes the selection to an insertion point positioned at the right end of the original selection.

The **CharRight**() function behaves the same as the statement and also returns the following values.

Value	Explanation
0 (zero)	If the insertion point or the active end of the selection cannot be moved to the right.
–1	If the insertion point or the active end of the selection is moved to the right by any number of characters, even if less than *Count*. For example, CharRight(10) returns –1 even if the insertion point is only three characters from the end of the document.

Examples

This example moves the insertion point to the start of the current sentence and then selects the first five characters to the right:

```
SentLeft
CharRight 5, 1
```

The following example first extends the selection five characters to the right, copies the selection, and then moves the insertion point five characters to the right of the selection. Note that CharRight 6 is used to move the selection five characters to the right of the selection. This instruction is equivalent to CharRight 1, which moves the insertion point to the right end of the selection, plus CharRight 5, which then moves it five characters.

```
CharRight 5, 1
EditCopy
CharRight 6
```

See Also

CharLeft, SentLeft, SentRight, WordLeft, WordRight

ChDefaultDir

Syntax   **ChDefaultDir** *Path$*, *Type*

Remarks   Sets one of the Word default folders to the specified path. Unlike
ToolsOptionsFileLocations, which saves default folder changes in
WINWORD6.INI (Windows 3.*x*), Word Settings (6) (Macintosh), or the registry
(Windows 95 and Windows NT), **ChDefaultDir** changes default folders for the
current Word session only. Changes made with **ChDefaultDir** are not reflected on
the File Locations tab in the Options dialog box (Tools menu).

Argument	Explanation
Path$	The path to which you want to set the default folder specified by *Type*
Type	A number corresponding to the default folder to set:

0   DOC-PATH

1   PICTURE-PATH

2   USER-DOT-PATH

3   WORKGROUP-DOT-PATH

4   INI-PATH

5   AUTOSAVE-PATH

6   TOOLS-PATH

7   CBT-PATH

8   STARTUP-PATH

15 The style-gallery–template path (this setting is ignored in Word
version 7.0)

Note that types 9 through 14 cannot be set with **ChDefaultDir**. To
return their values for the current Word session, use **DefaultDir$()**.

Example   This example creates the folder C:\BAK and then sets AUTOSAVE-PATH to that
folder for the current session. The instruction On Error Resume Next prevents an
error from stopping the macro if the folder already exists. On the Macintosh,
substitute a folder name such as HD:BACKUP.

```
On Error Resume Next
MkDir "C:\BAK"
Err = 0
ChDefaultDir "C:\BAK", 5
```

See Also   **ChDir**, **DefaultDir$()**, **Files$()**, **GetDirectory$()**, **ToolsOptionsFileLocations**

ChDir

Syntax   **ChDir** *Path$*

Remarks   Sets the current folder to the drive or folder specified by *Path$*. If the drive is omitted, the search for the specified path starts at the current folder. You can use **ChDir** to set the folder so that you do not have to specify the complete path when you use **FileOpen** to open a document.

Examples   This example changes the folder and then displays the Open dialog box so that you can open a document stored in that folder. You could create a macro like this for a folder you use often and assign the macro to a toolbar button for quick access. On the Macintosh, substitute a folder name such as HD:WORD 6:LETTERS.

```
ChDir "C:\WINWORD\LETTERS\PERSONAL"
Dim dlg As FileOpen
button = Dialog(dlg)
If button = -1 Then FileOpen dlg
```

The following Windows example determines whether the current folder is C:\WINWORD and changes to it if it is not.

```
If Files$(".") <> "C:\WINWORD" Then ChDir "C:\WINWORD"
```

Here is the same example, rewritten for the Macintosh:

```
If Files$(":") <> "HD:WORD 6" Then ChDir "HD:WORD 6"
```

See Also   **Connect**, **CountDirectories()**, **Files$()**, **GetDirectory$()**, **MkDir**, **RmDir**

CheckBox

Syntax   **CheckBox** *HorizPos*, *VertPos*, *Width*, *Height*, *Label$*, *.Identifier*

Remarks   Creates a check box in a custom dialog box.

Argument	Explanation
HorizPos, *VertPos*	The horizontal and vertical distance of the upper-left corner of the rectangle containing the check box and its associated label from the upper-left corner of the dialog box, in increments of 1/8 and 1/12 of the System font (Windows) or the dialog font (Macintosh).
Width, *Height*	The width and height of the check box, in increments of 1/8 and 1/12 of the System font (Windows) or the dialog font (Macintosh).

Argument	Explanation
Label$	The label associated with the check box. An ampersand (&) precedes the character in *Label$* that is the access key for selecting and clearing the check box.
.Identifier	Together with the dialog record name, *.Identifier* creates a variable whose value corresponds to the state of the check box. The form for this variable is *DialogRecord.Identifier* (for example, dlg.MyCheckBox). *DialogRecord.Identifier* can return the following values:

0 (zero)   The check box is cleared.

1   The check box is selected.

−1 The check box is filled with gray.

The identifier string (*.Identifier* minus the period) is also used by statements in a dialog function that act on the check box, such as **DlgEnable** and **DlgVisible**.

To see an example of **CheckBox** in a dialog box definition, see **Begin Dialog…End Dialog**.

See Also   **Begin Dialog…End Dialog**

CheckBoxFormField

Syntax   **CheckBoxFormField**

Remarks   Inserts a check box form field at the insertion point. **CheckBoxFormField** corresponds to the Check Box Form Field button on the Forms toolbar.

See Also   **DropDownFormField**, **InsertFormField**, **TextFormField**

ChooseButtonImage

Syntax   **ChooseButtonImage** [**.Face** = *number*,] **.Button** = *number*, [**.Context** = *number*,] [**.Text** = *text*,] **.Toolbar** = *text*

Remarks   Changes the image or text on the specified toolbar button.

Argument	Explanation
.Face	A number corresponding to an image for the button in the built-in set of button images, where 0 (zero) is no image (for a blank button), 1 is the first image, 2 is the second image, and so on. For a list of button images and their associated numbers, see "Toolbar Button Images and Numbers" in Help.
.Button	A number corresponding to the position of the button to change on the specified toolbar, where 1 is the first position, 2 is the second, and so on. Note that a list box or space counts as one position. If you specify a position that corresponds to a space, Word modifies the button to the right of the space.
.Context	Determines where the toolbar change is stored:
	0 (zero) or omitted Normal template
	1 Active template
.Text	The text you want to appear on the button. If you specify both .Face and .Text, .Text takes precedence.
.Toolbar	The name of the toolbar as listed in the Toolbars dialog box (View menu).

Note You can choose a button image for a list box on a toolbar; however, the button is displayed only when the toolbar is vertical.

Examples

This example changes the image on the Stop button on the Macro toolbar to button image 50:

```
ChooseButtonImage .Face = 50, .Button = 9, .Context = 0, \
        .Toolbar = "Macro"
```

The following example creates a dialog record for the Custom Button dialog box (Toolbar Customization shortcut menu) and then displays the dialog box so you can modify the third button on the Standard toolbar. Note that, unlike those for other dialog records, instructions that set values in a **ChooseButtonImage** dialog record must precede the **GetCurValues** instruction.

```
Dim dlg As ChooseButtonImage
dlg.Toolbar = "Standard"
dlg.Button = 3
GetCurValues dlg
Dialog dlg
ChooseButtonImage dlg
```

See Also   **AddButton**, **CopyButtonImage**, **EditButtonImage**, **MoveButton**, **PasteButtonImage**, **ResetButtonImage**

Chr$()

Syntax   **Chr$(***CharCode***)**

Remarks   Returns the character whose character code is *CharCode*.

Character codes in the range 0 (zero) to 31, inclusive, match the nonprinting characters of the standard ASCII code. For example, Chr$(13) is a carriage return character and Chr$(9) is a tab character. You can use Chr$(13) to create a new line within a message string used with **MsgBox** (but not **InputBox$()**).

The following table lists a few of the special characters you can produce using **Chr$()**.

Value	Character returned
Chr$(9)	Tab character
Chr$(11)	Newline character (SHIFT+ENTER)
Chr$(13)	Paragraph mark
	Note that paragraph marks in Windows text files and Word for Windows version 2.*x* documents have the value Chr$(13) + Chr$(10) until you save the file in Word Document format in Word version 6.0.
Chr$(30)	Nonbreaking hyphen
Chr$(31)	Optional hyphen
Chr$(32)	Space character
Chr$(34)	Quotation mark
Chr$(160)	Nonbreaking space (Windows)
Chr$(202)	Nonbreaking space (Macintosh)

The appearance of the symbol assigned to a given character code varies with the font used. Character codes in the range 127 to 255, inclusive, return different symbols, according to the font used.

Because the quotation mark is used to indicate the beginning or end of a string in WordBasic, you use Chr$(34) if you want to include a quotation mark in a string. For example, to create a message box with the message "Type "Yes" or "No"," you would use the following statement:

```
MsgBox "Type " + Chr$(34) + "Yes" + Chr$(34) + " or " + \
    Chr$(34) + "No" + Chr$(34)
```

Tip You can type pairs of quotation marks in an instruction and Word will convert them to the correct syntax using Chr$(34) the first time you run or save the macro. For example, Word converts MsgBox "Type ""Yes"" or ""No""" to the instruction shown previously. Similarly, tab characters are automatically converted to Chr$(9).

Examples

This example displays a message box with two lines:

```
MsgBox "This is the first line" + Chr$(13) + "This is the second line"
```

The following example creates a table of symbols between character codes 127 and 255 (often referred to as the extended character set). The first instruction asks the user to name the font for which he or she would like to see the symbols.

```
fontchoice$ = InputBox$("Please enter the Font Name ", \
                        "Symbol Table", "Symbol")
For i = 127 To 255
    Font "Times New Roman"
    Insert Str$(i) + Chr$(9)
    Font fontchoice$
    Insert Chr$(i)
    InsertPara
Next
```

See Also

Asc(), **Str$()**

CleanString$()

Syntax

CleanString$(**_Source$_)**

Remarks

Removes nonprinting characters and special Word characters from _Source$,_ or changes them to spaces (character code 32).

In Windows and on the Macintosh, the following characters are changed to spaces, unless otherwise noted.

Character code	Description
1–29	Nonprinting characters. Character 13 (paragraph mark) is not removed. Character 10 is converted to character 13, unless preceded by character 13, in which case character 10 is removed. Character 7 is removed, unless preceded by character 13, in which case character 7 is converted to character 9 (tab character).
31	Optional hyphen. Character 31 is removed rather than changed to a space.

In Windows, the following characters are converted as described.

Character code	Description
160	Nonbreaking space; changed to a space
172	Optional hyphen symbol; removed
176	Nonbreaking space symbol; changed to a space
182	Paragraph mark character; removed
183	Bullet character; changed to a space

On the Macintosh, the following characters converted as described.

Character code	Description
194	Optional hyphen symbol; removed
202	Nonbreaking space; changed to a space

If a field is included in the selection and the field codes are displayed, **CleanString$()** changes the field characters to spaces.

Example

This example uses **CleanString$()** to remove any nonprinting characters (except character 13) in the selected text:

```
temp$ = Selection$()
clean$ = CleanString$(temp$)
```

See Also

LTrim$(), RTrim$()

ClearAddIns

Syntax

ClearAddIns *RemoveFromList*

Remarks

Unloads all global templates and Word add-in libraries (WLLs) that appear in the list of global templates and add-ins in the Templates And Add-ins dialog box (Templates command, File menu).

Argument	Explanation
RemoveFromList	Specifies whether to remove the global templates and add-ins from the list in addition to unloading them:
	0 (zero) Global templates and add-ins remain in the list.
	1 Global templates and add-ins are removed from the list (except for those in the Startup folder).

See Also   **AddAddIn**, **AddInState()**, **CountAddIns()**, **DeleteAddIn**, **GetAddInId()**, **GetAddInName$()**

ClearFormField

Syntax   **ClearFormField**

Remarks   Clears the text in a text form field selected in a protected form document. **ClearFormField** behaves like the BACKSPACE key. Note that in an unprotected form document, **ClearFormField** deletes the selected text form field.

Example   This example is intended to run when the focus moves to a text form field. If the user moves to the form field using the TAB key, thereby selecting its contents, the condition GetSelStartPos() <> GetSelEndPos() is true and Word clears the form field. If the user clicks the form field with the mouse, the condition is false and Word takes no action.

```
If GetSelEndPos() <> GetSelStartPos() Then ClearFormField
```

See Also   **SetFormResult**, **TextFormField**

Close

Syntax   **Close** [[#]*FileNumber*]

Remarks   Closes an open sequential file. *FileNumber* is the number specified in the **Open** instruction that opened the file for input, output, or appending. If *FileNumber* is omitted, all files that were opened with **Open** are closed.

Sequential files, which are opened with **Open** and closed with **Close**, are not displayed in document windows. Although you can use **Open** to open any file, **Open** and **Close** are intended to be used with text files. **Close** does not display a prompt when it closes a file. For more information about sequential files, see Chapter 9, "More WordBasic Techniques," in Part 1, "Learning WordBasic."

Example

This example opens a file, inserts a list of AutoText entries in the Normal template and any loaded global templates, and then closes the file:

```
Open "AUTOTEXT.TXT" For Output As #1
For count = 1 To CountAutoTextEntries(0)
    Print #1, AutoTextName$(count)
Next count
Close #1
```

See Also

Eof(), **Input**, **Input$()**, **Line Input**, **Lof()**, **Open**, **Print**, **Read**, **Seek**, **Write**

ClosePane

Syntax

ClosePane

Remarks

Closes a pane. Use this statement to close the lower pane in a split document window, a footnote pane, or any other kind of pane. **ClosePane** generates a WordBasic error if no pane is open in the active document. Note that **ClosePane** does not close a document window.

Example

This example closes the lower pane in the active document if the window is split:

```
If DocSplit() Then ClosePane
```

See Also

DocSplit, **OtherPane**, **WindowPane()**

ClosePreview

Syntax

ClosePreview

Remarks

Returns the active document from print preview to the previous view. **ClosePreview** has no effect if the active document is not displayed in print preview.

See Also

FilePrintPreview

CloseUpPara

Syntax

CloseUpPara

Remarks

Removes the paragraph formatting that creates space before the selected paragraphs. **CloseUpPara** corresponds to setting to 0 (zero) the Before option on the Indents And Spacing tab in the Paragraph dialog box (Format menu).

Example	This macro toggles Before formatting between one line and no lines before the selected paragraphs:

```
Sub MAIN
    Dim dlg As FormatParagraph
    GetCurValues dlg
    If Val(dlg.Before) <> 0 Then
        CloseUpPara
    Else
        OpenUpPara
    End If
End Sub
```

See Also	**FormatParagraph, OpenUpPara**

CloseViewHeaderFooter

Syntax	**CloseViewHeaderFooter**
Remarks	Hides the Header And Footer toolbar and moves the insertion point to its previous location in the document area. If the insertion point is not in a header or footer, an error occurs.
See Also	**GoToHeaderFooter, ShowNextHeaderFooter, ShowPrevHeaderFooter, ViewHeader**

CmpBookmarks()

Syntax	**CmpBookmarks(**Bookmark1$, Bookmark2$**)**
Remarks	Compares the contents of two bookmarks. Use **CmpBookmarks()** with the predefined bookmarks in Word to check the location of the insertion point or to create a macro that operates only within an area marked with a bookmark. For example, using the "\Sel" (current selection) bookmark and the "\Para" bookmark, you can set up a macro to operate only within a particular paragraph. For more information about predefined bookmarks, see "Operators and Predefined Bookmarks" later in this part.

Argument	Explanation
Bookmark1$	The first bookmark
Bookmark2$	The second bookmark

This function returns the following values.

Value	Explanation
0 (zero)	*Bookmark1$* and *Bookmark2$* are equivalent.
1	*Bookmark1$* is entirely below *Bookmark2$*.
2	*Bookmark1$* is entirely above *Bookmark2$*.
3	*Bookmark1$* is below and inside *Bookmark2$*.
4	*Bookmark1$* is inside and above *Bookmark2$*.
5	*Bookmark1$* encloses *Bookmark2$*.
6	*Bookmark2$* encloses *Bookmark1$*.
7	*Bookmark1$* and *Bookmark2$* begin at the same point, but *Bookmark1$* is longer.
8	*Bookmark1$* and *Bookmark2$* begin at the same point, but *Bookmark2$* is longer.
9	*Bookmark1$* and *Bookmark2$* end at the same place, but *Bookmark1$* is longer.
10	*Bookmark1$* and *Bookmark2$* end at the same place, but *Bookmark2$* is longer.
11	*Bookmark1$* is below and adjacent to *Bookmark2$*.
12	*Bookmark1$* is above and adjacent to *Bookmark2$*.
13	One or both of the bookmarks do not exist.

Example   This example adds a string of characters in front of every line in a selection. The example first marks the selected text with a bookmark and then uses a **While…Wend** loop controlled by three **CmpBookmarks()** functions to add text in front of each line. The first **CmpBookmarks()** function tests whether the insertion point and the selection, stored in the "Temp" bookmark, begin at the same point; this is true when the loop begins. The second **CmpBookmarks()** function tests whether the insertion point is contained within "Temp"; this is true as long as the insertion point is within the original selection. The third **CmpBookmarks()** function tests whether the insertion point is at the end of the original selection. When the insertion point moves beyond the original selection, the loop ends. Within the **While…Wend** loop is yet another **CmpBookmarks()** instruction, which determines whether the selection is at the end of the document, a special case.

```
                    CopyBookmark "\Sel", "Temp"
                    SelType 1
                    While CmpBookmarks("\Sel", "Temp") = 8 \
                            Or CmpBookmarks("\Sel", "Temp") = 6 \
                            Or CmpBookmarks("\Sel", "Temp") = 10 \
                            And leaveloop <> 1
                        EndOfLine
                        If CmpBookmarks("\Sel", "\EndOfDoc") = 0 Then leaveloop = 1
                        StartOfLine
                        Insert "***"
                        LineDown
                    Wend
                    EditGoTo "Temp"
                    EditBookmark "Temp", .Delete
```

See Also   **CopyBookmark**, **EditBookmark**, **EmptyBookmark**

ColumnSelect

Syntax   **ColumnSelect**

Remarks   Turns on column selection mode to select a column of text, such as numbers
                    aligned at the same tab stop in two or more lines of text. **Cancel** or any command
                    acting on the column selection ends this mode. **ColumnSelect** does not select a
                    column in a Word table; use **TableSelectColumn** for this purpose.

Example   This example selects the numbers and tab characters in the current line and the
                    two subsequent lines of a list, as in the illustration that follows it:

```
                    StartOfLine
                    ColumnSelect
                    WordRight 2
                    LineDown 2
```

See Also   **Cancel**, **ExtendSelection**

ComboBox

Syntax   **ComboBox** *HorizPos*, *VertPos*, *Width*, *Height*, *ArrayVariable$( )*, *.Identifier*[$]

Remarks   Creates a combo box—a single control that is a combination of a list box and a text box—in a custom dialog box. A user can either select an item from the list or type a new item in the text box.

Argument	Explanation
HorizPos, *VertPos*	The horizontal and vertical distance of the upper-left corner of the combo box from the upper-left corner of the dialog box, in increments of 1/8 and 1/12 of the System font (Windows) or the dialog font (Macintosh).
Width, *Height*	The width and height of the combo box, in increments of 1/8 and 1/12 of the System font (Windows) or the dialog font (Macintosh).
ArrayVariable$( )	A text array containing the items to be listed in the combo box.
.Identifier[$]	Together with the dialog record name, *.Identifier*[$] creates a variable whose value corresponds to the text of the item chosen or the text typed in the combo box. The form for this variable is *DialogRecord.Identifier*[$] (for example, `dlg.MyComboBox$`). The dollar sign ($) is optional; you can use it to indicate that the variable is a string variable.
	The identifier string (*.Identifier*[$] minus the period) is also used by statements in a dialog function that act on the combo box, such as **DlgEnable** and **DlgVisible**.

The macro must define and assign values to the elements in *ArrayVariable$( )* before defining the dialog box containing a combo box. To see an example of **ComboBox** in a dialog box definition, see **Begin Dialog…End Dialog**.

See Also   **Begin Dialog…End Dialog**, **Dialog**, **Dim**

CommandValid()

Syntax   **CommandValid**(*CommandName$*)

Remarks   Indicates whether *CommandName$* is a valid WordBasic statement and, if so, whether it is available in the current context.

The **CommandValid()** function returns the following values.

Value	Explanation
-1	If *CommandName$* is valid and is available in the current context
0 (zero)	If *CommandName$* is valid but is not available in the current context
1	If *CommandName$* is not valid

Example

This example tests whether the Undo command (Edit menu) is available. If it is, the previous editing or formatting command is undone.

```
If CommandValid("EditUndo") = -1 Then
    EditUndo
End If
```

See Also   **IsMacro()**

Connect

Syntax   **Connect [.Drive** = *number*,**] .Path** = *text* **[, .Password** = *text***]**

Remarks   In Windows, establishes a connection to a network drive. On the Macintosh, **Connect** is not available and generates an error; use **MountVolume** instead.

Argument	Explanation
.Drive	A number corresponding to the letter you want to assign to the network drive, where 0 (zero) corresponds to the first available drive letter, 1 to the second available drive letter, and so on. If you don't specify .Drive, the next available letter is used.
.Path	The path for the network drive (for example, "\\PROJECT\INFO").
.Password	The password, if the network drive is protected with a password.

Example   This example establishes a connection to a network drive protected with the password "smiley" and assigns the network drive to the next available network drive letter:

```
Connect .Path = "\\PROJECT\INFO", .Password = "smiley"
```

See Also   **ChDir, CountDirectories(), GetDirectory$(), MountVolume**

ControlRun

Syntax   **ControlRun .Application** = *number*

Remarks   In Windows, runs either the Clipboard or the Control Panel. If you want to run a different program, use the **Shell** statement. On the Macintosh, **ControlRun** is not available and generates an error.

Argument	Explanation
.Application	The application to run:
	0 (zero) Clipboard (this value is not available and generates an error in Windows 95)
	1 Control Panel

Example   This example runs the Control Panel:

```
ControlRun .Application = 1
```

See Also   **Shell, ShowClipboard**

Converter$()

Syntax   **Converter$**(*FormatNumber*)

Remarks   Returns the class name of the file format associated with *FormatNumber*.

Argument	Explanation
FormatNumber	A number corresponding to a file format listed under Save File As Type in the Save As dialog box (File menu): 0 (zero) corresponds to the first format, 1 to the second format, and so on.
	FormatNumber can also be a value returned by **ConverterLookup**(). Note that in some cases, the format number returned by **ConverterLookup**() does not match the position of the format name in the list box. In Windows for example, `ConverterLookup("Excel Worksheet")` returns 101.

Example   This example inserts at the insertion point a list of file format class names available to Word. The instructions run until a$ is an empty string (""), indicating that the end of the list of available formats has been reached.

```
x = 0
a$ = Converter$(x)
While a$ <> ""
    Insert a$ + Chr$(13)
    x = x + 1
    a$ = Converter$(x)
Wend
```

See Also   ConverterLookup(), FileSaveAs

ConverterLookup()

Syntax   ConverterLookup(*FormatName$*)

Remarks   Returns a number corresponding to the file format specified by *FormatName$*.
                    You can use this number with the .Format argument in a **FileSaveAs** instruction
                    to save a file in a different format. If the specified format does not exist,
                    ConverterLookup() returns –1.

Argument	Explanation
FormatName$	The class name for the format as returned by **Converter$**(), or the name of a file format as it appears in the Save File As Type box in the Save As dialog box (File menu).

Examples   This Windows example saves the active document in rich-text format (RTF),
                    using the class name "MSRTF" to specify the format:

```
FileSaveAs .Name = "C:\RTF\TEST.RTF", \
        .Format = ConverterLookup("MSRTF")
```

The following Macintosh example also saves the active document in RTF, but
specifies the format using the name in the Save File As Type box in the Save As
dialog box instead of the class name:

```
FileSaveAs .Name = "HD:RTF:RTF TEST", \
        .Format = ConverterLookup("Rich Text Format")
```

See Also   Converter$(), FileSaveAs

ConvertObject

Syntax   **ConvertObject** [**.IconNumber** = *number*] [**, .ActivateAs** = *number*]
                    [**, .IconFilename** = *text*] [**, .Caption** = *text*] [**, .Class** = *text*]
                    [**, .DisplayIcon** = *number*]

Remarks   Converts the selected embedded object from one class to another, allows a different server application to edit the object, or changes how the object is displayed in the document. The arguments for the **ConvertObject** statement correspond to the options in the Convert dialog box (Object submenu, Edit menu).

Argument	Explanation
.IconNumber	If .DisplayIcon is set to 1, a number corresponding to the icon you want to use in the program file specified by .IconFilename. Icons appear in the Change Icon dialog box (Object command, Insert menu): 0 (zero) corresponds to the first icon, 1 to the second icon, and so on. If omitted, the first (default) icon is used.
	On the Macintosh, icons for embedded objects cannot be changed; this argument is ignored.
.ActivateAs	Specifies whether Word converts or sets the server application for the selected object:
	0 (zero) Converts the selected object to the object type specified by .Class.
	1 Uses the server application specified by .Class to edit the object. Note that this setting applies to all objects of the selected type and that Word uses the specified server application when inserting objects of the selected type.
.IconFilename	If .DisplayIcon is set to 1, the path and filename of the program file in which the icon to be displayed is stored.
	On the Macintosh, icons for embedded objects cannot be changed; this argument is ignored.
.Caption	If .DisplayIcon is set to 1, the caption of the icon to be displayed; if omitted, Word inserts the name of the object.
.Class	A class name specifying the object type to convert to or the server application for editing the object, depending on the setting for .ActivateAs. The class name for a Word document is Word.Document.6 and a Word picture is Word.Picture.6.
	To look up other class names, insert an object of the type to convert to in a document and view the field codes; the class name of the object follows the word "EMBED."
.DisplayIcon	Specifies whether or not to display the object as an icon:
	0 (zero) or omitted Object is not displayed as an icon.
	1 Object is displayed as an icon.

Example   This Windows example changes the display of the selected embedded object to an icon stored in PROGMAN.EXE.

```
ConvertObject .IconNumber = 28, .IconFilename = "PROGMAN.EXE", \
    .Caption = "Caption Text", .DisplayIcon = 1
```

See Also   **InsertObject**

CopyBookmark

Syntax   **CopyBookmark** *Bookmark1$*, *Bookmark2$*

Remarks   Sets *Bookmark2$* to the insertion point or range of text marked by *Bookmark1$*. You can use this statement with predefined bookmarks—such as "\StartOfSel" and "\EndOfSel"—to set bookmarks relative to the insertion point or selection. For more information about predefined bookmarks, see "Operators and Predefined Bookmarks" later in this part.

Example   This example selects the current section, then sets one bookmark at the start of the section and another bookmark at the end. You can use this technique to define starting points and end points between which your macro operates.

```
EditGoTo "\Section"
CopyBookmark "\StartOfSel", "SectionStart"
CopyBookmark "\EndOfSel", "SectionEnd"
```

See Also   **CmpBookmarks(), EditBookmark, SetEndOfBookmark, SetStartOfBookmark**

CopyButtonImage

Syntax   **CopyButtonImage** *Toolbar$*, *Tool* [, *Context*]

Remarks   Copies the face of the specified toolbar button so that the face can be pasted onto another button using **PasteButtonImage**.

Argument	Explanation
Toolbar$	The name of the toolbar, as it appears in the Toolbars dialog box (View menu).
Tool	A number corresponding to the button face to copy, where 1 is the first button on the specified toolbar, 2 is the second, and so on.
Context	Specifies which button face Word copies:
	0 (zero) or omitted The button face that is displayed when a document based on the Normal template is active.
	1 The button face that is currently displayed.
	Note that the button face that is displayed depends on the custom settings, if any of the active template, any loaded global templates, and the Normal template.

Example   This example pastes the face of the third button on the Standard toolbar (the Save button) onto the first button of a custom toolbar named "TestBar":

```
CopyButtonImage "Standard", 3
PasteButtonImage "TestBar", 1
```

See Also   **AddButton, ChooseButtonImage, EditButtonImage, MoveButton, PasteButtonImage, ResetButtonImage**

CopyFile

Syntax **CopyFile .FileName** = *text*, **.Directory** = *text*

Remarks Copies a file to the specified folder. **CopyFile** allows you to specify a new name when copying the file.

Argument	Explanation
.FileName	The name of the file to copy. If you do not specify the path, Word copies the file from the current folder.
.Directory	The path of the folder to which the file is copied. Include a filename if you want to rename the file in addition to copying it.

Examples This example copies the document JULY.DOC to the C:\WINWORD\MEMOS folder. On the Macintosh, substitute a folder name such as HD:WORD 6:MEMOS.

```
CopyFile "JULY.DOC", "C:\WINWORD\MEMOS"
```

This example displays a dialog box that prompts for the folder to which to copy the active document. The proposed folder is C:\BAK. On the Macintosh, substitute a default folder name such as HD:BACKUP.

```
a$ = FileName$()
Dim dlg As CopyFile
dlg.FileName = a$
dlg.Directory = "C:\BAK"
x = Dialog(dlg)
If x = -1 Then CopyFile dlg
```

See Also **FileSaveAs, Kill, Name**

CopyFormat

Syntax **CopyFormat**

Remarks Copies the character formatting of the first character of the selected text to another text selection. If a paragraph mark is selected, Word copies paragraph formatting in addition to character formatting. For **CopyFormat** to work, macro instructions must make a selection immediately before the **CopyFormat** instruction, make a new selection immediately following **CopyFormat**, and then use the **PasteFormat** statement to apply the formatting.

Example This example copies the character formatting of the first character of the current paragraph (selected using the predefined bookmark "\Para") to the paragraph immediately above it:

```
EditGoTo "\Para"
CopyFormat
ParaUp 2
ParaDown 1, 1
PasteFormat
```

See Also   **CopyText, PasteFormat**

CopyText

Syntax   **CopyText**

Remarks   Copies the selected text without putting it on the Clipboard (the same as pressing SHIFT+F2). For **CopyText** to work, macro instructions must make a selection immediately before the **CopyText** instruction, make a new selection immediately after **CopyText**, and then use the **OK** statement to copy the text.

Example   This example inserts a copy of the current paragraph (selected using the predefined bookmark "\Para") immediately below the current paragraph:

```
EditGoTo "\Para"
CopyText
ParaDown
OK
```

See Also   **Cancel, MoveText, OK**

CountAddIns()

Syntax   **CountAddIns()**

Remarks   Returns the number of global templates and Word add-in libraries (WLLs) in the list of global templates and add-ins in the Templates And Add-ins dialog box (Templates command, File menu).

Example   This example unloads all global templates whose filenames contain the text ".DOT" in the list of global templates and add-ins.

```
For i = 1 To CountAddIns()
    a$ = GetAddInName$(i)
    If InStr(a$, ".DOT") <> 0 Then
        AddInState a$, 0
    End If
Next i
```

See Also   **AddAddIn, AddInState, ClearAddIns, DeleteAddIn, GetAddInId(), GetAddInName$()**

CountAutoCorrectExceptions()

Syntax   **CountAutoCorrectExceptions**(*Tab*)

Remarks   Returns the number of exceptions listed on the specified tab in the AutoCorrect Exceptions dialog box (AutoCorrect command, Tools menu). In Word version 6.0, **CountAutoCorrectExceptions()** is unavailable and generates an error.

Argument	Explanation
Tab	The tab from which to return the number of exceptions:
	0 (zero) First Letter
	1 INitial CAps

For an example, see **GetAutoCorrectException$()**.

See Also   **GetAutoCorrectException$()**, **IsAutoCorrectException()**, **ToolsAutoCorrectExceptions**

CountAutoTextEntries()

Syntax   **CountAutoTextEntries**([*Context*])

Remarks   Returns the number of AutoText entries defined for the specified context.

Argument	Explanation
Context	The context in which to count AutoText entries:
	0 (zero) or omitted Normal template and any loaded global templates
	1 Active template
	Note that if *Context* is 1 and the active template is the Normal template, **CountAutoTextEntries()** returns 0 (zero).

For an example, see **AutoTextName$()**.

See Also   **AutoTextName$()**, **GetAutoText$()**

CountBookmarks()

Syntax   **CountBookmarks()**

Remarks   Returns the number of bookmarks in the active document. As the first example in this entry demonstrates, you can use this function to define an array containing every bookmark in a document.

Examples

This example creates an array containing the name of every bookmark in the active document:

```
size = CountBookmarks() - 1
Dim marks$(size)
For count = 0 To size
    marks$(count) = BookmarkName$(count + 1)
Next
```

The following example deletes all the bookmarks in the active document:

```
For n = 1 To CountBookmarks()
    EditBookmark .Name = BookmarkName$(CountBookmarks()), \
        .Delete
Next
```

See Also

BookmarkName$(), **EditBookmark**

CountDirectories()

Syntax

CountDirectories(*Directory$*)

Remarks

Returns the number of subfolders contained within *Directory$*. If *Directory$* is omitted, the current folder is assumed. If *Directory$* does not exist, **CountDirectories()** returns –1.

Example

This example determines whether there are any subfolders in the Word program folder. On the Macintosh, substitute a folder name such as HD:WORD 6.

```
dirNum = CountDirectories("C:\WINWORD")
If dirNum = 0 Then
    MsgBox "No subfolders."
Else
    MsgBox "There are" + Str$(dirNum) + " subfolders."
End If
```

See Also

Files$(), **GetDirectory$()**

CountDocumentProperties()

Syntax

CountDocumentProperties()

Remarks

Returns the total number of built-in and custom document properties defined for the current document. For a list of the built-in properties available in Word, see **DocumentPropertyName$()**. In Word version 6.0, **CountDocumentProperties()** is unavailable and generates an error.

For an example, see **DocumentPropertyName$()**.

See Also

DocumentPropertyName$(), **GetDocumentProperty()**

CountDocumentVars()

Syntax   **CountDocumentVars()**

Remarks   Returns the number of document variables set with **SetDocumentVar** or
                      SetDocumentVar() in the active document.

Example   This example resets each document variable in the active document to an empty
                      string (""). If the document contains no variables, a message box is displayed.

```
numVars = CountDocumentVars()
If numVars > 0 Then
    For i = 1 To CountDocumentVars()
        name$ = GetDocumentVarName$(1)
        SetDocumentVar name$, ""
    Next
Else
    MsgBox "No document variables to reset."
End If
```

See Also   **GetDocumentVar$()**, **GetDocumentVarName$()**, **SetDocumentVar**

CountFiles()

Syntax   **CountFiles()**

Remarks   Returns the number of filenames in the list of most recently used files at the
                      bottom of the File menu.

Example   This example opens the most recently used file. You could use this instruction in
                      an AutoExec macro. It uses **CountFiles()** to determine that at least one file is
                      listed on the File menu.

```
If CountFiles() Then File1 Else MsgBox "Sorry, no file listed."
```

See Also   **FileList**, **FileName$()**, **File***Number*

CountFonts()

Syntax   **CountFonts()**

Remarks   Returns the number of fonts available with the selected printer. This is the number
                      of fonts listed in the Font dialog box (Format menu) or in the Formatting toolbar's
                      font list.

                      The font list includes fonts installed on the printer, TrueType® fonts (if they are
                      installed), and system fonts.

Example	This example creates a new document and then inserts the available font names, each formatted with the corresponding font:

```
FileNewDefault
For count = 1 To CountFonts()
    Font Font$(count)
    Insert Font$(count)
    InsertPara
Next
```

See Also	**Font**

CountFoundFiles()

Syntax	**CountFoundFiles()**
Remarks	Returns the number of files found in the last search using **FileFind**. **CountFoundFiles()** returns 0 (zero) if no files were found in the last search or if a search has not been performed during the current Word session.
Example	This example determines whether the last **FileFind** search was successful:

```
If CountFoundFiles() = 0 Then MsgBox "No files found."
```

For another example, see **FileFind**.

See Also	**FileFind**, **FoundFileName$()**

CountKeys()

Syntax	**CountKeys([**_Context_**])**
Remarks	Returns the number of key assignments specified on the Keyboard tab in the Customize dialog box (Tools menu) that differ from the default assignments.

Argument	Explanation
Context	Specifies the template in which to count key assignments:
	0 (zero) or omitted Normal template
	1 Active template

For an example, see **KeyCode()**.

See Also	**KeyCode()**, **KeyMacro$()**, **ToolsCustomizeKeyboard**

CountLanguages()

Syntax   **CountLanguages**( )

Remarks   Returns the number of available language formats, including the No Proofing format (set with the instruction `Language "0"`). For the list of valid foreign language names, see **ToolsLanguage**.

Example   This example fills the array `langnames$( )` with the list of available language formats:

```
Dim langnames$(CountLanguages())
For count = 1 To CountLanguages()
    langnames$(count) = Language$(count)
Next
```

See Also   **Language**, **ToolsLanguage**

CountMacros()

Syntax   **CountMacros**([*Context*] [**,** *All*] [**,** *Global*])

Remarks   Returns the number of macros available in the specified context.

Argument	Explanation
Context	Specifies the template in which to count macros:
	0 (zero) or omitted Normal template
	1 Active template
	Note that if you specify 1 and Normal is the active template, **CountMacros**() returns 0 (zero).
All	If 1, all available macros, add-in commands, and built-in commands are included in the count.
Global	If 1, only macros stored in loaded global templates and add-in commands are counted.

Example   This example stores the number of built-in commands in `builtins` and then inserts in the active document a list of the names of the built-in commands:

```
loaded = CountMacros(0, 0, 1)
active = CountMacros(1)
normal = CountMacros(0)
templates = active + normal
nonbuiltins = loaded + templates
builtins = CountMacros(0, 1) - nonbuiltins
For count = 1 to builtins
    pos = count + nonbuiltins
    Insert Str$(count) + Chr$(9) + MacroName$(pos, 0, 1)
    InsertPara
Next count
```

See Also   **ListCommands, MacroName$()**

CountMenuItems()

Syntax   **CountMenuItems(***Menu$***,** *Type* **[,** *Context***])**

Remarks   Returns the number of menu items on the specified menu. Separators are counted as menu items. In several cases, a list of menu items is counted as one. You can identify these cases in the Position On Menu box on the Menus tab in the Customize dialog box (Tools menu). Examples include the list of filenames on the File menu, the list of windows on the Window menu, and the list of proofing tools on the Tools menu.

Argument	Explanation
Menu$	The name of a menu or a shortcut menu. Menu names appear in the Menu list box, which is on the Menus tab in the Customize dialog box (Tools menu).
	Including an ampersand (&) before the underlined letter in the menu name is optional (for example, you can specify either "File" or "&File"). Do not include the parenthetical phrases "(No Document)" and "(Shortcut)" even though that text appears in the Customize dialog box.
Type	The type of menu:
	0 (zero) Menus on the menu bar when a document is open
	1 Menus on the menu bar when no document is open
	2 Shortcut menus
Context	Specifies which menu items to count:
	0 (zero) The items that are displayed on the menu when a document based on the Normal template is active
	1 or omitted The items that are currently displayed on the menu
	Note that the items that are displayed on the menu depend on the custom settings, if any, of the active template, any loaded global templates, and the Normal template.

Example

This example inserts a tab-delimited list of the menu items on the Tools menu in the active template:

```
tab$ = Chr$(9)
For n = 1 To CountMenuItems("T&ools", 0, 1)
    Insert Str$(n) + tab$ + MenuItemText$("T&ools", 0, n, 1)
    InsertPara
Next
```

See Also

MenuItemMacro$(), **MenuItemText$()**

CountMenus()

Syntax

CountMenus(*Type* [, *Context*])

Remarks

Returns the number of menus of the specified type.

Argument	Explanation
Type	The type of menu to count:
	0 (zero) Menus on the menu bar when a document is open
	1 Menus on the menu bar when no document is open
	2 Shortcut menus
Context	Specifies which menus are counted:
	0 (zero) The menus that are available when a document based on the Normal template is active
	1 or omitted The menus that are currently available
	Note that the menus that are available depend on the custom settings, if any, of the active template, any loaded global templates, and the Normal template.

For an example, see **MenuText$()**.

See Also

CountMacros(), **CountMenuItems()**, **MenuText$()**

CountMergeFields()

Syntax

CountMergeFields()

Remarks

Returns the number of fields in the header record of the data source or in the header source attached to the active main document. **CountMergeFields()** returns 0 (zero) if the active document is not a main document, data source, or header source.

Example   This example inserts a list of merge field names in the active document:

```
For n = 1 To CountMergeFields()
    Insert MergeFieldName$(n)
    InsertPara
Next
```

See Also   **InsertMergeField**, **MergeFieldName$()**

CountStyles()

Syntax   **CountStyles(**[*Context*] [, *All*]**)**

Remarks   Returns the number of styles defined for the specified context.

Argument	Explanation
Context	Specifies the location of styles to count:
	0 (zero) or omitted Active document
	1 Active template
All	Specifies whether to include built-in styles:
	0 (zero) or omitted Built-in styles are excluded.
	1 Built-in styles are included.
	Note that Word contains 75 built-in styles, and that two of those built-in styles are defined by default: Default Paragraph Font and Normal.

Examples   This example returns the number of all built-in styles plus the number of user-created styles used in the template attached to the active document:

```
n = CountStyles(1, 1)
```

The following example merges styles into the active document from the attached template. Then, the macro finds the number of styles defined just for the document, if any, by subtracting the number of styles defined for the template from the number of styles defined for the document.

```
FormatStyle .Source = 1, .Merge
n = CountStyles(0, 0) - CountStyles(1, 0)
```

See Also   **StyleName$()**

CountToolbarButtons()

Syntax   **CountToolbarButtons(***Toolbar$* [, *Context*]**)**

Remarks   Returns the number of toolbar buttons on the specified toolbar. Note that spaces and list boxes are counted as "buttons."

Argument	Explanation
Toolbar$	The name of the toolbar as it appears in the Toolbars dialog box (View menu)
Context	Specifies which buttons to count:
	0 (zero) The buttons that are available when a document based on the Normal template is active
	1 or omitted The buttons that are currently available
	Note that the buttons that are available depend on the custom settings, if any, of the active template, any loaded global templates, and the Normal template.

For an example, see **CountToolbars()**.

See Also   **CountToolbars()**, **ToolbarButtonMacro$()**, **ToolbarName$()**

CountToolbars()

Syntax   **CountToolbars(**[*Context*]**)**

Remarks   Returns the number of toolbars listed in the Toolbars dialog box (View menu). Note that not all toolbars are listed in all circumstances. For example, the macro toolbar only appears in the Toolbars dialog box when at least one macro-editing window is open.

Argument	Explanation
Context	Specifies which toolbars to count:
	0 (zero) The toolbars that are available when a document based on the Normal template is active
	1 or omitted The toolbars that are currently available
	Note that the toolbars that are available depend on the custom settings, if any, of the active template, any loaded global templates, and the Normal template.

Example   This example creates a new document and then inserts a list of toolbar names followed by the number of buttons on each toolbar.

```
FileNewDefault
For i = 1 To CountToolbars(0)
    name$ = ToolbarName$(i)
    numbuttons = CountToolbarButtons(name$)
    Insert name$ + "," + Str$(numbuttons) + Chr$(13)
Next i
```

See Also   **CountToolbarButtons()**, **ToolbarButtonMacro$()**, **ToolbarName$()**

CountToolsGrammarStatistics()

Syntax	**CountToolsGrammarStatistics( )**
Remarks	Returns the number of statistics that are stored when you check grammar with the **ToolsGrammar** statement. You can use this number to define the size of a two-dimensional array that you fill using the **ToolsGrammarStatisticsArray** statement.
	For an example, see **ToolsGrammarStatisticsArray**.
See Also	**ToolsGrammar**, **ToolsGrammarStatisticsArray**, **ToolsOptionsGrammar**

CountWindows()

Syntax	**CountWindows( )**
Remarks	Returns the number of open document and macro-editing windows, which is also the number of windows listed on the Window menu.
Example	This macro arranges windows side by side instead of stacking them as the Arrange All command (Window menu) does:

```
Sub MAIN
yours$ = WindowName$()               'Note which window is active
If DocMaximize() Then DocRestore     'Can't resize if maximized
fullwidth = Val(AppInfo$(6))         'Get workspace width
fulldepth = Val(AppInfo$(7))         'Get workspace depth
width = fullwidth / CountWindows()
For wnd = 1 To CountWindows()        'Move each window, resize it
    x = width *(wnd - 1)
    If DocMinimize() Then DocRestore 'Can't resize if minimized
    DocMove x, 0
    DocSize width, fulldepth - 1
    NextWindow
Next wnd
Activate yours$                      'Reactivate original window
End Sub
```

See Also	**WindowName$( )**, **Window***Number*

CreateSubdocument

Syntax   **CreateSubdocument**

Remarks   Converts the selected outline headings into subdocuments. If the active document
                    is not in master document or outline view, or if the selection spans a subdocument
                    boundary, an error occurs. An error is also generated if the first paragraph selected
                    is not a heading.

See Also   **InsertSubdocument**, **MergeSubdocument**, **OpenSubdocument**,
                    RemoveSubdocument, **SplitSubdocument**, **ViewMasterDocument**

Date$()

Syntax

Date$([*SerialNumber*])

Remarks

Returns a date corresponding to *SerialNumber*, a decimal representation of the date, time, or both. If *SerialNumber* is omitted, **Date$()** returns today's date. For information about serial numbers, see **DateSerial()**.

The date format is determined by the "DateFormat=" line in the [Microsoft Word] section of WINWORD6.INI (Windows 3.*x*), Word Settings (6) (Macintosh), or the registry (Windows 95 and Windows NT). (In Windows 3.*x*, if there is no "DateFormat=" line, **Date$()** uses the "sShortDate" setting in the [intl] section of WIN.INI.) You can use **SetPrivateProfileString** to change the current date format.

Example

This Windows example displays the current date in a message box, in the form MMMM d, yyyy (which produces a date string such as "January 1, 1994"). The first instruction saves the original date format so that it may be restored in the last instruction. On the Macintosh, substitute "Word Settings (6)" for "WINWORD6.INI."

```
OriginalFormat$ = GetPrivateProfileString$("Microsoft Word", \
    "DateFormat", "WINWORD6.INI")
SetPrivateProfileString "Microsoft Word", "DateFormat", \
    "MMMM d, yyyy", "WINWORD6.INI"
MsgBox "Today is " + Date$() + "."
SetPrivateProfileString "Microsoft Word", "DateFormat", \
    OriginalFormat$, "WINWORD6.INI"
```

See Also

DateSerial(), **DateValue()**, **Day()**, **GetPrivateProfileString$()**, **Month()**, **Now()**, **SetPrivateProfileString**, **Time$()**, **Today()**, **Year()**

DateSerial()

Syntax

DateSerial(*Year*, *Month*, *Day*)

Remarks

Returns the serial number of the specified date. The serial number corresponds to the number of days between December 30, 1899, and the specified date, up to December 31, 4095. For example, the serial number 1 corresponds to December 31, 1899. **DateSerial()** generates an error if the specified date is beyond the allowable range.

Argument	Explanation
Year	A number between 0 (zero) and 4095, inclusive, or a numeric expression. To specify a year in the range 1900 to 1999, you can give the last two digits of the year; to specify the year 1899 or a year after 1999, give all four digits of the year.
Month	A number between 1 and 12, inclusive, or a numeric expression representing the month of the year.
Day	A number between 1 and 31, inclusive, or a numeric expression representing the day of the month.

Example

This example prompts the user to enter a date and then displays a message box to indicate the day of the week corresponding to that date:

```
Dim days$(7)
days$(1) = "Sunday" : days$(2) = "Monday" days$(3) = "Tuesday"
days$(4) = "Wednesday" days$(5) = "Thursday"
days$(6) = "Friday" days$(7) = "Saturday"
datestring$ = Inputbox$("Please enter the date for which " + \
        "you want to determine the weekday (mm/dd/yy):")
monthnum = Val(Left$(datestring$, 2))
daynum = Val(Mid$(datestring$, 4, 2))
yearnum = Val(Right$(datestring$, 2))
dayofweek = DateSerial(yearnum, monthnum, daynum)
MsgBox "The day of the week is " + days$(Weekday(dayofweek)) + "."
```

See Also

Date$(), **DateValue()**, **Day()**, **Month()**, **Now()**, **TimeSerial()**, **Today()**, **Year()**

DateValue()

Syntax

DateValue(*DateText$*)

Remarks

Returns the serial number of the date represented by *DateText$*. Use **DateValue()** to convert a date represented by text to a serial number. A serial number is a decimal representation of the date, time, or both. For information about serial numbers, see **DateSerial()**.

Argument	Explanation
DateText$	A string representing a date in a Word date format. For example, the following are each valid representations of July 8, 1991:
	7/8/91
	July 8, 1991
	8 July 1991
	If *DateText$* includes only numbers, **DateValue()** recognizes the order of the components of the date as month, day, year.

DateText$ must represent a date from December 30, 1899, to December 31, 4095. **DateValue()** generates an error if *DateText$* is out of this range. If the year portion of *DateText$* is omitted, **DateValue()** uses the current year from the computer's built-in calendar. **DateValue()** ignores time information in *DateText$*.

Example

This example prompts the user to enter an end date, and then displays the number of days between today and that date:

```
enddate$ = InputBox$("Please enter an end date:")
serialenddate = DateValue(enddate$)
numdays = serialenddate - Today()
numdays = Abs(numdays)
MsgBox "The number of days between now and " + enddate$ + \
    " is" + Str$(numdays) + "."
```

See Also

Date$(), **DateSerial()**, **Now()**, **TimeValue()**, **Today()**

Day()

Syntax

Day(*SerialNumber*)

Remarks

Returns an integer between 1 and 31, inclusive, corresponding to the day component of *SerialNumber*, a decimal representation of the date, time, or both. For information about serial numbers, see **DateSerial()**.

Argument	Explanation
SerialNumber	The serial number used by Word for date and time calculations. *SerialNumber* can represent a date or time (or both) from December 30, 1899, through December 31, 4095, where December 30, 1899, is 0 (zero).

Example

This example uses the **Day()** function to determine the day of the month, and then displays the result in a message box with the appropriate suffix (for example, "3rd"):

```
daynumber = Day(Now())
Select Case daynumber
    Case 1, 21, 31
        daysuffix$ = "st"
    Case 2, 22
        daysuffix$ = "nd"
    Case 3, 23
        daysuffix$ = "rd"
    Case Else
        daysuffix$ = "th"
End Select
MsgBox "Today is the" + Str$(daynumber) + \
        daysuffix$ + " day of the month."
```

See Also	DateSerial(), Hour(), Minute(), Month(), Now(), Second(), Today(), Weekday(), Year()

Days360()

Syntax	**Days360**(*StartDate*[*$*]**,** *EndDate*[*$*])
Remarks	Returns the number of days between two dates based on a 360-day year (twelve 30-day months). Use this function to help compute payments if your accounting system is based on twelve 30-day months. The arguments *StartDate* and *EndDate* are the two dates between which you want to know the number of days. If *StartDate* occurs after *EndDate*, **Days360**() returns a negative number.

Argument	Explanation
StartDate[*$*]	A text string or a serial number that represents the initial date. For information about available date formats in Word, see **DateValue**(). For information about serial numbers, see **DateSerial**().
EndDate[*$*]	A text string or a serial number that represents the end date.

Example	This example uses **Days360**() to determine the number of days between January 1, 1992, and February 1, 1993, assuming a 360-day year:

```
numdays = Days360("1/1/92","2/1/93")
```

See Also	**DateSerial**(), **DateValue**(), **Day**()

DDEExecute

Syntax	**DDEExecute** *ChanNum***,** *Command$*
Remarks	Sends a command or series of commands to an application through a dynamic-data exchange (DDE) channel.

Argument	Explanation
ChanNum	The channel number of the DDE conversation as returned by **DDEInitiate**(). If *ChanNum* doesn't correspond to an open channel, an error occurs.
Command$	A command or series of commands recognized by the server application. In Windows, you can also use the format described under **SendKeys** to send specific key sequences. If the server application can't perform the specified command, an error occurs.

In Microsoft Excel and many other applications that support DDE, *Command$* should be one or more statements or functions in the application's macro language. For example, in Microsoft Excel the XLM macro instruction to create a new worksheet is NEW(1). To send the same command through a DDE channel, you use the following instruction:

```
DDEExecute channel, "[NEW(1)]"
```

Note that some applications, including Microsoft Excel, require that each command received through a DDE channel be enclosed in brackets.

You can use a single **DDEExecute** instruction to send more than one command. For example, the following instruction tells Microsoft Excel to open and then close a worksheet:

```
DDEExecute channel, "[NEW(1)][FILE.CLOSE(0)]"
```

Note that there is no space between the bracketed commands; a space character between the commands would cause an error. The preceding instruction is equivalent to the following two instructions:

```
DDEExecute channel, "[NEW(1)]"
DDEExecute channel, "[FILE.CLOSE(0)]"
```

Many commands require arguments in the form of strings enclosed in quotation marks. Because quotation marks indicate the beginning and end of a string in WordBasic, you must use Chr$(34) to include a quotation mark in a command string. For example, the following instruction tells Microsoft Excel to open SALES.XLS:

```
DDEExecute channel, "[OPEN(" + Chr$(34) + "SALES.XLS" + Chr$(34) + ")]"
```

For more information on sending commands to Microsoft Excel and other applications, see Chapter 8, "Communicating with Other Applications" in Part 1, "Learning WordBasic."

Example

This example starts Microsoft Excel if it is not running and then opens a channel to Microsoft Excel and the System topic (for information on the System topic, see **DDERequest$( )**). The example then sends commands to open SALES.XLS (Windows) or BLUE SKY SALES (Macintosh) and go to cell R4C2. Unlike a document, which may or may not be open, the System topic is always available when Microsoft Excel is running.

Here is the Windows version of the example:

```
If AppIsRunning("Microsoft Excel") = 0 Then Shell "C:\EXCEL\EXCEL.EXE"
channel = DDEInitiate("Excel", "System")
q$ = Chr$(34)
cmd1$ = "[OPEN(" + q$ + "C:\EXCEL\EXAMPLES\SALES.XLS" + q$ + ")]"
cmd2$ = "[SELECT(" + q$ + " R4C2" + q$ + ", " + q$ + " R4C2" + q$ + ")]"
bothcmds$ = cmd1$ + cmd2$
DDEExecute channel, bothcmds$
```

And here is the Macintosh version:

```
If AppIsRunning(MacID$("XCEL")) = 0 Then Shell MacID$("XCEL")
channel = DDEInitiate("Excel", "System")
q$ = Chr$(34)
cmd1$ = "[OPEN(" + q$ + "HD1:EXCEL:EXAMPLES:BLUE SKY SALES" + q$ + ")]"
cmd2$ = "[SELECT(" + q$ + " R4C2" + q$ + ", " + q$ + " R4C2" + q$ + ")]"
bothcmds$ = cmd1$ + cmd2$
DDEExecute channel, bothcmds$
```

See Also   **DDEInitiate(), DDEPoke, DDERequest$(), DDETerminate, DDETerminateAll**

DDEInitiate()

Syntax   **DDEInitiate(***Application$, Topic$***)**

Remarks   Initiates a dynamic-data exchange (DDE) conversation with an application and opens a DDE channel through which the conversation takes place. If **DDEInitiate()** is able to open a channel, it returns the number of the open channel, which is an integer greater than 0 (zero). (The first DDE channel Word opens during a session is channel 1, the second is channel 2, and so on.) All subsequent DDE instructions during the DDE conversation use this number to specify the channel. **DDEInitiate()** returns 0 (zero) if it fails to open a channel.

Note In Word version 6.0 for Windows NT and Word version 7.0, you cannot depend on a program started with **Shell** to be finished loading before the instructions following the **Shell** statement in your macro are run. A **DDEInitiate** instruction that tries to communicate with an application that has not finished loading will generate errors. To avoid this problem, you can use a **For...Next** loop to delay the **DDEInitiate** instruction until the other application is loaded. For example:

```
If AppIsRunning("Microsoft Access") = 0 Then
    Shell "MSACCESS.EXE", 0
    For i = 1 to 2000
        x = i
    Next i
End IF
chan = DDEInitiate("MSAccess", "System")
```

Argument	Explanation
Application$	The name used to specify an application that supports DDE as a DDE server. In Windows, this is usually the name of the application's .EXE file without the .EXE filename extension. If the application is not running, **DDEInitiate( )** cannot open a channel and returns an error.
Topic$	The name of a topic recognized by *Application$*. An open document is a typical topic. (If *Topic$* is a document name, the document must be open.) If *Application$* doesn't recognize *Topic$*, **DDEInitiate( )** generates an error.
	Many applications that support DDE recognize a topic named System, which is always available and can be used to find out which other topics are available. For more information on the System topic, see **DDERequest$( )**.

The maximum number of channels that can be open simultaneously is determined by Microsoft Windows and your system's memory and resources. If you aren't using an open channel, you should conserve resources by closing the channel using **DDETerminate** or **DDETerminateAll**.

Examples

This example opens a channel to Microsoft Excel and the file SALES.XLS (Windows) or BLUE SKY SALES (Macintosh). The variable `channel` is assigned the channel number that is returned. If Microsoft Excel is not running or the file is not open, the function returns 0 (zero) and generates an error.

Here is the Windows version of the example:

```
channel = DDEInitiate("Excel", "C:\EXCEL\EXAMPLES\SALES.XLS")
```

And here is the Macintosh version:

```
channel = DDEInitiate("Excel", "HD1:EXCEL:EXAMPLES:BLUE SKY SALES")
```

The following example first ensures that Microsoft Excel is running, and then opens a channel to Microsoft Excel and the System topic and uses **DDERequest$( )** to get the Topics item. The Topics item, a standard item in the System topic that is always available, is a list of available topics, including the names of open documents.

Here is the Windows version of the example:

```
If AppIsRunning("Microsoft Excel") = 0 Then
   Shell "C:\EXCEL\EXCEL.EXE"
   AppActivate "Microsoft Word", 1
End If
channel = DDEInitiate("Excel", "System")
topics$ = DDERequest$(channel, "Topics")
If InStr(topics$, "Sheet1") <> 0 Then
    MsgBox "Sheet1 is an available topic."
End If
DDETerminate channel
```

And here is the Macintosh version:

```
If AppIsRunning(MacID$("XCEL")) = 0 Then
   Shell MacID$("XCEL")
   AppActivate MacID$("MSWD"), 1
End If
channel = DDEInitiate("Excel", "System")
topics$ = DDERequest$(channel, "Topics")
If InStr(topics$, "Sheet1") <> 0 Then
    MsgBox "Sheet1 is an available topic."
End If
DDETerminate channel
```

See Also   **DDEExecute**, **DDEPoke**, **DDERequest$()**, **DDETerminate**, **DDETerminateAll**

DDEPoke

Syntax   **DDEPoke** *ChanNum*, *Item$*, *Data$*

Remarks   Uses an open dynamic-data exchange (DDE) channel to send data to an application. When you start a DDE conversation using **DDEInitiate()**, you open a channel to a specific topic recognized by the server application. In Microsoft Excel, for example, each open document is a separate topic. When you send information to a topic in the server application, you must specify the item in that topic you want to send information to. In Microsoft Excel, for example, cells are valid items and they are referred to using either the "R1C1" format or named references.

DDEPoke sends data as a text string; you cannot send text in any other format, nor can you send graphics.

Argument	Explanation
ChanNum	The channel number of the DDE conversation as returned by **DDEInitiate()**. If *ChanNum* doesn't correspond to an open channel, an error occurs.
Item$	An item within a DDE topic. If the server application doesn't recognize *Item$*, an error occurs.
Data$	The string containing the data to send to the server application.

Examples

This example sends the value of the variable `Total$` to the second row and third column of the Sheet1 worksheet in Microsoft Excel. On the Macintosh, the application name used in the **DDEInitiate()** instruction should be `MacID$("XCEL")` rather than `"Excel"`.

```
channel — DDEInitiate ("Excel". "Sheet1")
DDEPoke channel, "R2C3", Total$
```

The following example sends the string "Total: $1,434" to the cell named "QuarterTotal" in the Sheet1 worksheet. On the Macintosh, the application name used in the **DDEInitiate()** instruction should be `MacID$("XCEL")` rather than `"Excel"`.

```
channel — DDEInitiate("Excel", "Sheet1")
DDEPoke channel, "QuarterTotal", "Total: $1,434"
```

See Also

DDEExecute, DDEInitiate(), DDERequest$(), DDETerminate, DDETerminateAll

DDERequest$()

Syntax

DDERequest$(*ChanNum***,** *Item$***)**

Remarks

Uses an open dynamic-data exchange (DDE) channel to request an item of information from an application. When you start a DDE conversation using **DDEInitiate()**, you open a channel to a specific topic recognized by the server application. In Microsoft Excel, for example, each open document is a separate topic. When you request information from the topic in the server application, you must specify the item in that topic whose contents you are requesting. In Microsoft Excel, for example, cells are valid items and they are referred to using either the "R1C1" format or named references.

DDERequest$() returns data as a text string only; if the function is unsuccessful, it returns an empty string (""). Text in any other format cannot be transferred, nor can graphics.

Argument	Explanation
ChanNum	The channel number of the DDE conversation as returned by **DDEInitiate**( ). If *ChanNum* doesn't correspond to an open channel, an error occurs.
Item$	The item within a DDE topic recognized by the server application. **DDERequest$**( ) returns the entire contents of the specified item. If the server application doesn't recognize *Item$*, an error occurs.

Microsoft Excel and other applications that support DDE recognize a topic named System. Three standard items in the System topic are described in the following table. Note that you can get a list of the other items in the System topic using the item SysItems.

Item in System topic	Effect
SysItems	Returns a list of all items in the System topic
Topics	Returns a list of available topics
Formats	Returns a list of all the Clipboard formats supported by Word

For an example that uses the System topic, see **DDETerminate**( ).

Example

This Windows example opens a channel to Microsoft Excel and SALES.XLS and then requests the contents of cell R4C2:

```
channel = DDEInitiate("Excel", "C:\EXCEL\EXAMPLES\SALES.XLS")
a$ = DDERequest$(channel, "R4C2")
MsgBox a$
```

Here is the same example for the Macintosh:

```
channel = DDEInitiate("Excel", "HD1:EXCEL:EXAMPLES:BLUE SKY SALES")
a$ = DDERequest$(channel, "R4C2")
MsgBox a$
```

See Also   **DDEExecute**, **DDEInitiate**( ), **DDEPoke**, **DDETerminate**, **DDETerminateAll**

DDETerminate

Syntax   **DDETerminate** *ChanNum*

Remarks   Closes the specified dynamic-data exchange (DDE) channel. To free system resources, you should close channels you aren't using.

Argument	Explanation
ChanNum	The channel number of the DDE conversation as returned by **DDEInitiate**( ). If *ChanNum* isn't an open channel number, an error occurs.

Example

This example opens a DDE channel to request a list of topics from Microsoft Excel. The instructions insert the requested list into the active Word document and then close the channel. On the Macintosh, the application name used in the **DDEInitiate()** instruction should be MacID$("XCEL") rather than "Excel".

```
channel = DDEInitiate("Excel", "System")
a$ = DDERequest$(channel, "Topics")
Insert a$
DDETerminate channel
```

See Also

DDEExecute, **DDEInitiate()**, **DDEPoke**, **DDERequest$()**, **DDETerminateAll**

DDETerminateAll

Syntax

DDETerminateAll

Remarks

Closes all dynamic-data exchange (DDE) channels opened by Word; **DDETerminateAll** does not close channels opened to Word by client applications. Using this statement is the same as using a **DDETerminate** statement for each open channel. **DDETerminateAll** does not cause an error if no DDE channels are open.

If you interrupt a macro that opens a DDE channel, you may inadvertently leave a channel open. Open channels are not closed automatically when a macro ends, and each open channel uses system resources. For this reason, it's a good idea to use **DDETerminateAll** while debugging a macro that opens one or more DDE channels.

See Also

DDEExecute, **DDEInitiate()**, **DDEPoke**, **DDERequest$()**, **DDETerminate**

Declare

Syntax

Declare Sub *SubName* **Lib** *LibName$* [(*ArgumentList*)] [**Alias** *Routine$*]

Declare Function *FunctionName*[$] **Lib** *LibName$* [(*ArgumentList*)] [**Alias** *Routine$*] **As** *Type*

Remarks

In Windows, makes available a routine stored in a Windows dynamic-link library (DLL), a Word add-in library (WLL), or the Windows operating system for use as a function or subroutine in a WordBasic macro. On the Macintosh, makes available a routine stored in a Word add-in library (WLL) only. The declaration specifies the name of the routine, the library file in which it is stored, and any arguments the routine takes. **Declare** instructions are usually placed at the start of a macro, before the main subroutine; they cannot be placed inside a subroutine or function.

Caution

- When experimenting with external routines, save your work often. An invalid argument passed to a routine could result in unpredictable behavior in Word or other applications.

- You cannot declare an external routine in a 16-bit library from a 32-bit application, such as Word for Windows 95 or Word version 6.0 for Windows NT. You must update macros that declare routines in 16-bit libraries to identify the 32-bit versions of those libraries.

- The names and locations of many Windows 3.*x* operating system routines (often referred to as API calls) changed in Windows 95 and Windows NT. You must update macros that declare Windows 3.*x* API calls to declare the correct routines in Windows 95 or Windows NT. Windows 3.*x* API function libraries are documented in the Microsoft Windows 3.1 Software Development Kit. Windows 95 and Windows NT function libraries are documented in the Microsoft Win32 Software Development Kit.

Argument	Explanation
Sub or **Function**	Use **Function** if the function you are declaring returns a value; use **Sub** if it does not.
SubName or *FunctionName*[$]	The name used in the macro to call the routine. This name does not have to be the actual name of the routine in the library. You can define the actual name using the **Alias** part of the statement. If *FunctionName* returns a string, it should include a dollar sign ($) like other string functions in WordBasic. Note that routine names are case sensitive in Windows 95 and Windows NT; if this name is the actual name of the routine in the library, it should match the documented case.
LibName$	The filename of the library containing the routine, in quotation marks. In Windows, use the entire filename, including the extension, to prevent ambiguity.
	In Windows, Word looks for the file in the current folder, the Windows folder, the Windows System folder, the Word program folder, and in the folders listed in the PATH environment variable. If the file is not stored in any of these folders, or is not a loaded add-in libarary (WLL), include the complete path with the filename. On the Macintosh, Word looks for the file in the current folder, the System folder, the Word program folder, the Word Dictionaries folder, and the Microsoft folder. If the file is not stored in any of these folders, or is not a loaded WLL, include the complete path with the filename.
ArgumentList	A list of variables representing arguments that are passed to the routine. See the following table for the syntax used within *ArgumentList*.

Argument	Explanation
Alias *Routine$*	The actual name of the routine in the library, in quotation marks. It is required only if the name specified after **Sub** or **Function** is not the actual name of the routine. Note that routine names are case sensitive in Windows 95 and Windows NT.
As *Type*	Declares the data type of the value returned by a function. The type is one of the following: **As Integer** for an integer or logical (BOOL) return type; **As String** for a string (LPSTR) return type; **As Long** for a long return type; **As Double** for a double return type.

The *ArgumentList* argument has the following syntax:

(*Variable*[$] [**As** *Type*] [, *Variable*[$] [**As** *Type*]] [, ...])

The following table describes the parts of *ArgumentList*.

Part	Explanation
Variable[$]	A WordBasic variable name. For string variables, adding a dollar sign ($) to the variable name is the same as specifying **As String**— for example, fileName$ is the same as fileName As String. If there is no **As** *Type*, and the variable name does not end in a dollar sign, the variable defaults to a WordBasic numeric variable (double precision floating-point number).
As *Type*	Declares the data type of the argument required by the routine: **As Integer** for integer or logical (BOOL) arguments; **As String** (or simply $ at the end of the variable name) for string (LPSTR) arguments; **As Long** for long arguments; **As Double** for double arguments.

Example

This Windows example uses the selection as a search keyword in Help. If there is one exact match, the macro displays the topic. If there is more than one match, the macro displays the Search dialog box (Windows 3.*x* Help) or the Help Topics dialog box (Windows 95 Help) with the keyword selected. If there is no match, the macro displays the Search or Help Topics dialog box, with the keyword list scrolled to the keyword closest in spelling to the selected word.

```
Declare Function WinHelp Lib "USER.EXE"(hWnd As Integer, lpHelpFile \
    As String, wCmd As Integer, dwData As String) As Integer
Declare Function GetActiveWindow Lib "USER.EXE"() As Integer
Sub MAIN
    hWnd = GetActiveWindow
    helpFile$ = "C:\WINWORD\WINWORD.HLP"
    wCmd = 261              'The decimal value for HELP_PARTIALKEY
    keyWord$ = Selection$()
    success = WinHelp(hWnd, helpFile$, wCmd, keyWord$)
    If success = 0 Then MsgBox "Could not start Windows Help"
End Sub
```

See Also   **Dim**

DefaultDir$()

Syntax   **DefaultDir$(***Type***)**

Remarks   Returns the path currently set for the default folder specified by *Type*, a number that corresponds to a default folder, as shown in the following table.

Type	**Explanation**
0	DOC-PATH
1	PICTURE-PATH
2	USER-DOT-PATH
3	WORKGROUP-DOT-PATH
4	INI-PATH
5	AUTOSAVE-PATH
6	TOOLS-PATH
7	CBT-PATH
8	STARTUP-PATH
9	The program-file path (PROGRAMDIR)
10	The graphics-filter path (fixed; cannot be changed)
11	The text-converter path (fixed; cannot be changed)
12	The proofing-tool path (fixed; cannot be changed)
13	The temporary-file path
14	The current folder
15	The style-gallery–template path (can be changed using **ChDefaultDir**)
16	The Trash folder (Macintosh only)
17	The Microsoft folder (Macintosh only)

Example	This example sets TOOLS-PATH to C:\TOOLS if it is not set already. On the Macintosh, substitute a folder name such as HD:TOOLS.

```
If DefaultDir$(6) = "" Then
    ChDefaultDir "C:\TOOLS", 6
End If
```

See Also	**ChDefaultDir**, **ChDir**

DeleteAddIn

Syntax	**DeleteAddIn** *AddIn*
	DeleteAddIn *AddIn$*
Remarks	Removes a global template or Word add-in library (WLL) from the list of global templates and add-ins in the Templates And Add-ins dialog box (Templates command, File menu).

Argument	Explanation
AddIn	A number corresponding to the global template or add-in's position in the list, where 1 is the first template or add-in, 2 is the second, and so on.
AddIn$	The path (if necessary) and filename of the global template or add-in.

See Also	**AddAddIn**, **AddInState()**, **ClearAddIns**, **CountAddIns()**, **GetAddInId()**, **GetAddInName$()**

DeleteBackWord

Syntax	**DeleteBackWord**
Remarks	Deletes the word immediately preceding the insertion point or the selection, but does not place it on the Clipboard.
	If there is a selection, **DeleteBackWord** behaves as if there were an insertion point; the statement does not delete the selection but deletes the word immediately preceding it. If the insertion point is in the middle of a word, **DeleteBackWord** deletes the characters between the insertion point and the start of the word.
	Note that if there is a space character between the word and the insertion point, **DeleteBackWord** deletes the space character as well as the word. Also, if the insertion point follows a punctuation mark, such as a comma or period, **DeleteBackWord** deletes the punctuation mark only.
See Also	**DeleteWord**, **EditClear**, **EditCut**, **WordLeft**

DeleteButton

Syntax   **DeleteButton** *Toolbar$,* *Position* [, *Context*]

Remarks   Removes a button, list box, or space from a toolbar.

Argument	Explanation
Toolbar$	The name of the toolbar as listed in the Toolbars dialog box (View menu).
Position	A number corresponding to the position of the item to remove, where 1 is the first position, 2 is the second, and so on. Note that a list box or space counts as one position.
Context	Determines where the change to the toolbar is stored:
	0 (zero) or omitted Normal template
	1 Active template

For an example, see **AddButton**.

See Also   **AddButton**, **ChooseButtonImage**, **CopyButtonImage**, **EditButtonImage**, **MoveButton**, **PasteButtonImage**, **ResetButtonImage**

DeleteDocumentProperty

Syntax   **DeleteDocumentProperty** *Name$*

Remarks   Removes the *Name$* custom property from the list of custom properties on the Custom tab in the Properties dialog box (Properties command, File menu). If the property specified by *Name$* is not a custom property, an error occurs. Use the **DocumentPropertyExists**() function to verify that the *Name$* property exists.

For a list of the built-in properties available in Word, see **DocumentPropertyName$**(). In Word version 6.0, **DeleteDocumentProperty** is unavailable and generates an error.

See Also   **DocumentPropertyExists**(), **GetDocumentProperty**(), **IsCustomDocumentProperty**(), **SetDocumentProperty**

DeleteWord

Syntax   **DeleteWord**

Remarks   Deletes the word immediately following the insertion point or the first word or part of a word included in the selection, but does not place it on the Clipboard. If the insertion point is in the middle of a word, **DeleteWord** deletes the characters following the insertion point to the end of the word.

Note that if there is a space character between the insertion point and the word, **DeleteWord** deletes the space character as well as the word. Also, if the insertion point precedes a punctuation mark, such as a comma or period, **DeleteWord** deletes the punctuation mark only.

See Also   **DeleteBackWord, EditClear, EditCut, WordRight**

DemoteList

Syntax   **DemoteList**

Remarks   Demotes the selected paragraphs by one level in a multilevel list. If the selected paragraphs are formatted as a bulleted list or as a numbered list that isn't

multilevel, **DemoteList** increases the indent. If the selected paragraphs are not already formatted as a numbered or bulleted list, an error occurs.

See Also   **FormatBulletsAndNumbering, PromoteList**

DemoteToBodyText

Syntax   **DemoteToBodyText**

Remarks   Demotes the selected headings to body text by applying the Normal style. **DemoteToBodyText** has no effect if the selected paragraphs are already formatted with Normal style.

See Also   **OutlineDemote, OutlineMoveDown, OutlinePromote**

Dialog, Dialog()

Syntax   **Dialog** *DialogRecord* [, *DefaultButton*] [, *TimeOut*]

                Dialog(*DialogRecord* [, *DefaultButton*] [, *TimeOut*])

Remarks   The **Dialog** statement and **Dialog**( ) function are both used to display the dialog box specified by *DialogRecord* in a preceding **Dim** instruction. The dialog box displayed can be a Word dialog box or one that you define within a macro.

                If you use the **Dialog** statement to display a dialog box and the user chooses the Cancel button, Word generates an error that an **On Error** instruction can trap. If you don't want or need to trap the error, you can use the **Dialog**() function to display the dialog box. In addition to displaying the dialog box, the **Dialog**() function returns a value corresponding to the button chosen. The return values are the same as those used to specify *DefaultButton*.

                When you display a dynamic dialog box, use **DisableInput** to make the ESC key cancel the dialog box properly. For more information, see **DisableInput**.

Argument	Explanation
DialogRecord	The name given to the dialog record in the **Dim** instruction.
DefaultButton	The default command button:
	−2 No default command button
	−1 The OK button
	0 (zero) The Cancel button
	> 0 (zero) A command button, where 1 is the first **PushButton** instruction in the definition, 2 is the second, and so on
	The default command button is chosen if the user presses ENTER when a dialog box control other than a command button has the focus. Unless you specify otherwise, the OK button is the default command button.
	DefaultButton is used only with custom dialog boxes. For *DefaultButton* to have any effect, the instruction for the specified button must be preceded in the dialog box definition by an instruction for a nonbutton dialog box control that can receive the focus, such as a list box or check box. (Note that because a text control cannot receive the focus, it does not meet this criterion.) Otherwise, the first button in the dialog box definition is the default command button. If the dialog box definition has a dialog function associated with it, *DefaultButton* may be overridden by a **DlgFocus$** statement. For information on creating dialog functions, see Chapter 5, "Working with Custom Dialog Boxes," in Part 1, "Learning WordBasic."
TimeOut	The amount of time, in milliseconds, the dialog box is displayed. If 0 (zero) or omitted, the dialog box is displayed until the user closes it.

Note   A macro can use any number of custom dialog boxes, but WordBasic supports only one custom dialog record at a time (you can define any number of dialog records for Word dialog boxes). This means that you can't define a series of custom dialog records, intending to use them later in the macro. Each custom dialog record overwrites the previous one. If your macro uses more than one custom dialog box and you need to store the values contained in a dialog record that will be overwritten, save the values in regular variables. For more information about using custom dialog records, see Chapter 5, "Working with Custom Dialog Boxes," in Part 1, "Learning WordBasic."

Examples

This example uses the **Dialog()** function to display the Font dialog box (Format menu) so the user can set different character-formatting options. The instruction x = Dialog(dlg) returns a value corresponding to the button the user chooses and removes the need for error handling. If the user chooses the OK button, the last instruction in the example, If x = -1 Then FormatFont dlg, implements the options that the user selected in the dialog box; if the user chooses the Cancel button, the options chosen are ignored. Without this statement, nothing happens, even though the dialog box has been displayed and the user has chosen the OK button.

```
Dim dlg As FormatFont
GetCurValues dlg
x = Dialog(dlg)
If x = -1 Then FormatFont dlg
```

The following example is the same as the previous one, except that it uses the **Dialog** statement to display the dialog box and includes error handling. If the user chooses the Cancel button, the resulting error is trapped and a message is displayed.

```
Dim dlg As FormatFont
GetCurValues dlg
On Error Goto trap
Dialog dlg
FormatFont dlg
Goto skiptrap
trap:
MsgBox "Dialog box closed -- no changes"
skiptrap:
```

The following example displays a simple custom dialog box with text box and command button controls. Since the text box control is the first control defined in the dialog box definition, it has the focus when the dialog box is displayed. The x = Dialog(dlg, 1) instruction makes the Find button the default command button (instead of the OK button).

```
Begin Dialog UserDialog 346, 90, "Social Security Macro"
    TextBox 9, 22, 192, 18, .secnum
    Text 9, 6, 183, 13, "Social Security Number:"
    OKButton 249, 4, 88, 21
    CancelButton 249, 28, 88, 21
    PushButton 249, 52, 88, 21, "Find..."
End Dialog
Dim dlg As UserDialog
x = Dialog(dlg, 1)
```

See Also

Begin Dialog…End Dialog, Dim, GetCurValues

DialogEditor

Syntax   **DialogEditor**

Remarks   Starts the Dialog Editor if it is not already running and makes it the active application. If the Dialog Editor is already running, the **DialogEditor** statement makes it the active application. If the Dialog Editor is shrunk to an icon, the **DialogEditor** statement restores and activates it. For more information about the Dialog Editor, see Chapter 5, "Working with Custom Dialog Boxes," in Part 1, "Learning WordBasic."

Dim

Syntax   **Dim** [**Shared**] *Var1* [(*Size1* [, *Size2*] [, ...])] [, *Var2* [(*Size1* [, *Size2*] [, ...])]] [, ...]

Dim *DialogRecord* **As** *DialogName*

Dim *DialogRecord* **As UserDialog**

Remarks   Declares variables to be shared by more than one subroutine, defines array variables, or defines a dialog record. **Dim** statements that declare shared variables must be placed outside the macro's subroutines—usually before the main subroutine.

Syntax	Purpose
Dim *Var*(*Size1* [, *Size2*] [, ...])	Defines an array variable. For one-dimensional arrays, *Size1* is the subscript of the last element in the array.
	For multidimensional arrays, each *Size* argument is the subscript of the last element for the dimension of the array to be defined.
	In WordBasic, the first element in an array is always numbered 0 (zero), so to define a one-dimensional array of seven elements—for example, the days of the week—*Size1* would be 6. To define a two-dimensional array of 12 rows by 31 columns—for example, the days of the year organized by month—*Size1* would be 11 and *Size2* would be 30.
Dim Shared *Var*[(*Size1* [, *Size2*] [, ...])]	Declares a string, numeric, or array variable to be shared by more than one subroutine. The **Dim** statement must be placed outside any subroutine. Usually, shared variable declarations are placed at the start of a macro, before the main subroutine.

Syntax	Purpose
Dim *DialogRecord* **As** *DialogName*	Defines a dialog record variable for a Word dialog box. *DialogName* can be any WordBasic statement that corresponds to a Word command or dialog box. For example, **FormatFont** or **FileOpen** are valid as *DialogName*.
Dim *DialogRecord* **As** **UserDialog**	Defines a dialog record for a user-defined dialog box.

Examples

This example declares three variables to be shared by multiple subroutines and would typically be placed before the Sub MAIN instruction.

```
Dim Shared numDocs, docName$, savePath$
```

The following example stores the names of the days of the week in the array Days$ and displays the third element of the array, "Tuesday," in the status bar:

```
Dim Days$(6)
Days$(0) = "Sunday" : Days$(1) = "Monday" : Days$(2) = "Tuesday"
Days$(3) = "Wednesday" : Days$(4) = "Thursday"
Days$(5) = "Friday" : Days$(6) = "Saturday"
Print Days$(2)
```

The following example stores the names of the days of the week and their Spanish translations in the two-dimensional array Days$. The last instruction displays "Martes," the element in the third row of the second column of the array, in the status bar:

```
Dim Days$(6, 1)
Days$(0, 0) = "Sunday" : Days$(0, 1) = "Domingo" : Days$(1, 0) =
"Monday"
Days$(1, 1) = "Lunes" : Days$(2, 0) = "Tuesday" : Days$(2, 1) = "Martes"
Days$(3, 0) = "Wednesday" : Days$(3, 1) = "Miércoles" : Days$(4, 0) =
"Thursday"
Days$(4, 1) = "Jueves" : Days$(5, 0) = "Friday" : Days$(6, 1) =
"Viernes"
Days$(5, 1) = "Saturday" : Days$(6, 0) = "Sábado"
Print Days$(2, 1)
```

The following example declares the variable num as shared, sets the variable to 6, and then calls the MyRoutine subroutine. The subroutine adds 10 to num, and the main subroutine displays the new value. Note that the instruction Dim Shared num must be placed outside both subroutines.

```
Dim Shared num                       'Declare num as shared
Sub MAIN
    num = 6                          'Set the value of num
    MyRoutine                        'Call the routine
    Print num                        'Display the new value of num
End Sub

Sub MyRoutine
    num = num + 10                   'Increase the value of num
End Sub
```

In the following example, **Dim** is used to define the dialog record TOVrec in which the values of the View tab in the Options dialog box (Tools menu) are stored. This macro toggles the setting of the Paragraph Marks check box.

```
Dim TOVrec As ToolsOptionsView      'Define dialog record
GetCurValues TOVrec                  'Get the current state
If TOVrec.Paras = 1 Then             'If on
    TOVrec.Paras = 0                 'turn off
Else                                 'Else
    TOVrec.Paras = 1                 'turn on
End If
ToolsOptionsView TOVrec              'Apply new setting
```

In the following example, **Dim** is used to define the dialog record Dlg for a user-defined dialog box:

```
Begin Dialog UserDialog 320, 57, "A Simple Dialog Box"
    Text 5, 16, 205, 18, "This is a simple dialog box."
    OKButton 220, 4, 88, 21
    CancelButton 220, 29, 88, 21
End Dialog
Dim Dlg As UserDialog                'Define the dialog record
Dialog Dlg                           'Display the dialog box
```

See Also   **Declare, Dialog, Let, Redim**

DisableAutoMacros

Syntax   **DisableAutoMacros** [*Disable*]

Remarks   Disables AutoOpen, AutoClose, AutoNew, and AutoExit macros until they are re-enabled with the instruction DisableAutoMacros 0 or until Word is started again. You can place a **DisableAutoMacros** statement before the line in your macro that triggers an auto macro—for example, a **FileNew** instruction that creates a document based on a template containing an AutoNew macro.

Argument	Explanation
Disable	Specifies whether to disable auto macros: 0 (zero) Enables auto macros 1 or omitted Disables auto macros

You cannot use **DisableAutoMacros** to disable an AutoExec macro or to disable the current macro. For example, you could not place a **DisableAutoMacros** statement in an AutoOpen macro to disable AutoOpen. To disable an AutoExec macro, hold down the SHIFT key while Word is loading or use the /m startup switch. For more information, see "Startup Switches" in Help.

Example

This example creates a new document based on the Memo template. Assume that the Memo template contains an AutoNew macro that presents a series of dialog boxes. The **DisableAutoMacros** statement prevents AutoNew from running.

```
DisableAutoMacros
FileNew .Template = "MEMO"
```

DisableInput

Syntax

DisableInput [*Disable*]

Remarks

Prevents the ESC key from interrupting a macro. **DisableInput** does not prevent ESC from canceling a dialog box.

Argument	Explanation
Disable	Determines whether or not to disable the ESC key: 0 (zero) Enables the ESC key to cancel the macro 1 or omitted Prevents the ESC key from canceling the macro

Note If the user presses ESC while a dynamic dialog box is displayed, a message stating that the macro was interrupted appears and the dialog box remains on screen. To make ESC behave properly when you display a dynamic dialog box, precede the **Dialog** or **Dialog()** instruction with the instruction `DisableInput 1`; follow with `DisableInput 0` to reset the original ESC key behavior.

Example

This example shows how you might use **DisableInput** instructions preceding and following an instruction that displays a dynamic dialog box.

```
DisableInput 1
button = Dialog(MyDynamicDlg)
DisableInput 0
```

DlgControlId()

Syntax   **DlgControlId**(*Identifier$*)

Remarks   Used within a dialog function to return the numeric identifier for the dialog box
control specified by *Identifier$*, the string identifier of the dialog box control.
Numeric identifiers are numbers, starting at 0 (zero), that correspond to the
positions of dialog box control instructions within a dialog box definition. For
example, consider the following instruction in a dialog box definition:

```
CheckBox 97, 54, 36, 12, "&Update", .MyCheckBox
```

The instruction `DlgControlId("MyCheckBox")` returns 0 (zero) if the **CheckBox**
instruction is the first instruction in the dialog box definition, 1 if it is the second
instruction, and so on.

In most cases, your dialog functions will perform actions based on the string
identifier of the control that was selected. However, dialog functions can use
numeric identifiers to manipulate more quickly a large number of controls (for
example, the number of controls found in a multiple-panel dialog box). Note that
if you change the order of instructions in a dialog box definition, the numeric
identifiers for the corresponding controls will change also.

For information about using a dialog function, see Chapter 5, "Working with
Custom Dialog Boxes," in Part 1, "Learning WordBasic."

Example   This macro displays a simple dialog box containing the OK and Cancel buttons
and a check box labeled "Test." The dialog function checks to see if the value for
`action` is 2, meaning a control has been selected or chosen. If so, the dialog
function then checks to see if the control selected is the first one defined—in other
words, if the numeric identifier returned by **DlgControlId**() is 0 (zero). If it is, a
message box is displayed in front of the dialog box, which remains on-screen.

```
Sub MAIN
Begin Dialog UserDialog 320, 50, "Test", .MyDlgFunction
    CheckBox 212, 10, 88, 19, "Test", .Test          '0
    OKButton 7, 10, 88, 21                           '1
    CancelButton 109, 10, 88, 21                     '2
End Dialog
Dim dlg As UserDialog
DisableInput 1
button = Dialog(dlg)
DisableInput 0
End Sub
```

```
Function MyDlgFunction(identifier$, action, suppvalue)
If action = 2 Then
    If DlgControlId(identifier$) = 0 Then
        MsgBox "You selected the first control " + \
                "defined in the dialog box definition."
    End If
End If
End Function
```

See Also   **DlgFocus, DlgValue**

DlgEnable, DlgEnable()

Syntax   **DlgEnable** *Identifier*[*$*] [, *On*]

DlgEnable(*Identifier*[*$*])

Remarks   The **DlgEnable** statement is used within a dialog function to enable or disable the
dialog box control identified by *Identifier*[*$*] while the dialog box is displayed.
When a dialog box control is disabled, it is visible in the dialog box, but is
dimmed and not functional.

For information about using a dialog function, see Chapter 5, "Working with
Custom Dialog Boxes," in Part 1, "Learning WordBasic."

Argument	Explanation
Identifier[*$*]	The string or numeric identifier of the dialog box control
On	Enables or disables the dialog box control:
	1 Enables the control
	0 (zero) Disables the control
	Omitted Toggles the control

The **DlgEnable()** function returns the following values.

Value	Explanation
−1	If the control is enabled
0 (zero)	If the control is disabled

Example   This example disables the dialog box control with the string identifier "Set" when
the dialog box is initially displayed. (The main subroutine that contains the dialog
box definition is not shown.)

```
Function MyDlgFunction(identifier$, action, suppvalue)
Select Case action
    Case 1                        'The dialog box is displayed
        DlgEnable "Set", 0
    Case 2                        'The user selects a control
        'Statements that perform actions based
        'on which control is selected go here
    Case 3                        'Text change (not applicable)
    Case Else
End Select
End Function
```

See Also   **DlgVisible**

DlgFilePreview, DlgFilePreview$()

Syntax   **DlgFilePreview** [*Identifier*[*$*]] [*, Filename$*]

        DlgFilePreview$()

Remarks   The **DlgFilePreview** statement is used within a dialog function to preview the first page of the document specified by *Filename$* (which does not have to be open). If you don't specify *Filename$*, **DlgFilePreview** previews the first page of the active document. The document is displayed in the box created with a **FilePreview** instruction in the dialog box definition. Because a custom dialog box can have only one file preview box, the use of *Identifier*[*$*] to specify the file preview box is optional.

The **DlgFilePreview$()** function returns the path and filename of the document displayed in the file preview box. If the active document has not been saved as a file (for example, a new document such as Document2 or a macro open for editing), **DlgFilePreview$()** returns the window name instead of the path and filename.

For information about using a dialog function, see Chapter 5, "Working with Custom Dialog Boxes," in Part 1, "Learning WordBasic."

Example   This example updates the file preview box according to the selection made in a list box containing filenames. (The main subroutine that contains the dialog box definition is not shown.)

```
Function PreviewFiles(identifier$, action, suppvalue)
If action = 1 Then                        'Preview first file in list
    previewfilename$ = DlgText$("ListBox1")
    DlgFilePreview$ previewfilename$
ElseIf action = 2 Then                    'The user selects a control
    If identifier$ = "ListBox1" Then      'Preview selected file
        previewfilename$ = DlgText$("ListBox1")
        DlgFilePreview$ previewfilename$
    End If
End If
End Function
```

See Also   **DlgSetPicture, DlgUpdateFilePreview, FilePreview, Picture**

DlgFocus, DlgFocus$()

Syntax   **DlgFocus** *Identifier*[*$*]

DlgFocus$()

Remarks   The **DlgFocus** statement is used within a dialog function to set the focus on the dialog box control identified by *Identifier*[*$*] while the dialog box is displayed. When a dialog box control has the focus, it is active and responds to keyboard input. For example, if a text box has the focus, any text you type appears in that text box.

The **DlgFocus$()** function returns the string identifier for the dialog box control that currently has the focus.

For information about using a dialog function, see Chapter 5, "Working with Custom Dialog Boxes," in Part 1, "Learning WordBasic."

Example   This example sets the focus on the control "MyControl1" when the dialog box is initially displayed. (The main subroutine that contains the dialog box definition is not shown.)

```
Function MyDlgFunction(identifier$, action, suppvalue)
Select Case action
    Case 1                      'The dialog box is displayed
        DlgFocus "MyControl1"
    Case 2                      'The user selects a control
        'Statements that perform actions based
        'on which control is selected go here
    Case 3                      'Text change (not applicable)
    Case Else
End Select
End Function
```

See Also   **DlgEnable, DlgVisible**

DlgListBoxArray, DlgListBoxArray()

Syntax **DlgListBoxArray** *Identifier[$]*, *ArrayVariable$( )*

DlgListBoxArray(*Identifier[$]* [, *ArrayVariable$( )*]**)**

Remarks The **DlgListBoxArray** statement is used within a dialog function to fill a list box, drop-down list box, or combo box with the contents of *ArrayVariable$( )*. You can use this statement to change the contents of a list box, drop-down list box, or combo box in a custom dialog box while the dialog box is displayed.

For information about using a dialog function, see Chapter 5, "Working with Custom Dialog Boxes," in Part 1, "Learning WordBasic."

Argument	Explanation
Identifier[$]	The string or numeric identifier of the dialog box control. The control must be a list box, drop-down list box, or combo box.
ArrayVariable$( )	A string array containing items to be displayed in the specified list box, drop-down list box, or combo box.

The **DlgListBoxArray( )** function fills *ArrayVariable$( )* with the contents of the list box, drop-down list box, or combo box specified by *Identifier[$]* and returns the number of entries in the list box, drop-down list box, or combo box. *ArrayVariable$( )* is optional with the **DlgListBoxArray( )** function; if *ArrayVariable$( )* is omitted, **DlgListBoxArray( )** returns the number of entries in the specified control.

Example This example changes the contents of a list box while the dialog box is displayed. The dialog box definition in the main subroutine (not shown) defines a dialog box containing a list box, the OK and Cancel buttons, and a Change button. When the user chooses the Change button, the **If** control structure in Case 2 of the dialog function takes over: A new string array is defined, **DlgListBoxArray** is used to replace the contents of the list box, and the Change button is disabled. By default, a custom dialog box is closed when the user chooses a command button such as the Change button; however, in this example, the keepDisplayed = 1 and dlgTest = keepDisplayed instructions keep the dialog box displayed (when a dialog function returns a value of 1, the dialog box remains displayed).

```
Function dlgTest(identifier$, action, suppvalue)
Select Case action
    Case 1                      'The dialog box is displayed
    Case 2                      'The user selects a control
        If identifier$ = "Change" Then
            Dim MyArray2$(1)
            MyArray2$(0) = "New first item"
            MyArray2$(1) = "New second item"
            DlgListBoxArray "MyListBox", MyArray2$()
            DlgFocus "MyListBox"
            DlgEnable "Change", 0
            keepDisplayed = 1
        End If
    Case 3                      'Text change (not applicable)
    Case Else
End Select
dlgTest = keepDisplayed
End Function
```

See Also   **DlgEnable, DlgFocus, DlgText**

DlgLoadValues, DlgLoadValues()

Syntax   **DlgLoadValues** *ValuesFile$,* *Identifier$*

DlgLoadValues(*ValuesFile$,* *Identifier$*)

Remarks   On the Macintosh, the **DlgLoadValues** statement retrieves values stored by a
DlgStoreValues instruction for controls in a custom dialog box.

Argument	Explanation
ValuesFile$	The name of the file in which the values are stored. *ValuesFile$* can include a path. If a path is not included, Word looks for *ValuesFile$* in the Preferences folder. If *ValuesFile$* does not exist, empty strings and null values are passed to the dialog box but no error occurs.
Identifier$	A string that identifies the set of stored values (the same string is used when storing values with **DlgStoreValues**).

The **DlgLoadValues**() behaves the same as the statement, and also returns the
following values:

Value	Explanation
0 (zero)	If either *ValuesFile$* or *Identifier$* does not exist, or if any of the stored values cannot be loaded (this can occur if the dialog definition has changed since the values were last stored).
-1	If the values were loaded successfully.

In Windows, **DlgLoadValues** and **DlgLoadValues**() are not available and generate errors.

Example

This Macintosh macro shows how you can use **DlgStoreValues** and **DlgLoadValues** in a dialog function to save settings for a variety of dialog box controls. During initialization of the dialog box, the **DlgLoadValues** instruction runs; when the user chooses OK, the **DlgStoreValues** instruction runs. Note that the identifier for the first check box ends in 0 (zero), preventing Word from performing its default action of saving the check box setting. The first time the dialog box is displayed, the file containing the settings (DLGVALS) does not exist. The file is created the first time the **DlgStoreValues** instruction runs.

```
Sub MAIN
Begin Dialog UserDialog 225, 167, "Test", .MyDlgFunction
    CheckBox 11, 48, 88, 19, "Test 1", .FirstBox0
    CheckBox 97, 48, 88, 19, "Test 2", .SecondBox
    OKButton 118, 124, 88, 21
    CancelButton 11, 124, 88, 21
    TextBox 11, 24, 197, 18, .TextBox1
    Text 11, 7, 46, 12, "Name:", .Text1
    GroupBox 11, 71, 197, 41, "Group Box"
    OptionGroup  .OptionGroup1
        OptionButton 17, 84, 89, 18, "Option A", .OptionA
        OptionButton 110, 84, 89, 18, "Option B", .OptionB
End Dialog
Dim dlg As UserDialog
DisableInput 1
button = Dialog(dlg)
DisableInput 0
End Sub


Function MyDlgFunction(identifier$, action, suppvalue)
Select Case action
    Case 1              'initialization
        DlgLoadValues "DLGVALS", "MyDlgFunction"
    Case 2              'button chosen or setting changed
        If identifier$ = "OK" Then
            DlgStoreValues "DLGVALS", "MyDlgFunction"
        End If
    Case Else
End Select
End Function
```

See Also   **DlgStoreValues**

DlgSetPicture

Syntax   **DlgSetPicture** *Identifier*[*$*]**,** *PictureName$***,** *PictureType*

Remarks   Used in a dialog function to set the graphic displayed by a **Picture** dialog box
control whose identifier is *Identifier*[*$*].

Argument	Explanation
Identifier[*$*]	The string or numeric identifier of the dialog box control.
PictureName$	The name of the graphics file, AutoText entry, or bookmark containing the graphic to be displayed. If the picture does not exist, Word displays the text "(missing picture)" within the rectangle that defines the picture area.
PictureType	A value indicating how the graphic is stored:

0 (zero)   *PictureName$* is a file.

1   *PictureName$* is an AutoText entry.

2   *PictureName$* is a bookmark.

3   *PictureName$* is ignored; the graphic is retrieved from the Clipboard.

4   *PictureName$* is a PICT file stored in the resource fork of the template containing the macro (Macintosh only). You can use the ResEdit program to add PICT files to the resource fork of a template.

Example   In this example, the user selects a person's name from a list box and a picture of
the person is displayed in the dialog box. The instructions assume that the
graphics file to display is in the C:\PHOTOS folder and that the filename is the
same as the selected name, followed by a .PIC filename extension. (On the
Macintosh, change the instruction that sets the pictureName$ variable to use the
value "HD:PHOTOS:" + name$.) The main subroutine that contains the dialog box
definition is not shown.

```
Function dlgTest(identifier$, action, suppvalue)
Select Case action
    Case 1                          'The dialog box is displayed
    Case 2                          'The user selects a control
       If identifier$ = "Name" Then
           name$ = DlgText$("Name")
           pictureName$ = "C:\PHOTOS\" + name$ + ".PIC"
           DlgSetPicture "Photo", pictureName$, 0
       End If
    Case 3                          'Text change (not applicable)
    Case Else
End Select
End Function
```

See Also   **Picture**

DlgStoreValues

Syntax   **DlgStoreValues** *ValuesFile$*, *Identifier$*

Remarks   On the Macintosh, stores string and numeric values for controls in custom dialog boxes so they may be retrieved later by **DlgLoadValues**. If you create a complex wizard, using **DlgStoreValues** and **DlgLoadValues** instead of **SetPrivateProfileString** and **GetPrivateProfileString$()** for storing and retrieving values entered by the user can improve performance significantly.

Argument	Explanation
ValuesFile$	The name of the file in which the values are stored. *ValuesFile$* can include a path. If a path is not specified, Word looks for *ValuesFile$* in the Preferences folder.
Identifier$	A string that identifies the set of stored values (this string is used when retrieving values with **DlgLoadValues**).
	Note that while you can store multiple sets of values for different dialog boxes in the same file, it is recommended for future cross-platform compatibility that you use one values file per dialog box.

The following rules determine which values Word stores:

- Values for the following items are stored by default: check boxes, option groups, text boxes, list boxes, drop-down list boxes, and combo boxes. Values for all other items are *not* stored by default.

- You can reverse the default behavior for most individual items by giving the item a string identifier that ends in 0 (zero). For example, you can store the value for a Text control (such as a tip in a wizard) or prevent the value for a check box from being stored. Note that .Item0 and .Item000 are examples of identifiers that end in 0 (zero), but .Item100 is not.

- You cannot store values for picture, file preview, option button, and push button controls.

In Windows, **DlgStoreValues** is unavailable and generates an error.

For an example, see **DlgLoadValues.**

See Also   **DlgLoadValues**

DlgText, DlgText$()

Syntax   **DlgText** *Identifier[$]*, *Text$*

DlgText$(***Identifier[$]*)**

Remarks   The **DlgText** statement is used in a dialog function to set the text or label for the dialog box control identified by *Identifier[$]*. The **DlgText** statement does not change the string identifier of a dialog box control.

For a text box or combo box, **DlgText** sets the text within the text box. For dialog box controls that have labels, such as check boxes, option buttons, option groups, and command buttons, **DlgText** sets the label. For list boxes, **DlgText** sets the selection to *Text$* or to the first item that begins with *Text$*.

For information about using a dialog function, see Chapter 5, "Working with Custom Dialog Boxes," in Part 1, "Learning WordBasic."

Argument	Explanation
Identifier[*$*]	The string or numeric identifier of the dialog box control
Text$	The text or label to set

The **DlgText$()** function returns the text or label of the dialog box control identified by *Identifier*[*$*]. If the dialog box control is a list box, the text of the selected item is returned. If the dialog box control is a text box or combo box, **DlgText$()** returns the text that appears in the text box.

Example

This example hides and displays a control in a dialog box, and, accordingly, toggles the label of a command button between "Hide Control" and "Show Control." (The main subroutine that contains the dialog box definition is not shown.) By default, a custom dialog box is closed when the user chooses a command button; however, in this example, the keepDisplayed = 1 and dlgTest = keepDisplayed instructions keep the dialog box displayed (when a dialog function returns a value of 1, the dialog box remains displayed).

```
Function dlgTest(identifier$, action, suppvalue)
Select Case action
    Case 1                          'The dialog box is displayed
    Case 2                          'The user chooses a button
        If identifier$ = "Hide" Then
            If DlgText$("Hide") = "Hide &Control" Then
                DlgVisible "Option1", 0
                DlgText$ "Hide", "Show &Control"
            Else
                DlgVisible "Option1", 1
                DlgText$ "Hide", "Hide &Control"
            End If
            keepDisplayed = 1
        End If
    Case 3                          'Text change (not applicable)
    Case Else
End Select
dlgTest = keepDisplayed
End Function
```

See Also   **DlgValue**

DlgUpdateFilePreview

Syntax   **DlgUpdateFilePreview** [*Identifier$*]

Remarks   Used within a dialog function to update a file preview box (created by a
FilePreview instruction in a dialog box definition). Since a dialog box can have
only one file preview box, *Identifier$* is optional.

Example   This example updates a file preview box after the user has selected a left indent
measurement for the selected text. After the user selects the measurement, the file
preview box shows the change in the indent. Note that the instruction
Val(DlgText$("DropListBox1") is necessary to remove the string "inch" from the
measurement; **FormatParagraph** does not accept "inch" as a valid measurement.

```
Sub MAIN
Dim indents$(3)
indents$(0) = ".5 inch" : indents$(1) = "1 inch"
indents$(2) = "1.5 inches" : indents$(3) = "2 inches"
Begin Dialog UserDialog 354, 258, "Change Indents", .dlgTest
    PushButton 255, 10, 88, 21, "Close", .close
    Text 15, 8, 151, 25, "Select a left indent:", .Text1
    FilePreview 15, 58, 219, 183, .fileprev
    DropListBox 15, 29, 179, 30, indents$(), .DropListBox1
End Dialog
Dim dlg As UserDialog
DisableInput 1
x = Dialog(dlg)
DisableInput 2
End Sub

Function dlgTest(identifier$, action, suppvalue)
Select Case action
Case 1                  'The dialog box is displayed
Case 2                  'The user selects a control
    If identifier$ = "DropListBox1" Then
        indent$ = Str$(Val(DlgText$("DropListBox1")))
        FormatParagraph .LeftIndent = indent$
        DlgUpdateFilePreview
    End If
Case Else
End Select
End Function
```

See Also   **DlgFilePreview**, **FilePreview**

DlgValue, DlgValue()

Syntax

DlgValue *Identifier*[*$*], *Value*

DlgValue(*Identifier*[*$*])

Remarks

The **DlgValue** statement is used in a dialog function to select or clear a dialog box control by setting the numeric value associated with the control specified by *Identifier*[*$*]. For example, DlgValue "MyCheckBox", 1 selects a check box, DlgValue "MyCheckBox", 0 clears a check box, and DlgValue "MyCheckBox", -1 fills the check box with gray. An error occurs if *Identifier*[*$*] specifies a dialog box control such as a text box or an option button that cannot be set with a numeric value.

For information about using a dialog function, see Chapter 5, "Working with Custom Dialog Boxes," in Part 1, "Learning WordBasic."

Argument	Explanation
Identifier[*$*]	The string or numeric identifier of the dialog box control. The **DlgValue** statement and **DlgValue**() function can be used with identifiers created by the following statements: **CheckBox**, **ComboBox**, **DropListBox**, **ListBox**, and **OptionGroup**.
Value	Numeric value to set the dialog box control identified by *Identifier*[*$*]

The **DlgValue**() function returns the numeric value of the check box, list box, drop-down list box, combo box, or option group identified by *Identifier*[*$*]. For example, DlgValue("MyCheckBox") returns 1 if the check box is selected, 0 (zero) if it is cleared, and -1 if it is filled with gray. The instruction DlgValue("MyListBox") returns 0 (zero) if the first item in the list box is selected, 1 if the second item is selected, and so on.

Example

This example is the portion of a dialog function that runs when the check box with the identifier "MyCheckBox" is selected. **DlgValue**() is used to determine whether the check box was turned on or off. If it was turned on, the instructions redefine an array and fill a list box with the items in the array.

```
Case 2                      'The user selects a control
   If identifier$ = "MyCheckBox" Then
      If DlgValue("MyCheckBox") = 1 Then
         ReDim MyArray$(1)
         MyArray$(0) = "Alberto"
         MyArray$(1) = "Gina"
         DlgListBoxArray "MyListBox", MyArray$()
      End If
   End If
```

See Also

DlgText

DlgVisible, DlgVisible()

Syntax   **DlgVisible** *Identifier*[$] [, *On*]

DlgVisible *FirstIdentifier*[$] , *LastIdentifier*[$], *On*

DlgVisible(*Identifier*[$])

Remarks   In Windows 3.*x*, the **DlgVisible** statement is used in a dialog function to make visible or to hide the dialog box control identified by *Identifier*[$]. On the Macintosh and in Windows 95 and Windows NT, the **DlgVisible** statement can be used to make visible or to hide a range of dialog box controls. You can use **DlgVisible** to hide little-used options until they are needed, or to create dialog boxes with multiple panels of controls.

Argument	Explanation
Identifier[$]	The string or numeric identifier of the dialog box control
FirstIdentifier[$]	The string or numeric identifier of the first dialog box control in a range of dialog box controls
LastIdentifier[$]	The string or numeric identifier of the last dialog box control in a range of dialog box controls. *LastIdentifier*[$] can be the same as *FirstIdentifier*[$].
On	Shows or hides the dialog box control *Identifier*[$] or the range of dialog box controls between *FirstIdentifier*[$] and *LastIdentifier*[$] as listed in a dialog box definition.
	1 Shows the control or range of controls
	0 (zero) Hides the control or range of controls
	Omitted Toggles the control between visible and hidden
	Note that the *On* argument cannot be omitted if *FirstIdentifier*[$] and *LastIdentifier*[$] are specified.

The **DlgVisible**() function returns the following values:

Value	Explanation
−1	If the control is visible
0 (zero)	If the control is hidden

For an example that uses **DlgVisible**, see **DlgText**.

See Also   **DlgEnable**, **DlgFocus**, **DlgText**

DocClose

Syntax

DocClose [*Save*]

Remarks

Closes the active document window. **DocClose** is not the same as **FileClose**: Whereas **FileClose** closes the active document and all associated windows, **DocClose** closes only the active document window. When a document is open in a single window, which is usually the case, **DocClose** and **FileClose** have the same effect.

Argument	Explanation
Save	Determines whether or not to save the document:
	0 (zero) or omitted Prompts the user to save if changes have been made in the document since the last time it was saved.
	1 Saves the document without prompting before closing it.
	2 Closes the window but does not save the document.
	The *Save* argument also controls whether a prompt appears if the document has a routing slip. A prompt appears if *Save* is 0 (zero) or omitted; otherwise, the document is closed without being routed.

Example

This example closes every open document window and prompts the user to save any unsaved changes:

```
While Window( ) <> 0
    DocClose 0
Wend
```

See Also

ClosePane, FileClose

DocMaximize, DocMaximize()

Syntax

DocMaximize [*State*]

DocMaximize()

Remarks

The **DocMaximize** statement maximizes or restores all document windows according to the value of *State*: 1 maximizes windows and 0 (zero) restores windows. If *State* is not specified, **DocMaximize** toggles document windows between restored and maximized states.

The **DocMaximize()** function returns the following values.

Value	Explanation
−1	If the document windows are maximized
0 (zero)	If the document windows are not maximized

See Also

AppMaximize, DocMinimize, DocRestore

DocMinimize, DocMinimize()

Syntax   **DocMinimize**

                    DocMinimize()

Remarks   The **DocMinimize** statement shrinks the active document window to an icon.

The **DocMinimize()** function returns the following values.

Value	Explanation
−1	If the active document window is minimized
0 (zero)	If the active document window is not minimized

See Also   **AppMinimize**, **DocMaximize**, **DocRestore**

DocMove

Syntax   **DocMove** *HorizPos*, *VertPos*

Remarks   Moves the active document window or icon to the specified location. If the active document is maximized, Word cannot perform this action and generates an error.

Argument	Explanation
HorizPos, *VertPos*	The horizontal (*HorizPos*) and vertical (*VertPos*) distance from the upper-left corner of the workspace to the upper-left corner of the document window, in points (72 points = 1 inch). Negative values are allowed.

Example   This example moves the document window to the position 20 points to the right and 40 points down from the upper-left corner of the workspace:

```
If DocMaximize() = 0 Then DocMove 20, 40
```

See Also   **AppMove**, **DocSize**, **DocWindowPosLeft**, **DocWindowPosTop**

DocRestore

Syntax   **DocRestore**

Remarks   Restores all document windows from a maximized state or restores a minimized document window. Unlike **DocMaximize**, which maximizes the document windows if restored and restores them if maximized, **DocRestore** only restores document windows. It generates an error if the active document is already restored.

There is no corresponding function for **DocRestore**. As the example for this entry demonstrates, however, you can use the **DocMaximize()** function to determine whether document windows are restored.

Example   This example restores document windows if they are maximized:

```
If DocMaximize() <> 0 Then DocRestore
```

See Also   **AppRestore, DocMaximize, DocMinimize**

DocSize

Syntax   **DocSize** *Width*, *Height*

Remarks   Sizes the active document window to the specified *Width* and *Height*, in points (72 points = 1 inch). If the active document is maximized or minimized, Word cannot perform this action and generates an error. Note that this statement must have arguments for both the width and height of the window. To size only the width or height of a window, use **DocWindowWidth** or **DocWindowHeight**

Example   This example ensures that the active document window is restored and then sizes it to half the width of the workspace:

```
If DocMaximize() or DocMinimize() Then DocRestore
DocSize(Val(AppInfo$(6)) / 2), Val(AppInfo$(7))
```

See Also   **AppInfo$(), AppSize, DocWindowHeight, DocWindowWidth**

DocSplit, DocSplit()

Syntax   **DocSplit** *Percentage*

DocSplit()

Remarks   The **DocSplit** statement splits the active document window at the given height, expressed as a percentage of the distance between the top and bottom of the document area.

The **DocSplit()** function returns the split position as a percentage of the active document area's height or returns 0 (zero) if the document window is not split.

The **DocSplit** statement accepts values between 0 (zero) and 100, but values near the ends of the range may not split the document window, depending on the screen elements that are displayed and the size of the window. Using the **WindowPane()** function, you can determine whether a window is split.

Example   This example splits the active document window in the middle:

```
DocSplit 50
```

See Also   **ClosePane, OtherPane, WindowPane()**

DocumentHasMisspellings()

Syntax   **DocumentHasMisspellings()**

Remarks   Returns information about the status of automatic spell checking in the active document. In Word version 6.0, **DocumentHasMisspellings()** is unavailable and generates an error.

The **DocumentHasMisspellings()** function returns the following values.

Value	Explanation
-1	If automatic spell checking is turned off (unless the document is empty), or if checking is in progress
0 (zero)	If the document has been completely checked and contains no misspellings, or if the document is empty
1	If the document has been completely checked and contains at least one misspelling

Example   This example enables automatic spell checking and finds the next misspelled word in the active document. (Errors are shown if the document either hasn't been checked for spelling errors or has been completely checked and contains misspellings.) When it locates the misspelled word, the example opens the shortcut menu containing spelling suggestions.

```
If DocumentHasMisspellings() <> 1 Then
    ToolsOptionsSpelling .AutomaticSpellChecking = 1,
.HideSpellingErrors = 0
End If
NextMisspelling
```

See Also   **NextMisspelling, ToolsGetSpelling, ToolsLanguage, ToolsOptionsSpelling**

DocumentPropertyExists()

Syntax   **DocumentPropertyExists(***Name$***)**

Remarks   Returns 1 if *Name$* is the name of an existing property or 0 (zero) if it is not. For a list of the built-in properties available in Word, see **DocumentPropertyName$()**. In Word version 6.0, **DocumentPropertyExists()** is unavailable and generates an error. For an example, see **SetDocumentProperty**.

See Also   **DeleteDocumentProperty, DocumentPropertyName$(),
DocumentPropertyType(), IsCustomDocumentProperty()**

DocumentPropertyName$()

Syntax   **DocumentPropertyName$(***PropertyNumber***)**

Remarks   Returns the name of the document property as specified by *PropertyNumber*.
Word lists the built-in properties first. The custom properties are appended at the
end the list. Use the **DocumentPropertyExists()** function to verify that the
property specified by *PropertyNumber* exists. In Word version 6.0,
DocumentPropertyName$() is unavailable and generates an error.

The following table lists the built-in properties available in Word for the active
document. The list indicates which of these properties are read-only.

Property name	Explanation
Title	The title of the document
Subject	The subject of the document
Author	The author of the document
Manager	The name of the manager
Company	The name of the company
Category	The category of the document
Keywords	The keywords used to identify the document
Comments	The comments about the document
Template	The document template (read-only)
CreateTime	The creation date (read-only)
LastSavedTime	The date the document was last saved (read-only)
LastPrinted	The date the document was last printed (read-only)
LastSavedBy	The name of the person who last saved the document (read-only)
RevisionNumber	The number of times that the document has been saved (read-only)
TotalEditingTime	The total time that the document has been open, in minutes, as a number (read-only)
Pages	The number of pages (read-only)
Paragraphs	The number of paragraphs (read-only)
Lines	The number of lines (read-only)
Words	The number of words (read-only)
Characters	The number of characters (read-only)

Property name	Explanation
Bytes	The size of the document, in the form "36,352 Bytes" (read-only)
NameOfApplication	The name of the associated application; for example, "Microsoft Word for Windows 95" (read-only)
Security	The level of document protection (read-only)

Example

This example inserts a list of all the document properties at the end of the current document. Property names are inserted with bold formatting, and each one is followed by its value.

```
EndOfDocument
InsertPara
For count = 1 To CountDocumentProperties()
    a$ = DocumentPropertyName$(count)
    Bold 1 : Insert a$
    InsertPara
    If DocumentPropertyType(a$) = 1 then
        b = GetDocumentProperty(a$)
        Bold 0 : Insert Str$(b)
        InsertPara : InsertPara
    Else
        b$ = GetDocumentProperty$(a$)
        Bold 0 : Insert b$
        InsertPara : InsertPara
    End If
Next
```

See Also

CountDocumentProperties(), **DocumentPropertyType()**, **GetDocumentProperty()**, **IsDocumentPropertyReadOnly()**, **SetDocumentProperty**

DocumentPropertyType()

Syntax

DocumentPropertyType(_Name$_**)**

Remarks

Returns a numeric value that indicates the type of the _Name$_ property. If _Name$_ is not a valid property, an error occurs. Use the **DocumentPropertyExists()** function to verify that the _Name$_ property exists.

For a list of the built-in properties available in Word, see **DocumentPropertyName$()**. In Word version 6.0, **DocumentPropertyType()** is unavailable and generates an error.

The **DocumentPropertyType()** function returns the following values.

Value	Explanation
0	The property is a string.
1	The property is a number.
2	The property is a date.
3	The property is a Yes or No value.

See Also

DocumentPropertyExists(), **DocumentPropertyName$()**,
IsCustomDocumentProperty(), **IsDocumentPropertyReadOnly()**

DocumentProtection()

Syntax

DocumentProtection()

Remarks

Returns a value specifying the protection mode of the active document. To change
the current protection mode, use **ToolsProtectDocument**. In Word version 6.0,
DocumentProtection() is unavailable and generates an error.

Value	Explanation
0 (zero)	The document is not protected.
1	Users can only select and modify text in form fields.
2	Users can only add annotations.
3	Users can select and edit text, but all changes are tracked with revision marks.

See Also

ToolsProtectDocument, **ToolsUnprotectDocument**

DocumentStatistics

Syntax

DocumentStatistics [.FileName = *text*] [, **.Directory** = *text*] [, **.Template** = *text*]
[, **.Title** = *text*] [, **.Created** = *text*] [, **.LastSaved** = *text*] [, **.LastSavedBy** = *text*]
[, **.Revision** = *text*] [, **.Time** = *text*] [, **.Printed** = *text*] [, **.Pages** = *text*]
[, **.Words** = *text*] [, **.Characters** = *text*] [, **.Paragraphs** = *text*] [, **.Lines** = *text*]
[, **.FileSize** = *text*]

Remarks

Used with a dialog record, **DocumentStatistics** returns information about the
active document. In Word version 6.0, the arguments for the **DocumentStatistics**
statement correspond to the information available in the Document Statistics
dialog box (Summary Info command, File menu). Also, the arguments are read-
only, which means that unlike other WordBasic statements, you cannot use
DocumentStatistics to set a value. Instead, you use the **DocumentStatistics**
dialog record in the same way you use a function: to return information.

In Word version 7.0, this statement is included for backward compatibility. You can use the document property statements and functions to access document statistics for the active document. For more information, see **GetDocumentProperty()**.

Argument	Explanation
.FileName	The name of the document (the path is not included)
.Directory	The path in which the document is kept
.Template	The path and filename of the template attached to the document
.Title	The document's title
.Created	The date and time the document was created
.LastSaved	The date and time the document was last saved
.LastSavedBy	The author of the document
.Revision	The number of times the document has been saved
.Time	The total time spent editing the document
.Printed	The date and time the document was last printed
.Pages	The number of pages in the document
.Words	The number of words in the document
.Characters	The number of characters in the document
.Paragraphs	The number of paragraphs in the document
.Lines	The number of lines in the document
.FileSize	The size of the document in the form "36,352 Bytes"

Note To ensure you get the most up-to-date information when using a **DocumentStatistics** dialog record to return document statistics, include the instruction `FileSummaryInfo .Update` before defining the dialog record.

Example

This example uses the **DocumentStatistics** dialog record to obtain the number of words in the active document. You can use this example as a model for how to obtain the value of any **DocumentStatistics** argument.

```
FileSummaryInfo .Update              'Update document statistics
Dim dlg As DocumentStatistics        'Create a dialog record
GetCurValues dlg                     'Fill record with values
MsgBox "Number of words: " + dlg.Words
```

See Also   **FileSummaryInfo, SelInfo()**

DocWindowHeight, DocWindowHeight()

Syntax

DocWindowHeight *Height*

DocWindowHeight()

Remarks

The **DocWindowHeight** statement sets the active document window to the specified *Height*, in points (72 points = 1 inch), without affecting its width. If the active document is maximized or minimized, Word cannot perform this action and generates an error. The **DocWindowHeight**() function returns the height of the active document window in points.

Example

This example restores the active document window if it is maximized or minimized, moves it to the upper-left corner of the workspace, and then sizes the window to 267 points high:

```
If DocMaximize() or DocMinimize() Then DocRestore
DocMove 0, 0
DocWindowHeight 267
```

See Also

AppWindowHeight, DocSize, DocWindowWidth

DocWindowPosLeft, DocWindowPosLeft()

Syntax

DocWindowPosLeft *Position*

DocWindowPosLeft()

Remarks

The **DocWindowPosLeft** statement positions the active document window or icon so that it is *Position* points from the left border of the workspace. If the active document is maximized, Word cannot perform this action and generates an error. The **DocWindowPosLeft**() function returns the horizontal position in points.

Example

This example displays the horizontal and vertical positions of the active document window relative to the border of the workspace:

```
horizpos = DocWindowPosLeft()
vertpos = DocWindowPosTop()
MsgBox "Points from left:" + Str$(horizpos) + Chr$(13) + \
    "Points from top:" + Str$(vertpos), "Doc Window Position"
```

See Also

AppWindowPosLeft, DocMove, DocSize, DocWindowHeight, DocWindowPosTop, DocWindowWidth

DocWindowPosTop, DocWindowPosTop()

Syntax   **DocWindowPosTop** *Position*

DocWindowPosTop()

Remarks   The **DocWindowPosTop** statement positions the active document window or icon so that it is *Position* points from the upper border of the workspace. If the active document is maximized, Word cannot perform this action and generates an error. The **DocWindowPosTop()** function returns the vertical position in points. For an example, see **DocWindowPosLeft**.

See Also   **AppWindowPosTop, DocMove, DocSize, DocWindowHeight, DocWindowPosTop, DocWindowWidth**

DocWindowWidth, DocWindowWidth()

Syntax   **DocWindowWidth** *Width*

DocWindowWidth()

Remarks   The **DocWindowWidth** statement sets the active document window to the specified *Width*, in points (72 points = 1 inch), without affecting its height. If the active document is maximized or minimized, Word cannot perform this action and generates an error. The **DocWindowWidth()** function returns the width of the active document window in points.

Example   This example maximizes the Word window (Windows) and restores document windows. If there are two open document windows, the windows are each sized to 240 points in width and are placed side by side.

```
If InStr(AppInfo$(1), "Macintosh") = 0 Then
    If AppMaximize() = 0 Then AppMaximize
End If
If CountWindows() = 2 Then
    If DocMaximize() Or DocMinimize() Then DocRestore
    DocMove 0, 0
    DocWindowWidth 240
    NextWindow
    If DocMinimize() Or DocMinimize() Then DocRestore
    DocMove 240, 0
    DocWindowWidth 240
End If
```

See Also   **AppWindowWidth, DocSize, DocWindowHeight**

DoFieldClick

Syntax   **DoFieldClick**

Remarks   Moves the insertion point to the location specified by the selected
GOTOBUTTON field, or runs the macro specified by the selected
MACROBUTTON field (the same as double-clicking the field or pressing
ALT+SHIFT+F9 (Windows) or OPTION+SHIFT+F9 (Macintosh) within the result of
the field).

DOSToWin$()

Syntax   **DOSToWin$**(*StringToTranslate$*)

Remarks   In Windows, translates a string from the original equipment manufacturer (OEM)
character set to the Windows character set. On the Macintosh, **DOSToWin$()**
performs no translation and returns the specified string unchanged.

The OEM character set is typically used by MS-DOS applications. Characters 32
through 127 are usually the same in the OEM and Windows character sets. The
other characters in the OEM character set (0 (zero) through 31 and 128 through
255) are generally different from the Windows characters.

Example   This example opens a sequential file created by an MS-DOS application,
translates each line to the Windows character set, and places the result in a new
sequential file:

```
ChDir "C:\TMP"
Open "DOS.TXT" For Input As #1
Open "WINDOWS.TXT" For Output As #2
While Not Eof(1)
    Line Input #1, temp$
    Print #2, DOSToWin$(temp$)
Wend
Close
```

See Also   **WinToDOS$()**

DottedUnderline, DottedUnderline()

Syntax   **DottedUnderline** [*On*]

DottedUnderline()

Remarks   The **DottedUnderline** statement adds or removes the dotted-underline character
format for the selected text, or controls dotted-underline formatting for characters
to be inserted at the insertion point.

Argument	Explanation
On	Specifies whether to add or remove the dotted-underline format:
	1 Formats the selection with the dotted-underline format
	0 (zero) Removes the dotted-underline format
	Omitted Toggles the dotted-underline format

The **DottedUnderline( )** function returns the following values.

Value	Explanation
0 (zero)	If none of the selection is in the dotted-underline format
−1	If part of the selection is in the dotted-underline format
1	If all the selection is in the dotted-underline format

See Also

DoubleUnderline, **FormatBordersAndShading**, **FormatFont**, **Underline**

DoubleUnderline, DoubleUnderline()

Syntax

DoubleUnderline [*On*]

DoubleUnderline( )

Remarks

The **DoubleUnderline** statement adds or removes the double-underline character format for the selected text, or controls double-underline formatting for characters to be inserted at the insertion point.

Argument	Explanation
On	Specifies whether to add or remove the double-underline format:
	1 Formats the selection with the double-underline format
	0 (zero) Removes the double-underline format
	Omitted Toggles the double-underline format

The **DoubleUnderline( )** function returns the following values.

Value	Explanation
0 (zero)	If none of the selection is in the double-underline format
−1	If part of the selection is in the double-underline format
1	If all the selection is in the double-underline format

See Also

DottedUnderline, **FormatBordersAndShading**, **FormatFont**, **Underline**

DrawAlign

Syntax

DrawAlign [**.Horizontal** = *number*] [**, .Vertical** = *number*]
[**, .RelativeTo** = *number*]

Remarks

Aligns the selected drawing objects. The arguments for the **Align** statement correspond to the options in the Align dialog box (Align Drawing Objects button, Drawing toolbar).

Argument	Explanation
.Horizontal	Specifies a horizontal alignment:
	0 (zero) None; existing horizontal positions are preserved
	1 Left
	2 Center
	3 Right
.Vertical	Specifies a vertical alignment:
	0 (zero) None; existing vertical positions are preserved
	1 Top
	2 Center
	3 Bottom
.RelativeTo	Specifies what the objects are aligned with:
	0 (zero) Each other
	1 Page

Example

This example left-aligns all drawing objects within the current paragraph. Using the predefined bookmark "\Para," **DrawSetRange** sets the drawing object range to the paragraph containing the insertion point. For more information about predefined bookmarks, see "Operators and Predefined Bookmarks" later in this part.

```
DrawSetRange "\Para"
For count = 1 To DrawCount()
    DrawExtendSelect count
Next count
DrawAlign .Horizontal = 1, .Vertical = 0, .RelativeTo = 0
```

See Also

DrawCount(), **DrawExtendSelect**, **DrawSelect**, **DrawSetRange**, **FormatDrawingObject**

DrawArc

Syntax   **DrawArc**

Remarks   Switches to page layout view and adds a default arc drawing object in front of the
current text layer. A default arc is shaped and oriented like the lower-left portion
of a circle and is inserted at the upper-left corner of the current page.

See Also   **DrawEllipse, DrawFlipHorizontal, DrawFlipVertical, DrawGetType(),
DrawLine, DrawRotateLeft, DrawRotateRight, FormatDrawingObject**

DrawBringForward

Syntax   **DrawBringForward**

Remarks   Moves the selected drawing object in front of the next one in a stack of drawing
objects. **DrawBringForward** does not move a drawing object from the layer
behind text to the layer in front of text. An error occurs if the selection is not a
drawing object.

See Also   **DrawBringInFrontOfText, DrawBringToFront, DrawSendBackward,
DrawSendBehindText, DrawSendToBack**

DrawBringInFrontOfText

Syntax   **DrawBringInFrontOfText**

Remarks   Moves the selected drawing object from the layer behind text to the layer in front
of text. The object is placed behind any other drawing objects already in front of
the text layer. An error occurs if the object is already part of the drawing layer
above text or if the selection is not a drawing object.

See Also   **DrawBringForward, DrawBringToFront, DrawSendBackward,
DrawSendBehindText, DrawSendToBack**

DrawBringToFront

Syntax   **DrawBringToFront**

Remarks   Moves the selected drawing object to the topmost position in a stack of drawing
objects. **BringToFront** does not move a drawing object from the layer behind
text to the layer in front of text. An error occurs if the selection is not a drawing
object.

See Also   **DrawBringForward, DrawBringInFrontOfText, DrawSendBackward,
DrawSendBehindText, DrawSendToBack**

DrawCallout

Syntax   **DrawCallout**

Remarks   Inserts a callout drawing object in front of the current text layer at the upper-left
corner of the document. A callout consists of a text box and a line segment within
a bounding rectangle. When you first insert a callout, the text box is the same size
as the bounding rectangle, so the line segment does not appear. You change the
size of the text box with the **DrawSetCalloutTextbox** statement.

To change the size and position of the rectangle bounding the callout, as well as
the fill color and line style, use **FormatDrawingObject**. You can change other
options for the callout with **FormatCallout**.

Example   This example inserts and formats a callout that points to the left. The
DrawCallout instruction inserts a default callout whose type is set by the
FormatCallout instruction. The **FormatDrawingObject** instruction then
positions and sizes the callout and adds a fill color. Coordinates for the text box
within the callout are defined in the two-dimensional array calloutpts$() and
then applied using **DrawSetCalloutTextbox**. Finally, text is inserted into the
callout.

```
DrawCallout
FormatCallout .Type = 1, .Gap = "10 pt", .Angle = 4, \
    .Drop = "Center", .Length = "100 pt", .Border = 1, \
    .AutoAttach = 0, .Accent = 0
FormatDrawingObject .FillColor = 0, .FillPatternColor = 7, \
    .FillPattern = 5, .ArrowStyle = 2, \
    .HorizontalPos = "173 pt", .HorizontalFrom = 1, \
    .VerticalPos = "100 pt", .VerticalFrom = 1, \
    .Height = "42 pt", .Width = "161 pt"
Dim calloutpts$(2, 2)
calloutpts$(1, 1) = "63 pt"
calloutpts$(1, 2) = "0 pt"
calloutpts$(2, 1) = "97 pt"
calloutpts$(2, 2) = "42 pt"
DrawSetCalloutTextbox calloutpts$()
Insert "This callout points to the left."
```

See Also   **DrawGetCalloutTextbox, DrawSetCalloutTextbox, DrawTextBox,
FormatCallout, FormatDrawingObject**

DrawClearRange

Syntax   **DrawClearRange**

Remarks   Clears a drawing range. For more information about drawing ranges, see
                  DrawSetRange.

See Also   **DrawSetRange**

DrawCount()

Syntax   **DrawCount**()

Remarks   Returns the number of drawing objects whose anchors are in the range set by
                  DrawSetRange.

Example   This example displays a message box showing the number of drawing objects in
                  the active document:

```
DrawSetRange "\Doc"
numobjects = DrawCount()
MsgBox "There are" + Str$(numobjects) + " drawing objects" + \
       " in the document."
```

See Also   **DrawGetType**(), **DrawSetRange**

DrawCountPolyPoints()

Syntax   **DrawCountPolyPoints**([*Object*])

Remarks   Returns the number of points in a freeform drawing object. If the specified object
                  is not a freeform shape, an error occurs.

Argument	Explanation
Object	Specifies a drawing object:
	Omitted The selected drawing object
	> 0 (zero) An object whose anchor is in a range set by the **DrawSetRange** statement, where 1 is the first object in the range, 2 is the second object, and so on. If the number is not in the range 1 to **DrawCount**(), an error occurs.

Example   This example determines whether the first two drawing objects in the document
                  are freeform shapes. If they are, the points of the first freeform drawing object are
                  loaded into the array pointsArray() and applied to the second freeform drawing
                  object.

```
DrawSetRange "\Doc"
If DrawGetType(1) = 7 And DrawGetType(2) = 7 Then
    size = DrawCountPolyPoints(1)
    Dim pointsArray(size, 2)
    DrawGetPolyPoints pointsArray(), 1
    DrawSetPolyPoints size, pointsArray(), 2
Else
    MsgBox "The first or second drawing object is " + \
        "not a freeform shape."
End If
```

See Also   **DrawFreeformPolygon**, **DrawGetPolyPoints**, **DrawSetPolyPoints**

DrawDisassemblePicture

Syntax   **DrawDisassemblePicture**

Remarks   Converts the selected graphic into a group of drawing objects. If the selected graphic cannot be disassembled, Word inserts it into a text box drawing object. If a graphic is not selected, an error occurs.

See Also   **DrawGroup**, **DrawUngroup**

DrawEllipse

Syntax   **DrawEllipse**

Remarks   Switches to page layout view and adds a default elliptical drawing object in front of the current text layer. A default elliptical drawing object is a circle and is inserted at the upper-left corner of the current page.

See Also   **DrawGetType()**, **DrawRoundRectangle**, **FormatDrawingObject**

DrawExtendSelect

Syntax   **DrawExtendSelect** *Count*

Remarks   Selects the drawing object specified by *Count*, whose anchor is within the drawing range set by the **DrawSetRange** statement. *Count* is the position of the drawing object relative to the text layer: 1 corresponds to the object closest to the text layer, 2 to the next object, and so on. If one or more drawing objects are already selected, the drawing object specified by *Count* is added to the group of selected objects. If no drawing range has been set, or if *Count* is greater than the number of objects whose anchors are within the range, an error occurs.

See Also   **DrawGroup**, **DrawSelect**

DrawFlipHorizontal

Syntax **DrawFlipHorizontal**

Remarks Flips the selected drawing object from left to right. **DrawFlipHorizontal** works only on objects drawn using the Drawing toolbar; an error occurs if the selected object is an embedded object.

See Also **DrawFlipVertical**, **DrawRotateLeft**, **DrawRotateRight**

DrawFlipVertical

Syntax **DrawFlipVertical**

Remarks Flips the selected drawing object from top to bottom. **DrawFlipVertical** works only on objects drawn using the Drawing toolbar; an error occurs if the selected object is an embedded object.

See Also **DrawFlipHorizontal**, **DrawRotateLeft**, **DrawRotateRight**

DrawFreeformPolygon

Syntax **DrawFreeformPolygon**

Remarks Switches to page layout view and adds a default freeform drawing object in front of the text layer. A default freeform shape consists of a single line segment and is inserted at the upper-left corner of the current page. To change the freeform shape, you use the **DrawSetPolyPoints** statement.

Example This example adds an N-shaped drawing object in front of the text layer by inserting a default freeform drawing object and then using **DrawSetPolyPoints** to change it. Because the lines in an N shape have four end points, eight elements must be assigned to the pointsArray$( ) array (four pairs of two values). End points are measured relative to the upper-left corner of the current page.

```
DrawFreeformPolygon
Dim pointsArray$(4, 2)
pointsArray$(1, 1) = "150 pt"
pointsArray$(1, 2) = "200 pt"
pointsArray$(2, 1) = "150 pt"
pointsArray$(2, 2) = "100 pt"
pointsArray$(3, 1) = "200 pt"
pointsArray$(3, 2) = "200 pt"
pointsArray$(4, 1) = "200 pt"
pointsArray$(4, 2) = "100 pt"
DrawSetPolyPoints 4, pointsArray$()
```

See Also **DrawCountPolyPoints()**, **DrawGetPolyPoints**, **DrawSetPolyPoints**, **FormatDrawingObject**

DrawGetCalloutTextbox

Syntax   **DrawGetCalloutTextbox** *TwoDimensionalArray*[$]( ) [, *Object*]

Remarks   Fills a two-dimensional array with coordinates that describe the position and size of the text area within the bounding rectangle of the specified callout drawing object.

Argument	Explanation
TwoDimensionalArray[$]( )	The predefined two-dimensional array to fill with the coordinates of the specified callout text box. *TwoDimensionalArray*[$]( ) may be a string or numeric array. A string array is filled with text measurements consisting of a number followed by the abbreviation for the default measurement unit. A numeric array is filled with the numbers only.
	For example, given an array pts( ) defined with the instruction Dim pts(2, 2), the instruction DrawGetCalloutTextbox pts( ) fills the array as follows:
	pts(1, 1) The horizontal position (the distance from the left edge of the bounding rectangle to the text area), in the default measurement unit
	pts(1, 2) The vertical position (the distance from the top edge of the bounding rectangle to the text area)
	pts(2, 1) The width of the text area
	pts(2, 2) The height of the text area
Object	Specifies a drawing object:
	Omitted The selected drawing object
	> 0 (zero) An object whose anchor is in a range set by the **DrawSetRange** statement, where 1 is the first object in the range, 2 is the second object, and so on. If the number is not in the range 1 to **DrawCount**( ), an error occurs.
	If the specified drawing object is not a callout, an error occurs.

Example

This example displays a message box showing the horizontal position, vertical position, width, and height of the text area within the selected callout:

```
Dim pts$(2, 2)
DrawGetCalloutTextbox pts$()
msg$ = "HorizPos: " + pts$(1, 1) + Chr$(13)
msg$ = msg$ + "VertPos: " + pts$(1, 2) + Chr$(13)
msg$ = msg$ + "Width: " + pts$(2, 1) + Chr$(13)
msg$ = msg$ + "Height: " + pts$(2, 2) + Chr$(13)
MsgBox msg$, "Text Area In Callout"
```

See Also   **DrawCallout, DrawSetCalloutTextbox, DrawSetInsertToTextbox**

DrawGetPolyPoints

Syntax   **DrawGetPolyPoints** *TwoDimensionalArray*[**$**]*( )* [**,** *Object*]

Remarks   Fills a two-dimensional array with coordinates of the end points in the specified freeform drawing object. If the specified object is not a freeform shape, an error occurs. You can use the array as an argument for **DrawSetPolyPoints** to apply the coordinates to another freeform drawing object. You must define the array before running **DrawGetPolyPoints**; use **DrawCountPolyPoints( )** to determine the appropriate size for the array.

Argument	Explanation
TwoDimensionalArray[**$**]*( )*	The predefined two-dimensional array to fill with the coordinates of the specified freeform drawing object. *TwoDimensionalArray*[**$**]*( )* may be a string or numeric array. A string array is filled with text measurements consisting of a number followed by the abbreviation for the default measurement unit. A numeric array is filled with the numbers only.
Object	Specifies a drawing object:
	Omitted The selected drawing object
	> 0 (zero) An object whose anchor is in a range set by the **DrawSetRange** statement, where 1 is the first object in the range, 2 is the second object, and so on. If the number is not in the range 1 to **DrawCount( )**, an error occurs.

Example

This example stores the coordinates of the selected freeform drawing object in the array pointsArray(). If a freeform drawing object is not selected, an error occurs.

```
If DrawGetType() = 7 Then
    size = DrawCountPolyPoints()
    Dim pointsArray(size, 2)
    DrawGetPolyPoints pointsArray()
Else
    MsgBox "The selected drawing object is not a freeform shape."
End If
```

For another example, see **DrawCountPolyPoints()**.

See Also

DrawCountPolyPoints(), **DrawFreeformPolygon**, **DrawSetPolyPoints**

DrawGetType()

Syntax

DrawGetType([*Count*]**)**

Remarks

Returns a number corresponding to the type of the drawing object specified by *Count*. *Count* is in the range 1 to **DrawCount()**, the number of objects within a range specified by **DrawSetRange**. If *Count* is omitted, the type of the selected drawing object is returned.

DrawGetType() returns the following values.

Value	Explanation
0 (zero)	*Count* is not specified and a drawing object is not selected.
1	*Count* is not specified and more than one drawing object is selected.
2	The drawing object is a line.
3	The drawing object is a text box.
4	The drawing object is a rectangle.
5	The drawing object is an ellipse.
6	The drawing object is an arc.
7	The drawing object is a freeform shape.
8	The drawing object is a callout.

Example   This example sets the drawing range to the entire document using the predefined bookmark "\Doc," counts the number of arcs in the document, and then displays the result in a message box:

```
DrawSetRange "\Doc"
numarcs = 0
For i = 1 To DrawCount()
    type = DrawGetType(i)
    If type = 6 Then numarcs = numarcs + 1
Next
MsgBox "The document contains" + Str$(numarcs) + " arc(s)."
```

See Also   **DrawCount(), DrawSelect, DrawSetRange**

DrawGroup

Syntax   **DrawGroup**

Remarks   Groups the selected drawing objects so they can be manipulated as a single object.

Example   This example sets the drawing range to the current paragraph and then selects each object whose anchor is in the range. If the number of objects in the range is greater than one, they are grouped together.

```
DrawSetRange "\Para"
numobjects = DrawCount()
For i = 1 To numobjects
    DrawExtendSelect i
Next i
If numobjects > 1 Then DrawGroup
```

See Also   **DrawDisassemblePicture, DrawExtendSelect, DrawSelect, DrawSetRange, DrawUngroup**

DrawInsertWordPicture

Syntax   **DrawInsertWordPicture**

Remarks   Opens a temporary document (a Word Picture object) and displays the Picture and Drawing toolbars. When the user closes the document or clicks Close Picture on the Picture toolbar, the object is embedded in the document that was active when **DrawInsertWordPicture** was run. The instruction DrawInsertWordPicture is the same as the instruction InsertObject .Class = "Word.Picture.6".

See Also   **InsertDrawing, InsertObject, InsertPicture**

DrawLine

Syntax   **DrawLine**

Remarks   Adds a default linear drawing object in front of the current text layer. The default line segment is inserted at the upper-left corner of the current page.

See Also   **DrawArc, DrawFlipHorizontal, DrawFlipVertical, DrawFreeformPolygon, DrawGetType(), DrawRotateLeft, DrawRotateRight, FormatDrawingObject**

DrawNudgeDown

Syntax   **DrawNudgeDown**

Remarks   Moves the selected drawing object or objects down 10 pixels or, if Snap To Grid is selected in the Snap To Grid dialog box (Drawing toolbar), moves the selected objects down by the measurement in the Vertical Spacing box.

See Also   **DrawNudgeDownPixel, DrawNudgeLeft, DrawNudgeRight, DrawNudgeUp, DrawSnapToGrid**

DrawNudgeDownPixel

Syntax   **DrawNudgeDownPixel**

Remarks   Moves the selected drawing object or objects down one pixel (the smallest unit on the screen).

See Also   **DrawNudgeDown, DrawNudgeLeftPixel, DrawNudgeRightPixel, DrawNudgeUpPixel**

DrawNudgeLeft

Syntax   **DrawNudgeLeft**

Remarks   Moves the selected drawing object or objects left 10 pixels or, if Snap To Grid is selected in the Snap To Grid dialog box (Drawing toolbar), moves the selected objects left by the measurement in the Horizontal Spacing box.

See Also   **DrawNudgeDown, DrawNudgeLeftPixel, DrawNudgeRight, DrawNudgeUp, DrawSnapToGrid**

DrawNudgeLeftPixel

Syntax   **DrawNudgeLeftPixel**

Remarks   Moves the selected drawing object or objects left one pixel (the smallest unit on the screen).

See Also   **DrawNudgeLeft**, **DrawNudgeDownPixel**, **DrawNudgeRightPixel**, **DrawNudgeUpPixel**

DrawNudgeRight

Syntax   **DrawNudgeRight**

Remarks   Moves the selected drawing object or objects right 10 pixels or, if Snap To Grid is selected in the Snap To Grid dialog box (Drawing toolbar), moves the selected objects right by the measurement in the Horizontal Spacing box.

See Also   **DrawNudgeDown**, **DrawNudgeLeft**, **DrawNudgeRightPixel**, **DrawNudgeUp**, **DrawSnapToGrid**

DrawNudgeRightPixel

Syntax   **DrawNudgeRightPixel**

Remarks   Moves the selected drawing object or objects right one pixel (the smallest unit on the screen).

See Also   **DrawNudgeDownPixel**, **DrawNudgeLeftPixel**, **DrawNudgeRight**, **DrawNudgeUpPixel**

DrawNudgeUp

Syntax   **DrawNudgeUp**

Remarks   Moves the selected drawing object or objects up 10 pixels or, if Snap To Grid is selected in the Snap To Grid dialog box (Drawing toolbar), moves the selected objects up by the measurement in the Vertical Spacing box.

See Also   **DrawNudgeDown**, **DrawNudgeLeft**, **DrawNudgeRight**, **DrawNudgeUpPixel**, **DrawSnapToGrid**

DrawNudgeUpPixel

Syntax	**DrawNudgeUpPixel**
Remarks	Moves the selected drawing object or objects up one pixel (the smallest unit on the screen).
See Also	**DrawNudgeDownPixel**, **DrawNudgeLeftPixel**, **DrawNudgeRightPixel**, **DrawNudgeUp**

DrawRectangle

Syntax	**DrawRectangle**
Remarks	Adds a default rectangular drawing object in front of the current text layer. A default rectangle is a square and is inserted at the upper-left corner of the current page.
See Also	**DrawFreeformPolygon**, **DrawRoundRectangle**, **DrawTextBox**, **FormatDrawingObject**

DrawResetWordPicture

Syntax	**DrawResetWordPicture**
Remarks	Resets the boundaries in a Word Picture object to include all drawing objects in the picture editing window. If the active window is not a picture editing window, an error occurs.
See Also	**DrawInsertWordPicture**, **FileClosePicture**

DrawReshape

Syntax	**DrawReshape**
Remarks	Toggles the handles on the selected freeform drawing object between the bounding rectangle (where you use the handles to scale or resize the object) and the vertices of the freeform shape (where you use the handles to reshape the object). You can select multiple freeform drawing objects before running **DrawReshape**. If a freeform drawing object is not selected, an error occurs.
See Also	**DrawFreeformPolygon**, **DrawGetType()**, **DrawSelect**

DrawRotateLeft

Syntax   **DrawRotateLeft**

Remarks   Rotates the selected drawing object counterclockwise 90 degrees.
DrawRotateLeft works only on objects drawn using the Drawing toolbar; an
error occurs if the selected object is an embedded object.

See Also   **DrawFlipHorizontal**, **DrawFlipVertical**, **DrawRotateRight**

DrawRotateRight

Syntax   **DrawRotateRight**

Remarks   Rotates the selected drawing object clockwise 90 degrees. **DrawRotateRight**
works only on objects drawn using the Drawing toolbar; an error occurs if the
selected object is an embedded object.

See Also   **DrawFlipHorizontal**, **DrawFlipVertical**, **DrawRotateLeft**

DrawRoundRectangle

Syntax   **DrawRoundRectangle**

Remarks   Adds a default rectangular drawing object with rounded corners in front of the
current text layer. A default rounded rectangle has sides of equal length and is
inserted at the upper-left corner of the current page.

See Also   **DrawEllipse**, **DrawFreeformPolygon**, **DrawRectangle**, **DrawTextBox**,
FormatDrawingObject

DrawSelect, DrawSelect()

Syntax   **DrawSelect** *Object*

        DrawSelect(*Object*)

Remarks   The **DrawSelect** statement selects the specified drawing object and deselects any
other selected drawing objects. To select a drawing object without deselecting
other objects, use the **DrawExtendSelect** statement. The **DrawSelect()** function
behaves the same as the statement and also returns −1 if the specified object was
selected.

Argument	Explanation
Object	Specifies a drawing object whose anchor is in a range set by **DrawSetRange**, where 1 is the first object in the range, 2 is the second object, and so on. If the number is not in the range 1 to **DrawCount()**, an error occurs.

Example	This example selects the last drawing object in the document and brings it to the topmost position among the drawing objects on the same drawing layer:

```
DrawSetRange "\Doc"
numobjects = DrawCount()
DrawSelect numobjects
DrawBringToFront
```

See Also	**DrawExtendSelect, DrawSetRange**

DrawSelectNext

Syntax	**DrawSelectNext**
Remarks	Selects the next drawing object, where "next" means next closest to the top in a stack of drawing objects. If the topmost object is selected, Word selects the bottommost object. If a drawing object is not selected when **DrawSelectNext** runs, an error occurs. Note that you do not need to set a drawing range with **DrawSetRange** to use **DrawSelectNext**.
See Also	**DrawExtendSelect, DrawSelect, DrawSelectPrevious**

DrawSelectPrevious

Syntax	**DrawSelectPrevious**
Remarks	Selects the previous drawing object, where "previous" means next closest to the bottom in a stack of drawing objects. If the bottommost object is selected, Word selects the topmost object. If a drawing object is not selected when **DrawSelectPrevious** runs, an error occurs. Note that you do not need to set a drawing range with **DrawSetRange** to use **DrawSelectPrevious**.
See Also	**DrawExtendSelect, DrawSelect, DrawSelectNext**

DrawSendBackward

Syntax	**DrawSendBackward**
Remarks	Moves the selected drawing object behind the previous one in a stack of drawing objects. **DrawSendBackward** does not move a drawing object from the layer in front of text to the layer behind text. An error occurs if a drawing object is not selected.
See Also	**DrawBringForward, DrawBringInFrontOfText, DrawBringToFront, DrawSendBehindText, DrawSendToBack**

DrawSendBehindText

Syntax   DrawSendBehindTextxxx

Remarks   Moves the selected drawing object from the layer in front of text to the layer behind text. The object is placed in front of any other drawing objects already behind the text layer. An error occurs if the object is already part of the drawing layer behind text or if a drawing object is not selected.

See Also   **DrawBringForward, DrawBringInFrontOfText, DrawBringToFront, DrawSendBackward, DrawSendToBack**

DrawSendToBack

Syntax   DrawSendToBack

Remarks   Moves the selected drawing object behind all previous ones in a stack of drawing objects. **DrawSendToBack** does not move a drawing object from the layer in front of text to the layer behind text. An error occurs if a drawing object is not selected.

See Also   **DrawBringForward, DrawBringInFrontOfText, DrawBringToFront, DrawSendBackward, DrawSendBehindText**

DrawSetCalloutTextbox

Syntax   **DrawSetCalloutTextbox** *TwoDimensionalArray*[$]*( )* [, *Object*]

Remarks   Applies the position and size stored in a two-dimensional array to the text area of the specified callout drawing object.

Argument	Explanation
TwoDimensionalArray[$]*( )*	A two-dimensional array containing coordinates for the position and size of the text area relative to the bounding rectangle of a callout drawing object. You can use a numeric array containing values in the default measurement unit or a string array containing text measurements.
	For information on how values are stored in the array, see **DrawGetCalloutTextbox**.

Argument	Explanation
Object	Specifies a drawing object:
	Omitted The selected drawing object
	> 0 (zero) An object whose anchor is in a range set by the **DrawSetRange** statement, where 1 is the first object in the range, 2 is the second object, and so on. If the number is not in the range 1 to **DrawCount( )**, an error occurs.
	If the specified drawing object is not a callout, an error occurs.

For an example, see **DrawCallout**.

See Also   **DrawCallout, DrawGetCalloutTextbox, DrawSetInsertToTextbox**

DrawSetInsertToAnchor

Syntax   **DrawSetInsertToAnchor** [*Object*]

Remarks   Moves the insertion point to the beginning of the paragraph to which the specified drawing object is anchored.

Argument	Explanation
Object	Specifies a drawing object:
	Omitted The selected drawing object
	> 0 (zero) An object whose anchor is in a range set by the **DrawSetRange** statement, where 1 is the first object in the range, 2 is the second object, and so on. If the number is not in the range 1 to **DrawCount( )**, an error occurs.

See Also   **DrawSetInsertToTextBox**

DrawSetInsertToTextbox

Syntax   **DrawSetInsertToTextbox** [*Object*]

Remarks   Moves the insertion point to the text area of the specified text box or callout drawing object. If the specified object is not a text box or callout drawing object, an error occurs.

Argument	Explanation
Object	Specifies a drawing object:
	Omitted The selected drawing object
	> 0 (zero) An object whose anchor is in a range set by the **DrawSetRange** statement, where 1 is the first object in the range, 2 is the second object, and so on. If the number is not in the range 1 to **DrawCount**(), an error occurs.

Example

This example sets the drawing range to the entire document and then selects the first drawing object. If the drawing object is a text box or callout, Word moves the insertion point to the text area and inserts some text.

```
DrawSetRange "\Doc"
Select Case DrawGetType(1)
   Case 3                         'Text box
      DrawSetInsertToTextbox 1
      Insert "Text box text"
   Case 8                         'Callout
      DrawSetInsertToTextbox 1
      Insert "Callout text."
   Case Else
End Select
```

See Also

DrawCallout, **DrawSelect**, **DrawSetInsertToAnchor**, **DrawTextBox**

DrawSetPolyPoints

Syntax

DrawSetPolyPoints *NumPoints*, *TwoDimensionalArray*[$]*( )* [, *Object*]

Remarks

Applies the coordinates stored in a two-dimensional array to the specified freeform drawing object. If the specified object is not a freeform shape, an error occurs.

Argument	Explanation
NumPoints	The number of coordinates in *TwoDimensionalArray*[$]*( )* to apply to the freeform drawing object. *NumPoints* cannot exceed the size of the array.
TwoDimensionalArray[$]*( )*	A two-dimensional array containing the coordinates of the end points in the freeform drawing object. You can use a numeric array containing values in the default measurement unit or a string array containing text measurements.
	For information on how values are stored in the array, see **DrawGetPolyPoints**.

Argument	Explanation
Object	Specifies a drawing object:
	Omitted The selected drawing object
	> 0 (zero) An object whose anchor is in a range set by **DrawSetRange**, where 1 is the first object in the range, 2 is the second object, and so on. If the number is not in the range 1 to **DrawCount**( ), an error occurs.

For an example, see **DrawCountPolyPoints**( ).

See Also   **DrawCountPolyPoints**( ), **DrawFreeformPolygon**, **DrawGetPolyPoints**, **DrawReshape**

DrawSetRange, DrawSetRange()

Syntax   **DrawSetRange** *Bookmark$*

DrawSetRange(*Bookmark$*)

Remarks   The **DrawSetRange** statement sets the drawing range to the bookmark specified by *Bookmark$*. A drawing range establishes the group of drawing objects that other drawing statements and functions operate on. For example, the **DrawCount**( ) function counts the number of drawing objects whose anchors are within the drawing range.

The **DrawSetRange**( ) function behaves the same as the statement and also returns –1 if the range was set or 0 (zero) if the range was not set (for example, if the specified bookmark does not exist).

It is often convenient to use predefined bookmarks when setting a drawing range. For example, you can set the drawing range to the entire document by using the instruction DrawSetRange "\Doc". For more information on predefined bookmarks, see "Operators and Predefined Bookmarks" later in this part.

Example   This example sets the drawing range to the current page, counts the number of drawing objects within the range, and then displays a message box with the result:

```
DrawSetRange "\Page"
n = DrawCount()
MsgBox "The current page contains" + Str$(n) + " drawing object(s)."
```

See Also   **DrawClearRange**, **DrawCount**( ), **DrawSelect**

DrawSnapToGrid

Syntax

DrawSnapToGrid .SnapToGrid = *number* [**, .XGrid** = *number or text*] [**, .YGrid** = *number or text*] [**, .XOrigin** = *number or text*] [**, .YOrigin** = *number or text*]

Remarks

Establishes a grid that restricts where drawing objects may be positioned and how they may be sized. A grid is useful when you want to align and connect drawing objects. The arguments for **DrawSnapToGrid** correspond to the options in the Snap To Grid dialog box (Snap To Grid button, Drawing toolbar).

Argument	Explanation
.SnapToGrid	If 1, activates the restriction on positioning drawing objects.
.XGrid	The distance, in points or a text measurement, between vertical gridlines (in other words, the increments in which drawing objects can be positioned horizontally).
.YGrid	The distance, in points or a text measurement, between horizontal gridlines (in other words, the increments in which drawing objects can be positioned vertically).
.XOrigin	The distance, in points or a text measurement, from the left edge of the page to the vertical gridline you want Word to use when laying out all other vertical gridlines. Specifying 0 (zero) or a multiple of the .XGrid measurement has no effect.
.YOrigin	The distance, in points or a text measurement, from the top edge of the page to the horizontal gridline you want Word to use when laying out all other horizontal gridlines. Specifying 0 (zero) or a multiple of the .YGrid measurement has no effect.

See Also   **DrawAlign**

DrawTextBox

Syntax   **DrawTextBox**

Remarks

Adds a default bounded area of text to the drawing layer in front of the current text layer. A default text box is one-inch square and is inserted at the upper-left corner of the current page.

See Also   **DrawCallout**, **DrawRectangle**, **DrawSetInsertToAnchor**, **DrawSetInsertToTextBox**, **FormatDrawingObject**

DrawUngroup

Syntax	**DrawUngroup**

Remarks   Removes the association that exists between drawing objects previously associated with the **DrawGroup** statement, so you can move and size each object independently. If a group of drawing objects is not selected, an error occurs.

See Also   **DrawExtendSelect**, **DrawGroup**, **DrawSelect**

DrawUnselect

Syntax   **DrawUnselect**

Remarks   Deselects the selected drawing object and moves the insertion point to the beginning of the paragraph containing the corresponding anchor. If more than one drawing object is selected, **DrawUnselect** moves the insertion point to the first paragraph containing an anchor for at least one of the selected objects.

See Also   **DrawExtendSelect**, **DrawSelect**, **DrawSelectNext**, **DrawSelectPrevious**

DropDownFormField

Syntax   **DropDownFormField**

Remarks   Inserts a drop-down form field at the insertion point. **DropDownFormField** corresponds to the Drop-Down Form Field button on the Forms toolbar.

See Also   **AddDropDownItem**, **CheckBoxFormField**, **InsertFormField**, **RemoveAllDropDownItems**, **RemoveDropDownItem**, **TextFormField**

DropListBox

Syntax   **DropListBox** *HorizPos*, *VertPos*, *Width*, *Height*, *ArrayVariable$( )*, *Identifier*

Remarks   Creates a drop-down list box from which a user can select an item within a user-defined dialog box. **DropListBox** has the same syntax as **ListBox**. When a drop-down list box is dropped down, the portion that is dropped down can cover other controls in the dialog box or fall outside the dialog box.

Argument	Explanation
HorizPos, *VertPos*	The horizontal and vertical distance of the upper-left corner of the drop-down list box from the upper-left corner of the dialog box in increments of 1/8 and 1/12 of the System font (Windows) or the dialog font (Macintosh).
Width, *Height*	The width and height of the list box, in increments of 1/8 and 1/1 of the System font (Windows) or the dialog font (Macintosh). *Height* is the height of the list box when it is dropped down.

Argument	Explanation
ArrayVariable$( )	A string array containing the items to be listed, one list box item per array element.
.Identifier	Together with the dialog record name, creates a variable whose value corresponds to the selected list box item. The form for this variable is *DialogRecord.Identifier* (for example, `dlg.MyList`). The identifier string (*.Identifier* minus the period) is also used by statements in a dialog function that act on the list box, such as **DlgEnable** and **DlgVisible**.

See the **ListBox** entry for an example of a list box.

To modify the example so that it displays a drop-down list box instead of a list box, change the **ListBox** instruction to **DropListBox**, and change the *Height* argument to the height of the drop-down list box when it is dropped down.

For an example of **DropListBox** used in a complete dialog box definition, see **Begin Dialog...End Dialog**.

See Also   **Begin Dialog...End Dialog**, **ComboBox**, **DlgListBoxArray**, **ListBox**

EditAutoText

Syntax

EditAutoText .Name = *text* [, **.Context** = *number*] [, **.InsertAs** = *number*] [, **.Insert**] [, **.Add**] [, **.Delete**]

Remarks

Inserts, adds, or deletes an AutoText entry. The arguments for the **EditAutoText** statement correspond to the options in the AutoText dialog box (Edit menu).

Argument	Explanation
.Name	The name of the AutoText entry.
.Context	A context for the new AutoText entry:
	0 (zero) or omitted Normal template
	1 Active template
	Note that .Context is used only when Word adds an AutoText entry. When inserting or deleting an entry, Word automatically looks for the entry first in the active template and then in the Normal template. When inserting an entry and no match is found in the active or Normal templates, Word looks in each loaded global template in the order listed in the Templates And Add-ins dialog box (File menu). You cannot delete an AutoText entry from a loaded global template.
.InsertAs	Used with .Insert to control whether the entry is inserted with its formatting:
	0 (zero) or omitted Entry is inserted with formatting.
	1 Entry is inserted as plain text.

You can specify only one of the following arguments.

Argument	Explanation
.Insert	Inserts the entry into the document
.Add	Stores the entry in the template (if there is no selection, an error occurs)
.Delete	Deletes the entry from the template

If you do not specify .Insert, .Add, or .Delete, Word inserts the AutoText entry.

Examples

This example selects the text of the first paragraph (not including the paragraph mark) and then defines it as an AutoText entry named "MainHead," stored in the Normal template:

```
StartOfDocument
EditGoTo "\Para"
CharLeft 1, 1
EditAutoText .Name = "MainHead", .Context = 0, .Add
```

The following example inserts the "MainHead" AutoText entry without formatting:

```
EditAutoText .Name = "MainHead", .InsertAs = 1, .Insert
```

See Also   **AutoText, AutoTextName$(), CountAutoTextEntries(), GetAutoText$(), InsertAutoText, SetAutoText**

EditBookmark

Syntax   **EditBookmark .Name** = *text* [, **.SortBy** = *number*] [, **.Add**] [, **.Delete**] [, **.Goto**]

Remarks   Adds, deletes, or selects the specified bookmark. The arguments for the **EditBookmark** statement correspond to the options in the Bookmark dialog box (Edit menu).

Argument	Explanation
.Name	The name of the bookmark
.SortBy	Controls how the list of bookmarks is sorted when you display the Bookmark dialog box with a **Dialog** or **Dialog()** instruction:

    0 (zero)   By name

    1   By location

You can specify only one of the following arguments.

Argument	Explanation
.Add	Adds a bookmark at the insertion point or selection
.Delete	Deletes the bookmark
.Goto	Moves the insertion point or selection to the bookmark

If you do not specify .Add, .Delete, or .Goto, Word adds the bookmark.

Example   This example searches for a paragraph containing only the word "Index" (that is, the heading for the index), and then, if the heading is found, adds a bookmark in front of it. You could use this bookmark in another **EditBookmark** instruction or with **EditGoTo** to move the insertion point to the index.

```
StartOfDocument
EditFind .Find = "^pIndex^p", .MatchCase = 1, \
    .Direction = 0, .Format = 0
If EditFindFound() Then
    CharLeft : CharRight
    EditBookmark .Name = "Index", .Add
End If
```

See Also   **BookmarkName$(), CmpBookmarks(), CopyBookmark, CountBookmarks(), EditGoTo, EmptyBookmark(), ExistingBookmark(), GetBookmark$(), SetEndOfBookmark, SetStartOfBookmark**

EditButtonImage

Syntax   **EditButtonImage** *Toolbar$*, *Position* [, *Context*]

Remarks   Runs the button image editor to modify the specified toolbar button image.

Argument	Explanation
Toolbar$	The name of the toolbar as listed in the Toolbars dialog box (View menu).
Position	A number corresponding to the position of the button whose image you want to edit, where 1 is the first position, 2 is the second, and so on. Note that a list box or space counts as one position.
Context	Determines where the new button image is stored:
	0 (zero) or omitted Normal template
	1 Active template

Example   This example opens the image editor and displays the first button image on the Standard toolbar for editing:

```
EditButtonImage "Standard", 1, 0
```

See Also   **ChooseButtonImage, CopyButtonImage, PasteButtonImage, ResetButtonImage**

EditClear

Syntax   **EditClear** [*Count*]

Remarks   Deletes the selection or a specified number of characters. Unlike **EditCut**, **EditClear** does not change the contents of the Clipboard.

Argument	Explanation
Count	Specifies the number and location of characters to delete:
	> 0 (zero) Deletes characters to the right of the insertion point.
	Omitted Deletes the selection or the character to the right of the insertion point.
	< 0 (zero) Deletes characters to the left of the insertion point.
	If *Count* is nonzero and there is a selection, Word deletes the selection and counts it as one character against *Count*.
	Note that EditClear 0 has no effect.

> **Note** In Word version 6.0, if **EditClear** deletes a paragraph mark, the combined paragraphs are formatted with the style of the remaining paragraph mark. In Word version 7.0, the combined paragraphs are formatted with the style of the deleted paragraph mark. For compatibility, in Word version 6.0 macros converted to Word version 7.0, the **EditClear** statement is changed to **WW6_EditClear**, which maintains the Word version 6.0 behavior.

Example This example deletes five characters to the right of the insertion point or, if there is a selection, deletes the selection plus four characters:

```
EditClear 5
```

See Also **EditCut**

EditConvertAllEndnotes

Syntax **EditConvertAllEndnotes**

Remarks Converts all endnotes in the active document to footnotes. An error occurs if there are no endnotes.

Example This example converts all endnotes to footnotes. If WordBasic error 509 ("This command is not available") occurs, the error handler displays the message "No endnotes to convert" instead of the standard WordBasic error message. Other error conditions generate standard messages.

```
On Error Goto trap
EditConvertAllEndnotes
trap:
Select Case Err
    Case 509 : MsgBox "No endnotes to convert."
    Case Else : Error Err
End Select
```

See Also **EditConvertAllFootnotes**, **EditConvertNotes**, **EditSwapAllNotes**

EditConvertAllFootnotes

Syntax **EditConvertAllFootnotes**

Remarks Converts all footnotes in the active document to endnotes. An error occurs if there are no footnotes. For an example using a similar statement, see **EditConvertAllEndnotes**.

See Also **EditConvertAllEndnotes**, **EditConvertNotes**, **EditSwapAllNotes**

EditConvertNotes

Syntax   **EditConvertNotes**

Remarks   Converts the selected footnotes to endnotes, or vice versa. An error occurs if the insertion point or selection is not in the footnote or endnote pane, or if there are no notes in the pane.

See Also   **EditConvertAllEndnotes, EditConvertAllFootnotes, EditSwapAllNotes**

EditCopy

Syntax   **EditCopy**

Remarks   Copies the selection to the Clipboard. If there is no selection, an error occurs.

See Also   **EditCut, EditPaste, EditPasteSpecial**

EditCopyAsPicture

Syntax   **EditCopyAsPicture**

Remarks   On the Macintosh, copies the selected text or object to the Clipboard as a picture. In Windows, **EditCopyAsPicture** is not available and generates an error.

See Also   **EditCopy, EditPasteSpecial**

EditCreatePublisher

Syntax   **EditCreatePublisher .FileName** = *text* [, **.Appearance** = *number*] [, **.Rtf** = *number*] [, **.Pict** = *number*]

Remarks   On the Macintosh, publishes the selected text in an edition, which you can then subscribe to in other documents. The arguments for the **EditCreatePublisher** statement correspond to the options in the Create Publisher dialog box (Publishing command, Edit menu). In Windows, **EditCreatePublisher** is not available and generates an error.

Argument	Explanation
.FileName	The path and filename for the new edition.
.Appearance	Specifies how the selection is published:
	0 (zero) or omitted As shown on screen
	1 As shown when printed
.Rtf	If 1, allows the publisher to export rich-text format (RTF).
.Pict	If 1, allows the publisher to export a picture format (PICT).

See Also   **EditLinks, EditPasteSpecial, EditPublishOptions, EditSubscribeOptions, EditSubscribeTo**

EditCut

Syntax   **EditCut**

Remarks   Removes the selection from the document and places it on the Clipboard. If there is no selection, an error occurs.

See Also   **EditClear, EditCopy, EditPaste, EditPasteSpecial, Spike**

EditFind

Syntax   **EditFind** [**.Find** = *text*] [**, .Replace** = *text*] [**, .Direction** = *number*]
[**, .WholeWord** = *number*] [**, .MatchCase** = *number*]
[**, .PatternMatch** = *number*] [**, .SoundsLike** = *number*]
[**, .FindAllWordForms** = *number*] [**, .Format** = *number*] [**, .Wrap** = *number*]

Remarks   Finds the next instance of the specified text, formatting, or both. The arguments for the **EditFind** statement correspond to the options in the Find dialog box (Edit menu). Used in a **While…Wend** loop, **EditFind** can be extremely useful when you need to repeat a series of instructions each time a certain piece of text or formatting is found in your document. Many examples in "Statements and Functions" illustrate this common use of **EditFind**.

Argument	Explanation
.Find	The text to find, or, to search for formatting only, an empty string (""). You can search for special characters, such as paragraph marks, by specifying appropriate character codes. For example, "^p" corresponds to a paragraph mark and "^t" corresponds to a tab character.
	If .PatternMatch is set to 1, you can specify wildcard characters and other advanced search criteria. For example, "*(ing)" finds any word ending in "ing."
	To search for a symbol character, specify the symbol's character code following a caret (^) and a zero (0). In Windows, for example, "^0151" corresponds to an em dash (—).
.Replace	You may need to set .Replace to an empty string ("") to avoid an error. For example, if you set .PatternMatch to 1 and the replacement text currently in the Replace dialog box is not valid with pattern matching on, an error occurs.
.Direction	The direction to search:
	0 (zero) Searches toward the end of the document.
	1 Searches toward the beginning of the document.
	The default is the direction used in the previous search or 0 (zero) the first time the Find or Replace command is run.
.WholeWord	If 1, corresponds to selecting the Find Whole Words Only check box.
.MatchCase	If 1, corresponds to selecting the Match Case check box.
.PatternMatch	If 1, Word evaluates .Find as a string containing advanced search criteria such as the asterisk (*) and question mark (?) wildcard characters (corresponds to selecting the Use Pattern Matching check box).
.SoundsLike	If 1, corresponds to selecting the Sounds Like check box.
.FindAllWordForms	If 1, corresponds to selecting the Find All Word Forms check box.
.Format	Finds formatting in addition to, or instead of, text:
	0 (zero) Ignores formatting
	1 Uses the specified formatting

Argument	Explanation
.Wrap	Controls what happens if the search begins at a point other than the beginning of the document and the end of the document is reached (or vice versa if .Direction is set to 1). The .Wrap argument also controls what happens if there is a selection and the search text is not found in the selection.

0 (zero) or omitted   The search operation ends and the macro continues.

1   If there is a selection, Word searches the remainder of the document. If the beginning or the end of the document is reached, Word continues the search from the opposite end.

2   If there is a selection, Word displays a message asking whether to search the remainder of the document. If the beginning or the end of the document is reached, Word displays a message asking whether to continue the search from the opposite end.

Formatting is not specified within the **EditFind** instruction itself. Instead, you precede **EditFind** with one or more **EditFindBorder**, **EditFindFont**, **EditFindLang**, **EditFindPara**, **EditFindStyle**, or **EditFindTabs** instructions. Then, in the **EditFind** instruction, you set .Format to 1. Note that **EditFindBorder** and **EditFindTabs** are available only on the Macintosh.

Here are some tips for using **EditFind** effectively:

- **EditFind** retains whatever settings were used in the most recent find or replace operation. For example, if the Find Whole Words Only check box was selected in the Find dialog box in the last find operation (or if the .WholeWord argument was set to 1), .WholeWord will still be set to 1 in the new find operation—unless you explicitly set it to 0 (zero). Before beginning a find operation, make sure to specify every option that can affect the outcome of a search.

- When you search for formatting, it's a good idea to include the statement **EditFindClearFormatting** before specifying the formats you want to find. That way, you clear any formats left over from previous find or replace operations.

- When repeating an operation for each occurrence of a piece of text or formatting in the document using a **While...Wend** loop, remember to use **StartOfDocument** before the first **EditFind** instruction. You should either omit the .Wrap argument or set it to 0 (zero). If you set .Wrap to 1, you may create an endless loop. If you set .Wrap to 2, Word displays a message asking if you'd like to continue from the beginning of the document; you must choose No to keep the macro running.

Examples

This example finds the next instance of "Trey Research" with single-underline formatting:

```
EditFindClearFormatting          'Clear leftover formats
EditFindFont .Underline = 1
EditFind .Find = "Trey Research", .Direction = 0, \
    .WholeWord = 0, .MatchCase = 0, .Format = 1
```

The following example inserts the string "Tip: " at the beginning of every Heading 6 paragraph. The instructions StartOfDocument and While EditFindFound() are key to any macro that repeats a series of actions each time the specified item is found.

```
StartOfDocument
EditFindClearFormatting
EditFindStyle .Style = "Heading 6"
EditFind .Find = "", .Direction = 0, .Format = 1, .Wrap = 0
While EditFindFound()
    StartOfLine
    Insert "Tip: "
    EditFindStyle .Style = "Heading 6"
    EditFind .Find = "", .Direction = 0, .Format = 1, .Wrap = 0
Wend
```

See Also

EditFindClearFormatting, EditFindBorder, EditFindFont, EditFindFound(), EditFindFrame, EditFindLang, EditFindPara, EditFindStyle, EditFindTabs, EditReplace

EditFindBorder

Syntax   **EditFindBorder** [**.ApplyTo** = *number*] [, **.Shadow** = *number*]
[, **.TopBorder** = *number*] [, **.LeftBorder** = *number*] [, **.BottomBorder** = *number*]
[, **.RightBorder** = *number*] [, **.HorizBorder** = *number*] [, **.VertBorder** = *number*]
[, **.TopColor** = *number*] [, **.LeftColor** = *number*] [, **.BottomColor** = *number*]
[, **.RightColor** = *number*] [, **.HorizColor** = *number*] [, **.VertColor** = *number*]
[, **.FineShading** = *number*] [, **.FromText** = *number or text*]
[, **.Shading** = *number*] [, **.Foreground** = *number*] [, **.Background** = *number*]
[, **.Tab** = *number*]

Remarks   On the Macintosh, when followed by an **EditFind** or **EditReplace** instruction in
which .Format is set to 1, specifies the borders or shading applied to the text you
want to find. For argument descriptions, see **FormatBordersAndShading**. In
Windows, **EditFindBorder** is not available and generates an error.

See Also   **EditFind**, **EditFindClearFormatting**, **EditFindFrame**, **EditFindLang**,
EditFindPara, **EditFindStyle**, **EditFindTabs**, **EditReplace**,
EditReplaceBorder, **FormatBordersAndShading**

EditFindClearFormatting

Syntax   **EditFindClearFormatting**

Remarks   Clears any formats specified for text to be found. Before specifying formats with
EditFindFont, **EditFindPara**, and so on, it's a good idea to include the
EditFindClearFormatting statement to ensure that any unwanted formats are not
included in the specification.

Example   The **EditFindClearFormatting** statement in this example ensures that the only
formats specified are bold and italic:

```
EditFindClearFormatting
EditFindFont .Bold = 1, .Italic = 1
EditFind .Find = "", .Format = 1
```

See Also   **EditFind**, **EditFindBorder**, **EditFindFont**, **EditFindFrame**, **EditFindLang**,
EditFindPara, **EditFindStyle**, **EditFindTabs**, **EditReplace**,
EditReplaceClearFormatting

EditFindFont

Syntax

EditFindFont [.**Points** = *number*] [, .**Underline** = *number*] [, .**Color** = *number*]
[, .**Strikethrough** = *number*] [, .**Superscript** = *number*] [, .**Subscript** = *number*]
[, .**Shadow** = *number*] [, .**Hidden** = *number*] [, .**SmallCaps** = *number*]
[, .**AllCaps** = *number*] [, .**Outline** = *number*] [, .**Spacing** = *number*]
[, .**Position** = *number or text*] [, .**Kerning** = *number*]
[, .**KerningMin** = *number or text*] [, .**Default**] [, .**Tab** = *number*] [, .**Font** = *text*]
[, .**Bold** = *number*] [, .**Italic** = *number*]

Remarks

When followed by an **EditFind** or **EditReplace** instruction in which .Format is
set to 1, specifies the character formatting of the text you want to find. You can
set .Strikethrough, .Superscript, .Subscript, .Shadow, .Hidden, .SmallCaps,
.AllCaps, .Outline, .Kerning, .Bold, and .Italic to one of the three following
values.

Use this value	To do this
–1	Find text regardless of whether it has the format
0 (zero)	Find text that does not have the format
1	Find text that has the format

Note that .Shadow and .Outline are available only on the Macintosh. For more
information on the arguments, see **FormatFont**.

Examples

This example finds the next instance of any text that is bold:

```
EditFindClearFormatting
EditFindFont .Bold = 1
EditFind .Find = "", .Format = 1
```

The following example finds the next instance of the word "Note" that is not bold:

```
EditFindClearFormatting
EditFindFont .Bold = 0
EditFind .Find = "Note", .Format = 1
```

The following example finds the next instance of "Note" whether or not it is bold.
Normally, you use **EditFindClearFormatting** to remove formatting
specifications from a search operation. With the instruction EditFindFont
.Bold = -1, you can remove the specification for bold without affecting other
search formats set previously.

```
EditFindFont .Bold = -1
EditFind .Find = "Note", .Format = 1
```

See Also	**EditFind**, **EditFindBorder**, **EditFindClearFormatting**, **EditFindFrame**, **EditFindLang**, **EditFindPara**, **EditFindStyle**, **EditFindTabs**, **EditReplace**, **EditReplaceFont**, **FormatFont**

EditFindFound()

Syntax	**EditFindFound**()

Remarks   Returns a value indicating whether the most recent **EditFind** operation was successful.

Value	Explanation
−1	The find operation was successful.
0 (zero)	The find operation was not successful.

Example   This macro counts the number of times "pillbox" occurs in a document and then displays the result in a message box. **EditFindFound**() is often used with a **While…Wend** loop to repeat a series of instructions each time the specified text or formatting is found.

```
Sub MAIN
count = 0
StartOfDocument
EditFind .Find = "pillbox", .WholeWord = 1, .Format = 0, .Wrap = 0
While EditFindFound()
    count = count + 1
    EditFind
Wend
MsgBox "The word " + Chr$(34) + "pillbox" + Chr$(34) + \
    " was found" + Str$(count) + " times."
End Sub
```

See Also	**EditFind**, **EditReplace**, **While…Wend**

EditFindFrame

Syntax EditFindFrame [.Wrap = *number*] [, .WidthRule = *number*]
[, .FixedWidth = *number or text*] [, .HeightRule = *number*]
[, .FixedHeight = *number or text*] [, .PositionHorz = *number or text*]
[, .PositionHorzRel = *number*] [, .DistFromText = *number or text*]
[, .PositionVert = *number or text*] [, .PositionVertRel = *number*]
[, .DistVertFromText = *number or text*] [, .MoveWithText = *number*]
[, .LockAnchor = *number*]

Remarks On the Macintosh, when followed by an **EditFind** or **EditReplace** instruction in which .Format is set to 1, specifies the frame formatting of the text you want to find. For information on the arguments, see **FormatFrame**. In Windows, **EditFindFrame** is not available and generates an error.

See Also **EditFind, EditFindBorder, EditFindFont, EditFindLang, EditFindPara, EditFindStyle, EditFindTabs, EditReplaceFrame, FormatFrame**

EditFindHighlight

Syntax **EditFindHighlight**

Remarks When followed by an **EditFind** or **EditReplace** instruction in which .Format is set to 1, specifies that the text you want to find is highlighted. Word finds any text that has been highlighted, even if different colors of highlight have been used in the same document. In Word version 6.0, **EditFindHighlight** is unavailable and generates an error.

Example This example finds all instances of highlighted text in the document, removes the highlight, and applies bold formatting to that text.

```
EditFindClearFormatting
EditReplaceClearFormatting
EditFindHighlight
EditReplaceFont .Bold = 1
EditReplaceNotHighlight
EditReplace .Find = "", .Replace = "", .Format = 1, .ReplaceAll
```

See Also **EditFind, EditReplaceHighlight, Highlight, HighlightColor, ToolsOptionsRevisions**

EditFindLang

Syntax   **EditFindLang .Language** = *text*

Remarks   When followed by an **EditFind** or **EditReplace** instruction in which .Format is
set to 1, specifies the language formatting of the text you want to find. Although
the Language command (Tools menu) lists the names of languages in their
English form, the text for .Language must be in the specified language and
include any accented characters (for example, Italian must be specified as
"Italiano" and French must be specified as "Français"). For a list of valid foreign
language names, see **ToolsLanguage**.

Example   This example formats all occurrences of German text with italic. Note that the
instruction `EditReplaceLang .Language = "Deutsch"` is required to preserve the
language formatting of the found text.

```
EditFindClearFormatting
EditReplaceClearFormatting
EditFindLang .Language = "Deutsch"
EditReplaceLang .Language = "Deutsch"
EditReplaceFont .Italic = 1
EditReplace .Find = "", .Replace = "", .Format = 1, \
    .ReplaceAll, .Wrap = 1
```

See Also   **EditFind, EditFindBorder, EditFindFont, EditFindFrame, EditFindPara,
EditFindStyle, EditFindTabs, EditReplace, EditReplaceLang, Language,
ToolsLanguage**

EditFindNotHighlight

Syntax   **EditFindNotHighlight**

Remarks   When followed by an **EditFind** or **EditReplace** instruction in which .Format is
set to 1, specifies that the text you want to find is not highlighted. In Word version
6.0, **EditFindNotHighlight** is unavailable and generates an error.

See Also   **EditFind, EditFindHighlight, Highlight, HighlightColor,
ToolsOptionsRevisions**

EditFindPara

Syntax

EditFindPara [**.LeftIndent** = *number or text*] [, **.RightIndent** = *number or text*]
[, **.Before** = *number or text*] [, **.After** = *number or text*]
[, **.LineSpacingRule** = *number*] [, **.LineSpacing** = *number or text*]
[, **.Alignment** = *number*] [, **.WidowControl** = *number*]
[, **.KeepWithNext** = *number*] [, **.KeepTogether** = *number*]
[, **.PageBreak** = *number*] [, **.NoLineNum** = *number*] [, **.DontHyphen** = *number*]
[, **.Tab** = *number*] [, **.FirstIndent** = *number or text*]

Remarks

When followed by an **EditFind** or **EditReplace** instruction in which .Format is
set to 1, specifies the paragraph formatting of the text you want to find. You can
set .WidowControl, .KeepWithNext, .KeepTogether, .PageBreak, .NoLineNum,
and .DontHyphen to one of the three following values.

Use this value	To do this
−1	Find text regardless of whether it has the format
0 (zero)	Find text that does not have the format
1	Find text that has the format

For more information on the arguments, see **FormatParagraph**. For an example,
see **EditReplacePara**.

See Also

**EditFind, EditFindBorder, EditFindFont, EditFindFrame, EditFindLang,
EditFindStyle, EditFindTabs, EditReplace, EditReplacePara,
FormatParagraph**

EditFindStyle

Syntax

EditFindStyle .Style = *text*

Remarks

When followed by an **EditFind** or **EditReplace** instruction in which .Format is
set to 1, specifies the style of the text you want to find. If the specified style does
not exist in the active document, or if the capitalization does not match that of the
actual style name, an error occurs.

Argument	Explanation
.Style	The name of the style you want to find; to remove a style from the specification, use an empty string ("").

Examples

This example finds and selects the next paragraph formatted with the Heading 2
style:

```
EditFindClearFormatting
EditFindStyle .Style = "Heading 2"
EditFind .Find = "", .Format = 1
```

The following example finds the next instance of the word "catnip" in a paragraph of any style. Normally, you use **EditFindClearFormatting** to remove formatting specifications from a search operation. With the instruction `EditFindStyle .Style = ""`, you can remove the style specification without affecting other search formats set previously.

```
EditFindStyle .Style = ""
EditFind .Find = "catnip", .Format = 1
```

See Also   **EditFind, EditFindBorder, EditFindFont, EditFindFrame, EditFindLang, EditFindPara, EditFindTabs, EditReplace, EditReplaceStyle, FormatStyle**

EditFindTabs

Syntax   **EditFindTabs [.Position =** *text*] [**, .Align =** *number*] [**, .Leader =** *number*]

Remarks   On the Macintosh, when followed by an **EditFind** or **EditReplace** instruction in which .Format is set to 1, specifies tab setting for the text you want to find. For argument descriptions, see **FormatTabs**. In Windows, **EditFindTabs** is not available and generates an error.

See Also   **EditFind, EditFindBorder, EditFindClearFormatting, EditFindFrame, EditFindLang, EditFindPara, EditFindStyle, EditReplace, EditReplaceTabs, FormatTabs**

EditGoTo

Syntax   **EditGoTo .Destination =** *text*

Remarks   Moves the insertion point or selection to the specified location or item, such as a page, bookmark, footnote, line, or field. To move the insertion point to a destination listed in the following table, use the corresponding identifier in combination with a number, the plus sign (+) or minus sign (−), or a string.

Destination	Identifier	Example text for .Destination
Page	p (or omitted)	The text "p5" or "5" goes to the fifth page.
Section	s	The text "s" goes to the next section.
Line	l	The text "l+5" goes to the fifth line after the current insertion point. The plus sign (+) means count forward from the insertion point.
Bookmark	(none)	The text "Temp" goes to the bookmark "Temp."
Annotation	a	The text "a'Sara Levine'" goes to the next mark for an annotation by Sara Levine.
Footnote	f	The text "f-" goes to the previous footnote reference mark. The minus sign (−) means count backward from the insertion point.

Destination	Identifier	Example text for .Destination
Endnote	e	The text "e5" goes to the fifth endnote reference mark.
Field	d	The text "d'TIME'" goes to the next TIME field. The single quotation marks separate the field type from the identifier.
Table	t	The text "t" goes to the next table.
Graphic	g	The text "g10" goes to the tenth graphic in the document.
Equation	q	The text "q-" goes to the previous equation.
Object	o	The text "o-'WordArt'" goes to the previous Microsoft WordArt object. The single quotation marks separate the object type from the identifier.

The following table summarizes the use of numbers and the plus sign or minus sign with destination identifiers in **EditGoTo** instructions. Numbers and the plus sign or minus sign can be used with every type of destination except bookmarks.

Identifier and this	Result
Number	Goes to an item according to its location within the document. For example, EditGoto "130" goes to the thirtieth line in a document; EditGoto "f200" goes to the two-hundredth footnote.
+[*Number*] or –[*Number*]	Goes to an item relative to the current location. For example, EditGoto "1+2" goes to the second line after the current line. Likewise, EditGoto "1-2" goes to the second line before the current line. The instruction EditGoto "1-" goes to the previous line; EditGoto "1+" goes to the next line.
Omitted	Goes to the next item specified. For example, EditGoto "s" goes to the next section in the document.

Example

This example counts the number of tables in the document. The bookmark "Temp" is defined at each successive insertion point location so **CmpBookmarks()** can determine whether the most recent **EditGoTo** (or **RepeatFind**) instruction has moved the insertion point. When **RepeatFind** no longer moves the insertion point—that is, when there are no more tables—Word exits the **While...Wend** loop.

```
StartOfDocument
EditBookmark "Temp", .Add
count = 0
If SelInfo(12) = - 1 Then count = 1
EditGoTo .Destination = "t"
While CmpBookmarks("\Sel", "Temp") <> 0
```

```
            EditBookmark "Temp", .Add
            count = count + 1
            RepeatFind
    Wend
    EditBookmark "Temp", .Delete
    MsgBox "There are" + Str$(count) + " tables in the document"
```

See Also   **EditFind**, **GoBack**, **GoToNext***Item*, **GoToPrevious***Item*, **NextField**,
NextObject, **NextPage**, **PrevField**, **PrevObject**, **PrevPage**, **RepeatFind**

EditLinks

Syntax   **EditLinks [.UpdateMode** = *number*,**] [.Locked** = *number*,**]**
[.SavePictureInDoc = *number*,**] [.UpdateNow,] [.OpenSource,] [.KillLink,]**
.Link = *text*, **.Application** = *text*, **.Item** = *text*, **.FileName** = *text*

Remarks   Sets options for the specified link. The arguments for the **Link** statement
correspond to the options in the Links dialog box (Edit menu).

Argument	Explanation
.UpdateMode	Specifies how the link is updated: 0 (zero) Automatically 1 Manually
.Locked	Specifies whether to lock or unlock the link: 0 (zero) Unlock the link 1 Lock the link
.SavePictureInDoc	If 1, saves a copy of the linked object in the Word document
.UpdateNow	Updates the specified link
.OpenSource	Opens the source of the specified link (for example, a Microsoft Excel worksheet)
.KillLink	Replaces the specified link with its most recent result
.Link	Specifies the link listed in the Links dialog box whose options are to be set: "1" corresponds to the first link in the list, "2" corresponds to the second, and so on. Note that the number must be enclosed in quotation marks. You can also use the "\Sel" predefined bookmark to specify the currently selected link.
.Application	The type of document supplying the link, as it appears in the LINK field codes—for example, "Word.Document.6" for a Word document or "Excel.Sheet.5" for a Microsoft Excel 5.0 worksheet.
.Item	Text that identifies the linked information (for example, a bookmark name such as "INTERN_LINK2" in a Word document, or a range of cells such as R1C1:R5C3 in a Microsoft Excel worksheet)
.FileName	The path and filename of the source document containing the linked item

The last three arguments correspond to choosing the Change Source button and setting options in the Change Source dialog box.

Examples

This example unlocks an existing link to a Microsoft Excel 5.0 worksheet and makes updating automatic. On the Macintosh, substitute a path and filename such as HD:WORKSHEETS:SALES.

```
EditLinks .UpdateMode = 0, .Locked = 0, .Link = "\Sel", \
    .Application = "Excel.Sheet.5", .Item = "Sales Report!R1C1:R5C3", \
    .FileName = "C:\EXCEL5\EXAMPLES\SALES.XLS"
```

The following example selects each link between the active document and a Microsoft Excel 5.0 worksheet and makes updating manual:

```
StartOfDocument
ViewFieldCodes 1
EditFind "^d LINK Excel.Sheet.5", .Format = 0, .Wrap = 0
While EditFindFound()
    Dim dlg As EditLinks
    GetCurValues dlg
    dlg.UpdateMode = 1
    EditLinks dlg
    CharRight
    RepeatFind
Wend
```

See Also

EditPasteSpecial, EditPublishOptions, EditSubscribeOptions, InsertField, LockFields, UnlinkFields, UnlockFlelds

EditObject

Syntax

EditObject

Remarks

Opens the selected object linking and embedding (OLE) object for editing in the application associated with the object. OLE objects include Equation Editor equations, font effects created with WordArt, Microsoft Excel charts, and so on.

Example

This example selects the next equation in the active document and opens it for editing in the Equation Editor:

```
EditGoTo .Destination = "o'Equation.2'"
EditObject
```

See Also

ActivateObject, EditGoTo, InsertObject

EditPaste

Syntax   **EditPaste**

Remarks   Inserts the contents of the Clipboard at the insertion point. **EditPaste** replaces the
                  selection if you select the Typing Replaces Selection check box on the Edit tab in
                  the Options dialog box (Tools menu).

See Also   **CopyText**, **EditCopy**, **EditCut**, **EditPasteSpecial**, **MoveText**

EditPasteSpecial

Syntax   **EditPasteSpecial** [**.IconNumber** = *number*] [**, .Link** = *number*]
                  [**, .DisplayIcon** = *number*] [**, .Class** = *text*] [**, .DataType** = *text*]
                  [**, .IconFilename** = *text*] [**, .Caption** = *text*]

Remarks   Inserts the contents of the Clipboard at the insertion point. The arguments for the
                  EditPasteSpecial statement correspond to the options in the Paste Special dialog
                  box (Edit menu). Unlike **EditPaste**, **EditPasteSpecial** allows you to control the
                  format of the pasted information and to establish a link with the information
                  source (for example, a Microsoft Excel worksheet).

Argument	Explanation
.IconNumber	If .DisplayIcon is set to 1, a number corresponding to the icon you want to use in the program file specified by .IconFilename. Icons appear in the Change Icon dialog box (Object command, Insert menu): 0 (zero) corresponds to the first icon, 1 to the second icon, and so on. If omitted, the first (default) icon is used.
	On the Macintosh, icons for embedded objects cannot be changed; this argument is ignored.
.Link	Specifies whether or not to create a link:
	0 (zero) or omitted No link is created.
	1 A link is created.
.DisplayIcon	Specifies whether or not to display a link as an icon:
	0 (zero) or omitted Link is not displayed as an icon.
	1 Link is displayed as an icon.
.Class	The object class of the Clipboard contents. This argument cannot be set. However, you can define a dialog record as **EditPasteSpecial** and then use the dialog record to return the current value of .Class.

Argument	Explanation
.DataType	Specifies a format for the pasted contents:
	Bitmap Bitmap (Windows only)
	DIB Device Independent Bitmap (Windows only)
	Object Object linking and embedding (OLE) object
	PICT Metafile (Windows) or Word Picture (Macintosh)
	RTF Rich-text format
	Text Unformatted text
	Styled Formatted text that preserves font formatting (Macintosh only)
.IconFilename	If .DisplayIcon is set to 1, the path and filename of the program file in which the icon to be displayed is stored.
	On the Macintosh, icons for embedded objects cannot be changed; this argument is ignored.
Caption	If .DisplayIcon is set to 1, the caption of the icon to be displayed; if omitted, Word inserts the name of the object.

Note Not all data types are available for each Clipboard item. For example, in Windows, if the Clipboard contains a text selection from a Word document, the available data types are "Object," "PICT, "RTF," and "Text." For a selection from a Microsoft Excel worksheet, the available formats are "Bitmap," "Object," "PICT," "RTF," and "Text." If you specify an unavailable data type, an error occurs.

See Also   **EditCopy**, **EditCreatePublisher**, **EditCut**, **EditLinks**, **EditPaste**, **EditSubscribeTo**, **InsertField**

EditPicture

Syntax   **EditPicture**

Remarks   Opens the selected graphic for editing.

Example   This example goes to the next graphic and opens it for editing.

```
ViewFieldCodes 0
EditGoTo "g"
CharRight 1,1
EditPicture
```

See Also   **EditObject**, **FormatPicture**, **InsertPicture**, **Picture**

EditPublishOptions

Syntax   **EditPublishOptions** [**.SendManually** = *number*] [, **.SendEditionNow** = *number*]
[, **.SendEditionWhenEdited** = *number*] [, **.Delete**] [, **.Appearance** = *number*]
[, **.Rtf** = *number*] [, **.Pict** = *number*]

Remarks   On the Macintosh, sets options for the selected publisher. The arguments for the
EditPublishOptions statement correspond to the options in the Publisher Options
dialog box (Publishing command, Edit menu). In Windows, **EditPublishOptions**
is not available and generates an error.

Argument	Explanation
.SendManually	Specifies how the edition is updated:
	0 (zero) or omitted On Save (the edition is updated whenever a change is made to the publisher)
	1 Manually (the edition is updated on demand)
.SendEditionNow	If 1, immediately updates the edition with changes in the publisher.
.SendEditionWhenEdited	If 1, updates the edition whenever changes are made to the publisher; .SendManually must be 0 (zero).
.Delete	Cancels the publisher.
.Appearance	Specifies how the publisher is published:
	0 (zero) or omitted As shown on screen
	1 As shown when printed
.Rtf	If 1, allows the publisher to export rich-text format (RTF).
.Pict	If 1, allows the publisher to export a picture format (PICT).

See Also   **EditCreatePublisher**, **EditLinks**, **EditSubscribeOptions**, **EditSubscribeTo**

EditRedo

Syntax   **EditRedo**

Remarks   Redoes the last action that was undone (reverses **EditUndo**).

See Also   **EditRepeat**, **EditUndo**

EditRepeat

Syntax   **EditRepeat**

Remarks   Repeats the most recent editing action, if possible.

See Also   **EditRedo**, **EditUndo**

EditReplace

Syntax

EditReplace [**.Find** = *text*] [, **.Replace** = *text*] [, **.Direction** = *number*]
[, **.MatchCase** = *number*] [, **.WholeWord** = *number*]
[, **.PatternMatch** = *number*] [, **.SoundsLike** = *number*] [, **.FindAllWordForms** =
number] [, **.FindNext**] [, **.ReplaceOne**] [, **.ReplaceAll**] [, **.Format** = *number*]
[, **.Wrap** = *number*]

Remarks

Replaces one or all instances of the specified text or formatting (or both) with
different text or formatting. If there is a selection and .Wrap is omitted or set to 0
(zero), the .Find text is replaced only within the selection. The arguments for the
EditReplace statement correspond to the options in the Replace dialog box.

Argument	Explanation
.Find	The text to find, or, to search for formatting only, an empty string (""). You can search for special characters, such as paragraph marks, by specifying appropriate character codes. For example, "^p" corresponds to a paragraph mark and "^t" corresponds to a tab character.
	If .PatternMatch is set to 1, you can specify wildcard characters and other advanced search criteria. For example, "*(ing)" finds any word ending in "ing."
	To search for a symbol character, specify the symbol's character code following a caret (^) and a zero (0). In Windows, for example, "^0151" corresponds to an em dash (—).
.Replace	The replacement text, or, to delete the text specified with .Find, an empty string (""). You specify special characters and advanced search criteria just as you do for .Find.
	To specify a graphic or other nontext item as the replacement, put the item on the Clipboard and specify "^c" for .Replace.
.Direction	The direction to search:
	0 (zero) Searches toward the end of the document
	1 Searches toward the beginning of the document
	The default is the direction used in the previous search or 0 (zero) the first time the Find or Replace command is run.
.MatchCase	If 1, corresponds to selecting the Match Case check box
.WholeWord	If 1, corresponds to selecting the Find Whole Words Only check box
.PatternMatch	If 1, Word evaluates .Find as a string containing advanced search criteria such as the asterisk (*) and question mark (?) wildcard characters (corresponds to selecting the Use Pattern Matching check box)

Argument	Explanation
.SoundsLike	If 1, corresponds to selecting the Sounds Like check box
.FindAllWordForms	If 1, corresponds to selecting the Find All Word Forms check box.
.FindNext	Finds the next instance of the text specified by .Find
.ReplaceOne	Replaces the first instance of the text specified by .Find
.ReplaceAll	Replaces all instances of the .Find text
.Format	Finds and replaces formatting in addition to, or instead of, text:
	0 (zero) Ignores formatting
	1 Uses the specified formatting
.Wrap	Controls what happens if the search begins at a point other than the beginning of the document and the end of the document is reached (or vice versa if .Direction is set to 1). The .Wrap argument also controls what happens if there is a selection and the search text is not found in the selection.
	0 (zero) The replace operation ends and the macro continues.
	1 If there is a selection, the replace operation continues in the remainder of the document. If the beginning or end of the document is reached, the replace operation continues from the opposite end.
	2 If there is a selection, Word displays a message asking whether to continue the replace operation in the remainder of the document. If the beginning or end of the document is reached, Word displays a message asking whether to continue the replace operation from the opposite end.

Formatting is not specified within the **EditReplace** instruction itself. Instead, you precede **EditReplace** with one or more of the following statements: **EditFindBorder**, **EditFindFont**, **EditFindLang**, **EditFindPara**, **EditFindStyle**, **EditFindTabs**, **EditReplaceBorder**, **EditReplaceFont**, **EditReplaceLang**, **EditReplacePara**, **EditReplaceStyle**, or **EditReplaceTabs**. Then, in the **EditReplace** instruction, you set .Format to 1. Note that **EditFindBorder**, **EditFindTabs**, **EditReplaceBorder**, and **EditReplaceTabs** are available only on the Macintosh.

Here are some tips for using **EditReplace** effectively:

- **EditReplace** retains whatever settings were used in the most recent find or replace operation. For example, if the Find Whole Words Only check box was selected in the Replace dialog box in the last replace operation (or if the .WholeWord argument was set to 1), .WholeWord will automatically be set to 1 in the new replace operation—unless you explicitly set it to 0 (zero). Before beginning a replace operation, make sure to specify every option that can affect the outcome of a search.

- When you search for and replace formatting, it's a good idea to include the statements **EditFindClearFormatting** and **EditReplaceClearFormatting** before specifying the formats you want to find and replace. That way, you clear any formats left over from previous find or replace operations.

Example

This example finds all instances of underlined text in the document and replaces the format with italic. Note that the instruction .Wrap = 1 means no **StartOfDocument** statement is required; instances both before and after the insertion point are replaced.

```
EditFindClearFormatting
EditReplaceClearFormatting
EditFindFont .Underline = 1
EditReplaceFont .Italic = 1, .Underline = 0
EditReplace .Find = "", .Replace = "", .Format = 1, \
    .ReplaceAll, .Wrap = 1
```

See Also

EditFind, **EditReplaceBorder**, **EditReplaceClearFormatting**, **EditReplaceFont**, **EditReplaceFrame**, **EditReplaceLang**, **EditReplacePara**, **EditReplaceStyle**, **EditReplaceTabs**

EditReplaceBorder

Syntax

EditReplaceBorder [**.ApplyTo** = *number*] [, **.Shadow** = *number*] [, **.TopBorder** = *number*] [, **.LeftBorder** = *number*] [, **.BottomBorder** = *number*] [, **.RightBorder** = *number*] [, **.HorizBorder** = *number*] [, **.VertBorder** = *number*] [, **.TopColor** = *number*] [, **.LeftColor** = *number*] [, **.BottomColor** = *number*] [, **.RightColor** = *number*] [, **.HorizColor** = *number*] [, **.VertColor** = *number*] [, **.FineShading** = *number*] [, **.FromText** = *number or text*] [, **.Shading** = *number*] [, **.Foreground** = *number*] [, **.Background** = *number*] [, **.Tab** = *number*]

Remarks	On the Macintosh, when followed by an **EditReplace** instruction in which .Format is set to 1, specifies border and shading formats for the replacement text. For argument descriptions, see **FormatBordersAndShading**. In Windows, **EditReplaceBorder** is not available and generates an error.
See Also	**EditFind, EditFindBorder, EditReplace, EditReplaceClearFormatting, EditReplaceFrame, EditReplaceLang, EditReplacePara, EditReplaceStyle, EditReplaceTabs, FormatBordersAndShading**

EditReplaceClearFormatting

Syntax	**EditReplaceClearFormatting**
Remarks	Clears any formats specified for replacement text. Before specifying replacement formats with **EditReplaceFont**, **EditReplacePara**, and so on, it's a good idea to include the **EditReplaceClearFormatting** statement to ensure that any unwanted formats are not included in the replacement formatting. For an example, see **EditReplace**.
See Also	**EditFindClearFormatting, EditReplace, EditReplaceBorder, EditReplaceFont, EditReplaceFrame, EditReplaceLang, EditReplacePara, EditReplaceStyle, EditReplaceTabs**

EditReplaceFont

Syntax	**EditReplaceFont** [**.Points** = *number*] [, **.Underline** = *number*] [, **.Color** = *number*] [, **.Strikethrough** = *number*] [, **.Superscript** = *number*] [, **.Subscript** = *number*] [, **.Shadow** = *number*] [, **.Hidden** = *number*] [, **.SmallCaps** = *number*] [, **.AllCaps** = *number*] [, **.Outline** = *number*] [, **.Spacing** = *number*] [, **.Position** = *number or text*] [, **.Kerning** = *number*] [, **.KerningMin** = *number or text*] [, **.Default**] [, **.Tab** = *number*] [, **.Font** = *text*] [, **.Bold** = *number*] [, **.Italic** = *number*]
Remarks	When followed by an **EditReplace** instruction in which .Format is set to 1, specifies the character formatting of the replacement text. You can set .Strikethrough, .Superscript, .Shadow, .Subscript, .Hidden, .SmallCaps, .AllCaps, .Outline, .Kerning, .Bold, and .Italic to one of the three following values.

Use this value	To do this
−1	Preserve the state of a given format in the found text
0 (zero)	Remove the given format from the found text
1	Apply the given format to the found text

Note that .Shadow and .Outline are available only on the Macintosh. For more information on the arguments, see **FormatFont**. For an example, see **EditFindLang**.

See Also   **EditFindFont**, **EditReplace**, **EditReplaceBorder**, **EditReplaceClearFormatting**, **EditReplaceLang**, **EditReplacePara**, **EditReplaceStyle**, **EditReplaceTabs**, **FormatFont**

EditReplaceFrame

Syntax   **EditReplaceFrame** [**.Wrap** = *number*] [, **.WidthRule** = *number*] [, **.FixedWidth** = *number or text*] [, **.HeightRule** = *number*] [, **.FixedHeight** = *number or text*] [, **.PositionHorz** = *number or text*] [, **.PositionHorzRel** = *number*] [, **.DistFromText** = *number or text*] [, **.PositionVert** = *number or text*] [, **.PositionVertRel** = *number*] [, **.DistVertFromText** = *number or text*] [, **.MoveWithText** = *number*] [, **.LockAnchor** = *number*]

Remarks   On the Macintosh, when followed by an **EditFind** or **EditReplace** instruction in which .Format is set to 1, specifies the frame formatting of the replacement text. For information on the arguments, see **FormatFrame**. In Windows, **EditReplaceFrame** is not available and generates an error.

See Also   **EditFindFrame**, **EditReplace**, **EditReplaceBorder**, **EditReplaceFont**, **EditReplaceLang**, **EditReplacePara**, **EditReplaceStyle**, **EditReplaceTabs**, **FormatFrame**

EditReplaceHighlight

Syntax   **EditReplaceHighlight**

Remarks   When followed by an **EditReplace** instruction in which .Format is set to 1, specifies that the replacement text is highlighted. In Word version 6.0, **EditReplaceHighlight** is unavailable and generates an error.

Example   This example highlights all instances of bold text in the document.

```
EditFindClearFormatting
EditReplaceClearFormatting
EditFindFont .Bold = 1
EditReplaceHighlight
EditReplace .Find = "", .Replace = "", .Format = 1 .ReplaceAll
```

See Also   **EditFindHighlight**, **EditReplace**, **Highlight**, **HighlightColor**, **ToolsOptionsRevisions**

EditReplaceLang

Syntax　　　　　**EditReplaceLang .Language** = *text*

Remarks　　　　When followed by an **EditReplace** instruction in which .Format is set to 1, specifies the language formatting of the replacement text. Although the Language command (Tools menu) lists the names of languages in their English form, the text for .Language must be in the specified language and include any accented characters (for example, Italian must be specified as "Italiano" and French must be specified as "Français"). For a list of valid foreign language names, see **ToolsLanguage**. For an example, see **EditFindLang**.

See Also　　　　**EditFindLang, EditReplace, EditReplaceBorder, EditReplaceClearFormatting, EditReplaceFont, EditReplaceFrame, EditReplacePara, EditReplaceStyle, EditReplaceTabs, ToolsLanguage**

EditReplaceNotHighlight

Syntax　　　　　**EditReplaceNotHighlight**

Remarks　　　　When followed by an **EditReplace** instruction in which .Format is set to 1, specifies that the replacement text is not highlighted. In Word version 6.0, **EditReplaceNotHighlight** is unavailable and generates an error.

See Also　　　　**EditFindNotHighlight, EditReplace, Highlight, HighlightColor, ToolsOptionsRevisions**

EditReplacePara

Syntax　　　　　**EditReplacePara** [**.LeftIndent** = *number or text*]
[**, .RightIndent** = *number or text*] [**, .Before** = *number or text*]
[**, .After** = *number or text*] [**, .LineSpacingRule** = *number*]
[**, .LineSpacing** = *number or text*] [**, .Alignment** = *number*]
[**, .WidowControl** = *number*] [**, .KeepWithNext** = *number*]
[**, .KeepTogether** = *number*] [**, .PageBreak** = *number*]
[**, .NoLineNum** = *number*] [**, .DontHyphen** = *number*] [**, .Tab** = *number*]
[**, .FirstIndent** = *number or text*]

Remarks　　　　When followed by an **EditReplace** instruction in which .Format is set to 1, specifies paragraph formatting for the replacement text. You can set .WidowControl, .KeepWithNext, .KeepTogether, .PageBreak, .NoLineNum, and .DontHyphen to one of the three following values.

Use this value	To do this
−1	Preserve the state of a given format in the found text
0 (zero)	Remove the given format from the found text
1	Apply the given format to the found text

For more information on the arguments, see **FormatParagraph**.

Example

This example applies a 2-inch left indent to all paragraphs in the active document that currently have a 1-inch left indent:

```
StartOfDocument
EditFindClearFormatting
EditReplaceClearFormatting
EditFindPara .LeftIndent = "1 in"
EditReplacePara .LeftIndent = "2 in"
EditReplace .Find = "", .Replace = "", .ReplaceAll, \
    .Format = 1, .Wrap = 0
```

See Also

EditFindPara, EditReplace, EditReplaceBorder, EditReplaceClearFormatting, EditReplaceFont, EditReplaceFrame, EditReplaceLang, EditReplaceStyle, EditReplaceTabs, FormatParagraph

EditReplaceStyle

Syntax

EditReplaceStyle .Style = *text*

Remarks

When followed by an **EditReplace** instruction in which .Format is set to 1, specifies a style for the replacement text. If the specified style does not exist in the active document, or if the capitalization does not match that of the actual style name, an error occurs.

Argument	Explanation
.Style	The name of the style for the replacement text; to remove a style from the replacement formatting, use an empty string ("").

Example

This example changes all Heading 4 paragraphs to Heading 3 paragraphs:

```
StartOfDocument
EditFindClearFormatting
EditReplaceClearFormatting
EditFindStyle .Style = "Heading 4"
EditReplaceStyle .Style = "Heading 3"
EditReplace .Find = "", .Replace = "", .ReplaceAll, \
    .Format = 1, .Wrap = 0
```

See Also

EditFindStyle, EditReplace, EditReplaceBorder, EditReplaceClearFormatting, EditReplaceFont, EditReplaceFrame, EditReplaceLang, EditReplacePara, EditReplaceTabs, FormatStyle

EditReplaceTabs

Syntax   **EditReplaceTabs** [**.Position** = *text*] [, **.Align** = *number*] [, **.Leader** = *number*]

Remarks   On the Macintosh, when followed by an **EditReplace** instruction in which .Format is set to 1, specifies tab setting for the replacement text. For argument descriptions, see **FormatTabs**. In Windows, **EditReplaceTabs** is not available and generates an error.

See Also   **EditFindTabs**, **EditReplace**, **EditReplaceBorder**, **EditReplaceClearFormatting**, **EditReplaceFrame**, **EditReplaceLang**, **EditReplacePara**, **EditReplaceStyle**, **FormatTabs**

EditSelectAll

Syntax   **EditSelectAll**

Remarks   Selects the entire document.

EditSubscribeOptions

Syntax   **EditSubscribeOptions** [**.GetManually** = *number*] [, **.GetEditionNow** = *number*] [, **.Format** = *number*] [, **.KeepFormatting** = *number*]

Remarks   On the Macintosh, sets options for the selected subscriber. The arguments for the **EditSubscribeOptions** statement correspond to the options in the Subscriber Options dialog box (Publishing command, Edit menu). In Windows, **EditSubscribeOptions** is not available and generates an error.

Argument	Explanation
.GetManually	Specifies how the subscriber is updated:
	0 (zero) or omitted Automatically (the subscriber is updated whenever a change is made to the edition)
	1 Manually (the subscriber is updated on demand)
.GetEditionNow	If 1, immediately updates the subscriber with changes in the current edition.
.Format	Specifies a format for subscribing to the edition:
	0 (zero) or omitted Best
	1 Formatted text (RTF)
	2 Unformatted text
	3 Picture
.KeepFormatting	If 1, preserves formatting changes made in the subscriber.

See Also   **EditCreatePublisher**, **EditLinks**, **EditPublishOptions**, **EditSubscribeTo**

EditSubscribeTo

Syntax

EditSubscribeTo .FileName = *text* [**, .Format** = *number*]
[**, .GetManually** = *number*]

Remarks

On the Macintosh, subscribes to a published edition. In Windows,
EditSubscribeTo is not available and generates an error.

Argument	Explanation
.FileName	The path and filename of the edition.
.Format	Specifies a format for subscribing to the edition:
	0 (zero) or omitted Best
	1 Formatted text (RTF)
	2 Unformatted text
	3 Picture
.GetManually	Specifies how the subscriber is updated:
	0 (zero) or omitted Automatically (the subscriber is updated whenever a change is made to the edition)
	1 Manually (the edition is updated on demand)

See Also

EditCreatePublisher, **EditLinks**, **EditPasteSpecial**, **EditPublishOptions**,
EditSubscribeOptions

EditSwapAllNotes

Syntax

EditSwapAllNotes

Remarks

Converts all footnotes in the document to endnotes and all endnotes to footnotes.
The insertion point may be in either the document window or the footnote or
endnote pane. If there are no footnotes or endnotes, an error occurs.

See Also

EditConvertAllEndnotes, **EditConvertAllFootnotes**, **EditConvertNotes**

EditTOACategory

Syntax   **EditTOACategory .Category** = *number*, **.CategoryName** = *text*

Remarks   Modifies the name of a category of citations for a table of authorities. The
arguments for the **EditTOACategory** command correspond to the options in the
Edit Category dialog box (Mark Citations dialog box, Index And Tables
command, Insert menu).

Argument	Explanation
.Category	The category you want to modify: 1 corresponds to the first name in the list, 2 to the second name, and so on.
.CategoryName	The new name for the category of citations.

Example   This example changes the ninth item in the list of categories to "Case Histories":

```
EditTOACategory .Category = 8, .CategoryName = "Case Histories"
```

See Also   **InsertTableOfAuthorities**, **MarkCitation**

EditUndo

Syntax   **EditUndo**

Remarks   Undoes the last action, if possible. Most editing and formatting actions can be
undone. Some actions, such as modifying a style, cannot be undone.

See Also   **EditRedo**, **EditRepeat**

EmptyBookmark()

Syntax   **EmptyBookmark**(*Name$*)

Remarks   Determines whether *Name$* is an "empty" bookmark. An empty bookmark marks
only a location for the insertion point in a document; it does not mark any text.
You can use **EmptyBookmark**() to verify that a bookmark (for example, a
bookmark referred to in a REF field) does indeed mark text.

This function returns the following values.

Value	Explanation
−1	If the bookmark is empty (that is, it marks no text)
0 (zero)	If the bookmark is not empty or does not exist

Example

This example verifies that the bookmark referred to in each REF field both exists and is not empty. If a reference to a nonexistent or empty bookmark is encountered, an appropriate message box is displayed.

```
StartOfDocument
ViewFieldCodes 1
EditFind .Find = "^d REF", .Format = 0, .Wrap = 0
While EditFindFound()
    CharLeft
    WordRight 2
    WordRight 1, 1
    mark$ = RTrim$(Selection$())
    If Not ExistingBookmark(mark$) Then
        MsgBox mark$ + " is not a bookmark."
    ElseIf EmptyBookmark(mark$) Then
        MsgBox mark$ + " is an empty bookmark."
    End If
    CharRight
    EditFind .Find = "^d REF", .Format = 0, .Wrap = 0
Wend
```

See Also

BookmarkName$(), CmpBookmarks(), CountBookmarks(), EditBookmark, ExistingBookmark(), GetBookmark$()

EnableFormField

Syntax

EnableFormField *BookmarkName$, Enable*

Remarks

Allows or prevents changes to the specified form field while the form is being filled in.

Argument	Explanation
BookmarkName$	The name of the bookmark that marks the form field.
Enable	Specifies whether the form field can be filled in or otherwise changed:
	0 (zero) The form field cannot be changed.
	1 The form field can be changed.

Example

This example allows or prevents changes to a form field based on the user name specified on the User Info tab in the Options dialog box (Tools menu). This macro could be part of an AutoNew macro that runs each time a document based on the form template is created.

```
Dim dlg As ToolsOptionsUserInfo
GetCurValues dlg
If dlg.Name = "Stella Richards" Then
    EnableFormField "TotalSales", 1
Else
    EnableFormField "TotalSales", 0
End If
```

See Also   **InsertFormField**

EndOfColumn, EndofColumn()

Syntax   **EndOfColumn** [*Select*]

EndOfColumn ([*Select*])

Remarks   The **EndOfColumn** statement moves the insertion point or extends the selection (if *Select* is nonzero) to the bottom of the table column containing the insertion point or selection. If the selection extends over more than one column, the insertion point moves or the selection is extended to the bottom of the rightmost column in the selection. If the insertion point or selection is not in a table, an error occurs.

Note If the last row in the table does not have a cell that corresponds to the column that contains the current selection—for example, if you have deleted or merged cells in the last row—**EndOfColumn** moves the insertion point or extends the selection to the end of the last row in the table.

The **EndOfColumn()** function behaves the same as the statement and also returns one of the following values.

Value	Explanation
0 (zero)	If the insertion point was not moved or the selection was not extended (that is, if it was already at the bottom of the column)
−1	If the insertion point was moved or the selection was extended

Example   This example moves the insertion point from anywhere in the table to the beginning of the last cell in the last row:

```
EndOfRow
EndOfColumn
```

See Also   **EndOfRow, StartOfColumn**

EndOfDocument, EndOfDocument()

Syntax   **EndOfDocument** [*Select*]

EndOfDocument([*Select*])

Remarks   The **EndOfDocument** statement moves the insertion point or, if *Select* is nonzero, the active end of the selection (the end that moves when you press CTRL+SHIFT+END) to the end of the document.

The **EndOfDocument()** function behaves the same as the statement and also returns one of the following values.

Value	Explanation
0 (zero)	If the insertion point or the active end of the selection was not moved (for example, if it was already at the end of the document)
–1	If the insertion point or the active end of the selection was moved

See Also   **AtEndOfDocument( )**, **StartOfDocument**

EndOfLine, EndOfLine()

Syntax   **EndOfLine** [*Select*]

EndOfLine ([*Select*])

Remarks   The **EndOfLine** statement moves the insertion point or, if *Select* is nonzero, the active end of the selection (the end that moves when you press SHIFT+END) to the end of the current line or the line that contains the active end of the selection. If there is a paragraph mark at the end of the line, EndOfLine positions the insertion point to the left of the paragraph mark; EndOfLine 1 moves the active end of the selection over the paragraph mark.

The **EndOfLine()** function behaves the same as the statement and also returns one of the following values.

Value	Explanation
0 (zero)	If the insertion point or the active end of the selection was not moved (that is, if it was already at the end of the line)
–1	If the insertion point or the active end of the selection was moved

Avoid using **EndOfLine** by itself to go to the end of a paragraph unless you are sure that the paragraph is a single line (for example, a word in a list of words). Instead, use the following instructions:

```
ParaDown    'Go to start of next paragraph
CharLeft    'Go back one character
```

Examples   This example selects the current line and the paragraph mark (if there is one at the end of the line). The instruction `EditGoTo "\Line"` has the same effect.

```
StartOfLine
EndOfLine 1
```

The following example selects the current line but not the paragraph mark (if there is one at the end of the line):

```
EndOfLine
StartOfLine 1
```

See Also   **EndOfRow, ParaDown, StartOfLine**

EndOfRow, EndOfRow()

Syntax   **EndOfRow** [*Select*]

EndOfRow ([*Select*])

Remarks   The **EndOfRow** statement moves the insertion point or extends the selection (if *Select* is nonzero) to the last cell of the table row containing the insertion point or selection. If the selection extends over more than one row, the insertion point moves or the selection is extended to the last cell of the last row in the selection. If the insertion point or selection is not in a table, an error occurs.

The **EndOfRow()** function behaves the same as the statement and also returns one of the following values.

Value	Explanation
0 (zero)	If the insertion point was not moved or the selection was not extended (that is, if it was already at the end of the row)
−1	If the insertion point was moved or the selection was extended

Example   This example deletes the selected cells or the cell containing the insertion point and all cells to the right:

```
EndOfRow 1
TableDeleteCells
```

See Also   **EndOfColumn, EndOfLine, StartOfRow**

EndOfWindow, EndOfWindow()

Syntax   **EndOfWindow** [*Select*]

                     EndOfWindow([*Select*])

Remarks   The **EndOfWindow** statement moves the insertion point or, if *Select* is nonzero, the active end of the selection (the end that moves when you press CTRL+SHIFT+PAGE DOWN) to the lower-right corner of the contents currently visible in the document window.

                     The **EndOfWindow**() function behaves the same as the statement and also returns one of the following values.

Value	Explanation
0 (zero)	If the insertion point or the active end of the selection was not moved (that is, if it was already at the lower-right corner of the window)
–1	If the insertion point or the active end of the selection was moved

                     For an example, see **StartOfWindow**.

See Also   **EndOfDocument**, **StartOfWindow**

Environ$()

Syntax   **Environ$**(*EnvironmentVariable$*)

Remarks   In Windows 3.*x* and Windows 95, returns a string associated with *EnvironmentVariable$*. For example, `tempdir$ = Environ$("TEMP")` returns the folder associated with the TEMP environment variable. On the Macintosh, **Environ$**() is not available and generates an error.

                     Environment variables are normally set using MS-DOS® batch files (such as AUTOEXEC.BAT) or the System option in Control Panel in Windows NT. For more information about environment variables, see your system documentation.

Example   This Windows example checks the PATH environment variable and displays one of two message boxes based on the number of characters in the path. (The limit is 127 characters.)

```
path$ = Environ$("PATH")
length = Len(path$)
avail = 127 - length
Select Case avail
    Case 127
        MsgBox "The PATH is empty."
    Case 0 To 126
        MsgBox "You can add" + Str$(avail) + \
                " character(s) to the PATH."
    Case Else
End Select
```

See Also   **AppInfo$()**, **GetProfileString$()**, **GetSystemInfo**

Eof()

Syntax   **Eof(**[#]*FileNumber***)**

Remarks   Determines whether the end of an open sequential file has been reached. *FileNumber* is the number specified in the **Open** instruction that opened the file for input. For more information about sequential files, see Chapter 9, "More WordBasic Techniques," in Part 1, "Learning WordBasic."

You cannot use this function to check for the end of a Word document open in a document window. To check for the end of a Word document, use the predefined bookmark "\EndOfDoc" with **CmpBookmarks()**. For more information about predefined bookmarks, see "Operators and Predefined Bookmarks" later in this part.

Eof() returns the following values.

Value	Explanation
−1	The end of the file specified by *FileNumber* has been reached.
0 (zero)	The end of the file has not been reached.

For an example, see **Read**.

See Also   **Close**, **Input**, **Input$()**, **Line Input**, **Lof()**, **Open**, **Print**, **Read**, **Seek**, **Write**

Err

Syntax   **Err = 0**

Error Err

ErrorNum = **Err**

Remarks   **Err** is a special variable whose value is the error code for the most recent error
                      condition.

- **Err = 0** is ued to reset error trapping after an error has occurred, normally at
  the end of an error trap.
- **Error Err** displays the message associated with the most recent error
  condition and stops the macro.
- *ErrorNum* = **Err** assigns the value of **Err** to the variable *ErrorNum*.

For more information on trapping errors, see **On Error**.

Example   This macro prompts the user to type a style name that is then applied to the
                      selected paragraphs. The macro contains an error handler that illustrates the use
                      of **Err** within a **Select Case** control structure. The **Select Case** control structure
                      in this macro can be described as follows:

- If the error code is 102 (which occurs if the **InputBox$** dialog box is
  canceled), the macro prevents the "Command failed" error message from
  being displayed.
- If the error code is 24 (which occurs if the style name does not exist), Word
  displays a custom message box in place of the "Bad parameter" error message,
  error trapping is reset with the instruction Err = 0, and the **InputBox$** dialog
  box is displayed again so the user can type another style name. Note that Case
  24 is the only case in which error trapping needs to be reset. In the other cases,
  the macro ends and there is no need for further error trapping.
- If the error code is neither 102 nor 24, the instruction Error Err displays the
  error.

```
Sub MAIN
On Error Goto trap
start:
apply$ = InputBox$("Type a style name:", "Apply Style")
Style apply$
trap:
Select Case Err
    Case 102            'Input box was canceled
    Case 24             'Bad parameter
        MsgBox "No such style; try another name."
        Err = 0
        Goto start
    Case Else           'Any other error condition
        Error Err
End Select
End Sub
```

See Also   **Error, Goto, On Error**

Error

Syntax   **Error Err**

Error *ErrorNumber*

Remarks   **Error Err** generates the most recent error condition and stops the macro. **Error** *ErrorNumber* generates the error condition associated with *ErrorNumber*. For WordBasic error conditions, which have numbers of less than 1000, **Error** displays an error message. For Word errors, which have numbers of 1000 or greater, **Error** generates an error condition, but does not display an error message. **Error** can be used to test an error trap.

For a list of errors and their numbers, see "Error Messages," later in this part. For more information on error trapping, see **On Error** and **Err**.

Example   This example generates WordBasic error condition 53 in order to test the handling of this error. When error condition 53 occurs, Word displays a custom message box; any other error runs the instruction Error Err, which displays the built-in message associated with the error number.

```
On Error Goto trap
Error 53              'Generate error condition
trap:
If Err = 53 Then
    MsgBox "Error 53 successfully trapped"
    Err = 0
Else
    Error Err
End If
```

See Also   **Err, Goto, On Error**

ExistingBookmark()

Syntax   **ExistingBookmark**(*Name$*)

Remarks   Indicates whether the bookmark specified by *Name$* exists in the active document. This function returns the following values.

Value	Explanation
–1	If the bookmark exists
0 (zero)	If the bookmark does not exist

Example   This macro displays a prompt in the status bar for the name of a bookmark to add. If the bookmark does not yet exist, it is added. If the bookmark already exists, Word displays a message box that asks whether to reset the bookmark. If the user answers No, the macro ends. Otherwise, the bookmark is reset.

```
Sub MAIN
Input "Bookmark to add", myMark$
If ExistingBookmark(myMark$) Then
    ans = MsgBox(myMark$ + " already exists; reset?", 36)
    If ans = 0 Then Goto bye
End If
EditBookmark myMark$, .Add
bye:
End Sub
```

See Also   **BookmarkName$()**, **CmpBookmarks()**, **CountBookmarks()**, **EditBookmark**, **EmptyBookmark()**, **GetBookmark$()**

ExitWindows

Syntax   **ExitWindows**

Remarks   In Windows 3.x, closes all open applications and quits Windows. In Windows 95 and Windows NT, **ExitWindows** logs the current user off. **ExitWindows** does not save changes or prompt you to save changes in Word documents; it does prompt you to save changes in other open Windows-based applications.

ExitWindows can be useful if you have an MS-DOS batch file that starts Word and runs a macro using the **/m**macroname startup switch. By including ExitWindows as the final instruction in the macro, you restore control to the MS-DOS batch file. If you are running a batch file that starts Word from a command prompt running within Windows 3.x, Windows 95, or Windows NT, use FileExit 2 instead of ExitWindows.

On the Macintosh, **ExitWindows** is not available and generates an error.

See Also   **FileExit**, **FileQuit**

ExtendMode()

Syntax   **ExtendMode()**

Remarks   Returns −1 if extend mode is on. In extend mode, actions that normally move the insertion point extend the selection. **ExtendMode()** does not indicate whether column selection mode is on.

Example   This example toggles the state of extend mode:

```
If ExtendMode() = 0 Then ExtendSelection Else Cancel
```

See Also   **Cancel**, **ColumnSelect**, **ExtendSelection**

ExtendSelection

Syntax   **ExtendSelection** [*Character$*]

Remarks   Performs one of the following actions:

- If extend mode is off, activates extend mode (in extend mode, actions that normally move the insertion point move the active end of the selection).

- If extend mode is already on, extends the selection to the next unit of text (the progression is as follows: word, sentence, paragraph, section, entire document).

- If *Character$* is specified, extends the selection from the insertion point or the fixed end of the current selection (the end of the selection that does not move when you press SHIFT+an arrow key) to the next instance of that character without activating or deactivating extend mode.

You can use **ExtendSelection** with **EditGoTo** and **EditFind** to extend the selection to a specific location or piece of text. Use the **Cancel** statement to deactivate extend mode.

Example   This example selects all text from the insertion point to and including the bookmark "MyMark":

```
ExtendSelection
EditGoTo "MyMark"
Cancel
```

See Also   **Cancel**, **ColumnSelect**, **ExtendMode()**, **ShrinkSelection**

FieldSeparator$, FieldSeparator$()

Syntax   **FieldSeparator$** *Separator$*

FieldSeparator$()

Remarks   The **FieldSeparator$** statement sets the separator character, *Separator$*, that Word recognizes when dividing text among cells in a **TextToTable** operation. For example, if you have data in which the items of information are delimited by percent signs (%), you can use the instruction FieldSeparator "%" before converting the data to a table. The **FieldSeparator$()** function returns the current separator character.

See Also   **TextToTable**

FileAOCEAddMailer

Syntax   **FileAOCEAddMailer**

Remarks   Adds a mailer to the active document. **FileAOCEAddMailer** is available only on the Macintosh and only if PowerTalk is installed.

See Also   **AOCEAddRecipient**, **AOCESetSubject**, **FileAOCEDeleteMailer**, **FileAOCEExpandMailer**

FileAOCEDeleteMailer

Syntax   **FileAOCEDeleteMailer**

Remarks   Removes the mailer from the active document. **FileAOCEDeleteMailer** is available only on the Macintosh and only if PowerTalk is installed.

See Also   **AOCEClearMailerField**, **FileAOCEAddMailer**, **FileAOCEExpandMailer**

FileAOCEExpandMailer

Syntax   **FileAOCEExpandMailer**

Remarks   Toggles the display of the mailer attached to the active document between the full mailer and a bar showing just the sender and subject. **FileAOCEExpandMailer** is available only on the Macintosh and only if PowerTalk is installed.

See Also   **FileAOCEAddMailer**, **FileAOCEDeleteMailer**

FileAOCEForwardMail

Syntax	**FileAOCEForwardMail**
Remarks	Adds a mailer for forwarding the active letter. The subject text is copied to the new mailer and prefixed by "Fwd> ". **FileAOCEForwardMail** is available only on the Macintosh and only if PowerTalk is installed.
See Also	**AOCESendMail**, **FileAOCEReplyMail**, **FileAOCESendMail**

FileAOCENextLetter

Syntax	**FileAOCENextLetter**
Remarks	Opens the next available letter in the In Tray. If there are no more letters to open, a message appears. **FileAOCENextLetter** is available only on the Macintosh and only if PowerTalk is installed.

FileAOCEReplyAllMail

Syntax	**FileAOCEReplyAllMail**
Remarks	Adds a mailer for replying to the active letter and specifies the sender and all recipients of the original letter as recipients. The subject text is copied from the original letter and prefixed with "Re> ". **FileAOCEReplyAllMail** is available only on the Macintosh and only if PowerTalk is installed.
See Also	**FileAOCEReplyMail**

FileAOCEReplyMail

Syntax	**FileAOCEReplyMail**
Remarks	Adds a mailer for replying to the active letter and specifies the sender of the original letter as the recipient. The subject text is copied from the original letter and prefixed with "Re> ". **FileAOCEReplyMail** is available only on the Macintosh and only if PowerTalk is installed.
See Also	**FileAOCEForwardMail**, **FileAOCEReplyAllMail**

FileAOCESendMail

Syntax   **FileAOCESendMail**

Remarks   Displays a dialog box in which you can set options for sending the active document to the the recipients specified in the attached mailer. Use **AOCESendMail** to set options and send the document without displaying a dialog box. **FileAOCESendMail** is available only on the Macintosh and only if PowerTalk is installed.

See Also   **AOCESendMail, FileAOCEForwardMail**

FileClose

Syntax   **FileClose** [*Save*]

Remarks   Closes the active document. All document windows containing the active document are closed. If the document is open in more than one window and you want to close only the active window, use **DocClose**.

Argument	Explanation
Save	Determines whether or not Word saves the document before closing it if the document is "dirty"—that is, if changes have been made since the last time the file was saved:
	0 (zero) or omitted Prompts the user to save the document.
	1 Saves the document before closing it.
	2 Closes the document without saving it.
	The *Save* argument also controls whether a prompt appears if the document has a routing slip. A prompt appears if *Save* is 0 (zero) or omitted; otherwise, the document is closed without being routed.

See Also   **ClosePane, DocClose, FileCloseAll, FileExit, IsDocumentDirty()**

FileCloseAll

Syntax   **FileCloseAll** [*Save*]

Remarks   Closes all open document windows.

Argument	Explanation
Save	Determines whether or not Word saves each document before closing it if it is "dirty"—that is, if changes have been made since the last time the file was saved:

0 (zero) or omitted   Prompts the user to save each changed document.

1   Saves each changed document before closing it.

2   Closes all documents without saving changed documents.

The *Save* argument also controls whether a prompt appears if a document has a routing slip. A prompt appears if *Save* is 0 (zero) or omitted; otherwise, the document is closed without being routed.

See Also   **DocClose, FileClose, FileExit, FileQuit**

FileClosePicture

Syntax   **FileClosePicture**

Remarks   Closes the picture editing window and embeds a Word Picture object in the document.

See Also   **DrawResetWordPicture**

FileConfirmConversions, FileConfirmConversions()

Syntax   **FileConfirmConversions** [*On*]

FileConfirmConversions()

Remarks   The **FileConfirmConversions** statement controls whether Word displays a confirmation dialog box when a file in a format other than Word Document or Document Template is opened. In Word version 6.0, **FileConfirmConversions** selects or clears the Confirm Conversions check box in the Open dialog box (File menu). In Word version 7.0, **FileConfirmConversions** selects or clears the Confirm Conversions At Open check box on the General tab in the Options dialog box (Tools menu).

Argument	Explanation
On	Specifies whether Word displays the confirmation dialog box:
	0 (zero) Does not display the dialog box.
	1 Displays the dialog box.
	Omitted Toggles the Confirm Conversions check box.

The **FileConfirmConversions**() function returns the following values.

Value	Explanation
0 (zero)	If the Confirm Conversions check box is cleared
−1	If the Confirm Conversions check box is selected

See Also   **MailMergeAskToConvertChevrons**

FileCreator$()

Syntax   **FileCreator$**(*File$*)

Remarks   On the Macintosh, returns the four-character application signature for the application that created *File$*, a path and filename. In Windows, **FileCreator$**() is not available and generates an error.

Example   This Macintosh example checks the creator before opening the file specified by openme$. If the application signature is not "MSWD," a message is displayed.

```
openme$ = "HD:GAMES:GAME RULES"
If FileCreator$(openme$) <> "MSWD" Then
    ans = MsgBox(openme$ + " was not created by Microsoft Word. " + \
        "Open anyway?", 4)
    If ans = 0 Then endmacro = -1
End If
If Not endmacro Then FileOpen .Name = openme$
```

See Also   **FileType$**(), **MacID$**(), **SetFileCreatorAndType**

FileDocumentLayout

Syntax

FileDocumentLayout [**.Tab** = *number*] [, **.TopMargin** = *number or text*]
[, **.BottomMargin** = *number or text*] [, **.LeftMargin** = *number or text*]
[, **.RightMargin** = *number or text*] [, **.Gutter** = *number or text*]
[, **.PageWidth** = *number or text*] [, **.PageHeight** = *number or text*]
[, **.Orientation** = *number*] [, **.FirstPage** = *number*] [, **.OtherPages** = *number*]
[, **.VertAlign** = *number*] [, **.ApplyPropsTo** = *number*] [, **.Default**]
[, **.FacingPages** = *number*] [, **.HeaderDistance** = *number or text*]
[, **.FooterDistance** = *number or text*] [, **.SectionStart** = *number*]
[, **.OddAndEvenPages** = *number*] [, **.DifferentFirstPage** = *number*]
[, **.Endnotes** = *number*] [, **.LineNum** = *number*] [, **.StartingNum** = *number*]
[, **.FromText** = *number or text*] [, **.CountBy** = *number*] [, **.NumMode** = *number*]

Remarks

On the Macintosh, sets page attributes such as margins and page width for the entire document or sections within the document. With the exception of .Tab, the arguments for **FileDocumentLayout** are the same as the arguments described for **FilePageSetup**. In Windows, use **FilePageSetup**.

Argument	Explanation
.Tab	Specifies which tab to select when you display the Document Layout dialog box with a **Dialog** or **Dialog**() instruction:

0 (zero)   Margins

1   If QuickDraw GX is installed, Paper Size; if not, Margins

2   Margins

3   Layout

Keep the following points in mind when using **FileDocumentLayout**:

- Setting page size and orientation does not override those set by the user in the Page Setup dialog box (supplied by the printer driver). For more information, see the note in **FileMacPageSetup**.

- Word does not have access to Macintosh paper source settings. Although settings for .FirstPage and .OtherPages are saved with the document, they are ignored when printing. If the document is printed in Windows, however, the options take effect.

See Also

FileMacPageSetup, **FileMacPageSetupGX**, **FileMacCustomPageSetupGX**, **FilePageSetup**, **FormatColumns**

FileExit

Syntax

FileExit [*Save*]

Remarks

Quits Word. **FileExit** (Windows) is the same as **FileQuit** (Macintosh).

Argument	Explanation
Save	Determines whether Word saves each document before closing it if it is "dirty"—that is, if changes have been made since the last time the file was saved:

0 (zero) or omitted   Prompts the user to save each changed document.

1   Saves all edited documents before quitting.

2   Quits without saving changed documents.

The *Save* argument also controls whether a prompt appears if a document has a routing slip or if Word is printing in the background. Prompts appear if *Save* is 0 (zero) or omitted; otherwise, Word quits without routing documents or finishing print jobs.

See Also

AppClose, ExitWindows, FileCloseAll, FileQuit

FileFind

Syntax

FileFind [**.SearchName** = *text*] [, **.SearchPath** = *text*] [, **.Name** = *text*]
[, **.SubDir** = *number*] [, **.Title** = text] [, **.Author** = *text*] [, **.Keywords** = *text*]
[, **.Subject** = *text*] [, **.Options** = *number*] [, **.MatchCase** = *number*] [, **.Text** = *text*]
[, **.PatternMatch** = *text*] [, **.DateSavedFrom** – *text*] [, **.DateSavedTo** = *text*]
[, **.SavedBy** = *text*] [, **.DateCreatedFrom** = *text*] [, **.DateCreatedTo** = *text*]
[, **.View** = *number*] [, **.SortBy** = *number*] [, **.ListBy** = *number*]
[, **.SelectedFile** = *number*] [, **.ShowFolders** = *number*] [, **.Add**] [, **.Delete**]

Remarks

Creates a list of files based on the search criteria specified by one or more of the arguments. In Word version 6.0, the arguments for the **FileFind** statement correspond to the options in the Search dialog box (Find File command, File menu).

In Word version 7.0, the .SearchName, .Options, .PatternMatch, .View, .SortBy, .ListBy, .SelectedFile, .ShowFolders, .Add, and .Delete arguments are ignored, and you cannot use a **Dialog** or **Dialog**() instruction to display the Word version 6.0 Find File dialog box.

Argument	Explanation
.SearchName	A name given to a group of search criteria you want to add to or remove from the Search dialog box (using .Add or .Delete). Note that when performing the search, Word ignores .SearchName; you must specify criteria using .SearchPath, .Name, and so on.
.SearchPath	A path or list of paths in which to search for files. In Word version 6.0, you can specify more than one path by separating them with semicolons (;). In Word version 7.0, you cannot specify more than one path.
.Name	The name of the document or, in Windows, a file specification. To find document templates, for example, the file specification would be "*.DOT". On the Macintosh, use **MacID$()** to specify a file type (for example, MacID$("WTBN") to find document templates).
.SubDir	If 1, Word searches subfolders of the folder or folders specified by .SearchPath.
.Title	Title in the Summary Info dialog box
.Author	Author in the Summary Info dialog box
.Keywords	Keywords used to identify the document in the Summary Info dialog box
.Subject	Subject in the Summary Info dialog box
.Options	Specifies how to list the found files: 0 (zero) Create a new list 1 Add matches to the existing file list 2 Search only in the existing file list
.MatchCase	Specifies whether to match the case of each letter in .Text: 0 (zero) Do not match the case (default) 1 Match the case
.Text	The text to search for in the document
.PatternMatch	If 1, Word evaluates .Text as a string containing advanced search criteria such as the asterisk (*) and question mark (?) wildcard characters. For more information, search for "search operators" in Word Help and choose "Advanced search criteria."
.DateSavedFrom	The document save date you want to search from
.DateSavedTo	The document save date you want to search to
.SavedBy	The name of the person who last saved the document

Argument	Explanation
.DateCreatedFrom	The document creation date you want to search from. The following are examples of valid date formats: 7/8/93 8-Jul-91 July 8, 1991
.DateCreatedTo	The document creation date you want to search to
.View	Specifies what to display on the right side of the dialog box when you display the Find File dialog box with a **Dialog** or **Dialog()** instruction: 0 (zero) File information (a line for each file) 1 A preview window of the contents of the selected file 2 Summary information for the selected file
.SortBy	Specifies how documents are sorted when you display the Find File dialog box with a **Dialog** or **Dialog()** instruction: 0 (zero) Alphabetically by author 1 By creation date, with the most recently created file listed first 2 Alphabetically by the name of the person who last saved the document 3 By the date last saved, with the most recently saved file listed first 4 Alphabetically by filename 5 By size, with the smallest file listed first
.ListBy	Specifies whether to list filenames or titles on the left side of the dialog box when you display the Find File dialog box with a **Dialog** or **Dialog()** instruction: 0 (zero) Filenames 1 Titles
.SelectedFile	When you've used a **Dialog** or **Dialog()** instruction to display the Find File dialog box, returns a number when the user closes the dialog box that corresponds to the file that was last selected. To retrieve the filename, pass this value to the **FoundFileName$()** function (for example, `FoundFileName$(dlg.SelectedFile)`).
.ShowFolders	If 1, groups filenames by folder when you display the Find File dialog box with a **Dialog** or **Dialog()** instruction.
.Add	Stores the specified search criteria under the name specified by .SearchName; may be used to create or modify a group of search criteria.
.Delete	Removes the group of search criteria specified by .SearchName.

If you specify multiple words for .Title, .Subject, .Author, .Keywords, .Path, and .Text, Word interprets the entire argument as a logical expression rather than as a multiple-word phrase. A comma serves as the logical operator OR, and a space or an ampersand (&) serves as the logical operator AND.

Examples

This Windows example searches a folder for files with the .RPT filename extension, defines an array to hold their names, and then uses **FoundFileName$()** to fill the array with the filenames.

```
FileFind .SearchPath = "C:\REPORTS", .Name = "*.RPT"
size = CountFoundFiles() - 1
If size >= 0 Then
    Dim mydocs$(size)
    For count = 0 To size
        mydocs$(count) = FoundFileName$(count + 1)
    Next
End If
```

The following Macintosh example creates a dialog record for the Find File dialog box, sets the search path and file type criteria, specifies that summary information be displayed for the found files, and then displays the list of found files.

```
Dim dlg As FileFind
dlg.SearchPath = "HD:MY DOCUMENTS"
dlg.Name = MacID$("W6BN")
dlg.View = 2
x = Dialog(dlg)
```

See Also

CountFoundFiles(), **FoundFileName$()**

FileList

Syntax

FileList *Number*

Remarks

Opens one of the files in the list of recently used files at the bottom of the File menu. (Word defines "used" as either opened or saved.) *Number* corresponds to the number next to the filename listed on the File menu (from 1 through 9) you want to open. If *Number* is greater than the number of files listed, an error occurs. If the specified file is already open, Word activates the document.

You can control the number of filenames that appear on the File menu with the Recently Used File List option on the General tab in the Options dialog box (Tools menu).

Example

This example opens the most recently used file. You can include these instructions in an AutoExec macro so that every time you start Word, the most recently used file is opened automatically. If there is no file listed on the File menu, On Error Resume Next prevents Word from displaying an error message.

```
On Error Resume Next
FileList 1
```

See Also

CountFiles(), FileName$(), File*Number*, FileOpen

FileMacCustomPageSetupGX

Syntax

FileMacCustomPageSetupGX [.PageWidth = *number or text*]
[, .PageHeight = *number or text*] [, .Orientation = *number*]
[, .ApplyPropsTo = *number*]

Remarks

On the Macintosh with QuickDraw GX installed, sets page width, height, and orientation for the entire document or sections within the document. For argument descriptions, see **FilePageSetup**.

In Windows, and on the Macintosh if QuickDraw GX is not installed, **FileMacCustomPageSetupGX** is not available and generates an error.

See Also

FileDocumentLayout, FileMacPageSetup, FileMacPageSetupGX,
FilePageSetup

FileMacPageSetup

Syntax

FileMacPageSetup [.PageWidth = *number or text*] [, .PageHeight = *number or text*] [, .Orientation = *number*] [, .ApplyPropsTo = *number*] [, .Default]

Remarks

On the Macintosh, sets page width, height, and orientation for the entire document or sections within the document. For argument descriptions, see **FilePageSetup**. If QuickDraw GX is installed, **FileMacPageSetup** generates an error; use **FileMacPageSetupGX** and **FileMacCustomPageSetupGX** instead.

Note Changing the page size with **FileMacPageSetup** is equivalent to setting a custom paper size in the Custom Paper Size dialog box (Page Setup command, File menu). In both cases, the custom settings override other page size settings in the Page Setup dialog box.

See Also

FileDocumentLayout, FileMacCustomPageSetupGX, FileMacPageSetupGX,
FilePageSetup

FileMacPageSetupGX

Syntax

FileMacPageSetupGX [**.PageWidth** = *number or text*] [**, .PageHeight** = *number or text*] [**, .Orientation** = *number*]

Remarks

On the Macintosh with QuickDraw GX installed, sets page width, height, and orientation for the default page setup. Note that only those sections with the default page format will be changed; sections whose page format has been changed with **FileDocumentLayout** or **FileMacCustomPageSetupGX** are unchanged. For argument descriptions, see **FilePageSetup**.

In Windows, and on the Macintosh if QuickDraw GX is not installed, **FileMacPageSetupGX** is not available and generates an error.

See Also

FileDocumentLayout, **FileMacCustomPageSetupGX**, **FileMacPageSetup**, **FilePageSetup**

FileName$()

Syntax

FileName$([*Number*]**)**

Remarks

Returns the path and filename of the active document or of a file in the list of recently used files at the bottom of the File menu.

Argument	Explanation
Number	The number of the file in the order listed on the File menu, from 1 through 9. If the number is 0 (zero) or omitted, **FileName$()** returns the name of the active document; if there is no active document, it returns an empty string(""). If *Number* is greater than the number of files listed on the File menu, an error occurs.
	You can control the number of filenames that appear on the File menu with the Recently Used File List option on the General tab in the Options dialog box (Tools menu).

Example	When run, this example demonstrates the difference between **FileName$()** and **WindowName$()**. **FileName$()** always returns a file's path and filename. **WindowName$()** returns the window title, which does not include the path and may include extra text such as "(Read-Only)" or ":2" after the filename.

```
MsgBox "File = " + FileName$() + Chr$(13) + \
    "Window = " + WindowName$()
```

See Also	**CountFiles()**, **FileList**, **FileNameFromWindow$()**, **File***Number*, **Files$()**, **WindowName$()**

FileNameFromWindow$()

Syntax	**FileNameFromWindow$**([*WindowNumber*])
Remarks	Returns the path and filename of the document in the specified window.

Argument	Explanation
WindowNumber	The position of the window on the Window menu, where 1 is the first position, 2 is the second position, and so on. If *WindowNumber* is 0 (zero) or omitted, **FileNameFromWindow$()** returns the path and filename of the active document; if the active document has never been saved, it returns an empty string ("").

See Also	**CountWindows()**, **FileName$()**, **WindowName$()**

FileNameInfo$()

Syntax	**FileNameInfo$**(*Filename$*, *InfoType*)
Remarks	Returns the part of *Filename$* specified by *InfoType*.

Argument	Explanation
Filename$	The path, if specified, and filename of a document. Though the path must exist, the filename does not have to be the name of an existing document. If the path does not exist, an error occurs.

Argument	Explanation
InfoType	The part of *Filename$* to return:

1   The full path and filename. In Windows, for example, `FileNameInfo$(FileName$(), 1)` might return "C:\DOCUMENT\TEST.DOC." If *Filename$* does not include a path, **FileNameInfo$()** returns a path made up of the current folder and *Filename$*, even if such a file does not yet exist.

2   The filename only, if *Filename$* is located in the current folder; otherwise, the full path and filename.

3   The filename. On the Macintosh, for example, `FileNameInfo$("HD:DOCUMENTS:TEST DOC", 3)` returns "TEST DOC."

4   The filename without a filename extension. In Windows, for example, `FileNameInfo$("C:\DOCUMENT\TEST.DOC", 4)` returns "TEST." On the Macintosh, setting *InfoType* to 4 returns the whole filename (same as setting *InfoType* to 3).

5   The full path, including the trailing backslash (\) (Windows) or colon (:) (Macintosh). On the Macintosh, for example, `FileNameInfo$("HD:DOCUMENTS:TEST DOC", 5)` returns "HD:DOCUMENTS:."

6   In Windows, returns the universal naming convention (UNC) network path and filename. For example, if TEST.DOC is located on a server with the network share name \\DOCUMENT\PUBLIC, then `FileNameInfo$("D:\DOCUMENT\TEST.DOC", 6)` returns "\\DOCUMENT\PUBLIC\DOCUMENT\TEST.DOC."

On the Macintosh, returns a string that begins with the zone and computer name. For example if INSTRUCTIONS is located in a shared folder named ART TOOLS, `FileNameInfo$("ART TOOLS:INSTRUCTIONS")` might return "PUBLIC:TOOLS:ART TOOLS:INSTRUCTIONS," where PUBLIC is the zone and TOOLS is the computer name.

If *Filename$* is not located on a network share, the full path and filename are returned.

Example

This Windows example uses **FileNameInfo$()** to change the filename extension of all the files in the current folder with the extension .DOC to .RTF and then saves the files in rich-text format (RTF):

```
file$ = Files$("*.DOC")
While file$ <> ""
    FileOpen .Name = file$
    noExtension$ = FileNameInfo$(file$, 4)
    FileSaveAs .Name = noExtension$ + ".RTF" , .format = 6
    FileClose 2
    file$ = Files$()
Wend
```

See Also   **FileName$(), FileNameFromWindow$()**

FileNew

Syntax   **FileNew [.Template = *text*] [, .NewTemplate = *number*]**

Remarks   Creates a new document or template based on the template you specify, or runs a
wizard. The arguments for the **FileNew** statement correspond to the options in the
New dialog box (File menu).

Argument	Explanation
.Template	The name of the template or document on which to base the new document or template, or the name of the wizard to run
.NewTemplate	Specifies whether to create a new document or a new template:
	0 (zero) or omitted Create a new document
	1 Create a new template

Examples   These examples create a new document based on a memo template. In Windows,
the .DOT filename extension is optional—you can specify either "MEMO1" or
"MEMO1.DOT."

```
FileNew .Template = "MEMO1"       'Windows
FileNew .Template = "MEMO 1"      'Macintosh
```

The following examples create a new template based on the existing Letter3
template:

```
FileNew .NewTemplate = 1, .Template = "LETTER3.DOT" 'Windows
FileNew .NewTemplate = 1, .Template = "LETTER 3"     'Macintosh
```

The following examples run the Resume wizard:

```
FileNew .Template = "RESUME.WIZ"       'Windows
FileNew .Template = "RESUME WIZARD"     'Macintosh
```

See Also   **FileNewDefault, FileOpen**

FileNewDefault

Syntax   **FileNewDefault**

Remarks   Creates a new document based on the Normal template.

See Also   **FileNew**

File*Number*

Syntax   **File***Number*

Remarks   Opens one of the files in the list of recently used files at the bottom of the File menu. (Word defines "used" as either opened or saved.) **File1** opens the first document in the list (the most recently used), **File2** opens the second document, and so on through **File9**. Nine is the maximum number of filenames that can be listed on the File menu. If no file is listed, or if *Number* is greater than the number of files listed, an error occurs. If the specified file is already open, Word activates the document.

You can control the number of files to be listed on the File menu with the Recently Used File List option on the General tab in the Options dialog box (Tools menu).

See Also   **CountFiles()**, **FileList**, **FileName$()**, **Window***Number*

FileOpen

Syntax   **FileOpen .Name** = *text* [, **.ConfirmConversions** = *number*]
[, **.ReadOnly** = *number*] [, **.AddToMru** = *number*] [, **.PasswordDoc** = *text*]
[, **.PasswordDot** = *text*] [, **.Revert** = number] [, **.WritePasswordDoc** = *text*]
[, **.WritePasswordDot** = *text*]

Remarks   Opens the specified document. If the document does not exist, or is not located in the specified folder, an error occurs. Most arguments for the **FileOpen** statement correspond to the options in the Open dialog box (File menu).

Argument	Explanation
.Name	The name of the document (paths are accepted). In Windows, you can specify multiple files by separating the filenames with spaces; on the Macintosh and in Windows NT, you can specify only one file per **FileOpen** instruction.
	If you use **Dialog** or **Dialog**() to display the Open dialog box, you can display files of a certain type by setting .Name to a file specification. To display text files, for example, the file specification would be `"*.TXT"` (Windows) or `MacID$("TEXT")` (Macintosh). For an example, see **MacID$()**.

Argument	Explanation
.ConfirmConversions	If 1, displays the Convert File dialog box if the file is not in Word format.
.ReadOnly	If 1, opens the document as read-only.
.AddToMru	If 1, adds the filename to the list of recently used files at the bottom of the File menu. (Note that MRU is an abbreviation for "most recently used.")
.PasswordDoc	The password to open the document, if required.
.PasswordDot	The password to open the template, if required.
.Revert	Controls what happens if .Name is the filename of an open document:
	0 (zero) Word activates the open document.
	1 Word discards any unsaved changes to the open document and reopens the file.
.WritePasswordDoc	The password to save changes to the document, if required.
.WritePasswordDot	The password to save changes to the template, if required.

In Windows 95 and Windows NT, if any part of the path or filename for a file specified by .Name contains a space character, the entire path and filename must be enclosed by Chr$(34) characters, as shown in the following example:

```
FileOpen .Name = Chr$(34) + "C:\DOCUMENTS\AUGUST REPORT" + Chr$(34)
```

You can specify multiple files using this technique as well. Each filename must be separated by a space character, as shown in the following example:

```
FileOpen .Name = Chr$(34) + "JUNE REPORT" + Chr$(34) + " " + \
        Chr$(34) + "JULY REPORT" + Chr$(34) + " " + \
        Chr$(34) + "AUGUST REPORT" + Chr$(34)
```

On the Macintosh, paths and filenames that contain spaces should not be enclosed by Chr$(34) characters. The following Macintosh example shows the correct way to specify a path and filename with spaces in them in a Macintosh **FileOpen** instruction:

```
FileOpen .Name = "HD:MONTHLY REPORTS:AUGUST REPORT"
```

Examples   This Windows example changes the current folder, and then opens a read-only copy of MYDOC.DOC:

```
ChDir "C:\WINWORD\DOCS"
FileOpen .Name = "MYDOC.DOC", .ReadOnly = 1
```

The following Macintosh example also opens MY DOCUMENT, but because the full path is specified, no **ChDir** instruction is required before the **FileOpen** instruction:

```
FileOpen .Name = "HD:WORD:MY DOCUMENT", .ReadOnly = 1
```

See Also   **FileConfirmConversions**, **FileFind**, **FileNew**, **MacID$( )**

FilePageSetup

Syntax   **FilePageSetup** [**.Tab** = *number*] [**, .TopMargin** = *number or text*]
[**, .BottomMargin** = *number or text*] [**, .LeftMargin** = *number or text*]
[**, .RightMargin** = *number or text*] [**, .Gutter** = *number or text*]
[**, .PageWidth** = *number or text*] [**, .PageHeight** = *number or text*]
[**, .Orientation** = *number*] [**, .FirstPage** = *number*] [**, .OtherPages** = *number*]
[**, .VertAlign** = *number*] [**, .ApplyPropsTo** = *number*] [**, .Default**]
[**, .FacingPages** = *number*] [**, .HeaderDistance** = *number or text*]
[**, .FooterDistance** = *number or text*] [**, .SectionStart** = *number*]
[**, .OddAndEvenPages** = *number*] [**, .DifferentFirstPage** = *number*]
[**, .Endnotes** = *number*] [**, .LineNum** = *number*] [**, .StartingNum** = *number*]
[**, .FromText** = *number or text*] [**, .CountBy** = *number*] [**, .NumMode** = *number*]

Remarks   In Windows, sets page attributes such as margins and page width for the entire document or sections within the document. The arguments for the **FilePageSetup** statement correspond to the options in the Page Setup dialog box (File menu). On the Macintosh, use **FileDocumentLayout**.

Argument	Explanation
.Tab	Specifies which tab to select when you display the Page Setup dialog box with a **Dialog** or **Dialog**( ) instruction:
	0 (zero) Margins
	1 Paper Size
	2 Paper Source
	3 Layout
	For details, see the second example in this entry.
.TopMargin	The distance between the top edge of the page and the top boundary of the body text in points or a text measurement
.BottomMargin	The distance between the bottom edge of the page and the bottom boundary of the body text in points or a text measurement
.LeftMargin	The distance between the left edge of the page and the left boundary of the body text in points or a text measurement

Argument	Explanation
.RightMargin	The distance between the right edge of the page and the right boundary of the body text in points or a text measurement
.Gutter	The extra margin space allowed for binding the document, in points or a text measurement
.PageWidth	The width of the page in points or a text measurement
.PageHeight	The height of the page in points or a text measurement
.Orientation	The orientation of the page: 0 (zero) Portrait 1 Landscape Note that unlike using the **TogglePortrait** statement, specifying a new orientation with **FilePageSetup** does not automatically adjust the page size and margins for the new orientation.
.FirstPage, .OtherPages	Selects the paper source for the first page and the other pages in the document: 0 (zero) Default Tray (determined by the printer driver) 1 Upper Tray 2 Lower Tray 4 Manual Feed (often used to override the default tray for the first page) 5 Envelope Other values may be available depending on your printer driver. To determine a value, record a macro that selects the option you want on the Paper Source tab in the Page Setup dialog box, and then review the values for .FirstPage and .OtherPages in the macro-editing window.
.VertAlign	Alignment of section on the page: 0 (zero) Top 1 Center 2 Justified
.ApplyPropsTo	The part of the document to apply the page setup properties to: 0 (zero) This Section 1 This Point Forward 2 Selected Sections 3 Selected Text 4 Whole Document
.Default	Makes the current page-setup properties the default for new documents based on the active template.

Argument	Explanation
.FacingPages	If 1, corresponds to selecting the Mirror Margins check box
.HeaderDistance	Distance of header from the top of the page
.FooterDistance	Distance of footer from the bottom of the page
.SectionStart	Determines the type of section break:
	0 (zero) Continuous
	1 New Column
	2 New Page
	3 Even Page
	4 Odd Page
.OddAndEvenPages	If 1, corresponds to selecting the Different Odd And Even check box
.DifferentFirstPage	If 1, corresponds to selecting the Different First Page check box
.Endnotes	If 1, corresponds to selecting the Suppress Endnotes check box
.LineNum	If 1, corresponds to selecting the Add Line Numbering check box
.StartingNum	The number at which to begin line numbering
.FromText	The distance from text, in points or a text measurement; 0 (zero) sets automatic spacing
.CountBy	The numeric increment used to print line numbers.
.NumMode	Determines how lines are numbered:
	0 (zero) Restart at each new page
	1 Restart at each new section
	2 Continuous

Examples

This Windows example sets the top margin to 1 inch for the entire document:

```
FilePageSetup .ApplyPropsTo = 4, .TopMargin = "1 in"
```

The following Windows example displays the Paper Source tab in the Page Setup dialog box, and then applies the settings the user selects:

```
Dim dlg As FilePageSetup
GetCurValues dlg
dlg.Tab = 2
Dialog dlg
FilePageSetup dlg
```

See Also

FileDocumentLayout, FileMacCustomPageSetupGX, FileMacPageSetup, FileMacPageSetupGX, FormatColumns, FormatSectionLayout

FilePost

Syntax	**FilePost** *Destination$*
Remarks	Posts the active document to a public folder in Microsoft Exchange. If the folder specified by *Destination$* isn't a valid public folder, an error occurs.
	The **FilePost** statement is available only in Microsoft Word for Windows 95 and only if running against Microsoft Exchange Server.
See Also	**FileRoutingSlip, FileSendMail**

FilePreview

Syntax	**FilePreview** *HorizPos, VertPos, Width, Height, .Identifier*
Remarks	Creates a file preview box—similar to the one in the Find File dialog box (File menu)—in a custom dialog box. A custom dialog box can have only one file preview box.

You cannot use the Dialog Editor to create a **FilePreview** instruction. A good workaround is to use another control as a stand-in. In the Dialog Editor, size and position the stand-in control as you want the file preview box to be sized and positioned. Then, after you paste the dialog box definition into your macro, convert the stand-in instruction to a **FilePreview** instruction.

The file preview box displays the first page of the document that is active when the dialog box is displayed. You can also control which document is displayed in the file preview box by using **DlgFilePreview** in a dialog function. For information about using a dialog function, see Chapter 5, "Working with Custom Dialog Boxes," in Part 1, "Learning WordBasic."

Argument	Explanation
HorizPos, VertPos	The horizontal and vertical distance of the upper-left corner of the file preview box from the upper-left corner of the dialog box, in increments of 1/8 and 1/12 of the System font (Windows) or the dialog font (Macintosh).
Width, Height	The width and height of the file preview box, in increments of 1/8 and 1/12 of the System font (Windows) or the dialog font (Macintosh).
.Identifier	An identifier used by a **DlgFilePreview** instruction in a dialog function to change the document displayed in the file preview box.

For an example, see **DlgUpdateFilePreview**.

See Also	**DlgFilePreview, DlgUpdateFilePreview, Picture**

FilePrint

Syntax

FilePrint [**.Background** = *number*] [, **.AppendPrFile** = *number*]
[, **.Range** = *number*] [, **.PrToFileName** = *text*] [, **.From** = *text*] [, **.To** = *text*]
[, **.Type** = *number*] [, **.NumCopies** = *number*] [, **.Pages** = *text*]
[, **.Order** = *number*] [, **.PrintToFile** = *number*] [, **.Collate** = *number*]
[, **.FileName** = *text*] [, **.OutputPrinter** = *text*]

Remarks

Prints all or part of the active document or a document you specify. The arguments for the **FilePrint** statement correspond to the options in the Print dialog box (File menu).

Argument	Explanation
.Background	If 1, the macro continues while Word prints the document. On the Macintosh, this argument is not available and generates an error.
.AppendPrFile	If you print to a file, specifies whether to overwrite or append to the file if it already exists:
	0 (zero) Overwrite
	1 Append
	On the Macintosh, this argument is ignored unless QuickDraw GX is installed.
.Range	The page range:
	0 (zero) Prints the entire document
	1 Prints the selection
	2 Prints the current page
	3 Prints the range of pages specified by .From and .To
	4 Prints the range of pages specified by .Pages
.PrToFileName	If you print to a file, the path and filename of the file to print to. This argument is not available on the Macintosh unless QuickDraw GX is installed.
.From	The starting page number when .Range is 3
.To	The ending page number when .Range is 3
.Type	The item to print:
	0 (zero) Document
	1 Summary Info
	2 Annotations
	3 Styles
	4 AutoText Entries
	5 Key Assignments

Argument	Explanation
.NumCopies	The number of copies to print
.Pages	The page numbers and page ranges you want to print, separated by commas. For example, "2, 6-10" prints page 2 and pages 6 through 10.
.Order	Further delimits the range of pages to print:
	0 (zero) Prints all pages in the range.
	1 Prints only odd pages in the range.
	2 Prints only even pages in the range.
.PrintToFile	If 1, sends printer instructions to a file. Make sure to specify a filename with .PrToFileName. This argument is not available on the Macintosh unless QuickDraw GX is installed.
.Collate	If 1, organizes pages when printing multiple copies of the document.
.FileName	The path and filename of the document to print. If omitted, Word prints the active document.
.OutputPrinter	On the Macintosh, if QuickDraw GX is installed, specifies the printer to print to. If the specified printer is not valid, Word prints to the printer selected in the Print dialog box or to the default desktop printer.

See Also   **FilePrintDefault, FilePrintOneCopy, FilePrintSetup, ToolsOptionsPrint**

FilePrintDefault

Syntax   **FilePrintDefault**

Remarks   Prints the active document using the current settings in the Print and Print Setup (Word version 6.0) dialog boxes (File menu) and on the Print tab in the Options dialog box (Tools menu).

See Also   **FilePrint, FilePrintOneCopy, FilePrintSetup, ToolsOptionsPrint**

FilePrintOneCopy

Syntax   **FilePrintOneCopy**

Remarks   On the Macintosh with QuickDraw GX installed, prints a single copy of the active document. This statement corresponds to the Print One Copy command that is added to the File menu if you install QuickDraw GX. In Windows, and on the Macintosh if QuickDraw GX is not installed, **FilePrintOneCopy** is not available and generates an error.

See Also   **FilePrint, FilePrintDefault**

FilePrintPreview, FilePrintPreview()

Syntax   **FilePrintPreview** [*On*]

FilePrintPreview()

Remarks   The **FilePrintPreview** statement switches the active document to and from print preview.

Argument	Explanation
On	Displays the document in print preview or the previous view:
	Omitted Toggles print preview
	0 (zero) Cancels print preview
	1 Switches to print preview

The **FilePrintPreview**() function returns the following values.

Value	Explanation
−1	If the active document is in print preview
0 (zero)	If the active document is in some other view

See Also   **ClosePreview**, **FilePrintPreviewFullScreen**, **FilePrintPreviewPages**, **ViewZoom**

FilePrintPreviewFullScreen

Syntax   **FilePrintPreviewFullScreen**

Remarks   Toggles the display of rulers, scroll bars, the status bar, and the menu bar in print preview. If the active document is not in print preview, an error occurs.

See Also   **ToolsOptionsView**

FilePrintPreviewPages, FilePrintPreviewPages()

Syntax   **FilePrintPreviewPages** *PagesAcross*

FilePrintPreviewPages()

Remarks   The **FilePrintPreviewPages** statement specifies whether to display one or two columns of pages in page layout view and print preview. *PagesAcross* can be 1 or 2 only; for more control over the grid of page images, use **ViewZoom**. The **FilePrintPreviewPages**() function returns the number of columns of pages currently displayed. If the active document is not in either page layout view or print preview, an error occurs.

See Also   **FilePrintPreview**, **ViewPage**, **ViewZoom**

FilePrintSetup

Syntax	**FilePrintSetup** [**.Printer** = *text*] [**, .Options**] [**, .DoNotSetAsSysDefault** = *number*]
Remarks	Changes the active printer or a printer's options. In Word version 6.0, the arguments for the **FilePrintSetup** statement correspond to the options in the Print Setup dialog box (Print command, File menu). On the Macintosh, **FilePrintSetup** is not available and generates an error.

Argument	Explanation
.Printer	The name of the new printer to be activated. Specify this argument exactly as it appears in the Printer Setup dialog box.
	To activate the system default printer, specify an empty string ("").
.Options	Displays a dialog box showing the options for .Printer. You can use the **SendKeys** statement to select options.
.DoNotSetAsSysDefault	If 0 (zero) or omitted, makes .Printer the system default printer.
	In Word version 6.0, this argument is unavailable and generates an error.

Examples	This Windows example changes the system default printer to the PostScript® printer attached to the COM2 port.

```
FilePrintSetup .Printer = "PostScript printer on COM2:"
```

The following Windows example uses the **SendKeys** statement to send the key sequence ALT+O, ALT+L, ENTER to the Options dialog box for the current printer. The instructions depend on the existence of an Orientation box whose access key is O and a Landscape button in that box whose access key is L.

```
SendKeys "%o%l{enter}"
FilePrintSetup .Options
```

See Also	**FilePrint, SendKeys, ToolsOptionsPrint**

FileProperties

Syntax	**FileProperties**
Remarks	Displays the Properties dialog box for the active document. For a list of the built-in properties available in Word, see **DocumentPropertyName$()**. In Word version 6.0, **FileProperties** is unavailable and generates an error.
	Use the document properties statements and functions to define custom properties and to return and change the values for available custom and built-in properties.
See Also	**DocumentPropertyName$(), GetDocumentProperty(), SetDocumentProperty**

FileQuit

Syntax   **FileQuit** [*Save*]

Remarks   Quits Word. **FileQuit** (Macintosh) is the same as **FileExit** (Windows). For
                  information on the *Save* argument, see **FileExit**.

See Also   **AppClose**, **ExitWindows**, **FileCloseAll**, **FileExit**

FileRoutingSlip

Syntax   **FileRoutingSlip** [**.Subject** = *text*] [, **.Message** = *text*] [, **.AllAtOnce** = *number*]
                  [, **.ReturnWhenDone** = *number*] [, **.TrackStatus** = *number*]
                  [, **.Protect** = *number*] [, **.AddSlip**] [, **.RouteDocument**] [, **.AddRecipient**]
                  [, **.OldRecipient**] [, **.ResetSlip**] [, **.ClearSlip**] [, **.ClearRecipients**]
                  [, **.Address** = *text*]

Remarks   Adds, removes, or changes the routing slip for the active document, or routes the
                  active document to the recipients specified by the routing slip. **FileRoutingSlip** is
                  available only if Microsoft Mail is installed. The arguments for **FileRoutingSlip**
                  correspond to the options in the Routing Slip dialog box (Add Routing Slip
                  command, File menu).

Argument	Explanation
.Subject	Text for the subject line of the electronic mail message
.Message	The message you want to precede the icon for the attached document
.AllAtOnce	Specifies how recipients receive the document:
	0 (zero) Sends the document to the first recipient specified by .Address
	1 Sends a copy of the document to all the recipients at the same time
.ReturnWhenDone	If 1, sends the document back to the original sender when the last recipient chooses the Send command from the File menu
.TrackStatus	If 1, sends a message back to the original sender each time the document is forwarded

Argument	Explanation
.Protect	Specifies a level of protection for the document:
	0 (zero) No protection
	1 All changes are tracked by revision marks.
	2 Recipients can add annotations only.
	3 Recipients can enter information in form fields only.
.Address	The address of a recipient for the document you are routing. To add multiple recipients, use multiple **FileRoutingSlip** instructions to add them one at a time. If you are routing the document to recipients one at a time, add recipient names in the order you want to route the document.

Only one of the following arguments can be specified for each **FileRoutingSlip** instruction.

Argument	Explanation
.AddSlip	Adds a routing slip to the active document.
	Note that when you close a document with an attached routing slip, Word displays a message asking if you want to route the document. To suppress this message in a macro that contains **DocClose**, **FileClose**, **FileCloseAll**, or **FileExit** instructions, set the .Save argument for those statements to 1 or 2. Word closes the document or documents without routing them.
.RouteDocument	Routes the active document.
.AddRecipient	Adds the address specified by .Address to the list of recipients.
.OldRecipient	Adds the address specified by .Address to the list of recipients only if the document has not already been routed. When you record a modification to a routing slip for a document that has already been routed, **FileRoutingSlip** instructions with .OldRecipient arguments are recorded for recipients who have already received the document.
.ResetSlip	Prepares the document to be rerouted to the recipients. If the document has not completed its first routing, Word displays a message.
.ClearSlip	Removes the routing slip from the active document.
.ClearRecipients	Removes all addresses from the list of recipients.

Example

This example adds a routing slip to the active document (which includes the current date in the subject line), adds two recipients, and then routes the document:

```
curdate$ = Date$(Now())
FileRoutingSlip .Subject = "Status Doc " + curdate$, \
    .Message = "Please fill in your status.", .AllAtOnce = 0, \
    .ReturnWhenDone = 1, .TrackStatus = 1, .Protect = 1, .AddSlip
FileRoutingSlip .Address = "Sara Levine", .AddRecipient
FileRoutingSlip .Address = "Carlos Alicea", .AddRecipient
FileRoutingSlip .RouteDocument
```

See Also

FileSendMail

Files$()

Syntax

**Files$**(*FileSpec$*)

Remarks

Returns the first filename that matches the file specification *FileSpec$*. If you specify a period (.) (Windows) or colon (:) (Macintosh) as the *FileSpec$*, **Files$**() returns the current path. In Windows, you can use the MS-DOS wildcard characters—the asterisk (*) and the question mark (?)—to specify files. On the Macintosh, you use **MacID$**() to specify files of a certain type.

Argument	Explanation
FileSpec$	The file specification. If you omit the file specification, the next file that matches the most recently used *FileSpec$* is returned.
	In Windows, you can specify a path as part of the file specification (for example, `C:\DOCS\*.TXT`). On the Macintosh, you produce the same result by changing the current folder with **ChDir** and then using **MacID$**() to specify files of a certain type (for example, `MacID$("TEXT")`).

By specifying *FileSpec$* on the first iteration and omitting it thereafter, you can use **Files$**() to generate a list of files that match *FileSpec$* (as in the final example in this reference entry). If no files match, an empty string ("") is returned.

Note that if the path or filename returned by **Files$**() contains one or more spaces, the entire return value is enclosed in quotation marks.

Examples

This Windows example returns the first file ending with the .DOC filename extension found in the current folder:

```
a$ = Files$("*.DOC")
```

The following is the same example, rewritten for the Macintosh. W6BN is the four-character sequence that specifies the Word Document file type.

```
a$ = Files$(MacID$("W6BN"))
```

The following examples return the current path (for example, "C:\WINWORD" or "HD:WORD 6:"):

```
CurDir$ = Files$(".")     'Windows example
CurDir$ = Files$(":")     'Macintosh example
```

If NOTE.DOC exists in the current folder, the following example opens the document. If NOTE.DOC does not exist, a message box is displayed.

```
If Files$("NOTE.DOC") <> "" Then
    FileOpen "NOTE.DOC"
Else
    MsgBox "File not found in current folder."
End If
```

The following example fills an array with the names of all files in the current folder. The instructions first count the files to determine the size of the array. Then they define the array, fill it with the filenames, and sort the elements. You could use this array to present a list of files in a user-defined dialog box or to open and perform an operation on each file in the array. On the Macintosh, substitute MacID$("****") for "*.*" in the file specifications.

```
temp$ = Files$("*.*")
count = - 1
While temp$ <> ""
    count = count + 1
    temp$ = Files$()
Wend
If count > -1 Then
    Dim list$(count)
    list$(0) = Files$("*.*")
    For i = 1 To count
        list$(i) = Files$()
    Next i
    SortArray list$()
    MsgBox Str$(count + 1) + " files; 1st in array is " + list$(0)
Else
    MsgBox "No files in current folder."
End If
```

See Also   **FileFind, MacID$()**

FileSave

Syntax   **FileSave**

Remarks   Saves the active document or template. If the document is not named, **FileSave** displays the Save As dialog box (File menu).

See Also   **FileSaveAll**, **FileSaveAs**, **IsDocumentDirty()**, **IsTemplateDirty()**

FileSaveAll

Syntax   **FileSaveAll** [*Save*] [**,** *OriginalFormat*]

Remarks   Saves all changed files, including the Normal template and any other templates attached to open documents that have changed. It's a good idea to include a **FileSaveAll** statement if your macro makes changes to AutoText entries, other macros, or keyboard, menu, and toolbar assignments.

Argument	Explanation
Save	Specifies whether or not to prompt the user to save each document or template if it is "dirty"—that is, if changes have been made since the last time the document or template was saved:
	0 (zero) Prompts the user to save each changed document or template.
	1 Saves all changed documents and templates automatically.
OriginalFormat	Specifies whether or not to prompt when saving a document opened from a foreign file format in which changes have been made that cannot be stored in the original format:
	0 (zero) Saves the document in Word Document format.
	1 Saves the document in its original format.
	2 or omitted Prompts the user to save in Word Document format.

See Also   **FileSave**, **FileSaveAs**, **IsDocumentDirty()**, **IsTemplateDirty()**

FileSaveAs

Syntax   **FileSaveAs** [**.Name** = *text*] [**, .Format** = *number*] [**, .LockAnnot** = *number*] [**, .Password** = *text*] [**, .AddToMru** = *number*] [**, .WritePassword** = *text*] [**, .RecommendReadOnly** = *number*] [**, .EmbedFonts** = *number*] [**, .NativePictureFormat** = *number*] [**, .FormsData** = *number*] [**, .SaveAsAOCELetter** = *number*]

Remarks   Saves the active document with a new name or format. The arguments for the **FileSaveAs** statement correspond to the options in the Save As dialog box (File menu).

Argument	Explanation
.Name	The new name. If you don't specify .Name, the current folder and name are the defaults. If the document has never been saved, Word saves to a default name such as DOC1.DOC (Windows) or DOCUMENT1 (Macintosh). Note that if a document with the new name or a default name already exists, Word overwrites that document without prompting.
.Format	Specifies the new format:
	0 (zero) Word document
	1 Document template
	2 Text Only (extended characters saved in ANSI character set)
	3 Text Only with Line Breaks (extended characters saved in ANSI character set)
	4 MS-DOS Text (extended characters saved in IBM® PC character set) (Windows only)
	5 MS-DOS Text with Line Breaks (extended characters saved in IBM PC character set) (Windows only)
	6 Rich-Text Format (RTF)
	You can return values appropriate for other formats by specifying a format name in a **ConverterLookup**( ) instruction.
.LockAnnot	If 1, locks the document for annotations. You can also lock a document with **ToolsProtectDocument**.
.Password	Sets a password for opening the document.
.AddToMru	If 1, places the document name first on the list of recently used files at the bottom of the File menu. (Note that MRU is an abbreviation for "most recently used.")
.WritePassword	Sets a password for saving changes to the document.
.RecommendReadOnly	If 1, displays a message upon opening the document suggesting that it be opened as read-only.
.EmbedFonts	If 1, embeds TrueType fonts in the document.
.NativePictureFormat	If 1, saves only the Windows version of imported graphics.
.FormsData	If 1, saves the data entered by a user in a form as a data record. Note the form must be unprotected or **FileSaveAs** generates an error.
.SaveAsAOCELetter	If the active document has an attached mailer, specifies how to save the document:
	0 (zero) As a Word document (mailer is not saved)
	1 or omitted As an AOCE letter (mailer is saved)
	This option is available only on the Macintosh and only if PowerTalk is installed.

Example	This example saves the active document in rich-text format (RTF) with the filename TEST.RTF:

```
FileSaveAs .Name = "TEST.RTF", .Format = 6
```

See Also	**Converter$()**, **ConverterLookup()**, **FileSave**, **FileSaveAll**, **Name**, **ToolsOptionsSave**, **ToolsProtectDocument**

FileSendMail

Syntax	**FileSendMail**
Remarks	Opens a message window for sending the active document through Microsoft Mail. Use the **ToolsOptionsGeneral** statement with the .SendMailAttach argument to control whether the document is sent as text in the message window or as an attachment. **FileSendMail** is available only if Microsoft Mail is installed.
See Also	**AOCESendMail**, **FileAOCESendMail**, **FileRoutingSlip**, **ToolsOptionsGeneral**

FileSummaryInfo

Syntax	**FileSummaryInfo** [**.Title** = *text*] [**, .Subject** = *text*] [**, .Author** = *text*] [**, .Keywords** = *text*] [**, .Comments** = *text*] [**, .FileName** = *text*] [**, .Directory** = *text*] [**, .Template** = *text*] [**, .CreateDate** = *text*] [**, .LastSavedDate** = *text*] [**, .LastSavedBy** = *text*] [**, .RevisionNumber** = *text*] [**, .EditTime** = *text*] [**, .LastPrintedDate** = *text*] [**, .NumPages** = *text*] [**, .NumWords** = *text*] [**, .NumChars** = *text*] [**, .NumParas** = *text*] [**, .NumLines** = *text*] [**, .Update**] [**, .FileSize** = *text*]
Remarks	Sets the summary information and allows access to document statistics for the active document. In Word version 6.0, the arguments for the **FileSummaryInfo** statement correspond to the options in the Summary Info dialog box (File menu) and the Document Statistics dialog box (Statistics button, Summary Info command). All the arguments corresponding to the options in the Document Statistics dialog box are read-only, with the exception of .EditTime.
	In Word version 7.0, this statement is included for backward compatibility. You can use the document property statements and functions to set or access summary information for the active document. For more information, see **GetDocumentProperty()** and **SetDocumentProperty**.

Argument	Explanation
.Title	The title of the document
.Subject	The subject of the document
.Author	The author of the document
.Keywords	The keywords used to identify the document

Argument	Explanation
.Comments	The comments about the document
.FileName	When using **FileSummaryInfo** as a statement, the name of the file to make summary information changes to (the file must be open); when returning information from a **FileSummaryInfo** dialog record, the filename of the active document (path not included)
.Directory	The document's location (read-only)
.Template	The document template (read-only)
.CreateDate	The creation date (read-only)
.LastSavedDate	The date the document was last saved (read-only)
.LastSavedBy	The name of the person last saving the document (read-only)
.RevisionNumber	The number of times the document has been saved (read-only)
.EditTime	The total time the document has been open, in minutes
.LastPrintedDate	The date the document was last printed (read-only)
.NumPages	The number of pages (read-only)
.NumWords	The number of words (read-only)
.NumChars	The number of characters (read-only)
.NumParas	The number of paragraphs (read-only)
.NumLines	The number of lines (read-only)
.Update	Updates the summary information
.FileSize	The size of the document in the form "36,352 Bytes" (read-only)

Note To ensure you get the most up-to-date information when using a **FileSummaryInfo** dialog record to return summary information or document statistics, include the instruction `FileSummaryInfo .Update` before defining the dialog record.

Examples

This example sets the title of the active document:

```
FileSummaryInfo .Title = "Exploration of the Upper Amazon."
```

The following example defines the variable `author$` as the author of the active document.

```
Dim dlg As FileSummaryInfo
GetCurValues dlg
author$ = dlg.Author
```

See Also

DocumentStatistics

FileTemplates

Syntax   **FileTemplates** [**.Template** = *text*] [**, .LinkStyles** = *number*]

Remarks   Changes the template attached to the active document. To add or remove global templates, use **AddAddIn**, **AddInState**, and **DeleteAddIn**. The arguments for the **FileTemplate** statement correspond to the options in the Templates And Add-ins dialog box (Templates command, File menu).

Argument	Explanation
.Template	The path and filename of the template to attach.
.LinkStyles	If 1, styles in the active document are linked to the active template; Word copies styles from the attached template each time the document is opened.

If you choose Templates from the File menu while recording a macro, Word records the .Store argument in the **FileTemplates** statement. This argument is recognized for backward compatibility with Word version 2.*x* macros. In Word version 6.0 or later, the .Store argument is ignored.

See Also   **AddAddIn**, **AddInState**, **DeleteAddIn**, **FileNew**, **Organizer**

FileType$()

Syntax   **FileType$**(*File$*)

Remarks   On the Macintosh, returns a four-character string identifying the file type of *File$* (a path and filename). In Windows, **FileType$()** is not available and generates an error.

Example   This Macintosh example displays a message box stating the file type of the file specified by checkfile$:

```
checkfile$ = "HD:WORK:TO DO LIST"
ftype$ = FileType$(checkfile$)
Select Case ftype$
    Case "W6BN" : a$ = "a Word document"
    Case "WDBN" : a$ = "a Word 5.1 document"
    Case "WTBN" : a$ = "a Word template"
    Case "TEXT" : a$ = "a text file"
    Case "XLS5" : a$ = "a Microsoft Excel worksheet"
    Case "APPL" : a$ = "an application"
    Case "WDLL" : a$ = "a Word add-in library"
    Case "WIZ!" : a$ = "a wizard"
    Case Else : a$ = ""
End Select
```

```
If a$ <> "" Then
    MsgBox checkfile$ + " is " + a$ + "."
Else
    MsgBox checkfile$ + " has file type " + ftype$ "."
End If
```

See Also　　**FileCreator$(), MacID$(), SetFileCreatorAndType**

Font, Font$()

Syntax

Font *Name$* [**,** *Size*]

Font$()

Font$(*Count***)**

Remarks

The **Font** statement applies the specified font to the selection.

Argument	Explanation
Name$	The name of the font to apply.
Size	The size of the font, in points. You can use this argument instead of following a **Font** instruction with a **FontSize** instruction.

The **Font$()** function returns the name of the font applied to the selection. If the selection contains more than one font, an empty string ("") is returned. If *Count* is specified, **Font$()** returns the name of the font at position *Count* in the current font list, in the range 1 to **CountFonts()**.

Examples

This example selects the paragraph containing the insertion point (using the predefined bookmark "\Para") and then applies 8-point Courier font:

```
EditGoTo "\Para"
Font "Courier", 8
```

The following example displays a message box if the paragraph containing the insertion point has more than one font:

```
EditGoTo "\Para"
If Font$() = "" Then
    MsgBox "Paragraph contains more than one font."
End If
```

See Also　　**CountFonts(), FontSize, FormatFont**

FontSize, FontSize()

Syntax   **FontSize** *Size*

                  FontSize( )

Remarks   The **FontSize** statement sets the font size of the selected text, in points.

                  The **FontSize( )** function returns the font size of the selected text. If the selection contains more than one font size, 0 (zero) is returned.

See Also   **Font**, **FontSizeSelect**, **FormatFont**

FontSizeSelect

Syntax   **FontSizeSelect**

Remarks   If the Formatting toolbar is displayed, moves the focus to the Font Size box; otherwise, displays the Font dialog box (Format menu), selects the Font tab, and then moves the focus to the Size box.

See Also   **Font**, **FontSize**, **FormatFont**

FontSubstitution

Syntax   **FontSubstitution .UnavailableFont** = *text*, **.SubstituteFont** = *text*

Remarks   Sets font-mapping options for the active document. The arguments for the **FontSubstitution** statement correspond to the options in the Font Substitution dialog box (Compatibility tab, Options dialog box, Tools menu).

Argument	Explanation
.UnavailableFont	The name of a font not available on your computer that you want to map to a different font for display and printing
.SubstituteFont	The name of a font available on your computer that you want to substitute for the unavailable font

See Also   **ToolsOptionsCompatibility**

For...Next

Syntax   **For** *CounterVariable* = *Start* **To** *End* [**Step** *Increment*]
                      Series of instructions
                  Next [*CounterVariable*]

Remarks   Repeats the series of instructions between **For** and **Next** while increasing *CounterVariable* by 1 (default) or *Increment* until *CounterVariable* is greater than *End*. If *Start* is greater than *End*, *Increment* must be a negative value; *CounterVariable* decreases by *Increment* until it is less than *End*.

If you place one or more **For...Next** loops within another, use a unique *CounterVariable* for each loop, as in the following instructions:

```
For I = 1 To 10
    For J = 1 To 10
        For K = 1 To 10
            'Series of instructions
        Next K
    Next J
Next I
```

For more information about **For...Next**, see Chapter 4, "Advanced WordBasic," in Part 1, "Learning WordBasic."

Examples   This example displays five message boxes in a row, each giving the current value of count:

```
For count = 1 To 5
    MsgBox "Current value of count is" + Str$(count)
Next count
```

The following example produces exactly the same effect as the previous example by decrementing the value of count in steps of −1:

```
For count = 5 To 1 Step -1
    MsgBox "Current value of count is" + Str$(count)
Next
```

The following example demonstrates how you can use WordBasic counting functions with a **For...Next** loop to perform an operation on all the items in a certain category. In this example, the names of all the bookmarks defined in the active document are stored in the array mark$().

```
numBookmarks = CountBookmarks()
arraySize = numBookmarks - 1
Dim mark$(arraySize)
For n = 0 To arraySize
    mark$(n) = BookmarkName$(n + 1)
Next
```

See Also   **Goto, If...Then...Else, Select Case, While...Wend**

FormatAddrFonts

Syntax   **FormatAddrFonts** [**.Points** = *number*] [, **.Underline** = *number*]
[, **.Color** = *number*] [, **.Strikethrough** = *number*] [, **.Superscript** = *number*]
[, **.Subscript** = *number*] [, **.Hidden** = *number*] [, **.SmallCaps** = *number*]
[, **.AllCaps** = *number*] [, **.Spacing** = *number*] [, **.Position** = *number or text*]
[, **.Kerning** = *number*] [, **.KerningMin** = *number or text*] [, **.Default**]
[, **.Tab** = *number*] [, **.Font** = *text*] [, **.Bold** = *number*] [, **.Italic** = *number*]

Remarks   Sets character formatting for the address on an envelope. Precede
ToolsCreateEnvelope with **FormatAddrFonts** to specify options corresponding
to those in the Font dialog box (Format menu). Include .Default to store the
options you specify as the default character formatting for the address. For
argument descriptions, see **FormatFont**.

See Also   **FormatFont**, **FormatRetAddrFonts**, **ToolsCreateEnvelope**

FormatAutoFormat

Syntax   **FormatAutoFormat**

Remarks   Automatically formats a document according to the options set with
ToolsOptionsAutoFormat. To control the look of the document, you can use
FormatStyleGallery to copy styles into the active document before or after
running **FormatAutoFormat**.

Example   This Windows example automatically formats the active document using styles in
REPORT1.DOT. On the Macintosh, substitute "REPORT 1" for "REPORT1."

```
FormatStyleGallery .Template = "REPORT1"
FormatAutoFormat
```

See Also   **FormatStyleGallery**, **ToolsOptionsAutoFormat**

FormatBordersAndShading

Syntax   **FormatBordersAndShading** [**.ApplyTo** = *number*] [, **.Shadow** = *number*]
[, **.TopBorder** = *number*] [, **.LeftBorder** = *number*] [, **.BottomBorder** = *number*]
[, **.RightBorder** = *number*] [, **.HorizBorder** = *number*] [, **.VertBorder** = *number*]
[, **.TopColor** = *number*] [, **.LeftColor** = *number*] [, **.BottomColor** = *number*]
[, **.RightColor** = *number*] [, **.HorizColor** = *number*] [, **.VertColor** = *number*]
[, **.FineShading** = *number*] [, **.FromText** = *number or text*]
[, **.Shading** = *number*] [, **.Foreground** = *number*] [, **.Background** = *number*]
[, **.Tab** = *number*]

Remarks   Sets border and shading formats for the selected paragraphs, table cells, or
graphic. The arguments for the **FormatBordersAndShading** statement
correspond to the options in the Borders And Shading dialog box (Format menu).

Argument	Explanation
.ApplyTo	If the selection consists of more than one of the following items, specifies to which item or items the border format is applied: 0 (zero) Paragraphs 1 Graphic 2 Cells 3 Whole table If .ApplyTo is omitted, the default for the selection is assumed.
.Shadow	Specifies whether to apply a shadow to the border of paragraphs or a graphic: 0 (zero) Does not apply a shadow. 1 Applies a shadow. You cannot apply a shadow to a table or table cells. If you want to apply a shadow to a paragraph or graphic, the item must have—or you must specify—matching right, left, top, and bottom borders. Otherwise, an error occurs.
.VertBorder	The line style for the vertical border between table cells, in the range 0 (zero), which is no border, through 11 (or 12 on the Macintosh). The border does not appear unless the table selection is at least two cells wide. (When applied to paragraphs, .VertBorder has the same effect as .LeftBorder.)
.TopColor, .LeftColor, .BottomColor, .RightColor, .HorizColor, .VertColor	The color to be applied to the specified borders, in the range from 0 (zero), which is Auto, through 16. For a list of colors and their values, see **CharColor**.
.FineShading	A shading pattern in the range 0 (zero) to 40 corresponding to a shading percentage in 2.5 percent increments. If .FineShading is anything but 0 (zero), .Shading is ignored.
.FromText	The distance of the border from adjacent text, in points or a text measurement. Valid only for paragraphs; otherwise, .FromText must be an empty string ("") or omitted or an error will occur.
.Shading	The shading pattern to be applied to the selection, in the range from 0 (zero), which is Clear, through 25. For a list of shading patterns and their values, see **ShadingPattern**.

Argument	Explanation
.Foreground	The color to be applied to the foreground of the shading, in the range from 0 (zero), which is Auto, through 16. For a list of colors and their values, see **CharColor**.
.Background	The color to be applied to the background of the shading, in the range from 0 (zero), which is Auto, through 16.
.Tab	Specifies which tab to select when you display the Borders And Shading dialog box with a **Dialog** or **Dialog**() instruction:
	0 (zero) Borders tab
	1 Shading tab

See Also   **BorderBottom, BorderInside, BorderLeft, BorderLineStyle, BorderNone, BorderOutside, BorderRight, BorderTop, EditFindBorder, EditReplaceBorder, ShadingPattern**

FormatBullet

Syntax   **FormatBullet** [**.Points** = *number*] [, **.Color** = *number*] [, **.Alignment** = *number*] [, **.Indent** = *number or text*] [, **.Space** = *number or text*] [, **.Hang** = *number*] [, **.CharNum** = *number*] [, **.Font** = *text*]

Remarks   Adds bullets to the selected paragraphs. The arguments for the **FormatBullet** statement correspond to the options in the Modify Bulleted List dialog box (Bulleted tab, Bullets And Numbering command, Format menu). You cannot display this dialog box using a **Dialog** or **Dialog**() instruction.

Argument	Explanation
.Points	The size of the bullets, in points
.Color	The color of the bullets (for a list of colors, see **CharColor**)
.Alignment	Specifies an alignment for the bullets within the space between the left indent and the first line of text; takes effect only if .Space is 0 (zero):
	0 (zero) or omitted Left
	1 Centered
	2 Right
.Indent	The distance between the left indent and the first line of text, in points or a text measurement
.Space	The distance between the bullet and the first line of text, in points or a text measurement

Argument	Explanation
.Hang	If 1, applies a hanging indent to the selected paragraphs
.CharNum	The sum of 31 and the number corresponding to the position of the symbol in the Symbol dialog box (Insert menu), counting from left to right. For example, to specify an omega (Ω), which is at position 56 on the table of symbols in the Symbol font, set .CharNum to 87.
.Font	The name of the font containing the symbol. Names of decorative fonts appear in the Font box in the Symbol dialog box.

See Also   **CharColor**, **FormatBulletsAndNumbering**, **FormatHeadingNumber**, **FormatMultilevel**, **FormatNumber**

FormatBulletDefault, FormatBulletDefault()

Syntax   **FormatBulletDefault** [*Add*]

FormatBulletDefault()

Remarks   The **FormatBulletDefault** statement adds bullets to or removes bullets from the selected paragraphs.

Argument	Explanation
Add	Specifies whether to add or remove bullets:
	0 (zero) Removes bullets. If the paragraph preceding or following the selection is not formatted as a list paragraph, the list format in the selection is removed along with the bullets.
	1 Adds bullets. If the paragraph preceding the selection already has bullets applied with the Bullets And Numbering command (Format menu), the selected paragraphs are formatted with matching bullets; otherwise, the default settings of the Bullets And Numbering dialog box (Format menu) are used.
	Omitted Toggles bullets.

The **FormatBulletDefault**() function returns the following values.

Value	Explanation
0 (zero)	If none of the selected paragraphs are bulleted or numbered
−1	If the selected paragraphs are not all bulleted, all "skipped," or all formatted with the same level of numbering
1	If all the selected paragraphs are bulleted

See Also   **FormatBulletsAndNumbering**, **FormatNumberDefault**, **SkipNumbering**

FormatBulletsAndNumbering

Syntax   **FormatBulletsAndNumbering** [**.Remove**] [**, .Hang** = *number*] [**, .Preset** = *number*]

Remarks   Adds bullets or numbers to the selected paragraphs based on the preset bullets or
numbering scheme you specify, or removes bullets and numbers. The arguments
for the **FormatBulletsAndNumbering** statement correspond to the options in the
Bullets And Numbering dialog box (Format menu). In Windows, you cannot
display this dialog box using a **Dialog** or **Dialog()** instruction. On the Macintosh,
you can display this dialog box using a **Dialog** or **Dialog()** instruction; however,
the Multilevel tab does not appear.

Argument	Explanation
.Remove	Removes bullets or numbering from the selection.
.Hang	If 1, applies a hanging indent to the selected paragraphs.
.Preset	A number corresponding to a bullets or numbering scheme in the Bullets And Numbering dialog box (Format menu)
	To determine the appropriate number, display the Bullets And Numbering dialog box and then select the tab with the scheme you want. Counting left to right, values for the preset schemes are:
	▪ 1 through 6 for the schemes on the Bulleted tab
	▪ 7 through 12 for the schemes on the Numbered tab
	▪ 13 through 18 for the schemes on the Multilevel tab

Example   This example adds diamond-shaped bullets to the selected paragraphs and formats
the paragraphs with a hanging indent:

```
FormatBulletsAndNumbering .Hang = 1, .Preset = 3
```

See Also   **FormatBulletDefault**, **FormatNumberDefault**, **RemoveBulletsNumbers**,
SkipNumbering

FormatCallout

Syntax   **FormatCallout** [**.Type** = *number*] [**, .Gap** = *number or text*] [**, .Angle** = *number*]
[**, .Drop** = *text*] [**, .Length** = *number or text*] [**, .Border** = *number*]
[**, .AutoAttach** = *number*] [**, .Accent** = *number*]

Remarks   Sets options for callout drawing objects. The arguments for the **FormatCallout**
statement correspond to the options in the Format Callout dialog box (Format
Callout button, Drawing toolbar).

Argument	Explanation
.Type	Specifies the type of callout:
	0 (zero) One line segment (vertical or horizontal)
	1 One line segment (vertical, horizontal, or diagonal)
	2 Two line segments
	3 Three line segments
.Gap	Specifies the distance between the callout line and the rectangle bounding the text area, in points or a text measurement.
.Angle	Specifies the angle for the callout line (affects the outermost line segment if .Type is set to 2 or 3):
	0 (zero) Any; Word adjusts the angle automatically as you move and size the callout.
	1 30 degrees
	2 45 degrees
	3 60 degrees
	4 90 degrees
.Drop	Specifies the starting position of the callout line with respect to the rectangle bounding the text area:
	Top Top of the text area (or if .Type is set to 1 and the line segment is horizontal, the right edge of the text area)
	Center Center of the text area
	Bottom Bottom of the text area (or if .Type is set to 1 and the line segment is horizontal, the left edge of the text area)
	You can also specify a positive text measurement for the distance between the top of the text area and the starting point of the callout line.
.Length	If .Type is set to 2 or 3, the length of the first segment in the callout line in twips (20 twips = 1 point) or a text measurement, or "Best Fit" if you want Word to adjust the length automatically as you size and position the callout.
.Border	If 1, applies a border around the callout text.
.AutoAttach	If 1, changes the starting position of the callout line automatically when the callout origin or the callout text is switched from left to right.
.Accent	If 1, adds a vertical line next to the text area.

For an example, see **DrawCallout**.

See Also   **DrawCallout, DrawGetCalloutTextBox, DrawSetCalloutTextBox, FormatDrawingObject**

FormatChangeCase

Syntax

FormatChangeCase [**.Type** = *number*]

Remarks

Changes the case of the selected text according to the specified type of capitalization. The arguments for the **FormatChangeCase** statement correspond to the options in the Change Case dialog box (Format menu).

Argument	Explanation
.Type	The type of capitalization you want to apply:
	0 (zero) or omitted Sentence case (capitalizes the first character in each selected sentence).
	1 lowercase (changes selected characters to lowercase).
	2 UPPERCASE (changes selected characters to uppercase).
	3 Title Case (capitalizes the first letter of each selected word).
	4 tOGGLE cASE (toggles the capitalization of each selected letter).

See Also

AllCaps, ChangeCase, LCase$(), SmallCaps, UCase$()

FormatColumns

Syntax

FormatColumns [**.Columns** = *number or text*] [**, .ColumnNo** = *text*]
[**, .ColumnWidth** = *text*] [**, .ColumnSpacing** = *text*] [**, .EvenlySpaced** = *number*]
[**, .ApplyColsTo** = *number*] [**, .ColLine** = *number*] [**, .StartNewCol** = *number*]

Remarks

Formats all or part of the document with the specified number of columns, or changes the width of and space between existing columns. The arguments for the **FormatColumns** statement correspond to the options in the Columns dialog box (Format menu).

Argument	Explanation
.Columns	The number of columns to apply to the portion of the document specified by .ApplyColsTo
.ColumnNo	If .EvenlySpaced is set to 0 (zero), the number of the column to format; if you are returning information from a **FormatColumns** dialog record, the column for which you want to return the width
	To set the width of any column independently of other columns, you need to include an additional **FormatColumns** instruction to set the width of the last column. If you include only one **FormatColumns** instruction, the resulting number of columns will be the same as .ColumnNo. For example, if you change the width of the first column in a section containing three columns, there will be only one column after the instruction runs. To preserve the three-column format, you need to include an additional **FormatColumns** instruction and set .ColumnNo to 3.

Argument	Explanation
.ColumnWidth	The width of the column specified by .ColumnNo, or if .EvenlySpaced is set to 1, the width of each column in the portion of the document specified by .ApplyColsTo
.ColumnSpacing	The space between columns
.EvenlySpaced	If 1, makes each column the same width
.ApplyColsTo	Specifies the portion of the document to apply the column format to:

0 (zero)   This section

1   This Point Forward

2   Selected Sections

3   Selected Text

4   Whole Document

Argument	Explanation
.ColLine	If 1, adds a line between columns
.StartNewCol	If 1, corresponds to selecting the Start New Column check box (effective only if This Point Forward is specified by .ApplyColsTo)

Example

This example formats the current section into three columns of equal width and specifies that a vertical line appear between columns:

```
FormatColumns .Columns = "3", .EvenlySpaced = 1, .ColLine = 1
```

See Also

TableColumnWidth

FormatDefineStyleBorders

Syntax

FormatDefineStyleBorders [**.ApplyTo** = *number*] [, **.Shadow** = *number*] [, **.TopBorder** = *number*] [, **.LeftBorder** = *number*] [, **.BottomBorder** = *number*] [, **.RightBorder** = *number*] [, **.HorizBorder** = *number*] [, **.VertBorder** = *number*] [, **.TopColor** = *number*] [, **.LeftColor** = *number*] [, **.BottomColor** = *number*] [, **.RightColor** = *number*] [, **.HorizColor** = *number*] [, **.VertColor** = *number*] [, **.FineShading** = *number*] [, **.FromText** = *number or text*] [, **.Shading** = *number*] [, **.Foreground** = *number*] [, **.Background** = *number*] [, **.Tab** = *number*]

Remarks

Sets border and shading formats for either the current style or the style specified in a **FormatStyle** instruction containing the .Define argument. Note that when modifying the style specified with **FormatStyle**, the **FormatDefineStyleBorders** instruction follows the **FormatStyle** instruction.

The arguments for the **FormatDefineStyleBorders** statement correspond to the options in the Borders And Shading dialog box (Format menu). For argument descriptions, see **FormatBordersAndShading**. For examples of how to use similar statements to define a style, see **FormatDefineStyleFont** and **FormatDefineStylePara**.

See Also   **FormatBordersAndShading**, **FormatDefineStyleFont**, **FormatDefineStylePara**, **FormatStyle**

FormatDefineStyleFont

Syntax   **FormatDefineStyleFont** [**.Points** = *number*] [, **.Underline** = *number*] [, **.Color** = *number*] [, **.Strikethrough** = *number*] [, **.Superscript** = *value*] [, **.Subscript** = *value*] [, **.Hidden** = *number*] [, **.SmallCaps** = *number*] [, **.AllCaps** = *number*] [, **.Spacing** = *value*] [, **.Position** = *number or text*] [, **.Kerning** = *number*] [, **.KerningMin** = *number or text*] [, **.Default**] [, **.Tab** = *number*] [, **.Font** = *text*] [, **.Bold** = *number*] [, **.Italic** = *number*]

Remarks   Sets character formats for either the current style or the style specified in a **FormatStyle** instruction containing the .Define argument. Note that when modifying the style specified with **FormatStyle**, the **FormatDefineStyleFont** instruction follows the **FormatStyle** instruction.

The arguments for the **FormatDefineStyleFont** statement correspond to options in the Font dialog box (Format menu). For argument descriptions, see **FormatFont**.

Example   This example defines the character formatting of the "TestMe" style as 10-point, bold, and small caps. Word creates the style if it does not already exist.

```
FormatStyle .Name = "TestMe", .Define
FormatDefineStyleFont .Points = "10", .Bold = 1, .SmallCaps = 1
```

See Also   **FormatFont**, **FormatStyle**

FormatDefineStyleFrame

Syntax   **FormatDefineStyleFrame** [**.Wrap** = *number*] [, **.WidthRule** = *number*] [, **.FixedWidth** = *number or text*] [, **.HeightRule** = *number*] [, **.FixedHeight** = *number or text*] [, **.PositionHorz** = *number or text*] [, **.PositionHorzRel** = *number*] [, **.DistFromText** = *number or text*] [, **.PositionVert** = *number or text*] [, **.PositionVertRel** = *number*] [, **.DistVertFromText** = *number or text*] [, **.MoveWithText** = *number*] [, **.LockAnchor** = *number*] [, **.RemoveFrame**]

Remarks   Sets frame formats for either the current style or the style specified in a
FormatStyle instruction containing the .Define argument. Note that when
modifying the style specified with **FormatStyle**, the **FormatDefineStyleFrame**
instruction follows the **FormatStyle** instruction.

The arguments for the **FormatDefineStyleFrame** statement correspond to the
options in the Frame dialog box (Format menu). For argument descriptions, see
FormatFrame. For examples of how to use similar statements to define a style,
see **FormatDefineStyleFont** and **FormatDefineStylePara**.

See Also   **FormatDefineStyleFont, FormatDefineStylePara, FormatFrame,**
FormatStyle

FormatDefineStyleLang

Syntax   **FormatDefineStyleLang .Language** = *text* [, **.Default**]

Remarks   Sets the language format for either the current style or the style specified in
a **FormatStyle** instruction containing the .Define argument. Note that when
modifying the style specified with **FormatStyle**, the **FormatDefineStyleLang**
instruction follows the **FormatStyle** instruction.

The arguments for the **FormatDefineStyleLang** statement correspond to the
options in the Language dialog box (Tools menu). For argument descriptions, see
ToolsLanguage. For examples of how to use similar statements to define a style,
see **FormatDefineStyleFont** and **FormatDefineStylePara**.

See Also   **FormatDefineStyleFont, FormatDefineStylePara, FormatStyle,**
ToolsLanguage

FormatDefineStyleNumbers

Syntax   **FormatDefineStyleNumbers** [**.Points** = *text*] [, **.Color** = *number*]
[, **.Before** = *text*] [, **.Type** = *number*] [, **.After** = *text*] [, **.StartAt** = *text*]
[, **.Include** = *number*] [, **.Alignment** = *number*] [, **.Indent** = *text*]
[, **.Space** = *number or text*] [, **.Hang** = *number*] [, **.Level** = *text*]
[, **.CharNum** = *text*] [, **.Font** = *text*] [, **.Strikethrough** = *number*]
[, **.Bold** = *number*] [, **.Italic** = *number*] [, **.Underline** = *number*]

Remarks   Sets number formats for either the current style or the style specified in a
FormatStyle instruction containing the .Define argument. Note that when
modifying the style specified with **FormatStyle**, the
FormatDefineStyleNumbers instruction follows the **FormatStyle** instruction.

The arguments for the **FormatDefineStyleNumbers** statement correspond to the options in the Modify List dialog box (Bullets And Numbering command, Format menu). For argument descriptions, see **FormatBullet**, **FormatMultilevel**, and **FormatNumber**. For examples of how to use similar statements to define a style, see **FormatDefineStyleFont** and **FormatDefineStylePara**.

See Also   **FormatBullet**, **FormatDefineStyleFont**, **FormatDefineStylePara**, **FormatMultilevel**, **FormatNumber**, **FormatStyle**

FormatDefineStylePara

Syntax   **FormatDefineStylePara** [**.LeftIndent** = *number or text*]
[**, .RightIndent** = *number or text*] [**, .Before** = *number or text*]
[**, .After** = *number or text*] [**, .LineSpacingRule** = *number*]
[**, .LineSpacing** = *number or text*] [**, .Alignment** = *number*]
[**, .WidowControl** = *number*] [**, .KeepWithNext** = *number*]
[**, .KeepTogether** = *number*] [**, .PageBreak** = *number*]
[**, .NoLineNum** = *number*] [**, .DontHyphen** = *number*] [**, .Tab** = *number*]
[**, .FirstIndent** = *number or text*]

Remarks   Sets paragraph formats for either the current style or the style specified in a **FormatStyle** instruction containing the .Define argument. Note that when modifying the style specified with **FormatStyle**, the **FormatDefineStylePara** instruction follows the **FormatStyle** instruction.

The arguments for the **FormatDefineStylePara** statement correspond to the options in the Paragraph dialog box (Format menu). For argument descriptions, see **FormatParagraph**.

Example   This example adds 4 points of Before formatting and 4 points of After formatting to the definition of the style "TestMe":

```
FormatStyle .Name = "TestMe", .Define
FormatDefineStylePara .Before = "4 pt", .After = "4 pt"
```

See Also   **FormatParagraph**, **FormatStyle**

FormatDefineStyleTabs

Syntax   **FormatDefineStyleTabs** [**.Position** = *text*] [**, .DefTabs** = *number or text*]
[**, .Align** = *number*] [**, .Leader** = *number*] [**, .Set**] [**, .Clear**] [**, .ClearAll**]

Remarks   Sets tab formats for either the current style or the style specified in a **FormatStyle** instruction containing the .Define argument. Note that when modifying the style specified with **FormatStyle**, the **FormatDefineStyleTabs** instruction follows the **FormatStyle** instruction.

The arguments for the **FormatDefineStyleTabs** statement correspond to the options in the Tabs dialog box (Format menu). For argument descriptions, see **FormatTabs**. For examples of how to use similar statements to define a style, see **FormatDefineStyleFont** and **FormatDefineStylePara**.

See Also   **FormatDefineStyleFont**, **FormatDefineStylePara**, **FormatStyle**, **FormatTabs**

FormatDrawingObject

Syntax   **FormatDrawingObject** [**.Tab** = *number*] [**, .FillColor** = *number or text*]
[**, .LineColor** = *number or text*] [**, .FillPatternColor** = *number or text*]
[**, .FillPattern** = *number or text*] [**, .LineType** = *number*] [**, .LineStyle** = *number*]
[**, .LineWeight** = *number or text*] [**, .ArrowStyle** = *number*]
[**, .ArrowWidth** = *number*] [**, .ArrowLength** = *number*] [**, .Shadow** = *number*]
[**, .RoundCorners** = *number*] [**, .HorizontalPos** = *number or text*]
[**, .HorizontalFrom** = *number*] [**, .VerticalPos** = *number or text*]
[**, .VerticalFrom** = *number*] [**, .LockAnchor** = *number*]
[**, .Height** = *number or text*] [**, .Width** = *number or text*]
[**, .InternalMargin** = *number or text*]

Remarks   Changes the fill color, line style, size, and position of the selected drawing object or objects. The arguments for the **FormatDrawingObject** statement correspond to the options in the Drawing Object dialog box (Format menu).

Argument	Explanation
.Tab	Specifies the tab to select when you display the Drawing Object dialog box with a **Dialog** or **Dialog**( ) instruction:
	0 (zero) Fill tab
	1 Line tab
	2 Size And Position tab
.FillColor	Specifies a fill color. To specify a percentage of gray, double the percentage of gray you want and make it negative (for example, for 5 percent gray, specify –10; for 37.5 percent gray, specify –75). To specify a color, use a value between 1 and 16, as described in **CharColor**, where 0 (zero) indicates no color.
.LineColor	Specifies a line color. For values, see .FillColor.
.FillPatternColor	Specifies the pattern color. For values, see .FillColor.
.FillPattern	Specifies the fill pattern:
	0 (zero) Sets both .FillColor and .FillPattern to "None."
	1 through 25 Specifies an item in the Patterns box on the Fill tab: 1 corresponds to the first item ("None"), 2 to the second, and so on.

Argument	Explanation
.LineType	Specifies whether to show the line:
	0 (zero) Hides the line; only the fill and the arrowheads (if any) show.
	1 Shows the line defined by .LineColor, .LineStyle, and .LineWeight.
.LineStyle	Specifies a line style in the Style box on the Line tab, where 0 (zero) is the first item, 1 is the second item, and so on through 4.
.LineWeight	The line width, in points or a text measurement.
.ArrowStyle	Specifies the arrow style for a linear drawing object: 0 (zero) corresponds to the first item (no arrowheads) in the Style box under Arrow Head, 1 to the second item, and so on through 6.
.ArrowWidth	Specifies the width of the arrowhead for a linear drawing object:
	0 (zero) Narrow
	1 Medium
	2 Thick
.ArrowLength	Specifies the length of the arrowhead for a linear drawing object:
	0 (zero) Short
	1 Medium
	2 Long
.Shadow	If 1, applies a shadow effect to the drawing object.
.RoundCorners	If 1, rounds the corners of a rectangular drawing object.
.HorizontalPos	The distance, in points or a text measurement, between the reference point specified by .HorizontalFrom and the drawing object.
.HorizontalFrom	Specifies the reference point from which the horizontal position of the drawing object is measured:
	0 (zero) Margin
	1 Page
	2 Column
.VerticalPos	The distance, in points or a text measurement, between the reference point specified by .VerticalFrom and the drawing object.
.VerticalFrom	Specifies the reference point from which the vertical position of the drawing object is measured:
	0 (zero) Margin
	1 Page
	2 Paragraph

Argument	Explanation
.LockAnchor	If 1, the drawing-object anchor remains fixed when the associated drawing object is repositioned. A locked anchor cannot be repositioned.
.Height	The height of the drawing object, in points or a text measurement.
.Width	The width of the drawing object, in points or a text measurement.
.InternalMargin	A measurement, in twips (20 twips = 1 point) or a text measurement, for the internal margin within a text box or callout drawing object.

Example

This example moves the selected drawing object down 10 points and to the right 10 points, assuming that points is the current unit of measurement:

```
Dim dlg As FormatDrawingObject
GetCurValues dlg
dlg.HorizontalPos = Val(dlg.HorizontalPos) + 10
dlg.VerticalPos = Val(dlg.VerticalPos) + 10
FormatDrawingObject dlg
```

See Also

DrawAlign, **DrawReshape**, **DrawSnapToGrid**

FormatDropCap

Syntax

FormatDropCap [**.Position** = *number*] [**, .Font** = *text*]
[**, .DropHeight** = *number or text*] [**, .DistFromText** = *number or text*]

Remarks

Inserts a frame for the first character of the current paragraph so that it becomes a dropped capital letter. The arguments for the **FormatDropCap** statement correspond to the options in the Drop Cap dialog box (Format menu).

Argument	Explanation
.Position	Specifies the positioning for the dropped capital letter or removes dropped capital letter formatting.
	0 (zero) or omitted No dropped capital letter formatting
	1 Dropped (lines in the paragraph wrap around the dropped capital letter)
	2 In Margin (lines in the paragraph remain flush)
.Font	The font you want for the dropped capital letter
.DropHeight	The height of the dropped capital letter specified in lines of surrounding text
.DistFromText	The distance between the dropped capital letter and the rest of the paragraph in points or a text measurement

Example

This example makes the first character of every section a dropped capital letter. The instruction `.EditGoTo .Destination = "s"` moves the insertion point to the beginning of the following section. As soon as the function `CmpBookmarks("tmp", "\Sel")` returns a value of 0 (zero), indicating that the insertion point did not move and that there are no more sections, the temporary bookmark is deleted and the macro ends.

```
StartOfDocument
FormatDropCap .Position = 1, .DropHeight = "3"
EditBookmark .Name = "temp", .Add
EditGoTo .Destination = "s"
While CmpBookmarks("temp", "\Sel") <> 0
    FormatDropCap .Position = 1, .DropHeight = "3"
    CharLeft
    EditBookmark .Name = "temp", .Add
    EditGoTo .Destination = "s"
Wend
EditBookmark .Name = "temp", .Delete
```

See Also

FormatFrame, InsertFrame

FormatFont

Syntax

FormatFont [**.Points** = *number*] [, **.Underline** = *number*] [, **.Color** = *number*] [, **.Strikethrough** = *number*] [, **.Superscript** = *number*] [, **.Subscript** = *number*] [, **.Shadow** = *number*] [, **.Hidden** = *number*] [, **.SmallCaps** = *number*] [, **.AllCaps** = *number*] [, **.Outline** = *number*] [, **.Spacing** = *number*] [, **.Position** = *number or text*] [, **.Kerning** = *number*] [, **.KerningMin** = *number or text*] [, **.Default**] [, **.Tab** = *number*] [, **.Font** = *text*] [, **.Bold** = *number*] [, **.Italic** = *number*]

Remarks

Applies character formatting to the selected text. The arguments for the **FormatFont** statement correspond to the options in the Font dialog box (Format menu).

Argument	Explanation
.Points	The font size, in points
.Underline	Applies a type of underlining:
	0 (zero) None
	1 Single
	2 Words Only
	3 Double
	4 Dotted
.Color	Color of the text (for a list of colors, see **CharColor**).

Argument	Explanation
.Strikethrough	If 1, applies strikethrough formatting.
.Superscript	If 1, applies superscript formatting.
.Shadow	If 1, applies shadow formatting (Macintosh only).
.Subscript	If 1, applies subscript formatting.
.Hidden	If 1, applies hidden formatting.
.SmallCaps	If 1, applies small caps formatting.
.AllCaps	If 1, applies all caps formatting.
.Outline	If 1, applies outline formatting (Macintosh only).
.Spacing	The spacing between characters, in twips (20 twips = 1 point; 72 points = 1 inch) or a text measurement: 0 (zero) Normal >0 Expanded by the specified distance <0 Condensed by the specified distance
.Position	The character's position relative to the baseline, in units of 0.5 point or a text measurement: 0 (zero) Normal >0 Raised by the specified distance <0 Lowered by the specified distance
.Kerning	If 1, enables automatic kerning (character spacing).
.KerningMin	If .Kerning is set to 1, sets a minimum font size, in points, for automatic kerning.
.Default	Sets the character formats of the Normal style.
.Tab	Specifies which tab to select when you display the Font dialog box with a **Dialog** or **Dialog**() instruction: 0 (zero) Font tab 1 Character Spacing tab
.Font	The name of the font
.Bold	If 1, applies bold formatting.
.Italic	If 1, applies italic formatting.

Example

This example demonstrates how measurements other than twips or points may be used in **FormatFont** instructions by specifying a text measurement. This instruction positions the selected characters .25 centimeter above the baseline.

```
FormatFont .Position = ".25 cm"
```

See Also   **AllCaps, Bold, CharColor, DoubleUnderline, EditFindFont, EditReplaceFont, Font, FontSize, FormatChangeCase, FormatDefineStyleFont, GrowFont, Hidden, Italic, Outline, ResetChar, Shadow, ShrinkFont, SmallCaps, Strikethrough, Subscript, Superscript, Underline, WordUnderline**

FormatFrame

Syntax   **FormatFrame** [**.Wrap** = *number*] [**, .WidthRule** = *number*]
[**, .FixedWidth** = *number or text*] [**, .HeightRule** = *number*]
[**, .FixedHeight** = *number or text*] [**, .PositionHorz** = *number or text*]
[**, .PositionHorzRel** = *number*] [**, .DistFromText** = *number or text*]
[**, .PositionVert** = *number or text*] [**, .PositionVertRel** = *number*]
[**, .DistVertFromText** = *number or text*] [**, .MoveWithText** = *number*]
[**, .LockAnchor** = *number*] [**, .RemoveFrame**]

Remarks   Positions and sets options for the selected frame. If the insertion point or selection is not within a frame, an error occurs. The arguments for the **FormatFrame** statement correspond to the options in the Frame dialog box (Format menu).

Argument	Explanation
.Wrap	Specifies a Text Wrapping option:
	0 (zero) Text does not wrap around the frame.
	1 Text wraps around the frame.
.WidthRule	The rule used to determine the width of the frame:
	0 (zero) Auto (determined by paragraph width).
	1 Exactly (width will be exactly .FixedWidth).
.FixedWidth	If .WidthRule is 1, the width of the frame in points or a text measurement.
.HeightRule	The rule used to determine the height of the frame:
	0 (zero) Auto (determined by paragraph height).
	1 At Least (height will be no less than .FixedHeight).
	2 Exactly (height will be exactly .FixedHeight).
.FixedHeight	If .HeightRule is 1 or 2, the height of the frame in points or a text measurement (72 points = 1 inch).
.PositionHorz	Horizontal distance, in points or a text measurement, from the edge of the item specified by .PositionHorzRel. You can also specify "Left," "Right," "Center," "Inside," and "Outside" as text arguments.

Argument	Explanation
.PositionHorzRel	Specifies that the horizontal position is relative to: 0 (zero) Margin 1 Page 2 Column
.DistFromText	Distance between the frame and the text to its left, right, or both, in points or a text measurement.
.PositionVert	Vertical distance, in points or a text measurement, from the edge of the item specified by .PositionVertRel. You can also specify "Top," "Bottom," and "Center" as text arguments.
.PositionVertRel	Specifies that the vertical position is relative to: 0 (zero) Margin 1 Page 2 Paragraph
.DistVertFromText	Distance between the frame and the text above, below, or both, in points or a text measurement.
.MoveWithText	If 1, the frame moves as text is added or removed around it.
.LockAnchor	If 1, the frame anchor (which indicates where the frame will appear in normal view) remains fixed when the associated frame is repositioned. A locked frame anchor cannot be repositioned.
.RemoveFrame	Removes the frame format from the selected text or graphic.

Example

This example selects and frames the current paragraph and then formats the frame as left-aligned, relative to the current column, with a 0.13-inch gap between the frame and text above and below:

```
EditGoTo "\Para"
InsertFrame
FormatFrame .PositionHorz = 0, .PositionHorzRel = 2, \
    .DistVertFromText = "0.13 in"
```

See Also

EditFindFrame, EditReplaceFrame, FormatDefineStyleFrame, InsertFrame, RemoveFrames

FormatHeaderFooterLink

Syntax

FormatHeaderFooterLink

Remarks

Replaces the current header or footer with the corresponding header or footer from the previous section. An error occurs if the previous section does not contain a corresponding header or footer.

See Also

ShowNextHeaderFooter, ShowPrevHeaderFooter, ToggleHeaderFooterLink, ViewHeader

FormatHeadingNumber

Syntax

FormatHeadingNumber [.**Points** = *number*] [, .**Color** = *number*]
[, .**Before** = *text*] [, .**Type** = *number*] [, .**After** = *text*] [, .**StartAt** = *number*]
[, .**Include** = *number*] [, .**Alignment** = *number*] [, .**Indent** = *number or text*]
[, .**Space** = *number or text*] [, .**Hang** = *number*] [, .**RestartNum** = *number*]
[, .**Level** = *number*] [, .**Font** = *text*] [, .**Strikethrough** = *number*]
[, .**Bold** = *number*] [, .**Italic** = *number*] [, .**Underline** = *number*]

Remarks

Applies numbers to all paragraphs in the document formatted with one of the nine built-in heading level styles, or changes numbering options for a specified heading level. The arguments for the **FormatHeadingNumber** statement correspond to the options in the Modify Heading Numbering dialog box (Heading Numbering command, Format menu).

Argument	Explanation
.Points, .Color, .Font, .Strikethrough, .Bold, .Italic, .Underline	Apply character formatting to numbers at the specified level. For argument descriptions, see **FormatFont**.
.Before, .After, .Alignment, .Indent, .Space, .Hang	Set options for numbers at the specified level. For argument descriptions, see **FormatNumber**.
.Type	Specifies a format for numbering headings at the specified level:
	0 (zero) 1, 2, 3, 4
	1 I, II, III, IV
	2 i, ii, iii, iv
	3 A, B, C, D
	4 a, b, c, d
	5 1st, 2nd, …
	6 One, Two, …
	7 First, Second, …
.StartAt	The number for the first heading in each sequence of headings of the specified level. If .Type is 3 or 4, .StartAt corresponds to the position in the alphabet of the starting letter.
.Include	Specifies whether to include numbers and position options from the previous headings for numbers at the specified level:
	0 (zero) Includes neither numbers nor position options.
	1 Includes a series of numbers from higher-level headings before the numbers at the specified level.
	2 Includes both numbers from higher-level headings and position options from the previous level.

Argument	Explanation
.RestartNum	If 1, restarts heading numbering at each new section.
.Level	A number from 1 through 9 corresponding to the heading level whose numbering options you want to change.

See Also   **FormatBullet, FormatHeadingNumbering, FormatMultilevel, FormatNumber**

FormatHeadingNumbering

Syntax   **FormatHeadingNumbering [.Remove] [, .Preset** = *number*]

Remarks   Adds or removes numbers for the headings in the selection. A heading is a paragraph formatted with one of the nine built-in heading styles.

Argument	Explanation
.Remove	Removes numbers from the headings in the selection.
.Preset	A number corresponding to a numbering scheme in the Heading Numbering dialog box (Format menu).
	To determine the appropriate number, open the Heading Numbering dialog box and determine the number of the scheme. From left to right, the preset schemes are numbered 1 through 6.

See Also   **FormatBulletsAndNumbering**

FormatMultilevel

Syntax   **FormatMultilevel [.Points** = *number*] [, **.Color** = *number*] [, **.Before** = *text*] [, **.Type** = *number*] [, **.After** = *text*] [, **.StartAt** = *number*] [, **.Include** = *number*] [, **.Alignment** = *number*] [, **.Indent** = *number or text*] [, **.Space** = *number or text*] [, **.Hang** = *number*] [, **.Level** = *number*] [, **.Font** = *text*] [, **.Strikethrough** = *number*] [, **.Bold** = *number*] [, **.Italic** = *number*] [, **.Underline** = *number*]

Remarks   Applies multilevel list numbers to the selected paragraphs or changes numbering options for a specified level. The arguments for the **FormatMultilevel** statement correspond to the options in the Modify Multilevel List dialog box (Multilevel tab, Bullets And Numbering command, Format menu). You cannot display this dialog box using a **Dialog** or **Dialog**() instruction.

Argument	Explanation
.Level	A number from 1 through 9 corresponding to the heading level whose numbering options you want to change.
	Note that if you specify .Level, the options you set in the **FormatMultilevel** instruction are not applied. To apply the settings, include a second **FormatMultilevel** instruction in which .Level is not specified.
.Points, .Color, .Font, .Strikethrough, .Bold, .Italic, .Underline	Apply character formatting to numbers at the specified level. For individual argument descriptions, see **FormatFont**.
.Before, .After, .Alignment, .Indent, .Space, .Hang	Set options for numbers at the specified level. For argument descriptions, see **FormatNumber**.
.Type	Specifies a format for numbering headings at the specified level:
	0 (zero) 1, 2, 3, 4
	1 I, II, III, IV
	2 i, ii, iii, iv
	3 A, B, C, D
	4 a, b, c, d
	5 1st, 2nd, …
	6 One, Two, …
	7 First, Second, …
.StartAt	The number for the first heading in each sequence of headings of the specified level. If .Type is 3 or 4, .StartAt corresponds to the position in the alphabet of the starting letter.
.Include	Specifies whether to include numbers and position options from the previous headings for numbers at the specified level:
	0 (zero) Includes neither numbers nor position options.
	1 Includes a series of numbers from higher-level headings before the numbers at the specified level.
	2 Includes both numbers from higher level-headings and position options from the previous level.

See Also   **FormatBullet**, **FormatBulletsAndNumbering**, **FormatHeadingNumber**, **FormatNumber**

FormatNumber

Syntax

FormatNumber [**.Points** = *number*] [, **.Color** = *number*] [, **.Before** = *text*]
[, **.Type** = *number*] [, **.After** = *text*] [, **.StartAt** = *number*] [, **.Include** = *number*]
[, **.Alignment** = *number*] [, **.Indent** = *number or text*] [, **.Space** = *number or text*]
[, **.Hang** = *number*] [, **.Font** = *text*] [, **.Strikethrough** = *number*]
[, **.Bold** = *number*] [, **.Italic** = *number*] [, **.Underline** = *number*]

Remarks

Numbers the selected paragraphs. The arguments for the **FormatNumber**
statement correspond to the options in the Modify Numbered List dialog box
(Numbered tab, Bullets And Numbering command, Format menu). You cannot
display this dialog box using a **Dialog** or **Dialog()** instruction.

Argument	Explanation
.Points, .Color, .Font, .Strikethrough, .Bold, .Italic, .Underline	Apply character formatting to numbers at the specified level. For argument descriptions, see **FormatFont**.
.Before	The text, if any, you want to appear before each number.
.Type	Specifies a format for numbering lists:
	0 (zero) 1, 2, 3, 4
	1 I, II, III, IV
	2 i, ii, iii, iv
	3 A, B, C, D
	4 a, b, c, d
.After	The text, if any, you want to appear after each number.
.StartAt	The number for the first selected paragraph. If .Type is 3 or 4, .StartAt corresponds to the position in the alphabet of the starting letter.
.Include	Specifies whether to include numbers and position options from the previous headings for numbers at the specified level:
	0 (zero) Includes neither numbers nor position options.
	1 Includes a series of numbers from higher-level headings before the numbers at the specified level.
	2 Includes both numbers from higher-level headings and position options from the previous level.
.Alignment	Specifies an alignment for the numbers within the space between the left indent and the first line of text; takes effect only if .Space is 0 (zero):
	0 (zero) or omitted Left
	1 Centered
	2 Right

Argument	Explanation
.Indent	The distance between the left indent and the first line of text, in points or a text measurement.
.Space	The distance between the number and the first line of text, in points or a text measurement.
.Hang	If 1, applies a hanging indent to the selected paragraphs.

See Also   **FormatBullet**, **FormatBulletsAndNumbering**, **FormatHeadingNumber**, **FormatMultilevel**

FormatNumberDefault, FormatNumberDefault()

Syntax   **FormatNumberDefault** [*On*]

FormatNumberDefault()

Remarks   The **FormatNumberDefault** statement adds numbers to or removes numbers from the selected paragraphs.

Argument	Explanation
On	Specifies whether to add or remove numbers:
	0 (zero) Removes numbers. If the paragraph preceding or following the selection is not formatted as a list paragraph, the list format in the selection is removed along with the numbers.
	1 Adds numbers. If the paragraph preceding or following the selection already has numbers applied with the Bullets And Numbering command (Format menu), the selected paragraphs are formatted with the same numbering scheme; otherwise, the default settings of the Bullets And Numbering dialog box are used.
	Omitted Toggles numbers.

The **FormatNumberDefault**() function returns the following values.

Value	Explanation
0 (zero)	If none of the selected paragraphs are numbered or bulleted
−1	If the selected paragraphs are not all bulleted, all "skipped," or all formatted with the same level of numbering
1–9	If all the selected paragraphs are numbered with the same level of numbering in a multilevel list

Value	Explanation
10	If all the selected paragraphs are numbered with one of the six schemes on the Numbered tab in the Bullets And Numbering dialog box
11	If all the selected paragraphs are bulleted
12	If all the selected paragraphs are "skipped"

See Also **FormatBulletDefault**, **FormatBulletsAndNumbering**, **SkipNumbering**

FormatPageNumber

Syntax **FormatPageNumber** [**.ChapterNumber** = *number*] [, **.NumRestart** = *number*] [, **.NumFormat** = *number*] [, **.StartingNum** = *number*] [, **.Level** = *number*] [, **.Separator** = *number*]

Remarks Determines the format of the page numbers used in the current section. The arguments for the **FormatPageNumber** statement correspond to the options in the Page Number Format dialog box (Page Numbers command, Insert menu).

Argument	Explanation
.ChapterNumber	If 1, includes the chapter number with the page number.
.NumRestart	Determines whether or not a different starting number can be set:
	0 (zero) Selects the Continue From Previous Section option (the setting for .StartingNum has no effect).
	1 Selects the Start At option (numbering begins at the number set for .StartingNum).
.NumFormat	The format for the page numbers:
	0 (zero) 1 2 3…
	1 a b c…
	2 A B C…
	3 i ii iii…
	4 I II III…
.StartingNum	The current section's starting page number (if .NumRestart is set to 1).

Argument	Explanation
.Level	A number corresponding to the heading level applied to the first paragraph in each chapter (for including the chapter number with the page number).
.Separator	If you specify .ChapterNumber, specifies the separator between the chapter number and the page number:

0 (zero) Hyphen

1 Period

2 Colon

3 Em dash

4 En dash

See Also   **InsertPageNumbers**

FormatParagraph

Syntax

FormatParagraph [**.LeftIndent** = *number or text*]
[**, .RightIndent** = *number or text*] [**, .Before** = *number or text*]
[**, .After** = *number or text*] [**, .LineSpacingRule** = *number*]
[**, .LineSpacing** = *number or text*] [**, .Alignment** = *number*]
[**, .WidowControl** = *number*] [**, .KeepWithNext** = *number*]
[**, .KeepTogether** = *number*] [**, .PageBreak** = *number*]
[**, .NoLineNum** = *number*] [**, .DontHyphen** = *number*] [**, .Tab** = *number*]
[**, .FirstIndent** = *number or text*]

Remarks

Applies paragraph formatting to the selected paragraphs. The arguments for the **FormatParagraph** statement correspond to the options in the Paragraph dialog box (Format menu).

Argument	Explanation
.LeftIndent	The left indent in points or a text measurement
.RightIndent	The right indent in points or a text measurement
.Before	The space before the paragraph in points or a text measurement

Argument	Explanation
.After	The space after the paragraph in points or a text measurement
.LineSpacingRule	The rule used to determine line spacing:
	0 (zero) or omitted Single
	1 1.5 Lines
	2 Double
	3 At Least
	4 Exactly
	5 Multiple
	If you specify Single, 1.5 Lines, or Double, and also specify a value for .LineSpacing, the .LineSpacing value takes precedence.
.LineSpacing	The spacing for all lines within the paragraph (used when .LineSpacingRule is At Least, Exactly, or Multiple)
.Alignment	Sets a paragraph alignment:
	0 (zero) Left
	1 Centered
	2 Right
	3 Justified
.WidowControl	If 1, prevents a page break from leaving a single line of the paragraph at the top or bottom of a page (corresponds to selecting the Widow/Orphan Control check box)
.KeepWithNext	If 1, keeps the paragraph on the same page as the paragraph that follows (corresponds to selecting the Keep With Next check box)
.KeepTogether	If 1, keeps all lines in the paragraph on the same page (corresponds to selecting the Keep Lines Together check box)
.PageBreak	If 1, makes the paragraph always appear at the top of a new page (corresponds to selecting the Page Break Before check box)
.NoLineNum	If 1, turns off line numbering for the paragraph (corresponds to selecting the Suppress Line Numbers check box)
.DontHyphen	If 1, excludes the paragraph from automatic hyphenation (corresponds to selecting the Don't Hyphenate check box)
.Tab	Specifies which tab to select when you display the Paragraph dialog box with a **Dialog** or **Dialog**() instruction:
	0 (zero) Indents And Spacing tab
	1 Text Flow tab
.FirstIndent	The first-line indent in points or a text measurement

Example   This example sets justified alignment and adds 1 inch of space above and below each paragraph in the selection:

```
FormatParagraph .Alignment = 3, .Before = "1 in", .After = "1 in"
```

See Also   **EditFindPara, EditReplacePara, FormatBordersAndShading, FormatDefineStylePara, FormatStyle, FormatTabs, ParaKeepLinesTogether, ParaKeepWithNext, ParaPageBreakBefore, ParaWidowOrphanControl, Style**

FormatPicture

Syntax   **FormatPicture** [**.SetSize** = *number*] [, **.CropLeft** = *number or text*] [, **.CropRight** = *number or text*] [, **.CropTop** = *number or text*] [, **.CropBottom** = *number or text*] [, **.ScaleX** = *number or text*] [, **.ScaleY** = *number or text*] [, **.SizeX** = *number or text*] [, **.SizeY** = *number or text*]

Remarks   Applies formatting to the selected graphic. If the current selection is not a graphic or contains a mixture of text and graphics, an error occurs. The arguments for the **FormatPicture** statement correspond to the options in the Picture dialog box (Format menu).

Argument	Explanation
.SetSize	Indicates what arguments are used to determine the size of the graphic when both the scale and size are specified:
	0 (zero) .ScaleX and .ScaleY are used to format the graphic.
	1 .SizeX and .SizeY are used to format the graphic.
.CropLeft, .CropRight, .CropTop, .CropBottom	Amount to crop the graphic, in points (72 points = 1 inch) or a text measurement. If you specify a negative value, the graphic is not cropped. Instead, the amount of white space around the graphic is increased.
.ScaleX, .ScaleY	The horizontal and vertical proportions of the graphic, as percentages of the original width and height.
.SizeX, .SizeY	The horizontal and vertical dimensions of the graphic, in points or a text measurement.

Example   This example resizes the selected graphic to 75 percent of the original width and height:

```
FormatPicture .ScaleX = "75%", .ScaleY = "75%"
```

See Also   **InsertPicture**

FormatRetAddrFonts

Syntax

FormatRetAddrFonts [**.Points** = *number*] [, **.Underline** = *number*]
[, **.Color** = *number*] [, **.Strikethrough** = *number*] [, **.Superscript** = *number*]
[, **.Subscript** = *number*] [, **.Hidden** = *number*] [, **.SmallCaps** = *number*]
[, **.AllCaps** = *number*] [, **.Spacing** = *number*] [, **.Position** = *number or text*]
[, **.Kerning** = *number*] [, **.KerningMin** = *number or text*] [, **.Default**]
[, **.Tab** = *number*] [, **.Font** = *text*] [, **.Bold** = *number*] [, **.Italic** = *number*]

Remarks

Sets character formatting for the return address on an envelope. Precede
ToolsCreateEnvelope with **FormatRetAddrFonts** to specify options
corresponding to those in the Font dialog box (Format menu). Include .Default to
store the options you specify as the default character formatting for the return
address. For argument descriptions, see **FormatFont**.

See Also

FormatAddrFonts, FormatFont, ToolsCreateEnvelope

FormatSectionLayout

Syntax

FormatSectionLayout [**.SectionStart** = *number*] [, **.VertAlign** = *number*]
[, **.Endnotes** = *number*] [, **.LineNum** = *number*] [, **.StartingNum** = *number*]
[, **.FromText** = *text*] [, **.CountBy** = *text*] [, **.NumMode** = *number*]

Remarks

Applies section formatting to the selected sections. This command exists for
compatibility with earlier versions of Word. The arguments for the
FormatSectionLayout statement are duplicated in **FilePageSetup**.

See Also

FilePageSetup

FormatStyle

Syntax

FormatStyle .Name = *text* [, **.Delete**] [, **.Merge**] [, **.NewName** – *text*]
[, **.BasedOn** = *text*] [, **.NextStyle** = *text*] [, **.Type** = *number*] [, **.FileName** = *text*]
[, **.Source** = *number*] [, **.AddToTemplate** = *number*] [, **.Define**] [, **.Rename**]
[, **.Apply**]

Remarks

Creates, modifies, redefines, applies, or deletes the specified style. You can also
use **FormatStyle** to merge styles into the active document from its attached
template. The arguments for the **FormatStyle** statement correspond to the options
in the Style dialog box (Format menu).

To define formats for the style, follow the **FormatStyle** instruction with one or
more of the following instructions: **FormatDefineStyleBorders**,
**FormatDefineStyleFont, FormatDefineStyleFrame, FormatDefineStyleLang,
FormatDefineStyleNumbers, FormatDefineStylePara,
FormatDefineStyleTabs**.

To copy styles, use **Organizer**.

Argument	Explanation
.Name	The name of the style.
.Delete	Deletes the specified style.
.Merge	Merges styles to or from the document or template specified by .FileName, depending on the value specified for .Source.
.NewName	Specifies a new name for the style; used with .Rename.
.BasedOn	Specifies an existing style on which to base the specified style.
.NextStyle	Specifies the style to be applied automatically to the new paragraph after pressing ENTER in a paragraph formatted with the style specified by .Name.
.Type	When creating a new style, specifies the type:
	0 (zero) or omitted Paragraph
	1 Character
.FileName	The document or template to merge styles to or from. If .FileName is omitted and .Source is set to 1, styles are merged from the active template to the active document.
.Source	Specifies whether to merge styles to or from the active document:
	0 (zero) From the active document to the file specified by .FileName
	1 From the file specified by .FileName to the active document
.AddToTemplate	If 1, corresponds to selecting the Add To Template check box.
.Define	Redefines an existing style or creates a new style with the formats specified in subsequent instructions.
.Rename	Renames the style specified by .Name to the name specified by .NewName.
.Apply	Applies the style to the selected paragraphs.

Examples

This example applies the Normal style to the selected paragraphs and is equivalent to the **NormalStyle** statement:

```
FormatStyle .Name = "Normal", .Apply
```

The following example defines the character formatting of the "TestMe" style as 10-point, bold, and small caps. Word creates the style if it does not already exist.

```
FormatStyle .Name = "TestMe", .Define
FormatDefineStyleFont .Points = "10", .Bold = 1, .SmallCaps = 1
```

See Also   **CountStyles(), Organizer, FormatDefineStyleBorders, FormatDefineStyleFont, FormatDefineStyleFrame, FormatDefineStyleLang, FormatDefineStyleNumbers, FormatDefineStylePara, FormatDefineStyleTabs, NormalStyle, Style, StyleName$()**

FormatStyleGallery

Syntax   **FormatStyleGallery .Template** = *text* [**, .Preview** = *number*]

Remarks   Copies the styles from the specified template to the active document. Existing styles are updated.

Argument	Explanation
.Template	The template containing the styles you want to use. Paths are allowed. In Windows, including the .DOT filename extension is not required.
.Preview	Specifies what to preview in the StyleGallery dialog box when you display the dialog box with a **Dialog** or **Dialog()** instruction:

0 (zero)   Active document

1   Example document

2   List of styles and samples

For an example, see **FormatAutoFormat**.

See Also   **FormatAutoFormat, FormatStyle, ToolsOptionsAutoFormat**

FormatTabs

Syntax   **FormatTabs** [**.Position** = *text*] [**, .DefTabs** = *number or text*] [**, .Align** = *number*] [**, .Leader** = *number*] [**, .Set**] [**, .Clear**] [**, .ClearAll**]

Remarks   Sets and clears tab stops for the selected paragraphs. The arguments for the **FormatTabs** statement correspond to the options in the Tabs dialog box (Format menu).

Argument	Explanation
.Position	Position of the tab stop in a text measurement
.DefTabs	Position for default tab stops in the document in points or a text measurement

Argument	Explanation
.Align	Alignment of the tab stop:
	0 (zero) Left
	1 Center
	2 Right
	3 Decimal
	4 Bar
.Leader	The leader character for the tab stop:
	0 (zero) None
	1 Period
	2 Hyphen
	3 Underscore
.Set	Sets the specified custom tab stop.
.Clear	Clears the specified custom tab stop.
.ClearAll	Clears all custom tab stops.

Examples   This example sets a right-aligned tab stop at 1.5 inches:

```
FormatTabs .Position = "1.5 in", .Align = 2, .Set
```

The following example clears all custom tab stops:

```
FormatTabs .ClearAll
```

See Also   **EditFindTabs, EditReplaceTabs, FormatDefineStyleTabs, NextTab(), PrevTab(), TabLeader$(), TabType()**

FormFieldOptions

Syntax   **FormFieldOptions** [**.Entry** = *text*] [**, .Exit** = *text*] [**, .Name** = *text*]
[**, .Enable** = *number*] [**, .TextType** = *number*] [**, .TextWidth** = *number or text*]
[**, .TextDefault** = *text*] [**, .TextFormat** = *text*] [**, .CheckSize** = *number*]
[**, .CheckWidth** = *number or text*] [**, .CheckDefault** = *number*]
[**, .Type** = *number*] [**, .OwnHelp** = *number*] [**, .HelpText** = *text*]
[**, .OwnStat** = *number*] [**, .StatText** = *text*]

Remarks Changes the properties of a selected form field. The arguments for the **FormFieldOptions** statement correspond to the options in the dialog box that Word displays when you select a form field and click the Form Field Options button on the Forms toolbar or choose Form Field Options from the shortcut menu. If more than one form field is selected, **FormFieldOptions** changes the properties of the first form field in the selection. If no form field is selected, or if you attempt to set options that are inappropriate for the selected form field, an error occurs.

Argument	Explanation
.Entry	The macro that runs when the form field receives the focus
.Exit	The macro that runs when the form field loses the focus
.Name	The name of the bookmark that will mark the form field
.Enable	If 1, allows the form field to be changed as the form is filled in
.TextType	For a text form field, specifies the type:
	0 (zero) Regular Text
	1 Number
	2 Date
	3 Current Date
	4 Current Time
	5 Calculation
.TextWidth	For a text form field, specifies a maximum width:
	0 (zero) Unlimited
	> 0 A maximum width, in characters
.TextDefault	The default text for a text form field
.TextFormat	For a text form field, specifies a format appropriate for .TextType. If .TextType is set to 0 (zero) for Regular Text, the following values are available: Uppercase, Lowercase, First Capital, Title Case. For formats available to other text types, review the items in the Text Format box in the Text Form Field Options dialog box.
.CheckSize	For a check box form field, specifies whether to set a fixed size:
	0 (zero) Auto (the size is determined by the font size of the surrounding text).
	1 Exactly (the size is fixed to that specified by .CheckWidth).
.CheckWidth	For a check box form field, and if .CheckSize is set to 1, specifies a fixed width and height in points or a text measurement.
.CheckDefault	For a check box form field, specifies whether the check box should be cleared or selected by default:
	0 (zero) Cleared
	1 Selected

Argument	Explanation
.Type	Specifies the type of form field:
	0 (zero) or omitted Text form field
	1 Check box form field
	2 Drop-down form field
.OwnHelp	If 1, allows .HelpText to be specified.
.HelpText	The text that is displayed in a message box when the form field has the focus and the user presses F1 (Windows) or COMMAND+/ or HELP (Macintosh).
.OwnStat	If 1, allows .StatText to be specified.
.StatText	The text that is displayed in the status bar when the form field has the focus.

You can use the **FormFieldOptions** dialog record to retrieve information about the selected form field. For details, see the second example in this entry.

Examples

This example specifies help text for the selected form field. Help text is specified for both the status bar and the box that Word displays when the user presses F1 (Windows) or COMMAND+/ or HELP (Macintosh).

```
FormFieldOptions .OwnHelp = 1, .HelpText = "Briefly summarize " + \
    "your favorite activity. Provide specific details.", \
    .OwnStat = 1, .StatText = "What you like to do best..."
```

This example uses the **FormFieldOptions** dialog record to define the variable curType with a number that corresponds to the .Type setting for the selected form field. You can use this example as a model for how to return information on any of the options you can set with **FormFieldOptions**.

```
Dim dlg As FormFieldOptions
GetCurValues dlg
curType = dlg.Type
```

See Also   **EnableFormField, InsertFormField**

FormShading, FormShading()

Syntax   **FormShading** [*On*]

FormShading()

Remarks   The **FormShading** statement controls shading for form fields in the active document.

Argument	Explanation
On	Specifies whether to display form fields with or without shading.
	1 Displays form fields with shading.
	0 (zero) Displays form fields without shading.
	Omitted Toggles form-field shading.

The **Formhading()** function returns 0 (zero) if form fields are not shaded and –1 if they are.

See Also   **FormFieldOptions**

FoundFileName$()

Syntax   **FoundFileName$**(*Number*)

Remarks   Returns the name of a file found in the most recent **FileFind** operation. The argument *Number* is a number between 1 and **CountFoundFiles()**. For an example, see **FileFind**.

See Also   **CountFoundFiles()**, **FileFind**

Function...End Function

Syntax   **Function** *FunctionName*[$][(*ArgumentList*)]
   Series of instructions to determine a value
   FunctionName[$] = *value*
End Function

Remarks   Defines a function—a series of instructions that returns a single value. To return a string value, the function name must end with a dollar sign ($). Note that unlike the names of built-in WordBasic functions, the names of user-defined functions that do not specify *ArgumentList* do not end with empty parentheses; if you include empty parentheses, an error will occur.

ArgumentList is a list of variables, separated by commas, that are passed to the function by the statement calling the function. String variables must end with a dollar sign. *ArgumentList* cannot include values; constants should be declared as variables and passed to the function through variable names.

For more information about creating functions, see Chapter 4, "Advanced WordBasic," in Part 1, "Learning WordBasic."

Example

This macro prompts the user to type a number of degrees Fahrenheit, which is passed to the ConvertTemp( ) function through the variable fahrenheit. The function converts fahrenheit to degrees Celsius, and then the main subroutine displays this value in a message box.

```
Sub MAIN
    On Error Resume Next
    tmp$ = InputBox$("Type a Fahrenheit temperature:")
    fahrenheit = Val(tmp$)
    celsius = ConvertTemp(fahrenheit)
    MsgBox tmp$ + " Fahrenheit =" + Str$(celsius) + " Celsius"
End Sub
Function ConvertTemp(fahrenheit)
    tmp = fahrenheit
    tmp = ((tmp - 32) * 5) / 9
    tmp = Int(tmp)
    ConvertTemp = tmp
End Function
```

See Also

Sub...End Sub

GetAddInID()

Syntax

GetAddInID(*AddIn$*)

Remarks

Returns a number corresponding to the specified global template or add-in's position in the list of global templates and add-ins in the Templates And Add-ins dialog box (Templates command, File menu): 1 corresponds to the first template or add-in, 2 to the second, and so on. If *AddIn$* is not currently a global template or add-in, **GetAddInID**() returns 0 (zero).

Argument	Explanation
AddIn$	The path (if necessary) and filename of the global template or Word add-in library (WLL).

Example

This example displays one of two messages, depending on whether the specified template is currently loaded. On the Macintosh, substitute a path and filename such as HD:TEMPLATES:MY TEMPLATE.

```
id = GetAddInID("C:\TEMPLATES\MYDOT.DOT")
If id > 0 Then
    MsgBox "MYDOT.DOT is global template number" + Str$(id) + "."
Else
    MsgBox "MYDOT.DOT is not currently a global template."
End If
```

See Also

AddAddIn, AddInState, ClearAddIns, CountAddIns(), DeleteAddIn, GetAddInName$()

GetAddInName$()

Syntax

GetAddInName$(*AddInID*)

Remarks

Returns the path and filename of the global template or add-in whose position in the list of global templates and add-ins in the Templates And Add-ins dialog box (Templates command, File menu) corresponds to *AddInID*: 1 corresponds to the first template or add-in, 2 to the second, and so on.

Example

This example displays a list of the current global templates and add-ins in a message box:

```
size = CountAddIns() - 1
Dim GlobalAddIns$(size)
For i = 0 To size
    GlobalAddIns$(i) = GetAddInName$(i + 1)
    msg$ = msg$ + GlobalAddIns$(i) + Chr$(13)
Next
MsgBox msg$, "Current Global Templates and Add-ins"
```

See Also   **AddAddIn, AddInState, ClearAddIns, CountAddIns(), DeleteAddIn, GetAddInID()**

GetAddress$()

Syntax   **GetAddress$(**[*Name$*], [*AddressProperties$*], [*UseAutoText*], [*DisplaySelectDialog*], [*SelectDialog*], [*CheckNamesDialog*], [*MRUChoice*], [*UpdateMRU*]**)**

Remarks   Returns an address from the default address book. **GetAddress$()** is available only if you have Windows 95 and either Microsoft Exchange or Schedule+ version 2.0 installed. In Word version 6.0, **GetAddress$()** is unavailable and generates an error.

Argument	Explanation
Name$	The name of the addressee, as specified in the Search Name dialog box in the address book.
AddressProperties$	If *UseAutoText* is set to 1, *AddressProperties$* specifies the name of an AutoText entry that defines a sequence of address book properties.
	If *UseAutoText* is set to 0 (zero) or omitted, *AddressProperties$* defines a custom layout. Valid address book property name or sets of property names are surrounded by angle brackets ("<" and ">") and separated by a space or a paragraph mark (for example, "<PR_GIVEN_NAME> <PR_SURNAME>" + Chr$(13) + "<PR_OFFICE_TELEPHONE_NUMBER>".)
	If *AddressProperties$* is omitted, Word looks for the default AutoText entry, "AddressLayout". If "AddressLayout" hasn't been defined, Word uses the following layout definition for the address: "<PR_GIVEN_NAME> <PR_SURNAME>" + Chr$(13) + "<PR_STREET_ADDRESS>" + Chr$(13) + "<PR_LOCALITY>" + ", " + "<PR_STATE_OR_PROVINCE>" + " " + "<PR_POSTAL_CODE>" + Chr$(13) + "<PR_COUNTRY>".
	For a list of the valid address book property names, see **AddAddress**.

Argument	Explanation
UseAutoText	Indicates the value that *AddressProperties$* specifies: 0 (zero) or omitted Defines the layout of the address book properties. 1 Specifies the name of the AutoText entry that defines the layout of the address book properties.
DisplaySelectDialog	Specifies whether the Select Name dialog box is displayed: 0 (zero) The Select Name dialog box is not displayed. 1 or omitted The Select Name dialog box is displayed. 2 The Select Name dialog box is not displayed, but no search for a specific name is performed. The address returned by **GetAddress$()** will be the previously selected address.
SelectDialog	Specifies how the Select Name dialog box should be displayed: 0 (zero) or omitted In Browse mode 1 In Compose mode, with only the To: box 2 In Compose mode, with both the To: and CC: boxes
CheckNamesDialog	Specifies whether to display the Check Names dialog box when the value of *Name$* is not specific enough: 0 (zero) The Check Names dialog box is not displayed. 1 or omitted The Check Names dialog box is displayed. This parameter is ignored if *DisplaySelectDialog* is nonzero. If *SelectDialog* is set to 1 or 2, all names are resolved before the Select Names dialog box is closed.
MRUChoice	Specifies which list of most recently used addresses to use as the address list: 0 (zero) or omitted The list of delivery addresses 1 The list of return addresses
UpdateMRU	Specifies whether the new address is added to the list of most recently used addresses: 0 (zero) or omitted The address is not added. 1 The address is added. If *SelectDialog* is set to 1 or 2, *UpdateMRU* is ignored.

Examples

This example sets the variable `letterAddress$` to John Smith's address, moves the insertion point to the beginning of the document, and inserts the address. The inserted address will include the default address book properties.

```
letterAddress$ = GetAddress$("John Smith", "", 0, 0)
StartOfDocument
Insert letterAddress$
```

The following example inserts John Smith's address, using the "My Address Layout" AutoText entry as the layout definition. "My Address Layout" is defined in the active template and contains a set of address properties assigned to the `text$` variable. The example also adds John Smith's address to the list of most recently used addresses.

```
text$ = "<PR_GIVEN_NAME> <PR_SURNAME>" + Chr$(13) + \
    "<PR_STREET_ADDRESS>" + Chr$(13) + "<PR_LOCALITY>" + \
    ", " + "<PR_STATE_OR_PROVINCE>" + "   " + "<PR_POSTAL_CODE>" + \
    Chr$(13) + "<PR_OFFICE_TELEPHONE_NUMBER>"
SetAutoText "My Address Layout", text$, 1
letterAddress$ = GetAddress$("John Smith", "My Address Layout",
    \ 1, , , , , 1)
StartOfDocument
Insert letterAddress$
```

The following example inserts information from the same address at two different locations in the active document, using a different set of properties for each location. In this example, the second **GetAddress$()** instruction does not display the Select Name dialog box of the address book.

```
letterAddress$ = GetAddress$("John Smith", \
    "<PR_GIVEN_NAME> <PR_SURNAME>" + Chr$(13) + \
    "<PR_STREET_ADDRESS>" + Chr$(13) + "<PR_LOCALITY>" + \
    ", " + "<PR_STATE_OR_PROVINCE>" + "   " + "<PR_POSTAL_CODE>" + \
    Chr$(13) + "<PR_OFFICE_TELEPHONE_NUMBER>", 0, 0)
letterGivenName$ = GetAddress$( , "<PR_GIVEN_NAME>", , 2)
StartOfDocument
Insert letterAddress$
InsertPara
Insert "Dear "
Insert letterGivenName$
InsertPara
```

See Also

AddAddress, AutoText, InsertAddress, ToolsCreateEnvelope, ToolsCreateLabels

GetAttr()

Syntax

GetAttr(*Filename$*)

Remarks

Returns a number corresponding to the file attributes set for *Filename$*, the path and filename of the file on which you want information. In Windows, the attributes correspond to those you can set using the Properties command (File menu) in File Manager (Windows 3.*x* and Windows NT) or Windows Explorer (Windows 95). For definitions of the attributes, display the Properties dialog box and choose the Help button. On the Macintosh, only the Read Only and Hidden attributes are available (Read Only corresponds to the Locked check box in the Get Info dialog box (File menu) in the Finder). The values returned by **GetAttr**( ) are additive. For example, if both Read Only and Archive are selected, the return value is 33 (the sum of 1 and 32).

Value	Explanation
0 (zero)	None of the file attributes are selected.
1	The Read Only attribute is selected.
2	The Hidden attribute is selected.
4	The System attribute is selected (not availble on the Macintosh).
32	The Archive attribute is selected (not available on the Macintosh).

For an example, see **SetAttr**.

See Also

SetAttr

GetAutoCorrect$()

Syntax

**GetAutoCorrect$**(*AutoCorrectEntry$*)

Remarks

Returns the replacement text for the specified entry in the Replace column of the AutoCorrect dialog box (Tools menu). If *AutoCorrectEntry$* doesn't exist, **GetAutoCorrect$**() returns an empty string ("").

Argument	Explanation
AutoCorrectEntry$	The text specified in the Replace column for an AutoCorrect entry in the AutoCorrect dialog box. *AutoCorrectEntry$* is not case-sensitive. For example, you can specify an entry "GW" as either "GW" or "gw."

Example

This example checks the replacement text for the AutoCorrect entry "uk." If the replacement text doesn't match "United Kingdom," the AutoCorrect entry is modified to do so.

```
If GetAutoCorrect$("uk") <> "United Kingdom" Then
    ToolsAutoCorrect .Replace = "uk", \
        .With = "United Kingdom", .Add
End If
```

See Also   **ToolsAutoCorrect**

GetAutoCorrectException$()

Syntax   **GetAutoCorrectException$(***Tab***,** *EntryNumber***)**

Remarks

Returns the text of the exception that corresponds to *EntryNumber* on the specified tab in the AutoCorrect Exceptions dialog box (AutoCorrect command, Tools Menu). In Word version 6.0, **GetAutoCorrectException$()** is unavailable and generates an error.

Argument	Explanation
Tab	The tab where Word looks for the exception list entry:
	0 (zero) First Letter
	1 INitial CAps
EntryNumber	The number of the exception list entry, from 1 to the number returned by **CountAutoCorrectExceptions()**

Example

This example creates the array exceptions$(), which contains all the exceptions listed on the INitial CAps tab in the AutoCorrect Exceptions dialog box (AutoCorrect command, Tools Menu):

```
size = CountAutoCorrectExceptions(1) - 1
Dim exceptions$(size)
For count = 0 To size
    exceptions$(count) = GetAutoCorrectException$(1, count + 1)
Next
```

The following example deletes all the exceptions listed on the INitial CAps tab in the AutoCorrect Exceptions dialog box (AutoCorrect command, Tools Menu):

```
For n = 1 To CountAutoCorrectExceptions(1)
    ac$ = GetAutoCorrectException$(1, 1)
    ToolsAutoCorrectExceptions .Tab = 1, .Name = ac$, .Delete
Next
```

See Also   **CountAutoCorrectExceptions()**, **IsAutoCorrectException()**,
ToolsAutoCorrectExceptions

GetAutoText$()

Syntax **GetAutoText$**(*Name$* [, *Context*])

Remarks Returns the unformatted text of the specified AutoText entry.

Argument	Explanation
Name$	The name of the AutoText entry
Context	Where the AutoText entry is stored:
	0 (zero) or omitted Normal template and any loaded global templates
	1 Active template
	Note that if *Context* is 1 and the active template is the Normal template, **GetAutoText$**() returns an empty string ("").

Example This example displays a message box containing the text of the AutoText entry named "Welcome," which is stored in the active template:

```
MsgBox GetAutoText$("Welcome", 1)
```

See Also **AutoText**, **AutoTextName$()**, **CountAutoTextEntries()**, **EditAutoText**, **InsertAutoText**, **SetAutoText**

GetBookmark$()

Syntax **GetBookmark$**(*Name$*)

Remarks Returns the text (unformatted) marked by the specified bookmark. If *Name$* is not the name of a bookmark in the active document, **GetBookmark$**() returns an empty string ("").

Examples This example sets the variable first$ to the text of the first bookmark in the document:

```
first$ = GetBookmark$(BookmarkName$(1))
```

The following example sets the variable paratext$ to the text of the paragraph containing the insertion point:

```
paratext$ = GetBookmark$("\Para")
```

The bookmark "\Para" is one of several predefined bookmarks that Word defines and updates automatically. For more information, see "Operators and Predefined Bookmarks" later in this part.

See Also **BookmarkName$()**, **CountBookmarks()**, **EditBookmark**

GetCurValues

Syntax   **GetCurValues** *DialogRecord*

Remarks   Stores in *DialogRecord* the current values for a previously defined dialog record
for a Word dialog box. You use **Dim** to define a dialog record (for example, `Dim dlg As ToolsOptionsSave`), **GetCurValues** to store the settings (for example, `GetCurValues dlg`), and the syntax *DialogRecord.ArgumentName* to return specific settings (for example, `save = dlg.FastSaves`). You do not need to use **GetCurValues** with a dialog record for a custom dialog box; if you do, the instruction has no effect.

Example   This Word version 6.0 example uses **GetCurValues** to retrieve the date the active document was created from the Document Statistics dialog box (Summary Info command, File menu). The instructions then use date functions to calculate the number of days since the document was created and display a message box according to the result.

```
Dim dlg As DocumentStatistics
GetCurValues dlg
docdate$ = dlg.Created
age = Now() - DateValue(docdate$)
age = Int(age)
Select Case age
    Case 0
        MsgBox "This document is less than a day old."
    Case Is > 0
        MsgBox "This document was created" + Str$(age) + " day(s) ago."
    Case Else
        MsgBox "Check your computer's date and time."
End Select
```

For an example that uses **GetCurValues** and shows how to toggle any check box, see **Abs()**.

See Also   **Dialog**, **Dim**

GetDirectory$()

Syntax   **GetDirectory$**([*Directory$*,] *Count*)

Remarks   Returns the name of the subfolder specified by *Count* in the specified folder.

Argument	Explanation
Directory$	The path of the folder containing the subfolder; if omitted, the current folder is assumed.
Count	A number in the range 1 to **CountDirectories()**, where 1 corresponds to the first subfolder, 2 to the second, and so on.

Example

This example defines an array with the names of the subfolders in the current folder. In a dialog box definition, you could specify this array in a **ListBox** instruction to present a list of the subfolders.

```
Dim subdirs$(CountDirectories())
For i = 1 To CountDirectories()
    subdirs$(i) = LCase$(GetDirectory$(i))
Next
```

See Also

CountDirectories()

GetDocumentProperty(), GetDocumentProperty$()

Syntax

GetDocumentProperty(*Name$* [, *CustomOrBuiltIn*])

**GetDocumentProperty$**(*Name$* [, *CustomOrBuiltIn*])

Remarks

GetDocumentProperty() returns the numeric representation of the *Name$* property defined in the active document. This can be a built-in property or a custom property. If the *Name$* property is a string or a date, or if it is not defined, an error occurs. Yes or No properties are returned as 1 or 0 (zero), respectively.

GetDocumentProperty$() returns the string representation of the *Name$* property defined in the active document. This can be a built-in property or a custom property. **GetDocumentProperty$()** returns an error if the *Name$* property is a number or is not defined. Date properties are returned in the default date format, and Yes or No properties are returned as "Y" or "N". Use the **DocumentPropertyExists()** function to verify that the *Name$* property exists.

For a list of the built-in properties available in Word, see **DocumentPropertyName$()**. In Word version 6.0, **GetDocumentProperty()** and **GetDocumentProperty$()** are unavailable and generate errors.

Argument	Explanation
Name$	The name of the property.
CustomOrBuiltIn	Specifies whether *Name$* is a built-in property or a custom property:
	0 (zero) or omitted Word looks in the list of built-in and custom properties and returns the first matching value.
	1 *Name$* is a built-in property.
	2 *Name$* is a custom property.

See Also

DocumentPropertyName$(), **DocumentPropertyType()**, **SetDocumentProperty**

GetDocumentVar$()

Syntax   **GetDocumentVar$**(*VariableName$*)

Remarks   Returns the string associated with *VariableName$*, which was previously set for
the active document with the **SetDocumentVar** statement. If the insertion point is
not in a document—for example, if the macro-editing window is active—an error
occurs.

Example   This AutoOpen macro determines whether there is a reminder note and, if so,
displays it:

```
Sub MAIN
worknote$ = GetDocumentVar$("reminder")
If worknote$ <> "" Then
    MsgBox worknote$, "Note from last time"
End If
End Sub
```

For an example that prompts for a reminder note to store with a document before
closing it, see **SetDocumentVar**.

See Also   **SetDocumentVar**

GetDocumentVarName$()

Syntax   **GetDocumentVarName$**(*VariableNumber*)

Remarks   Returns the name of a document variable set with **SetDocumentVar** or
SetDocumentVar().

Argument	Explanation
VariableNumber	The number of the document variable, from 1 to the total number of document variables stored in the active document (you can obtain the total using **CountDocumentVars()**).

For an example, see **CountDocumentVars()**.

See Also   **CountDocumentVars()**, **GetDocumentVar$()**, **SetDocumentVar**

GetFieldData$()

Syntax   **GetFieldData$()**

Remarks   When the insertion point is within an ADDIN field, retrieves text data stored internally within the field. Data stored within an ADDIN field is not visible, even when field codes are showing. If there is a selection, it must begin at an ADDIN field; otherwise, an error occurs.

See Also   **PutFieldData**

GetFormResult(), GetFormResult$()

Syntax   **GetFormResult(***BookmarkName$***)**

             GetFormResult$(***BookmarkName$*)**

Remarks   **GetFormResult()** returns a number corresponding to the setting of a check box form field or drop-down form field marked by the bookmark *BookmarkName$*. (Word adds a bookmark automatically when you insert a form field.) **GetFormResult()** returns values as follows:

- For a check box form field, returns 0 (zero) if the check box is cleared or 1 if it is selected.
- For a drop-down form field, returns 0 (zero) if the first item is selected, 1 if the second item is selected, and so on.

Note that an error occurs if you use **GetFormResult()** with a text form field.

GetFormResult$() returns a string corresponding to the setting of the form field marked by the bookmark *BookmarkName$*. **GetFormResult$()** returns values as follows:

- For a check box form field, returns "0" (zero) if the check box is cleared or "1" if it is selected.
- For a drop-down form field, returns the item that is currently selected.
- For a text form field, returns the current text.

Example   This is an example of an "on-exit" macro that tests the item selected in a drop-down form field as soon as the user moves the focus to another form field. If the item is "Paris," a message box is displayed. The on-exit macro is assigned to the field marked by the bookmark "Dropdown1."

```
Sub MAIN
city$ = GetFormResult$("Dropdown1")
If city$ = "Paris" Then
    MsgBox "We offer daily excursions to Versailles!"
End If
End Sub
```

For more information about on-exit macros, see Chapter 9, "More WordBasic Techniques," in Part 1, "Learning WordBasic."

See Also   **SetFormResult**

GetMergeField$()

Syntax   **GetMergeField$**(*FieldName$*)

Remarks   Returns the contents of the specified merge field in the current data record. If the main document is not the active document or *FieldName$* doesn't exist, **GetMergeField$**() returns an empty string ("").

Example   This example displays the contents of the FirstName field for the current data record:

```
MsgBox GetMergeField$("FirstName")
```

See Also   **CountMergeFields**(), **MergeFieldName$**()

GetPrivateProfileString$()

Syntax   **GetPrivateProfileString$**(*Section$*, *KeyName$*, *Filename$*)

Remarks   Returns a setting in a settings file, a file that your macros can use to store and retrieve settings. For example, you can store the name of the active document when you quit Word so that it can be reopened automatically the next time you start Word. In Windows, a settings file is a text file such as WIN.INI. On the Macintosh, a settings file is a resource file such as Word Settings (6).

In Windows 95 and Windows NT, you can use **GetPrivateProfileString$**() to return a setting in the registry.

Argument	Explanation
Section$	The name of the section in the settings file that contains *KeyName$*. In Windows, the section name appears between brackets before the associated keys (do not include the brackets with *Section$*).
	If you are using **GetPrivateProfileString$()** in Windows 95 or Windows NT to return a setting in the registry, *Section$* should be the complete path to the key, including the root (for example, "HKEY_CURRENT_USER\Software\Microsoft\Word\7.0\Options").
KeyName$	The key whose setting you want to retrieve. In a Windows settings file, the key name is followed by an equal sign (=) and the setting.
	If you are using **GetPrivateProfileString$()** in Windows 95 or Windows NT to return a value from the registry, *KeyName$* should be the name of the value in the key specified by *Section$* (for example, "MessageBeeps").
Filename$	The filename for the settings file. If a path is not specified, the Windows folder (Windows) or the Preferences folder (Macintosh) is assumed.
	If you are using **GetPrivateProfileString$()** in Windows 95 or Windows NT to return a value from the registry, *Filename$* must be an empty string ("").

If a specified section, key, or file does not exist, **GetPrivateProfileString$()** returns an empty string ("").

Example

This example sets the variable artdir$ to the path specified by the PICTURE-PATH key in the [Microsoft Word] section of WINWORD6.INI and, if the setting exists, changes the current folder accordingly. The last two instructions display the Insert Picture dialog box (Picture command, Insert menu). On the Macintosh, substitute Word Settings (6) for WINWORD6.INI. In Windows 95 and Windows NT, substitute the full path to the Options key for "Microsoft Word," and substitute an empty string ("") for WINWORD6.INI.

```
artdir$ = GetPrivateProfileString$("Microsoft Word", \
    "PICTURE-PATH", "WINWORD6.INI")
If artdir$ <> "" Then ChDir artdir$
Dim dlg As InsertPicture
x = Dialog(dlg)
```

For another example, see **SetPrivateProfileString**.

See Also

GetProfileString$(), **SetPrivateProfileString**, **SetProfileString**

GetProfileString$()

Syntax   **GetProfileString$(**[*Section$*,] *KeyName$*)

Remarks   In Windows 3.*x*, returns a setting in WIN.INI, or if *Section$* is "Microsoft Word 2.0," "Microsoft Word," "MSWord Text Converters," or "MSWord Editable Sections," returns the setting from WINWORD6.INI instead. These exceptions are made for compatibility with Word for Windows version 2.*x* macros. On the Macintosh, **GetProfileString$()** returns settings from the Word Settings (6) file. In Windows or on the Macintosh, it is generally preferable to use **GetPrivateProfileString$()**, which allows you to specify a settings file from which to return information.

Argument	Explanation
Section$	The name of the section in the settings file that contains *KeyName$*. In Windows, the section name appears between brackets before the associated keys (do not include the brackets with *Section$*). If omitted, "Microsoft Word" is assumed.
KeyName$	The key whose setting you want to retrieve. In Windows, the key name is followed by an equal sign (=) and the setting.

If a specified section or key does not exist, **GetProfileString$()** returns an empty string ("").

Note In Windows 95 and Windows NT, settings are stored in the registry. You can still use **SetProfileString** and **GetProfileString$()** to set and return settings from a text file with the name WIN.INI, but neither the system nor Word uses these settings. To access and change values in the registry from within WordBasic, you need to use **GetPrivateProfileString$()** and **SetPrivateProfileString$()**.

See Also   **GetPrivateProfileString$()**, **SetPrivateProfileString**, **SetProfileString**

GetSelEndPos()

Syntax   **GetSelEndPos()**

Remarks   Returns the character position of the end of the selection relative to the start of the document, which has a character position of 0 (zero). The end of the selection is defined as the end farthest from the start of the document. All characters, including nonprinting characters, are counted. Hidden characters are counted even if they are not displayed.

Example

This macro displays a message box if there is no selection. The user-defined function checksel compares the character positions at the start and end of the selection. If the positions are equal, indicating there is no selection, the function returns 0 (zero) and the message box is displayed.

```
Sub MAIN
    If checksel = 0 Then MsgBox "There is no selection."
End Sub

Function checksel
    If GetSelStartPos() = GetSelEndPos() Then
        checksel = 0
    Else
        checksel = 1
    End If
End Function
```

See Also

GetSelStartPos(), **GetText$()**, **SetSelRange**

GetSelStartPos()

Syntax

GetSelStartPos()

Remarks

Returns the character position of the start of the selection relative to the start of the document, which has a character position of 0 (zero). The start of the selection is defined as the end closest to the start of the document. All characters, including nonprinting characters, are counted. Hidden characters are counted even if they are not displayed.

For an example, see **GetSelEndPos()**.

See Also

GetSelEndPos(), **GetText$()**, **SetSelRange**

GetSystemInfo, GetSystemInfo$()

Syntax

GetSystemInfo *Array$( )*

GetSystemInfo$(*Type*)

Remarks

The **GetSystemInfo** statement fills a previously defined string array with information about the environment in which Word is running. In Windows, the size of the array should be 12 elements; on the Macintosh, 15 elements.

The **GetSystemInfo$()** function returns one piece of information about the environment in which Word is running. *Type* is one of the following numeric codes, specifying the type of information to return. In Windows, *Type* is a value from 21 to 32. Note that *Type* 23, 25, and 27 return meaningful values in Windows 3.*x* only.

Type	Explanation
21	The environment (for example, "Windows" or "Windows NT")
22	The type of central processing unit, or CPU (for example, "80286," "80386," "i486," or "Unknown")
23	The MS-DOS version number
24	The Windows version number
25	The percent of system resources available
26	The amount of available disk space, in bytes
27	The mode under which Windows is running: "Standard" or "386-Enhanced"
28	Whether a math coprocessor is installed: "Yes" or "No"
29	The country setting
30	The language setting
31	The vertical display resolution, in pixels
32	The horizontal display resolution, in pixels

On the Macintosh, *Type* is a value from 512 to 526.

Type	Explanation
512	The environment ("Macintosh")
513	The folder for storing settings files (for example, "HD:System Folder:Preferences:")
514	Whether the current display is color: "Yes" or "No"
515	The processor type (for example, "68000", "68040", or "PowerPC™")
516	The computer type (for example, "Macintosh IIci" or "PowerBook™ 145")
517	System software version (for example, "7.1")
518	The Macintosh name as set in the Sharing Setup control panel
519	Whether QuickDraw GX is installed: "Yes" or "No"
520	Whether Balloon Help™ is on: "Yes" or "No"
521	The vertical display resolution, in pixels
522	The horizontal display resolution, in pixels
523	The country setting
524	Whether a math coprocessor is installed: "Yes" or "No"

Type	Explanation
525	Total memory available for running applications, in bytes
526	Free disk space, in bytes

If you are writing a macro to run both in Windows and on the Macintosh, use the **AppInfo$()** function to determine the current platform before running a **GetSystemInfo$()** instruction.

Examples

This Windows example creates a table of system information in a new document. First, the example defines and fills an array with labels for each type of system information. Second, the example opens a new document and defines the info$() array, which **GetSystemInfo** then fills with the system information. Finally, the **For...Next** loop inserts the table of information. This example could be easily modified for the Macintosh by increasing the size of the array to 14 and changing the labels.

```
Dim a$(11)
a$(0) = "Environment" : a$(1) = "CPU" : a$(2) = "MS-DOS"
a$(3) = "Windows" : a$(4) = "% Resources" : a$(5) = "Disk Space"
a$(6) = "Mode" : a$(7) = "Coprocessor" : a$(8) = "Country"
a$(9) = "Language" : a$(10) = "Pixels High" : a$(11) = "Pixels Wide"
Dim info$(11)
GetSystemInfo info$()
FileNewDefault
FormatTabs .Position = "1.5 in", .Set
For i = 0 To 11
    Insert a$(i) + Chr$(9) + info$(i)
    InsertPara
Next
```

The following Macintosh example displays in a message box the total amount of available disk space:

```
space$ = GetSystemInfo$(526)
MsgBox "Available disk space: " + space$ + " bytes."
```

See Also

AppInfo$()

GetText$()

Syntax

GetText$(*CharPos1***, ***CharPos2***)**

Remarks

Returns the text (unformatted) from *CharPos1* through *CharPos2*. Note that **GetText$()** does not return hidden text that is not displayed even though Word counts hidden characters when determining the range of text to return. Though **GetText$()** can be handy if you need to return document text without changing the selection, special document elements such as fields, tables, and page breaks within the specified range can produce unpredictable results.

Argument	Explanation
CharPos1	The character position that defines the beginning of the range, relative to the start of the document, which has a character position of 0 (zero)
CharPos2	The character position that defines the end of the range

Example

This example sets the variable a$ to the first 10 characters in the document:

```
a$ = GetText$(0, 10)
```

See Also

GetSelEndPos( ), **GetSelStartPos( )**, **SetSelRange**

GoBack

Syntax

GoBack

Remarks

Moves the insertion point among the last four locations where editing occurred (the same as pressing SHIFT+F5).

Example

An AutoExec macro such as the following runs each time you start Word. If there is at least one document listed at the bottom of the File menu, this macro opens the document and moves the insertion point to the most recent editing location.

```
Sub MAIN
If FileName$(1) <> "" Then
    FileList 1
    GoBack
End If
End Sub
```

See Also

EditGoTo

Goto

Syntax

Goto *Label*

Remarks

Redirects a running macro from the **Goto** instruction to the specified *Label* anywhere in the same subroutine or function. The macro continues running from the instruction that follows the label. Keep the following in mind when placing a label in a macro:

- Labels must be the first text on a line and cannot be preceded by spaces or tab characters.

- Labels must be followed by a colon (:). (Do not include the colon in the **Goto** instruction.)

- Labels that contain letters must begin with a letter and can contain letters and numbers up to a maximum length of 40 characters, not counting the colon.

- You can use a number that appears at the beginning of a line instead of a label. Line numbers are supported primarily for compatibility with Basic programs created in older versions of the Basic programming language that required line numbers. The line number can be as high as 32,759 and does not need a colon following it.

Example

This macro displays a message box, with Yes, No, and Cancel buttons, asking if the user wants to continue the macro. If the user chooses No or Cancel, the macro branches to the label bye immediately before End Sub, and the macro ends.

```
Sub MAIN
ans = MsgBox("Continue macro?", 3)
If ans = 0 Or ans = 1 Then Goto bye
'Series of instructions to run if the user chooses Yes
bye:
End Sub
```

See Also   For...Next, If...Then...Else, Select Case, While...Wend

GoToAnnotationScope

Syntax   GoToAnnotationScope

Remarks   Selects the range of document text associated with the annotation containing the insertion point. If the insertion point is not within an annotation in the annotation pane, an error occurs.

The range, or "scope," of the annotation is defined as the text that was selected when the annotation mark was inserted. This text appears shaded when the insertion point is within the annotation in the annotation pane. If no text was selected when the annotation was inserted, **GoToAnnotationScope** moves the insertion point to the position immediately preceding the annotation mark in the document text.

Example   This example copies to the Clipboard the document text associated with the annotation containing the insertion point. The first **If** instruction ensures that the annotation pane is open and the insertion point is within it. Then **GoToAnnotationScope** selects the associated document text. The second **If** instruction ensures that text is selected before running **EditCopy**.

```
If ViewAnnotations() = -1 And WindowPane() = 3 Then
    GoToAnnotationScope
    If SelType() = 2 Then
        EditCopy
    Else
        MsgBox "No text to select."
    End If
    OtherPane
Else
    MsgBox "Please place the insertion point in an annotation."
End If
```

See Also   **GoToNext***Item*, **GoToPrevious***Item*, **OtherPane**, **ViewAnnotations()**,
WindowPane()

GoToHeaderFooter

Syntax   **GoToHeaderFooter**

Remarks   Moves the insertion point from a header to a footer, or vice versa. If the insertion
point is not in a header or footer, an error occurs.

See Also   **CloseViewHeaderFooter**, **ShowNextHeaderFooter**, **ShowPrevHeaderFooter**,
ViewFooter, **ViewHeader**

GoToNext*Item*

Syntax   **GoToNext***Item*

Remarks   Moves the insertion point to the next item specified by *Item*.

Argument	Explanation
Item	The item you want to go to. The following statements are available:
	GoToNextAnnotation
	GoToNextEndnote
	GoToNextFootnote
	GoToNextPage
	GoToNextSection
	GoToNextSubdocument

See Also   **EditGoTo**, **GoToHeaderFooter**, **GoToPrevious***Item*

GoToPrevious*Item*

Syntax   **GoToPrevious***Item*

Remarks   Moves the insertion point to the previous item specified by *Item*.

Argument	Explanation
Item	The item you want to go to. The following statements are available: **GoToPreviousAnnotation** **GoToPreviousEndnote** **GoToPreviousFootnote** **GoToPreviousPage** **GoToPreviousSection** **GoToPreviousSubdocument**

See Also   **EditGoTo, GoBack, GoToNext***Item*

GroupBox

Syntax   **GroupBox** *HorizPos*, *VertPos*, *Width*, *Height*, *Label$* [, *.Identifier*]

Remarks   Creates a box in a custom dialog box that you can use to enclose a group of related option buttons or check boxes.

Argument	Explanation
HorizPos, VertPos	The horizontal and vertical distance from the upper-left corner of the group box to the upper-left corner of the dialog box, in increments of 1/8 and 1/12 of the System font (Windows) or the dialog font (Macintosh).
Width, Height	The width and height of the group box, in increments of 1/8 and 1/12 of the System font (Windows) or the dialog font (Macintosh).
Label$	The label displayed in the upper-left corner of the group box. An ampersand (&) precedes the character in *Label$* that is the access key for moving to the group box.
.Identifier	An optional identifier used by statements in a dialog function that act on the group box. For example, you can use this identifier with **DlgText** to change *Label$* while the dialog box is displayed.

For an example, see **OptionGroup**.

See Also   **Begin Dialog…End Dialog, DlgText, OptionGroup**

GrowFont

Syntax   GrowFont

Remarks   Increases the font size of the selected text (or text to be inserted at the insertion point) to the next size supported by the selected printer. If more than one font size is included in the selection, each size is increased to the next available setting. If there is no selection, the larger font size will be applied to new text.

See Also   FontSize, FormatFont, GrowFontOnePoint, ShrinkFont, ShrinkFontOnePoint

GrowFontOnePoint

Syntax   GrowFontOnePoint

Remarks   Increases the font size of the selected text (or text to be inserted at the insertion point) by 1 point, whether or not the new size is supported by the selected printer. If more than one font size is included in the selection, each size is increased by 1 point.

See Also   FontSize, FormatFont, GrowFont, ShrinkFont, ShrinkFontOnePoint

HangingIndent

Syntax   **HangingIndent**

Remarks   Applies a hanging indent to the selected paragraphs, or increases the current hanging indent to the next tab stop of the first paragraph in the selection.

See Also   **Indent**, **UnHang**, **UnIndent**

Help

Syntax   **Help**

Remarks   In Word version 6.0, displays Help for the selected context. If no context is active —for example, if the insertion point is in a Word document and not in a field— **Help** displays the Word Help Contents screen.

In Word version 7.0, **Help** displays the Answer Wizard tab in the Help Topics dialog box.

See Also   **HelpActiveWindow**, **HelpTool**

HelpAbout

Syntax   **HelpAbout** [**.AppName** = *text*] [, **.AppCopyright** = *text*] [, **.AppUserName** = *text*] [, **.AppOrganization** = *text*] [, **.AppSerialNumber** = *text*]

Remarks   Without any arguments, displays the About Microsoft Word dialog box (Help menu), which gives the Word version number, the serial number, copyright information, and the name of the licensed user.

The arguments for the **HelpAbout** statement are read-only, which means that unlike other WordBasic statements, **HelpAbout** cannot be used to set a value. Instead, you define a dialog record as **HelpAbout** and then use the dialog record in the same way you use a function: to return information. In this case, the dialog record can return information from the About Microsoft Word dialog box.

Argument	Explanation
.AppName	The name and version number of Word as they appear in the About Microsoft Word dialog box
.AppCopyright	The copyright notice for Word
.AppUserName	The name of the person to whom the active copy of Word is licensed
.AppOrganization	The organization name provided when Word was installed
.AppSerialNumber	The serial number of the active copy of Word

Example   This example defines a dialog record for the About Microsoft Word dialog box, stores the current values in the dialog record, and then displays in a message box the value for the serial number:

```
Dim dlg As HelpAbout
GetCurValues dlg
MsgBox "Serial number: " + dlg.AppSerialNumber
```

See Also   **AppInfo$()**, **DocumentStatistics**, **GetSystemInfo**, **MicrosoftSystemInfo**

HelpActiveWindow

Syntax   **HelpActiveWindow**

Remarks   Displays a Help topic describing the command associated with the active view or pane.

See Also   **Help**, **HelpTool**

HelpContents

Syntax   **HelpContents**

Remarks   Displays either the Help Topics dialog box (Word version 7.0) or the contents for Help (Word version 6.0).

See Also   **Help**, **HelpIndex**

HelpExamplesAndDemos

Syntax   **HelpExamplesAndDemos**

Remarks   Displays a screen from which you can access all the examples and demonstrations in Help. Note that in Windows 95 and Windows NT, the examples and demonstrations are not available and **HelpExamplesAndDemos** generates an error.

See Also   **HelpQuickPreview**

HelpIndex

Syntax   **HelpIndex**

Remarks   Displays either the Help Topics dialog box (Word version 7.0) or the index for Help (Word version 6.0).

See Also   **Help**, **HelpContents**

HelpKeyboard

Syntax   **HelpKeyboard**

Remarks   Displays a list of Help topics about keyboard and mouse shortcuts.

HelpMSN

Syntax   **HelpMSN**

Remarks   Displays a dialog box from which users can connect to forums on The Microsoft
                    Network for information about Microsoft Word. **HelpMSN** is available only in
                    Word for Windows 95 and only if the Microsoft Network is installed.

See Also   **Help**

HelpPSSHelp

Syntax   **HelpPSSHelp**

Remarks   Displays information in Help about the support services available for Microsoft
                    Word.

HelpQuickPreview

Syntax   **HelpQuickPreview**

Remarks   Starts a tutorial that introduces Microsoft Word. Note that in Windows 95 and
                    Windows NT, the Quick Preview demos are not available and
                    HelpQuickPreview generates an error.

See Also   **HelpExamplesAndDemos**

HelpSearch

Syntax   **HelpSearch**

Remarks   Displays either the Help Topics dialog box (Word version 7.0) or the Search
                    dialog box for performing a keyword search in Help (Word version 6.0).

HelpTipOfTheDay

Syntax   **HelpTipOfTheDay .StartupTips** = *number*

Remarks   Controls whether the Tip Of The Day dialog box appears when you start Word.
                    This statement is ignored in Word version 7.0.

Argument	Explanation
.StartupTips	If 1, displays the Tip Of The Day dialog box each time you start Word. This argument is not available in Word version 7.0.

HelpTool

Syntax   **HelpTool**

Remarks   Changes the mouse pointer to a question mark, indicating you will get context-
                    sensitive Help on the next command you choose or the next element of the Word
                    screen you click. If you click text, Word displays a box describing current
                    paragraph and character formats.

See Also   **Help**, **HelpActiveWindow**

HelpUsingHelp

Syntax   **HelpUsingHelp**

Remarks   Displays a list of Help topics that describe how to use Help.

HelpWordPerfectHelp

Syntax   **HelpWordPerfectHelp**

Remarks   In Windows, used with a **Dialog** or **Dialog**() instruction to display the Help For
                    WordPerfect® Users dialog box (Help menu), as shown in the example for this
                    entry. On the Macintosh, **HelpWordPerfectHelp** is not available and generates
                    an error.

Example   This Windows example displays the Help For WordPerfect Users dialog box:

```
Dim dlg As HelpWordPerfectHelp
x = Dialog (dlg)
```

See Also   **HelpWordPerfectHelpOptions**

HelpWordPerfectHelpOptions

Syntax

HelpWordPerfectHelpOptions [**.CommandKeyHelp** = *number*]
[, **.DocNavKeys** = *number*] [, **.MouseSimulation** = *number*]
[, **.DemoGuidance** = *number*] [, **.DemoSpeed** = *number*] [, **.HelpType** = *number*]

Remarks

In Windows, sets options in the Help for WordPerfect Users feature. The
arguments for **HelpWordPerfectHelpOptions** correspond to the options in the
Help Options dialog box (Help For WordPerfect Users command, Help menu).
On the Macintosh, **HelpWordPerfectHelpOptions** is not available and generates
an error.

Argument	Explanation
.CommandKeyHelp	If 1, Word evaluates keystrokes as WordPerfect keystrokes.
.DocNavKeys	If 1, the arrow keys and the PAGE UP, PAGE DOWN, HOME, END, and ESC keys function as they would in WordPerfect.
.MouseSimulation	If 1, the mouse pointer moves as Help for WordPerfect Users selects options during demonstrations.
.DemoGuidance	If 1, Help for WordPerfect Users displays help text when user input is required during demonstrations.
.DemoSpeed	Controls the speed of demonstrations:
	0 (zero)　Fast
	1　Medium
	2　Slow
.HelpType	Specifies whether Help for WordPerfect Users displays help text or demonstrates the WordPerfect command you choose:
	0 (zero)　Help text
	1　Demonstration

Hidden, Hidden()

Syntax

Hidden [*On*]

Hidden()

Remarks

The **Hidden** statement adds or removes the hidden character format for the
current selection, or controls hidden formatting for characters to be inserted at the
insertion point. You can control the display of hidden text with the Hidden Text
check box, an option on the View tab in the Options dialog box (Tools menu).

Argument	Explanation
On	Specifies whether to add or remove the hidden format:
	1 Adds the hidden format.
	0 (zero) Removes the hidden format.
	Omitted Toggles the hidden format.

The **Hidden**() function returns the following values.

Value	Explanation
0 (zero)	If none of the selection is formatted as hidden
–1	If part of the selection is formatted as hidden
1	If all the selection is formatted as hidden

See Also   **FormatFont**

Highlight

Syntax   **Highlight**

Remarks   Highlights the selected text. If the selection is already highlighted, **Highlight** removes the highlight formatting. If no text is selected, the **Highlight** statement has no effect. In Word version 6.0, **Highlight** is unavailable and generates an error.

Use the **HighlightColor** statement to change the highlight color for the selected text, or use the **ToolsOptionsRevisions** statement to change the default highlight color.

See Also   **EditFindHighlight**, **EditReplaceHighlight**, **HighlightColor**, **ToolsOptionsRevisions**

HighlightColor, HighlightColor()

Syntax   **HighlightColor** *Color*

HighlightColor()

Remarks   The **HighlightColor** statement sets the highlight color for the selected text. If no text is selected, the **HighlightColor** statement has no effect. Use the **ToolsOptionsRevisions** statement to change the default highlight color.

In Word version 6.0, **HighlightColor** and **HighlightColor**() are unavailable and generate errors.

Argument	Explanation
Color	The highlight color. For a list of colors and their values, see **CharColor**.
	If *Color* is set to 0 (zero), highlight formatting is removed.

The **HighlightColor()** function returns the following values.

Value	Explanation
-1	If the selection contains text with different highlight colors.
0 (zero)	If the selection contains no highlight formatting.
n	A number indicating the highlight color. For a list of colors and their corresponding numeric values, see **CharColor**.

See Also   **EditFindHighlight**, **EditReplaceHighlight**, **Highlight**, **ToolsOptionsRevisions**

HLine

Syntax   **HLine** [*Count*]

Remarks   Scrolls the active document horizontally. A "line" corresponds to clicking a scroll arrow on the horizontal scroll bar once.

Argument	Explanation
Count	The amount to scroll, in lines:
	Omitted One line to the right
	> 0 (zero) The specified number of lines to the right
	< 0 (zero) The specified number of lines to the left; scrolls into the left margin only if there is text in the margin

See Also   **HPage**, **HScroll**, **VLine**

Hour()

Syntax   **Hour**(*SerialNumber*)

Remarks   Returns an integer between 0 (zero) and 23, inclusive, corresponding to the hours component of *SerialNumber*, a decimal representation of the date, time, or both. For information about serial numbers, see **DateSerial()**.

Example   This example sets the variable thishour to the hours component of the current time:

```
thishour = Hour(Now())
```

See Also   **DateSerial()**, **Day()**, **Minute()**, **Month()**, **Now()**, **Second()**, **Today()**, **Weekday()**, **Year()**

HPage

Syntax   **HPage** [*Count*]

Remarks   Scrolls the active document horizontally. **HPage** corresponds to clicking the horizontal scroll bar to the left or right of the scroll box.

Argument	Explanation
Count	The amount to scroll, in document-window widths:
	Omitted One width to the right
	> 0 (zero) The specified number of widths to the right
	< 0 (zero) The specified number of widths to the left

See Also   **HLine**, **HScroll**, **VPage**

HScroll, HScroll()

Syntax   **HScroll** *Percentage*

HScroll()

Remarks   The **HScroll** statement scrolls horizontally to the specified percentage of the document width. **HScroll** corresponds to dragging the scroll box on the horizontal scroll bar.

The **HScroll**() function returns the current horizontal scroll position as a percentage of the document width. **HScroll**() does not return negative values; if the document is scrolled into the left margin, **HScroll**() returns 0 (zero).

See Also   **HLine**, **HPage**, **VScroll**

If...Then...Else

Syntax   **If** *Condition* **Then** *Instruction* [**Else** *Instruction*]

If *Condition1* **Then**
    Series of instructions
[**ElseIf** *Condition2* **Then**
    Series of instructions]
[**Else**
    Series of instructions]
End If

Remarks   Runs instructions conditionally. In the simplest form of the **If** conditional—**If** *Condition* **Then** *Instruction*—the *Instruction* runs if *Condition* is true. In WordBasic, "true" means the condition evaluates to –1 and "false" means the condition evaluates to 0 (zero).

You can write an entire **If** conditional on one line if you specify one condition following **If** and one instruction following **Then** (and one instruction following **Else**, if included). Do not conclude this form of the conditional with **End If**. Note that it is possible to specify multiple instructions using this form if you separate the instructions with colons, as in the following conditional:

```
If Bold() = 1 Then Bold 0 : Italic 1
```

In general, if you need to specify a series of conditional instructions, the full syntax is preferable to separating instructions with colons. With the full syntax, you can use **ElseIf** to include a second condition nested within the **If** conditional. You can add as many **ElseIf** instructions to an **If** conditional as you need.

For more information about **If...Then...Else**, see Chapter 3, "WordBasic Fundamentals," in Part 1, "Learning WordBasic."

Examples   This example applies bold formatting to the entire selection if the selection is partially bold:

```
If Bold() = -1 Then Bold 1
```

The following example applies italic formatting if the selection is entirely bold; otherwise, underline formatting is applied:

```
If Bold() = 1 Then Italic 1 Else Underline 1
```

The following example shows how you can use a compound expression as the condition (in this case, whether the selection is both bold and italic):

```
If Bold() = 1 And Italic() = 1 Then ResetChar
```

The following example uses the full syntax available with the **If** conditional. The conditional could be described as follows: "If the selection is entirely bold, make it italic. If the selection is partially bold, reset the character formatting. Otherwise, make the selection bold."

```
If Bold() = 1 Then
    Italic 1
ElseIf Bold() = -1 Then
    ResetChar
Else
    Bold 1
End If
```

See Also   **For…Next, Goto, Select Case, While…Wend**

Indent

Syntax   **Indent**

Remarks   Moves the left indent of the selected paragraphs to the next tab stop of the first paragraph in the selection. **Indent** maintains the setting of a first-line or hanging indent.

See Also   **FormatParagraph, HangingIndent, UnIndent**

Input

Syntax   **Input** #*FileNumber, Variable1*[$] [, *Variable2*[$]] [, *Variable3*[$]] [, …]

Input [*Prompt$,*] *Variable1*[$] [, *Variable2*[$]] [, *Variable3*[$]] [, …]

Remarks   Retrieves string or numeric values from a sequential file, typically containing data added with the **Print** statement, and assigns the values to variables. *FileNumber* is the number specified in the **Open** instruction that opened the file for input. For more information about sequential files, see Chapter 9, "More WordBasic Techniques," in Part 1, "Learning WordBasic."

Input is similar to **Read** in that it retrieves comma-delimited values from sequential files, but unlike **Read**, it does not remove quotation marks from string values. **Input** can accept strings with as many as 65,280 characters. Longer strings are truncated. For more information, see **Read**.

If *FileNumber* is omitted, the user is prompted with a question mark (?) in the status bar to type one or more values, separated by commas. The user presses ENTER to end keyboard input. If *Prompt$* is specified, the question mark follows the string.

Examples

This Windows example opens for input a list of files to save in rich-text format (RTF). Assume that FILES.TXT is a text file in which each paragraph contains two string values: the filename to open and the filename to save. The instructions open each file in turn and save it in RTF. On the Macintosh, substitute folder names such as HD:WORD DOCS: and HD:RTF DOCS:.

```
Open "C:\DOCS\FILES.TXT" For Input As #1
While Not Eof(#1)
    Input #1, docname$, rtfname$
    FileOpen "C:\DOCS\" + docname$
    FileSaveAs .Name = "C:\RTF\" + rtfname$, .Format = 6
    FileClose 2
Wend
Close #1
```

The following example displays the prompt "RTF filename?" in the status bar and defines the variable rtfname$ with the text the user types:

```
Input "RTF filename", rtfname$
```

See Also

Close, Eof(), Input$(), InputBox$(), Line Input, Lof(), Open, Read, Print, Seek, Write

Input$()

Syntax

Input$(*NumChars***, [#]***FileNumber***)**

Remarks

Reads *NumChars* characters (as many as 32,767) from an open sequential file. *FileNumber* is the number specified in the **Open** instruction that opened the file for input.

Example

This example defines the variable filecode$ with the first 10 characters in the text file INFO.TXT:

```
Open "INFO.TXT" For Input As #1
filecode$ = Input$(10, #1)
Close #1
```

See Also

Close, Eof(), Input, InputBox$(), Line Input, Lof(), Open, Print, Read, Seek, Write

InputBox$()

Syntax

InputBox$(***Prompt$* [, *Title$*] [, *Default$*])**

Remarks

Displays a dialog box requesting a single piece of information and returns the text entered in the dialog box when the user chooses the OK button. If the user chooses the Cancel button, an error occurs. You can use the **On Error** statement to trap the error.

Argument	Explanation
Prompt$	Text displayed in the dialog box indicating the kind of information requested. If *Prompt$* is longer than 255 characters, an error occurs.
Title$	Text displayed in the title bar of the dialog box (if omitted, Word uses the title "Microsoft Word").
Default$	Text that initially appears in the text box of the dialog box. This value is returned if the user types nothing before choosing OK. If *Default$* is longer than 255 characters, an error occurs.

In Windows, if the user presses ENTER to start a new line while the dialog box is displayed, **InputBox$()** returns text containing Chr$(11) + Chr$(10) (a newline character followed by a paragraph mark) where the line break was made. For a method of removing the newline character, see the third example for this entry. On the Macintosh, if the user presses RETURN to start a new line, Chr$(13) is returned.

To choose the OK button in an input box using keys, press ENTER (Macintosh), or press TAB to move to the OK button, and then press ENTER (Windows).

Examples

This example asks the user to type a word, which is assigned to the variable word$. You could use this variable in a macro that counts the occurrences of a given word in the active document (as in the example for **EditFindFound()**).

```
word$ = InputBox$("Count instances of:", "WordCounter")
```

The following example prompts the user to type a number from 1 to 10. **InputBox$()** returns what the user types as a string, which the **Val()** function converts to a number to assign to the numeric variable num. Note that if the user spells out "Ten" instead of typing "10," **Val()** returns 0.

```
num = Val(InputBox$("Type a number from 1 to 10:"))
```

This example asks the user to type multiple lines, which are assigned to the variable a$. The **CleanString$()** function removes any extra newline characters (returned in Windows) so that line breaks are preserved as entered by the user.

```
a$ = InputBox$("Type multiple lines:")
a$ = CleanString$(a$)
```

See Also   **Input, MsgBox, On Error, Val()**

Insert

Syntax   **Insert** *Text$*

Remarks	Inserts the specified text at the insertion point. You can insert characters such as quotation marks, tab characters, nonbreaking hyphens, and newline characters using the **Chr$()** function with **Insert**. You can insert numbers by first converting them to text with the **Str$()** function.
Examples	This example inserts the text "Hamlet" (without quotation marks) at the insertion point:

```
Insert "Hamlet"
```

The following example inserts the text "Hamlet" enclosed in quotation marks at the insertion point:

```
Insert Chr$(34) + "Hamlet" + Chr$(34)
```

This example inserts the text "GroupA:35" at the insertion point. To create the number portion of the string, **Str$()** converts a numeric variable to a string, and **LTrim$()** removes the leading space that is automatically added by **Str$()**.

```
num = 35
num$ = LTrim$(Str$(num))
Insert "GroupA:" + num$
```

See Also	**Chr$()**, **InsertPara**, **LTrim$()**, **Str$()**

InsertAddCaption

Syntax	**InsertAddCaption [.Name =** *text*]
Remarks	Adds a new item to the Label box in the Caption dialog box (Insert menu). The new item becomes a valid string for the .Label argument in an **InsertCaption** instruction.

Argument	Explanation
.Name	The name for the new caption label

Example	This example adds "Diagram" to the list of available caption labels:

```
InsertAddCaption .Name = "Diagram"
```

See Also	**InsertAutoCaption, InsertCaption, InsertCaptionNumbering**

InsertAddress

Syntax	**InsertAddress**
Remarks	Opens the Address Book window of the default Personal Address Book and inserts the selected address at the insertion point.

InsertAddress is available only if Windows 95 and either Microsoft Exchange or Schedule+ version 2.0 are installed. In Word version 6.0, **InsertAddress** is unavailable and generates an error.

See Also   **AddAddress**, **GetAddress$()**, **ToolsCreateEnvelope**, **ToolsCreateLabels**

InsertAnnotation

Syntax   **InsertAnnotation**

Remarks   Inserts an annotation mark at the insertion point, opens the annotation pane, and places the insertion point in the annotation pane. If text is selected, the annotation mark is inserted immediately after the selected text, which appears shaded when the insertion point is in the associated annotation in the annotation pane. If the document window is too small to display the annotation pane, an error occurs.

See Also   **GoToAnnotationScope**, **InsertFootnote**, **ShowAnnotationBy**, **ViewAnnotations**

InsertAutoCaption

Syntax   **InsertAutoCaption [.Clear] [, .ClearAll] [, .Object** = *text*] **[, .Label** = *text*] **[, .Position** = *number*]

Remarks   Specifies a caption to insert automatically whenever an object of the specified type is inserted. The arguments for the **InsertAutoCaption** statement correspond to the options in the AutoCaption dialog box (Caption command, Insert menu).

Argument	Explanation
.Clear	Cancels adding captions automatically for the type of object specified by .Object.
.ClearAll	Cancels adding captions automatically for all types of objects.
.Object	The name of the object type for which you want to establish an automatic caption, as it appears in the Add Caption When Inserting box.
.Label	The caption label to insert automatically. If the label has not yet been defined, the instruction has no effect. Use **InsertAddCaption** to define new labels.
.Position	The position of the caption:
	0 (zero) Above Item
	1 Below Item

Example   This example creates a new caption label, "Picture," and specifies that whenever a Microsoft Word Picture object is inserted, this label is automatically inserted:

```
InsertAddCaption .Name = "Picture"
InsertAutoCaption .Object = "Word.Picture.6", \
        .Label = "Picture"
```

See Also   **InsertAddCaption, InsertCaption, InsertCaptionNumbering**

InsertAutoText

Syntax   **InsertAutoText**

Remarks   Attempts to match the current selection or the text before or surrounding the insertion point with an AutoText entry and insert the entry (including its formatting, if any). Word looks for the entry first in the active template, then in the Normal template, and finally in each loaded global template in the order listed in the Templates And Add-ins dialog box (File menu). If no match can be made, an error occurs.

See Also   **AutoText, AutoTextName$( ), CountAutoTextEntries( ), EditAutoText, GetAutoText$( ), SetAutoText**

InsertBreak

Syntax   **InsertBreak [.Type** = *number*]

Remarks   Inserts a page, column, or section break at the insertion point. The values available for the .Type argument correspond to the options in the Break dialog box (Insert menu).

Argument	Explanation
.Type	The type of break to insert:
	0 (zero) or omitted Page break
	1 Column break
	2 Next Page section break
	3 Continuous section break
	4 Even Page section break
	5 Odd Page section break
	6 Line break (newline character)

Example   This example inserts a page break before each Heading 1 paragraph in the active document:

```
StartOfDocument
EditFindClearFormatting
EditFindStyle .Style = "Heading 1"
EditFind .Find = "", .Direction = 0, .Wrap = 0
While EditFindFound()
    CharLeft
    InsertBreak .Type = 0
    EditFind .Find = "", .Direction = 0, .Wrap = 0
Wend
```

See Also   **InsertColumnBreak, InsertPageBreak, InsertSectionBreak, ParaPageBreakBefore, TableSplit**

InsertCaption

Syntax   **InsertCaption [.Label** = *text*] [, **.TitleAutoText** = *text*] [, **.Title** = *text*] [, **.Delete**] [, **.Position** = *number*]

Remarks   Inserts a caption above or below a selected item. The arguments for the **InsertCaption** statement correspond to the options in the Caption dialog box (Insert menu).

Argument	Explanation
.Label	The caption label to insert. If the label has not yet been defined, an error occurs. Use **InsertAddCaption** to define new labels.
.TitleAutoText	The AutoText entry whose contents you want to insert after the label in the caption (overrides any text specified for .Title).
.Title	The text to insert after the label in the caption (ignored if .TitleAutoText is specified).
.Delete	Removes the specified Label from the label box. Built-in labels (such as "Figure") cannot be deleted; if .Label specifies a built-in label, an error occurs.
.Position	When an item is selected, specifies whether to insert the caption above or below the item:
	0 (zero) Above Selected Item
	1 Below Selected Item

Example   This example inserts a caption with the label "Figure" and the title ": WordArt Object" after each WordArt object in the active document. **GetSelStartPos()** returns the character position of the insertion point before and after the **EditGoTo** instruction. When the character positions are the same, indicating there are no more WordArt objects, the **While…Wend** loop is exited.

```
StartOfDocument
cp1 = GetSelStartPos()
EditGoTo "o'MSWordArt.2'"
cp2 = GetSelStartPos()
While cp1 <> cp2
    CharRight 1, 1
    InsertCaption .Label = "Figure", \
            .Title = ": WordArt Object", .Position = 1
    cp1 = GetSelStartPos()
    EditGoTo "o'MSWordArt.2'"
    cp2 = GetSelStartPos()
Wend
```

See Also   **InsertAddCaption, InsertAutoCaption, InsertCaptionNumbering**

InsertCaptionNumbering

Syntax   **InsertCaptionNumbering** [**.Label** = *text*] [, **.FormatNumber** = *number*]
[, **.ChapterNumber** = *number*] [, **.Level** = *number*] [, **.Separator** = *text*]

Remarks   Defines a format for sequence numbers in captions for a specific type of item. The
arguments for the **InsertCaptionNumbering** statement correspond to the options
in the Caption Numbering dialog box (Caption command, Insert menu).

Argument	Explanation
.Label	The label for which you want to define a sequence number format. If the label has not yet been defined, an error occurs. Use **InsertAddCaption** to define new labels.
.FormatNumber	Specifies a default format for the sequence number in captions containing the specified label:
	0 (zero) 1, 2, 3, …
	1 a, b, c, …
	2 A, B, C, …
	3 i, ii, iii, …
	4 I, II, III, …
.ChapterNumber	If 1, a chapter number is included by default in captions containing the specified label. Chapters are determined by the heading style specified by .Level.
.Level	A number corresponding to the heading style used for chapter headings in the active document: 1 corresponds to Heading 1, 2 corresponds to Heading 2, and so on.
.Separator	The character to use as a separator between the chapter number and the sequence number.

Example   This example defines a number format for captions containing the "Figure" label. Chapter numbers are excluded from the sequence number.

```
InsertCaptionNumbering .Label = "Figure", .FormatNumber = 3, \
        .ChapterNumber = 0
```

See Also   **InsertAddCaption**, **InsertAutoCaption**, **InsertCaption**

InsertChart

Syntax   **InsertChart**

Remarks   Starts Microsoft Graph and displays a default chart for editing. When the user exits Microsoft Graph, the chart is embedded in the active document. The instruction `InsertChart` is the same as the instruction `InsertObject` `.Class = "MSGraph"`.

See Also   **InsertDrawing**, **InsertExcelTable**, **InsertObject**

InsertColumnBreak

Syntax   **InsertColumnBreak**

Remarks   Inserts a column break at the insertion point. If the insertion point is in a table, **InsertColumnBreak** splits the table by inserting a paragraph mark above the row containing the insertion point. The instruction `InsertColumnBreak` is the same as the instruction `InsertBreak .Type = 1`.

See Also   **InsertBreak**, **InsertPageBreak**, **InsertSectionBreak**, **TableSplit**

InsertCrossReference

Syntax   **InsertCrossReference [.ReferenceType** = *text*] [, **.ReferenceKind** = *text*] [, **.ReferenceItem** = *text*]

Remarks   Inserts a cross-reference to a heading, bookmark, footnote, endnote, or an item for which a caption label is defined (for example, an equation, figure, or table). The arguments for the **InsertCrossReference** statement correspond to the options in the Cross-reference dialog box (Insert menu).

Argument	Explanation
.ReferenceType	The type of item to which you want to insert a cross-reference, as it appears in the Reference Type box.

Argument	Explanation
.ReferenceKind	A number specified as text corresponding to the information you want the cross-reference to include. See the following table for available values.
.ReferenceItem	If .ReferenceType is "Bookmark", a bookmark name. For all other reference types, a number specified as text corresponding to an item in the For Which [Reference Type] box: "1" corresponds to the first item, "2" corresponds to the second item, and so on.

The following table shows the values available for .ReferenceKind based on the setting for .ReferenceType.

.ReferenceType	Values available for .ReferenceKind	
Heading	0 (zero)	Heading Text
	7	Page Number
	8	Heading Number
Bookmark	1	Bookmark Text
	7	Page Number
	9	Paragraph Number
Footnote	5	Footnote Number
	7	Page Number
Endnote	6	Endnote Number
	7	Page Number
An item for which a caption label is defined	2	Entire Caption
	3	Only Label And Number
	4	Only Caption Text
	7	Page Number

Example

This example inserts a sentence containing two cross references to a diagram: one to the caption and another to the page containing the diagram. A typical sentence inserted with these instructions might be, "For a diagram of a widget, see 'Figure 1: Standard Widget' on page 5."

```
Insert "For a diagram of a widget, see " + Chr$(34)
InsertCrossReference .ReferenceType = "Figure", \
        .ReferenceKind = "2", .ReferenceItem = "1"
Insert Chr$(34) + " on page "
InsertCrossReference .ReferenceType = "Figure", \
        .ReferenceKind = "7", .ReferenceItem = "1"
Insert "."
```

See Also   **InsertCaption**

InsertDatabase

Syntax

InsertDatabase [.**Format** = *number*] [, .**Style** = *number*]
[, .**LinkToSource** = *number*] [, .**Connection** = *text*] [, .**SQLStatement** = *text*]
[, .**SQLStatement1** = *text*] [, .**PasswordDoc** = *text*] [, .**PasswordDot** = *text*]
[, .**DataSource** = *text*] [, .**From** = *text*] [, .**To** = *text*] [, .**IncludeFields** = *number*]

Remarks

Retrieves data from a data source (for example, a separate Word document, a Microsoft Excel worksheet, or a Microsoft Access database) and inserts it into the active document as a table.

Argument	Explanation
.Format	Specifies a format listed under Formats in the Table AutoFormat dialog box (Table menu): 0 (zero) corresponds to the first format in the list ("none"), 1 corresponds to the second format, and so on.
.Style	Specifies which attributes of the format specified by .Format to apply to the table. Use the sum of any combination of the following values:

0	None
1	Borders
2	Shading
4	Font
8	Color
16	Auto Fit
32	Heading Rows
64	Last Row
128	First Column
256	Last Column

Argument	Explanation
.LinkToSource	If 1, establishes a link between the new table and the data source.
.Connection	Specifies a range within which to perform the query. How you specify the range depends on how data is retrieved. For example:

- When retrieving data using ODBC (Windows only), you specify a connection string.
- When retrieving data from Microsoft Excel using dynamic data exchange (DDE), you specify a named range.
- When retrieving data from Microsoft Access (Windows only), you specify the word "Table" or "Query" followed by the name of a table or query.

Argument	Explanation
.SQLStatement	An optional query string that retrieves a subset of the data in a primary data source to insert into the document (Windows only).
.SQLStatement1	If the query string is longer than 255 characters, .SQLStatement specifies the first portion of the string and .SQLStatement1 specifies the second portion (Windows only).
.PasswordDoc	The password (if any) required to open the data source.
.PasswordDot	If the data source is a Word document, the password (if any) required to open the attached template.
.DataSource	The path and filename of the data source.
.From	The number of the first data record in the range of records you want to insert.
.To	The number of the last data record in the range of records you want to insert.
.IncludeFields	If 1, field names from the data source appear in the first row of the new table.

Note To generate the connection and query strings automatically, record the actions you take in the Database dialog box (Insert menu) as a macro.

See Also   **InsertExcelTable, MailMergeCreateDataSource**

InsertDateField

Syntax   **InsertDateField**

Remarks   Inserts a DATE field at the insertion point. The date format matches the last format chosen using the Date And Time command (Insert Menu).

See Also   **InsertDateTime, InsertField, InsertPageField, InsertTimeField**

InsertDateTime

Syntax   **InsertDateTime [.DateTimePic** = *text*] [, **.InsertAsField** = *number*]

Remarks   Inserts the current date, time, or both, as either text or a TIME field.

Argument	Explanation
.DateTimePic	A string describing the format used for displaying the date, time, or both. If omitted, Word uses the format specified by the "DateFormat=" line in the [Microsoft Word] section of WINWORD6.INI (Windows 3.*x*), Word Settings (6) (Macintosh), or the registry (Windows 95 and Windows NT). In Windows 3.*x*, if there is no "DateFormat=" line, Word uses the "sShortDate" setting in the [intl] section of WIN.INI.
.InsertAsField	Specifies whether Word inserts the information as a TIME field:
	0 (zero) Word inserts the information as text.
	1 Word inserts the information as a TIME field.
	Omitted Word inserts the information according to the current setting of the Insert As Field check box in the Date And Time dialog box (Insert menu).

Example

This example inserts a TIME field for the current date in the form "3 September, 1993":

```
InsertDateTime .InsertAsField = 1, .DateTimePic = "d MMMM, yyyy"
```

See Also   **InsertDateField, InsertField, InsertPageField**

InsertDrawing

Syntax   **InsertDrawing**

Remarks   If Microsoft Draw is installed on your computer, starts Microsoft Draw and displays a blank window. When the user exits Microsoft Draw, the drawing is embedded in the active document. The instruction `InsertDrawing` is the same as the instruction `InsertObject .Class = "MSDraw"`.

See Also   **DrawInsertWordPicture, InsertChart, InsertEquation, InsertExcelTable, InsertObject, InsertPicture, InsertSound, InsertWordArt**

InsertEquation

Syntax   **InsertEquation**

Remarks   If Microsoft Equation Editor is installed on your computer, starts Equation Editor. When the user exits Equation Editor, the equation is embedded in the active document. The instruction `InsertEquation` is the same as the instruction `InsertObject .Class = "Equation.2"`.

See Also   **ActivateObject, EditObject, InsertChart, InsertDrawing, InsertExcelTable, InsertWordArt**

InsertExcelTable

Syntax

InsertExcelTable

Remarks

Starts Microsoft Excel and displays a new worksheet. When the user exits Microsoft Excel, the worksheet is embedded in the active document. The instruction `InsertExcelTable` is the same as the instruction `InsertObject .Class = "Excel.Sheet.5"`.

See Also

InsertChart, **InsertDatabase**, **InsertObject**

InsertField

Syntax

InsertField .Field = *text*

Remarks

Inserts the specified field at the insertion point.

Argument	Explanation
.Field	The field type and instructions to insert. For information on a specific field, including syntax and examples, select the field name in the Field dialog box (Insert menu), and then press F1 (Windows) or HELP (Macintosh). The .Field argument accepts a maximum of 255 characters.

Do not include the field characters ({ }), but follow all other syntax rules for field codes. To insert quotation marks in field codes, use `Chr$(34)`.

Examples

This example inserts an AUTHOR field:

```
InsertField .Field = "AUTHOR"
```

The following example nests a FILLIN field within a COMMENTS field. The instructions display all field codes, insert a COMMENTS field using **InsertField**, then insert the FILLIN field using **InsertFieldChars**.

```
ToolsOptionsView .FieldCodes = 1
InsertField .Field = "COMMENTS"
CharLeft
InsertFieldChars
Insert "FILLIN " + Chr$(34) + "Type your comment" + Chr$(34)
```

See Also

InsertFieldChars

InsertFieldChars

Syntax   **InsertFieldChars**

Remarks   Inserts field characters ({}) at the insertion point and then positions the insertion
                  point between the field characters.

See Also   **InsertField**

InsertFile

Syntax   **InsertFile .Name** = *text* [, **.Range** = *text*] [, **.ConfirmConversions** = *number*]
                  [, **.Link** = *number*]

Remarks   Inserts all or part of the specified file at the insertion point.

Argument	Explanation
.Name	The path and filename of the file to insert. If the path is not specified, the current folder is assumed.
.Range	If the file specified by .Name is a Word document, .Range is a bookmark. If the file is another type (for example, a Microsoft Excel worksheet), .Range refers to a named range or cell range (for example, R1C1:R3C4). If Word cannot recognize .Range, an error occurs.
.ConfirmConversions	Specifies whether Word displays the Convert File dialog box when inserting files in formats other than Word Document format.
.Link	If 1, inserts an INCLUDETEXT field instead of the contents of the file itself.

Examples   This example inserts the contents of PRICES.DOC into the active document. On
                  the Macintosh, substitute a path and filename such as HD:PRICES:PRICE LIST.

```
InsertFile .Name = "C:\PRICES\PRICES.DOC"
```

The following example inserts the portion of PRICES.DOC marked with the
bookmark "sportscars" into the active document:

```
InsertFile .Name = "PRICES.DOC", .Range = "sportscars"
```

The following Windows example creates a new document and then inserts one INCLUDETEXT field for each file in the folder C:\TMP with the filename extension .TXT:

```
FileNewDefault
ChDir "C:\TMP"
name$ = Files$("*.TXT")
While name$ <> ""
    InsertFile name$, .Link = 1, .ConfirmConversions = 0
    InsertPara
    name$ = Files$()
Wend
```

To change the previous example for the Macintosh, substitute `ChDir "HD:TEMP FILES"` and `name$ = Files$(MacID$("TEXT"))` for the second and third instructions, respectively.

See Also   **InsertDatabase**, **InsertField**

InsertFootnote

Syntax   **InsertFootnote [.Reference = *text*] [, .NoteType = *number*]**

Remarks   Inserts a footnote or endnote reference mark at the insertion point, opens the footnote or endnote pane, and places the insertion point in the pane. The arguments for the **InsertFootnote** statement correspond to the options in the Footnote And Endnote dialog box (Footnote command, Insert menu).

Argument	Explanation
.Reference	A custom reference mark. If omitted, Word inserts an automatically numbered reference mark.
	To specify a symbol, use the syntax {*FontName CharNum*}. *FontName* is the name of a font containing the symbol. Names of decorative fonts appear in the Font box in the Symbol dialog box (Insert menu). *CharNum* is the sum of 31 and the number corresponding to the position of the symbol you want to insert, counting from left to right in the table of symbols. For example, to specify an omega (Ω) at position 56 in the table of symbols in the Symbol font, include the argument `.Reference = "{Symbol 87}"`.
.NoteType	Specifies whether to insert a footnote or endnote:
	0 (zero) Footnote
	1 Endnote
	Omitted The type that was inserted most recently

Example

This example inserts an automatically numbered footnote reference mark at the insertion point, inserts a footnote, and then closes the footnote pane:

```
InsertFootnote .NoteType = 0
Insert "Sara Levine, "
Italic 1 : Insert "The Willow Tree"
Italic 0 : Insert " (Lone Creek Press, 1993)."
ClosePane
```

See Also

InsertAnnotation, **NoteOptions**, **ViewFootnoteArea**, **ViewFootnotes**

InsertFormField

Syntax

InsertFormField [**.Entry** = *text*] [, **.Exit** = *text*] [, **.Name** = *text*]
[, **.Enable** = *number*] [, **.TextType** = *number*] [, **.TextDefault** = *text*]
[, **.TextWidth** = *number or text*] [, **.TextFormat** = *text*] [, **.CheckSize** = *number*]
[, **.CheckWidth** = *number or text*] [, **.CheckDefault** = *number*]
[, **.Type** = *number*] [, **.OwnHelp** = *number*] [, **.HelpText** = *text*]
[, **.OwnStat** = *number*] [, **.StatText** = *text*]

Remarks

Inserts a form field at the insertion point. The arguments for the **InsertFormField** statement correspond to the options in the Form Field (Insert menu) and Form Field Options dialog boxes.

Argument	Explanation
.Entry	The macro that runs when the form field receives the focus.
.Exit	The macro that runs when the form field loses the focus.
.Name	A name for a bookmark that will mark the form field.
.Enable	If 1, allows the form field to be changed as the form is filled in.
.TextType	When inserting a text form field, specifies the type:
	0 (zero) Regular Text
	1 Number
	2 Date
	3 Current Date
	4 Current Time
	5 Calculation
.TextDefault	The default text for a text form field.
.TextWidth	When inserting a text form field, specifies a maximum width:
	0 (zero) Unlimited
	> 0 A maximum width, in characters

Argument	Explanation
.TextFormat	When inserting a text form field, specifies a format appropriate for .TextType. If .TextType is set to 0 (zero) for Regular Text, the following values are available: Uppercase, Lowercase, First Capital, Title Case.
	For formats available to other text types, review the items in the Text Format box in the Text Form Field Options dialog box.
.CheckSize	When inserting a check box form field, specifies whether to set a fixed size:
	0 (zero) Auto (the size is determined by the font size of the surrounding text).
	1 Exactly (the size is fixed to that specified by .CheckWidth).
.CheckWidth	When inserting a check box form field, and if .CheckSize is set to 1, specifies a fixed width and height in points or a text measurement.
.CheckDefault	When inserting a check box form field, specifies whether the check box should be cleared or selected by default:
	0 (zero) Cleared
	1 Selected
.Type	Specifies the type of form field to insert:
	0 (zero) or omitted Text form field
	1 Check box form field
	2 Drop-down form field
.OwnHelp	Specifies the source of the text that is displayed in a message box when the form field has the focus and the user presses the F1 key (Windows) or COMMAND+/ or HELP (Macintosh):
	0 (zero) None
	1 The text of the AutoText entry specified by .HelpText
	2 The text specified by .HelpText
.HelpText	If .OwnHelp is set to 1, the name of an AutoText entry containing help text for the form field. If .OwnHelp is set to 2, help text.
.OwnStat	Specifies the source of the text that is displayed in the status bar when the form field has the focus:
	0 (zero) None
	1 The text of the AutoText entry specified by .StatText
	2 The text specified by .StatText
.StatText	If .OwnStat is set to 1, the name of an AutoText entry containing status bar text for the form field. If .OwnHelp is set to 2, the text to be displayed in the status bar.

Examples   This example inserts a drop-down form field for which status bar text is specified and then adds the names of three cities to the form field:

```
InsertFormField .Name = "Cities", .Enable = 1, .Type = 2, \
        .OwnStat = 1, .StatText = "Select a city."
AddDropDownItem "Cities", "Bonn"
AddDropDownItem "Cities", "Paris"
AddDropDownItem "Cities", "Tokyo"
```

The following example inserts a check box form field that is 8 points high and wide and is selected by default. WriteSettings is specified as the "on-exit" macro that runs when the check box loses the focus. In a macro, instructions following this one could use **GetFormResult()** and **SetPrivateProfileString** to record in a text file whether the user selects or clears the check box.

```
InsertFormField .Exit = "WriteSettings", .Name = "Check1", \
        .Enable = 1, .CheckSize = 1, .CheckWidth = "8 pt", \
        .CheckDefault = 1, .Type = 1
```

The following example inserts a text form field. The argument .TextType = 1 specifies that the text is a number, and .TextFormat = "0%" specifies that the number be shown as a percentage. The default percentage is 100 percent.

```
InsertFormField .Name = "PercentComplete", .Enable = 1, \
        .TextType = 1, .TextWidth = "4", \
        .TextDefault = "100%", .TextFormat = "0%", .Type = 0
```

See Also   **AddDropDownItem, CheckBoxFormField, DropDownFormField, EnableFormField, FormFieldOptions, RemoveAllDropDownItems, RemoveDropDownItem, TextFormField**

InsertFrame

Syntax   **InsertFrame**

Remarks   Inserts an empty frame, or frames the selected text, graphic, or both. If there is no selection, Word inserts a 1-inch–square frame at the insertion point (the frame appears as a square in page layout view). You can change the dimensions of the frame with **FormatFrame**.

Example   This example inserts a frame and then positions it in the margin to the left of the current paragraph, so the user can type a margin note in it. If the active document is not in page layout view, Word displays a message box asking if the user wants to switch to page layout view.

```
SelType 1
If ViewPage() = 0 Then
    ans = MsgBox("Switch to page layout view?", \
            "Insert Margin Note", 36)
    If ans = - 1 Then ViewPage
End If
InsertFrame
FormatFrame .Wrap = 1, .WidthRule = 1, .FixedWidth = ".75 in", \
        .PositionHorz = "Left", .PositionHorzRel = 1, \
        .DistFromText = "0.13 in", .PositionVert = "0", \
        .PositionVertRel = 2, .DistVertFromText = "0"
SelType 1 : FontSize 8 : Italic 1
ToolsOptionsView .HScroll = 1
HScroll 0
```

See Also   **FormatFrame**, **RemoveFrames**

InsertIndex

Syntax   **InsertIndex** [.**HeadingSeparator** = *number*] [, .**Replace** = *number*]
[, .**Type** = *number*] [, .**RightAlignPageNumbers** = *number*]
[, .**Columns** = *number*]

Remarks   Compiles and inserts an index at the insertion point or replaces an existing index.
The index is the result of an INDEX field that you can update when index entries
change.

Argument	Explanation
.HeadingSeparator	Specifies the heading separator:
	0 (zero) or omitted None
	1 Blank Line
	2 Letter
.Replace	Specifies whether to replace the index, if it already exists:
	0 (zero) or omitted The existing index is not replaced (the instruction has no effect other than to select the index).
	1 The existing index is replaced.
.Type	Specifies the type of index:
	0 (zero) or omitted Indented
	1 Run-in
.RightAlignPageNumbers	If 1, aligns page numbers with the right edge of the column.
.Columns	The number of columns you want in the index.

Example

This example inserts a simple, indented index that replaces the current index, if one exists:

```
InsertIndex .Type = 0, .HeadingSeparator = 0, .Replace = 1
```

See Also

AutoMarkIndexEntries, **MarkIndexEntry**

InsertMergeField

Syntax

InsertMergeField .MergeField = *text*

Remarks

Inserts a MERGEFIELD field that Word updates in each merge document during a mail merge. If the active document is not a main document, an error occurs.

Argument	Explanation
.MergeField	A merge field name corresponding to the type of information you want to insert. Field names appear in the first record of the data source or in the header source (if a header source is attached to the main document).

Example

This example inserts a MERGEFIELD field that is updated with the city name from the data source during a mail merge:

```
InsertMergeField .MergeField = "City"
```

See Also

InsertField, **MailMergeInsertAsk**, **MailMergeInsertFillIn**, **MailMergeInsertIf**, **MailMergeInsertMergeRec**, **MailMergeInsertMergeSeq**, **MailMergeInsertNext**, **MailMergeInsertNextIf**, **MailMergeInsertSet**, **MailMergeInsertSkipIf**

InsertObject

Syntax

InsertObject [**.IconNumber** = *number*] [**, .FileName** = *text*] [**, .Link** = *number*] [**, .DisplayIcon** = *number*] [**, .Tab** = *number*] [**, .Class** = *text*] [**, .IconFilename** = *number*] [**, .Caption** = *text*]

Remarks

Starts an object linking and embedding (OLE) application in which the user creates an object, or immediately creates an embedded object using a specified file. In either case, **InsertObject** inserts an EMBED field at the insertion point.

Argument	Explanation
.IconNumber	If .DisplayIcon is set to 1, a number corresponding to the icon you want to use in the program file specified by .IconFilename. Icons appear in the Change Icon dialog box (Object command, Insert menu): 0 (zero) corresponds to the first icon, 1 to the second icon, and so on. If omitted, the first (default) icon is used.
	Note that on the Macintosh, icons for embedded objects cannot be changed and this argument is ignored.
.FileName	The path and filename of the file you want to store as an embedded object in the active document.
	If you specify .Filename, you must set .Tab to 1 and specify .Class. For an example of inserting an existing file as an object, see the second example in this entry.
.Link	If 1, links the embedded object to the file specified by .FileName. When the file changes, Word updates the embedded object.
.DisplayIcon	Specifies whether or not to display a link as an icon:
	0 (zero) or omitted Link is not displayed as an icon.
	1 Link is displayed as an icon.
.Tab	Specifies which tab to select when you display the Object dialog box with a **Dialog** or **Dialog( )** instruction.
	0 (zero) Create New tab
	1 Create From File tab
.Class	The class name of a new object to insert. To look up class names, insert an object in a document and view the field codes; the class name of the object follows the word "EMBED."
.IconFilename	If .DisplayIcon is set to 1, the path and filename of the program file in which the icon to be displayed is stored.
	Note that on the Macintosh, icons for embedded objects cannot be changed and this argument is ignored.
.Caption	If .DisplayIcon is set to 1, the caption of the icon to be displayed; if omitted, Word inserts the name of the object.

Examples

This Windows example starts Paintbrush®. When the user chooses Exit & Return from the File menu, Word inserts the following field at the insertion point: {EMBED PBrush * MERGEFORMAT}.

```
InsertObject .Class = "PBrush"
```

The following Windows example inserts an embedded object that is linked to the file FLOCK.BMP:

```
InsertObject .FileName = "C:\WIN31\FLOCK.BMP", .Link = 1, \
    .Tab = 1, .Class = "Pbrush"
```

The following Macintosh example inserts an embedded object that is linked to the file APRIL SALES:

```
InsertObject .FileName = "HD1:MICROSOFT WORD:CHARTS:APRIL SALES", \
    .Link = 1, .Tab = 1, .Class = "MSGraph"
```

See Also   **ActivateObject, EditObject, InsertChart, InsertDrawing, InsertExcelTable**

InsertPageBreak

Syntax   **InsertPageBreak**

Remarks   Inserts a page break at the insertion point. The instruction InsertPageBreak is the same as the instruction InsertBreak .Type = 0.

See Also   **InsertBreak, InsertColumnBreak, InsertSectionBreak, ParaPageBreakBefore, TableSplit**

InsertPageField

Syntax   **InsertPageField**

Remarks   Inserts a PAGE field without any field instructions at the insertion point.

See Also   **InsertDateField, InsertField, InsertPageNumbers, InsertTimeField**

InsertPageNumbers

Syntax   **InsertPageNumbers** [**.Type** = *number*] [**, .Position** = *number*]
[**, .FirstPage** = *number*]

Remarks   Inserts a PAGE field inside a frame in the header or footer and positions the frame as specified. The arguments for the **InsertPageNumbers** statement correspond to the options in the Page Numbers dialog box (Insert menu).

Argument	Explanation
.Type	Specifies where to add the page field:
	0 (zero) Header
	1 Footer
.Position	Specifies the position of the framed PAGE field:
	0 (zero) Left
	1 Center
	2 Right
	3 Inside (left on odd pages and right on even pages)
	4 Outside (right on odd pages and left on even pages)
.FirstPage	If 1, the field is included in the header or footer on the first page.

Example

This example adds a right-aligned page number to the header and specifies that the page number not appear on the first page:

```
InsertPageNumbers .Type = 0, .Position = 2, .FirstPage = 0
```

See Also

FormatPageNumber, InsertPageField, ViewHeader

InsertPara

Syntax

InsertPara

Remarks

Inserts a paragraph mark at the insertion point.

See Also

Chr$(), Insert

InsertPicture

Syntax

InsertPicture .Name = *text* [, **.LinkToFile** = *number*] [, **.New**]

Remarks

Inserts a graphic at the insertion point. If .LinkToFile is set to 1 or 2, the graphic is inserted as an INCLUDEPICTURE field that you can update when the graphics file changes.

Argument	Explanation
.Name	The path and filename of the graphic to insert. If the path is omitted, the current folder is assumed.
.LinkToFile	Specifies whether to insert the graphic as a field and whether to save graphic data in the document:
	0 (zero) or omitted Inserts the graphic specified in the .Name argument.
	1 Inserts an INCLUDEPICTURE field at the insertion point and saves graphic data in the document.
	2 Inserts an INCLUDEPICTURE field at the insertion point and prevents graphic data from being stored in the document by adding a \d switch.
.New	Inserts a 1-inch–square empty metafile graphic, surrounded by a border.

Example

This example inserts an INCLUDEPICTURE field whose result is the Windows bitmap WINLOGO.BMP:

```
InsertPicture .Name = "WINLOGO.BMP", .LinkToFile = 1
```

The following example inserts an INCLUDEPICTURE field whose result is the PICT-format bitmap Artist:

```
InsertPicture .Name = "Artist", .LinkToFile = 1
```

See Also   **InsertDrawing**, **InsertFile**, **InsertObject**

InsertSectionBreak

Syntax   **InsertSectionBreak**

Remarks   Inserts a section break with the same formatting as the section containing the insertion point.

See Also   **InsertBreak**, **InsertColumnBreak**, **InsertPageBreak**

InsertSound

Syntax   **InsertSound**

Remarks   Starts Sound Recorder in Windows or Microsoft Voice Annotation on the Macintosh so the user can record or insert a sound. When the user exits the sound application, the sound is embedded in the active document. If the computer is not sound enabled, an error occurs.

See Also   **InsertChart**, **InsertDrawing**, **InsertExcelTable**, **InsertObject**

InsertSpike

Syntax   **InsertSpike**

Remarks   Empties the special AutoText entry "Spike" and inserts its contents at the insertion point. For an example, see **Spike**.

See Also   **EditAutoText**, **InsertAutoText**, **Spike**

InsertSubdocument

Syntax   **InsertSubdocument .Name** = *text* [, **.ConfirmConversions** = *number*] [, **.ReadOnly** = *number*] [, **.PasswordDoc** = *text*] [, **.PasswordDot** = *text*] [, **.Revert** = *number*] [, **.WritePasswordDoc** = *text*] [, **.WritePasswordDot** = *text*]

Remarks   Adds the specified file as a subdocument in the active master document. If the active document is not in outline or master document view, an error occurs. For argument descriptions, see **FileOpen**.

Example   This example adds the document SUB1.DOC to the beginning of the active document as a read-only, or locked, subdocument. On the Macintosh, substitute a path such as HD:MY DOCS:SUBDOC 1.

```
StartOfDocument
ViewMasterDocument
InsertSubdocument .Name = "C:\MYDOCS\SUB1.DOC", .ReadOnly = 1
```

See Also   **CreateSubdocument**, **FileOpen**, **MergeSubdocument**, **OpenSubdocument**, **RemoveSubdocument**, **SplitSubdocument**, **ViewMasterDocument**

InsertSymbol

Syntax   **InsertSymbol .Font** = *text*, **.Tab** = *number*, **.CharNum** = *number or text*

Remarks   Inserts a symbol at the insertion point. Note that **InsertSymbol** does not insert a SYMBOL field as in Word for Windows version 2.*x*. The arguments for the **InsertSymbol** statement correspond to the options in the Symbol dialog box (Insert menu).

Argument	Explanation
.Font	The name of the font containing the symbol. Names of decorative fonts appear in the Font box in the Symbol dialog box.

Argument	Explanation
.Tab	Specifies which tab to select when you display the Symbol dialog box with a **Dialog** or **Dialog**() instruction:
	0 (zero) Symbols tab
	1 Special Characters tab
.CharNum	The sum of 31 and the number corresponding to the position of the symbol on the table of symbols, counting from left to right. For example, to specify an omega (Ω) at position 56 on the table of symbols in the Symbol font, set .CharNum to 87.

Example   This example inserts a double-headed arrow at the insertion point:

```
InsertSymbol .Font = "Symbol", .CharNum = "171"
```

See Also   **Chr$()**

InsertTableOfAuthorities

Syntax   **InsertTableOfAuthorities** [**.Replace** = *number*] [, **.Passim** = *number*] [, **.KeepFormatting** = *number*] [, **.Category** = *number*]

Remarks   Collects citations from TA (Table of Authorities Entry) fields and inserts a TOA (Table of Authorities) field at the insertion point.

Argument	Explanation
.Replace	Specifies whether to replace a previously compiled table of authorities:
	0 (zero) or omitted The existing table of authorities is not replaced (the instruction has no effect other than selecting the field result).
	1 The existing table of authorities is replaced.
.Passim	If 1, Word replaces five or more different page references to the same authority with "passim."
.KeepFormatting	If 1, Word retains the formatting of long citations.
.Category	A number corresponding to an item in the Category box that specifies the type of citations to collect: 0 (zero) corresponds to the first item ("All"), 1 corresponds to the second item, and so on.

See Also   **InsertTableOfContents**, **InsertTableOfFigures**, **MarkCitation**

InsertTableOfContents

Syntax

InsertTableOfContents [**.Outline** = *number*] [**, .Fields** = *number*]
[**, .From** = *number*] [**, .To** = *number*] [**, .TableId** = *text*] [**, .AddedStyles** = *text*]
[**, .Replace** = *number*] [**, .RightAlignPageNumbers** = *number*]

Remarks

Collects table-of-contents entries from headings, TC (Table of Contents Entry) fields, or both, and inserts a TOC (Table of Contents) field at the insertion point.

Argument	Explanation
.Outline	If 1, collects table-of-contents entries from heading styles.
.Fields	If 1, collects table-of-contents entries from TC (Table of Contents Entry) fields.
.From	If .Outline is 1, the highest level of heading style to collect.
.To	If .Outline is 1, the lowest level of heading style to collect.
.TableId	The entry identifier specified in those TC fields you want to include in the table of contents.
.AddedStyles	Styles to collect in addition to the heading styles indicated by .From and .To. Use the following syntax when specifying .AddedStyles:
	StyleToCollect1,*TOC#*[,*StyleToCollect2*,*TOC#*][,…]
	You can specify any number of styles to collect, though the length of the string value cannot be longer than 256 characters. For example, .AddedStyles = "NoteStyle,3" causes text formatted with a style called "NoteStyle" to be collected into a table of contents and formatted with the TOC 3 style.
.Replace	Specifies whether to replace a previously compiled table of contents:
	0 (zero) or omitted The existing table of contents is not replaced (the instruction has no effect other than to select the table).
	1 The existing table of contents is replaced.
.RightAlignPageNumbers	If 1, aligns page numbers with the right margin.

Examples

This example inserts a table of contents using Heading 1 through Heading 3 styles. TC fields, if any, are excluded.

```
InsertTableOfContents .Outline = 1, .From = 1, .To = 3, \
        .Fields = 0, .RightAlignPageNumbers = 1, .Replace = 1
```

The following example inserts a table of contents using Heading 1 through Heading 3 styles and Heading 5 styles (Heading 4 styles are skipped). Note that headings formatted with the Heading 5 style are formatted with the TOC 4 style in the table of contents.

```
InsertTableOfContents .Outline = 1, .From = 1, .To = 3, \
    .AddedStyles = "Heading 5,4", .RightAlignPageNumbers = 1, \
    .Replace = 0
```

The following example inserts a table of contents based on text formatted with the "Intro," "Main heading," "Summary," and "Subhead" styles. Text formatted with the Intro, Main heading, and Summary styles is mapped to the TOC 1 style; text formatted with the Subhead style is mapped to the TOC 2 style.

```
custom$ = "Intro,1,Summary,1,Main heading,1,Subhead,2"
InsertTableOfContents .Outline = 0, .AddedStyles = custom$, \
        .RightAlignPageNumbers = 1, .Replace = 0
```

See Also   **InsertTableOfAuthorities, InsertTableOfFigures, MarkTableOfContentsEntry**

InsertTableOfFigures

Syntax   **InsertTableOfFigures** [**.Outline** = *number*][, **.From** = *number*] [, **.To** = *number*] [, **.Caption** = *text*] [, **.Label** = *number*] [, **.RightAlignPageNumbers** = *number*] [, **.Replace** = *number*]

Remarks   Collects captions with the specified label and inserts them at the insertion point.

Argument	Explanation
.Outline	If 1, includes text from outline headings in the table of figures; set .Outline to 0 (zero) to collect captions only.
.From	If .Outline is 1, the highest level of heading style to collect.
.To	If .Outline is 1, the lowest level of heading style to collect.
.Caption	The label that identifies the items for which you want to create a table.
.Label	If 1, includes labels and sequence numbers with captions in the table of figures.
.RightAlignPageNumbers	If 1, aligns page numbers with the right margin.
.Replace	Specifies whether to replace a previously compiled table of figures:
	0 (zero) or omitted The existing table of figures is not replaced (the instruction has no effect other than to select the table).
	1 The existing table of figures is replaced.

Example

This example inserts a table of figures marked by captions with the label "Diagram." If a table of diagrams already exists, it is replaced.

```
InsertTableOfFigures .Outline = 0, .Caption = "Diagram", .Label = 1, \
            .RightAlignPageNumbers = 1, .Replace = 1
```

See Also

InsertAutoCaption, InsertCaption, InsertTableOfAuthorities, InsertTableOfContents

InsertTimeField

Syntax

InsertTimeField

Remarks

Inserts a TIME field without any field instructions at the insertion point.

See Also

InsertDateField, InsertDateTime, InsertField, InsertPageField

InsertWordArt

Syntax

InsertWordArt

Remarks

If Microsoft WordArt is installed on your computer, starts WordArt. When the user exits WordArt, the WordArt object is embedded in the active document. The instruction `InsertWordArt` is the same as the instruction `InsertObject` `.Class = "MSWordArt.2"`.

See Also

ActivateObject, EditObject, InsertChart, InsertDrawing, InsertEquation, InsertExcelTable

InStr()

Syntax

InStr([*Index,*] *Source$*, *Search$***)**

Remarks

Returns the character position in *Source$* at which *Search$* begins, where 1 corresponds to the first character, 2 to the second character, and so on. If *Source$* does not contain *Search$*, **InStr()** returns 0 (zero).

Argument	Explanation
Index	The character position in *Source$* at which to begin the search
Source$	The text to be searched
Search$	The text to search for

Examples

This example sets the variable pos to 7:

```
list$ = "Bonn, Paris, Tokyo"
city$ = "Paris"
pos = InStr(list$, city$)
```

The following example sets pos to 15. Note that if *Index* were not specified, pos would be 2.

```
pos = InStr(3, "Bonn, Paris, Tokyo", "o")
```

The following example, which assigns an MS-DOS filename with a filename extension to name$, defines prefix$ as the filename without the extension:

```
name$ = "SUMMARY.DOC"
dot = InStr(name$, ".")
If dot > 1 Then prefix$ = Left$(name$, dot - 1)
```

See Also   **Left$(), Len(), LTrim$(), Mid$(), Right$(), RTrim$()**

Int()

Syntax   **Int(*n*)**

Remarks   Returns the integer part of a decimal number *n*. If *n* is greater than or equal to 32,768 or less than or equal to –32,769, an error occurs.

Examples   This example sets the variable x to 98:

```
x = Int(98.6)
```

The following example sets x to –9.

```
x = Int(-9.6)
```

The following function rounds a decimal number to the nearest whole number.

```
Function fRoundOff(x)
    fRoundOff = Int(x + 0.5 * Sgn(x))
End Function
```

See Also   **Abs(), Rnd(), Sgn()**

IsAutoCorrectException()

Syntax   **IsAutoCorrectException(*Tab*, *Exception$*)**

Remarks   Returns a value indicating whether *Exception$* appears in the list of of AutoCorrect exceptions on the specified tab in the AutoCorrect Exceptions dialog box (AutoCorrect command, Tools Menu). In Word version 6.0, **IsAutoCorrectException()** is unavailable and generates an error.

Argument	Explanation
Tab	The tab where Word looks for *Exception$*:
	0 (zero) First Letter
	1 INitial CAps
Exception$	The text to find as an entry on the specified tab.

The **IsAutoCorrectException**() function returns the following values.

Value	Explanation
-1	*Exception$* is an exception list entry.
0	*Exception$* is not an exception list entry.

See Also   **CountAutoCorrectExceptions**(), **GetAutoCorrectException$**(), **ToolsAutoCorrectExceptions**

IsCustomDocumentProperty()

Syntax   **IsCustomDocumentProperty**(*Name$*)

Remarks   Returns 1 if the *Name$* property is a custom property, or returns 0 (zero) if it is not a custom property or is not valid. Use the **DocumentPropertyExists**() function to verify that the *Name$* property exists.

For a list of the built-in properties available in Word, see **DocumentPropertyName$**(). In Word version 6.0, **IsCustomDocumentProperty**() is unavailable and generates an error.

See Also   **CountDocumentProperties**(), **DocumentPropertyExists**(), **DocumentPropertyType**(), **IsDocumentPropertyReadOnly**()

IsDocumentDirty()

Syntax   **IsDocumentDirty**()

Remarks   Returns a value indicating whether the active document has changed since it was last saved (that is, if it is "dirty"). Whether a document is dirty determines if Word displays a prompt to save changes when the document is closed.

Value	Explanation
0 (zero)	If the document has not changed since it was last saved
−1	If the document has changed since it was last saved

Example

This example saves the active document if there are unsaved changes:

```
If IsDocumentDirty() = -1 Then FileSave
```

See Also

IsTemplateDirty(), **SetDocumentDirty**, **SetTemplateDirty**

IsDocumentPropertyReadOnly()

Syntax

IsDocumentPropertyReadOnly(*Name$* [, *CustomOrBuiltIn*])

Remarks

Returns 1 if the *Name$* property is read-only. If *Name$* is not a valid property, an error occurs. Use the **DocumentPropertyExists()** function to verify that the *Name$* property exists.

For a list of the built-in properties available in Word, see **DocumentPropertyName$()**. In Word version 6.0, **IsDocumentPropertyReadOnly()** is unavailable and generates an error.

Argument	Explanation
Name$	The name of the property.
CustomOrBuiltIn	Specifies whether *Name$* is a custom property or a built-in property:
	0 (zero) or omitted *Name$* is a custom property unless it appears in the list of built-in properties.
	1 *Name$* is a built-in property. If it is not one of the built-in properties, an error occurs.
	2 *Name$* is a custom property, regardless of whether a built-in property with the same name already exists.

See Also

DocumentPropertyExists(), **DocumentPropertyName$()**, **DocumentPropertyType()**, **IsCustomDocumentProperty()**

IsExecuteOnly()

Syntax

IsExecuteOnly([*Macro$*])

Remarks

Returns 0 (zero) if the specified macro can be edited or –1 if the macro is execute-only. Macros that cannot be edited are sometimes referred to as *encrypted*. You can make a macro execute-only using **MacroCopy**.

Argument	Explanation
Macro$	The name of a macro. Use the following syntax:
	[*TemplateName*:]*MacroName$*
	If *TemplateName* is omitted, Word looks for the macro in the Normal template and loaded global templates. If *TemplateName* is specified, the template must be open in a document window, attached to an open document, or loaded as a global template; otherwise **IsExecuteOnly()** generates an error.
	If both *TemplateName* and *MacroName$* are omitted, the macro containing the **IsExecuteOnly()** instruction is assumed.

Example

This example determines whether the global macro Test is execute-only. If it isn't, Word displays the macro in the macro-editing window.

```
encrypted = IsExecuteOnly("NORMAL:Test")
If encrypted = 0 Then ToolsMacro .Name = "Test", .Show = 1, .Edit
```

See Also

IsMacro(), **MacroCopy**

IsMacro()

Syntax

IsMacro([*WindowNumber*\]**)**

Remarks

Returns –1 if the window specified by *WindowNumber* is a macro-editing window and 0 (zero) if it is not.

Argument	Explanation
WindowNumber	Specifies a window on the Window menu: 1 corresponds to the first window, 2 to the second window, and so on. If *WindowNumber* is 0 (zero) or omitted, the active window is assumed. If *WindowNumber* does not correspond to a number on the Window menu, an error occurs.

Example

This example creates a new document if the active window is a macro-editing window:

```
If IsMacro() = -1 Then FileNewDefault
```

See Also

MacroFileName$(), **MacroNameFromWindow$()**, **SelInfo()**

IsTemplateDirty()

Syntax

IsTemplateDirty()

Remarks

Returns a value indicating whether the active template has changed since it was last saved (that is, if it is "dirty"). Whether a template is dirty determines if Word displays a prompt to save changes when the template is closed.

Value	Explanation
0 (zero)	If the template has not changed since it was last saved
−1	If the template has changed since it was last saved

Example

This example saves the active template if there are unsaved changes:

```
If IsTemplateDirty() = -1 Then SaveTemplate
```

See Also

IsDocumentDirty, **SaveTemplate**, **SetDocumentDirty()**, **SetTemplateDirty**

Italic, Italic()

Syntax

Italic [*On*]

Italic()

Remarks

The **Italic** statement adds or removes the italic character format for the selected text, or controls italic formatting for characters to be inserted at the insertion point.

Argument	Explanation
On	Specifies whether to add or remove the italic format:
	1 Formats the selection as italic.
	0 (zero) Removes the italic format.
	Omitted Toggles the italic format.

The **Italic()** function returns the following values.

Value	Explanation
0 (zero)	If none of the selection is formatted as italic
−1	If part of the selection is formatted as italic
1	If all the selection is formatted as italic

See Also

FormatFont

JustifyPara, JustifyPara()

Syntax   JustifyPara

JustifyPara()

Remarks   The **JustifyPara** statement justifies the selected paragraphs. The **JustifyPara()** function returns the following values.

Value	Explanation
0 (zero)	If none of the selection is justified
−1	If part of the selection is justified or there is a mix of alignments
1	If all the selection is justified

See Also   **CenterPara, FormatParagraph, LeftPara, RightPara**

KeyCode()

Syntax   **KeyCode**(*Count* [, *Context*] [, *FirstOrSecond*])

Remarks   Returns a number representing a key assignment that differs from the default assignment. For tables of key codes and the keys they represent, see **ToolsCustomizeKeyboard$**.

Argument	Explanation
Count	A number in the range 1 to **CountKeys**() specifying the custom key assignment for which you want to return a key code
Context	The template containing the custom key assignment:
	0 (zero) or omitted Normal template
	1 Active template
FirstOrSecond	If the key assignment is a sequence of two key combinations (for example, if you've assigned CTRL+S, N to **NormalStyle**), specifies which key combination to return a code for:
	1 The first key combination in the sequence
	2 The second key combination in the sequence
	If you specify 2 and the key assignment is not a key sequence, **KeyCode**() returns 255 (the null key code).

Example   This example inserts a table of key codes and macro names for key assignments in the active template that differ from the default assignments:

```
If CountKeys(1) = 0 Then
    MsgBox "No custom key assignments in active template."
    Goto bye
End If
FormatTabs .ClearAll
FormatTabs .Position = "1in", .Set
Bold 1 : Underline 1
Insert "Key Code" + Chr$(9) + "Macro"
Bold 0 : Underline 0
For i = 1 To CountKeys(1)
    Insert Chr$(13) + Str$(KeyCode(i, 1))
    combo2 = KeyCode(i, 1, 2)
    If combo2 <> 255 Then Insert "," + Str$(combo2)
    Insert Chr$(9) + KeyMacro$(i, 1)
Next i
bye:
```

See Also   **CountKeys**(), **KeyMacro$**()

KeyMacro$()

Syntax

KeyMacro$(*Count* [, *Context*]**)**

Remarks

Returns the name of a macro or built-in command with a key assignment that differs from the default assignment.

Argument	Explanation
Count	A number in the range 1 to **CountKeys( )** specifying the custom key assignment for which you want to return the command or macro name
Context	The template containing the custom key assignment:
	0 (zero) or omitted Normal template
	1 Active template

For an example, see **KeyCode( )**.

See Also

CountKeys( ), **KeyCode( )**, **MenuItemMacro$( )**

Kill

Syntax

Kill *FileSpec$*

Remarks

Deletes the specified file or files. If *FileSpec$* specifies an open document, an error occurs.

Argument	Explanation
FileSpec$	The file specification. In Windows, you can use the MS-DOS wildcard characters—the asterisk (*) and the question mark (?)—to specify files. You can also specify a path as part of the file specification (for example, C:\DOCS*.TXT).
	On the Macintosh, you can use **MacID$( )** to specify files of a certain type (for example, MacID$("TEXT")); to specify a path, precede the **Kill** instruction with a **ChDir** instruction.

Examples

This example deletes a file in C:\WORD\LETTERS. On the Macintosh, substitute a path and filename such as HD:WORD:LETTERS:DRAFT.

```
Kill "C:\WORD\LETTERS\DRAFT.DOC"
```

The following Windows example deletes all the files in the C:\DELETE folder:

```
Kill "C:\DELETE\*.*"
```

The previous example could be rewritten for the Macintosh as follows:

```
ChDir "HD:DELETE"
Kill MacID$("****")
```

See Also   **CopyFile, MacID$(), RmDir**

Language, Language$()

Syntax   **Language** *Language$*

Language$([*Count*])

Remarks   The **Language** statement identifies the selected text as being in a specific language. The proofing tools use dictionaries of the specified language on this text. Although the Language dialog box (Tools menu) lists language names in their English form, *Language$* must be in the specified language and include any accented characters. For example, Italian must be specified as "Italiano" and French must be specified as "Français." For a list of valid foreign language names, see **ToolsLanguage**.

If *Count* is 0 (zero) or omitted, the **Language$**() function returns the language format of the first character of the selected text. If there is no selection, **Language$**() returns the language format of the character to the left of the insertion point.

If *Count* is greater than 0 (zero), **Language$**() returns the name of the language *Count*, where *Count* is the position of the language in an internal list of untranslated language names. Note that the list of untranslated language names does not match the list in the Language dialog box (Tools menu) because in the dialog box, language names are translated into English and sorted alphabetically. The *Count* argument is in the range 1 to **CountLanguages**().

Examples   These instructions show three different uses for the **Language** statement. The first marks the selection as British English, the second as whatever language is twelfth, and the third as No Proofing. The proofing tools skip over text marked as No Proofing.

```
Language "English (UK)"
Language Language$(12)
Language "0"
```

The following macro creates a two-column list in the active document showing all valid **Language$**(*Count*) instructions and the corresponding language names that each value of *Count* returns. The returned language names are all valid arguments for the **Language** statement.

```
Sub MAIN
For i = 1 To CountLanguages()
    If i > 1 Then InsertPara
    Insert "Language$(" + Right$(Str$(i), Len(Str$(i))-1) + ")" \
        + Chr$(9) + Language$(i)
Next
End Sub
```

See Also   **CountLanguages**(), **ToolsLanguage**

LCase$()

Syntax   **LCase$(***Source$***)**

Remarks   Returns a string in which all letters of *Source$* have been converted to lowercase.

Example   This example displays the string assigned to the name$ variable in lowercase:

```
name$ = "Stella Richards"
MsgBox LCase$(name$)
```

See Also   **ChangeCase**, **UCase$()**

Left$()

Syntax   **Left$(***Source$***,** *Count***)**

Remarks   Returns the leftmost *Count* characters of *Source$*.

Examples   This example displays the text "Legal" in the status bar:

```
a$ = "Legal File List"
Print Left$(a$, 5)
```

The following example uses **Left$()** to return the first part of a hyphenated word. **InStr()** is used to determine the position of the hyphen (-) character. **Left$()** is then used to return all the characters to the left of the hyphen.

```
wholeWord$ = "fade-out"
hyphen = InStr(wholeWord$, "-")
firstWord$ = Left$(wholeWord$, (hyphen - 1))
MsgBox "First part of word: " + firstWord$
```

A similar set of instructions can be used to return the characters before the filename extension in an MS-DOS filename. Instead of determining the position of the hyphen, you would use **InStr()** to return the position of the period (.) character. This can be useful if you want to save a copy of the active document with a different filename extension. For an example, see **InStr()**.

See Also   **InStr()**, **Len()**, **LTrim$()**, **Mid$()**, **Right$()**, **RTrim$()**

LeftPara, LeftPara()

Syntax   **LeftPara**

                    LeftPara()

Remarks   The **LeftPara** statement aligns the selected paragraphs with the left indent.

The **LeftPara()** function returns the following values.

Value	Explanation
0 (zero)	If none of the selection is left-aligned
−1	If part of the selection is left-aligned
1	If all the selection is left-aligned

See Also   **CenterPara**, **FormatParagraph**, **JustifyPara**, **RightPara**

Len()

Syntax   **Len**(*Source$*)

Remarks   Returns the number of characters in *Source$*.

Example   This example prompts the user to type a name for an AutoText entry and then uses **Len()** to determine whether the name exceeds the 32-character limit. The **On Error** instruction prevents the "Command failed" message from appearing if the user cancels the **InputBox$()** dialog box.

```
On Error Goto Finish
Start:
a$ = InputBox$("Type a name for the AutoText entry.")
If Len(a$) > 32 Then
    MsgBox "Please type no more than 32 characters."
    Goto Start
End If
Finish:
```

See Also   **InStr()**, **Left$()**, **LTrim$()**, **Mid$()**, **Right$()**, **RTrim$()**

Let

Syntax   [**Let**] *Var = Expression*

Remarks   Assigns the value of an expression to a variable. The use of **Let** is optional.

Example   Each of the following instructions assigns the value 100 to the variable A:

```
Let A = 100
A = 100
```

See Also   **Dim**

Line Input

Syntax

Line Input #*FileNumber***,** *Variable***$**

Line Input [*Prompt$,*] *Variable***$**

Remarks

Reads an entire line from an open sequential file and places it into a string variable. In a sequential file, a line is terminated by the carriage-return (ANSI 13) and linefeed (ANSI 10) characters. *FileNumber* is the number specified by the **Open** instruction that opened the file for input. For more information about sequential files, see Chapter 9, "More WordBasic Techniques," in Part 1, "Learning WordBasic."

Line Input is similar to the **Input** and **Read** statements, but **Line Input** does not break the line into separate values at commas. It places the entire line into a single string variable. **Line Input** can accept lines as long as 65,280 characters. Longer lines are truncated. Unlike **Read**, which takes only the text within quotation marks, **Line Input** does not distinguish between quotation marks and other characters.

If #*FileNumber* is omitted, the user is prompted with a question mark (?) in the status bar to type a value. The user presses ENTER to end keyboard input. If *Prompt$* is specified, the question mark is not displayed.

Examples

This example places one line from the file designated as #1 into the variable sample$:

```
Line Input #1, sample$
```

The following example displays the default prompt (a question mark) in the status bar. The variable key$ is defined as the text entered after the question mark.

```
Line Input key$
```

The following example displays the prompt "Search text: " in the status bar. The variable target$ is defined as the text entered after the prompt.

```
Line Input "Search text: ", target$
```

See Also

Close, Eof(), Input, Input$(), Lof(), Open, Print, Read, Seek, Write

LineDown, LineDown()

Syntax

LineDown [*Count*] [**,** *Select*]

LineDown([*Count*] [**,** *Select*]**)**

Remarks

The **LineDown** statement moves the insertion point or the active end of the selection (the end that moves when you press SHIFT+DOWN ARROW) down by the specified number of lines.

Argument	Explanation
Count	The number of lines to move down; if omitted, 1 is assumed. Negative values move the insertion point or the active end of the selection up.
Select	Specifies whether to select text:

0 (zero) or omitted   Text is not selected. If there is already a selection, **LineDown** moves the insertion point *Count* lines below the selection.

Nonzero   Text is selected. If there is already a selection, **LineDown** moves the active end of the selection toward the end of the document.

In a typical selection made from left to right, where the active end of the selection is closer to the end of the document, **LineDown** extends the selection. In a selection made from right to left, it shrinks the selection.

The **LineDown()** function behaves the same as the statement and also returns the following values.

Value	Explanation
0 (zero)	If the insertion point or the active end of the selection cannot be moved down.
−1	If the insertion point or the active end of the selection is moved down by any number of lines, even if less than *Count*. For example, LineDown(10) returns −1 even if the insertion point is only three lines above the end of the document.

Examples

This example moves the insertion point down five lines:

```
LineDown 5
```

The following example uses **LineDown()** to count the lines in a document:

```
StartOfDocument
lines = 1
While LineDown()
    lines = lines + 1
Wend
MsgBox "There are" + Str$(lines) + " lines in the document."
```

See Also

LineUp, ParaDown, ParaUp

LineUp, LineUp()

Syntax   **LineUp** [*Count*] [, *Select*]

LineUp([*Count*] [, *Select*])

Remarks   The **LineUp** statement moves the insertion point or the active end of the selection (the end that moves when you press SHIFT+UP ARROW) up by the specified number of lines.

Argument	Explanation
Count	The number of lines to move up; if omitted, 1 is assumed. Negative values move the insertion point or the active end of the selection down.
Select	Specifies whether to select text:
	0 (zero) or omitted Text is not selected. If there is already a selection, **LineUp** moves the insertion point *Count* lines above the selection.
	Nonzero Text is selected. If there is already a selection, **LineUp** moves the active end of the selection toward the beginning of the document.
	In a typical selection made from left to right, where the active end of the selection is closer to the end of the document, **LineUp** shrinks the selection. In a selection made from right to left, it extends the selection.

The **LineUp()** function behaves the same as the statement and also returns the following values.

Value	Explanation
0 (zero)	If the insertion point or the active end of the selection cannot be moved up.
−1	If the insertion point or the active end of the selection is moved up by any number of lines, even if less than *Count*. For example, LineUp(10) returns −1 even if the insertion point is three lines below the start of the document.

Examples   This example moves the insertion point up 20 lines:

```
LineUp 20
```

The following example displays a message box if the insertion point is in the first line of the document:

```
If LineUp() = 0 Then MsgBox "No lines above here."
```

See Also   **LineDown, ParaDown, ParaUp**

ListBox

Syntax

ListBox *HorizPos*, *VertPos*, *Width*, *Height*, *ArrayVariable$( )*, *.Identifier*

Remarks

Creates a list box from which a user can select an item in a custom dialog box.

Argument	Explanation
HorizPos, *VertPos*	The horizontal and vertical distance from the upper-left corner of the list box to the upper-left corner of the dialog box, in increments of 1/8 and 1/12 of the System font (Windows) or the dialog font (Macintosh).
Width, *Height*	The width and height of the list box, in increments of 1/8 and 1/12 of the System font (Windows) or the dialog font (Macintosh).
ArrayVariable$( )	A string array containing the list, one list box item per array element.
.Identifier	Together with the dialog record name, *.Identifier* creates a variable whose value corresponds to the number of the selected list box item. The form for this variable is *DialogRecord.Identifier* (for example, dlg.MyList).
	The identifier string (*.Identifier* minus the period) is also used by statements in a dialog function that act on the list box, such as **DlgEnable** and **DlgVisible**.

Example

This macro displays a list of menu names. First, it creates an array of menu names to be presented in a list box, then it defines a dialog box containing the list box, and finally it displays the dialog box.

```
Sub MAIN
Dim MyList$(CountMenus(1) - 1)
For i = 1 To CountMenus(1)
    MyList$(i - 1) = MenuText$(1, i)
Next i
Begin Dialog UserDialog 320, 118, "List Box Example"
    Text 27, 0, 120, 13, "This is a list box:"
    ListBox 29, 25, 160, 84, MyList$(), .MyList
    OKButton 226, 5, 88, 21
    CancelButton 226, 29, 88, 21
End Dialog
Dim dlg As UserDialog
x = Dialog(dlg)
End Sub
```

See Also

Begin Dialog...End Dialog, **ComboBox**, **DlgListBoxArray**, **DropListBox**

ListCommands

Syntax   **ListCommands**

Remarks   Creates a new document and inserts a table of built-in Word commands that also
shows shortcut keys and menu assignments. In Word version 6.0c for Windows,
ListCommands is not available and generates an error.

See Also   **CountMacros()**, **MacroName$()**

LockDocument, LockDocument()

Syntax   **LockDocument** [*Lock*]

LockDocument()

Remarks   The **LockDocument** statement adds or removes read-only protection for an entire
master document or one of its subdocuments. If the insertion point is within a
master document but not within a subdocument, **LockDocument** locks or unlocks
the entire document. If the insertion point is within a subdocument,
LockDocument locks or unlocks the subdocument only.

Argument	Explanation
Lock	Specifies whether to add or remove read-only protection for the subdocument or master document:
	0 (zero) Removes read-only protection. Note that if you unlock an entire master document, Word unlocks all subdocuments that were previously locked.
	1 Adds read-only protection.
	Omitted Toggles read-only protection.

The **LockDocument()** function returns –1 if the subdocument or master
document is read-only and 0 (zero) if it is not. Note that when the insertion point
is in a subdocument, **LockDocument()** returns information about the read-only
state of the subdocument only, not of the entire master document.

See Also   **ToolsProtectDocument**, **ToolsProtectSection**, **ToolsUnprotectDocument**

LockFields

Syntax   **LockFields**

Remarks   Prevents the fields within the selection from being updated.

Example   This example inserts a DATE field and then immediately locks the field. This is
useful if you want Word to insert the date for you, but you don't want the date to
be updated each time you print the document.

```
InsertDateField
PrevField
LockFields
```

See Also   **UnlinkFields, UnlockFields, UpdateFields**

Lof()

Syntax   **Lof(**[#]*FileNumber*)

Remarks   Returns the length of an open sequential file, in bytes. *FileNumber* is the number specified in the **Open** instruction that opened the file for input. For more information about sequential files, see Chapter 9, "More WordBasic Techniques," in Part 1, "Learning WordBasic."

Example   This example uses **Open** to prepare the file MYDATA.TXT for sequential input and then displays the size of the file MYDATA.TXT in the status bar:

```
Open "MYDATA.TXT" For Input As #1
    Size = Lof(1)
    Print Size; " bytes"
Close #1
```

See Also   **Close, Eof(), Input, Input$(), Line Input, Open, Print, Read, Seek, Write**

LTrim$()

Syntax   **LTrim$(**Source$)

Remarks   Returns *Source$* minus any leading spaces (spaces to the left of the first character). **LTrim$()** is especially useful for removing the leading space from numeric values that have been converted to strings and for cleaning up user input.

Example   This example converts the numeric variable code to a string and then removes the leading space that was automatically added by **Str$()**. The variable lastName$ is then joined with code$ and stored in the variable license$.

```
lastName$ = "Peterson"
code = 1234
code$ = Str$(code)
code$ = LTrim$(code$)
license$ = lastName$ + code$
```

See Also   **InStr(), Left$(), Mid$(), Right$(), RTrim$()**

MacID$()

Syntax

> **MacID$(***Identifier$***)**

Remarks

On the Macintosh, converts an application signature or a file type to a value that can be used with instructions (such as **AppClose**, **Files$()**, or **Shell**) that require either an application filename or a file type. In Windows, **MacID$()** is not available and generates an error.

MacID$() provides a way to specify an application without specifying the application filename, which the user can change. **MacID$()** can be used to specify an application with the following instructions: **AppActivate**, **AppClose**, **AppCount**, **AppGetNames**, **AppGetNames()**, **AppIsRunning()**, **Shell**.

MacID$() can be used with **Files$()**, **FileOpen**, and **Kill** to specify a Macintosh file type. Because the Macintosh does not support the MS-DOS asterisk (*) and question mark (?) wildcard characters, you use a file type to identify groups of files. For example, the following statement returns a text filename from the current folder:

```
textfile1$ = Files$(MacID$("TEXT"))
```

Note You cannot specify multiple files in a specific folder by concatenating a path and a **MacID$()** file type. For example, the following instruction produces unexpected results:

```
textfile1$ = Files$("HD:TEXT FILES:" + MacID$("TEXT"))
```

Instead, you use a **ChDir** instruction to change the current folder, and then use **MacID$()** in an instruction to specify a file type.

Argument	Explanation
Identifier$	An application signature or file type.
	An application signature is a four-character sequence that uniquely identifies an application. For example, MSWD is the application signature for Word; XCEL is the application signature for Microsoft Excel.
	A file type is a four-character sequence that identifies a file format. For example, W6BN is the file type for files created by Microsoft Word 6.0 for the Macintosh and TEXT is the file type for text files (and files created in Windows, such as Word 6.0 for Windows files). You can use "****" to indicate all files in a folder.
	Note that application signatures and file types are case sensitive. For example, "MSWD" is the application signature for Word, but "Mswd" is not. For a given filename, you can use **FileCreator$()** to determine the signature of the application that created the file, and you can use **FileType$()** to determine the file type.

Examples

This example uses **MacID$()** with **AppIsRunning()** and **Shell** to determine whether Microsoft Excel is running and to start Microsoft Excel if it is not running.

```
If AppIsRunning(MacID$("XCEL")) = 0 Then Shell MacID$("XCEL")
```

The following example uses **MacID$()** with **FileOpen** to display the Open dialog box and list the Word templates in the current folder.

```
Dim FOdlg as FileOpen
GetCurValues FOdlg
FOdlg.Name = MacID$("WTBN")
choice= Dialog(FOdlg)
If choice = -1 Then FileOpen FOdlg
```

The following example uses **MacID$()** with **Files$()** to insert a list of text files in the current folder into the active window:

```
textfilename$ = Files$(MacID$("TEXT"))
While textfilename$ <> ""
    Insert textfilename$
    textfilename$ = Files$()
    InsertPara
Wend
```

See Also

AppActivate, AppClose, AppCount(), AppGetNames, AppIsRunning(), FileCreator$(), FileOpen, Files$(), FileType$(), Kill, SetFileCreatorAndType, Shell

MacroCopy

Syntax

MacroCopy [*Template1*:]*Macro1$*, [*Template2*:]*Macro2$* [, *ExecuteOnly*]

Remarks

Copies a macro from one open template to another. **MacroCopy** cannot replace an open macro. A template is open if it is attached to an open document, open in a document window, or loaded as a global template. If you make the new macro execute-only, it cannot be edited.

Argument	Explanation
Template1, Template2	The open template containing the macro you want to copy and the open template to which you want to copy the macro, respectively. In Windows, if you do not include the filename extension in the template name, .DOT is assumed.
	Include paths if the templates are not in the folder specified by User Templates in the File Types box on the File Locations tab in the Options dialog box (Tools menu).
Macro1$, Macro2$	The name of the macro to copy and the name of the new macro, respectively.
ExecuteOnly	If nonzero, makes the destination macro execute-only. Note that this action cannot be reversed. It is a good idea to make a copy of a macro before making the original execute-only.

If you don't specify a source or destination template, the Normal template is assumed. You can use the syntax **Global:***MacroName$* to specify the Normal template as the source or destination in a **MacroCopy** instruction. For example:

```
MacroCopy "MyTemp:DelStylesTest", "Global:DelStyles"
```

Though not required, including "Global:" can make **MacroCopy** instructions affecting the Normal template easier to read.

Example

This example copies the MyTest macro from the MYTEMP template to the Normal template. The new macro is given the name MyFinal.

```
MacroCopy "MYTEMP:MyTest", "Global:MyFinal"
```

See Also

IsExecuteOnly()

MacroDesc$()

Syntax

MacroDesc$(***Name$*)**

Remarks

Returns the description associated with the macro *Name$*. The same text is displayed in the Description box when you select the macro in the Macro dialog box (Tools menu) and in the status bar when you select a macro assigned to a menu or toolbar. You can set macro descriptions with **ToolsMacro**.

If *Name$* does not exist in the active template or the Normal template, an error occurs. If *Name$* exists in both the active template and the Normal template, the description for the macro in the active template is returned.

Example

This example prints a list of macros in the Normal template and their descriptions. To print a similar list for the active template, substitute CountMacros(1) and MacroName$(count, 1) in the first and second instructions, respectively.

```
For count = 1 To CountMacros(0)
    name$ = MacroName$(count, 0)
    Bold 1
    Insert name$ + Chr$(9)
    Bold 0
    Insert MacroDesc$(name$)
    InsertPara
Next count
```

See Also

CountMacros(), KeyMacro$(), MacroName$(), MenuItemMacro$(), ToolsMacro

MacroFileName$()

Syntax

MacroFileName$([*MacroName$*])

Remarks

Returns the path and filename of the template containing the macro specified by *MacroName$*. Word first looks for the macro in the active template (if different from Normal), then in the Normal template, then in any loaded global templates (in alphabetic order), and finally in built-in commands (the same order Word would look for the macro when running it). If *MacroName$* is omitted, **MacroFileName$()** returns the path and filename of the template containing the macro that is running. If *MacroName$* does not exist, **MacroFileName$()** returns an empty string ("").

See Also

MacroDesc$(), MacroName$(), MacroNameFromWindow$()

MacroName$()

Syntax

MacroName$(*Count* [, *Context*] [, *All*] [, *Global*])

Remarks

Returns the name of the macro defined in the specified context.

Argument	Explanation
Count	A number representing a position in the internal list of macros in the given context. Unlike lists in the Macro dialog box (Tools menu), the order is not alphabetic. The number can range from 1 to the number returned by **CountMacros()** in the given context.
	If you specify 0 (zero) for *Count*, **MacroName$()** returns the name of the macro in the active (or most recently active) macro-editing window.
Context	Specifies the template from which the internal list of macros is generated:
	0 (zero) Normal template
	1 Active template
	Note that if you specify 1 when Normal is the active template and *Count* is greater than 0, an error occurs.
All	If 1, all available macros, add-in commands, and built-in commands are listed in the following order: macros stored in the active template, macros stored in the Normal template, macros stored in loaded global templates, add-in commands, and built-in commands.
Global	If 1, only macros stored in loaded global templates and add-in commands are listed.

For an example that uses **MacroName$()**, see **MacroDesc$()**.

See Also   **CountMacros()**, **ListCommands**

MacroNameFromWindow$()

Syntax   **MacroNameFromWindow$(**[*WindowNumber*]**)**

Remarks   Returns the name of the macro in the specified macro-editing window. If the specified window is not a macro-editing window, **MacroNameFromWindow$()** returns an empty string ("").

Argument	Explanation
WindowNumber	Specifies a window on the Window menu: 1 corresponds to the first window, 2 to the second window, and so on. If *WindowNumber* is 0 (zero) or omitted, the active window is assumed. If *WindowNumber* does not correspond to a number on the Window menu, an error occurs.

See Also   **IsMacro()**, **MacroFileName$()**, **MacroName$()**

MacScript, MacScript$()

Syntax

MacScript *Script$*

**MacScript$**(*Script$*)

Remarks

The **MacScript** statement runs an existing AppleScript script resource, or passes the specified string to the default scripting language to compile and run.

Argument	Explanation
Script$	The path and filename of a script file, or a string to compile and run. If you specify a script file, Word loads the file and runs the first script resource.

The **MacScript$**() function behaves the same as the statement and also returns a string that corresponds to the value returned by the specified script. If the script returns a number, it is converted to a string. If the script does not return a value, **MacScript$**() returns an empty string ("").

In Windows, **MacScript** and **MacScript$**() are not available and generate errors.

Example

The following macro refers to a script called CalculateString. Suppose that this script takes the selected string in a Word document and sends it to Microsoft Excel, where Microsoft Excel attempts to evaluate the string as a formula. If Microsoft Excel can evaluate the formula, the script returns the value to Word as a string. Word can then replace the selection with the result.

```
Sub MAIN
result$ = MacScript$("HD:APPLESCRIPT:SCRIPTS:CALCULATESTRING")
If result$ <> "" Then
    EditCut
    Insert result$
End If
End Sub
```

For more information on extending Word and WordBasic with AppleScript script resources, see Appendix D, "AppleScript," in Part 3, "Appendixes."

See Also

Call, **Declare**

Magnifier, Magnifier()

Syntax   **Magnifier** [*On*]

Magnifier()

Remarks   The **Magnifier** statement changes the mouse pointer from the standard pointer to a pointer resembling a magnifying glass, or vice versa, in print preview. When the mouse pointer is a magnifying glass, the user can zoom in on a particular area of the page or zoom out to see an entire page or pages.

Argument	Explanation
On	Specifies the mouse pointer to display in print preview:
	0 (zero) Displays the standard pointer.
	1 Displays the magnifying glass pointer.
	Omitted Toggles the mouse pointer.

The **Magnifier**() function returns –1 if the mouse pointer is a magnifying glass and 0 (zero) if it is the standard pointer.

See Also   **FilePrintPreview**, **ViewZoom**

MailCheckNames

Syntax   **MailCheckNames**

Remarks   Validates the addresses that appear in the To:, Cc:, and Bcc: lines in the active WordMail message. **MailCheckNames** is available only in Word for Windows 95 and only if Microsoft Exchange is installed.

See Also   **MailHideMessageHeader**, **MailSelectNames**

MailHideMessageHeader

Syntax   **MailHideMessageHeader**

Remarks   Toggles the display of the header of the active WordMail message. **MailHideMessageHeader** is available only in Word for Windows 95 and only if Microsoft Exchange is installed.

See Also   **MailCheckNames**, **MailSelectNames**

MailMerge

Syntax

MailMerge [**.CheckErrors** = *number*] [, **.Destination** = *number*]
[, **.MergeRecords** = *number*] [, **.From** = *number*] [, **.To** = *number*]
[, **.Suppression** = *number*] [, **.MailMerge**] [, **.MailSubject** = *text*]
[, **.MailAsAttachment** = *number*] [, **.MailAddress** = *text*]

Remarks

Sets options for a mail merge, merges the main document with the specified data records, or both. If the active document is not a main document, an error occurs.

Argument	Explanation
.CheckErrors	Specifies how to check and report mail-merge errors:
	0 (zero) Simulates the mail merge and reports errors in a new document.
	1 Performs a mail merge, pausing to report each error as it occurs.
	2 Performs a mail merge and reports any errors in a new document.
.Destination	Specifies where to send the merge documents:
	0 (zero) New document
	1 Printer
	2 Electronic mail; messaging application programming interface (MAPI), vendor independent messaging (VIM), and Apple Open Collaboration Environment (AOCE) are supported.
	3 Fax
.MergeRecords	Specifies whether or not to merge a subset of the data records:
	0 (zero) Merges all data records.
	1 Merges the range of data records specified by .From and .To.
.From	The number of the first data record to merge.
.To	The number of the last data record to merge.
.Suppression	Specifies whether or not to print blank lines for empty merge fields:
	0 (zero) Does not print blank lines.
	1 Prints blank lines.
.MailMerge	Performs the mail merge (omit .MailMerge if you want to set options only).

Argument	Explanation
.MailSubject	If the destination is electronic mail, specifies the subject text.
.MailAsAttachment	If 1, and if the destination is electronic mail or fax, sends the merge documents as attachments.
.MailAddress	If the destination is electronic mail or fax, specifies the name of the merge field that contains the electronic mail address or fax number.

Example

This example merges the main document with data records 50 to 100 and sends the merge documents to a new document:

```
MailMerge .CheckErrors = 2, .Destination = 0, .MergeRecords = 1, \
    .From = 50, .To = 100, .MailMerge
```

See Also

MailMergeCheck, **MailMergeQueryOptions**, **MailMergeToDoc**, **MailMergeToPrinter**

MailMergeAskToConvertChevrons, MailMergeAskToConvertChevrons()

Syntax

MailMergeAskToConvertChevrons [*Prompt*]

MailMergeAskToConvertChevrons()

Remarks

When you open a document created in Word for the Macintosh version 5.*x* or 4.0 that contains chevrons (« »), the **MailMergeAskToConvertChevrons** statement controls whether or not Word displays a prompt asking if you want to convert text enclosed by chevrons to merge fields.

Argument	Explanation
Prompt	Specifies whether or not to display a prompt:
	0 (zero) Does not display the prompt; whether Word converts merge fields is controlled by **MailMergeConvertChevrons**.
	1 Displays the prompt.
	Omitted Toggles the option to display the prompt.

The **MailMergeAskToConvertChevrons**() function returns −1 if Word will display the prompt and 0 (zero) if it will not.

See Also

MailMergeConvertChevrons

MailMergeCheck

Syntax   **MailMergeCheck .CheckErrors** = *number*

Remarks   Checks for errors and reports any that are found. You can check for errors with or without performing a mail merge.

Argument	Explanation
.CheckErrors	Specifies whether or not to perform a mail merge when checking for errors:
	0 (zero) Simulates the mail merge and reports errors in a new document.
	1 Performs a mail merge, pausing to report each error as it occurs.
	2 Performs a mail merge and reports any errors in a new document.

See Also   **MailMerge**

MailMergeConvertChevrons, MailMergeConvertChevrons()

Syntax   **MailMergeConvertChevrons** [*Convert*]

MailMergeConvertChevrons()

Remarks   When you open a document created in Word for the Macintosh version 5.*x* or 4.0 that contains chevrons (« ») and **MailMergeAskToConvertChevrons()** returns 0 (zero), **MailMergeConvertChevrons** controls whether or not Word converts text enclosed by chevrons to merge fields. If **MailMergeAskToConvertChevrons()** returns 1, **MailMergeConvertChevrons** controls which button is the default when Word displays a prompt asking if you want to convert chevrons.

Argument	Explanation
Convert	Controls whether or not to convert chevrons (or which button is the default if the prompt appears):
	0 (zero) Does not convert chevrons (or sets the default button in the prompt to No).
	1 Converts chevrons (or sets the default button in the prompt to Yes).
	Omitted Toggles the setting that determines whether chevrons are converted (or toggles the default button in the prompt).

The **MailMergeConvertChevrons()** function returns 0 (zero) if the default button is No and −1 if the default button is Yes.

See Also   **MailMergeAskToConvertChevrons**

MailMergeCreateDataSource

Syntax

MailMergeCreateDataSource .FileName = *text* [, **.PasswordDoc** = *text*]
[, **.HeaderRecord** = *text*] [, **.MSQuery**] [, **.SQLStatement** = *text*]
[, **.SQLStatement1** = *text*] [, **.Connection** = *text*] [, **.LinkToSource** = *number*]

Remarks

Creates a Word document that stores data for a mail merge.
MailMergeCreateDataSource attaches the new data source to the active
document, which becomes a main document if it is not one already.

To create a new data source with a table you can fill in later, specify only
.FileName and .HeaderRecord (and .PasswordDoc if you want to protect the new
data source).

Argument	Explanation
.FileName	The path and filename for the new data source
.PasswordDoc	A password to protect the new data source
.HeaderRecord	Field names for the header record. If omitted, the standard header record is used: "Title, FirstName, LastName, JobTitle, Company, Address1, Address2, City, State, PostalCode, Country, HomePhone, WorkPhone." To separate field names in Windows, use the character specified by the "sList" setting in the [intl] section of your WIN.INI file. (In Windows 95 and Windows NT, this setting is stored in the registry.)
.MSQuery	Launches Microsoft Query, if installed (Windows only). The .FileName, .PasswordDoc, and .HeaderRecord arguments a re ignored.

The .SQLStatement, .SQLStatement1, and .Connection arguments have no effect
in **MailMergeCreateDataSource** instructions. If you display the Create Data
Source dialog box using a dialog record and a **Dialog** or **Dialog**() instruction, you
can return the values of these arguments. For more information about returning
these values, see **MailMergeDataSource$**(). The .LinkToSource argument is
ignored.

See Also

MailMergeCreateHeaderSource, **MailMergeDataSource$**(),
MailMergeEditDataSource, **MailMergeOpenDataSource**

MailMergeCreateHeaderSource

Syntax

MailMergeCreateHeaderSource [**.FileName** = *text*] [**.PasswordDoc** = *text*]
[, **.HeaderRecord** = *text*]

Remarks

Creates a Word document that stores a header record that is used in place of the
data source header record in a mail merge. **MailMergeCreateHeaderSource**
attaches the new header source to the active document, which becomes a main
document if it is not one already.

Argument	Explanation
.FileName	The path and filename for the new header source
.PasswordDoc	A password to protect the new header source
.HeaderRecord	Field names for the header record. If omitted, the standard header record is used: "Title, FirstName, LastName, JobTitle, Company, Address1, Address2, City, State, PostalCode, Country, HomePhone, WorkPhone." To separate field names in Windows, use the character specified by the "sList" setting in the [intl] section of your WIN.INI file. (In Windows 95 and Windows NT, this setting is stored in the registry.)

See Also **MailMergeCreateDataSource, MailMergeEditHeaderSource, MailMergeOpenHeaderSource**

MailMergeDataForm

Syntax **MailMergeDataForm**

Remarks Displays the Data Form dialog box for entering a new data record. You can use **MailMergeDataForm** in a main document, a data source, or any document containing data delimited by table cells or separator characters.

See Also **MailMergeEditDataSource**

MailMergeDataSource$()

Syntax **MailMergeDataSource$(***Type***)**

Remarks Returns information about the data or header source, the means of data retrieval, or the current connection or query string.

Type	Values and descriptions
0	The path and filename of the data source
1	The path and filename of the header source
2	A number, returned as text, indicating how data is being supplied for the mail-merge operation:
	0 From a Word document or through a Word file converter
	1 Dynamic data exchange (DDE) from Microsoft Access (Windows only)
	2 DDE from Microsoft Excel
	3 DDE from Microsoft Query (Windows only)
	4 Open database connectivity (ODBC) (Windows only)
3	A number, returned as text, indicating how the header source is being supplied for the mail-merge operation. See values and descriptions for *Type* 2.

Type	Values and descriptions
4	The connection string for the data source
5	The query string (SQL statement)

See Also   **MailMergeCreateDataSource**, **MailMergeEditDataSource**, **MailMergeOpenDataSource**

MailMergeEditDataSource

Syntax   **MailMergeEditDataSource**

Remarks   Performs one of the following when a main document is active:

- If the data source is a Word document, opens the data source (or activates the data source if it is already open).

- If Word is accessing the data through dynamic data exchange (DDE)—using an application such as Microsoft Excel or Microsoft Access—displays the data source in that application.

- If Word is accessing the data through open database connectivity (ODBC) (Windows only), displays the data in a Word document. Note that if Microsoft Query is installed, a message appears providing the option to display Microsoft Query instead of converting data.

See Also   **MailMergeCreateDataSource**, **MailMergeEditMainDocument**, **MailMergeOpenDataSource**

MailMergeEditHeaderSource

Syntax   **MailMergeEditHeaderSource**

Remarks   Opens the header source attached to the active main document or activates the header source if it is already open. If the active document is not a main document, or if a header source is not attached, an error occurs.

See Also   **MailMergeCreateHeaderSource**, **MailMergeEditDataSource**, **MailMergeOpenHeaderSource**

MailMergeEditMainDocument

Syntax   **MailMergeEditMainDocument**

Remarks   Activates the mail-merge main document associated with the active header source or data source. If there is no main document associated with the active header or data source, or if the main document is not open, an error occurs.

See Also   **MailMergeEditDataSource**

MailMergeFindRecord

Syntax   **MailMergeFindRecord .Find** = *text*, **.Field** = *text*

Remarks   If a main document is active and merged data is visible, displays a merge document for the first data record containing the specified text in the given field. If a data source is active and is a Word document, **MailMergeFindRecord** selects the first row that matches the specified criteria. You can use **MailMergeFindRecord** in a main document, a data source, or any document containing data delimited by table cells or separator characters.

Argument	Explanation
.Find	Text you want to find in the specified field.
.Field	Limits the search to the specified field name.

Example   This example displays a merge document for the first data record in which the last name is "Perez." If the data record is found, the number of the record is stored in the variable numRecord.

```
MailMergeFindRecord .Find = "Perez", .Field = "LastName"
If MailMergeFoundRecord() Then
    numRecord = MailMergeGotoRecord()
End If
```

See Also   **MailMergeFirstRecord, MailMergeFoundRecord(), MailMergeGotoRecord, MailMergeLastRecord, MailMergeNextRecord, MailMergePrevRecord, MailMergeViewData**

MailMergeFirstRecord

Syntax   **MailMergeFirstRecord**

Remarks   If merged data is visible in the main document, displays a merge document for the first data record in the query result (or the first record in the data source if no query options are in effect). This statement is valid only when a main document is active.

See Also   **MailMergeFindRecord, MailMergeGotoRecord, MailMergeLastRecord, MailMergeNextRecord, MailMergePrevRecord, MailMergeViewData**

MailMergeFoundRecord()

Syntax   **MailMergeFoundRecord()**

Remarks   Returns a value indicating whether the most recent **MailMergeFindRecord** operation was successful.

Value	Explanation
−1	The find operation was successful.
0 (zero)	The find operation was not successful.

For an example, see **MailMergeFindRecord**.

See Also   **MailMergeFindRecord**

MailMergeGotoRecord, MailMergeGotoRecord()

Syntax   **MailMergeGotoRecord** *RecordNumber*

MailMergeGotoRecord()

Remarks   If merged data is visible in the main document, the **MailMergeGotoRecord** statement displays a merge document for the data record corresponding to *RecordNumber*. Note that *RecordNumber* is the position of the record in the query result produced by the current query options, and is therefore not necessarily the position of the record in the data source.

The **MailMergeGotoRecord**() function returns the number of the data record currently displayed. If the active document is not a main document, both the statement and the function generate an error. For an example using **MailMergeGotoRecord**(), see **MailMergeFindRecord**.

See Also   **MailMergeFindRecord**, **MailMergeFirstRecord**, **MailMergeLastRecord**, **MailMergeNextRecord**, **MailMergePrevRecord**, **MailMergeViewData**

MailMergeHelper

Syntax   **MailMergeHelper**

Remarks   Used with a **Dialog** or **Dialog**() instruction to display the Mail Merge Helper dialog box (Mail Merge command, Tools menu), with which you can set up a main document, create and edit a data source, and perform a mail merge.

Example   This example displays the Mail Merge Helper dialog box.

```
Dim dlg As MailMergeHelper
GetCurValues dlg
x = Dialog(dlg)
```

See Also   **MailMerge**

MailMergeInsertAsk

Syntax

MailMergeInsertAsk .Name = *text* [, **.Prompt** = *text*]
[, **.DefaultBookmarkText** = *text*] [, **.AskOnce** = *number*]

Remarks

Inserts an ASK field into a main document at the insertion point. When updated, an ASK field displays a dialog box that prompts for text to assign to the specified bookmark.

Argument	Explanation
.Name	The name of the bookmark to which you want to assign the text typed in the dialog box.
.Prompt	A prompt that appears in the dialog box (for example, "Your Initials:").
.DefaultBookmarkText	Default text to assign to the bookmark.
.AskOnce	If 1, Word displays the prompt once at the beginning of the merge instead of once for each data record.

See Also

InsertField, MailMergeInsertFillIn, MailMergeInsertSet

MailMergeInsertFillIn

Syntax

MailMergeInsertFillIn [.**Prompt** = *text*] [, **.DefaultFillInText** = *text*]
[, **.AskOnce** = *number*]

Remarks

Inserts a FILLIN field into a main document at the insertion point. When updated, a FILLIN field displays a dialog box that prompts for text to insert into the document at the location of the field.

Argument	Explanation
.Prompt	A prompt that appears in the dialog box (for example, "Your Initials:").
.DefaultFillInText	Default text to insert at the field location.
.AskOnce	If 1, Word displays the prompt once at the beginning of the merge operation instead of once for each data record.

See Also

InsertField, MailMergeInsertAsk, MailMergeInsertSet

MailMergeInsertIf

Syntax   **MailMergeInsertIf .MergeField** = *text*, **.Comparison** = *number*
[, **.CompareTo** = *text*] [, **.TrueAutoText** = *text*] [, **.TrueText** = *text*]
[, **.FalseAutoText** = *text*] [, **.FalseText** = *text*]

Remarks   Inserts an IF field into a main document at the insertion point. When updated, an
IF field compares a field in a data record to a specified value, and then inserts the
appropriate text according to the result of the comparison.

Argument	Explanation
.MergeField	The name of the merge field you want to compare to the text specified by .CompareTo.
.Comparison	Specifies the operator for the comparison:
	0 (zero) = (equal to)
	1 <> (not equal to)
	2 < (less than)
	3 > (greater than)
	4 <= (less than or equal to)
	5 >= (greater than or equal to)
	6 = " " (is blank)
	7 <> " " (is not blank)
.CompareTo	Text to compare to the merge field. This argument is required unless .Comparison is set to 6 (is blank) or 7 (is not blank).
.TrueAutoText	An AutoText entry containing the text to insert if the comparison is true (.TrueText is ignored).
.TrueText	Text to insert if the comparison is true.
.FalseAutoText	An AutoText entry containing the text to insert if the comparison is false (.FalseText is ignored).
.FalseText	Text to insert if the comparison is false.

See Also   **InsertField**, **MailMergeInsertNext**, **MailMergeInsertNextIf**,
MailMergeInsertSkipIf

MailMergeInsertMergeRec

Syntax   **MailMergeInsertMergeRec**

Remarks   Inserts a MERGEREC field into a main document at the insertion point. A
MERGEREC field inserts the number of the current data record (the position of
the data record in the current query result) during a mail merge.

See Also   **InsertField**, **MailMergeInsertMergeSeq**

MailMergeInsertMergeSeq

Syntax   **MailMergeInsertMergeSeq**

Remarks   Inserts a MERGESEQ field into a main document at the insertion point. A
MERGESEQ field inserts a number based on the sequence in which data records
are merged (for example, when merging records 50 to 100, inserts 1 when
merging record number 50).

See Also   **InsertField, MailMergeInsertMergeRec**

MailMergeInsertNext

Syntax   **MailMergeInsertNext**

Remarks   Inserts a NEXT field into a main document at the insertion point. A NEXT field
advances to the next data record so that data from more than one record can be
merged into the same merge document (for example, a sheet of mailing labels).

See Also   **InsertField, MailMergeInsertNextIf**

MailMergeInsertNextIf

Syntax   **MailMergeInsertNextIf .MergeField** = *text*, **.Comparison** = *number*,
.CompareTo = *text*

Remarks   Inserts a NEXTIF field into a main document at the insertion point. If the
comparison in the NEXTIF field is true, Word merges the next data record into
those merge fields in the current merge document that follow the NEXTIF field.
Otherwise, Word merges the next data record into a new merge document. In
general, it is preferable to specify query options instead of using NEXTIF fields.
For argument descriptions, see **MailMergeInsertIf**.

See Also   **InsertField, MailMergeInsertIf, MailMergeInsertNext,
MailMergeInsertSkipIf**

MailMergeInsertSet

Syntax   **MailMergeInsertSet .Name** = *text* [, **.ValueText** = *text*]
[, **.ValueAutoText** = *text*]

Remarks   Inserts a SET field into a main document at the insertion point. A SET field
defines the text of the specified bookmark.

Argument	Explanation
.Name	The name of the bookmark to define
.ValueText	Text to assign the bookmark to
.ValueAutoText	The AutoText entry whose text you want to assign the bookmark to (.ValueText is ignored)

See Also   InsertField, MailMergeInsertAsk, MailMergeInsertFillIn

MailMergeInsertSkipIf

Syntax   MailMergeInsertSkipIf .MergeField = *text* , .Comparison = *number*
[, .CompareTo = *text*]

Remarks   Inserts a SKIPIF field into a main document at the insertion point. If the comparison in the SKIPIF field is true, Word cancels the current merge document and skips to the next data record. In general, it is preferable to specify query options instead of using SKIPIF fields. For argument descriptions, see **MailMergeInsertIf**.

See Also   InsertField, MailMergeInsertIf, MailMergeInsertNext, MailMergeInsertNextIf

MailMergeLastRecord

Syntax   MailMergeLastRecord

Remarks   If merged data is visible in the main document, displays a merge document for the last data record in the current query result (or the last record in the data source if no query options are in effect). This statement is valid only when a main document is active.

See Also   MailMergeFindRecord, MailMergeFirstRecord, MailMergeGotoRecord, MailMergeNextRecord, MailMergePrevRecord, MailMergeViewData

MailMergeMainDocumentType, MailMergeMainDocumentType()

Syntax   MailMergeMainDocumentType *Type*

MailMergeMainDocumentType()

Remarks   The **MailMergeMainDocumentType** statement makes the active window a main document. Note that if the active document is already a main document, Word removes the attached data source, if any.

Argument	Explanation
Type	The type of merge documents you will create with the main document:

0 (zero) or omitted   Form letters

1   Mailing labels

2   Envelopes

3   Catalog documents

The **MailMergeMainDocumentType( )** function returns one of the *Type* values if the active document is a main document, or −1 if it is a regular Word document.

See Also   **MailMergeCreateDataSource**, **MailMergeOpenDataSource**, **MailMergeReset**

MailMergeNextRecord

Syntax   **MailMergeNextRecord**

Remarks   If merged data is visible in the main document, displays a merge document for the next record in the current reply (or the next record in the data source if no query options are in effect). This statement is valid only when a main document is active.

See Also   **MailMergeFindRecord**, **MailMergeFirstRecord**, **MailMergeGotoRecord**, **MailMergeLastRecord**, **MailMergePrevRecord**, **MailMergeViewData**

MailMergeOpenDataSource

Syntax   **MailMergeOpenDataSource .Name** = *text* [, **.ConfirmConversions** = *number*] [, **.ReadOnly** = *number*] [, **.LinkToSource** = *number*] [, **.AddToMru** = *number*] [, **.PasswordDoc** = *text*] [, **.PasswordDot** = *text*] [, **.Revert** = number] [, **.WritePasswordDoc** = *text*] [, **.WritePasswordDot** = *text*] [, **.Connection** = *text*] [, **.SQLStatement** = *text*] [, **.SQLStatement1** = *text*]

Remarks   Attaches the specified data source to the active document, which becomes a main document if it is not one already.

Argument	Explanation
.Name	The name of the data source. In Windows, you can specify a Microsoft Query (.QRY) file instead of a specifying a data source, a connection string, and a query string.
.LinkToSource	If 1, the query specified by .Connection and .SQLStatement is performed each time the main document is opened.

Argument	Explanation
.Connection	Specifies a range within which to perform the query specified by .SQLStatement. How you specify the range depends on how data is retrieved. For example:
	• When retrieving data through ODBC (Windows only), you specify a connection string.
	• When retrieving data from Microsoft Excel using dynamic data exchange (DDE), you specify a named range.
	• When retrieving data from Microsoft Access (Windows only), you specify the word "Table" or "Query" followed by the name of a table or query.
.SQLStatement	Defines query options for retrieving data.
.SQLStatement1	If the query string is longer than 255 characters, .SQLStatement specifies the first portion of the string and .SQLStatement1 specifies the second portion.

Note To determine the connection and query strings, set query options manually, and then use **MailMergeDataSource$()** to return the strings.

For descriptions of other arguments, see **FileOpen**.

See Also **FileOpen**, **MailMergeCreateDataSource**, **MailMergeEditDataSource**, **MailMergeOpenHeaderSource**

MailMergeOpenHeaderSource

Syntax **MailMergeOpenHeaderSource .Name** = *text* [, **.ConfirmConversions** = *number*] [, **.ReadOnly** = *number*] [, **.AddToMru** = *number*] [, **.PasswordDoc** = *text*] [, **.PasswordDot** = *text*] [, **.Revert** = number] [, **.WritePasswordDoc** = *text*] [, **.WritePasswordDot** = *text*]

Remarks Attaches the specified header source to the active document, which becomes a main document if it is not one already. The header record in the header source is used in place of the header record in the data source. For argument descriptions, see **FileOpen**.

See Also **MailMergeCreateHeaderSource**, **MailMergeEditHeaderSource**, **MailMergeOpenDataSource**

MailMergePrevRecord

Syntax   **MailMergePrevRecord**

Remarks   If merged data is visible in the main document, displays a merge document for the previous record in the current query result (or the previous record in the data source if no query options are in effect). This statement is valid only when a main document is active.

See Also   **MailMergeFindRecord, MailMergeFirstRecord, MailMergeGotoRecord, MailMergeLastRecord, MailMergeNextRecord**

MailMergeQueryOptions

Syntax   **MailMergeQueryOptions .SQLStatement** = *text* [**, .SQLStatement1** = *text*]

Remarks   Specifies the query options for a mail merge. You can use **MailMergeQueryOptions** to change the query options established with a **MailMergeCreateDataSource** or **MailMergeOpenDataSource** instruction. If the active document is not a main document, an error occurs.

Argument	Explanation
.SQLStatement	An optional query string that retrieves a subset of the data in a primary data source.
.SQLStatement1	If the string is longer than 255 characters, .SQLStatement specifies the first portion of the string and .SQLStatement1 specifies the second portion.

Note To determine the query string, set query options manually, and then use **MailMergeDataSource$()** to return the string.

See Also   **MailMergeCreateDataSource, MailMergeDataSource$(), MailMergeOpenDataSource**

MailMergeReset

Syntax   **MailMergeReset**

Remarks   Detaches the data and header sources from the main document and resets it to a regular Word document. If the active document is not a main document, an error occurs.

See Also   **MailMergeMainDocumentType**

MailMergeState()

Syntax   **MailMergeState(***Type***)**

Remarks   Returns one of four different types of information about the current state of a
mail-merge setup. *Type* 1, *Type* 2, and *Type* 3 return –1 if the active document is
not a main document, data source, or header source.

Type	Values and descriptions
0 (zero)	Returns information about the active document:
	0 (zero) Regular Word document
	1 Main document with no data or header source attached
	2 Main document with an attached data source
	3 Main document with an attached header source
	4 Main document with both a data and header source attached
	5 Data source or header source; associated main document is open
1	Returns the kind of main document:
	0 (zero) Form letters
	1 Mailing labels
	2 Envelopes
	3 Catalog
2	Returns information about the selected mail-merge options:
	0 (zero) Neither blank-line suppression nor query options are enabled.
	1 Blank-line suppression is enabled.
	2 Query options are enabled.
	3 Both blank-line suppression and query options are enabled.
3	Returns the mail-merge destination:
	0 (zero) New document
	1 Printer
	2 Electronic mail
	3 Fax

Example   This example checks the state of the active document before performing a mail
merge. If the active document is not a main document, Word displays a message
box. If the document is a main document but has no attached data source, a data
source is attached. In any other case, the mail merge begins immediately.

```
Select Case MailMergeState(0)
    Case 0
        MsgBox "Not a mail merge main document."
        quitmacro = 1
    Case 1, 3
        MailMergeOpenDataSource .Name = "C:\DATA\DATA.DOC"
    Case Else
End Select
If quitmacro = 1 Then Goto bye
MailMergeToPrinter
bye:
```

See Also   **MailMergeMainDocumentType**

MailMergeToDoc

Syntax   **MailMergeToDoc**

Remarks   Merges data records with the main document and sends the resulting merge documents to a new document. If the most recent mail merge specified a range of data records to merge, only those records are merged.

See Also   **MailMerge, MailMergeToPrinter**

MailMergeToPrinter

Syntax   **MailMergeToPrinter**

Remarks   Merges data records with the main document and prints the resulting merge documents. If the most recent mail merge specified a range of data records to merge, only those records are merged.

See Also   **MailMerge, MailMergeToDoc**

MailMergeUseAddressBook

Syntax   **MailMergeUseAddressBook .AddressBookType** = *text*

Remarks   Selects the address book to be used as the data source for a mail merge.

MailMergeUseAddressBook is available only if Windows 95 and either Microsoft Exchange or Schedule+ version 2.0 are installed. In Word version 6.0, **MailMergeUseAddressBook** is unavailable and generates an error.

Argument	Explanation
.AddressBookType	Specifies the address book to be used as the data source:
	scd Schedule+ Contact List
	pab Microsoft Exchange Personal Address Book

See Also   AddAddress, GetAddress$()

MailMergeViewData, MailMergeViewData()

Syntax   **MailMergeViewData** [*DisplayResults*]

MailMergeViewData()

Remarks   The **MailMergeViewData** statement controls the display of merge fields in a main document. If the active document is not a main document, an error occurs.

Argument	Explanation
DisplayResults	Specifies whether to display merge field names in chevrons (« ») or information from the current data record in place of the merge fields:
	0 (zero) Merge field names
	1 Information from the current data record

The **MailMergeViewData()** function returns 0 (zero) if merge field names are displayed and 1 if information from the current data record is displayed.

See Also   **MailMergeEditDataSource**

MailMessageDelete

Syntax   **MailMessageDelete**

Remarks   Deletes the active WordMail message. **MailMessageDelete** is available only in Word for Windows 95 and only if Microsoft Exchange is installed.

See Also   **MailMessageMove, MailMessageNext, MailMessagePrevious**

MailMessageForward

Syntax   **MailMessageForward**

Remarks   Opens a new WordMail message with an empty To: line for forwarding the active message. **MailMessageForward** is available only in Word for Windows 95 and only if Microsoft Exchange is installed.

See Also   **MailMessageReply, MailMessageReplyAll**

MailMessageMove

Syntax

MailMessageMove

Remarks

Displays the Move dialog box in which the user can specify a new location for the active WordMail message in an available message store. **MailMessageMove** is available only in Word for Windows 95 and only if Microsoft Exchange is installed.

See Also

MailMessageDelete, **MailMessageNext**, **MailMessagePrevious**

MailMessageNext

Syntax

MailMessageNext

Remarks

Closes the active WordMail message and displays the next message, if available. **MailMessageNext** is available only in Word for Windows 95 and only if Microsoft Exchange is installed.

See Also

MailMessageDelete, **MailMessageMove**, **MailMessagePrevious**

MailMessagePrevious

Syntax

MailMessagePrevious

Remarks

Closes the active WordMail message and displays the previous message, if available. **MailMessagePrevious** is available only in Word for Windows 95 and only if Microsoft Exchange is installed.

See Also

MailMessageDelete, **MailMessageMove**, **MailMessageNext**

MailMessageProperties

Syntax

MailMessageProperties

Remarks

Displays the Properties dialog box for the active WordMail message. **MailMessageProperties** is available only in Word for Windows 95 and only if Microsoft Exchange is installed.

See Also

FileProperties

MailMessageReply

Syntax   **MailMessageReply**

Remarks   Opens a new WordMail message with the sender's address on the To: line for
                    replying to the active message. **MailMessageReply** is available only in Word for
                    Windows 95 and only if Microsoft Exchange is installed.

See Also   **MailMessageForward**, **MailMessageReplyAll**

MailMessageReplyAll

Syntax   **MailMessageReplyAll**

Remarks   Opens a new WordMail message with the sender and all other recipients'
                    addresses on the To: and Cc: lines, as appropriate, for replying to the active
                    message. **MailMessageReplyAll** is available only in Word for Windows 95 and
                    only if Microsoft Exchange is installed.

See Also   **MailMessageForward**, **MailMessageReply**

MailSelectNames

Syntax   **MailSelectNames**

Remarks   Displays the Select Names dialog box in which the user can add addresses to the
                    To:, Cc:, and Bcc: lines of the active unsent WordMail message.
                    MailSelectNames is available only in Word for Windows 95 and only if
                    Microsoft Exchange is installed

See Also   **MailCheckNames**, **MailHideMessageHeader**

MarkCitation

Syntax   **MarkCitation** [**.LongCitation** = *text*] [, **.LongCitationAutoText** = *text*]
                    [, **.Category** = *number*] [, **.ShortCitation** = *text*] [, **.NextCitation**] [, **.Mark**]
                    [, **.MarkAll**]

Remarks   Inserts a TA (Table of Authorities Entry) field next to the text you select or next
                    to every instance of the selected text.

                    The arguments for the **MarkCitation** statement correspond to the options in the
                    Mark Citation dialog box (Table Of Authorities tab, Index And Tables command,
                    Insert menu).

Argument	Explanation
.LongCitation	The long citation for the entry as it will appear in the table of authorities.
.LongCitationAutoText	The name of an AutoText entry containing the long citation text you want to appear in the table of authorities (.LongCitation is ignored).
.Category	The number of the category (in the order of the list of categories in the Mark Citation dialog box) to associate with the entry: 1 corresponds to the first category in the list, 2 to the second category, and so on.
.ShortCitation	The short citation for the entry as it will appear in the list under Short Citation in the Mark Citation dialog box.
.NextCitation	Finds the next instance of the text specified by .ShortCitation.
.Mark	Inserts a TA (Table of Authorities Entry) field to the right of the selected text.
.MarkAll	Inserts a TA (Table of Authorities Entry) field to the right of all instances of the selected text.

If you don't specify .NextCitation, .Mark, or .MarkAll, Word inserts a TA field to the right of the selected text.

See Also   **InsertTableOfAuthorities, MarkIndexEntry, MarkTableOfContentsEntry**

MarkIndexEntry

Syntax   **MarkIndexEntry [.MarkAll]** [, **.Entry** = *text*] [, **.Range** = *text*]
[, **.Bold** = *number*] [, **.Italic** = *number*] [, **.CrossReference** = *text*]
[, **.EntryAutoText** = *text*] [, **.CrossReferenceAutoText** = *text*]

Remarks   Inserts an XE (Index Entry) field next to the text you select or next to every instance of the selected text. The arguments for the **MarkIndexEntry** statement correspond to the options in the Mark Index Entry dialog box (Index tab, Index And Tables command, Insert menu).

Argument	Explanation
.MarkAll	Inserts an XE field after each instance of the selected text.
.Entry	The text you want to appear in the index in the form *MainEntry*[:*Subentry*].
.Range	The name of a bookmark marking the range of pages you want to appear in the index. If you don't specify .Range, the number of the page containing the XE field appears in the index.

Argument	Explanation
.Bold	If 1, page numbers for the entry are bold in the index.
.Italic	If 1, page numbers for the entry are italic in the index.
.CrossReference	A cross-reference that will appear in the index.
.EntryAutoText	The name of an AutoText entry containing the text you want to appear in the index (.Entry is ignored).
.CrossReferenceAutoText	The name of an AutoText entry containing the text for a cross-reference (.CrossReference is ignored).

See Also　　**InsertIndex**, **MarkCitation**, **MarkTableOfContentsEntry**

MarkTableOfContentsEntry

Syntax　　**MarkTableOfContentsEntry** [**.Entry** = *text*] [**, .EntryAutoText** = *text*] [**, .TableId** = *text*] [**, .Level** = *text*]

Remarks　　Inserts a TC (Table of Contents Entry) field next to the selected text.

Argument	Explanation
.Entry	The text you want to appear in the table of contents
.EntryAutoText	The name of an AutoText entry containing the text you want to appear in the table of contents (.Entry is ignored)
.TableId	A one-letter identifier for the type of item (for example, "i" for an illustration)
.Level	A level for the entry in the table of contents

See Also　　**InsertTableOfContents**, **MarkCitation**, **MarkIndexEntry**

MenuItemMacro$()

Syntax　　**MenuItemMacro$**(*Menu$*, *Type*, *Item* [, *Context*])

Remarks　　Returns the name of the macro or built-in command associated with the specified menu item.

Argument	Explanation
Menu$	The name of a menu or shortcut menu. Menu names are listed in the Change What Menu box on the Menus tab in the Customize dialog box (Tools menu).
	Including an ampersand (&) before the underlined letter in the menu name is optional (for example, you can specify either "File" or "&File"). Do not include the parenthetical phrases "(No Document)" and "(Shortcut)", even though that text appears in the Customize dialog box.

Argument	Explanation
Type	The type of menu:
	0 Menus on the menu bar when a document is open
	1 Menus on the menu bar when no document is open
	2 Shortcut menus
Item	A number representing the item's position on the menu. The number can range from 1 to the number returned by **CountMenuItems()**. Separators between commands are considered items, and if *Item* represents the position of a separator, **MenuItemMacro$()** returns the string "(Separator)."
	Note that lists such as the list of recently used files on the File menu or proofing tools on the Tools menu correspond to a single item. If you specify the position of a list, **MenuItemMacro$()** returns an empty string ("").
Context	Specifies the menu assignment for which you want to return the macro or command name:
	0 (zero) or omitted The assignment that is available when a document based on the Normal template is active
	1 The assignment that is currently available
	Note that the assignment that is available depends on the custom settings, if any, of the active template, any loaded global templates, and the Normal template.

Example

This example defines an array variable containing the names of commands and macros assigned to the File menu in the current working environment. To define a similar array for the File menu of the active template, substitute CountMenuItems("File", 0, 1) in the first instruction and MenuItemMacro$("File", 0, count, 1) in the fourth instruction.

```
numItems = CountMenuItems("File", 0, 0)
Dim fileItem$(numItems - 1)
For count = 1 To numItems
    fileItem$(count - 1) = MenuItemMacro$("File", 0, count, 0)
Next count
```

See Also

CountMacros(), KeyMacro$(), MacroDesc$(), MacroName$(), MenuItemText$(), ToolsCustomizeMenus

MenuItemText$()

Syntax   **MenuItemText$**(*Menu$*, *Type*, *Item* [, *Context*])

Remarks   Returns the menu text associated with a macro or built-in command assigned to the specified menu. You can change the menu text with **ToolsCustomizeMenus**.

Note The menu text for a subset of built-in commands changes depending on the current conditions of the Word environment. For these commands, **MenuItemText$()** returns the command name instead of the menu text. The commands include **EditCopy**, **EditPaste**, **EditRedoOrRepeat**, **EditUndo**, **FileClose**, **FileCloseAll**, **FileCloseOrCloseAll**, **FileExit**, **FileQuit**, **FileSave**, **FileSaveAll**, **FileSaveAs**, **FormatFrameOrFramePicture**, **TableDeleteGeneral**, **TableInsertGeneral**, **TableSort**, **TableToOrFromText**, and **ToolsProtectUnprotectDocument**.

Argument	Explanation
Menu$	The name of a menu or shortcut menu. Menu names are listed in the Change What Menu box on the Menus tab in the Customize dialog box (Tools menu).
	Including an ampersand (&) before the underlined letter in the menu name is optional (for example, you can specify either "File" or "&File"). Do not include the parenthetical phrases "(No Document)" and "(Shortcut)", even though that text appears in the Customize dialog box.
Type	The type of menu:
	0 (zero) Menus on the menu bar when a document is open
	1 Menus on the menu bar when no document is open
	2 Shortcut menus
Item	A number representing the item's position on the menu. The number can range from 1 to the number returned by **CountMenuItems()**. Separators between commands are considered items, and if *Item* represents the position of a separator, **MenuItemText$()** returns the string "(Separator)."
	Note that lists such as the list of recently used files on the File menu or proofing tools on the Tools menu correspond to a single item. If you specify the position of a list, **MenuItemText$()** returns a parenthetical phrase describing the list—for example, "(List of Recently Used Files)" or "(List of Proofing Tools)".

Argument	Explanation
Context	Specifies the menu assignments for which you want to return the menu text:
	0 (zero) or omitted The assignments that are available when a document based on the Normal template is active
	1 The assignments that are currently available
	Note that the assignments that are available depend on the custom settings, if any, of the active template, any loaded global templates, and the Normal template.

Example

This example displays a message box with the menu text of the first Word-related item on the Help menu when no document is open (on the Macintosh, this is the first item after the Show Balloons command):

```
MsgBox MenuItemText$("Help", 1, 1, 0)
```

See Also

CountMenuItems(), **CountMenus()**, **MenuItemMacro$()**, **MenuText$()**, **ToolsCustomizeMenus**

MenuMode

Syntax   **MenuMode**

Remarks   Activates the menu bar. **MenuMode** corresponds to pressing the ALT key (Windows) or the DECIMAL (.) key on the numeric keypad when Num Lock is off (Macintosh).

MenuText$()

Syntax   **MenuText$(***Type***, ***MenuNumber* [, *Context*]**)**

Remarks   Returns the name of a shortcut menu or a menu on the menu bar. If there is an underlined letter in the menu name, **MenuText$()** includes an ampersand (&) before the letter in the returned text. (On the Macintosh, the underlined letters in menu and command names appear only in menu mode.)

Argument	Explanation
Type	The type of menu:
	0 (zero) Menus on the menu bar when a document is open
	1 Menus on the menu bar when no document is open
	2 Shortcut menus
MenuNumber	A number in the range 1 to **CountMenus**() for the specified type. If *Type* is 0 (zero) or 1, *MenuNumber* represents a position on the menu bar from left to right (where 1 corresponds to the File menu). If *Type* is 2, *MenuNumber* represents a position in the series of shortcut menus in the Change What Menu box on the Menus tab in the Customize dialog box (Tools menu): The first shortcut menu in the series is 1, the second is 2, and so on.
Context	Specifies the template that contains the name of menu *MenuNumber* you want to return:
	0 (zero) or omitted Normal template
	1 Active template

Example

This example defines an array to fill with the names of the shortcut menus available in the Normal template and then fills the array:

```
size = CountMenus(2, 0) - 1
Dim shortcutMenus$(size)
For count = 0 To size
    shortcutMenus$(count) = MenuText$(2, count + 1, 0)
Next count
```

See Also

CountMenuItems(), **CountMenus**(), **MenuItemMacro$**(), **MenuItemText$**(), **ToolsCustomizeMenus**

MergeFieldName$()

Syntax

MergeFieldName$(*Count*)

Remarks

Returns a field name in a data source or header source. In a data source set up as a Word table, the field names are in the first row as column headings. In a data source set up as delimited lists, the field names are in the first paragraph. An error occurs if you run **MergeFieldName$**() when the active document is not a main document.

Argument	Explanation
Count	The number corresponding to the field name in the data source or header source, where 1 is the first field name, 2 is the second, and so on.

Example	This example defines an array containing the field names available to a main document (which must be active when the example is run):

```
numFields = CountMergeFields()
Dim mmFields$(numFields - 1)
For count = 1 To numFields
    mmFields$(count - 1) = MergeFieldName$(count)
Next count
```

See Also	**CountMergeFields(), InsertMergeField**

MergeSubdocument

Syntax	**MergeSubdocument**
Remarks	Merges the selected subdocuments of a master document into one subdocument. If only one subdocument is selected, or if the active document is not in master document or outline view, an error occurs.
See Also	**CreateSubdocument, InsertSubdocument, OpenSubdocument, RemoveSubdocument, SplitSubdocument, ViewMasterDocument**

MicrosoftApplication

Syntax	**Microsoft***Application*
Remarks	Starts the specified Microsoft application if it is not running or switches to the application if it is already running.

Argument	Explanation
Application	The application you want to go to. The following statements are available:
	MicrosoftAccess (not available on the Macintosh)
	MicrosoftExcel
	MicrosoftFoxPro
	MicrosoftMail
	MicrosoftPowerPoint
	MicrosoftProject
	MicrosoftPublisher (not available on the Macintosh)
	MicrosoftSchedule (not available on the Macintosh)
	MicrosoftSystemInfo

See Also	**AppActivate, AppIsRunning()**

Mid$()

Syntax   **Mid$**(*Source$*, *Start* [, *Count*])

Remarks   Returns a portion of *Source$* starting at a given character position.

Argument	Explanation
Source$	The original string.
Start	The character position in *Source$* where the string you want to return begins.
Count	The number of characters in the string you want to return. If you do not specify *Count*, the number of characters to the end of the string is assumed.

Example   This example returns the second word of a two-word string:

```
wholeName$ = "Sanjeev Reddy"
space = InStr(wholeName$, " ")
lastName$ = Mid$(wholeName$, space + 1)
```

See Also   **InStr()**, **Left$()**, **Len()**, **LTrim$()**, **Right$()**, **RTrim$()**

Minute()

Syntax   **Minute**(*SerialNumber*)

Remarks   Returns an integer between 0 (zero) and 59, inclusive, corresponding to the minutes component of *SerialNumber*, a decimal representation of the date, time, or both. For information about serial numbers, see **DateSerial()**.

Example   This example displays the minutes component of the current time:

```
mins = Minute(Now())
MsgBox "It is" + Str$(mins) + " minute(s) after the hour."
```

See Also   **DateSerial()**, **Day()**, **Hour()**, **Month()**, **Now()**, **Second()**, **Today()**, **Weekday()**, **Year()**

MkDir

Syntax   **MkDir** *Name$*

Remarks   Creates the folder specified by *Name$*. An error occurs if the folder already exists. If you don't specify a path, *Name$* is interpreted relative to the current folder. On the Macintosh, note that if *Name$* begins with a colon, *Name$* is a relative path; if *Name$* contains a colon elsewhere in the folder specification, *Name$* is an absolute path.

Examples

This example creates the folder "OUTPUT" by specifying a path. Note that the TEST folder must already exist; **MkDir** cannot create both folders at the same time. On the Macintosh, substitute a folder name such as HD:TEST:OUTPUT.

```
MkDir "C:\TEST\OUTPUT"
```

Each of the following examples creates a subfolder within the current folder:

```
MkDir "OUTPUT"      'Windows or Macintosh
MkDir ".\OUTPUT"    'Windows
MkDir ":OUTPUT"     'Macintosh
```

The following Windows example creates a folder at the same level as the current folder:

```
MkDir "..\OUTPUT"
```

The following is the Macintosh equivalent of the previous example:

```
MkDir "::OUTPUT"
```

See Also

ChDir, **CountDirectories()**, **Files$()**, **GetDirectory$()**, **Name**, **RmDir**

Month()

Syntax

Month(*SerialNumber*)

Remarks

Returns an integer between 1 and 12, inclusive, corresponding to the month component of *SerialNumber*, a decimal representation of the date, time, or both. For information about serial numbers, see **DateSerial()**.

Example

This example displays the number of full months between the current month and the new year:

```
months = Month(Now())
MsgBox Str$(12 - months) + " full month(s) left in the year."
```

See Also

DateSerial(), **Day()**, **Hour()**, **Minute()**, **Now()**, **Second()**, **Today()**, **Weekday()**, **Year()**

MountVolume, MountVolume()

Syntax

MountVolume *Zone$*, *Server$*, *Volume$* [, *User$*] [, *UserPassword$*] [, *VolumePassword$*]

MountVolume(*Zone$*, *Server$*, *Volume$* [, *User$*] [, *UserPassword$*] [, *VolumePassword$*])

Remarks   On the Macintosh, the **MountVolume** statement connects to a disk or folder shared across the network.

Argument	Explanation
Zone$	The zone that the computer you want to connect to is in.
Server$	The name of the computer.
Volume$	The name of the shared disk or folder.
User$	Your user name, as registered by the shared computer. If you do not specify a user name, you are connected as a guest.
UserPassword$	The password, if any, required to connect to the specified computer.
VolumePassword$	The password, if any, required to access the specified disk or folder.

The **MountVolume()** function behaves the same as the statement, and also returns one of the following values.

Value	Explanation
0 (zero)	The instruction was successful or the connection already exists.
−28	AppleTalk is not available (for example, your computer is not connected to a network).
−35	The specified volume was not found.
−50	The instruction contains and invalid argument (for example, the zone, server, or volume name is missing, or the user name is not recognized).
−58	An external file system error occurred.
−108	There was not enough memory to make the connection.
−5000	Access was denied.
−5002	The method used to authenticate the user is unknown.
−5003	The AppleTalk Filing Protocol (AFP) on the server is incompatible with **MountVolume**.
−5016	The specified server is not responding.
−5023	The user was not authenticated; this usually occurs because the password is incorrect.
−5042	The password has expired.
−5061	The computer is already connected to the maximum number of volumes.
−5063	The specified server is the same as the computer running the instruction.

Note **MountVolume** cannot connect to volumes that the Finder cannot connect to using an alias.

In Windows, **MountVolume** and **MountVolume( )** are not available and generate errors; use **Connect** instead.

Example

This example connects to a shared folder as a guest:

```
MountVolume "Public", "Tools", "Art Tools"
```

See Also

Connect

MoveButton

Syntax

MoveButton *SourceToolbar$*, *SourcePosition*, *TargetToolbar$*, *TargetPosition* [, *Copy*] [, *Context*]

Remarks

Moves or copies a toolbar button, list box, or space to another toolbar or to another position on the same toolbar.

Argument	Explanation
SourceToolbar$	The name of the toolbar containing the item you want to move or copy, as listed in the Toolbars dialog box (View menu).
SourcePosition	The position of the item you want to move or copy, where 1 is the first position, 2 is the second, and so on. Note that a list box or space counts as one position.
TargetToolbar$	The name of the toolbar to which you want to move or copy the item.
TargetPosition	The position to which you want to move or copy the item.
Copy	If 1, copies instead of moves the toolbar item.
Context	Determines where the change to the toolbar or toolbars is stored.
	0 (zero) or omitted Normal template
	1 Active template

Example

This example copies the Show/Hide ¶ button from the Standard toolbar to the end of the Macro toolbar (assuming these toolbars have not been customized already):

```
MoveButton "Standard", 26, "Macro", 18, 1, 0
```

See Also

AddButton, ChooseButtonImage, CopyButtonImage, DeleteButton, EditButtonImage, PasteButtonImage, ResetButtonImage

MoveText

Syntax

MoveText

Remarks

Moves text without changing the contents of the Clipboard (the same as pressing the F2 key in Windows). For **MoveText** to work, macro instructions must make a selection immediately before the **MoveText** instruction, make a new selection immediately after **MoveText**, and then use the **OK** statement to move the text.

Example

This example moves the line containing the insertion point to the beginning of the document:

```
StartOfLine
EndOfLine 1
MoveText
StartOfDocument
OK
```

See Also

CopyFormat, CopyText, OK

MoveToolbar

Syntax

MoveToolbar *Toolbar$*, *Dock*, *HorizPos*, *VertPos*

Remarks

Moves the specified toolbar. If the specified toolbar is not displayed, an error occurs.

Argument	Explanation
Toolbar$	The name of the toolbar to move, as it is listed in the Toolbars dialog box (View menu).
Dock	Specifies whether to anchor the toolbar at the top, bottom, or either side of the Word window or to set it as a floating toolbar over the document window:
	0 (zero) The toolbar floats over the document window.
	1 The toolbar is anchored at the top of the Word window.
	2 The toolbar is anchored at the left of the Word window.
	3 The toolbar is anchored at the right of the Word window.
	4 The toolbar is anchored at the bottom of the Word window.
HorizPos, VertPos	If *Dock* is 0 (zero), the horizontal (*HorizPos*) and vertical (*VertPos*) distance from the upper-left corner of the Word window to the upper-left corner of the toolbar, in pixels.
	If *Dock* is nonzero, you must still specify *HorizPos* and *VertPos*. Word moves the toolbar to the nearest available position in the series of docked toolbars.

Example

This example displays the Forms toolbar and moves it to the lower-right corner of the Word window. The **If** conditional prevents the **AppMaximize** instruction from running and generating an error on the Macintosh.

```
If InStr(AppInfo$(1), "Macintosh") = 0 Then AppMaximize 1
ViewToolbars .Toolbar = "Forms", .Show
MoveToolbar "Forms", 0, 520, 410
```

See Also

ToolbarName$(), ToolbarState(), ViewToolbars

MsgBox, MsgBox()

Syntax

MsgBox *Message$* [, *Title$*] [, *Type*]

MsgBox(*Message$* [, *Title$*] [, *Type*])

Remarks

The **MsgBox** statement displays a message in a message box. You can also display a message with the **MsgBox()** function, which returns a value according to the command button the user chooses in the message box. Use **MsgBox()** if you need your macro to take action based on the user's response.

Argument	Explanation
Message$	The message to be displayed in the message box. If *Message$* is longer than 255 characters, an error occurs.
Title$	The title of the message box. In Windows, if *Title$* is omitted or is an empty string (""), "Microsoft Word" is the default title. On the Macintosh, if *Title$* is an empty string (""), a title bar does not appear in the message box.
Type	A value representing the symbol and buttons displayed in the box.

Type is the sum of three values, one from each of the following groups.

Group	Value	Meaning
Button	0 (zero)	OK button (default)
	1	OK and Cancel buttons
	2	Abort, Retry, and Ignore buttons
	3	Yes, No, and Cancel buttons
	4	Yes and No buttons
	5	Retry and Cancel buttons
Symbol	0 (zero)	No symbol (default)
	16	Stop symbol
	32	Question symbol (Windows) or attention symbol (Macintosh)
	48	Attention symbol
	64	Information symbol
Button action	0 (zero)	First button is the default
	256	Second button is the default
	512	Third button is the default

By specifying *Type* as –1, –2, or –8, you can display the message in the status bar instead of a message box. This is similar to using the **Print** statement, but gives you more control over how long the message is displayed. Specifying *Type* as –1 displays the message until another message replaces it; specifying –2 displays the message until a mouse or keyboard action occurs; and specifying –8 displays the message in the entire status bar width until a mouse or keyboard action occurs.

Because the **MsgBox** statement does not return a value, the use of button values other than 0 (zero) is not recommended. To make use of buttons other than the OK button, use the **MsgBox()** function. **MsgBox()** returns the following values.

Return value	Button chosen	Button text
–1	First (leftmost) button	OK
		Yes
		Abort
0 (zero)	Second button	Cancel
		No
		Retry
1	Third button	Cancel
		Ignore

If *Type* is a negative value—that is, if you use **MsgBox()** to display a message in the status bar—**MsgBox()** always returns 0 (zero).

Examples

In this example, the **MsgBox** instruction displays a message box containing the message "Unable to find file," the title "MyTest Macro," an OK button, and a Stop symbol (0 + 16 + 0 = 16):

```
MsgBox "Unable to find file.", "MyTest Macro", 16
```

In the following macro, the **If** conditional checks whether or not there is a selection before proceeding. If there is no selected text, the **MsgBox()** function displays a message box asking if the user wants to continue anyway. The second **If** conditional tests the return value. If it's 0 (zero), which means the second button (No) was chosen, the macro ends without running subsequent instructions.

```
Sub MAIN
'Series of instructions that select text
If SelType() <> 2 Then
   button = MsgBox("There is no selection. Continue anyway?", 36)
   If button = 0 Then Goto bye
End If
'Series of instructions that act on the selection
bye:
End Sub
```

See Also   **InputBox$(), Print**

Name

Syntax

Name *OldName$* **As** *NewName$*

Remarks

Renames a file. If you do not include paths with the *OldName$* and *NewName$* arguments, **Name** assumes the current folder—the one selected in the Open dialog box (File menu). In Windows, you can move a file to a different folder by including a different path for *NewName$*; however, you cannot use **Name** to move folders or to move a file to a different drive. On the Macintosh, the path for *OldName$* must match the path for *NewName$* or an error occurs.

Argument	Explanation
OldName$	The previous name of the file. If the filename specified by *OldName$* does not exist or is open, an error occurs.
NewName$	The new name of the file. If the filename specified by *NewName$* already exists, an error occurs.

The *OldName$* and *NewName$* arguments do not accept wildcard characters—the asterisk (*) and question mark (?).

Examples

This example uses **ChDir** to set the current folder, and then renames the file COGS.DOC as COGS88.DOC in that folder. Without the **ChDir** instruction preceding it, the **Name** instruction would need to specify the complete path for each filename. On the Macintosh, substitute a folder name such as HD:DOCS:MEMOS:JULY in the **ChDir** instruction.

```
ChDir "C:\MYDOCS\MEMOS\JULY"
Name "COGS.DOC" As "COGS88.DOC"
```

The following Windows example moves the file COGS.DOC to a different folder and leaves the filename unchanged:

```
Name "C:\TMP\COGS.DOC" As "C:\DOCS\COGS.DOC"
```

See Also

ChDir, **CopyFile**, **FileSaveAs**, **Kill**, **MkDir**, **RmDir**

NewToolbar

Syntax

NewToolbar .Name = *text* [, **.Context** = *number*]

Remarks

Creates a new toolbar to which you can add buttons using the **AddButton** and **MoveButton** statements.

Argument	Explanation
.Name	A name for the new toolbar (spaces are allowed).
.Context	The template in which you want to store the toolbar:

0 (zero) or omitted   Normal template; the toolbar always appears in the Toolbars dialog box (View menu).

1   Active template; the toolbar only appears in the Toolbars dialog box when the template is active.

See Also   **AddButton**, **CountToolbars()**, **MoveButton**, **ToolbarName$()**, **ViewToolbars**

NextCell, NextCell()

Syntax   **NextCell**

NextCell()

Remarks   The **NextCell** statement selects the contents of the next table cell (the same as pressing TAB in a table). If more than one cell is selected, **NextCell** selects the contents of the first cell in the selection. If the insertion point or selection is in the last cell of the table, **NextCell** adds a new row.

The **NextCell()** function behaves the same as the statement except when the insertion point or selection is completely within the last cell. In that case, the function returns 0 (zero) without enlarging the section, whereas the statement adds a new row.

Note You can use `EditGoTo .Destination = "\Cell"` to select the contents of the current cell. The predefined bookmark "\Cell" and a number of others are set and updated automatically. For information on predefined bookmarks, see "Operators and Predefined Bookmarks" later in this part.

Examples   This example moves the selection to the next cell, and then uses **SelType()** to determine if the cell is empty. If **SelType()** returns 1 (the value for the insertion point, indicating the cell is empty), a message box appears.

```
NextCell
If SelType() = 1 Then MsgBox "Empty cell!"
```

The following example uses the **NextCell()** function to determine if the insertion point is in the last cell. If the current cell is the last cell, the entire table is selected. If the current cell is not the last cell, the next cell is selected.

```
If NextCell() = 0 Then TableSelectTable
```

See Also   **PrevCell**

NextField, NextField()

Syntax   **NextField**

NextField()

Remarks   The **NextField** statement selects the next field, regardless of whether the field is showing its codes or results. **NextField** skips over the following fields, which are formatted as hidden text: XE (Index Entry), TA (Table of Authorities Entry), TC (Table of Contents Entry), and RD (Referenced Document).

The **NextField()** function behaves the same as the statement and also returns the following values.

Value	Explanation
0 (zero)	If there is no next field (in other words, if the selection is not moved)
1	If the selection is moved

With field codes displayed, you can use **EditFind** to go to the next field of any type, including XE, TA, TC, and RD fields, provided that hidden text is displayed. Specify "^d" (the code for a field character) as the text for the .Find argument, as shown in the following instructions:

```
ViewFieldCodes 1
EditFind .Find = "^d", .Direction = 0, .Format = 0
```

To find only XE fields, specify "^d XE" as the text to find.

Example   This example counts the number of fields in the document (excluding XE, TA, TC, and RD fields) and displays the result in a message box. Note that the **While...Wend** loop does not include a **NextField** statement because the While NextField() instruction also moves the selection.

```
StartOfDocument
count = 0
While NextField()
    count = count + 1
Wend
MsgBox "Number of fields in the document:" + Str$(Count)
```

See Also   **PrevField**

NextMisspelling

Syntax	**NextMisspelling**
Remarks	Finds the next misspelled word. If automatic spell checking is turned on, **NextMisspelling** opens the shortcut menu containing spelling suggestions. For an example, see **DocumentHasMisspellings()**. In Word version 6.0, **NextMisspelling** is unavailable and generates an error.
See Also	**DocumentHasMisspellings()**, **ToolsGetSpelling**, **ToolsLanguage**, **ToolsOptionsSpelling**

NextObject

Syntax **NextObject**

Remarks Moves the insertion point to the next document object on the current page in page layout view (the same as pressing ALT+DOWN ARROW (Windows) or OPTION+DOWN ARROW (Macintosh)). Document objects include text columns, table cells, footnotes, and frames.

From the top of the first text column on a page, the **NextObject** statement moves through document objects in the following order:

- Each text column, in order from first to last (if there is more than one), moving through all table cells and then all footnotes that appear within the text column
- Frames, if any appear, in the order that they appear in normal view, from the previous page break to the following page break

NextObject finally moves to the top of the first text column before cycling through the document objects again.

Keep the following points in mind when using **NextObject**:

- You can identify document objects by selecting the Text Boundaries check box, on the View tab in the Options dialog box (Tools menu), when the active document is in page layout view.
- Word does not consider OLE objects, such as embedded drawings and charts, to be document objects unless they are framed.
- If the insertion point is in a header or footer, **NextObject** moves between the header and footer.
- Make sure to switch to page layout view before using **NextObject**.

Example

This example moves the insertion point to the first document object on the current page. The `EditGoTo "\Page"` instruction selects the current page, and `SelType 1` cancels the selection, leaving the insertion point at the top of the page. The `NextObject` instruction moves the insertion point to the first document object.

```
ViewPage
EditGoTo "\Page"
SelType 1
NextObject
```

See Also

PrevObject

NextPage, NextPage()

Syntax

NextPage

NextPage()

Remarks

The **NextPage** statement scrolls forward one page in page layout view without moving the insertion point (the same as clicking the Page Forward button at the bottom of the vertical scroll bar in page layout view). If you want to move the insertion point after scrolling, include a **StartOfWindow** statement following **NextPage** in your macro.

NextPage scrolls from the current location on one page to the same relative location on the next page. To scroll to the beginning of the next page regardless of what portion of the current page appears, use the instruction `EditGoTo .Destination = "p"` instead of **NextPage**. Note, however, that **EditGoTo** also moves the insertion point.

The **NextPage()** function behaves the same as the statement and also returns the following values.

Value	Explanation
0 (zero)	If there is no next page (in other words, if the document doesn't scroll)
1	If the document scrolls

Note **NextPage** and **NextPage()** are available only in page layout view and generate an error if run in another view.

Example

This example scrolls forward one page and positions the insertion point at the top of the document window. If the document has scrolled as far as possible, a message box is displayed.

```
                    ViewPage
                    If NextPage() = 0 Then
                        MsgBox "Can't scroll!"
                    Else
                        StartOfWindow
                    End If
```

See Also   **EditGoTo**, **PageDown**, **PrevPage**, **ViewPage**, **VPage**

NextTab()

Syntax   **NextTab(***Position***)**

Remarks   Returns the position of the next tab stop to the right of *Position*, in points, for the first paragraph of the selection.

Use the following list of conversions as an aid in converting from points to other measurements:

- 1 inch = 72 points
- 1 centimeter = 28.35 points
- 1 pica = 12 points

Example   This example uses **NextTab()** with **TabType()** to return a value corresponding to the alignment of the first tab stop in the selection:

```
firstTabType = TabType(NextTab(0))
```

See Also   **FormatTabs**, **PrevTab()**, **TabLeader$()**, **TabType()**

NextWindow

Syntax   **NextWindow**

Remarks   Moves the window at the front of the internal order of open windows to the back. This statement does nothing if there is only one open window.

See Also   **Activate**, **ChDir**, **PrevWindow**, **Window()**, **WindowList**, **WindowName$()**, **Window***Number*

NormalFontPosition

Syntax   **NormalFontPosition**

Remarks   Restores the selected characters to the baseline if they have been raised or lowered.

See Also   **FormatFont**, **NormalFontSpacing**

NormalFontSpacing

Syntax   **NormalFontSpacing**

Remarks   Restores the selected characters to Normal character spacing if their current spacing is expanded or condensed.

See Also   **FormatFont**, **NormalFontPosition**

NormalStyle

Syntax   **NormalStyle**

Remarks   Applies the Normal style to the selected paragraphs. There is not a corresponding function for **NormalStyle**; however, you can use the **StyleName$()** function to determine the current style. For example, the instruction `If StyleName$() = "Normal" Then MsgBox "Normal paragraph"` displays a message box if the current paragraph is in the Normal style.

Example   This example selects the current paragraph, and if it contains the string "Comments:", applies the Normal style. The bookmark "\Para" is one of several predefined bookmarks that Word sets and updates automatically. For information on predefined bookmarks, see "Operators and Predefined Bookmarks" later in this part.

```
EditGoTo .Destination = "\Para"
If InStr(Selection$(), "Comments:") Then NormalStyle
```

See Also   **FormatStyle**, **ResetPara**, **Style**, **StyleName$()**

NormalViewHeaderArea

Syntax   **NormalViewHeaderArea** [**.Type** = *number*] [, **.FirstPage** = *number*]
[, **.OddAndEvenPages** = *number*] [, **.HeaderDistance** = *text*]
[, **.FooterDistance** = *text*]

Remarks   Opens the header/footer pane (normal and outline views) or displays the header or footer area (page layout view) and sets options for headers and footers. You can display the header/footer pane to edit any type of header or footer, regardless of the number of pages in the document.

The arguments for the **NormalViewHeaderArea** statement correspond to the options in the Header/Footer dialog box in Word version 2.*x*. Note that these options are usually set using **FilePageSetup** in Word version 6.0 and 7.0. Although you can retrieve information from the **NormalViewHeaderArea** dialog record, you cannot use this statement to display the Word version 2.*x* dialog box.

Argument	Explanation
.Type	Specifies whether to display the header or footer area. The possible values of .Type depend on the settings of .FirstPage and .OddAndEvenPages.
	If both .FirstPage and .OddAndEvenPages are set to 0 (zero):
	0 (zero) Header
	1 Footer
	If .FirstPage is set to 1 and .OddAndEvenPages is set to 0 (zero):
	0 (zero) Header
	1 Footer
	2 First header
	3 First footer
	If .FirstPage is set to 0 (zero) and .OddAndEvenPages is set to 1:
	0 (zero) Even header
	1 Even footer
	2 Odd header
	3 Odd footer
	If both .FirstPage and .OddAndEvenPages are set to 1:
	0 (zero) First header
	1 First footer
	2 Even header
	3 Even footer
	4 Odd header
	5 Odd footer
.FirstPage	If 1, allows a header or footer for the first page that differs from the rest of the pages in the section.
.OddAndEvenPages	If 1, allows one header or footer for even-numbered pages and a different header or footer for odd-numbered pages.
.HeaderDistance	The distance from the top of the page to the header.
.FooterDistance	The distance from the bottom of the page to the footer.

See Also   **FilePageSetup**, **ViewFooter**, **ViewHeader**

NoteOptions

Syntax

NoteOptions [**.FootnotesAt** = *number*] [**, .FootNumberAs** = *number*]
[**, .FootStartingNum** = *text*] [**, .FootRestartNum** = *number*]
[**, .EndnotesAt** = *number*] [**, .EndNumberAs** = *number*]
[**, .EndStartingNum** = *text*] [**, .EndRestartNum** = *number*]

Remarks

Specifies the placement and formatting of footnotes and endnotes. The arguments for the **NoteOptions** statement correspond to the options in the Note Options dialog box (Footnote command, Insert menu).

Argument	Explanation
.FootnotesAt	Specifies where to place footnotes:
	0 (zero) Bottom Of Page
	1 Beneath Text
.FootNumberAs	Specifies the format for footnote reference marks:
	0 (zero) 1, 2, 3,…
	1 a, b, c,…
	2 A, B, C,…
	3 i, ii, iii,…
	4 I, II, III,…
	5 *, †, ‡, §,…
.FootStartingNum	The starting number for footnotes; if .FootStartingNum is not 1, .FootRestartNum must be set to 0 (zero).
.FootRestartNum	Specifies how to number footnotes after page breaks or section breaks:
	0 (zero) Continuous
	1 Restart Each Section
	2 Restart Each Page
.EndnotesAt	Specifies where to place endnotes:
	0 (zero) End Of Section
	1 End Of Document
.EndNumberAs	Specifies the format for endnote reference marks. For values, see the .FootNumberAs argument.
.EndStartingNum	The starting number for endnotes; if .EndStartingNum is not 1, .EndRestartNum must be set to 0 (zero).
.EndRestartNum	Specifies how to number endnotes after section breaks:
	0 (zero) Continuous
	1 Restart Each Section

Example

This example places footnotes beneath text, using the "A, B, C" format and starting with "A"; footnote numbers restart with each new section:

```
NoteOptions .FootnotesAt = 1, .FootNumberAs = 2, \
        .FootStartingNum = "1", .FootRestartNum = 1
```

See Also

InsertFootnote

Now()

Syntax   Now()

Remarks   Returns a serial number that represents the current date and time according to the computer's system date and time. Numbers to the left of the decimal point represent the number of days between December 30, 1899 and the current date; numbers to the right represent the time as a fraction of a day. For more information about serial numbers, see **DateSerial()**.

Example   This example displays a message box stating the number of days until the new year. The number of days is calculated by subtracting the serial number for the current date and time from the serial number for January 1 of the following year.

```
yr = Year(Now())
rightNow = Now()
jan1 = DateSerial(yr + 1, 1, 1)
MsgBox "Days until the new year:" + Str$(jan1 - rightNow)
```

Fractions of a day appear in the result after the decimal point. To return strictly the number of days with no decimal fraction, substitute **Today()** in place of **Now()** in the preceding example.

See Also   **DateSerial()**, **Date$()**, **DateValue()**, **Today()**

OK

Syntax   **OK**

Remarks   Completes a **CopyText** or **MoveText** operation (the same as pressing ENTER while the operation is in progress).

Example   This example copies the line containing the insertion point to the beginning of the document without changing the contents of the Clipboard:

```
StartOfLine
EndOfLine 1
CopyText
StartOfDocument
OK
```

See Also   **Cancel**, **CopyText**, **MoveText**

OKButton

Syntax   **OKButton** *HorizPos*, *VertPos*, *Width*, *Height* [, *Identifier*]

Remarks   Creates an OK button in a custom dialog box. If the user chooses the OK button, the dialog box closes and its settings are applied.

Argument	Explanation
HorizPos, *VertPos*	The horizontal and vertical distance of the upper-left corner of the OK button from the upper-left corner of the dialog box, in increments of 1/8 and 1/12 of the System font (Windows) or the dialog font (Macintosh).
Width, *Height*	The width and height of the OK button, in increments of 1/8 and 1/12 of the System font (Windows) or the dialog font (Macintosh).
Identifier	An optional identifier used by statements in a dialog function that act on the OK button, such as **DlgEnable** and **DlgVisible**. If omitted, "OK" is the default identifier.

Note that choosing the OK button in a custom dialog box always returns –1 and choosing the Cancel button always returns 0 (zero). For example, in a dialog box displayed with the instruction x = Dialog(dlg), choosing OK sets the value of x to –1. The return value of other buttons is determined by the relative order of the **PushButton** statements in the dialog box definition.

For an example of **OKButton** used in a complete dialog box definition, see **Begin Dialog...End Dialog**.

See Also   **Begin Dialog...End Dialog**, **CancelButton**, **PushButton**

On Error

Syntax	**On Error Goto** *Label*
	On Error Resume Next
	On Error Goto 0

Remarks

Establishes an "error handler"—typically, a series of instructions that takes over when an error occurs. When an error occurs in a macro that does not contain the **On Error** statement, an error message is displayed and the macro quits.

This form	Performs this action
On Error Goto *Label*	Jumps from the line where the error occurred to the specified label. The instructions following this label can then determine the nature of the error (using the special variable **Err**) and take some appropriate action to correct or resolve the problem. For more information, see **Err**.
On Error Resume Next	Continues running the macro from the line that follows the line where the error occurred and resets **Err** to 0 (zero). In effect, the error is ignored.
On Error Goto 0	Disables the error trapping established by an earlier **On Error Goto** or **On Error Resume Next** statement and sets **Err** to 0 (zero).

Once an error triggers an error handler, no further error handling occurs until **Err** is reset to 0 (zero). Usually, you should place an Err = 0 instruction at the end of your error handler. Do not include Err = 0 in the middle of an error handler or you risk creating an endless loop if an error occurs within the handler.

Note that an error handler established in the main subroutine is not in effect when control passes to another subroutine. To trap all errors, each subroutine must have its own **On Error** statement and error handler. After control is returned to the main subroutine, the main **On Error** instruction is again in effect.

WordBasic generates errors with numbers less than 1000; Word itself generates errors with numbers 1000 or greater. Error handlers can trap both WordBasic and Word errors. However, if a Word error occurs, an error message is displayed, and the user must respond before the macro can continue. When the user chooses the OK button, control passes to the error handler.

For a complete list of all WordBasic and Word error messages and error numbers, see "Error Messages" later in this part.

Examples

This example shows a common use of **On Error Resume Next** to avoid WordBasic error number 102, "Command failed," when a user cancels a dialog box or prompt:

```
On Error Resume Next
A$ = InputBox$("Your name please:")
```

The following macro prompts the user to specify a sequential file for input (for example, a text-only file containing a list of Word documents). If the file cannot be found, the instructions following the label specified by **On Error Goto** *Label* suggest a reason corresponding to the error number.

```
Sub MAIN
On Error Goto ErrorHandler
DocName$ = InputBox$("Filename for input:", "", DocName$)
Open DocName$ For Input As #1
'Statements that use the input go here
Close #1
Goto Done                    'If there is no error, skip the error handler
ErrorHandler:
Select Case Err
    Case 53 : MsgBox "The file " + DocName$ + " does not exist."
    Case 64 : MsgBox "The specified drive is not available."
    Case 76 : MsgBox "The specified folder does not exist."
    Case 102               'If the user cancels the dialog box
    Case Else : MsgBox "Error" + Str$(Err) + " occurred."
End Select
Err = 0
Done:
End Sub
```

See Also

Err, **Error**, **Goto**, **Select Case**

OnTime

Syntax

OnTime *When*[*$*]*, Name$* [*, Tolerance*]

Remarks

Sets up a background timer that runs a macro at the time specified by *When*[*$*]. If Word is occupied at the specified time—for example, if a dialog box is displayed or Word is performing a large sort operation—the macro runs as soon as Word is idle.

If you close Word before *When*[*$*], the timer is canceled and is not reactivated when you start Word. To reset the timer each time you start Word—for example, if you want to automatically set an alarm macro at your next Word session (see the example in this entry)—name the macro that includes the **OnTime** instruction "AutoExec." For information about AutoExec and other auto macros, see Chapter 2, "Getting Started with Macros," in Part 1, "Learning WordBasic."

Argument	Explanation
When[*$*]	The time the macro is to be run, expressed as text in a 24-hour format (*hours*:*minutes*:*seconds*) or as a serial number, a decimal representation of the date, time, or both. For more information on serial numbers, see **DateSerial( )**.
	When you specify the time as text, including *seconds* is optional. For example, 2:37 P.M. is expressed as "14:37" and 2:37 A.M. is expressed as "02:37" or "2:37." Midnight is "00:00:00."
	You can include a string representing the date before the time. There are several available date formats. You can control the default date format by choosing the International option in Control Panel (Windows) or by using a control panel such as Date & Time (Macintosh). If the date is not specified, the macro runs at the first occurrence of the specified time.
Name$	The name of the macro to be run. For the macro to run, it must be available both when the **OnTime** instruction is run and when the specified time has arrived. For this reason, it is best to specify a macro in the global template, NORMAL.DOT. The format *MacroName.SubroutineName* is not allowed.
Tolerance	If *Name$* has not yet started within *Tolerance* seconds after *When*, Word will not run the macro. If *Tolerance* is 0 (zero) or omitted, Word always runs the macro, regardless of how many seconds elapse before Word is idle and can run the macro.

Note   Word can run only one **OnTime** macro at a time. If you start a second, the first **OnTime** macro is canceled.

Example

This example sets up a simple alarm clock function in Word. The first macro in the example sets up the background timer.

```
'Alarm program: Prompts user to input time for alarm to sound
'Current time appears in title bar of input box
Sub MAIN
Alarm$ = InputBox$("Time? (HH:mm:ss), 24hr", "Alarm " + Time$())
'Set background timer to run macro called Beeper
'No tolerance is set, so alarm will always sound
OnTime Alarm$, "Beeper"
End Sub
```

The following macro sounds an alarm and displays an alert message in response to the timer set up by the preceding macro. This macro must be named "Beeper" to work properly with the preceding macro.

```
Sub MAIN                        'Beeper program
For count = 1 To 7
    Beep
    Beep
    For TL = 1 To 100           'Adds a delay between beeps
    Next
Next
MsgBox "Preset alarm sounded", "Beeper " + Time$(), 48
End Sub
```

See Also   **Date$()**, **DateSerial()**, **DateValue()**, **Day()**, **Month()**, **Now()**, **TimeValue()**, **Today()**, **Year()**

Open

Syntax   **Open** *Name$* **For** *Mode$* **As** [#]*FileNumber*

Remarks   Opens a sequential file for input or output of text. You can use sequential files to supply values for macro variables or to store data generated by macros.

Sequential files, which are opened with **Open** and closed with **Close**, are not displayed in document windows. Although you can use **Open** to open any file, **Open** and **Close** are intended to be used with text files. For more information about sequential files, see Chapter 9, "More WordBasic Techniques," in Part 1, "Learning WordBasic."

Argument	Explanation
Name$	The name of the file to open
Mode$	The mode in which the file is opened:
	Input Opens the text file so that data may be read from the file into the macro. When you open a file for input, you can use **Read**, **Input**, **Line Input**, and **Input$()** instructions to read from the file. If *Name$* does not exist, an error occurs.
	Output Opens the text file so that data may be written from the macro to the file. When you open a file for output, you can use **Write** and **Print** instructions to write to the file. If *Name$* does not exist, Word creates it. If *Name$* already exists, Word deletes its contents.
	Append Opens the text file so that data may be written from the macro to the file. When you open a file to append, you can use **Write** and **Print** instructions to write to the file. The existing contents of the file remain and the information you write is added to the end of the file. If *Name$* does not exist, Word creates it.
FileNumber	A number to assign the file, from 1 through 4

Example

This macro saves a rich-text format (RTF) copy of each document listed in the text file CONVERT.TXT. The **Open** instruction opens CONVERT.TXT for input as a sequential file. The instructions in the **While...Wend** loop run once for each document, assigning the filename listed next in CONVERT.TXT to curdoc$, opening the document, saving an RTF copy, and then closing the document.

```
Sub MAIN
Open "CONVERT.TXT" For Input As #1
While Not Eof(1)
    Line Input #1, curdoc$
    FileOpen .Name = curdoc$
    FileSaveAs .Name = curdoc$, .Format = 6
    FileClose 2
Wend
Close #1
End Sub
```

See Also

Close, Eof(), Input, Input$(), Line Input, Lof(), Print, Read, Seek, Write

OpenSubdocument

Syntax

OpenSubdocument

Remarks

Opens the subdocument identified by the location of the insertion point or the beginning of the selection in a master document. Word opens the subdocument in a separate document window. If the active document is not a master document, or if the master document is not in master document or outline view, an error occurs.

See Also

CreateSubdocument, FileOpen, InsertSubdocument, MergeSubdocument, RemoveSubdocument, SplitSubdocument, ViewMasterDocument

OpenUpPara

Syntax

OpenUpPara

Remarks

Sets the Before option on the Indents And Spacing tab in the Paragraph dialog box (Format menu) to "12 pt."

Example

If there is no space before the current paragraph, this example sets the Before option to "12 pt":

```
Dim dlg As FormatParagraph
GetCurValues dlg
If dlg.Before = "0 pt" Then OpenUpPara
```

See Also

CloseUpPara, FormatParagraph

OptionButton

Syntax   **OptionButton** *HorizPos*, *VertPos*, *Width*, *Height*, *Label$* [, *.Identifier*]

Remarks   Creates an option button in a custom dialog box. An **OptionGroup** instruction is required for each series of related **OptionButton** instructions, which must be positioned directly following the **OptionGroup** instruction. Within a group of option buttons, only one button can be selected at a time.

Argument	Explanation
HorizPos, *VertPos*	The horizontal and vertical distance of the upper-left corner of the rectangle containing both the option button and its associated text from the upper-left corner of the dialog box, in increments of 1/8 and 1/12 of the System font (Windows) or the dialog font (Macintosh).
Width, *Height*	The width and height of the rectangle, in increments of 1/8 and 1/12 of the System font (Windows) or the dialog font (Macintosh).
Label$	The label associated with the option button. An ampersand (&) precedes the character in *Label$* that is the access key for selecting the option button.
.Identifier	An optional identifier used by statements in a dialog function that act on the option button. If omitted, the default identifier is the first two words in *Label$* (or the entire string if *Label$* is only one word). You should specify *.Identifier* because the identifier you assign remains the same regardless of changes you make to *Label$*.

For an example of **OptionButton** used in a complete dialog box definition, see **OptionGroup**.

See Also   **CheckBox**, **GroupBox**, **OptionGroup**, **PushButton**

OptionGroup

Syntax   **OptionGroup** *.Identifier*

Remarks   Defines a series of related option buttons in a dialog box definition. An **OptionGroup** instruction is required for each series of related **OptionButton** instructions, which must be positioned directly following the **OptionGroup** instruction. Within the group, only one option button can be selected at a time. The **OptionGroup** identifier returns a value corresponding to the selected option button.

Argument	Explanation
.Identifier	Together with the dialog record name, *.Identifier* creates a variable whose value corresponds to the selected option button, where 0 (zero) is the first option button in the group, 1 is the second, and so on. The form for this variable is *DialogRecord.Identifier* (for example, dlg.Brk).
	The identifier string (*.Identifier* minus the period) is also used by statements in a dialog function that act on the option group, such as **DlgEnable** and **DlgVisible**.

Example

This macro creates the dialog box shown following it and then inserts either a page break or column break according to the option button the user selects. The identifier defined for the option group is .Brk. Note how the second **If** instruction performs an action based on the value of the dlg.Brk variable.

```
Sub MAIN
Begin Dialog UserDialog 292, 78, "Example"
    OKButton 188, 14, 88, 21
    CancelButton 188, 38, 88, 21
    GroupBox 12, 6, 164, 60, "Break"
    OptionGroup .Brk
        OptionButton 22, 23, 117, 16, "&Page Break"
        OptionButton 22, 41, 133, 16, "&Column Break"
End Dialog
Dim dlg As UserDialog
If Dialog(dlg) Then
    If dlg.Brk = 0 Then InsertPageBreak Else InsertBreak .Type = 1
End If
End Sub
```

See Also

Begin Dialog…End Dialog, **GroupBox**, **ListBox**, **OptionButton**

Organizer

Syntax

Organizer [.Copy,] [.Delete,] [.Rename,] [.Source = *text***,]**
[.Destination = *text***,] .Name =** *text* **[, .NewName =** *text***] [, .Tab =** *number***]**

Remarks

Deletes and renames styles, AutoText entries, toolbars, and macros, and copies these elements between templates. The arguments for the **Organizer** statement correspond to the options in the Organizer dialog box (Macro command, Tools menu).

Argument	Explanation
.Copy	Copies the specified item from the source to the destination.
.Delete	Deletes the specified item from the source.
.Rename	Renames the specified item in the source.
.Source	The filename of the document or template containing the item you want to copy, delete, or rename. Paths are accepted.
.Destination	The filename of the document or template to which you want to copy the item. Paths are accepted.
.Name	The name of the style, AutoText entry, toolbar, or macro you want to copy, delete, or rename.
.NewName	A new name for the specified item; used with .Rename.
.Tab	The kind of item you want to copy, delete, or rename:

0 (zero)   Styles

1   AutoText

2   Toolbars

3   Macros

You also use these values to specify which tab to select when you display the Organizer dialog box with a **Dialog** or **Dialog()** instruction.

Note When you use **Organizer** to make a change to a file that is not open, Word opens the file in the background, saves changes, and then closes the file. If you need to make a large number of changes, your macro will run faster if it opens the file first, performs the **Organizer** instructions, and then closes the file using the instruction FileClose 1 to save changes.

Example This Word macro copies the AutoText entries from the active template to the Normal template. First, the name of the active template is retrieved from the Templates And Add-ins dialog box (Templates command, File menu). If the Document Template text box is blank, indicating the active document is a template, the template's filename is retrieved from the Document Statistics dialog box (Statistics button, Summary Info command, File menu). Then, the number of AutoText entries stored in the active template is returned. Finally, using a **For**...**Next** loop, the **Organizer** instruction is repeated once for each AutoText entry.

```
Sub MAIN
Dim dlg As FileTemplates
GetCurValues dlg
template$ = dlg.Template
If template$ = "" Then
    Redim dlg As DocumentStatistics
    GetCurValues dlg
    template$ = dlg.Directory + "\" + dlg.FileName
End If
num = CountAutoTextEntries(1)
If num = 0 Then Goto bye
For count = 1 To num
    Organizer .Copy, .Source = template$, \
        .Destination = "C:\WINWORD\TEMPLATE\NORMAL.DOT", \
        .Name = AutoTextName$(count, 1), .Tab = 1
Next count
bye:
End Sub
```

See Also   **EditAutoText, FileTemplates, FormatStyle, NewToolbar, ToolsMacro**

OtherPane

Syntax   **OtherPane**

Remarks   Moves the insertion point to its most recent position in the next pane of the active window. **OtherPane** is often used in macros that open the annotation or footnote panes.

Example   This example inserts a footnote and then returns the insertion point to the footnote reference mark. In page layout view, where footnotes are not inserted in a separate pane, the instruction GoBack returns the insertion point to the reference mark. In normal view or outline view, the instruction OtherPane returns the insertion point.

```
FntText$ = "This is the footnote text"
InsertFootnote
Insert FntText$
If ViewPage() Then
    GoBack
Else
    OtherPane
End If
```

See Also   **ClosePane, DocSplit, WindowPane()**

Outline, Outline()

Syntax   **Outline** [*On*]

Outline()

Remarks   On the Macintosh, the **Outline** statement adds or removes the outline character format for the current selection, or controls outline formatting for characters to be inserted at the insertion point.

Argument	Explanation
On	Specifies whether to add or remove the outline format:
	1 Formats the selection with outline
	0 (zero) Removes the outline format
	Omitted Toggles the outline format

The **Outline**() function returns the following values.

Value	Explanation
0 (zero)	If none of the selection is formatted with outline
−1	If part of the selection is formatted with outline
1	If all the selection is formatted with outline

In Windows, **Outline** and **Outline**() are not available and generate errors.

See Also   **FormatFont**

OutlineCollapse

Syntax   **OutlineCollapse**

Remarks   Collapses one level of heading or body text under the selected headings. If the active document is not in outline or master document view, an error occurs.

Example   This example collapses every heading in the document by one level:

```
ViewOutline
EditSelectAll
OutlineCollapse
```

See Also   **OutlineExpand, ShowAllHeadings**

OutlineDemote

Syntax   **OutlineDemote**

Remarks   Applies the next heading level style to the selected headings (Heading 1 through
Heading 8) or body text.

Example   This example demotes each paragraph in the document that follows a Heading 2:

```
StartOfDocument : ViewOutline
EditFindClearFormatting
EditFindStyle .Style = "Heading 2"
EditFind .Find = "", .Direction = 0, .Format = 1, .Wrap = 0
While EditFindFound()
    ParaDown
    OutlineDemote
    EditFind .Direction = 0
Wend
```

See Also   **OutlineMoveDown, OutlinePromote**

OutlineExpand

Syntax   **OutlineExpand**

Remarks   Expands one level of heading or body text under the selected headings. If the
active document is not in outline or master document view, an error occurs.

Example   This example expands every heading in the document by one level:

```
ViewOutline
EditSelectAll
OutlineExpand
```

See Also   **OutlineCollapse, ShowAllHeadings**

OutlineLevel()

Syntax   **OutlineLevel()**

Remarks   Returns a number corresponding to the heading level of the selected paragraph.
Returns 0 (zero) if the style of the selected paragraph is not a built-in heading
level style. If multiple paragraphs are selected, **OutlineLevel()** returns the
heading level of the first paragraph in the selection.

Example   This example deletes all paragraphs in a document that are not formatted with a built-in heading level style:

```
StartOfDocument
ViewNormal
While ParaDown()
    ParaUp                          'Go to each paragraph in turn.
    If OutlineLevel() = 0 Then      'If it's not a heading,
        ParaDown 1, 1               'select it, then
        EditClear                   'delete it.
    Else                            'If it is a heading,
        ParaDown                    'go to the next paragraph
    End If
Wend                                'and begin the process again.
```

See Also   **FormatStyle, StyleName$()**

OutlineMoveDown

Syntax   **OutlineMoveDown**

Remarks   Moves the selected paragraphs below the next visible paragraph. Body text moves with a heading only if the body text is selected or collapsed.

See Also   **OutlineMoveUp, OutlineDemote**

OutlineMoveUp

Syntax   **OutlineMoveUp**

Remarks   Moves the selected paragraphs above the next visible paragraph. Body text moves with a heading only if the body text is selected or collapsed.

See Also   **OutlineMoveDown, OutlinePromote**

OutlinePromote

Syntax   **OutlinePromote**

Remarks   Applies the previous heading level style to the selected headings (Heading 2 through Heading 9) or body text.

Example   This example promotes the heading level style of the current paragraph if each character in the paragraph, including the paragraph mark, is bold:

```
ViewOutline
EditGoTo "\Para"
If Bold() = 1 Then OutlinePromote
```

See Also   **OutlineDemote**, **OutlineMoveUp**

OutlineShowFirstLine, OutlineShowFirstLine()

Syntax   **OutlineShowFirstLine** [*On*]

OutlineShowFirstLine()

Remarks   The **OutlineShowFirstLine** statement controls the display of body text in outline view. You can use this statement to make the document easier to scan by hiding all but the first line of body text. If the active document is not in outline or master document view, an error occurs.

Argument	Explanation
On	Specifies whether or not to display the first line of body text:
	0 (zero) All body text is shown.
	1 or omitted Only the first line of body text is shown.

The **OutlineShowFirstLine()** function returns the following values.

Value	Explanation
0 (zero)	All lines of body text are displayed.
−1	Only the first line of body text is displayed.

See Also   **OutlineCollapse**, **OutlineShowFormat**

OutlineShowFormat

Syntax   **OutlineShowFormat**

Remarks   Displays character formatting in outline view or, if character formatting is already displayed, hides it. If the active document is not in outline or master document view, an error occurs.

See Also   **OutlineShowFirstLine**, **ViewDraft**

Overtype, Overtype()

Syntax

Overtype [*On*]

Overtype()

Remarks

The **Overtype** statement switches between overtype and insert modes. In overtype mode, characters you type replace existing characters one by one; in insert mode, characters you type move existing text to the right.

Argument	Explanation
On	Specifies the mode:
	0 (zero)　Switches to insert mode.
	1　Switches to overtype mode ("OVR" appears in status bar).
	Omitted　Switches between overtype and insert modes.

The **Overtype**() function returns the following values.

Value	Explanation
0 (zero)	If overtype mode is off
−1	If overtype mode is on

Note that text you insert with the **Insert** statement will not overwrite text in the document, regardless of whether the document is in insert or overtype mode.

Example

If overtype mode is active, this example displays a message box with Yes and No buttons asking if overtype should be deactivated. If the user chooses Yes, which returns a value of −1, overtype is deactivated.

```
If Overtype() = -1 Then
    Button = MsgBox("Overtype is on. Turn off?", 4)
    If button = -1 Then Overtype 0
End If
```

See Also

ToolsOptionsGeneral

PageDown, PageDown()

Syntax

PageDown [*Count*] [, *Select*]

PageDown([*Count*] [, *Select*])

Remarks

The **PageDown** statement moves the insertion point or the active end of the selection (the end that moves when you press SHIFT+PAGE DOWN) down by the specified number of screens, where one screen is equal to the height of the active window. If there is not a full screen between the insertion point or the selection and the end of the document, **PageDown** moves the insertion point or the active end of the selection to the end of the document.

Argument	Explanation
Count	The number of screens to move; if omitted, 1 is assumed. Negative values move the insertion point or the active end of the selection up.
Select	Specifies whether to select text:
	0 (zero) or omitted Text is not selected. If there is already a selection, **PageDown** moves the insertion point *Count*–1 screens below the selection.
	Nonzero Text is selected. If there is already a selection, **PageDown** moves the active end of the selection toward the end of the document.
	In a typical selection made from left to right, where the active end of the selection is closer to the end of the document, **PageDown** extends the selection. In a selection made from right to left, it shrinks the selection.

The **PageDown()** function behaves the same as the statement and also returns the following values:

Value	Explanation
0 (zero)	If the insertion point or the active end of the selection cannot be moved down.
–1	If the insertion point or the active end of the selection is moved down by any number of screens, even if less than *Count*. For example, PageDown(2) returns –1 even if the insertion point is only one screen from the end of the document.

Examples

This example extends the selection down two screens from the insertion point:

```
PageDown 2, 1
```

The following example counts the number of screens between the insertion point and the end of the document. The **PageDown**() function is used to detect when the end of the document is reached.

```
n = 0
While PageDown()
    n = n + 1
Wend
MsgBox "Number of screens:" + Str$(n)
```

See Also   **EditGoTo, HPage, HScroll, NextPage, PageUp, VPage, VScroll**

PageUp, PageUp()

Syntax   **PageUp** [*Count*] [, *Select*]

PageUp([*Count*] [, *Select*])

Remarks   The **PageUp** statement moves the insertion point or the active end of the selection (the end that moves when you press SHIFT+PAGE UP) up by the specified number of screens, where one screen is equal to the height of the active window. If there is not a full screen between the insertion point or the selection and the beginning of the document, **PageUp** moves the insertion point or the active end of the selection to the beginning of the document.

Argument	Explanation
Count	The number of screens to move; if omitted, 1 is assumed. Negative values move the insertion point or the active end of the selection down.
Select	Specifies whether to select text:
	0 (zero) or omitted Text is not selected. If there is already a selection, **PageUp** moves the insertion point *Count*–1 screens above the selection.
	Nonzero Text is selected. If there is already a selection, **PageUp** moves the active end of the selection toward the beginning of the document.
	In a typical selection made from left to right, where the active end of the selection is closer to the end of the document, **PageUp** shrinks the selection. In a selection made from right to left, it extends the selection.

The **PageUp**() function behaves the same as the statement and also returns the following values.

Value	Explanation
0 (zero)	If the insertion point or the active end of the selection cannot be moved up.
−1	If the insertion point or the active end of the selection is moved up by any number of screens, even if less than *Count*. For example, PageUp(2) returns −1 even if a single **PageUp** instruction brings the beginning of the document into view.

Example

This example selects one screen up from the insertion point. If there is less than one screen above the insertion point, the message "Selected to start of document" appears in the status bar.

```
PageUp 1, 1
If CmpBookmarks("\StartOfSel", "\StartOfDoc") = 0 Then
    Print "Selected to start of document."
End If
```

See Also

EditGoTo, HPage, HScroll, PageDown, PrevPage, VPage, VScroll

ParaDown, ParaDown()

Syntax

ParaDown [*Count*] [, *Select*]

ParaDown([*Count*] [, *Select*])

Remarks

The **ParaDown** statement moves the insertion point or the active end of the selection (the end that moves when you press CTRL+SHIFT+DOWN ARROW (Windows) or COMMAND+SHIFT+DOWN ARROW (Macintosh)) down by the specified number of paragraphs.

Regardless of the position of the insertion point within a paragraph or whether there is a selection within a paragraph, the instruction ParaDown moves the insertion point to the start of the next paragraph. The only exception is when the insertion point is in the last paragraph of the document; in that case, ParaDown moves the insertion point to the end of the paragraph. If the current selection extends over multiple paragraphs, the instruction ParaDown moves the insertion point to the beginning of the first paragraph following the end of the selection.

Argument	Explanation
Count	The number of paragraphs to move; if omitted, 1 is assumed. Negative values move the insertion point or the active end of the selection up.
Select	Specifies whether to select text:
	0 (zero) or omitted Text is not selected. If there is already a selection, **ParaDown** moves the insertion point *Count* paragraphs below the selection.
	Nonzero Text is selected. If there is already a selection, **ParaDown** moves the active end of the selection toward the end of the document.
	In a typical selection made from left to right, where the active end of the selection is closer to the end of the document, **ParaDown** extends the selection. In a selection made from right to left, it shrinks the selection.

The **ParaDown()** function behaves the same as the statement and also returns the following values.

Value	Explanation
0 (zero)	If the insertion point or the active end of the selection cannot be moved down.
−1	If the insertion point or the active end of the selection is moved down by any number of paragraphs, even if less than *Count*. For example, ParaDown(2) returns −1 even if the insertion point is at the beginning of the last paragraph in the document.

Example

This example inserts three asterisks (***) before each paragraph in the document. Because the While ParaDown() instruction eventually moves the insertion point to the end of the last paragraph, where the asterisks are not appropriate, the **If** control structure uses **CmpBookmarks()** to detect that condition and exit the **While…Wend** loop.

```
StartOfDocument
Insert "***"
While ParaDown()
    If CmpBookmarks("\Sel", "\EndOfDoc") <> 0 Then
        Insert "***"
    End If
Wend
```

See Also   **LineDown, PageDown, ParaUp**

ParaKeepLinesTogether, ParaKeepLinesTogether()

Syntax   **ParaKeepLinesTogether** [*On*]

ParaKeepLinesTogether()

Remarks   The **ParaKeepLinesTogether** statement adds or removes the Keep Lines
Together paragraph format for the selected paragraphs. All lines in a paragraph
formatted with Keep Lines Together remain on the same page when Word
repaginates the document.

Argument	Explanation
On	Specifies whether to add or remove the Keep Lines Together format:
	1 Adds the Keep Lines Together format.
	0 (zero) Removes the Keep Lines Together format.
	Omitted Toggles the Keep Lines Together format.

The **ParaKeepLinesTogether**() function returns the following values.

Value	Explanation
0 (zero)	If none of the selected paragraphs are formatted with Keep Lines Together
−1	If some of the selected paragraphs are formatted with Keep Lines Together
1	If all the selected paragraphs are formatted with Keep Lines Together

See Also   **FormatParagraph, ParaKeepWithNext, ParaPageBreakBefore**

ParaKeepWithNext, ParaKeepWithNext()

Syntax   **ParaKeepWithNext** [*On*]

ParaKeepWithNext()

Remarks   The **ParaKeepWithNext** statement adds or removes the Keep With Next
paragraph format for the selected paragraphs. A paragraph formatted with Keep
With Next remains on the same page as the paragraph it follows when Word
repaginates the document.

Argument	Explanation
On	Specifies whether to add or remove the Keep With Next format:
	1 Adds the Keep With Next format.
	0 (zero) Removes the Keep With Next format.
	Omitted Toggles the Keep With Next format.

The **ParaKeepWithNext**() function returns the following values.

Value	Explanation
0 (zero)	If none of the selected paragraphs are formatted with Keep With Next
–1	If some of the selected paragraphs are formatted with Keep With Next
1	If all the selected paragraphs are formatted with Keep With Next

See Also   **FormatParagraph**, **ParaKeepLinesTogether**, **ParaPageBreakBefore**

ParaPageBreakBefore, ParaPageBreakBefore()

Syntax   **ParaPageBreakBefore** [*On*]

ParaPageBreakBefore()

Remarks   The **ParaPageBreakBefore** statement adds or removes the Page Break Before paragraph format for the selected paragraphs. A paragraph formatted with Page Break Before appears at the top of a new page whenever the document is printed.

Argument	Explanation
On	Specifies whether to add or remove the Page Break Before format:
	1 Adds the Page Break Before format.
	0 (zero) Removes the Page Break Before format.
	Omitted Toggles the Page Break Before format.

The **ParaPageBreakBefore**() function returns the following values.

Value	Explanation
0 (zero)	If none of the selected paragraphs are formatted with Page Break Before
–1	If some of the selected paragraphs are formatted with Page Break Before
1	If all the selected paragraphs are formatted with Page Break Before

See Also   **FormatParagraph**, **ParaKeepLinesTogether**, **ParaKeepWithNext**

ParaUp, ParaUp()

Syntax   **ParaUp** [*Count*] [**,** *Select*]

ParaUp([*Count*] [**,** *Select*])

Remarks

The **ParaUp** statement moves the insertion point or the active end of the selection (the end that moves when you press CTRL+SHIFT+UP ARROW (Windows) or COMMAND+SHIFT+UP ARROW (Macintosh)) up by the specified number of paragraphs.

If the insertion point is at the beginning of a paragraph, the instruction ParaUp moves the insertion point to the beginning of the previous paragraph. If the insertion point is not at the beginning of the paragraph, or if there is a selection, ParaUp moves the insertion point to the beginning of the current paragraph. If the current selection extends over multiple paragraphs, the instruction ParaUp moves the insertion point to the beginning of the first selected paragraph.

Argument	Explanation
Count	The number of paragraphs to move; if omitted, 1 is assumed. Negative values move the insertion point or the active end of the selection down.
Select	Specifies whether to select text:
	0 (zero) or omitted Text is not selected. If there is already a selection, **ParaUp** moves the insertion point *Count*–1 paragraphs above the selection.
	Nonzero Text is selected. If there is already a selection, **ParaUp** moves the active end of the selection toward the beginning of the document.
	In a typical selection made from left to right, where the active end of the selection is closer to the end of the document, **ParaUp** shrinks the selection. In a selection made from right to left, it extends the selection.

The **ParaUp()** function behaves the same as the statement and also returns the following values.

Value	Explanation
0 (zero)	If the insertion point or the active end of the selection cannot be moved up.
–1	If the insertion point or the active end of the selection is moved up by any number of paragraphs, even if less than *Count*. For example, ParaUp(2) returns –1 even if the insertion point is at the end of the first paragraph in the document.

Example

This example finds the next occurrence of the phrase "Press F1 for Help" and then selects the entire text of the surrounding paragraph:

```
EditFind .Find = "Press F1 for Help"
ParaUp
ParaDown 1, 1
```

Note that you can also use the predefined bookmark "\Para" in the instruction
`EditGoTo "\Para"` to select the paragraph containing the insertion point or
selection. For more information on predefined bookmarks, see "Operators and
Predefined Bookmarks" later in this part.

See Also   **LineUp**, **PageUp**, **ParaDown**

ParaWidowOrphanControl, ParaWidowOrphanControl()

Syntax   **ParaWidowOrphanControl** [*On*]

ParaWidowOrphanControl()

Remarks   The **ParaWidowOrphanControl** statement adds or removes the Widow/Orphan
Control paragraph format for the selected paragraphs. A paragraph formatted with
Widow/Orphan Control prevents a page break from leaving a single line of the
paragraph at the top or bottom of a page.

Argument	Explanation
On	Specifies whether to add or remove the Widow/Orphan Control format:
	1 Adds the Widow/Orphan Control format.
	0 (zero) Removes the Widow/Orphan Control format.
	Omitted Toggles the Widow/Orphan Control format.

The **ParaWidowOrphanControl**() function returns the following values.

Value	Explanation
0 (zero)	If none of the selected paragraphs are formatted with Widow/Orphan Control
−1	If some of the selected paragraphs are formatted with Widow/Orphan Control
1	If all the selected paragraphs are formatted with Widow/Orphan Control

See Also   **FormatParagraph**, **ParaKeepLinesTogether**, **ParaKeepWithNext**,
ParaPageBreakBefore

PasteButtonImage

Syntax   **PasteButtonImage** *Toolbar$*, *Tool* [, *Context*]

Remarks   Sets the face of the specified toolbar button to the graphic on the Clipboard.

Argument	Explanation
Toolbar$	The name of the toolbar, as it appears in the Toolbars dialog box (View menu).
Tool	A number corresponding to the button face to change, where 0 (zero) is the first button on the specified toolbar, 1 is the second, and so on.
Context	Determines where the change is stored:

0 (zero) or omitted   Normal template

1   Active template

For an example that uses **PasteButtonImage**, see **CopyButtonImage**.

See Also   **ChooseButtonImage**, **CopyButtonImage**, **EditButtonImage**, **ResetButtonImage**

PasteFormat

Syntax   **PasteFormat**

Remarks   Applies formatting copied with **CopyFormat** to the selection. If a paragraph mark was selected when **CopyFormat** was run, Word applies paragraph formatting in addition to character formatting.

Example   This example copies both character and paragraph formats from the current paragraph (selected using the predefined bookmark "\Para"), and then applies only the paragraph formats to the next paragraph. Character formats are not applied because no text is selected when PasteFormat runs. **ResetChar** ensures that any new text typed at the insertion point has the font characteristics of the current style.

```
SelType 1                'Cancel selection, if any
EditGoTo "\Para"
CopyFormat
ParaDown
PasteFormat
ResetChar
```

See Also   **CopyFormat**, **ResetChar**, **ResetPara**

PathFromMacPath$()

Syntax   **PathFromMacPath$**(*Path$*)

Remarks   Converts the Macintosh path and filename specified by *Path$* to a valid path and filename for the current operating system.

In Windows 3.x, each foldername and filename may contain up to eight characters, followed by an optional filename extension (a period and up to three characters). When converting a Macintosh path to a valid Windows 3.x path, Word does the following to each Macintosh folder name and filename:

- Removes spaces.
- Adds an exclamation point (!) before the folder name or filename if spaces or extra characters are removed.
- If the folder name or filename is longer than eight characters, adds a period and removes extra characters to form a valid Windows 3.x folder name or filename with an extension; for example, the Macintosh folder name "Employee Addresses" becomes the Windows 3.x folder name "!Employe.ead".
- Uses the first period, if any, to determine where the extension begins in the Windows folder name or filename, removing any unusable characters; for example, the Macintosh filename "PC text file.text" becomes the Windows 3.x filename "!PCtextf.tex".
- If there is more than one period, removes all characters between the first and the last period; for example, the Macintosh filename "chapter1.rev.3" becomes the Windows 3.x filename "!chapter.3".

Example

In Word for Windows, this example returns the path and filename "\HD80\Reports\!FinalRe.por".

```
winpath$ = PathFromMacPath$("HD80:Reports:Final Report")
```

See Also

PathFromWinPath$()

PathFromWinPath$()

Syntax

PathFromWinPath$(***Path$*)**

Remarks

Converts the Windows path and filename specified by *Path$* to a valid path and filename for the current operating system.

On the Macintosh, drive names, folder names, and filenames are separated by colons (:) instead of backslashes. When converting a Windows path to a valid Macintosh path, Word does the following:

- Substitutes colons for backslashes.
- Substitutes Macintosh drive names for drive letters or root folder specifications: "C:" is replaced by the name of the startup disk; "A:" and "B:" are replaced by the names of the disks in the first and second floppy disk drives, respectively; "D:", "E:", "F:", and so on are replaced by the names of other hard drives. For example, C:\DOCS\STORY.DOC or \DOCS\STORY.DOC might become HD:DOCS:STORY.DOC.

- Removes server names. For example, \\COMMON\TOOLS\ART becomes TOOLS:ART.

- Substitutes colons (:) to represent relative paths (for example, LETTERS\ALICE.DOC becomes :LETTERS:ALICE.DOC and ..\LETTERS\ALICE.DOC becomes ::LETTERS:ALICE.DOC).

Because all Windows filenames are valid on the Macintosh, **PathFromWinPath$( )** does not change the filenames themselves.

See Also **PathFromMacPath$( )**

PauseRecorder

Syntax **PauseRecorder**

Remarks Stops and restarts macro recording. **PauseRecorder** is the built-in Word command that runs when the user chooses the Pause Recorder button on the Macro toolbar; this statement would not typically appear in a macro.

Picture

Syntax **Picture** *HorizPos*, *VertPos*, *Width*, *Height*, *PictureName$*, *Type*, *.Identifier*

Remarks Displays a graphic in a custom dialog box. Word automatically sizes the graphic to fit within the *Width* and *Height* you have specified.

Argument	Explanation
HorizPos, *VertPos*	The horizontal and vertical distance of the upper-left corner of the rectangle containing the graphic from the upper-left corner of the dialog box, in increments of 1/8 and 1/12 of the System font (Windows) or the dialog font (Macintosh).
Width, *Height*	The width and height of the rectangle, in increments of 1/8 and 1/12 of the System font (Windows) or the dialog font (Macintosh).
PictureName$	The name of the graphics file, AutoText entry, or bookmark containing the graphic that is initially displayed. You can reset *PictureName$* with **DlgSetPicture** in a dialog function when the dialog box is displayed.

Argument	Explanation
Type	A value indicating how the graphic is stored:
	0 (zero) *PictureName$* is a graphics file. Paths are allowed.
	1 *PictureName$* is an AutoText entry. The AutoText entry must contain a single graphic only (no text or paragraph marks) and must be stored either in the Normal template or the template attached to the active document.
	2 *PictureName$* is a bookmark in the active document. The bookmark must mark a single graphic only (no text or paragraph marks).
	3 *PictureName$* is ignored and the graphic is retrieved from the Clipboard. Include empty quotation marks ("") in place of *PictureName$*. The Clipboard must contain a single graphic only. If the Clipboard contains any text from a Word document, the Microsoft Word icon is displayed in the dialog box.
	4 *PictureName$* is a PICT file stored in the resource fork of the template containing the macro (Macintosh only). You can use the ResEdit program to add PICT files to the resource fork of a template.
.Identifier	An identifier used by statements in a dialog function that act on the graphic. For example, you can use this identifier with **DlgSetPicture** to display a different graphic.

Note If the specified picture does not exist, Word displays the text "(missing picture)" within the rectangle that defines the picture area. You can change this behavior by adding 16 to the value for *Type*. If *Type* is 16, 17, 18, or 19 and the specified picture does not exist, Word displays an error (which may be trapped with **On Error**) and displays neither the text "(missing picture)" nor a rectangle in the dialog box.

Example

This example defines a square area at the upper-left corner of the dialog box and inserts the graphic stored in the AutoText entry "Smiley." The dialog box control is identified as .Graphic. For an example of a complete dialog box definition, see **Begin Dialog...End Dialog**.

```
Picture 7, 7, 50, 50, "Smiley", 1, .Graphic
```

See Also   **DlgSetPicture**

PrevCell, PrevCell()

Syntax   **PrevCell**

PrevCell()

Remarks   The **PrevCell** statement selects the contents of the previous cell (the same as pressing SHIFT+TAB in a table). If there is already a selection including multiple cells, **PrevCell** selects the first cell in the selection.

The **PrevCell()** function behaves the same as the statement and also returns the following values.

Value	Explanation
0 (zero)	If the selection is wholly contained in the leftmost cell of the first row (in other words, if the selection is not moved)
−1	If the selection is moved

Example   This example moves the selection to the previous cell; if the selection is in the first cell, the entire table is selected.

```
If PrevCell() = 0 Then TableSelectTable
```

See Also   **NextCell**

PrevField, PrevField()

Syntax   **PrevField**

PrevField()

Remarks   The **PrevField** statement selects the previous field, regardless of whether the field is showing its codes or result. **PrevField** skips over the following fields, which are formatted as hidden text: XE (Index Entry), TA (Table of Authorities Entry), TC (Table of Contents Entry), and RD (Referenced Document).

The **PrevField()** function behaves the same as the statement and also returns the following values.

Value	Explanation
0 (zero)	If there is no previous field (in other words, if the selection is not moved)
1	If the selection is moved

With field codes displayed, you can use **EditFind** to go to the previous field of any type, including XE, TA, TC, and RD fields, provided that hidden text is displayed. Simply specify "^d" (the code for a field character) as the text for the .Find argument and 1 for the .Direction argument, as shown in the following instructions:

```
ViewFieldCodes 1
EditFind .Find = "^d", .Direction = 1, .Format = 1
```

To find only XE fields, specify "^d XE" as the text to find.

Example

This macro counts the number of fields above the insertion point (excluding XE, TA, TC, and RD fields) and displays the result in a message box:

```
Sub MAIN
    count = 0
    While PrevField()
        count = count + 1
    Wend
    MsgBox "Fields above the insertion point:" + Str$(count)
End Sub
```

See Also

NextField

PrevObject

Syntax

PrevObject

Remarks

Moves the insertion point to the previous document object on the current page in page layout view (the same as pressing ALT+UP ARROW (Windows) or OPTION+UP ARROW (Macintosh)). Document objects include frames, footnotes, table cells, and text columns.

From the top of the first text column on a page, the **PrevObject** statement moves through document objects in the following order:

- Frames, if any appear, in the order that they appear in normal view, from the following page break to the previous page break

- Each text column, in order from last to first (if there is more than one), moving through all footnotes and then all table cells that appear within the text column

PrevObject finally moves to the top of the first text column before cycling through the document objects again.

Keep the following points in mind when using **PrevObject**:

- You can identify document objects by selecting the Text Boundaries check box on the View tab in the Options dialog box (Tools menu).
- Word does not consider OLE objects, such as embedded drawings and charts, to be document objects unless they are framed.
- If the insertion point is in a header or footer, **PrevObject** moves between the header and footer.
- Make sure to switch to page layout view before using **PrevObject**.

See Also   **NextObject**

PrevPage, PrevPage()

Syntax   **PrevPage**

PrevPage()

Remarks   The **PrevPage** statement scrolls back one page in page layout view without moving the insertion point (the same as clicking the Page Back button at the bottom of the vertical scroll bar in page layout view). If you want to move the insertion point after scrolling, include a **StartOfWindow** statement following **PrevPage** in your macro.

PrevPage scrolls from the current location on one page to the same relative location on the previous page. To scroll to the beginning of the previous page regardless of what portion of the current page appears, use the instruction `EditGoTo .Destination = "p-1"` instead of **PrevPage**. Note, however, that **EditGoTo** also moves the insertion point.

The **PrevPage()** function behaves the same as the statement and also returns the following values.

Value	Explanation
0 (zero)	If there is no previous page (in other words, if the document doesn't scroll)
1	If the document scrolls

Note **PrevPage** and **PrevPage()** are available only in page layout view and generate an error if run in another view.

Example	This example ensures the document is in page layout view, scrolls to the previous page, and moves the insertion point to the top of the window:

```
ViewPage
PrevPage
StartOfWindow
```

See Also   **EditGoTo**, **NextPage**, **PageUp**, **ViewPage**, **VPage**

PrevTab()

Syntax   **PrevTab**(*Position*)

Remarks   Returns the position of the next tab stop to the left of *Position*, in points, for the first paragraph in the selection.

Use the following list of conversions as an aid in converting from points to other measurements:

- 1 inch = 72 points
- 1 centimeter = 28.35 points
- 1 pica = 12 points

Example   This example displays a message box stating the position, in inches, of the last tab stop in the current paragraph. In the first instruction, PrevTab(8.5 * 72) returns the position of the last tab in points, given a page width of 8.5 inches and 72 points per inch. The value is divided by 72 to give the position in inches. The next three instructions prepare the number for display in a message box, with a maximum of two digits after the decimal point.

```
LastPos = PrevTab(8.5 * 72) / 72
LastPos$ = Str$(LastPos)
dot = InStr(LastPos$, ".")
LastPos$ = Left$(LastPos$, dot + 2)
MsgBox "Position of last tab stop: " + LastPos$ + " inches"
```

See Also   **FormatTabs**, **NextTab()**, **TabLeader$()**, **TabType()**

PrevWindow

Syntax   **PrevWindow**

Remarks   Moves the window at the back of the internal order of open windows to the front. This statement does nothing if there is only one open window.

See Also   **Activate**, **ChDir**, **NextWindow**, **Window()**, **WindowList**, **WindowName$()**, **Window***Number*

Print

Syntax   **Print** [**#***FileNumber*,] *Expression1*[*$*] [**;** *or* **,** *Expression2*[*$*] [**;** or , ...]

Remarks   Displays the specified expressions in the status bar, or if you specify *FileNumber*,
sends the expressions to the sequential file associated with that number. Unlike
MsgBox, which accepts only strings, **Print** accepts strings, string variables,
numbers, and numeric variables, and allows you to mix all these types.

You can join strings and string variables with the plus sign (+). You can join
strings and numbers with a semicolon (;) or a comma (,). A comma inserts a tab
between values.

Note **Print** automatically adds a space before positive numeric values; there is no
need to include an extra space in a string that precedes one. **Print** does not add a
space before negative numeric values.

Like **Write**, the **Print** statement can send expressions to a sequential file.
However, the expressions are formatted differently in the file, as illustrated in the
following table. Note that **Print** separates the expressions with a tab character.

WordBasic instruction	Line created in sequential file #1
`Print #1, "Phil", "Teacher"`	`Phil    Teacher`
`Write #1, "Phil", "Teacher"`	`"Phil","Teacher"`

Examples   This example displays the following sentence in the status bar: "March sales were
2500 and May sales were 3600 for a total of 6100."

```
mar = 2500
may = 3600
Print "March sales were"; mar ; " and May sales were" \
    ; may ; " for a total of" ; mar + may ; "."
```

The following example displays this line on the status bar: "Juan Garcia 32 1234".

```
name$ = "Juan Garcia"
age = 32
employeeNum = 1234
Print name$; age; employeeNum
```

The following example sets up a sequential file for use as a text-only data source
in a mail-merge operation. The first **Print** instruction inserts column headings; the
second adds a data record. Items in a given **Print** instruction are inserted into a
single paragraph and are separated by tabs. Note that WordBasic doesn't have a
sequential-file-access instruction that can read tab-delimited data. To see the
results, you must open the sequential file as you would any Word document.

```
Open "DATA.TXT" For Output As #1
Print #1, "Name", "Address", "Occupation"
Print #1, "Juan Garcia", "123 Main St", "Accountant"
Close #1
```

See Also   **Close, Eof(), Input, Input$(), Line Input, Lof(), MsgBox, Open, Read, Seek, Write**

PromoteList

Syntax   **PromoteList**

Remarks   Promotes the selected paragraphs by one level in a multilevel list. If the selected paragraphs are formatted as a bulleted list or as a numbered list that isn't multilevel, **PromoteList** decreases the indent. If the selected paragraphs are not already formatted as a numbered or bulleted list, an error occurs.

See Also   **DemoteList, FormatBulletsAndNumbering**

PushButton

Syntax   **PushButton** *HorizPos*, *VertPos*, *Width*, *Height*, *Label$* [, *.Identifier*]

Remarks   Creates a command button in a custom dialog box. When the command button is chosen, the **Dialog()** instruction that displays the dialog box (for example, button = Dialog(dlg)) returns a value corresponding to the relative order of that **PushButton** instruction among the other **PushButton** instructions: 1 for the first command button, 2 for the second, and so on.

Argument	Explanation
HorizPos, VertPos	The horizontal and vertical distance of the upper-left corner of the command button from the upper-left corner of the dialog box, in increments of 1/8 and 1/12 of the System font (Windows) or the dialog font (Macintosh).
Width, Height	The width and height of the command button, in increments of 1/8 and 1/12 of the System font (Windows) or the dialog font (Macintosh).
Label$	The label associated with the command button. An ampersand (&) precedes the character in *Label$* that is the access key for choosing the command button.
.Identifier	An optional identifier used by statements in a dialog function that act on the command button. If omitted, the default identifier is the first two words in *Label$* (or the entire string if *Label$* is only one word). You should specify *.Identifier* because the identifier you assign remains the same regardless of changes you make to *Label$*.

Example

This example creates a command button with the text "Create Link," whose identifier is "Link." For an example of **PushButton** used in a complete dialog box definition, see **Begin Dialog...End Dialog**.

```
PushButton 10, 54, 108, 21, "&Create Link", .Link
```

See Also

Begin Dialog...End Dialog, **CancelButton**, **OKButton**, **OptionButton**

PutFieldData

Syntax

PutFieldData *FieldData$*

Remarks

When the insertion point is within an ADDIN field, stores the text data specified by *FieldData$* in the field. The data is stored internally in the field and is not visible, even when field codes are showing. If there is a selection, it must begin at an ADDIN field; otherwise, an error occurs.

See Also

GetFieldData$()

Read

Syntax

Read #*FileNumber*, *Variable1*[$] [, *Variable2*[$]] [, *Variable3*[$]] [, ...]

Remarks

Retrieves string or numeric values from an open sequential file, typically containing data added with the **Write** statement, and assigns the values to variables. *FileNumber* is the number specified in the **Open** instruction that opened the file for output. For more information about sequential files, see Chapter 9, "More WordBasic Techniques," in Part 1, "Learning WordBasic."

Read is similar to **Input**, but removes quotation marks from strings. For example, a text-only paragraph created with a **Write** instruction might appear as follows:

```
"Michelle Levine", 26,"Dancer"
```

Whereas **Input** interprets the first value as "Michelle Levine", **Read** takes only the text within the quotation marks: Michelle Levine.

Example

This example reads each paragraph in the sequential file in turn and defines name$ as the first item and age as the second item. For each paragraph, the values are displayed in a message box.

```
Open "DATA.TXT" For Input As #1
While Not Eof(1)
    Read #1, name$, age
    MsgBox name$ + " is" + Str$(age) + " years old."
Wend
Close #1
```

See Also

Close, **Eof()**, **Input**, **Input$()**, **Line Input**, **Lof()**, **Open**, **Print**, **Seek**, **Write**

Redim

Syntax

Redim [**Shared**] *Var1*[(*Size1* [, *Size2*] [, ...])] [, *Var2*[(*Size1* [, *Size2*] [, ...])]]

Redim *Var* **As** *DialogName*

Redim *Var* **As** **UserDialog**

Remarks

Empties array variables so that the array elements can be redefined. **Redim** stands for "redimension"—you can specify new *Size* values when redefining array variables. Note that whenever you use **Redim**, existing array contents are lost. **Redim** can also redefine a dialog record for a Word dialog box or a custom dialog box. For descriptions of arguments used with **Redim**, see **Dim**.

Examples

This example illustrates how you might use **Redim** to recycle the storage space in an array variable when you have finished using the first set of values. This helps conserve system resources.

```
Dim BigArray$(100)
BigArray$(0) = "A long text string"
'Series of statements that define array elements 1 through 99
BigArray$(100) = "Another long text string"
'Series of statements that make use of the values in BigArray$()
Redim BigArray$(100)
'Series of statements that define and make use of new array elements
```

The following macro retrieves the author name from the Summary Info dialog box (File menu) and the user name from the User Info tab in the Options dialog box (Tools menu), and then compares the two values. If they are different, a message box is displayed.

The **Dim** statement stores the array of values from the Summary Info dialog box in the dialog record dlg. After the author name is retrieved, these values are no longer needed. **Redim** can therefore recycle the dialog record dlg to store the values from the User Info tab (Options dialog box).

```
Sub MAIN
Dim dlg As FileSummaryInfo
GetCurValues dlg
Author$ = dlg.Author
Redim dlg As ToolsOptionsUserInfo
GetCurValues dlg
UserName$ = dlg.Name
If Author$ <> UserName$ Then
    MsgBox "Author does not match user."
End If
End Sub
```

See Also

Dim, Let

REM

Syntax

REM *Comments*

'*Comments*

Remarks

Designates explanatory text, which Word ignores when the macro is run. You can use an apostrophe (') instead of **REM**. Each notation has its advantages and disadvantages: **REM** makes it easier to distinguish comments from WordBasic instructions, but requires more space than an apostrophe.

Example   This example demonstrates four ways to include a comment in a macro:

```
REM MyMacro Title -- MyName Here
'More about MyMacro
ParaDown      'Move to start of next paragraph
ParaUp            REM Moves to start of previous paragraph
```

RemoveAllDropDownItems

Syntax   **RemoveAllDropDownItems** *BookmarkName$*

Remarks   Removes all items from a drop-down form field.

Argument	Explanation
BookmarkName$	The name of the bookmark that marks the drop-down form field. If you specify a bookmark that does not mark a drop-down form field, an error occurs.

See Also   **AddDropDownItem**, **DropDownFormField**, **RemoveDropDownItem**

RemoveBulletsNumbers

Syntax   **RemoveBulletsNumbers**

Remarks   Removes bullets or numbers as well as list formatting from the selected paragraphs in a bulleted or numbered list created with the Bullets And Numbering command (Format menu). Subsequent bulleted or numbered paragraphs start a new list and restart the numbering in the case of a numbered list. **RemoveBulletsNumbers** corresponds to the Remove button in the Bullets And Numbering dialog box (Format menu).

See Also   **FormatBulletsAndNumbering**, **SkipNumbering**

RemoveDropDownItem

Syntax   **RemoveDropDownItem** *BookmarkName$*, *ItemText$*

Remarks   Removes an item from a drop-down form field.

Argument	Explanation
BookmarkName$	The name of the bookmark that marks the drop-down form field. If you specify a bookmark that does not mark a drop-down form field, an error occurs.
ItemText$	The item to remove from the drop-down form field.

Example	This example removes three items from the drop-down form field marked by the bookmark "Dropdown1":

```
RemoveDropDownItem "Dropdown1", "Red"
RemoveDropDownItem "Dropdown1", "Blue"
RemoveDropDownItem "Dropdown1", "Green"
```

See Also	**AddDropDownItem**, **DropDownFormField**, **RemoveAllDropDownItems**

RemoveFrames

Syntax	**RemoveFrames**
Remarks	Removes all frames in the selection. Note that borders, applied automatically when you insert a frame around text, are not removed.
Example	This example removes all frames from the entire document:

```
EditSelectAll
RemoveFrames
```

See Also	**FormatBordersAndShading**, **FormatFrame**, **InsertFrame**

RemoveSubdocument

Syntax	**RemoveSubdocument**
Remarks	Merges the contents of the selected subdocuments into the master document and removes the subdocuments. **RemoveSubdocument** does not delete subdocument files. If the active document is not in master document or outline view, or the insertion point is not in a subdocument, an error occurs.
See Also	**CreateSubdocument**, **InsertSubdocument**, **MergeSubdocument**, **OpenSubdocument**, **SplitSubdocument**, **ViewMasterDocument**

RenameMenu

Syntax	**RenameMenu** *Menu$*, *NewName$*, *Type* [, *Context*]
Remarks	Renames the specified menu. If *Menu$* is not one of the menus of the given *Type*, an error occurs.

Argument	Explanation
Menu$	The name of a menu as it appears on the menu bar. Including an ampersand (&) before the access key in the menu name is optional (for example, you can specify either "File" or "&File").
NewName$	The new menu name. An ampersand (&) before a character in the menu name sets the access key for displaying the menu.

Argument	Explanation
Type	The type of menu:
	0 (zero) Menus on the menu bar when a document is open.
	1 Menus on the menu bar when no document is open.
	Note that you cannot rename shortcut menus.
Context	Specifies where the new menu name is stored:
	0 (zero) or omitted Normal template (the new menu name appears regardless of which template is active).
	1 Active template (the new menu name appears only when the template is active).

Example

This example renames the Tools menu "Other Tasks" and makes ALT, T (Windows) or COMMAND﹢TAB, T (Macintosh) the key sequence that activates the menu:

```
RenameMenu "Tools", "Other &Tasks", 0
```

See Also

MenuText$( ), ToolsCustomizeMenus

RepeatFind

Syntax

RepeatFind

Remarks

Repeats the most recent **EditFind** or **EditGoTo** operation. Note that when an **EditFind** instruction is repeated, settings for .Direction, .WholeWord, .MatchCase, .PatternMatch, .Format, and .Wrap are all repeated.

Example

This example counts the number of times the word "success" occurs in the active document and then displays the result in a message box:

```
StartOfDocument
EditFind .Find = "success", .Direction = 0, .WholeWord = 1, \
    .MatchCase = 0, .Format = 0, .Wrap = 0
While EditFindFound()
    count = count + 1
    RepeatFind
Wend
MsgBox "The word " + Chr$(34) + "success" + Chr$(34) \
    + " occurs" + Str$(Count) + " times."
```

See Also

EditFind, EditGoTo, EditRepeat

ResetButtonImage

Syntax   **ResetButtonImage** *Toolbar$*, *Tool* [, *Context*]

Remarks   Resets the face of the specified toolbar button to the graphic originally associated
with the command the button runs.

Argument	Explanation
Toolbar$	The name of the toolbar, as it appears in the Toolbars dialog box (View menu)
Tool	A number corresponding to the button face to reset, where 1 is the first button on the specified toolbar, 2 is the second, and so on
Context	Determines where the change is stored:
	0 (zero) or omitted Normal template
	1 Active template

See Also   **ChooseButtonImage**, **CopyButtonImage**, **EditButtonImage**,
PasteButtonImage, **ViewToolbars**

ResetChar, ResetChar()

Syntax   **ResetChar**

                   ResetChar()

Remarks   The **ResetChar** statement removes manual character formatting (formatting not
defined in the selected paragraph styles) from the selected text. For example, if
you manually format a word or phrase in a paragraph as bold text and the
paragraph style is plain text, **ResetChar** would remove the bold format.

The **ResetChar**() function returns the following values without resetting
character formats.

Value	Explanation
0 (zero)	If the selected text contains any manual character formatting
1	If the selected text contains no manual character formatting

Example   If the current paragraph is formatted as Normal, this example selects the entire paragraph (using the predefined bookmark "\Para") and removes any character formatting not defined as part of the style:

```
If StyleName$() = "Normal" Then
    EditGoTo "\Para"
    ResetChar
End If
```

See Also   **FormatFont**, **ResetPara**

ResetNoteSepOrNotice

Syntax   **ResetNoteSepOrNotice**

Remarks   Resets the separator, the continuation notice, or the continuation separator for footnotes or endnotes to the default. **ResetNoteSepOrNotice** generates an error unless you first open a separator pane.

Example   This example opens the footnote continuation notice pane and then determines if there is a continuation notice. If the pane contains anything more than a paragraph mark, ResetNoteSepOrNotice removes the notice. Without the **If** conditional, the example would generate an error if the notice were already set to the default.

```
ViewFootnoteContNotice
EditSelectAll
paraMark$ = Chr$(13)
If Selection$() <> paraMark$ Then ResetNoteSepOrNotice
ClosePane
```

See Also   **NoteOptions**, **ViewEndnoteContNotice**, **ViewEndnoteContSeparator**, **ViewEndnoteSeparator**, **ViewFootnoteContNotice**, **ViewFootnoteContSeparator**, **ViewFootnoteSeparator**

ResetPara, ResetPara()

Syntax   **ResetPara**

ResetPara()

Remarks   The **ResetPara** statement removes paragraph formatting not defined in the current paragraph style from the selected text. For example, if you format a paragraph with a half-inch left indent and the style applied to the paragraph has no left indent, **ResetPara** would remove the indent.

The **ResetPara()** function returns the following values without removing paragraph formatting.

Value	Explanation
0 (zero)	If the first paragraph in the selection contains formatting that differs from the formatting defined for the applied paragraph style
−1	If the first paragraph in the selection contains no formatting that differs from the formatting defined for the applied paragraph style

Example

If the current paragraph is formatted as Normal, this example removes any paragraph formatting not defined as part of the style:

```
If StyleName$() = "Normal" Then ResetPara
```

See Also

FormatParagraph, **NormalStyle**, **ResetChar**

Right$()

Syntax

**Right$**(*Source$*, *Count*)

Remarks

Returns the rightmost *Count* characters of *Source$*.

Example

This example prompts the user to enter his or her first and last name in an **InputBox$()** dialog box. By subtracting the position of the space (located between the first and last name) from the length of the full name, the instructions determine the number of characters after the space. **Right$()** is then able to retrieve the last name from the single string.

```
fullName$ = InputBox$("Please type your first and last name.")
length = Len(fullName$)
space = InStr(fullName$, " ")
lastName$ = Right$(fullName$, length - space)
MsgBox "Last name is " + lastName$ + "."
```

See Also

InStr(), **Left$()**, **Len()**, **LTrim$()**, **Mid$()**, **RTrim$()**

RightPara, RightPara()

Syntax

RightPara

RightPara()

Remarks

The **RightPara** statement aligns the selected paragraphs with the right indent.

The **RightPara( )** function returns the following values.

Value	Explanation
0 (zero)	If none of the selection is right-aligned
−1	If part of the selection is right-aligned
1	If all the selection is right-aligned

Example

This example formats each right-aligned paragraph with a left indent of 2 inches:

```
StartOfDocument
While ParaDown()                    'Check each paragraph one by one,
    ParaUp                          'including the first paragraph
    If RightPara() = 1 Then         'If right-aligned, then indent left
        FormatParagraph .LeftIndent = "2 in"
    End If
    ParaDown
Wend
```

See Also

CenterPara, **FormatParagraph**, **JustifyPara**, **LeftPara**

RmDir

Syntax

RmDir *Name$*

Remarks

Removes the specified folder. *Name$* can be a full or relative path. For this statement to work, the folder must contain no files or subfolders. **RmDir** cannot remove the current folder.

Examples

This Windows example deletes all files from a folder and then deletes the folder:

```
Kill "C:\WORD\FCCPROJ\*.*"
RmDir "C:\WORD\FCCPROJ"
```

The following is the same example, rewritten for the Macintosh:

```
curfolder$ = Files$(":")
ChDir "HD:WORD:FCC PROJECT"
Kill MacID$("****")
ChDir curfolder$
RmDir "HD:WORD:FCC PROJECT"
```

The following example deletes a subfolder within the current folder:

```
RmDir "FCCPROJ"
```

The following examples delete a folder at the same level as the current folder:

```
RmDir "..\FCCPROJ"      'Windows example
RmDir "::FCC PROJECT"   'Macintosh example
```

See Also   **ChDir**, **Files$()**, **Kill**, **MacID$()**, **MkDir**

Rnd()

Syntax   **Rnd**()

Remarks   Returns a random real number greater than or equal to 0 (zero) and less than 1. To generate a random integer between *a* and *b*, use the following syntax:

$$\text{Int}(\text{Rnd}() * ((b + 1) - a) + a)$$

Example   This example defines the variable num as a random integer between 50 and 100 and then displays the number in a message box:

```
a = 50
b = 100
num = Int(Rnd() * (b - a) + a)
MsgBox "The random number is" + Str$(num)
```

See Also   **Abs()**, **Int()**, **Sgn()**

RTrim$()

Syntax   **RTrim$**(*Source$*)

Remarks   Returns *Source$* minus any trailing spaces (spaces to the right of the last character). **RTrim$()** is especially useful for cleaning up user-defined variables before passing them to other parts of a macro.

Example   This example prompts the user for his or her last name and then removes extra spaces the user may have typed at the end of the name:

```
lastName$ = InputBox$("Please enter your last name.")
lastName$ = RTrim$(lastName$)
```

See Also   **InStr()**, **Left$()**, **LTrim$()**, **Mid$()**, **Right$()**

RunPrintManager

Syntax   **RunPrintManager**

Remarks   In Windows, starts Print Manager if it is not running or switches to Print Manager if it is already running. On the Macintosh, **RunPrintManager** is not available and generates an error.

See Also   **AppActivate**, **AppIsRunning()**, **ControlRun**

SaveTemplate

Syntax   SaveTemplate

Remarks   Saves changes to the active template unless the active template is the Normal template. If your macro includes changes to items such as AutoText entries or keyboard, toolbar, and menu assignments for a template other than Normal, it's a good idea to include a **SaveTemplate** instruction to preserve the changes. To save changes to all documents and templates, including the Normal template, use **FileSaveAll**.

SaveTemplate does not request confirmation before saving changes. You may want to use **MsgBox()** to confirm that changes should be saved before running **SaveTemplate**.

See Also   **FileSave**, **FileSaveAll**

ScreenRefresh

Syntax   ScreenRefresh

Remarks   Updates the display on your monitor to show the current screen display. You can use **ScreenRefresh** in a macro after a **ScreenUpdating** instruction has turned off screen updating. **ScreenRefresh** turns on screen updating for just one instruction and then immediately turns it off. Subsequent instructions do not update the screen until screen updating is turned on again with another **ScreenUpdating** instruction. You can use **ScreenRefresh** and **ScreenUpdating** to create a series of screen "snapshots." During a long process, the screen can be updated from time to time to indicate the macro's progress.

Note On the Macintosh, document windows are hidden when screen updating is turned off. A **ScreenRefresh** instruction displays updated document windows for an instant, but then the document windows are hidden again. Therefore, on the Macintosh, you may want to use **ScreenUpdating** instead of **ScreenRefresh** to turn screen updating on and off.

For an example, see **ScreenUpdating**.

See Also   **ScreenUpdating**

ScreenUpdating, ScreenUpdating()

Syntax

ScreenUpdating [*On*]

ScreenUpdating()

Remarks

The **ScreenUpdating** statement controls most display changes on the monitor while a macro is running. When screen updating is turned off, toolbars remain visible and Word still allows the macro to display or retrieve information using status bar prompts, input boxes, dialog boxes, or message boxes. You can increase the speed of some macros by preventing screen updates. Screen updating is restored when the macro finishes or when it stops after an error.

Argument	Explanation
On	Specifies whether to show screen updates:
	0 (zero) The screen does not update while the macro is running.
	1 The screen updates normally while the macro is running.
	Omitted Toggles screen updating.

The **ScreenUpdating**() function returns the following values.

Value	Explanation
0 (zero)	Screen updating is turned off.
1	Screen updating is turned on.

Example

This example arranges document windows in three different ways. A **ScreenUpdating** statement is used to turn off screen updating while the windows are being arranged. When the windows are arranged, a **ScreenRefresh** statement displays them. Note that the instructions TileDocWindowsVertically and CascadeDocWindows call subroutines (not shown here) that tile and cascade document windows.

```
ScreenUpdating 0
TileDocWindowsVertically
ScreenRefresh
MsgBox "Windows are tiled vertically."
CascadeDocWindows
ScreenRefresh
MsgBox "Windows are cascaded."
WindowArrangeAll
ScreenUpdating 1
MsgBox "Windows are tiled horizontally."
```

See Also

ScreenRefresh

Second()

Syntax   **Second**(*SerialNumber*)

Remarks   Returns an integer between 0 (zero) and 59, inclusive, corresponding to the
seconds component of *SerialNumber*, a decimal representation of the date, time,
or both. For information about serial numbers, see **DateSerial**().

Example   This example produces a beep five seconds after the macro is started. Note that
Second(Now()) returns the seconds component of the current time according to
your computer's built-in clock.

```
n = Second(Now())
beepTime = n + 5
If beepTime > 59 Then beepTime = beepTime - 60
While Second(Now()) <> beepTime
Wend
Beep
```

See Also   **DateSerial**(), **Day**(), **Hour**(), **Minute**(), **Month**(), **Now**(), **Today**(),
Weekday(), **Year**()

Seek, Seek()

Syntax   **Seek** [#]*FileNumber*, *Count*

Seek([#]*FileNumber*)

Remarks   The **Seek** statement controls where data is retrieved from a sequential file open
for input, or where data is inserted into a file open for output or appending. For
more information about sequential files, see Chapter 9, "More WordBasic
Techniques," in Part 1, "Learning WordBasic."

Argument	Explanation
FileNumber	The number specified in the **Open** instruction that opened the file for input, output, or appending.
Count	The character position where data retrieval or insertion occurs. Note that line breaks and other delimiters, such as commas, are counted as characters.

The **Seek**() function returns the current character position in the sequential file.
You can use the **Seek**() function to store the current character position before you
close a sequential file, and the **Seek** statement to return to that position when you
reopen the file.

Example

This example finds the first line beginning with the letter "P" in DATA.TXT and then displays a message box showing the entry and its character position in the file:

```
Open "DATA.TXT" For Input As #1
Input #1, name$
While Left$(name$, 1) <> "P"
    If Eof(1) Then
        MsgBox "No P names in the file."
        Goto finish
    End If
    n = Seek(#1)
    Input #1, name$
Wend
MsgBox "First P name is " + name$ + " at position" + Str$(n)
finish:
Close #1
```

See Also

Close, **Eof()**, **Input**, **Input$()**, **Line Input**, **Lof()**, **Open**, **Print**, **Read**, **Write**

Select Case

Syntax

Select Case *Expression*
    Case *CaseExpression*
        Series of instruction(s)
    [**Case Else**
        Series of instruction(s)]
End Select

Remarks

Runs one of several series of instructions according to the value of *Expression*. *Expression* is compared with each *CaseExpression* in turn. When a match is found, the instructions following that **Case** *CaseExpression* are run, and then control passes to the instruction following **End Select**. If there is no match, the instructions following **Case Else** are run. If there is no match and there is no **Case Else** instruction, an error occurs.

The **Select Case** control structure is an important part of most dialog functions. For more information about dialog functions, see Chapter 5, "Working with Custom Dialog Boxes," in Part 1, "Learning WordBasic."

Keep the following points in mind when using **Select Case**:

- Use the **Is** keyword to compare *CaseExpression* with *Expression* using a relational operator. For example, the instruction `Case Is > 8` tests for any value greater than 8. Do not use the **Is** keyword without a relational operator or an error will occur; for example, `Case Is 8` generates an error.

- Use the **To** keyword to test for a value that falls within a specified range. For example, the instruction `Case 4 To 8` tests for any value greater than or equal to 4 and less than or equal to 8.

- If you include a **Goto** instruction to go to a label outside the **Select Case** control structure, an error will occur.

Examples

This example goes to each paragraph in the document and inserts either a bullet or a hyphen, depending on whether the paragraph's style is "ListItem1" or "ListItem2." If a paragraph that is not formatted with either of these styles is found, the instruction following **Case Else** displays a message box.

```
StartOfDocument
While CmpBookmarks("\Sel", "\EndOfDoc") <> 0
    Select Case StyleName$()
        Case "ListItem1"
            ToolsBulletsNumbers .Type = 0
        Case "ListItem2"
            Insert "-" + Chr$(9)
        Case Else
            MsgBox "Not a list style"
    End Select
    ParaDown
Wend
```

The following example illustrates how **Select Case** may be used to evaluate numeric expressions. The **Select Case** instruction generates a random number between –5 and 5, and the subsequent **Case** instructions run depending on the value of that numeric expression.

```
Select Case Int(Rnd() * 10) - 5
    Case 1,3
        Print "One or three"
    Case Is > 3
        Print "Greater than three"
    Case -5 To 0
        Print "Between -5 and 0 (inclusive)"
    Case Else
        Print "Must be 2"
End Select
```

See Also

For…Next, Goto, If…Then…Else, While…Wend

SelectCurAlignment

Syntax   **SelectCurAlignment**

Remarks   Extends the selection forward until text with a different paragraph alignment is encountered. There are four types of paragraph alignment: left, centered, right, and justified.

Example   This example positions the insertion point at the beginning of the first subsequent paragraph that does not have the same alignment as the current paragraph. If the alignment is the same to the end of the document, Word displays a message box.

```
SelectCurAlignment
CharRight
If CmpBookmarks("\Sel", "\EndOfDoc") = 0 Then
    MsgBox "No variation in alignment found."
End If
```

See Also   **CenterPara**, **FormatParagraph**, **JustifyPara**, **LeftPara**, **RightPara**, **SelectCurIndent**, **SelectCurSpacing**, **SelectCurTabs**

SelectCurColor

Syntax   **SelectCurColor**

Remarks   Extends the selection forward until text with a different color is encountered.

Example   This example extends the selection from the beginning of the document to the first character formatted with a different color and then displays the number of characters in the selection:

```
StartOfDocument
SelectCurColor
n = Len(Selection$())
MsgBox "Contiguous characters with the same color:" + Str$(n)
```

See Also   **CharColor**, **FormatFont**, **SelectCurFont**

SelectCurFont

Syntax   **SelectCurFont**

Remarks   Extends the selection forward until text in a different font or font size is encountered.

Example   This example extends the selection to the first character in a different font or font size and then increases the font size to the next available setting:

```
SelectCurFont
GrowFont
```

See Also   **Font, FontSize, FormatFont, SelectCurColor**

SelectCurIndent

Syntax   **SelectCurIndent**

Remarks   Extends the selection forward from the insertion point until text with different left or right paragraph indents is encountered.

Example   This example determines whether all the paragraphs in the document are formatted with the same left and right indents and then displays a message box indicating the result:

```
StartOfDocument
SelectCurIndent
LineDown
If LineDown() = 0 Then
    MsgBox "All paragraphs share the same left and right indents."
Else
    MsgBox "Not all paragraphs share the same left and right indents."
End If
```

See Also   **FormatParagraph, Indent, SelectCurAlignment, SelectCurSpacing, SelectCurTabs, UnIndent**

SelectCurSentence

Syntax   **SelectCurSentence**

Remarks   Selects the entire sentence containing the insertion point or selection, including the trailing space. If the selection is larger than a sentence when **SelectCurSentence** is run, an error occurs.

Example   This example defines the variable a$ as the text in the current sentence. To avoid an error if there is a selection that extends over multiple sentences, the first instruction cancels the selection if there is one.

```
If SelType() = 2 Then SelType 1     'Cancel selection, if any
SelectCurSentence
a$ = Selection$()
```

See Also   **SelectCurWord, SentLeft, SentRight**

SelectCurSpacing

Syntax   **SelectCurSpacing**

Remarks   Extends the selection from the insertion point forward until a paragraph with different line spacing is encountered.

Example   This example demonstrates a quick way to jump to the beginning of the next paragraph whose line spacing is different from that of the current paragraph. If the spacing is the same to the end of the document, Word displays a message box.

```
SelectCurSpacing
CharRight
If CmpBookmarks("\Sel", "\EndOfDoc") = 0 Then
    MsgBox "No variation in spacing found."
End If
```

See Also   **FormatParagraph, SelectCurAlignment, SelectCurIndent, SelectCurTabs, SpacePara1, SpacePara15, SpacePara2**

SelectCurTabs

Syntax   **SelectCurTabs**

Remarks   Extends the selection forward from the insertion point until a paragraph with different tab stops is encountered.

Example   This example determines the position of the first tab stop in the current paragraph, and then sets the same tab stop for the next series of paragraphs that have tab settings different from those in the original paragraph. Because **NextTab()** returns a position in points, points are also used in the **FormatTabs** instruction.

```
n = NextTab(0)
SelectCurTabs
CharRight
SelectCurTabs
FormatTabs .Position = Str$(n) + "pt"
```

See Also   **FormatTabs, SelectCurAlignment, SelectCurIndent, SelectCurSpacing**

SelectCurWord

Syntax   **SelectCurWord**

Remarks   Selects the entire word containing the insertion point or selection. Whereas double-clicking a word selects both the word and the trailing space (if any), **SelectCurWord** does not select the trailing space. If the selection is larger than a word when **SelectCurWord** is run, an error occurs.

Example   This example defines the variable a$ as the characters in the word containing the
insertion point. If there is a selection, the first instruction cancels it, so in effect,
a$ is defined as the first word in the selection.

```
If SelType() = 2 Then SelType 1      'Cancel selection, if any
SelectCurWord
a$ = Selection$()
```

See Also   **SelectCurSentence, WordLeft, WordRight**

SelectDrawingObjects

Syntax   **SelectDrawingObjects**

Remarks   Toggles the mouse pointer shape between the standard mouse pointer and the
pointer for selecting drawing objects. You drag a dotted rectangle to enclose the
drawing objects you want to select.

See Also   **DrawExtendSelect, DrawSelect**

Selection$()

Syntax   **Selection$()**

Remarks   Returns the plain, unformatted text of the selection. **Selection$()** can return as
many as 65,280 characters or the maximum that available memory can hold. If the
selection is too large, an error occurs and no text is returned. If no text is selected,
Selection$() returns the character following the insertion point.

Example   This example selects the first heading in the document and then uses the
Selection$() function to define the variable heading$ with the selected text:

```
StartOfDocument
EditFindClearFormatting
EditFindStyle .Style = "heading 1"
EditFind .Find = "", .WholeWord = 0, .MatchCase = 0, .Direction = 0, \
    .Format = 1, .Wrap = 0
If EditFindFound() <> 0 Then
    heading$ = Selection$()
End If
```

See Also   **ExtendSelection, SelInfo(), SelType, ShrinkSelection**

SelectionFileName$()

Syntax   **SelectionFileName$()**

Remarks   Returns the full path and filename of the active document if it has been saved. If
the document has not been saved, or if the active window is a macro-editing
window, **SelectionFileName$()** returns the current path followed by a backslash
(\) (Windows) or colon (:) (Macintosh).

Example   This example checks to see if the active window is a macro-editing window. If
not, the example checks the last character in the text returned by
SelectionFileName$(). If the last character is a backslash (\) or colon (:),
indicating the document has never been saved, a message is displayed.

```
a$ = SelectionFileName$()
If SelInfo(27) = -1 Then
    MsgBox "A macro-editing window is active."
    Goto bye
End If
end$ = Right$(a$, 1)
If end$ = "\" Or end$ = ":" Then
    MsgBox "The active document has never been saved."
End If
bye:
```

See Also   **FileName$()**, **FileNameInfo$()**, **GetDirectory$()**

SelInfo()

Syntax   **SelInfo(***Type***)**

Remarks   Returns one of 37 types of information about the selection, where *Type* is one of
the values described in the following tables. In the explanations, the active end of
the selection refers to the end that moves when you press SHIFT+an arrow key.

Type	Explanation
1	Number of the page containing the active end of the selection. If you set a starting page number or make other manual adjustments, returns the adjusted page number (unlike SelInfo(3)).
	If the selection is in a header or footer pane in normal view, returns −1. If the selection is in a footnote or annotation pane, returns the page number of the first footnote or annotation in the selection.
2	Number of the section containing the active end of the selection.
3	Number of the page containing the active end of the selection, counting from the beginning of the document. Any manual adjustments to page numbering are disregarded (unlike SelInfo(1)).
4	Number of pages in the document.

Type 5 is valid only in page layout view. Type 6 is valid in page layout view or in normal view if you select the Background Repagination check box on the General tab and clear the Draft Font check box on the View tab in the Options dialog box (Tools menu).

Type	**Explanation**
5	Horizontal position of the selection; distance between the left edge of the selection and the left edge of the page, in twips (20 twips = 1 point, 72 points = 1 inch). Returns –1 if the selection is not visible.
6	Vertical position of the selection; distance between the top edge of the selection and the top edge of the page, in twips (20 twips = 1 point, 72 points = 1 inch). Returns –1 if the selection is not visible in the document window.

Types 7 and 8 are most useful in page layout view, where you can display text boundaries by selecting the Text Boundaries check box on the View tab in the Options dialog box (Tools menu). Text boundaries include table cells, frames, the edges of the page, text columns, and so on. For a complete list of text boundaries, see **NextObject**.

Type	**Explanation**
7	Horizontal position of the selection, relative to the left edge of the nearest text boundary enclosing it, in twips (20 twips = 1 point, 72 points = 1 inch). Returns –1 if selection is not visible.
8	Vertical position of the selection, relative to the upper edge of the nearest text boundary enclosing it, in twips (20 twips = 1 point, 72 points = 1 inch). Especially useful for determining the position of the insertion point within a frame or table cell. For a complete list of text boundaries, see **NextObject**. Returns –1 if the selection is not visible.
9	Character position of the first character in the selection or, if no text is selected, the character to the right of the insertion point (same as the character column number displayed in the status bar after "Col").
10	Line number of the first character in the selection; if Background Repagination is cleared or if Draft Font is selected, returns –1.
11	Returns –1 if the selection is an entire frame.
12	Returns –1 if the selection is within a table.

Types 13 through 18 apply only if the selection is within a table; if the selection is not within a table, the function returns –1.

Type	**Explanation**
13	The row number containing the beginning of the selection.
14	The row number containing the end of the selection.
15	The number of rows in the table.

Type	**Explanation**
16	The table column number containing the beginning of the selection.
17	The table column number containing the end of the selection.
18	The greatest number of columns within any row in the selection.

Types 19 through 37 return miscellaneous information.

Type	**Explanation**
19	The current percentage of magnification as set by **ViewZoom**.
20	The current selection mode: returns 0 (zero) for normal selection, 1 for extended selection, and 2 for column selection. Corresponds to the box in the status bar that reads either "EXT" or "COL."
21	Returns –1 if Caps Lock is in effect.
22	Returns –1 if Num Lock is in effect.
23	Returns –1 if Word is in overtype mode.
24	Returns –1 if revision marking is in effect.
25	Returns –1 if the selection is in the footnote or endnote pane, or in a footnote or endnote in page layout view. See also values 35 and 36.
26	Returns –1 if the selection is in an annotation pane.
27	Returns –1 if the selection is in a macro-editing window.
28	Returns –1 if the selection is in the header or footer pane or in a header or footer in page layout view.
29	The number of the bookmark enclosing the start of the selection; 0 (zero) if none or invalid. The number corresponds to the position of the bookmark in the document—1 for the first bookmark, 2 for the second, and so on.
30	The number of the last bookmark that starts before or at the same place as the selection; returns 0 (zero) if none or invalid.
31	Returns –1 if the insertion point is at the end-of-row mark in a table.
32	Returns one of the following values, depending on where the selection is in relation to a footnote, endnote, or annotation reference:

    –1   If the selection includes but is not limited to a footnote, endnote, or annotation reference

    0 (zero)   If the selection is not in a footnote, endnote, or annotation reference

    1   If the selection is in a footnote reference

    2   If the selection is in an endnote reference

    3   If the selection is in an annotation reference

Type	Explanation
33	The kind of header or footer containing the selection:
	−1 None (the selection is not in a header or footer)
	0 (zero) Even-page header
	1 Odd-page header (or the only header if there are not odd and even headers)
	2 Even-page footers
	3 Odd-page footer (or the footer if there are not odd and even footers)
	4 First-page header
	5 First-page footer
34	Returns −1 if the active document is a master document (that is, if it contains at least one subdocument)
35	Returns −1 if the selection is in the footnote pane or in a footnote in page layout view.
36	Same as 35, but for endnotes.
37	Returns one of the following values, depending on whether the current selection is in a WordMail message:
	0 (zero) If the selection is not in a WordMail message
	1 If the selection is in a WordMail send note
	2 If the selection is in a WordMail read note

Examples

This example determines whether the current selection extends over a page break, either manual or automatic. Note that SelInfo(3) is used twice: once to return the page number of the end of the selection, and again to return the page number of the beginning of the selection. The macro is then able to compare these values to determine how many page breaks are in the selection.

```
ToolsRepaginate
EditBookmark .Name = "Tmp"
endPage = SelInfo(3)
SelType 1
startPage = SelInfo(3)
EditGoTo .Destination = "Tmp"
numBreaks = endPage - startPage
If numBreaks = 1 Then
    MsgBox "Selection extends over one page break."
ElseIf numBreaks > 1 Then
    MsgBox "Selection extends over" + Str$(numBreaks) + \
        " page breaks."
End If
EditBookmark .Name = "Tmp", .Delete
```

The following example increases the view magnification by 10 percent:

```
n = SelInfo(19)
If n < 190 Then
    ViewZoom .ZoomPercent = n + 10
ElseIf n = 200 Then
    MsgBox "Already zoomed to maximum."
Else
    ViewZoom .ZoomPercent = 200
End If
```

See Also   Selection$(), SelType

SelType, SelType()

Syntax   **SelType** *Type*

SelType( )

Remarks   The **SelType** statement specifies how the insertion point or selected text is indicated in your document. For example, you can specify that selected text appear with a dotted underline instead of in reverse video, which may be preferable on some video displays.

SelType is more commonly used to position the insertion point at the beginning of the current selection. For this result, **SelType** has advantages over **CharLeft** because if there is no current selection, the insertion point does not move left.

Argument	Explanation
Type	The type of highlight:
	1 Solid insertion point (default)
	2 Solid selection (default)
	4 Dotted selection or insertion point (whichever is current)
	Note that the **SelType**() function never returns this value because 5 and 6 provide more specific information.
	5 Dotted insertion point (visible in **CopyText** and **MoveText** modes)
	6 Dotted selection (visible in **CopyText** and **MoveText** modes)

The **SelType**() function returns a number corresponding to the type of highlight.

Example   This example selects the next occurrence of the word "background" and then cancels the selection, leaving the insertion point at the beginning of the word:

```
EditFind .Find = "background", .Direction = 0
If EditFindFound( ) Then SelType 1
```

See Also   Selection$(), SelInfo()

SendKeys

Syntax

SendKeys *Keys$*, *Wait*

Remarks

Sends the keystrokes specified by *Keys$* to the active application, just as if they were typed at the keyboard. To send keys to a Word dialog box, **SendKeys** must precede instructions that display the dialog box so that those keystrokes are in memory when the macro pauses.

On the Macintosh, a **SendKeys** instruction can send no more than 10 keystrokes, and can send them only to Word; **SendKeys** cannot be used with another application.

Note Use **SendKeys** to operate other applications only when there is no alternative, and then use it with caution. In general, dynamic data exchange (DDE) is a better way for Word to interact with other applications because DDE provides a channel for two-way communication between applications and provides a path for detecting and dealing with errors in the other application. You should test even the simplest use of **SendKeys** under a variety of conditions to avoid unpredictable results, data loss, or both.

When stepping through a macro (using the Step or Step Subs button on the Macro toolbar) that contains a **SendKeys** instruction, note that the macro may not perform as expected unless the **SendKeys** instruction and the instruction that activates the target application or dialog box are on the same line, separated by a colon.

Argument	Explanation
Keys$	A key or key sequence, such as "a" for the letter *a,* or "{enter}{tab}" for the ENTER key followed by the TAB key.
Wait	If Word is not the active application and *Wait* is –1, Word waits for all keys to be processed before proceeding.
	For example, in Windows, if you run the following instructions to send *Keys$* to Microsoft Excel, a beep occurs in Word only after text is inserted into all 10 cells. If *Wait* were 0 (zero), the beep would occur as text was inserted into the first cell.

```
AppActivate "Microsoft Excel"
For i = 1 To 10
    SendKeys "Testing{down}", -1
Next i
Beep
```

The following table lists non-character keys available to send in Windows and on the Macintosh.

Key	Code
ENTER	{enter} or ~
ESC	{escape} or {esc}
SPACE	{ }
TAB	{tab}

The following table lists non-character keys available to send only in Windows.

Key	Code
BACKSPACE	{backspace} or {bs} or {bksp}
BREAK	{break}
CAPS LOCK	{capslock}
CLEAR	{clear}
DEL	{delete} or {del}
DOWN ARROW	{down}
END	{end}
HELP	{help}
HOME	{home}
INS	{insert}
LEFT ARROW	{left}
NUM LOCK	{numlock}
PAGE DOWN	{pgdn}
PAGE UP	{pgup}
RIGHT ARROW	{right}
UP ARROW	{up}
F1, F2, F3,...F16	{F1}, {F2}, {F3},...{F16}

In addition to the key codes listed above, you can specify any key code listed in **ToolsCustomizeKeyboard**. To do so, use the syntax {*Code*}. For example, the instruction SendKeys "{13}" sends the key code for ENTER and SendKeys "{32}" sends the key code for SPACE.

To repeat a character, use the syntax {*Character Number*}. For example, SendKeys "{s 10}" repeats the letter *s* 10 times. Remember to put a space between the key and the number. To repeat a key whose code already includes braces, add a space and a number within the braces, for example: SendKeys "{enter 10}". (You cannot repeat **ToolsCustomizeKeyboard** key codes in this way.)

In Windows, to send a key combination that includes SHIFT, ALT, or CTRL, use the following symbols. (On the Macintosh, you can send a SHIFT key combination using the plus sign (+), but you cannot send key combinations including OPTION or COMMAND.)

To combine with	Precede the key code by
SHIFT	+ (plus sign)
ALT (Windows) or COMMAND (Macintosh)	% (percent sign)
CTRL (Windows) or CONTROL (Macintosh)	^ (caret)
OPTION (Macintosh)	# (pound sign)

For example, in Windows, "%{enter}" sends the code for ALT+ENTER. You can group keys with parentheses and precede the group with the key code for a SHIFT, ALT, or CTRL key. For example, the code "+(wordbasic)" specifies WORDBASIC (but you can also simply use the uppercase letters WORDBASIC, without using the plus sign). To send a plus sign (+), a percent sign (%), a caret (^), or a pound sign (#) as literal text, enclose the character in braces. For example, to send a plus sign, use the instruction SendKeys "{+}". You can also use braces to send parentheses.

Note In Windows, when sending key combinations that include the ALT key, make it a rule to send lowercase characters. For example, to open the File menu (ALT, F), use "%f." Using "%F" is equivalent to pressing ALT+SHIFT+F.

Examples

One use of **SendKeys** is to insert text or select items in a Word dialog box (for example, to provide default text or initially select a specific item). This Windows example displays the Open dialog box (File menu) and inserts the default text "TESTFILE" into the File Name box. You can produce the same effect with the single instruction SendKeys "%foTESTFILE".

```
SendKeys "TESTFILE"
Dim dlg As FileOpen
x = Dialog(dlg)
```

The following Windows example starts Microsoft Excel with the worksheet MARCH.XLS and then performs the equivalent to pressing the PAGE DOWN key 20 times:

```
SendKeys "{pgdn 20}"
Shell "C:\EXCEL\MARCH.XLS", 1
```

See Also   **AppActivate, DDEExecute, DDEInitiate(), DDEPoke**

SentLeft, SentLeft()

Syntax

SentLeft [*Count,*] [*Select*]

SentLeft([*Count,*] [*Select*])

Remarks

The **SentLeft** statement moves the insertion point or the active end of the selection (the end that moves when you press SHIFT+an arrow key) to the left by the specified number of sentences.

Argument	Explanation
Count	The number of sentences to move; if less than one or omitted, 1 is assumed.
Select	Specifies whether to select text:
	0 (zero) or omitted Text is not selected. If there is already a selection, **SentLeft** moves the insertion point *Count*–1 sentences to the left of the selection.
	Nonzero Text is selected. If there is already a selection, **SentLeft** moves the active end of the selection toward the beginning of the document.
	In a typical selection made from left to right, where the active end of the selection is closer to the end of the document, **SentLeft** shrinks the selection. In a selection made from right to left, it extends the selection.

Note that Word counts empty table cells as "sentences," and that, regardless of length or punctuation, Word considers every paragraph to contain at least one sentence.

The **SentLeft()** function behaves the same as the statement and also returns the following values.

Value	Explanation
0 (zero)	If the insertion point or the active end of the selection cannot be moved to the left.
–1	If the insertion point or the active end of the selection is moved to the left by any number of sentences, even if less than *Count*. For example, SentLeft(10) returns –1 even if the insertion point is only three sentences from the start of the document.

Example

This example deletes all sentences in the document containing the phrase "see page." In other words, the example deletes all cross-references to other pages. Note that you could substitute SelectCurSentence for the pair of instructions SentLeft and SentRight 1, 1.

```
StartOfDocument
EditFind .Find = "see page", .WholeWord = 1, .Direction = 0, .Format = 0
While EditFindFound()
    SentLeft
    SentRight 1, 1
    EditClear
    EditFind .Find = "see page", .WholeWord = 1, .Direction = 0, \
        .Format = 0
Wend
```

See Also   **CharLeft**, **ParaUp**, **SelectCurSentence**, **SentRight**, **StartOfLine**, **WordLeft**

SentRight, SentRight()

Syntax   **SentRight** [*Count,*] [*Select*]

              SentRight([*Count,*] [*Select*])

Remarks   The **SentRight** statement moves the insertion point or the active end of the
              selection (the end that moves when you press SHIFT+an arrow key) to the right by
              the specified number of sentences.

Argument	Explanation
Count	The number of sentences to move; if less than one or omitted, 1 is assumed.
Select	Specifies whether to select text: 0 (zero) or omitted Text is not selected. If there is already a selection, **SentRight** moves the insertion point *Count*–1 sentences to the right of the selection. Nonzero Text is selected. If there is already a selection, **SentRight** moves the active end of the selection toward the end of the document. In a typical selection made from left to right, where the active end of the selection is closer to the end of the document, **SentRight** extends the selection. In a selection made from right to left, it shrinks the selection.

Note that Word counts empty table cells as "sentences," and that, regardless of
length or punctuation, Word considers every paragraph to contain at least one
sentence.

The **SentRight()** function behaves the same as the statement and also returns the following values.

Value	Explanation
0 (zero)	If the insertion point or the active end of the selection cannot be moved to the right.
−1	If the insertion point or the active end of the selection is moved to the right by any number of sentences, even if less than *Count*. For example, `SentRight(10)` returns −1 even if the insertion point is only three sentences from the end of the document.

Example

This example counts the number of sentences in the document (excluding paragraph marks) and displays the result in a message box:

```
StartOfDocument
count = 0
While SentRight(1, 1) <> 0
    If Right$(Selection$(), 1) <> Chr$(13) Then count = count + 1
Wend
MsgBox "Number of sentences in document:" + Str$(count)
```

See Also

CharRight, EndOfLine, ParaDown, SelectCurSentence, SentLeft, WordRight

SetAttr

Syntax

SetAttr *Filename$*, *Attribute*

Remarks

Sets file attributes for *Filename$*. In Windows, the attributes correspond to those you can set using the Properties command (File menu) in File Manager Windows 3.*x* and Windows NT) or the Windows Explorer (Windows 95). For definitions of the attributes, display the Properties dialog box and choose the Help button. On the Macintosh, only the Read Only and Hidden attributes are available (Read Only corresponds to the Locked check box in the Get Info dialog box (File menu) in the Finder). The file whose attributes you want to set must be closed; an error occurs if you try to set an attribute for an open document.

Argument	Explanation
Filename$	The path and filename of the file whose attribute you want to set
Attribute	Specifies the attribute:

0 (zero)   Clears all attributes except System

1   Read Only

2   Hidden

4   System (not available on the Macintosh)

32 Archive (not available on the Macintosh)

Note Attribute values are additive. For example, to set both the Read Only and Archive attributes, *Attribute* would be 33 (the sum of 1 and 32). For a way to set the Read Only attribute independently, see the example for this entry. You cannot set the System attribute in combination with the Archive attribute.

Example

This example makes the file C:\TEST\TEST.DOC read-only without affecting the file's other attributes. First, **GetAttr**() returns the current *Attribute* value. Then the **If** conditional uses the MOD operator to determine whether the *Attribute* value is odd, which means the file's Read Only attribute is already selected. In that case, Word displays a message box. If *Attribute* is an even value or 0 (zero), the **SetAttr** instruction sets the Read Only attribute. On the Macintosh, substitute a path and filename such as HD:TEST:TEST DOCUMENT.

```
attribs = GetAttr("C:\TEST\TEST.DOC")
Print attribs
If attribs MOD 2 Then
        MsgBox "File is already read-only."
Else
        SetAttr "C:\TEST\TEST.DOC", 1
End If
```

See Also   **GetAttr**()

SetAutoText

Syntax   **SetAutoText** *Name$*, *Text$* [, *Context*]

Remarks   Defines a text-only AutoText entry. Unlike an **EditAutoText** instruction that uses .Add, **SetAutoText** does not require a selection.

Argument	Explanation
Name$	The name of the new entry
Text$	The text to be associated with the entry
Context	Specifies the availability of the entry:
	0 (zero) or omitted Normal template (available to all documents)
	1 Active template (available only to documents based on the active template)
	Note that if *Context* is 1 and the active template is the Normal template, **SetAutoText** generates an error.

Example

This example defines the AutoText entry "Disclaim" in the active template; "Disclaim" contains the text assigned to text$:

```
text$ = "No warranty is either expressed or implied."
SetAutoText "Disclaim", text$, 1
```

See Also

AutoText, **AutoTextName$()**, **CountAutoTextEntries()**, **EditAutoText**, **GetAutoText$()**, **InsertAutoText**

SetDocumentDirty

Syntax

SetDocumentDirty [*Dirty*]

Remarks

Controls whether Word recognizes a document as "dirty"—that is, changed since the last time the document was saved. When a dirty document is closed, Word displays a prompt asking if changes should be saved.

If you change a document and then set *Dirty* to 0 (zero), Word recognizes the document as unchanged, or "clean." When you close the document, Word neither displays a prompt nor saves changes.

Argument	Explanation
Dirty	Specifies whether to make the active document dirty:
	0 (zero) The document is treated as clean.
	1 or omitted The document is recognized as dirty.

Example

This example assumes that a main document for a mail merge is active. The instructions print form letters to a document, which is then made clean. When the document is closed, Word will not display a prompt or save changes.

```
MailMergeToDoc
SetDocumentDirty 0
```

See Also

IsDocumentDirty(), **IsTemplateDirty()**, **SetTemplateDirty**

SetDocumentProperty

Syntax   **SetDocumentProperty** *Name$,* *Type,* *Value[$],* *CustomOrBuiltIn*

Remarks   Defines a document property for the active document. If *Name$* is a built-in property that doesn't match the type specified by *Type,* or if it is a read-only property, an error occurs. Use the **DocumentPropertyExists**() function to determine whether a property called *Name$* already exists.

For a list of the built-in properties available in Word, see **DocumentPropertyName$**(). In Word version 6.0, **SetDocumentProperty** is unavailable and generates an error.

Argument	Explanation
Name$	The name of the property. *Name$* can be a built-in property or a custom property.
Type	The type of the property to be defined:
	0 (zero) String
	1 Number
	2 Date
	3 Yes or No
	If *Name$* is a built-in property and doesn't match the type specified by *Type,* an error occurs.
Value[$]	The property value. *Value[$]* must match the type specified by *Type.*
	If *Value[$]* doesn't match the type specified by *Type,* an error occurs.
CustomOrBuiltIn	Specifies whether *Name$* is a custom property or a built-in property:
	0 (zero) or omitted *Name$* is a custom property unless it appears in the list of built-in properties. If *Name$* is a built-in property, **SetDocumentProperty** will update its value.
	1 *Name$* is a built-in property. If it is not one of the built-in properties, an error occurs.
	2 *Name$* is a custom property, regardless of whether a built-in property with the same name already exists.

Example

This example asks the user to insert the name of a customer and then assigns the name to the variable customerName$. The **SetDocumentProperty** instruction defines the custom property "Customer" with the value of customerName$. Note that this is done only if the custom property "Customer" is not already defined.

```
customerName$ = InputBox$("Please type the name of the customer",
"Customer Name")
If DocumentPropertyExists("Customer") = 0 Then
    SetDocumentProperty("Customer", 0, customerName$, 2)
End If
```

See Also

DocumentPropertyExists(), GetDocumentProperty(), IsCustomDocumentProperty(), IsDocumentPropertyReadOnly(), SetDocumentPropertyLink

SetDocumentPropertyLink

Syntax

SetDocumentPropertyLink *Name$, Source$*

Remarks

Defines a custom property for the active document and links it to an existing bookmark named *Source$*. If *Source$* doesn't exist, an error occurs. Use the **DocumentPropertyExists()** function to verify that the *Name$* property exists.

For a list of the built-in properties available in Word, see **DocumentPropertyName$()**. In Word version 6.0, **SetDocumentPropertyLink** is unavailable and generates an error.

Argument	Explanation
Name$	The name of the property. *Name$* can be a built-in property or a custom property.
Source$	The name of the bookmark.

Example

This example inserts a DATE field at the insertion point, defines the DateOfLetter bookmark, and defines a custom property for the active document. This property is linked to the DateOfLetter bookmark.

```
InsertField .Field = "DATE"
EditGoto .Destination = "d- 'DATE'"
UnlinkFields
EditBookmark .Name = "DateOfLetter", .Add
SetDocumentPropertyLink("Date of letter","DateOfLetter")
```

See Also

GetDocumentProperty(), SetDocumentProperty

SetDocumentVar, SetDocumentVar()

Syntax

SetDocumentVar *VariableName$*, *VariableText$*

SetDocumentVar(*VariableName$*, *VariableText$*)

Remarks

The **SetDocumentVar** statement associates the string *VariableText$* with the active document. You use the *VariableName$* argument with the function **GetDocumentVar$()** to return the associated string when the document is active. The variable is saved with the document. You can set multiple document variables for a single document. To delete a document variable, specify an empty string ("") for *VariableText$*. If the insertion point is not in a document—for example, if the macro-editing window is active—an error occurs.

The **SetDocumentVar()** function behaves the same as the statement, and also returns –1 if the variable is set successfully.

Example

This example prompts for a reminder note to store with a document before closing it. If the macro were named FileClose, it would run each time the user chose Close from the File menu (the instruction FileClose runs the built-in command).

The instruction On Error Goto CloseNow ensures that a WordBasic error doesn't appear if the user cancels the **InputBox$()** dialog box. The instructions Err = 0 and On Error Resume Next reset error handling and ensure that an error doesn't appear if the user cancels the prompt to save changes.

```
On Error Goto CloseNow
worknote$ = InputBox$("Type a note for next time:")
SetDocumentVar "reminder", worknote$
CloseNow:
Err = 0
On Error Resume Next
FileClose
```

For an example of an AutoOpen macro that displays the most recent reminder note each time the document is opened, see **GetDocumentVar$()**.

See Also

GetDocumentVar$()

SetEndOfBookmark

Syntax

SetEndOfBookmark *Bookmark1$* [, *Bookmark2$*]

Remarks

Marks the end point of *Bookmark1$* with *Bookmark2$*. If *Bookmark2$* is omitted, *Bookmark1$* is set to its own end point.

Example	This example marks the end of the current selection with the bookmark "EndPoint":

```
SetEndOfBookmark "\Sel", "EndPoint"
```

The bookmark "\Sel" is one of several predefined bookmarks that Word defines and updates automatically. For more information, see "Operators and Predefined Bookmarks" later in this part.

See Also   **CopyBookmark**, **EditBookmark**, **SetStartOfBookmark**

SetFileCreatorAndType

Syntax   **SetFileCreatorAndType** *File$*, *Creator$* [, *Type$*]

Remarks   On the Macintosh, sets the creator (application signature) and file type for the specified file.

Argument	Explanation
File$	The path and filename of the file whose creator and type you want to set.
Creator$	A four-character application signature (for example, MSWD for Word) or a string returned by the **MacID$()** function.
Type$	A four-character string specifying a file type (for example, W6BN for a Word document) or a string returned by the **MacID$()** function.

In Windows, **SetFileCreatorAndType** is not available and generates an error.

See Also   **FileCreator$()**, **FileType$()**, **MacID$()**

SetFormResult

Syntax   **SetFormResult** *BookmarkName$*, *Result*[*$*] [, *DefaultResult*]

Remarks   Sets the result of the form field marked by the bookmark *BookmarkName$* or updates any fields embedded within the specified form field. Depending on the type of form field, you specify *Result*[*$*] as a string or number, as follows:

- For a check box form field, specify 0 (zero) to clear the check box or 1 to select it.
- For a drop-down form field, specify 0 (zero) to select the first item, 1 to select the second item, and so on. You can also specify the item itself as a string.
- For a text form field, specify a string.

If you do not specify *Result[$]*, **SetFormResult** updates any fields within the specified form field.

If *DefaultResult* is 1, the result becomes the default result for the field. The default result is displayed each time the document containing the form field is protected for forms.

Examples

The following example is an AutoNew macro that runs each time a form is created. It sets the default results for the text form field "NameText," the check box form field "AgeCheck," and the drop-down form field "PreferencesList." It then protects the document for forms.

```
Sub MAIN
SetFormResult "NameText", "John Jones", 1
SetFormResult "AgeCheck", 1, 1
SetFormResult "PreferencesList", 2, 1
ToolsProtectDocument .Type = 2
End Sub
```

The following example updates a text form field identified by the bookmark "DateField." The form field contains a date field, which is updated by the SetFormResult instruction.

```
SetFormResult "DateField"
```

See Also   **GetFormResult()**

SetPrivateProfileString, SetPrivateProfileString()

Syntax   **SetPrivateProfileString** *Section$*, *KeyName$*, *Setting$*, *Filename$*

SetPrivateProfileString(*Section$*, *KeyName$*, *Setting$*, *Filename$*)

Remarks

Defines or redefines a setting in a settings file, a file that your macros can use for storing and retrieving settings. For example, you can store the name of the active document when you quit Word so that it can be reopened automatically the next time you start Word. In Windows, a settings file is a text file such as WINWORD6.INI. On the Macintosh, a settings file is a resource file such as Word Settings (6). In Windows 95 and Windows NT, you can use **SetPrivateProfileString** to assign a setting to a value in the registry.

Argument	Explanation
Section$	The name of the section in the settings file that contains the key you want to set. In Windows, this is the name that appears between brackets before the associated keys (do not include the brackets with *Section$*).
	If you are using **SetPrivateProfileString** in Windows 95 or Windows NT to assign a setting to a value in the registry, *Section$* should be the complete path to the key, including the root (for example, "HKEY_CURRENT_USER\Software\Microsoft\Word\6.0\Options".
KeyName$	The key to set. In a Windows settings file, the key name is followed by an equal sign (=) and the setting.
	If you are using **SetPrivateProfileString** in Windows 95 or Windows NT to assign a setting to a value in the registry, *KeyName$* should be the name of the value in the key specified by *Section$* (for example, "MessageBeeps").
Setting$	The new setting.
Filename$	The filename for the settings file. If a path is not specified, the Windows folder (Windows) or the Preferences folder (Macintosh) is assumed. If the file does not already exist, Word creates it.
	If you are using **S etPrivateProfileString** in Windows 95 or Windows NT to assign a setting to a value in the registry, *Filename$* must be an empty string ("").

The **SetPrivateProfileString**() function behaves the same as the statement and also returns a value indicating whether the action was successful: −1 means the key was set, 0 (zero) means the key was not set. Keys cannot be set if the settings file is read-only.

Example

This pair of auto macros automatically opens the document that was active the last time you quit Word. On the Macintosh, substitute a settings filename such as MY SETTINGS for MY.INI.

The following is the AutoExit macro. If the active window is a macro-editing window, the **If** conditional prevents Word from writing the macro name to the settings file. This prevents an error from occurring in the AutoExec macro.

```
Sub MAIN
If SelInfo(27) <> -1 Then a$ = FileName$()
check = SetPrivateProfileString("Word Info", "LastActive", a$, \
    "MY.INI")
If check = 0 Then MsgBox "Could not set INI option."
End Sub
```

The following is the AutoExec macro:

```
Sub MAIN
name$ = GetPrivateProfileString$("Word Info", "LastActive", \
    "MY.INI")
If name$ <> "" Then FileOpen .Name = name$
End Sub
```

See Also   **GetProfileString$()**, **GetPrivateProfileString$()**, **SetProfileString**,
ToolsAdvancedSettings

SetProfileString

Syntax   **SetProfileString** *Section$*, *KeyName$*, *Setting$*

Remarks   In Windows, creates a key and defines a setting for it, or redefines the setting of an existing key in WIN.INI. If *Section$* is "Microsoft Word 2.0," "Microsoft Word," "MSWord Text Converters," or "MSWord Editable Sections," **SetProfileString** redefines the setting in WINWORD6.INI. These exceptions are made for compatibility with Word for Windows version 2.*x* macros. On the Macintosh, **SetProfileString** defines settings in the Word Settings (6) file. It is generally preferable to use **SetPrivateProfileString**, which allows you to specify a settings file to modify.

Argument	Explanation
Section$	The name of the section in the settings file that contains the key you want to set. In Windows, this is the name that appears between brackets before the associated keys (do not include the brackets with *Section$*).
KeyName$	The key to set. In Windows, the key name is followed by an equal sign (=) and the setting.
Setting$	The new setting.

Note In Windows 95 and Windows NT, settings are stored in the registry. You can still use **SetProfileString** and **GetProfileString$()** to set and return settings from a text file with the name WIN.INI, but neither the system nor Word uses these settings. To access and change values in the registry from within WordBasic, you need to use **GetPrivateProfileString$()** and **SetPrivateProfileString**.

Example

This Windows example uses **GetSystemInfo$()** to determine the "sCountry" setting in the [intl] section of WIN.INI; **SetProfileString** changes the key's setting to "Sweden" if it does not already have that setting.

```
If GetSystemInfo$(29) <> "Sweden" Then
    SetProfileString "intl", "sCountry", "Sweden"
End If
```

See Also

GetPrivateProfileString$(), **GetProfileString$()**, **SetPrivateProfileString**, **ToolsAdvancedSettings**

SetSelRange

Syntax

SetSelRange *Pos1*, *Pos2*

Remarks

Selects the characters between character position *Pos1* and character position *Pos2*. The character position at the start of the document is 0 (zero), the position after the first character is 1, the position after the second character is 2, and so on. All characters, including nonprinting characters, are counted. Hidden characters are counted even if they are not displayed. Note that the document does not scroll even if the selected characters are not visible in the document window.

Example

This example selects the first 20 characters in the document:

```
SetSelRange 0, 20
```

See Also

GetSelEndPos(), **GetSelStartPos()**, **GetText$()**

SetStartOfBookmark

Syntax **SetStartOfBookmark** *Bookmark1$* [, *Bookmark2$*]

Remarks Marks the starting point of *Bookmark1$* with *Bookmark2$*. If *Bookmark2$* is omitted, *Bookmark1$* is set to its own starting point.

Example This example marks either end of the current paragraph with bookmarks:

```
SetStartOfBookmark "\Para", "BeginPara"
SetEndOfBookmark "\Para", "EndPara"
```

The bookmark "\Para" is one of several predefined bookmarks that Word defines and updates automatically. For more information, see "Operators and Predefined Bookmarks" later in this part.

See Also **CopyBookmark, EditBookmark, SetEndOfBookmark**

SetTemplateDirty

Syntax **SetTemplateDirty** [*Dirty*]

Remarks Controls whether Word recognizes a template as "dirty"—that is, changed since the last time the template was saved. When a dirty template is closed, Word displays a prompt asking if changes should be saved.

If you change a template and then set *Dirty* to 0 (zero), Word recognizes the template as unchanged, or "clean." When you close the template, Word neither displays a prompt nor saves changes.

Argument	Explanation
Dirty	Specifies whether to make the active template dirty:
	0 (zero) The template is treated as clean.
	1 or omitted The template is recognized as dirty.

Example

This example makes a temporary change in the active template's keyboard assignments (assigns the **SmallCaps** command to CTRL+SHIFT+C (Windows) or COMMAND+SHIFT+C (Macintosh)) and then makes the template clean. When the template is closed, Word does not display a prompt or save changes.

```
ToolsCustomizeKeyboard .KeyCode = 835, .Context = 1, \
    .Name = "SmallCaps", .Add
SetTemplateDirty 0
```

See Also

IsDocumentDirty(), **IsTemplateDirty()**, **SetDocumentDirty**

Sgn()

Syntax

Sgn(n**)**

Remarks

Determines whether n is positive, negative, or 0 (zero).

Value	Explanation
0 (zero)	If n is 0 (zero)
−1	If n is a negative number
1	If n is a positive number

Example

This example compares two values. If the difference is negative, a message box is displayed.

```
maySales = 1200
juneSales = 1000
difference = juneSales - maySales
If Sgn(difference) = -1 Then
    MsgBox "Sales fell by" + Str$(Abs(difference)) + " dollars!"
End If
```

See Also

Abs(), **Int()**, **Rnd()**

ShadingPattern, ShadingPattern()

Syntax

ShadingPattern *Type*

ShadingPattern()

Remarks

The **ShadingPattern** statement applies a shading format to the selected paragraphs, table cells, or frame.

Argument	Explanation
Type	The shading format to apply:

0	☐	13	▨
1	■	14	▤
2	▨	15	Ⅲ
3	▨	16	▧
4	▨	17	▨
5	▨	18	▨
6	▨	19	▨
7	▨	20	▤
8	▨	21	Ⅲ
9	▨	22	▧
10	▨	23	▨
11	▨	24	▦
12	▨	25	▨

On the Macintosh, formats 35 through 61 apply shading patterns in 2.5% increments:

35	2.5%	49	55%
36	7.5%	50	57.5%
37	12.5%	51	62.5%
38	15%	52	65%
39	17.5%	53	67.5%
40	22.5%	54	72.5%
41	27.5%	55	77.5%
42	32.5%	56	82.5%
43	35%	57	85%
44	37.5%	58	87.5%
45	42.5%	59	92.5%
46	45%	60	95%
47	47.5%	61	97.5%
48	52.5%		

The **ShadingPattern()** function returns the following values.

Value	Explanation
0 (zero)	If none of the selection is shaded (the shading pattern is Clear)
−1	If the selection contains a mixture of shading patterns
1 through 25 or 35 through 61	If all the selection is formatted with the same shading pattern

See Also   **FormatBordersAndShading**

Shadow, Shadow()

Syntax   **Shadow** [*On*]

Shadow()

Remarks   On the Macintosh, the **Shadow** statement adds or removes the shadow character format for the current selection, or controls shadow formatting for characters to be inserted at the insertion point.

Argument	Explanation
On	Specifies whether to add or remove the shadow format:
	1 Formats the selection with shadow
	0 (zero) Removes the shadow format
	Omitted Toggles the shadow format

The **Shadow()** function returns the following values.

Value	Explanation
0 (zero)	If none of the selection is formatted with shadow
−1	If part of the selection is formatted with shadow
1	If all the selection is formatted with shadow

In Windows, **Shadow** and **Shadow()** are not available and generate errors.

See Also   **FormatFont**

Shell

Syntax

Shell *Application$* [, *WindowStyle*]

Remarks

Starts another application (such as Microsoft Excel) or process (such as an MS-DOS batch file or executable file). In Windows, if the specified application is already running, **Shell** starts another instance of the same application; on the Macintosh, **Shell** activates the instance that is already running.

Note In Word version 6.0 for Windows NT and Word version 7.0, you cannot depend on a program started with **Shell** to be finished loading before the instructions following the **Shell** statement in your macro are run. Any instructions that try to communicate with an application that has not finished loading will generate errors or unexpected results. To avoid this problem, you can use a **For...Next** loop to delay the instructions until the other application is loaded. For an example, see **DDEInitiate**.

Argument	Explanation
Application$	In Windows, the path and filename required to find the application, as well as any valid switches or arguments you choose to include, just as you would type them in the Run dialog box. To display a command window, specify Environ$("COMSPEC") (Windows 3.*x*), Environ$("COMMAND") (Windows 95), or Environ$("CMD") (Windows NT) as *Application$*.
	On the Macintosh, *Application$* is the application name or the signature returned by the **MacID$()** function. It is generally preferable to use the signature instead of the application name (for example, MacID$("XCEL") instead of "Microsoft Excel") because, unlike the application name, the signature never changes.
	Application$ can be a document filename by itself, provided the file is associated with an application. (In Windows, a filename is associated with an application if its extension is registered in the [Extensions] section of the WIN.INI file (or the registry in Windows 95 and Windows NT). On the Macintosh, associations between filenames and applications are created automatically; you can use **SetFileCreatorAndType** to change an association.) **Shell** starts the associated application and opens the document.

Argument	Explanation
WindowStyle	In Windows, how the window containing the application should be displayed (some applications ignore this):
	0 (zero) Minimized window (icon)
	1 Normal window (current window size, or previous size if minimized)
	2 Minimized window (for Microsoft Excel compatibility)
	3 Maximized window
	4 Deactivated window
	On the Macintosh, *WindowStyle* 0 (zero), 1, 2, and 3 are effectively the same: The application window (which has only one size) is activated. Set *WindowStyle* to 4 to start an application but leave Word active.

Examples

This Windows example starts Notepad and loads the document TORT.TXT:

```
Shell "Notepad TORT.TXT"
```

The following Macintosh example starts Microsoft Excel but leaves Word active:

```
Shell MacID$("XCEL"), 4
```

The following Windows example creates a text-only file (DOCLIST.TXT) that lists documents with the filename extension .DOC in the C:\WINWORD folder. You might use an instruction like this to create a file you can open later for sequential input. The "/c" switch ensures that control is returned to Word after the command line following "/c" is run.

```
Shell Environ$("COMSPEC") + " /c dir /b C:\WINWORD\*.DOC > DOCLIST.TXT"
```

See Also

AppActivate, **DDEInitiate()**, **Environ$()**, **MacID$()**, **SetFileCreatorAndType**

ShowAll, ShowAll()

Syntax

ShowAll [*On*]

ShowAll()

Remarks

The **ShowAll** statement displays all nonprinting characters, such as hidden text, tab marks, space marks, and paragraph marks. **ShowAll** corresponds to the All check box on the View tab in the Options dialog box (Tools menu).

Argument	Explanation
On	Specifies whether to hide or display all nonprinting characters:
	1 Displays nonprinting characters.
	0 (zero) Hides nonprinting characters.
	Omitted Toggles the display.

If your macro depends on nonprinting characters being visible in the document, it's a good idea to include ShowAll 1 as one of the first instructions.

The **ShowAll()** function returns the following values.

Value	Explanation
0 (zero)	The All check box is selected.
−1	The All check box is cleared.

Example

This example displays all nonprinting characters and then searches for hidden text:

```
ShowAll 1
EditFindClearFormatting
EditFindFont .Hidden = 1
EditFind .Find = "", .Format = 1
```

See Also   **ToolsOptionsView**

ShowAllHeadings

Syntax   **ShowAllHeadings**

Remarks

In outline view, toggles between showing all text (headings and body text) and showing only headings. To be sure to display all text, include a **ShowHeading9** instruction to display all headings without body text before running a **ShowAllHeadings** instruction.

ShowAllHeadings is available only in outline view and master document view; an error occurs if the statement is run in another view.

Example

This example switches to outline view and displays all text:

```
ViewOutline
ShowHeading9
ShowAllHeadings
```

See Also   **OutlineCollapse**, **OutlineExpand**, **OutlineShowFirstLine**, **ShowHeading***Number*

ShowAnnotationBy

Syntax

ShowAnnotationBy *ReviewerName$*

Remarks

Displays the annotations by *ReviewerName$* when the annotation pane is open. To display all annotations, specify "All Reviewers" as *ReviewerName$*. If *ReviewerName$* does not match a reviewer in the list at the top of the annotation pane, Word displays all annotations.

Example

This example instructs Word to display annotations by Sara Levine only, and then displays the annotation pane:

```
ShowAnnotationBy "Sara Levine"
ViewAnnotations 1
```

See Also

ViewAnnotations

ShowClipboard

Syntax

ShowClipboard

Remarks

On the Macintosh, displays the Clipboard and its contents. In Windows, **ShowClipboard** is not available and generates an error; you can display the Clipboard with the **ControlRun** statement.

See Also

ControlRun

ShowHeadingNumber

Syntax

ShowHeading*Number*

Remarks

In outline view, shows all headings up to the specified heading level and hides subordinate headings and body text. *Number* is an integer from 1 to 9; you cannot use a variable in place of *Number*.

ShowHeading*Number* is available only in outline view and master document view; an error occurs if the statement is run in another view.

Example

This example takes advantage of outline view to easily reorder sections of the document. Consider an alphabetic reference whose headings, formatted as Heading 1 paragraphs, have gotten out of order; this macro can quickly alphabetize the sections. Collapsed headings and body text move with the Heading 1 paragraphs.

```
ViewOutline
ShowHeading1
EditSelectAll
TableSort .Order = 0
```

See Also   **OutlineCollapse**, **OutlineExpand**, **OutlineShowFirstLine**, **ShowAllHeadings**

ShowMe

Syntax   **ShowMe**

Remarks   Displays Help when there's more information available. The **ShowMe** statement corresponds to the Show Me button on the TipWizard® toolbar. In Word version 6.0, **ShowMe** is unavailable and generates an error.

See Also   **AutomaticChange**, **Help**

ShowNextHeaderFooter

Syntax   **ShowNextHeaderFooter**

Remarks   If the insertion point is in a header, moves to the next header within the current section (for example, from an odd header to an even header) or to the first header in the following section. If the insertion point is in a footer, **ShowNextHeaderFooter** moves to the next footer. If the insertion point is in the last header or footer in the last section of the document, or is not in a header or footer, an error occurs.

See Also   **CloseViewHeaderFooter**, **FormatHeaderFooterLink**, **GoToHeaderFooter**, **ShowPrevHeaderFooter**, **ToggleHeaderFooterLink**, **ViewFooter**, **ViewHeader**

ShowPrevHeaderFooter

Syntax   **ShowPrevHeaderFooter**

Remarks   If the insertion point is in a header, moves to the previous header within the current section (for example, from an even header to an odd header) or to the last header in the previous section. If the insertion point is in a footer, **ShowNextHeaderFooter** moves to the previous footer. If the insertion point is in the first header or footer in the first section of the document, or is not in a header or footer, an error occurs.

See Also   **CloseViewHeaderFooter**, **FormatHeaderFooterLink**, **GoToHeaderFooter**, **ShowNextHeaderFooter**, **ToggleHeaderFooterLink**, **ViewFooter**, **ViewHeader**

ShowVars

Syntax	**ShowVars**
Remarks	Displays a list of variables and their current values to help you debug the active macro. With **ShowVars** instructions, you can pause the macro and check the variables at exactly the points you want.
Example	This example defines the variables name$ and age as the items in the first line of the text file DATA.TXT. The variables are displayed in a dialog box where the values may be modified.

```
Open "DATA.TXT" For Input As #1
Input #1, Name$, Age
ShowVars
```

See Also	**MsgBox**, **Print**, **Stop**

ShrinkFont

Syntax	**ShrinkFont**
Remarks	Decreases the size of the selected text to the next available font size supported by the assigned printer. If the selection contains characters of varying font sizes, each size is reduced to the next available setting. If there is no selection, the smaller font size will be applied to new text.
Example	This macro inserts a line of increasingly smaller Z characters. Note how you can use a colon to place separate instructions on the same line. In this macro, **ShrinkFont** is executed three times in a single line.

```
Sub MAIN
FontSize 45
For count = 1 To 7
    Insert "Z"
    ShrinkFont : ShrinkFont : ShrinkFont
Next count
End Sub
```

See Also	**Font, FontSize, FormatFont, GrowFont, ResetChar, ShrinkFontOnePoint**

ShrinkFontOnePoint

Syntax   **ShrinkFontOnePoint**

Remarks   Decreases the font size of the selected text (or text to be inserted at the insertion
point) by 1 point, whether or not the new size is supported by the selected printer.
If more than one font size is included in the selection, each size is decreased by
1 point.

See Also   **GrowFontOnePoint, ShrinkFont**

ShrinkSelection

Syntax   **ShrinkSelection**

Remarks   Shrinks the selection to the next smaller unit of text. The progression is as
follows: entire document, section, paragraph, sentence, word, insertion point.
The insertion point is the beginning of the original selection. Running
ShrinkSelection when there is no selection produces a beep.

Unlike **ExtendSelection, ShrinkSelection** does not activate or require extend
mode.

See Also   **ExtendMode( ), ExtendSelection**

SizeToolbar

Syntax   **SizeToolbar** *Toolbar$*, *Width*

Remarks   Sizes a floating toolbar to the available width nearest the specified width. If the
specified toolbar is anchored at the top, bottom, or either side of the Word
window, **SizeToolbar** has no effect.

Argument	Explanation
Toolbar$	The name of the toolbar as listed in the Toolbars dialog box (View menu)
Width	The width of the toolbar, in pixels

Example   This example sizes the Standard toolbar such that the buttons are displayed in two
horizontal rows.

```
MoveToolbar "Standard", 0, 0, 40
SizeToolbar "Standard", 368
```

See Also   **MoveToolbar**

SkipNumbering, SkipNumbering()

Syntax   **SkipNumbering**

SkipNumbering()

Remarks   The **SkipNumbering** statement skips bullets or numbers for the selected
paragraphs in a bulleted or numbered list created with the Bullets And Numbering
command (Format menu). Subsequent bulleted or numbered paragraphs continue
the current list, rather than starting a new list (and restarting the numbering in the
case of a numbered list).

The **SkipNumbering()** function returns the following values.

Value	Explanation
0 (zero)	If the selected paragraphs are not skipped. The selected paragraphs may or may not be part of a bulleted or numbered list.
−1	If some of the selected paragraphs are skipped and some are not, or the selection includes more than one level in a multilevel list.
1	If all the selected paragraphs are skipped.

Example   This example selects the current paragraph and uses **SkipNumbering()** to
determine whether the paragraph is skipped. If it is, numbering is reapplied to the
paragraph.

```
EditGoTo "\Para"
If SkipNumbering() = 1 Then
    FormatBulletsAndNumbering
End If
```

See Also   **DemoteList, FormatBulletsAndNumbering, PromoteList,
RemoveBulletsNumbers**

SmallCaps, SmallCaps()

Syntax   **SmallCaps** [*On*]

SmallCaps()

Remarks   The **SmallCaps** statement adds or removes the small caps character format for the
current selection, or controls small caps formatting for characters to be inserted at
the insertion point.

Argument	Explanation
On	Specifies whether to add or remove the small caps format:
	1 Formats the selection as small caps.
	0 (zero) Removes the small caps format.
	Omitted Toggles the small caps format.

The **SmallCaps()** function returns the following values.

Value	Explanation
0 (zero)	If none of the selection is formatted as small caps
–1	If part of the selection is formatted as small caps
1	If all the selection is formatted as small caps

Example

If the current paragraph (selected using the predefined bookmark "\Para") has any small caps formatting, this example formats the entire paragraph as small caps:

```
SelType 1                         'Cancel selection, if any
EditGoTo "\Para"
If SmallCaps() = -1 Then SmallCaps 1
```

See Also

AllCaps, ChangeCase, FormatFont, UCase$()

SortArray

Syntax

SortArray *ArrayName[$]()* [, *Order*] [, *From*] [, *To*] [, *SortType*] [, *SortKey*]

Remarks

Performs an alphanumeric sort on the elements in the specified array. **SortArray** is especially useful for sorting arrays that fill list boxes in a custom dialog box. **SortArray** can sort one-dimensional or two-dimensional arrays; an error occurs if the specified array has more than two dimensions.

Argument	Explanation
ArrayName[$]()	The one-dimensional or two-dimensional array to be sorted. Arrays with more than two dimensions are not sorted.
Order	The sorting order:
	0 (zero) or omitted Ascending
	1 Descending
From	Number of the first element to sort. The default is 0 (zero).
To	Number of the last element to sort (must be greater than *From*).
SortType	The kind of sort to perform (applies only to two-dimensional arrays):
	0 (zero) or omitted Sort the "rows" in the array matrix.
	1 Sort the "columns" in the array matrix.

Argument	Explanation
SortKey	The number of the row or column to sort by (applies only to two-dimensional arrays): 0 (zero) indicates the first row or column, 1 indicates the second, and so on. The default is 0 (zero).
	If *SortType* is 0 (zero), indicating a row sort, *SortKey* specifies the column that determines the sort. If *SortType* is 1, indicating a column sort, *SortKey* specifies the row that determines the sort.

Here are some examples of **SortArray** instructions, with descriptions of their effect.

Instruction	Description
SortArray ArrayTest( )	Sort all the element(s) in the array ArrayTest( ) in ascending order, beginning with the element(s) numbered 0 (zero). If the array is two-dimensional, sort the rows of the array matrix, using the first column as the sort key.
SortArray List$( ), 0, 1, 10	Sort the elements numbered 1 through 10 in the array List$( ) in ascending order.
SortArray MailingList$( ), 1, 1, 20, 0, 1	Sort the elements numbered 1 through 20 in the two-dimensional array MailingList$( ) in descending order. Sort rows, using the second column as the sort key
SortArray Table( ), 0, 0, 10, 1, 3	Sort the elements numbered 0 (zero) through 10 in the two-dimensional array Table( ) in ascending order. Sort columns, using the fourth row as the sort key.

Note Although the **SortArray** arguments other than *ArrayName*[$]( ) are optional, you cannot omit arguments between arguments that you do include. For example, SortArray Test( ), 0, 0, 2, 0, 1 is a valid instruction, but SortArray Test( ), 0, , , , 1 is not valid and will not sort the array.

Examples

This example creates an array containing the names of all the bookmarks in the active document and then sorts the names. When first defined, the variable marks$(0) represents the name of the first bookmark added to the document. After the array is sorted, marks$(0) represents the first name in an alphabetic list of the bookmark names.

```
size = CountBookmarks() - 1
Dim marks$(size)
For count = 0 To size
    marks$(count) = BookmarkName$(count + 1)
Next
SortArray(marks$())
```

The following example opens a text file containing a list of 100 names and addresses. There are five fields for the names and addresses: the first field is for the name, the second for the street address, the third for the city or town, the fourth for the state or province, and the fifth for the postal code. The array MailList$() is defined to accommodate the names and addresses, which are read into the array. The array is then sorted by postal code in descending order (so that rows with the highest postal code are first). The sorted names and addresses are then written back to the file. Note that you could perform the same sort by opening the file in a document window and using the **TableSort** statement.

```
Open "LIST.TXT" For Input As #1
Dim MailList$(99, 4)
For x = 0 To 99
    Read #1, MailList$(x, 0), MailList$(x, 1), MailList$(x, 2), \
        MailList$(x, 3), MailList$(x, 4)
Next
Close #1
SortArray MailList$(), 1, 0, 99, 0, 4
Open "NEWLIST.TXT" For Output As #1
For x = 0 To 99
    Write #1, MailList$(x, 0), MailList$(x, 1), MailList$(x, 2), \
            MailList$(x, 3), MailList$(x, 4)
Next
Close #1
```

See Also   **Dim**, **TableSort**

SpacePara1, SpacePara1()

Syntax   **SpacePara1**

             SpacePara1()

Remarks   The **SpacePara1** statement single-spaces the selected paragraphs. The exact spacing is determined by the font size of the largest characters in the paragraph.

The **SpacePara1()** function returns the following values.

Value	Explanation
0 (zero)	If none of the selection is single-spaced
−1	If part of the selection is single-spaced
1	If all the selection is single-spaced

See Also   **CloseUpPara, FormatParagraph, OpenUpPara, SpacePara15, SpacePara2**

SpacePara15, SpacePara15()

Syntax   **SpacePara15**

SpacePara15( )

Remarks   The **SpacePara15** statement formats the selected paragraphs with 1.5 line spacing. The exact spacing is determined by the font size of the largest characters in the paragraph plus 6 points.

The **SpacePara15()** function returns the following values.

Value	Explanation
0 (zero)	If none of the selection is formatted with 1.5 line spacing
−1	If part of the selection is formatted with 1.5 line spacing
1	If all the selection is formatted with 1.5 line spacing

See Also   **CloseUpPara, FormatParagraph, OpenUpPara, SpacePara1, SpacePara2**

SpacePara2, SpacePara2()

Syntax   **SpacePara2**

SpacePara2( )

Remarks   The **SpacePara2** statement double-spaces the selected paragraphs. The exact spacing is determined by the point size of the largest characters in the paragraph plus 12 points.

The **SpacePara2()** function returns the following values.

Value	Explanation
0 (zero)	If none of the selection is double-spaced
−1	If part of the selection is double-spaced
1	If all the selection is double-spaced

See Also   **CloseUpPara, FormatParagraph, OpenUpPara, SpacePara1, SpacePara15**

SpellChecked, SpellChecked()

Syntax   **SpellChecked** [*On*]

SpellChecked()

Remarks   The **SpellChecked** statement identifies the selected text as either checked for
spelling errors or not checked. If no text is selected, **SpellChecked** and
SpellChecked() have no effect.

In Word version 6.0, **SpellChecked** and **SpellChecked**() are unavailable and
generate errors.

Argument	Explanation
On	Specifies whether to identify the selection as checked or not checked for spelling errors:
	1 Identifies the selection as checked
	0 (zero) Identifies the selection as not checked
	Omitted Toggles the setting

The **SpellChecked**() function returns the following values.

Value	Explanation
0 (zero)	If the selection is not checked for spelling
-1	If only part of the selection is checked for spelling
1	If all the selection is checked for spelling

See Also   **ToolsSpelling**, **DocumentHasMisspellings**()

Spike

Syntax   **Spike**

Remarks   Deletes the current selection and adds it to a built-in AutoText entry called the
Spike. Items added to the Spike are separated by paragraph marks.

You can use the Spike to collect text and graphics from various locations in one
or more documents and then insert them all together using **InsertSpike**, which
clears the Spike. To insert the Spike contents without clearing the Spike, you use
EditAutoText.

Example   This example opens RESEARCH.DOC, uses **Spike** to collect all the Heading 1
paragraphs, closes RESEARCH.DOC without saving changes, and then inserts
the headings into the active document. On the Macintosh, substitute a path such as
HD:DOCUMENTS:RSRCH PAPER.

```
FileOpen .Name = "C:\DOCS\RESEARCH.DOC", .ReadOnly = 1
EditFindClearFormatting
EditFindStyle .Style = "Heading 1"
EditFind .Find = "", .Direction = 0, .Format = 1
While EditFindFound()
    Spike
    ParaDown
    EditFind .Find = "", .Direction = 0, .Format = 1
Wend
FileClose 2                  'Close without saving
InsertSpike                  'Empty the Spike at insertion point
```

See Also   **EditAutoText, EditCut, InsertSpike**

SplitSubdocument

Syntax   **SplitSubdocument**

Remarks   Divides an existing subdocument into two subdocuments at the same level in master document or outline view. The division is made at the insertion point (or the beginning of the selection, if there is one). If the active document is not in master document or outline view, or the insertion point is not at the beginning of a paragraph within a subdocument, an error occurs.

See Also   **CreateSubdocument, InsertSubdocument, MergeSubdocument, OpenSubdocument, RemoveSubdocument, ViewMasterDocument**

StartOfColumn, StartOfColumn()

Syntax   **StartOfColumn** [*Select*]

              StartOfColumn([*Select*])

Remarks   The **StartOfColumn** statement moves the insertion point or extends the selection (if *Select* is nonzero) to the top of the table column containing the insertion point or selection. If the selection extends over more than one column, the insertion point moves to the top of the column containing the end of the selection. If the insertion point or selection is not in a table, an error occurs.

Note If the first row in the table does not have a cell that corresponds to the column that contains the current selection—for example, if you have deleted or merged cells in the first row—**StartOfColumn** moves the insertion point to the end of the first row in the table.

The **StartOfColumn()** function behaves the same as the statement and also returns one of the following values.

Value	Explanation
0 (zero)	If the insertion point was not moved or the selection was not extended (that is, if it was already at the top of the column)
−1	If the insertion point was moved or the selection was extended

If the insertion point is not in a table, **StartOfColumn** and **StartOfColumn()** generate an error.

Example

This example moves the insertion point from anywhere in the table to the end of the first row:

```
TableSelectRow
StartOfColumn
```

See Also

EndOfColumn, **StartOfRow**

StartOfDocument, StartOfDocument()

Syntax

StartOfDocument [*Select*]

StartOfDocument([*Select*])

Remarks

The **StartOfDocument** statement moves the insertion point or, if *Select* is nonzero, the active end of the selection (the end that moves when you press CTRL+SHIFT+HOME (Windows) or COMMAND+SHIFT+HOME (Macintosh)) to the beginning of the document.

The **StartOfDocument()** function behaves the same as the statement and also returns one of the following values.

Value	Explanation
0 (zero)	If the insertion point or the active end of the selection was not moved (for example, if it was already at the start of the document)
−1	If the insertion point or the active end of the selection was moved

Example

This example moves the insertion point to the start of the document and then prepares Word to begin a replace operation:

```
StartOfDocument
EditFindClearFormatting
EditReplaceClearFormatting
'Instructions that perform a replace operation go here
```

See Also

AtStartOfDocument(), **EndOfDocument**

StartOfLine, StartOfLine()

Syntax

StartOfLine [*Select*]

StartOfLine ([*Select*])

Remarks

The **StartOfLine** statement moves the insertion point or, if *Select* is nonzero, the active end of the selection (the end that moves when you press SHIFT+HOME) to the beginning of the current line or the line that contains the active end of the selection.

The **StartOfLine**() function behaves the same as the statement and also returns one of the following values.

Value	Explanation
0 (zero)	If the insertion point or the active end of the selection was not moved (that is, if it was already at the beginning of the line)
−1	If the insertion point or the active end of the selection was moved

Avoid using **StartOfLine** by itself to go to the beginning of a paragraph unless you are sure that the paragraph is a single line (for example, a word in a list of words).

Example

This example moves the insertion point to the start of the current paragraph regardless of the length of the paragraph or the position of the insertion point within it. The first instruction selects the entire paragraph.

```
EditGoTo "\Para"
StartOfLine
```

The bookmark "\Para" is one of several predefined bookmarks that Word defines and updates automatically. For more information on predefined bookmarks, see "Operators and Predefined Bookmarks" later in this part.

See Also

EndOfLine, ParaUp, StartOfRow

StartOfRow, StartOfRow()

Syntax

StartOfRow [*Select*]

StartOfRow ([*Select*])

Remarks

The **StartOfRow** statement moves the insertion point or extends the selection (if *Select* is nonzero) to the beginning of the first cell in the table row containing the insertion point. If the selection extends over more than one row, the insertion point moves or the selection is extended to the first cell of the first row in the selection. If the insertion point or selection is not in a table, an error occurs.

The **StartOfRow()** function behaves the same as the statement and also returns one of the following values.

Value	Explanation
0 (zero)	If the insertion point was not moved or the selection was not extended (that is, if it was already at the beginning of the row)
−1	If the insertion point was moved or the selection was extended

Example

This example moves the insertion point from anywhere in the table to the beginning of the first cell:

```
StartOfRow
StartOfColumn
```

See Also

EndOfRow, StartOfColumn, StartOfLine

StartOfWindow, StartOfWindow()

Syntax

StartOfWindow [*Select*]

StartOfWindow([*Select*])

Remarks

The **StartOfWindow** statement moves the insertion point or, if *Select* is nonzero, the active end of the selection (the end that moves when you press CTRL+SHIFT+PAGE UP (Windows) or COMMAND+SHIFT+PAGE UP (Macintosh)) to the upper-left corner of the contents currently visible in the document window.

The **StartOfWindow()** function behaves the same as the statement and also returns one of the following values.

Value	Explanation
0 (zero)	If the insertion point or the active end of the selection was not moved (that is, if it was already at the upper-left corner of the window)
−1	If the insertion point or the active end of the selection was moved

Example

This example selects the visible contents of the active document window:

```
StartOfWindow
EndOfWindow 1
```

See Also

EndOfWindow, StartOfDocument

Stop

Syntax

Stop [*SuppressMessage*]

Remarks

Stops a running macro. If *SuppressMessage* is –1, no message appears. Otherwise, Word displays a message box that says the macro was interrupted. When Word encounters a **Stop** instruction in a macro that is open in a macro-editing window, you can click the Continue button on the Macro toolbar to continue running the macro.

See Also

ShowVars

Str$()

Syntax

Str$(*n*)

Remarks

Returns the string representation of the value *n*. If *n* is a positive number, **Str$**() returns a string with a leading space. To remove the leading space, use **LTrim$**().

Examples

This example uses **Str$**() to make a numeric variable acceptable as part of a string in a message box. Note that no space is needed after "were" because **Str$**() has included a space at the beginning of a$.

```
sales = 2400
a$ = Str$(sales)
MsgBox "Sales this week were" + a$ + " dollars."
```

You can use the following function to return string representations of numeric variables without the leading space:

```
Function MyString$(Num)
    If Num >= 0 Then
        MyString$ = LTrim$(Str$(Num))
    Else
        MyString$ = Str$(Num)
    End If
End Function
```

In another subroutine, `String1$ = MyString$(25)` is an example of an instruction that calls the preceding function.

See Also

Chr$**(), **InStr**(), **Left$(), **LTrim$**(), **Mid$**(), **Right$**(), **RTrim$**(), **String$**(), **Val**()

Strikethrough, Strikethrough()

Syntax

Strikethrough [*On*]

Strikethrough()

Remarks

The **Strikethrough** statement adds or removes the strikethrough character format for the current selection, or controls strikethrough formatting for characters to be inserted at the insertion point.

Argument	Explanation
On	Specifies whether to add or remove the strikethrough format:
	1 Formats the selection as strikethrough.
	0 (zero) Removes the strikethrough format.
	Omitted Toggles the strikethrough format.

The **Strikethrough**() function returns the following values.

Value	Explanation
0 (zero)	If none of the selection is formatted as strikethrough
−1	If part of the selection is formatted as strikethrough
1	If all the selection is formatted as strikethrough

When revision marking is activated, Word uses strikethrough to mark deleted text. However, Word does not recognize text formatted with the **Strikethrough** statement as deleted. If you want to mark the selected text as deleted for the purpose of revision marks, use the following instructions:

```
ToolsRevisions .MarkRevisions = 1
EditClear
```

See Also

FormatFont, ToolsRevisions

String$()

Syntax

String$(*Count*, *Source$*)

String$(*Count*, *CharCode*)

Remarks

Returns the first character in *Source$* or the character corresponding to the character code *CharCode*, repeated *Count* times. *Count* can be as large as 65,280.

Examples	This instruction prints the text "ddddd" in the status bar:

```
Print String$(5, 100)
```

This example inserts a row of 40 characters with the character code 164 before the first selected paragraph:

```
SelType 1 : ParaDown : ParaUp      'Go to start of paragraph
Insert String$(40, 164)            'Insert character string
InsertPara                         'Insert a paragraph mark
```

See Also   **Asc()**, **Chr$()**, **InStr()**, **Str$()**

Style

Syntax   **Style** *StyleName$*

Remarks   Applies a style to the selected paragraphs. If *StyleName$* does not exist, an error occurs. To create a style, use **FormatStyle**.

Example   This example finds the first instance of the word "Overview" followed by a paragraph mark and applies the Heading 1 style:

```
StartOfDocument
EditFind .Find = "Overview^p", .Direction = 0, .MatchCase = 1, \
    .Format = 0
If Edit.FindFound() Then Style "Heading 1"
```

See Also   **FormatStyle**, **NormalStyle**, **StyleName$()**

StyleDesc$()

Syntax   **StyleDesc$(***StyleName$***)**

Remarks   Returns the description of the specified style in the active document. For example, a typical description for the Heading 1 style is "Normal + Arial®, 14 pt, Bold, Space Before 12 pt After 3 pt." If *StyleName$* does not exist, **StyleDesc$()** returns an empty string ("").

Example   This example displays the description of the Heading 1 style in a message box:

```
infostyle$ = "Heading 1"
MsgBox StyleDesc$(infostyle$), "Description for " + infostyle$
```

See Also   **CountStyles()**, **FormatStyle**, **StyleName$()**

StyleName$()

Syntax

StyleName$([*Count,*] [*Context,*] [*All*]**)**

Remarks

Returns the name of the specified style or, if no style is specified, the name of the style applied to the first paragraph in the selection. Note that if the insertion point or selection is within text formatted with a character style, **StyleName$()** returns the name of the character style (not the paragraph style). For a method of returning the paragraph style in this case, see the second example in this reference entry.

Argument	Explanation
Count	The position of the style in an alphabetic list of styles for the document or template, according to the value of *Context*. The number can range from 1 to **CountStyles()**, which returns the total number of styles (both character and paragraph) in the specified context. If *Count* is 0 (zero) or omitted, the name of the current style is returned.
Context	The list of styles to use:
	0 (zero) or omitted Active document
	1 Active template
All	Specifies whether to include built-in styles:
	0 (zero) or omitted Built-in styles are excluded.
	1 Built-in styles are included.
	Note that Word contains 75 built-in styles, and that two of those built-in styles are defined by default: Default Paragraph Font and Normal.

Examples

This example checks to see if the first style in the list of document styles is used in the document. If the style is not used, a message box is displayed:

```
FirstStyle$ = StyleName$(1)
StartOfDocument
EditFindClearFormatting
EditFindStyle .Style = FirstStyle$
EditFind .Find = "", .WholeWord = 0, .MatchCase = 0, .Direction = 0, \
    .Format = 1, .Wrap = 0
If EditFindFound() = 0 Then
    MsgBox "Style " + FirstStyle$ + " is not in use."
End If
```

The following example ensures that **StyleName$()** returns the underlying paragraph style, regardless of any character styles applied to the current selection:

```
EditBookmark "tmp"
SelType 1
reset$ = StyleName$()
Style "Default Paragraph Font"
parastyle$ = StyleName$()
Style reset$
EditGoto "tmp"
EditBookmark "tmp", .Delete
```

See Also   **CountStyles()**, **FormatStyle**, **StyleDesc$()**

Sub...End Sub

Syntax   **Sub** *SubName*[(*ArgumentList*)]
         Series of instructions
         End Sub

Remarks   Defines a subroutine. A subroutine is a series of instructions that can be called repeatedly from the main subroutine and can make your macros shorter and easier to debug.

Argument	Explanation
SubName	The name of the subroutine.
ArgumentList	A list of arguments, separated by commas. You can then use these arguments in the subroutine. Values, string and numeric variables, and array variables are all valid arguments.

Subroutines must appear outside the main subroutine—generally, you add subroutines after the **End Sub** instruction that ends the main subroutine. You can call a subroutine not only from the macro's main subroutine, but also from other subroutines and even other macros. For more information about using subroutines, including how to share variables and pass arguments between subroutines, see Chapter 4, "Advanced WordBasic," in Part 1, "Learning WordBasic."

Example   In this macro, the main subroutine calls the GoBeep subroutine, passing the number of times to beep through the variable numBeeps:

```
Sub MAIN
    numBeeps = 3
    GoBeep(numBeeps)
End Sub
```

```
Sub GoBeep(count)
    For n = 1 To count
        Beep
        For t = 1 To 100 : Next      'Add time between beeps
    Next
End Sub
```

If the GoBeep subroutine were in a macro named LibMacros, the call to the subroutine would be as follows:

```
Sub MAIN
    numBeeps = 3
    LibMacros.GoBeep(numBeeps)
End Sub
```

For more information about using subroutines in different macros, see Chapter 4, "Advanced WordBasic," in Part 1, "Learning WordBasic."

See Also   **Call, Function…End Function**

Subscript, Subscript()

Syntax   **Subscript** [*On*]

Subscript()

Remarks   The **Subscript** statement adds or removes the subscript character format for the current selection, or controls subscript formatting for characters to be inserted at the insertion point.

Argument	Explanation
On	Specifies whether to add or remove the subscript format:
	1 Formats the selection as subscript.
	0 (zero) Removes the subscript format.
	Omitted Toggles the subscript format.

The **Subscript()** function returns the following values.

Value	Explanation
0 (zero)	If none of the selection is formatted as subscript
−1	If part of the selection is formatted as subscript
1	If all the selection is formatted as subscript

See Also   **FormatFont, Superscript**

Superscript, Superscript()

Syntax

Superscript [*On*]

Superscript()

Remarks

The **Superscript** statement adds or removes the superscript character format for the current selection, or controls superscript formatting for characters to be inserted at the insertion point.

Argument	Explanation
On	Specifies whether to add or remove the superscript format:
	1 Formats the selection as superscript.
	0 (zero) Removes the superscript format.
	Omitted Toggles the superscript format.

The **Superscript()** function returns the following values.

Value	Explanation
0 (zero)	If none of the selection is formatted as superscript
−1	If part of the selection is formatted as superscript
1	If all the selection is formatted as superscript

See Also

FormatFont, Subscript

SymbolFont

Syntax

SymbolFont [*TextToInsert$*]

Remarks

Formats the selected text with the Symbol font or inserts the specified text formatted with the Symbol font at the insertion point. If no text is specified or selected, the **SymbolFont** statement has no effect.

See Also

FormatFont, InsertSymbol

TabLeader$()

Syntax   **TabLeader$(***Pos***)**

Remarks   Returns the leader character of the custom tab stop at the position *Pos*, which is given in points (72 points = 1 inch). If more than one paragraph is selected, **TabLeader$()** evaluates the settings in the first paragraph.

There are three cases in which **TabLeader$()** returns an empty string (""): if there is no tab stop at the position *Pos*, if the tab stop is a default tab stop, or if the document is in outline view. If there is a custom tab stop at *Pos*, **TabLeader$()** returns one of the following values.

Value	Explanation
(space)	No leader (corresponds to a tab leader set to "None")
.	Period
-	Hyphen
_	Underscore

To change the tab leader, use **FormatTabs**.

Example   This example determines whether a tab stop at the three-fourths–inch position has an underscore leader character. If it does, the **FormatTabs** instruction changes the leader character to "None."

```
ViewNormal
If TabLeader$(54) = "_" Then
    FormatTabs .Position = "54 pt", .Leader = 0
End If
```

See Also   **FormatTabs, NextTab(), PrevTab(), TabType()**

TableAutoFormat

Syntax   **TableAutoFormat [.Format =** *number***] [, .Borders =** *number***]
[, .Shading =** *number***] [, .Font =** *number***] [, .Color =** *number***]
[, .AutoFit =** *number***] [, .HeadingRows =** *number***] [, .FirstColumn =** *number***]
[, .LastRow =** *number***] [, .LastColumn =** *number***]**

Remarks   Applies a predefined look to a table. The arguments for the **TableAutoFormat** statement correspond to the options in the Table AutoFormat dialog box (Table menu).

Argument	Explanation
.Format	The format to apply: 0 (zero) corresponds to the first format listed in the Formats list box ("none"), 1 corresponds to the second format, and so on.
.Borders	If 1, applies the border properties of the specified format.
.Shading	If 1, applies the shading properties of the specified format.
.Font	If 1, applies the font properties of the specified format.
.Color	If 1, applies the color properties of the specified format.
.AutoFit	If 1, decreases the width of the table columns as much as possible without changing the way text wraps in the cells.
.HeadingRows	If 1, applies the heading-row properties of the specified format.
.FirstColumn	If 1, applies the first-column properties of the specified format.
.LastRow	If 1, applies the last-row properties of the specified format.
.LastColumn	If 1, applies the last-column properties of the specified format.

Example

This example applies all the properties of the Classic 2 table format to the table containing the insertion point. If the insertion point is not in a table, a message box is displayed.

```
If SelInfo(12) = -1 Then     'If insertion point is in a table
    TableAutoFormat .Format = 5, .Borders = 1, .Shading = 1, \
    .Font = 1, .Color = 1, .AutoFit = 1, .HeadingRows = 1, \
    .FirstColumn = 1, .LastRow = 0, .LastColumn = 1
Else
    MsgBox "The insertion point is not in a table."
End If
```

See Also

TableColumnWidth, **TableHeadings**, **TableRowHeight**, **TableUpdateAutoFormat**

TableAutoSum

Syntax   **TableAutoSum**

Remarks   Inserts an = (Formula) field that calculates and displays the sum of the values in table cells above or to the left of the cell containing the insertion point. For information on how Word determines which values to add, see **TableFormula**.

See Also   **TableFormula**

TableColumnWidth

Syntax

TableColumnWidth [**.ColumnWidth** = *number or text*]
[**, .SpaceBetweenCols** = *number or text*] [**, .PrevColumn**] [**, .NextColumn**]
[**, .AutoFit**] [**, .RulerStyle** = *number*]

Remarks

Sets the column width and the space between columns for the selected cells. The arguments for the **TableColumnWidth** statement correspond to the options on the Column tab in the Cell Height And Width dialog box (Table menu).

Argument	Explanation
.ColumnWidth	The width to apply to the selected cells or columns, in points or a text measurement (.RulerStyle specifies how other columns are affected).
.SpaceBetweenCols	The distance between the text in each column, in points or a text measurement.
.PrevColumn	After the actions (if any) specified by the preceding arguments are carried out, selects the previous column.
.NextColumn	After the actions (if any) specified by the preceding arguments are carried out, selects the next column.
.AutoFit	Decreases the width of the selected cells as much as possible without changing the way text wraps in the cells.
.RulerStyle	Specifies how Word adjusts the table:
	0 (zero) If there is a selection, only the selected cells are changed. Row width is not preserved. If there is no selection, Word sizes all cells in the selected column.
	1 Word preserves row width by adjusting all cells to the right of the selection in proportion to their widths.
	2 Word preserves row width by adjusting cells in the column immediately to the right of the selection only.
	3 Word preserves row width by adjusting all cells to the right of the selection, assigning them each the same width.
	4 Only the cell containing the insertion point (or the first cell in the selection) is changed. Row width is not preserved.

Example

For each table in the document, this example adjusts the width of the first column to 2 inches and the second column to 3 inches. The first **TableColumnWidth** instruction both formats the first column and moves the selection to the second column.

```
StartOfDocument
While ParaDown()
    If SelInfo(12) =  - 1 Then    'If insertion point is in a table
        StartOfRow
        TableSelectColumn
        TableColumnWidth .ColumnWidth = "2 in", .RulerStyle = 0, \
                .NextColumn
        If SelInfo(18) > 1 Then 'If more than one column
                TableColumnWidth .ColumnWidth = "3 in", .RulerStyle = 0
        End If
        LineDown
    End If
Wend
```

See Also   **SelInfo(), TableDeleteColumn, TableRowHeight, TableSelectColumn**

TableDeleteCells

Syntax   **TableDeleteCells .ShiftCells** = *number*

Remarks   Deletes the selected cells. If the insertion point or selection is not within a table, an error occurs.

Argument	Explanation
.ShiftCells	Sets the direction to shift the remaining cells:
	0 (zero) or omitted Shift the cells left.
	1 Shift the cells up.
	2 Delete the entire row.
	3 Delete the entire column.

Example   This example deletes the first cell in a table if the table contains more than two rows:

```
If SelInfo(15) > 2 Then
    TableSelectTable
    StartOfRow
    TableDeleteCells
End If
```

See Also   **SelInfo(), TableDeleteColumn, TableDeleteRow**

TableDeleteColumn

Syntax   **TableDeleteColumn**

Remarks   Deletes the table column containing the insertion point, or deletes all columns
               containing part of the selection. If the insertion point or selection is not within a
               table, an error occurs.

Example   This example deletes the first column in a table:

```
StartOfRow
TableDeleteColumn
```

See Also   **SelInfo()**, **TableDeleteCells**, **TableDeleteRow**

TableDeleteRow

Syntax   **TableDeleteRow**

Remarks   Deletes the row containing the insertion point, or deletes all rows containing part
               of the selection. If the insertion point or selection is not within a table, an error
               occurs.

Example   This example deletes the last row in a table if the table contains more than two
               rows:

```
If SelInfo(15) > 2 Then
    EndOfColumn
    TableDeleteRow
End If
```

See Also   **SelInfo()**, **TableDeleteCells**, **TableDeleteColumn**

TableFormula

Syntax   **TableFormula [.Formula** = *text*] **[, .NumFormat** = *text*]

Remarks   Inserts an = (Formula) field containing the specified formula at the insertion
               point. If the insertion point is in a table cell that already contains an = (Formula)
               field, the existing field is replaced with a field containing the specified formula.

Argument	Explanation
.Formula	The mathematical formula you want the = (Formula) field to evaluate. Spreadsheet-type references to table cells are valid. For example, `"=SUM(a4:c4)"` specifies the first three values in the fourth row.
	For more information on valid formulas, display the Formula dialog box (Table menu), and then choose the Help button.
.NumFormat	A format for the result of the = (Formula) field. For sample formats, choose Formula from the Table menu and review the list in the Number Format box.

If the insertion point is in a table, specifying .Formula is optional so long as there is at least one cell containing a value above or to the left of the cell containing the insertion point. If the cells above contain values, the inserted field is {=SUM(ABOVE)}; if the cells to the left contain values, the inserted field is {=SUM(LEFT)}. If the cells above and the cells to the left contain values, Word uses the following rules to determine which SUM function to insert:

- If the cell immediately above the insertion point contains a value, Word inserts {=SUM(ABOVE)}.

- If the cell immediately above does not contain a value and the cell immediately to the left does, Word inserts {=SUM(LEFT)}.

- If neither adjoining cell contains a value, Word inserts {=SUM(ABOVE)}.

If you don't specify .Formula and all the cells above and to the left of the insertion point are empty, a field error occurs.

Example   This example adds a row to the end of the table, moves the insertion point to the last cell, and then inserts an = (Formula) field that adds the values in the last column:

```
TableSelectTable
EndOfRow
NextCell
EndOfRow
TableFormula .Formula = "=SUM(ABOVE)"
```

See Also   **InsertField, TableAutoSum, ToolsCalculate**

TableGridlines, TableGridlines()

Syntax   **TableGridlines** [*On*]

TableGridlines()

Remarks   The **TableGridlines** statement displays or hides table gridlines.

Argument	Explanation
On	Specifies whether to display or hide table gridlines:
	0 (zero) Hides table gridlines.
	1 Displays table gridlines.
	Omitted Toggles the option on or off.

The **TableGridlines()** function returns the following values.

Value	Explanation
0 (zero)	If table gridlines are hidden
−1	If table gridlines are displayed

Example   This example displays table gridlines if they are not already showing. You could use this instruction as part of an AutoOpen macro, so that whenever documents based on a certain template are opened, table gridlines are displayed.

```
If Not TableGridlines() Then TableGridlines 1
```

See Also   **ToolsOptionsView**

TableHeadings, TableHeadings()

Syntax   **TableHeadings** [*On*]

TableHeadings()

Remarks   The **TableHeadings** statement adds or removes the table heading format for the selected rows. Rows formatted as table headings are repeated when a table spans more than one page.

Argument	Explanation
On	Specifies whether to add or remove the table heading format:
	0 (zero) Removes the table heading format.
	1 Adds the table heading format.
	Omitted Toggles the table heading format.

The **TableHeadings**( ) function returns the following values.

Value	Explanation
0 (zero)	If none of the selected rows are formatted as table headings
−1	If one or more but not all of the selected rows are formatted as table headings
1	If all the selected rows are formatted as table headings

See Also   **TableRowHeight**

TableInsertCells

Syntax   **TableInsertCells** [**.ShiftCells** = *number*]

Remarks   Inserts cells above or to the left of the selected range of cells in a table. If the insertion point or selection is not in a table, an error occurs.

Argument	Explanation
.ShiftCells	Sets the direction to shift the cells in the selected range:
	0 (zero) Shift the cells right.
	1 or omitted Shift the cells down.
	2 Insert an entire row.
	3 Insert an entire column.

Example   This example selects the current cell (using the predefined bookmark "\Cell") and the cell below it, and then inserts two new cells. The existing cells are shifted to the right. The **If** control structure makes sure the selection is entirely within a table before running **TableInsertCells**.

```
EditGoTo "\Cell"
LineDown 1, 1
If SelInfo(12) = -1 Then
    TableInsertCells .ShiftCells = 0
Else
    MsgBox "Selection extends outside the table."
End If
```

See Also   **SelInfo()**, **TableInsertColumn**, **TableInsertRow**

TableInsertColumn

Syntax   **TableInsertColumn**

Remarks   Inserts a column to the left of the column that contains the insertion point, or inserts as many columns as are selected to the left of the selection. If the insertion point or selection is not in a table, an error occurs.

Example   This example adds a column to the end of the table containing the insertion point:

```
TableSelectTable        'Select the entire table
StartOfColumn           'Move to the end of the first row
TableInsertColumn       'Add a new column
```

See Also   **TableInsertCells**, **TableInsertRow**

TableInsertRow

Syntax   **TableInsertRow** [**.NumRows =** *number*]

Remarks   Inserts a row above the selected rows or above the row that contains the insertion point. If the insertion point or any part of the selection is not in a table, an error occurs. If the insertion point immediately follows a table, **TableInsertRow** inserts a row at the end of the table.

Argument	Explanation
.NumRows	The number of rows you want to add. If .NumRows is 0 (zero) or omitted, **TableInsertRow** inserts above the selection as many rows as are selected.

Examples

The following example adds a row to the end of a table:

```
TableSelectTable
CharRight
TableInsertRow
```

This example adds two new rows at the top of a table:

```
TableSelectTable
StartOfRow
TableInsertRow .NumRows = 2
```

See Also

TableInsertCells, TableInsertColumn

TableInsertTable

Syntax

TableInsertTable [.**ConvertFrom** = *number*] [, .**NumColumns** = *number*] [, .**NumRows** = *number*] [, .**InitialColWidth** = *number or text*] [, .**Wizard**] [, .**Format** = *number*] [, .**Apply** = *number*]

Remarks

Converts a series of selected paragraphs into a table or inserts an empty table if there is no selection. If the insertion point is already in a table, an error occurs.

Argument	Explanation
.ConvertFrom	Specifies the character used to separate items of text into cell contents:
	0 (zero) Paragraph marks (Word places every other paragraph in the second column)
	1 Tab characters
	2 Commas
.NumColumns	Number of columns in the table.

Argument	Explanation
.NumRows	Number of rows in the table.
.InitialColWidth	The initial width for each column, in points or a text measurement. If omitted, column width is calculated so that the table stretches from margin to margin.
.Wizard	Runs the Table wizard.
.Format	One of the predefined formats listed in the Table AutoFormat dialog box (Table menu): 0 (zero) corresponds to the first format listed in the Formats box ("none"), 1 corresponds to the second format, and so on.
.Apply	Specifies which attributes of the format specified by .Format to apply to the table. Use the sum of any combination of the following values:

0	None
1	Borders
2	Shading
4	Font
8	Color
16	AutoFit
32	Heading Rows
64	Last Row
128	First Column
256	Last Column

Example

This example inserts a three-column, five-row table:

```
TableInsertTable .NumColumns = 3, .NumRows = 5, \
          .InitialColWidth = "2 in"
```

See Also

TableAutoFormat, **TableToText**, **TextToTable**

TableMergeCells

Syntax

TableMergeCells

Remarks

Merges selected table cells in the same row into a single cell. Selections can extend over multiple rows; however, Word only merges cells in the same row. **TableMergeCells** generates an error if Word cannot merge cells—for example, if only one cell is selected.

Example   This example either merges the currently selected cells or displays a message box if the command cannot be performed:

```
On Error Goto No
TableMergeCells
No:
If Err = 509 Then
    MsgBox "Sorry, can't merge."
End If
```

See Also   **TableSplitCells**

TableRowHeight

Syntax   **TableRowHeight** [**.RulerStyle** = *text*] [, **.LineSpacingRule** = *number*]
[, **.LineSpacing** = *number or text*] [, **.LeftIndent** = *number or text*]
[, **.Alignment** = *number*] [, **.AllowRowSplit** = *number*] [, **.PrevRow**]
[, **.NextRow**]

Remarks   Sets formats for the selected rows in a table. The arguments for the **TableRowHeight** statement correspond to the options on the Row tab in the Cell Height And Width dialog box (Table menu).

Argument	Explanation
.RulerStyle	When the left indent is changed, specifies how Word adjusts the table:
	0 (zero) Word moves cells to the right.
	1 Word preserves the position of the right edge of the table by narrowing all cells in the selected rows in proportion to their widths.
	2 Word preserves the position of the right edge of the table by narrowing cells in the first column only.
	3 Word preserves the position of the right edge of the table by narrowing all cells in the selected rows, assigning them each the same width.
	4 Word indents only the row containing the insertion point (or the first row in the selection).
	When row height is changed, specifies which rows are affected:
	0 (zero), 1, 2, or 3 If there is a selection, only the selected rows are affected. If there is no selection, all rows are affected.
	4 Only the row containing the insertion point or the first row in the selection is affected.

Argument	Explanation
.LineSpacingRule	The rule for determining the height of the rows:
	0 (zero) Auto
	1 At Least
	2 Exactly
.LineSpacing	The height of the rows, in points or a text measurement.
.LeftIndent	The distance between the left edge of the text and the left margin, in points or a text measurement.
.Alignment	The alignment of the rows:
	0 (zero) Left
	1 Center
	2 Right
.AllowRowSplit	If 1, allows text in the row to be divided at a page break.
.PrevRow	Selects the previous row for formatting.
.NextRow	Selects the next row for formatting.

Example

This example sets a minimum row height of 2 lines for the selected rows and indents them 1 inch from the left margin:

```
TableRowHeight .RulerStyle = "0", .LeftIndent = "1 in", \
    .LineSpacingRule = 1, .LineSpacing = "2 li", .Alignment = 0
```

See Also   **TableColumnWidth**, **TableHeadings**, **TableSelectRow**

TableSelectColumn

Syntax   **TableSelectColumn**

Remarks   Selects the table column containing the insertion point, or selects all columns containing the selection. If the insertion point or selection is not in a table, an error occurs.

Example   This example adds two new columns before the first column in a table:

```
TableSelectTable          'Select the entire table
StartOfRow                'Go to the first cell
TableSelectColumn         'Select the first column
CharRight 1, 1            'Extend selection to the second column
TableInsertColumn         'Insert two new columns
```

See Also   **TableSelectRow**, **TableSelectTable**

TableSelectRow

Syntax   **TableSelectRow**

Remarks   Selects the table row containing the insertion point, or selects all rows containing the selection. If the insertion point or selection is not in a table, an error occurs.

See Also   **TableSelectColumn**, **TableSelectTable**

TableSelectTable

Syntax   **TableSelectTable**

Remarks   Selects the entire table containing the insertion point. If the insertion point or selection is not in a table, an error occurs. As the examples in this entry demonstrate, you can use **TableSelectTable** in combination with other WordBasic statements to move the insertion point reliably to the first cell in a table or to the first character after a table.

Examples   This example moves the insertion point to the first cell in a table:

```
TableSelectTable
StartOfRow
```

The following example moves the insertion point to the end-of-row mark in the first row in a table. When the insertion point is at this position, you can use **TableInsertColumn** to add a column to the end of a table.

```
TableSelectTable
StartOfColumn
```

The following example moves the insertion point to the first character after a table:

```
TableSelectTable
CharRight
```

See Also   **TableSelectColumn**, **TableSelectRow**

TableSort

Syntax   **TableSort [.DontSortHdr** = *number*] **[, .FieldNum** = *number*]
[, .Type = *number*] **[.Order** = *number*] **[, .FieldNum2** = *number*]
[, .Type2 = *number*] **[, .Order2** = *number*] **[, .FieldNum3** = *number*]
[, .Type3 = *number*] **[, .Order3** = *number*] **[, .Separator** = *number*]
[, .SortColumn = *number*] **[, .CaseSensitive** = *number*]

Remarks Sorts the selected paragraphs or table rows. If you want to sort paragraphs within a table cell, select only the paragraphs and not the end-of-cell mark; if you select the end-of-cell mark and then sort, Word displays a message stating that it found no valid records to sort. The arguments for the **TableSort** statement correspond to the options in the Sort dialog box (Table menu).

Argument	Explanation
.DontSortHdr	If 1, excludes the first paragraph or table row from the sort operation.
.FieldNum, .FieldNum2, .FieldNum3	The number of the fields (text or table columns) to sort by. Word sorts by .FieldNum, then by .FieldNum2, and then by .FieldNum3.
.Type, .Type2, .Type3	The respective sort types for .FieldNum, .FieldNum2, and .FieldNum3:
	0 (zero) Alphanumeric
	1 Numeric
	2 Date
.Order, .Order2, .Order3	The sorting order to use when sorting .FieldNum, .FieldNum2, and .FieldNum3:
	0 (zero) Ascending
	1 Descending
.Separator	The type of separator (irrelevant for table rows):
	0 (zero) Comma
	1 Tab
	2 Other (the character that appears in the Other box in the Sort Options dialog box)
.SortColumn	If 1, sorts only the selected column (requires a column selection).
.CaseSensitive	If 1, sorts with case sensitivity.

Example This example sorts table rows in ascending alphanumeric order, first by the first column, and then by the second column. The first row is excluded from the sort operation.

```
Select Case SelInfo(15)
    Case -1
        MsgBox "Please place the insertion point in a table."
    Case 1
        MsgBox "Sorry, can't sort a single-row table."
    Case Else
        TableSelectTable
        TableSort .Order = 0, .FieldNum = "1", .Type = 0, \
                .Order2 = 0, .FieldNum2 = "2", .Type2 = 0, \
                .DontSortHdr = 1
End Select
```

The following illustration shows a table before and after sorting by the preceding example.

Last	First
Quinn	Steve
Smith	Peter
Alicea	Juanita
Smith	Eileen
Alicea	Carlos

Last	First
Alicea	Carlos
Alicea	Juanita
Quinn	Steve
Smith	Eileen
Smith	Peter

A table before sorting ...   and after sorting.

See Also   **TableSortAToZ**, **TableSortZToA**

TableSortAToZ

Syntax   **TableSortAToZ**

Remarks   Sorts the paragraphs or table rows in the active document in ascending alphanumeric order. If the first paragraph or table row is a valid header record, it is not included in the sort. **TableSortAToZ** is intended for sorting mail-merge data sources.

See Also   **MailMergeEditDataSource**, **TableSort**, **TableSortZToA**

TableSortZToA

Syntax   **TableSortZToA**

Remarks   Sorts selected paragraphs or table rows in descending alphanumeric order. If the first paragraph or table row is a valid header record, it is not included in the sort. **TableSortZToA** is intended for sorting mail-merge data sources.

See Also   **MailMergeEditDataSource**, **TableSort**, **TableSortAToZ**

TableSplit

Syntax   **TableSplit**

Remarks   Inserts an empty paragraph above the current row in the table. In addition to splitting a table, you can use **TableSplit** to insert an empty paragraph above a table when the table is the first object in the document. If the insertion point or selection is not in a table, an error occurs.

Example   This example splits a table above the fourth row if the table contains more than three rows:

```
If SelInfo(15) > 3 Then
    StartOfColumn
    For i = 1 To 3
        TableSelectRow
        LineDown
    Next
    TableSplit
End If
```

See Also   **TableSplitCells**

TableSplitCells

Syntax   **TableSplitCells [.NumColumns = *text*]**

Remarks   Splits each selected table cell. Word generates an error if the selection or insertion point is not within a table.

Argument	Explanation
.NumColumns	Specifies the number of cells to split each selected table cell into. If omitted, Word splits each cell into two cells.

See Also   **TableMergeCells**, **TableSplit**

TableToText

Syntax   **TableToText [.ConvertTo =*number*]**

Remarks   Converts the selected rows to normal text. All the cells in the rows you want to convert must be selected; otherwise, an error occurs. The argument for the **TableToText** statement corresponds to the options in the Convert Table To Text dialog box (Table menu).

Argument	Explanation
.ConvertTo	Determines the character used to separate the contents of each cell:

0 (zero)   Paragraph marks

1 or omitted   Tab characters (each row ends with a paragraph mark)

2   Commas (each row ends with a paragraph mark)

3   Other (the character that appears in the Other box in the Convert Table To Text dialog box)

Example

This example converts the selected cells to a tabbed table:

```
TableToText
```

See Also

TableInsertTable, TextToTable

TableUpdateAutoFormat

Syntax

TableUpdateAutoFormat

Remarks

Updates the table containing the insertion point with the characteristics of a predefined table format. For example, if you apply a table format with **TableAutoFormat** and then insert rows and columns, the table may no longer match the predefined look. **TableUpdateAutoFormat** restores the format.

See Also

TableAutoFormat

TabType()

Syntax

TabType(*Pos***)**

Remarks

Returns the alignment of the custom or default tab stop at the position *Pos*, which is given in points (72 points = 1 inch). If more than one paragraph is selected, **TabType()** evaluates the setting in the first paragraph.

If there is no tab stop at the position *Pos*, **TabType()** returns –1. If there is a tab stop at *Pos*, **TabType()** returns one of the following values.

Value	Explanation
0 (zero)	Left-aligned or default
1	Centered
2	Right-aligned
3	Decimal
4	Bar

Example

This example determines whether a tab stop at the three-fourths–inch position is centered. If it is, the **FormatTabs** instruction changes the alignment to left alignment.

```
If TabType(54) = 1 Then
    FormatTabs .Position = "54 pt", .Align = 0
End If
```

See Also

FormatTabs, **NextTab()**, **PrevTab()**, **TabLeader$()**

Text

Syntax

Text *HorizPos*, *VertPos*, *Width*, *Height*, *Label$* [, *.Identifier*]

Remarks

Creates a text label in a custom dialog box. If you want to use the text control to define an access key for a list box or text box, the **Text** instruction must precede the instruction for the list box or text box control.

Although you cannot type multiple-line text labels in the Dialog Editor, you can size a text label to hold more than one line and use a variable for *Label$* that holds more than one line of text (use Chr$(13) to indicate a line break within a string).

Argument	Explanation
HorizPos, *VertPos*	The horizontal and vertical distance of the upper-left corner of the text control rectangle from the upper-left corner of the dialog box, in increments of 1/8 and 1/12 of the System font (Windows) or the dialog font (Macintosh).
Width, *Height*	The width and height of the rectangle, in increments of 1/8 and 1/12 of the System font (Windows) or the dialog font (Macintosh).
Label$	The label to display in the dialog box. An ampersand (&) precedes the character in *Label$* that is the access key for the control following the **Text** instruction. If *Label$* is longer than 255 characters, an error occurs.
.Identifier	An optional identifier used by statements in a dialog function that act on the text control. For example, you can use this identifier with **DlgText** to change *Label$* while the dialog box is displayed.

Examples

In this example, the **Text** instruction results in the label "Sample Text," which indicates that "S" is the access key for the text box defined in the next instruction.

```
Begin Dialog UserDialog 320, 84, "Sample Dialog Macro"
    Text 10, 6, 160, 12, "&Sample Text", .myTextControl
    TextBox 10, 21, 236, 18, .TextBox1
    OKButton 9, 58, 88, 21
    CancelButton 115, 58, 88, 21
End Dialog
```

The following example displays the first 255 characters of the current selection in the text label.

```
textlabel$ = Left$(Selection$(), 255)
Begin Dialog UserDialog 621, 251, "Show Selection Text"
    OKButton 409, 220, 88, 21
    CancelButton 509, 220, 88, 21
    Text 10, 6, 586, 203, textlabel$, .Text1
End Dialog
```

See Also   **Begin Dialog...End Dialog**, **TextBox**

TextBox

Syntax   **TextBox** *HorizPos*, *VertPos*, *Width*, *Height*, *.Identifier*[$] [, *MultiLine*]

Remarks   Creates a single-line or multiple-line text box into which the user can enter information in a custom dialog box. You can insert as many as 255 characters into a text box control.

Argument	Explanation
HorizPos, *VertPos*	The horizontal and vertical distance of the upper-left corner of the text box from the upper-left corner of the dialog box, in increments of 1/8 and 1/12 of the System font (Windows) or the dialog font (Macintosh).
Width, *Height*	The width and height of the text box, in increments of 1/8 and 1/12 of the System font (Windows) or the dialog font (Macintosh).
.Identifier [$]	Together with the dialog record name, *.Identifier*[$] creates a variable whose value corresponds to the text in the text box. The form for this variable is *DialogRecord.Identifier*[$] (for example, dlg.MyTextBox$). The dollar sign ($) is optional; you can use it to indicate that the variable is a string variable.
	The identifier string (*.Identifier*[$] minus the period) is also used by statements in a dialog function that act on the text box, such as **DlgEnable** and **DlgVisible**.
MultiLine	Specifies whether the text box is a single-line or multiple-line text box:
	0 (zero) Single-line text box
	1 Multiple-line text box
	In a multiple-line text box, the user can press ENTER or SHIFT+ENTER to begin new lines when typing text into the box. Note that multiple-line text boxes do not contain scroll bars; however, the user may scroll through text using the arrow keys. If the user presses ENTER or SHIFT+ENTER to begin a new line, the string returned by the identifier will contain a paragraph mark.

Example

In this example, text entered in the multiple-line text box created with the **TextBox** instruction is stored in the `dlg.TextBox1` variable:

```
Begin Dialog UserDialog 290, 152, "Sample Dialog Macro"
    Text 10, 6, 260, 12, "&Sample Text: Press ENTER"
    Text 10, 22, 143, 12, "to start a new line."
    TextBox 10, 43, 236, 64, .TextBox1, 1
    OKButton 10, 117, 88, 21
    CancelButton 117, 117, 88, 21
End Dialog
Dim dlg As UserDialog
Dialog dlg
```

See Also

Begin Dialog…End Dialog, **Text**

TextFormField

Syntax

TextFormField

Remarks

Inserts a text form field at the insertion point. **TextFormField** corresponds to the Text Form Field button on the Forms toolbar.

See Also

CheckBoxFormField, **DropDownFormField**, **InsertFormField**

TextToTable

Syntax

TextToTable [.ConvertFrom = *number*] [**, .NumColumns** = *number*]
[**, .NumRows** = *number*] [**, .InitialColWidth** = *number or text*]
[**, .Format** = *number*] [**, .Apply** = *number*]

Remarks

Converts the selected text to a table based on the separator character you specify. If you run **TextToTable** without any arguments, Word uses tab characters as the separator if there are no commas, or commas if there are no tab characters, or paragraph marks if there are no tab characters or commas, or if there is a mixture of tab characters and commas. The arguments for the **TextToTable** statement correspond to the options in the Convert Text To Table dialog box (Table menu).

Argument	Explanation
.ConvertFrom	Specifies the character that separates text elements:
	0 (zero) Paragraph marks
	1 Tab characters
	2 Commas
	3 Other (the character that appears in the Other box in the Convert Text To Table dialog box)
.NumColumns	The number of columns to create.

Argument	Explanation
.NumRows	The number of rows to create.
.InitialColWidth	The width of the columns in points or a text measurement. If omitted, column width is calculated so that the table stretches from margin to margin.
.Format	One of the predefined formats listed in the Table AutoFormat dialog box (Table menu): 0 (zero) corresponds to the first format listed in the Formats box ("none"), 1 corresponds to the second format, and so on.
.Apply	Specifies which attributes of the format specified by .Format to apply to the table. For a list of attributes and their values, see **TableInsertTable**.

See Also   **TableAutoFormat**, **TableInsertTable**, **TableToText**

Time$()

Syntax   **Time$([**SerialNumber**])**

Remarks   Returns a time corresponding to *SerialNumber*, a decimal representation of the date, time, or both. If *SerialNumber* is omitted, **Time$()** returns the current time. For information about serial numbers, see **DateSerial()**.

The time format is determined by the "TimeFormat=" line in the [Microsoft Word] section of WINWORD6.INI (Windows 3.*x*), Word Settings (6) (Macintosh), or the registry (Windows 95 and Windows NT). (In Windows 3.*x*, if there is no "TimeFormat=" line, **Time$()** uses the time settings in the [intl] section of WIN.INI.) Within a macro, you can use **SetPrivateProfileString** to change the current time format.

Example   When included at the end of a macro, this example displays a message box showing the time the macro finished running:

```
MsgBox "The macro finished at " + Time$()
```

See Also   **Date$()**, **DateSerial()**, **GetPrivateProfileString$()**, **Hour()**, **Minute()**, **Now()**, **Second()**, **SetPrivateProfileString**, **TimeSerial()**, **TimeValue()**

TimeSerial()

Syntax   **TimeSerial(**Hour**,** Minute**,** Second**)**

Remarks   Returns the serial number of the specified time. Because serial numbers are decimal numbers representing a number of days, **TimeSerial()** returns a decimal number from 0 to 0.99998842592593. For more information about serial numbers, see **DateSerial()**.

Argument	Explanation
Hour	A number between 0 and 23, inclusive, or a numeric expression
Minute	A number between 0 and 59, inclusive, representing the minutes after the hour, or a numeric expression
Second	A number between 0 and 59, inclusive, representing the seconds after the minute, or a numeric expression

Example

This example displays a message box with a decimal number corresponding to the fraction of the current day that has passed:

```
h = Hour(Now())
m = Minute(Now())
s = Second(Now())
fraction = TimeSerial(h, m, s)
MsgBox Left$(Str$(fraction), 5) + " of this day is over."
```

See Also

DateSerial(), **Day()**, **Month()**, **Now()**, **Time$()**, **TimeValue()**, **Today()**, **Year()**

TimeValue()

Syntax

TimeValue(*TimeText$*)

Remarks

Returns the serial number of the time represented by *TimeText$*. Use **TimeValue()** to convert a time represented by text to a serial number. A serial number is a decimal representation of the date, time, or both. For information about serial numbers, see **DateSerial()**.

Argument	Explanation
TimeText$	A string representing the time. For example, the following are each valid representations of 4:30 P.M.:
	16:30:00
	4:30 pm
	4:30 PM
	TimeText$ must represent a time between 00:00:00 and 23:59:59 on the 24-hour clock. **TimeValue()** generates an error if *TimeText$* is out of this range.

Example

This example displays the serial number for the current time in the status bar:

```
Print TimeValue(Time$())
```

See Also

DateSerial(), **DateValue()**, **Day()**, **Month()**, **Now()**, **Time$()**, **TimeSerial()**, **Today()**, **Year()**

TipWizard

Syntax   **TipWizard**

Remarks   Displays or hides the TipWizard toolbar. In Word version 6.0, **TipWizard** is unavailable and generates an error.

See Also   **AutomaticChange**, **Help**, **ShowMe**

Today()

Syntax   **Today()**

Remarks   Returns a serial number that represents the current date according to the computer's system date. Unlike **Now()**, which returns a serial number in which the digits after the decimal point represent the time as a fraction of a day, **Today()** returns strictly whole numbers. For more information about serial numbers, see **DateSerial()**.

Example   This example displays a message box stating the number of days until the new year. The number of days is calculated by subtracting the serial number for the current date from the serial number for January 1 of the following year.

```
yr = Year(Today())
rightNow = Today()
jan1 = DateSerial(yr + 1, 1, 1)
MsgBox "Days until the new year:" + Str$(jan1-rightNow)
```

See Also   **Date$()**, **DateSerial()**, **DateValue()**, **Day()**, **Month()**, **Now()**, **Time$()**, **TimeSerial()**, **TimeValue()**, **Year()**

ToggleFieldDisplay

Syntax   **ToggleFieldDisplay**

Remarks   Toggles the display of the fields in the selection between field codes and field results. If the selection does not contain at least one field, an error occurs. The exception to this rule is in page layout view, where **ToggleFieldDisplay** toggles the display of all fields.

Example   This example uses the **ViewFieldCodes** statement to change the display of all fields to field results, and then changes the display of fields in the current paragraph (selected using the predefined bookmark "\Para") back to field codes:

```
ViewFieldCodes 0
EditGoTo .Destination = "\Para"
ToggleFieldDisplay
```

See Also   **ViewFieldCodes**

ToggleFull

Syntax   **ToggleFull**

Remarks   Toggles full screen mode on and off.

See Also   **ToolsOptionsView**, **ViewToolbars**

ToggleHeaderFooterLink

Syntax   **ToggleHeaderFooterLink**

Remarks   If the current header or footer is not linked to the previous section, replaces the header or footer with the corresponding header or footer from the previous section and establishes a link. If the current header or footer is already linked, **ToggleHeaderFooterLink** breaks the link so you can modify the headers or footers independently. If the insertion point is not in a header or footer, an error occurs.

See Also   **FormatHeaderFooterLink**, **ShowNextHeaderFooter**, **ShowPrevHeaderFooter**, **ViewHeader**

ToggleMainTextLayer

Syntax   **ToggleMainTextLayer**

Remarks   Toggles the display of the main text layer when headers and footers are displayed. If headers and footers are not displayed, an error occurs.

See Also   **ViewHeader**

TogglePortrait

Syntax   **TogglePortrait**

Remarks   Switches the selected sections between portrait and landscape page orientations. If the selected sections have different page orientations, an error occurs.

See Also   **FilePageSetup**

ToggleScribbleMode

Syntax   **ToggleScribbleMode**

Remarks   In Windows, toggles hand annotation mode on and off. When you activate hand annotation mode, Word switches the active document to page layout view. This statement is for use with Windows for Pen Computing only. On the Macintosh, **ToggleScribbleMode** is not available and generates an error.

ToolbarButtonMacro$()

Syntax   **ToolbarButtonMacro$(***Toolbar$*, *Position* [, *Context*]**)**

Remarks   Returns the name of the built-in command, macro, font, AutoText entry, or style assigned to the specified toolbar button. If you specify a position that corresponds to a space, **ToolbarButtonMacro$()** returns an empty string ("").

Argument	Explanation
Toolbar$	The name of the toolbar as it appears in the Toolbars dialog box (View menu).
Position	A number corresponding to the position of the button on the specified toolbar, where 1 is the first position, 2 is the second position, and so on. Note that a list box or space counts as one position.
Context	Specifies the button for which to return the name:
	0 (zero) The button displayed on the toolbar when a document based on the Normal template is active.
	1 or omitted The button currently displayed on the toolbar.
	Note that the button displayed on the toolbar depends on the custom settings, if any, of the active template, any loaded global templates, and the Normal template.

Example   This example fills an array with the names of commands assigned to the Standard toolbar when a document based on the Normal template is active.

```
size = CountToolbarButtons("Standard", 0) - 1
Dim standardmacro$(size)
For i = 0 To size
    standardmacro$(i) = ToolbarButtonMacro$("Standard", i + 1, 0)
Next i
```

See Also   **CountToolbarButtons(), CountToolbars(), ToolbarName$()**

ToolbarName$()

Syntax   **ToolbarName$(***Toolbar* [, *Context*]**)**

Remarks   Returns the name of the specified toolbar as it appears in the Toolbars dialog box (View menu).

Argument	Explanation
Toolbar	A number in the range 1 to **CountToolbars()**, corresponding to the toolbar whose name you want to return
Context	Specifies the list of toolbars from which to return a name for *Toolbar*:

0 (zero)   The list of toolbars available to all documents, including those from loaded global templates

1 or omitted   The list of all toolbars currently available, including those available only to documents based on the active template

For an example, see **CountToolbars()**.

See Also   **CountToolbarButtons()**, **CountToolbars()**, **ToolbarButtonMacro$()**

ToolbarState()

Syntax   **ToolbarState(*Toolbar$*)**

Remarks   Returns −1 if the toolbar specified by *Toolbar$* is displayed and 0 (zero) if it is not.

Example   This example switches to page layout view if the Drawing toolbar is displayed.

```
If ToolbarState("Drawing") Then ViewPage
```

See Also   **ToolbarName$()**, **ViewRibbon**, **ViewRuler**, **ViewStatusBar**, **ViewToolbars**

ToolsAddRecordDefault

Syntax   **ToolsAddRecordDefault**

Remarks   Adds an empty record to the end of a data source. For example, **ToolsAddRecordDefault** adds an empty row to the bottom of a table in a Word document containing data for a mail merge. **ToolsAddRecordDefault** can be used with any document that could be used as a data source during a mail merge.

See Also   **MailMergeEditDataSource**, **ToolsRemoveRecordDefault**

ToolsAdvancedSettings

Syntax   **ToolsAdvancedSettings .Application** = *text*, **.Option** = *text* , **.Setting** = *text* [, **.Delete**] [, **.Set**]

Remarks

Changes settings in a settings file, such as WINWORD6.INI (Windows 3.*x*) or Word Settings (6) (Macintosh), or a private settings file. The arguments for **ToolsAdvancedSettings** correspond to the options in the Advanced Settings dialog box, which you can display by choosing Macro from the Tools menu and running the Word command **ToolsAdvancedSettings**. Note that in Windows 95 and Windows NT, settings are stored in the registry and you cannot use**ToolsAdvancedSettings** to change them.

Argument	Explanation
.Application	The name of a section in a settings file, as listed in the Categories box.
	Note that by following the section name with a space and the name of a settings file in parentheses, you can set a key in any settings file. In Windows for example, "Macro Settings (MY.INI)" specifies the [Macro Settings] section of the MY.INI file in the Windows folder. On the Macintosh, "Macro Settings (MY SETTINGS)" specifies the [Macro Settings] section of the MY SETTINGS file in SYSTEM FOLDER:PREFERENCES.
.Option	The key to set.
.Setting	The new setting.
.Delete	Deletes the key.
.Set	Sets the key.

For more information about changing settings in a settings file, see **SetPrivateProfileString**.

Example

This example sets the date format in the [Microsoft Word] section of the Word settings file:

```
ToolsAdvancedSettings .Application = "Microsoft Word", \
        .Option = "DateFormat", .Setting = "M/D/YYYY", .Set
```

See Also

GetPrivateProfileString$(), **GetProfileString$()**, **SetPrivateProfileString**, **SetProfileString**, **ToolsOptionsFileLocations**

ToolsAutoCorrect

Syntax

ToolsAutoCorrect [.InitialCaps = *number*] [**, .SentenceCaps** = *number*] [**, .Days** = *number*] [**, .CapsLock** = *number*] [**, .ReplaceText** = *number*] [**, .Formatting** = *number*] [**, .Replace** = *text*] [**, .With** = *text*] [**, .Add**] [**, .Delete**] [**, .SmartQuotes** = *number*]

Remarks

Sets AutoCorrect options. The arguments for the **ToolsAutoCorrect** statement correspond to the options in the AutoCorrect dialog box (Tools menu).

Argument	Explanation
.InitialCaps	If 1, Word corrects words in which the first two letters are capitalized. For example, "WOrd" becomes "Word."
.SentenceCaps	If 1, Word capitalizes the first letter of new sentences.
.Days	If 1, Word capitalizes the days of the week. For example, "tuesday" becomes "Tuesday."
.CapsLock	If 1, Word corrects typing with CAPS LOCK on.
.ReplaceText	If 1, activates automatic replacement of text.
.Formatting	If 1, formatting is stored with the replacement text when a replacement entry is added; available only if text is selected before running **ToolsAutoCorrect**.
.Replace	The text you want to replace automatically with the text specified by .With (for example, a person's initials).
.With	The text you want to insert automatically when the text specified by .Replace is typed (for example, a person's full name).
.Add	Adds the text specified by .Replace and .With to the list of replacement entries.
.Delete	Deletes the replacement entry specified by .Replace.
.SmartQuotes	If 1, Word inserts "smart" quotation marks (" " and ' ') and apostrophes (').

Example

This example adds a replacement entry and activates automatic replacement of text:

```
ToolsAutoCorrect .ReplaceText = 1, .Replace = "sr", \
        .With = "Stella Richards", .Add
```

See Also

ToolsAutoCorrectCapsLockOff, **ToolsAutoCorrectDays**, **ToolsAutoCorrectInitialCaps**, **ToolsAutoCorrectReplaceText**, **ToolsAutoCorrectSentenceCaps**, **ToolsAutoCorrectSmartQuotes**

ToolsAutoCorrectCapsLockOff, ToolsAutoCorrectCapsLockOff()

Syntax

ToolsAutoCorrectCapsLockOff [*On*]

ToolsAutoCorrectCapsLockOff()

The **ToolsAutoCorrectCapsLockOff** statement selects or clears the Correct Accidental Usage Of cAPS LOCK Key check box in the AutoCorrect dialog box (Tools menu). The **ToolsAutoCorrectCapsLockOff()** function returns information about the state of the check box. For information about arguments and return values, see **ToolsAutoCorrectDays**.

Remarks	In Word version 6.0, **ToolsAutoCorrectCapsLockOff** and **ToolsAutoCorrectCapsLockOff( )** are unavailable and generate errors.
See Also	**ToolsAutoCorrect**, **ToolsAutoCorrectInitialDays**

ToolsAutoCorrectDays, ToolsAutoCorrectDays()

Syntax	**ToolsAutoCorrectDays** [*On*]
	ToolsAutoCorrectDays( )
Remarks	The **ToolsAutoCorrectDays** statement selects or clears the Capitalize Names Of Days check box in the AutoCorrect dialog box (Tools menu).

Argument	Explanation
On	Specifies whether to select or clear the check box:
	1 Selects the check box.
	0 (zero) Clears the check box.
	Omitted Toggles the check box.

The **ToolsAutoCorrectDays( )** function returns the following values.

Value	Explanation
0 (zero)	If the Capitalize Names Of Days check box is cleared
–1	If the Capitalize Names Of Days check box is selected

See Also	**ToolsAutoCorrect**

ToolsAutoCorrectExceptions

Syntax	**ToolsAutoCorrectExceptions** [**.Tab** = *number*] [, **.Name** = *text*] [, **.AutoAdd** = *number*] [, **.Add**] [, **.Delete**]
Remarks	Adds words to or deletes words from the list of AutoCorrect exceptions. The arguments for the **ToolsAutoCorrectExceptions** statement correspond to the options in the AutoCorrect Exceptions dialog box (AutoCorrect command, Tools menu). In Word version 6.0, **ToolsAutoCorrectExceptions** is unavailable and generates an error.

Argument	Explanation
.Tab	The tab where the exception is added or deleted: 0 (zero) First Letter 1 INitial CAps
.Name	The exception list entry to be added or deleted.
.AutoAdd	If 1, Word adds to the list of exceptions any word that the user changes back to its original spelling or capitalization after it has been automatically corrected.
.Add	Adds .Name to the exception list specified by .Tab.
.Delete	Deletes .Name from the exception list specified by .Tab.

See Also   **CountAutoCorrectExceptions()**, **GetAutoCorrectException$()**,
IsAutoCorrectException()

ToolsAutoCorrectInitialCaps, ToolsAutoCorrectInitialCaps()

Syntax   **ToolsAutoCorrectInitialCaps** [*On*]

ToolsAutoCorrectInitialCaps()

Remarks   The **ToolsAutoCorrectInitialCaps** statement selects, clears, or toggles the
Correct TWo INitial CApitals check box in the AutoCorrect dialog box (Tools
menu). The **ToolsAutoCorrectInitialCaps()** function returns information about
the state of the check box. For information on arguments and return values, see
ToolsAutoCorrectDays.

See Also   **ToolsAutoCorrect**, **ToolsAutoCorrectDays**

ToolsAutoCorrectReplaceText, ToolsAutoCorrectReplaceText()

Syntax   **ToolsAutoCorrectReplaceText** [*On*]

ToolsAutoCorrectReplaceText()

Remarks   The **ToolsAutoCorrectReplaceText** statement selects, clears, or toggles the
Replace Text As You Type check box in the AutoCorrect dialog box (Tools
menu). The **ToolsAutoCorrectReplaceText()** function returns information about
the state of the check box. For information on arguments and return values, see
ToolsAutoCorrectDays.

See Also   **ToolsAutoCorrect**, **ToolsAutoCorrectDays**

ToolsAutoCorrectSentenceCaps, ToolsAutoCorrectSentenceCaps()

Syntax   ToolsAutoCorrectSentenceCaps [*On*]

ToolsAutoCorrectSentenceCaps()

Remarks   The **ToolsAutoCorrectSentenceCaps** statement selects, clears, or toggles the Capitalize First Letter Of Sentences check box in the AutoCorrect dialog box (Tools menu). The **ToolsAutoCorrectSentenceCaps()** function returns information about the state of the check box. For information on arguments and return values, see **ToolsAutoCorrectDays**.

See Also   **ToolsAutoCorrect, ToolsAutoCorrectDays**

ToolsAutoCorrectSmartQuotes, ToolsAutoCorrectSmartQuotes()

Syntax   ToolsAutoCorrectSmartQuotes [*On*]

ToolsAutoCorrectSmartQuotes()

Remarks   The **ToolsAutoCorrectSmartQuotes** statement selects, clears, or toggles the Change 'Straight Quotes' To 'Smart Quotes' check box in the AutoCorrect dialog box (Tools menu). The **ToolsAutoCorrectSmartQuotes()** function returns information about the state of the check box. For information on arguments and return values, see **ToolsAutoCorrectDays**.

See Also   **ToolsAutoCorrect, ToolsAutoCorrectDays**

ToolsBulletListDefault

Syntax   **ToolsBulletListDefault**

Remarks   Adds bullets and tab characters to the selected paragraphs and formats the paragraphs with a hanging indent. Bullets are inserted as SYMBOL fields.

Note The **ToolsBulletListDefault** statement corresponds to the Bulleted List button on the Toolbar in Word for Windows version 2.*x*. In Word version 6.0, the Bullets button is on the Formatting toolbar and its corresponding WordBasic statement is **FormatBulletDefault**.

See Also   **FormatBulletDefault, FormatBulletsAndNumbering, FormatNumberDefault, ToolsBulletsNumbers, ToolsNumberListDefault**

ToolsBulletsNumbers

Syntax

ToolsBulletsNumbers [**.Replace** = *number*] [, **.Font** = *text*] [, **.CharNum** = *text*]
[, **.Type** = *number*] [, **.FormatOutline** = *text*] [, **.AutoUpdate** = *number*]
[, **.FormatNumber** = *number*] [, **.Punctuation** = *text*] [, **.StartAt** = *text*]
[, **.Points** = *number or text*] [, **.Hang** = *number*] [, **.Indent** = *number or text*]
[, **.Remove**]

Remarks

Sets formats for bulleted, numbered, and outline-numbered paragraphs. This
statement is included for compatibility with the previous version of Word for
Windows; the arguments for **ToolsBulletsNumbers** correspond to the options in
the Bullets And Numbering dialog box (Tools menu) in Word for Windows
version 2.*x*. Not every argument applies to each type of list.

Argument	Explanation
.Replace	If 1, Word updates bullets only for paragraphs that are already bulleted, or updates numbers only for paragraphs that are already numbered.
.Font	The font for the numbers or the bullet character in a list.
.CharNum	The character or ANSI code for the character to use as the bullet. Bullets are inserted as SYMBOL fields.
.Type	The type of list to create: 0 (zero) Bulleted list 1 Numbered list 2 Outline-numbered list
.FormatOutline	A format for numbering outlines. The available formats are Legal, Outline, Sequence, Learn, and Outline All. The Learn format applies a format based on the first number for each level in the selection.
.AutoUpdate	If 1, numbers are inserted as fields that update automatically when the sequence of paragraphs changes.
.FormatNumber	Specifies a format for numbering lists: 0 (zero) 1, 2, 3, 4 1 I, II, III, IV 2 i, ii, iii, iv 3 A, B, C, D 4 a, b, c, d
.Punctuation	The separator character or characters for numbers in a list. If you specify one character, it follows each number; if you specify two characters, they enclose each number.
.StartAt	The starting number or letter for the list.

Argument	Explanation
.Points	The size of the bullet character, in points, in a bulleted list.
.Hang	If 1, sets a hanging indent for the list.
.Indent	If .Hang is set to 1, the width of the left indent in points or a text measurement.
.Remove	Removes existing bullets or numbers.

Example

This example formats the selection as a bulleted list, with the bullet defined as character code 183 in the Symbol font, at 10 points in size:

```
ToolsBulletsNumbers .Font = "Symbol", .CharNum = "183", .Type = 0, \
    .Points = 10, .Hang = 1, .Indent = "0.25 in", .Replace = 0
```

See Also

FormatBulletDefault, **FormatBulletsAndNumbering**, **FormatNumberDefault**, **ToolsBulletListDefault**, **ToolsNumberListDefault**

ToolsCalculate, ToolsCalculate()

Syntax

ToolsCalculate

ToolsCalculate([*Expression$*])

Remarks

The **ToolsCalculate** statement evaluates the selection as a mathematical expression, and then displays the result in the status bar. The result is also placed on the Clipboard.

If *Expression$* is not specified, the **ToolsCalculate**() function acts just like the statement except that it returns the result instead of displaying it in the status bar and placing it on the Clipboard. If you do specify *Expression$*, it is evaluated as a mathematical expression; *Expression$* can include bookmark names and simple cell references (such as a5).

Example

In this example, the **ToolsCalculate**() function adds values from two table cells and returns the result in the variable total. The insertion point must be within the table containing the values.

```
total = ToolsCalculate("a5 + b5")
```

See Also

TableAutoSum, **TableFormula**

ToolsCompareVersions

Syntax

ToolsCompareVersions .Name = *text*

Remarks

Displays revision marks indicating where the active document differs from the specified document. **ToolsCompareVersions** corresponds to the Compare Versions dialog box (Revisions command, Tools menu).

Argument	Explanation
.Name	The name of the document to which the active document is compared; include a path if the document is not in the current folder.

Example

This example compares the active document to C:\DRAFT\REV1DOC.DOC. On the Macintosh, substitute a path such as HD:DRAFT:FIRST REV.

```
ToolsCompareVersions .Name = "C:\DRAFT\REV1DOC.DOC"
```

See Also   **ToolsOptionsRevisions**, **ToolsRevisions**

ToolsCreateEnvelope

Syntax

ToolsCreateEnvelope [.ExtractAddress = *number*] [, **.EnvAddress** = *text*]
[, **.EnvOmitReturn** = *number*] [, **.EnvReturn** = *text*]
[, **.PrintBarCode** = *number*] [, **.EnvWidth** = *number or text*]
[, **.EnvHeight** = *number or text*] [, **.EnvPaperSize** = *number*]
[, **.PrintFIMA** = *number*] [, **.LabelAutoText** = *text*] [, **.UseEnvFeeder** = *number*]
[, **.AddrFromLeft** = *number or text*] [, **.AddrFromTop** = *number or text*]
[, **.RetAddrFromLeft** = *number or text*] [, **.RetAddrFromTop** = *number or text*]
[, **.PrintEnvLabel**] [, **.AddToDocument**]

Remarks

Creates an envelope that is printed with the active document. The arguments for the **ToolsCreateEnvelope** statement correspond to the options on the Envelopes tab in the Envelopes And Labels dialog box (Tools menu). To specify address formatting, use **FormatAddrFonts** and **FormatRetAddrFonts**.

Argument	Explanation
.ExtractAddress	Specifies whether or not to use the text marked by the "EnvelopeAddress" bookmark (a user-defined bookmark) as the recipient's address:
	0 (zero) The "EnvelopeAddress" bookmark is not used.
	1 The "EnvelopeAddress" bookmark is used.
.EnvAddress	Text specifying the recipient's address (ignored if .ExtractAddress is specified).
.EnvOmitReturn	Specifies whether or not to omit the return address:
	0 The return address is not omitted.
	1 The return address is omitted.
.EnvReturn	Text specifying the return address.
.PrintBarCode	Specifies whether or not to add a POSTNET bar code: 1 adds the bar code, 0 (zero) does not. For U.S. mail only.

Argument	Explanation
.EnvWidth, .EnvHeight	The width and height of the envelope, in points or a text measurement, when .EnvPaperSize corresponds to Custom Size.
.EnvPaperSize	Corresponds to a size in the Envelope Size box in the Envelope Options dialog box: 0 (zero) corresponds to the first size, 1 to the second size, and so on.
.PrintFIMA	Specifies whether or not to add a Facing Identification Mark (FIM A) for use in presorting courtesy reply mail: 1 adds the FIM A, 0 (zero) does not. For U.S. mail only.
.LabelAutoText	The name of an AutoText entry in which the address fields for a data source are stored (only recorded when creating envelopes in a mail merge).
.UseEnvFeeder	A number corresponding to the envelope source listed in the Feed From box: 0 (zero) corresponds to the first source, 1 to the second source, and so on.
.AddrFromLeft	The distance, in the current default unit or a text measurement, between the left edge of the envelope and the recipient's address.
.AddrFromTop	The distance, in the current default unit or a text measurement, between the top edge of the envelope and the recipient's address.
.RetAddrFromLeft	The distance, in the current default unit or a text measurement, between the left edge of the envelope and the return address.
.RetAddrFromTop	The distance, in the current default unit or a text measurement, between the top edge of the envelope and the return address.
.PrintEnvLabel	Prints the envelope.
.AddToDocument	Adds a section with the recipient's address and the return address to the beginning of the document.

Example

This example adds an envelope to the active document with addresses specified in the variables to$ and from$. The recipient's address is bold.

```
rtn$ = Chr$(13)
to$ = "Jane Doe"  + rtn$ + "123 Skye St." + \
        rtn$ + "OurTown, WA 98107"
from$ = "John Doe" + rtn$ + "456 Erde Lane" + \
        rtn$ + "OurTown, WA 98107"
FormatAddrFonts .Bold = 1
ToolsCreateEnvelope .EnvAddress = to$, .EnvReturn = from$, \
        .AddToDocument
```

See Also

FormatAddrFonts, FormatRetAddrFonts, ToolsCreateLabels

ToolsCreateLabels

Syntax

ToolsCreateLabels [**.ExtractAddress** = *number*] [, **.LabelListIndex** = *number*]
[, **.LabelIndex** = *number*] [, **.LabelDotMatrix** = *number*]
[, **.LabelTray** = *number*] [, **.LabelAcross** = *number*] [, **.LabelDown** = *number*]
[, **.SingleLabel** = *number*] [, **.LabelRow** = *number*] [, **.LabelColumn** = *number*]
[, **.LabelAutoText** = *text*] [, **.LabelText** = *text*] [, **.PrintEnvLabel**]
[, **.AddToDocument**] [, **.LabelTopMargin** = *number or text*]
[, **.LabelSideMargin** = *number or text*] [, **.LabelVertPitch** = *number or text*]
[, **.LabelHorPitch** = *number or text*] [, **.LabelHeight** = *number or text*]
[, **.LabelWidth** = *number or text*]

Remarks

Creates a label or a sheet of labels that is printed with the active document. The
arguments for the **ToolsCreateLabels** statement correspond to the options on the
Labels tab in the Envelopes And Labels dialog box (Tools menu).

Argument	Explanation
.ExtractAddress	Specifies whether or not to use the text marked by the "EnvelopeAddress" bookmark (a user-defined bookmark) as the label text:
	0 (zero) The "EnvelopeAddress" bookmark is not used.
	1 The "EnvelopeAddress" bookmark is used.
.LabelListIndex	For dot matrix printers, the values are:
	1 Avery® Standard
	3 Avery Intl (UK)
	4 Avery Intl (France)
	6 CoStar LabelWriter
	For laser printers, the values are:
	0 (zero) Avery Standard
	2 Avery Pan European
	5 Other
.LabelIndex	Corresponds to an item in the Product Number box in the Label Options dialog box: 0 (zero) corresponds to the first item, 1 to the second item, and so on.
.LabelDotMatrix	Specifies the kind of printer:
	0 (zero) Laser
	1 Dot matrix
.LabelTray	Corresponds to a tray listed in the Tray list box in the Label Options dialog box: 0 (zero) corresponds to the first tray in the list, 1 to the second, and so on. Available only if .LabelDotMatrix is set to 0 (zero).

Argument	Explanation
.SingleLabel	If 1, allows you to print a single label on a page of labels by specifying .LabelRow and .LabelColumn.
.LabelRow	If .SingleLabel is set to 1, the row containing the label you want to print.
.LabelColumn	If .SingleLabel is set to 1, the column containing the label you want to print.
.LabelAutoText	The name of an AutoText entry in which the label text is stored (ignored if .ExtractAddress is specified).
.LabelText	The text to print on the labels (ignored if .ExtractAddress or .LabelAutoText is specified).
.PrintEnvLabel	Prints the labels.
.AddToDocument	Creates a new document with label text ready for printing.

The following arguments are for creating custom labels and need not be specified (and are ignored) if the combination of .LabelListIndex, .LabelIndex, and .LabelDotMatrix specifies valid labels.

Argument	Explanation
.LabelAcross	The number of labels in a row
.LabelDown	The number of labels in a column
.LabelTopMargin	The width of the top margin on the page of labels, in the current default unit or a text measurement
.LabelSideMargin	The width of the side margins on the page of labels, in the current default unit or a text measurement
.LabelVertPitch	The distance from the top of one label to the top of the next label down, in the current default unit or a text measurement
.LabelHorPitch	The distance from the left edge of one label to the left edge of the next label across, in the current default unit or a text measurement
.LabelHeight	The height of the labels, in the current default unit or a text measurement.
.LabelWidth	The width of the labels, in the current default unit or a text measurement.

Example

This example creates a new document with label text arranged for printing onto a sheet of Avery labels. The argument .LabelListIndex = 0 specifies Avery Standard as the label product, and .LabelIndex = 4 specifies product number 5160 (for addresses). The label text is retrieved from the AutoText entry "MyLabelAddress."

```
ToolsCreateLabels .LabelListIndex = 0, .LabelIndex = 10, \
    .LabelDotMatrix = 0, .LabelTray = 1, .AddToDocument, \
    .LabelAutoText = "MyLabelAddress"
```

See Also

ToolsCreateEnvelope

ToolsCustomize

Syntax

ToolsCustomize [**.Tab** = *number*]

Remarks

Displays the Customize dialog box (Tools menu) with the specified tab selected.

Argument	Explanation
.Tab	The tab to select:
	0 (zero) Toolbars
	1 Menus
	2 Keyboard

See Also

AddButton, ToolsCustomizeKeyboard, ToolsCustomizeMenuBar, ToolsCustomizeMenus

ToolsCustomizeKeyboard

Syntax

ToolsCustomizeKeyboard [**.KeyCode** = *number*] [, **.KeyCode2** = *number*] [, **.Category** = *number*] [, **.Name** = *text*] [, **.Add**] [, **.Remove**] [, **.ResetAll**] [, **.CommandValue** = *text*] [, **.Context** = *number*]

Remarks

Assigns and reassigns shortcut keys to built-in commands, macros, fonts, AutoText entries, styles, or common symbols. The arguments for the **ToolsCustomizeKeyboard** statement correspond to the options on the Keyboard tab in the Customize dialog box (Tools menu).

Argument	Explanation
.KeyCode	A number representing the key combination, as listed later in this entry.
.KeyCode2	A number representing the second key combination in a key sequence. For example, to assign the key sequence CTRL+S, 1 (on the Macintosh, COMMAND+S, 1) to the Heading 1 style, you set .KeyCode to 339 (for CTRL+S or COMMAND+S) and .KeyCode2 to 49 (for 1).
.Category	Specifies the kind of item to assign a shortcut key:
	1 or omitted Built-in commands
	2 Macros
	3 Fonts
	4 AutoText entries
	5 Styles
	6 Common symbols

Argument	Explanation
.Name	The name of the command, macro, or other item. If .Category is set to 6, you can specify a symbol by typing or pasting it into the macro-editing window or using a **Chr$()** instruction such as Chr$(167).
.Add	Adds the key assignment or assignments to the specified item.
.Remove	If the specified key code is currently assigned, removes the assignment such that the associated key combination has no effect. If the specified key code is not assigned, .Remove resets the key code to its default action. Note that specifying .Name is not required when removing or resetting a key assignment.
.ResetAll	Resets all key assignments to their defaults.
.CommandValue	Additional text required for the command specified by .Name, if any. For example, if .Name is set to Color, .CommandValue specifies the color. For more information, see the table of settings for .CommandValue in **ToolsCustomizeMenus**.
.Context	Determines where new key assignments are stored: 0 (zero) or omitted Normal template 1 Active template

The following tables list the values you need to specify the appropriate number for .KeyCode. The first table contains values you add to values in the second table when specifying a key combination (for example, you would specify CTRL+S (on the Macintosh, COMMAND+S) as the sum of 256 and 83, or 339).

Add this	To combine with this key
256	CTRL (Windows) or COMMAND (Macintosh)
512	SHIFT
1024	ALT (Windows) or OPTION (Macintosh)
2048	CONTROL (Macintosh)

In Windows, function keys F11 through F16 are equivalent to ALT+F1 through ALT+F6. Therefore, the key code corresponding to F11 has the same effect as a key code corresponding to ALT+F1. Similarly, specifying ALT+F11—effectively ALT+ALT+F1—is no different from specifying ALT+F1.

This key code	Corresponds to
8	BACKSPACE
9	TAB
12	5 on the numeric keypad when Num Lock is off
13	ENTER
19	PAUSE

This key code	Corresponds to
27	ESC
32	SPACEBAR
33	PAGE UP
34	PAGE DOWN
35	END
36	HOME
45	INS
46	DEL
48	0
49	1
50	2
51	3
52	4
53	5
54	6
55	7
56	8
57	9
65	A
66	B
67	C
68	D
69	E
70	F
71	G
72	H
73	I
74	J
75	K
76	L
77	M
78	N
79	O
80	P

This key code	Corresponds to
81	Q
82	R
83	S
84	T
85	U
86	V
87	W
88	X
89	Y
90	Z
96	0 on the numeric keypad
97	1 on the numeric keypad
98	2 on the numeric keypad
99	3 on the numeric keypad
100	4 on the numeric keypad
101	5 on the numeric keypad
102	6 on the numeric keypad
103	7 on the numeric keypad
104	8 on the numeric keypad
105	9 on the numeric keypad
106	* on the numeric keypad
107	+ on the numeric keypad
109	− on the numeric keypad
110	. on the numeric keypad
111	/ on the numeric keypad
112	F1
113	F2
114	F3
115	F4
116	F5
117	F6
118	F7
119	F8
120	F9

This key code	Corresponds to
121	F10
122	F11
123	F12
124	F13
125	F14
126	F15
127	F16
145	SCROLL LOCK
186	;
187	=
188	,
189	-
190	.
191	/
192	`
219	[
220	\
221	]
222	'

Examples

This example assigns CTRL+SHIFT+F (Windows) or COMMAND+SHIFT+F (Macintosh) to **FileFind**:

```
ToolsCustomizeKeyboard .Category = 1, .Name = "FileFind", \
    .KeyCode = 838, .Add
```

The following example removes the key assignment from **FileFind**:

```
ToolsCustomizeKeyboard .Category = 1, .Name = "FileFind", \
    .KeyCode = 838, .Remove
```

See Also

CountKeys( ), **KeyCode( )**, **KeyMacro$( )**

ToolsCustomizeMenuBar

Syntax

ToolsCustomizeMenuBar [**.Context** = *number*] [**, .Position** = *number*]
[**, .MenuType** = *number*] [**, .MenuText** = *text*] [**, .Menu** = *text*] [**, .Add**]
[**, .Remove**] [**, .Rename**]

Remarks

Adds, removes, or renames menus on the menu bar. Arguments for the
ToolsCustomizeMenuBar statement correspond to options in the Menu Bar
dialog box (Menus tab, Customize command, Tools menu).

Argument	Explanation
.Context	Determines where the menu change is stored:
	0 (zero) or omitted Normal template
	1 Active template
.Position	Specifies where to add a new menu: 0 (zero) corresponds to the first (leftmost) position, 1 to the second, and so on. To add a menu to the rightmost position, set .Position to –1.
.MenuType	Specifies which menu bar to change:
	0 or omitted The menu bar when a document is open
	1 The menu bar when no document is open
.MenuText	A new name for the menu; used with .Add and .Rename. Place an ampersand (&) in front of the access key, if any. Note that a menu bar can have only one menu of a given name (irrespective of ampersands).
.Menu	The name of the menu you want to change; used with .Rename and .Remove. Including an ampersand (&) before the access key in the menu name is optional (for example, you can specify either "File" or "&File").
.Add	Adds the menu specified by .MenuText to the menu bar.
.Remove	Removes the specified menu.
.Rename	Renames the specified menu.

If you do not specify .Add, .Remove, or .Rename, Word adds the menu.

To reset menu bars, use the .ResetAll argument with **ToolsCustomizeMenus**.
Note that this resets all menu assignments to their defaults.

Example

This example adds a new menu named Macros to the right of the Help menu
(Windows) or Window menu (Macintosh):

```
ToolsCustomizeMenuBar .MenuText = "&Macros", .Add, .Position = -1
```

See Also

ToolsCustomizeMenus

ToolsCustomizeMenus

Syntax   **ToolsCustomizeMenus** [**.MenuType** = *number*] [, **.Position** = *number*]
[, **.Category** = *number*] [, **.Name** = *text*] [, **.Menu** = *text*] [, **.AddBelow** = *text*]
[, **.MenuText** = *text*] [, **.Rename**] [, **.Add**] [, **.Remove**] [, **.ResetAll**]
[, **.CommandValue** = *text*] [, **.Context** = *number*]

Remarks   Changes menu assignments for built-in commands, macros, fonts, AutoText
entries, and styles. The arguments for the **ToolsCustomizeMenus** statement
correspond to the options on the Menus tab in the Customize dialog box (Tools
menu).

Argument	Explanation
.MenuType	The type of menu you want to modify:
	0 or omitted Menus on the menu bar when a document is open
	1 Menus on the menu bar when no document is open
	2 Shortcut menus
.Position	The position on the menu where you want to add or remove an item:
	−1 or omitted Automatically determines an appropriate position for adding the item.
	−2 Adds the item to the bottom of the menu.
	n Adds, removes, or renames the item at the specified position, where 1 is the first position, 2 is the second position, and so on. When adding an item, if *n* is greater than the number of existing menu items plus one, the item is added to the bottom of the menu.
	Note that separators are considered items and that in some cases, a set of menu items is counted as one. For more information, see CountMenuItems( ).
.Category	The type of item to be assigned:
	1 or omitted Built-in commands
	2 Macros
	3 Fonts
	4 AutoText entries
	5 Styles

Argument	Explanation
.Name	The name of the built-in command, macro, font, AutoText entry, or style whose menu assignment you want to change. When adding or removing a separator, specify "(Separator)."
.Menu	The menu you want to change. Menu names are listed in the Change What Menu list box.
	Including an ampersand (&) before the access key in the menu name is optional (for example, you can specify either "File" or "&File"). Do not include the parenthetical phrases "(No Document)" and "(Shortcut)" even though that text appears in the Customize dialog box.
.AddBelow	The text of or command name associated with the menu item after which you want to add the new item.
	Note that you do not need to specify this argument if you specify .Position. If you specify both arguments, .AddBelow takes precedence.
.MenuText	The text as it will appear on the menu. Place an ampersand (&) in front of the access key, if any. On the Macintosh, access keys are displayed only in menu mode, which is activated by pressing the DECIMAL (.) key on the numeric keypad (Num Lock off).
	If you want an ampersand to appear in the menu text, include two ampersands. For example, setting .MenuText to "&Examples && Practices" creates the menu item "Examples & Practices."
.Rename	Renames the menu item specified by .Menu and .Name (and .Position, if specified), with the text specified by .MenuText.
.Add	Adds the item to the menu.
.Remove	Removes the item from the menu.
.ResetAll	Resets all menu assignments to their defaults. Note that this argument resets changes made with **ToolsCustomizeMenuBar** as well as **ToolsCustomizeMenus**.
.CommandValue	Additional text required for the command specified by .Name, if any. For example, if .Name is set to Color, .CommandValue specifies the color. For more information, see the next table in this entry.
.Context	Determines where the new menu assignment is stored:
	0 (zero) or omitted Normal template
	1 Active template

When removing or renaming menu items, you must specify .Name and .Menu. Word starts at the bottom of the specified menu and moves up until it finds an item that performs the action specified by .Name. You can also specify .Position and .MenuText if you need to be sure that the menu item you are changing is at a specific position and has specific menu text. Note that if Word can't find an item that matches each of the specified criteria, an error occurs.

The following table lists in the left column commands that require a command value and describes in the right column how to specify .CommandValue. The equivalent action in the Customize dialog box (Tools menu) to specifying .CommandValue is selecting an item in the list box that appears when you select one of the following commands in the Commands box.

If .Name is set to	.CommandValue must be
Borders, Color, or Shading	A number—specified as text—corresponding to the position of the setting in the list box containing values, where 0 (zero) is the first item, 1 is the second item, and so on.
Columns	A number between 1 and 45—specified as text—corresponding to the number of columns you want to apply.
Condensed	A text measurement between 0.1 pt and 12.75 pt specified in 0.05-point increments (72 points = 1 inch).
Expanded	A text measurement between 0.1 pt and 12.75 pt specified in 0.05-point increments (72 points = 1 inch).
FileOpenFile	The path and filename of the file to open. If the path is not specified, the current folder is assumed.
Font Size	A positive text measurement, specified in 0.5-point increments (72 points = 1 inch).
Lowered, Raised	A text measurement between 1 pt and 64 pt specified in 0.5-point increments (72 points = 1 inch).
Symbol	A string created by concatenating a **Chr$()** instruction and the name of a symbol font (for example, Chr$(167) + "Symbol").

Example

This example adds the macro TestMacro to the Help menu. The menu item for this macro is Test, which appears immediately after Index. Because .AddBelow is specified, .Position is not required.

```
ToolsCustomizeMenus .Category = 2, .Name = "TestMacro", \
        .MenuType = 0, .Menu = "Help", .MenuText = "&Test", \
        .AddBelow = "Index", .Context = 0, .Add
```

See Also

CountMenuItems(), **MenuItemMacro$()**, **MenuText$()**, **ToolsCustomizeMenuBar**

ToolsGetSpelling, ToolsGetSpelling()

Syntax

ToolsGetSpelling *FillArray$*() [, *Word$*] [, *MainDic$*] [, *SuppDic$*] [, *Mode*]

ToolsGetSpelling(*FillArray$*() [, *Word$*] [, *MainDic$*] [, *SuppDic$*] [, *Mode*])

Remarks

The **ToolsGetSpelling** statement fills an array with the words suggested as replacements for a misspelled word. Suggestions are assigned to elements of the array in the order they appear in the spelling checker.

Argument	Explanation
FillArray$	The array—which must be defined before **ToolsGetSpelling** is run—to fill with suggested replacements.
Word$	The word for which you want suggested replacements. If *Word$* is omitted, Word uses the word closest to the insertion point.
MainDic$	A text string that represents the language name for the main dictionary in the specified language. For a list of valid foreign language names, see **ToolsLanguage**. If you specify neither a word nor a main dictionary, Word uses the main dictionary that corresponds to the language formatting of the word closest to the insertion point.
SuppDic$	A path and filename for a custom dictionary (for example, "C:\WINWORD\USER1.DIC" (Windows) or "HD:WORD:MY TERMS" (Macintosh)). If *Word$* is found in the custom dictionary, **ToolsGetSpelling** puts no words in the array. If .SuggestFromMainDictOnly (**ToolsOptionsSpelling** statement) is 0 (zero), suggested replacements are retrieved from the custom dictionary as well as the main dictionary. Note that anagrams are retrieved from the main dictionary only.
Mode	Specifies how Word makes suggestions for *Word$*:
	0 or omitted Returns suggested correct spellings for *Word$*.
	1 Returns suggested replacements that match the search criteria when *Word$* contains the question mark (?) and asterisk (*) wildcard characters.
	2 Returns anagrams for *Word$* (words composed of the same letters as *Word$*). Word does not return anagrams from a custom dictionary. Note that this functionality may not be available if you are using a spelling checker other than the one shipped with Word.

The **ToolsGetSpelling**() function returns the number of replacements suggested by the spelling checker. If the word is spelled correctly, 0 (zero) is returned.

Example   This example checks the spelling of the word "kolor," and then displays up to five
                     suggested replacements in a series of message boxes:

```
Dim suggest$(4)
ToolsGetSpelling suggest$(), "kolor"
For count = 0 To 4
    If suggest$(count) <> "" Then MsgBox suggest$(count)
Next
```

See Also   **ToolsGetSynonyms**, **ToolsLanguage**, **ToolsOptionsSpelling**

ToolsGetSynonyms, ToolsGetSynonyms()

Syntax   **ToolsGetSynonyms** *FillArray$*() [, *Word$*] [, *MainDic$*]

                     ToolsGetSynonyms(*FillArray$*() [, *Word$*] [, *MainDic$*])

Remarks   The **ToolsGetSynonyms** statement fills an array with synonyms for a word.

Argument	Explanation
FillArray$	The array—which must be defined before **ToolsGetSynonyms** is run—to fill with synonyms.
Word$	The word for which you want synonyms. If *Word$* is omitted, Word uses the word closest to the insertion point.
MainDic$	A text string that represents the language name for the main dictionary in the specified language. For a list of valid foreign language names, see **ToolsLanguage**. If you specify neither a word nor a main dictionary, Word uses the main dictionary that corresponds to the language formatting of the word closest to the insertion point.

The **ToolsGetSynonyms**() function returns the following values.

Value	Explanation
0 (zero)	If there are no synonyms available
−1	If one or more synonyms are available

Example

This example prompts the user for a word, and then displays up to five synonyms for that word in a message box:

```
word$ = InputBox$("Display synonyms for: ", "Get Synonyms")
Dim synonyms$(4)
ToolsGetSynonyms synonyms$(), word$
list$ = synonyms$(0)
For count = 1 To 4
    If synonyms$(count) <> "" Then
        list$ = list$ + ", " + synonyms$(count)
    End If
Next
MsgBox list$, "Synonyms for " + word$
```

See Also

ToolsGetSpelling

ToolsGrammar

Syntax

ToolsGrammar

Remarks

Displays the Grammar dialog box (Tools menu) and begins checking grammar in the active document.

Example

This example displays a message box that asks whether or not to check grammar. If the user chooses the Yes button (returning a value of –1), Word begins checking grammar.

```
ans = MsgBox("Check grammar now?", 3)
If ans = -1 Then ToolsGrammar
```

See Also

ToolsSpelling

ToolsGrammarStatisticsArray

Syntax

ToolsGrammarStatisticsArray *TwoDimensionalArray$( )*

Remarks

Performs a grammar check, and then fills a two-dimensional array with the available grammar statistics for the active document.

Argument	Explanation
TwoDimensionalArray$( )	The two-dimensional array—which must be defined before **ToolsGrammarStatisticsArray** is run—to fill with the names of counts, averages, and indexes (the first dimension) and their associated statistics (the second dimension).

Example

This example defines a two-dimensional array for storing grammar statistics, fills the array with grammar statistics for the active document, and then inserts a two-column list of statistics at the insertion point (names of counts, averages, and indexes on the left and their associated statistics on the right, separated by tab characters):

```
numstats = CountToolsGrammarStatistics()
size = numstats -1
Dim docstats$(size, 1)
ToolsGrammarStatisticsArray docstats$()
For count = 0 To size
    InsertPara
    Insert docstats$(count, 0) + Chr$(9) + docstats$(count, 1)
Next
```

See Also   **CountToolsGrammarStatistics()**

ToolsHyphenation

Syntax   **ToolsHyphenation** [**.AutoHyphenation** = *number*] [**.HyphenateCaps** = *number*]
[, **.HyphenationZone** = *number or text*]
[, **.LimitConsecutiveHyphens** = *number*]

Remarks   Hyphenates the selected text or the entire document. The arguments for the **ToolsHyphenation** statement correspond to the options in the Hyphenation dialog box (Tools menu).

Argument	Explanation
.AutoHyphenation	If 1, hyphenates without prompting for verification.
.HyphenateCaps	If 1, allows hyphenation of words in all capital letters.
.HyphenationZone	A measurement for the hyphenation zone in points or a text measurement. The hyphenation zone is the maximum amount of space to allow between the end of a line and the right margin.
.LimitConsecutiveHyphens	The maximum number of consecutive lines that can end with hyphens (or 0 (zero) for No Limit).

Example   This example begins hyphenation, allowing hyphenation of words in all capital letters and setting a hyphenation zone of 24 points:

```
ToolsHyphenation .AutoHyphenation = 1, .HyphenateCaps = 1, \
        .HyphenationZone = "24 pt"
```

See Also   **ToolsHyphenationManual**

ToolsHyphenationManual

Syntax   **ToolsHyphenationManual**

Remarks   Hyphenates the document, displaying the Manual Hyphenation dialog box
(Manual button, Hyphenation dialog box, Tools menu) each time Word proposes
that a word be hyphenated so the user can manually adjust the placement of
hyphens. To set hyphenation options before running **ToolsHyphenationManual**,
use the **ToolsHyphenation** statement and set .AutoHyphenation to 0 (zero).

Example   This example sets a hyphenation zone of 16 points before running
ToolsHyphenationManual. An error handler prevents error 102 ("Command
failed") from appearing if the user cancels the Manual Hyphenation dialog box.

```
ToolsHyphenation .AutoHyphenation = 0, .HyphenationZone = 16
On Error Goto trap
ToolsHyphenationManual
trap:
If Err = 102 Then Goto bye Else Error Err
bye:
```

See Also   **ToolsHyphenation**

ToolsLanguage

Syntax   **ToolsLanguage .Language =** *text* [**, .Default**]

Remarks   Sets the language format for the selected text. The language format identifies the
text for the proofing tools in Word so that rules appropriate to the specified
language are used.

Argument	Explanation
.Language	The name of the language
.Default	Adds the specified language format to the definition of the active template's Normal style

The following list includes valid settings for .Language. Note that languages
marked with an asterisk (*) are valid only in Word version 7.0.

To specify this language	Set .Language to this text
(no proofing)	0 (zero)
	Do not include the text "(zero)"
Basque *	Euskera
Brazilian Portuguese	Português (BR)
Catalan	Català

To specify this language	Set .Language to this text
Czech *	Èeština
Danish	Dansk
Dutch	Nederlands
Dutch (preferred)	Nederlands (voorkeur)
English (AUS)	English (AUS)
English (UK)	English (UK)
English (US)	English (US)
Finnish	Suomi
French	Français
French Candien	Canadien Français
German	Deutsch
Greek *	ÅëëçíêÜ
Hungarian *	Magyar
Italian	Italiano
Norwegian Bokmål	Norsk Bokmål
Norwegian Nynorsk	Norsk Nynorsk
Polish *	Polski
Portuguese	Português (POR)
Russian *	Ðóññêèé
Slovenian *	Slovenian
Spanish	Español
Swedish	Svenska
Swiss German	Deutsch (Schweiz)
Turkish *	Türkçe

Example

This example makes Brazilian Portuguese an attribute of the Normal style:

```
ToolsLanguage .Language = "Português (BR)", .Default
```

See Also   **CountLanguages(), FormatDefineStyleLang, Language**

ToolsMacro

Syntax

ToolsMacro .Name = *text* [, **.Run**] [, **.Edit**] [, **.Show** = *number*] [, **.Delete**]
[, **.Rename**] [, **.Description** = *text*] [, **.NewName** = *text*] [, **.SetDesc**]

Remarks

Runs or records a macro, sets the description of a macro, renames a macro, or opens a new or existing macro in a macro-editing window. The arguments for the **ToolsMacro** statement correspond to the options in the Macro dialog box (Tools menu). Note that the .Rename and .NewName arguments are included for compatibility with previous versions of Word.

Argument	Explanation
.Name	The name of the macro.
.Run	Runs the macro.
.Edit	Opens a macro-editing window containing the macro specified by .Name.
.Show	Specifies the context:
	0 (zero) All available macros; includes macros in loaded global templates
	1 Macros in the Normal template
	2 Built-in commands
	3 If the active document is not based on the Normal template, macros in the active template; otherwise, macros in the first loaded global template (global templates are listed in alphabetic order)
	> 3 Macros in the remaining loaded global templates (in alphabetic order)
	Omitted Word looks for the macro in whatever context was last selected in the Macro dialog box. To ensure that the correct macro runs, especially if a macro naming conflict between templates is possible, you should specify a value for .Show.
.Delete	Deletes the specified macro.
.Rename	Renames the specified macro.
.Description	Specifies a new description for the macro; used with .SetDesc. If the macro is assigned to a menu or toolbar and is selected or pointed to, the description is displayed in the status bar.
.NewName	A new name for the macro; used with .Rename.
.SetDesc	Sets a new description for the macro.

Example	This example opens a macro-editing window for the macro Test stored in the Normal template:

```
ToolsMacro .Name = "Test", .Show = 1, .Edit
```

See Also	**CountMacros(), IsMacro(), KeyMacro$(), MacroDesc$(), MacroFileName$(), MacroNameFromWindow$(), MenuItemMacro$(), Organizer, PauseRecorder**

ToolsManageFields

Syntax	**ToolsManageFields** [**.FieldName** = *text*] [, **.Add**] [, **.Remove**] [, **.Rename**] [, **.NewName** = *text*]
Remarks	Adds, removes, or renames a field name in a mail-merge data source or header source. If the active document does not contain a table with the specified field in the first row of the table, an error occurs.

Argument	Explanation
.FieldName	The field name you want to add, remove, or rename
.Add	Adds the specified field name to a new table column
.Remove	Removes the specified field name and the associated table column
.Rename	Renames the specified field name
.NewName	A new name for the field; used with .Rename

Example	This example renames the "Name1" field to "FirstName":

```
ToolsManageFields .FieldName = "Name1", .NewName = "FirstName", \
          .Rename
```

See Also	**MailMergeEditDataSource**

ToolsMergeRevisions

Syntax	**ToolsMergeRevisions .Name** = *text*
Remarks	Merges the revision marks from the active document into the specified document, which Word opens if it is not open already. If the active document minus revision marks is not equivalent to the specified document minus revision marks, an error occurs. You can use a series of **FileOpen** instructions followed by **ToolsMergeRevisions** instructions to collect revision marks from multiple review copies into one document.

Argument	Explanation
.Name	The path and filename of the document from which you want to merge revisions

Example

This example opens REVISE1.DOC, merges revision marks into ORIGINAL.DOC, and then performs the same action with REVISE2.DOC:

```
FileOpen .Name = "REVISE1.DOC"
ToolsMergeRevisions .Name = "ORIGINAL.DOC"
FileOpen .Name = "REVISE2.DOC"
ToolsMergeRevisions .Name = "ORIGINAL.DOC"
```

See Also

ToolsCompareVersions, ToolsOptionsRevisions, ToolsReviewRevisions, ToolsRevisions

ToolsNumberListDefault

Syntax

ToolsNumberListDefault

Remarks

Adds numbers and tab characters to the selected paragraphs and formats the paragraphs with a hanging indent.

Note   The **ToolsNumberListDefault** statement corresponds to the Numbered List button on the Toolbar in Word for Windows version 2.*x*. In Word version 6.0, the Numbering button is on the Formatting toolbar and its corresponding WordBasic statement is **FormatNumberDefault**.

See Also

FormatBulletDefault, FormatBulletsAndNumbering, FormatNumberDefault, ToolsBulletListDefault, ToolsBulletsNumbers

ToolsOptions

Syntax

ToolsOptions .Tab = *number*

Remarks

Displays the Options dialog box (Tools menu) with the specified tab selected. Unless you precede **ToolsOptions** with an **On Error** instruction, Word displays an error message if the dialog box is canceled.

Argument	Explanation
.Tab	The tab to select:
	0 (zero) View
	1 General
	2 Edit
	3 Print
	4 Save
	5 Spelling
	6 Grammar
	7 AutoFormat
	8 Revisions
	9 User Info
	10 Compatibility
	11 File Locations

Example

This example displays the View tab in the Options dialog box. The On Error Resume Next instruction prevents Word from displaying an error message if the user chooses Cancel.

```
On Error Resume Next
ToolsOptions .Tab = 0
```

See Also   **ToolsCustomize**

ToolsOptionsAutoFormat

Syntax

ToolsOptionsAutoFormat [**.PreserveStyles** = *number*]
[, **.ApplyStylesHeadings** = *number*] [, **.ApplyStylesLists** = *number*]
[, **.ApplyStylesOtherParas** = *number*] [, **.AdjustParaMarks** = *number*]
[, **.AdjustTabsSpaces** = *number*] [, **.AdjustEmptyParas** = *number*]
[, **.ReplaceQuotes** = *number*] [, **.ReplaceSymbols** = *number*]
[, **.ReplaceBullets** = *number*] [, **.ApplyBulletedLists** = *number*] [,
.ReplaceOrdinals = *number*] [, **.ReplaceFractions** = *number*] [, **.ApplyBorders**
= *number*] [, **.ApplyNumberedLists** = *number*] [, **.ShowOptionsFor** = *number*]

Remarks

Sets automatic formatting options for **FormatAutoFormat** or the AutoFormat As You Type feature (Word version 7.0 only). The arguments for the **ToolsOptionsAutoFormat** statement correspond to the options on the AutoFormat tab in the Options dialog box (Tools menu). Note that the .ReplaceBullets, .AdjustParaMarks, .AdjustTabsSpaces, and .AdjustEmptyParas arguments are retained for backward compatibility with Word version 6.0 macros.

Argument	Explanation
.PreserveStyles	If 1, preserves previously applied styles.
	In Word version 7.0, this argument is ignored when .ShowOptionsFor is set to 0 (zero).
.ApplyStylesHeadings	If 1, applies automatic styles to headings.
	In Word version 7.0, this argument is ignored when .ShowOptionsFor is set to 0 (zero).
.ApplyStylesLists	If 1, applies automatic styles to lists.
	In Word version 7.0, this argument is ignored when .ShowOptionsFor is set to 0 (zero).
.ApplyStylesOtherParas	If 1, applies automatic styles to paragraphs.
.AdjustParaMarks	If 1, adds or removes paragraph marks in a document (for example, removes extra paragraph marks from lines of text copied from an electronic mail message).
.AdjustTabsSpaces	If 1, adjusts tab settings and spaces automatically.
.AdjustEmptyParas	If 1, removes empty paragraph marks used to add space between paragraphs.
.ReplaceQuotes	If 1, replaces straight double quotation marks (" "), single quotation marks (' '), and apostrophes (') with "smart" quotation marks (" " or ' ') and apostrophes (').
.ReplaceSymbols	If 1, replaces "(r)", "(c)", and "(tm)" with the ®, ©, and ™ symbols from the Symbol dialog box (Insert menu).
.ReplaceBullets	If 1, replaces bullet characters with bullets from the Bullets And Numbering dialog box (Format menu).
	If -1, the setting specified by .ApplyBulletedLists is used.
	This argument is ignored when .ShowOptionsFor is set to 0 (zero).
.ApplyBulletedLists	If 1, replaces bullet characters with bullets from the Bullets And Numbering dialog box (Format menu), according to what is typed. For example, "➡>" is replaced with "▷".
	This argument is available only in Word version 7.0.
.ReplaceOrdinals	If 1, replaces "st", "nd", "rd", or "th" in ordinal numbers with the same letters in superscript. For example, "1st" is replaced with "1st."

Argument	Explanation
.ReplaceFractions	If 1, replaces typed fractions with fractions from the current character set. For example, 1/2 is replaced with ½.
.ApplyBorders	If 1, applies borders by replacing a series of three or more minus signs (-), equal signs (=), or underlines (_) with a specific border line. For example, a series of three or more equal signs (=) is replaced by a double border line.
	This argument is available only in Word version 7.0. It is ignored when .ShowOptionsFor is set to 1 or is omitted.
.ApplyNumberedLists	If 1, interprets and formats paragraphs as numbered lists with a numbering scheme from the Bullets And Numbering dialog box (Format menu), according to what is typed. For example, if a paragraph starts with "1.1" and a tab, Word automatically inserts "1.2" and a tab after the ENTER key is pressed.
	This argument is available only in Word version 7.0. It is ignored when .ShowOptionsFor is set to 1 or is omitted.
.ShowOptionsFor	Specifies which group of options are set by the **ToolsOptionsAutoFormat** statement:
	0 (zero) AutoFormat As You Type feature
	1 or omitted **FormatAutoFormat** statement
	This argument is available only in Word version 7.0.

See Also   **FormatAutoFormat, ToolsAutoCorrect**

ToolsOptionsCompatibility

Syntax   **ToolsOptionsCompatibility** [**.Product** = *text*] [**, .Default**]
[**, .NoTabHangIndent** = *number*] [**, .NoSpaceRaiseLower** = *number*]
[**, .PrintColBlack** = *number*] [**, .WrapTrailSpaces** = *number*]
[**, .NoColumnBalance** = *number*] [**, .ConvMailMergeEsc** = *number*]
[**, .SuppressSpBfAfterPgBrk** = *number*] [**, .SuppressTopSpacing** = *number*]
[**, .OrigWordTableRules** = *number*] [**, .TransparentMetafiles** = *number*]
[**, .ShowBreaksInFrames** = *number*] [**, .SwapBordersFacingPages** = *number*]
[**, .LeaveBackslashAlone** = *number*] [**, .ExpandShiftReturn** = *number*]
[**, .DontULTrailSpace** = *number*] [**, .DontBalanceSbDbWidth** = *number*]
[**, .SuppressTopSpacingMac5** = *number*] [**, .SpacingInWholePoints** = *number*]
[**, .PrintBodyTextBeforeHeader** = *number*] [**, .NoLeading** = *number*]
[**, .NoSpaceForUL** = *number*] [**, .MWSmallCaps** = *number*]
[**, .NoExtraLineSpacing** = *number*] [**, .TruncateFontHeight** = *number*]
[**.SubFontBySize** = *number*]

Remarks   Adjusts the display of certain elements in the active document to mimic the
display in other word-processing applications. For example, you can specify that
spaces at the end of a line wrap to the next line as they do in WordPerfect. The
arguments for the **ToolsOptionsCompatibility** statement correspond to the
options on the Compatibility tab in the Options dialog box (Tools menu).

Argument	Explanation
.Product	The name of the product whose display you want to mimic, as listed in the Recommended Options For box. If you specify .Product, display options are determined automatically.
.Default	Makes the display options you specify the default for new documents based on the active template.
.NoTabHangIndent	If 1, a tab stop is not added automatically to a paragraph formatted with a hanging indent.
.NoSpaceRaiseLower	If 1, extra line spacing is not added for raised and lowered characters.
.PrintColBlack	If 1, colors are printed as black on printers that don't support color.
.WrapTrailSpaces	If 1, spaces at the end of lines wrap to the next line.
.NoColumnBalance	If 1, text columns are not balanced above continuous section breaks.
.ConvMailMergeEsc	If 1, correctly interprets characters preceded by backslashes (\) in Word version 2.x mail-merge data sources. For example, \" is interpreted as ".
.SuppressSpBfAfterPgBrk	If 1, space before or after hard page and column breaks is removed.
.SuppressTopSpacing	If 1, extra line spacing at the top of the page is removed.
.OrigWordTableRules	If 1, table borders are combined as in Word for the Macintosh version 5.x.
.TransparentMetafiles	If 1, the area behind metafile pictures is not blanked.
.ShowBreaksInFrames	If 1, Word displays manual, or "hard," page or column breaks in any frames that contain them.
.SwapBordersFacingPages	If 1, Word prints a left paragraph border (not a box) on the right on odd numbered pages if either the Different Odd And Even or Mirror Margins check box (Page Setup dialog box, File menu) is selected.
.SuppressTopSpacingMac5	If 1, extra line spacing at the top of the page is handled as in Word for the Macintosh version 5.x.

Argument	Explanation
.SpacingInWholePoints	If 1, rounds character spacing measurements to the nearest whole number.
.PrintBodyTextBeforeHeader	If 1, the main text layer prints before the header/footer layer (the reverse of the default order). This allows Word to process PostScript codes in the main text layer the same as Word for the Macintosh version 5.*x.*
.NoLeading	If 1, displays lines of text without leading as in Word for the Macintosh version 5.*x.*
.NoSpaceForUL	If 1, no extra space for underlines is added.
	This argument is available only in Word version 7.0.
.MWSmallCaps	If 1, Word applies small caps formatting as in Word for the Macintosh version 5.*x* (which produces slightly larger small caps).
.NoExtraLineSpacing	If 1, line spacing is handled as in WordPerfect version 5.*x.*
	This argument is available only in Word version 7.0.
.TruncateFontHeight	If 1, font size is rounded up or down as in WordPerfect version 6.*x* for Windows.
	This argument is available only in Word version 7.0.
.SubFontBySize	If 1, fonts are substituted based on the font size in WordPerfect version 6.0 documents.
	This argument is available only in Word version 7.0.

Note The arguments .LeaveBackslashAlone, .ExpandShiftReturn, .DontULTrailSpace, and .DontBalanceSbDbWidth affect only the Japanese version of Word and are otherwise ignored.

If you specify .Product and at least one other display option, the display option settings take precedence.

See Also   **FontSubstitution**

ToolsOptionsEdit

Syntax   **ToolsOptionsEdit** [**.ReplaceSelection** = *number*] [, **.DragAndDrop** = *number*]
[, **.AutoWordSelection** = *number*] [, **.InsForPaste** = *number*]
[, **.Overtype** = *number*] [, **.SmartCutPaste** = *number*]
[, **.AllowAccentedUppercase** = *number*] [, **.PictureEditor** = *text*]
[, **.TabIndent** = *number*]

Remarks   Sets editing options. The arguments for the **ToolsOptionsEdit** statement correspond to the options on the Edit tab in the Options dialog box (Tools menu).

Argument	Explanation
.ReplaceSelection	If 1, replaces selected text with typed text.
.DragAndDrop	If 1, allows drag-and-drop editing.
.AutoWordSelection	If 1, dragging selects one word at a time instead of one character at a time.
.InsForPaste	If 1, allows the INS key to be used for pasting the Clipboard contents.
.Overtype	If 1, replaces text following the insertion point with typed text.
.SmartCutPaste	If 1, automatically adjusts spacing between words and punctuation when cutting and pasting.
.AllowAccentedUppercase	If 1, allows proofing tools and the Change Case feature to suggest that Word add an accent mark to an uppercase letter.
.PictureEditor	The name of the application you want to use to edit pictures, as it appears in the Picture Editor box.
.TabIndent	If 1, TAB and BACKSPACE can be used to add or remove list formatting.
	This argument is available only in Word version 7.0.

Example

This example toggles the Drag-And-Drop Text Editing check box:

```
Dim dlg As ToolsOptionsEdit
GetCurValues dlg
If dlg.DragAndDrop Then
    dlg.DragAndDrop = 0
Else
    dlg.DragAndDrop = 1
End If
ToolsOptionsEdit dlg
```

See Also   Overtype

ToolsOptionsFileLocations

Syntax   **ToolsOptionsFileLocations .Path** = *text* , **.Setting** = *text*

Remarks   Sets default folders. The arguments for the **ToolsOptionsFileLocations** statement correspond to the options on the File Locations tab in the Options dialog box (Tools menu). The new setting takes effect immediately.

Argument	Explanation
.Path	One of the following settings in the [Microsoft Word] section of WINWORD6.INI (Windows 3.x), Word Settings (6) (Macintosh), or the registry (Windows 95 and Windows NT):
	DOC-PATH
	PICTURE-PATH
	USER-DOT-PATH
	WORKGROUP-DOT-PATH
	INI-PATH
	AUTOSAVE-PATH
	TOOLS-PATH
	CBT-PATH
	STARTUP-PATH
.Setting	The path for the default folder, or an empty string ("") to remove the setting from WINWORD6.INI (Windows), Word Settings (6) (Macintosh), or the registry (Windows 95 and Windows NT).

Example

This example sets the default folder for documents to C:\MYDOCS. On the Macintosh, substitute a folder name such as HD:WORD DOCS.

```
ToolsOptionsFileLocations .Path = "DOC-PATH", \
        .Setting = "C:\MYDOCS"
```

See Also

SetPrivateProfileString

ToolsOptionsGeneral

Syntax

ToolsOptionsGeneral [**.Pagination** = *number*] [, **.WPHelp** = *number*] [, **.WPDocNavKeys** = *number*] [, **.BlueScreen** = *number*] [, **.ErrorBeeps** = *number*] [, **.Effects3d** = *number*] [, **.UpdateLinks** = *number*] [, **.SendMailAttach** = *number*] [, **.RecentFiles** = *number*] [, **.RecentFileCount** = *number*] [, **.Units** = *number*] [, **.ButtonFieldClicks** = *number*] [, **.ShortMenuNames** = *number*] [, **.RTFInClipboard** = *number*] [, **.ConfirmConversions** = *number*] [, **.TipWizardActive** = *number*]

Remarks

Sets general options. The arguments for the **ToolsOptionsGeneral** statement correspond to the options on the General tab in the Options dialog box (Tools menu).

Argument	Explanation
.Pagination	If 1, allows background repagination.
.WPHelp	If 1, enables WordPerfect Help (ignored on the Macintosh).

Argument	Explanation
.WPDocNavKeys	If 1, enables WordPerfect document navigation keys (ignored on the Macintosh).
.BlueScreen	If 1, changes the document window to display white text on a blue background.
.ErrorBeeps	If 1, Word beeps when an action occurs that generates an error.
.Effects3d	If 1, Word displays dialog boxes with three-dimensional effects.
	This argument is ignored in Word version 7.0.
.UpdateLinks	If 1, automatically updates linked information when you open documents.
.SendMailAttach	If 1, the Send command (File menu) sends the active document as an attachment instead of text in an electronic mail message.
.RecentFiles	If 1, lists recently used files above the Exit command on the File menu.
.RecentFileCount	A number from 1 to 9 corresponding to the maximum number of recently used files you want to be listed.
.Units	Sets the default unit of measurement:
	0 (zero) Inches
	1 Centimeters
	2 Points
	3 Picas
.ButtonFieldClicks	Sets the number of clicks (1 or 2) required to run a macro with a MACROBUTTON field.
.ShortMenuNames	If 1, on the Macintosh, substitutes "Ins" for "Insert," "Fmt" for "Format," and "Wnd" for "Window" on the menu bar. In Windows, this argument produces an error.
.RTFInClipboard	If 1, on the Macintosh, text copied to the Clipboard retains its character and paragraph formatting. In Windows, this argument produces an error.
.ConfirmConversions	If 1, displays the Convert File dialog box if the file you want to open is not in Word format.
	This argument is available only in Word version 7.0.
.TipWizardActive	If 1, activates the TipWizard. If the TipWizard is already activated, resets the TipWizard (the TipWizard may display tips that you have already seen).
	This argument is available only in Word verison 7.0.

Example

Before opening TEST.DOC, this example ensures that no filename will be "bumped off" the list of recently used files when changes are saved to TEST.DOC (unless the list already contains the maximum of nine filenames):

```
Dim dlg As ToolsOptionsGeneral
GetCurValues dlg
num = CountFiles()
If num < 9 Then
    num$ = LTrim$(Str$(num))
    If dlg.RecentFileCount = num$ Then
        dlg.RecentFileCount = num + 1
        ToolsOptionsGeneral dlg
    End If
End If
FileOpen .Name = "TEST.DOC"
```

See Also

Beep, **CountFiles()**, **HelpWordPerfectHelpOptions**, **ToolsRepaginate**

ToolsOptionsGrammar

Syntax

ToolsOptionsGrammar [**.Options** = *number*] [**.CheckSpelling** = *number*] [, **.ShowStatistics** = *number*]

Remarks

Sets grammar checking options. The arguments for the **ToolsOptionsGrammar** statement correspond to the options on the Grammar tab in the Options dialog box (Tools menu).

Argument	Explanation
.Options	Specifies which set of grammar rules to use:
	0 (zero) All rules
	1 Rules for business writing
	2 Rules for casual writing
	3 First custom settings
	4 Second custom settings
	5 Third custom settings
.CheckSpelling	If 1, checks spelling during grammar checking.
.ShowStatistics	If 1, readability statistics are displayed when the grammar check is complete.

Example

This example specifies that spelling be checked with grammar, and then starts the grammar checker:

```
ToolsOptionsGrammar .CheckSpelling = 1, .ShowStatistics = 1
ToolsGrammar
```

See Also

ToolsGrammar

ToolsOptionsPrint

Syntax

ToolsOptionsPrint [**.Draft** = *number*] [**, .Reverse** = *number*]
[**, .UpdateFields** = *number*] [**, .Summary** = *number*] [**, .ShowCodes** = *number*]
[**, .Annotations** = *number*] [**, .ShowHidden** = *number*]
[**, .EnvFeederInstalled** = *number*] [**, .UpdateLinks** = *number*]
[**, .Background** = *number*] [**, .DrawingObjects** = *number*]
[**, .FormsData** = *number*] [**, .DefaultTray** = *text*]
[**, .FractionalWidths** = *number*] [**, .PSOverText** = *number*]

Remarks

Sets options for printing a document. The arguments for the **ToolsOptionsPrint**
statement correspond to the options on the Print tab in the Options dialog box
(Tools menu).

Argument	Explanation
.Draft	If 1, prints in draft output (ignored on the Macintosh).
.Reverse	If 1, prints pages in reverse order.
.UpdateFields	If 1, updates all fields in the document when printed.
.Summary	If 1, prints summary information with the document.
.ShowCodes	If 1, prints field codes instead of field results.
.Annotations	If 1, prints annotations with the document.
.ShowHidden	If 1, prints all hidden text with the document.
.EnvFeederInstalled	If 1, indicates that an envelope feeder is installed.
.UpdateLinks	If 1, automatically updates all linked information when you print documents.
.Background	If 1, allows background printing (ignored on the Macintosh).
.DrawingObjects	If 1, prints Word drawing objects with the document.
.FormsData	If 1, prints only the data entered by the user in an online form onto a preprinted form.
.DefaultTray	Specifies the default paper tray as it appears in the Default Tray box.
.FractionalWidths	If 1, improves the character spacing in proportionally spaced fonts when printing on a LaserWriter® (Macintosh only).
.PSOverText	If 1, prints the result of PRINT field instructions (such as PostScript commands) on top of text or other graphics when printing on a LaserWriter (Macintosh only).

Example

This example specifies that documents be printed in reverse page order:

```
ToolsOptionsPrint .Reverse = 1
```

See Also

FilePrint, FilePrintSetup

ToolsOptionsRevisions

Syntax

ToolsOptionsRevisions [**.InsertedTextMark** = *number*]
[, **.InsertedTextColor** = *number*] [, **.DeletedTextMark** = *number*]
[, **.DeletedTextColor** = *number*] [, **.RevisedLinesMark** = *number*]
[, **.RevisedLinesColor** = *number*] [, **.HighlightColor** = *number*]

Remarks

Sets options for marking revisions. The arguments for the **ToolsOptionsRevisions** statement correspond to the options on the Revisions tab in the Options dialog box (Tools menu). The options affect documents in which revision marking is active, and documents you compare to other documents with the Compare Versions command (Revisions dialog box, Tools menu).

Argument	Explanation
.InsertedTextMark	The format for inserted text:
	0 (zero) None
	1 Bold
	2 Italic
	3 Underline
	4 Double underline
.DeletedTextMark	The format for deleted text:
	0 (zero) Hidden
	1 Strikethrough
.RevisedLinesMark	The position for revision lines:
	0 (zero) None
	1 Left border
	2 Right border
	3 Outside border
.InsertedTextColor, .DeletedTextColor, .RevisedLinesColor	The colors for inserted text, deleted text, and revision lines. If omitted, the color is set to "Auto." For a list of values, see **CharColor**.
.HighlightColor	The color for highlighting. The highlighting color remains the current color unless a different one is specified. If .HighlightColor is set to 0 (zero), no highlighting is applied.
	For a list of values, see **CharColor**.
	This argument is available only in Word version 7.0.

Example

When revision marking is active, this example instructs Word to format inserted text with a double underline and to add blue revision lines in the left margin:

```
ToolsOptionsRevisions .InsertedTextMark = 4, \
        .RevisedLinesMark = 1, .RevisedLinesColor = 2
```

See Also

ToolsCompareVersions, ToolsRevisions

ToolsOptionsSave

Syntax

ToolsOptionsSave [.CreateBackup = *number*] [**, .FastSaves** = *number*]
[**, .SummaryPrompt** = *number*] [**, .GlobalDotPrompt** = *number*]
[**, .NativePictureFormat** = *number*] [**, .EmbedFonts** = *number*]
[**, .FormsData** = *number*] [**, .AutoSave** = *number*] [**, .SaveInterval** = *text*]
[**, .Password** = *text*] [**, .WritePassword** = *text*]
[**, .RecommendReadOnly** = *number*]

Remarks

Sets options for saving documents. The arguments for the **ToolsOptionsSave** statement correspond to the options on the Save tab in the Options dialog box (Tools menu).

Argument	Explanation
.CreateBackup	If 1, creates a backup copy every time you save, and fast saves are not allowed.
.FastSaves	If 1, allows fast saves.
.SummaryPrompt	If 1, prompts for summary information when you save a new document.
.GlobalDotPrompt	If 1 and you make changes to the Normal template, displays a message box asking if you want save the changes when you quit Word; if 0 (zero), changes to the Normal template are saved automatically.
.NativePictureFormat	If 1, saves imported graphics in the format of the current platform only (for example, in Windows, saves only the Windows version of graphics imported from the Macintosh).
.EmbedFonts	If 1, embeds TrueType fonts when you save.
.FormsData	If 1, saves the data entered by a user in a form as a tab-delimited record for use in a database.
.AutoSave	If 1, allows automatic saving.
.SaveInterval	Specifies the time interval for saving documents automatically, in minutes; available only if .AutoSave has been set to 1.
.Password	The password for opening the document.
.WritePassword	The password for saving changes to the document.
.RecommendReadOnly	If 1, displays a message box upon opening the document suggesting that it be opened as read-only.

Example   This example sets an interval of 10 minutes between automatic saves:

```
ToolsOptionsSave .AutoSave = 1, .SaveInterval = "10"
```

See Also   **FileSave, FileSaveAll, FileSaveAs**

ToolsOptionsSpelling

Syntax   **ToolsOptionsSpelling [.AlwaysSuggest** = *number*]
[, **.SuggestFromMainDictOnly** = *number*] [, **.IgnoreAllCaps** = *number*]
[, **.IgnoreMixedDigits** = *number*] [, **.ResetIgnoreAll**] [, **.Type** = *number*]
[, **.CustomDict***n* = *text*] [, **.AutomaticSpellChecking** = *number*] [,
.HideSpellingErrors = *number*] [, **.RecheckDocument**]

Remarks   Sets options for checking spelling in a document. The arguments for the
ToolsOptionsSpelling statement correspond to the options on the Spelling tab in
the Options dialog box (Tools menu).

Argument	Explanation
.AlwaysSuggest	If 1, always suggests a replacement spelling for each misspelled word.
.SuggestFromMainDictOnly	If 1, draws spelling suggestions from the main dictionary only.
.IgnoreAllCaps	If 1, ignores words in all capital letters.
.IgnoreMixedDigits	If 1, ignores words that contain numbers.
.ResetIgnoreAll	Resets the Ignore All list so that Word will not ignore words for which you chose Ignore All while checking spelling during the current Word session.
.Type	Type of dictionary being searched:
	0 (zero) Normal
	2 Complete
	3 Medical
	4 Legal
	Note that if you specify 2, 3, or 4 and have not installed the corresponding dictionary, an error occurs. For information on how to purchase supplemental dictionaries, contact Microsoft Customer Service.
.CustomDict*n*	The path and filename of a custom dictionary to create or add; include a separate .CustomDict*n* argument for each custom dictionary, up to 10.

Argument	Explanation
.AutomaticSpellChecking	If 1, enables automatic checking for spelling in the current document.
	This argument is available only in Word version 7.0.
.HideSpellingErrors	If 1, hides spelling error underlines in the active document.
	This argument is available only in Word version 7.0.
.RecheckDocument	Rechecks the entire document for spelling errors. This ensures that words that have already been reviewed and corrected are checked for spelling errors again.
	This argument is available only in Word version 7.0.

Example

This example performs a spelling check in which words in all capital letters and words that contain numbers are not checked. The custom dictionary MYTERMS.DIC is used with the main dictionary. On the Macintosh, substitute a path such as HD:WORD:MY TERMS.

```
ToolsOptionsSpelling .IgnoreAllCaps = 1, .IgnoreMixedDigits = 1,\
        Type = 0, .CustomDict1 = "C:\WINWORD\MYTERMS.DIC"
ToolsSpelling
```

See Also

DocumentHasMisspellings, NextMisspelling, ToolsSpelling, ToolsSpellSelection

ToolsOptionsUserInfo

Syntax

ToolsOptionsUserInfo [**.Name** = *text*] [**, .Initials** = *text*] [**, .Address** = *text*]

Remarks

Changes user information. The arguments for the **ToolsOptionsUserInfo** statement correspond to the options on the User Info tab in the Options dialog box (Tools menu).

Argument	Explanation
.Name	The name of the current user
.Initials	The initials of the current user
.Address	The mailing address of the current user

Example

This example sets the current user name and initials:

```
ToolsOptionsUserInfo .Name = "Gina Fiori", .Initials = "GF"
```

See Also

DocumentStatistics, FileSummaryInfo

ToolsOptionsView

Syntax

ToolsOptionsView [**.DraftFont** = *number*] [, **.WrapToWindow** = *number*]
[, **.PicturePlaceHolders** = *number*] [, **.FieldCodes** = *number*]
[, **.BookMarks** = *number*] [, **.FieldShading** = *number*] [, **.StatusBar** = *number*]
[, **.HScroll** = *number*] [, **.VScroll** = *number*]
[, **.StyleAreaWidth** = *number or text*] [, **.Tabs** = *number*] [, **.Spaces** = *number*]
[, **.Paras** = *number*] [, **.Hyphens** = *number*] [, **.Hidden** = *number*]
[, **.ShowAll** = *number*] [, **.Drawings** = *number*] [, **.Anchors** = *number*]
[, **.TextBoundaries** = *number*] [, **.VRuler** = *number*] [, **.Highlight** = *number*]

Remarks

Displays or hides various elements in the active document or macro-editing
window and the Word window. With the exception of .StatusBar, which controls
the display of the status bar no matter which window is active, the arguments for
ToolsOptionsView control the display of elements on a window-by-window
basis. The arguments correspond to the options on the View tab in the Options
dialog box (Tools menu). As indicated in the following table, not all arguments
are available in every view or in the macro-editing window. Specifying an
argument that is not available in the active view generates an error.

Argument	Explanation	Available in these views
.DraftFont	If 1, shows all text in the same font without formatting.	Normal, outline, macro
.WrapToWindow	If 1, Word wraps text within document windows; column formatting is ignored.	Normal, outline, macro
.PicturePlaceHolders	If 1, displays placeholders for graphics.	Normal, outline, page layout
.FieldCodes	If 1, displays field codes.	Normal, outline, page layout
.BookMarks	If 1, displays bold brackets around text marked with a bookmark.	Normal, outline, page layout
.FieldShading	Specifies when to display fields with shading: 0 (zero) Never 1 Always 2 When Selected	Normal, outline, page layout
.StatusBar	If 1, displays the status bar.	All
.HScroll	If 1, displays horizontal scroll bars in document windows.	All

Argument	Explanation	Available in these views
.VScroll	If 1, displays vertical scroll bars in document windows.	All
.StyleAreaWidth	Sets the width of the style area in twips (20 twips = 1 point; 72 points = 1 inch) or a text measurement.	Normal, outline
.Tabs	If 1, displays tab marks.	All
.Spaces	If 1, displays space marks.	All
.Paras	If 1, displays paragraph marks.	All
.Hyphens	If 1, displays optional hyphens.	All
.Hidden	If 1, displays hidden text.	All
.ShowAll	If 1, displays all nonprinting characters.	All
.Drawings	If 0 (zero), hides any drawing objects you've created in your documents	Page layout
.Anchors	If 1, displays anchors next to items that may be positioned.	Page layout
.TextBoundaries	If 1, displays text boundaries.	Page layout
.VRuler	If 1, displays the vertical ruler.	Page layout
.Highlight	If 1, displays highlight formatting that has been applied to text. This argument is available only in Word version 7.0.	Normal, outline, page layout

Example

This example toggles the display of hidden text:

```
Dim dlg As ToolsOptionsView
GetCurValues dlg
dlg.ShowAll = 0
If dlg.Hidden Then
    dlg.Hidden = 0
Else
    dlg.Hidden = 1
End If
ToolsOptionsView dlg
```

See Also

ShowAll, **TableGridlines**, **ToggleFull**, **ToolsOptionsCompatibility**, **ViewDraft**, **ViewRibbon**, **ViewRuler**, **ViewStatusBar**

ToolsProtectDocument

Syntax   **ToolsProtectDocument** [**.DocumentPassword** = *text*] [**, .NoReset** = *number*] [**, .Type** = *number*]

Remarks   Protects the document from changes. According to the value of .Type, the user can make limited changes such as adding annotations or revision marks. If the document is already protected, an error occurs.

Argument	Explanation
.DocumentPassword	The password required to "unprotect" the document after choosing Unprotect Document (Tools menu).
.NoReset	If 1, Word does not reset form fields to their default results when a form is protected from changes using **ToolsProtectDocument** (applies only if .Type is 2). This option allows the form designer to create an "on entry" or "on exit" macro that removes protection from the form, modifies the form, and then protects it again without resetting form fields. Note that form fields are always reset when you protect a form using the Forms toolbar or the Protect Document dialog box (Tools menu).
.Type	The type of protection:

0 (zero) or omitted   Users can select and edit text, but all changes are tracked with revision marks.

1   Users can only add annotations.

2   Users can only select and modify text in form fields.

   To specify which sections of a multiple-section form should be protected and which should not, use **ToolsProtectSection**.

Unlike **FileSaveAs** or **ToolsOptionsSave**, which you can use to protect a document from being opened or saved, **ToolsProtectDocument** controls what the user is allowed to do while the document is open.

See Also   **DocumentProtection()**, **FileSaveAs**, **ToolsOptionsSave**, **ToolsProtectSection**, **ToolsUnprotectDocument**

ToolsProtectSection

Syntax   **ToolsProtectSection .Protect** = *number* [**, .Section** = *number*]

Remarks   Enables or disables protection for sections within a document when the document is protected for forms with **ToolsProtectDocument**. **ToolsProtectSection** has no effect if the document is protected for annotations or revision marks.

Argument	Explanation
.Protect	Specifies whether to enable or disable protection for the specified section:
	0 (zero) or omitted Disables protection.
	1 Enables protection.
.Section	The section for which you want to enable or disable protection: 1 corresponds to the first section, 2 to the second section, and so on.

Example

This example protects a document for forms, but disables protection for the second section of the document:

```
ToolsProtectDocument .Type = 2
ToolsProtectSection .Section = 2, .Protect = 0
```

See Also

DocumentProtection(), **ToolsProtectDocument**, **ToolsUnprotectDocument**

ToolsRemoveRecordDefault

Syntax

ToolsRemoveRecordDefault

Remarks

Removes the data record containing the insertion point—for example, removes the table row containing the insertion point. **ToolsRemoveRecordDefault** can be used with any document that could be used as a data source during a mail merge.

See Also

MailMergeEditDataSource, **ToolsAddRecordDefault**

ToolsRepaginate

Syntax

ToolsRepaginate

Remarks

Forces repagination of the entire document.

Example

This example repaginates the document if it has been changed since the last time it was saved:

```
If IsDocumentDirty() Then ToolsRepaginate
```

See Also

ToolsOptionsGeneral

ToolsReviewRevisions

Syntax

ToolsReviewRevisions [.ShowMarks] [, .HideMarks] [, .Wrap = *number*] [, .FindPrevious] [, .FindNext] [, .AcceptRevisions] [, .RejectRevisions]

Remarks

Searches for revision marks or accepts or rejects the selected revisions. The arguments for **ToolsReviewRevisions** correspond to the options in the Review Revisions dialog box (Revisions command, Tools menu).

You can use only one of the following arguments per **ToolsReviewRevisions** instruction.

Argument	Explanation
.ShowMarks	Displays revision marks in the active document.
.HideMarks	Hides revision marks in the active document.
.Wrap	Controls what happens if the search begins at a point other than the beginning of the document and the end of the document is reached: 0 (zero) or omitted The search operation ends and the macro continues. 1 The search continues from the beginning of the document to the point where the search began. 2 Word displays a message box asking whether to continue the search from the beginning of the document.
.FindPrevious	Searches toward the beginning of the document and selects the nearest text with revision marks.
.FindNext	Searches toward the end of the document and selects the nearest text with revision marks.
.AcceptRevisions	Accepts the revisions to the selected text.
.RejectRevisions	Cancels the revisions to the selected text.

Example

This example displays revision marks, selects the next marked text, and then accepts the revisions:

```
ToolsReviewRevisions .ShowMarks
ToolsReviewRevisions .FindNext
ToolsReviewRevisions .AcceptRevisions
```

See Also

ToolsCompareVersions, **ToolsOptionsRevisions**, **ToolsRevisions**, **ToolsRevisionType**()

ToolsRevisionAuthor$()

Syntax

ToolsRevisionAuthor$()

Remarks

Returns the name of the person who made the selected revision. If the selection does not include revision marks, **ToolsRevisionAuthor$()** returns an empty string (**""**).

Example

This example finds the next revision and checks the revision author. If the revision author is Stella Richards, the revision is accepted.

```
ToolsRevisions .ViewRevisions = 1
ToolsReviewRevisions .FindNext
If ToolsRevisionAuthor$() = "Stella Richards" Then
    ToolsReviewRevisions .AcceptRevisions
End If
```

See Also   **ToolsReviewRevisions, ToolsRevisionDate$(), ToolsRevisions, ToolsRevisionType()**

ToolsRevisionDate()

Syntax   **ToolsRevisionDate()**

Remarks   Returns a serial number corresponding to the date and time the selected revision was made, or −1 if the selection contains no revisions. For information on serial numbers, see **DateSerial()**.

Example   This example finds the next revision and checks the revision date. The revision is rejected if it was made more than 10 days before the current date.

```
ToolsRevisions .ViewRevisions = 1
ToolsReviewRevisions .FindNext
If (Now() - ToolsRevisionDate()) > 10 Then
    ToolsReviewRevisions .RejectRevisions
End If
```

See Also   **ToolsReviewRevisions, ToolsRevisionAuthor$(), ToolsRevisionDate$(), ToolsRevisions, ToolsRevisionType()**

ToolsRevisionDate$()

Syntax   **ToolsRevisionDate$()**

Remarks   Returns the date and time the selected revision was made. If the selection does not include revision marks, **ToolsRevisionDate$()** returns an empty string ("").

Example   This example uses the **ToolsRevisionType()** function to determine whether the selection contains a revision. If so, a message box displays the date and time the selected revision was made. If the selected text contains no revision, Word displays an appropriate message box.

```
If ToolsRevisionType() <> 0 Then
    MsgBox "Revision made " + ToolsRevisionDate$() + "."
Else
    MsgBox "No revisions are selected."
End If
```

See Also   **ToolsReviewRevisions, ToolsRevisionAuthor$(), ToolsRevisionDate(), ToolsRevisions, ToolsRevisionType()**

ToolsRevisions

Syntax   **ToolsRevisions** [**.MarkRevisions** = *number*] [, **.ViewRevisions** = *number*]
[, **.PrintRevisions** = *number*] [, **.AcceptAll**] [, **.RejectAll**]

Remarks   Specifies how revisions are marked and reviewed in the active document. The
arguments for the **ToolsRevisions** statement correspond to the options in the
Revisions dialog box (Tools menu).

Argument	Explanation
.MarkRevisions	If 1, activates revision marking.
.ViewRevisions	If 1, revision marks appear in the document when you edit it with revision marking on.
.PrintRevisions	Specifies whether or not to include revision marks in the printed document:
	0 (zero) Revision marks do not appear (revisions are printed as if they were accepted).
	1 Revision marks appear.
.AcceptAll	Accepts all revisions in the active document.
.RejectAll	Rejects all revisions in the active document.

Example   This example activates revision marking in the active document, but prevents the
revision marks from appearing while the document is edited:

```
ToolsRevisions .MarkRevisions = 1, .ViewRevisions = 0
```

See Also   **ToolsCompareVersions, ToolsMergeRevisions, ToolsOptionsRevisions,
ToolsReviewRevisions, ToolsRevisionType( )**

ToolsRevisionType( )

Syntax   **ToolsRevisionType( )**

Remarks   Returns one of the following values, corresponding to the type of revision made to
the selected text.

Value	Explanation
0 (zero)	If the selection contains no revisions
1	If all or part of the selection contains text marked as inserted
2	If all or part of the selection contains text marked as deleted
3	If the selection contains a replacement (text marked as inserted followed immediately by text marked as deleted)
4	If the selection contains more than one revision

For an example, see the entry for **ToolsRevisionDate$()**.

See Also   **ToolsReviewRevisions**, **ToolsRevisionAuthor$()**, **ToolsRevisionDate()**, **ToolsRevisionDate$()**, **ToolsRevisions**

ToolsShrinkToFit

Syntax   **ToolsShrinkToFit**

Remarks   Attempts to decrease the font size of text just enough to fit the active document on one fewer pages. **ToolsShrinkToFit** is handy for saving paper when printing if the last page contains only a few lines of text. If Word is unable to perform the operation, a message box is displayed.

See Also   **ViewZoomWholePage**

ToolsSpelling

Syntax   **ToolsSpelling**

Remarks   Checks spelling in the current selection or, if there isn't a selection, checks spelling from the location of the insertion point to the end of the document.

Example   This example asks whether or not to check spelling, and then checks spelling if the user chooses the Yes button:

```
ans = MsgBox("Check spelling now?", 3)
If ans = -1 Then
    StartOfDocument
    ToolsSpelling
End If
```

See Also   **ToolsOptionsSpelling**, **ToolsSpellSelection**

ToolsSpellingRecheckDocument

Syntax   **ToolsSpellingRecheckDocument**

Remarks   Rechecks the entire document for spelling errors, ensuring that words that have already been reviewed and corrected are checked for spelling errors again. In Word version 6.0, **ToolsSpellingRecheckDocument** is unavailable and generates an error.

See Also   **DocumentHasMisspellings()**, **NextMisspelling**, **SpellChecked**, **ToolsSpelling**, **ToolsSpellSelection**

ToolsSpellSelection

Syntax   **ToolsSpellSelection**

Remarks   Checks spelling in the current selection. If the selection is only part of a word, or
                    if the insertion point is at the end of a word, the selection is extended to include
                    the whole word. If the insertion point isn't in or doesn't follow a word, the next
                    word is checked.

Example   This example asks whether or not to check the spelling of the current selection,
                    and then checks spelling if the user chooses the Yes button:

```
ans = MsgBox("Check spelling of selection?", 3)
If ans = -1 Then ToolsSpellSelection
```

See Also   **ToolsOptionsSpelling, ToolsSpelling**

ToolsThesaurus

Syntax   **ToolsThesaurus**

Remarks   Displays the Thesaurus dialog box (Tools menu), which lists alternatives for the
                    selected word.

See Also   **ToolsGetSynonyms**

ToolsUnprotectDocument

Syntax   **ToolsUnprotectDocument [.DocumentPassword =** *text*]

Remarks   Removes protection from the active document. If the document is not protected,
                    an error occurs.

Argument	Explanation
.DocumentPassword	The password, if any, used to protect the document. Note that passwords are case-sensitive.
	If the document is protected with a password and you don't specify .DocumentPassword, a dialog box prompts the user for the password.

See Also   **DocumentProtection(), ToolsProtectDocument, ToolsProtectSection**

ToolsWordCount

Syntax	**ToolsWordCount** [**.CountFootnotes** = *number*] [, **.Pages** = *text*] [, **.Words** = *text*] [, **.Characters** = *text*] [, **.Paragraphs** = *text*] [, **.Lines** = *text*]
Remarks	Counts the number of pages, words, characters, paragraphs, and lines in the active document. The .CountFootnotes argument is the only one that can be set; the remaining arguments are read-only and can be used with a dialog record to return information about the active document. For more information, see the example for this entry. For information about dialog records, see Chapter 4, "Advanced WordBasic," in Part 1, "Learning WordBasic."

Argument	Explanation
.CountFootnotes	If 1, text in footnotes and endnotes is included in the count.
.Pages	The number of pages in the document.
.Words	The number of words in the document.
.Characters	The number of characters in the document.
.Paragraphs	The number of paragraphs in the document.

Example	This example counts the number of pages, words, characters, paragraphs, and lines in the active document—including text in footnotes and endnotes—and then displays the word count in a message box:

```
ToolsWordCount .CountFootnotes = 1
Dim dlg As ToolsWordCount
GetCurValues dlg
MsgBox "Current word count: " + dlg.Words
```

See Also	**DocumentStatistics**, **FileSummaryInfo**

UCase$()

Syntax	**UCase$**(*Source$*)
Remarks	Returns a string in which all letters of *Source$* have been converted to uppercase.
Example	This example displays an **InputBox$** dialog box that prompts the user to type an acronym. When the user chooses OK, the text is stored in the variable acronym$, which is then converted to uppercase.

```
acronym$ = InputBox$("Please enter an acronym.")
acronym$ = UCase$(acronym$)
```

See Also	**ChangeCase, LCase$**()

Underline, Underline()

Syntax	**Underline** [*On*]
	Underline()
Remarks	The **Underline** statement adds or removes the single-underline character format for the selected text, or controls single-underline formatting for characters to be inserted at the insertion point.

Argument	Explanation
On	Specifies whether to add or remove the single-underline format:
	1 Formats the selection with the single-underline format.
	0 (zero) Removes the single-underline format.
	Omitted Toggles the single-underline format.

The **Underline**() function returns the following values.

Value	Explanation
0 (zero)	If none of the selection is in the single-underline format
−1	If part of the selection is in the single-underline format
1	If all the selection is in the single-underline format

See Also	**DottedUnderline, DoubleUnderline, FormatFont, WordUnderline**

UnHang

Syntax	**UnHang**
Remarks	Removes a hanging indent from the selected paragraphs, or reduces the current hanging indent to the previous tab stop of the first paragraph in the selection.

See Also	**HangingIndent**, **UnIndent**

UnIndent

Syntax	**UnIndent**
Remarks	Moves the left indent of the selected paragraphs to the previous tab stop of the first paragraph in the selection. **UnIndent** maintains the setting of a first-line or hanging indent.
See Also	**Indent**, **UnHang**

UnlinkFields

Syntax	**UnlinkFields**
Remarks	Replaces the selected fields with their most recent results. When you unlink a field, it is converted to regular text or graphics and can no longer be updated automatically. Note that some fields cannot be unlinked—for example, XE (Index Entry) fields, which show no result. If the selection does not contain fields that can be unlinked, an error occurs.
Example	This example unlinks all fields in the active document. First, Word displays a message box giving the user the option to update all fields before unlinking. Then, depending on the user's response, Word carries out the appropriate action.

```
answer = MsgBox("Update all fields before unlinking?", \
    "Unlink All Fields", 35)
On Error Goto trap
Select Case answer
    Case -1                 'Yes
        EditSelectAll
        UpdateFields
        UnlinkFields
    Case 0                  'No
        EditSelectAll
        UnlinkFields
    Case 1                  'Cancel
        Goto bye
trap:
    If Err = 102 Then MsgBox "No fields to unlink." Else Error Err
bye:
End Select
```

See Also	**LockFields**, **UnlockFields**, **UpdateFields**

UnlockFields

Syntax   **UnlockFields**

Remarks   Allows selected fields that were previously locked with **LockFields** to be
                    updated.

See Also   **LockFields**, **UnlinkFields**, **UpdateFields**

UpdateFields

Syntax   **UpdateFields**

Remarks   Updates the selected fields.

See Also   **LockFields**, **UnlinkFields**, **UnlockFields**

UpdateSource

Syntax   **UpdateSource**

Remarks   Saves the changes made to the result of an INCLUDETEXT field back to the
                    source document. The source document must be formatted as a Word document.

See Also   **UpdateFields**

Val()

Syntax

Val(*a$*)

Remarks

Returns the numeric value of *a$*. A common use of **Val()** is to convert strings containing digit characters to numbers so they may be used in mathematical formulas. If *a$* does not begin with a digit character, **Val()** returns 0 (zero). The *a$* string can be as long as 255 characters.

Note Whereas raw numbers in a WordBasic instruction are not affected by the current settings for decimal and thousands separators, the **Val()** function is. For example, if the thousands separator is a period, the instruction a = 1.001 sets a to 1.001 but the instruction a = Val("1.001") sets a to 1001.

Examples

In both of the following instructions, **Val()** returns 10:

```
num = Val("10")
num = Val("10 Apples")
```

In both of the following instructions, **Val()** returns 0 (zero):

```
num = Val("ten")
num = Val("Apartment 10")
```

The following example prompts the user to type a number, which the **InputBox$()** function returns as a string. **Val()** converts the string to a number and multiplies it by 12. **Str$()** converts the product to a string so that it can be displayed in a message box.

```
a$ = InputBox$("How many dozen apples?")
total = Val(a$) * 12
MsgBox a$ + " dozen equals" + Str$(total)
```

See Also

Str$()

ViewAnnotations, ViewAnnotations()

Syntax

ViewAnnotations [*On*]

ViewAnnotations()

Remarks

The **ViewAnnotations** statement opens or closes the annotation pane. An error occurs if there are no annotations in the active document.

Argument	Explanation
On	Specifies whether to open or close the annotation pane:
	0 (zero) Closes the annotation pane.
	1 Opens the annotation pane.
	Omitted Toggles the display of the annotation pane.

The **ViewAnnotations**() function returns the following values.

Value	Explanation
0 (zero)	If the annotation pane is closed
−1	If the annotation pane is open

See Also   **InsertAnnotation, ViewEndnoteArea, ViewFootnoteArea, ViewFootnotes**

ViewBorderToolbar

Syntax   **ViewBorderToolbar**

Remarks   Displays the Borders toolbar if it is hidden or hides the Borders toolbar if it is displayed.

See Also   **ViewDrawingToolbar, ViewToolbars**

ViewDraft, ViewDraft()

Syntax   **ViewDraft** [*On*]

ViewDraft()

Remarks   The **ViewDraft** statement turns draft mode on or off for the active document or macro-editing window. Draft mode is specified by the Draft Font check box on the View tab in the Options dialog box (Tools menu).

Argument	Explanation
On	Specifies whether to turn draft mode on or off:
	0 (zero) Turns draft mode off.
	1 Turns draft mode on.
	Omitted Toggles draft mode.

The **ViewDraft()** function returns the following values.

Value	Explanation
0 (zero)	If draft mode is off
−1	If draft mode is on

See Also   **ToolsOptionsView**

ViewDrawingToolbar

Syntax   **ViewDrawingToolbar**

Remarks   Displays the Drawing toolbar if it is hidden or hides the Drawing toolbar if it is displayed.

See Also   **ViewBorderToolbar**, **ViewToolbars**

ViewEndnoteArea, ViewEndnoteArea()

Syntax   **ViewEndnoteArea** [*On*]

ViewEndnoteArea()

Remarks   In normal and outline views, the **ViewEndnoteArea** statement opens or closes the endnote pane. In page layout view, **ViewEndnoteArea** moves the insertion point to or from the endnote area. If there are no endnotes in the active document, this statement has no effect.

Argument	Explanation
On	Specifies whether to open or close the endnote pane:
	0 (zero) In normal and outline views, closes the endnote pane; in page layout view, has no effect.
	1 In normal and outline views, opens the endnote pane; in page layout view, moves the insertion point between an endnote and its associated reference mark in the document text.
	Omitted In normal and outline views, toggles the display of the endnote pane; in page layout view, moves the insertion point between an endnote and its associated reference mark in the document text.

The **ViewEndnoteArea()** function returns the following values.

Value	Explanation
0 (zero)	If the endnote pane is closed
−1	If the endnote pane is open

See Also   **ViewAnnotations**, **ViewFootnoteArea**, **ViewFootnotes**

ViewEndnoteContNotice

Syntax   **ViewEndnoteContNotice**

Remarks   Opens a pane containing the endnote continuation notice, which indicates that an endnote is continued on the following page.

See Also   **ResetNoteSepOrNotice**, **ViewEndnoteContSeparator**, **ViewEndnoteSeparator**, **ViewFootnoteContNotice**

ViewEndnoteContSeparator

Syntax   **ViewEndnoteContSeparator**

Remarks   Opens a pane containing the endnote continuation separator, which appears before endnote text that is continued from the previous page.

See Also   **ResetNoteSepOrNotice**, **ViewEndnoteContNotice**, **ViewEndnoteSeparator**, **ViewFootnoteContSeparator**

ViewEndnoteSeparator

Syntax   **ViewEndnoteSeparator**

Remarks   Opens a pane containing the endnote separator, which appears between document text and the endnotes.

See Also   **ResetNoteSepOrNotice**, **ViewEndnoteContNotice**, **ViewEndnoteContSeparator**, **ViewFootnoteSeparator**

ViewFieldCodes, ViewFieldCodes()

Syntax   **ViewFieldCodes** [*On*]

ViewFieldCodes()

Remarks   The **ViewFieldCodes** statement controls the display of all fields in the active document. The display of field codes is specified by the Field Codes check box on the View tab in the Options dialog box (Tools menu). You can control the display of selected fields with the **ToggleFieldDisplay** statement.

Argument	Explanation
On	Specifies how to display fields:
	0 (zero) Displays field results.
	1 Displays field codes.
	Omitted Toggles the display of fields.

The **ViewFieldCodes**() function returns the following values.

Value	Explanation
0 (zero)	If field results are displayed
−1	If field codes are displayed

See Also   **ToggleFieldDisplay**, **ToolsOptionsView**

ViewFooter, ViewFooter()

Syntax   **ViewFooter**

ViewFooter()

Remarks   The **ViewFooter** statement switches the active document to page layout view, positions the insertion point in the footer area, and then displays the Header And Footer toolbar. If the Header And Footer toolbar is already displayed, **ViewFooter** hides it and moves the insertion point to the document area.

The **ViewFooter**() function returns the following values.

Value	Explanation
0 (zero)	If the insertion point is not in the footer area
−1	If the insertion point is in the footer area

See Also   **CloseViewHeaderFooter**, **ViewHeader**

ViewFootnoteArea, ViewFootnoteArea()

Syntax   **ViewFootnoteArea** [*On*]

ViewFootnoteArea()

Remarks   The **ViewFootnoteArea** statement opens or closes the footnote pane (in normal view) and moves the insertion point between the document area and the footnote area. If there are no footnotes in the active document, this statement has no effect.

Argument	Explanation
On	Specifies whether to display the footnote area:
	0 (zero) Closes the footnote pane (in normal view) and moves the insertion point to the appropriate reference mark in the document area.
	1 Opens the footnote pane (in normal view) and moves the insertion point between a footnote and its associated reference mark in the document text.
	Omitted Toggles the display of the footnote pane (in normal view) and moves the insertion point from the document area to the footnote area, or vice versa.

The **ViewFootnoteArea**() function returns the following values.

Value	Explanation
0 (zero)	If the footnote pane is closed
−1	If the footnote pane is open

See Also   **ViewAnnotations**, **ViewEndnoteArea**, **ViewFootnotes**

ViewFootnoteContNotice

Syntax   **ViewFootnoteContNotice**

Remarks   Opens a pane containing the footnote continuation notice, which indicates that a footnote is continued on the following page.

See Also   **ResetNoteSepOrNotice**, **ViewEndnoteContNotice**, **ViewFootnoteContSeparator**, **ViewFootnoteSeparator**

ViewFootnoteContSeparator

Syntax   **ViewFootnoteContSeparator**

Remarks   Opens a pane containing the footnote continuation separator, which appears before footnote text that is continued from the previous page.

See Also   **ResetNoteSepOrNotice**, **ViewEndnoteContSeparator**, **ViewFootnoteContNotice**, **ViewFootnoteSeparator**

ViewFootnotes, ViewFootnotes()

Syntax   **ViewFootnotes**

ViewFootnotes( )

Remarks   In normal view, the **ViewFootnotes** statement opens or closes the footnote pane or endnote pane according to the following rules:

- If the document contains footnotes, opens the footnote pane.
- If the document contains endnotes, but no footnotes, opens the endnote pane.
- If the footnote pane or endnote pane is already open, closes the pane.

In page layout view, **ViewFootnotes** moves the insertion point according to the following rules:

- If the document has only footnotes, moves the insertion point to the footnote area; if it has only endnotes, moves the insertion point to the endnote area.
- If the document has both footnotes and endnotes, displays a dialog box that asks the user to choose between the footnote and endnote area.
- If the insertion point is already in a footnote or endnote area, moves the insertion point to the document area.

If the document contains no footnotes or endnotes, **ViewFootnotes** has no effect.

The **ViewFootnotes( )** function returns the following values.

Value	Explanation
0 (zero)	If neither the footnote nor endnote pane is open
−1	If either the footnote or endnote pane is open

See Also   **ViewEndnoteArea**, **ViewFootnoteArea**

ViewFootnoteSeparator

Syntax   **ViewFootnoteSeparator**

Remarks   Opens a pane containing the footnote separator, which appears between document text and the footnotes.

See Also   **ResetNoteSepOrNotice**, **ViewEndnoteSeparator**, **ViewFootnoteContNotice**, **ViewFootnoteContSeparator**

ViewHeader, ViewHeader()

Syntax   **ViewHeader**

ViewHeader( )

Remarks   The **ViewHeader** statement switches the active document to page layout view, positions the insertion point in the header area, and then displays the Header And Footer toolbar. If the Header And Footer toolbar is already displayed, **ViewHeader** hides it and moves the insertion point to the document area.

The **ViewHeader()** function returns the following values.

Value	Explanation
0 (zero)	If the insertion point is not in the header area
−1	If the insertion point is in the header area

See Also   **ViewFooter**

ViewMasterDocument, ViewMasterDocument()

Syntax   **ViewMasterDocument**

ViewMasterDocument( )

Remarks   The **ViewMasterDocument** statement switches the active document to master document view. The **ViewMasterDocument()** function returns the following values.

Value	Explanation
0 (zero)	If the active document is not in master document view
−1	If the active document is in master document view

See Also   **ViewOutline**, **ViewToggleMasterDocument**

ViewMenus()

Syntax   **ViewMenus( )**

Remarks   Returns a value that indicates which menu bar is displayed: the full menu bar when a document window is open, or the abbreviated menu bar when no document window is open. You can use **ViewMenus()** as an alternative to **CountWindows()** to determine whether at least one document window is open.

Value	Explanation
0 (zero)	If the full menu bar is displayed
1	In Windows, if only the File, Help, and application Control menus are displayed; on the Macintosh, if only the Apple, File, Help, and Application menus are displayed. Note that other menus may be available if they've been added with **ToolsCustomizeMenuBar**

Note These values correspond to values allowed for the .MenuType argument when you customize menus with **ToolsCustomizeMenus** and **ToolsCustomizeMenuBar**.

See Also   **ToolsCustomizeMenus**, **ToolsCustomizeMenuBar**

ViewNormal, ViewNormal()

Syntax   **ViewNormal**

ViewNormal( )

Remarks   The **ViewNormal** statement switches the active document to normal view. The **ViewNormal**() function returns the following values.

Value	Explanation
0 (zero)	If the active document is not in normal view
−1	If the active document is in normal view

See Also   **FilePrintPreview**, **ViewDraft**, **ViewMasterDocument**, **ViewOutline**, **ViewPage**

ViewOutline, ViewOutline()

Syntax   **ViewOutline**

ViewOutline( )

Remarks   The **ViewOutline** statement switches the active document to outline view. The **ViewOutline**() function returns the following values.

Value	Explanation
0 (zero)	If the active document is not in outline view
−1	If the active document is in outline view

See Also   **FilePrintPreview**, **ViewDraft**, **ViewMasterDocument**, **ViewNormal**, **ViewPage**

ViewPage, ViewPage()

Syntax	**ViewPage**
	ViewPage( )

Remarks   The **ViewPage** statement switches the active document to page layout view. The **ViewPage( )** function returns the following values.

Value	Explanation
0 (zero)	If the active document is not in page layout view
−1	If the active document is in page layout view

See Also   **FilePrintPreview, ViewDraft, ViewMasterDocument, ViewNormal, ViewOutline**

ViewRibbon, ViewRibbon()

Syntax	**ViewRibbon** [*On*]
	ViewRibbon( )

Remarks   The **ViewRibbon** statement displays or hides the Formatting toolbar. This statement is included for compatibility with the previous version of Word.

Argument	Explanation
On	Specifies whether to display or hide the Formatting toolbar:
	0 (zero) Hides the Formatting toolbar.
	1 Displays the Formatting toolbar.
	Omitted Toggles the Formatting toolbar on and off.

The **ViewRibbon( )** function returns the following values.

Value	Explanation
0 (zero)	If the Formatting toolbar is hidden
−1	If the Formatting toolbar is displayed

See Also   **ToolsOptionsView, ViewRuler, ViewStatusBar, ViewToolbars**

ViewRuler, ViewRuler()

Syntax	**ViewRuler** [*On*]
	ViewRuler( )

Remarks   The **ViewRuler** statement displays or hides the rulers. If the active document is in outline or master document view, an error occurs.

Argument	Explanation
On	Specifies whether to display or hide the rulers:
	0 (zero) Hides the rulers.
	1 Displays the rulers.
	Omitted Toggles the rulers on and off.

The **ViewRuler**() function returns the following values.

Value	Explanation
0 (zero)	If the rulers are hidden
−1	If the rulers are displayed

See Also   **ToolsOptionsView, ViewRibbon, ViewStatusBar, ViewToolbars**

ViewStatusBar, ViewStatusBar()

Syntax   **ViewStatusBar** [*On*]

ViewStatusBar()

Remarks   The **ViewStatusBar** statement displays or hides the status bar.

Argument	Explanation
On	Specifies whether to display or hide the status bar:
	0 (zero) Hides the status bar.
	1 Displays the status bar.
	Omitted Toggles the status bar on and off.

The **ViewStatusBar**() function returns the following values.

Value	Explanation
0 (zero)	If the status bar is hidden
−1	If the status bar is displayed

See Also   **ToolsOptionsView, ViewRibbon, ViewRuler, ViewToolbars**

ViewToggleMasterDocument

Syntax   **ViewToggleMasterDocument**

Remarks   Switches the active document from outline view to master document view or from master document view to outline view. If the document is in normal view, page layout view, or print preview, an error occurs.

See Also   **ViewMasterDocument, ViewOutline**

ViewToolbars

Syntax

ViewToolbars [**.Toolbar** = *text*] [, **.Context** = *number*]
[, **.ColorButtons** = *number*] [, **.LargeButtons** = *number*] [, **.ToolTips** = *number*]
[, **.ToolTipsKey** = *number*] [, **.Reset**] [, **.Delete**] [, **.Show**] [, **.Hide**]

Remarks

The arguments for the **ViewToolbars** statement correspond to the options in the
Toolbars dialog box (View menu).

Argument	Explanation
.Toolbar	The name of the toolbar you want to reset, delete, display, or hide, as listed in the Toolbars box.
.Context	Specifies a template in which to reset an existing toolbar:
	0 (zero) or omitted Normal template
	1 Active template
.ColorButtons	If 1, displays color toolbar buttons.
.LargeButtons	If 1, displays enlarged toolbar buttons.
.ToolTips	If 1, displays the button name beneath a button when the mouse pointer is over it.
.ToolTipsKey	If 1, displays the shortcut key assigned to the toolbar button in the button's ToolTip.
.Reset	Restores the specified toolbar to its default configuration of buttons.
.Delete	Deletes the specified toolbar.
.Show	Displays the specified toolbar.
.Hide	Hides the specified toolbar.

See Also

NewToolbar, **ToolsOptionsView**, **ViewRibbon**, **ViewRuler**, **ViewStatusBar**

ViewZoom

Syntax

ViewZoom [**.AutoFit**] [, **.TwoPages**] [, **.FullPage**] [, **.NumColumns** = *number*]
[, **.NumRows** = *number*] [, **.ZoomPercent** = *text*]

Remarks

Changes the magnification for the active document and new documents in the
current view. The arguments for **ViewZoom** correspond to the options in the
Zoom dialog box (View menu). If the active document is not in page layout view
and you specify .TwoPages, .FullPage, .NumColumns, or .NumRows, an error
occurs.

Argument	Explanation
.AutoFit	Sets magnification so the entire width of the page is visible.
.TwoPages	In page layout view, sets magnification so two entire pages are visible.

Argument	Explanation
.FullPage	In page layout view, sets magnification so the entire page is visible.
.NumColumns	When displaying multiple pages in grid formation, the number of columns in the grid.
.NumRows	When displaying multiple pages in grid formation, the number of rows in the grid.
.ZoomPercent	The percentage of magnification relative to the default display (100 percent).

See Also   **ViewZoom100, ViewZoom200, ViewZoom75, ViewZoomPageWidth, ViewZoomWholePage**

ViewZoom100

Syntax   **ViewZoom100**

Remarks   Switches to normal view and sets magnification to 100 percent for the active document and new documents.

See Also   **ViewZoom, ViewZoom200, ViewZoom75, ViewZoomPageWidth, ViewZoomWholePage**

ViewZoom200

Syntax   **ViewZoom200**

Remarks   Switches to normal view and sets magnification to 200 percent for the active document and new documents.

See Also   **ViewZoom, ViewZoom100, ViewZoom75, ViewZoomPageWidth, ViewZoomWholePage**

ViewZoom75

Syntax   **ViewZoom75**

Remarks   Switches to normal view and sets magnification to 75 percent for the active document and new documents.

See Also   **ViewZoom, ViewZoom100, ViewZoom200, ViewZoomPageWidth, ViewZoomWholePage**

ViewZoomPageWidth

Syntax   **ViewZoomPageWidth**

Remarks   Sets magnification so the entire width of the page is visible.

See Also   **ViewZoom, ViewZoom100, ViewZoom200, ViewZoom75, ViewZoomWholePage**

ViewZoomWholePage

Syntax   **ViewZoomWholePage**

Remarks   Sets magnification so the entire page is visible in page layout view. **ViewZoomWholePage** switches to page layout view if the active document is in another view.

See Also   **ViewZoom, ViewZoom100, ViewZoom200, ViewZoom75, ViewZoomPageWidth**

VLine

Syntax   **VLine** [*Count*]

Remarks   Scrolls the active document vertically. A "line" corresponds to clicking a scroll arrow on the vertical scroll bar once.

Argument	Explanation
Count	The amount to scroll, in lines:
	Omitted One line down
	> 0 (zero) The specified number of lines down
	< 0 (zero) The specified number of lines up

See Also   **HLine, VPage, VScroll**

VPage

Syntax   **VPage** [*Count*]

Remarks   Scrolls the active document vertically. **VPage** corresponds to clicking the vertical scroll bar above or below the scroll box.

Argument	Explanation
Count	The amount to scroll, in screens:
	Omitted One screen down
	> 0 (zero) The specified number of screens down
	< 0 (zero) The specified number of screens up

See Also   **HPage**, **VLine**, **VScroll**

VScroll, VScroll()

Syntax   **VScroll** *Percentage*

VScroll()

Remarks   The **VScroll** statement scrolls vertically to the specified percentage of the document length. **VScroll** corresponds to dragging the scroll box on the vertical scroll bar.

The **VScroll**() function returns the current vertical scroll position as a percentage of the document length.

Example   This example scrolls to the middle of the active document:

```
VScroll 50
```

See Also   **HScroll**, **VLine**, **VPage**

WaitCursor

Syntax

WaitCursor *Wait*

Remarks

Changes the mouse pointer from the current pointer to an hourglass or watch, or vice versa. Control of the pointer is restored to Word when the macro ends.

Argument	Explanation
Wait	Specifies the mouse pointer to display:
	0 (zero) The current pointer
	1 The hourglass pointer (Windows) or watch pointer (Macintosh)

Example

This example suppresses the hourglass or watch pointer for the first half of the total iterations of a **For**...**Next** loop and then displays the hourglass or watch for the second half:

```
WaitCursor 0
For i = 1 To 1000
    If i = 500 Then WaitCursor 1
Next I
```

Weekday()

Syntax

Weekday(*SerialNumber*)

Remarks

Returns an integer between 1 and 7, inclusive, corresponding to the day of the week (where 1 is Sunday) on which the date represented by *SerialNumber* falls. A serial number is a decimal representation of the date, time, or both. For information about serial numbers, see **DateSerial**().

Example

This example defines an array containing the names of the days of the week, returns a number corresponding to the current weekday, and then uses this number with the array to return the name of the current weekday. This name is then displayed in a message box.

```
Dim days$(7)
days$(1) = "Sunday" : days$(2) = "Monday" : days$(3) = "Tuesday"
days$(4) = "Wednesday" : days$(5) = "Thursday"
days$(6) = "Friday" : days$(7) = "Saturday"
thisday = Weekday(Now())
MsgBox "Would you believe it's " + days$(thisday) + " already?"
```

See Also

DateSerial(), **Day()**, **Hour()**, **Minute()**, **Month()**, **Now()**, **Second()**, **Today()**, **Year()**

While...Wend

Syntax

While *Condition*
    Series of instructions
Wend

Remarks

Repeats a series of instructions between **While** and **Wend** while the specified condition is true. The **While...Wend** control structure is often used in WordBasic to repeat a series of instructions each time a given piece of text or formatting is found in a Word document. For an example of this use of **While...Wend**, see **EditFind**.

Example

This Windows example uses the **Files$()** function within a **While...Wend** loop to insert a list of files in the current folder whose filenames end with the .DOC filename extension. The instruction a$ = Files$("*.DOC") returns the first filename with a .DOC extension and a$ = Files$() returns the next filename with a .DOC extension each time the instructions within the loop run. As soon as Files$() returns an empty string (""), indicating there are no other .DOC files in the current folder, the condition a$ <> "" is false and Word exits the **While...Wend** loop.

```
FileNewDefault
currdir$ = Files$(".")
a$ = Files$("*.DOC")
While a$ <> ""
    count = count + 1
    a$ = FileNameInfo$(a$, 3)
    InsertPara : Insert a$
    a$ = Files$()
Wend
StartOfDocument : Bold 1
Insert currdir$ + " contains" + Str$(count) + " files."
```

On the Macintosh, you can use a similar example to create a list of Word documents in the current folder by modifying the instruction that sets the currdir$ variable and by specifying a signature instead of "*.DOC" as the file specification. Replace the first two **Files$()** instructions in the previous example with the following instructions:

```
currdir$ = Files$(":")
a$ = Files$(MacID$("W6BN"))
```

See Also

For...Next, Goto, If...Then...Else, Select Case

Window()

Syntax   **Window( )**

Remarks   Returns a number that corresponds to the position of the active window on the
                  Window menu, where 1 corresponds to the first position, 2 to the second position,
                  and so on. If there are no open windows, **Window**() returns 0 (zero). Word lists
                  windows on the Window menu in alphabetic order.

See Also   **WindowList, WindowName$( ), Window***Number***, WindowPane( )**

WindowArrangeAll

Syntax   **WindowArrangeAll**

Remarks   Arranges all open windows so they do not overlap.

See Also   **DocMove, DocRestore, DocSize**

WindowList

Syntax   **WindowList** *Number*

Remarks   Activates a window listed on the Window menu. The instruction WindowList 1
                  activates the first window in the list, WindowList 2 activates the second window,
                  and so on through the number of open windows. If no windows are listed, or if
                  Number is greater than the number of open windows, an error occurs.

Example   This example activates the first window containing the document TEST.DOC.
                  The **InStr( )** function checks for the string "TEST.DOC" in the window name,
                  which may include extra text such as "(Read-Only)" if the document is read-only,
                  or ":2" if the document is open in more than one window.

```
numwin = CountWindows( )
If numwin <> 0 Then
    i = 1
    While i <= numwin And leave <> 1
        winname$ = WindowName$(i)
        If InStr(winname$, "TEST.DOC") Then leave = 1
        If leave <> 1 Then i = i + 1
    Wend
End If
If InStr(winname$, "TEST.DOC") Then
    WindowList i
Else
    MsgBox "There is no window containing TEST.DOC."
End If
```

See Also	**CountWindows()**, **Window()**, **WindowName$()**, **Window***Number*, **WindowPane()**

WindowName$()

Syntax	**WindowName$(***Number***)**
Remarks	Returns the title of the open window listed at position *Number* on the Window menu, where 1 corresponds to the first position, 2 to the second position, and so on. If *Number* is 0 (zero) or omitted, **WindowName$()** returns the title of the active window.
	For an example, see **WindowList**.
See Also	**CountWindows()**, **Window()**, **WindowList**, **Window***Number*, **WindowPane()**

WindowNewWindow

Syntax	**WindowNewWindow**
Remarks	Opens a new window containing the active document. Word adds a colon (:) and a number to the titles of windows containing a document that is open in more than one window. For example, if the window title of the active document is TEST.DOC and you run **WindowNewWindow**, Word opens a new window titled TEST.DOC:2 and changes the original window title to TEST.DOC:1.
See Also	**DocSplit**, **WindowArrangeAll**, **WindowName$()**

Window*Number*

Syntax	**Window***Number*
Remarks	Activates a window listed on the Window menu. **Window1** activates the first window in the list, **Window2** activates the second window, and so on through **Window9**. If no windows are listed, or if *Number* is greater than the number of windows listed, an error occurs.

Note You cannot use a variable in place of *Number*; you must use an integer. **WindowList** provides the same functionality as **Window***Number* but accepts a numeric variable to specify the window to activate.

See Also	**Activate**, **CountWindows()**, **Window()**, **WindowList**, **WindowName$()**, **WindowPane()**

WindowPane()

Syntax   **WindowPane( )**

Remarks   Returns the following values.

Value	Explanation
1	If the active window is not split or if the insertion point is in the top pane of the active window
3	If the insertion point is in the bottom pane of the active window (for example, the footnote pane, the annotation pane, or the lower of two document panes)

Example   This example moves the insertion point to the top pane of the active document if the active window is split and the insertion point is in the bottom pane:

```
If WindowPane() = 3 Then OtherPane
```

See Also   **DocSplit, OtherPane, ViewAnnotations( ), ViewFootnoteArea( )**

WinToDOS$()

Syntax   **WinToDOS$(***StringToTranslate$***)**

Remarks   In Windows, translates a string from the Windows character set to the original equipment manufacturer (OEM) character set. On the Macintosh, **WinToDOS$( )** performs no translation and returns the specified string unchanged.

The OEM character set is typically used by MS-DOS applications. Characters 32 through 127 are usually the same in the OEM and Windows character sets. The other characters in the OEM character set (0 through 31 and 128 through 255) are generally different from the Windows characters.

Example   This example opens a sequential file created by a Windows-based application, translates each line to the OEM character set, and places the result in a new sequential file:

```
ChDir "C:\TMP"
Open "WINDOWS.TXT" For Input As #1
Open "DOS.TXT" For Output As #2
While Not Eof(1)
    Line Input #1, temp$
    Print #2, WinToDOS$(temp$)
Wend
Close
```

See Also   **DOSToWin$( )**

WordLeft, WordLeft()

Syntax   **WordLeft** [*Count,*] [*Select*]

WordLeft([*Count,*] [*Select*])

Remarks   The **WordLeft** statement moves the insertion point or the active end of the selection (the end that moves when you press CTRL+SHIFT+LEFT ARROW (Windows) or COMMAND+SHIFT+LEFT ARROW (Macintosh)) to the left by the specified number of words.

Argument	Explanation
Count	The number of words to move; if less than one or omitted, 1 is assumed.
Select	Specifies whether to select text:
	0 (zero) or omitted Text is not selected. If there is already a selection, **WordLeft** moves the insertion point *Count*–1 words to the left of the selection.
	Nonzero Text is selected. If there is already a selection, **WordLeft** moves the active end of the selection toward the beginning of the document.
	In a typical selection made from left to right, where the active end of the selection is closer to the end of the document, **WordLeft** shrinks the selection. In a selection made from right to left, it extends the selection.

Note that Word includes spaces following a word as part of the word. However, Word counts punctuation, tab characters, and paragraph marks as "words." For example, if a word is enclosed in quotation marks, moving the insertion point from the position following the closing quotation mark to the position preceding the opening quotation mark using **WordLeft** would require the instruction WordLeft 3.

The **WordLeft**() function behaves the same as the statement and also returns the following values.

Value	Explanation
0 (zero)	If the insertion point or the active end of the selection cannot be moved to the left.
–1	If the insertion point or the active end of the selection is moved to the left by any number of words, even if less than *Count*. For example, WordLeft(10) returns –1 even if the insertion point is only three words from the start of the document.

See Also   **CharLeft, SelectCurWord, SentLeft, WordRight**

WordRight, WordRight()

Syntax

WordRight [*Count,*] [*Select*]

WordRight([*Count,*] [*Select*])

Remarks

The **WordRight** statement moves the insertion point or the active end of the selection (the end that moves when you press CTRL+SHIFT+RIGHT ARROW (Windows) or COMMAND+SHIFT+RIGHT ARROW (Macintosh)) to the right by the specified number of words.

Argument	Explanation
Count	The number of words to move; if less than one or omitted, 1 is assumed.
Select	Specifies whether to select text:
	0 (zero) or omitted Text is not selected. If there is already a selection, **WordRight** moves the insertion point *Count*–1 words to the right of the selection.
	Nonzero Text is selected. If there is already a selection, **WordRight** moves the active end of the selection toward the end of the document.
	In a typical selection made from left to right, where the active end of the selection is closer to the end of the document, **WordRight** extends the selection. In a selection made from right to left, it shrinks the selection.

Note that Word includes spaces following a word as part of the word. However, Word counts punctuation, tab characters, and paragraph marks as "words."

The **WordRight()** function behaves the same as the statement and also returns the following values.

Value	Explanation
0 (zero)	If the insertion point or the active end of the selection cannot be moved to the right.
–1	If the insertion point or the active end of the selection is moved to the right by any number of characters, even if less than *Count*. For example, WordRight(10) returns –1 even if the insertion point is only three words from the end of the document.

Example

This example counts the number of words (including punctuation, tab characters, and paragraph marks) in the selection and then displays the result in a message box:

```
EditBookmark "CountMe", .Add
SelType 1
While CmpBookmarks("\Sel", "CountMe") = 6 \
        Or CmpBookmarks("\Sel", "CountMe") = 8
    WordRight
    count = count + 1
Wend
EditGoTo "CountMe"
EditBookmark "CountMe", .Delete
MsgBox "There are" + Str$(count) + " words in the selection."
```

See Also

CharRight, **SelectCurWord**, **SentRight**, **WordLeft**

WordUnderline, WordUnderline()

Syntax

WordUnderline [*On*]

WordUnderline()

Remarks

The **WordUnderline** statement adds or removes the word-underline character format for the selected text, or controls word-underline formatting for characters to be inserted at the insertion point.

Argument	Explanation
On	Specifies whether to add or remove the word-underline format.
	1 Formats the selection with the word-underline format.
	0 (zero) Removes the word-underline format.
	Omitted Toggles the word-underline format.

The **WordUnderline()** function returns the following values.

Value	Explanation
0 (zero)	If none of the selection is in the word-underline format
−1	If part of the selection is in the word-underline format
1	If all the selection is in the word-underline format

See Also

DottedUnderline, **DoubleUnderline**, **FormatFont**, **Underline**

Write

Syntax   **Write** #*FileNumber*, *Expression1*[$] [, *Expression2*[$]] [, ...]

Remarks   Writes the specified expressions to an open sequential file. *FileNumber* is the
                  number specified in the **Open** instruction that opened the file for output or
                  appending. For more information about sequential files, see Chapter 9, "More
                  WordBasic Techniques," in Part 1, "Learning WordBasic."

                  Write is similar to the **Print** statement, but instead of separating the expressions
                  with tab characters, **Write** separates them with commas; also, **Write** encloses
                  strings in quotation marks. This allows the resulting values to be read by a **Read**
                  instruction. For an illustration of the respective output of the **Print** and **Write**
                  statements, see **Print**.

Example   This example opens a sequential file for output (creating it if it does not already
                  exist), prompts the user for three pieces of data, and then uses the **Write** statement
                  to insert the data into the sequential file:

```
Open "DATAFILE.TXT" For Output As #1
name$ = InputBox$("Enter name:")
age = Val(InputBox$("Enter age:"))
job$ = InputBox$("Enter occupation:")
Write #1, name$, age, job$
Close #1
```

                  The following is an example of a paragraph in DATAFILE.TXT inserted by the
                  Write statement:

```
"Michelle Levine", 26,"Dancer"
```

See Also   **Close, Eof(), Input, Input$(), Line Input, Lof(), Open, Print, Read, Seek**

Year()

Syntax

Year(*SerialNumber*)

Remarks

Returns an integer between 1899 and 4095, inclusive, corresponding to the year component of *SerialNumber*, a decimal representation of the date, time, or both. For information about serial numbers, see **DateSerial()**.

Example

This example returns the year component of the current date, converts it to a string, and then shortens the string to only the final two digits:

```
years - Year(Now())
years$ = Str$(years)
years$ = Right$(years$, 2)
```

See Also

DateSerial(), **Day()**, **Hour()**, **Minute()**, **Month()**, **Now()**, **Second()**, **Today()**, **Weekday()**

Operators and Predefined Bookmarks

The following sections provide detailed information about WordBasic operators and predefined bookmarks.

Operators

An expression is any valid combination of operators, variables, numbers, strings, and WordBasic functions that can be evaluated to a single result. Depending on the kind of operator and values used, the result of an expression can be a number, string, or logical value, where the numbers −1 and 0 (zero) represent the logical values true and false, respectively. In WordBasic, there are four categories of operators to use with values to form expressions: arithmetic, string concatenation, comparison, and logical. This section describes the operators within these categories in order of operator precedence.

Operator Precedence

When several operations occur in an expression, each part is evaluated and resolved in a predetermined order known as operator precedence. Parentheses can be used to override the order of precedence and force some parts of an expression to be evaluated before others. Operations within parentheses are always performed before those outside parentheses.

Within parentheses, however, normal operator precedence is maintained. When expressions contain operators from more than one category, arithmetic operators (including the string concatenation operator) are evaluated first, comparison operators are evaluated next, and logical operators are evaluated last.

Within an expression, multiplication and division operations are evaluated before addition and subtraction operations. When multiplication and division occur together in an expression, each operation is evaluated as it occurs from left to right. Likewise, when addition and subtraction occur together in an expression, each operation is evaluated in order of appearance from left to right. All comparison operators have equal precedence; that is, they are evaluated in the left-to-right order in which they appear in an expression.

The string concatenation operator (+) is not really an arithmetic operator, but in precedence it does fall after all arithmetic operators and before all comparison operators.

Arithmetic Operators

Use these operators to generate any numeric value to assign to a variable or to use in input, output, or loops.

Operator	Description
– (Negation)	Indicates that the operand is a negative value. The operand can be any numeric expression.
* (Multiplication)	Multiplies two numbers. The operands can be any numeric expressions.
/ (Division)	Divides two numbers. The operands can be any numeric expressions.
MOD (Modular division)	Divides two operands and returns only the remainder. For example, the result of the expression 19 MOD 7 (which can be read as 19 modulo 7) is 5. The operands can be any numeric expressions.
+ (Addition)	Sums two numbers. The operands can be any numeric expressions.
	Note that you also use + as the string concatenation operator.
– (Subtraction)	Finds the difference between two numbers. The operands can be any numeric expressions.

The String Concatenation Operator

Use the string concatenation operator to link literal strings and string variables.

Operator	Description
+ (String concatenation)	Concatenates two strings. For example, the result of "Microsoft " + "Word" is "Microsoft Word". You must ensure that spaces are included in the strings being concatenated to avoid running words or characters together.
	If you use the **Str$()** function to return numbers as strings, note that the function adds a space before positive numbers (for example, Str$(47) returns " 47"), but not before negative numbers (for example, Str$(-47) returns "-47").
	Note that you also use + as the addition operator.

Comparison Operators

Use these operators, also known as relational operators, to compare two expressions (numeric or string) and return true (–1) or false (0) values for use in control structures such as **If** conditionals and **While...Wend** loops. The following table lists the comparison operators and the conditions that determine whether the result is true or false.

Operator	True	False
= (Equal to)	*exp1 = exp2*	*exp1 <> exp2*
<> (Not equal to)	*exp1 <> exp2*	*exp1 = exp2*
< (Less than)	*exp1 < exp2*	*exp1 >= exp2*
> (Greater than)	*exp1 > exp2*	*exp1 <= exp2*
<= (Less than or equal to)	*exp1 <= exp2*	*exp1 > exp2*
>= (Greater than or equal to)	*exp1 >= exp2*	*exp1 < exp2*

Logical Operators

Use these operators in combination with comparison expressions to create compound logical expressions that return true (–1) or false (0) values.

Operator	Description
AND	If, and only if, both expressions evaluate true, the result is true. If either expression evaluates false, the result is false. The result is determined as follows:

True AND True	True
False AND True	False
True AND False	False
False AND False	False

Operator	Description
OR	If either or both expressions evaluate true, the result is true. The result is determined as follows:

True OR True	True
False OR True	True
True OR False	True
False OR False	False

Operator	Description
NOT	The result is determined as follows:

NOT False	True
NOT True	False

Note that a NOT compound expression evaluates as described only when the operands are comparisons or numeric true and false values, where true is –1 and false is 0 (zero).

True, False, and Bitwise Comparisons

In WordBasic, "true" is represented by the number –1, and "false" by the number 0 (zero). When WordBasic recognizes the number –1 as true and 0 (zero) as false, it is actually recognizing the values of each bit in the bytes that represent those numbers: –1 is the byte 1111 1111 and 0 (zero) is the byte 0000 0000. In fact, if WordBasic finds at least one "1" bit in any byte that represents a number, it recognizes the byte as true. Therefore, any nonzero number can represent true because the bytes for all nonzero numbers, both positive and negative, include at least one "1" bit. Only the byte for the number 0 (zero) contains all "0" bits and is therefore considered false.

When WordBasic evaluates a comparison—such as "A" = "A" or 5 < 2— it returns the standard true or false byte. But when WordBasic evaluates a compound expression (using one of the logical operators AND, OR, or NOT), it returns the byte for whatever number results from the eight "bitwise" comparisons that the logical operator makes with the original numbers. In a bitwise comparison, the operator compares each corresponding bit in the bytes that represent the values in the expression.

For example, in an AND bitwise comparison, if the first bit in each byte is set to 1, the first bit in the resulting byte is set to 1; otherwise, the bit is set to 0 (zero). In the expression "A" = "A" AND 5 < 2, the byte that represents "A" = "A" is 1111 1111 (the byte for –1, or true), and the byte that represents 5 < 2 is 0000 0000 (the byte for 0, or false). So WordBasic makes the following eight bitwise comparisons.

Bit in "A" = "A"	Bit in 5 < 2	Bit in AND result
1	0	0
1	0	0
1	0	0
1	0	0
1	0	0
1	0	0
1	0	0
1	0	0

The resulting byte is 0000 0000, which is the number 0 (zero). Therefore, because WordBasic considers the value 0 (zero) to be false, the result of "A" = "A" AND 5 < 2 is false.

Note If the eight bitwise comparisons are made with bytes other than those representing −1 and 0 (zero), unexpected results may occur. (Remember that WordBasic recognizes any nonzero value as true because every nonzero value contains at least one "1" bit.) For example, with the compound expression 5 AND 2, where the byte for 5 is 0000 0101 and the byte for 2 is 0000 0010, the resulting byte is 0000 0000, which is the number 0 (zero). Because WordBasic always considers 0 (zero) to be false, the result of 5 AND 2 is false, even though the nonzero values 5 and 2 are considered "true" on their own.

In a compound expression, the three logical operators AND, OR, and NOT make the following bitwise comparisons for each bit in the bytes that represent the values in the expression.

AND

This operator returns the "1" bit if, and only if, both bits in the bytes being compared are "1" bits.

Bit in first byte	Bit in second byte	Bit in AND result
0	0	0
0	1	0
1	0	0
1	1	1

OR

This operator returns the "1" bit if either bit in the bytes being compared is a "1" bit.

Bit in first byte	Bit in second byte	Bit in OR result
0	0	0
0	1	1
1	0	1
1	1	1

NOT

This operator converts each bit in a single byte to its opposite bit in the result.

Bit in byte	Bit in NOT result
0	1
1	0

You can get unexpected results using the NOT operator with true values other than –1. For example, the number 1 evaluates true, but the expression NOT 1 also evaluates true. The result is true because 1 is the byte 0000 0001, and the NOT operator changes each bit to its opposite value; thus, the result of NOT 1 is the byte 1111 1110, which is the number –2. Just as WordBasic recognizes 1 as a numeric value for true, it also recognizes –2 as a numeric value for true.

A number of WordBasic functions can return the value 1. For example, **Bold**() returns 1 if all the current selection is bold and –1 if some of the current selection is bold. Consider the following instruction:

```
If Bold() Then MsgBox "Some or all of the selection is bold."
```

This instruction works reliably because both 1 and –1 evaluate true. But the following instruction will not work reliably:

```
If NOT Bold() Then MsgBox "None of the selection is bold."
```

If none of the selection is bold, **Bold**() returns 0 (zero), and the message box is displayed as expected. Likewise, if some of the selection is bold, **Bold**() returns –1, and the message box is not displayed. But if all the selected text is bold, **Bold**() returns 1; because NOT 1 is true (as shown earlier), the message box will be displayed, even though the selection is bold. To avoid unexpected results with NOT, you should use only the values –1 and 0 (zero) to represent true and false.

Predefined Bookmarks

Word sets and automatically updates a number of reserved bookmarks. You can use these predefined bookmarks just as you use the ones that you place in documents, except that you don't have to set them and they are not listed in the Go To dialog box (Edit menu). The following table describes the predefined bookmarks available in Word.

Bookmark	Description
\Sel	Current selection or the insertion point.
\PrevSel1	Most recent selection where editing occurred; going to this bookmark is equivalent to running the **GoBack** statement once.
\PrevSel2	Second most recent selection where editing occurred; going to this bookmark is equivalent to running the **GoBack** statement twice.
\StartOfSel	Start of the current selection.
\EndOfSel	End of the current selection.
\Line	Current line or the first line of the current selection. If the insertion point is at the end of a line that is not the last line in the paragraph, the bookmark includes the entire next line.
\Char	Current character, which is the character following the insertion point if there is no selection, or the first character of the selection.
\Para	Current paragraph, which is the paragraph containing the insertion point or, if more than one paragraph is selected, the first paragraph of the selection. Note that if the insertion point or selection is in the last paragraph of the document, the "\Para" bookmark does not include the paragraph mark.
\Section	Current section, including the break at the end of the section, if any. The current section contains the insertion point or selection. If the selection contains more than one section, the "\Section" bookmark is the first section in the selection.
\Doc	Entire contents of the active document, with the exception of the final paragraph mark.
\Page	Current page, including the break at the end of the page, if any. The current page contains the insertion point. If the current selection contains more than one page, the "\Page" bookmark is the first page of the selection. Note that if the insertion point or selection is in the last page of the document, the "\Page" bookmark does not include the final paragraph mark.
\StartOfDoc	Beginning of the document.
\EndOfDoc	End of the document.

Bookmark	Description
\Cell	Current cell in a table, which is the cell containing the insertion point. If one or more cells of a table are included in the current selection, the "\Cell" bookmark is the first cell in the selection.
\Table	Current table, which is the table containing the insertion point or selection. If the selection includes more than one table, the "\Table" bookmark is the entire first table of the selection, even if the entire table is not selected.
\HeadingLevel	The heading that contains the insertion point or selection, plus any subordinate headings and text. If the current selection is body text, the "\HeadingLevel" bookmark includes the preceding heading, plus any headings and text subordinate to that heading.

The following macro demonstrates a typical use of predefined bookmarks. The macro moves line by line through a document from the current line and removes any leading spaces from the lines. The **While...Wend** instruction uses the "\Sel" (current selection) and "\EndofDoc" bookmarks with the **CmpBookmarks()** function to determine whether the selection is at the end of the document. When the end of the document is reached, Word displays a message to alert the user.

```
Sub MAIN
StartOfLine
While CmpBookmarks("\Sel", "\EndOfDoc")
    A$ = GetBookmark$("\Line")
    B = Asc(A$)
    If B = 32 Then DeleteWord
    EndOfLine
    CharRight
Wend
MsgBox "End of document."
End Sub
```

The **CmpBookmarks()** function compares two bookmarks and can return a number of different values according to the relative location and size of the bookmarks. For more information on **CmpBookmarks()**, see the entry in "Statements and Functions" earlier in this part.

For other examples of predefined bookmarks used in WordBasic macros, see the following entries in "Statements and Functions" earlier in this part: **CmpBookmarks()**, **CopyBookmark**, **ParaDown**, **Select Case**.

Error Messages

The following list of Microsoft Word error messages and their corresponding error codes is divided into two parts: WordBasic error messages and Word error messages. The list is included for use in error trapping using the WordBasic statements **On Error**, **Err**, and **Error**. For more information, see the corresponding entries in "Statements and Functions."

WordBasic Error Messages

When you run a macro and an error occurs, you can get more information by choosing the Help button in the error message box. For information about an error message at any time, see "Error Messages" in Help. Choose an error from the list to display the corresponding Help topic. The following list of macro errors includes error numbers you can use with the **Error** statement.

Note In Windows, if an untrapped error occurs in a macro while Word is minimized, the macro halts, Word remains minimized, and the Word icon flashes. When Word is maximized, an error message that indicates the nature of the error is displayed.

Error Number	Error Message
5	Illegal function call
6	Overflow
7	Out of memory
9	Subscript out of range
11	Division by zero
14	Out of string space
22	Invalid array dimension
24	Bad parameter
25	Out of memory (stack space)
26	Dialog needs End Dialog or a push button

Error Number	Error Message
28	Directory already exists
39	CASE ELSE expected
51	Internal error
52	Bad file name or number
53	File not found
54	Bad file mode
55	File already open
57	Device I/O error
62	Input past end of file
64	Bad file name
67	Too many files
74	Rename across disks
75	Path/File access error
76	Path not found
100	Syntax error
101	Comma missing
102	Command failed
103	Dialog record variable expected
104	ELSE without IF
105	END IF without IF
109	INPUT missing
111	Expression too complex
112	Identifier expected
113	Duplicate label
114	Label not found
115	Right parenthesis missing
116	Argument-count mismatch
117	Missing NEXT or WEND
118	Nested SUB or FUNCTION definitions
119	NEXT without FOR
120	Array already dimensioned
122	Type mismatch
123	Undefined dialog record field
124	Unknown Command, Subroutine, or Function
125	Unexpected end of macro

Error Number	Error Message
126	WEND without WHILE
127	Wrong number of dimensions
129	Too many nested control structures
130	SELECT without END SELECT
131	Illegal Redim to dialog record
132	External call caused string overflow
133	Wrong number or type of arguments for DLL call
134	An argument to a function contained an illegal date or time.
135	The () statement is not available in Word for ().
136	The () statement is not available in Word for ().
137	The specified path is not a valid path option.
138	The current selection cannot be modified by this command.
139	Only one user dialog may be up at any time.
140	Dialog control identifier does not match any current control.
141	The () statement is not available on this dialog control type.
142	Specified application is not currently running
143	The dialog control with the focus may not be disabled or hidden.
144	Focus may not be set to a hidden or disabled control.
149	The () command cannot be called as a function.
150	Dialog control identifier is already defined.
152	This command is not available because no document is open.
155	The selection does not start in a field.
157	The field cannot contain data.
158	The value of one of the fields is too low.
159	The value of one of the fields is too high.
160	Wrong number of parameters
161	Cannot change dialogs when focus is changing (action 4)
162	The () command can only be called as a function.
163	This statement can only be used when a user dialog is active.
164	Array variable has not been initialized.
500	Cannot initiate link
501	Invalid channel number
502	Application does not respond
503	Process failed in other application
504	Window does not exist

Error Number	Error Message
505	Cannot activate application
506	Cannot send keys
508	Other application is busy
509	The () command is not available because ().
511	No such macro or command
512	Value out of range
513	String too long
514	Document not open
528	Unable to load spelling checker
529	Cannot open dictionary
530	Dialog box description too complex
535	Macro cannot be run because it is already running.
536	There is no macro with that name.
537	Unable to run macro specified
538	Unable to edit macro specified
539	Unable to rename macro specified
540	Unable to delete macro specified
541	Unable to set description of macro specified
543	Unable to open specified library
544	Unable to execute the scroll command; the scroll bar is not active.
545	The () statement is currently disabled.
546	Footnotes or endnotes must start at 1 if numbering is not continuous.
547	Network Permission Error
549	The specified menu or menu item does not exist.
551	Word is unable to perform this action because the specified template is locked.
552	Word is unable to perform this action because the specified template does not exist.
553	Unable to create macro specified
554	No drawing range has been set.
555	The bookmark specified for the drawing range is invalid.
556	Wrong drawing object type for this command
557	Could not insert the drawing object
558	At least one subdocument in this master document is locked. No changes can be made to any locked subdocuments.
559	The current selection is a block.

Error Number	Error Message
560	The revision marks are not visible.
561	Document is protected
562	ToolsGrammarStatisticsArray cannot be run on a document that contains more than one language format.
563	The document is not a master document.
564	There are no subdocuments in that direction.
565	The specified document is not in the Add-in list.
566	The specified Word library cannot be unloaded because it is in use.
567	Cannot add more than 25 items in the dropdown list box
568	The specified font doesn't exist
569	PatternMatch and SoundsLike parameters cannot both be set to 1
570	Cannot sort arrays with more than two dimensions
574	Address not found
575	MAPI returned error
576	Cannot add address to Personal Address Book
577	You must specify display name for a new address
578	Unknown document property
579	Cannot delete a built-in document property
580	Unknown link
581	Cannot change the value of a read-only document property
582	Unable to load specified library
583	Illegal function name

Word Error Messages

These error messages are generated outside WordBasic, by Word itself. Word always displays an error message box for these messages and waits for the user to choose the OK button, regardless of whether a macro contains error-trapping statements. Once the user responds, Word returns control to the WordBasic macro, and the error can be trapped and handled like any other. Note that the **Error** statement cannot create these error conditions, nor can it be used to display these error messages.

Error Number	Error Message
1001	There is insufficient memory. Save the document now.
1003	You can specify only one line, footnote, endnote, annotation, or field at a time.

Error Number	Error Message
1005	This bookmark does not exist.
1006	You entered multiple destinations for a page, line, footnote, endnote, or annotation.
1008	Word cannot insert a section break here.
1009	The bookmark name is not valid.
1011	There is not enough memory to compile the index.
1013	There is not enough memory to run the DDE application.
1014	There is not enough memory to run the application.
1015	This command is not available in Word for the Macintosh.
1016	There is not enough memory to complete the operation.
1017	There is not enough memory to update the display.
1018	There is not enough memory to define the AutoText entry.
1019	There is not enough memory to merge the styles.
1020	There is not enough memory to display the outline.
1021	There is not enough memory to display the ruler.
1022	The name you typed is not a valid AutoText entry. Use the AutoText button on the Standard toolbar to define AutoText entries that can be inserted as a long piece of text or a graphic.
1023	There is a serious disk error on file ().
1024	The file () is not available.
1025	Word cannot open the document.
1026	This style name does not exist.
1027	There is insufficient memory, and Word cannot perform the replace operation.
1028	The search item was not found.
1029	There is not enough memory to display or print the picture.
1030	The dimensions after cropping are too small or too large.
1031	The dimensions after resizing are too small or too large.
1032	The file is too large to save. Delete some text and try again.
1033	Word cannot use the DOT-PATH specified in the File Locations panel because it is not valid.
1034	Word cannot use the INI-PATH specified in the File Locations panel because it is not valid.
1035	Word cannot use the TOOLS-PATH specified in the File Locations panel because it is not valid.
1036	Word cannot start the converter ().
1037	There is not enough memory to run this converter.

Error Number	Error Message
1038	The password is incorrect. Word cannot overwrite the document.
1039	This is not a valid hyphenation zone measurement.
1041	This document template does not exist.
1042	Settings you chose for the left and right margins, column spacing, or paragraph indents are too large for the page width in some sections.
1043	This tab stop is too large.
1044	Word cannot print.
1045	This is not a valid print range.
1046	Word cannot print due to a problem with the current printer.
1047	There is not enough memory to repaginate or print this document.
1048	Windows needs more disk space to print this document.
1049	Another window cannot be opened until one is closed.
1050	This is not a valid number.
1051	This is not a valid measurement.
1052	The number must be between () and ().
1053	The measurement must be between () and ().
1054	Word cannot write to file ().
1055	The document name or path is not valid.
1056	This is not a valid filename.
1057	Word cannot give a document the same name as an open document.
1058	You cannot save a template file to non-template format.
1059	This file is read-only.
1060	Word cannot save or create this file. Make sure the disk is not write protected.
1062	Fields are nested too deeply.
1066	There is not enough memory to run Word.
1069	Word cannot open the existing ().
1070	This is not a valid date.
1071	This is not a valid style name.
1072	The style sheet is full. Word cannot define the new style.
1073	You cannot base a style on itself.
1074	The Based On style name does not exist or is of incorrect type.
1075	The Next style name does not exist or is of incorrect type.
1076	Word cannot merge the style sheet from the active template.
1077	This style name already exists or is reserved for a built-in style.

Error Number	Error Message
1078	This file could not be found.
1079	There is not enough memory for such a large Clipboard.
1080	The indent size is too large.
1081	The paragraph is too wide.
1083	The command name must have an extension.
1084	Word cannot open this document template.
1085	The document template is not valid.
1090	The style sheet is full. The style of some paragraphs may become Normal.
1091	Word cannot insert a file into itself.
1093	There is not enough memory to run the thesaurus.
1094	Word cannot start the thesaurus.
1095	There is not enough memory to run the spelling checker.
1097	Word cannot start the spelling checker.
1103	Word cannot find the file WORDCBT.CBT.
1104	This is not a valid tab stop.
1105	There are too many tab stops set in this paragraph.
1106	There are too many tab stops to clear at one time.
1107	Word found no XE (Index Entry) fields for the index.
1108	Word cannot create a work file.
1109	A settings file is not valid. Word will use the defaults.
1111	Word cannot open a window for the result. Close some open windows and try again.
1112	You cannot insert DATA, NEXT, NEXTIF, or SKIPIF fields inside other fields.
1113	You cannot include DATA, NEXT, NEXTIF, or SKIPIF fields in annotations, headers, footers, footnotes or endnotes.
1114	A DATA field must be the first field in the main document.
1115	A DATA field does not contain a data filename.
1116	There is a syntax error in a field condition.
1117	Word does not recognize the filename in the data source you typed.
1118	Word does not recognize the filename in the header source you typed.
1119	The requested record is beyond the end of the mail merge data source.
1120	There is a printer error.

Error Number	Error Message
1121	Word cannot change printers. No printers are installed.
1122	The number in the Start At box is not valid.
1123	The number in the Format box is not valid.
1124	The numbers in the Start At and Format boxes are not valid.
1125	Word found no TC (Table of Contents Entry) fields for the table of contents.
1126	Word found no paragraphs with heading styles to include in the table of contents.
1127	Make a selection first.
1128	This is not a valid selection.
1129	The document is too large to save. Delete some text before saving.
1130	The document is too large for Word to handle.
1132	There is insufficient memory. Close an application.
1133	This search list is not valid
1134	This search expression is not valid.
1138	The window is too small.
1140	This is not a valid action for endnotes.
1142	Word found no revision marks.
1143	This document has too many styles. Word discarded some styles.
1144	Word cannot read the formatting in this document.
1145	Word found no footnotes.
1146	Word found no annotations.
1147	There is insufficient memory. The fonts in the copied text may be incorrect.
1151	Word cannot move text containing a section break to the selected destination.
1152	Word cannot move footnote, endnote, or annotation references to the selected destination.
1153	Word cannot replace footnote, endnote, or annotation references.
1154	There are too many edits in the document. This operation will be incomplete. Save your work.
1155	This is not a valid action for the end of a row.
1156	This is not a valid action for footnotes.
1157	Word did not save the document.
1158	The original file may be damaged due to a serious disk error. Save it with a new filename.

Error Number	Error Message
1159	You are working without a Word work file and memory is nearly full. Save your work.
1160	The Word work file and memory are nearly full. Save your work.
1161	This exceeds the maximum number of columns.
1162	This exceeds the maximum width.
1163	The end of a row cannot be deleted.
1164	You cannot insert this selection into a table.
1170	You cannot paste this selection into a table.
1172	Word cannot paste text containing a section break.
1175	The Paste command failed because the copy and paste areas are different shapes.
1176	There is insufficient memory. Close extra windows and save your work.
1177	The document name or path is not valid.
1179	This is not a valid action for annotations.
1180	The value is out of range.
1181	Word could not create a work file.
1182	There is not enough memory to sort.
1183	Word cannot sort fields in the selection.
1184	Word found no valid records to sort.
1185	The style you want to create is based on too many styles.
1186	There is insufficient memory. Word is closing the saved document.
1190	There is an unrecoverable disk error on file ().
1191	The disk is full trying to write to (). Free some space on this drive or save the document on a different disk.
1194	You cannot close a running macro.
1195	() is not a valid macro or command name.
1196	There is not enough memory to record the command.
1198	Cannot run Word: incorrect system version.
1200	Word cannot start Examples and Demos.
1202	There is not enough memory to run Examples and Demos.
1208	Word cannot rename or delete a macro that is open for editing.
1209	You cannot edit a macro while it is being recorded.
1210	This macro line is too long.
1211	You cannot record over a macro that is open for editing.

Error Number	Error Message
1215	There is insufficient memory. Close extra windows and try again.
1217	One or more rows are too wide to split.
1218	The recorded macro was too long and has been truncated.
1219	One or more rows are too wide for this operation.
1220	Word cannot find or run the application.
1225	You cannot copy or move this selection.
1226	There is insufficient memory. Word cannot display the requested font.
1227	Word cannot open the graphics file.
1229	This style has a circular Based On list.
1234	Records with an incorrect number of fields will be skipped.
1235	There is not enough memory to complete the operation.
1236	There is insufficient memory. The list may be incomplete.
1237	You cannot quit Microsoft Word because a dialog is active. Switch to Microsoft Word first and close the dialog.
1240	You cannot repaginate until a printer is installed.
1241	Word is opening a Word for OS/2 document. (This document may be fully converted by saving it as a Word for Windows document from within Word for OS/2.)
1245	Word cannot display this picture format.
1246	The specified data type is unavailable.
1247	Word cannot start the file converter () because it is being used by another Word session.
1248	Word cannot locate the server application for () objects. Install the server application with the Setup program.
1249	Word cannot obtain the data for the () link.
1250	Word cannot change the function of the specified key.
1251	The key name is not valid.
1255	The spelling checker is in use.
1256	The link does not exist.
1257	You cannot save while the file is in use by another process. Try saving the file with a new name.
1260	Word cannot save this file because it is already open elsewhere.
1261	Word cannot open this file because it is being updated by another process.
1262	You cannot modify a specified link.

Error Number	Error Message
1263	You have tried to open too many custom dictionaries. Word can have up to 10 custom dictionaries open at the same time.
1264	The server application, source file, or item cannot be found.\rMake sure the application is properly installed, and that it has not been deleted, moved, or renamed.
1265	You cannot change printer orientation with the current printer installed.
1266	Line spacing must be at least ().
1267	Word cannot create the custom dictionary ().
1268	Word cannot open custom dictionary ().
1269	Word cannot edit the ().
1270	Word cannot use the AUTOSAVE-PATH specified in the File Locations panel because it is not valid.
1271	Word cannot recognize this language.
1272	There is not enough memory to run Help for WordPerfect Users.
1273	Word cannot start Help for WordPerfect Users.
1275	The object () is locked for editing.
1276	No text or formatting is in the Find box.
1277	The custom dictionary is full. The word was not added.
1278	The custom dictionary () is too large. Try dividing it in half.
1279	A spelling checker error occurred. Word is ending the current session.
1280	The custom dictionary () is not available.
1282	The number in the Position box must be positive.
1283	This file was not recognized by the specified graphics filter.
1284	The graphics file is too large to be converted.
1285	This graphics file may be damaged and cannot be converted.
1286	The graphics filter was unable to convert this file.
1287	Word cannot start the graphics filter.
1289	The grammar checker is in use.
1290	There is not enough memory to run the grammar checker.
1291	Word cannot start the grammar checker.
1292	Word cannot read this file. Install Graphics filters by running setup.
1293	Word does not recognize the object ().
1295	The item name "()" of link () cannot be found.
1297	The setting does not exist or cannot be deleted.

Error Number	Error Message
1298	This document could not be registered.
1299	The list of paths is full.
1300	Word cannot save the document while the backup file is open. Clear the backup option or save the document with a new name.
1302	The operation is cancelled.
1304	There is not enough memory to hyphenate the document.
1305	Word cannot locate the hyphenator file.
1306	The file viewer could not be initialized.
1309	There is not enough memory to create the hand annotation.
1310	Make the list separator and the decimal separator different before calculating.
1311	The thesaurus is in use.
1312	The password is incorrect. Word cannot open the document.
1313	Word cannot make the current document into both a mail merge main document and a data document.
1314	The disk drive is not valid.
1315	The path is not valid.
1316	This action will not change the default page number format. To change the default page number format for this section, use Insert Page Number and choose the Format button.
1317	The disk is full.
1318	There is not enough memory to display the Mail Merge toolbar.
1319	The disk search failed. Word has restored the previous search path.
1320	The setting could not be created.
1321	The directory or folder is not valid.
1323	Word cannot find the () ().
1324	Word cannot find the () for ().
1325	The style name contains a character that is not valid.
1326	The style name is too long. The maximum number of characters allowed is 253.
1327	Word cannot create the specified destination file.
1328	This file is empty or does not contain a graphic image.
1331	A grammar checker error occurred. Word is ending the current session.
1332	The path cannot contain any periods as path elements.
1333	Word is unable to start Help.

Error Number	Error Message
1334	You cannot edit the result of a link or embedded object.
1335	Word cannot convert graphics files because no printer has been selected in File Print.
1336	Word cannot create the () file because no field names were specified.
1338	The maximum number of fields allowed is 31.
1339	Word cannot write to the settings file.
1340	The destination document did not accept the update.
1341	This filename is not valid or it contains a path.
1342	Graphics files can be inserted using the Picture option from the Insert menu.
1343	Word is hyphenating another document.
1345	You cannot print a graphics file using the Find File command.
1346	You cannot attach a document template as a data or header source.
1347	A hyphenation error occurred. Word is ending the current session.
1348	A thesaurus error occurred. Word is ending the current session.
1349	Word cannot use the DOC-PATH specified in the File Locations panel because it is not valid.
1351	Word cannot search for paragraph marks in Outline View.
1352	Word cannot delete the old backup file because it is read-only or another user has it open.
1353	Word cannot open the () for ().
1354	There are too many characters in the selection for the edit text window.
1355	The selection contains characters that cannot be edited using the edit text window.
1356	Word has finished searching the (). The search item was not found.
1357	Word has finished searching the ().
1358	Word cannot use the PICTURE-PATH specified in the File Locations panel because it is not valid.
1359	The directory or folder name is not valid.
1360	You do not have network permissions for this action.
1361	This file is in use by another application or user.
1362	There are too many open files.
1363	Cannot delete the current working directory or folder.
1364	A file error has occurred.
1366	There is no picture available at the specified location.

Error Number	Error Message
1367	A directory or folder of the proposed name already exists.
1368	A file of the proposed name already exists.
1369	Word cannot rename the file.
1371	You must type some text for a custom footnote or endnote mark.
1372	The AutoText name is not valid.
1373	The AutoText name already exists.
1374	The macro name is not valid.
1375	The macro name already exists.
1376	The organizer was unable to rename the () ().
1377	The built in () () cannot be deleted.
1378	A built in style cannot be renamed.
1380	The password is too long.
1381	Word detected an error while trying to bring up the Connect Network dialog box.
1382	There is not enough memory to edit a macro.
1383	You cannot close Microsoft Word because a dialog is active.\rSwitch to Microsoft Word first and close the dialog.
1385	There is not enough memory to convert the macros in this file.
1386	The organizer was unable to copy the () ().
1387	Word could not determine the destination.
1388	Word cannot add the entry because AutoCorrect entries cannot be blank.
1389	The password is incorrect.
1391	Word cannot complete the save due to a file permission error.
1392	Unable to add because AutoCorrect entries are limited to 31 characters in length.
1394	Unable to add entry to AutoCorrect because there is insufficient memory.
1395	AutoCorrect cannot replace text which contains a space character. Please remove the space, or replace it with something else.
1396	Word could not save the language setting in the custom dictionary.
1397	The active document is not a valid mail merge main document.
1398	Word did not update the source file.
1399	Dropdown list form fields must have at least one item in their list.
1400	Check the floppy drive to make sure the door is closed and it contains the correct disk.

Error Number	Error Message
1402	There is not enough memory to save the entire Ignore All list.
1405	The document is locked and cannot be opened.
1406	The disk is full or too many files are open.
1407	Word cannot replace the found item with text containing a break.
1408	This version of the spelling checker does not understand the language formatting of custom dictionary ().
1409	Column widths cannot be less than ().
1410	One or more columns or column spaces with zero width were found and removed.
1411	There must be at least one column defined.
1412	The linked document in () is unavailable.
1413	This font style name does not exist.
1414	You cannot put drawing objects into a text box, callout, annotation, footnote, endnote, or macro.
1415	The requested envelope size is not valid.
1419	The page height for some sections is greater than the maximum allowable page height.
1420	The top/bottom margins are too large for the page height in some sections.
1422	Increasing left margin causes first column to become too narrow in some sections having unevenly spaced columns.
1423	Increasing right margin causes last column to become too narrow in some sections having unevenly spaced columns.
1424	The network drive cannot be connected because there are no free drive letters.
1425	The network drive cannot be accessed without a password.
1426	The network path is not valid.
1427	The network password is not valid.
1428	Word has finished searching the (). () replacements were made.
1429	Word has finished searching the (). () replacement was made.
1431	() is not a valid () file.
1432	() is an incorrect version of the () file.
1433	There is not enough memory to make the indicated changes to the menu.
1434	Word cannot find the designated menu.
1435	There is no header layer for this page. All available layers will be displayed.

Error Number	Error Message
1436	The number must be between () and ().
1437	This caption label is not valid.
1438	You can have no more than 25 items in your drop-down list box.
1439	Word could not finish merging these documents or inserting this database.
1440	This command is available only from a macro.
1441	This AutoCorrect entry does not exist.
1442	Word could not shrink the document by one page because the document is already only one page.
1443	After several attempts, Word was unable to shrink the document by one page.
1444	Word could not successfully convert the picture into drawing objects.
1445	There are not enough system resources to complete the operation.
1446	The new toolbar must have a name.
1447	The formula is empty.
1448	The default directory or folder for this item cannot be on a floppy drive. Please choose a directory or folder on a hard drive.
1449	That toolbar already exists in the specified context. Please choose a different name.
1450	The document contains a character set that is not supported by this version of Word.
1451	Word found no TA (Table of Authorities Entry) fields for the table of authorities.
1452	Word cannot open () as a data or header source because it contains no data.
1453	The name you have chosen is already used for a built-in toolbar. Please choose a different name.
1454	Word cannot save the mail file.
1455	The new menu name cannot be the same as an existing menu name.
1456	The selection does not consist of heading levels.
1457	An unlocked subdocument already exists in another master document.
1458	The file cannot be opened with write privileges.
1459	The master document needs to be saved. Please save it now and try the operation again.
1460	Word could not save the subdocument. Please try a full save of the master document.

Error Number	Error Message
1461	Unknown mail address.
1462	Ambiguous mail address. There are two or more people whose mail addresses match the one specified.
1463	Word was unable to mail your document.
1464	The Find What text contains a Pattern Match expression which is not valid.
1465	The field delimiter cannot be the same as the record delimiter.
1466	The row or column value is too large or small for this sheet of labels.
1467	The margins, label size, and number across or down values produce a page that is larger than the label page size.
1468	Horizontal and vertical pitch must be greater than or equal to the label width and height, respectively.
1469	Label width and height must be positive values.
1470	Word could not recognize the field and record delimiter you specified.
1471	This save format is not valid.
1472	Word cannot save a document as form data only with the same name as an open document.
1475	Your mail system does not support certain services needed for document routing.
1474	Word cannot print because there is no default printer selected. Please select a printer.
1476	Too many mail sessions. Log off other mail sessions and try again.
1477	General mail failure. Close Microsoft Word, restart the mail system, and try again.
1478	The entry is empty.
1479	No citation was found.
1480	The Update Source command cannot be used to update a master document.
1481	Word cannot rename a file to another drive.
1482	The Find What text for a Sounds Like search can only contain non-accented alphabetic letters.
1483	Word found no captions to include in the table of figures.
1484	Word cannot load help because the Microsoft Help application or the () file was not found.
1485	The operation cannot be completed because a master document cannot contain more than 9 levels of subdocuments.

Error Number	Error Message
1486	There has been a network or file permission error. The network connection may be lost.
1487	Too many files are open. Please close a window.
1488	Too many DDE channels are open. Please close a window.
1489	Too many Word documents are open. Please close a window.
1490	The template cannot be customized because it is locked for editing.
1491	The style () refers to more than one style in the destination document.
1492	This menu item is automatically added by Word and cannot be removed from the menu.
1493	A proofing tool menu item is automatically added when Word detects that the tool has been installed. This item cannot be removed from the menu.
1494	The Find What text contains a range that is not valid.
1495	This command supports only table and paragraph-delimited lists.
1496	Record () contained too many field delimiters (()).
1497	Record () contained too few field delimiters (()).
1498	Word found no endnotes.
1499	Word could not load this add-in program.
1500	Start At must be between () and () for this format.
1502	Word cannot attach a document to a protected template.
1503	You cannot record a macro to a locked file.
1504	No index entries were marked.
1505	Word cannot insert a database that has no field names selected.
1506	Word cannot update the index.
1507	Subdocument () cannot be inserted because it is the current master document or because it contains the current master document as a subdocument.
1508	The maximum length value must be equal to or greater than the length of the default text, () characters.
1509	Word cannot create a subdocument within a field code or result.
1510	Word cannot create a subdocument within a table.
1511	Word cannot create a subdocument within a frame.
1512	() is not a style name.
1513	() refers to more than one style.

Error Number	Error Message
1515	Word cannot copy style () because it matches a style of a different type.
1516	Word cannot find the graphics filter, or there is not enough memory to load it.
1517	Word cannot find the designated menu item.
1518	The macro () cannot be renamed or deleted because it is currently open for editing or recording.
1519	Word cannot load the Button Editor, COMMTB.DLL.
1520	Mail is not installed on your system.
1521	Word has already routed this message. Reset the routing slip and try again.
1522	Word cannot run a macro until it has finished routing this document.
1523	The document does not have a routing slip. Add a routing slip and try again.
1524	Word for Windows cannot open a Word for the Macintosh glossary file.
1525	Word did not update the source file because it is protected or is an open subdocument.
1526	You must type a character for the custom separator.
1527	The Replace With text contains a group number which is out of range.
1528	() is not a valid special character for the Replace With box.
1529	() is not a valid special character for the Find What box.
1530	The current selection does not contain a valid table or list.
1531	Word cannot read the header or footer in this document. Save the document in Rich Text Format, close it, and then reopen it.
1532	Word cannot create a master document from these Word for the Macintosh files. Perhaps there is not enough memory.
1533	The list of filenames is too long. Word cannot open this many files at one time.
1534	Word cannot merge documents that can be distributed by mail or fax without a valid mail address. Choose the Setup button to select a mail address data field.
1535	Word could not merge the main document with the data source because the data records were empty or no data records matched your query options.
1536	Word cannot find or run the Print Manager.
1537	A valid date or time is required.

Error Number	Error Message
1538	A valid number is required.
1539	Word found no paragraphs with the styles needed to compile a table of figures.
1540	Word found no paragraphs with the styles needed to compile a table of contents.
1541	Word found no TC (Table of Contents Entry) fields for the table of figures.
1542	Word could not parse your query options into a valid SQL string.
1543	You can type no more than 32 characters in the Text Before and Text After boxes.
1544	Word could not re-establish a DDE connection to () to complete the current task.
1545	This is not a valid filename '()'.
1546	Word could not retrieve a SQL string from the active data source.
1547	This document cannot be opened in the Organizer dialog box.
1548	The default menu for this command does not exist. Use the Customize command to add this command to a menu.
1549	Word has increased the envelope height or width because it was too small. The minimum envelope dimensions are () by ().
1550	This toolbar name is not valid.
1551	This toolbar name already exists.
1552	The built-in styles Normal and Default Paragraph Font cannot be based on any style.
1553	Word could not open () because it didn't contain a valid database
1554	This command is unavailable because the form field was not inserted with the Forms toolbar or by using the Insert Form Field dialog box.
1555	Word cannot switch applications.
1556	Word could not locate or start ().
1557	The organizer could not delete the () ().
1558	The () () does not exist.
1559	Word could not restore an automatically saved document from the last session.
1560	Word could not replace the selection with the specified database.
1561	Word cannot start the grammar checker.
1562	No citations were marked.
1563	Word cannot open () as a data or header source because it is a mail merge main document.

Error Number	Error Message
1564	The document cannot be locked.
1565	You cannot send a catalog created by merging documents directly to mail, fax, or a printer.
1566	Word could not merge these documents or insert this database.
1567	Microsoft Mail Local Fax is not installed on your system.
1568	The registration database file is not valid. You can correct it with Word's Setup program.
1569	Word cannot complete the current operation because the Microsoft OLE Extension is missing or there is insufficient memory to use it.
1570	There is not enough available disk space to run Word.
1571	You cannot paste form fields into annotations, headers, footers, footnotes, endnotes, or text boxes.
1572	The formatting in this document is too complex. Please full save the document now.
1573	Word cannot undo this action because a subdocument or master document is locked.
1574	You cannot change a locked subdocument or master document.
1575	A valid date format is required.
1576	A valid number format is required.
1577	The add-in template is not valid.
1578	This entry is not valid for sorting. Please type or select another entry from the list.
1579	Word cannot sort this table or selection because all of its rows are table headings.
1580	Word cannot sort these numbers because it does not recognize the list separator, number format, or currency format settings used in (). To see the current settings, double-click the International icon in the () Control Panel.
1581	Word cannot start the Quick Preview.
1582	Word cannot find the requested bookmark.
1583	These query options are too complex for Microsoft Access version 1.0. Please upgrade to a later version of Microsoft Access to perform these query options.
1584	Word cannot sort Microsoft Access queries. You must sort the query in Microsoft Access.
1585	The global template, Normal, is already open as an add-in program.

Error Number	Error Message
1586	Word is opening a Word version 1.x for Windows template. Macros from Word 1.x for Windows cannot be converted and will be lost if this file is saved in Word 6.0 for Windows format.
1587	This page contains too many drawing objects to update the display.
1588	You cannot put section breaks into a header, footer, footnote, endnote, annotation, text box, callout, or macro.
1589	The operation cannot be completed because the subdocument is open in another window.
1590	The operation cannot be completed because the subdocument has a different type of protection from the master document. Make the protection the same for the master document and the subdocuments.
1591	The operation cannot be completed because the master document or subdocument contains an open embedded object. You must update and close these objects before you can continue.
1592	Word cannot make the requested network connection.
1593	There are too many characters in the form field.
1594	The selection is marked as deleted text.
1595	Word cannot search for paragraph marks in master document view.
1596	() is not a valid special character for the Find What box or is not supported when the Use Pattern Matching checkbox is selected
1597	There is not enough memory to display the menus. Save all changes and close Word.
1598	You cannot edit a picture that is not saved in the document.
1599	The selected drawing objects will not fit in a single group.
1600	You cannot copy text to another document before you finish reviewing changes made with the AutoFormat command.
1601	Word could not insert the results because your query generated an empty result.
1602	Word cannot open () as a header file because it cannot be converted to a Word file format.
1603	There is no grammar checker available for English.
1605	Word is still active. Save your document and close Word before shutting down.
1609	Apple PowerTalk (AOCE) is not installed.
1610	Before sending a letter, you must fill in a subject and add at least one recipient.
1611	There are no more letters that Word can open.
1612	Word cannot open the letter unless Apple PowerTalk is installed.

Error Number	Error Message
1613	There is not enough memory available to run the application.
1614	Word cannot find the application.
1615	Word cannot place a subscription there.
1616	Word was unable to create a publisher.
1617	The original file for this alias could not be found.
1618	() contains () Publishers to the Edition (). If there is more than one Publisher to an Edition, the Edition's contents aren't predictable.
1620	There is another Publisher open to the Edition (). If there is more than one Publisher to an Edition, the Edition's contents aren't predictable.
1621	There is not enough memory to run Apple PowerTalk.
1623	Word is unable to connect to the edition file for this publisher/subscriber.
1624	Word can only convert Word 5.0 and 5.1 settings files.
1625	Word cannot find the application (). Run Setup to install ().
1627	Apple PowerTalk is not fully initialized. Try restarting Word after your Mailbox appears.
1629	A document with a PowerTalk Mailer cannot be shown in multiple windows.
1630	Changes to the PowerTalk Mailer cannot be recorded.
1631	The server application can edit only one object each time. Close the application before you insert a new object.
1633	There is not enough memory to convert the side-by-side paragraphs to tables.
1691	Word cannot start help because the help application or help file was not found. Choose Microsoft Word Help from the Help menu to locate help.
1692	Word needs the Helvetica® 9 point font to display properly on this Macintosh. Please install this font to obtain the best results.
1693	Word was unable to write some of the embedded objects due to insufficient memory.
1694	There was an error reading from the file.
1695	Word cannot convert this document.
1696	The file appears to be corrupted.
1697	The file is not the right file type.
1698	There was an error opening the file.
1699	There was an error saving the file.

Error Number	Error Message
1700	Word cannot save the file here because the path name is too long.
1701	Word will not be able to save this file in its current directory. It will be opened Read Only.
1702	Address Book failure: ()
1703	Logon failed. You must log on to Microsoft Exchange to access your address book.
1704	Cannot load Extended MAPI library ()
1705	() is an invalid Extended MAPI library
1707	Extended MAPI initialization failed.
1708	Word was unable to post your document.
1709	The AutoCorrect Exception name contains invalid or no characters.
1710	Unable to add the AutoCorrect Exception name to the list.
1711	Unable to delete the AutoCorrect Exception name from the list.
1712	AutoCorrect Exception .Tab value out of range (0-1).

PART 3

Appendixes

A P P E N D I X   A

Workgroup Extensions for Microsoft Word

Note to User

WBMAPI.DLL is not supported by Microsoft Corporation. It is provided "as is" because we believe it may be useful to you. We regret that Microsoft is unable to support or assist you, should you have problems using this tool or any code that relies on this tool.

With the workgroup extensions for Microsoft Word, Word developers can include electronic mail (*e-mail*) in their custom applications. With the workgroup extensions and WordBasic, you can access the messaging application programming interface (MAPI) to create applications in Word that can:

- Send messages and attached files to multiple users.
- Search for messages in your Mail Inbox.
- Read or delete messages in your Mail Inbox.

To use the workgroup extensions, you must have Microsoft Word version 6.0 for Windows and one of the following:

- Microsoft Windows version 3.1 or later and Microsoft Mail for PC Networks version 3.0 or later
- Microsoft Windows for Workgroups version 3.1 or later

You can also use the workgroup extensions if you have Microsoft Word version 6.0 for Windows NT and Microsoft Windows NT version 3.5 or later, or Microsoft Word version 7.0 and Microsoft Windows 95 or Microsoft Windows NT version 3.51 or later.

The WordBasic MAPI functions of the workgroup extensions consist of *wrapper* and *helper* functions. Wrapper functions mirror the arguments, data types, and functionality of corresponding MAPI functions. Helper functions read individual fields within MAPI data types or construct the aggregate data types that MAPI requires. The names of helper functions begin with "MAPISet" or "MAPIQuery."

For more in-depth information about MAPI, see the *Microsoft Mail Technical Reference* in your Microsoft Mail for PC Networks package.

Note The workgroup extensions described in this appendix are not available on the Macintosh. For information about using messaging services in WordBasic on the Macintosh, see the AOCE statements and functions in Part 2, "WordBasic Reference."

Loading the Workgroup Extensions

The WordBasic MAPI functions are provided in WBMAPI.DLL, a Windows dynamic-link library (DLL) provided on the Microsoft Word Developer's Kit disk. Copy WBMAPI.DLL from either the WIN16 (Windows 3.*x*) or the WIN32 (Windows 95 and Windows NT) subfolder in the WBMAPI folder to the user's Windows System folder, or to any folder recognized automatically by the operating system. Every user of a workgroup application based on WBMAPI.DLL must have this file installed.

All of the **Declare** statements for the WBMAPI.DLL functions documented in this appendix, as well as useful constants, are included in the aaAllDeclarations macro, which is stored in WBMAPI.DOT, a template in the WBMAPI folder on the Microsoft Word Developer's Kit disk. Copy these declarations from the macro and include them in every macro you create that uses the WBMAPI.DLL functions.

In addition to aaAllDeclarations, many example macros are contained in WBMAPI.DOT; they provide a good starting point for building new applications that use the workgroup extensions. Users do not require WBMAPI.DOT.

Understanding the Workgroup Extensions

The workgroup extensions for Word provide functions that mirror MAPI functions. Since WordBasic cannot directly manipulate MAPI data types such as messages or recipient lists, the MAPI data types are managed by the WBMAPI.DLL library. The library, in turn, provides WordBasic handles to the MAPI data types. All references to MAPI data types are made by referencing handles. The WBMAPI.DLL library provides functions to create and destroy MAPI data types, as well as to examine and manipulate fields within MAPI data types.

When a WBMAPI.DLL function is successful, it returns a handle as a non-negative value. When a function is not successful, it returns a MAPI error value as a negative integer.

Understanding Mail Sessions

The workgroup extensions for Word messaging functions require that a Mail session is established before they are used. A Mail session validates the identity of the user and indicates which message store to use when finding and saving messages.

Because the current version of WordBasic does not support global variables, a Mail session cannot remain open when a macro completes execution. To open and close a Mail session, include both **MAPILogon** and **MAPILogoff** in every macro that uses the workgroup extensions.

Subroutines and functions can use the Mail session established by a calling procedure or function if you pass the Mail session handle to the subroutine or function. The following example passes the session handle from the main subroutine to the DisplayOriginator subroutine:

```
Sub MAIN
    Session = MAPILogon(0, "", "", 0, 0)
    DisplayOriginator Session
    result = MAPILogoff(Session, 0, 0, 0)
End Sub

Sub DisplayOriginator(MainSession)
    Dim MessageID$, Originator$, Address$
    result = MAPIFindNext(MainSession, 0, "", "", 0, 0, MessageID$)
    result = MAPIReadMail(MainSession, 0, MessageID$, 0, 0)
    result = MAPIQueryOriginator(Originator$, Address$)
    MsgBox Originator$ + " @ " + Address$
End Sub
```

Understanding Messages

The Current Messages

The workgroup extensions for Word maintain two *current messages* in memory. The *current outbound message* is the message you are preparing to send with **MAPISendMail** or to save with **MAPISaveMail**. The *current inbound message* is the message you most recently read with **MAPIReadMail**. MAPISet helper functions update the current outbound message, while MAPIQuery helper functions retrieve information from the current inbound message.

To send the current outbound message, use **MAPISendMail**. To save the current outbound message in the Mail Inbox without sending it, use **MAPISaveMail**. To retrieve a message from the Inbox and make it the current inbound message, use **MAPIFindNext** and **MAPIReadMail**.

The workgroup extensions for Word initialize both current messages when your macro calls the **MAPILogon** function. It removes both current messages from memory when your macro ends.

Recipients

Messages are sent to a recipient list. Each recipient is identified with a *friendly name* and an *address*. A friendly name is the descriptive name of the user. Friendly names can be ambiguous, so additional information is required to guarantee unique addressing. The address is a unique string that contains the account name of the user and must be unambiguous. The address string format varies depending on the configuration of the Mail transport system and must be obtained from the workgroup extensions before it can be used. The workgroup extensions return both strings for recipients that are selected using the Mail Address Book.

When setting message recipients, use both the name and address strings to avoid problems with ambiguous names. If you do not supply an address string, the recipient is treated as unresolved. When sending a message, the workgroup extensions will automatically attempt to resolve unresolved recipients and will return an error if it cannot resolve all recipients. You can use **MAPIResolveName** to force resolution before sending.

WBMAPI.DLL initializes a recipient list for the current outbound message when your macro calls the **MAPILogon** function. It removes the recipient list from memory when your macro ends.

Working with MAPI Data Types

Handle

A handle is a short, signed integer. A valid handle is a non-negative integer. In the current release of MAPI, 0 (zero) is a valid session handle. A negative value for a handle indicates an error. The errors returned are the negative values of the MAPI errors documented in the *Microsoft Mail Technical Reference*. For example, the MAPI error MAPI_E_INVALID_RECIPS is returned as –25. SUCCESS_SUCCESS is returned as 0 (zero).

MapiFile

The MapiFile data type is not supported in WordBasic. To retrieve the information about the file attachments of a message, use the **MAPIQueryAttachments** helper function. To add file attachments, use **MAPISetAttachment**.

MapiMessage

The MapiMessage data type is broken into its component data types. After **MAPIReadMail** returns successfully, use **MAPIQuerySubject**, **MAPIQueryOriginator**, and **MAPIQueryDateReceived** to retrieve envelope information about a message. Use **MAPIQueryNoteText** to retrieve the text of the message. Use successive calls to **MAPIQueryNoteText** to retrieve the text in usable chunks, since the message text can be longer than 65,280 characters, the maximum length of a WordBasic string.

MapiRecip

Several functions use or return a handle to a **MapiRecip** data type, which contains the recipient list of a message. To add addresses to new messages, follow this general procedure:

1. Use **MAPIAddress** to allow the user to specify a recipient list.
2. Use **MAPIQueryRecipientList** to retrieve information about recipients in the recipient list.
3. Use **MAPIResolveName** to resolve ambiguous names in a recipient list.
4. Finally, use **MAPISetRecipient** to add recipients to the current outbound message.

See "MAPIQueryRecipientList" later in this appendix for an example of addressing messages and resolving names.

Other helper functions, which you will probably use infrequently, provide greater detail and additional functionality. **MAPISetRecipientList** adds a complete recipient list to the current outbound message, but the function is useful only if the list does not contain any unresolved names. **MAPIQueryRecipientListCount** returns the number of names in a recipient list, and **MAPIQueryRecipientListElement** retrieves information about a specific recipient in the list.

WordBasic MAPI Functions

Consider the following for all the WBMAPI.DLL functions:

- To use a function described in this section, you must include the corresponding **Declare** statement, which you can copy directly from the aaAllDeclarations macro in WBMAPI.DOT. For more information, see "Loading the Workgroup Extensions" earlier in this appendix.

- **MAPILogon** must be called successfully to open a MAPI session before any other function call. End each WordBasic macro with **MAPILogoff** to close the MAPI session.

- You should usually pass 0 (zero) for the *UIParam* argument in the function declarations later in this appendix. Although it is unlikely that dialog box pointers could be useful to the typical WordBasic programmer, the argument is still represented to support the full generality of MAPI.

- Always pass 0 (zero) for the *Reserved* argument in the functions declarations. The current version of MAPI does not support this argument.

- Add flag values to set multiple flags for a function call. The following example calls **MAPILogon** with two flags:

```
MAPI_LOGON_UI = 1
MAPI_NEW_SESSION = 2
Flags = MAPI_LOGON_UI + MAPI_NEW_SESSION
Session = MAPILogon(0, "", "", Flags, 0)
```

MAPIAddress

Syntax   **MAPIAddress**(*Session*, *UIParam*, *Caption$*, *EditFields*, *Label$*, *Flags*, *Reserved*)

Remarks   Addresses a mail message. With this function, users can create a set of address list entries using the Mail Address Book, a standard address list dialog box. The dialog box cannot be suppressed, but function arguments allow the caller to set characteristics of the dialog box.

The call is made with the recipient list of the current outbound message, which can be empty. Users can add new entries to the set. **MAPIAddress** returns a handle to a recipient list. Use **MAPIQueryRecipientList** to retrieve names, addresses, or recipient classes from the recipient list. Use **MAPISetRecipient** to copy recipients to the current outbound message.

In addition to choosing names from the Address Book list, users can type names in the Address Book fields. Use **MAPIResolveName** to resolve these names before sending the message.

Argument	Explanation
Session	An opaque session handle whose value represents a session with the messaging system. The session handle is returned by **MAPILogon** and invalidated by **MAPILogoff**. If the value is 0 (zero), the messaging system initiates a session from a system default session (if one exists) or presents a log-in dialog box. In all cases, the messaging system returns to its state before the call.
UIParam	The parent window handle for the dialog box. A value of 0 (zero) specifies that any dialog box displayed is application modal.
Caption$	The caption of the Address Book dialog box.
EditFields	The number of edit controls that should be present in the address list. The values 0 (zero) to 4 are valid. If *EditFields* is 0 (zero), only address list browsing is allowed. *EditFields* values of 1 to 3 control the number of edit controls present. Entries selected for the different controls are differentiated by the *RecipClass* field of the returned recipient list. If *EditFields* is 4, each recipient class supported by the underlying messaging system has an edit control.
Label$	A string used as an edit control label in the address list dialog box. This argument is ignored and should be an empty string ("") except when *EditFields* is 1. An ampersand (&) in the *Label$* argument marks the following character as the access key for the field.
	If you want the label to be the default control label "To:", *Label$* should be an empty string ("").
Flags	A bitmask of flags. Unspecified flags should always be set to 0 (zero). Undocumented flags are reserved. The following flags are defined:
	`MAPI_LOGON_UI = 1` `MAPI_NEW_SESSION = 2`
	Set MAPI_LOGON_UI if the function should display a log-in dialog box (if required). When this flag is not set, the function does not display a dialog box and returns an error if the user is not logged in. If the session passed in *Session* is not 0 (zero), this flag is ignored.
	Set MAPI_NEW_SESSION to establish a session other than the current one. For instance, if the Mail client application is already running, another MAPI application can piggyback on the session created by the Mail client application. Do not set this flag if you want the default session (if it still exists). If the session passed in *Session* is not 0 (zero), this flag is ignored.
Reserved	Reserved for future use. This argument must be 0 (zero).

The following table lists the possible return values of the **MAPIAddress** function and their meanings.

Value	Name	Meaning
Positive integer		A handle to a recipient list. **MAPIAddress** was successful.
–2	MAPI_E_FAILURE	One or more unspecified errors occurred while addressing the mail. No list of entries was returned.
–3	MAPI_E_LOGIN_FAILURE	There was no default log-in, and the user failed to log in successfully when the log-in dialog box was displayed. No list of entries was returned.
–5	MAPI_E_INSUFFICIENT_MEMORY	There was insufficient memory to proceed. No list of entries was returned.
–17	MAPI_E_INVALID_MESSAGE	An invalid message ID was used for the *MessageID$* argument. No list of entries was returned.
–19	MAPI_E_INVALID_SESSION	An invalid session handle was used for the *Session* argument. No list of entries was returned.
–24	MAPI_E_INVALID_EDITFIELDS	The value of *EditFields* was outside the range of 0 (zero) to 4. No list of entries was returned.
–25	MAPI_E_INVALID_RECIPIENTS	One or more of the recipients in the address list were not valid. No list of entries was returned.
–26	MAPI_E_NOT_SUPPORTED	The operation was not supported by the underlying messaging system.
–1	MAPI_USER_ABORT	The user canceled the process. No list of entries was returned.

Example   The following example displays the Address Book dialog box with one edit field. The dialog box title is "Submit Report" and the edit field label is "Manager:". Users can press ALT+M to access the edit field.

```
Sub MAIN
MAPI_LOGON_UI = 1
Session = MAPILogon(0, "", "", MAPI_LOGON_UI, 0)
RecipList = MAPIAddress(Session, 0, "Submit Report", 1, "&Manager:",\
        0, 0)
result = MAPILogoff(Session, 0, 0, 0)
End Sub
```

MAPIDeleteMail

Syntax

MAPIDeleteMail(*Session*, *UIParam*, *MessageID$*, *Flags*, *Reserved*)

Remarks

Deletes a message from the Inbox. Before calling **MAPIDeleteMail**, use
MAPIFindNext to verify that the correct message will be deleted.

Argument	Explanation
Session	An opaque session handle whose value represents a session with the messaging system. The session handle is returned by **MAPILogon** and invalidated by **MAPILogoff**. If the value is 0 (zero), the messaging system establishes a session from a system default session (if one exists) or presents a log-in dialog box. In all cases, the messaging system returns to its state before the call.
UIParam	The parent window handle for the dialog box. A value of 0 (zero) specifies that any dialog box displayed is application modal.
MessageID$	The messaging system's string identifier for the message being deleted. The string identifier is returned by **MAPIFindNext** or **MAPISaveMail**. Applications should assume that this identifier is invalid after **MAPIDeleteMail** returns successfully.
Flags	A bitmask of flags. All flags are reserved and should be set to 0 (zero).
Reserved	Reserved for future use. This argument must be 0 (zero).

The following table lists the possible return values of the **MAPIDeleteMail**
function and their meanings.

Value	Name	Meaning
–2	MAPI_E_FAILURE	One or more unspecified errors occurred while deleting the mail. No mail was deleted.
–5	MAPI_E_INSUFFICIENT_MEMORY	There was insufficient memory to proceed. No mail was deleted.

Value	Name	Meaning
–17	MAPI_E_INVALID_MESSAGE	An invalid message ID was used for the *MessageID$* argument. No mail was deleted.
–19	MAPI_E_INVALID_SESSION	An invalid session handle was used for the *Session* argument. No mail was deleted.
–1	MAPI_USER_ABORT	The user canceled the process. No mail was deleted.
0	SUCCESS_SUCCESS	The function returned successfully.

Examples

The following example finds and deletes the first message in the Inbox.

```
Sub MAIN
MAPI_LOGON_UI = 1
Session = MAPILogon(0, "", "", MAPI_LOGON_UI, 0)
Dim MessageID$
result = MAPIFindNext(Session, 0, "", "", 0, 0, MessageID$)
result = MAPIDeleteMail(Session, 0, MessageID$, 0, 0)
result = MAPILogoff(Session, 0, 0, 0)
End Sub
```

The following example saves a message in the Inbox, reads it, then deletes it. Use this example to determine the name of the current user.

```
Sub MAIN
MAPI_LOGON_UI = 1
Session = MAPILogon(0, "", "", MAPI_LOGON_UI, 0)
Dim MessageID$, UserName$, Address$
result = MAPISaveMail(Session, 0, "New Subject", "New Message",\
    0, 0, MessageID$)
result = MAPIReadMail(Session, 0, MessageID$, 0, 0)
result = MAPIQueryOriginator(UserName$, Address$)
result = MAPIDeleteMail(Session, 0, MessageID$, 0, 0)
result = MAPILogoff(Session, 0, 0, 0)
MsgBox "Current user: " + UserName$ + " @ " + Address$
End Sub
```

MAPIDetails

Syntax

MAPIDetails(*Session, UIParam, Recipients, RecipIndex, Flags, Reserved*)

Remarks

Displays a dialog box that provides the details of a recipient in a recipient list. Use the *RecipIndex* argument to specify which recipient to display. Use **MAPIQueryRecipientListCount** to determine the number of recipients in a list.

The dialog box cannot be suppressed. The caller can make the entry either modifiable or fixed. The call works only for recipients that have been resolved either as the recipients of read mail, resolved entries returned by **MAPIAddress**, or entries returned by **MAPIResolveName**.

The folder the entry belongs to determines the amount of information presented in the details dialog box. It contains at least the friendly name and address of the recipient.

Argument	Explanation
Session	An opaque session handle whose value represents a session with the messaging system. Session handles are returned by **MAPILogon** and invalidated by **MAPILogoff**. If the value is 0 (zero), the messaging system sets up a session from a system default session (if one exists) or presents a log-in dialog box. In all cases, the messaging system returns to its state before the call.
UIParam	The parent window handle for the dialog box. A value of 0 (zero) specifies that any dialog box displayed is application modal.
Recipients	A handle to the recipient list containing the entry whose details are to be displayed.
RecipIndex	The index of the recipient to display. Recipients are numbered from 0 (zero) to **MAPIQueryRecipientListCount** minus 1.
Flags	A bitmask of flags. Unspecified flags should always be set to 0 (zero). Undocumented flags are reserved. The following flags are defined:

```
MAPI_LOGON_UI = 1
MAPI_NEW_SESSION = 2
MAPI_AB_NOMODIFY = 1024
```

Set MAPI_LOGON_UI if the function should display a log-in dialog box (if required). When this flag is not set, the function does not display a dialog box and returns an error if the user is not logged in.

Set MAPI_NEW_SESSION if you want to establish a session other than the current one. For instance, if a mail client is already running, another MAPI e-mail client can piggyback on the session created by the mail client application. Do not set this flag if you want the default session (if it still exists). If the session passed in *Session* is not 0 (zero), this flag is ignored.

Set MAPI_AB_NOMODIFY if the details of the entry should not be modifiable even if the entry belongs to the personal address book.

Reserved	Reserved for future use. This argument must be 0 (zero).

The following table lists the possible return values of the **MAPIDetails** function and their meanings.

Value	Name	Meaning
–21	MAPI_E_AMBIGUOUS_RECIPIENT	The recipient is not a resolved recipient. No dialog box was displayed.
–2	MAPI_E_FAILURE	One or more unspecified errors occurred while matching the message type. The call failed before message type matching could take place.
–5	MAPI_E_INSUFFICIENT_MEMORY	There was insufficient memory to proceed. No dialog box was displayed.
–3	MAPI_E_LOGIN_FAILURE	There was no default log-in, and the user failed to log in successfully when the log-in dialog box was displayed. No dialog box was displayed.
–26	MAPI_E_NOT_SUPPORTED	The operation was not supported by the underlying messaging system.
–1	MAPI_USER_ABORT	The user canceled the process. No dialog box was displayed.
0	SUCCESS_SUCCESS	The function returned successfully.

Example

The following example displays a standard Mail Address Book dialog box, then the details for the last recipient selected by the user. The user cannot modify the details.

```
Sub MAIN
MAPI_LOGON_UI = 1
Session = MAPILogon(0, "", "", MAPI_LOGON_UI, 0)
RecipList = MAPIAddress(Session, 0, "Address Book", 4, "", 0, 0)
RecipCount = MAPIQueryRecipientListCount(RecipList)
MAPI_AB_NOMODIFY = 1024
result = MAPIDetails(Session, 0, RecipList, RecipCount - 1,\
    MAPI_AB_NOMODIFY, 0)
result = MAPILogoff(Session, 0, 0, 0)
End Sub
```

MAPIFindNext

Syntax

MAPIFindNext(*Session*, *UIParam*, *MessageType$*, *SeedMessageID$*, *Flags*, *Reserved*, *MessageID$*)

Remarks

Returns the ID of the next (or first) message of a specified type. This function allows an application to enumerate messages of a given type. It returns message identifiers that can be used in subsequent MAPI function calls to retrieve and delete messages. **MAPIFindNext** is for processing incoming mail, not for managing received mail. **MAPIFindNext** looks for messages in the folder in which new messages of the specified type are delivered. **MAPIFindNext** calls can be made only in the context of a valid MAPI session established with **MAPILogon**.

When provided an empty *SeedMessageID$*, **MAPIFindNext** returns the ID of the first message specified with *MessageType$*. When provided a non-empty *SeedMessageID$*, **MAPIFindNext** returns the next matching message of the type specified with *MessageType$*. Repeated calls to **MAPIFindNext** ultimately result in a return of MAPI_E_NO_MESSAGES, which means the enumeration of the matching message types is complete.

Message identifiers are not guaranteed to remain valid, because other applications can move or delete messages. Applications must be able to handle calls to **MAPIFindNext**, **MAPIDeleteMail**, and **MAPIReadMail** that fail because they are for invalid message IDs. The ordering of messages is system specific. Message ID strings must be dynamic strings.

Message type matching is done against message type strings. All message types whose names match (up to the length of the *MessageType$* argument) are returned. If the *MessageType$* argument begins with "IPM.", matching occurs in the Inbox. If the *MessageType$* argument begins with "IPC.", matching is performed in the hidden application mail folder. IPM messages are interpersonal messages; IPC messages are interprocess communication messages that are not visible to the user. If the message type is an empty string (""), the list includes all messages in the Inbox.

Argument	Explanation
Session	An opaque session handle whose value represents a session with the messaging system. Session handles are returned by **MAPILogon** and invalidated by **MAPILogoff**. If the value is 0 (zero), **MAPIFindNext** returns MAPI_E_INVALID_SESSION. In all cases, the messaging system returns to its state before the call.
UIParam	The parent window handle for the dialog box. A value of 0 (zero) specifies that any dialog box displayed is application modal.

Argument	Explanation
MessageType$	A string that is the message type. To specify normal interpersonal messages, use an empty string ("").
SeedMessageID$	A string that is the message identifier seed for the request. If the identifier is an empty string (""), the first message matching the type specified in the *MessageType$* argument is returned. Message IDs are system specific and opaque. Message IDs might be invalidated at any time if another application moves or deletes a message.

Flags	A bitmask of flags. Unspecified flags should always be set to 0 (zero). Undocumented flags are reserved. The following flags are defined:
	
	`MAPI_UNREAD_ONLY = 32`
	`MAPI_NEW_SESSION = 2`
	`MAPI_GUARANTEE_FIFO = 256`
	
	Set MAPI_UNREAD_ONLY if the function should enumerate only unread messages. When this flag is not set, all messages of the given type are returned.
	
	Set MAPI_NEW_SESSION if you want to establish a session other than the current one . For instance, if a mail client is already running, another MAPI e-mail client can piggyback on the session created by the mail client application. Do not set this flag if you want the default session (if it still exists). If the session passed in *Session* is not 0 (zero), this flag is ignored.
	
	Set MAPI_GUARANTEE_FIFO if you want the message IDs returned in the order the messages were received. **MAPIFindNext** calls may take longer if this flag is set.

Reserved	Reserved for future use. This argument must be 0 (zero).
MessageID$	A variable-length string that is the message identifier. Message IDs are system specific, nonprintable, and opaque. Message ID strings must be dynamic strings. Message IDs might be invalidated at any time if another application deletes or moves a message.

The following table lists the possible return values of the **MAPIFindNext** function and their meanings.

Value	Name	Meaning
–2	MAPI_E_FAILURE	One or more unspecified errors occurred while matching the message type. The call failed before message type matching could take place.
–5	MAPI_E_INSUFFICIENT_MEMORY	There was insufficient memory to proceed. No mail was found.

Value	Name	Meaning
−17	MAPI_E_INVALID_MESSAGE	An invalid message ID was used for the *SeedMessageID$* argument. No mail was found.
−19	MAPI_E_INVALID_SESSION	An invalid session handle was used for the *Session* argument. No mail was found.
−16	MAPI_E_NO_MESSAGES	The **MAPIFindNext** function could not find a matching message.
−1	MAPI_USER_ABORT	The user canceled the process. No mail was found.
0	SUCCESS_SUCCESS	The function returned successfully.

Examples

The following example finds and displays the subject of messages in the Inbox that belong to the message type, "IPM.Sample.Report".

```
Sub MAIN
MAPI_LOGON_UI = 1
Session = MAPILogon(0, "", "", MAPI_LOGON_UI, 0)
Dim MessageID$, Subject$
result = MAPIFindNext(Session, 0, "IPM.Sample.Report", "",\
        0, 0, MessageID$)
While result = 0
    result = MAPIReadMail(Session, 0, MessageID$, 0, 0)
    result = MAPIQuerySubject(Subject$)
    MsgBox Subject$
    result = MAPIFindNext(Session, 0, "IPM.Sample.Report", MessageID$,\
        0, 0, MessageID$)
Wend
result = MAPILogoff(Session, 0, 0, 0)
End Sub
```

The following example finds and deletes all IPC messages.

```
Sub MAIN
MAPI_LOGON_UI = 1
Session = MAPILogon(0, "", "", MAPI_LOGON_UI, 0)
Dim MessageID$
result = MAPIFindNext(Session, 0, "IPC.", "", 0, 0, MessageID$)
While result = 0
    result = MAPIDeleteMail(Session, 0, MessageID$, 0, 0)
    result = MAPIFindNext(Session, 0, "IPC.", MessageID$, 0, 0,\
        MessageID$)
Wend
result = MAPILogoff(Session, 0, 0, 0)
End Sub
```

MAPILogoff

Syntax   **MAPILogoff**(*Session*, *UIParam*, *Flags*, *Reserved*)

Remarks   Ends a session with the messaging system.

Argument	Explanation
Session	An opaque session handle whose value represents a session with the messaging system. Session handles are returned by **MAPILogon** and invalidated by **MAPILogoff**.
UIParam	The parent window handle for the dialog box. A value of 0 (zero) specifies that any dialog box displayed is application modal.
Flags	Reserved for future use. This argument must be 0 (zero).
Reserved	Reserved for future use. This argument must be 0 (zero).

The following table lists the possible return values of the **MAPILogoff** function and their meanings.

Value	Name	Meaning
–5	MAPI_E_INSUFFICIENT_MEMORY	There was insufficient memory to proceed. The session was not terminated.
–19	MAPI_E_INVALID_SESSION	An invalid session handle was used for the *Session* argument. The session was not terminated.
0	SUCCESS_SUCCESS	The function returned successfully.

Example   The following example begins and ends a Mail session.

```
Sub MAIN
MAPI_LOGON_UI = 1
Session = MAPILogon(0, "", "", MAPI_LOGON_UI, 0)
result = MAPILogoff(Session, 0, 0, 0)
End Sub
```

MAPILogon

Syntax

MAPILogon(*UIParam*, *User$*, *Password$*, *Flags*, *Reserved*)

Remarks

Begins a session with the messaging system. You can log in to the messaging system in two ways, using simple MAPI mail calls:

- Implicitly log in.

  Any MAPI function call made outside an established MAPI session generates a log-in dialog box, which the calling application can suppress. In this case, when the call returns, the session is terminated and the messaging system returns to its state before the call was made. For example, a user logged off from the messaging system before the call would also be logged off after the call was completed.

- Explicitly log in using the **MAPILogon** function (and log off using **MAPILogoff**).

  If you want to maintain a session over a number of simple MAPI calls, you can use the **MAPILogon** function to provide a session handle to the messaging system. This session handle can be used in subsequent MAPI calls to explicitly provide user credentials to the messaging system. A flag is available to display a log-in dialog box if the credentials presented fail to validate the session. You can pass an empty password, although it may not validate the mail session.

MAPILogon returns a session handle. A negative value for the handle indicates an error. Currently, 0 (zero) is a valid session handle.

Argument	Explanation
UIParam	The parent window handle for the dialog box. A value of 0 (zero) specifies that any dialog box displayed is application modal.
User$	A client account-name string, limited to 256 characters or fewer. An empty string ("") indicates that a log-in dialog box with an empty name field should be generated (if the appropriate flag is set).
Password$	A credential string, limited to 256 characters or fewer. An empty string ("") indicates that a log-in dialog box with an empty password field should be generated (if the appropriate flag is set) or that the messaging system does not require password credentials.

Argument	Explanation
Flags	A bitmask of flags. Unspecified flags should always be set to 0 (zero). Undocumented flags are reserved. The following flags are defined:

```
MAPI_LOGON_UI = 1
MAPI_NEW_SESSION = 2
MAPI_FORCE_DOWNLOAD = 4096
```

Set MAPI_LOGON_UI if the function should display a dialog box to prompt for name and password (if required). When this flag is not set, the **MAPILogon** function does not display a log-in dialog box and returns an error if the user is not logged in.

Set MAPI_NEW_SESSION to establish a session other than the current one. For instance, if a mail client is already running, another MAPI e-mail client can piggyback on the session created by the mail client application. Do not set this flag if you want the default session (if it still exists).

Set MAPI_FORCE_DOWNLOAD to force a download of all new messages from the mail server to a user's Inbox during the log-in process. Use this flag so an application can deal with the user's complete set of messages when it logs in. When this flag is set, a progress indicator is displayed, and is automatically removed when the process is complete. Use of this flag may increase processing time.

Argument	Explanation
Reserved	Reserved for future use. This argument must be 0 (zero).

The following table lists the possible return values of the **MAPILogon** function and their meanings.

Value	Name	Meaning
–2	MAPI_E_FAILURE	One or more unspecified errors occurred during log-in. No session handle was returned.
–5	MAPI_E_INSUFFICIENT_MEMORY	There was insufficient memory to proceed. No session handle was returned.
–3	MAPI_E_LOGIN_FAILURE	There was no default log-in, and the user failed to log in successfully when the log-in dialog box was displayed. No session handle was returned.
–8	MAPI_E_TOO_MANY_SESSIONS	The user had too many sessions open at once. No session handle was returned.

Value	Name	Meaning
−1	MAPI_USER_ABORT	The user canceled the process. No session handle was returned.
0	SUCCESS_SUCCESS	The function returned successfully.

Example   The following example begins a Mail session and downloads new mail into the Inbox.

```
Sub MAIN
MAPI_LOGON_UI = 1
MAPI_FORCE_DOWNLOAD = 4096
Flags = MAPI_LOGON_UI + MAPI_FORCE_DOWNLOAD
Session = MAPILogon(0, "", "", Flags, 0)
result = MAPILogoff(Session, 0, 0, 0)
End Sub
```

MAPIQueryAttachments

Syntax   **MAPIQueryAttachments**(*PathName$*, *FileName$*, *Position$*)

Remarks   Retrieves information about the file attachments of the current inbound message. First use **MAPIReadMail** to make a message the current inbound message, then successively call **MAPIQueryAttachments** to enumerate the attachments of the message. **MAPIQueryAttachments** returns either the type of the attachment or −1 to indicate no more attachments.

MAPIReadMail automatically creates a temporary file for every attachment unless you call **MAPIReadMail** with the MAPI_ENVELOPE_ONLY or MAPI_SUPPRESS_ATTACH flag. The temporary files are not deleted automatically by the workgroup extensions. You must use **MAPIQueryAttachments** to enumerate the attachments and delete the temporary files.

Argument	Explanation
PathName$	The full path of a temporary file that contains a copy of the attached file.
FileName$	The filename seen by the recipient. This name can differ from the filename in *PathName$* if temporary files are being used. If *FileName$* is empty, the filename from *PathName$* is used. If the attachment is an OLE object, *FileName$* contains the class name of the object; for example, "Microsoft Excel Worksheet."
Position$	An integer formatted as a string indicating where the attachment is placed in the message body.

The following table lists the possible return values of the **MAPIQueryAttachments** function and their meanings.

Value	Name	Meaning
0		Attachment is a data file, not an OLE object.
1	MAPI_OLE	Attachment is an embedded OLE object.
2	MAPI_OLE_STATIC	Attachment is a static OLE object.
−1		Message contains no attachments or all attachments have been queried.

Example

The following example successively displays the filename of each attachment of the first message in the Inbox:

```
Sub MAIN
MAPI_LOGON_UI = 1
Session = MAPILogon(0, "", "", MAPI_LOGON_UI, 0)
Dim MessageID$, PathName$, MailFileName$, Position$
result = MAPIFindNext(Session, 0, "", "", 0, 0, MessageID$)
result = MAPIReadMail(Session, 0, MessageID$, 0, 0)
While result >= 0
    result = MAPIQueryAttachments(PathName$, MailFileName$, Position$)
    If result >= 0 Then
        MsgBox MailFileName$
        Kill PathName$
    End If
Wend
result = MAPILogoff(Session, 0, 0, 0)
End Sub
```

MAPIQueryDateReceived

Syntax

MAPIQueryDateReceived(*DateReceived$*)

Remarks

Returns the date and time of the current inbound message.

Argument	Explanation
DateReceived$	A string indicating the date and time a message is received. The format is YYYY/MM/DD HH:MM; hours are measured on a 24-hour clock.

Example

The following example displays the date and time of the first message in the Inbox.

```
Sub MAIN
MAPI_LOGON_UI = 1
Session = MAPILogon(0, "", "", MAPI_LOGON_UI, 0)
Dim MessageID$, MailDate$
result = MAPIFindNext(Session, 0, "", "", 0, 0, MessageID$)
MAPI_ENVELOPE_ONLY = 64
MAPI_PEEK = 128
Flags = MAPI_ENVELOPE_ONLY + MAPI_PEEK
result = MAPIReadMail(Session, 0, MessageID$, Flags, 0)
result = MAPIQueryDateReceived(MailDate$)
MsgBox MailDate$
result = MAPILogoff(Session, 0, 0, 0)
End Sub
```

MAPIQueryNoteText

Syntax   **MAPIQueryNoteText(***NoteText$***,** *Size***)**

Remarks   Returns the text of the current inbound message. Of the current inbound message,
MAPIQueryNoteText returns at most the number of characters specified in the
Size argument. The function returns 1 if there is more text, or 0 (zero) if there is
not.

Use successive calls to **MAPIQueryNoteText** to retrieve the text in usable
chunks since the message text can be longer than 65,280 characters, the maximum
length of a WordBasic string.

Argument	Explanation
NoteText$	A string containing text in the message
Size	The maximum number of characters to return

The following table lists the possible return values of the **MAPIQueryNoteText**
function and their meanings.

Value	Meaning
1	The message contains additional text.
0	The message contains no additional text.

Example   The following example creates a new Word document, and copies to the
document all the text of the first message in the Inbox. The text is copied in
chunks of 1,024 characters.

```
Sub MAIN
FileNew
MAPI_LOGON_UI = 1
Session = MAPILogon(0, "", "", MAPI_LOGON_UI, 0)
Dim MessageID$, NoteText$
result = MAPIFindNext(Session, 0, "", "", 0, 0, MessageID$)
MAPI_SUPPRESS_ATTACH = 2048
MAPI_PEEK = 128
Flags = MAPI_SUPPRESS_ATTACH + MAPI_PEEK
result = MAPIReadMail(Session, 0, MessageID$, Flags, 0)
result = 1
While result = 1
    NoteText$ = String$(1024, 32)
    result = MAPIQueryNoteText(NoteText$, Len(NoteText$))
    Insert NoteText$
Wend
result = MAPILogoff(Session, 0, 0, 0)
End Sub
```

MAPIQueryOriginator

Syntax   **MAPIQueryOriginator**(*OrigName$*, *Address$*)

Remarks   Returns the friendly name of the originator of the current inbound message.

Argument	Explanation
OrigName$	The friendly name of the originator of the current inbound message
Address$	The address of the originator of the current inbound message

Example   The following example displays the friendly name and address of the originator of the first message in the Inbox.

```
Sub MAIN
MAPI_LOGON_UI = 1
Session = MAPILogon(0, "", "", MAPI_LOGON_UI, 0)
Dim MessageID$, Originator$, Address$
result = MAPIFindNext(Session, 0, "", "", 0, 0, MessageID$)
MAPI_ENVELOPE_ONLY = 64
MAPI_PEEK = 128
Flags = MAPI_ENVELOPE_ONLY + MAPI_PEEK
result = MAPIReadMail(Session, 0, MessageID$, Flags, 0)
result = MAPIQueryOriginator(Originator$, Address$)
MsgBox Originator$ + " @ " + Address$
result = MAPILogoff(Session, 0, 0, 0)
End Sub
```

MAPIQueryRecipientList

Syntax   **MAPIQueryRecipientList**(*Recipients*, *RecipName$*, *Address$*)

Remarks   Retrieves information about recipients in a recipient list. On the first call to **MAPIQueryRecipientList**, *Recipients* must be a handle to a recipient list of the type returned by **MAPIAddress**. The **MAPIQueryRecipientList** function returns –1 to indicate that there are no more recipients. Otherwise, it returns the recipient class of the recipient.

Argument	Explanation
Recipients	A handle to a recipient list on the first call to **MAPIQueryRecipientList**. Use 0 (zero) for succeeding calls.
RecipName$	The friendly name of the recipient as displayed by the messaging system.
Address$	Provider-specific message delivery data. This field can be used by the message system to identify recipients who are not in an address list (custom recipients).

The following table lists the possible return values of the **MAPIQueryRecipientList** function and their meanings.

Value	Name	Meaning
0	MAPI_ORIG	The recipient is the originator of the message.
1	MAPI_TO	The recipient is a To recipient of the message.
2	MAPI_CC	The recipient is a carbon-copy (CC) recipient of the message.
3	MAPI_BCC	The recipient is a blind carbon-copy (BCC) recipient of the message.
–1		Either the recipient list contains no recipients or all recipients have been queried.

Example   The following example displays the Mail Address Book, which returns a handle to a recipient list. The example then prompts the user to resolve any unresolved names in the list. Finally, all resolved names are added to a new message.

```
Sub MAIN
MAPI_LOGON_UI = 1
MAPI_DIALOG = 8
Session = MAPILogon(0, "", "", MAPI_LOGON_UI, 0)
RecipList = MAPIAddress(Session, 0, "", 4, "", 0, 0)
```

```
If RecipList >= 0 Then
    'Query the first recipient
    RecipClass = 0
    RecipName$ = ""
    Address$ = ""
    RecipClass = MAPIQueryRecipientList(RecipList, RecipName$, Address$)
    While RecipClass >= 0
        'Process the recipient
        If Address$ <> "" Then
            result = MAPISetRecipient(RecipClass, RecipName$, Address$)
        Else
            ResolveList = MAPIResolveName(Session, 0, RecipName$, \
              Address$, MAPI_DIALOG, 0)
            If ResolveList >= 0 Then
                result = MAPIQueryRecipientListElement(ResolveList, 0, \
                  RecipName$, Address$)
                result = MAPISetRecipient(RecipClass, RecipName$, \
                  Address$)
            Else
                result = MAPISetRecipient(RecipClass, RecipName$, "")
            End If
        End If
        'Query the next recipient
        RecipClass = 0
        RecipName$ = ""
        Address$ = ""
        RecipClass = MAPIQueryRecipientList(0, RecipName$, Address$)
    Wend
    'Display the Send Note dialog
    result = MAPISendMail(Session, 0, "", "", MAPI_DIALOG, 0)
End If
result = MAPILogoff(Session, 0, 0, 0)
End Sub
```

MAPIQueryRecipientListCount

Syntax   **MAPIQueryRecipientListCount(*Recipients*)**

Remarks   Returns the number of names in a recipient list.

Argument	Explanation
Recipients	A handle to a recipient list

The following table lists the possible return values of the **MAPIQueryRecipientListCount** function and their meanings.

Value	Meaning
0	*Recipients* is not a valid handle to a recipient list, or the recipient list is empty.
Positive integer	The number of recipients in the recipient list.

Example

The following example displays the Mail Address Book, and then the number of resolved recipients selected by the user.

```
Sub MAIN
MAPI_LOGON_UI = 1
Session = MAPILogon(0, "", "", MAPI_LOGON_UI, 0)
RecipList = MAPIAddress(Session, 0, "", 4, "", 0, 0)
TotalCount = MAPIQueryRecipientListCount(RecipList)
ResolvedCount = 0
For i = 0 To TotalCount - 1
    RecipName$   ""
    Address$ = ""
    result = MAPIQueryRecipientListElement(RecipList, i, RecipName$,\
      Address$)
    If Address$ <> "" Then ResolvedCount = ResolvedCount + 1
Next
MsgBox Str$(ResolvedCount) + " of " + Str$(TotalCount) + " recipients
resolved"
result = MAPILogoff(Session, 0, 0, 0)
End Sub
```

MAPIQueryRecipientListElement

Syntax

MAPIQueryRecipientListElement(*Recipients, RecipIndex, RecipName$, Address$*)

Remarks

Retrieves information about one recipient in a recipient list. **MAPIQueryRecipientList** and **MAPIQueryRecipientListElement** return the same information about recipients. **MAPIQueryRecipientList** steps through the recipient list one-at-a-time in order, while **MAPIQueryRecipientListElement** retrieves information about one recipient anywhere in the list.

Recipients must be a handle to a recipient list of the type returned by **MAPIAddress**. Use *RecipIndex* to specify which recipient to query.

Argument	Explanation
Recipients	A handle to a recipient list.
RecipIndex	The index of the recipient to query. Recipients are numbered from 0 (zero) to **MAPIQueryRecipientListCount** minus 1.
RecipName$	The friendly name of the recipient as displayed by the messaging system.
Address$	Provider-specific message delivery data. This field can be used by the message system to identify recipients who are not in an address list (custom recipients).

The following table lists the possible return values of the
MAPIQueryRecipientListElement function and their meanings.

Value	Name	Meaning
0	MAPI_ORIG	The recipient is the originator of the message.
1	MAPI_TO	The recipient is a To recipient of the message.
2	MAPI_CC	The recipient is a carbon-copy (CC) recipient of the message.
3	MAPI_BCC	The recipient is a blind carbon-copy (BCC) recipient of the message.

Example   The following example displays the Mail Address Book, and then the name and address of the last name selected by the user.

```
Sub MAIN
MAPI_LOGON_UI = 1
Session = MAPILogon(0, "", "", MAPI_LOGON_UI, 0)
RecipList = MAPIAddress(Session, 0, "", 4, "", 0, 0)
RecipCount = MAPIQueryRecipientListCount(RecipList)
Dim RecipName$, Address$
result = MAPIQueryRecipientListElement(RecipList, RecipCount - 1, \
        RecipName$, Address$)
MsgBox RecipName$ + " @ " + Address$
result = MAPILogoff(Session, 0, 0, 0)
End Sub
```

MAPIQuerySubject

Syntax   **MAPIQuerySubject**(*Subject$*)

Remarks   Returns the subject text of the current inbound message.

Argument	Explanation
Subject$	The subject text, limited to 256 characters. (Messages saved with **MAPISaveMail** are not limited to 256 characters.) An empty string ("") indicates no subject text.

Example

The following example displays the subject of the first message in the Inbox.

```
Sub MAIN
MAPI_LOGON_UI = 1
Session = MAPILogon(0, "", "", MAPI_LOGON_UI, 0)
Dim MessageID$, Subject$
result = MAPIFindNext(Session, 0, "", "", 0, 0, MessageID$)
MAPI_ENVELOPE_ONLY = 64
MAPI_PEEK = 128
Flags = MAPI_ENVELOPE_ONLY + MAPI_PEEK
result = MAPIReadMail(Session, 0, MessageID$, Flags, 0)
result = MAPIQuerySubject(Subject$)
MsgBox Subject$
result = MAPILogoff(Session, 0, 0, 0)
End Sub
```

MAPIReadMail

Syntax

MAPIReadMail(*Session*, *UIParam*, *MessageID$*, *Flags*, *Reserved*)

Remarks

Reads a mail message and makes it the current inbound message. Before calling **MAPIReadMail**, use **MAPIFindNext** to verify that the correct message will be read. Use the MAPIQuery helper functions to retrieve information about the message. Use the MAPISet helper functions and **MAPISaveMail** to change the message. Use the MAPISet helper functions and **MAPISendMail** to forward or reply to the message.

MAPIReadMail automatically creates a temporary file for every attachment unless you call **MAPIReadMail** with the MAPI_ENVELOPE_ONLY or MAPI_SUPPRESS_ATTACH flag. The temporary files are not deleted automatically by the workgroup extensions. You must use **MAPIQueryAttachments** to enumerate the attachments and delete the temporary files.

Recipients, attachments, and contents are copied from the message before the function returns to the caller, so later changes to these elements do not affect the contents of the message unless changes are explicitly saved with **MAPISaveMail** or **MAPISendMail**.

Argument	Explanation
Session	An opaque session handle whose value represents a session with the messaging system. If the value is 0 (zero), **MAPIReadMail** returns MAPI_E_INVALID_SESSION.
UIParam	The parent window handle for the dialog box. A value of 0 (zero) specifies that any dialog box displayed is application modal.
MessageID$	A variable-length string that is the message identifier of the message to be read. Message IDs are system specific, nonprintable, and opaque. Message IDs can be obtained from the **MAPIFindNext** and **MAPISaveMail** functions.

Flags	A bitmask of flags. Unspecified flags should always be set to 0 (zero). Undocumented flags are reserved. The following flags are defined:
	
	`MAPI_ENVELOPE_ONLY = 64`
	`MAPI_SUPPRESS_ATTACH = 2048`
	`MAPI_BODY_AS_FILE = 512`
	`MAPI_PEEK = 128`
	
	Set MAPI_ENVELOPE_ONLY if you don't want the function to copy attachments to temporary files or return the note text. All other message information (except temporary filenames) is returned. Setting this flag usually reduces the processing time required for the function.
	
	Set MAPI_SUPPRESS_ATTACH if you don't want **MAPIReadMail** to copy attachments but just to return note text. If MAPI_ENVELOPE_ONLY is set, this flag is ignored. The flag should reduce the time required by the **MAPIReadMail** function.
	
	Set MAPI_BODY_AS_FILE if you want the message body written to a temporary file and added to the attachment list as the first attachment, instead of using **MAPIQueryNoteText** to retrieve the message body (the default behavior). The *Position* argument of a body attachment is –1.
	
	Set MAPI_PEEK if you don't want **MAPIReadMail** to mark the message as read. Any unsuccessful return leaves the message unread.

Reserved	Reserved for future use. This argument must be 0 (zero).

The following table lists the possible return values of the **MAPIReadMail** function and their meanings.

Value	Name	Meaning
−13	MAPI_E_ATTACHMENT_WRITE_FAILURE	An attachment could not be written to a temporary file. Check folder permissions.
−4	MAPI_E_DISK_FULL	The disk was full.
−2	MAPI_E_FAILURE	One or more unspecified errors occurred while reading the mail. No mail was read.
−5	MAPI_E_INSUFFICIENT_MEMORY	There was insufficient memory to proceed. No mail was read.
−17	MAPI_E_INVALID_MESSAGE	The message ID was invalid. It may have been deleted or changed by another process.
−19	MAPI_E_INVALID_SESSION	An invalid session handle was used for the *Session* argument. No mail was read.
−26	MAPI_E_NOT_SUPPORTED	The operation was not supported by the underlying messaging system.
−9	MAPI_E_TOO_MANY_FILES	Too many file attachments were contained in the message. No mail was read.
−10	MAPI_E_TOO_MANY_RECIPIENTS	There were too many recipients of the message. No mail was read.
0	SUCCESS_SUCCESS	The function returned successfully.

Example

The following example displays the subject of the first message in the Inbox. The **MAPIReadMail** function in the example does not retrieve the note text or attachments of the message, and it does not mark the message as read.

```
Sub MAIN
MAPI_LOGON_UI = 1
Session = MAPILogon(0, "", "", MAPI_LOGON_UI, 0)
Dim MessageID$, Subject$
result = MAPIFindNext(Session, 0, "", "", 0, 0, MessageID$)
MAPI_ENVELOPE_ONLY = 64
MAPI_PEEK = 128
Flags = MAPI_ENVELOPE_ONLY + MAPI_PEEK
result = MAPIReadMail(Session, 0, MessageID$, Flags, 0)
result = MAPIQuerySubject(Subject$)
MsgBox Subject$
result = MAPILogoff(Session, 0, 0, 0)
End Sub
```

MAPIResolveName

Syntax   **MAPIResolveName**(*Session*, *UIParam*, *RecipName$*, *Address$*, *Flags*, *Reserved*)

Remarks   Displays a dialog box to resolve an ambiguous recipient name. This function resolves a mail recipient's name (as entered by a user) to an unambiguous address list entry. **MAPIResolveName** prompts the user to choose between ambiguous entries, if necessary. A recipient list containing fully resolved information about the entry is allocated and returned.

Some *RecipName$* strings cannot be resolved. Some strings may produce too many matches or no matches at all, or the user can cancel the Resolve Name dialog box.

MAPIResolveName returns a handle to a recipient list.

Argument	Explanation
Session	An opaque session handle whose value represents a session with the messaging system. The session handle is returned by **MAPILogon** and invalidated by **MAPILogoff**. If the value is 0 (zero), the messaging system initiates a session from a system default session (if one exists) or presents a log-in dialog box. In all cases, the messaging system returns to its state before the call.
UIParam	The parent window handle for the dialog box. A value of 0 (zero) specifies that any dialog box displayed is application modal.
RecipName$	A string containing the name to be resolved.

Argument	Explanation
Address$	Provider-specific Mail address of the recipient.
Flags	A bitmask of flags. Unspecified flags should always be set to 0 (zero). Undocumented flags are reserved. The following flags are defined:

```
MAPI_LOGON_UI = 1
MAPI_NEW_SESSION = 2
MAPI_DIALOG = 8
MAPI_AB_NOMODIFY = 1024
```

Set MAPI_LOGON_UI if the function should display a log-in dialog box (if required). When this flag is not set, the function does not display a dialog box and returns an error if the user is not logged in.

Set MAPI_NEW_SESSION if you want to establish a session other than the current one. For instance, if a mail client is already running, another MAPI e-mail client can piggyback on the session created by the mail client application. Do not set this flag if you want the default session (if it still exists). If the session passed in *Session* is not 0 (zero), this flag is ignored.

Set MAPI_DIALOG if **MAPIResolveName** should attempt to resolve names by displaying a name resolution dialog box to the user. If this flag is not set, resolutions which do not result in a single name return MAPI_E_AMBIGUOUS_RECIPIENT.

Set MAPI_AB_NOMODIFY if the details of the entry should not be modifiable even if the entry belongs to the personal address book. Part of the resolution dialog box could involve displaying details about the various entries that match the *RecipName$* argument. Set this flag if these details should not be modifiable. This flag is ignored if MAPI_DIALOG is not set.

Reserved	Reserved for future use. This argument must be 0 (zero).

The following table lists the possible return values of the **MAPIResolveName** function and their meanings.

Value	Name	Meaning
–21	MAPI_E_AMBIGUOUS_RECIPIENT	One or more recipients were specified ambiguously. The name was not resolved.
–2	MAPI_E_FAILURE	One or more unspecified errors occurred while addressing the mail. The name was not resolved.

Value	Name	Meaning
−5	MAPI_E_INSUFFICIENT_MEMORY	There was insufficient memory to proceed. The name was not resolved.
−3	MAPI_E_LOGIN_FAILURE	There was no default log-in, and the user failed to log in successfully when the log-in dialog box was displayed. The name was not resolved.
−26	MAPI_E_NOT_SUPPORTED	The operation was not supported by the underlying messaging system.
−1	MAPI_USER_ABORT	The user canceled the process. The name was not resolved.
Positive integer		A handle to a recipient list.

Example

The following example resolves a name.

```
Sub MAIN
MAPI_LOGON_UI = 1
MAPI_DIALOG = 8
Session = MAPILogon(0, "", "", MAPI_LOGON_UI, 0)
RecipName$ = "carlos"
Address$ = ""
ResolveList = MAPIResolveName(Session, 0, RecipName$, Address$,\
    MAPI_DIALOG, 0)
If ResolveList > 0 Then MsgBox Address$
result = MAPILogoff(Session, 0, 0, 0)
End Sub
```

MAPISaveMail

Syntax

MAPISaveMail(*Session*, *UIParam*, *Subject$*, *NoteText$*, *Flags*, *Reserved*, *MessageID$*)

Remarks

Saves the current outbound message in the Mail Inbox, optionally replacing an existing message. Before calling **MAPISaveMail**, use **MAPIFindNext** to verify that the correct message will be saved. *MessageID$* must be a variable-length string. The elements of the message identified by the *MessageID$* argument are replaced by the elements of the current outbound message. If the *MessageID$* argument is empty, a new message is created. The new message ID is returned in the *MessageID$* argument on completion of the call. All replaced messages are saved in their appropriate folders. New messages are saved in the folder appropriate for incoming messages of that class.

The **MAPISaveMail** function uses the recipients and file attachments that you previously specified with the **MAPISetRecipient**, **MAPISetRecipientList**, **MAPISetMessageType** and **MAPISetAttachment** functions.

Argument	Explanation
Session	An opaque session handle whose value represents a session with the messaging system. Session handles are returned by **MAPILogon** and invalidated by **MAPILogoff**. If the value is 0 (zero) and *MessageID* is an empty string (""), the messaging system establishes a session from a system default session (if one exists) or presents a log-in dialog box. Otherwise, calls with *Session* equal to 0 (zero) return MAPI_E_INVALID_SESSION.
UIParam	The parent window handle for the dialog box. A value of 0 (zero) specifies that any dialog box displayed is application modal.
Subject$	The subject text, limited to 256 characters. (Messages saved with **MAPISaveMail** are not limited to 256 characters.) An empty string ("") indicates no subject text.
NoteText$	A string containing the text of the message.

Flags	A bitmask of flags. Unspecified flags should always be set to 0 (zero). Undocumented flags are reserved. The following flags are defined:
	
	`MAPI_LOGON_UI = 1`
	`MAPI_NEW_SESSION = 2`
	
	Set MAPI_LOGON_UI if the function should display a log-in dialog box (if required). When this flag is not set, the function does not display a dialog box and returns an error if the user is not logged in.
	
	Set MAPI_NEW_SESSION if you want to establish a session other than the current one. For instance, if a mail client is already running, another MAPI e-mail client can piggyback on the session created by the mail client application. Do not set this flag if you want the default session (if it still exists). If the session passed in *Session* is not 0 (zero), this flag is ignored.

Reserved	Reserved for future use. This argument must be 0 (zero).
MessageID$	The variable-length string identifier for this message. It is returned by the **MAPIFindNext** function or a previous call to **MAPISaveMail**. If a new message is to be created, this argument should be an empty string (""). Message ID strings must be dynamic strings.

The following table lists the possible return values of the **MAPISaveMail** function and their meanings.

Value	Name	Meaning
−4	MAPI_E_DISK_FULL	The disk was full.
−2	MAPI_E_FAILURE	One or more unspecified errors occurred while saving the mail. No mail was saved.
−5	MAPI_E_INSUFFICIENT_MEMORY	There was insufficient memory to proceed. No mail was saved.
−17	MAPI_E_INVALID_MESSAGE	An invalid message ID was used for the *MessageID$* argument. No mail was saved.
−19	MAPI_E_INVALID_SESSION	An invalid session handle was used for the *Session* argument. No mail was saved.
−3	MAPI_E_LOGIN_FAILURE	There was no default log-in, and the user failed to log in successfully when the log-in dialog box was displayed. No mail was saved.
−26	MAPI_E_NOT_SUPPORTED	The operation was not supported by the underlying messaging system.
−1	MAPI_USER_ABORT	The user canceled the process. No mail was saved.
0	SUCCESS_SUCCESS	The function returned successfully.

Example

The following example saves a message in the Inbox with two unresolved recipients.

```
Sub MAIN
MAPI_LOGON_UI = 1
Session = MAPILogon(0, "", "", MAPI_LOGON_UI, 0)
Dim MessageID$
result= MAPISetRecipient(1,"Anita Kopf","")
result= MAPISetRecipient(2,"Roger Selva","")
result = MAPISaveMail(Session, 0, "Monthly Summary",\
    "We will quickly satisfy all orders for clamps.", 0, 0, MessageID$)
result = MAPILogoff(Session, 0, 0, 0)
End Sub
```

MAPISendDocuments

Syntax

MAPISendDocuments(*UIParam*, *DelimChar$*, *FilePaths$*, *FileNames$*, *Reserved*)

Remarks

Sends a standard mail message. Calling the function displays a Send Note dialog box, which prompts the user to send a mail message with data file attachments. Attachments can include the active document or all the currently open documents. The function is used primarily for calls from a macro or scripting language, often found in applications such as spreadsheet or word-processing programs.

If the user is not currently logged in, a standard log-in dialog box appears. After the user logs in successfully, the Send Note dialog box appears.

The user's default messaging options are used as the default dialog box values. The function caller is responsible for deleting temporary files created when using this function.

Argument	Explanation
UIParam	The parent window handle for the dialog box. A value of 0 (zero) specifies that the Send Note dialog box is application modal.
DelimChar$	A string containing the character used to delimit the names in the *FilePaths$* and *FileNames$* arguments. This character should not be a character that your operating system uses or allows in filenames.
FilePaths$	A string containing the list of full paths (including drive letters) for the attached files. The list is formed by concatenating correctly formed paths separated by the character specified in the *DelimChar$* argument. For example:
	`C:\TMP\TEMP1.DOC;C:\TMP\TEMP2.DOC`
	The files specified in this argument are added to the message as file attachments.
	If this argument contains an empty string (""), the Send Note dialog box is displayed with no attached files.
FileNames$	A string containing the list of the original filenames (in 8.3 format) as they should be displayed in the message. When multiple names are specified, the list is formed by concatenating the filenames separated by the character specified in the *DelimChar$* argument. For example:
	`MEMO.DOC;EXPENSES.DOC`
	Note that the icon displayed for a file is based on the filename extension supplied in this argument. For example, a filename with an .XLS extension is displayed with a Microsoft Excel icon. Mail also relies on the file extension when opening and saving a file. If an attached file has no extension, append the default extension for your application's document type.
Reserved	Reserved for future use. This argument must be 0 (zero).

The following table lists the possible return values of the **MAPISendDocuments** function and their meanings.

Value	Name	Meaning
−12	MAPI_E_ATTACHMENT_ OPEN_FAILURE	One or more files in the *FilePaths$* argument could not be located. No mail was sent.
−4	MAPI_E_DISK_FULL	The disk was full.
−2	MAPI_E_FAILURE	One or more unspecified errors occurred while sending the mail. It is not known if the mail was sent.
−5	MAPI_E_INSUFFICIENT_MEMORY	There was insufficient memory to proceed.
−3	MAPI_E_LOGIN_FAILURE	There was no default log-in, and the user failed to log in successfully when the log-in dialog box was displayed. No mail was sent.
−1	MAPI_USER_ABORT	The user canceled the process (from the send dialog box). No mail was sent.
0	SUCCESS_SUCCESS	The mail was successfully sent. The caller is responsible for deleting any temporary files referenced in the *FilePaths$* argument.

Example   The following example displays the Send Note dialog box with two attachments.

```
Sub MAIN
result = MAPISendDocuments(0, ";",\
    "C:\DOCUMENT\THANKYOU.DOC;C:\WGTPLATE\CONTRACT.DOC" \
    "THANKYOU.DOC;CONTRACT.DOC",0)
End Sub
```

MAPISendMail

Syntax   **MAPISendMail**(*Session*, *UIParam*, *Subject$*, *NoteText$*, *Flags*, *Reserved*)

Remarks   Sends a mail message, allowing greater flexibility than **MapiSendDocuments** in message generation. This function sends the current outbound message as a standard mail message. It can, if you choose, prompt for user input with a dialog box or proceed without any user interaction.

You can optionally provide a list of subject or note text when you call **MAPISendMail**. The **MAPISendMail** function uses the recipients and file attachments that you previously specified with the **MAPISetRecipient**, **MAPISetRecipientList**, or **MAPISetAttachment** functions.

If you provide recipient names, file attachments, or note text, the function can send the files or note without prompting users. If the optional arguments are specified and a dialog box is requested with the MAPI_DIALOG flag, the arguments provide the initial values for the Send Note dialog box.

File attachments are copied to the message before the function returns; therefore, later changes to the files do not affect the contents of the message. The files must be closed when they are copied.

Argument	Explanation
Session	An opaque session handle whose value represents a session with the messaging system. If the value is 0 (zero), the messaging system sets up a session either from a system default session (if one exists) or by presenting a log in dialog box. In all cases, the messaging system returns to its state before the call.
UIParam	The parent window handle for the dialog box. A value of 0 (zero) specifies that any dialog box displayed is application modal.
Subject$	The subject text, limited to 256 characters. An empty string ("") indicates no subject text. Some implementations may truncate subject lines that are too long or contain carriage returns, linefeeds, or other control characters.
NoteText$	A string containing the text of the message. An empty string ("") indicates no text. The implementation wraps lines as appropriate. Implementations may place limits on the size of the text. A return of MAPI_E_TEXT_TOO_LARGE is generated if this limit is exceeded.

Argument	Explanation

Flags	A bitmask of flags. Unspecified flags should always be set to 0 (zero). Undocumented flags are reserved. The following flags are defined:
	
	`MAPI_LOGON_UI = 1`
	`MAPI_NEW_SESSION = 2`
	`MAPI_DIALOG = 8`
	
	Set MAPI_LOGON_UI if the function should display a dialog box to prompt for log-in (if required). When this flag is not set, the function does not display a dialog box and returns an error if the user is not logged in.
	
	Set MAPI_NEW_SESSION if you want to establish a session other than the current one. For instance, if a mail client is already running, another MAPI e-mail client can piggyback on the session created by the mail client application. Do not set this flag if you want the default session (if it still exists). If the session passed in *Session* is not 0 (zero), this flag is ignored.
	
	Set MAPI_DIALOG if the function should display a dialog box to prompt the user for recipients and other sending options. When you do not set this flag, the function does not display a dialog box, but at least one recipient must be specified.

Reserved	Reserved for future use. This argument must be 0 (zero).

The following table lists the possible return values of the **MAPISendMail** function and their meanings.

Value	Name	Meaning
−21	MAPI_E_AMBIGUOUS_RECIPIENT	A recipient matched more than one of the recipient descriptor types, and MAPI_DIALOG was not set. No mail was sent.
−11	MAPI_E_ATTACHMENT_ NOT_FOUND	The specified attachment was not found. No mail was sent.
−15	MAPI_E_BAD_RECIPTYPE	The type of a recipient was not MAPI_TO, MAPI_CC, or MAPI_BCC. No mail was sent.
−4	MAPI_E_DISK_FULL	The disk was full. No mail was sent.
−2	MAPI_E_FAILURE	One or more unspecified errors occurred while sending the mail. No mail was sent.

Value	Name	Meaning
–5	MAPI_E_INSUFFICIENT_MEMORY	There was insufficient memory to proceed. No mail was sent.
–19	MAPI_E_INVALID_SESSION	An invalid session handle was used for the *Session* argument. No mail was sent.
–3	MAPI_E_LOGIN_FAILURE	There was no default log-in, and the user failed to log in successfully when the log-in dialog box was displayed. No mail was sent.
–18	MAPI_E_TEXT_TOO_LARGE	The text in the message was too large to be sent. No mail was sent.
–9	MAPI_E_TOO_MANY_FILES	There were too many file attachments. No mail was sent.
–10	MAPI_E_TOO_MANY_RECIPIENTS	There were too many message recipients specified. No mail was sent.
–8	MAPI_E_TOO_MANY_SESSIONS	The user had too many sessions open at once. No mail was sent.
–14	MAPI_E_UNKNOWN_RECIPIENT	The recipient did not appear in the address list. No mail was sent.
–1	MAPI_USER_ABORT	The user canceled the process from the send dialog box. No mail was sent.
0	SUCCESS_SUCCESS	The function returned successfully.

Examples

The following example sends a message to two unresolved recipients. **MAPISendMail** will return an error if the names cannot be resolved unambiguously.

```
Sub MAIN
MAPI_LOGON_UI = 1
Session = MAPILogon(0, "", "", MAPI_LOGON_UI, 0)
result = MAPISetRecipient(1, "Anne Gabor", "")
result = MAPISetRecipient(2, "Roger Selva", "")
result = MAPISendMail(Session, 0, "Monthly Summary",\
    "We will quickly satisfy all orders for clamps.", 0, 0)
result = MAPILogoff(Session, 0, 0, 0)
End Sub
```

The following example prepares a message for sending to two recipients, then displays the Send Note dialog box to allow the user to modify, cancel, or send the message.

```
Sub MAIN
MAPI_LOGON_UI = 1
Session = MAPILogon(0, "", "", MAPI_LOGON_UI, 0)
Dim MessageID$
result = MAPISetRecipient(1, "Phillipe Tran", "AF:TBU/WGAM/PHILT")
result = MAPISetRecipient(1, "Patricia Loren", "AF:TBU/WGAM/PATL")
MAPI_DIALOG = 8
result = MAPISendMail(Session, 0, "Monthly Summary",\
    "We will quickly satisfy all orders for clamps.", MAPI_DIALOG, 0)
result = MAPILogoff(Session, 0, 0, 0)
End Sub
```

MAPISetAttachment

Syntax

MAPISetAttachment(*FileName$*, *PathName$*, *Position*, *Flags*, *Reserved*)

Remarks

Attaches a file to the current outbound message. A message can include multiple attachments. **MAPISetAttachment** attaches Word documents or any other data file, but the function does not support OLE objects.

Errors in attachment processing are not returned until the message is actually sent with **MAPISendMail**.

Argument	Explanation
FileName$	The filename seen by the recipient. This name can differ from the filename in *PathName$*. If *FileName$* is empty, the filename from *PathName$* is used.
PathName$	The full path of the file to be attached.
Position	An integer indicating where the attachment is placed in the message body. The first position is 0 (zero), and the last position is the length of the note text minus 1. The file attachment overwrites the existing character in its position.
	Use –1 for *Position* to insert the attachment at the beginning of the message without overwriting an existing character.
Flags	Reserved for future use. This argument must be 0 (zero).
Reserved	Reserved for future use. This argument must be 0 (zero).

Example

This example attaches two files to the current outbound message, then sends the message. One file is attached at the beginning of the message, the other at the end.

```
Sub MAIN
MAPI_LOGON_UI = 1
Session = MAPILogon(0, "", "", MAPI_LOGON_UI, 0)
Dim NoteText$
NoteText$ = "We will quickly satisfy all orders for clamps. "
result = MAPISetRecipient(1, "Phillipe Tran", "AF:TBU/WGAM/PHILT")
result = MAPISetRecipient(2, "Patricia Loren", "AF:TBU/WGAM/PATL")
result = MAPISetAttachment("THANKYOU.DOC", "C:\DOCUMENT\THANKYOU.DOC",\
    - 1, 0, 0)
result = MAPISetAttachment("CONTRACT.DOC", "C:\WGTPLATE\CONTRACT.DOC",\
    Len(NoteText$) - 1, 0, 0)
result = MAPISendMail(Session, 0, "Monthly Summary", NoteText$, 0, 0)
result = MAPILogoff(Session, 0, 0, 0)
End Sub
```

MAPISetMessageType

Syntax

MAPISetMessageType(*MessageType$*)

Remarks

Sets the message type of the current outbound message. Message types allow custom messages within Mail. You can use custom messages to associate messages with specific projects or applications. Messages can be interpersonal messages that appear in the user's Inbox, or interprocess communication messages that are invisible to the user. The *MessageType$* argument begins with "IPM." for interpersonal messages or with "IPC." for interprocess communication messages. The standard format for message types is "IPM.Vendor.Application" or "IPC.Vendor.Application."

Use **MAPIFindNext** to retrieve messages using the message type. This procedure is faster and more reliable than retrieving every message in the Inbox or searching for certain strings within the message subject or note text.

Message types are optional. For normal interpersonal messages, do not use **MAPISetMessageType**, or specify an empty string ("").

If your application generates IPC messages, you should provide users or administrators with a utility to find and delete outdated IPC messages in the Inbox. For an example, see **MAPIFindNext**.

Argument	Explanation
MessageType$	A string that is the message type

Example

The following example sends a message with a custom message type.

```
Sub MAIN
MAPI_LOGON_UI = 1
Session = MAPILogon(0, "", "", MAPI_LOGON_UI, 0)
result = MAPISetRecipient(1, "Michael Ranwez", "")
result = MAPISetMessageType("IPM.Sample.Report")
result = MAPISendMail(Session, 0, "Monthly Summary",\
    "We will quickly satisfy all orders for clamps.", 0, 0)
result = MAPILogoff(Session, 0, 0, 0)
End Sub
```

MAPISetRecipient

Syntax

MAPISetRecipient(*RecipClass*, *RecipName$*, *Address$*)

Remarks

Adds one recipient to the current outbound message. Use **MAPISetRecipientList** to add a recipient list with one or more recipients to the current outbound message.

Either *RecipName* or *Address* can be an empty string (""). If *Address* is an empty string (""), the recipient is treated as unresolved, and **MAPISendMail** automatically attempts resolution when the message is sent. If *RecipName* cannot be resolved unambiguously, **MAPISendMail** returns an error.

Argument	Explanation
RecipClass	Classifies the recipient of the message.
	The following *RecipClass* values are defined:
	`MAPI_ORIG = 0`
	`MAPI_TO = 1`
	`MAPI_CC = 2`
	`MAPI_BCC = 3`
	Set MAPI_TO to specify a To recipient.
	Set MAPI_CC to specify a carbon-copy (CC) recipient.
	Set MAPI_BCC to specify a blind carbon-copy (BCC) recipient.
	Do not set MAPI_ORIG. The messaging system automatically establishes the originator.
RecipName$	The friendly name of the recipient as displayed by the messaging system.
Address$	Provider-specific message delivery data. This field can be used by the message system to identify recipients who are not in an address list (custom recipients).

Example

The following example adds two recipients to the current outbound message, then sends the message. The To recipient is resolved, and the CC recipient is unresolved. If the unresolved recipient cannot be resolved unambiguously, **MAPISendMail** returns an error.

```
Sub MAIN
MAPI_LOGON_UI = 1
Session = MAPILogon(0, "", "", MAPI_LOGON_UI, 0)
MAPI_TO = 1
MAPI_CC = 2
result = MAPISetRecipient(MAPI_TO, "Phillipe Tran", \
    "AF:TBU/WGAM/PHILT")
result = MAPISetRecipient(MAPI_CC, "Patricia Loren", "")
result = MAPISendMail(Session, 0, "Monthly Summary",\
    "We will quickly satisfy all orders for clamps.", 0, 0)
result = MAPILogoff(Session, 0, 0, 0)
End Sub
```

MAPISetRecipientList

Syntax   **MAPISetRecipientList**(*Recipients*)

Remarks   Copies a recipient list with one or more recipients to the current outbound
                    message. The function replaces the existing recipient list of the current outbound
                    message. Use **MAPISetRecipient** to add one recipient to the current outbound
                    message without removing existing recipients.

                    Use **MAPIAddress** to allow users to add users to a recipient list.

                    If any recipients within the recipient list are unresolved, **MAPISendMail**
                    automatically attempts resolution when the message is sent. If all recipients
                    cannot be resolved unambiguously, **MAPISendMail** returns an error.

Argument	Explanation
Recipients	A handle to a recipient list

Example   The following example displays the Mail Address Book dialog box, then copies
                    the recipient list to a new message.

```
Sub MAIN
MAPI_LOGON_UI = 1
Session = MAPILogon(0, "", "", MAPI_LOGON_UI, 0)
RecipList = MAPIAddress(Session, 0, "Address Book", 4, "", 0, 0)
If RecipList >= 0 Then
    result = MAPISetRecipientList(RecipList)
    MAPI_DIALOG = 8
    result = MAPISendMail(Session, 0, "", "", MAPI_DIALOG, 0)
End If
result = MAPILogoff(Session, 0, 0, 0)
End Sub
```

APPENDIX B

ODBC Extensions for Microsoft Word

> **Note to User**
>
> WBODBC.WLL is not supported by Microsoft Corporation. It is provided "as is" because we believe it may be useful to you. We regret that Microsoft is unable to support or assist you, should you have problems using this tool or any code that relies on this tool.

With the functions provided in the ODBC add-in library for Microsoft Word, you can create WordBasic macros that can access data in any database management system (DBMS) that supports the open database connectivity (ODBC) application programming interface (API) standard. With the ODBC extensions, you can:

- Update data or add new data to a DBMS data source.

    For example, employees can update personnel records in a DBMS by filling in a form in Word. Or you can add a table of data created in Word as a new data source in an existing database.

- Retrieve data for use as a mail-merge data source and insert tables of data in a document.

    With the ODBC extensions, you can access data directly from a DBMS through Structured Query Language (SQL) statements. If you are retrieving large amounts of data or retrieving data from large databases, bypassing the Word command interface can speed data access.

- Retrieve data for use in calculations by other WordBasic functions.

    For example, you can create a macro to retrieve the daily price of commodities and interest rates from your company's database and then use the values as variables in calculating projected expenses.

- Interactively compose and issue queries and retrieve results from the database.

Information in this appendix is intended only for WordBasic programmers. If you are developing C language or Visual Basic applications that support the ODBC API, you can obtain the Microsoft ODBC Software Development Kit version 2.10 as part of a Level 2 membership in the Microsoft Developer Network (MSDN). To join MSDN in the United States and Canada, call (800) 759-5474 from 6:30 A.M. to 5:30 P.M. (Pacific time), Monday through Friday. Outside North America, contact your local Microsoft subsidiary, or call (303) 684-0914 in the United States to obtain local contact information. The ODBC SDK isn't required to use the ODBC extensions in the WBODBC.WLL add-in that is provided in the *Microsoft Word Developer's Kit.*

Note The ODBC extensions described in this appendix are not available on the Macintosh.

Understanding the ODBC Extensions

Open database connectivity (ODBC) is an application programming interface that uses structured query language (SQL) to access and manipulate data in database management systems such as dBASE®, Paradox®, and Microsoft Access.

SQL is a widely accepted industry standard for storing, maintaining, and retrieving information from a DBMS. A particular DBMS may support different SQL functions and grammar to take advantage of unique, proprietary features. For that reason, if SQL statements are used to access data directly, an application would require separate programs, each targeted to a specific DBMS, to work with external data.

Using ODBC API functions, however, a single application can access data in diverse DBMSs without supporting multiple implementations of SQL. To access a particular DBMS, an application supporting ODBC uses software components called *drivers*, which perform all interaction between an application and a specific DBMS. The following illustration shows the relationship between the dBASE ODBC driver and an application accessing dBASE database files.

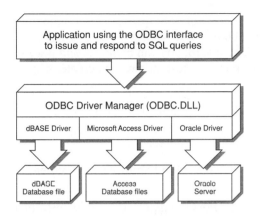

To provide the same interoperability for WordBasic macros, the WBODBC.WLL add-in provides functions you can call from WordBasic that mirror ODBC functions. With these functions, you can create a macro that can access data in any ODBC-supporting DBMS for which you have an ODBC driver.

In C programs, ODBC API functions provide a standard interface to SQL statements. The functions in the WBODBC.WLL in turn mirror the ODBC functions for WordBasic.

The ODBC Extensions and SQL

After establishing a data source connection through a call to **SQLOpen**, you issue SQL queries to an ODBC-supporting DBMS by calls to the WordBasic ODBC extensions **SQLExecQuery** or **SQLQueryExec**. The SQL statements in the query should conform to SQL grammar. If the SQL grammar is supported by the ODBC API, the query is interpreted by the ODBC driver. The ODBC Driver Manager (ODBC.DLL) then calls the appropriate ODBC API functions to execute the query.

If the query contains SQL grammar that is not supported by the ODBC driver, the query is passed directly to the DBMS without further processing by ODBC API functions. In this way, a driver can support a superset of SQL, including vendor-specific grammar.

You can see some examples of SQL queries in the sample macros in the WBODBC.DOT, which is included on the Microsoft Word Developer's Kit disk. When you run the Exec macro, you can compose and issue queries interactively; you can also use this macro to test queries you create before including the query strings in other macros.

To learn more about the SQL grammar supported by a specific ODBC driver, see the online Help file provided with each driver. For more information about SQL, the following standards are available:

- Database Language – SQL with Integrity Enhancement, ANSI, 1989 ANSI X3.135-1989.
- X/Open and SQL Access Group SQL CAE draft specification (1991).
- Database Language SQL: ANSI X3H2 and ISO/IEC JTC1,SC21,WG3 (draft international standard).

In addition to standards and the SQL documentation provided with the DBMS you are using, there are many books that describe SQL, including:

- *Microsoft ODBC Programmer's Reference,* provided with the Microsoft ODBC Software Development Kit version 2.10.
- Date, C. J.: *A Guide to the SQL Standard* (Addison-Wesley, 1989).
- Emerson, Sandra L., Darnovsky, Marcy, and Bowman, Judith S.: *The Practical SQL Handbook* (Addison-Wesley, 1989).
- Groff, James R. and Weinberg, Paul N.: *Using SQL* (Osborne McGraw-Hill, 1990).
- Gruber, Martin: *Understanding SQL* (Sybex, 1990).
- Hursch, Jack L. and Carolyn J.: *SQL, The Structured Query Language* (TAB Books, 1988).
- Pascal, Fabian: *SQL and Relational Basics* (M & T Books, 1990).
- Trimble, J. Harvey, Jr. and Chappell, David: *A Visual Introduction to SQL* (Wiley, 1989).
- Van der Lans, Rick F.: *Introduction to SQL* (Addison-Wesley, 1988).
- Vang, Soren: *SQL and Relational Databases* (Microtrend Books, 1990).
- Viescas, John: *Quick Reference Guide to SQL* (Microsoft Corp., 1989).

Tip If you use Microsoft Query, you can create a query in the Query window and then copy the equivalent SQL statements to your WordBasic macro.

ODBC SQL Data Types

Each ODBC driver has different naming syntax for its own SQL data types. A given ODBC driver maps its native SQL data types to ODBC SQL data types. Information about data-type mapping for a specific ODBC driver is provided in the online Help file for each installed driver. For example, the following table shows how the ODBC driver for Paradox maps native Paradox data types.

Paradox data type	ODBC SQL data type
Alphanumeric	SQL_CHAR
Date	SQL_DATE
Number	SQL_DOUBLE
Short	SQL_SMALLINT

A given driver and ODBC data source do not necessarily support all ODBC SQL data types. For complete information about ODBC SQL data types, see the *Microsoft ODBC Programmer's Reference* in the Microsoft ODBC Software Development Kit version 2.10.

The extensions in WBODBC.WLL allow you to create and delete ODBC tables, as well as to examine and manipulate fields within ODBC tables. When using the SQL statements CREATE TABLE and ALTER TABLE, you must specify the data types native to that particular DBMS. For example, if you are adding a column to a table in Microsoft FoxPro and the data type of the column is "Date," you must specify "Date" as the column data type in the ALTER TABLE statement, not the ODBC SQL data type "SQL_DATE." To determine the appropriate data type for the DBMS you are using, use the WordBasic ODBC function **SQLGetTypeInfo$**. For any valid SQL data type, this function returns the corresponding data type for the DBMS of the current data source.

Note that the ODBC extensions for Word cannot directly manipulate ODBC SQL data types; the ODBC extensions use only string data types. Numbers are formatted and manipulated as strings.

Before You Begin

Before you use the add-in functions described in this chapter, you must do the following:

- Install the appropriate ODBC driver needed to access the DBMS you are using. Each DBMS requires a different driver.
- Define specific data sources you want to access in the selected DBMS. You must have previously created the specific database file or table in the DBMS before defining the data source.

- Install the WBODBC.WLL add-in library.
- Load the WBODBC.WLL add-in library by using the Templates command on the File menu.

Installing ODBC Drivers

An ODBC driver is a dynamic-link library (DLL) that an application supporting ODBC can use to gain access to a particular DBMS, such as dBASE or Microsoft Access. The ODBC driver implements ODBC API function calls that are compatible with the SQL statements used by a particular DBMS and performs all interaction with a data source.

Installing the ODBC Drivers Provided with Word

You can install the ODBC drivers for DBMSs such as Microsoft Access, Microsoft FoxPro, Paradox, and dBASE when you install Word or any time you run the Setup program with the Custom installation option. All the provided ODBC drivers are installed unless you change the Data Access options. The ODBC drivers must be installed in your Windows System folder or in a folder recognized automatically by the operating system.

Installing Additional ODBC Drivers

To install other Microsoft or third-party ODBC drivers you purchase after installing Word, you can use the ODBC installer provided with the ODBC drivers. Install the drivers to your Windows System folder or a folder recognized automatically by the operating system.

If you've already installed at least one ODBC driver on your hard disk, you can use the ODBC Administrator program to install additional third-party ODBC drivers. (ODBC drivers provided by Word must be installed by using the Word Setup program.) To start the ODBC Administrator program, double-click the ODBC icon in the Control Panel. Then choose the Drivers button in the Data Sources dialog box.

Note The ODBC driver you install may share some of the same dynamic-link libraries (DLLs) as other drivers installed on your computer. If so, you may be asked if you want to overwrite the driver you specified, whether or not it has been installed. Choose the Yes button to install the driver.

Setting Up Data Sources

After you install an ODBC driver, you must set up the *data sources* you want to access in a particular DBMS. A data source is a specific set of data in a DBMS and any information about the network or operating system (or both) needed to access the data. The following are examples of data sources:

- A Microsoft Access database file in a public folder of a colleague's computer running Windows 95.

- An ORACLE® DBMS running on an OS/2® operating system, accessed by Novell® NetWare®.

- A dBASE file on your computer hard disk; in this case a network and remote operating system are not included in the data source.

- A Tandem NonStop SQL DBMS running on the Guardian™ 90 operating system, accessed through a gateway.

You add, change, or delete a data source by using the ODBC Administrator program. To start the program, double-click the ODBC icon in the Control Panel or run ODBCADM.EXE (Windows 3.x) or ODBCAD32.EXE (Windows 95 and Windows NT). You can add any data source to the list in the Data Sources dialog box, providing the driver it uses is already installed on your machine.

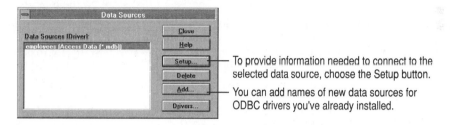

To provide information needed to connect to the selected data source, choose the Setup button.

You can add names of new data sources for ODBC drivers you've already installed.

When you add a new data source, the setup information you provide is stored in the ODBC.INI file (Windows 3.x) or the registry (Windows 95 and Windows NT) and is used each time you access the data source. The minimum connection information typically includes the name of the data source, a user ID, and a password. Some ODBC drivers allow you to specify additional required information, such as a network address or additional passwords. For information about the connection options for a particular ODBC driver, choose the Help button in the Setup dialog box.

If you don't provide sufficient information when you set up the data source, you can provide the needed connection arguments in calls to the add-in function **SQLOpen**. You may also want to specify the connection string arguments to override the arguments stored during setup. If sufficient connection information is not provided in calls to **SQLOpen**, the ODBC driver may display a dialog box for entering the missing information, depending on the value of the *DriverPrompt* argument in the **SQLOpen** instruction.

Installing and Loading WBODBC.WLL

The ODBC extensions for WordBasic are provided in WBODBC.WLL, a Word add-in library (WLL) on the Microsoft Word Developer's Kit disk. To install the add-in library, copy the WBODBC.WLL file from the WIN16 (Windows 3.*x*) or WIN32 (Windows 95 and Windows NT) subfolder in the WBODBC folder to your Template folder.

Before running a macro that uses the ODBC extensions, you must load the add-in in Word. To load the add-in library, use the Templates command (File menu) to add the WBODBC.WLL to the list of global templates and add-ins. If you will frequently use the ODBC extensions in macros, you can load the add-in automatically each time you start Word by storing the WBODBC.WLL file in the STARTUP folder in your Word program folder.

The WBODBC.DOT and INVOICE3.DOT templates in the WBODBC folder on the Microsoft Word Developer's Kit disk contain the example macros described in this appendix. Copy the templates to your Template folder to use, copy, and modify those macros. If you have installed the Microsoft Access ODBC driver provided with Word, you can copy the TEST.MDB database (also located in the WBODBC folder on the Microsoft Word Developer's Kit disk) to your hard disk and set it up as an ODBC data source to use when running the example macros.

Using the ODBC Extensions

This section contains basic information on using the ODBC extensions. Three example macros included in WBODBC.DOT illustrate the use of the functions. The sample form, INVOICE3.DOT, which shows how you can automate Word forms to take advantage of the ODBC extensions, is described at the end of this section.

Declaring the Functions

To indicate that the ODBC extensions are located in the WBODBC.WLL add-in library, you must declare the functions prior to calling them in a macro. All of the **Declare** statements for the WBODBC.WLL functions documented in this appendix are included in the AllDeclarations macro stored in the WBODBC.DOT template. Copy these declarations into every macro that uses the WBODBC.WLL functions.

Sequence of Use

To retrieve data, you must first establish a connection with a data source by using **SQLOpen**. A successful call to **SQLOpen** returns a unique connection identification number. The connection ID identifies the specified data source until the connection is closed by using **SQLClose** or **SQLCloseAll**. The connection ID is used by **SQLExecQuery** or **SQLQueryExec** to send a query, and the SQL retrieve functions then use the same connection ID to retrieve the query results.

You can use the following SQL retrieve functions with **SQLExecQuery**: **SQLRetrieveColumns**, **SQLRetrieveFlush**, **SQLRetrieveItem$**, **SQLRetrieveRows**, **SQLRetrieveToDocument**.

You can use the following SQL retrieve functions with **SQLQueryExec**: **SQLQueryFetch**, **SQLQueryRetrieve**, **SQLRetrieveColSize**, **SQLRetrieveColumns**, **SQLRetrieveFlush**, **SQLSetRowPos**.

Mapping the Structure of a Database

Before sending a query with **SQLExecQuery** or **SQLQueryExec**, you might want to determine the underlying structure, or schema, of a DBMS. This is called *mapping* the database. For example, you might want to know whether the database is organized as "tables" or "files." Once you've mapped the database, you can more easily write macros to manipulate the data.

You map a database by using the **SQLGetSchema** and **SQLGetSchemaItem$** functions. With **SQLGetSchema**, you specify the type of information, or property, that you want to learn about the DBMS. You then use **SQLGetSchemaItem$** to retrieve a specific description of the property. The third example macro described later in this section shows how to use these functions.

Checking for Error Conditions

After a call to any ODBC extension that returns a numeric value, you should check for a returned error condition, which is indicated by a 0 (zero) or a negative integer. The ODBC extensions include functions for examining errors. First you call **SQLCountErrors**, which returns a count of the number of lines of error information stored in memory after a preceding WordBasic ODBC function call returned an error value. If **SQLCountErrors** returns a positive integer, you then call **SQLErrorText$** to return each line of error message text. The returned error message text can then be evaluated by an error trap or displayed to the user.

ODBC Examples

The macros shown in the following examples are available in WBODBC.DOT, the template provided on the Microsoft Word Developer's Kit disk. Only portions of the macros are included here; to review the complete code for an example, open the macro in a macro-editing window.

Example 1: Issuing SQL queries interactively

When you run the Exec example macro, you type the SQL query in a dialog box. If the query string results in an error, the `ParseErrors` subroutine is called to display the error message. The query is then redisplayed in a dialog box so that you can edit the query string. Successful queries are stored in a new document so that you can reuse them in other macros.

```
While quit = 0
    s$ = InputBox$("SQL> ", "SQL Interactive Interpreter", prompt$)
    If Len(s$) = 0 Then
        quit = 1
    Else
        ret = SQLExecQuery(connect_num, s$)
        If ret <= 0 Then
            prompt$ = s$
            x$ = "Error: " + Str$(ret) + "," + Str$(SQLErrorCount)
            MsgBox x$
            ParseErrors
        Else
            If FirstLog <> 0 Then
                FileNew
                FirstLog = 0
            EndIf
            LogString(s$)
            prompt$ = ""
        EndIf
    EndIf
Wend
```

And here is the `ParseErrors` subroutine:

```
Sub ParseErrors
nerrors = SQLCountErrors()
For i = 1 To nerrors
    MsgBox "error: class(" + SQLErrorClass(i) + ") code(" + \
            Str$(SQLErrorCode(i)) + "): " + SQLErrorText(i)
Next
End Sub
```

Example 2: Retrieving data and inserting it into a table

The Report example macro opens a Microsoft Access data source named "test.mdb," a data source set up from the Microsoft Access database TEST.MDB that is provided on the Microsoft Word Developer's Kit disk.

The SQL query string sent with the **SQLExecQuery** function selects each row, or record, of information for which there is an entry in the "name" field. (Note that the Quote2$( ) user-defined function, not shown here, returns the string "name" preceded and followed by Chr$(34), the ANSI character code for a double quotation mark.) Next, the macro creates a table in a new Word document and inserts each data item retrieved by **SQLRetrieveItem$** into the appropriate table cell. If the amount in any account field is less than 1, that amount is formatted as bold. If an ODBC extension returns an error value, control is passed to the MyError error handler.

```
connect_num = SQLOpen("DSN=test.mdb", output_ref$, 0)
If connect_num <= 0 Then Goto MyError
ret = SQLExecQuery(connect_num, "Select * from table4 " + \
        Quote2$("name"))
If ret <= 0 Then Goto MyError
col = SQLRetrieveColumns(connect_num)
row = SQLRetrieveRows(connect_num)
If col <= 0 Or row <= 0 Then Goto MyError
FileNew
TableInsertTable  .ConvertFrom = 0, .NumColumns = col, .NumRows = row
For i = 1 To row
        For j = 1 To Col
        item$ = SQLRetrieveItem$(connect_num, j, i)
        If (j = 1) Then
            Insert item$
        Else
            v = Val(item$)
            s$ = Str$(v / 100)
            Insert s$
            If (v < 100) Then
                ParaUp 1, 1
                Bold(1)
                CharRight 1, 0
            End If
        End If
        If j <> col Or i <> row Then NextCell
    Next
Next
ret = SQLClose(connect_num)
If ret > 0 Then Goto MyEnd
```

Example 3: Mapping the database structure

The Schema example macro displays a dynamic dialog box in which you can select an option corresponding to a database property to see a description of that property. The macro uses **SQLGetSchema** and **SQLGetSchemaItem$** to build a shared array of the strings describing the database properties. The array, called combobox1$( ), is then displayed in the dialog box.

In the main subroutine (not shown here), the connection information for **SQLOpen**—the name of a data source, the database name, and any other required connection string arguments—is entered in response to dialog boxes.

After the custom dialog box is defined, it is displayed. The following subroutine, GetDBInfoWithQualifier, is called by the dialog function (or by the intermediate function GetDBInfo if there is no value for the qual$ argument) every time the user selects a different property in the dialog box. The dialog function then uses the shared array combobox1$( ) to update the custom dialog box.

```
Function GetDBInfoWithQualifier(itemid, qual$)
i = SQLGetSchema(connect_num, itemid, qual$)
If i > 0 Then
    For j = i - 1 To MaxItem
        combobox1$(j) = ""
    Next
    For j = 0 To i - 1
        s$ = SQLGetSchemaText(connect_num, j + 1)
        combobox1$(j) = s$
    Next
Else
    MsgBox "No Information"
End If
GetDBInfoWithQualifier = i
End Function
```

Example of Automating Forms Using ODBC

The INVOICE3.DOT template included in the WBODBC folder on the Microsoft Word Developer's Kit disk contains an integrated collection of macros similar to the INVOICE2.DOT macros described in Chapter 9, "More WordBasic Techniques," in Part 1, "Learning WordBasic." The primary difference between the two templates is that INVOICE2.DOT uses dynamic data exchange (DDE) to retrieve data from and write data to a data source in a running application (a workbook open in Microsoft Excel), while INVOICE3.DOT uses the ODBC extensions to retrieve data from and write data to a data source in a DBMS (an .MDB file created in Microsoft Access).

The advantages of using the ODBC extensions to automate Word forms are simple: the ODBC functions are faster than comparable DDE commands; the ODBC functions require only a data source, not both a data source and the application that was used to create it; and the ODBC functions can be used to read and modify data sources created by DBMSs that do not support DDE. In general, the ODBC error reporting functions make debugging and handling ODBC errors more flexible than handling and debugging comparable DDE errors in WordBasic.

The following table shows a comparison of the steps that macros using DDE versus macros using the ODBC extensions must carry out to automate a form.

DDE macro steps	ODBC macro steps
Determine whether required application is running; start the application if it is not running.	Not required.
Locate the file that will act as the data source and open it in the running application.	Connect to an established ODBC data source (previously set up using the ODBC Administrator program).
Execute a query in the form of the application's programming language with **DDEExecute**.	Execute a query in ODBC SQL using **SQLExecQuery** or **SQLQueryExec**.
Retrieve data as strings using **DDERequest**; parse as required by the application's DDE and database functionality.	With **SQLExecQuery**, retrieve data items as strings using row and column notation with **SQLRetrieveItem$**, or retrieve the entire query and insert it as a table with **SQLRetrieveToDocument**. With **SQLQueryExec**, move through rows using **SQLQueryFetch** or **SQLSetRowPos** and return data from columns using **SQLQueryRetrieve**.
Close the DDE channel using **DDETerminate**.	Close the data source channel using **SQLClose**.

For comparison, open the macros in the two templates on the Microsoft Word Devleeper's Kit disk: INVOICE2.DOT in the WRDBASIC folder and INVOICE3.DOT in the WBODBC folder. Looking at the areas in the macros that retrieve and write data, you can compare and contrast the amount of code, the data parsing routines, and the error handling routines required by ODBC and DDE. Create a new document based on each form and use it to run the macros and demonstrate the differences in speed.

For complete information about the purpose and functionality of the Invoice form itself and the use of form fields to trigger WordBasic macros, see "Automating Forms" in Chapter 9, "More WordBasic Techniques," in Part 1, "Learning WordBasic."

Note To run the macros in the INVOICE3.DOT template, you must have access to the NWIND.MDB or NORTHWIND.MDB file (shipped with Microsoft Access version 2.0 and version 7.0, respectively) and you must create a data source called "Northwind" associated with that database. For information about creating ODBC data sources, see "Setting Up Data Sources," earlier in this appendix.

WordBasic ODBC Functions

Consider the following for all the WordBasic ODBC functions:

- To use a function described in this section, you must include the corresponding **Declare** statement, which you can copy directly from the AllDeclarations macro in WBODBC.DOT. For more information, see "Using the ODBC Extensions" earlier in this appendix.

- In general, an *error value* is an integer that is less than or equal to zero. A return value of 0 (zero) implies a general error, for which more information can be obtained using the error functions.

- A return value of –1 (SQL_NoMoreData) implies that the logical end of a file has been reached.

- A return value of –2 (SQL_StillExecuting) during asynchronous processing implies that an ODBC operation is still in progress.

- If a string function cannot return a value from a data source, it returns an empty string ("").

SQLClose

Syntax

SQLClose(*ConnectNum*)

Remarks

Terminates a connection with an external data source. If the call is successful, then **SQLClose** will terminate the specified data source connection.

Argument	Explanation
ConnectNum	The unique connection ID of the data source from which you want to disconnect. *ConnectNum* was returned by a previously executed **SQLOpen** function. If *ConnectNum* is not valid, **SQLClose** returns an error value.

If the connection is successfully terminated, **SQLClose** returns 1, and the connection ID number is no longer valid. If **SQLClose** is unable to disconnect from the data source, it returns an error value and places error information in memory for the error functions, if such information is available.

SQLCloseAll

Syntax

SQLCloseAll()

Remarks

Terminates all connections with external data sources. If the call is successful, then **SQLCloseAll** terminates all data source connections. This is useful when you want to ensure that any existing connections are closed before a macro or subroutine runs.

If the connections are successfully terminated, **SQLCloseAll** returns 1, and no connection ID numbers are valid. If **SQLCloseAll** is unable to disconnect from any single data source, it returns an error value and places error information in memory for the error functions, if such information is available.

SQLCountErrors

Syntax

SQLCountErrors()

Remarks

Returns the number of rows of detailed error information available. Each available row can be retrieved by calling **SQLErrorText$** and passing a row number from 1 through the value returned by **SQLCountErrors** (1 is the first available row). For information about the structure of error rows, see **SQLErrorText$**.

A return value of 0 (zero) indicates no error information is available. A return value greater than 0 (zero) indicates the number of rows of error information available. Note that **SQLErrorCount** does not return information on itself.

SQLErrorClass$

Syntax

SQLErrorClass$(*ErrorNum*)

Remarks

Determines the ODBC SQLSTATE class and subclass of the specified error. For errors that occur in the data source, the ODBC driver maps the returned native error to the appropriate SQLSTATE. For errors that are detected by the driver or the Driver Manager, the driver or Driver Manager generates the appropriate SQLSTATE.

SQLSTATE values are specified by the X/Open and SQL Access Group SQL CAE specification (1992). For complete information on ODBC error codes and the ODBC API SQLError function, see the *Microsoft ODBC Programmer's Reference* in the Microsoft ODBC Software Development Kit version 2.10.

Argument	Explanation
ErrorNum	A row number between 1 and the value returned by the **SQLCountErrors** function (1 is the first available item).

SQLSTATE, the five-character string value returned by **SQLErrorClass$**, consists of a two-character class value followed by a three-character subclass value. If the error class is not available for the type of error that was encountered, this function returns an empty string ("").

Example   The following example parses the five-character SQLSTATE value returned by
                     SQLErrorClass$ into its class and subclass components.

```
SQLSTATE$ = SQLErrorClass$(connect_num)
class$ = Left$(2,SQLSTATE$)
subclass$ = Right$(3,SQLSTATE$)
```

SQLErrorCode

Syntax   **SQLErrorCode**(*ErrorNum*)

Remarks   Determines the native error code in the data source for the specified error. Native
                     errors are generated and returned from the DBMS of the data source on
                     a given connection. For information about particular native error codes, see the
                     documentation for the appropriate DBMS.

Argument	Explanation
ErrorNum	A row number between 1 and the value returned by the **SQLCountErrors** function (1 is the first available item).

This function returns the numeric native error code for errors generated in the data
source. For errors detected by the driver or the Driver Manager, **SQLErrorCode**
returns a native error of 0 (zero).

SQLErrorFlush

Syntax   **SQLErrorFlush**()

Remarks   Removes error information for the current error. Although you can use
                     SQLErrorFlush to deliberately remove current error information, note that all
                     error information is automatically removed whenever an ODBC high-level
                     function completes successfully.

                     If the error information could not be flushed, the **SQLErrorFlush** function
                     returns a negative error value.

SQLErrorText$

Syntax   **SQLErrorText$**(*ErrorNum*)

Remarks   Retrieves a row of available error information. **SQLErrorText$** returns a single
                     string that contains a delimited list of error information that can be evaluated by
                     an error trap or displayed to the user.

Argument	Explanation
ErrorNum	A row number between 1 and the value returned by the **SQLCountErrors** function (1 is the first available item).

Each row of error information has the following four fields:

- The vendor
- The ODBC component
- The name of the data source
- A text message describing the error

If one or more of these fields is not available for the type of error that was encountered, those fields are left blank. For more information about ODBC error messages, see the *Microsoft ODBC Programmer's Reference* in the Microsoft ODBC Software Development Kit version 2.10. For information about specific return values, see the Help file for the appropriate ODBC driver.

Example

The following example demonstrates a simple loop for displaying error information to the user in a message box. After the number of lines of error information is returned by **SQLCountErrors**, a **For…Next** loop displays the errors.

```
count = SQLCountErrors()
for msgs = 1 to count
    MsgBox SQLErrorText$(count), "ODBC Error", 48
next count
```

SQLExecQuery

Syntax

SQLExecQuery(*ConnectNum*, *Query$*)

Remarks

Sends a query to a data source using an existing connection and stores the entire query result in memory.

Note Unlike **SQLExecQuery**, **SQLQueryExec** does not store the entire query result in memory. To avoid resource problems when creating complex database solutions using the ODBC add-in library, use **SQLQueryExec**.

Before calling **SQLExecQuery**, a connection must be established with a data source using **SQLOpen**. A successful call to **SQLOpen** returns a unique connection ID number. **SQLExecQuery** uses that connection ID number to send SQL language queries to the data source.

SQLExecQuery only executes a query; results generated from the query are not returned. Retrieving results is handled by the **SQLRetrieveColumns**, **SQLRetrieveItem$**, and **SQLRetrieveRows** functions. If **SQLExecQuery** is called using an existing connection ID number, all pending results on that connection will automatically be discarded. The connection ID will then refer to the new query and its results.

Argument	Explanation
ConnectNum	The unique connection ID of the data source you want to query returned by a previously executed **SQLOpen** function. If *ConnectNum* is not valid, **SQLExecQuery** returns 0 (zero).
Query$	The SQL language query that is to be executed on the data source. The query should follow SQL grammar; the Help file for the appropriate ODBC driver also describes any SQL language limitations or modifications for the given DBMS.
	If **SQLExecQuery** is unable to execute *Query$* on the specified data source, **SQLExecQuery** returns 0 (zero). The exact error can be obtained from the error functions.

If **SQLExecQuery** is able to successfully execute the query on the specified connection, it will return one of three values, depending on the type of SQL statement that was executed.

SQL statement	Return value
SELECT	The number of result columns available
UPDATE, INSERT or DELETE	The number of rows affected by the statement
Other	A positive value

If there was an error executing the query, SQLExecQuery returns a negative error value.

Example

The following example sends a simple SELECT query to an established data source connection during asynchronous processing. While **SQLExecQuery** continues to return the value –2, the query is still being processed; the macro should wait for a final return value from **SQLExecQuery** before determining whether an error occurred.

```
ret = -2
While ret = -2
    ret = SQLExecQuery(connect_num, "select * from authors")
Wend
If ret <= 0 Then Goto ParseErrors
```

SQLGetSchema

Syntax

SQLGetSchema(*ConnectNum*, *Type*, *Qualifier$*)

Remarks

Establishes a pseudo-query on a data source connection to provide information about the schema (structure) of the data source. After **SQLGetSchema** establishes a pseudo-query and returns a value describing the available information, use **SQLGetSchemaItem$** one or more times to return the available string or strings of information about the data source structure. **SQLGetSchema** works with the ODBC API functions SQLGetInfo and SQLTables to find the requested information; for complete information about these API functions, see the *Microsoft ODBC Programmer's Reference* in the Microsoft ODBC Software Development Kit version 2.10.

For a complete example macro using **SQLGetSchema**, see the third example macro described in "Using the ODBC Extensions" earlier in this appendix.

Arguments	Explanation
ConnectNum	The unique connection ID of the data source you want information about, returned by a previously executed **SQLOpen** function. If *ConnectNum* is not valid, **SQLGetSchema** returns 0 (zero).
Type	A value between 1 and 14 that specifies the type of information you want returned. For descriptions of the information that can be returned, see the table of return values, following.
Qualifier$	A text string used to qualify the search for the requested information. This string should be enclosed by quotation marks. Note that *Qualifier$* is only included for *Type* values of 3, 4, and 5. For other *Type* values, *Qualifier$* should be an empty string (**""**).
	If *Type* is 3, *Qualifier$* should be the name of a database in the current data source. **SQLGetSchema** will then only return the number of table owners in that database. If you specify an empty string (**""**), the function will return the number of all owners of all databases on *ConnectNum*.
	If *Type* is 4, *Qualifier$* should be both a database name and an owner name. The syntax of *Qualifier$* is "*Database.Owner*". **SQLGetSchema** will then return the number of tables that are located in the given database and owned by the given owner. If you specify an empty string (**""**), the function will return the number of all table names in all databases owned by all owners on *ConnectNum*.
	If *Type* is 5, *Qualifier$* should be the name of a table. Information about the columns in that table will be returned.

The numeric value returned by the **SQLGetSchema** function depends on the value of the *Type* argument that was passed, as described in the following table. Use **SQLGetSchemaItem$** one or more times to return the available string or strings, as indicated by the numeric return value of **SQLGetSchema**.

Type	**Meaning of return value**
1	Number of available data sources.
2	Number of databases on the current connection.
3	Number of owners in a database on the current connection. This *Type* requires that a value be specified for *Qualifier$*.
4	Number of tables for a given owner and database on the current connection. This *Type* requires that a value be specified for *Qualifier$*.
5	Number describing a two-dimensional array listing the columns in a particular table and their data types. The return value is the total number of string values available. The odd-numbered items are the names of the columns. The even-numbered items are the data types of the columns. This *Type* requires that a value be specified for *Qualifier$*.
6	If a non-error value, the user ID of the current user is available.
7	If a non-error value, the name of the current database is available.
8	If a non-error value, the name of the data source as given in the ODBC.INI file (Windows 3.*x*) or the registry (Windows 95 and Windows NT) is available.
9	If a non-error value, the name of the data source DBMS (i.e. Oracle, SQL Server, etc.) is available.
10	If a non-error value, the name of the server name for the data source is available.
11	If a non-error value, the terminology used by the data source to refer to owners (i.e. "owner", "Authorization ID", "Schema", etc.) is available.
12	If a non-error value, the terminology used by the data source to refer to tables (i.e. "table", "file", etc.) is available.
13	If a non-error value, the terminology used by the data source to refer to qualifiers (i.e. "database" or "directory") is available.
14	If a non-error value, the terminology used by the data source to refer to procedures (i.e. "database procedure", "stored procedure", or "procedure") is available.

> **Note** The **SQLGetSchema** function should not overwrite the pending results of another query sent to the same data source. To avoid overwriting pending query results, establish a new connection to the data source using **SQLOpen,** and specify the resulting connection ID for **SQLGetSchema.**

SQLGetSchemaItem$

Syntax

SQLGetSchemaItem$(*ConnectNum,* *Item*)

Remarks

Returns a string that provides information about the schema (structure) of the data source on a particular connection. After a successful call to **SQLGetSchema,** you can use **SQLGetSchemaItem$** one or more times to return the string value or values that **SQLGetSchema** indicates are available for a particular aspect of the data source structure. The values available from **SQLGetSchemaItem$** depend on the type of information that was requested.

For a complete example macro using **SQLGetSchemaItem$**, see the third example macro described in "Using the ODBC Extensions" earlier in this appendix.

Argument	Explanation
ConnectNum	The unique connection ID of the data source you want information about, returned by a previously executed **SQLOpen** function. If *ConnectNum* is not valid, **SQLGetSchemaItem$** returns 0 (zero).
Item	Specifies the item of information you want returned. Note that *Item* should be a value between 1 and the number returned by **SQLGetSchema** for an established pseudo-query.

The string values available from this function depend on the type of information that was requested. See the table of return values for **SQLGetSchema** for descriptions.

SQLGetTypeInfo$

Syntax

**SQLGetTypeInfo$**(*ConnectNum,* *Type$*)

Remarks

Maps a known data type into an acceptable native data type. When using the SQL statements CREATE TABLE and ALTER TABLE, you must specify the data types native to that particular DBMS. To determine an appropriate data type for the DBMS you are using, you use the **SQLGetTypeInfo$** function. For more information about data-type mapping for a given ODBC driver, see the corresponding Help file.

Argument	Explanation
ConnectNum	The unique connection ID of the data source to which you want to map a known data type to a native data type. The connection ID is returned by a previously executed **SQLOpen** function. If *ConnectNum* is not valid, **SQLGetTypeInfo$** returns an error value.
Type$	A data type for which you want to know the equivalent DBMS native data type.

For any valid SQL data type, this function returns the corresponding data type for the DBMS of the current data source.

Example

This example demonstrates how **SQLGetTypeInfo$** can be used to make WordBasic ODBC macros portable to multiple DBMSs. Here, **SQLGetTypeInfo$** stores native data types in variables; as a result, the SQL CREATE TABLE query specified in **SQLExecQuery** works regardless of the DBMS in which the data source was created.

```
int$ = SQLGetTypeInfo$(connect_num,"integer")
txt$ = SQLGetTypeInfo$(connect_num,"text")
ret = SQLExecQuery(connect_num, \
        "create table emp_id(id " + int$ + ", name" + txt$ + "(32))")
```

SQLOpen

Syntax

SQLOpen(*Connect$*, *Output$*, *DriverPrompt*)

Remarks

Establishes a connection with a data source. A connection established with **SQLOpen** can be used throughout a macro until the connection is closed with **SQLClose**. Note that **SQLOpen** can prompt the user for additionally needed connection information.

Argument	Explanation
Connect$	The information necessary to establish a connection to a data source. Note that any data-source name that is used in *Connect$* must be an existing data-source name defined with ODBC Setup or the ODBC Administration Utility. For more information on how to define data-source names, see "Setting Up Data Sources" earlier in this appendix.
	Note that *Connect$* should follow the format described in the Help file for the appropriate ODBC driver. This string may require the data-source name, one or more user IDs, one or more passwords, and any other information necessary to successfully connect to the particular DBMS.
Output$	A predefined string variable where you want the completed connection string to be placed. If *Output$* is omitted, a completed connection string will not be returned.

Argument	Explanation
DriverPrompt	A number from 1 to 4 specifying if, and how, the driver should display prompts. This sets the fDriverCompletion flag in the ODBC API SQLDriverConnect function.

    1   Always display a dialog box. The flag is set to SQL_DRIVER_PROMPT.

    2   Display a dialog box only if there is not enough information to connect. The driver uses information from the connection string and from the data source specification as its defaults. The flag is set to SQL_DRIVER_COMPLETE.

    3   Same as 2, but the driver grays and disables any unnecessary prompts. The flag is set to SQL_DRIVER_COMPLETE_REQUIRED.

    4   If the connection string is unsuccessful, do not display a dialog box. The flag is set to SQL_DRIVER_NOPROMPT.

If the connection is successfully established, **SQLOpen** returns a connection ID number. Use the connection ID number with other functions to reference that connection.

If **SQLOpen** is unable to connect with the information provided, it returns the error value 0 (zero). In such cases, and if more information is available, **SQLOpen** places error information in memory for the error functions to return, if such information is available.

Examples

This example uses **SQLOpen** to create a connection to a Microsoft Access data source without displaying unnecessary prompts.

```
connect_num = SQLOpen("mydata.mdb", output_string$, 2)
```

The following example uses **SQLOpen** with a complex *Connect$*.

```
connect_num = SQLOpen("DSN = MyServer; UID = dbayer; PWD = 123; \
    Database = pubs", output_string$, 1)
```

SQLQueryExec

Syntax

SQLQueryExec(*ConnectNum*, *Query$*)

Remarks

Sends a query to a data source using an existing connection.

Note Unlike **SQLExecQuery**, **SQLQueryExec** does not store the entire query result in memory. To avoid resource problems when creating complex database solutions using the ODBC add-in library, use **SQLQueryExec**.

Before calling **SQLQueryExec**, a connection must be established with a data source using **SQLOpen**. A successful call to **SQLOpen** returns a unique connection ID number. **SQLQueryExec** uses that connection ID number to send SQL language queries to the data source.

SQLQueryExec only executes a query; results generated from the query are not returned. Retrieving results is handled by the **SQLQueryFetch**, **SQLQueryRetrieve**, **SQLRetrieveColSize**, and **SQLSetRowPos** functions. If **SQLQueryExec** is called using an existing connection ID number, all pending results on that connection will automatically be discarded. The connection ID will then refer to the new query and its results.

You cannot use **SQLRetrieveItem$** or **SQLRetrieveToDocument** to return data from a **SQLQueryExec** instruction.

Argument	Explanation
ConnectNum	The unique connection ID of the data source you want to query returned by a previously executed **SQLOpen** function. If *ConnectNum* is not valid, **SQLQueryExec** returns 0 (zero).
Query$	The SQL language query that is to be executed on the data source. The query should follow SQL grammar; the Help file for the appropriate ODBC driver also describes any SQL language limitations or modifications for the given DBMS.
	If **SQLQueryExec** is unable to execute *Query$* on the specified data source, **SQLQueryExec** returns 0 (zero). The exact error can be obtained from the error functions.

If **SQLQueryExec** is able to successfully execute the query on the specified connection, it will return one of three values, depending on the type of SQL statement that was executed.

SQL statement	Return value
SELECT	The number of result columns available
UPDATE, INSERT or DELETE	The number of rows affected by the statement
Other	A positive value

If there was an error executing the query, **SQLQueryExec** returns a negative error value.

Note If **SQLQueryExec** successfully executes the query but the result of the query contains no data, the function will return 0 (zero). To determine whether this return value indicates an error or simply that the result contains no data, check for error messages with **SQLCountErrors**. If **SQLCountErrors** returns 0 (zero), then **SQLQueryExec** successfully executed the SQL query but the result is empty.

Example

The following example sends a simple SELECT query to an established data source connection during asynchronous processing. While **SQLQueryExec** continues to return the value –2, the query is still being processed; the macro should wait for a final return value from **SQLQueryExec** before determining whether an error occurred.

```
ret = -2
While ret = -2
    ret = SQLQueryExec(connect_num, "select * from authors")
Wend
If ret <= 0 Then Goto ParseErrors
```

SQLQueryFetch

Syntax

SQLQueryFetch(*ConnectNum*)

Remarks

Positions the cursor at the next row of data in the query result of **SQLQueryExec**. The cursor cannot be moved backward. To use **SQLQueryFetch**, a macro must have already established a connection using **SQLOpen**. Also, a query must have already been executed using **SQLQueryExec**, and results must be pending.

Use **SQLQueryRetrieve** to return data from the row of data at which the cursor is positioned.

You cannot use **SQLQueryFetch** in combination with **SQLRetrieveItem$** or **SQLRetrieveToDocument** to return data from a data source.

Argument	Explanation
ConnectNum	The unique connection ID for a data source. The data source specified must have pending query results. If *ConnectNum* is not valid, **SQLQueryExec** would have returned an error value. In such a case, **SQLQueryExec** places error information in memory for the error functions, if such information is available.

If the cursor was moved, **SQLQueryFetch** returns 1; if the cursor is already positioned at the last row of data, it returns –1 (SQL_NoMoreData). Otherwise, **SQLQueryFetch** returns 0 (zero) or a negative error value.

Example

The following example uses a **While...Wend** loop to return the data in each column of each row of the pending data source until **SQLQueryFetch** returns a value indicating that the cursor is already at the last row of the query results.

```
cols = SQLRetrieveColumns(connect_no)
ret = SQLQueryFetch(connect_no)
While ret = 1
    For i = 1 To cols
        storsize = SQLRetrieveColSize(connect_no, i)
        stor$ = String$(storsize, 50)
        SQLQueryRetrieve(connect_no, i, stor$, storsize)
        ' Statement block that processes the value of stor$
    Next i
ret = SQLQueryFetch(connect_no)
Wend
```

SQLQueryRetrieve

Syntax

SQLQueryRetrieve(*ConnectNum*, *Column*, *DataVar$*, *DataSize*)

Remarks

Assigns to the *DataVar$* variable the data in the specified *Column* of the current row (the row where **SQLQueryFetch** or **SQLSetRowPos** positioned the cursor) of the query result. To use **SQLQueryRetrieve**, a macro must have already established a connection using **SQLOpen**. Also, a query must have already been executed using **SQLQueryExec**, and results must be pending.

You cannot use **SQLQueryRetrieve** to return data from a query executed by **SQLExecQuery**.

Caution **SQLQueryRetrieve** assigns the data to the characters in *DataVar$*, up to the number of characters specified by *DataSize*. If the number of characters assigned to *DataVar$* before it is used by **SQLQueryRetrieve** is less than *DataSize*, **SQLQueryRetrieve** may cause memory errors.

To avoid memory errors, the macro must ensure that the value of *DataVar$* is at least *DataSize* characters long before it is used in a **SQLQueryRetrieve** instruction.

Argument	Explanation
ConnectNum	The unique connection ID for a data source. The data source specified must have pending query results. If *ConnectNum* is not valid, **SQLQueryExec** would have returned an error value. In such a case, **SQLQueryRetrieve** places error information in memory for the error functions, if such information is available.
Column	The number of a column in the data source from which to retrieve data. Use **SQLRetrieveColumns** to determine the valid range of values. If the column value is out of range, **SQLQueryRetrieve** returns 0 (zero) and places the error information in memory for the error functions.
DataVar$	The variable to which **SQLQueryRetrieve** assigns the data, up to the number of characters specified by *DataSize*. Before the **SQLQueryRetrieve** instruction is run, the value of *DataVar$* must be at least *DataSize* characters long. Otherwise, memory errors may occur.
DataSize	Specifies the width of the data at *Column*. To determine the value for *DataSize*, use **SQLRetrieveColSize**. If the length of the data in *Column* exceeds *DataSize*, **SQLQueryRetrieve** truncates the data.

If the data cannot be returned successfully, **SQLQueryRetrieve** returns 0 (zero) or a negative error value.

Example

The following example uses a **While...Wend** loop to return the data in each column of each row in the pending data source with **SQLQueryRetrieve** so it can be processed.

```
cols = SQLRetrieveColumns(connect_no)
ret = SQLQueryFetch(connect_no)
While ret - 1
    For i = 1 To cols
        storsize = SQLRetrieveColSize(connect_no, 1)
        stor$ - String$(storsize, 50)
        SQLQueryRetrieve(connect_no, i, stor$, storsize)
        ' Statement block that processes the value of stor$
    Next i
ret = SQLQueryFetch(connect_no)
```

SQLRetrieveColSize

Syntax   SQLRetrieveColSize(*ConnectNum*, *ColNum*)

Remarks   Determines the maximum width of the string values in the specified column of the data source. To use **SQLRetrieveColSize**, a macro must have already established a connection using **SQLOpen**. Also, a query must already have been executed using **SQLQueryExec**, and results must be pending. Use the value returned by **SQLRetrieveColSize** in a **String$()** instruction to create a variable large enough to contain the value assigned to it by subsequent **SQLQueryRetrieve** instructions.

You cannot use **SQLRetrieveColSize** to determine the width of a column in the query results returned by **SQLExecQuery**.

Argument	Explanation
ConnectNum	The unique connection ID for a data source. If *ConnectNum* is not valid, **SQLQueryExec** would have returned an error value. In such a case, **SQLRetrieveColSize** places error information in memory for the error functions, if such information is available.

SQLRetrieveColSize returns the maximum width of the specified column in the data source. Note that the column size is one-based; that is, the first column is 1, not 0 (zero).

SQLRetrieveColSize returns 0 (zero) if it cannot determine the maximum width of the column, and places error information in memory for the error functions, if such information is available.

If there are no results pending on the connection, no data was found, or there is no data, **SQLRetrieveColSize** returns –1 (SQL_NoMoreData).

Example   The following example uses the value returned by **SQLRetrieveColSize** in a **String$()** instruction to make the variable stor$ large enough to use in the subsequent **SQLQueryRetrieve** instruction. The value returned by **SQLRetrieveColSize** is also used in the **SQLQueryRetrieve** instruction to indicate how many characters to return from specified column of the data source.

```
storsize = SQLRetrieveColSize(connect_no, 1)
stor$ = String$(storsize, 35)        'creates a string # characters
SQLQueryRetrieve(connect_no, 1, stor$, storsize)
```

SQLRetrieveColumns

Syntax

SQLRetrieveColumns(*ConnectNum*)

Remarks

Determines the number of columns available in the data source. To use **SQLRetrieveColumns**, a macro must have already established a connection using **SQLOpen**. Also, a query must already have been executed using **SQLExecQuery** or **SQLQueryExec**, and results must be pending.

Argument	Explanation
ConnectNum	The unique connection ID for a data source. If *ConnectNum* is not valid, **SQLExecQuery** or **SQLQueryExec** would have returned an error value. In such a case, **SQLRetrieveColumns** places error information in memory for the error functions, if such information is available.

SQLRetrieveColumns returns the number of columns in the data source. Note that the column count is one-based; that is, the first column is 1, not 0 (zero).

If there are no results pending on the connection, no data was found, or there is no data, **SQLRetrieveColumns** returns –1 (SQL_NoMoreData).

SQLRetrieveFlush

Syntax

SQLRetrieveFlush(*ConnectNum*)

Remarks

Flushes the current query and frees any resources held. In general, data from old queries is flushed when a new query is established, but you can use **SQLRetrieveFlush** to deliberately remove current query results. To use **SQLRetrieveFlush**, a macro must have already established a connection using **SQLOpen**. Also, a query must already have been executed using **SQLExecQuery** or **SQLQueryExec**, and results must be pending.

Argument	Explanation
ConnectNum	The unique connection ID for a data source. The data source specified must have pending query results. If *ConnectNum* is not valid, **SQLExecQuery** or **SQLQueryExec** would have returned an error value. In such a case, **SQLRetrieveFlush** places error information in memory for the error functions, if such information is available.

If the current query could not be flushed, the **SQLErrorFlush** function returns a negative error value.

SQLRetrieveItem$

Syntax   **SQLRetrieveItem$**(*ConnectNum*, *Column*, *Row*)

Remarks   Extracts an available data item from a data source. To use **SQLRetrieveItem$**, a macro must have already established a connection using **SQLOpen**. Also, a query must have already been executed using **SQLExecQuery**, and results must be pending.

You cannot use **SQLRetrieveItem$** to return data from a **SQLQueryExec** instruction.

For a complete example macro using **SQLRetrieveItem$** and the other functions used to retrieve information from a data source, see the second example macro described in "Using the ODBC Extensions" earlier in this appendix.

Argument	Explanation
ConnectNum	The unique connection ID for a data source. The data source specified must have pending query results. If *ConnectNum* is not valid, **SQLExecQuery** would have returned an error value. In such a case, **SQLRetrieveItem$** places error information in memory for the error functions, if such information is available.
Column	The number of a column in the data source. Use **SQLRetrieveColumns** to determine the valid range of values. If the column value is out of range, **SQLRetrieveItem$** returns an empty string ("").
Row	The number of a row in the data source. Use **SQLRetrieveRows** to determine the valid range of values. If the row value is out of range, **SQLRetrieveItem$** returns an empty string ("").

SQLRetrieveItem$ returns the specified data item as a string.

SQLRetrieveRows

Syntax   **SQLRetrieveRows**(*ConnectNum*)

Remarks   Determines the number of rows available in the data source. To use **SQLRetrieveRows**, a macro must have already established a connection using **SQLOpen**. Also, a query must have already been executed using **SQLExecQuery**, and results must be pending.

Argument	Explanation
ConnectNum	The unique connection ID for a data source. If *ConnectNum* is not valid, **SQLExecQuery** would have returned an error value. In such a case, **SQLRetrieveRows** places error information in memory for the error functions, if such information is available.

Returns the number of rows in the data source. Note that the row count is one-based; that is, the first row is 1, not 0 (zero).

SQLRetrieveRows returns 0 (zero) if used to determine the number of rows in the query result of a **SQLQueryExec** instruction.

If there are no results pending on the connection, no data was found, or there is no data, **SQLRetrieveRows** returns –1 (SQL_NoMoreData).

SQLRetrieveToDocument

Syntax

SQLRetrieveToDocument(*ConnectNum*)

Remarks

Retrieves the results of a query and places the entire contents into a table in the active document. To use **SQLRetrieveToDocument**, a macro must have already established a connection using **SQLOpen**. Also, a query must already have been executed using **SQLExecQuery**, and results must be pending.

You cannot use **SQLRetrieveToDocument** to return data from a **SQLQueryExec** instruction.

Argument	Explanation
ConnectNum	The unique connection ID of the data source you want to query returned by a previously executed **SQLOpen** function. If *ConnectNum* is not valid, **SQLRetrieveToDocument** returns 0 (zero).

If the pending query result cannot be returned successfully, **SQLRetrieveToDocument** returns a negative error value.

Example

The following example establishes a connection to a data source, queries the data source to select every record, and then uses **SQLRetrieveToDocument** to insert the entire data source in a table in a new Word document.

```
connect_num - SQLOpen("DSN-test.mdb", output_ref$, 0)
ret = SOLExecQuery(connect_num. "Select * from table4 " + \
      Quote2$("name"))
FileNew
ret = SQLRetrieveToDocument(connect_num)
ret = SQLClose(connect_num)
```

SQLSetRowPos

Syntax   **SQLSetRowPos**(*ConnectNum*, *Row*)

Remarks   Positions the cursor at a specified row of the query results of **SQLQueryExec**. To use **SQLSetRowPos**, a macro must have already established a connection using **SQLOpen**. Also, a query must have already been executed using **SQLQueryExec**, and results must be pending.

Note Not all DBMSs can move the cursor to an arbitrary row of a query result. If a **SQLOpen** instruction returned a connection to a DBMS that cannot use move the cursor arbitrarily, **SQLSetRowPos** returns 0 (zero).

Use **SQLQueryRetrieve** to return data from the row of data at which the cursor is positioned.

You cannot use **SQLSetRowPos** to return data from a **SQLExecQuery** instruction.

Argument	Explanation
ConnectNum	The unique connection ID for a data source. The data source specified must have pending query results. If *ConnectNum* is not valid, **SQLQueryExec** would have returned an error value. In such a case, **SQLSetRowPos** places error information in memory for the error functions, if such information is available.
Row	The number of a row in the data source. If the row value is out of range, **SQLSetRowPos** returns 0 (zero).
	You cannot use **SQLRetrieveRows** to determine the number of rows in a query result from a **SQLQueryExec** instruction. Therefore, you must use one of the following two methods to determine valid values for *Row*:
	Create a **While...Wend** loop to call **SQLQueryFetch** and increment a counter variable until **SQLQueryFetch** returns –1. Then use any value between 1 and the counter variable for *Row*.
	Use any value and then determine whether **SQLQueryFetch** succeeded: if it didn't, try another value; if it did, process the data in the row at which the cursor was successfully positioned.

If the cursor was moved, **SQLSetRowPos** returns 1. If an error occurred, **SQLSetRowPos** returns 0 (zero) or a negative error value.

If the DBMS specified by the **SQLOpen** instruction that returned *ConnectNum* does not support this functionality, **SQLSetRowPos** returns 0 (zero).

SQLSynchronize

Syntax

SQLSynchronize(*Flag*)

Remarks

Specifies whether to allow ODBC functions to be called asynchronously. Several of the functions in the ODBC API can be called asynchronously. The ODBC extensions for Microsoft Word take advantage of this functionality. Not all ODBC drivers can handle asynchronous calls, but the ODBC API was designed so that the calling convention is the same for all drivers.

For complete information on asynchronous processing, see "Requesting Asynchronous Processing" in Chapter 6, "Executing SQL Statements," in the *Microsoft ODBC Programmer's Reference* in the Microsoft ODBC Software Development Kit version 2.0.

Argument	Explanation
Flag	Specifies whether to enable or disable asynchronous processing:

0 (zero)   Enables asynchronous processing; subsequently, SQL functions may return –2 (SQL_StillExecuting) if activity on the connection is not complete.

1   Disables asynchronous processing.

If **SQLSynchronize** is unsuccessful, the function returns a negative error value.

Example

The following example demonstrates the calling convention for asynchronous ODBC functions.

```
err = SQLSynchronize(0)
status = SQLExecQuery(connection, query_string$)
While SQLRetrieveRows(connection) = -2
    'Series of statements to perform other processing
Wend
```

The ODBC functions used in the WBODBC.WLL can be called in this manner after asynchronous processing is enabled.

APPENDIX C

Microsoft Word Application Programming Interface

The Microsoft Word application programming interface (Word API) is the doorway into the internal functionality of Microsoft Word. Using a programming language such as Microsoft Visual C++ (Windows) or Symantec® THINK C (Macintosh), the Word API, and the tools provided on the Microsoft Word Developer's Kit disk, you can create add-ins that interact directly with Microsoft Word. This appendix covers the concepts, tools, and methods for programming Word add-in libraries (WLLs).

Why Use the Word API?

The WordBasic macro language provides one method of controlling Word through programming. WordBasic can access all of Word's functionality, and, in Windows, can even call Windows API functions directly, which provides a significant degree of power and flexibility. However, the Word API goes beyond WordBasic, providing even more flexibility and better performance.

Word API programming has several advantages over WordBasic. You can write code that is fast, efficient, and flexible. You can use pre-existing libraries of external code, or create new code using any compiler suitable for creating code modules. There are few limitations to the complexity or sophistication of WLLs that you can design and create for Word.

In Windows, a Word add-in library is a special form of a standard Windows dynamic-link library (DLL). On the Macintosh, a Word add-in library is a WDLL code resource designed to be available directly to WordBasic. You can use any language that can create a Windows DLL or Macintosh code resource, such as C, Pascal, or Assembler. However, C is the language of choice for most people.

Note In this appendix, the term "WLL" is used to refer to a Word add-in library developed for either Windows or the Macintosh.

What You Need to Know

Before using the Word API, you should know the basics of creating a DLL (Windows) or a code resource (Macintosh). You should also be familiar with Word and the WordBasic macro language.

Requirements

Windows 3.*x*, Windows 95, or Windows NT To develop WLLs in Windows 3.*x*, Windows 95, or Windows NT, you need the following:

- Microsoft Word Developer's Kit
- Microsoft Word version 6.0 for Windows or Windows NT, or Word version 7.0
- Microsoft Windows version 3.1 or later, Microsoft Windows 95, or Microsoft Windows NT version 3.5 or later
- A compiler that can produce Windows-compatible DLL files (for example, Microsoft Visual C++)

Macintosh To develop WLLs on the Macintosh, you need the following:

- Microsoft Word Developer's Kit
- Microsoft Word version 6.0 or later for the Macintosh
- Apple Macintosh System 7.0 or later
- A compiler that can produce Macintosh code resources (for example, Symantec THINK C)

Installation

The files necessary to build WLLs are located in the CAPI folder on the Microsoft Word Developer's Kit disk. Within the CAPI folder, the SAMPLE subfolder contains the files needed to build a sample WLL in Visual C++ (Windows) or Symantec THINK C (Macintosh). This sample code provides a good starting point for developing your own WLLs.

Windows, Windows 95, or Windows NT From the Microsoft Word Developer's Kit disk, copy the entire CAPI subfolder to an appropriate location in your compiler folder structure. The CAPI subfolder contains the following files, which need to be available to each WLL project you create:

- CAPILIB.C, a collection of helper functions described in the section "Using the CAPILIB Functions" later in this appendix
- CAPILIB.H, the header file defining the CAPILIB functions
- WDCAPI.H, the header file defining the functions, data structures, and constants needed to program WLLs

- CONFIG.H, the header file required to compile WLLs correctly on either 16-bit or 32-bit platforms

- WDCMDS.H, the header file defining all of the Word commands and functions available through the Word API

- WDERROR.H, the header file defining the Word API error codes returned by Word

- WDFID.H, the header file defining all of the arguments taken by the Word commands listed in WDCMDS.H

Macintosh   From the Microsoft Word Developer's Kit disk, drag the CAPI folder to an appropriate location in your compiler folder. The CAPI folder contains files similar to those described for the Windows disk; these files need to be available to each WLL project you create.

Overview of Add-ins and WLLs

External functions in a library are called add-ins, or add-in functions. Add-in functions for Word are faster and more efficient than equivalent WordBasic macros because they are written in C and compiled, and can take advantage of the full functionality of the operating system. You can declare and call external add-in functions in a WLL from WordBasic, or they can be registered with Word using the functions in the Word API.

What Is a Word Add-in Library?

In Windows, a Word add-in library (WLL) is a stand-alone dynamic-link library (DLL) with the filename extension .WLL (once built, the DLL filename extension is renamed to WLL so that the file can be identified as a Word add-in library). On the Macintosh, a WLL is a WDLL code resource, which is designed especially for Word. The rules for compiling, linking, and building a WLL are the same as those for creating a DLL (Windows) or code resource (Macintosh). What sets a WLL apart are the special functions that Word looks for and calls automatically when the WLL is loaded and unloaded: **wdAutoOpen** and **wdAutoRemove**.

Word uses these two functions as automatic points of entry into a WLL. Word calls the **wdAutoOpen** function when the WLL is loaded. This is where the WLL should register its functions and customize Word so that the functions can be called from menu items or toolbar buttons. After doing so, the function returns a value to Word indicating success or failure (on the Macintosh, the function must return the value to the main routine, which in turn returns the value to Word). Here is the syntax:

```
// Windows
short FAR PASCAL wdAutoOpen( short DocID );

// Macintosh
short wdAutoOpen( short DocID );
```

Word calls the optional **wdAutoRemove** function, if included, when the WLL is being unloaded, either by the user or when Word shuts down. Here is the syntax:

```
// Windows
void FAR PASCAL wdAutoRemove( void );

// Macintosh
void wdAutoRemove( void );
```

This function can be used to free dynamically allocated memory when the WLL is unloaded. In addition, if your WLL makes permanent changes to the Normal or active template, you should include the **wdAutoRemove** function to remove any customization that you don't want the template to retain. If your WLL does not specify permanent changes, the Normal or active template is not "dirtied" by the WLL; all customization is temporary and is automatically removed when the WLL is unloaded. In that case, the **wdAutoRemove** function is not necessary.

For descriptions of the other WLL-specific functions that Word makes available through the Word API, see "Word API Functions" later in this appendix.

WordBasic and the Word API

For the most part, there's a one-to-one correspondence between the statements and functions in WordBasic and those that can be called from an add-in function in a WLL. However, the Word API is intended to provide word-processing functionality rather than to duplicate WordBasic functionality. Therefore, elements of the WordBasic language such as control structures, variable declarations, basic file I/O, and custom dialog boxes cannot be called from an add-in function in a WLL. Also note that you can run existing WordBasic macros through the Word API just as you would use the WordBasic **ToolsMacro** statement, but you cannot access the functionality of the WordBasic **Call** statement to pass arguments or run specific subroutines or functions.

In addition to **wdAutoOpen** and **wdAutoRemove**, described earlier, there are a handful of Word functions that are available only to WLLs through the Word API. For information on these Windows and Macintosh functions and their use in WLLs, see "Word API Functions" later in this appendix.

Loading a WLL

There are several ways to load a WLL, either directly by the user or automatically when Word is started or a WordBasic macro is run.

Templates command   From the File menu, choose Templates. Word displays the Templates And Add-ins dialog box. Under Global Templates And Add-ins, choose the Add button. In the Add Template dialog box, select Word Add-ins in the list of file types, and then select a WLL. Choose OK to add the WLL to the list of selected add-ins. When you close the Templates And Add-ins dialog box, Word loads the WLL.

Open command   From the File menu, choose Open. Type the path and filename of the WLL to load it. To see a list that includes all WLLs in the selected folder, type ***.wll** in the File Name box and choose OK (Windows) or select All Files in the List Files Of Type box (Macintosh).

AddAddIn statement   A WLL can be loaded from any WordBasic macro, or from a function in another WLL, by calling **AddAddIn**. This statement and others used in WordBasic macros to work with Word add-in libraries are described in Part 2, "WordBasic Reference."

Auto macros   If a WordBasic auto macro, such as AutoExec, AutoNew, or AutoOpen, is available, Word runs it automatically. You can use the **AddAddIn** statement in any auto macro to automatically load a WLL. For example, an AutoExec macro in the Normal template can automatically load a WLL every time Word is started.

Startup folder   All WLLs located in Word's designated startup folder will automatically load when Word is started. To set the startup folder, choose Options from the Tools menu, select the File Locations tab, and then specify the folder for the Startup option.

Command line   In Windows, you can load a WLL when Word is started by adding an /l command line switch to the command line for a Microsoft Word program item in Program Manager (Windows 3.x and Windows NT) or a Microsoft Word shortcut in Windows Explorer (Windows 95). The following example command line loads CAPI.WLL when Word is started.

c:\winword\winword.exe /lc:\winword\templates\capi.wll

On the Macintosh, you can modify the Word Switches setting in Word Settings (6) to load a WLL when Word is started. For information about modifying this setting, see "Startup Switches" in WordBasic Help.

Note It is also possible for a WordBasic macro to declare and then directly call a function in a WLL, but this doesn't guarantee that the WLL will be loaded as expected. Unless the WLL is loaded in one of the ways described above, the **wdAutoOpen** function does not have the chance to register other functions, and any intended modifications to menus or toolbars will not be made.

Calling Word from a WLL

To call Word with the Word API, a WLL fills WDOPR data structures with data that is meaningful to a Word function, and then sends the structures through the **wdCommandDispatch** function, which identifies the Word function to use. The WDOPR data structure and **wdCommandDispatch** are discussed in detail in the following sections. The CAPILIB functions provided on the Microsoft Word Developer's Kit disk wrap up many of the steps required to build arrays of WDOPRs, and they help perform common WLL tasks, such as customizing Word.

Use the sections on **wdCommandDispatch** ("The wdCommandDispatch Function"), WDOPRs ("The Word Operator (WDOPR)"), and basic Word API techniques ("Techniques for Successful Calling") to learn about the Word API in general and some platform-specific issues. Then use the section on CAPILIB ("Using the CAPILIB Functions") to get an overview of the helper functions you can use to program WLLs quickly and efficiently.

The wdCommandDispatch Function

An add-in library function accesses Word by calling the **wdCommandDispatch** function. This is the only function in Word that your add-ins will call. The **wdCommandDispatch** function lets you call virtually all WordBasic statements and functions. It passes the same arguments as those described for WordBasic statements and functions in Part 2, "WordBasic Reference."

Here is the syntax for the **wdCommandDispatch** function:

```
// Windows
short FAR PASCAL wdCommandDispatch( short CommandID, short DlgOptions,
    short cArgs, LPWDOPR lpwdoprArgs, LPWDOPR lpwoprReturn );
```

```
// Macintosh
pascal short (*wdCommandDispatch) ( short CommandID, short DlgOptions,
    short cArgs, LPWDOPR lpwoprArgs, LPWDOPR lpwoprReturn );
```

For platform-specific details about declaring **wdCommandDispatch** in your WLL code, see "Platform-Specific Notes About wdCommandDispatch" later in this section.

Step by Step Through the Parameters

Understanding each of the parameters of the **wdCommandDispatch** function is important. The following paragraphs detail the purpose and use of each parameter.

CommandID

This is the WordBasic command Word is to execute. The names of available functions are provided as constants in the header file WDCMDS.H. Most of these command names closely parallel their WordBasic equivalents.

DlgOptions

This is the "dialog options" parameter, and is only necessary for WordBasic commands that correspond to Word dialog boxes. This parameter is ignored if the command doesn't involve a dialog box. The following constants for this parameter are defined in WDCAPI.H.

CommandDefaults Returns default values for the dialog box's fields, without actually activating the dialog box. This is similar to the **GetCurValues** statement in WordBasic.

CommandDialog Activates the dialog box. This is similar to the **Dialog** statement in WordBasic. If the function is set to return values from Word, the field settings are just returned to the calling code, and no implied action takes place.

CommandAction Causes the action indicated by the dialog box to actually take place. When combined with CommandDialog, the dialog box will first be displayed, letting the user make any desired changes to the fields, and then the dialog box's action will take place.

cArgs

This is the number of Word arguments being passed. (Arguments for Word commands are wrapped in a data structure called a WDOPR.) The next parameter, lpwdoprArgs, points to an array of WDOPR arguments; cArgs simply provides the count for this array.

lpwdoprArgs

This is a pointer to an array of WDOPR arguments passed to the function dispatcher; in other words, these are the actual arguments for the Word command. Building up this array of arguments is an important part of preparing to call **wdCommandDispatch**. The next section explains this parameter in greater detail.

lpwdoprReturn

This parameter points to a single WDOPR data structure that returns one data item from a WordBasic function. The returned data item can be any of the supported WDOPR data types. When using **wdCommandDispatch** to execute WordBasic statements that correspond to dialog boxes, you should set this parameter to lpwdoprNil. If you are calling a WordBasic statement that can also be called as a function—for example, **Bold** and **Bold()**—this parameter must correspond to how you want to use the statement: as a statement or as a function.

Platform-Specific Notes About wdCommandDispatch

The following topics address specific issues about accessing **wdCommandDispatch** and the Word API on the Windows 3.*x*, Windows 95, Windows NT, and Macintosh platforms.

Windows 3.*x*

In Windows 3.*x*, a WLL imports **wdCommandDispatch** directly from Word version 6.0 for Windows. By declaring the function as described earlier in this section and including the function in the IMPORTS section of the .DEF file for you WLL, your add-in library will work correctly in Windows 3.*x*.

Windows 95 and Windows NT

In Windows 95 and Windows NT, importing functions directly from applications (as Windows 3.*x* allows) is discouraged. To use **wdCommandDispatch** successfully in Windows 95 and Windows NT, your WLL should declare the following function:

```
static unsigned int (*pfn_wdCommandDispatch) () = NULL;
{
    if (pfn_wdCommandDispatch == NULL)
        pfn_wdCommandDispatch = GetProcAddress(GetModuleHandle(NULL),
        "wdCommandDispatch");
    return ((*pfn_wdCommandDispatch)
        (CommandID, DlgOptions, cArgs, lpwdoprArgs, lpwdoprRetrun));
}
```

After declaring this function, the WLL should behave the same as one created for Windows 3.*x*. However, bear the following details in mind when programming 32-bit WLLs or migrating 16-bit WLLs to 32-bit WLLs:

- Any code that assumes an int or stack is 16 bits will cause problems in Windows 95 or Windows NT. This is especially important when calling functions in which you are expecting a variable number of parameters; the mechanism to get the parameters cannot assume a 16-bit stack.

- For Windows NT on x86 platforms, make sure that you use standard calling conventions (__stdcall) for all the functions you export to or import from Word. For Windows NT on a MIPS® or Alpha AXP™ platform, use the C calling convention (__cdecl). One way to handle this is to not use any calling convention prefix at all and control stdcall or cdecl from the .MAK file by using the appropriate switch (for example, in Microsoft Visual C++, -Gz on x86 platforms and default on MIPS or Alpha AXP).

- Several 32-bit Windows API functions with default unicode support have a suffix: W or A. For ANSI, you need to pick the one with suffix A (for example, CallWindowProcA instead of CallWindowProcW).

Passing Floating-Point Parameters on a RISC Platform

If you are writing external DLLs or WLLs to run in Word version 6.0 for Windows NT or Word version 7.0 on a RISC platform, you should be aware of the following issue. Although some processor architectures define a special mechanism for supplying floating-point parameters to functions, WordBasic always passes parameters to external functions using the method for integers, pointers, and structures. Therefore, if your code includes functions with floating-point parameters that will be declared and called by WordBasic macros, you need to use a special technique for passing the parameters.

To access floating-point parameters within a DLL or WLL, you must declare them as structures, and then copy them into a local variable for use within your routine. You can use the following structure and macro definition to accomplish this.

```
struct WORDARGDBL
{
    char x[sizeof(double)];
};

#define DblArgValue(a)      (*(double*)&(a))
```

Here is an example of how you can use this structure and definition in a WLL function:

```
double WINAPI AbsCapi (struct WORDARGDBL arg1)
{
    InitWCB (&wcb, TypeDouble, NULL, 0);
    AddDoubleParam (&wcb, DblArgValue(arg1));
    err = wdCommandDispatch (wdAbs, 0, wcb.cArgs, wcb.wdoprArgs,
        &wcb.wdoprReturn);
    return wcb.wdoprReturn.Double;
}
```

Macintosh

A Macintosh code resource cannot import a function directly from an application. Therefore, the application must provide the resource with a pointer to the parameters for **wdCommandDispatch**. Every time Word calls the WLL, it passes a pointer to a WCDB structure. Here is the structure:

```
typedef struct _WCDB
{
    short          cac;
    char           fLock;
    char           fPurge;
    char           szFunction[66];
    pascal short   (*pfnWordCapi)();
    short          *prgParams;
    union
    {
        long    Short;
        long    Long;
        double     Double;
        uchar      *String;
    } retval;
} WCDB;
```

Element	Description
cac	CAPI Call, the action to be taken by the main function. The defined actions are cacCallFunction, cacCallTimer, cacTerminate, cacWdAutoOpen, cacWdAutoRemove, and cacWindEvent.
fLock	Specifies whether the WLL should remain locked after being called.
fPurge	Specifies whether the WLL should be purged after being called.
szFunction	The function being called from WordBasic; cac is cacCallFunction. On the Macintosh, if the function being called does not exist in the WLL, the WLL should return CAPINoSuchFunction (5) to Word.
pfnWordCapi	A pointer to **wdCommandDispatch**.
prgParams	A pointer to the parameter list passed to szFunction.
retval (union)	The return value of szFunction, if any, as one of the data types specified in the union.

In the main function of the WLL, the dispatcher must be based on the value of the CAPI Call (cac) passed by Word. Apart from this behavior, a Macintosh WLL should work the same as a Windows WLL.

Note On the Macintosh, WordBasic passes function names to a WLL in all uppercase. For simplicity and speed, a WLL should be written to perform a case-insensitive comparison to determine which function in the WLL is being called.

At the same time Word passes a pointer to the WCDB for a WLL to use, it passes a pointer to lUser, a long that holds global data for the WLL. Word initializes this value to 0 (zero); a WLL can modify the data at any time, and Word will return the current data in lUser each time it calls the WLL.

The Word Operator (WDOPR)

The lpwdoprArgs parameter of **wdCommandDispatch** is a pointer to an array of Word operator (WDOPR) data structures. The WDOPR structure lets you pass one of several types of data, and even lets you pass entire arrays of strings or double-precision floating-point values.

For efficiency, several types of data can be passed in the same memory location through the union part of the WDOPR structure; the Type field determines how the data is to be interpreted. Other bit fields in the WDOPR data structure convey to and from the Word API function important information about the argument.

Here is the Windows WDOPR and LPWDOPR type definition, which is found in WDCAPI.H:

```
typedef struct
{
    union
        {
        short       Short;
        long        Long;
        double      Double;
        LPUCHAR     String;
        struct
            {
            ARRAY_DEF far *  ArrayDef;
            union
                {
                double far *        DoubleArray;
                LPUCHAR far *       StringArray;
                };
            };
        };
    ushort BufferSize;
    ushort Type       :4;
    ushort IsArray    :1;
    ushort ForInput   :1;
    ushort ForOutput  :1;
    ushort BufferTooSmall :1;
    ushort :8;
    ushort FieldId;
} WDOPR, far * LPWDOPR;
```

Note On the Macintosh, the corresponding type definition has named unions, Macintosh-specific types (for example, StringPtr instead of LPUCHAR), and a different bit-field order. Otherwise, the information for the Macintosh is the same as the information given for Windows in the following sections. For the complete Macintosh WDOPR data structure, see WDCAPI.H on the Microsoft Word Developer's Kit disk (Macintosh).

Step by Step Through the Data Structure

The following paragraphs describe in detail each part of the WDOPR data structure.

The Type Union

The WDOPR structure starts with a union of several data types. Each WDOPR argument is set up to pass one of these data types at a time. In addition to passing a single short, long, double, or string value, you can also pass arrays of doubles or strings. If an array is passed, the WDOPR structure contains a pointer to the array and to a data structure that defines the dimensions of the array. For complete information about arrays in the Word operator, see "Specifics on Arrays" later in this section.

BufferSize

This field specifies the length of a string handled for input or output. If the argument is set for input, the BufferSize field can be set to one of two ways:

- If BufferSize is set to 0 (zero), the string is passed as a null-terminated string.
- If BufferSize is set to a nonzero value, that exact number of characters, including null characters, is passed from the string. If the WDOPR holds an array of strings, BufferSize indicates the length of each string in the array, which means that all array strings should have the same maximum length.

If the argument is set for output, the BufferSize field indicates the size of the buffer allocated for the returned string. If the allocated buffer is not large enough, or if you deliberately set BufferSize to 0 (zero), an error occurs, the BufferTooSmall bit field is set to 1, and BufferSize is set to the required size. For information about handling returned strings, see "Techniques for Successful Calling" later in this appendix.

The Bit Fields

The following bit fields in the WDOPR data structure convey important information about the argument.

Type   These 4 bits indicate the type of the WDOPR's data. The constants TypeVoid, TypeShort, TypeLong, TypeDouble, and TypeString are defined in WDCAPI.H for use in this field.

In Part 2, "WordBasic Reference," statement and function arguments and return types are specified as "number" (TypeShort, TypeLong, TypeDouble) or "text" (TypeString). To determine the appropriate WDOPR type for a "number" argument or return type, cross-reference the WordBasic topic with WBTYPE.TXT (Windows) or WBTYPE (Macintosh), a text file included in the CAPI folder on the Microsoft Word Developer's Kit disk; if the statement or function does not appear in the list of those that use TypeDouble or TypeLong, then the WDOPR type should be TypeShort.

IsArray   This bit should be set to 1 if the WDOPR is passing an array of the indicated data type. Note that it is the responsibility of the calling function to handle the allocation of memory for WDOPR arrays. For more information, see "Specifics on Arrays" later in this section.

ForInput   ForInput indicates that the contents of the WDOPR argument are intended as input to a dialog box's field settings. This bit is ignored if the command does not correspond to a dialog box.

ForOutput   ForOutput indicates that the WDOPR has been set up to return the value of one field of a dialog box. Set this bit if you are using the CommandDefaults constant for DlgOptions in your **wdCommandDispatch** function. This bit is ignored if the command does not correspond to a dialog box.

BufferTooSmall   If the allocated buffer space is too small to hold the field's data, **wdCommandDispatch** generates an error that sets BufferTooSmall to 1 (true) upon return from calling the command. It is important to clear this bit when making any call. The calling routine is responsible for checking this bit field and taking corrective action. Note that you can check this flag, reallocate the buffer (using the required size returned in BufferSize), and try the call again. If this occurs after calling a command that corresponds to a dialog box where the ForOutput bit was set before the call, this bit should be checked in all WDOPRs to determine which buffer was too small.

FieldID

FieldID is an identifier for the named field parameters passed in each WDOPR. Constants are provided in WDFID.H for this field, and they correspond closely to the parameters that can be passed in WordBasic, as described in Part 2, "WordBasic Reference." For example, in WordBasic the **FormatFont** statement takes the .Bold argument. The corresponding FieldID constant used to pass a short value of 1 in a WDOPR argument is fidBold. This WDOPR would, of course, be constructed and passed as part of a **wdFormatFont** command to the **wdCommandDispatch** function.

Specifics on Arrays

The WDOPR data structure is set up to facilitate the passing of either arrays of strings or arrays of doubles. These arrays can have one or more dimensions.

One of the data types in the union part of the WDOPR is a nested set of structures for passing arrays. Several pieces of information about each array are passed in the appropriate variables. The ARRAY_DEF structure passes information on the number of dimensions in the array and the size of each of those dimensions. Like the WDOPR structure, the ARRAY_DEF structure is also defined in WDCAPI.H, and is listed here for reference.

```
typedef struct
{
    short    cArrayDimensions;
    short    ArrayDimensions[];
} ARRAY_DEF;
```

The remaining part of the WDOPR's array-passing structure is a union of two pointers. In the first case, the pointer is to the first value in an array of double-precision floating-point values. In the second case, the pointer is to an area of memory containing a list of pointers to null-terminated strings.

Keep the following points in mind when building WDOPR arguments to pass arrays:

- ARRAY_DEF must be loaded with data about each dimension of the array.
- For doubles, DoubleArray must be loaded with a pointer to the array.
- For strings, StringArray must be loaded with a pointer to a list of pointers to each string in the array.
- You must set IsArray to 1.

- When passing an array of strings on output, you must specify the length of the array; if the array length is 0 (zero), the Word API will assume that the buffer length is 0 (zero).
- On output, the length of strings in an array is determined by BufferSize. If you pass a string longer than BufferSize, the Word API will write into at most the first BufferSize–1 locations.

Note   There is a subtle difference in the way WordBasic and C arrays are dimensioned. In WordBasic, an array has elements 0 (zero) through n, whereas in C, an array has elements 0 (zero) through n–1, where n is the value given in the array's declaration. The following two arrays, for example, will be allocated the same amount of memory, with elements 0 (zero) through 5 in both cases:

```
' WordBasic array definition
Dim Array (5)

// C array definition
double Array[6];
```

Keep this in mind when working with WordBasic arrays in your Word API code.

Techniques for Successful Calling

It is important to make your Word API code robust because a problem in your Word API code can cause problems in Word. Any possible error conditions should be accounted for, and proper allocation and deallocation of memory should be verified, especially when passing strings.

Handling Errors

The **wdCommandDispatch** function returns an error code that should always be checked. Error constants are defined in WDERROR.H, and errors specific to the Word API are listed in "Word API Errors" later in this appendix. Any nonzero returned value indicates a problem, and your code should accommodate all cases.

In Windows, you should also be careful with function calls into other Windows DLLs, and take appropriate action for any unexpected conditions. A good working knowledge of Windows programming techniques will help make your Word API programming successful.

Allocating Memory

It is the responsibility of the WLL to allocate and deallocate required memory. This means you must declare or allocate appropriate memory space for all string buffers, arrays, and so on. For dynamically allocated variables you must also remember to deallocate the memory later on.

There are two general approaches to allocating enough space for strings returned by Word API commands:

Fixed size   In general, 256 bytes is sufficient for virtually all returned strings, so you can declare or allocate character buffers of this length for most purposes.

Double calling   Another useful technique is to first set BufferSize to 0 (zero), which guarantees that the command will fail. Upon return, however, BufferSize contains the number of bytes required to successfully return the string. You can then allocate a buffer of the exact size required and repeat the call.

Deallocating Memory

It is important to correctly deallocate all memory dynamically allocated by your WLL. Sometimes you can deallocate immediately after a function call. In other cases the returned data will need to be passed back to Word, or kept for future reference by your WLL. In these cases, you are responsible for keeping track of and eventually deallocating these blocks of memory. For example, you might set a flag that can be checked in **wdAutoRemove** to indicate that a specific buffer is to be deallocated.

Working with Strings

When a string is passed from WordBasic to a WLL function, it is automatically lengthened to a minimum of 256 bytes (including the null character) by Word. The WLL can always safely write up to 256 bytes into a passed string. If you need to pass back a longer string, you must take special steps to prevent overwriting the wrong parts of memory. For example, you might add another parameter to your function and insist that WordBasic passes the actual string length. The following WordBasic instructions demonstrate how this might work:

```
strsize = 500
x$ = String$( strsize, "x" )
rtn = MyNewCAPIFunction( strsize, x$ )
```

It is the ultimate responsibility of your WLL code to make sure the string is long enough before overwriting its contents.

Using the CAPILIB Functions

CAPILIB provides a toolbox of functions to simplify your Word API programming tasks. This section takes a close look at these functions and how to use them to build Word operators, pass arrays, and customize Word.

The Word Command Buffer (WCB)

WCB is a data structure defined in WDCAPI.H. This structure is used by the various functions in CAPILIB to help build up the array of WDOPR parameters to be passed to the **wdCommandDispatch** function. The constant MaxArgs, found in WDCAPI.H, determines the maximum number of WDOPR parameters that can be built up. MaxArgs is safely set to 34, an argument count much greater than you'll probably ever need. cArgs is automatically incremented as WDOPR arguments are built up by the CAPILIB functions, and contains the actual count of the WDOPR arguments.

```
typedef struct
{
    short   cArgs;
    WDOPR   wdoprReturn;
    WDOPR   wdoprArgs[MaxArgs];
} WCB;
```

Functions in CAPILIB

There are eighteen functions in CAPILIB, which can be grouped into seven categories:

- Initialize WCB
- Add dialog fields
- Add parameters
- Define arrays
- Call a Word command
- Register functions in Word
- Assign functions in Word

You should include the header file CAPILIB.H in modules that call these functions.

Initialize WCB

The first function initializes the WCB structure before building up the WDOPR
arguments. The InitWCB function sets the cArgs count to 0 (zero) and sets up the
return type. It is very important to call this function first; if cArgs is not initialized
and set to the proper count, **wdCommandDispatch** will behave unpredictably.

```
// Windows
void InitWCB( WCB far *lpwcb, ushort retType, LPUCHAR lpBuffer,
    ushort cBufferSize );

// Macintosh
void InitWCB( WCB *lpwcb, ushort retType, StringPtr lpBuffer,
    ushort cBufferSize );
```

The parameters to InitWCB are as follows.

Parameter	Description
lpwcb	A pointer to the WCB to be initialized.
retType	The return type of the command. This lets the InitWCB function prepare the return WDOPR's contents.
lpBuffer	Pointer to the start of buffer. If the returned information will be a string buffer, the return WDOPR will only contain a pointer to a buffer.
cBufferSize	The return buffer's allocated length.

Add Dialog Fields

After InitWCB has been called, you build up WDOPR arguments one at a time by
calling the other functions. Each of these functions increments the cArgs count
and initializes the fields in a single WDOPR argument.

These four functions add field parameters for dialog commands:

```
// Windows
void AddShortDlgField( WCB far *lpwcb, short ShortVal, ushort FieldId,
    ushort fMode );
void AddLongDlgField( WCB far *lpwcb, long LongVal, ushort FieldId,
    ushort fMode );
void AddDoubleDlgField( WCB far *lpwcb, double DoubleVal,
    ushort FieldId, short fMode );
void AddStringDlgField( WCB far *lpwcb, LPUCHAR lpStr, ushort FieldId,
    ushort fMode, ushort cBufferSize );
```

```
// Macintosh
void AddShortDlgField( WCB *lpwcb, short ShortVal, ushort FieldId,
    ushort fMode );
void AddLongDlgField( WCB    *lpwcb, long LongVal, ushort FieldId,
    ushort fMode );
void AddDoubleDlgField( WCB *lpwcb, double DoubleVal, ushort FieldId,
    ushort fMode );
void AddStringDlgField( WCB *lpwcb, StringPtr lpStr, ushort FieldId,
    ushort fMode, ushort cBufferSize );
```

Here's a description of each of the parameters of these functions.

Parameter	Description
lpwcb	The address of the WCB structure.
ShortVal	The field's data, of the type indicated in the name of each function.
FieldId	The field's ID. A list of field ID constants is provided in WDFID.H, which should be included in modules calling the Word API functions. These constants have names that closely parallel the dialog command field names in WordBasic.
fMode	Indicates the input/output mode for the given dialog command field. Set this field using the constants INPUT, OUTPUT, or both.
cBufferSize	The allocated space for the string buffer.

Add Parameters

The next group of functions is called to build parameters for statements other than those that correspond to dialog boxes. The WDOPR argument in this case doesn't have field names, and the input/output information is irrelevant. For these reasons, only two parameters are passed to these functions: the WCB address, and the WDOPR argument data of the type indicated in the function's name.

```
// Windows
void AddShortParam( WCB far *lpwcb, short ShortVal );
void AddLongParam( WCB far *lpwcb, long LongVal );
void AddDoubleParam( WCB far *lpwcb, double DoubleVal );
void AddStringParam( WCB far *lpwcb, LPUCHAR lpStr );

// Macintosh
void AddShortParam( WCB *lpwcb, short ShortVal );
void AddLongParam( WCB *lpwcb, long LongVal );
void AddDoubleParam( WCB *lpwcb, double DoubleVal );
void AddStringParam( WCB *lpwcb, StringPtr lpStr );
```

Define Arrays

Three functions are provided to help you set up WDOPR arguments that pass arrays.

```
// Windows
ARRAY_DEF far * SetArrayDef( HANDLE *phArrDef, short cDimensions, ... );
void AddStringArray( WCB far *lpwcb, ARRAY_DEF far *ArrayDef,
    LPUCHAR far *lpStrArray, ushort cBufferSize );
void AddDoubleArray( WCB far *lpwcb, ARRAY_DEF far *ArrayDef,
    double far *lpdblArray );

// Macintosh
ARRAY_DEF * SetArrayDef( Handle *phArrDef, short cDimensions, ... );
void AddStringArray( WCB *lpwcb, ARRAY_DEF *ArrayDef, StringPtr
    *lpStrArray, ushort cBufferSize );
void AddDoubleArray( WCB *lpwcb, ARRAY_DEF *ArrayDef, double
    *lpdblArray );
```

The first function, SetArrayDef, builds the ArrayDef parameter required in the WDOPR when arrays are passed. ARRAY_DEF contains information on the number of dimensions and the size of each dimension for an array. The other two functions, AddStringArray and AddDoubleArray, build the WDOPR argument, filling in the data structure with pointers to an array and its associated ARRAY_DEF. When adding a string array, one additional parameter is passed to indicate the allocated size of each string in the array. Note that all strings in an array are allocated to the same maximum size, although the actual null-terminated strings may be of a shorter length.

Note SetArrayDef allocates memory. After using an array, your WLL function needs to free that memory. For example, given the array hArrayDef, a function should deallocate memory as follows:

```
// Windows
GlobalUnlock( hArrayDef );
GlobalFree( hArrayDef );

// Macintosh
HUnlock( hArrayDef );
DisposHandle( hArrayDef );
```

The following stripped-down Windows code fragments demonstrate how SetArrayDef can be used to build the array definition table for an array of strings. Note that this code is extracted from the example code on the Microsoft Word Developer's Kit disk; you might want to study the example in its entirety.

```
HANDLE           hArrayDef;
ARRAY_DEF far * ArrayDef;
LPSTR            lpStrArray[ARRAYSIZE];
char             strArray[ARRAYSIZE][64];

ArrayDef = SetArrayDef( &hArrayDef, 1, ARRAYSIZE );

InitWCB( &wcb, TypeShort, NULL, 0 );
AddStringArray( &wcb, ArrayDef, lpStrArray, 64 );
```

Call a WordBasic Statement or Function

This function uses a subset of the other CAPILIB functions to fill a WCB for a WordBasic statement or function that does not correspond to a dialog box; it then dispatches the command to Word and returns the result. You can use this as an efficient way to dispatch WordBasic statements and functions in your WLL.

```
// Windows
short CallCapi( LPWCB far *wcb, short CommandID, ushort retType, LPSTR
lpBuffer, ushort cBufferSize, LPSTR lpszFormat, ... );

//Macintosh
short CallCapi( WCB *wcb, short CommandID, ushort retType, StringPtr
lpBuffer, ushort cBufferSize, StringPtr lpszFormat, ... );
```

Parameter	Description
*wcb	Pointer to the WCB structure.
CommandID	The WordBasic statement or function to be called; CommandID cannot correspond to a dialog box.
retType	The return type of the WordBasic statement or function.
lpBuffer	Buffer to store the return string, if any.
cBufferSize	Size of the buffer specified by lpBuffer.
lpszFormat	String describing the type of the arguments passed to CommandID. This list should be a string of characters that identify the type of each argument that follows. Use the following characters:
	i Integer
	l Long
	d Double
	s String
	For example, if the statement or function takes a string argument followed by an integer argument, lpszFormat would be "si"; the following argument list would be a string argument and an integer. CallCapi automatically parses this list and fills the WCB with the data in the specified order.
...	The list of arguments to dispatch with the statement, in the order specified by lpszFormat.

The following Macintosh example demonstrates how you can use CallCapi to dispatch the **wdMsgBox** statement in a single instruction.

```
CallCapi (&wcb, wdMsgBox, TypeVoid, NULL, 0, "ss", "Timer Hit!", "Examp
WLL");
```

Register Functions in Word

The final group of functions provided in CAPILIB provides help with several common programming tasks in your WLL. These functions set up their WDOPR arguments and call **wdCommandDispatch** in the same way your code will. For this reason they provide excellent working examples of the use of the other CAPILIB functions.

To be callable from Word, functions must be registered with Word. The CAPIRegister function simplifies this task for you. The DocID parameter (passed in to **wdAutoOpen**), the name of your new function, and a description are the only parameters to this function.

```
// Windows
short CAPIRegister( short DocID, LPUCHAR lpszFunctionName, LPUCHAR
    lpszDescription );

// Macintosh
short CAPIRegister( short DocID, StringPtr lpszFunctionName, StringPtr
    lpszDescription );
```

DocID is a document identifier. It is used to register functions in Word and to customize Word to assign registered functions to toolbar buttons, menus, and shortcut keys.

Just as you choose the names for macros in Word templates, the name you choose for each registered add-in function should be unique to avoid naming conflicts during a Word session. If two or more add-in functions in two or more WLLs are registered under the same name, Word will run the function in the WLL listed first in the list of loaded global templates and add-ins in the Templates And Add-ins dialog box (Templates command, File menu).

A description is not required. If you specify a null value for lpszDescription, CAPIRegister ignores that parameter.

Assign Functions in Word

The final group of functions helps you assign registered functions to toolbar buttons, menus, or shortcut keys. Other than the DocID, the parameters all correspond closely to parameters for the equivalent WordBasic statements **AddButton**, **NewToolbar**, **ToolsCustomizeMenu**, **ToolsCustomizeMenuBar**, and **ToolsCustomizeKeyboard**.

```
// Windows
short CAPIAddButton( short DocID, LPUCHAR lpszToolbar, short cPosition,
    LPUCHAR lpszMacro, LPUCHAR lpszFace );
short CAPIAddToolbar( short DocID, LPUCHAR lpszToolbar )
short CAPIAddMenu( short DocID, LPUCHAR lpszMenuName, short Position,
    short MenuType );
short CAPIAddMenuItem( short DocID, LPUCHAR lpszMenu, LPUCHAR lpszName,
    LPUCHAR lpszMenuText, short Position, short MenuType );
short CAPIAddKey( short DocID, short KeyCode, LPUCHAR lpszName );

// Macintosh
short CAPIAddButton( short DocID, StringPtr lpszToolbar, short
    cPosition, StringPtr lpszMacro, StringPtr lpszFace );
short CAPIAddToolbar( short DocID, StringPtr lpszToolbar );
short CAPIAddMenu( short DocID, StringPtr lpszMenuName, short
    Position, short MenuType );
short CAPIAddMenuItem( short DocID, StringPtr lpszMenu, StringPtr
    lpszName, StringPtr lpszMenuText, short Position, short MenuType );
short CAPIAddKey( short DocID, short KeyCode, StringPtr lpszName );
```

When a WLL passes DocID as the context in which to customize Word, all customization is temporary; the template is not "dirtied" and all customization is removed automatically when the WLL is unloaded.

Note If you want to make customization in Word permanent, pass the numeric value 0 (zero) to modify the Normal template or 1 to modify the active template (if other than the Normal template) instead of DocID. Note, however, that if you pass a context other than DocID, the template will be dirtied; you should include a **wdAutoRemove** function in your WLL to deliberately clean up the Word environment when the WLL is unloaded.

For more information about these functions, see "Customizing Word with CAPILIB" later in this section.

Building Word Operators with CAPILIB

The following example code demonstrates the steps in building two WDOPR arguments for a call to **wdCommandDispatch**. The two WDOPR arguments pass the number of columns and the number of rows for a new table created by the WordBasic **TableInsertTable** statement. The WCB structure named wcb is first initialized by a call to InitWCB, the two WDOPR string field arguments are built up, and then **wdCommandDispatch** is called to perform the **TableInsertTable** statement. When activated, this block of code inserts a 4 by 12 table in the current document.

```
// Initialize the WCB - this zero's the WDOPR count
InitWCB( &wcb, TypeVoid, NULL, 0 );

// Build WDOPR arguments for number of columns and rows
AddStringDlgField( &wcb, "4", fidNumColumns, fMode, 0 );
AddStringDlgField( &wcb, "12", fidNumRows, fMode, 0 );

// Call into Word's TableInsertTable command
err = wdCommandDispatch ( wdTableInsertTable, CommandAction,
    wcb.cArgs, wcb.wdoprArgs, lpwdoprNil );
```

The last parameter to **wdCommandDispatch** is lpwdoprNil. Take a look in
WDCAPI.H to see how the lpwdoprNil data type is defined as a WDOPR pointer
to a zero. Use this when the Word API command doesn't return a WDOPR
argument in the last parameter to **wdCommandDispatch**.

Passing Arrays with CAPILIB

To use the CAPILIB functions to build a WDOPR that passes an array, follow this
general procedure:

- Call SetArrayDef to set up the number and size of the array's dimensions.
- For doubles, call AddDoubleArray, passing the ArrayDef and the double array.
- For strings, call AddStringArray, passing the ArrayDef, the string array, and
  an array of pointers to each string in the array.

Example of Passing a Double Array

The following Windows code fragments demonstrate the passing of an array of
doubles in a Word API function, using CAPILIB functions. Note that ArrayDef,
in this case, is set up for a one-dimension array sized ARRAYSIZE. In the case of
a multiple-dimensional array, you would pass different values to the SetArrayDef
function.

```
// Related declarations
HANDLE          hArrayDef;
ARRAY_DEF far * ArrayDef;
double          array[ARRAYSIZE];

// Set the array definition
ArrayDef = SetArrayDef( &hArrayDef, 1, ARRAYSIZE );

// Build a double array WDOPR
InitWCB( &wcb, TypeVoid, NULL, 0 );
AddDoubleArray( &wcb, ArrayDef, array );
```

```
// Use wdCommandDispatch here

// Free allocated ArrayDef
GlobalUnlock( hArrayDef );
GlobalFree( hArrayDef );
```

Example of Passing a String Array

The following lines of Windows code illustrate the general procedure for handling string arrays using the CAPILIB module functions. The important concept to grasp here is the way the various parts of the WDOPR's data structure are loaded with the appropriate data. The string contents are contained in the character array strArray, pointers to each of these strings are loaded into lpStrArray, and the string array's dimensions and sizes are loaded into ArrayDef. Each of these parts of the WDOPR data structure must be loaded correctly for passing string array data.

```
// Related declarations
HANDLE          hArrayDef;
ARRAY_DEF far * ArrayDef;
LPSTR           lpStrArray[ARRAYSIZE];
char          strArray[ARRAYSIZE][MAXLENGTH];

// Set the array definition
ArrayDef = SetArrayDef( &hArrayDef, 1, ARRAYSIZE );

// Set the array of LPSTR to point to a buffer
for( i = 0; i < ARRAYSIZE; i++ )
    lpStrArray[i] = strArray[i];

// Build a string array WDOPR
InitWCB( &wcb, TypeShort, NULL, 0 );
AddStringArray( &wcb, ArrayDef, lpStrArray, MAXLENGTH );

// Use wdCommandDispatch here

// Free allocated ArrayDef
GlobalUnlock( hArrayDef );
GlobalFree( hArrayDef );
```

Customizing Word with CAPILIB

A WLL function registered in Word can be called from any WordBasic macro, just like any built-in statement. You also can assign a new Word API function to a toolbar button, menu item, or shortcut key. The proper place to make such an assignment is in the **wdAutoOpen** function. This function runs automatically when the WLL is loaded, making your function associations automatic. There are several **wdCommandDispatch** commands that let you make these assignments in a manner analogous to the way WordBasic works. Specific CAPILIB functions simplify the process even further.

Adding a Command

An add-in function registered in Word extends WordBasic and is immediately available as a new command that can be included as an instruction in any macro. Use the CAPIRegister function in CAPILIB to register your add-in function.

Note A WLL function that requires arguments from a WordBasic macro cannot be registered in Word. This kind of function must be declared in the WordBasic macro with the WordBasic **Declare** statement.

Adding a Toolbar Button

The following lines of code demonstrate how a toolbar button labeled "Table," assigned to the new function MyTable, can be added to the standard toolbar using the appropriate CAPILIB function. This line of code would normally go in the **wdAutoOpen** function of a WLL to create the button when the WLL is loaded.

```
err = CAPIAddButton( DocID, "Standard", cPosition, "MyTable",
    "Table" );
```

A related function in CAPILIB, CAPIAddToolbar, lets you add your own toolbar, to which you can then add buttons. For example:

```
err = CAPIAddToolbar( DocID, "MyToolbar" );
```

Adding a Menu Item

You can easily add a menu item and assign a registered function to it. The CAPIAddMenuItem function in CAPILIB simplifies the process. For example, the following line of code adds a new menu item labeled "String Array Test" to the end of the File menu and assigns the function StringArray to it:

```
err = CAPIAddMenuItem( DocID, "File", "StringArray", "String Array
    Test", -1, 0 );
```

A related function, CAPIAddMenu, lets you add a new menu to the main menu bar and assign to it a name that can be used to further build the menu with CAPIAddMenuItem.

Adding a Shortcut Key

A registered Word API function can also be assigned to a shortcut key using the CAPIAddKey function provided in CAPILIB. For example:

```
err = CAPIAddKey( DocID, KeyCode, "MyNewFunction" );
```

This line of code assigns the Word API function MyNewFunction to the shortcut key indicated by KeyCode in the current document. For a complete description of the various KeyCode integers, see **ToolsCustomizeKeyboard** in Part 2, "WordBasic Reference."

Calling Word from Another Application

It is not possible to call a WLL from an application other than Word and then have the called WLL drive Word. The CAPI messaging interface (CMI) is a way to get around this problem.

Windows 3.*x*

To call **wdCommandDispatch**, a WLL must be called by Word; otherwise stack problems occur, resulting in a general protection fault. When making a Word API call, the calling application can send a message to Word (WM_WDCAPI) instead of calling **wdCommandDispatch**. As a result, Word calls **wdCommandDispatch** from its own stack (avoiding stack problems) when it processes the message.

To use the CAPI messaging interface, follow this general procedure.

1. Include the following in a header file:

```
#include "wdcapi.h"
#define WM_WDCAPI    (WM_USER | 0x0300)
typedef struct
{
    short    CommandID;
    short    DlgOptions;
    short    cArgs;
    LPWDOPR  lpwdoprArgs;
    LPWDOPR  lpwdoprReturn;
} CMI;
typedef CMI far *LPCMI;
```

2. Fill the CMI structure.

3. Call SendMessage in the following way:

```
err = (int)SendMessage( hWordWnd, WM_WDCAPI, 0, (LPARAM)(LPCMI)&cmi
);
```

Windows 95 and Windows NT

To access the CMI from Windows 95 or Windows NT, you call **cmiCommandDispatch** instead of sending the WM_WORDCAPI message to Word (in Windows 95 and Windows NT, WM_WORDCAPI returns CAPIBadMessage). To call **cmiCommandDispatch**, you can either link your application with the WIN32CMI.LIB file, or load the WIN32CMI.DLL with LoadLibrary and then call GetProcAddress to get the address of the function. The **cmiCommandDispatch** function has the same prototype as **wdCommandDispatch**; see the CMI header file (WIN32CMI.H) for this prototype.

The WIN32CMI.LIB and WIN32CMI.DLL files are located in the CAPI\WIN32CMI folder on the Microsoft Word Developer's Kit disk. The folder includes the source files required to build the LIB and DLL (a Microsoft Visual C++ version 2.0 project file is provided). If you are programming on a RISC platform, you will need to build the LIB and DLL for your platform using the source files provided.

Macintosh

On the Macintosh, you can use the CMI to drive Word from an application or code resource that is not directly called by Word. CMI on the Macintosh uses Apple Events to dispatch commands to Word instead of calling **wdCommandDispatch** directly from the Word API.

To make a CMI call on the Macintosh, you calling application or code resource needs to build an Apple Event that contains all the information normally passed by **wdCommandDispatch**. After it sends the event to Word, it needs to unpack the reply event.

To use the CMI on the Macintosh, use the CMILIB.C and CMILIB.H files included in the CMI folder in the CAPI folder on the Microsoft Word Developer's Kit disk instead of the CAPILIB.C and CAPILIB.H described earlier in this appendix. With these files added to your project, you can simply make calls to **cmiCommandDispatch** instead of **wdCommandDispatch**; all of the Apple Event construction is handled by the CMI files. Review the sample provided in the CMI:SAMPLE foler to see how the CMI is used.

Word API Functions

There are some functions in Word available to WLLs but not to WordBasic. These functions fill special needs of WLLs in Windows and on the Macintosh, as the following topics explain.

General Functions

Note that the following four WordBasic functions can only be called from a WLL.

wdAddCommand

Registers add-in functions in Word. It takes three arguments: the DocID (which is passed by Word to **wdAutoOpen**), the name of the function to be registered, and a description.

wdPrint

Same as the WordBasic **Print** statement; it prints a string in the status bar.

wdGetInst

Returns the handle (a long value) of the instance of Word (Windows only).

wdGetHwnd

Returns the handle (a long value) of the Word window (Windows only).

Timer Messages

On the Macintosh, the single function **wdSetTimer** supplies timer messages from Word for a WLL to use. When a timer message happens, the WLL gets called from Word with cacCallTimer. Here is the syntax:

```
short wdSetTimer( short DocID, long Timer);
```

Parameter	Description
DocID	Identifies which WLL the timer message should be sent to
Timer	The number of milliseconds to set the timer for

A WLL can have a single timer set at any time; calling **wdSetTimer** clears the old timer before setting a new one. Calling with a Timer value of 0 (zero) clears the old timer.

WLL Windows

On the Macintosh, the following group of functions should be used for WLLs that need windows created for them that Word will send messages to.

After a WLL window has been established, events are handled as follows:

- MouseDown and mouseUp events are sent to all WLL windows.
- Update events are sent to the appropriate WLL window.
- KeyDown events are sent to the appropriate WLL window only if **wdCaptureKeyDown** has been done for that window.

wdOpenWindow

This function opens and displays a WLL window, and returns the window pointer in a long to use in the other WLL window functions. Here is the syntax:

```
long wdOpenWindow( short DocID, short x, short y, short dx,
    short dy, long lData, short fFloat);
```

Parameter	Description
DocID	Identifies which WLL to send messages to
x, y, dx, dy	Specifies the position and size of the window in pixels

Parameter	Description
lData	Contains user data
fFloat	If fTrue, uses altDBoxProc for the window type; otherwise, uses documentProc (does not actually cause the window to float or not float)

wdCloseWindow

Closes a CAPI window, and returns a short containing fTrue or fFalse to indicate success or failure. The function takes the window pointer as a long parameter. Here is the syntax:

```
short wdCloseWindow( long *Window);
```

wdCaptureKeyDown

Starts mode in which KeyDown messages are sent to the CAPI window, and returns a short containing fTrue or fFalse to indicate success or failure. This function takes the window pointer as a long parameter. Here is the syntax:

```
short wdCaptureKeyDown( long *Window);
```

wdReleaseKeyDown

Stops mode in which KeyDown messages are sent to the CAPI window, and returns a short containing fTrue or fFalse to indicate success or failure. This function takes the window pointer as a long parameter. Here is the syntax:

```
short wdReleaseKeyDown( long *Window);
```

Word API Errors

The following errors, shown here with their names and descriptions, are the Word-API–specific errors defined in WDERROR.H, where error 0 (zero) is CAPINoError.

Error	Name	Description
5001	CAPIBadCommandId	Command ID is invalid
5002	CAPIOddParamBlock	Parameter block has an odd number of bytes
5003	CAPICmdNotAvailable	Command is not available
5004	CAPIBadArgCount	Too many or too few arguments
5005	CAPIInternalError	Internal data-handling error
5006	CAPIByteCountMismatch	Parameter block doesn't have an acceptable number of bytes
5007	CAPINotFunction	Non-function called as a function
5008	CAPIBadType	Parameter type passed or expected is wrong

Error	Name	Description
5009	CAPIStringTooLong	String is longer than 255 characters
5010	CAPINullReturnBuffer	Pointer for output is nil
5011	CAPICantLock	Can't lock global handle
5012	CAPICantAllocate	Can't allocate global handle
5013	CAPINoDialog	Commmand has no dialog box
5014	CAPIOutOfMemory	Word API is out of memory
5015	CAPIFieldIdOutOfRange	Too many parameters passed to function
5016	CAPIBadFieldId	FieldID not in dialog box
5017	CAPIBadHandle	Handle has not been allocated
5018	CAPIArrayExpected	Parameter takes an array only
5019	CAPITooManyDimensions	Too many dimensions for array
5020	CAPIExpectedNumericType	Parameter passed was not a short, long, or numeric type
5021	CAPIExpectedStringType	Parameter passed was not a string type
5022	CAPIParameterOutOfRange	Parameter value was out of an acceptable range
5023	CAPICantReturnString	String type requested for numeric-only field
5024	CAPICantReturnNumeric	Numeric type requested for string-only field
5025	CAPIReturnOverflow	Buffer for return string is too small
5026	CAPIArrayOverflow	String array buffer is too small
5027	CAPIDlgCommandOverflow	Dialog-box command string buffer is too small
5028	CAPIOverflowNotHandled	BufferTooSmall bit set on input
5029	CAPICantParse	String passed can't be parsed
5030	CAPIBadMessage	Bad pointer in message
5031	CAPICommandFailed	Word API command failed
5032	CAPIBadDocRef	Document reference number (DocID) is invalid
5033	CAPIInsufficientStack	Minimum stack not available
5034	CAPIUninitializedString	0 (zero) was passed as string pointer

A P P E N D I X   D

AppleScript

Word supports AppleScript scripting on the Apple Macintosh. Word supports the Required, Core, Table, and Text suites of Apple Events, as defined by the Apple Event Registry. In addition, Word defines four objects, one event, and approximately 68 properties for use in AppleScript scripts that interact with Word.

To use AppleScript with Word, you must have the following:

- Microsoft Word version 6.0
- Apple Macintosh System 7 or later
- AppleScript extension version 1.1
- Apple Script Editor or another scripting application compatible with Open Scripting Architecture (OSA)

Note This appendix assumes that you are using Script Editor, the application provided in the AppleScript Developer's Toolkit from Apple Computer, Inc. Any OSA-compatible script editing application can use the same information to create scripts for Microsoft Word version 6.0.

To use this appendix, you should already be familiar with AppleScript and scripting on the Macintosh. The reference section of this appendix describes only the new objects, events, and properties created for use with Word version 6.0. The remaining objects, events, and properties that Word shares with other scriptable applications are described in your scripting documentation. For more information about AppleScript, see *Getting Started with AppleScript* and *AppleScript Language Guide*, both included in the AppleScript Developer's Tookit version 1.1 from Apple Computer, Inc.

Supported Suites

With all of the objects and events listed in this section, users can create, format, change, and print Word documents from AppleScript.

Word recognizes the following standard objects, as defined by the Apple Event Registry.

Suite	Objects
Core	Application, Character, Document, File, Selection-Object, Text, Text Style Info, Window, Insertion Point
Text	Line, Paragraph, Text, Text Flow, Word
Table	Cell, Column, Row, Table

Word responds to the following standard events, as described in the Apple Event Registry.

Suite	Events
Required	Open, Print, Quit, Run
Core	Close, Count, Data Size, Delete, Duplicate, Exists, Get, Make, Move, Open, Print, Quit, Save, Set
Miscellaneous	Activate, Begin Transaction, Copy, Cut, Do Script, End Transaction, Paste, Redo, Revert, Undo

To determine the properties that Word supports for these standard objects, or to determine the arguments required by these supported events, refer to the AppleScript dictionary for Microsoft Word, accessible through the Open Dictionary command (File menu) in the Script Editor (or a comparable feature of your scripting application). For detailed information about supported objects and their properties, as well as supported events, see your scripting documentation.

In addition to the standard events and objects described above, Word defines four new objects and one new event.

Word Objects   Paragraph Style, Range, Section, Sentence

Word Event   Select

For detailed information about these objects and events, see "Extensions to Supported Suites" later in this appendix.

Object Hierarchy

The object hierarchy determines which objects are related to each other within a particular class of objects. The following table shows 16 object classes (the first column) and their corresponding elements (the second column). Within an object class, elements are grouped together by their valid reference forms (the third column). In other words, from an object in the first column, you can use a reference form in the third column to refer to an element in the second column.

An object that is the element of another object class may appear as its own object class later in the table. In some cases, an object can be an element of its own class; for example, a paragraph object is an element of the paragraph object class. In other cases, an object may appear as an element of an object class that would at first seem too small to contain the specified element; for example, because, technically, a word can be one character long, the word object is an element of the character object class.

Word supports the following reference forms:

- Property
- Index
- Relative
- Name
- Middle/Arbitrary/Every Element
- Range
- Filter

Word does not support the ID reference form. For complete descriptions of these reference forms, refer to your AppleScript documentation.

Object Class	Element	Valid Reference Forms
Application	Window, Document	Index, Name, Filter
	Character, Word, Sentence, Line, Paragraph, Section, Table	Index, Filter
	Text Flow	Name
	Paragraph Style	Name
Document	Window	Index, Name, Filter
	Character, Word, Sentence, Line, Paragraph, Section, Table	Index, Filter
	Text Flow	Name
	Paragraph Style	Name

Object Class	Element	Valid Reference Forms
Window	Window	Relative
	Character, Word, Sentence, Line, Paragraph, Section, Table	Index, Filter
	Text Flow	Name
	Paragraph Style	Name
Character, Word, Sentence, Line, Paragraph, Section, Table	Character, Word, Sentence, Line, Paragraph, Section, Table	Index, Filter, Relative
	Text	Range
Text	Character, Word, Sentence, Line, Paragraph, Section, Table	Index, Filter, Relative
Table	Row, Column, Cell	Index, Filter
	Range	Name
Row	Row	Relative
	Cell, Column	Index, Filter
	Range	Range
Column	Column	Relative
	Cell, Row	Index, Filter
	Range	Range
Cell	Character, Word, Sentence, Line, Paragraph, Section, Table	Index, Filter, Relative
	Range	Range
Range	Cell, Row, Column	Index, Filter

The following paragraphs suggest some techniques you can use for handling and referencing objects in Word. These techniques will help you get the best performance out of your script applications.

Index through bigger objects

Word does not maintain internal indices to all text objects. To find the AppleScript object `word 200`, Word must scan through all the words in the document until it finds the two-hundredth word. Scanning through bigger objects is quicker, so scripts that reference larger objects first will execute more rapidly. For example, assuming the 1000th word is also the third word in the fifth paragraph of the third section, the reference `word 1000` will execute much more slowly than the reference `word 3 of paragraph 5 of section 3,` even though each references the same word.

Use the filter reference form sparingly

To support the wide variety of filter reference cases supported by AppleScript, Word uses a set of operating system utilities that perform much of the bookkeeping involved with complex filter expressions. With this implementation, the operating system repeatedly asks for individual objects from Word during the processing of a filter reference. Then tests are performed on the objects to see if they meet the given filter criteria. This back-and-forth process of getting objects and then performing tests can be slow.

If you must use the filter reference form, use it in conjunction with a index reference qualifier (for example, the first word where character 1 is "w") to speed up the script. Avoid the qualifier "every"; it forces Word to filter all the text within a parent object.

Use bookmarks

As noted previously, using the index reference form can be slow. But even more problematic, as documents change, the indices of specific words or paragraphs will also change. If the document being accessed by a script is subject to change, the script cannot rely on fixed indices to locate particular text objects. The filter reference form can be used to find particular objects, but this method can be slow.

The best way to maintain persistent references to text and table objects in Word is to use bookmarks. Bookmarks are names that you can assign to any selected text. Even if the document is changed, the bookmark still refers to the original selection. For example, if a bookmark named "xref" is created for the third word of a document, and then a new word is inserted at the beginning of the document, the bookmark "xref" will refer to the fourth word.

Bookmarks are exposed to AppleScript through the Text Flow object, which is only accessible by name from a document. For example, the following reference refers to the text associated with the bookmark "xref":

```
set selection to text flow "xref"
```

Any valid text event can be performed on a Text Flow object. Text Flow objects can also reference Range objects if the bookmark for the range is contained in a Word table.

Extensions to Supported Suites

Word adds four objects, one event, and many properties that extend the standard suites that Word supports, identified earlier in this appendix and described in your AppleScript documentation. This section provides a reference to these Word-specific objects, events, and properties.

Word Objects

Word defines four new objects: Paragraph Style, Range, Section, and Sentence.

Paragraph Style

Paragraphs within Word documents all have an associated "style," which determines many of their default properties. This is different than the AppleScript notion of style, which only describes a few basic text properties (such as bold and italic). To avoid conflict with AppleScript's notion of style, Word defines the object Paragraph Style to be a named set of most text properties.

A Paragraph Style object has all the properties of any text object, but does not have any text elements. To change a property for all the paragraphs of a particular style, you can simply change that property of the appropriate paragraph style object.

```
tell app "Microsoft Word"
    set font of paragraph style "Heading 1" to "Helvetica"
end tell
```

Note that every paragraph has a Paragraph Style property, which is the name of that paragraph's Word style. A script can change any paragraph's style by setting this property:

```
tell app "Microsoft Word"
    set paragraph style of second paragraph to "Heading 2"
end tell
```

Range

Microsoft Excel defines a Range object to simplify access to Table objects. The standard Table, Row, and Column objects use complex records for returning their data. The Range object, however, returns a simple list of the cells of the given range.

Within word, a Range can be any contiguous part of a table: a row, a column, the whole table, or some rectangular part of the table. A Range object is referenced through the Name form.

```
tell app "Microsoft Word"
    get range "R2C3:R4C5" of table 1
end tell
```

Section

Word exposes the Section object as a simple extension to all the other standard text objects (for example, Word and Paragraph). In the text stream of a document, a section is bounded by section breaks or a section break and the beginning or end of the document. A document with no section breaks contains one section.

Sentence

Word exposes the Sentence object as simple extension to all the other standard text objects (for example, Word and Paragraph). In the text stream of a document, a sentence is usually bounded by terminating punctuation (period, exclamation point, question mark), excluding any leading white space. However, a paragraph composed of a stream of text and no punctuation (for example, a heading) is considered to contain one sentence (all of the text).

Word Event

Word defines one new event: Select.

Select

The Select event applies to any text object. The Select event is just a shorthand for setting the selection of the application to a particular AppleScript object.

The two instructions in the following script are equivalent:

```
tell app "Microsoft Word"
    set selection to second paragraph
    select second paragraph
end tell
```

Here is the syntax for the Select event:

select *reference*

The *reference* argument is a valid reference to the object to select.

The Select event is supported by Word because the usual purpose of WordBasic macros is to manipulate the current selection. The most efficient way to perform actions on text within Word is to select the text with the Select event, and then perform complex formatting using WordBasic through the Do Script event. With this scenario, a user can use AppleScript's expressive object references while also taking advantage of WordBasic's efficiency. For more information on using the Do Script event with WordBasic, see "Extending WordBasic with AppleScript" later in this appendix.

Word Properties

Virtually all text properties in Word are exposed to native AppleScript. These properties can be broken down into three categories: character, paragraph, and section. Character properties are generally those available in the Font dialog box (Format menu); paragraph properties are usually found in the Paragraph dialog box (Format menu); section properties are found scattered throughout other dialog boxes (such as Columns on the Format menu and Page Setup on the File Menu).

All of these properties can be accessed from any text object. That is, a paragraph property can be read from a word or sentence object. However, changing these properties often implies changing them for an entire parent object. For example, setting the Justification property of a word object actually changes the justification of the entire paragraph object that contains the word. Similarly, getting the Number Columns property of a paragraph actually returns the number of columns for the section that contains the paragraph. Character properties only affect the exact text object being referenced.

The following topics describe the character, paragraph, and section properties that are exposed by Word.

Note You can set Word properties that take Boolean values with one of the following three values: true, false, or toggle. The toggle value reverses the current value of the property; for example, if the bold property of the specified text object is true, the following instruction sets it to false:

```
set bold of textobject to toggle
```

Character Properties

All of the properties described in the following table apply to each character of the referenced object in a Word document.

Property	Description	Data type
All Caps	Returns or sets a value that specifies whether the object is formatted with all capital letters.	Boolean
Bold	Returns or sets a value that specifies whether the object is formatted as bold.	Boolean
Character Position	Returns or sets the vertical position of characters for the object.	Points
Character Spacing	Returns or sets the amount of spacing between characters for an object.	Points

Property	Description	Data type
Hidden	Returns or sets a value specifying whether the text of the object is hidden.	Boolean
Italic	Returns or sets a value that specifies whether the text of the object is italic.	Boolean
Kerning Size	Returns or specifies the smallest font size to kern for the object.	Points
Language	Returns or specifies the language for the object.	String
Length	Returns the number of characters contained in the object	Integer
Outline	Returns or sets a value that specifies whether the object is formatted as outline.	Boolean
Plain	Returns or sets a value that specifies whether there are no character styles applied to the object.	Boolean
Shadow	Returns or sets a value that specifies whether the object is formatted with shadow.	Boolean
Small Caps	Returns or sets a value that specifies whether the object is formatted with small capital letters.	Boolean
Strikethrough	Returns or sets a value that specifies whether the object is formatted with strikethrough.	Boolean
Subscript	Returns or sets a value that specifies whether the object is formatted as subscript.	Boolean
Superscript	Returns or sets a value that specifies whether the object is formatted as superscript.	Boolean
Underline	Returns or specifies the type of underlining for the object.	One of the following values: none, single, words only, double, dotted, hidden

Paragraph Properties

All of the properties described in the following table apply to the paragraph or paragraphs related to the referenced object in a Word document.

Property	Description	Data type
After Spacing	Returns or sets the spacing after paragraphs for the object.	Points
Before Spacing	Returns or sets the spacing before paragraphs for the object.	Points
Top Border Color, Left Border Color, Bottom Border Color, Right Border Color, and Between Border Color	Return or set the color of a border of the object.	An RGB color
Top Border Distance, Left Border Distance, Bottom Border Distance, Right Border Distance, and Between Border Distance	Return or set the distance from text of a border of the object.	Points
Border Shadow	Returns or sets a value that specifies whether the object has shadowed borders.	Boolean
Top Border, Left Border, Bottom Border, Right Border, and Between Border	Return or set the type of a border for an object.	One of the following values: none, hair, thin, medium, thick, thicker, thickest, double, thick double, thicker double, dotted, dashed
Dont Hyphenate	Returns or sets a value that specifies whether automatic hyphenation is suppressed for the object.	Boolean
First Line Indent	Returns or sets the amount of indent for the first line of the paragraph (also known as the hanging indent) for the object.	Current application units (points, picas, centimeters, inches)
Justification	Returns or specifies the paragraph justification for the object.	One of the following values: left, right, center, full

Property	Description	Data type
Keep Lines Together	Returns or sets a value that specifies whether the lines in a paragraph or paragraphs of the object are kept together.	Boolean
Keep With Next	Returns or sets a value that specifies whether a paragraph or paragraphs of the object are kept on the same page with their following paragraphs.	Boolean
Left Indent	Returns or specifies the width of the left paragraph indent for the object.	Current application units (points, picas, centimeters, inches)
Line Spacing Amount	Returns or specifies the line spacing for the object (when Line Spacing Type is multiple).	Lines
Line Spacing Type	Returns or specifies the type of line spacing for the object.	One of the following values: single, lines1pt5, double, at least, exactly, multiple
Page Break Before	Returns or sets a value that specifies whether page breaks are made before paragraphs for the object.	Boolean
Right Indent	Returns or specifies the width of the right paragraph indent for the object.	Current application units (points, picas, centimeters, inches)
Shade Background Color	Returns or specifies the background color of paragraph shading for the object.	An RGB color
Shade Foreground Color	Returns or specifies the foreground color of paragraph shading for the object.	An RGB color

Property	Description	Data type
Shade Pattern	Returns or specifies the shading pattern for the object.	One of the following values: clear, solid, p5, p10, p20, p25, p30, p40, p50, p60, p70, p75, p80, p90, dark horizontal, dark vertical, dark down diagonal, dark up diagonal, dark grid, dark trellis, light horizontal, light vertical, light down diagonal, light up diagonal, light grid, light trellis
Suppress Line Numbers	Returns or sets a value that specifies whether line numbers are suppressed for the object.	Boolean
Tab Alignments	Returns or specifies the alignment of each nondefault tab stop for the object.	A list of the following values: left, center, right, decimal, bar
Tab Leaders	Returns or specifies the leader style of each nondefault tab stop for the object.	A list of the following values: none, dot, hyphen, single, heavy
Tab Positions	Returns or specifies the position of each nondefault tab stop for the object.	Current application units (points, picas, centimeters, inches)
Widow Orphan Control	Returns or sets a value that specifies whether widow and orphan control is active for the object.	Boolean

Section Properties

All of the properties described in the following table apply to the section or sections related to the referenced object in a Word document.

Property	Description	Data type
Bottom Margin	Returns or sets the width of the bottom margin for the object.	Current application units (points, picas, centimeters, or inches)
Column Spacings	Returns or sets the sizes of spaces between columns for an object.	Current application units (points, picas, centimeters, or inches)

Property	Description	Data type
Column Widths	Returns or sets the widths of columns for an object.	Current application units (points, picas, centimeters, or inches)
Equal Width Columns	Returns or sets a value that specifies whether the columns are the same width for the object.	Boolean
First Paper Source	Returns the paper source for the first page of the object. Read only.	One of the following values: none, upper, lower, middle, manual, envelope, envelope manual, auto, tractor, small format, large format, large capacity, cassette, manual PostScript
Gutter Margin	Returns or sets the width of the gutter margin for the object.	Current application units (points, picas, centimeters, inches)
Left Margin	Returns or specifies the width of the left margin for the object.	Current application units (points, picas, centimeters, inches)
Line Between Columns	Returns or sets a value that specifies whether there are lines between columns for the object.	Boolean
Number Columns	Returns or specifies the number of columns for the object.	Integer
Other Paper Source	Returns the paper source for pages other than the first page for the object. Read only.	One of the following values: none, upper, lower, middle, manual, envelope, envelope manual, auto, tractor, small format, large format, large capacity, cassette, manual PostScript
Page Height	Returns the height of the page for the object. Read only.	Current application units (points, picas, centimeters, inches)
Page Orientation	Returns the orientation of the page for the object. Read only.	One of the following values: none, portrait, landscape, mixed

Property	Description	Data type
Page Width	Returns the page width for the object. Read only.	Current application units (points, picas, centimeters, inches)
Right Margin	Returns or specifies the width of the right margin for the object.	Current application units (points, picas, centimeters, inches)
Top Margin	Returns or specifies the width of the top margin for the object.	Current application units (points, picas, centimeters, inches)

Extending WordBasic with AppleScript

When combined, AppleScript and WordBasic can be used to customize the Macintosh in many ways. A script can control Word and other scriptable applications, while WordBasic can run scripts that in turn do work and return data to Word. With AppleScript recording turned on, you can easily record scripts from within Word. You can also write simple macros and customize the Word interface to expose external scripts, so any user can take advantage of compiled script applications without leaving Word.

Recording Scripts

AppleScript can record Word. That is, Word will generate Apple Events for all user actions when recording has been turned on for an entire Macintosh. These events can then be recorded by AppleScript.

In Word, AppleScript recording is based on the internal WordBasic recording mechanism. Because of this, WordBasic macros and AppleScript scripts cannot be recorded at the same time. If Word is in the process of recording a WordBasic macro, it will ignore requests to record from AppleScript. Similarly, if Word is recording Apple Events, the user will not be able to start WordBasic macro recording.

Just as a subset of the functionality in Word is exposed to AppleScript, only a small segment of user actions are recorded as native AppleScript. That is, most simple editing, formatting, and file manipulation actions will be recorded as one of the basic events acting on an Apple Event object (for example, opening a file or setting the style of the selection to bold). All other actions are recorded as Do Script events with the appropriate WordBasic instructions, much as the actions would be recorded within a WordBasic macro.

Using the Do Script Event

Much of Word's functionality is *not* exposed directly to AppleScript because the standard suites are meant to be a common interface for objects across many applications. However, scripts can still control Word completely by using the Do Script event. With Do Script, a script can run the same WordBasic instructions that Word macros use to control the application. This effectively gives a script access to all the functionality of Word.

WordBasic is the native programming language of Word, and Word is optimized to use WordBasic. Therefore, to get the fastest performance from Word, AppleScript programmers should consider using Do Script events to control Word as much as possible.

Here is the syntax for the Do Script event:

do script *WordBasic$*

Note that *WordBasic$* is either one instruction to execute or a list of instructions. The result of a Do Script event in a script is either one value, if Word was passed one WordBasic instruction, or a list of values, if Word was passed a list of instructions.

For example, here is a simple WordBasic macro:

```
Sub MAIN
    FileOpen "Hard Drive:Microsoft Word:Sample Document"
    EditFindStyle .Style = "Heading 2"
    EditReplaceStyle .Style = "Heading 3"
    EditReplace .Direction = 0, .ReplaceAll, .Format = 1, .Wrap = 1
    FileClose 1
End Sub
```

In AppleScript, scripting commands and objects could be used to duplicate the functionality of the original WordBasic macro, as follows:

```
tell application "Microsoft Word"
    open "Hard Drive:Microsoft Word:Sample Document"
    set countpara to count paragraphs of document "Sample Document"
    repeat with n from 1 to countpara
        if paragraph style of paragraph n = "Heading 2" then
            set paragraph style of paragraph n to "Heading 3"
        end if
    end repeat
    save document "Sample Document"
    close document "Sample Document"
end tell
```

However, an AppleScript script can use a single Do Script event to take the most advantage of the internal functionality of Word to duplicate the original macro:

```
tell application "Microsoft Word"
    Do Script ¬
        "FileOpen \"Hard Drive:Microsoft Word:Sample Document\"
        EditFindStyle .Style = \"Heading 2\"
        EditReplaceStyle .Style = \"Heading 3\"
        EditReplace .Direction = 0, .ReplaceAll, .Format = 1, .Wrap = 1
        FileClose 1"
end tell
```

Attaching Scripts

A limited form of AppleScript "attachability" within Word is provided through the WordBasic **MacScript** statement and **MacScript$()** function. With these, any interface element in Word that can be attached to a macro (for example, menu commands and toolbar buttons) can run a script.

Note that this does not provide arbitrary script object attachability. Word does not provide for attachment of scripts to any object. Thus, it is not possible to write a script which handles particular Apple Events for an attached object. For example, a script cannot be attached to a window so that the script can handle the Close event.

Here is the syntax for the **MacScript** statement:

MacScript *Script$*

MacScript accepts a string parameter which may be either a path to a file, or a portion of text in the default scripting language. If the string is a path to a compiled script file or standalone script application, that file is opened and the first script resource is run. Otherwise, the string itself is passed to the default scripting language for compilation and execution.

Here is the syntax for the **MacScript$()** function:

MacScript$(***Script$*)**

MacScript$() performs exactly as **MacScript**, except that it returns a string value. If the executed script returns a value, it is coerced into a string and returned. If the executed script does not return a value, an empty string ("") is returned.

For more information, see **MacScript** in Part 2, "WordBasic Reference."

APPENDIX E

Microsoft Word Operating Limits

Some of the limits listed in the following tables are determined by the amount of memory available.

WordBasic Limits

Operating parameter	Limit
Macro size	Limited only by available memory
Length of variable, subroutine, and user-defined function names	40 characters (Word version 6.0) 80 characters (Word version 7.0)
Length of string variables	65,280 characters
Highest number	$1.7976931348623 \times 10^{308}$
Number of arguments that can be passed to a subroutine or function	20

Word Limits

Operating parameter	Limit
Number of open windows	Limited only by available memory
Maximum file size	32 megabytes (not including graphics)
Number of words in custom dictionaries	10,000
Length of bookmark names	20 characters (Word version 6.0) 40 characters (Word version 7.0)
Number of bookmarks per document	32,000
Length of AutoText entry names (including spaces)	31 characters
Length of style names	253 characters
Number of styles per document or template	4,093
Number of fields per document	32,000

Operating parameter	Limit
Number of general switches in a field	10
Number of field-specific switches in a field	10
Number of nesting levels for fields	20
Number of subdocuments in a master document	Limited only by available memory
Number of columns in a table	31
Number of newspaper-style columns	100
Number of tabs set in a paragraph	50
Minimum page height	3 inches
Number of custom toolbars	Limited only by available memory
Number of custom toolbar buttons	Limited only by available memory
Number of characters per line	768
Font size	1,637 pt (22 inches)
Number of fonts per document	32,767
Amount of space between characters	1,637 pt
Distance text can be raised or lowered	1,637 pt

Index

' (apostrophe) 41–42, 712–13
– (minus sign) 48–49
– (negation) arithmetic operator 890
– (subtraction) arithmetic operator 890
" " (quotation marks) 42, 44, 45, 146
$ (dollar sign) 46
( ) (parentheses) 43, 146, 889–90
* (asterisk) 48–49
* (multiplication) arithmetic operator 890
, (comma) 146
. (period) 146
/ (division) arithmetic operator 890
/ (slash) 48–49
: (colon) 40, 53
[ ] (square brackets), use of, in this manual xvi, 285–86
\ Sel predefined bookmark 63–64, 895–96
\ Cell predefined bookmark 63–64, 895–96
\ Char predefined bookmark 63–64, 895 96
\ Doc predefined bookmark 63–64, 895–96
\ EndOfDoc predefined bookmark 63–64, 895–96
\ EndOfSel predefined bookmark 63–64, 895–96
\ HeadingLevel predefined bookmark 63–64, 895–96
\ Line predefined bookmark 63–64, 895–96
\ Page predefined bookmark 63–64, 895–96
\ Para predefined bookmark 63–64, 895–96
\ PrevSel1 predefined bookmark 63–64, 895–96
\ PrevSel2 predefined bookmark 63–64, 895–96
\ Section predefined bookmark 63–64, 895–96
\ StartOfDoc predefined bookmark 63–64, 895–96
\ StartOfSel predefined bookmark 63–64, 895–96
\ Table predefined bookmark 63–64, 895–96
+ (plus sign) 48–49, 890, 891
< (less than) 50, 891
<= (less than or equal to) 50, 891
<> (not equal to) 50, 891
= (equal to) 47, 50, 891
= (Expression) field See = (Formula) field
= (Formula) field 781, 784–85
> (greater than) 50, 891
>= (greater than or equal to) 50, 891
¶ (paragraph mark), displaying and hiding 757–58, 850–51
3D dialog effects 102

A

About Microsoft Word dialog box, displaying 569–70
Abs() function 287
absolute values 287
accents, adding to uppercase letters 840–41

access keys 111
Access, Microsoft
    as a DDE server 177–79
    DDE application name for 167
actions See operations
Activate statement 287
ActivateObject statement 288
activating
    applications 299–300, 305–8
    menu bar 657
    Microsoft applications 659
    windows 287, 305–6, 672, 707, 880–81
Add/Remove REM button 153–54
AddAddIn statement and function 288–89
AddAddress statement 289–92
AddButton statement 292–93
AddDropDownItem statement 293
adding
    annotations 582
    bookmarks 434–35
    check boxes to dialog boxes 333–34
    check-box form fields to forms 334, 594–96
    drop-down form fields to forms 431
    fields to forms 594–96
    footnotes and endnotes 593–94
    items to custom dialog boxes 102–5
    items to drop-down form fields 293
    menu items 824–26
    menus 823
    numbers 781, 784–85, 813
    text form fields to forms 800
add-ins See Word add-in libraries (WLLs)
AddInState statement and function 294
addition 48–49, 781, 784–85, 813
address books
    adding addresses to 289–92
    inserting addresses from 581–82
    returning addresses from 548–50
    using in mail merge 649–50
addresses, formatting for envelopes 512, 539
aligning
    drawing objects 411
    items in dialog boxes 106–8, 113
    pages 480, 492–94
    rows in tables 791–92
    text See alignment, paragraph; tab stops
alignment, paragraph
    centered 327, 522, 536–38
    justified 522, 536–38, 613

alignment, paragraph *(continued)*
    left 522, 536–38, 618–19
    right 522, 536–38, 718–19
all caps character format 295, 443–44, 458–59, 518, 520, 526–28, 763–64
AllCaps statement and function 295
alphanumeric sort 793–95
ALT key *See* MenuMode statement
America Online, product support via 8
anchors
    drawing object, moving insertion point to 427
    frame, locking 520–21, 528–29
    hiding and displaying 850–51
AND logical operator 56–57, 891–94
AnnotationRefFromSel$() function 295–96
annotations
    displaying 759, 863–64
    document text associated with, selecting 565–66
    going to next or previous 567
    going to specific 448–50, 566
    inserting 582
    locking document for 504–6, 852
    marks, returning 295–96
    moving insertion point to 686
    pane, opening and closing 863–64
    pen 804
    printing 496–97
    protecting document while making 504–6, 852
    range (scope) of text associated with, selecting 565–66
    statements and functions related to, list of 276
    unprotecting documents protected for 858
ANSI codes 311–12, 336–37
AOCE (Apple Open Collaboration Environment) 193
AOCEAddRecipient statement 296
AOCEAuthenticateUser() function 296
AOCEClearMailerField statement 297
AOCECountRecipients() function 297
AOCEGetRecipient$() function 297–98
AOCEGetSender$() function 298
AOCEGetSubject$() function 298
AOCESendMail statement 298–99
AOCESetSubject statement 299
apostrophe (') 41–42, 712–13
AppActivate statement 299–300
AppClose statement 301
AppCount() function 301
appending to data files 681–82
AppGetNames statement and function 302
AppHide statement 302
AppInfo$() function 303–4
AppIsRunning() function 168–69, 170, 305
Apple Open Collaboration Environment (AOCE) 193
AppleScript
    overview of Word support 1035–36
    Paragraph Style object 1040

AppleScript *(continued)*
    Range object 1040
    recording scripts 1048
    reference forms 1037
    requirements 1035
    running scripts from WordBasic 631, 1050
    Section object 1041
    Select event 1041
    Sentence object 1041
    techniques for writing scripts 1038–39
    using to send WordBasic instructions 1049–50
    Word character properties 1042–43
    Word object hierarchy 1037–38
    Word paragraph properties 1044–46
    Word section properties 1046–48
application control statements and functions 265–66
application names for DDE conversations 167
application signatures 479, 626–27, 747
application windows
    displaying hidden 309
    listing open 302
    moving 307, 310, 311
    position of, returning 310, 311
    sizing 309–10, 311
    testing if maximized 305–6
    testing if minimized 306–7
    testing if restored 307–8
applications
    activating 299–300, 305–8, 659
    closing 301, 473
    closing DDE channels to 372–73
    communicating with *See* communicating with other
        applications
    determining if running 305
    exchanging data between *See* dynamic-data exchange
        (DDE); object linking and embedding (OLE)
    hidden, displaying 309
    hiding 302
    Microsoft *See* individual application names
    open, counting 301, 302
    opening channels to, via DDE 168–71, 368–70
    quitting 473
    requesting information from, via DDE 168–71, 371–72
    restoring 305–8
    sending commands to, via DDE 172–73, 366–68
    sending data to, via DDE 171–72, 370–71
    sending keystrokes to 736–38
    sending Windows messages to 308–9
    sharing information with other 165–93
    starting 626–27, 756–57
    windows *See* application windows
AppMaximize statement and function 305–6
AppMinimize statement and function 306–7
AppMove statement 307

AppRestore statement and function 307–8
AppSendMessage statement 308–9
AppShow statement 309
AppSize statement 309–10
AppWindowHeight statement and function 310
AppWindowPosLeft statement and function 310
AppWindowPosTop statement and function 311
AppWindowWidth statement and function 311
archived files 551, 741–42
arcs
    creating 412
    testing for 419–20
argument mismatch errors 147
arguments
    for statements 20, 42
    for subroutines 85–88
    for user-defined functions 85–88, 545–46
arithmetic operators 890
arranging windows 880
array variables 77–81
arrays
    checking contents of 134, 155
    defining (dimensioning) 78, 382–84, 711–12
    for contents of list, combo, and drop-down list boxes
        117–18
    passing with the Word API 1016–17
    resizing 79
    sorting 81, 764–66
    using functions in CAPILIB 1022–23, 1026–27
arrows, on drawing object lines 523–25
art See graphics
Asc() function 311–12
ASK field 641
assigning
    macros to menus, shortcut keys, toolbars 13–14
    values to variables 619
assistance, customer See Microsoft Product Support Services
asterisk (*) 48–49
AtEndOfDocument() function 65, 312
AtStartOfDocument() function 312
attaching templates 508
attributes, file 551, 741–42
author 405–6, 506–7
authorities, tables of See tables of authorities
auto macros
    See also specific macro name
    disabling 384–85
    in forms 213
    using to load a WLL 1007
AutoCaption 582–83
AutoClose macro 35, 37
AutoCorrect
    adding and deleting entries 807–8
    adding exceptions 809–10
    counting exceptions 352

AutoCorrect (continued)
    deleting exceptions 809–10
    determining exceptions 608–9
    enabling/disabling replacement of entries 810
    options, toggling 807–9, 810, 811
    returning exceptions 552
    returning replacement text 551–52
    statements and functions related to, list of 266
AutoExec macro 35–36
AutoExit macro 35, 37
AutoFormat
    formatting documents with 512
    formatting tables 780–81, 797
    setting options 836–38
AutoMarkIndexEntries statement 312
AutomaticChange statement 313
AutoNew macro 35, 36
AutoOpen macro 35, 36
autosave files, default folders for 332, 376–77, 841–42
AutoSave option 847–48
AutoSum 781
AutoText
    See also AutoCorrect; Spike statement
    assigning entries to menus, shortcut keys, toolbars
        292–93, 818–22, 824–26
    copying entries 684–86
    counting entries 352
    creating entries 313, 433–34, 742–43
    deleting entries 433–34, 684–86
    displaying entries in picture dialog box control 393,
        702–3
    inserting entries 313, 433–34, 583, 584–85
    listing defined entries 313–14, 352
    printing entries 496–97
    renaming entries 684–86
    returning text of entries 553
    saving entries 722
    statements and functions related to, list of 266
    storing instructions as 150
    storing variable values in 205
AutoText statement 313
AutoTextName$() function 313–14
available disk space, memory 303–4, 561–63

B

BACKSPACE key
    See also DeleteBackWord statement; DeleteWord
        statement
    using while recording macros 15
backup files, saving automatically 847–48
batch files, running 473, 756–57
Beep statement 315–16

Begin Dialog...End Dialog statement 316–18
bitwise comparisons 892–94
block selection *See* selecting; extending selections
bold
    character format 319, 443–44, 458–59, 520, 526–28
    use of, in this manual xvi, 285–86
Bold statement and function 319
BookmarkName$() function 319–20
bookmarks
    adding 434–35
    beginning of, setting 752
    contents of, comparing 341–43
    contents of, returning 553
    copying 349
    counting 352–53
    creating 434–35
    cross-references to, inserting 586–87
    deleting 434–35
    displaying bookmarked graphics in dialog boxes 393,
      702–3
    empty 464–65
    end of, setting 746–47
    going to specific 434–35, 448–50
    hiding and displaying 850–51
    inserting in Mail Merge main documents 643–44
    names of, returning 319–20
    predefined 63–64, 895–96
    restricting operation of macros by using 63–64
    setting beginnings of 752
    setting ends of 746–47
    statements and functions related to, list of 267
    testing for existence of 472–73, 553
    testing if empty 464–65
books about WordBasic 9
BorderBottom statement and function 320–21
BorderInside statement and function 321
BorderLeft statement and function 322
BorderLineStyle statement and function 322–23
BorderNone statement and function 323
BorderOutside statement and function 323–24
BorderRight statement and function 324
borders
    bottom 320–21
    formatting 442, 457–58, 512–14, 519–20
    inside 321
    left 322
    line style 322–23, 442, 457–58, 512–14, 519–20
    outside 323–24
    removing 323
    right 324
    specifying in styles 519–20
    statements and functions related to, list of 267
    table 780–81, 797
    top 324
Borders toolbar 864

BorderTop statement and function 324
boxes
    See also borders
    grouping option buttons and check boxes within 567
boxes, check *See* check boxes
boxes, dialog *See* dialog boxes, custom
braces ({ }) *See* field characters
brackets ([ ]), use of, in this manual xvi, 285–86
branching
    to subroutines 82–83, 325
    within subroutines or functions 82–83, 564–65
breaks
    column 586
    page 600
    section 480, 492–94, 583–84, 602
built-in dialog boxes *See* dialog boxes, built-in
bulleted lists
    See also lists
    adding and removing bullets 514–15, 516, 531–32, 713,
      811, 812–13
    formatting bullets 514–15, 516, 531–32, 812–13
    skipping bullets 763
    statements and functions related to, list of 267–68
    testing for bullets 515
buttons
    See also dialog boxes, custom; specific button name
    adding to dialog boxes 316–18
    Cancel 96–97, 100, 326, 665–66
    command, adding to custom dialogs 709–10
    default, in dialog boxes 316–18, 379–81, 389
    detecting user's choice of 665–66
    displaying and hiding in dialog boxes 398
    OK, adding to dialog boxes 677
    option *See* option buttons
    setting and changing labels of 394–95
    toolbar *See* toolbar buttons

C

calculations 781, 784–85, 813
Call statement 83, 85, 88, 325
calling
    dialog functions 127
    Microsoft *See* Microsoft Product Support Services
callouts
    formatting 516–17
    inserting 413
    moving insertion point to 427–28
    size and position of 417–18, 426–27
    testing for 419–20
Cancel button
    adding to custom dialog boxes 326
    description of 100

Cancel button *(continued)*
    detecting choice of 665–66
    value returned by 96–97
Cancel statement 325–26
CancelButton statement 326
CAPI messaging interface (CMI), using 1029–30
CAPILIB
    building WDOPRs (Word operator data structures) with
        1025–26
    calling a WordBasic statement or function 1023–24
    customization functions in 1024–25
    fields, adding to dialog box equivalents 1020–21
    functions in 1019–25
    overview of 1019–27
    parameters, adding to commands 1021
    registering functions 1024
    using array functions in 1022–23, 1026–27
    Word Command Buffer (WCB), initializing 1020
    Word Command Buffer (WCB), overview of 1019
capital letters
    See also capitalization
    adding accents to 840–41
    all caps character format 763–64
    dropped, inserting 525–26
    finding and replacing 443–44, 458–59
capitalization
    all caps character format 295, 518, 520, 526–28
    changing 295, 327–28, 518, 520, 526–28, 618, 860
    correcting automatically 807–9, 810, 811
    determining 327–28
    initial caps 327–28, 807–8, 810
    sentence-style caps 327–28, 807–8, 811
    small caps character format 520, 526–28, 763–64
    use of, in this manual xvi
CAPS LOCK key 808–9
captions
    AutoCaption 582–83
    cross-references to, inserting 586–87
    inserting 582–83, 584–85
    labels, creating 581
    numbering format, specifying 585–86
    tables of *See* tables of figures
case control structure 725–26 *See also* Select Case statement
case, text *See* capitalization
cells, table
    deleting 783
    going to 670–71, 705–6
    inserting 787–88
    merging 790–91
    selecting 668, 704
    splitting 796
center alignment tab stops 448, 462, 522–23, 541–42, 797–98
centering paragraphs 327, 522, 536–38
CenterPara statement and function 327
central processing unit (CPU), returning type of 561–63

ChangeCase statement and function 327–28
changes, allowing and preventing *See* protecting;
    unprotecting
channels, DDE
    closing 174, 372–73
    opening 168–71, 368–70
    requesting data from other applications 171–72, 371–72
    sending commands through 173–74, 366–68
    sending data through 172–73, 370–71
character formatting
    See also fonts; paragraph formatting; styles
    all caps 295, 518, 520, 526–28, 763–64
    bold 319, 520, 526–28
    case 295, 327–28, 518, 520, 526–28, 618, 860
    color 328–29, 443–44, 458–59, 520, 526–28
    condensed 673
    copying 350–51, 700
    displaying in outline view 690
    dropped caps 525–26
    expanded 673
    finding and replacing 438–41, 442, 443–44, 455–57,
        458–59
    font 509, 510, 520, 526–28, 779
    Font dialog box, initializing 526–28
    font size 568, 761, 762, 857
    for envelope addresses 512, 539
    hidden text 520, 526–28, 573–74
    italic 520, 526–28, 612
    kerning 520, 526–28
    language 356, 521, 617, 831–32
    lowercase 518
    outline 687
    pasting 700
    removing 716–17
    shadow 755
    size 510, 520, 568, 761, 762, 857
    small caps 443–44, 458–59, 520, 526–28, 763–64,
        763–64
    spacing 520, 526–28, 673
    statements and functions related to, list of 269
    strikethrough 520, 526–28, 774
    styles 539–41
    subscript 520, 526–28, 672, 778
    superscript 520, 526–28, 672, 779
    symbols 779
    underline 409–10, 520, 526–28, 860, 885
    uppercase 295, 518, 520, 526–28, 763–64
character sets, translating strings between 409, 882
characters
    See also character formatting
    ANSI codes for 311–12, 336–37
    baseline, restoring to 672
    counting 405–6, 506–7, 619, 859

characters *(continued)*
deleting 435–36
Font dialog box, initializing 526–28
formatting *See* character formatting
inserting 580–81
lowering 672 *See also* character formatting; subscripts
nonprinting 337–38, 580–81, 757–58, 850–51
raising 672 *See also* character formatting; superscripts
repeated, returning string of 774–75
selecting by 329–31, 474
spacing between 520, 526–28, 673
symbols, inserting 580–81, 603–4
CharColor statement and function 328–29
CharLeft statement and function 329–30
CharRight statement and function 330–31
charts, inserting 586
ChDefaultDir statement 332
ChDir statement 333
check box form fields
adding 334, 594–96
formatting 542–44
returning setting of 557–58
selecting and clearing 747–48
setting default value 747–48
check boxes
See also check box form fields; controls, dialog box;
option buttons
adding to custom dialog boxes 333–34, 683
boxing groups of 567
description of 100
displaying and hiding 398
labels of, setting and changing 394–95
returning value of 121, 397
selecting and clearing 132–33, 397
setting value of 118–19
toggling values of 93–94
CheckBox statement 333–34
CheckboxFormField statement 334
checking
See also proofing documents
grammar 361, 829–30, 844
spelling 827–28, 844, 848–49, 857, 858
chevrons (« »), converting to merge field markers 634, 635
ChooseButtonImage statement 334–36
Chr$() function 45, 336–37
circles 415 *See also* drawing objects; option buttons
citations
changing category names of 464
marking as Table of Authorities entries 652–53
CleanString$() function 337–38
ClearAddIns statement 338–39
ClearFormField statement 339
clearing
See also deleting
add-ins 338–39

clearing *(continued)*
check boxes and option buttons 397
drawing ranges 414
form fields 339
tab stops 522–23, 541–42
clients 166
Clipboard
copying and cutting to 437, 438
displaying contents in picture dialog box control 393, 702–3
pasting from 452–53, 840–41
running 346, 759
Close statement 339–40
ClosePane statement 340
ClosePreview statement 340
CloseUpPara statement and function 340–41
CloseViewHeaderFooter statement 354
closing
See also stopping; terminating
annotation pane 863–64
applications 301, 473
DDE channels 174, 372–73
dialog boxes 326, 677
documents 399, 477, 481, 500
documents 478
files 210, 339–40, 399, 477
footnote/endnote pane 865–66, 867–68, 869
header/footer 354
Microsoft Windows 473
panes 340
sequential files 339–40
windows 399, 477, 478
CMI (CAPI messaging interface), using 1029–30
CmpBookmarks() function 66, 341–43
codes, ANSI 311–12, 336–37
codes, error
Word API, list of 1032–33
Word, list of 901–21
WordBasic, list of 897–901
collapsing outlines 687
collating pages when printing 496–97
colon (:) 40, 53
color
See also character formatting, color
in tables 780–81, 797
of borders 442, 457–58, 512–14
of drawing objects 523–25
toolbar buttons 874
column breaks, inserting 583–84, 586
columns
deleting in tables 784
going to next or previous 670–71, 705–6
inserting in tables 788
selecting 343, 466, 769–70, 792
spacing between in tables 782–83

columns *(continued)*
    text columns, creating and formatting 518–19
    width of text columns 518–19
    width of, in tables 782–83
ColumnSelect statement 343
combining strings 48–49
combo boxes
    See also dialog boxes, custom; drop-down list boxes; list
      boxes
    adding to custom dialog boxes 344
    contents of, setting and returning 394–95
    contents of, updating 390–91
    description of 100
    displaying and hiding 398
    placing items into 117–18
    responding to selected items in 133–34
    responding to typing in 136–37
    returning number of entries in 390–91
    value stored in dialog record 121
ComboBox statement 344
comma (,) 146
comma-delimited input, reading 578–79, 711
comma-delimited output, writing 886
command buttons
    See also dialog boxes, custom
    adding to custom dialog boxes 709–10
    displaying and hiding 398
    labels of, setting and changing 394–95
command line, using to load a WLL 1007–8
COMMAND+OPTION+X key combination *See* MoveText
  statement
commands
    assigning to menus, shortcut keys, toolbar buttons
      292–93, 818–22, 824–26
    checking availability of 344–45
    displaying Help for 572
    executing by sending keystrokes 736–38
    key combinations for, returning 615
    menu text, returning 656–57
    modifying 31–34
    printing list of 624
    restoring modified 34–35
    sending to other applications via DDE 366–68
CommandValid() function 344–45
commenting out instructions in macros 153–54
comments 41–42, 712–13
communicating information with other applications 165–93
comparing
    contents of bookmarks 341–43
    documents 813–14, 834–35
    files 834–35
    strings 51
comparison operators 891
compatibility options 838–40
compound expressions 56–58

CompuServe, product support via 8
condensed character format 673
condition testing
    documents, to see if saved 609–10
    macros, to see if editable 610–11
    templates, to see if saved 611–12
conditional statements 49–58, 53–55, 74–75, 577–78, 725–26
Connect statement 345
connecting to network drives 345, 661–63
consultation services from Microsoft 9
contents, tables of *See* tables of contents
context-sensitive Help, displaying 569, 570, 572
control characters, sending to applications 736–38
Control Panel, running 346
control structures
    For...Next 510–11
    If...Then...Else 577–78
    Select Case 725–26
    While...Wend 879
controlling other applications via DDE 366–68
ControlRun statement 346
controls, dialog box
    See also buttons; check boxes; combo boxes; drop-down
      list boxes; list boxes; option buttons; text, in dialog
      boxes, custom; text boxes
    disabling and enabling 125, 132–33, 387–88
    hiding and displaying 138–40, 398
    labels of, setting and changing 137–38, 394–95
    returning identifiers of 386–87
    returning values of, for Word dialogs 554
    setting and returning focus 137–38, 379–81, 389
    setting and returning value of 117–20, 397
conventions, documentation xvi, 285–86
conversations, DDE 166, 168–71, 174
Converter$() function 346–47
ConverterLookup() function 347
converting
    files *See* converting files
    graphics to drawing objects 415
    numbers to and from strings 386–87, 625, 773, 863
    tables to text 796–97
    text to tables 475, 789–90, 800–801
    Word for the Macintosh Mail Merge documents 634, 635
converting files
    compatibility options 838–40
    confirming conversions 478–79
    listing available converters 346–47
    opening from other format 490–92
    saving to other format 504–6
ConvertObject statement 347–48
CopyBookmark statement 349
CopyButtonImage statement 349
CopyFile statement 350
CopyFormat statement 350–51

copying
  AutoText entries 684–86
  bookmarks 349
  character formatting 350–51, 700
  code examples 21–22
  dialog boxes to macros 111–12
  files 350
  macros 30–31, 628, 684–86
  paragraph formatting 350–51, 700
  selections 351, 437
  styles 541, 684–86
  syntax from Help 149
  text 351, 437
  to the Clipboard 437
  toolbar button faces 349
  toolbar buttons and list boxes 663
  toolbars 684–86
copyright notice, displaying 569–70
CopyText statement 351
CountAddIns() function 351
CountAutoCorrectExceptions() function 352
CountAutoTextEntries() function 352
CountBookmarks() function 352–53
CountDirectories() function 353
CountDocumentProperties() function 353
CountDocumentVars() function 201, 354
CountFiles() function 354
CountFonts() function 354–55
CountFoundFiles() function 355
counting
  AutoCorrect exceptions 352
  AutoText entries in templates 352
  bookmarks 352–53
  custom key assignments 355, 614
  document properties 353
  drawing objects 414
  fonts, available 354–55
  language formats, available 356
  menu items 357–58
  menus 358
  open applications 301, 302
  points in freeform drawing objects 414–15
  subfolders in a folder 353
  toolbar buttons 359–60
  toolbars 360
  words, lines, etc. 859
CountKeys() function 355
CountLanguages() function 356
CountMacros() function 356–57
CountMenuItems() function 357–58
CountMenus() function 358
CountMergeFields() function 358–59
country setting, returning from WIN.INI file 561–63
CountStyles() function 359
CountToolbarButtons() function 359–60

CountToolbars() function 360
CountToolsGrammarStatistics() function 361
CountWindows() function 361
CPU (central processing unit), returning type of 561–63
CreateSubdocument statement 362
creating
  AutoText entries 313, 433–34, 742–43
  bookmarks 434–35
  cross-references 586–87
  custom dialog boxes 102–14, 316–18, 382
  documents 489, 490
  dynamic dialog boxes 125–43
  envelopes 814–15
  file preview boxes in custom dialogs 495
  folders 660–61
  indexes 597–98
  macros 833–34
  mailing labels 816–17
  paragraphs, new 601
  styles 539–41
  tables 475, 789–90, 800–801
  tables of authorities 604
  tables of contents 605–6
  tables of figures 606–7
  templates 489
  toolbars 667–68
  wizards 218–27
creator, file 479, 626–27, 747
cropping graphics 538
cross-references
  in indexes 653–54
  inserting 586–87
currency symbol, returning from WIN.INI file 303–4
cursor See insertion point; mouse pointers
custom dialog boxes See dialog boxes, custom
custom functions 545–46
customer assistance See Microsoft Product Support Services
Customize dialog box, displaying 818
customizing
  keyboard key assignments 355, 614, 615, 818–22
  menus 357–58, 656–58, 714–15, 818, 823, 824–26
  statements and functions related to, list of 268–69
  toolbar buttons 334–36, 349, 359–60, 435, 663, 699–700, 716, 805
  toolbars 292–93, 360, 378, 805–6, 818, 874
cutting
  text to the Clipboard 438
  text to the Spike 768–69

D

data
  See also databases
  appending to data files 681–82

data *(continued)*
    files *See* data files
    input from sequential access files 578–79, 620, 711
    inserting from databases 588–89, 591
    passing with the Word API *See* Word operator data
        structure (WDOPR)
    reading from sequential access files 578–79, 620, 711
    requesting from other applications 171–72, 371–72
    sending keystrokes to applications 736–38
    sending to other applications via DDE 370–71
    user-input, prompting for 579–80
    user-input, returning from forms 557–58
    writing to sequential access files 708–9, 886
data files
    See also sequential access files
    opening 681–82
    reading from 578–79
data records, Mail Merge *See* Mail Merge; Mail Merge fields
data sources
    Mail Merge *See* Mail Merge; Mail Merge fields
    ODBC (open database connectivity) 974–75
databases
    accessing data in *See* ODBC extensions for Microsoft
        Word
    connecting to forms 214
    inserting data from 588–89 *See also* ODBC extensions
        for Microsoft Word
    updating data in *See* ODBC extensions for Microsoft
        Word
DATE field 589
Date$() function 363
dates
    See also time
    converting from serial numbers 363
    converting to serial numbers 363–65
    current 363, 676, 803
    day, extracting from serial number 365–66
    format of 303–4, 363, 589–90
    inserting 589–90
    month, extracting from serial number 661
    of last printing or revision 405–6, 506–7
    statements and functions related to, list of 269
    weekday, extracting from serial number 878
    year, extracting from serial number 887
DateSerial() function 363–64
DateValue() function 364–65
Day() function 365–66
days
    See also dates
    of the month, extracting from dates 365–66
    of the week, capitalizing 807–8, 809
    of the week, extracting from dates 878
Days360() function 366

DDE (dynamic data exchange)
    application names 167
    channels 166, 366–70, 372–73
    clients 166
    compared with send keys 736–38
    compared with sending raw keystrokes 736–38
    conversations 166, 168–71, 174
    items 168
    Microsoft Access as a server for 177–79
    Microsoft Excel as a server for 174–77
    Microsoft Word as a server for 179–82
    requesting data from other applications 171–72, 371–72
    sending commands to other applications 366–68
    sending data to other applications 172–73, 370–71
    servers 166
    statements and functions related to, list of 273
    topics 167–68
DDEExecute statement 173–74, 366–68
DDEInitiate() function 170–71, 368–70
DDEPoke statement 172, 178, 370–71
DDERequest$() function 171–72, 371–72
DDETerminate statement 174, 372–73
DDETerminateAll statement 174, 373
deactivating instructions in macros 153–54
debugging macros 24–25, 145–56, 470–71, 472, 761, 773
decimal tab stops 448, 462, 522–23, 541–42, 797–98
decimals, truncating 608
Declare statement 228–29, 230–31, 373–76
default
    check box values 118–19
    command button in dialog boxes 121
    element in dialog boxes, specifying 316–18
    folders 332, 376–77, 841–42
    font, for envelope addresses 512, 539
    font, of Normal style 520, 526–28
    form field results, setting 747–48
    tab in dialog boxes 522, 526–28, 536–38
    text in text boxes 118–19
DefaultDir$ statement 376–77
defining *See* creating
DELETE key
    See also DeleteBackWord statement; DeleteWord
        statement; deleting
    using while recording macros 15
DeleteAddIn statement 377
DeleteBackWord statement 377
DeleteButton statement 378
DeleteDocumentProperty statement 378
DeleteWord statement 378–79
deleting
    See also Redim statement
    add-ins 377
    AutoText entries 433–34, 684–86
    bookmarks 434–35
    cells in tables 783

deleting *(continued)*
  characters 435–36
  columns in tables 784
  document properties 378
  files 615–16
  items from custom dialog boxes 110
  macros 30–31, 684–86, 833–34
  menu items 824–26
  menus 823
  rows in tables 784
  selections 435–36, 438
  styles 539–41, 684–86
  text 377, 378–79, 435–36, 438
  toolbar buttons and list boxes 378
  toolbars 684–86
  words 377, 378–79
delimiter characters, field 475
demonstrations
  for WordPerfect users, running 573
  Microsoft Word, running 570
DemoteList statement 379
DemoteToBodyText statement 379
demoting
  headings in outlines 688
  headings to body text 379
  list items in multilevel lists 379
deselecting drawing objects 431
diagrams *See* drawing objects; graphs, inserting
dialog box control identifiers 114, 127–28
dialog box controls
  See also buttons; check boxes; combo boxes; list boxes;
    drop-down list boxes; text boxes; option buttons
  defined 114
  disabling and enabling 387–88
  hiding and displaying 398
  labels of, setting and changing 394–95
  returning identifiers of 386–87
  returning values of, for built-in dialog boxes 554
  setting and returning focus 379–81, 389
  setting and returning value of 397
dialog box definitions 114, 115–17
dialog box settings 140–41
dialog boxes, built-in
  See also dialog boxes, custom; dialog boxes, dynamic
  changing settings in 92–94
  closing 96–97, 677
  controls, returning identifiers of 386–87
  defined 114
  dialog records for 91–97, 382–84
  displaying 95–97, 379–81
  displaying messages in 59–60
  returning values of controls in 554
  selecting and clearing options in 397
  statements and functions related to, list of 269–70

dialog boxes, built-in *(continued)*
  trapping errors in 379–81
  wizard 221–27
dialog boxes, custom
  See also dialog boxes, built-in; dialog boxes, dynamic
  adding comments in dialog box definitions of 111
  adding items to 102–5
  aligning items in 106–8, 113
  Cancel button in 100, 326
  canceling 326
  check boxes in 100, 118–19, 121, 333–34, 567
  combo boxes in 100, 117–18, 121, 344
  command buttons in 709–10
  control identifiers for 127–28
  controls in, hiding and displaying 398
  controls in, returning identifiers of 386–87
  controls in, setting and returning value of 397
  copying to macros 111–12
  creating 102–14, 316–18, 382, 579–80
  default button, specifying 316–18, 379–81, 389
  default command button in, specifying 121
  defined 114
  deleting items from 110
  dialog box definitions for 115–17
  dialog records 117
  dialog records, defining 382–84
  disabling and enabling controls in 387–88
  displaying 120–21, 379–81
  displaying graphics in 393, 702–3
  drop-down list boxes in 100, 117–18, 121, 431–32
  entering text in 101
  File Preview boxes in 105
  filling list or combo boxes in 390–91
  focus in, setting and returning 389
  group boxes in 101, 103–4, 113
  identifiers for 110–11
  labels and identifiers in 110–11, 394–95, 798–99
  list boxes in 100, 117–18, 121, 623
  moving around in 119
  multiple dialog boxes in a macro 379–81
  multiple-line text boxes in 105
  OK buttons in 100, 677
  option buttons in 101, 103–4, 683
  option groups in 121, 567, 683–84
  pictures in 101, 104
  placing values in 117–20
  positioning items in 105–9, 113
  previewing documents in 388–89, 396, 495
  prompting for user input 579–80
  push buttons in 100, 121
  retrieving values from 121–23
  setting focus and tab order in 119, 316–18, 379–81
  size of 109
  sizing items in 106–9
  text boxes in 101, 105, 118–19, 121, 799–800

dialog boxes, custom *(continued)*
    text, adding static (fixed) 798–99
    trapping errors 379–81
dialog boxes, dynamic
    See also dialog boxes, built-in; dialog boxes, custom
    canceling 131
    capabilities of 123–25
    change of focus in 137–38
    check boxes in 132–33
    combo boxes in 133–34, 136–37
    creating 125–43
    defined 114
    disabling options in 125
    drop-down list boxes in 133–34
    enabling options in 125
    function techniques 131–41
    hiding options on initialization of 138–40
    initializing 126–27, 138–40
    list boxes in 133–34
    loading values in 391–92
    multiple panels of controls in 138–40
    push buttons in 135–36
    storing settings of 140–41
    storing values for 394
    text boxes in 136–37
    updating text continuously in 140–41
Dialog Editor
    See also dialog boxes, built-in; dialog boxes, custom;
        dialog boxes, dynamic
    adding items by using 102–5
    aligning items by using 106–8
    changing labels and identifiers by using 110–11
    copying dialog boxes to macros by using 111–12
    deleting items by using 110
    editing dialog boxes by using 112
    exiting 112
    Information dialog box 110–11
    positioning items by using 105–9
    sizing items by using 106–9
    starting 102, 382
    tips for using 112–13
dialog functions
    calling 127
    defined 114
    how to use 125–43
    responding to user actions by using 132–38
    statements and functions used in 142–43
    storing dialog box settings 140–41
    syntax 128–30
    updating text in dialog boxes continuously 140–41
    value of variables defined in 131
dialog records
    checking status of 154, 155
    defined 114
    defining 92, 117, 382–84, 711–12

dialog records *(continued)*
    how to use 91–97
    obtaining and storing values of controls 554
Dialog statement and function 95–97, 120–21, 379–81
DialogEditor statement 382
differences across versions of Word 253–63
differences between Microsoft Windows and the Macintosh
    253–63
Dim Shared instruction 84–85
Dim statement 78, 84–85, 92, 117, 382–84
dirty flag, setting and testing 609–10, 611–12, 743, 752–53
DisableAutoMacros statement 163, 384–85
DisableInput statement 163, 385
disabling
    auto-executing macros 384–85
    controls in dialog boxes 125, 387–88
    the ESC key 385
disk space, available, returning amount of 303–4, 561–63
display
    resolution of, returning 561–63
    updating 722, 723
displaying
    annotations 759, 863–64
    Borders toolbar 864
    dialog box controls 387–88, 398
    dialog boxes 379–81
    draft mode 864–65
    Drawing toolbar 865
    error messages 472
    field codes or results 803, 866–67
    footnotes and endnotes 865–66, 869
    graphics in dialog boxes 393, 702–3
    gridlines in tables 786
    header/footer 760, 867, 870
    headings in outline view 759–60
    hidden applications 309
    hidden text 757–58, 850–51
    highlight formatting 850–51
    merge fields 650
    messages 58–61, 665–66
    nonprinting characters 757–58, 850–51
    optional hyphens 757–58, 850–51
    paragraph marks (¶) 757–58, 850–51
    revision marks 853–55, 856
    rulers 872–73
    space marks 757–58, 850–51
    status bar 850–51, 873
    tab characters 757–58, 850–51
    text in the status bar 708–9
    toolbars 806, 874
    windows 672, 707
division 48–49, 890
DlgControlId statement 386–87
DlgEnable statement and function 387–88
DlgFilePreview statement and function 388–89

DlgFocus statement and function 389
DlgListBoxArray statement and function 390–91
DlgLoadValues statement and function 391–92
DlgSetPicture statement 393
DlgStoreValues statement 394
DlgText statement and function 394–95
DlgUpdateFilePreview statement 396
DlgValue statement and function 397
DlgVisible statement and function 398
DLLs (dynamic-link libraries)
    See also Word add-in libraries (WLLs)
    calling routines in 228–34
    converting declarations for 233–34
    creating *See* Word API (Microsoft Word Application
        Programming Interface)
    making functions available to macros 373–76
    ODBC drivers 974
    WBMAPI.DLL 926
DocClose statement 399
docking toolbars 664
DocMaximize statement and function 399
DocMinimize statement and function 400
DocMove statement 400
DocRestore statement 400–401
DocSize statement 401
DocSplit statement and function 401–2
document layout
    initializing dialog box 480
    options, specifying 480
document properties
    built in, list of 403–4
    counting 353
    custom, identifying 609
    deleting 378
    displaying 499
    existing, identifying 402–3
    read-only, identifying 610
    returning 555
    returning names of 403–4
    setting 744–45
    setting links 745
    statements and functions related to, list of 271–72
    storing variable values in 203–5
    type, determining 404–5
document variables 201–3, 354, 556, 746
document windows
    closing 399, 477, 478
    maximizing 399
    minimizing 400
    positioning 407
documentation conventions xvi, 285–86
DocumentHasMisspellings() function 402
DocumentPropertyExists() function 402–3
DocumentPropertyName$() function 403–4
DocumentPropertyType() function 404–5

DocumentProtection() function 405
documents
    See also files; master documents; sequential access files
    annotating *See* annotations
    binding together *See* master documents
    changes to, allowing and preventing 504–6, 624, 741–42,
        847–48, 852, 858
    closing 399, 477, 478, 481, 500
    comparing 813–14, 834–35
    compatibility options 838–40
    converting file formats 346–47, 478–79, 490–92, 504–6,
        838–40
    copying 350
    creating 489, 490
    default folders for 332, 376–77, 841–42
    deleting 615–16
    detecting if saved 609–10, 743
    ends of 65–66, 312, 467
    finding 355, 481–84, 545
    formatting *See* character formatting; paragraph
        formatting
    formatting, statements and functions related to, list of
        281
    including within documents 862 *See also* master
        documents
    information about, returning 405–6, 506–7
    inserting 592–93, 603
    inserting AutoText entries in 313, 433–34, 583
    inserting text into 62
    laying out *See* page setup
    listing, in current folder 502–3
    magnifying 632, 874–75, 876
    master *See* master documents
    merging *See* Mail Merge
    most recently used list 354, 484–85, 490
    moving 667
    multiple windows for 881
    names of, returning 405–6, 486–89, 506–7, 731
    opening 484–85, 490–92
    paths of, returning 405–6, 486–89, 506–7, 731
    previewing in custom dialog boxes 388–89, 396, 495
    previewing in print preview 340, 498
    printing 496–97
    protecting 405, 504–6, 624, 741–42, 847–48, 852
    removing protection from 858
    renaming 504–6, 667
    routing 500–502
    saving 504–6, 609–10, 743, 847–48
    scrolling in *See* scrolling
    selecting entire 462, 474
    sending via electronic mail 500–502, 506
    shrinking to fit on fewer pages 857
    size, returning 405–6, 506–7
    statements and functions related to, list of 270–71
    statistics on 405–6, 506–7

documents *(continued)*
    summary information about 506–7
    unprotecting 858
    windows *See* windows
DocumentStatistics statement 405–6
DocWindowHeight statement and function 407
DocWindowPosLeft statement and function 407
DocWindowPosTop statement and function 408
DocWindowWidth statement and function 408
DoFieldClick statement 409
dollar sign ($) 46
DOSToWin$() function 409
dot (.) 146
dotted-underline character format 409–10
DottedUnderline statement and function 409–10
double-underline character format 410
DoubleUnderline statement and function 410
DOWN ARROW key *See* LineDown statement and function
Download Service, Microsoft 8
draft mode 864–65
drag-and-drop editing option 840–41
DrawAlign statement 411
DrawArc statement 412
DrawBringForward statement 412
DrawBringInFrontOfText statement 412
DrawBringToFront statement 412
DrawCallout statement 413
DrawClearRange statement 414
DrawCount() function 414
DrawCountPolyPoints() function 414–15
DrawDisassemblePicture statement 415
DrawEllipse statement 415
DrawExtendSelect statement 415
DrawFlipHorizontal statement 416
DrawFlipVertical statement 416
DrawFreeformPolygon statement 416
DrawGetCalloutTextbox statement 417–18
DrawGetPolyPoints statement 418–19
DrawGetType() function 419–20
DrawGroup statement 420
drawing layer
    adding text to 430
    moving objects backward 425, 426
    moving objects behind text layer 426
    moving objects forward 412
    moving objects in front of text layer 412
drawing objects
    See also Microsoft Draw
    aligning 411
    anchors, moving insertion point to 427
    arcs 412
    callouts 413, 417–18, 426–28, 516–17, 523–25
    circles 415
    creating from graphics 415
    deselecting 431

drawing objects *(continued)*
    ellipses 415
    flipping 416
    formatting 523–25
    freeform 414–15, 416, 418–19, 423, 428–29
    grouping 420
    lines 421
    moving backward in drawing layer 425, 426
    moving behind text layer 426
    moving forward in drawing layer 412
    moving horizontally 421, 422
    moving in front of text layer 412
    moving vertically 421, 422, 423
    positioning 523–25
    rectangles 423, 424
    returning number of 414
    rotating 424
    selecting 415, 424–25, 730
    snapping to grid when moving 430
    statements and functions related to, list of 272–73
    testing if selected 424–25
    text boxes 427–28, 430
    type of, returning 419–20
    ungrouping 431
    Word Picture objects 420, 423, 478
drawing range 414, 429
Drawing toolbar, hiding and displaying 865
drawings *See* drawing objects; graphics
DrawInsertWordPicture statement 420
DrawLine statement 421
DrawNudgeDown statement 421
DrawNudgeDownPixel statement 421
DrawNudgeLeft statement 421
DrawNudgeLeftPixel statement 422
DrawNudgeRight 422
DrawNudgeRightPixel statement 422
DrawNudgeUp statement 422
DrawNudgeUpPixel statement 423
DrawRectangle statement 423
DrawResetWordPicture statement 423
DrawReshape statement 423
DrawRotateLeft statement 424
DrawRotateRight statement 424
DrawRoundRectangle statement 424
DrawSelect statement and function 424–25
DrawSelectNext statement and function 425
DrawSelectPrevious statement and function 425
DrawSendBackward statement 425
DrawSendBehindText statement 426
DrawSendToBack statement 426
DrawSetCalloutTextbox statement 426–27
DrawSetInsertToAnchor statement 427
DrawSetInsertToTextbox statement 427–28
DrawSetPolyPoints statement 428–29
DrawSetRange statement and function 429

DrawSnapToGrid statement 430
DrawTextBox statement 430
DrawUngroup statement 431
DrawUnselect statement 431
drivers, ODBC, installing 974
drives, connecting to network 345, 661–63
drop-down form fields
    adding 431, 594–96
    adding items to 293
    formatting 542–44
    removing items from 713–14
    returning setting of 557–58
    setting result and default value 747–48
drop-down list boxes 100, 117–18, 133–34, 431–32
  See also combo boxes; dialog boxes, custom; drop-down
  form fields; list boxes
DropDownFormField statement 431
DropListBox statement 431–32
dropped caps, inserting 525–26
duplicate label errors 148
dynamic data exchange (DDE)
    application names 167
    channels 166, 366–70, 372–73
    clients 166
    compared with send keys 736–38
    compared with sending raw keystrokes 736–38
    conversations 166, 168–71, 174
    items 168
    Microsoft Access as a server for 177–79
    Microsoft Excel as a server for 174–77
    Microsoft Word as a server for 179–82
    requesting data from other applications 171–72, 371–72
    sending data to other applications 172–73, 366–68,
      370–71
    servers 166
    statements and functions related to, list of 273
    topics 167–68
dynamic dialog boxes *See* dialog boxes, dynamic
dynamic-link libraries (DLLs)
    See also Word add-in libraries (WLLs)
    calling routines in 228–34
    converting declarations for 233–34
    creating *See* Word API (Microsoft Word Application
      Programming Interface)
    making functions available to macros 373–76
    ODBC drivers 974
    WBMAPI.DLL 926

E

echoing (refreshing the screen) 722, 723
EditAutoText statement 433–34
EditBookmark statement 434–35
EditButtonImage statement 435

EditClear statement 435–36
EditConvertAllEndnotes statement 436
EditConvertAllFootnotes statement 436
EditConvertNotes statement 437
EditCopy statement 437
EditCopyAsPicture statement 437
EditCreatePublisher statement 437–38
EditCut statement 438
EditFind statement 438–41
EditFindBorder statement 442
EditFindClearFormatting statement 442
EditFindFont statement 443–44
EditFindFound() function 56, 444
EditFindFrame statement 445
EditFindHighlight statement 445
EditFindLang statement 446
EditFindNotHighlight statement 446
EditFindPara statement 447
EditFindStyle statement 447–48
EditFindTabs statement 448
EditGoTo statement 448–50
editing
    See also copying; cutting; inserting; pasting
    allowing and preventing 504–6, 610–11, 624, 741–42,
      852–53, 858
    AutoText entries 433–34
    dialog boxes 110–11, 112, 382
    embedded objects 288, 451
    graphics 453
    linked objects 450–51
    macros 19–26, 610–11, 833–34
    options 840–41
    repeating last operation 454
    statements and functions related to, list of 273–74,
      275–76
    undoing 464
edition
    publishing 437–38, 454
    subscribing to 462, 463
EditLinks statement 450–51
EditObject statement 451
EditPaste statement 452
EditPasteSpecial statement 452–53
EditPicture statement 453
EditPublishOptions statement 454
EditRedo statement 454
EditRepeat statement 454
EditReplace statement 455–57
EditReplaceBorder statement 457–58
EditReplaceClearFormatting statement 458
EditReplaceFont statement 458–59
EditReplaceFrame statement 459
EditReplaceHighlight statement 459
EditReplaceLang statement 460

EditReplaceNotHighlight statement 460
EditReplacePara statement 460–61
EditReplaceStyle statement 461
EditReplaceTabs statement 462
EditSelectAll statement 462
EditSubscribeOptions statement 462
EditSubscribeTo statement 463
EditSwapAllNotes statement 463
EditTOACategory statement 464
EditUndo statement 464
electronic forms *See* forms
electronic mail
    Apple Open Collaboration Environment (AOCE) 296,
      297–99, 475, 476, 477
    including in custom applications 925–67
    retrieving messages from 193
    sending documents via 475, 476, 477, 500–502, 506
    sending messages via 193
    statements and functions related to, list of 274
elements 78
ellipses
    drawing 415
    formatting 523–25
    testing for 419–20
EMBED field 598–600
embedded objects
    See also embedding; object linking and embedding (OLE)
    application for editing, specifying 347–48
    editing 288, 451
    going to specific 448–50
embedding
    See also embedded objects; object linking and embedding
      (OLE)
    any object 598–600
    documents within documents *See* inserting documents
      within documents; master documents
    Equation Editor objects 590
    fonts 504–6, 847–48
    Microsoft Access objects 588–89
    Microsoft Draw objects 590
    Microsoft Excel objects 588–89, 591
    Microsoft Graph objects 586
    Sound Recorder objects 602
    Word Picture objects 420, 478
    WordArt graphics 607
EmptyBookmark() function 464–65
EnableFormField statement 465–66
enabling
    controls in custom dialog boxes 387–88
    options in dialog boxes 125
encrypting macros 610–11
end of document, checking for 65–66, 312
end of file function 470
ending *See* closing; stopping; terminating
endnotes *See* footnotes and endnotes

EndOfDocument statement and function 467
EndOfLine statement and function 467–68
EndOfRow statement and function 468
EndOfWindow statement and function 469
ENTER key *See* OK statement
envelopes
    creating 814–15
    formatting addresses 512, 539
    printing 814–15
Environ$() function 469–70
environment
    options 842–44
    returning information about 303–4, 561–63
    statements and functions related to, list of 274–75
    variables 469–70
Eof() function 210–11, 470
equal sign (=) 47, 50
Equation Editor objects, inserting 590
equations
    cross-references to, inserting 586–87
    going to specific 448–50
    inserting 590
Err variable 161, 470–71
error handling *See* errors, trapping and handling
error messages
    common errors 145–48
    duplicate label errors 148
    parameter errors 148
    parameter number 147, 148
    syntax errors 146
    type mismatch errors 147
    undefined dialog record field 147–48
    unknown command, subroutine, function 147
    Word 158–59, 901–21
    Word API 1032–33
    WordBasic 145–48, 158–59, 897–901
Error statement 162, 472
error trapping *See* errors, trapping and handling
errors
    checking macros for 24–25
    duplicate label errors 148
    messages *See* error messages
    numbering of messages 158
    parameter errors 147, 148
    syntax 146
    trapping and handling 157–62, 379–81, 470–71, 472,
      635, 678–79
    type mismatch 147
    undefined dialog record field 147–48
    unknown command, subroutine, function 147
    user input 579–80
    ways to avoid 148–50
    Word 158–59, 901–21
    Word API 1032–33
    WordBasic 145–48, 158–59, 897–901

ESC key 385 *See also* Cancel statement
examples
    for form fields, creating 594–96
    running Microsoft Word 570
    syntax, copying from Help 21–22, 149
EXAMPLES.DOT 5–7
Excel, Microsoft *See* Microsoft Excel
exchanging data with other applications *See* dynamic data
  exchange (DDE); object linking and embedding (OLE)
executable functions, declaring to macros 373–76
execute-only macros 610–11, 628
executing
    commands for other applications via DDE 366–68
    macros 16–18, 23–24
ExistingBookmark() function 472–73
exiting
    applications 301, 473
    Dialog Editor 112
    Microsoft Windows 473
    Microsoft Word 473, 481, 500
ExitWindows statement 473
expanded character format 673
expanding outlines 688
exporting *See* converting files; output
Expression field *See* = (Formula) field
expressions 48–49
extending selections
    by characters 329–31, 474
    by columns 343, 466, 769–70
    by lines 467–68, 620–21, 622, 771
    by pages 692–94
    by paragraphs 474, 693–95, 697–99
    by progressive increments 474
    by rows 468, 771–72
    by sections 474
    by sentences 474, 739–41
    by table cells 668, 704
    by words 474, 883, 884–85
    canceling 325–26
    extend mode, activating 474
    testing for extend mode 473
    to a specified character 474
    to beginning or end of document 467, 770
    to top or bottom of window 469, 772
    until different formats are encountered 727–28, 729
ExtendMode() function 473
ExtendSelection statement 474

F

F10 key *See* MenuMode statement
F2 key *See* MoveText statement
false comparisons 892–94
false, value of 52

field codes, displaying and hiding 803, 850–51, 866–67
fields
    = (Formula) 781, 784–85
    ASK 641
    converting to results 861
    DATE 589
    delimiter characters 475
    displaying codes or results 803, 850–51, 866–67
    double-clicking on, equivalent statement 409
    field characters { }. inserting 592
    FILLIN 641
    form *See* form fields
    going to specific 448–50, 669, 704–5
    GOTOBUTTON 409
    IF 642
    INCLUDEPICTURE 601–2
    INCLUDETEXT 592–93, 862
    inserting 591
    locking and unlocking 624–25, 862
    MACROBUTTON 213, 409
    Mail Merge *See* Mail Merge fields
    MERGEFIELD 598, 650
    MERGEREC 642
    MERGESEQ 643
    NEXT 643
    NEXTIF 643
    protecting and unprotecting 624–25, 862
    selecting 669, 704–5
    separator characters 475
    SET 643–44
    SKIPIF 644
    statements and functions related to, list of 275
    TIME 589–90, 607
    unlinking 861
    updating 624–25, 861, 862
FieldSeparator$ statement and function 475
figures
    See also drawing objects; graphs, inserting
    captions for *See* captions
    cross-references to, inserting 586–87
    tables of *See* tables of figures
file creator 479, 626–27, 747
file formats, converting 347, 478–79, 490–92, 504–6, 838–40
file names *See* filenames
file pointer, setting in data file 724–25
file preview boxes
    adding to custom dialog boxes 105, 495
    displaying and hiding 398
    initializing 388–89
    updating 396
file types 508–9, 626–27, 747
FileAOCEAddMailer statement 475
FileAOCEDeleteMailer statement 475
FileAOCEExpandMailer statement 475
FileAOCEForwardMail statement 476

FileAOCENextLetter statement 476
FileAOCEReplyAllMail statement 476
FileAOCEReplyMail statement 476
FileAOCESendMail statement 477
FileClose statement 477
FileCloseAll statement 478
FileClosePicture statement 478
FileConfirmConversions statement and function 478–79
FileCreator$() function 479
FileDocumentLayout statement 480
FileExit statement 481
FileFind statement 481–84
FileList statement 484–85
FileMacCustomPageSetupGX statement 485
FileMacPageSetup statement 485
FileMacPageSetupGX statement 486
filename extension, finding files by 502–3
FileName$() function 486–87
FileNameFromWindow$() function 487
FileNameInfo$() function 487–89
filenames
    changing 504–6, 667
    Macintosh, translating for Windows 700–701
    returning 405–6, 486–89, 506–7, 547–48, 629, 731
    Windows, translating for the Macintosh 701–2
FileNew statement 489
FileNewDefault statement 490
FileNumber statement 490
FileOpen statement 490–92
FilePageSetup statement 492–94
FilePost statement 495
FilePreview statement 495
FilePrint statement 496–97
FilePrintDefault statement 497
FilePrintOneCopy statement 497
FilePrintPreview statement and function 498
FilePrintPreviewFullScreen statement 498
FilePrintSetup statement 499
FileProperties statement 499
FileQuit statement 500
FileRoutingSlip statement 500–502
files
    See also documents
    archived 551, 741–42
    attributes 551, 741–42
    closing 210, 339–40, 477, 478
    comparing 813–14
    converting file formats 347, 478–79, 490–92, 504–6,
        838–40
    copying 350
    creating 489, 490
    data See databases; Mail Merge; sequential access files
    default folders for 332, 376–77, 841–42
    deleting 615–16
    detecting if saved 609–10, 743, 752–53

files (continued)
    end of file function 470
    EXAMPLES.DOT 5–7
    finding 355, 481–84, 502–3, 545
    hidden 551, 741–42
    initialization 558–59, 560, 748–51, 806–7
    input, reading 578–79, 620
    inserting 592–93, 603
    INVOICE FORM template 5–7
    INVOICE2.DOT 5–7
    listing, in current folder 502–3
    MACRO EXAMPLES 5–7
    MKWIZARD.WIZ 5–7
    most recently used list 354, 484–85, 490–92
    moving 667
    names of See filenames
    NORTHWIND DATABASE 5–7
    NWIND.XLS 5–7
    ODBCAD32.EXE 975
    ODBCADM.EXE 975
    opening 484–85, 490–92, 681–82 See also files,
        converting file formats
    opening for sequential file access 206–7
    output, writing 708–9, 886
    POSITION.TXT 5–7
    previewing in custom dialog boxes 388–89, 495
    previewing in print preview 340, 498
    printing 496–97
    protecting 504–6, 741–42, 847–48, 852
    reading from 208–10
    read-only 551, 741–42
    renaming 504–6, 667
    sample 5–7
    saving 504–6
    sequential See sequential access files
    setting input/output point in 724–25
    settings 196–99
    size of, returning 405–6, 506–7, 625
    STARTER WIZARD 5–7
    STARTER.WIZ 5–7
    system 551, 741–42
    TEST.MDB 976
    text See sequential access files
    WBMAPI.DLL 193, 926–27
    WBMAPI.DOT 926
    WBODBC.DOT 976
    WBODBC.WLL 971, 973, 976
    WBTYPE.TXT 1015
    WIN.INI 199, 806–7
    WIN16API.TXT 6
    WIN32API.TXT 6
    WINWORD6.INI 199, 806–7
    WIZARD MAKER wizard 5–7
    Word Settings (6) 199
    writing to 207–8

Files$() function 502–3
FileSave statement 504
FileSaveAll statement 504
FileSaveAs statement 504–6
FileSendMail statement 506
FileSummaryInfo statement 506–7
FileTemplate statement 508
FileType$() function 508–9
FILLIN field 641
filling in forms automatically 212–18
finding
    See also going to
    author of revisions 854–55
    date of revisions 855
    documents 355, 481–84, 545
    files 355, 481–84, 502–3, 545
    formatting 438–41, 442, 443–44, 445, 446, 447, 448,
        455–57, 458–59, 460–61, 462
    repeating operations 715
    results of operation, returning 444
    revision marks 853–54
    search operators and options 438–41
    strings 607–8
    styles 438–41, 447–48, 461
    tab stops 672, 707
    text 438–41
first-line indent 522, 536–38
focus in dialog boxes 119–20, 389
folders
    creating 660–61
    current, setting 333
    default, returning 376–77
    default, setting 332, 841–42
    listing files in current folder 502–3
    listing subfolders in 353, 554–55
    removing 719–20
    renaming 667
Font dialog box, initializing 526–28
Font statement and function 509
fonts
    See also character formatting
    assigning to menus, shortcut keys, toolbar buttons
        292–93, 818–22, 824–26
    changing and returning 509, 520, 526–28
    counting available 354–55
    decreasing size of 761, 762
    embedding 504–6, 847–48
    for envelope addresses 512, 539
    in tables 780–81, 797
    increasing size of 568
    kerning 520, 526–28
    position *See* subscripts; superscripts
    size 509, 510, 568, 761, 762, 857
    substituting for missing fonts 510

fonts *(continued)*
    symbol, applying 779
    use of, in this manual xvi, 285–86
FontSize statement and function 510
FontSizeSelect statement 510
FontSubstitution statement 510
footers
    closing 354
    displaying 673–74, 867
    formatting 480, 492–94, 673–74
    linking to previous 529, 804
    moving insertion point to 566, 670–71, 686, 705–6, 760
    pane, opening and closing 340
footnotes and endnotes
    continuation notice and separator 717, 866, 868
    converting endnotes to footnotes 436, 437, 463
    converting footnotes to endnotes 436, 437, 463
    cross-references to, inserting 586–87, 586–87
    displaying 865–66, 867–68, 869
    going to specific 448–50, 566, 567, 670–71, 705–6
    inserting 593–94
    moving insertion point to 686
    numbering 674–75
    pane, opening and closing 340, 865–66, 867–68, 869
    positioning 674–75
    reference marks, formatting 593–94, 674–75
    separator line 717, 866, 869
    statements and functions related to, list of 276
    suppressing endnotes 480, 492–94
For...Next loop 71–73
For...Next statement 510–11
foreign languages *See* language formatting
form fields
    See also forms
    adding 213, 594–96
    allowing changes to 852–53, 858
    changing properties of 542–44
    check boxes 334, 747–48
    clearing 339
    drop-down 213, 293, 431, 713–14, 747–48
    formatting 542–44
    help on, creating 542–44, 594–96
    preventing changes to 465–66
    protecting and unprotecting 465–66, 852–53, 858
    returning settings of 557–58
    setting results and default values 747–48
    shading 544–45
    text, adding 747–48, 800
FormatAddrFonts statement 512
FormatAutoFormat statement 512
FormatBordersAndShading statement 512–14
FormatBullet statement 514–15
FormatBulletDefault statement and function 515
FormatBulletsAndNumbering statement 516
FormatCallout statement 516–17

FormatChangeCase statement 518
FormatColumns statement 518–19
FormatDefineStyleBorders statement 519–20
FormatDefineStyleFont statement 520
FormatDefineStyleFrame statement 520–21
FormatDefineStyleLang statement 521
FormatDefineStyleNumbers statement 521–22
FormatDefineStylePara statement 522
FormatDefineStyleTabs statement 522–23
FormatDrawingObject statement 523–25
FormatDropCap statement 525–26
FormatFont statement 526–28
FormatFrame statement 528–29
FormatHeaderFooterLink statement 529
FormatHeadingNumber statement 530–31
FormatHeadingNumbering statement 531
FormatMultilevel statement 531–32
FormatNumber statement 533–34
FormatNumberDefault statement and function 534–35
FormatPageNumber statement 535–36
FormatParagraph statement 536–38
FormatPicture statement 538
FormatRetAddrFonts statement 539
FormatSectionLayout statement 539
FormatStyle statement 539–41
FormatStyleGallery statement 541
FormatTabs statement 541–42
formatting
    See also AutoFormat; character formatting; paragraph
        formatting; styles; templates
    automatically See AutoFormat
    borders See borders
    callouts 516–17, 523–25
    caption numbers 585–86
    characters See character formatting
    copying 350–51, 700
    direct, removing 716–18
    displaying and hiding 864–65
    displaying in outline view 690
    drawing objects 523–25
    finding and replacing 438–41, 442, 443–44, 445, 446,
        447, 448, 455–59, 460–61, 462
    footnotes and endnote reference marks 593–94, 674–75
    form fields 542–44
    frames 520–21, 528–29
    graphics 538
    hiding and displaying 850–51
    indenting See indents
    indexes 597–98, 653–54
    language 356, 521, 617, 831–32
    lines 523–25
    lists 514–15, 516, 521–22, 531–32, 713, 812–13
    paragraphs See paragraph formatting
    pasting 700
    pictures 538

formatting (continued)
    removing nonstyle formatting 716–18
    sections 518–19, 529, 535–36, 539, 804
    shading 442, 457–58, 512–14, 519–20, 753–55
    statements and functions related to, list of 268, 280, 282
    tables 780–81, 786–87, 789–90, 791–92, 797, 800–801
    undoing 464
Formatting toolbar, hiding and displaying 872
FormFieldOptions statement 542–44
forms
    changes to, allowing and preventing 465–66, 852–53,
        858
    check boxes in 334
    connecting databases to 214
    drop-down fields in 293, 431, 713–14
    fields See form fields
    fields in 339, 465–66, 542–45, 557–58, 594–96, 747–48
    filling in automatically 212–18
    macros for automating 212–18
    obtaining user-input from 557–58
    protecting and unprotecting 405, 465–66, 852–53, 858
    results of, returning 557–58
    saving user data 504–6, 847–48
    text fields in, adding 800
FormShading statement and function 544–45
Formula field 781, 784–85
forward slash (/) 48–49
FoundFileName$() function 545
FoxPro, Microsoft, DDE application names for 167
frames
    anchors, hiding and displaying 850–51
    formatting 445, 459, 520–21, 528–29
    going to next or previous 670–71, 705–6
    inserting 596–97
    positioning 520–21, 528–29
    removing 520–21, 528–29, 714
    sizing 520–21, 528–29
    statements and functions related to, list of 267
freeform drawing objects
    coordinates of end points 418–19, 428–29
    creating 416
    formatting 523–25
    handles for, toggling 423
    number of points in, returning 414–15
    testing for type of 419–20
full screen mode 804
function keys See keys
Function...End Function statement 545–46
functions
    See also individual function names
    add-in (WLL) See Word add-in libraries (WLLs)
    custom 545–46
    declaring DLL, WLL, and EXE functions 373–76
    defined 41
    dialog box 142–43

functions *(continued)*
    lists of 265–84
    overview 43–44
    user-defined 82, 316–18

G

GEnie, product support via 8
GetAddInID() function 547
GetAddInName$() function 547–48
GetAddress$() function 548–50
GetAttr() function 551
GetAutoCorrect$() function 551–52
GetAutoCorrectException$() function 552
GetAutoText$() function 205, 553
GetBookmark$() function 65, 553
GetCurValues statement 554
GetDirectory$() function 554–55
GetDocumentProperty$() function 555
GetDocumentProperty() function 555
GetDocumentVar$() function 201–3, 556
GetDocumentVarName$() function 556
GetFieldData$() function 557
GetFormResult$() function 557–58
GetFormResult() function 557–58
GetMergeField$() function 558
GetPrivateProfileString$() function 197, 558–59
GetProfileString$() function 560
GetSelEndPos() function 560–61
GetSelStartPos() function 561
GetSystemInfo statement and function 561–63
GetText$() function 563–64
global templates *See* templates
Glossary *See* AutoText
GoBack statement 564
going to
    a specific place in a document 448–50, 715
    beginning or end of document 467, 770
    beginning or end of line 467–68, 771
    beginning or end of row 468, 771–72
    bookmarks 434–35
    end of column 466
    fields 669, 704–5
    header or footer 566, 760
    next or previous specified item 566, 567, 670–72, 705–7
    previous locations of the insertion point 564
    repeating operations 715
    table cells 668, 704
    top of column 769–70
    top or bottom of window 469, 772
Goto statement 76, 564–65
GoToAnnotationScope statement 565–66
GOTOBUTTON field 409
GoToHeaderFooter statement 566

GoToNextItem statement 566
GoToPreviousItem statement 567
grammar checking
    checking spelling concurrently 844
    returning statistics after 361, 828–30, 844
    specifying rules set 844
    starting 829–30
    synonyms, returning 828–29, 858
graphics
    See also borders; drawing objects; frames; pictures
    converting to drawing objects 415
    cropping 538
    cross-references to, inserting 586–87
    default folders for 332, 376–77, 841–42
    displaying and hiding 850–51
    editing 453, 840–41
    finding 438–41
    formatting 538
    going to specific 448–50
    in dialog boxes 101, 104, 393, 702–3
    inserting 601–2, 607
    linking and embedding from other files *See* object linking and embedding (OLE)
    sizing and scaling 538
    toolbar button faces *See* toolbar buttons
graphs, inserting 586
greater-than sign (>) 50
greater-than-or-equal-to sign (>=) 50
gridlines in tables 786
grids, drawing object 430
group boxes 101, 103–4, 113
GroupBox statement 567
grouping
    drawing objects 420
    options in custom dialog boxes 567, 683–84
GrowFont statement 568
GrowFontOnePoint statement 568
gutter margins, setting 480, 492–94

H

halting macros 385, 773
handles on freeform drawing objects 423
handles, MAPI data type 928
hanging paragraph indent 569, 860–61
HangingIndent statement 569
Header And Footer toolbar 867, 870
headers
    closing 354
    displaying 673–74, 870
    formatting 480, 492–94, 673–74
    linking to previous 529, 804
    moving insertion point to 566, 686, 760
    pane 340, 804

heading rows in tables 786–87
headings
  cross-references to, inserting 586–87
  in outlines, collapsing 687
  in outlines, converting to body text 379
  in outlines, demoting 688
  in outlines, displaying specific heading level 759–60
  in outlines, expanding 688
  in outlines, moving 689
  in outlines, promoting 689–90
  in outlines, returning heading level 688–89
  numbering 530–31
height
  of application windows 309–10
  of dialog boxes 316–18
  of drawing objects 523–25
  of frames 520–21, 528–29
  of graphics 538
  of pages 480, 485, 486, 492–94
  of windows 309–10, 407
Help
  copying syntax and examples from 149
  displaying 569, 570, 572
  examples and demonstrations 570
  for form fields, creating 542–44
  for WordBasic 21–22
  Help on using 572
  index 570
  keyboard guide 571
  on product support 7–9, 571
  searching with keywords 571
  statements and functions related to, list of 276–77
  Tip of the Day 572
  TipWizard 313, 760, 803
  tutorial, running 571
  WordPerfect Help, settting options for 573
Help statement 569
HelpAbout statement 569–70
HelpActiveWindow statement 570
HelpContents statement 570
helper functions 926
HelpExamplesAndDemos statement 570
HelpIndex statement 570
HelpKeyboard statement 571
HelpMSN statement 571
HelpPSSHelp statement 571
HelpQuickPreview statement 571
HelpSearch statement 571
HelpTipOfTheDay statement 572
HelpTool statement 572
HelpUsingHelp statement 572
HelpWordPerfectHelp statement 572
HelpWordPerfectHelpOptions statement 573

hidden
  application windows 301, 302
  applications, displaying 309
  files 551, 741–42
  text 443–44, 458–59, 520, 526–28, 573–74, 757–58, 850–51
Hidden statement and function 573–74
hiding
  application windows 302
  body text in outline view 687, 690, 758
  Borders toolbar 864
  dialog box controls 398
  Drawing toolbar 865
  gridlines in tables 786
  hidden text 757–58, 850–51
  highlight formatting 850–51
  nonprinting characters 757–58, 850–51
  optional hyphens 757–58, 850–51
  options in dialog boxes 138–40
  paragraph marks (¶) 757–58, 850–51
  revision marks 853–54, 856
  rulers 872–73
  space marks 757–58, 850–51
  status bar 850–51, 873
  tab characters 757–58, 850–51
  text See hidden text
  toolbars 806, 874
highlight formatting
  adding and removing 574–75
  determining color of 574–75
  displaying and hiding 850–51
  finding and replacing 445, 446, 459, 460
  specifying color of 574–75, 846–47
Highlight statement 574
HighlightColor statement and function 574–75
HLine statement 575
horizontal ruler, displaying and hiding 872–73
horizontal scroll bar
  displaying and hiding 850–51
  macro equivalents of using 575, 576
horizontally, flipping drawing objects 416
Hour() function 575
hour, extracting from time 575
hourglass mouse pointer 878
HPage statement 576
HScroll statement and function 575
hyphenation 522, 536–38, 830, 831
hyphens, displaying and hiding 757–58, 850–51

I

icons for linked and embedded objects 288, 347–48, 452–53, 598–600
identifiers 110–11

If conditional 53–55
IF field 642
If...Then...Else statement 577–78
illustrations *See* graphics
IMPORT field *See* INCLUDEPICTURE field
INCLUDE field *See* INCLUDETEXT field
INCLUDEPICTURE field 601–2
INCLUDETEXT field 592–93, 862
Indent statement 578
indents
    first line 522, 536–38
    hanging 569, 860–61
    in tables 791–92
    left and right 522, 536–38, 578, 861
INDEX field 597–98
index, Help 570
indexes
    creating and inserting 312, 597–98
    entries for, marking text as 653–54
    formatting 597–98, 653–54
    updating 597–98
information, document summary 506–7
initial caps 327–28, 807–8, 810
initialization files 750–51 *See also* settings files
initializing
    dialog boxes 126–27, 138–40, 397, 818
    Font dialog box 526–28
    Paragraph dialog box 522, 536–38
initiating DDE conversations 168–71
input
    comma-delimited, reading 209, 578–79
    opening files for 206–7, 681–82
    prompting for, with dialog box 579–80
    reading from sequential access files 208–10, 578–79, 620, 711
    returning user-input from forms 557–58
    sending keystrokes to applications 736–38
    setting input point in a data file 212, 724–25
Input statement 58, 61, 209, 578–79
Input$() function 209–10, 579
input, user 58–61
InputBox$() function 58, 60, 579–80
insert mode 691, 840–41
Insert statement 62, 580–81
InsertAddCaption statement 581
InsertAddress function 581–82
InsertAnnotation statement 582
InsertAutoCaption statement 582–83
InsertAutoText statement 583
InsertBreak statement 583–84
InsertCaption statement 584–85
InsertCaptionNumbering statement 585–86
InsertChart statement 586
InsertColumnBreak statement 586
InsertCrossReference statement 586–87

InsertDatabase statement 588–89
InsertDateField statement 589
InsertDateTime statement 589–90
InsertDrawing statement 590
InsertEquation statement 590
InsertExcelTable statement 591
InsertField statement 591
InsertFieldChars statement 592
InsertFile statement 592–93
InsertFootnote statement 593–94
InsertFormField statement 594–96
InsertFrame statement 596–97
InsertIndex statement 597–98
inserting
    addresses from address books 581–82
    annotations 582
    AutoText entries 313, 433–34, 583
    breaks (page, column, or section) 583–84, 602
    captions 582–83, 584–85
    cells in tables 787–88
    column breaks 586
    columns in tables 788
    contents of Clipboard 452–53
    contents of Spike 603
    cross-references 586–87
    data from databases 588–89, 591
    dates and times 589–90, 607
    documents within documents 603
    drawing objects *See* drawing objects
    equations 590
    field characters { } 592
    fields 591
    files 592–93
    footnotes and endnotes 593–94
    form fields 594–96
    frames 596–97
    graphics 601–2
    graphs 586
    indexes 597–98
    objects 452–53, 586, 588–89, 590, 598–600, 601–2, 607
    page breaks 600
    paragraph marks 601
    rows in tables 788–89
    sounds 602
    symbols 580–81, 603–4, 779
    tables 789–90, 800–801
    tables of authorities 604
    tables of contents 605–6
    tables of figures 606–7
    text and numbers 580–81
    WordArt 607
insertion point
    appearance of, changing 735
    locating 312, 341–43
    marking location of, with bookmark 464–65

insertion point *(continued)*
    moving *See* insertion point, moving
    moving between header and footer 566, 686
    moving by characters 329–31
    moving by columns 466, 670–71, 705–6, 769–70
    moving by lines 467–68, 620–21, 622, 771
    moving by pages 692–94
    moving by paragraphs 694–95, 697–99
    moving by rows 468, 771–72
    moving by sentences 739–41
    moving by words 883, 884–85
    moving to beginning of window 469, 772
    moving to beginning or end of document 467, 770
    moving to bookmarks 434–35, 448–50
    moving to callouts 427–28
    moving to drawing object anchor 427
    moving to next or previous field 669, 704–5
    moving to next or previous footnote 670–71, 705–6
    moving to next or previous frame 670–71, 705–6
    moving to next or previous header/footer 760
    moving to next or previous specified item 566, 567, 670–72, 706–7
    moving to next or previous table cells 668, 670–71, 704, 705–6
    moving to previous editing locations 564
    moving to specific page 671–72
    moving to text boxes 427–28
    repeating go to operations 715
    setting bookmarks relative to 349
    statements and functions related to, list of 278–79
InsertMergeField statement 598
InsertObject statement 598–600
InsertPageBreak statement 600
InsertPageField statement 600
InsertPageNumbers statement 600–601
InsertPara statement 601
InsertPicture statement 601–2
InsertSectionBreak statement 602
InsertSound statement 602
InsertSpike statement 603
InsertSubdocument statement 603
InsertSymbol statement 603–4
InsertTableOfAuthorities statement 604
InsertTableOfContents statement 605–6
InsertTableOfFigures statement 606–7
InsertTimeField statement 607
InsertWordArt statement 607
installing
    files to build WLLs 1004–5
    ODBC drivers 974
    sample files 6
InStr() function 607–8
instructions, storing as AutoText entries 150
Int() function 608
integers, truncating decimals to 608

international settings in WIN.INI file, returning 303–4, 561–63
Internet, product support via 8
interrupting macros 385, 773
inverting drawing objects 416
INVOICE FORM 5–7
INVOICE2.DOT 5–7
IsAutoCorrectException() function 608–9
IsCustomDocumentProperty() function 609
IsDocumentDirty function 609–10
IsDocumentPropertyReadOnly() function 610
IsExecuteOnly() function 610–11
IsMacro() function 611
IsTemplateDirty() function 611–12
italic
    character format 443–44, 458–59, 520, 526–28, 612
    use of, in this manual xvi, 285–86
Italic statement and function 612
items
    adding to drop-down form fields 293
    in topics for DDE conversations 168
    removing from drop-down form fields 713–14

J

justified alignment 522, 536–38, 613
JustifyPara statement and function 613

K

keep lines together paragraph format 522, 536–38, 696
keep with next paragraph format 522, 536–38, 696–97
key combinations, sending to applications 736–38
keyboard guide, using Help 571
KeyCode() function 614
KeyMacro$() function 615
keys
    access 111
    counting custom key assignments 355, 614
    customizing key assignments 818, 1028
    displaying Help for 571
    printing key assignments 496–97, 624
    resetting default key assignments 818–22
    returning commands and macros for key assignments 615
    saving changes to key assignments 722
    sending keystrokes to applications 736–38
    WordPerfect settings, enabling 573
Kill statement 615–16

L

labels
    in dialog boxes 110–11, 394–95
    mailing 643, 816–17

landscape page orientation 480, 485, 486, 492–94, 804
language
    setting in WIN.INI file, returning 561–63
    version of Word, returning 303–4
language formatting
    counting available types of 356
    defining for styles 521
    finding and replacing 438–41, 442, 446, 455–57, 458,
        460
    setting and returning 617, 831–32
Language statement and function 617
layers *See* drawing layer; text layer
layout, document 480
layout, page *See* page setup
LCase$() function 618
leader characters, tab 448, 462, 522–23, 541–42, 780
learning WordBasic 4–5
left alignment
    by using tab stops 448, 462, 522–23, 541–42, 797–98
    of paragraphs 522, 536–38, 578, 618–19, 861
left paragraph indent 578
Left$() function 618
LeftPara statement and function 618–19
legal citations *See* citations; tables of authorities
Len() function 619
length
    of files, returning 625
    of strings, returning 619
less-than sign (<) 50
less-than-or-equal-to sign (<=) 50
Let statement 619
Line Input statement 209, 620
line numbers paragraph format 522, 536–38
line spacing
    in paragraphs 766–67
    in tables 791–92
LineDown statement and function 620–21
lines
    borders on paragraphs and tables *See* borders
    counting 405–6, 506–7, 859
    drawing 421
    extending selection by 467–68, 620–21, 622, 771
    formatting 523–25
    going to specific 448–50
    keeping together in paragraphs 522, 536–38, 696
    numbering 480, 492–94, 522, 536–38
    selecting 467–68, 771
    testing for 419–20
    vertical, drawing with bar tab stops 522–23, 541–42
    widow and orphan, controlling 522, 536–38, 699
LineUp statement and function 622
linking
    any object 452–53, 598–600
    editing and setting options for linked objects 450–51
    graphics files 601–2

linking *(continued)*
    locking and unlocking 450–51
    updating 450–51
list boxes
    See also combo boxes; dialog boxes, custom; drop-down
        list boxes
    adding button image for vertical toolbar 334–36
    contents of, setting and returning 117–18, 121, 394–95,
        397
    contents of, updating 390–91
    copying or moving on toolbars 663
    creating in custom dialog boxes 431–32, 623
    deleting from toolbars 378
    displaying and hiding 398
    in dialog boxes, overview 100
    in dynamic dialog boxes 133–34
    returning number of entries in 390–91
    selecting and returning entries in 397
ListBox statement 623
ListCommands statement 624
listing
    application window names 302
    bookmarks in the active document 319–20, 352–53
    files in current folder 502–3
    subfolders in folders 353, 554–55
lists
    bulleted 514–15, 516, 531–32, 713, 763, 811, 812–13
    creating in custom dialogs 431–32
    demoting list items 379
    formatting bullets and numbers 521–22
    in custom dialog boxes *See* list boxes; drop-down list
        boxes; drop-down form fields
    interrupting 763
    multilevel 531–32
    numbered 516, 531–32, 533–35, 713, 763, 812–13, 835
    promoting list items 709
    removing formatting from 713
    statements and functions related to, list of 267–68
loading dialog box settings 140–41
loading sample files 6
locating
    insertion point 312, 341–43
    strings within strings 607–8
LockDocument statement and function 624
LockFields statement 624–25
locking
    documents from changes 624, 852
    fields from updates 624–25
    form fields from changes 465–66
    forms from changes 852–53
    links 450–51
Lof() function 211, 625
logical operators 56–58, 891–94

loop statements
    For...Next 510–11
    While...Wend 879
lowercase
    changing to and from 327–28
    character format 518
    converting strings to 618
    testing for 327–28
lowering characters 526–28, 672 *See also* character
    formatting; subscripts
LTrim$() function 625

M

MacID$() function 168–70, 626–27
Macintosh paths and filenames, translating for Windows
    700–701
Macintosh, differences between Microsoft Windows and
    253–63
MACRO EXAMPLES template 5–7
Macro Text style 25
Macro toolbar 22–23, 150
MACROBUTTON field 213, 409
MacroCopy statement 628
MacroDesc$() function 628–29
macro-editing windows 19–26
MacroFileName$() function 629
MacroName$() function 629–30
MacroNameFromWindow$() function 630
macros
    assigning to menus, shortcut keys, toolbar buttons 13–14,
        292–93, 818–22, 824–26
    Auto 35–37, 213
    AutoClose 35, 37
    AutoExec 35–36
    auto-executing 384–85
    AutoExit 35, 37
    AutoNew 35, 36
    AutoOpen 35, 36
    branching 325, 564–65
    cleaning up after 163–64
    commenting out instructions in 153–54
    comments in 41–42, 712–13
    copying 30–31, 628, 684–86
    copying code examples into 21–22
    copying dialog boxes to 111–12
    creating 11–15, 26, 702, 833–34
    deactivating instructions in 153–54
    debugging 24–25, 145–56, 470–71, 472, 761, 773
    deleting 30–31, 684–86, 833–34
    descriptions of, setting and returning 628–29, 833–34
    developing for more than one platform 234–42
    distributing 242–47
    editing 19–26, 833–34

macros *(continued)*
    execute-only 610–11, 628
    executing at a specific time 679–81
    for filling in forms automatically 212–18
    getting help with 21–22
    interrupting 385, 773
    key combinations for, returning 615
    limitations on recording 15
    menu item assignments, setting and returning 654–55
    moving 30–31
    names of, returning 629–30
    naming 12
    number of in template 356–57
    on-entry 213
    on-exit 213
    optimizing 247–50
    pausing 26
    protecting 610–11
    recording 11–15, 26, 702, 833–34
    refreshing screen during execution 722, 723
    renaming 30–31, 684–86
    restricting operation of, by using bookmarks 63–64
    running 16–18, 23–24, 90, 833–34
    sample 5–7
    saving 26–30, 722
    StartWizard 219–21
    statements and functions related to, list of 277
    stepping through 151–52
    stopping 26, 154, 385, 773
    subroutines in 82–83, 84–91, 325, 777–78
    template containing, returning path and filename of 629
    tracing through 150–51
    trapping errors in 157–62
    undoing actions while recording 15
    user-defined functions in 82, 83–91
    windows, detecting 611
    writing 19
MacScript statement and function 631, 1050
Magnifier statement and function 632
magnifying documents 632, 874–75, 876
mail *See* electronic mail; Mail Merge; Mail, Microsoft,
    communicating with
Mail Merge
    conditional instructions 642, 643, 644
    data records, adding 637, 806
    data records, finding 639–40
    data records, multiple in a merge document 643
    data records, removing 853
    data records, returning field information from 558
    data records, selecting 633–34, 645–46, 647
    data sources, attaching 645–46
    data sources, creating 636
    data sources, detaching 647
    data sources, editing 638
    data sources, returning field names 658–59

Mail Merge *(continued)*
   documents created in Word for the Macintosh 634, 635
   error checking 635
   fields *See* Mail Merge fields
   header source, activating and editing 638
   header source, attaching 646
   header source, creating 636–37
   header source, detaching 647
   header source, returning field names 658–59
   inserting merge fields in documents 598
   Mail Merge Helper dialog box 640
   main documents, activating and editing 638
   main documents, creating 644–46
   main documents, setting bookmarks in 643–44
   merged documents, displaying 639, 640, 644, 645, 647
   merging 633–34, 649
   prompting for user input during 641
   query options 647
   returning information about 637–38, 648–49
   setting options 633–34
   statements and functions related to, list of 277–78
Mail Merge fields
   See also Mail Merge
   adding and removing 834
   data and header source, returning names 658–59
   data, returning from current record 558
   displaying 650
   in header, number of 358–59
   renaming 834
Mail, Microsoft, communicating with 193
MailCheckNames statement 632
MailHideMessageHeader statement 632
mailing labels 643, 816–17
MailMerge statement 633–34
MailMergeAskToConvertChevrons statement and function
   634
MailMergeCheck statement 635
MailMergeConvertChevrons statement and function 635
MailMergeCreateDataSource statement 636
MailMergeCreateHeaderSource statement 636–37
MailMergeDataForm statement 637
MailMergeDataSource$() function 637–38
MailMergeEditDataSource statement 638
MailMergeEditHeaderSource statement 638
MailMergeEditMainDocument statement 638
MailMergeFindRecord statement 639
MailMergeFirstRecord statement 639
MailMergeFoundRecord() function 639–40
MailMergeGotoRecord statement and function 640
MailMergeHelper statement 640
MailMergeInsertAsk statement 641
MailMergeInsertFillIn statement 641
MailMergeInsertIf statement 642
MailMergeInsertMergeRec statement 642
MailMergeInsertMergeSeq statement 643

MailMergeInsertNext statement 643
MailMergeInsertNextIf statement 643
MailMergeInsertSet statement 643–44
MailMergeInsertSkipIf statement 644
MailMergeLastRecord statement 644
MailMergeMainDocumentType statement and function
   644–45
MailMergeNextRecord statement 645
MailMergeOpenDataSource statement 645–46
MailMergeOpenHeaderSource statement 646
MailMergePrevRecord statement 647
MailMergeQueryOptions statement 647
MailMergeReset statement 647
MailMergeState() function 648–49
MailMergeToDoc statement 649
MailMergeToPrinter statement 649
MailMergeUseAddressBook statement 649–50
MailMergeViewData statement and function 650
MailMessageDelete statement 650
MailMessageForward statement 650
MailMessageMove statement 651
MailMessageNext statement 651
MailMessagePrevious statement 651
MailMessageProperties statement 651
MailMessageReply statement 652
MailMessageReplyAll statement 652
MailMessageSelectNames statement 652
MAPI (messaging application programming interface) 193,
   925–67
MAPIAddress function 930–33
MAPIDeleteMail function 933–34
MAPIDetails function 934–36
MapiFile data type 929
MAPIFindNext function 928, 937–39
MAPILogoff function 927, 930, 940
MAPILogon function 927, 928, 930, 941–43
MapiMessage data type 929
MAPIQueryAttachments function 943–44
MAPIQueryDateReceived function 944–45
MAPIQueryNoteText function 945–46
MAPIQueryOriginator function 946
MAPIQueryRecipientList function 947–48
MAPIQueryRecipientListCount function 948–49
MAPIQueryRecipientListElement function 949–50
MAPIQuerySubject function 950–51
MAPIReadMail function 927, 951–53
MapiRecip data type 929
MAPIResolveName function 928, 954–56
MAPISaveMail function 927, 956–58
MAPISendDocuments function 959–60
MAPISendMail function 927, 960–64
MAPISetAttachment function 964–65
MAPISetMessageType function 965–66
MAPISetRecipient function 966–67
MAPISetRecipientList function 967

mapping fonts 510
margins, setting 480, 492–94
MarkCitation statement 652–53
MarkIndexEntry statement 653–54
marking text and graphics *See* bookmarks; revision marks;
  selecting
MarkTableOfContentsEntry statement 654
master documents
    inserting subdocuments in 603
    merging subdocuments together 659
    opening subdocuments in 682
    protecting as read-only 624
    splitting subdocuments 769
    statements and functions related to, list of 279–80
    subdocuments, converting headings to 362
    subdocuments, converting to regular text 714
    view, switching to and from 870, 873
matching AutoText entries, hierarchy of 313, 433–34, 583
math coprocessor, testing for presence of 303–4, 569–70
mathematical formulas 781, 784–85, 813
mathematical operators 48–49
maximizing windows 305–6, 399
memory
    available, returning amount of 303–4, 561–63, 569–70
    freeing 373
    freeing following DDE conversations 372–73
    managing when creating WLLs 1017–18
menu bar
    activating 657
    customizing 823
    displaying and hiding 870–71
MenuItemMacro$() function 654–55
MenuItemText$() function 656–57
MenuMode statement 657
menus
    activating 657
    adding 823
    adding items to 824–26
    commands, checking availability of 344–45
    customizing 818, 1028
    defaults, resetting to 824–26
    deleting items from 824–26
    displaying and hiding 870–71
    macros assigned to 654–55
    printing menu assignments 624
    removing 823
    removing items from 824–26
    renaming 714–15, 823
    renaming items on 824–26
    returning names of items on 656–57
    returning number of 358
    returning number of menu items on 357–58
    returning text of names of 657–58
    saving changes to 722
MenuText$() function 657–58

merge files *See* Mail Merge
MERGEFIELD field 598
MergeFieldName$() function 658–59
MERGEREC field 642
MERGESEQ field 643
MergeSubdocument statement 659
merging
    See also Mail Merge
    cells in tables 790–91
    revision marks 834–35
    styles 539–41
    subdocuments together in master documents 659
messages
    displaying 58–61
    displaying in message boxes 665–66
    displaying in status bar 665–66, 708–9
    error 145–48, 158–59, 897–921
    mail, in custom applications 925–67
    numbering of 158
    parameter number 147
    syntax errors 146
    type mismatch errors 147
    undefined dialog record field 147–48
    unknown command, subroutine, function 147
    Windows, sending to applications 308–9
    Word, list of 901–21
    WordBasic, list of 897–901
messaging application programming interface (MAPI) 193,
  925–67
Microsoft Access
    as a DDE server 177–79
    DDE application name for 167
    inserting data from 588–89
    starting and switching to 659
Microsoft DOS *See* MS-DOS
Microsoft Download Service (MSDL) 8
Microsoft Draw
    editing pictures 453
    embedding objects 590
Microsoft Excel
    as a DDE server 174–77
    controlling with DDE 366–68
    DDE application names for 167
    DDE channel, closing 372–73
    DDE channel, opening 368–70
    inserting data from 588–89
    inserting worksheets 591
    requesting data from 371–72
    sending data to, from Word 370–71
    starting and switching to 659
Microsoft folder 376–77
Microsoft FoxPro
    DDE application names for 167
    starting and switching to 659
Microsoft Graph, inserting charts from 586

Microsoft Mail
    communicating with 193
    sending documents via 500–502, 506
    starting and switching to 659
Microsoft PowerPoint, starting and switching to 659
Microsoft Product Support Services 7–9, 571
Microsoft Program Manager (Microsoft Windows 3.*x*), DDE
    application name for 167
Microsoft Project
    DDE application names for 167
    starting and switching to 659
Microsoft Publisher, starting and switching to 659
Microsoft Schedule+, starting and switching to 659
Microsoft Solution Providers program 9
Microsoft SystemInfo, starting and switching to 659
Microsoft Visual Basic 191–93
Microsoft Windows
    DDE application name for 167
    exiting 473
Microsoft Word
    application programming interface for *See* Word API
        (Microsoft Word Application Programming Interface)
    as a DDE server 179–82
    as an OLE Automation server 182–93
    DDE application names for 167
    examples and demonstrations, running 570
    exiting 473, 481, 500
    Help for, displaying 569, 572
    Help, instructions for using 572
    information about, returning 303–4
    initialization files 558–59, 560, 748–50
    licensed user of, returning 569–70
    ODBC extensions for 969–1001
    operating limits 1051–52
    product support information, displaying 571
    program folder 376–77
    quitting 473, 481, 500
    Tip of the Day, displaying 572
    tutorial, running 571
    version and serial number of, returning 303–4, 569–70
    Workgroup Extensions for 925–67
MicrosoftAccess statement 659
MicrosoftExcel statement 659
MicrosoftFoxPro statement 659
MicrosoftMail statement 659
MicrosoftPowerPoint statement 659
MicrosoftProject statement 659
MicrosoftPublisher statement 659
MicrosoftSchedule statement 659
MicrosoftSystemInfo statement 659
Mid$() function 660
minimizing windows 306–7, 400
minus sign (–) 48–49
Minute() function 660
minutes, extracting from times 660

mirror margins 480, 492–94
MkDir statement 660–61
MKWIZARD.WIZ 5–7, 218–27
MOD (modular division) 48–49, 890
mode, Windows 561–63
modems, product support via *See* Microsoft Download
    Service (MSDL)
modular division 48–49, 890
monitor *See* display
month
    See also dates
    30-day, computing dates based on 366
    extracting from dates 661
Month() function 661
most recently used files list 354, 484–85, 490–92
mounting volumes 661–63
MountVolume statement and function 661–63
mouse
    pointers 572, 730, 878
    recording macros with 15
    testing for presence of 303–4
MoveButton statement 663
MoveText statement 663–64
MoveToolbar statement 664
moving
    application windows 307, 310, 311
    around in dialog boxes 119
    document windows 400, 407, 408
    drawing objects backward 425, 426
    drawing objects behind text layer 426
    drawing objects forward 412
    drawing objects gridwise 430
    drawing objects horizontally 421, 422
    drawing objects in front of text layer 412
    drawing objects vertically 421, 422, 423
    files 667
    insertion point *See* insertion point, moving
    items in dialog boxes 105–9, 113
    macros 30–31
    paragraphs in outlines 689
    selections 663–64
    text 663–64 *See also* copying; deleting; pasting
    text and graphics by using the Spike 768–69
    toolbar buttons and list boxes 663
    toolbars 664
MSDL (Microsoft Download Service) 8
MS-DOS
    environment variables, returning 469–70
    version number, returning 561–63
MsgBox statement and function 58, 59–60, 154, 665–66
multilevel lists *See* lists
multiplication 48–49

N

Name statement 667
names
    application, for DDE conversations 167
    current user 849
    of AutoText entries 313–14
    of bookmarks 319–20
    of document properties 403–4
    of document variables 556
    of macros 12
    of macros, returning 629–30
    of menus and menu items 656–58, 714–15, 823, 824–26
    of styles, returning 776–77
    of toolbars 805–6
networks, connecting to 345, 661–63
newline characters, ANSI codes for 336–37
NewToolbar statement 667–68
NEXT field 643
NextCell statement and function 668
NextField statement and function 669
NEXTIF field 643
NextMisspelling() function 670
NextObject statement 670–71
NextPage statement and function 671–72
NextTab() function 672
NextWindow statement 672
nonbreaking hyphens, ANSI codes for 336–37
nonbreaking spaces, ANSI codes for 336–37
nonprinting characters
    changing to spaces 337–38
    displaying and hiding 757–58, 850–51
normal view 871
NormalFontPosition statement 672
NormalFontSpacing statement 673
NormalStyle statement 673
NormalViewHeaderArea statement 673–74
NOT logical operator 57, 58, 891–94
NoteOptions statement 674–75
not-equal-to sign (<>) 50
Now() function 676
number
    of AutoCorrect exceptions 352
    of AutoText entries 352
    of bookmarks 352–53
    of characters, words, lines, paragraphs, and pages 405–6, 506–7, 619, 859
    of custom key assignments 355, 614
    of document properties 353
    of document variables 354
    of fields in mail merge header 358–59
    of fonts available 354–55
    of global templates and add-ins 351
    of language formats available 356
    of lines 859

number (continued)
    of macros in template 356–57
    of menu items 357–58
    of menus 358
    of open windows 361
    of pages 859
    of paragraphs 859
    of styles 359
    of subfolders in a folder 353
    of toolbar buttons 359–60
    of toolbars 360
    of words 859
numbered lists
    See also lists
    adding and removing numbers 516, 531–32, 533–35, 713, 812–13, 835
    formatting numbers 516, 521–22, 531–32, 533–34, 812–13
    skipping numbers 763
    statements and functions related to, list of 267–68
    testing for numbers 534–35
numbering
    captions 585–86
    error messages 158
    footnotes and endnotes 674–75
    headings 530–31
    lines 480, 492–94, 522, 536–38
    lists See numbered lists
    pages 535–36, 600–601
    paragraphs 516, 531–32, 533–34, 812–13, 835
numbers
    adding up 781, 784–85, 813
    converting to and from strings 386–87, 625, 773, 863
    error message 158
    in lists See numbered lists
    page See page numbers
    random, generating 720
    returning sign of 753
    statements and functions related to, list of 281
    truncating 608
    using in WordBasic 44–48
numeric
    data, reading from input files 578–79, 620, 711
    data, writing to output files 708–9, 886
    equivalents of string identifiers, returning 386–87
    formats, returning from WIN.INI file 303–4
    identifiers 128
    variables 46, 382–84, 711–12

O

object linking and embedding (OLE)
    editing objects 288, 450–51
    icons for objects 347–48, 452–53

object linking and embedding (OLE) *(continued)*
   inserting objects 420, 452–53, 586, 588–89, 590,
     598–600, 601–2, 607
   link options 450–51
   object class, changing 347–48
   OLE Automation 182–93
   statements and functions related to, list of 279
   updating links 450–51
objects
   changing class (type) of 347–48
   drawing *See* drawing objects
   embedding *See* object linking and embedding (OLE)
   going to specific 448–50
   linking *See* object linking and embedding (OLE)
obtaining user input
   from forms 557–58
   with dialog box 579–80
ODBC (open database connectivity) extensions for Microsoft
  Word 969–1001
ODBCAD32.EXE 975
ODBCADM.EXE 975
OK buttons
   adding to dialog box 677
   detecting choice of 665–66
   overview 100
   value returned by 96–97
OK statement 677
OKButton statement 677
OLE *See* object linking and embedding (OLE)
On Error statement
   On Error Goto 678–79
   On Error Goto 0 160
   On Error Goto Label 159, 161, 678–79
   On Error Resume Next 159–60, 678–79
on-entry macro 213
on-exit macro 213
online forms *See* forms
online Help
   About Microsoft Word dialog box, displaying 569–70
   copying syntax and examples from 149
   displaying 569, 572
   displaying contents screen 570
   displaying for active windows or panes 570
   displaying for commands and screen elements 572
   displaying index 570
   examples and demonstrations 570
   Help on using 572
   keyboard guide 571
   on product support 7–9, 571
   searching by using keywords 571
   Tip of the Day, displaying 572
   tutorial, running 571
   WordPerfect Help, setting options for 573
OnTime statement 679–81

open database connectivity (ODBC) extensions for Microsoft
  Word 969–1001
Open statement 206–7, 681–82
opening
   annotation pane 863–64
   DDE channels 368–70
   documents 484–85, 490–92
   files 484–85, 490–92, 681–82 *See also* converting files
   files for sequential file access 206–7, 681–82
   footnote/endnote pane 865–66, 867–68, 869
   from other file formats *See* converting files
   new windows 881
   subdocuments from master documents 682
   templates 490–92
OpenSubdocument statement 682
OpenUpPara statement 682
operating limits
   Word 1051–52
   WordBasic 1051
operating system
   environment variables, returning 469–70
   returning information about 303–4, 561–63
operations
   completing 677
   repeating 454
   undoing 464
operators
   comparison 891
   logical 56–58, 891–94
   mathematical 48–49, 890
   relational 50, 891
   WordBasic 889–94
option buttons
   See also check boxes; dialog boxes, custom
   adding to custom dialog boxes 103–4, 333–34, 683
   displaying and hiding 398
   groups of 567, 683–84
   labels of, setting and changing 394–95
   overview 101
   selecting 397
optional hyphens
   ANSI codes for 336–37
   displaying and hiding 757–58, 850–51
OptionButton statement 683
OptionGroup statement 683–84
options
   See also check boxes; dialog boxes, custom; option
    buttons
   general 835–36, 842–44
   how settings affect macros 163
   print 845
   revision 846–47, 856
   save 847–48
   view 26

Options command (Tools menu) 163
Options dialog box, displaying 835–36
OR logical operator 56–57, 891–94
ordered lists *See* numbered lists
organization, returning name of user's 569–70
Organizer dialog box 30–31
Organizer statement 684–86
orientation, page 480, 485, 486, 492–94
orphans, preventing and allowing 522, 536–38, 699
OtherPane statement 686
outline character format 687
Outline statement and function 687
outline view
    displaying character formatting in 690
    switching to 871
OutlineCollapse statement 687
OutlineDemote statement 688
OutlineExpand statement 688
OutlineLevel() function 688–89
OutlineMoveDown statement 689
OutlineMoveUp statement 689
OutlinePromote statement 689–90
outlines
    collapsing 687
    converting headings to body text 379
    converting headings to subdocuments 362
    converting subdocuments to regular text 714
    demoting headings in 688
    expanding 688
    heading levels, displaying up to specific 759–60
    heading levels, returning 688–89
    hiding body text in 687, 690, 758
    moving headings and body text in 689
    promoting headings in 689–90
    statements and functions related to, list of 279–80
OutlineShowFirstLine statement and function 690
OutlineShowFormat statement 690
output
    comma-delimited, writing 886
    opening files for 681–82
    setting output point data file 724–25
    tab-delimited, writing 708–9
    writing to data files 708–9, 886
overtype mode 691, 840–41
Overtype statement and function 691

P

Page Back button *See* PrevPage statement and function
page breaks
    before paragraphs, inserting 522, 536–38, 697
    inserting 583–84, 600
    preventing 522, 536–38, 536–38, 696–97, 699
PAGE field 600–601

page layout *See* page setup
page layout view 498, 872
page numbers
    formatting 535–36
    going to specific 448–50
    inserting 600
    repaginating 853
page setup
    initializing dialog box 492–94
    options, specifying 485, 486, 492–94
PageDown statement and function 692–93
pages
    counting 405–6, 506–7, 859
    extending selection by 692–94
    going to next or previous 566, 567, 671–72, 692–94, 706–7
    going to specific 448–50
    laying out *See* page setup
    numbering 535–36, 600–601
    orientation of 480, 485, 486, 492–94, 804
    printing specific 496–97
    size of 480, 485, 486, 492–94
PageUp statement and function 693–94
panes
    activating 287
    annotation 863–64
    closing 340
    footnote and endnote 865–66, 867–68, 869
    Help on active 570
    moving insertion point to 686
    moving to other 686
    returning current 882
paper source, specifying 480, 492–94
ParaDown statement and function 694–95
Paragraph dialog box, initializing 522, 536–38
paragraph formatting
    See also character formatting; styles
    alignment, center 327, 522, 536–38
    alignment, justified 522, 536–38, 613
    alignment, left 522, 536–38, 618–19
    alignment, right 522, 536–38, 718–19
    borders *See* borders
    copying 350–51
    finding and replacing 438–41, 442, 447, 455–57, 458, 460–61
    hanging indents 536–38
    hyphenation 522, 536–38
    in lists *See* lists
    indents, first line 522, 536–38
    indents, hanging 522, 569, 860–61
    indents, left and right 522, 536–38, 578, 861
    keeping lines together 522, 536–38, 696
    keeping paragraphs together 522, 536–38, 696–97
    line numbering 522, 536–38
    line spacing 522, 536–38, 766–67

paragraph formatting *(continued)*
    page breaks before, inserting 522, 536–38, 697
    Paragraph dialog box, initializing 522, 536–38
    pasting 700
    removing nonstyle formatting from 717–18
    spacing before and after 340–41, 522, 536–38, 682
    spacing, line 536–38, 766–67
    statements and functions related to, list of 280
    styles 673, 775
    unindenting 861
    widow and orphan control 522, 536–38, 699
paragraph marks (¶)
    ANSI codes for 336–37
    displaying and hiding 757–58, 850–51
    in text files 336–37
    in Word for Windows 2.x documents 336–37
    inserting 601
paragraphs
    See also paragraph formatting
    aligning *See* paragraph formatting
    applying styles to 673
    borders *See* borders
    converting to tables 789–90, 800–801
    counting 405–6, 506–7, 859
    creating new 601
    extending selection by 694–95, 697–99
    going to next or previous 694–95, 697–99
    hyphenation in 522, 536–38
    in lists *See* lists
    indenting *See* paragraph formatting
    inserting between rows in tables 796
    keeping with next 522, 536–38, 696–97
    line numbering in 522, 536–38
    moving in outlines 689
    numbering 516, 531–32, 533–35, 812–13, 835
    page breaks before 697
    page breaks before, inserting 522, 536–38
    page breaks between 696–97
    page breaks between, preventing 522, 536–38
    page breaks within 696, 699
    page breaks within, preventing 522, 536–38
    Paragraph dialog box, initializing 522, 536–38
    removing nonstyle formatting from 716–18
    selecting by 474
    shading *See* shading
    sorting 793–95
    spacing *See* paragraph formatting
    spacing, line 767
    starting new 601
    widow and orphan lines, controlling 522, 536–38, 699
ParaKeepLinesTogether statement and function 696
ParaKeepWithNext statement and function 696–97
parameter errors 148
parameter number errors 147
ParaPageBreakBefore statement and function 697

ParaUp statement and function 697–99
ParaWidowOrphanControl statement and function 699
parentheses (( )) 43, 146, 889–90
parsing strings 607–8, 618, 660, 718
passing values between subroutines 85–88
passwords for protecting documents 490–92, 504–6, 847–48, 852, 858
PasteButtonImage statement 699–700
PasteFormat statement 700
pasting
    Clipboard contents into document 452–53
    formatting 700
    selections 452
    text and graphics 452
    toolbar button faces 699–700
PathFromMacPath$() function 700–701
PathFromWinPath$() function 701–2
paths
    add-in library, returning 547–48
    document, returning 405–6, 486–89, 506–7, 731
    Macintosh, translating for Windows 700–701
    template, returning 405–6, 506–7, 547–48, 629
    Windows, translating for the Macintosh 701–2
patterns, fill 523–25
PauseRecorder statement 702
pausing
    macro recording 702
    macros 26
pen, annotating with 804
period (.) 146
phone support *See* Microsoft Product Support Services
phonetic search criteria 438–41, 455–57
Picture statement 702–3
pictures
    See also borders; captions; frames; graphics
    converting to drawing objects 415
    copying contents as 437
    cropping 538
    cross-references to, inserting 586–87
    displaying and hiding 702–3, 850–51
    editing 453, 840–41
    formatting 538
    in dialog boxes 101, 104, 393, 398, 702–3
    inserting 601–2, 607
    linking and embedding *See* object linking and embedding (OLE)
    sizing and scaling 538
    Word Picture objects, creating 420
playing sounds and video files 288
plus sign (+) 48–49
point size 509, 510, 568, 761, 762, 857
pointers
    hourglass 878
    question mark 572
    standard and drawing, toggling 730

polygons *See* freeform drawing objects
portrait page orientation 480, 485, 486, 492–94, 804
POSITION.TXT 5–7
positioning
    document windows 407, 408
    drawing objects 523–25
    frames 520–21, 528–29
    items in dialog boxes 105–9, 113
    text and graphics 596–97 *See also herein* frames
    toolbars 664
    windows 407, 880
precedence of WordBasic operators 889–90
predefined bookmarks 63–64, 895–96
PrevCell statement and function 704
preventing
    changes to form fields 465–66
    changes to forms 852–53
    page breaks 522, 536–38, 696–97, 699
    screen updates 723
PrevField statement and function 704–5
previewing documents
    in custom dialog boxes 388–89, 396, 495
    in print preview 340, 498
PrevObject statement 705–6
PrevPage statement and function 706–7
PrevTab() function 707
PrevWindow statement 707
Print Manager, starting and switching to 721
Print Merge *See* Mail Merge
print preview 340, 498
Print statement 58–59, 155, 207, 208, 708–9
printing
    annotations 496–97
    AutoText entries 496–97
    date and time of last 405–6, 506–7
    documents 496–97
    envelopes 814–15
    key assignments 496–97
    monitoring 721
    options 845
    selecting printers 499
    shrinking documents to fit on fewer pages 857
    specifying paper source 480, 492–94
    styles 496–97
    summary information 496–97
    to files 496–97
PrintPreview *See* FilePrintPreview statement and function
private initialization files (.INI) 806–7
product support *See* Microsoft Product Support Services
profiles, startup *See* initialization files
Program Manager (Microsoft Windows 3.*x*), DDE application name for 167
Project, Microsoft, DDE application names for 167
PromoteList statement 709

promoting
    headings in outlines 689–90
    list items in multilevel lists 709
prompting
    for user input 61, 578–80, 620
    for user response with message box 60, 579–80, 665–66
    Save changes? prompt 743, 752–53
proofing documents
    See also spelling checking; grammar checking
    statements and functions related to, list of 280–81
properties
    changing form field 542–44
    document 203–5
    file 551, 741–42
protecting
    documents 405, 504–6, 610–11, 624–25, 741–42, 847–48, 852
    fields 624–25, 861, 862
    form fields 465–66
    forms 405, 852–53
    macros 610–11
    master documents and subdocuments 624
    sections 852–53
publisher, creating 437–38
Publishing and subscribing
    EditCreatePublisher statement 437–38
    EditPublishOptions statement 454
    EditSubscribeOptions statement 462
    EditSubscribeTo statement 463
push buttons 100, 121, 135–36 *See also* command buttons; dialog boxes, custom; option buttons
PushButton statement 709–10
PutFieldData statement 710

Q

question mark pointer 572
questions, asking user, with message box 579–80, 665–66
Quick Preview tutorial, running 571
QuickDraw GX
    FileMacCustomPageSetupGX statement 485
    FileMacPageSetupGX statement 486
    FilePrintOneCopy statement 497
quitting
    applications 301, 473
    Microsoft Windows 473
    Microsoft Word 481, 500
quotation marks (" ")
    ANSI codes for 336–37
    enclosing strings in 44, 45, 146
    in arguments 42
    inserting in field codes 591
    straight and curved, toggling 807–8, 811

R

radio buttons *See* option buttons
raising characters 526–28, 672 *See also* character formatting; superscripts
random numbers, generating 720
Read statement 209, 711
reading from files 208–10
read-only files 490–92, 504–6, 551, 741–42, 847–48
    See also protecting
REC (recording) 15
Record Next Command button 26, 148–49
recording
    macros 11–15, 26, 702, 833–34
    sounds 602
records
    dialog *See* dialog records
    for storing values in dialog boxes 117
rectangles
    drawing 423, 424
    formatting 523–25
    testing for 419–20
ReDim statement 711–12
redoing operations 454
refreshing the screen
    updating entire screen 722, 723
    updating file preview boxes 396
registry
    defining settings in 200, 748–50
    returning values from 200, 558–59
relational operators 50
REM statement 41–42, 712–13
remarks *See* comments
RemoveAllDropDownItems statement 713
RemoveBulletsNumbers statement 713
RemoveDropDownItem statement 713–14
RemoveFrames statement 714
RemoveSubdocument statement 714
removing
    borders on paragraphs and tables 323
    bullets from bulleted lists 713
    character formatting 716–17
    folders 719–20
    frames 520–21, 528–29, 714
    items from drop-down form fields 713–14
    menu items 824–26
    menus 823
    numbers from numbered lists 713
    paragraph formatting 717–18
    protection from documents 858
    spaces from strings 625, 720
RenameMenu statement 714–15
renaming
    AutoText entries 684–86
    documents 504–6, 667

renaming *(continued)*
    files 667
    macros 30–31, 684–86
    menu items 824–26
    menus 714–15, 823
    styles 539–41, 684–86
    toolbars 684–86
repaginating 853
RepeatFind statement 715
repeating
    characters 774–75
    last editing operation 454
    last find operation 715
    last go to operation 715
replacing
    formatting 455–59, 460–61
    search operators and options 455–57
    styles 455–57, 461
    text 455–57, 807–8, 810
requesting data from other applications 171–72, 371–72
requesting information in DDE conversations 171–72
ResetButtonImage statement 716
ResetChar statement and function 716–17
ResetNoteSepOrNotice statement 717
ResetPara statement and function 717–18
resizing
    application windows 309–10, 311
    callouts 426–27
    dialog boxes 109
    frames 520–21, 528–29
    items in dialog boxes 106–9
    toolbars 762
resolution, display, returning 561–63
restoring
    applications 305–8
    modified Word commands 34–35
    windows 305–8, 400–401
resuming macro recording 702
retrieving
    electronic mail messages 193
    values from dialog boxes 121–23
revision marks
    accepting or rejecting revisions 853–54, 856
    author, returning 854–55
    date and time of, returning 855
    finding 853–54
    formatting 846–47
    merging 834–35
    options 846–47, 856
    protecting documents using 405, 852
    type of, returning 856–57
    unprotecting documents protected for 858
revision, number of and date of last 405–6, 506–7
ribbon *See* Formatting toolbar, hiding and displaying
Right$() function 718

right-aligning paragraphs 522, 536–38, 718–19
right-alignment tab stops 448, 462, 522–23, 541–42, 797–98
RightPara statement and function 718–19
RmDir statement 719–20
Rnd() function 720
rotating drawing objects 424
rounded rectangles 424
routing documents 500–502
rows
    converting to normal text 796–97
    deleting 784
    formatting 791–92
    inserting 788–89
    merging cells in 790–91
    selecting 468, 771–72, 793
    sorting 793–95
RTrim$() function 720
rulers, displaying and hiding 850–51, 872–73
running
    Clipboard 346
    Control Panel 346
    Dialog Editor 382
    macros 16–18, 23–24, 90, 833–34
    Print Manager 721
    Windows-based applications 756–57
RunPrintManager statement 721

S

sample files 5–7
Save Copy As command 30
Save Template command 30
saved flag 609–10, 611–12, 743, 752–53
SaveTemplate statement 722
saving
    See also storing
    dirty flag, setting and testing 609–10, 611–12, 743, 752–53
    documents 504–6, 609–10, 743, 847–48
    macros 26–30, 722
    options 847–48
    templates 504, 722, 752–53
    to other file formats *See* converting files
scaling graphics 538
screen
    Help for screen elements, displaying 572
    information about, returning 303–4, 561–63
    refreshing 396, 722, 723
ScreenRefresh statement 722
ScreenUpdating statement and function 723
scripts
    See also AppleScript
    recording 1048
    running from WordBasic 631, 1050

scripts *(continued)*
    techniques for writing 1038–39
    using to send WordBasic instructions 1049–50
scroll bars, displaying and hiding 850–51
scrolling
    horizontally 575, 576, 575
    to a specific place 448–50
    vertically 671–72, 692–95, 697–99, 706–7, 876–77
search operators and options
    finding 438–41
    replacing 455–57
searching
    See also finding
    online Help by using keywords 571
Second() function 724
seconds, extracting from times 724
sections
    breaks between 480, 492–94, 583–84, 602
    formatting 518–19, 529, 535–36, 539, 804
    formatting, statements and functions related to, list of 281
    going to next or previous 566, 567
    going to specific 448–50
    page setup for, specifying 480, 485, 486, 492–94
    protecting from changes 852–53
    selecting by 474
Seek statement and function 212, 724–25
Select Case statement 74–75, 725–26
SelectCurAlignment statement 727
SelectCurColor statement 727
SelectCurFont statement 727–28
SelectCurIndent statement 728
SelectCurSentence statement 728
SelectCurSpacing statement 729
SelectCurTabs statement 729
SelectCurWord statement 729–30
SelectDrawingObjects statement 730
selecting
    See also deselecting drawing objects; extending selections; selections
    between two character positions 751
    by characters 329–31, 474
    by columns 343, 466, 769–70
    by lines 467–68, 620–21, 622, 771
    by pages 692–93
    by paragraphs 694–95, 697–99
    by rows 468, 771–72
    by sections 474
    by sentences 474, 739–41
    by table cells 668, 704
    by windows 469, 772
    by words 474, 840–41, 883, 884–85
    check boxes and option buttons 397
    columns in tables 792
    drawing objects 415, 424–25, 730

selecting *(continued)*
ending selection 325–26
entire document 462, 474
fields 669, 704–5
printers 499
rows in tables 793
sentences 728, 739–41
statements and functions related to, list of 278–79
tables 793
to the beginning of a document 770
to the end of a document 467
words 729–30
Selection$() function 65, 730
SelectionFileName$() function 731
selections
adding to the Spike 768–69
appearance of, changing 735
beginning of, returning 561
canceling 325–26
copying 351, 437
cutting to Clipboard 438
deleting 435–36, 438
end of, returning 560–61
extend mode, testing for 473
extending *See* extending selections
information about, returning 731–35
moving 663–64
moving by using the Spike 603
pasting 452
reducing by progressive increments 762
returning 563–64, 730
setting bookmarks for 434–35, 746–47, 752
shrinking 762
SelInfo() function 64, 162, 731–35
SelType statement and function 162, 735
sending
commands to other applications via DDE 173–74,
366–68
documents via electronic mail 500–502, 506
electronic mail messages 193
information in DDE conversations 172–73
Windows messages to applications 308–9
WordBasic instructions by using OLE Automation
182–93
SendKeys statement 736–38
sentences, selecting 474, 728, 739–41
sentence-style capitalization 327–28, 807–8, 811
SentLeft statement and function 739–40
SentRight statement and function 740–41
separator characters 303–4, 475
sequential access files
closing 339–40
end of file, detecting 470
opening 681–82
reading from 578–79, 620, 711

sequential access files *(continued)*
setting file pointer in 724–25
size of, returning 625
using 205–12
writing to 708–9, 886
serial number of Word, returning 569–70
serial numbers, date and time *See* dates; time
servers 166
services, support *See* Microsoft Product Support Services
SET field 643–44
SetAttr statement 741–42
SetAutoText statement 205, 742–43
SetDocumentDirty statement 743
SetDocumentProperty statement 203–5, 744–45
SetDocumentPropertyLink statement 745
SetDocumentVar statement and function 201–3, 746
SetEndOfBookmark statement 746–47
SetFileCreatorAndType statement 747
SetFormResult statement 747–48
SetPrivateProfileString statement and function 196, 748–50
SetProfileString statement 750–51
SetSelRange statement 751
SetStartOfBookmark statement 752
SetTemplateDirty statement 752–53
setting
drawing range 429
tab stops 522–23, 541–42
settings files
using 196–99
WIN.INI 199, 806–7
WINWORD6.INI 199, 806–7
Word Settings (6) 199
Sgn() function 753
shading
borders 442, 457–58, 512–14
form fields 544–45
specifying in styles 519–20
table 780–81, 797
ShadingPattern statement and function 753–55
shadow character format 755
Shadow statement and function 755
sharing
information with other applications 165–93
variables 84–88, 382–84, 711–12
Shell statement 169–70, 756–57
SHIFT+DOWN ARROW key combination *See* LineDown
statement and function
SHIFT+UP ARROW key combination *See* LineUp statement
and function
shortcut keys *See* keys
shortcut menus *See* menus
Show Variables button 152–53
ShowAll statement and function 757–58
ShowAllHeadings statement 758
ShowAnnotationBy statement 759

ShowClipboard statement 759
ShowHeadingNumber statement 759–60
showing *See* displaying
ShowMe statement 760
ShowNextHeaderFooter statement 760
ShowPrevHeaderFooter statement 760
ShowVars statement 154, 761
ShrinkFont statement 761
ShrinkFontOnePoint statement 762
ShrinkSelection statement 762
sign of numbers, returning 753
signatures, application 479, 626–27, 747
single underline character format 860, 885
size
    font 510, 568, 761, 762, 857
    of dialog boxes 109
    of documents 405–6, 506–7
    of files, returning 625
    of frames 520–21, 528–29
    of graphics 538
    of items in dialog boxes 106–9
    of tables 780–81, 797
    of toolbars 762
    of windows, changing 309–10, 311, 401, 407, 408
    of windows, returning 310, 311, 407, 408
SizeToolbar statement 762
SKIPIF field 644
SkipNumbering statement and function 763
slash (/) 48–49
small caps
    character format 443–44, 458–59, 520, 526–28, 763–64
    use of, in this manual xvi
SmallCaps statement and function 763–64
smart quotes 807–8, 811
snap-to-grid option 430
Solution Providers program, Microsoft 9
SortArray statement 764–66
sorting 764–66, 793–95
Sound Recorder objects, inserting 602
sounds
    beep 315–16
    inserting and recording 602
    playing 288
space characters, ANSI codes for 336–37
space marks, displaying and hiding 757–58, 850–51
SpacePara1 statement and function 766–67
SpacePara15 statement and function 767
SpacePara2 statement and function 767
spacing
    before and after paragraphs 340–41, 522, 536–38, 682
    between characters 520, 526–28, 673
    between columns in tables 782–83
    between paragraphs 522, 536–38
    between rows in tables 791–92
    between text columns 518–19

spacing *(continued)*
    kerning, font 520, 526–28, 673
    line 522, 536–38, 766–67
special characters
    changing to spaces 337–38
    field ({ }) 592
    inserting 580–81, 603–4, 779
    sending to applications 736–38
SpellChecked statement and function 768
spelling checking
    automatic 402, 670, 768, 857
    during grammar checking 844
    setting options 848–49
    specifying dictionaries 848–49
    starting 857, 858
    suggested replacements, returning 827–28
Spike AutoText entries 603, 768–69
Spike statement 768–69
SplitSubdocument statement 769
splitting
    document windows 401–2
    table cells 796
    tables 791–92, 796
SQL (structured query language), accessing databases
  by using 588–89, 970–73
SQLClose function 977, 982
SQLCloseAll function 977, 982–83
SQLCountErrors function 977, 983
SQLErrorClass$ function 983–84
SQLErrorCode function 984
SQLErrorFlush function 984
SQLErrorText$ function 977, 984–85
SQLExecQuery function 977, 985–86
SQLGetSchema function 977, 987–89
SQLGetSchemaItem$ function 977, 989
SQLGetTypeInfo$ function 973, 989–90
SQLOpen function 975, 977, 990–91
SQLQueryExec function 977, 991–93
SQLQueryFetch function 993–94
SQLQueryRetrieve function 994–95
SQLRetrieveColSize function 996
SQLRetrieveColumns function 997
SQLRetrieveFlush function 997
SQLRetrieveItem$ function 998
SQLRetrieveRows function 998–99
SQLRetrieveToDocument function 999
SQLSetRowPos function 1000–1001
SQLSynchronize function 1001
square brackets ([ ]), use of, in this manual xvi, 285–86
star (*) 48–49
start of document, checking for 312
Starter Wizard 218–27
STARTER WIZARD template 5–7
STARTER.WIZ 5–7, 218–27

starting
batch or executable files 756–57
DDE conversations 168–71
Dialog Editor 102, 382
Microsoft applications 659
Windows-based applications 756–57
StartOfColumn statement and function 769–70
StartOfDocument statement and function 770
StartOfLine statement and function 771
StartOfRow statement and function 771–72
StartOfWindow statement and function 772
Startup folder, using to load a WLL 1007
startup profiles *See* initialization files
StartWizard macro 219–21
statements
conditional 49–58, 74–75
debugging 154–55
error handling 159–62
lists of 265–84
loop 49
used in dialog functions 142–43
statistics, document 405–6, 506–7
status bar
displaying and hiding 850–51, 873
displaying help for form fields in 542–44, 594–96
displaying messages in 58–59, 665–66, 708–9
prompting for user input 620
Step button 151–52
Step Subs button 152
stepping through macros 151–52
Stop statement 154, 773
stopping
See also closing; terminating
DDE conversations 174
macro recording 702
macros 26, 154, 385, 773
storing
See also saving
dialog box settings 140–41
values of Word dialog box controls 554
Str$() function 773
straight quotes 807–8, 811
strikethrough character format 443–44, 458–59, 520, 526–28, 774
Strikethrough statement and function 774
string concatenation operator 891
string identifiers of dialog box controls, numeric equivalents, returning 386–87
string variables 46
String$() function 774–75
strings
changing case of 618, 860
comparing 51
converting to and from numbers 386–87, 625, 773, 863
finding 607–8

strings *(continued)*
length of 619
nonprinting and special characters in, changing to spaces 337–38
parsing 607–8, 618, 660, 718
passing with the Word API 1018
reading from input files 578–79, 620, 711
removing spaces from 625, 720
statements and functions related to, list of 281
translating to OEM character set 882
translating to Windows character set 409
user-input, prompting for 579–80
user-input, returning from forms 557–58
using in WordBasic 44–48
variables, defining 711–12
structured query language (SQL), accessing databases by using 588–89, 970–73
Style area, displaying and hiding 850–51
Style statement 775
StyleDesc$() function 775
StyleName$() function 776–77
styles
adding to templates 539–41
applying 673, 775
assigning to menus, shortcut keys, toolbar buttons 292–93, 818–22, 824–26
border and shading formats 519–20
character formats 520
copying 541, 684–86
creating 539–41, 539–41
deleting 539–41, 684–86
finding and replacing 438–41, 442, 447–48, 455–57, 458, 461
formatting instructions, returning 775
frame formats 520–21
in macro-editing windows 25
language formats 521
merging from template or document 539–41
names of, returning 776–77
Normal 673
number of, returning 359
numbering formats 521–22
paragraph formatting 522
printing 496–97
removing nonstyle formatting 716–18
renaming 539–41, 684–86
saving 722
statements and functions related to, list of 282
tab settings for 522–23
Sub...End Sub statement 777–78
subdocuments
See also master documents
creating from outline headings 362
going to next or previous 566, 567
inserting in master documents 603

subdocuments *(continued)*
    merging into document 659
    opening from master document 682
    splitting 769
subfolders *See* folders
subroutines 82–83, 84–91, 325, 777–78
subscribing, to an edition 462, 463
Subscript statement and function 778
subscripts 78, 443–44, 458–59, 520, 526–28, 778
substituting fonts in documents 510
subtraction 48–49
summary information 496–97, 506–7, 847–48
summing numbers 781, 784–85, 813
Superscript statement and function 779
superscripts 443–44, 458–59, 520, 526–28, 672, 779
support services *See* Microsoft Product Support Services
switching
    to a Microsoft application 659
    to outline view 871
SymbolFont statement 779
symbols
    assigning to shortcut keys 818–22
    finding and replacing 438–41, 455–57
    inserting 603–4, 779
synonyms, finding 828–29, 858
syntax
    conventions for statements and functions 285–86
    copying from Help 149
    errors 146
system
    files 551, 741–42
    information, returning 303–4, 561–63
    resources 372–73
System topic 168

T

TA field 604, 652–53
tab characters, displaying and hiding 757–58, 850–51
tab order of dialog box elements 316–18
tab stops
    clearing 522–23, 541–42
    finding 672, 707
    leader characters 522–23, 541–42, 780
    returning position of next or previous 672, 707
    setting 522–23, 541–42
    type of, returning 797–98
tab-delimited output, writing 708–9
TabLeader$() function 780
TableAutoFormat statement 780–81
TableAutoSum statement 781
TableColumnWidth statement 782–83
TableDeleteCells statement 783
TableDeleteColumn statement 784

TableDeleteRow statement 784
TableFormula statement 784–85
TableGridlines statement and function 786
TableHeadings statement and function 786–87
TableInsertCells statement 787–88
TableInsertColumn statement 788
TableInsertRow statement 788–89
TableInsertTable statement 789–90
TableMergeCells statement 790–91
TableRowHeight statement 791–92
tables
    aligning rows in 791–92
    borders *See* borders
    captions *See* captions
    column width in 782–83
    converting to text 796–97
    creating 475, 789–90, 800–801
    cross-references to, inserting 586–87
    deleting cells, columns, rows in 783, 784
    formatting 780–81, 782–83, 786–87, 789–90, 791–92, 797, 800–801
    going to specific 448–50
    gridlines, displaying and hiding 786
    heading rows in 786–87
    indenting rows in 791–92
    inserting cells in 787–88
    inserting columns in 788
    inserting paragraphs between rows 796
    inserting rows in 788–89
    merging cells in 790–91
    moving insertion point in 466, 468, 668, 670–71, 704, 705–6, 769–70, 771–72
    of authorities *See* tables of authorities
    of captions *See* tables of figures
    of contents *See* tables of contents
    of figures *See* tables of figures
    of tables *See* tables of figures
    selecting 793
    selecting in 466, 468, 668, 704, 769–70, 771–72, 792, 793
    size of 780–81, 797
    sorting in 793–95
    spacing between columns in 782–83
    splitting 791–92, 796
    splitting cells in 796
    statements and functions related to, list of 282
    summation in 781, 784–85
    tables of *See* tables of figures
tables of authorities
    changing names of citation categories 464
    creating 604
    marking citations for inclusion in 652–53
tables of contents
    creating 605–6
    entries, marking text as 654

tables of figures 606–7
TableSelectColumn statement 792
TableSelectRow statement 793
TableSelectTable statement 793
TableSort statement 793–95
TableSortAToZ statement 795
TableSortZToA statement 795
TableSplit statement 796
TableSplitCells statement 796
TableToText statement 796–97
TableUpdateAutoFormat statement 797
tabs *See* tab stops
TabType() function 797–98
TC field 605–6, 654
technical support *See* Microsoft Product Support Services
telephone numbers
    Microsoft Download Service 8
    Microsoft Product Support Services 7–9
telephone support *See* Microsoft Product Support Services
templates
    attaching 508
    AutoText entries in 313–14, 352, 553, 583
    copying elements between 628, 684–86
    creating 489, 504–6
    default folders for 332, 376–77, 841–42
    detecting if saved 611–12, 752–53
    for wizards 219
    global, adding to list 288–89
    global, creating 28–29
    global, deleting from list 338–39, 377
    global, loading and unloading 288–89, 294, 338–39
    global, returning number in list 351
    global, returning paths and filenames 547–48
    global, returning position in list 547
    opening 490–92
    paths of, returning 405–6, 506–7, 629
    saving 504–6, 722, 752–53
    saving macros to 26–29
    statements and functions related to, list of 270–71
    styles in, counting 359
    WBODBC.DOT 976
terminating
    See also closing; stopping
    DDE conversations 174
TEST.MDB database 976
text
    See also editing; text form fields
    adding to drawing layer 430
    adding to the Spike 768–69
    aligning *See* aligning; tab stops
    between two points, returning 563–64
    between two points, selecting 751
    bookmarked, returning 553
    boxes *See* text boxes
    color *See* character formatting; color

text *(continued)*
    comparing two bookmarked sections 341–43
    converting table rows to 796–97
    converting to tables 475, 789–90, 800–801
    copying 351, 437
    deleting 377, 378–79, 435–36, 438
    finding 438–41
    frames *See* frames
    hidden 520, 526–28, 573–74
    hyphenating 522, 536–38, 830, 831
    in dialog boxes 110–11, 394–95, 798–800 *See also*
        dialog boxes, custom
    indenting *See* paragraph formatting
    inserting 580–81
    inserting from other files 592–93
    inserting into documents 62
    inserting, with the Spike 603
    linking and embedding from other files *See* object linking
        and embedding (OLE)
    moving 603, 663–64, 768–69
    moving in outlines 689
    of AutoText entries, assigning 742–43
    of AutoText entries, inserting 313, 583
    of AutoText entries, returning 553
    opening files for input/output 681–82
    overtyping 691, 840–41
    pasting 452–53
    reading from input files 578–79, 620, 711
    replacing 455–57, 807–8, 810
    requesting from other applications 371–72
    returning 64–65
    returning from dialog box controls 394–95
    scrolling *See* scrolling
    selecting *See* selecting; selections
    sending to other applications via DDE 370–71
    setting bookmarks in 434–35
    size *See* character formatting
    special characters 779
    user input, prompting for 579–80
    wrapping 850–51
    writing to output files 708–9, 886
text boxes
    See also combo boxes; dialog boxes, custom; text form
        fields
    adding to custom dialog boxes 105, 799–800
    contents of, setting and returning 118–19, 121, 394–95
    creating on drawing layer 430
    formatting 523–25
    in dynamic dialog boxes 136–37
    moving insertion point to 427–28
    overview 101
    testing for 419–20
text files
    See also sequential access files
    opening 681–82

text form fields
    adding to forms 594–96, 800
    formatting 542–44
    returning contents of 557–58
    setting result and default value 747–48
text layer 804
Text statement 798–99
TextBox statement 799–800
TextFormField statement 800
TextToTable statement 800–801
The Microsoft Network, product support via 8, 571
thesaurus, displaying 858
time
    See also dates
    converting from serial number 801
    converting to serial number 801–2
    current 676, 801
    executing macro at a specific time 679–81
    format 589–90, 801
    formats, returning from WIN.INI file 303–4
    hour, extracting from 575
    inserting 589–90, 607
    minutes, extracting from 660
    of last printing or revision 405–6, 506–7
    seconds, extracting from 724
    statements and functions related to, list of 269
TIME field 589–90, 607
Time$() function 801
timer 679–81
TimeSerial() function 801–2
TimeValue() function 802
Tip of the Day dialog box, displaying 572
TipWizard statement 803
TOA field 604
TOC field 605–6
Today() function 803
ToggleFieldDisplay statement 803
ToggleFull statement 804
ToggleHeaderFooterLink statement 804
ToggleMainTextLayer statement 804
TogglePortrait statement 804
ToggleScribbleMode statement 804
toolbar buttons
    adding 292–93
    assignments, returning 805
    deleting 378
    displaying Help for 572
    editing face image 334–36, 349, 435, 699–700, 716
    enlarging 874
    moving 663
    resetting button image to default 716
ToolbarButtonMacro$() function 805
ToolbarName$() function 805–6

toolbars
    adding buttons to 292–93
    Borders 864
    buttons See toolbar buttons
    copying 684–86
    creating 667–68
    customizing See customizing toolbars
    deleting 684–86
    displaying and hiding 806, 874
    displaying Help for 572
    Drawing 865
    Formatting 872
    Header And Footer 867, 870
    list boxes See toolbar buttons
    Macro 22–23, 150
    moving 664
    number of, returning 360
    renaming 684–86
    resetting to default 874
    resizing 762
    saving changes to 722
    toolbar names, returning 805–6
ToolbarState() function 806
ToolsAddRecordDefault statement 806
ToolsAdvancedSettings statement 806–7
ToolsAutoCorrect statement 807–8
ToolsAutoCorrectCapsLockOff statement and function 808–9
ToolsAutoCorrectDays statement and function 809
ToolsAutoCorrectExceptions statement 809–10
ToolsAutoCorrectInitialCaps statement and function 810
ToolsAutoCorrectReplaceText statement and function 810
ToolsAutoCorrectSentenceCaps statement and function 811
ToolsAutoCorrectSmartQuotes statement and function 811
ToolsBulletListDefault statement 811
ToolsBulletsNumbers statement 812–13
ToolsCalculate statement and function 813
ToolsCompareVersions statement 813–14
ToolsCreateEnvelope statement 814–15
ToolsCreateLabels statement 816–17
ToolsCustomize statement 818
ToolsCustomizeKeyboard statement 818–22
ToolsCustomizeMenuBar statement 823
ToolsCustomizeMenus statement 824–26
ToolsGetSpelling statement and function 827–28
ToolsGetSynonyms statement and function 828–29
ToolsGrammar statement 829
ToolsGrammarStatisticsArray statement 829–30
ToolsHyphenation statement 830
ToolsHyphenationManual statement 831
ToolsLanguage statement 831–32
ToolsMacro statement 833–34
ToolsManageFields statement 834
ToolsMergeRevisions statement 834–35
ToolsNumberListDefault statement 835

ToolsOptions statement 835–36
ToolsOptionsAutoFormat statement 836–38
ToolsOptionsCompatibility statement 838–40
ToolsOptionsEdit statement 840–41
ToolsOptionsFileLocations statement 841–42
ToolsOptionsGeneral statement 842–44
ToolsOptionsGrammar statement 844
ToolsOptionsPrint statement 845
ToolsOptionsRevisions statement 846–47
ToolsOptionsSave statement 847–48
ToolsOptionsSpelling statement 848–49
ToolsOptionsUserInfo statement 849
ToolsOptionsView statement 850–51
ToolsProtectDocument statement 852
ToolsProtectSection statement 852–53
ToolsRemoveRecordDefault statement 853
ToolsRepaginate statement 853
ToolsReviewRevisions statement 853–54
ToolsRevisionAuthor$( ) function 854–55
ToolsRevisionDate$() function 855
ToolsRevisionDate() function 855
ToolsRevisions statement 856
ToolsRevisionType() function 856–57
ToolsShrinkToFit statement 857
ToolsSpelling statement 857
ToolsSpellingRecheckDocument statement 857
ToolsSpellSelection statement 858
ToolsThesaurus statement 858
ToolsUnprotectDocument statement 858
ToolsWordCount 859
ToolTips 874
topics for DDE conversations 167–68
Trace button 150–51
tracing through macros 150–51
training services from Microsoft 9
trapping errors 157–62, 678–79
Trash folder 376–77
troubleshooting See Help; Microsoft Product Support
    Services
true comparisons 892–94
true, value of 52
truncating decimals 608
tutorial 571
type mismatch errors 147
typing over text 691, 840–41
typographic conventions xvi, 285–86

U

UCase$() function 860
undefined dialog record field errors 147–48
underline character format 409–10, 443–44, 458–59, 520,
    526–28, 860, 885
Underline statement and function 860

undoing actions 15, 454, 464
ungrouping drawing objects 431
UnHang statement 860–61
UnIndent statement 861
unindenting paragraphs 861
unknown command, subroutine, function errors 147
UnlinkFields statement 861
unlinking fields 861
UnlockFields statement 862
unlocking
    documents from changes 858
    fields 862
    forms from changes 858
    links 450–51
unprotecting
    documents 405, 858
    fields 862
    form fields 465–66
    forms 405, 858
    links 450–51
unselecting See deselecting
UP ARROW key See LineUp statement and function
UpdateFields statement 862
UpdateSource statement 862
updating
    fields 624–25, 861, 862
    file preview boxes in custom dialog boxes 396
    included documents 862
    links 450–51
    screen 722, 723
    text in dialog boxes continuously 140–41
uppercase
    changing to and from 327–28
    character format 295, 518, 520, 526–28, 763–64
    converting strings to 860
    testing for 327–28
    use of, in this manual xvi
user dialog boxes See dialog boxes, custom
user information, changing 849
user input
    prompting for 578–80, 620
    requesting 58–61
    returning, from forms 557–58
user, returning name of licensed 569–70
user-defined functions 82, 83–91, 545–46

V

Val() function 863
values
    absolute 287
    argument 20
    of variables, displaying 761
    passing between subroutines 85–88

variables
    array 77–81 *See also* arrays
    assigning values 619
    changing values of 152–53
    dialog record 91–97
    document 201–3, 354, 556, 746
    Err 161
    shared, defining 711–12
    sharing 84–88, 382–84
    viewing values of 152–53, 154, 155, 761
version number of Word, returning 303–4, 569–70
vertical ruler, displaying and hiding 872–73
vertical scroll bar
    displaying and hiding 850–51
    macro equivalents of using 671–72, 692–94, 706–7,
        876–77
vertically, flipping drawing objects 416
video file, playing 288
View options 26
ViewAnnotations statement and function 863–64
ViewBorderToolbar statement 864
ViewDraft statement and function 864–65
ViewDrawingToolbar statement 865
ViewEndnoteArea statement and function 865–66
ViewEndnoteContNotice statement 866
ViewEndnoteContSeparator statement 866
ViewEndnoteSeparator statement 866
ViewFieldCodes statement and function 866–67
ViewFooter statement and function 867
ViewFootnoteArea statement and function 867–68
ViewFootnoteContNotice statement 868
ViewFootnoteContSeparator statement 868
ViewFootnotes statement and function 869
ViewFootnoteSeparator statement 869
ViewHeader statement and function 870
ViewMasterDocument statement and function 870
ViewMenus() function 870–71
ViewNormal statement and function 871
ViewOutline statement and function 871
ViewPage statement and function 872
ViewRibbon statement and function 872
ViewRuler statement and function 872–73
views
    closing 340, 354
    draft 864–65
    full screen 804
    header/footer 354, 760, 867, 870
    Help on active 570
    master document 870, 873
    normal 871
    outline 871
    page layout 498, 872
    print preview 340, 498
    statements and functions related to, list of 283–84
ViewStatusBar statement and function 873

ViewToggleMasterDocument statement 873
ViewToolbars statement 874
ViewZoom statement 874–75
ViewZoom100 statement 875
ViewZoom200 statement 875
ViewZoom75 statement 875
ViewZoomPageWidth statement 876
ViewZoomWholePage statement 876
Visual Basic 191–93
VLine statement 876
volumes, mounting 661–63
VPage statement 876–77
VScroll statement and function 877

W

WaitCursor statement 878
WBMAPI.DLL 193, 926–27
WBMAPI.DOT template 926
WBODBC.DOT 976
WBODBC.WLL 971, 973, 976
WBTYPE.TXT 1015
wdAddCommand command (Word API) 1030
wdAutoOpen function (Word API) 1005–6
wdAutoRemove function (Word API) 1005–6
wdCaptureKeyDown command (Word API) 1032
wdCloseWindow command (Word API) 1032
wdCommandDispatch function (Word API) 1008–13
wdGetHwnd command (Word API) 1031
wdGetInst command (Word API) 1031
wdOpenWindow command (Word API) 1031–32
WDOPR (Word operator data structure)
    See also Word API (Microsoft Word Application
        Programming Interface)
    arrays, passing 1016–17
    building with CAPILIB 1025–26
    overview of 1013
    parts of 1014–16
    strings, passing 1018
    type definition of 1013
wdPrint command (Word API) 1030
wdReleaseKeyDown command (Word API) 1032
wdSetTimer command (Word API) 1031
Weekday() function 878
weekday, extracting from date 878
While loop 55–56
While...Wend statement 879
widows, preventing and allowing 522, 536–38, 699
width
    dialog box, specifying 316–18
    drawing object 523–25
    frame 520–21, 528–29
    graphics 538
    of application windows 309–10, 311

width *(continued)*
    of columns in tables 782–83
    page 480, 485, 486, 492–94
    text column 518–19
    window 408
WIN.INI file
    international settings in, returning 303–4, 561–63
    modifying settings in 806–7
    overview 199
    returning settings from 558–59, 560, 748–51
WIN16API.TXT 6
WIN32API.TXT 6
Window() function 880
WindowArrangeAll statement 880
WindowList statement 880–81
WindowName$() function 881
WindowNewWindow statement 881
WindowNumber statement 881
WindowPane() function 882
windows
    activating 287, 299–300, 305–8, 672, 707, 880–81
    arranging 880
    closing 399, 477, 478
    current pane, returning 882
    height of 309–10, 311, 407
    Help on active 570
    hidden, displaying 309
    hiding 302
    information about, returning 303–4
    listing open window names 302
    macro, detecting 611
    macro-editing 19–26
    maximizing 305–6, 399
    minimizing 306–7, 400
    moving 307, 310, 311, 400
    open, returning number of 361
    opening multiple, for active document 881
    position of, returning 310, 311
    positioning 407, 408, 880
    restoring 305–8, 400–401
    returning identifiers of 880, 881
    scrolling in *See* scrolling
    selecting to beginning or end of 469, 772
    sizing 401, 407, 408
    splitting 401–2
    statements and functions related to, list of 284
    testing if minimized or maximized 305–7
    testing if restored 307–8
    width of, changing 309–10
Windows paths and filenames, translating for the Macintosh 701–2
Windows, Microsoft
    character set 409, 882
    DDE application name for 167
    differences between the Macintosh and 253–63

Windows, Microsoft *(continued)*
    exiting 473
    messages, sending to applications 308–9
    mode, returning 561–63
    quitting 473
    version number, returning 303–4, 561–63
WinToDos$() function 882
WINWORD6.INI file 199, 558–59, 560, 750–51, 806–7
WIZ! file type 219
WIZARD MAKER wizard 5–7, 218–27
wizards
    creating 218–27
    loading values in 391–92
    running 489
    sample 5–7
    storing values for 394
WLLs (Word add-in libraries)
    See also Word API (Microsoft Word Application Programming Interface)
    adding functions to menus 1028
    adding functions to shortcut keys 1028
    adding functions to toolbars 1028
    calling routines in 228–34
    converting declarations 233–34
    list of, adding to 288–89
    list of, deleting from 338–39, 377
    list of, returning number in 351
    list of, returning position in 547
    loading and unloading 288–89, 294, 338–39, 1007–8
    making functions available to macros 373–76, 1028
    overview of 1005–6
    statements and functions related to, list of 270–71
    WBODBC.WLL 971, 973, 976
Word
    application programming interface for *See* Word API (Microsoft Word Application Programming Interface)
    as a DDE server 179–82
    as an OLE Automation server 182–93
    DDE application names for 167
    initialization files 558–59, 560, 748–51
    ODBC extensions for 969–1001
    operating limits 1051–52
    Workgroup Extensions for 925–67
Word add-in libraries (WLLs)
    See also Word API (Microsoft Word Application Programming Interface)
    adding functions to menus 1028
    adding functions to shortcut keys 1028
    adding functions to toolbars 1028
    calling routines in 228–34
    converting declarations 233–34
    list of, adding to 288–89
    list of, deleting from 338–39, 377
    list of, returning number in 351
    list of, returning position in 547

Word add-in libraries (WLLs) *(continued)*
    loading and unloading 288–89, 294, 338–39, 1007–8
    making functions available to macros 373–76, 1028
    overview of 1005–6
    paths and filenames of, returning 547–48
    statements and functions related to, list of 270–71
    WBODBC.WLL 971, 973, 976
Word API (Microsoft Word Application Programming
  Interface)
    advantages over WordBasic 1003
    arrays, passing 1016–17
    calling WordBasic statements and functions with
      1008 13
    CAPILIB, using 1019–27
    data structures *See* Word operator data structure
      (WDOPR)
    error codes 1032–33
    installing files to build WLLs 1004–5
    making functions available to macros 1028
    memory, managing 1017–18
    menu item, adding 1028
    overview of 1003
    platform specific details 1010 13
    relationship to WordBasic 1006
    requirements for developing WLLs 1004
    shortcut key, adding 1028
    strings, passing 1018
    toolbar button, adding 1028
    wdAddCommand command 1030
    wdAutoOpen function 1005–6
    wdAutoRemove function 1005–6
    wdCaptureKeyDown command 1032
    wdCloseWindow command 1032
    wdCommandDispatch function 1008–13
    wdGetHwnd command 1031
    wdGetInst command 1031
    wdOpenWindow command 1031–32
    wdPrint command 1030
    wdReleaseKeyDown command 1032
    wdSetTimer command 1031
Word operator data structure (WDOPR)
    See also Word API (Microsoft Word Application
      Programming Interface)
    arrays, passing 1016–17
    building with CAPILIB 1025–26
    overview of 1013
    parts of 1014–16
    strings, passing 1018
    type definition of 1013
Word Picture objects 420, 423, 478
Word Settings (6) file 199
Word settings, obtaining values of Word dialog box controls
  554
word underline character format 885
WordArt objects, inserting 607

WordBasic
    books about 9
    calling with the Word API 1008–13
    features of 3–4
    learning 4–5
    operating limits 1051
    relationship to Word API 1006
    sample files 5–7
WordLeft statement and function 883
WordMail
    deleting messages 650
    displaying message properties 651
    displaying next message 651
    displaying previous message 651
    forwarding messages 650
    hiding and showing header 632
    moving messages 651
    replying to messages 652
    selecting names 652
    validating names 632
WordPerfect Help 573, 842–44
WordRight statement and function 884–85
words
    See also text
    counting 405–6, 506–7, 859
    deleting 377, 378–79
    hyphenating 830, 831
    selecting by 474, 729–30, 883, 884–85
    underlining 885
WordUnderline statement and function 885
Workgroup Extensions for Microsoft Word 925–67
wrapper functions 926
Write statement 207, 886
writing macros 19
writing to files 207–8
WW6_EditClear statement 435–36

X

X units 108
XE field 653–54

Y

Y units 108
year
    See also dates
    360-day, computing dates based on 366
    extracting from date 887
Year() function 887

Z

zooming 632, 874–75, 876